AF676622

Recent Advances in Anticancer Strategies

Recent Advances in Anticancer Strategies

Topic Editors

Hassan Bousbaa
Zhiwei Hu

MDPI

Basel • Beijing • Wuhan • Barcelona • Belgrade • Novi Sad • Cluj • Manchester

Topic Editors
Hassan Bousbaa
UNIPRO—Oral Pathology and Rehabilitation Research Unit
University Institute of Health Sciences (IUCS)
Cooperativa de Ensino Superior Politécnico e Universitário (CESPU)
Gandra
Portugal

Zhiwei Hu
Pelotonia Institute for Immuno-Oncology
The Arthur G. James Comprehensive Cancer Center
The Ohio State University College of Medicine
Columbus
USA

Editorial Office
MDPI AG
Grosspeteranlage 5
4052 Basel, Switzerland

This is a reprint of the Topic, published open access by the journals *Biomedicines* (ISSN 2227-9059), *Cancers* (ISSN 2072-6694), *Pharmaceutics* (ISSN 1999-4923) and *Current Oncology* (ISSN 1718-7729), freely accessible at: https://www.mdpi.com/topics/A8U6WXLXT6.

For citation purposes, cite each article independently as indicated on the article page online and as indicated below:

Lastname, A.A.; Lastname, B.B. Article Title. *Journal Name* **Year**, *Volume Number*, Page Range.

ISBN 978-3-7258-4217-9 (Hbk)
ISBN 978-3-7258-4218-6 (PDF)
https://doi.org/10.3390/books978-3-7258-4218-6

© 2025 by the authors. Articles in this book are Open Access and distributed under the Creative Commons Attribution (CC BY) license. The book as a whole is distributed by MDPI under the terms and conditions of the Creative Commons Attribution-NonCommercial-NoDerivs (CC BY-NC-ND) license (https://creativecommons.org/licenses/by-nc-nd/4.0/).

Contents

About the Editors . . . . **ix**

Preface . . . . **xi**

Zhiwei Hu and Hassan Bousbaa
Recent Advances in Anticancer Strategies
Reprinted from: *Cancers* **2025**, *17*, 173, https://doi.org/10.3390/cancers17020173 . . . . **1**

Lara Biny, Evgeniia Gerasimovich, Alexander Karaulov, Alyona Sukhanova and Igor Nabiev
Functionalized Calcium Carbonate-Based Microparticles as a Versatile Tool for Targeted Drug Delivery and Cancer Treatment
Reprinted from: *Pharmaceutics* **2024**, *16*, 653, https://doi.org/10.3390/pharmaceutics16050653 . **6**

João P. N. Silva, Bárbara Pinto, Luís Monteiro, Patrícia M. A. Silva and Hassan Bousbaa
Coupling Kinesin Spindle Protein and Aurora B Inhibition with Apoptosis Induction Enhances Oral Cancer Cell Killing
Reprinted from: *Cancers* **2024**, *16*, 2014, https://doi.org/10.3390/cancers16112014 . . . . **30**

Samir Fasih, Stephen Welch and Ana Elisa Lohmann
Antibody–Drug Conjugates: A Start of a New Era in Gynecological Cancers
Reprinted from: *Curr. Oncol.* **2024**, *31*, 7088–7106, https://doi.org/10.3390/curroncol31110522 . **49**

Bárbara Pinto, João P. N. Silva, Patrícia M. A. Silva, Daniel José Barbosa, Bruno Sarmento, Juliana Carvalho Tavares and Hassan Bousbaa
Maximizing Anticancer Response with MPS1 and CENPE Inhibition Alongside Apoptosis Induction
Reprinted from: *Pharmaceutics* **2024**, *16*, 56, https://doi.org/10.3390/pharmaceutics16010056 . . **68**

Andrea Cunha, Patrícia M. A. Silva, Bruno Sarmento and Odília Queirós
Targeting Glucose Metabolism in Cancer Cells as an Approach to Overcoming Drug Resistance
Reprinted from: *Pharmaceutics* **2023**, *15*, 2610, https://doi.org/10.3390/pharmaceutics15112610 . **89**

Mafalda Calheiros-Lobo, João P. N. Silva, Leonor Delgado, Bárbara Pinto, Luís Monteiro, Carlos Lopes, et al.
Targeting the EGFR and Spindle Assembly Checkpoint Pathways in Oral Cancer: A Plausible Alliance to Enhance Cell Death
Reprinted from: *Cancers* **2024**, *16*, 3732, https://doi.org/10.3390/cancers16223732 . . . . **118**

Ab Majeed Ganai, Eirinaios I. Vrettos, Stavroula G. Kyrkou, Vasiliki Zoi, Tabasum Khan Pathan, Rajshekhar Karpoormath, et al.
Design Principles and Applications of Fluorescent Kinase Inhibitors for Simultaneous Cancer Bioimaging and Therapy
Reprinted from: *Cancers* **2024**, *16*, 3667, https://doi.org/10.3390/cancers16213667 . . . . **147**

Joana Pereira-Vieira, Daniela D. Weber, Sâmia Silva, Catarina Barbosa-Matos, Sara Granja, Rui Manuel Reis, et al.
Glucose Metabolism as a Potential Therapeutic Target in Cytarabine-Resistant Acute Myeloid Leukemia
Reprinted from: *Pharmaceutics* **2024**, *16*, 442, https://doi.org/10.3390/pharmaceutics16040442 . **180**

Nadia de Gruil, Stefan Böhringer, Stefanie de Groot, Hanno Pijl, Judith R. Kroep and Jesse J. Swen
IGF1 and Insulin Receptor Single Nucleotide Variants Associated with Response in HER2-Negative Breast Cancer Patients Treated with Neoadjuvant Chemotherapy with or without a Fasting Mimicking Diet (BOOG 2013-04 DIRECT Trial)
Reprinted from: *Cancers* **2023**, *15*, 5872, https://doi.org/10.3390/cancers15245872 . . . . **197**

Siyuan Liu, Yi Hu, Fei Liu, Yizheng Jiang, Hongrui Wang, Xusheng Wu and Dehua Hu
Identifying Key Genes as Progression Indicators of Prostate Cancer with Castration Resistance Based on Dynamic Network Biomarker Algorithm and Weighted Gene Correlation Network Analysis
Reprinted from: *Biomedicines* **2024**, *12*, 2157, https://doi.org/10.3390/biomedicines12092157 . . **206**

Hasan Slika, Paolo Alimonti, Divyaansh Raj, Chad Caraway, Safwan Alomari, Eric M. Jackson and Betty Tyler
The Neurodevelopmental and Molecular Landscape of Medulloblastoma Subgroups: Current Targets and the Potential for Combined Therapies
Reprinted from: *Cancers* **2023**, *15*, 3889, https://doi.org/10.3390/cancers15153889 . . . . **231**

Zsuzsanna Suba
DNA Damage Responses in Tumors Are Not Proliferative Stimuli, but Rather They Are DNA Repair Actions Requiring Supportive Medical Care
Reprinted from: *Cancers* **2024**, *16*, 1573, https://doi.org/10.3390/cancers16081573 . . . . **275**

Junrui Tian and Jian Ma
The Value of Microbes in Cancer Neoantigen Immunotherapy
Reprinted from: *Pharmaceutics* **2023**, *15*, 2138, https://doi.org/10.3390/pharmaceutics15082138 . **303**

Liqin Yao, Qingqing Wang and Wenxue Ma
Navigating the Immune Maze: Pioneering Strategies for Unshackling Cancer Immunotherapy Resistance
Reprinted from: *Cancers* **2023**, *15*, 5857, https://doi.org/10.3390/cancers15245857 . . . . **323**

Miguel T. Campos, Filipa A. L. S. Silva, José Ramiro Fernandes, Susana G. Santos, Fernão D. Magalhães, Maria J. Oliveira and Artur M. Pinto
New MoS_2/Tegafur-Containing Pharmaceutical Formulations for Selective LED-Based Skin Cancer Photo-Chemotherapy
Reprinted from: *Pharmaceutics* **2024**, *16*, 360, https://doi.org/10.3390/pharmaceutics16030360 . **341**

Roxana Loriana Negrut, Adrian Cote, Vasile Aurel Caus and Adrian Marius Maghiar
Systematic Review and Meta-Analysis of Laparoscopic versus Robotic-Assisted Surgery for Colon Cancer: Efficacy, Safety, and Outcomes—A Focus on Studies from 2020–2024
Reprinted from: *Cancers* **2024**, *16*, 1552, https://doi.org/10.3390/cancers16081552 . . . . **364**

Tianyi Yin, Jingrun Han, Yuying Cui, Dong Shang and Hong Xiang
Prospect of Gold Nanoparticles in Pancreatic Cancer
Reprinted from: *Pharmaceutics* **2024**, *16*, 806, https://doi.org/10.3390/pharmaceutics16060806 . **382**

Qijun Su, Junqian Pan, Chunxin Wang, Meng Zhang, Haixin Cui and Xiang Zhao
Curcumin and Baicalin Co-Loaded Nanoliposomes for Synergistic Treatment of Non-Small Cell Lung Cancer
Reprinted from: *Pharmaceutics* **2024**, *16*, 973, https://doi.org/10.3390/pharmaceutics16080973 . **400**

Haobin Zhao, Ruining Han, Zhankun Wang, Junfang Xian and Xiaosu Bai
Colorectal Cancer Stem Cells and Targeted Agents
Reprinted from: *Pharmaceutics* **2023**, *15*, 2763, https://doi.org/10.3390/pharmaceutics15122763 . **418**

Saloni Malla, Angelique Nyinawabera, Rabin Neupane, Rajiv Pathak, Donghyun Lee, Mariam Abou-Dahech, et al.
Novel Thienopyrimidine-Hydrazinyl Compounds Induce DRP1-Mediated Non-Apoptotic Cell Death in Triple-Negative Breast Cancer Cells
Reprinted from: *Cancers* **2024**, *16*, 2621, https://doi.org/10.3390/cancers16152621 . . . . **435**

Daria Kalenichenko, Irina Kriukova, Alexander Karaulov, Igor Nabiev and Alyona Sukhanova
Cytotoxic Effects of Doxorubicin on Cancer Cells and Macrophages Depend Differently on the Microcarrier Structure
Reprinted from: *Pharmaceutics* **2024**, *16*, 785, https://doi.org/10.3390/pharmaceutics16060785 . **467**

Sarkar Siddique, Harry E. Ruda and James C. L. Chow
FLASH Radiotherapy and the Use of Radiation Dosimeters
Reprinted from: *Cancers* **2023**, *15*, 3883, https://doi.org/10.3390/cancers15153883 . . . . **482**

Paolo Bonome, Donato Pezzulla, Valentina Lancellotta, Anna Rita Scrofani, Gabriella Macchia, Elena Rodolfino, et al.
Combination of Local Ablative Techniques with Radiotherapy for Primary and Recurrent Lung Cancer: A Systematic Review
Reprinted from: *Cancers* **2023**, *15*, 5869, https://doi.org/10.3390/cancers15245869 . . . . **498**

Francesca Corti, Roberta Elisa Rossi, Pietro Cafaro, Gaia Passarella, Antonella Turla, Sara Pusceddu, et al.
Emerging Treatment Options for Neuroendocrine Neoplasms of Unknown Primary Origin: Current Evidence and Future Perspectives
Reprinted from: *Cancers* **2024**, *16*, 2025, https://doi.org/10.3390/cancers16112025 . . . . **512**

Baoshan Zhang, Jong-Mu Sun, Myung-Ju Ahn and Sin-Ho Jung
Randomized Phase II Cancer Clinical Trials to Validate Predictive Biomarkers
Reprinted from: *Biomedicines* **2024**, *12*, 2185, https://doi.org/10.3390/biomedicines12102185 . . **539**

Klijs J. de Koning, Carleen M. E. M. Adriaansens, Rob Noorlag, Remco de Bree and Robert J. J. van Es
Intraoperative Techniques That Define the Mucosal Margins of Oral Cancer In-Vivo: A Systematic Review
Reprinted from: *Cancers* **2024**, *16*, 1148, https://doi.org/10.3390/cancers16061148 . . . . **548**

Laurence Morin, Louis-Philippe Grenier, Nicolas Foucault, Éric Lévesque, François Fabi, Eve-Lyne Langlais, et al.
Comparison of Weekly Paclitaxel Regimens in Recurrent Platinum-Resistant Ovarian Cancer: A Single Institution Retrospective Study
Reprinted from: *Curr. Oncol.* **2024**, *31*, 4624–4631, https://doi.org/10.3390/curroncol31080345 . **568**

Fabio Volpe, Carmela Nappi, Emilia Zampella, Erica Di Donna, Simone Maurea, Alberto Cuocolo and Michele Klain
Current Advances in Radioactive Iodine-Refractory Differentiated Thyroid Cancer
Reprinted from: *Curr. Oncol.* **2024**, *31*, 3870–3884, https://doi.org/10.3390/curroncol31070286 . **576**

Kim N. Chi, Steven M. Yip, Glenn Bauman, Stephan Probst, Urban Emmenegger, Christian K. Kollmannsberger, et al.
^{177}Lu-PSMA-617 in Metastatic Castration-Resistant Prostate Cancer: A Review of the Evidence and Implications for Canadian Clinical Practice
Reprinted from: *Curr. Oncol.* **2024**, *31*, 1400–1415, https://doi.org/10.3390/curroncol31030106 . **591**

Akinori Minato, Nobuki Furubayashi, Yujiro Nagata, Toshihisa Tomoda, Hiroyuki Masaoka, Yoohyun Song, et al.
Prognostic Impact of Histologic Subtype and Divergent Differentiation in Patients with Metastatic Urothelial Carcinoma Treated with Enfortumab Vedotin: A Multicenter Retrospective Study
Reprinted from: *Curr. Oncol.* **2024**, *31*, 862–871, https://doi.org/10.3390/curroncol31020064 . . . **607**

About the Editors

Hassan Bousbaa

Dr. Hassan Bousbaa is a cancer researcher at the Oral Pathology and Rehabilitation Research Unit (UNIPRO) and an Associate Professor of Cellular and Molecular Biology at the Instituto Universitário de Ciências da Saúde—CESPU, Portugal. His research interests focus on targeted anticancer therapy, mitosis-targeting strategies, antimitotic agents, and the biological evaluation of both natural and synthetic compounds, as well as cancer biomarkers. He currently serves as a Section Editor for the journal *Pharmaceutics*.

Zhiwei Hu

Dr. Zhiwei Hu is a cancer researcher and senior scientist at the Pelotonia Institute for Immuno-Oncology of The Ohio State University (OSU) Comprehensive Cancer Center—James, where he helps establish and lead a new center for antibody therapeutics. He served as a research associate professor in the Division of Surgical Oncology Department of Surgery at OSU College of Medicine during his tenure from 2012 to 2024 and at Yale University School of Medicine from 2002 to 2012. His research interests focus on targeting cancer cells, cancer stem cells, and pathological neovasculature using tissue factor-targeted antibodies, CAR-NK immunotherapy, and photodynamic therapy approaches. He currently serves as an Editor for the journal *Life* and an Associate Editor for *Frontiers in Oncology* and *Frontiers in Immunology*, as well as a committee member for the Society for Immunotherapy of Cancer (SITC) Membership Committee.

Preface

The Topic "Recent Advances in Anticancer Strategies" aims to provide a comprehensive overview of the latest advancements in the field of cancer treatment. Cancer remains one of the leading causes of death worldwide, and researchers have been working to develop more effective and targeted treatments to improve outcomes for patients. Existing cancer therapies sometimes suffer from severe side effects and drug resistance, contributing to the rising incidence and mortality of cancer globally. Hence, there is an unmet need to develop and discover novel therapeutic strategies that offer more effective and less toxic treatment options for cancer patients. Novel anticancer approaches are emerging, including—but not limited to—ligand-/receptor-based targeting, controlled drug delivery, gene therapy, gene delivery, immunotherapy, targeted anticancer prodrugs and conjugates (such as photoactivatable caged prodrugs and antibody–drug conjugates), magnetic and ultrasound-mediated drug targeting, cancer stem cell therapy, and strategies aimed at targeting cancer signaling cascades and the tumor microenvironment. These approaches have the potential to selectively identify and eliminate cancerous cells while minimizing harm to healthy tissues.

To tackle this issue, the Topic features thirty high-quality original research and review articles, as well as one editorial, all focused on the emerging challenges and advances in experimental and translational cancer research. The contributions cover a wide range of key areas, such as the tumor microenvironment, mechanisms of drug resistance, identification of novel molecular targets, and strategies for enhancing treatment efficacy—including immunotherapy and targeted approaches. Drawn from four MDPI journals—*Biomedicines*, *Cancers*, *Current Oncology*, and *Pharmaceutics*—this collection offers a cross-disciplinary perspective that bridges preclinical discoveries and clinical applications. This first edition serves as an insightful resource for a general audience, researchers, and physicians interested in recent advances in cancer treatment and/or the translation of biological findings into innovative therapies. We would like to thank all the authors, reviewers, and the editorial team for their hard work in supporting the ongoing effort to find better treatments or a cure for cancer. The success of this first edition has led to the launch of a second edition of the Topic, which is currently ongoing and welcomes further research on recent advances in anticancer strategies, highlighting the potential impact of these innovative approaches on cancer treatment and patient outcomes.

Hassan Bousbaa and Zhiwei Hu
Topic Editors

cancers

MDPI

Editorial

Recent Advances in Anticancer Strategies

Zhiwei Hu [1,*] and Hassan Bousbaa [2,*]

1 Pelotonia Institute for Immuno-Oncology, The Arthur G. James Comprehensive Cancer Center, The Ohio State University College of Medicine, Columbus, OH 43210, USA
2 UNIPRO—Oral Pathology and Rehabilitation Research Unit, University Institute of Health Sciences (IUCS), Cooperativa de Ensino Superior Politécnico e Universitário (CESPU), Rua Central de Gandra, 1317, 4585-116 Gandra, Portugal
* Correspondence: zhiwei.hu@osumc.edu (Z.H.); hassan.bousbaa@iucs.cespu.pt (H.B.)

Due to the intricate nature of cancer development and progression, various types of cancer are increasingly prevalent worldwide. Despite radiotherapy and chemotherapy remaining the primary treatment options, their conventional approaches are plagued by significant toxicity and resistance issues, resulting in incomplete tumor eradication [1]. This presents a distinct challenge for researchers and clinicians alike. Therefore, there is an urgent need for new anticancer drugs and innovative drug delivery strategies to address these shortcomings and potentially offer more effective and safer therapeutic alternatives. This first edition of the topic "Recent Advances in Anticancer Strategies" (https://www.mdpi.com/topics/A8U6WXLXT6; accessed on 16 December 2024), focuses on pioneering research into the development and validation of novel anticancer approaches that could have a significant clinical impact in the near future.

Thirty papers were published, comprising thirteen articles and seventeen reviews, showcasing the latest advancements in novel anticancer approaches. This Editorial provides a concise summary of the findings and key highlights from these publications.

Antibody–drug conjugates (ADCs) represent a transformative approach in cancer therapy, utilizing antibodies to deliver cytotoxic drugs directly to cancer cells [2]. Research has highlighted advancements in ADCs for the treatment of gynecological cancers, dual inhibition strategies for oral cancer, and innovative drug delivery systems using functionalized calcium carbonate-based microparticles. These developments aim to enhance therapeutic outcomes by reducing off-target effects and improving the specificity and efficiency of drug delivery (Contributions 1–3).

The field of targeted therapies continues to advance with the development of kinase inhibitors for cancer bioimaging and therapy, as well as strategies targeting EGFR and glucose metabolism [3]. These approaches demonstrate potential in overcoming drug resistance and improving treatment outcomes. The synergistic targeting of EGFR and spindle assembly checkpoint pathways in oral cancer, alongside the utilization of fluorescent kinase inhibitors, are key examples of how precision medicine can be integrated into cancer care (Contributions 4–7).

Genetic and epigenetic research is uncovering biomarkers that could significantly impact cancer treatment [4]. Studies have identified key genes associated with prostate cancer progression, HER2-negative breast cancer responses, and cytarabine resistance in acute myeloid leukemia. These findings pave the way for more personalized therapies based on individual genetic profiles, optimizing treatment regimens and enhancing survival rates (Contributions 8–10). Slika et al. provide a comprehensive overview of the molecular and genetic underpinnings of medulloblastoma, detailing the distinct neurodevelopmental pathways and genetic mutations associated with different subgroups of the disease. They

https://doi.org/10.3390/cancers17020173

highlight how these molecular features can be leveraged to identify new therapeutic targets and inform treatment strategies (Contribution 11). Suba examines the role of DNA damage responses in tumors, emphasizing their impact on cellular processes beyond mere proliferation and highlighting the necessity for supportive medical care (Contribution 12).

Cancer immunotherapy is increasingly focusing on the development of bispecific antibodies, immune cell engagers, chimeric antigen receptor (CAR)-modified T and NK cells (CAR-T and CAR-NK), overcoming resistance mechanisms and harnessing the immune system's full potential [5,6]. Strategies include the use of immune checkpoint inhibitors, microbial contributions to neoantigen immunity, and restoring apoptosis in cancers such as colorectal cancer. These approaches represent a shift towards leveraging the body's immune defenses to fight cancer, offering new hope for patients with otherwise resistant forms of the disease (Contributions 13, 14).

Innovations in pharmacology and drug delivery are crucial for improving cancer treatment outcomes [7]. The research highlights the potential of gold nanoparticles for targeted pancreatic cancer therapy, as well as the benefits of laparoscopic versus robotic-assisted surgery for colon cancer. New formulations for LED-based photo-chemotherapy are also showing promise, providing more effective drug delivery and treatment options for skin cancer (Contributions 15–17). Su et al. explore the synergistic therapeutic potential of curcumin and baicalin co-loaded nanoliposomes for the treatment of non-small cell lung cancer, emphasizing the importance of formulation strategies for enhancing drug efficacy and overcoming resistance (Contribution 18).

Understanding the underlying mechanisms of cancer cell biology is essential for the development of new therapeutic strategies [8]. Recent studies have explored the cytotoxic effects of doxorubicin on cancer cells and the role of mitochondrial dynamics in non-apoptotic cell death, and targeted cancer stem cells in colorectal cancer. These insights are crucial for developing therapies that address the complexity of cancer cell biology (Contributions 19–21). FLASH radiotherapy involves the high-dose-rate delivery of radiation in very short pulses, which minimizes damage to surrounding healthy tissues while potentially increasing the radiosensitivity of cancer cells. The review article by Siddique et al. discusses the use of advanced radiation dosimeters to measure these high-dose rates accurately, which is critical for optimizing therapy and understanding the biological effects of FLASH radiotherapy (Contribution 22).

Optimizing treatment outcomes through clinical trials and novel therapies remains a priority [9]. The research includes the validation of predictive biomarkers used in cancer clinical trials, the management of neuroendocrine neoplasms of unknown primary origin, and the use of combination therapies involving local ablative techniques with radiotherapy. These studies aim to refine therapeutic strategies, enhance efficacy, and improve patient quality of life (Contributions 23–25). Koning et al. reviewed various intraoperative techniques used to accurately define the mucosal margins of oral cancer, thereby assisting surgeons in achieving complete resection (Contribution 26). Morin et al. present a single-institution retrospective study comparing weekly paclitaxel regimens in recurrent platinum-resistant ovarian cancer. Their analysis offers valuable insights into the efficacy and outcomes of different treatment schedules, which are crucial for optimizing therapeutic strategies and improving patient prognosis in gynecological cancers (Contribution 27). Volpe et al. discuss the latest advances in managing radioactive iodine-refractory differentiated thyroid cancer, focusing on new therapeutic strategies and their implications for patient outcomes. This research is crucial for optimizing treatment protocols and improving prognosis for patients with this challenging cancer type (Contribution 28).

Clinical trials and real-world evidence are vital for validating new cancer therapies and improving patient care [10]. Advances in radioligand therapy for metastatic castration-resistant prostate cancer, comparisons of laparoscopic versus robotic-assisted surgery for colon cancer, and an understanding of the prognostic factors in metastatic urothelial carcinoma are all critical areas of focus. These studies contribute valuable data, informing clinical practice and guiding treatment decisions (Contributions 16, 29, and 30).

This inaugural edition of the topic "Recent Advances in Anticancer Strategies" highlights groundbreaking research and diverse perspectives within the field of cancer treatment. The integration of novel therapies, targeted interventions, and innovative approaches discussed in these papers reflects the dynamic landscape of oncology. The success of this first edition not only demonstrates the depth of the scientific inquiry and collaboration in this area but also motivates us to continue advancing this discourse. We are pleased to announce that the call for submissions for the second edition is already open (https://www.mdpi.com/topics/1MJ7OBGQ2R; accessed on 18 December 2024); researchers are invited to contribute their latest findings and ideas, including but not limited to the discovery of novel tumor targets and cancer cell pathways, new bi/multi-specific antibodies, immune cell engagers, ADCs, tumor-specific CAR or T cell receptor (TCR)-modified immune cells, tumor-targeting photodynamic and radiation diagnoses and therapies, new approaches to eliminating immune suppressor cells (such as regulatory T cells, Treg; tumor-associated macrophages, TAM; myeloid-derived suppressor cells, MDSC; cancer-associated fibroblast, and CAF), cancer stem cells, and tumor neovasculature, to further shape the future of cancer research and clinical practice.

Funding: H.B. received funding from CESPU—Cooperativa de Ensino Superior Politécnico e Universitário under the projects "BeatCancer_GI2-CESPU-2023", and "FlavScreen_GI2-CESPU-2023". Z.H. received two Pelotonia Idea Awards "IRP00915" and "IRP01207" from The Ohio State University Comprehensive Cancer Center Intramural Research Program, and a Pilot Award from The Ohio State University Breast Cancer Translational Research Program.

Conflicts of Interest: The authors declare no conflicts of interest.

List of Contributions:

1. Biny, L.; Gerasimovich, E.; Karaulov, A.; Sukhanova, A.; Nabiev, I. Functionalized Calcium Carbonate-Based Microparticles as a Versatile Tool for Targeted Drug Delivery and Cancer Treatment. *Pharmaceutics* **2024**, *16*, 653. https://doi.org/10.3390/PHARMACEUTICS16050653.
2. Silva, J.P.N.; Pinto, B.; Monteiro, L.; Silva, P.M.A.; Bousbaa, H. Coupling Kinesin Spindle Protein and Aurora B Inhibition with Apoptosis Induction Enhances Oral Cancer Cell Killing. *Cancers* **2024**, *16*, 2014. https://doi.org/10.3390/CANCERS16112014.
3. Fasih, S.; Welch, S.; Lohmann, A.E. Antibody–Drug Conjugates: A Start of a New Era in Gynecological Cancers. *Curr. Oncol.* **2024**, *31*, 7088–7106. https://doi.org/10.3390/CURRONCOL31110522.
4. Pinto, B.; Silva, J.P.N.; Silva, P.M.A.; Barbosa, D.J.; Sarmento, B.; Tavares, J.C.; Bousbaa, H. Maximizing Anticancer Response with MPS1 and CENPE Inhibition Alongside Apoptosis Induction. *Pharmaceutics* **2024**, *16*, 56. https://doi.org/10.3390/PHARMACEUTICS16010056.
5. Cunha, A.; Silva, P.M.A.; Sarmento, B.; Queirós, O. Targeting Glucose Metabolism in Cancer Cells as an Approach to Overcoming Drug Resistance. *Pharmaceutics* **2023**, *15*, 2610. https://doi.org/10.3390/PHARMACEUTICS15112610.
6. Calheiros-Lobo, M.; Silva, J.P.N.; Delgado, L.; Pinto, B.; Monteiro, L.; Lopes, C.; Silva, P.M.A.; Bousbaa, H. Targeting the EGFR and Spindle Assembly Checkpoint Pathways in Oral Cancer: A Plausible Alliance to Enhance Cell Death. *Cancers* **2024**, *16*, 3732. https://doi.org/10.3390/CANCERS16223732.
7. Ganai, A.M.; Vrettos, E.I.; Kyrkou, S.G.; Zoi, V.; Khan Pathan, T.; Karpoormath, R.; Bouziotis, P.; Alexiou, G.A.; Kastis, G.A.; Protonotarios, N.E.; et al. Design Principles and Applications of Fluorescent Kinase Inhibitors for Simultaneous Cancer Bioimaging and Therapy. *Cancers* **2024**, *16*, 3667. https://doi.org/10.3390/CANCERS16213667.

8. Pereira-Vieira, J.; Weber, D.D.; Silva, S.; Barbosa-Matos, C.; Granja, S.; Reis, R.M.; Queirós, O.; Ko, Y.H.; Kofler, B.; Casal, M.; et al. Glucose Metabolism as a Potential Therapeutic Target in Cytarabine-Resistant Acute Myeloid Leukemia. *Pharmaceutics* **2024**, *16*, 442. https://doi.org/10.3390/PHARMACEUTICS16040442.
9. de Gruil, N.; Böhringer, S.; de Groot, S.; Pijl, H.; Kroep, J.R.; Swen, J.J. IGF1 and Insulin Receptor Single Nucleotide Variants Associated with Response in HER2-Negative Breast Cancer Patients Treated with Neoadjuvant Chemotherapy with or without a Fasting Mimicking Diet (BOOG 2013-04 DIRECT Trial). *Cancers* **2023**, *15*, 5872. https://doi.org/10.3390/CANCERS15245872.
10. Liu, S.; Hu, Y.; Liu, F.; Jiang, Y.; Wang, H.; Wu, X.; Hu, D. Identifying Key Genes as Progression Indicators of Prostate Cancer with Castration Resistance Based on Dynamic Network Biomarker Algorithm and Weighted Gene Correlation Network Analysis. *Biomedicines* **2024**, *12*, 2157. https://doi.org/10.3390/BIOMEDICINES12092157.
11. Slika, H.; Alimonti, P.; Raj, D.; Caraway, C.; Alomari, S.; Jackson, E.M.; Tyler, B. The Neurodevelopmental and Molecular Landscape of Medulloblastoma Subgroups: Current Targets and the Potential for Combined Therapies. *Cancers* **2023**, *15*, 3889. https://doi.org/10.3390/CANCERS15153889.
12. Hu, Z.; Suba, Z. DNA Damage Responses in Tumors Are Not Proliferative Stimuli, but Rather They Are DNA Repair Actions Requiring Supportive Medical Care. *Cancers* **2024**, *16*, 1573. https://doi.org/10.3390/CANCERS16081573.
13. Tian, J.; Ma, J. The Value of Microbes in Cancer Neoantigen Immunotherapy. *Pharmaceutics* **2023**, *15*, 2138. https://doi.org/10.3390/PHARMACEUTICS15082138.
14. Yao, L.; Wang, Q.; Ma, W. Navigating the Immune Maze: Pioneering Strategies for Unshackling Cancer Immunotherapy Resistance. *Cancers* **2023**, *15*, 5857. https://doi.org/10.3390/CANCERS15245857.
15. Campos, M.T.; Silva, F.A.L.S.; Fernandes, J.R.; Santos, S.G.; Magalhães, F.D.; Oliveira, M.J.; Pinto, A.M. New MoS2/Tegafur-Containing Pharmaceutical Formulations for Selective LED-Based Skin Cancer Photo-Chemotherapy. *Pharmaceutics* **2024**, *16*, 360. https://doi.org/10.3390/PHARMACEUTICS16030360.
16. Negrut, R.L.; Cote, A.; Caus, V.A.; Maghiar, A.M. Systematic Review and Meta-Analysis of Laparoscopic versus Robotic-Assisted Surgery for Colon Cancer: Efficacy, Safety, and Outcomes—A Focus on Studies from 2020–2024. *Cancers* **2024**, *16*, 1552. https://doi.org/10.3390/CANCERS16081552.
17. Yin, T.; Han, J.; Cui, Y.; Shang, D.; Xiang, H. Prospect of Gold Nanoparticles in Pancreatic Cancer. *Pharmaceutics* **2024**, *16*, 806. https://doi.org/10.3390/PHARMACEUTICS16060806.
18. Su, Q.; Pan, J.; Wang, C.; Zhang, M.; Cui, H.; Zhao, X. Curcumin and Baicalin Co-Loaded Nanoliposomes for Synergistic Treatment of Non-Small Cell Lung Cancer. *Pharmaceutics* **2024**, *16*, 973. https://doi.org/10.3390/PHARMACEUTICS16080973.
19. Zhao, H.; Han, R.; Wang, Z.; Xian, J.; Bai, X. Colorectal Cancer Stem Cells and Targeted Agents. *Pharmaceutics* **2023**, *15*, 2763. https://doi.org/10.3390/PHARMACEUTICS15122763.
20. Malla, S.; Nyinawabera, A.; Neupane, R.; Pathak, R.; Lee, D.; Abou-Dahech, M.; Kumari, S.; Sinha, S.; Tang, Y.; Ray, A.; et al. Novel Thienopyrimidine-Hydrazinyl Compounds Induce DRP1-Mediated Non-Apoptotic Cell Death in Triple-Negative Breast Cancer Cells. *Cancers* **2024**, *16*, 2621. https://doi.org/10.3390/CANCERS16152621.
21. Kalenichenko, D.; Kriukova, I.; Karaulov, A.; Nabiev, I.; Sukhanova, A. Cytotoxic Effects of Doxorubicin on Cancer Cells and Macrophages Depend Differently on the Microcarrier Structure. *Pharmaceutics* **2024**, *16*, 785. https://doi.org/10.3390/PHARMACEUTICS16060785.
22. Siddique, S.; Ruda, H.E.; Chow, J.C.L. FLASH Radiotherapy and the Use of Radiation Dosimeters. *Cancers* **2023**, *15*, 3883. https://doi.org/10.3390/CANCERS15153883.
23. Bonome, P.; Pezzulla, D.; Lancellotta, V.; Scrofani, A.R.; Macchia, G.; Rodolfino, E.; Tagliaferri, L.; Kovács, G.; Deodato, F.; Iezzi, R. Combination of Local Ablative Techniques with Radiotherapy for Primary and Recurrent Lung Cancer: A Systematic Review. *Cancers* **2023**, *15*, 5869. https://doi.org/10.3390/CANCERS15245869.
24. Corti, F.; Rossi, R.E.; Cafaro, P.; Passarella, G.; Turla, A.; Pusceddu, S.; Coppa, J.; Oldani, S.; Guidi, A.; Longarini, R.; et al. Emerging Treatment Options for Neuroendocrine Neoplasms of

Unknown Primary Origin: Current Evidence and Future Perspectives. *Cancers* **2024**, *16*, 2025. https://doi.org/10.3390/CANCERS16112025.
25. Zhang, B.; Sun, J.M.; Ahn, M.J.; Jung, S.H. Randomized Phase II Cancer Clinical Trials to Validate Predictive Biomarkers. *Biomedicines* **2024**, *12*, 2185. https://doi.org/10.3390/BIOMEDICINES12102185.
26. de Koning, K.J.; Adriaansens, C.M.E.M.; Noorlag, R.; de Bree, R.; van Es, R.J.J. Intraoperative Techniques That Define the Mucosal Margins of Oral Cancer In-Vivo: A Systematic Review. *Cancers* **2024**, *16*, 1148. https://doi.org/10.3390/CANCERS16061148.
27. Morin, L.; Grenier, L.P.; Foucault, N.; Lévesque, É.; Fabi, F.; Langlais, E.L.; Sebastianelli, A.; Lavoie, M.; Lalancette, M.; Plante, M.; et al. Comparison of Weekly Paclitaxel Regimens in Recurrent Platinum-Resistant Ovarian Cancer: A Single Institution Retrospective Study. *Curr. Oncol.* **2024**, *31*, 4624–4631. https://doi.org/10.3390/CURRONCOL31080345.
28. Volpe, F.; Nappi, C.; Zampella, E.; Di Donna, E.; Maurea, S.; Cuocolo, A.; Klain, M. Current Advances in Radioactive Iodine-Refractory Differentiated Thyroid Cancer. *Curr. Oncol.* **2024**, *31*, 3870–3884. https://doi.org/10.3390/CURRONCOL31070286.
29. Chi, K.N.; Yip, S.M.; Bauman, G.; Probst, S.; Emmenegger, U.; Kollmannsberger, C.K.; Martineau, P.; Niazi, T.; Pouliot, F.; Rendon, R.; et al. 177Lu-PSMA-617 in Metastatic Castration-Resistant Prostate Cancer: A Review of the Evidence and Implications for Canadian Clinical Practice. *Curr. Oncol.* **2024**, *31*, 1400–1415. https://doi.org/10.3390/CURRONCOL31030106.
30. Minato, A.; Furubayashi, N.; Nagata, Y.; Tomoda, T.; Masaoka, H.; Song, Y.; Hori, Y.; Kiyoshima, K.; Negishi, T.; Kuroiwa, K.; et al. Prognostic Impact of Histologic Subtype and Divergent Differentiation in Patients with Metastatic Urothelial Carcinoma Treated with Enfortumab Vedotin: A Multicenter Retrospective Study. *Curr. Oncol.* **2024**, *31*, 862–871. https://doi.org/10.3390/CURRONCOL31020064.

References

1. Anand, U.; Dey, A.; Chandel, A.K.S.; Sanyal, R.; Mishra, A.; Pandey, D.K.; De Falco, V.; Upadhyay, A.; Kandimalla, R.; Chaudhary, A.; et al. Cancer Chemotherapy and beyond: Current Status, Drug Candidates, Associated Risks and Progress in Targeted Therapeutics. *Genes Dis.* **2022**, *10*, 1367. [CrossRef] [PubMed]
2. Marei, H.E.; Cenciarelli, C.; Hasan, A. Potential of Antibody–Drug Conjugates (ADCs) for Cancer Therapy. *Cancer Cell Int.* **2022**, *22*, 255. [CrossRef] [PubMed]
3. Bai, J.W.; Qiu, S.Q.; Zhang, G.J. Molecular and Functional Imaging in Cancer-Targeted Therapy: Current Applications and Future Directions. *Signal Transduct. Target. Ther.* **2023**, *8*, 89. [CrossRef] [PubMed]
4. Gao, J.; Shi, W.; Wang, J.; Guan, C.; Dong, Q.; Sheng, J.; Zou, X.; Xu, Z.; Ge, Y.; Yang, C.; et al. Research Progress and Applications of Epigenetic Biomarkers in Cancer. *Front. Pharmacol.* **2024**, *15*, 1308309. [CrossRef] [PubMed]
5. Peng, L.; Sferruzza, G.; Yang, L.; Zhou, L.; Chen, S. CAR-T and CAR-NK as Cellular Cancer Immunotherapy for Solid Tumors. *Cell Mol. Immunol.* **2024**, *21*, 1089–1108. [CrossRef] [PubMed]
6. Waldman, A.D.; Fritz, J.M.; Lenardo, M.J. A Guide to Cancer Immunotherapy: From T Cell Basic Science to Clinical Practice. *Nat. Rev. Immunol.* **2020**, *20*, 651–668. [CrossRef]
7. Karahmet Sher, E.; Alebić, M.; Marković Boras, M.; Boškailo, E.; Karahmet Farhat, E.; Karahmet, A.; Pavlović, B.; Sher, F.; Lekić, L. Nanotechnology in Medicine Revolutionizing Drug Delivery for Cancer and Viral Infection Treatments. *Int. J. Pharm.* **2024**, *660*, 124345. [CrossRef]
8. Gao, D.; Ge, G. Exploring the Underlying Biology of Cancer and Potential Therapeutic Strategies: A Special Issue Focused on Mechanism-Based Studies. *Acta Biochim. Biophys. Sin.* **2023**, *55*, 891. [CrossRef]
9. Joshi, D.C.; Sharma, A.; Prasad, S.; Singh, K.; Kumar, M.; Sherawat, K.; Tuli, H.S.; Gupta, M. Novel Therapeutic Agents in Clinical Trials: Emerging Approaches in Cancer Therapy. *Discov. Oncol.* **2024**, *15*, 342. [CrossRef] [PubMed]
10. Tang, M.; Pearson, S.A.; Simes, R.J.; Chua, B.H. Harnessing Real-World Evidence to Advance Cancer Research. *Curr. Oncol.* **2023**, *30*, 1844. [CrossRef] [PubMed]

Disclaimer/Publisher's Note: The statements, opinions and data contained in all publications are solely those of the individual author(s) and contributor(s) and not of MDPI and/or the editor(s). MDPI and/or the editor(s) disclaim responsibility for any injury to people or property resulting from any ideas, methods, instructions or products referred to in the content.

pharmaceutics

MDPI

Review

Functionalized Calcium Carbonate-Based Microparticles as a Versatile Tool for Targeted Drug Delivery and Cancer Treatment

Lara Biny [1], Evgeniia Gerasimovich [2,3], Alexander Karaulov [4], Alyona Sukhanova [1,*] and Igor Nabiev [1,2,3,4,*]

1 Université de Reims Champagne-Ardenne, BIOSPECT, 51100 Reims, France; lara.biny@univ-reims.fr
2 Life Improvement by Future Technologies (LIFT) Center, Laboratory of Optical Quantum Sensors, Skolkovo, 143025 Moscow, Russia; ewgenia-gerasimowitch@yandex.ru or i.krukova@lift.center
3 Laboratory of Nano-Bioengineering, National Research Nuclear University MEPhI (Moscow Engineering Physics Institute), 115409 Moscow, Russia
4 Department of Clinical Immunology and Allergology, Institute of Molecular Medicine, Sechenov First Moscow State Medical University (Sechenov University), 119146 Moscow, Russia; drkaraulov@mail.ru
* Correspondence: alyona.sukhanova@univ-reims.fr (A.S.); igor.nabiev@univ-reims.fr (I.N.)

Abstract: Nano- and microparticles are increasingly widely used in biomedical research and applications, particularly as specific labels and targeted delivery vehicles. Silica has long been considered the best material for such vehicles, but it has some disadvantages limiting its potential, such as the proneness of silica-based carriers to spontaneous drug release. Calcium carbonate ($CaCO_3$) is an emerging alternative, being an easily available, cost-effective, and biocompatible material with high porosity and surface reactivity, which makes it an attractive choice for targeted drug delivery. $CaCO_3$ particles are used in this field in the form of either bare $CaCO_3$ microbeads or core/shell microparticles representing polymer-coated $CaCO_3$ cores. In addition, they serve as removable templates for obtaining hollow polymer microcapsules. Each of these types of particles has its specific advantages in terms of biomedical applications. $CaCO_3$ microbeads are primarily used due to their capacity for carrying pharmaceutics, whereas core/shell systems ensure better protection of the drug-loaded core from the environment. Hollow polymer capsules are particularly attractive because they can encapsulate large amounts of pharmaceutical agents and can be so designed as to release their contents in the target site in response to specific stimuli. This review focuses first on the chemistry of the $CaCO_3$ cores, core/shell microbeads, and polymer microcapsules. Then, systems using these structures for the delivery of therapeutic agents, including drugs, proteins, and DNA, are outlined. The results of the systematic analysis of available data are presented. They show that the encapsulation of various therapeutic agents in $CaCO_3$-based microbeads or polymer microcapsules is a promising technique of drug delivery, especially in cancer therapy, enhancing drug bioavailability and specific targeting of cancer cells while reducing side effects. To date, research in $CaCO_3$-based microparticles and polymer microcapsules assembled on $CaCO_3$ templates has mainly dealt with their properties in vitro, whereas their in vivo behavior still remains poorly studied. However, the enormous potential of these highly biocompatible carriers for in vivo applications is undoubted. This last issue is addressed in depth in the Conclusions and Outlook sections of the review.

Keywords: calcium carbonate; microparticles; microcapsules; core/shell structures; targeted delivery; anticancer treatment

1. Introduction

Microparticles are widely used in various fields of research and drug delivery applications [1,2]. Among the various materials used for microparticle fabrication, silica has long been considered the best candidate, but it has several disadvantages that limit its clinical potential, especially in preventing spontaneous drug release [3]. Calcium carbonate ($CaCO_3$) is an abundant, inexpensive, biocompatible material with suitable chemical and physical properties, such as a small size of particles with a large surface area [4]. These properties make it an attractive material for numerous biomedical applications and an ideal choice for targeted cancer immunotherapy [5]. There are three polymorphs of $CaCO_3$ particles: calcite, aragonite, and vaterite crystals. Though less thermodynamically stable than the others, vaterite crystals are spherical, composed of nanodomains, and highly porous, which makes them a good candidate for use in drug delivery systems [6,7].

The most common methods of synthesis of $CaCO_3$ microparticles are solid–liquid–gas carbonation [8] and chemical precipitation through the reaction of $CaCl_2$ with Na_2CO_3 in an aqueous medium [9]. There are also other methods of synthesis of $CaCO_3$ microparticles [10], such as supercritical fluid technology [11] and emulsion techniques [12,13]. In the course of synthesis, the temperature, pH, reagent concentrations, and other parameters can be controlled to optimize the size, morphology, and composition of the microparticles. It has been shown that the gradual addition of a calcium nitrate solution to the sodium carbonate solution allows controlling the saturation of the reaction medium and obtaining smaller $CaCO_3$ particles after prolonged agitation. Overall, temperature influences particle morphology and polymorphism, whereas the calcium and carbonate ion concentrations determine their size [14]. These different techniques of synthesis offer flexible approaches for obtaining $CaCO_3$ particles suitable for various therapeutic applications. $CaCO_3$-based microparticles have a wide range of potential applications, particularly in targeted drug delivery. Their use can offer significant advantages in terms of efficiency, cost-effectiveness, and sustainability compared to existing materials.

Three main types of $CaCO_3$-based microparticles with sizes ranging from about 0.2 to 6 μm have been extensively studied: core-only microparticles, polymer-coated cores (or core/shell microparticles), and hollow (shell) polymer capsules, for which $CaCO_3$ particles are used as sacrificial templates [2,15,16] (Figure 1). Each of these types possesses unique characteristics suitable for specific applications in cancer treatment.

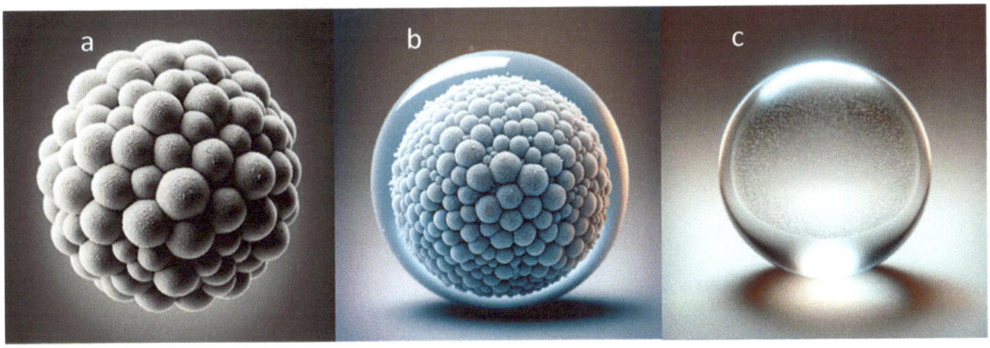

Figure 1. Spherical $CaCO_3$-based microparticles for targeted cancer therapy: (**a**) a $CaCO_3$ core-only microparticle; (**b**) a $CaCO_3$ core/shell microparticle; (**c**) a polyelectrolyte shell-only microcapsule without a core.

Core-only microparticles are primarily used due to their capacity for absorbing and carrying therapeutic agents. Their simple, porous structure also ensures drug release. However, their use is limited by their lack of targeting specificity and insufficient resistance to the potentially aggressive factors of the biological microenvironment. Additional strategies may be necessary to prevent their degradation or aggregation during the delivery [17].

Core/shell structures are considerably more advantageous because their polyelectrolyte shell provides enhanced protection of the encapsulated compound compared to core-only systems and can be functionalized to ensure specific targeting. Current research focuses on developing new strategies to enhance stability, targeting, and release control by coating microparticles with polymers [18] or lipids [19]. These microparticles can be designed to respond to specific stimuli, such as changes in pH [20,21] or temperature [22], by releasing their contents. They are commonly fabricated by means of layer-by-layer (LbL) deposition of alternating anionic and cationic polyelectrolytes, depending on the charge of the template microparticle [23,24].

Polymer microcapsules [16,25] are particularly interesting because of their capacity for encapsulating therapeutic agents while avoiding the adverse effect of $CaCO_3$ on the cellular calcium balance. They also can be designed to respond to specific stimuli, allowing for targeted drug release within tumors [26,27]. Polymeric microcapsules are synthesized on the basis of $CaCO_3$ templates, which are usually dissolved by ethylenediaminetetraacetic acid (EDTA) after LbL assembly of polyelectrolytes [28]. The EDTA concentration determines the dissolution rate and the final properties of the microparticles, including size, porosity, and stability.

Various therapeutic agents, including low-molecular-weight drugs, proteins, and nucleic acids, can be encapsulated by loading into $CaCO_3$ cores through absorption or chemical co-precipitation during the formation of the cores [29]. The loading capacity of these systems depends on several factors, such as the porosity and specific surface area of the $CaCO_3$ particles and the chemical properties of the drug. Studies have shown significant effectiveness of low-molecular-weight drug encapsulation [30] and their controlled release from $CaCO_3$ cores [31], sometimes with a reduced cytotoxicity [32]. The efficiency of encapsulation and stability of encapsulated molecules have been also demonstrated for proteins [33] and nucleic acids [34]. Drug release from delivery systems based on $CaCO_3$ microparticles can be activated by external stimuli, such as a change in pH [35] (slightly acidic in tumors) or temperature [22]. For targeted drug delivery, $CaCO_3$ microparticles can be functionalized with recognition molecules, usually antibodies, interacting with specific receptors on target cells [36]. Moreover, in vivo studies of a nasal drug delivery system based on $CaCO_3$ microparticles has shown improved bioavailability of the active substance [37]. Recently, in vivo applications of $CaCO_3$ particles using various administration routes have been intensely studied and proven to be promising [38].

In conclusion, the loading of drugs into calcium carbonate cores, core/shell microparticles based on them, or microcapsules is a promising technique in the field of drug delivery, especially for cancer therapy. $CaCO_3$-based microparticles efficiently encapsulate various therapeutic agents, improving their bioavailability and specifically targeting cancer cells while reducing side effects. In this review, we will first discuss the methods of synthesis of calcium carbonate cores and the fabrication of $CaCO_3$-based microparticles and microcapsules. Then, we explore the systems for the delivery of small-molecule drugs, proteins, and DNAs based on each of these structures, and finally address the potential uses and key challenges of these microstructures in cancer treatment.

2. Core-Only $CaCO_3$ Microparticles

Calcium carbonate cores have been used as containers over the past two decades [39] and offer numerous advantages for the delivery of pharmacological compounds, such as biocompatibility, a high loading capacity, and maintenance of the properties of the loaded molecules [40]. Their size and shape vary depending on synthesis conditions, including temperature, reactant concentrations, viscosity of the medium, and reaction time, which allows obtaining cores with desired properties [1,6,7]. The internal porous structure of functionalized calcium carbonate cores is also an important factor influencing drug loading, which has recently been elucidated by mercury intrusion porosimetry and scanning electron microscopy with a focused ion beam [41]. A reduced pore size has been found to be associated with an increased maximum payload, i.e., a higher capacity for retaining compounds within the particles.

2.1. Loading Methods

Calcium carbonate cores are used for the loading of small molecules [21,42], proteins [43,44], nucleic acids [34], and radionuclides [45,46]. The substances are loaded into the $CaCO_3$ cores either by co-synthesis, when the proteins are captured by the $CaCO_3$ cores during their growth, or by the adsorption of loading molecules onto the matrix surface of preformed $CaCO_3$ cores [47]. An alternative drug loading method by solvent evaporation is suitable for small molecules with different solubilities [42]. The adsorption of poorly soluble drugs onto the $CaCO_3$ particles may help overcome the low bioavailability of drugs [48], whereas loading during co-synthesis leads to the aggregation of proteins [43]. The co-precipitation method has proven to have a high loading efficiency for both small-molecule drugs and proteins [18,49]. The loading efficiency depends on the drug diffusion through the pores at the pH and ionic strength suited to each particular compound, while ensuring the preservation of its bioactivity. For example, the loading of superoxide dismutase into vaterite $CaCO_3$ crystals at pH 8.5 was highly efficient, with its activity retained, whereas at pH 9.5, only a 30% retention was achieved [43].

The enhancement of protein encapsulation into 6.9 μm $CaCO_3$ microparticles using protein–polysaccharide interactions has been shown [50]. The chitin-binding domain (ChBD) was inserted into a β-lactamase protein (BlaP) to obtain a chimeric protein, BlaPChBD, exhibiting an affinity for hyaluronic acid (HA). In the presence of HA, the particle size was decreased to 4.5 μm, which indicated a templating effect of HA on $CaCO_3$. The chitin-binding domain (ChBD) ensured a more stable interaction between the protein and HA, reducing aggregation and decreasing the particle size. The use of supercritical CO_2 ($ScCO_2$) technology in the presence of HA ensured successful encapsulation of BlaPChBD in vaterite $CaCO_3$ microparticles, increasing protein encapsulation sixfold compared to BlaP alone. In addition, thrombin cleavage sites were introduced to facilitate protein release by protease cleavage, the release rate being increased from less than 20% to 87% within 36 h. The β-lactamase encapsulation rate was below 1%, apparently due to unfavorable electrostatic interactions at pH 6.5, and was slightly increased (to 1.2%) after the insertion of the chitin-binding domain. The use of HA significantly increased the encapsulation of BlaPChBD (to 6.27%) due to protein–polysaccharide interactions. The results demonstrate the efficacy of using HA for enhancing the encapsulation and controlled release of proteins in $CaCO_3$-based delivery systems, offering a promising approach to the development of biodegradable and targeted drug delivery systems.

2.2. Demonstration and Limitations

The loading of three therapeutic proteins (insulin, catalase, and aprotinin) into vaterite $CaCO_3$ cores has shown that the protein loading capacity is independent of their molecular weight and depends only on inter-protein interactions [44]. The tested proteins differ from one another in adsorption kinetics, which indicates differences in the adsorption mechanisms.

The efficiencies of loading catalase into $CaCO_3$ vaterite crystals by means of absorption into preformed crystals (ADS) and co-synthesis (COS) [51] have been compared. COS has been shown to be more efficient, as in the case of the loading of small molecules [18], with a protein content of 20.3% versus 3.5% loaded by the ADS method. The high loading capacity of COS, with a local protein concentration of about 550 mg/mL, was due to $CaCl_2$-induced inter-protein interactions resulting in aggregation. The adsorption isotherms better fitted the Langmuir and Brunauer–Emmett–Teller (BET) models than the Freundlich model, which indicated aggregation in solution followed by absorption of aggregates into the crystals. Furthermore, catalase was found to retain about 79% of its specific activity after ADS loading. The stability of the aggregates in the crystals was confirmed by the fact that catalase loaded by the COS method could not be effectively removed by a single washing, unlike catalase loaded by the ADS method. This study highlights the high potential of the COS method for loading large amounts of active proteins into $CaCO_3$ crystals, offering a new approach to the encapsulation of therapeutic proteins [51]. One of the main problems with vaterite $CaCO_3$ particles is their aggregation [25]. However, stabilizers, such as SDS, successfully overcome this problem [21].

The $CaCO_3$-based delivery systems are often designed to be pH-dependent. Calcium carbonate/hyaluronate/glutamate submicron hollow spheres loaded with doxorubicin (DOX) [52] released 59.97% of DOX within 14 days at pH 7.4, 87.89% at pH 6.0, and 99.15%

at pH 5.0, with a loading efficiency of 85%. Specific binding of these particles to cancer cells was provided by the ligand–receptor interaction between HA and CD44 receptors, overexpressed on cancer cells. The IC_{50} of DOX-loaded microspheres was much lower than that of free DOX when tested on HeLa cancer cells (Figure 2).

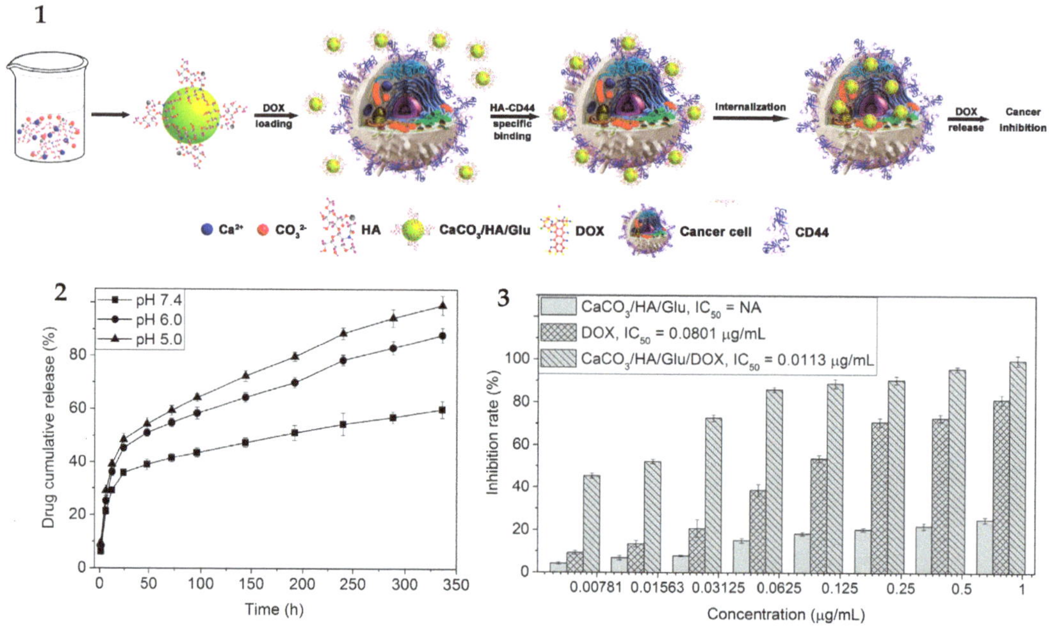

Figure 2. (**1**) Preparation of $CaCO_3$/HA/Glu MHSs, efficient loading of DOX, targeted delivery, specific internalization, and significant inhibition of cancer cells. (**2**) In vitro release profiles of $CaCO_3$/HA/Glu/DOX under different pH. Data represent the mean ± S.D.; n = 3. (**3**) Cytotoxic effects of free DOX, CaCO3/HA/Glu, and $CaCO^3$/HA/Glu/DOX on HeLa cells after 3 d treatment. Data represent the mean ± S.D.; n = 3. Abbreviations: HA, hyaluronate; Glu, glutamate; MHSs, mesoporous hollow spheres; DOX, doxorubicin. Adapted with permission from Guo, Y. et al., J. Coll. Interf. Sci.; published by Elsevier, 2017 [52].

Pneumolysin (PLY)-loaded $CaCO_3$ particles (0.95 μm) containing ovalbumin as a model antigen have been developed as a multimodal antigen delivery system for antitumor vaccines. OVA/$CaCO_3$/PLY nanoparticles obtained by physical adsorption of OVA and PLY on $CaCO_3$ promoted lysosomal degradation, cytoplasmic release, and cross-presentation of antigens, enhancing cellular immunity. The OVA/$CaCO_3$/PLY system induced efficient lysosomal leakage and cytoplasmic delivery of OVA in vitro [53].

The kinetics of drug release from the systems based on $CaCO_3$ cores is often bimodal, with initially rapid release due to the dissolution of aggregates followed by sustained release [54]. As the vaterite crystals destabilize, their morphology changes into the calcite one, making the release irreversible. The presence of aggregates within the matrix and the high loading rate by the co-synthesis method, especially for proteins, indicate the limitations of the application of the loading method by adsorption [51]. Nevertheless, other $CaCO_3$-based particle systems are being developed and exhibit a high efficiency in substance delivery. Table 1 summarizes the characteristics of the systems based on $CaCO_3$ cores as vehicles for the delivery of small molecules, proteins, DNAs, and radionuclides.

Table 1. The key characteristics and results obtained with the $CaCO_3$ core-only and $CaCO_3$-based core/shell microparticles and shell-only microcapsules.

Particle Type	Size	Cargo Type	Encapsulated Molecule	Results/Conclusions of the Cited Study	Shell Composition	Ref.
Core	1 µm	Small molecule	Doxorubicin	The IC50 value of doxorubicin for HeLa cancer cells is 0.0113 µg/mL, much lower than that of the free doxorubicin (0.0801 µg/mL).	Hyaluronate/glutamate	[52]
Core	0.6–3.2 µm	-	-	The thermal expansion of vaterite is reported for the first time; vaterite is not converted to calcite in the dilatometric test.	-	[6]
Core	0.43 µm	Fluorescent dye	Rhodamine 6G	Submicron vaterite containers enable controlled loading and release of active substances via calcite recrystallization in water.	-	[40]
Core	0.52 µm	-	-	The optimal salt concentrations, reaction time, and organic additives for ensuring controllable and reliable $CaCO_3$ particle design have been estimated.	-	[1]
Core	0.4–2.7 µm	-	-	Submicron vaterite particles have been synthesized by the drop precipitation method from saturated solutions of $NaCO_3$ and $CaCl_2$ in the presence of ethylene glycol with an EG-to-H_20 ratio of 4:1.	-	[7]
Core	n/a	Protein	BSA	Imaging the internal structure of functionalized $CaCO_3$ using FIB-SEM combined with MIP has distinguished between open, blocked, and drug-laden pores.	-	[41]
Core	17.9 µm	Small molecule	Ibuprofen, nifedipine, losartan potassium, and metronidazole benzoate	Drug loading by solvent evaporation is simple, fast, and efficient.	-	[48]
Core	3.1–23.5 µm	Small molecule	Aspirin, vanillin	The mechanism of adsorption of active ingredients onto functionalized $CaCO_3$ particles has been discovered, which could enable tailored loading without altering the efficacy of the ingredients when released.	-	[42]
Core	17.9 µm	Protein	Lysozyme, BSA	Functionalized $CaCO_3$ particles are a suitable pharmaceutical excipient for the delivery of proteins, such as lysozyme, with a loading efficiency of over 90%.	-	[49]
Core	3.4 µm	Protein	Superoxide dismutase	Superoxide dismutase (SOD) can be efficiently loaded into vaterite $CaCO_3$ crystals, with a content in the crystals as high as 380 mg/mL (10^{-2} M). SOD co-synthesis at pH 8.5 fully preserves SOD bioactivity.	-	[43]

Table 1. *Cont.*

Particle Type	Size	Cargo Type	Encapsulated Molecule	Results/Conclusions of the Cited Study	Shell Composition	Ref.
Core	10 µm	Protein	Catalase, insulin, aprotinin	The loading of three therapeutic proteins (250 kDa catalase, 5.8 kDa insulin, and 6.5 kDa aprotinin) into crystals of different porosities have shown that protein loading capacity depends solely on inter-protein interactions in the bulk solution in the presence of crystals and within the crystals.	-	[44]
Core	0.8–1.6 µm	Small molecule	Doxorubicin	Vaterite $CaCO_3$ crystals release drugs, the initial release as low as <10% within 24 h at pH 6. These vaterites exhibit prolonged drug release: ~40% over 8 days at pH 6.	-	[21]
Core	4–5 µm	Protein	Catalase	Extremely large capacity of loading by co-synthesis (~550 mg/mL) is explained by intermolecular protein interactions, i.e., formation of protein aggregates induced by $CaCl_2$ during co-synthesis.	-	[51]
Core	1 µm	Protein	Ovalbumin, pneumolysin	Multimodal delivery systems for $CaCO_3$/PLY antigens have been developed. OVA/$CaCO_3$/PLY vaccine formulations promote antigen cross-presentation, boost cellular and humoral immune responses, and offer promising preventive and therapeutic antitumor efficacy.	-	[53]
Core	5.45 µm	Protein	β-lactamase	β-Lactamase can associate with hyaluronic acid and be successfully loaded into vaterite $CaCO_3$ microparticles using the supercritical CO_2 technology aided by the templating effect of hyaluronic acid on $CaCO_3$.	-	[50]
Core	1.3 µm	-	-	Intravenous injection of $CaCO_3$ particles at a dose of 50 mg/kg significantly disrupted red blood cells but did not induce visible abnormalities in the tissue structures of key organs.	-	[55]
Core	4–7 µm	Radionuclide	^{224}Ra	^{224}Ra-labeled $CaCO_3$ microparticles are a promising agent for therapy against cancer dissemination in body cavities. A significant therapeutic effect has been obtained at specific activities from 0.4 to 4.6 kBq/mg.	-	[45]
Core	1–3, 3–15 µm	Radionuclide	^{224}Ra	^{224}Ra-labeled $CaCO_3$ microparticles remain in the peritoneal cavity, with a modest distribution of ^{224}Ra systemically, when administered at a relevant microparticle dose.	-	[46]

Table 1. *Cont.*

Particle Type	Size	Cargo Type	Encapsulated Molecule	Results/Conclusions of the Cited Study	Shell Composition	Ref.
Core	0.2–1.1 µm	Nucleic acid	DNA	$CaCO_3$/calcium phosphate (CaP)/DNA nanoparticles have a reduced size, better stability, and significantly higher gene transfection efficiency compared to $CaCO_3$/DNA and CaP/DNA ones.	-	[34]
Core/shell	2 µm	Small molecule	Doxorubicin	Doxorubicin has been loaded into $CaCO_3$ microparticles coated with poly-L-ornithine/fucoidan with a loading efficiency as high as 69.7%. Controlled release of doxorubicin significantly inhibits the proliferation of breast cancer cells.	Poly-L-ornithine/fucoidan	[56]
Core/shell	0.2 µm	Small molecule	Doxorubicin	PEG/oleic acid–amorphous calcium carbonate improves the stability of $CaCO_3$-core microparticles in aqueous media and controls drug release in cancer cells, thereby achieving an anticancer efficacy comparable to that of free drugs.	Oleic acid/PEG	[57]
Core/shell	3 µm	Small molecule	Doxorubicin	$CaCO_3$ microparticles loaded with herbal medicinal products exhibit excellent biocompatibility and pH sensitivity, which demonstrates their potential as effective drug carriers.	PDDA/PSS	[58]
Core/shell	~10 µm	Protein	Ovalbumin, cancer cell lysate	$CaCO_3$ microparticles are capable of delivering vaccines to cancer cell lysates and exhibit lower cytotoxicity and greatly enhanced cellular uptake leading to improved cross-presentation efficiency.	Poly(HPMA-APMA) with TLR7/8 agonists	[59]
Core/shell	0.65, 3.2 µm	Radionuclide	^{225}Ac	$CaCO_3$ core-shell particles effectively retain large amounts of ^{225}Ac and its daughter isotopes (^{221}Fr and ^{213}Bi). The kidney accumulation of ^{213}Bi after administration of ^{225}Ac encapsulated in $CaCO_3$ core/shell particles was low, unlike with non-encapsulated ^{225}Ac.	HSA/TA	[60]
Core/shell	~2 µm	Protein	BSA	A $CaCO_3$-to-pneumolysin (PLA) mass ratio of 0.8 is optimal in terms of a large protein payload of the microparticles and their stability against dissolution. Bioactive cargos remain intact in pores of PLA-coated $CaCO_3$ microparticles.	PLA	[61]
Core/shell	2–4 µm	Fluorescent dye	Nile Red, rhodamine 110	Oil-in-water emulsion droplets and phospholipid bilayer liposomes have been coated with $CaCO_3$ to obtain core/shell particles accommodating both hydrophobic and hydrophilic active agents.	$CaCO_3$	[62]

Table 1. *Cont.*

Particle Type	Size	Cargo Type	Encapsulated Molecule	Results/Conclusions of the Cited Study	Shell Composition	Ref.
Core/shell, shell	2–2.5 μm	Small molecule	Doxorubicin	Doxorubicin can be effectively incorporated into $CaCO_3$ microbeads via co-precipitation during their synthesis and into polymer microcapsules via spontaneous loading in an alkaline medium with a Cl^- counterion.	PAH/PSS/QD	[18]
Shell	4.75 μm	Protein	Lactalbumine, lysozyme, horseradish peroxidase, chymotrypsin	A new method of protein encapsulation by adsorption into microcapsules obtained through layer-by-layer deposition onto $CaCO_3$ cores has been proposed.	-	[39]
Shell	5.4 μm	-	-	Calcium, cadmium, and manganese carbonate crystals have been used as core materials to fabricate hollow polyelectrolyte capsules using layer-by-layer assembly.	PAH/PSS	[63]
Shell	9 μm	-	-	The structure–property relationships have been evaluated for 16 types of capsules made of different biopolymers and the mechanism of capsule formation has been inferred.	PLL, PR, DA, COL/HA, CS, DS, HS	[15]
Shell	3–6 μm	Protein	Insulin	Insulin is released from the microcapsules faster at pH 9.0 and 7.4 than in acidic solutions due to the difference in PAH charge density.	PAH/PSS, PVS, DS	[20]
Shell	5 μm	Fluorescent dye	FITC-dextran	Hyaluronic acid (HA)/poly(L-lysine (PLL) and HA/poly(allylamine) (PAH) capsules are rapidly internalized into endo-/lysosomatic vesicles upon addition to a macrophage culture.	HA/PAH, PLL	[64]
Shell	3 μm	Fluorescent dye	FITC-dextran	Polyelectrolyte capsules containing an enzymatically or hydrolytically degradable polycation degrade spontaneously in VERO-1 cells.	pARG/DS, p(HPMA-DMAE)/PSS, PAH/PSS	[65]
Shell	~1 μm	Fluorescent dye, protein	Rhodamine B, methylene blue, insulin	Polysaccharide-based glucose-receptive capsules have been made reactive to glucose by attaching a phenylboronic moiety to alginate.	Phenylboronic –modified alginate/PVPON	[66]
Shell	1.8–3.8 μm	-	-	Polyarginine/dextran sulfate (pArg/DS) capsules shrink and densify when heated, with their thermal response unaffected by the initial size, number of layers, or layer sequence.	pArg/DS	[67]

Table 1. *Cont.*

Particle Type	Size	Cargo Type	Encapsulated Molecule	Results/Conclusions of the Cited Study	Shell Composition	Ref.
Shell	0.5 μm	Small molecule	Doxorubicin	Capsules loaded with doxorubicin and modified with DR5 are 2–3 times more cytotoxic than the capsules without doxorubicin.	pArg/DS	[32]
Shell	3–5 μm	Extract	*Gratiola officinalis* extract	Encapsulated extract kills 100% of SKBR-3 breast cancer cells and 34% of HeLa cervical cancer cells.	PAH/PSS/DS	[68]
Shell	4 μm	Small molecule	Apigenin, ascorbic acid	The encapsulation efficiency is 20% for both apigenin and ascorbic acid. The release rate is 32–35% within 2 h at physiological pH.	PAH/DS	[69]
Shell	0.25–0.5 μm	Small molecule	Gemcitabine, clodronate	Gemcitabine and clodronate encapsulated in biodegradable polymer multilayer capsules effectively target lung cancer.	pArg/DS	[70]
Shell	3.3–4.8 μm	Protein	BSA, chymotrypsin, lysozyme	α-Chymotrypsin retains ~85% of its original enzymatic activity upon encapsulation.	PAH/PSS	[71]
Shell	5.0–8.3 μm	Small molecule	Tetracycline hydrochloride	Polymer microcapsules have a pectin loading capacity greater than 220 mg/g.	PAH/pectin	[72]
Shell	5.0 μm	Cells	*Escherichia coli*	After encapsulation, ~40% of the cells remain alive.	PAH/PSS	[73]
Shell	4.5 μm	Small molecule	Doxorubicin, nimbin	The IC_{50} for THP-1 cells are 75 and 1.8 μM for nimbin and doxorubicin, respectively. Release of the drugs is remotely activated by NIR laser irradiation.	PAH/PMA/NR	[74]
Shell	5.0 μm	Small molecule	Vitamin B12	Nanoengineered polymer capsules and soft lipid nanovectors are effective carriers for vitamin B_{12}.	PAH/PSS	[75]
Shell	5.0 μm	Protein	BSA	A high concentration of NaCl causes considerable dissociation of poly(allylamine) (PAH), apparently due to the action of ionic force.	PAH/PSS	[76]
Shell	4.2–6.3 μm	-	-	A method of surface activation of microcapsules containing the monoclonal antibody trastuzumab has been developed.	PAH/PSS/QD	[36]
Shell	3–4 μm	Protein	Ovalbumin, horseradish peroxidase	Lyophilized microcapsules are candidate adjuvants for antigen delivery; higher immune activation in both in vitro and in vivo assays compared to free antigen has been shown.	pArg/DS	[77]
Shell	3 μm	Nucleic acid	G-quadruplex DNA, double stranded DNA	Poly(methacrylic acid)/poly(N-vinylpyrrolidone) $(PMAA/PVPON)_n$ multilayer hydrogel capsules can encapsulate and release ~450 kDa double-stranded DNA.	PMA/PVPON	[29]

Table 1. *Cont.*

Particle Type	Size	Cargo Type	Encapsulated Molecule	Results/Conclusions of the Cited Study	Shell Composition	Ref.
Shell	0.65, 3.3 μm	Nucleic acid	mRNA, siRNA	Submicrometer-sized polymer capsules are more efficient in transferring siRNA than micrometer-sized ones used for eGFP mRNA transport.	pArg/DS	[78]
Shell	~3 μm	Nucleic acid	mRNA, pDNA, plasmid	Microcarriers mediate more efficient transfection than a commercially available liposome-based transfection reagent (>70% vs. <50% for mRNA, >40% vs. 20% for plasmid DNA).	pArg/DS/SiO_2	[79]
Shell	1–4 μm	Fluorescent dye	Tetramethylrhodamine dextran	Among the four types of DNA capsules studied, the smallest ones with the most integral DNA envelope exhibit the lowest leakage, highest affinity for ATP, and better kinetics and trigger sensitivity.	PAH/DNA	[80]
Shell	2.84 μm	Labeled protein	BSA-Cy7	The localization efficiency of the fluorescent dye in the target kidney after intra-arterial administration is 9 times higher than that in the other kidney and after intravenous injection. After 24 h, no microcapsules are observed in the target kidney.	pArg/DS	[81]
Shell	3–5 μm	Small molecule	Doxorubicin	Microcapsules intensely concentrate positively charged doxorubicin, subsequently releasing it in a controlled manner to effectively induce apoptosis of HepG2 tumor cells.	Chitosan/alginate	[82]
Shell	3–6 μm	Labeled protein	FITC-BSA	Substantially more BSA is loaded at pH 3.8 than at pH 5.0 (i.e., the pI of BSA), and the release of BSA is faster at a higher pH.	PLL/CS	[83]

3. CaCO$_3$-Based Core/Shell Systems

3.1. Methods of Fabrication

The CaCO$_3$ particles coated with a polyelectrolyte shell are better suited for the delivery of drugs and proteins. Polyelectrolytes are deposited onto the cores by the LbL method [63,84] or by electrospray [85]. Variation of the number of cationic/anionic bilayers deposited on the particle surface allows better control of the kinetics of substance delivery to the target. Application of these polymers is driven by electrostatic interaction, through covalent or hydrogen bonds, which explains how the release of loaded molecules can be induced by different stimuli, such as pH, ionic strength, temperature change, or ultrasound.

For the encapsulation of therapeutic agents, adsorption or co-synthesis can be used, and the choice of method determines their location: on the surface, between the layers, or within the matrix. Figure 3 summarizes the data on the fabrication of CaCO$_3$ core-only and core/shell microparticles.

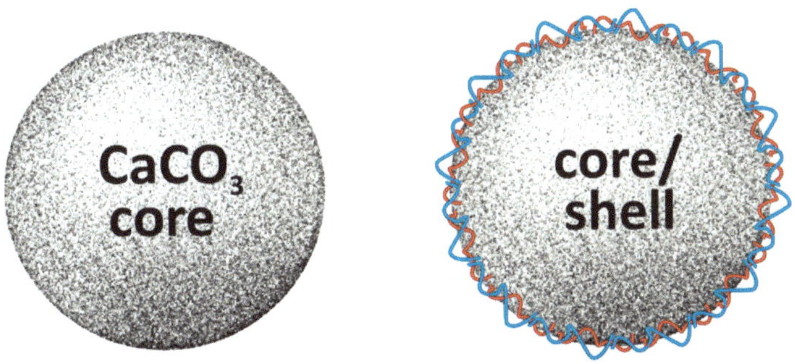

Figure 3. Summary of data on fabrication of porous CaCO$_3$ core-only and CaCO$_3$ core/shell microparticles. **On the left:** the pore size diameters for differently fabricated CaCO$_3$ cores are shown to be in the range of 2–50 nm [21], 5–30 nm [43], 10–60 nm [44] or 20–500 nm [49]. **On the right:** the shells on the CaCO$_3$ cores may be fabricated by the deposition of different polymers such as poly-L-ornithine/fucoidan [56]; poly(ethylene glycol)/oleic acid [57]; hyaluronic acid/glutamate [52]; hyaluronic acid/tannic acid [60]; ovalbumin/platelet lysate [53]; poly(diallyldimethylammonium chloride)/poly(sodium 4-styrenesulfonate) [58]; hyaluronic acid [50]; polylactic acid [61]; poly(acrylic acid) [62].

3.2. Delivery of Small Molecules

In the development of systems for small-molecule delivery based on microparticles, DOX is often used as a model anticancer drug. Efficient loading of DOX has been shown for core/shell microparticles composed of ~2 µm CaCO$_3$ cores coated with poly-L-ornithine and fucoidan. The release of DOX from these particles was confirmed by a significant antiproliferative effect on MCF-7 breast cancer cells [56]. DOX-loaded CaCO$_3$ microparticles modified with oleic acid (OA) and polyethylene glycol (PEG) exhibited a 70% drug release within 2 h in cancer cells in response to their specific environment, whereas their stability and drug retention in various other aqueous media were enhanced. Hybrid CaCO$_3$ microspheres have also been obtained using yeast cells as the organic matrix and the polyelectrolytes poly(diallyldimethylammonium chloride) (PDDA) and sodium poly(styrene sulfonate) (PSS) as shell components, with subsequent calcination and DOX loading [58]. Drug release tests showed an accelerated release of DOX in an acidic environment (pH 4.8) typical of cancer tissues compared with a neutral medium (pH 7). Cytotoxicity tests have shown a good biocompatibility of CaCO$_3$ microparticles 3 µm in diameter loaded with herbal medicinal products (HMPs) (Figure 4). Gradual decomposition of the coated particles in the acidic microenvironment of tumors ensures the targeted release of the drug directly into the cancer cells, thereby improving the efficacy of the treatment and minimizing the side effects on the surrounding healthy tissue. Thus, the feasibility of the delivery of small molecules using the core/shell system has been demonstrated.

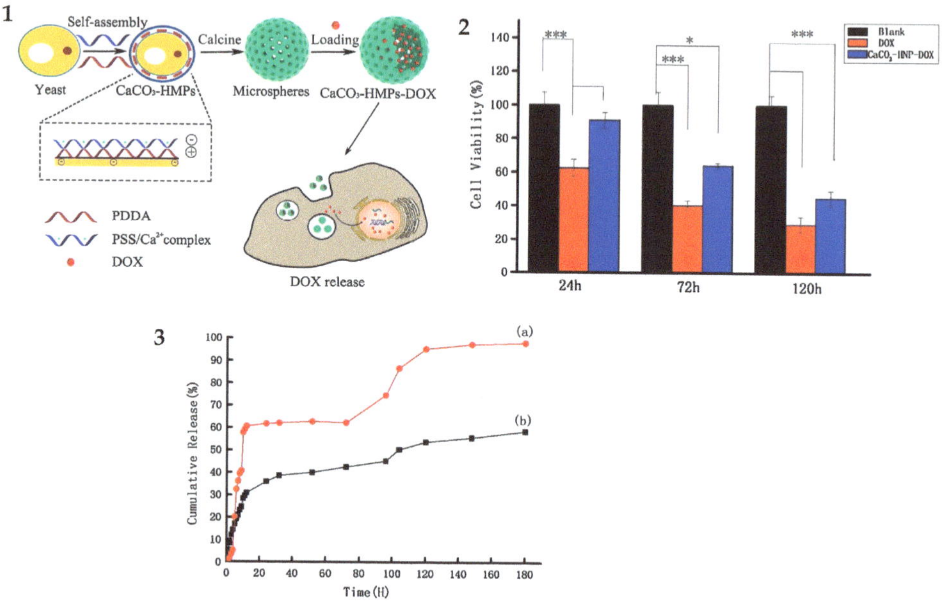

Figure 4. (**1**) Assembly schematic: the preparation of $CaCO_3$-HMPs through self-assembly of two oppositely charged polyelectrolytes, PDDA and PSS, on the surface of yeast cells, as dual templates for drug loading and release. (**2**) Cytotoxicity tests of $CaCO_3$-HMPs, DOX, and the $CaCO_3$-HMPs-DOX drug-delivery system (* $p < 0.05$, *** $p < 0.001$); (**3**) Cumulative release curve of DOX in different environments: (a) pH = 4.8 and (b) pH = 7. Abbreviations: HMPs, herbal medicinal products; PDDA, poly(diallyldimethylammonium chloride); PSS, poly(sodium 4-styrenesulfonate); DOX, doxorubicin. Reproduced with permission from Wei, Y., et al. Coll. Surf. B Biointerf.; published by Elsevier, 2021 [58].

3.3. Delivery of Proteins

Calcium carbonate microparticles containing cancer cell lysate and coated with polymer substituted with the low-molecular-weight TLR7/8 agonist have been developed, which could serve as novel personalized anticancer vaccines [62].

The solid-in-oil-in-water emulsion method for the manufacture of $CaCO_3$/polylactic acid core/shell microparticles about 1.11 μm in size has been designed as a tool for the controlled transport and release of water-soluble bioactive molecules. This technology could be used for developing more effective drug delivery systems [61].

The biomimetic approach has been used to obtain core/shell microparticles with a liquid core consisting of charged emulsion droplets or liposomes and a $CaCO_3$ shell, which can also be used as delivery vehicles [62].

Overall, these techniques improve the encapsulation and release of proteins, offering promising advances for drug delivery systems.

3.4. Delivery of Nucleic Acids

Although encapsulation of nucleic acids in core/shell systems has not yet been reported, some studies envisage it. For example, Bewernitz et al. [62] explore the manufacture of liquid-core/solid-shell microcapsules representing $CaCO_3$-coated emulsions and liposomes. These microcapsules, ranging in size from 2 to 10 μm, have been designed for potential applications in the controlled release of substances, including DNA molecules.

The method relies on the precipitation of $CaCO_3$ to form a shell around emulsion droplets or liposomes. This approach could be used to engineer a promising system for the protection and targeted delivery and release of DNA in biomedical applications due to the possibility of controlling the permeability and degradation of the $CaCO_3$ shell.

Applications of $CaCO_3$ core-based core/shell microparticles are summarized in Table 1.

4. $CaCO_3$-Based Hollow Microcapsules

4.1. Methods of Fabrication

Calcium carbonate-based hollow (or shell) microcapsules represent a fascinating area of research in medical nanotechnology, providing unique opportunities for targeted cancer treatment [29]. These microcapsules with encapsulated therapeutic agents are often designed to interact directly with tumors by functionalization of their surface with antibodies, peptides, proteins, hyaluronic acid, or nucleic acids to ensure controlled, targeted drug delivery [86].

The fabrication of these microcarriers is based on the LbL assembly of polyelectrolytes, a technique first tested on metformin particles [24], which allows the construction of multilayer films with nanometric precision by alternating the immersion of a substrate in solutions of polyelectrolytes of opposite charges. $CaCO_3$ cores, whose synthesis was considered above, are used as templates for the fabrication of microcapsules. Then, the cores are dissolved with a chelating agent, e.g., EDTA, and washed, and hollow spherical polyelectrolyte capsules are thus formed. Polyelectrolytes in different combinations, such as poly(allylamine hydrochloride) (PAH) and PSS [18,87], PAH and poly(vinyl sulfate) (PVS) [20], chitosan (Chi) and alginate (Alg) [82], HA and PAH/poly-L-lysine (PLL) [64], and poly-L-arginine (pArg) and dextran sulfate (DS) [65], are particularly effective in forming these multilayers on vaterite $CaCO_3$ cores. Detailed comparison of the stabilities, shrinkabilities, and internal structures of capsules made of different biopolymers have been performed [15]. These polymers, selected for their capability for self-assembling, ensure high stability and functionality of the microcapsules, making it possible to modulate their properties, such as solubility, reactivity, and biological compatibility, for the purposes of biomedical engineering and formation of protective coatings and sensors [88]. Figure 5 summarizes the methods for obtaining shell microcapsules.

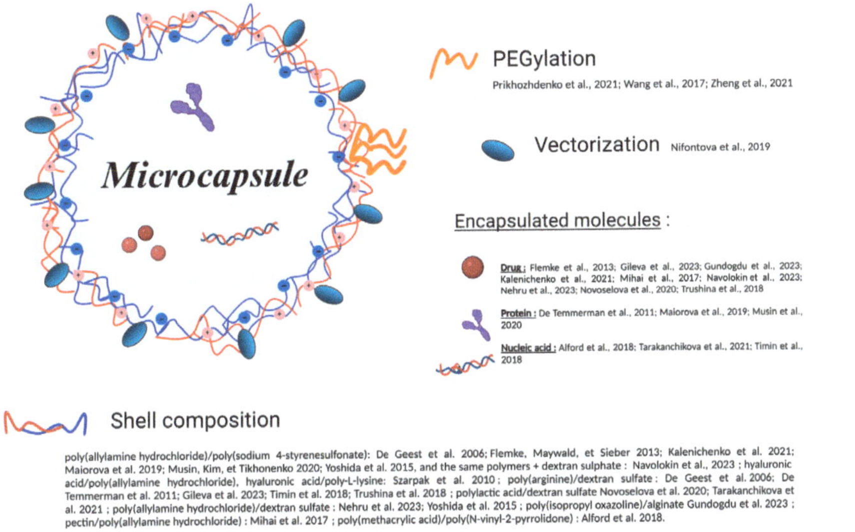

Figure 5. Summary of data on fabrication of microcapsules initially based on the $CaCO_3$ microparticles [18,20,22,29,32,36,57,64,65,67–70,72,73,75–79,81,89].

4.2. Delivery of Small Molecules

The capability of multilayered polyelectrolyte capsules to host low-molecular-weight drugs for cancer targeting has been recently demonstrated [30]. These smart polymer capsules exhibit considerable versatility, paving the way for future developments in medical nanotechnology and personalized medicine [66]. In recent years, uniformly sized microcapsules obtained on the basis of $CaCO_3$ cores as removable templates, have been loaded with gemcitabine and clodronate [70], DOX [18], apigenin and ascorbic acid [69], curcumin and ciprofloxacin [22], and *Gratiola officinalis* extract [68] as model drugs for cancer and other diseases.

Different encapsulation approaches are used with small-molecule drugs. Microcapsules fabricated using the PAH and PSS polyelectrolytes on $CaCO_3$ cores have exhibited efficiencies of DOX loading by co-precipitation and spontaneous loading of about 73 and 65%, respectively, due to optimized pH and salt concentration [18]. PAH/dextran sulfate (DS) polymer microcapsules designed for the delivery of apigenin and ascorbic acid exhibited a loading efficiency of about 20% for each substance after incubation of the microcapsules in the presence of the drugs [69]. The gemcitabine loading efficiency of submicron pArg/DS microcapsules was about 47% [70].

The microcapsules are designed so as to release the loaded drugs in response to specific stimuli. In the case of PAH/DS capsules containing apigenin and ascorbic acid, in vitro release was 45% and 40%, respectively, after 2 h at the physiological pH [69]. This study has also shown that the chemical composition of the capsules strongly affects the drug solubility and rate of its release. The release of DOX by diffusion from PAH/PSS microcapsules was prolonged at pH 6.0 and 7.4, corresponding to the pH values in tumor and normal tissues, respectively. The cumulative release of DOX within 48 h did not exceed 70% [18].

In in vitro experiments, pArg/DS microcapsules loaded with gemcitabine were internalized at a rate higher than 75% by macrophages and lung and liver epithelial cells [70]. Experiments in mouse models showed the specificity of microcapsule delivery: they were better retained by lung tumor than by healthy lung tissue. The efficiency of encapsulated gemcitabine estimated by the MTT assay was lower than that of the free drug after 24 and 48 h of incubation and equal to it after 72 h of incubation, which confirmed the prolonged, gradual release of the drug (Figure 6).

Microcapsules are commonly developed to reduce the side effects of drugs and to allow a more prolonged and targeted action of, e.g., DOX, thereby improving the efficacy of the treatment. It can be co-administered, thus compensating for the rapidity of elimination from the body [32]. Also, the microcapsules containing *Gratiola officinalis* extract were shown to effectively release the drug, causing the death of 100% of cultured cancer cells through overcoming protective autophagy [68].

Hollow polymeric microcapsules are also used for the encapsulation of live *E. coli* cells. $CaCO_3$ cores containing *E. coli* cells were obtained by co-precipitation and coated with different polyelectrolytes. Then, $CaCO_3$ cores were dissolved in EDTA to obtain capsules with a size of about 5 μm. Encapsulation reduced cell viability, the effect being mainly accounted for PAH, with only minor contributions from the other components. The encapsulated cells exhibited a prolonged lag phase of growth while retaining the ability to produce green fluorescent protein. About 40% of cells were alive after the encapsulation. This method has potential applications in the high-throughput screening of biocatalyst libraries, requiring optimization to improve cell survival [73].

Composite microcapsules based on $CaCO_3$ have been developed that contain various types of pectin with different degrees of methylation and amide content, as well as mixtures of polyelectrolyte complexes, including poly(allylamine) hydrochloride. These $CaCO_3$/pectin capsules were used as matrices for the loading of tetracycline hydrochloride (TCH), with analysis of drug release kinetics using the Higuchi and Korsmeyer–Peppas models. In vitro assays demonstrated the influence of $CaCO_3$ polymorphs on the drug release process, with 22–27% of TCH released within 10 h at pH 7.4 [72].

The potential of using $CaCO_3$-templated PAH/PSS polymer capsules for the targeted delivery of vitamin B12 has also been demonstrated [75]. The successful encapsulation of vitamin B12 was confirmed by optical absorption spectroscopy, transmission electron microscopy, and atomic force microscopy data. Experimental data on the specific encapsulation capacity of these polymer capsules for vitamin B12 show their potential as targeted vectors for nutrient delivery, highlighting the effectiveness of the PAH/PSS system in developing biocompatible and stable drug-delivery vectors.

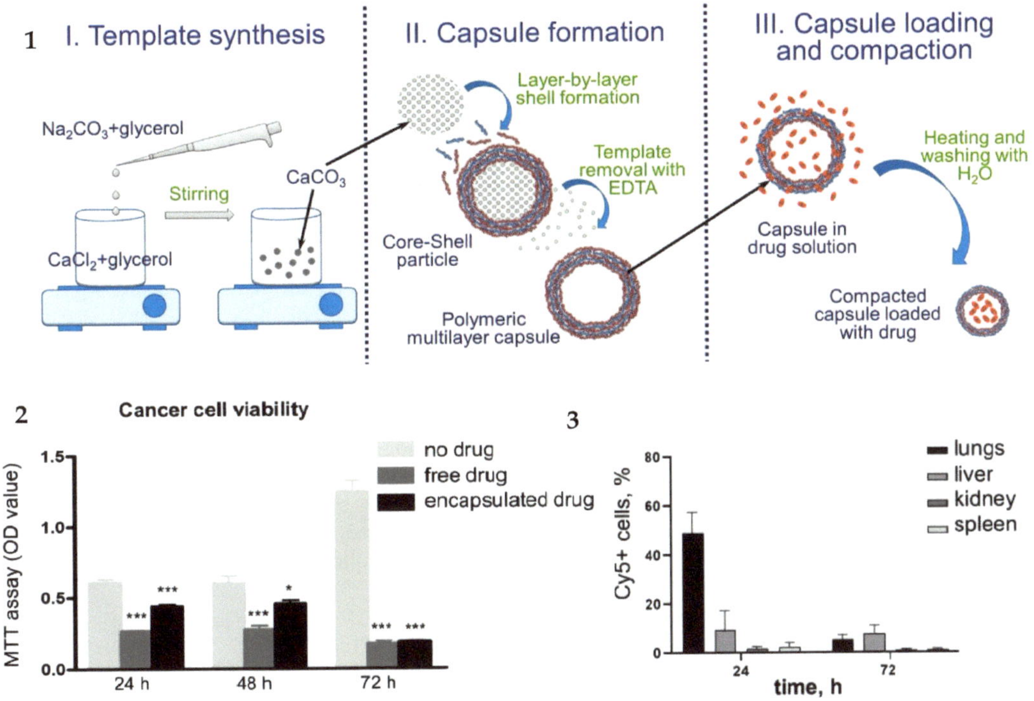

Figure 6. (**1**) Scheme of the stepwise capsule assembly, compaction, and loading. (**2**) Lung cancer cell viability in the presence of 20 μM free or encapsulated gemcitabine; MTT assay at the indicated time points. (**3**) Number of cells in the lungs, liver, kidney, and spleen with internalized Cy5-labeled capsules relative to the total amount of cells in the respective organs 24 and 72 h after intravenous injection of PMC. Abbreviation: PMC, polymeric multilayer capsules. Adapted with permission from Novoselova, M. V., et al. ACS Appl. Mater. Interfaces; published by American Chemical Society, 2020 [70].

4.3. Delivery of Proteins

Proteins can also be transported and released by polyelectrolyte capsule systems assembled on $CaCO_3$ cores [90]. The chemical methods for the fabrication and post-modification of hollow polymer capsules for protein delivery, including covalent bonding, electrostatic attachment, and hydrogen bonding, have been described [91]. Proteins can be encapsulated by physical adsorption on preformed $CaCO_3$ cores or by co-precipitation during the $CaCO_3$ particle synthesis. The latter approach has been shown to be five times more efficient [71]. Horseradish peroxidase (HRP) and ovalbumin serving as model antigens have been encapsulated in $CaCO_3$-based pArg/DS polymer capsules by co-precipitation. After lyophilization in the presence of polyols, HRP retained up to 70% of its enzymatic activity. Ovalbumin-loaded microcapsules were used as a model vaccine formulation. Ovalbumin encapsulated in polyelectrolyte microcapsules caused enhanced antigen presentation and amplification of T-cell proliferation compared to soluble ovalbumin. The immunological activity of lyophilized microcapsules was preserved according to the results of in vitro T-cell proliferation assay [77].

The effect of pH on the degradation of polyelectrolyte microcapsules formed on $CaCO_3$ particles with proteins encapsulated by adsorption was also studied [76]. An increase in pH led to an increase in protein yield and PAH detachment, apparently because the acidity of the medium (pH 7) was close to the charge exchange point of the PAH amino group. A high concentration of NaCl (2 M) caused considerable PAH dissociation and release of the protein.

4.4. Delivery of Nucleic Acids

Studies using polymeric capsules for delivering genetic material into cells are also carried out. $CaCO_3$-based microcapsules made from biodegradable biopolymers were used for the delivery of all CRISPR-Cas9 components to cells [79]. The efficiency of transfection indicated by a loss of red fluorescence in dTomato-expressing HEK293T reached 70%. Submicro- and microcapsules with pArg/DS shells were successfully used as carriers for messenger RNA (mRNA) and small interfering RNA (siRNA) [78]. This study demonstrated that the package efficiency of RNA molecules, delivery efficiency, and biodistribution strongly depended on the size of the capsules. Both studies highlight the importance of developing safe and effective delivery systems for gene therapy and genome editing. The use of microcarriers offers a promising alternative to viral vectors, reducing the associated risks and potentially enhancing the clinical acceptance of these technologies. The delivery systems based on microcapsules are summarized in Table 1.

Finally, the use of $CaCO_3$-based microcapsules in various medical applications, especially in immunotherapy and targeted cancer treatment, appears a promising approach. Ongoing research and innovations in this field could transform cancer treatment, offering more effective and less invasive solutions, notably through the release of small molecules, proteins, and nucleic acids encapsulated in these polyelectrolyte capsules by physical absorption or co-precipitation, thus marking a significant evolution in therapeutic strategies.

5. Conclusions

$CaCO_3$ microparticles are promising tools for anticancer therapy for several reasons: they are capable of incorporating a wide spectrum of active substances, both low-molecular-weight ones and biological macromolecules, and their size and pH sensitivity can be varied, which is advantageous for the controlled delivery of drugs, including gene therapy agents. Of special importance for targeted cancer therapy is the enhanced permeability and retention (EPR) effect of $CaCO_3$ microparticles ensuring their ready penetration into tumors and subsequent degradation and release of the loaded agent in the acidic microenvironment characteristic of malignant tumors [92,93]. $CaCO_3$ particles have been shown to cause the reprogramming of cancer cells and inhibition of tumor growth [5].

$CaCO_3$ submicro- and microparticles have considerable potential as vectors for targeted drug delivery, particularly in cancer treatment. Their controlled dissolution depending on pH ensures targeted drug release in the acidic areas of tumors while maintaining stability in the more neutral circulatory system. Different configurations of the delivery system, core-only and core/shell microparticles and microcapsules, offer solutions for the transport and controlled release of various therapeutic substances, including small molecules, proteins, and nucleic acids. Other materials have been studied in this respect, including metformin, manganese carbonate ($MnCO_3$), and cadmium carbonate ($CdCO_3$). However, metformin is insufficiently biocompatible, and both $MnCO_3$ and $CdCO_3$ microparticles are considerably smoother than $CaCO_3$ ones and may be toxic. In contrast, $CaCO_3$ microparticles are highly biocompatible, the roughness and porosity of their surface enabling adhesion of polymer layers to form a thick shell. For example, a $(PAH/PSS)_4$ is about two times thicker than the shells that can be deposited onto $MnCO_3$ and $CdCO_3$

cores, with polymer layers formed not only over the particle, but also on the inner surface of the pores [63].

Vaterite $CaCO_3$ cores are effective for loading small molecules through techniques such as co-precipitation, allowing for their subsequent controlled release. However, their rapid degradation in vivo can lead to premature release and disrupt the cellular calcium balance. To address this issue, core/shell particles have been developed, where the $CaCO_3$ core is coated with a shell of polyelectrolytes, which regulates its degradation, thus allowing sustained and controlled drug release while minimizing cell damage. This system can also be modified to specifically target cells or tissues, improving therapeutic efficacy and reducing side effects.

Finally, $CaCO_3$-based polyelectrolyte capsules overcome the issues entailed with $CaCO_3$ particles. Removal of the core through calcium chelation limits the destabilization of the tumor microenvironment by the increase in intracellular Ca^{2+} and ultimately controlling the pH. The capsules are particularly promising for the encapsulation and controlled release of small molecules, nucleic acids, and proteins, due to their ability to degrade under specific intracellular conditions. Although the delivery of biomacromolecular therapeutic agents presents a huge challenge compared to the delivery of small molecules due to both their high molecular weight and fragile structure, these problems can be solved by using polymer delivery systems [94]. In summary, $CaCO_3$-based particles offer a versatile platform for more effective therapeutic treatments, particularly for complex diseases, such as cancer, due to their adaptability and capability for targeted and controlled drug delivery and release.

6. Outlook: In Vivo Studies

6.1. Modulation of the pH of Tumor Environment

Submicron $CaCO_3$ particles offer a promising tool to counteract the characteristic acidity of tumors, a known factor in promoting their aggressiveness and metastatic potential. The targeting of tumors with 20 to 300 nm calcium carbonate particles allows for the gradual increase of the tumor pH to neutrality. This pH modulation is crucial, because a less acidic environment can inhibit the growth and spread of cancer cells, thereby reducing their virulence. Particularly, 100 nm particles stand out for their ability to sustain a prolonged pH elevation. This highlights the importance of particle size optimization in maximizing the treatment efficacy. Tests on animal models have shown a significant reduction of tumor growth, attesting to the therapeutic potential of this method. However, further research is required to optimize the dosage, evaluate the synergy with other treatments, and predict side effects. This advancement shows a way for improving cancer treatment strategies by targeting a fundamental aspect of tumor biology [95].

6.2. Biodistribution and Biocompatibility

The in vivo biodistribution of capsules is a major issue for the development of safe and effective drug carriers. Fluorescent $CaCO_3$-based pArg/DS capsules have been developed for kidney targeting via the renal artery [81]. The high efficiency of delivery to the area of interest was provided by the optimization of the administration protocol and dosage.

6.3. Retention, Stability, and Toxicity

$CaCO_3$ particles labeled with ^{224}Ra were proposed for the local therapy of disseminated tumors using intraperitoneal administration [46]. The results showed a targeted localization of microparticles, with moderate systemic payload release. Biodistribution studies showed that radioactivity was primarily localized in the peritoneal area after administration, with the highest activity associated with intraperitoneal adipose tissue and the parietal peritoneum. The release of ^{224}Ra from the particles was relatively limited, as evidenced by reduced absorption in the skeleton compared to the administration of free ^{224}Ra. Non-abdominal organs, such as the heart, muscles, and brain, displayed radioactivity levels below 100 Bq/g, which indicated a limited radiation exposure outside the abdominal area. These results indicate that radiolabeled $CaCO_3$ particles possess a high retention capacity and targeted bioavailability, making them potentially useful for targeted medical applications, minimizing non-target tissue exposure to radiation. The antitumor effect of $CaCO_3$ microparticles labeled with the alpha-emitting ^{224}Ra was shown in mice [45]. This study highlights the advantage of using $CaCO_3$ as a carrier of therapeutic agents and shows a particularly promising therapeutic strategy for tumors located in the abdominal cavity.

$CaCO_3$ core/shell particles 0.8 μm in size were used for the encapsulation of the alpha-emitting ^{225}Ac in order to enhance its retention and reduce systemic toxicity during alpha therapy [60]. The study showed a 93–94% retention of ^{225}Ac after 20 days, with the majority of ^{225}Ac microparticles localized in the lungs, which indicated a reduced renal toxicity potential. In vivo tests on Wistar rats confirmed the high retention efficiency of the particles, underscoring the effectiveness of ^{225}Ac-doped core/shell particles in safely retaining alpha emitters used for cancer treatment.

The wide potential applications of $CaCO_3$ nanoparticles in various sectors, including medicine, calls for a thorough evaluation of their toxicity. In vitro experiments on NIH 3T3 and MCF7 cells treated with $CaCO_3$ nanoparticles at different concentrations (1–50 μg/mL) for 12 to 72 h showed no cytotoxicity, oxidative stress, or DNA damage, indicating excellent biocompatibility. In vivo studies with zebrafish treated with $CaCO_3$ nanoparticles at doses as high as 200 μg/mL showed an absence of significant toxic effects on embryonic development. These results underscore the safety of $CaCO_3$ nanoparticles, suggesting their applicability in medicine and other fields, without cytotoxic or genotoxic risks to biological systems [96].

Various administration routes have been used for submicrometer- and micrometer-sized $CaCO_3$ microparticles, including intranasal [97,98], inhalatory [99], and transdermal [100] ones. The efficiency of drug delivery to the brain by $CaCO_3$ carriers administered intranasally has been demonstrated by in vivo functional tests [97]. Submicron (0.65 μm) $CaCO_3$-based particles administered by inhalation exhibited the highest efficiency of delivery to the blood and the respiratory part of the lung [99]. The transdermal administration of $CaCO_3$-based particles has also been tested. Prolonged drug release and the possibility of both targeted and systemic delivery have been demonstrated [100].

6.4. Vaccinal Applications

$CaCO_3$ microparticles are better than currently used vaccine delivery vehicles, including liposomes, synthetic copolymer systems, and metal nanoparticles, in several respects. Applications of liposomes for vaccine delivery are being developed, some of them being already available. However, their use is seriously limited because liposomes are prone to aggregation, premature vaccine release, and collapse under the conditions encountered in vivo. They sometimes poorly penetrate through biological membranes, and liposomes consisting of positively charged lipids may be toxic [101,102].

In addition, the production of liposome drug delivery systems is much more expensive than the production of conventional drugs: the production cost of 1 g of $CaCO_3$ is estimated to be as small as $0.2–0.4, whereas the production of 1 g of liposomes costs over $100 [103]. Therefore, alternative vaccine delivery tools are needed. Mineral microparticles, in particular, calcium carbonate beads, are more stable, biocompatible, and/or biodegradable and are less expensive to produce [103].

Recent studies illustrate the innovative use of vaccines in anticancer immunotherapy, highlighting the in vivo efficacy of formulations based on submicron- and micron-sized $CaCO_3$ particles. The physical adsorption of an antigen (ovalbumin) into $CaCO_3$ particles with adsorbed pneumolysin, the key virulence factor of *Streptococcus pneumoniae*, significantly amplified cellular and humoral immunity, demonstrating preventive and therapeutic antitumor efficacy [53]. The 0.95 μm $CaCO_3$ particles degraded into Ca^{2+} and CO_2 in the acidic lysosomal environment, promoting cross-presentation of antigens. This biodegradability of the particles was confirmed by the detection of intracellular Ca^{2+}, with the highest levels observed for the ovalbumin/$CaCO_3$/pneumolysin group. This study illustrates the induction of a robust immune response, offering an effective platform based on submicron- and micron-sized $CaCO_3$ particles for the development of anticancer immunotherapy through vaccination.

The last but not the least, it is well known that the translation from experiments to clinical trials is hindered not only by high production costs and the problems with scale-up, but also by safety issues and complicated procedures of obtaining approval by drug administration authorities. However, this problem does not exist in the case of calcium carbonate microparticles because their safety is guaranteed by the fact that they are already marketed as an FDA-approved antacid medication, as well as a digestive, antidiarrheal, and weight control drug [104].

Author Contributions: Conceptualization, A.S. and I.N.; writing—original draft preparation, L.B. and E.G.; writing—review and editing, E.G., L.B., A.S., I.N. and A.K.; supervision, I.N.; funding acquisition, A.K. and I.N. All authors have read and agreed to the published version of the manuscript.

Funding: This research was funded by the ITMO Cancer of Aviesan within the framework of the 2021–2030 Cancer Control Strategy, on funds administered by the French National Institute of Health and Medical Research, grant No. 22CP174-00 "Smart-Nano", and by the Université de Reims Champagne-Ardenne (I.N., A.S.). L.B. was supported by the Graduate School NANO-PHOT (École Universitaire de Recherche, PIA3, contract ANR-18-EURE-0013). The Russian Science Foundation (RSF) grant No. 22-75-10103 in the part of the work related to the synthesis of microparticles (E.G.), grant No. 23-75-30016 in the part of the work related to the synthesis of microcapsules (A.K.), and grant No. 21-79-30048 in the part of the work related to the microparticles and microcapsules functionalization are also acknowledged.

Acknowledgments: A.S., I.N. and L.B. acknowledge the support of the French Ministry of Higher Education, Research and Innovation, and the University of Reims Champagne-Ardenne. We also thank Vladimir Ushakov for proofreading the manuscript.

Conflicts of Interest: The authors declare no conflicts of interest. The funders had no role in the design of the study; in the collection, analyses, or interpretation of data; in the writing of the manuscript; or in the decision to publish the results. The company Life Improvement by Future Technologies (LIFT) Center had no role in the design of the study; in the collection, analyses, or interpretation of data; in the writing of the manuscript; or in the decision to publish the results.

References

1. Bahrom, H.; Goncharenko, A.A.; Fatkhutdinova, L.I.; Peltek, O.O.; Muslimov, A.R.; Koval, O.Y.; Eliseev, I.E.; Manchev, A.; Gorin, D.; Shishkin, I.I.; et al. Controllable synthesis of calcium carbonate with different geometry: Comprehensive analysis of particle formation, cellular uptake, and biocompatibility. *ACS Sustain. Chem. Eng.* **2019**, *7*, 19142–19156. [CrossRef]
2. Trushina, D.B.; Bukreeva, T.V.; Antipina, M.N. Size-controlled synthesis of vaterite calcium carbonate by the mixing method: Aiming for nanosized particles. *Cryst. Growth Des.* **2016**, *16*, 1311–1319. [CrossRef]
3. Vostrikova, A.V.; Prikhozhdenko, E.S.; Mayorova, O.A.; Goryacheva, I.Y.; Tarakina, N.V.; Sukhorukov, G.B.; Sapelkin, A.V. Thermal carbonization in nanoscale reactors: Controlled formation of carbon nanodots inside porous $CaCO_3$ microparticles. *Sci. Rep.* **2018**, *8*, 9394. [CrossRef] [PubMed]
4. Trofimov, A.D.; Ivanova, A.A.; Zyuzin, M.V.; Timin, A.S. Porous inorganic carriers based on silica, calcium carbonate and calcium phosphate for controlled/modulated drug delivery: Fresh outlook and future perspectives. *Pharmaceutics* **2018**, *10*, 167. [CrossRef] [PubMed]
5. Lam, S.F.; Bishop, K.W.; Mintz, R.; Fang, L.; Achilefu, S. Calcium carbonate nanoparticles stimulate cancer cell reprogramming to suppress tumor growth and invasion in an organ-on-a-chip system. *Sci. Rep.* **2021**, *11*, 9246. [CrossRef] [PubMed]
6. Ševčík, R.; Šašek, P.; Viani, A. Physical and nanomechanical properties of the synthetic anhydrous crystalline $CaCO_3$ polymorphs: Vaterite, aragonite and calcite. *J. Mater. Sci.* **2018**, *53*, 4022–4033. [CrossRef]
7. Svenskaya, Y.I.; Fattah, H.; Inozemtseva, O.A.; Ivanova, A.G.; Shtykov, S.N.; Gorin, D.A.; Parakhonskiy, B.V. Key parameters for size- and shape-controlled synthesis of vaterite particles. *Cryst. Growth Des.* **2018**, *18*, 331–337. [CrossRef]
8. Han, C.; Hu, Y.; Wang, K.; Luo, G. Preparation and in-situ surface modification of $CaCO_3$ nanoparticles with calcium stearate in a microreaction system. *Powder Technol.* **2019**, *356*, 414–422. [CrossRef]
9. Niu, Y.Q.; Liu, J.H.; Aymonier, C.; Fermani, S.; Kralj, D.; Falini, G.; Zhou, C.H. Calcium carbonate: Controlled synthesis, surface functionalization, and nanostructured materials. *Chem. Soc. Rev.* **2022**, *51*, 7883–7943. [CrossRef]
10. Fadia, P.; Tyagi, S.; Bhagat, S.; Nair, A.; Panchal, P.; Dave, H.; Dang, S.; Singh, S. Calcium carbonate nano- and microparticles: Synthesis methods and biological applications. *3 Biotech* **2021**, *11*, 457. [CrossRef]

11. Byrappa, K.; Ohara, S.; Adschiri, T. Nanoparticles synthesis using supercritical fluid technology—Towards biomedical applications. *Adv. Drug Deliv. Rev.* **2008**, *60*, 299–327. [CrossRef]
12. Pai, R.K.; Pillai, S. Nanoparticles of amorphous calcium carbonate by miniemulsion: Synthesis and mechanism. *CrystEngComm* **2008**, *10*, 865–872. [CrossRef]
13. Anton, N.; Benoit, J.P.; Saulnier, P. Design and production of nanoparticles formulated from nano-emulsion templates—A review. *J. Control. Release* **2008**, *128*, 185–199. [CrossRef] [PubMed]
14. Babou-Kammoe, R.; Hamoudi, S.; Larachi, F.; Belkacemi, K. Synthesis of $CaCO_3$ nanoparticles by controlled precipitation of saturated carbonate and calcium nitrate aqueous solutions. *Can. J. Chem. Eng.* **2012**, *90*, 26–33. [CrossRef]
15. Campbell, J.; Abnett, J.; Kastania, G.; Volodkin, D.; Vikulina, A.S. Which biopolymers are better for the fabrication of multilayer capsules? A comparative study using vaterite $CaCO_3$ as templates. *ACS Appl. Mater.* **2021**, *13*, 3259–3269. [CrossRef] [PubMed]
16. Chesneau, C.; Larue, L.; Belbekhouche, S. Design of tailor-made biopolymer-based capsules for biological application by combining porous particles and polysaccharide assembly. *Pharmaceutics* **2023**, *15*, 1718. [CrossRef] [PubMed]
17. Tan, C.; Dima, C.; Huang, M.; Assadpour, E.; Wang, J.; Sun, B.; Kharazmi, M.S.; Jafari, S.M. Advanced $CaCO_3$-derived delivery systems for bioactive compounds. *Adv. Colloid Interface Sci.* **2022**, *309*, 102791. [CrossRef] [PubMed]
18. Kalenichenko, D.; Nifontova, G.; Karaulov, A.; Sukhanova, A.; Nabiev, I. Designing functionalized polyelectrolyte microcapsules for cancer treatment. *Nanomaterials* **2021**, *11*, 3055. [CrossRef] [PubMed]
19. Li, G.; Zhao, Y.; Zhang, J.; Hao, J.; Xu, D.; Cao, Y. $CaCO_3$ Loaded lipid microspheres prepared by the solid-in-oil-in-water emulsions technique with propylene glycol alginate and xanthan gum. *Front. Nutr.* **2022**, *9*, 961326. [CrossRef]
20. Yoshida, K.; Ono, T.; Kashiwagi, Y.; Takahashi, S.; Sato, K.; Anzai, J.I. pH-dependent release of insulin from layer-by-layer-deposited polyelectrolyte microcapsules. *Polymers* **2015**, *7*, 1269–1278. [CrossRef]
21. Dou, J.; Zhao, F.; Fan, W.; Chen, Z.; Guo, X. Preparation of non-spherical vaterite $CaCO_3$ particles by flash nano precipitation technique for targeted and extended drug delivery. *J. Drug Deliv. Sci.* **2020**, *57*, 101768. [CrossRef]
22. Gundogdu, D.; Alemdar, C.; Turan, C.; Husnugil, H.H.; Banerjee, S.; Erel-Goktepe, I. Tuning stimuli-responsive properties of alginate hydrogels through layer-by-layer functionalization for dual-responsive dual drug release. *Colloids Surf. A Physicochem. Eng. Asp.* **2023**, *676*, 132213. [CrossRef]
23. Decher, G.; Hong, J.D.; Schmitt, J. Buildup of ultrathin multilayer films by a self-assembly process: III. Consecutively alternating adsorption of anionic and cationic polyelectrolytes on charged surfaces. *Thin Solid Films* **1992**, *210–211*, 831–835. [CrossRef]
24. Decher, G.; Hong, J.-D. Buildup of ultrathin multilayer films by a self-assembly process: I. Consecutive adsorption of anionic and cationic bipolar amphiphiles on charged surfaces. *Makromol. Chem. Macromol. Symp.* **1991**, *46*, 321–327. [CrossRef]
25. Vikulina, A.S.; Campbell, J. Biopolymer-based multilayer capsules and beads made via templating: Advantages, hurdles and perspectives. *Nanomaterials* **2021**, *11*, 2502. [CrossRef] [PubMed]
26. Volodkin, D.V.; Madaboosi, N.; Blacklock, J.; Skirtach, A.G.; Möhwald, H. Surface-supported multilayers decorated with bio-active material aimed at light-triggered drug delivery. *Langmuir* **2009**, *25*, 14037–14043. [CrossRef] [PubMed]
27. De Geest, B.G.; Skirtach, A.G.; Mamedov, A.A.; Antipov, A.A.; Kotov, N.A.; De Smedt, S.C.; Sukhorukov, G.B. Ultrasound-triggered release from multilayered capsules. *Small* **2007**, *3*, 804–808. [CrossRef] [PubMed]
28. Déjugnat, C.; Sukhorukov, G.B. pH-responsive properties of hollow polyelectrolyte microcapsules templated on various cores. *Langmuir* **2004**, *20*, 7265–7269. [CrossRef] [PubMed]
29. Alford, A.; Tucker, B.; Kozlovskaya, V.; Chen, J.; Gupta, N.; Caviedes, R.; Gearhart, J.; Graves, D.; Kharlampieva, E. Encapsulation and ultrasound-triggered release of G-quadruplex DNA in multilayer hydrogel microcapsules. *Polymers* **2018**, *10*, 1342. [CrossRef]
30. Campbell, J.; Kastania, G.; Volodkin, D. Encapsulation of low-molecular-weight drugs into polymer multilayer capsules templated on vaterite $CaCO_3$ crystals. *Micromachines* **2020**, *11*, 717. [CrossRef]
31. Li, S.; Lian, B. Application of calcium carbonate as a controlled release carrier for therapeutic drugs. *Minerals* **2023**, *13*, 1136. [CrossRef]
32. Gileva, A.; Trushina, D.; Yagolovich, A.; Gasparian, M.; Kurbanova, L.; Smirnov, I.; Burov, S.; Markvicheva, E. Doxorubicin-loaded polyelectrolyte multilayer capsules modified with antitumor DR5-specific TRAIL variant for targeted drug delivery to tumor cells. *Nanomaterials* **2023**, *13*, 902. [CrossRef] [PubMed]
33. Fujiwara, M.; Shiokawa, K.; Araki, M.; Ashitaka, N.; Morigaki, K.; Kubota, T.; Nakahara, Y. Encapsulation of proteins into $CaCO_3$ by phase transition from vaterite to calcite. *Cryst. Growth Design* **2010**, *10*, 4030–4037. [CrossRef]
34. Zhao, D.; Wang, C.Q.; Zhuo, R.X.; Cheng, S.X. Modification of nanostructured calcium carbonate for efficient gene delivery. *Colloids Surf. B Biointerfaces* **2014**, *118*, 111–116. [CrossRef]
35. Popova, V.; Poletaeva, Y.; Chubarov, A.; Dmitrienko, E. pH-responsible doxorubicin-loaded Fe_3O_4@$CaCO_3$ nanocomposites for cancer treatment. *Pharmaceutics* **2023**, *15*, 771. [CrossRef] [PubMed]
36. Nifontova, G.; Ramos-Gomes, F.; Baryshnikova, M.; Alves, F.; Nabiev, I.; Sukhanova, A. Cancer cell targeting with functionalized quantum dot-encoded polyelectrolyte microcapsules. *Front. Chem.* **2019**, *7*, 34. [CrossRef] [PubMed]
37. Trushina, D.B.; Borodina, T.N.; Belyakov, S.; Antipina, M.N. Calcium carbonate vaterite particles for drug delivery: Advances and challenges. *Mater. Today Adv.* **2022**, *14*, 100214. [CrossRef]
38. Ishikawa, F.; Murano, M.; Hiraishi, M.; Yamaguchi, T.; Tamai, I.; Tsuji, A. Insoluble powder formulation as an effective nasal drug delivery system. *Pharm. Res.* **2002**, *19*, 1097–1104. [CrossRef]

39. Volodkin, D.V.; Larionova, N.I.; Sukhorukov, G.B. Protein encapsulation via porous $CaCO_3$ microparticles templating. *Biomacromolecules* **2004**, *5*, 1962–1972. [CrossRef]
40. Parakhonskiy, B.V.; Haase, A.; Antolini, R. Sub-micrometer vaterite containers: Synthesis, substance loading, and release. *Angew. Chem. Intl. Ed.* **2012**, *51*, 1195–1197. [CrossRef]
41. Farzan, M.; Roth, R.; Québatte, G.; Schoelkopf, J.; Huwyler, J.; Puchkov, M. Loading of porous functionalized calcium carbonate microparticles: Distribution analysis with focused ion beam electron microscopy and mercury porosimetry. *Pharmaceutics* **2019**, *11*, 32. [CrossRef] [PubMed]
42. Levy, C.L.; Matthews, G.P.; Laudone, G.M.; Beckett, S.; Turner, A.; Schoelkopf, J.; Gane, P.A.C. Mechanism of adsorption of actives onto microporous functionalized calcium carbonate (FCC). *Adsorption* **2017**, *23*, 603–612. [CrossRef]
43. Binevski, P.V.; Balabushevich, N.G.; Uvarova, V.I.; Vikulina, A.S.; Volodkin, D. Bio-Friendly Encapsulation of superoxide dismutase into vaterite $CaCO_3$ crystals. Enzyme activity, release mechanism, and perspectives for ophthalmology. *Colloids Surf. B Biointerfaces* **2019**, *181*, 437–449. [CrossRef] [PubMed]
44. Feoktistova, N.A.; Balabushevich, N.G.; Skirtach, A.G.; Volodkin, D.; Vikulina, A.S. Inter-protein interactions govern protein loading into porous vaterite $CaCO_3$ crystals. *Phys. Chem. Chem. Phys.* **2020**, *22*, 9713–9722. [CrossRef]
45. Li, R.G.; Napoli, E.; Jorstad, I.S.; Bønsdorff, T.B.; Juzeniene, A.; Bruland, Ø.S.; Larsen, R.H.; Westrøm, S. Calcium carbonate microparticles as carriers of ^{224}Ra: Impact of specific activity in mice with intraperitoneal ovarian cancer. *Curr. Radiopharm.* **2020**, *14*, 145–153. [CrossRef] [PubMed]
46. Westrøm, S.; Malenge, M.; Jorstad, I.S.; Napoli, E.; Bruland, Ø.S.; Bønsdorff, T.B.; Larsen, R.H. Ra-224 labeling of calcium carbonate microparticles for internal α-therapy: Preparation, stability, and biodistribution in mice. *J. Label. Compd. Radiopharm.* **2018**, *61*, 472–486. [CrossRef] [PubMed]
47. Feoktistova, N.A.; Vikulina, A.S.; Balabushevich, N.G.; Skirtach, A.G.; Volodkin, D. Bioactivity of catalase loaded into vaterite $CaCO_3$ crystals via adsorption and co-synthesis. *Mater. Des.* **2020**, *185*, 108223. [CrossRef]
48. Preisig, D.; Haid, D.; Varum, F.J.O.; Bravo, R.; Alles, R.; Huwyler, J.; Puchkov, M. Drug loading into porous calcium carbonate microparticles by solvent evaporation. *Eur. J. Pharm. Biopharm.* **2014**, *87*, 548–558. [CrossRef] [PubMed]
49. Roth, R.; Schoelkopf, J.; Huwyler, J.; Puchkov, M. Functionalized calcium carbonate microparticles for the delivery of proteins. *Eur. J. Pharm. Biopharm.* **2018**, *122*, 96–103. [CrossRef]
50. Ramalapa, B.; Crasson, O.; Vandevenne, M.; Gibaud, A.; Garcion, E.; Cordonnier, T.; Galleni, M.; Boury, F. Protein-polysaccharide complexes for enhanced protein delivery in hyaluronic acid templated calcium carbonate microparticles. *J. Mater. Chem. B* **2017**, *5*, 7360–7368. [CrossRef]
51. Vikulina, A.S.; Feoktistova, N.A.; Balabushevich, N.G.; Skirtach, A.G.; Volodkin, D. The mechanism of catalase loading into porous vaterite $CaCO_3$ crystals by co-synthesis. *Phys. Chem. Chem. Phys.* **2018**, *20*, 8822–8831. [CrossRef]
52. Guo, Y.; Li, H.; Shi, W.; Zhang, J.; Feng, J.; Yang, X.; Wang, K.; Zhang, H.; Yang, L. Targeted delivery and pH-responsive release of doxorubicin to cancer cells using calcium carbonate/hyaluronate/glutamate mesoporous hollow spheres. *J. Colloid Interface Sci.* **2017**, *502*, 59–66. [CrossRef]
53. Lu, J.; Jiao, Y.; Cao, G.; Liu, Z. Multimode $CaCO_3$/pneumolysin antigen delivery systems for inducing efficient cellular immunity for anti-tumor immunotherapy. *Chem. Eng. J.* **2021**, *420*, 129746. [CrossRef]
54. Balabushevich, N.G.; Kovalenko, E.A.; Le-Deygen, I.M.; Filatova, L.Y.; Volodkin, D.; Vikulina, A.S. Hybrid $CaCO_3$-mucin crystals: Effective approach for loading and controlled release of cationic drugs. *Mater. Des.* **2019**, *182*, 108020. [CrossRef]
55. Lin, J.; Huang, L.; Xiang, R.; Ou, H.; Li, X.; Chen, A.; Liu, Z. Blood compatibility evaluations of $CaCO_3$ particles. *Biomed. Mater. Res.* **2021**, *16*, 055010. [CrossRef]
56. Wang, P.; Kankala, R.K.; Fan, J.; Long, R.; Liu, Y.; Wang, S. Poly-L-ornithine/fucoidan-coated calcium carbonate microparticles by layer-by-layer self-assembly technique for cancer theranostics. *J. Mater. Sci. Mater. Med.* **2018**, *29*, 68. [CrossRef] [PubMed]
57. Wang, C.; Chen, S.; Yu, Q.; Hu, F.; Yuan, H. Taking advantage of the disadvantage: Employing the high aqueous instability of amorphous calcium carbonate to realize burst drug release within cancer cells. *J. Mater. Chem. B* **2017**, *5*, 2068–2073. [CrossRef] [PubMed]
58. Wei, Y.; Sun, R.; Su, H.; Xu, H.; Zhang, L.; Huang, D.; Liang, Z.; Hu, Y.; Zhao, L.; Lian, X. Synthesis and characterization of porous $CaCO_3$ microspheres templated by yeast cells and the application as pH value-sensitive anticancer drug carrier. *Colloids Surf. B Biointerfaces* **2021**, *199*, 111545. [CrossRef] [PubMed]
59. Lybaert, L.; Ryu, K.A.; Nuhn, L.; De Rycke, R.; De Wever, O.; Chon, A.C.; Esser-Kahn, A.P.; De Geest, B.G. Cancer cell lysate entrapment in $CaCO_3$ engineered with polymeric TLR-agonists: Immune-modulating microparticles in view of personalized antitumor vaccination. *Chem. Mater.* **2017**, *29*, 4209–4217. [CrossRef]
60. Muslimov, A.R.; Antuganov, D.; Tarakanchikova, Y.V.; Karpov, T.E.; Zhukov, M.V.; Zyuzin, M.V.; Timin, A.S. An investigation of calcium carbonate core-shell particles for incorporation of 225Ac and sequester of daughter radionuclides: In vitro and in vivo studies. *J. Control. Release* **2021**, *330*, 726–737. [CrossRef]
61. Kudryavtseva, V.L.; Zhao, L.; Tverdokhlebov, S.I.; Sukhorukov, G.B. Fabrication of PLA/$CaCO_3$ hybrid micro-particles as carriers for water-soluble bioactive molecules. *Colloids Surf. B Biointerfaces* **2017**, *157*, 481–489. [CrossRef] [PubMed]
62. Bewernitz, M.A.; Lovett, A.C.; Gower, L.B. Liquid–solid core-shell microcapsules of calcium carbonate coated emulsions and liposomes. *Appl. Sci.* **2020**, *10*, 8551. [CrossRef]

63. Antipov, A.A.; Shchukin, D.; Fedutik, Y.; Petrov, A.I.; Sukhorukov, G.B.; Möhwald, H. Carbonate microparticles for hollow polyelectrolyte capsules fabrication. *Colloids Surf. A Physicochem. Eng. Asp.* **2003**, *224*, 175–183. [CrossRef]
64. Szarpak, A.; Cui, D.; Dubreuil, F.; De Geest, B.G.; De Cock, L.J.; Picart, C.; Auzély-Velty, R. Designing hyaluronic acid-based layer-by-layer capsules as a carrier for intracellular drug delivery. *Biomacromolecules* **2010**, *11*, 713–720. [CrossRef] [PubMed]
65. De Geest, B.G.; Vandenbroucke, R.E.; Guenther, A.M.; Sukhorukov, G.B.; Hennink, W.E.; Sanders, N.N.; Demeester, J.; De Smedt, S.C. Intracellularly degradable polyelectrolyte microcapsules. *Adv. Mater.* **2006**, *18*, 1005–1009. [CrossRef]
66. Belbekhouche, S.; Charaabi, S.; Carbonnier, B. Glucose-sensitive capsules based on hydrogen-bonded (poly-vinylpyrrolidone/ phenylboronic–modified alginate) system. *Colloids Surf. B Biointerfaces* **2019**, *177*, 416–424. [CrossRef] [PubMed]
67. Trushina, D.B.; Bukreeva, T.V.; Borodina, T.N.; Belova, D.D.; Belyakov, S.; Antipina, M.N. Heat-driven size reduction of biodegradable polyelectrolyte multilayer hollow capsules assembled on $CaCO_3$ template. *Colloids Surf. B Biointerfaces* **2018**, *170*, 312–321. [CrossRef] [PubMed]
68. Navolokin, N.; Lomova, M.; Bucharskaya, A.; Godage, O.; Polukonova, N.; Shirokov, A.; Grinev, V.; Maslyakova, G. Antitumor effects of microencapsulated gratiola officinalis extract on breast carcinoma and hu-man cervical cancer cells in vitro. *Materials* **2023**, *16*, 1470. [CrossRef] [PubMed]
69. Nehru, S.; Guru, A.; Pachaiappan, R.; Hatamleh, A.A.; Al-Dosary, M.A.; Arokiyaraj, S.; Sundaramurthy, A.; Arockiaraj, J. Co-encapsulation and release of apigenin and ascorbic acid in polyelectrolyte multilayer capsules for targeted polycystic ovary syndrome. *Int. J. Pharm.* **2023**, *651*, 123749. [CrossRef]
70. Novoselova, M.V.; Loh, H.M.; Trushina, D.B.; Ketkar, A.; Abakumova, T.O.; Zatsepin, T.S.; Kakran, M.; Brzozowska, A.M.; Lau, H.H.; Gorin, D.A.; et al. Biodegradable polymeric multilayer capsules for therapy of lung cancer. *ACS Appl. Mater. Interfaces* **2020**, *12*, 5610–5623. [CrossRef]
71. Petrov, A.I.; Volodkin, D.V.; Sukhorukov, G.B. Protein-calcium carbonate coprecipitation: A tool for protein encapsulation. *Biotechnol. Prog.* **2005**, *21*, 918–925. [CrossRef] [PubMed]
72. Mihai, M.; Racovita, S.; Vasiliu, A.-L.; Doroftei, F.; Barbu-Mic, C.; Schwarz, S.; Steinbach, C.; Simon, F. Auto-template microcapsules of $CaCO_3$/pectin and nonstoichiometric complexes as sustained tetracycline hydrochloride delivery carriers. *ACS Appl. Mater. Interfaces* **2017**, *9*, 37264–37278. [CrossRef]
73. Flemke, J.; Maywald, M.; Sieber, V. Encapsulation of living *E. coli* cells in hollow polymer microspheres of highly defined size. *Biomacromolecules* **2013**, *14*, 207–214. [CrossRef]
74. Sharma, V.; Vijay, J.; Ganesh, M.R.; Sundaramurthy, A. Multilayer capsules encapsulating nimbin and doxorubicin for cancer chemo-photothermal therapy. *Int. J. Pharm.* **2020**, *582*, 119350. [CrossRef]
75. Maiorova, L.A.; Erokhina, S.I.; Pisani, M.; Barucca, G.; Marcaccio, M.; Koifman, O.I.; Salnikov, D.S.; Gromova, O.A.; Astolfi, P.; Ricci, V.; et al. Encapsulation of vitamin B12 into nanoengineered capsules and soft matter nanosystems for targeted delivery. *Colloids Surf. B Biointerfaces* **2019**, *182*, 110366. [CrossRef] [PubMed]
76. Musin, E.V.; Kim, A.L.; Tikhonenko, S.A. Destruction of polyelectrolyte microcapsules formed on $CaCO_3$ microparticles and the release of a protein included by the adsorption method. *Polymers* **2020**, *12*, 520. [CrossRef]
77. De Temmerman, M.-L.; Rejman, J.; Grooten, J.; De Beer, T.; Vervaet, C.; Demeester, J.; De Smedt, S.C. Lyophilization of protein-loaded polyelectrolyte microcapsules. *Pharm. Res.* **2011**, *28*, 1765–1773. [CrossRef]
78. Tarakanchikova, Y.V.; Muslimov, A.R.; Zyuzin, M.V.; Nazarenko, I.; Timin, A.S.; Sukhorukov, G.B.; Lepik, K.V. Layer-by-layer-assembled capsule size affects the efficiency of packaging and delivery of different genetic cargo. *Part. Part. Syst. Charact.* **2021**, *38*, 2000228. [CrossRef]
79. Timin, A.S.; Muslimov, A.R.; Lepik, K.V.; Epifanovskaya, O.S.; Shakirova, A.I.; Mock, U.; Riecken, K.; Okilova, M.V.; Sergeev, V.S.; Afanasyev, B.V.; et al. Efficient gene editing via non-viral delivery of CRISPR–Cas9 system using polymeric and hybrid microcarriers. *Nanomed. NBM* **2018**, *14*, 97–108. [CrossRef]
80. Lin, Y.-H.; Singuru, M.M.R.; Marpaung, D.S.S.; Liao, W.-C.; Chuang, M.-C. Ethylene glycol-manipulated syntheses of calcium carbonate particles and DNA capsules toward efficient ATP-responsive cargo release. *ACS Appl. Bio Mater.* **2023**, *6*, 3351–3360. [CrossRef]
81. Prikhozhdenko, E.S.; Gusliakova, O.I.; Kulikov, O.A.; Mayorova, O.A.; Shushunova, N.A.; Abdurashitov, A.S.; Bratashov, D.N.; Pyataev, N.A.; Tuchin, V.V.; Gorin, D.A.; et al. Target delivery of drug carriers in mice kidney glomeruli via renal artery. *J. Control. Release* **2021**, *329*, 175–190. [CrossRef] [PubMed]
82. Zhao, Q.; Han, B.; Wang, Z.; Gao, C.; Peng, C.; Shen, J. Hollow chitosan-alginate multilayer microcapsules as drug delivery vehicle: Doxorubicin loading and in vitro and in vivo studies. *Nanomed. NBM* **2007**, *3*, 63–74. [CrossRef] [PubMed]
83. Zhao, Q.; Li, B. pH-controlled drug loading and release from biodegradable microcapsules. *Nanomed. NBM* **2008**, *4*, 302–310. [CrossRef] [PubMed]
84. Lvov, Y.; Antipov, A.A.; Mamedov, A.; Möhwald, H.; Sukhorukov, G.B. Urease encapsulation in nanoorganized microshells. *Nano Lett.* **2001**, *1*, 125–128. [CrossRef]
85. Finnegan, M.; Mallon, G.; Leach, A.; Themistou, E. Electrosprayed cysteine-functionalized degradable amphiphilic block copolymer microparticles for low pH-triggered drug delivery. *Polym. Chem.* **2019**, *10*, 5814–5820. [CrossRef]
86. Nifontova, G.; Tsoi, T.; Karaulov, A.; Nabiev, I.; Sukhanova, A. Structure-function relationships in polymeric multilayer capsules designed for cancer drug delivery. *Biomater. Sci.* **2022**, *10*, 5092–5115. [CrossRef] [PubMed]

87. Nifontova, G.; Zvaigzne, M.; Baryshnikova, M.; Korostylev, E.; Ramos-Gomes, F.; Alves, F.; Nabiev, I.; Sukhanova, A. Next-generation theranostic agents based on polyelectrolyte microcapsules encoded with semiconductor nanocrystals: Development and functional characterization. *Nanoscale Res.* **2018**, *13*, 30. [CrossRef] [PubMed]
88. Ariga, K.; Lvov, Y.M.; Kawakami, K.; Ji, Q.; Hill, J.P. Layer-by-layer self-assembled shells for drug delivery. *Adv. Drug Deliv. Rev.* **2011**, *63*, 762–771. [CrossRef] [PubMed]
89. Zheng, P.; Ding, B.; Shi, R.; Jiang, Z.; Xu, W.; Li, G.; Ding, J.; Chen, X. A multichannel Ca^{2+} nanomodulator for multilevel mitochondrial destruction-mediated cancer therapy. *Adv. Mater.* **2021**, *33*, 2007426. [CrossRef]
90. Svenskaya, Y.; Garello, F.; Lengert, E.; Kozlova, A.; Verkhovskii, R.; Bitonto, V.; Ruggiero, M.R.; German, S.; Gorin, D.; Terreno, E. Biodegradable polyelectrolyte/magnetite capsules for MR imaging and magnetic targeting of tumors. *Nanotheranostics* **2021**, *5*, 362–377. [CrossRef]
91. Borbora, A.; Manna, U. Impact of chemistry on the preparation and post-modification of multilayered hollow microcapsules. *Chem. Commun.* **2021**, *57*, 2110–2123. [CrossRef] [PubMed]
92. Maleki Dizaj, S.; Sharifi, S.; Ahmadian, E.; Eftekhari, A.; Adibkia, K.; Lotfipour, F. An update on calcium carbonate nanoparticles as cancer drug/gene delivery system. *Exp. Opin. Drug Deliv.* **2019**, *16*, 331–345. [CrossRef] [PubMed]
93. Zhao, Y.; Luo, Z.; Li, M.; Qu, Q.; Ma, X.; Yu, S.-H.; Zhao, Y. A preloaded amorphous calcium carbonate/doxorubicin@silica nanoreactor for pH-responsive delivery of an anticancer drug. *Angew. Chem. Intl. Ed.* **2015**, *54*, 919–922. [CrossRef] [PubMed]
94. Machtakova, M.; Thérien-Aubin, H.; Landfester, K. Polymer nano-systems for the encapsulation and delivery of active biomacromolecular therapeutic agents. *Chem. Soc. Rev.* **2022**, *51*, 128–152. [CrossRef]
95. Som, A.; Raliya, R.; Tian, L.; Akers, W.; Ippolito, J.E.; Singamaneni, S.; Biswas, P.; Achilefu, S. Monodispersed calcium carbonate nanoparticles modulate local pH and inhibit tumor growth in vivo. *Nanoscale* **2016**, *8*, 12639–12647. [CrossRef] [PubMed]
96. D'Amora, M.; Liendo, F.; Deorsola, F.A.; Bensaid, S.; Giordani, S. Toxicological profile of calcium carbonate nanoparticles for industrial applications. *Colloids Surf. B Biointerfaces* **2020**, *190*, 110947. [CrossRef]
97. Borodina, T.; Marchenko, I.; Trushina, D.; Volkova, Y.; Shirinian, V.; Zavarzin, I.; Kondrakhin, E.; Kovalev, G.; Kovalchuk, M.; Bukreeva, T. A Novel formulation of zolpidem for direct nose-to-brain delivery: Synthesis, encapsulation and intranasal administration to mice. *J. Pharm. Pharmacol.* **2018**, *70*, 1164–1173. [CrossRef]
98. Marchenko, I.; Borodina, T.; Trushina, D.; Rassokhina, I.; Volkova, Y.; Shirinian, V.; Zavarzin, I.; Gogin, A.; Bukreeva, T. Mesoporous particle-based microcontainers for intranasal delivery of imidazopyridine drugs. *J. Microencapsul.* **2018**, *35*, 657–666. [CrossRef] [PubMed]
99. Gusliakova, O.; Atochina-Vasserman, E.N.; Sindeeva, O.; Sindeev, S.; Pinyaev, S.; Pyataev, N.; Revin, V.; Sukhorukov, G.B.; Gorin, D.; Gow, A.J. Use of submicron vaterite particles serves as an effective delivery vehicle to the respiratory portion of the lung. *Front. Pharmacol.* **2018**, *9*, 559. [CrossRef]
100. Svenskaya, Y.I.; Genina, E.A.; Parakhonskiy, B.V.; Lengert, E.V.; Talnikova, E.E.; Terentyuk, G.S.; Utz, S.R.; Gorin, D.A.; Tuchin, V.V.; Sukhorukov, G.B. A simple non-invasive approach toward efficient transdermal drug delivery based on biodegradable particulate system. *ACS Appl. Mater. Interfaces* **2019**, *11*, 17270–17282. [CrossRef]
101. Wang, E.Y.; Sarmadi, M.; Ying, B.; Jaklenec, A.; Langer, R. Recent advances in nano- and micro-scale carrier systems for controlled delivery of vaccines. *Biomaterials* **2023**, *303*, 122345. [CrossRef]
102. He, H.; Lu, Y.; Qi, J.; Zhu, Q.; Chen, Z.; Wu, W. Adapting liposomes for oral drug delivery. *Acta Pharm. Sin. B.* **2019**, *9*, 36–48. [CrossRef]
103. Vikulina, A.; Voronin, D.; Fakhrullin, R.; Vinokurov, V.; Volodkin, D. Naturally derived nano- and micro-drug delivery vehicles: Halloysite, vaterite and nanocellulose. *New J. Chem.* **2020**, *44*, 5638–5655. [CrossRef]
104. Garg, V.; Narang, P.; Taneja, R. Antacids Revisited: Review on contemporary facts and relevance for self-management. *J. Int. Med. Res.* **2022**, *50*, 3000605221086457. [CrossRef]

Disclaimer/Publisher's Note: The statements, opinions and data contained in all publications are solely those of the individual author(s) and contributor(s) and not of MDPI and/or the editor(s). MDPI and/or the editor(s) disclaim responsibility for any injury to people or property resulting from any ideas, methods, instructions or products referred to in the content.

cancers

MDPI

Article

Coupling Kinesin Spindle Protein and Aurora B Inhibition with Apoptosis Induction Enhances Oral Cancer Cell Killing

João P. N. Silva [1], Bárbara Pinto [1], Luís Monteiro [1], Patrícia M. A. Silva [1,2,3,*] and Hassan Bousbaa [1,*]

[1] UNIPRO—Oral Pathology and Rehabilitation Research Unit, University Institute of Health Sciences (IUCS), Cooperativa de Ensino Superior Politécnico e Universitário (CESPU), Rua Central de Gandra, 1317, 4585-116 Gandra, Portugal; joaosilva_06@hotmail.com (J.P.N.S.); barbara_fernandes_pinto@hotmail.com (B.P.); luis.monteiro@iucs.cespu.pt (L.M.)

[2] Associate Laboratory i4HB, Institute for Health and Bioeconomy, University Institute of Health Sciences-CESPU, 4585-116 Gandra, Portugal

[3] UCIBIO—Applied Molecular Biosciences Unit, Translational Toxicology Research Laboratory, University Institute of Health Sciences (1H-TOXRUN, IUCS-CESPU), 4585-116 Gandra, Portugal

* Correspondence: patricia.silva@cespu.pt (P.M.A.S.); hassan.bousbaa@iucs.cespu.pt (H.B.); Tel.: +351-224157189 (P.M.A.S.); +351-224157186 (H.B.)

Simple Summary: Scientists are studying proteins like kinesin spindle protein and Aurora B, crucial for cell division and potential targets in cancer treatment. Drugs aimed at these proteins show promise in lab tests for killing cancer cells, but in clinical trials alone, they are not always effective, possibly due to varied cancer cell responses. To enhance their efficacy, researchers are exploring combinations with other cell-killing drugs. Our study focused on Navitoclax, an inducer of cancer cell death, tested alongside Ispinesib and Barasertib, targeting kinesin spindle protein and Aurora B, respectively. Together, these drugs induced significant cancer cell death, mainly through apoptosis. Moreover, imaging techniques revealing their combined effects suggest that combining these drugs could be a potent cancer treatment strategy, warranting further investigation in clinical trials.

Abstract: Many proteins regulating mitosis have emerged as targets for cancer therapy, including the kinesin spindle protein (KSP) and Aurora kinase B (AurB). KSP is crucial for proper spindle pole separation during mitosis, while AurB plays roles in chromosome segregation and cytokinesis. Agents targeting KSP and AurB selectively affect dividing cells and have shown significant activity in vitro. However, these drugs, despite advancing to clinical trials, often yield unsatisfactory outcomes as monotherapy, likely due to variable responses driven by cyclin B degradation and apoptosis signal accumulation networks. Accumulated data suggest that combining emerging antimitotics with various cytostatic drugs can enhance tumor-killing effects compared to monotherapy. Here, we investigated the impact of inhibiting anti-apoptotic signals with the BH3-mimetic Navitoclax in oral cancer cells treated with the selective KSP inhibitor, Ispinesib, or AurB inhibitor, Barasertib, aiming to potentiate cell death. The combination of BH3-mimetics with both KSP and AurB inhibitors synergistically induced substantial cell death, primarily through apoptosis. A mechanistic analysis underlying this synergistic activity, undertaken by live-cell imaging, is presented. Our data underscore the importance of combining BH3-mimetics with antimitotics in clinical trials to maximize their effectiveness.

Keywords: KSP inhibitor; Aurora B inhibitor; Navitoclax; oral cancer; antimitotics; combination treatment

1. Introduction

Cancer of the oral cavity and lip is the most common type of head and neck cancer with 377,713 new cases and 177,757 deaths reported in 2020 according to GLOBOCAN [1]. Approximately 90% of all oral cancers are oral squamous cell carcinomas (OSCCs) [2].

The most common origin sites for OSCC are the tongue and the floor of the mouth [2,3]. The emergence of this type of malignancy is mainly associated with tobacco and alcohol consumption. Nonetheless, other factors such as human papillomavirus infection can also lead to OSCC development [4,5]. Despite the different therapeutic strategies, small improvements in the treatment of oral cancer have been reported and high mortality rates for advanced disease are still observed [6]. Thus, new treatment options are needed.

Combinatorial approaches have risen as a hallmark in the treatment of cancer since they can lead to prolonged responses with lower toxicity and potential synergistic effects [7]. Microtubule-targeting agents (MTAs) have been extensively explored and some, such as paclitaxel and docetaxel, have been approved and are used for the treatment of head and neck squamous cell carcinoma (HNSCC) mostly in combination with platinum, 5-fluorouracil, and cetuximab [8]. Nonetheless, MTAs are associated with some disadvantages, including high toxicity due to low specificity and therapeutic resistance [9]. To overcome these issues, drugs that target specific proteins involved in mitosis, known as antimitotic agents, such as kinesins, like kinesin spindle protein (KSP), and kinases, like Aurora B, have been investigated [10].

KSP, also known as Eg5 and Kif11, is a kinesin-5 family member essential for bipolar mitotic spindle formation, microtubule cross-linking, and chromosome alignment [11–13]. The overexpression of KSP is associated with poor outcomes in breast and laryngeal cancers and its inhibition leads to the formation of monopolar spindles, activation of the spindle assembly checkpoint (SAC), and consequently, mitotic arrest followed by cell death [11,14].

Aurora B is a part of the Aurora kinase family that includes Aurora A and Aurora C and it plays a role in chromosome segregation and cytokinesis [15]. The overexpression of Aurora B was reported for metastatic and poorly differentiated OSCC suggesting this kinase is involved in OSCC progression [16]. In addition, Aurora B inhibition can lead to polyploidy, and consequently cell death [15,17].

Even though the inhibition of these proteins in preclinical trials showed promising results, their inhibitors have shown disappointing results as monotherapy in clinical trials, due mainly to the lack of efficacy [18–22]. Different possibilities have been suggested for this lack of efficacy. For instance, the fact that antimitotics act only during mitosis leads to low efficacy due to the administration schedules since only a low fraction of tumor cells will be undergoing mitosis at any given point in time. Additionally, mitotic slippage, a phenomenon wherein cells exit mitosis without division, culminating in aneuploidy and fostering cancer cell survival, has also been pointed as one of the major causes of antimitotic treatment resistance [23]. According to a recently proposed model, cell fate during mitotic arrest is defined by the duration of SAC activity, level of BCL-xL, and cyclin B1 degradation [24]. In this model, the increased duration of SAC activity enhances the probability of cell death. The level of BCL-xL also plays an important role. For instance, when cells are arrested in mitosis, the apoptotic signaling threshold is reached when cells present the low activity or inhibition of BCL-xL, leading to death in mitosis. On the contrary, high levels of BCL-xL allow the cyclin B1 degradation threshold to be reached, and mitotic slippage occurs. Post-slippage death occurs when the level of BCL-xL is high enough to allow mitotic exit but not enough to block the apoptotic threshold to be reached. BCL-xL is a prosurvival protein involved in the suppression of the intrinsic apoptotic pathway through the inhibition of cytochrome-c release from mitochondria, and its overexpression in OSCC is associated with poor prognosis [25]. Apoptosis is an important mechanism to prevent cancer development since it reduces the risk of genomic instability occurrence [26,27]. However, cancer cells acquire resistance to cell death by overexpressing prosurvival proteins, including BCL-2, BCL-xL, and BCL-w, while downregulating pro-apoptotic ones [28]. Thus, the addition of an inhibitor of BCL-xL to antimitotics should increase the apoptotic signaling and lead to increased cell death in mitosis preventing mitotic slippage or increasing post-slippage death. Accordingly, in several types of cancer cells, it was shown that the combination of the inhibitors of the prosurvival BCL-2 family members with antimitotics enhanced their efficacy by promoting apoptosis [29–32].

Therefore, in this work, we analyzed the effects of the addition of Navitoclax, an BCL-2 and BCL-xL inhibitor, with Ispinesib, a KSP inhibitor, or Barasertib, an Aurora B inhibitor, on oral cancer cells and showed that it enhanced the therapeutic potential of KSP and Aurora B targeting by increasing cell death during mitosis or post-slippage, respectively.

2. Materials and Methods

2.1. Small Molecule Inhibitors

The inhibitors of KSP (Ispinesib and Filanesib), Aurora B (Barasertib and SP-96), and BCL-2/BCL-xL (Navitoclax and ABT-737) were obtained from MedChem Express (Shanghai, China). Stock concentrations of 5 or 10 mM were prepared by resuspending the inhibitors in sterile dimethyl sulfoxide (DMSO, Sigma-Aldrich Co., Ltd., St. Louis, MO, USA). Multiple aliquots were made and stored at −20 °C to avoid the necessity of repeated freezing and thawing cycles. To mitigate potential DMSO toxicity, the working solutions were prepared in a fresh medium and used to make solutions with the desired concentrations.

2.2. Cell Culture

SCC25 (tongue squamous cell carcinoma; The Global Bioresource Center-ATCC® CRL-1628) and SCC09 (tongue squamous cell carcinoma; The Global Bioresource Center-ATCC® CRL-1629) tumor cell lines were grown in DMEM/F12 culture medium (Dulbecco's Modified Eagle Medium/Nutrient Mixture F-12, PAN-Biotech, Aidenbach, Germany), supplemented with 10% of the heat-inactivated fetal bovine serum (FBS, Biochrom, Berlin, Germany) and 1% of Pen/Strep (Biochrom). The non-tumor cell line HOK (human oral keratinocyte, ScienCell Research Laboratories, Carlsbad, CA, USA) was grown in OKM culture medium (oral keratinocyte medium, Innoprot, Bizkaia, Spain). The cell lines were kept at 37 °C with 5% CO_2 in an incubator (Hera Cell, Heraeus, Hanau, Germany) while ensuring humidity was maintained.

2.3. RNA Extraction, cDNA Synthesis, and Real-Time PCR

Total RNA was extracted from the cell lines HOK, SCC09, and SCC25, and cDNA was synthetized as previously described [33]. iQ™ SYBR Green Supermix Kit (Bio-Rad, Laboratories, Inc., Hercules, CA, USA) was used for DNA amplification on an iQ Thermal Cycler (Bio-Rad) using the following program: initial denaturing step at 95.0 °C for 3 min; 38 cycles at 94.0 °C for 20 s; 60.0 °C for 30 s and 72.0 °C for 30 s. The melting curve encompassed temperatures ranging from 65.0 to 95.0 °C, with 0.5 °C increments for 5 s each. The primers used, at a concentration of 10 μM, were as follows: KSP: forward 5′-GAACAATCATTAGCAGCAGAA-3′ and reverse 5′-TCAGTATAGACACCACAGTTG-3′; Aurora B: forward 5′-AGAAGGAGAACTCCTACCCCT-3′ and reverse 5′-CGCGTTAAGAT GTCGGGTG-3′; 18S: forward 5′-CAACATCGATGGGCGGCGGA-3′ and reverse 5′-CCCGC CCTCTTGGTGAGGTC-3′; GAPDH: forward 5′-ACAGTCAGCCGCATCTTC-3′ and reverse 5′-GCCCAATACGACCAAATCC-3′; Actin: forward 5′-AATCTGGCACCACACCTTC TA-3′ and reverse 5′-ATAGCACAGCCTGGATAGCAA-3′. The data were analyzed using the CFX ManagerTM Software (version 1.0, BioRad), and the relative quantification was calculated using the ΔΔCT method. The data were normalized against the housekeeping genes Actin and 18S for KSP and Actin and GAPDH for Aurora B.

2.4. Protein Extraction and Western Blotting

The HOK, SCC09, and SCC25 cell line total protein extraction was performed by first centrifuging the cells and then resuspending them in a lysis buffer containing 50 mM Tris pH 7.5, 150 mM NaCl, 1 mM EDTA, and 1% Triton-100, supplemented with a protease inhibitor cocktail (Sigma–Aldrich (St. Louis, MO, USA)). The proteins were then quantified by using the BCA™ Protein Assay Kit (Pierce Biotechnology (Rockford, IL, USA)) according to the manufacturer's instructions. Subsequently, 15 μg of protein lysate was resuspended with SDS-sample buffer consisting of 375 mM Tris pH 6.8, 12% SDS, 60% Glycerol, 0.12% Bromophenol Blue, and 600 nM DTT, and denatured for 3 min at 95 °C. The proteins were then separated using the SDS–PAGE gels of 7.5% to resolve high molecular weight proteins such as KSP (120–130 kDa), and 10% to resolve low molecular weight proteins such as Aurora B (39–45 kDa). Protein transfer from the gels onto nitrocellulose membranes (Amersham (Staffordshire, UK)) was carried out using the Trans-Blot Turbo Transfer System from Bio-Rad. Afterwards, 5% non-fat dried milk in TBST (50 mM Tris pH 7.5, 150 mM NaCl, 0.05% Tween-20) was used to block the membranes. Then, the membranes were incubated overnight at 4 °C with the following primary antibodies diluted in TBST: mouse anti-α-tubulin (1:5000, T568 Clone B-5-1-2, Sigma–Aldrich), rabbit anti-KSP (1:1000, abcam), and rabbit anti-Aurora B (1:1000, Sigma-Aldrich). After washing the membranes with TBST containing 1% skim milk three times for 5 min each, they were incubated with suitable horseradish peroxidase-conjugated secondary antibodies (1:1500, Vector) for 1 h at room temperature. Protein detection was carried out using the Enhanced Chemiluminescence (ECL) method with a ChemiDOc system (Bio-Rad). Protein signal intensity was quantified using the Image Lab 6.1v software. The normalization of protein values was performed using the expression levels of α-tubulin.

2.5. Indirect Immunofluorescence

The SCC25 cells were seeded at a density of 0.1×10^6 cells/mL on poly-L-lysine-coated coverslips in a complete culture medium for 24 h. Following this, the cells were treated with 1.875 nM Ispinesib, 1000 nM Barasertib, as well as 3000 nM Navitoclax. After 24 h, the cells were fixed with methanol (Sigma-Aldrich, Co., Ltd., Gillingham, UK) at −20 °C for 10 min and then washed three times with PBS for 5 min each. Subsequently, the cells were blocked with 10% FBS in PBST (0.05% Tween-20 in PBS) for 30 min at room temperature, followed by a 1 h incubation with primary antibodies (mouse anti-α-tubulin, 1:2500, Sigma-Aldrich Co., Ltd., Gillingham, UK; human anti-CREST [34], 1:4000, gift from E. Bronze-da-Rocha, University of Porto, Portugal) diluted in PBST with 5% FBS. After three washes with PBST, the cells were incubated with Alexa Fluor 488- and 568-conjugated secondary antibodies (1:1500, Molecular Probes, Eugene, OR, USA). The staining of DNA was accomplished using 2 μg/mL of 4′,6-diamidino-2-phenylindole (DAPI, Sigma-Aldrich) diluted in Vectashield mounting medium (Vector, H-1000, Burlingame, CA, USA).

2.6. MTT Assay

To evaluate cell viability, a cytotoxicity assay using the tetrazolium salt 3-(4,5-dimethylthiazol-2-yl)-2,5-diphenyltetrazolium bromide (MTT) was performed. For seeding, 0.05×10^6 SCC25 cells/mL and 0.1×10^6 SCC09 cells/mL were plated in 96-well plates. The cells were allowed to adhere to the wells for 24 h with only medium. Subsequently, the culture medium was replaced with fresh medium containing the 2-fold serial dilutions of the inhibitors: 1.875 nM to 30 nM for Ispinesib, 1000 nM to 16,000 nM for Barasertib, 1500 nM to 24,000 nM for Navitoclax, 0.9375 nM to 15 nM for Filanesib, 1000 nM to 16,000 nM for SP-96, and 1500 nM to 24,000 nM for ABT-737 for SCC25 cells, and 3.75 nM to 60 nM for Ispinesib, 4000 nM to 64,000 nM for Barasertib, and 1000 nM to 16,000 nM for Navitoclax for SCC09 cells. After 48 h of exposure, 200 μL of non-supplemented medium and 20 μL of MTT tetrazolium salt solution (5 mg/mL PBS) were added to each well, followed by incubation for 2–4 h at 37 °C. Subsequently, the medium was aspirated, and 100 μL of DMSO was added to dissolve the resulting formazan crystals. Optical density was measured at 570 nm using a microplate reader (Biotek Synergy 2, Winooski, VT, USA) equipped with the Gen5 software (version 1.07.5, Biotek, Winooski, VT, USA). The IC_{50} values were calculated using GraphPad Prism version 8 (GraphPad Software Inc., San Diego, CA, USA) using the non-linear regression analysis. The effects of combinations were evaluated using the Combenefit Software (version 2.021, Cancer Research UK Cambridge Institute, Cambridge, UK) with a dual-drug crosswise concentration analysis.

2.7. Apoptosis Detection Using Annexin V/PI Staining

To evaluate apoptotic cell death, the Annexin V-FITC Apoptosis Detection Kit (eBioscience, Vienna, Austria) was employed according to the manufacturer's guidelines. Briefly, the SCC25 cells at a concentration of 0.1×10^6 cells/mL were seeded into 6-well plates and, after 24 h, treated with Ispinesib and Barasertib alone or in combination with Navitoclax or Filanesib and SP-96 alone or in combination with ABT-737 at synergistic concentrations. Following a 48 h incubation period, the cells were harvested, centrifuged at 1000 rpm for 5 min, and suspended in 1× binding buffer. Annexin V-FITC was then added and incubated at room temperature for 10 min in the dark. After washing, the cells were suspended in 1x binding buffer, and Propidium Iodide (PI) at a concentration of 20 μg/mL was added. A BD Accuri™ C6 Plus Flow cytometer (BD Biosciences, Qume Drive, San Jose, CA, USA) was used to measure the fluorescence. The data were then analyzed using the BD Accuri TM C6 Plus software, version 1.0.27.1. The sample processing followed the manufacturer's instructions for the "Annexin V-FITC Apoptosis Detection Kit", with a minimum of 20,000 events collected per sample.

2.8. Mitotic Index Determination

In total, 0.1×10^6 SCC25 cells were seeded in six-well dishes. After 24 h, Ispinesib alone or combined with Navitoclax or Filanesib alone or in combination with ABT-737 at the synergistic point concentrations were added. Positive controls for antimitotic activity were established by treating the cells with 1 μM of the microtubule depolymerizing agent nocodazole. The control groups included untreated cells and cells treated with DMSO, serving to evaluate solvent-induced cytotoxicity. The mitotic index, calculated as the percentage of mitotic cells within the overall cell population, was determined through the observation of cell rounding under phase-contrast microscopy after the 24 h treatment from ten random microscope fields.

2.9. Time-Lapse Microscopy

In total, 0.08×10^6 SCC25 cells were seeded onto LabTek II chambered cover glass (Nunc, Penfield, NY, USA). The remaining wells were filled with sterile water to maintain a humidified atmosphere. Following overnight incubation at 37 °C under 5% CO_2, the medium was replaced with fresh medium containing Ispinesib/Barasertib alone or in combination with Navitoclax at synergistic concentrations. To capture time-lapse images at 5 min intervals over 48 h, an Axio Observer Z.1 SD inverted microscope (Carl Zeiss (Oberkochen, Germany)) equipped with an incubation chamber set to 37 °C and 5% CO_2 using differential interference contrast (DIC) optics and a 63× objective was used. Time-lapse image sequences were compiled into movies using the ImageJ software (version 1.47, Rasband (New York, NY, USA), W.S., ImageJ, U. S. National Institutes of Health, Bethesda, MD, USA).

2.10. Phase-Contrast and Fluorescence Microscopy Images

Phase-contrast microscopy images were obtained using a Nikon TE 2000-U microscope (Nikon, Amsterdam, The Netherlands) with a 10× objective, connected to a DXM1200F digital camera controlled by Nikon ACT-1 software version 2.63 (Melville, NY, USA). An Axio Observer Z.1 SD microscope (Carl Zeiss, Jena, Germany) with an AxioCam MR3 equipped with a Plan Apochromatic 63×/NA 1.4 objective was used to capture fluorescence images. ImageJ version 1.47 was used to process fluorescence images.

2.11. Colony Formation Assay

A total of 850 SCC25 cells were seeded in six-well plates. After 24 h of incubation, Ispinesib or Barasertib alone or in combination with Navitoclax, at the respective synergistic point concentrations, were added. The control groups included untreated cells and cells treated with DMSO. After 48 h, the medium was removed and DMEM F12 medium without drugs was added. The cells were then incubated for a duration of 6 days. Next, colony fixation was performed by the addition of 100% methanol at −20 °C for 20 min. The staining was performed by the addition of violet crystal (Merck) 0.05% (*w*/*v*) in distilled water for 30 min. At least three independent experiments were used to obtain the number of colonies for each condition. Plating efficiency (PE) was determined by calculating the percentage of grown colonies over the number of cells seeded in the control. The survival fraction for each condition was then calculated as the ratio of the number of colonies to the number of cells seeded, multiplied by 1/PE.

2.12. Statistical Analysis

All experiments were conducted in triplicate, and a minimum of three independent experiments were performed. The data are expressed as mean ± standard deviation (SD). Statistical analyses were conducted using GraphPad Prism Software Inc. (La Jolla, CA, USA) v8, employing one-way or two-way ANOVA with Tukey's multiple comparison test. The values of * $p < 0.05$, ** $p < 0.01$, *** $p < 0.001$, and **** $p < 0.0001$ were deemed statistically significant.

3. Results

3.1. KSP and Aurora B Proteins Are Overexpressed in Oral Squamous Carcinoma Cells

KSP is a plus-end directed kinesin essential for bipolar spindle formation, and it was suggested that its overexpression in mice can lead to genomic instability and tumor development [12,14]. Its inhibition leads to the formation of monopolar spindles, activation of SAC, and consequently, mitotic arrest typically followed by cell death [11,14]. While Aurora B is a serine-threonine protein kinase member of the Aurora kinases family involved in correct chromosomal segregation and was shown to be overexpressed in poorly differentiated and metastasized OSCC [16,35]. Aurora B inhibition can lead to polyploidy, and consequently cell death [15,36].

Thus, we analyzed the mRNA and protein expression levels of these targets in two squamous cell carcinoma (SCC) cell lines, SCC25 and SCC09, through qRT-PCR and Western blot, respectively. The results show that the mRNA levels of both proteins are overexpressed in SCC25 and SCC09 when compared to the non-tumoral cell HOK (Figure 1a,c). The KSP and Aurora B protein expression levels also demonstrated an increase in both cell lines (Figure 1b,d).

These results show that these proteins can be potential targets for the treatment of oral cancer.

Next, we proceeded to target KSP and Aurora B and searched for possible synergism in oral cancer killing when combined with apoptosis targeting.

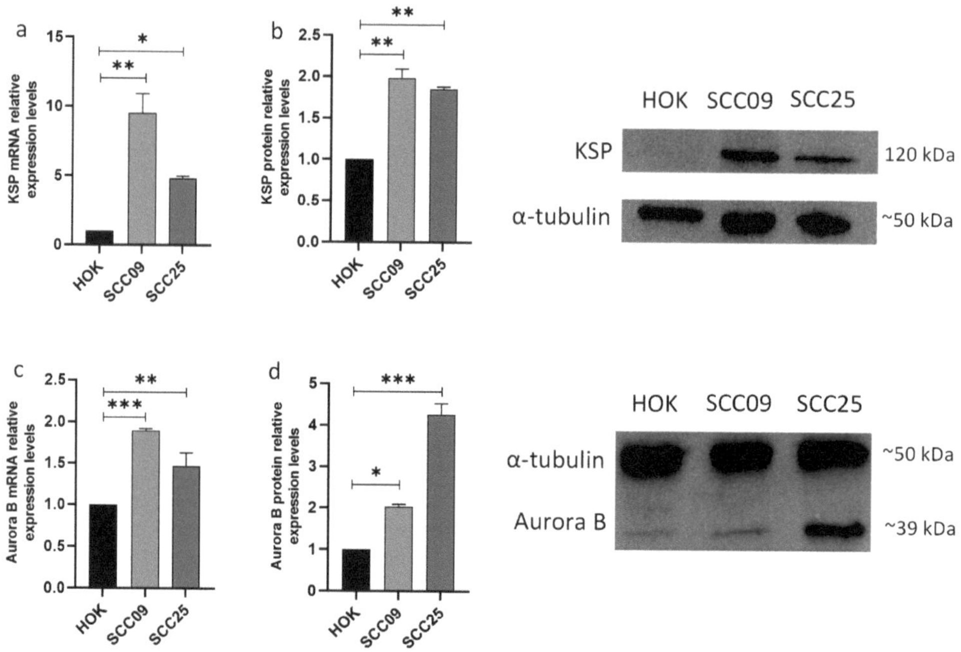

Figure 1. KSP and Aurora B show increased expression in oral squamous carcinoma cell lines. The mRNA expression levels of KSP (**a**) and Aurora B (**c**) were assessed through qRT-PCR in the oral cancer cell lines SCC09 and SCC25 and compared to the non-tumor human oral keratinocyte (HOK) cells. The quantification of the protein levels of KSP (**b**, left) and Aurora B (**d**, left) was performed by the Western blotting assay, with the protein α-tubulin as control. The representative Western blot images for KSP (**b**, right) and Aurora B (**d**, right) are presented. The data presented indicate the mean value along with the standard deviation (mean ± SD) obtained from three independent experiments. Statistical analysis was performed using one-way ANOVA followed by Tukey's multiple comparisons test. The significance levels were as follows: * for $p < 0.05$, ** for $p < 0.01$, and *** for $p < 0.001$. Original western blots are presented in File S1.

3.2. The Combinatorial Approaches with Ispinesib and Navitoclax and Barasertib with Navitoclax Show Synergistic Effects in Oral Cancer Cells

Firstly, to confirm the specificity of the inhibitors under study, the phenotype of the cells treated with Ispinesib, Barasertib, and Navitoclax was assessed by immunofluorescence microscopy. All the drugs showed the expected phenotype with Ispinesib leading to a monopolar spindle phenotype in the cells arrested in mitosis, while the addition of Barasertib led to misalignment of chromosomes during metaphase and to a multinucleated phenotype after cell division (Figure 2a,b). The cells treated with Navitoclax maintained a bipolar spindle configuration.

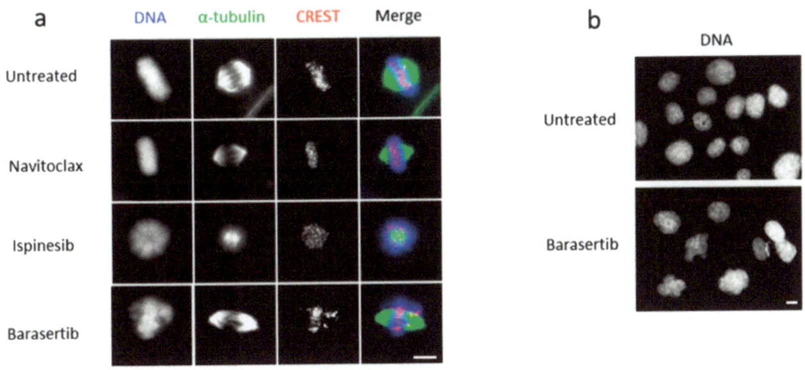

Figure 2. Mitotic defects induced by KSP and Aurora B inhibition. Illustrative immunofluorescence images showing SCC25 cells phenotype after 24 h treatment with 1.875 nM of Ispinesib or 1000 nM of Barasertib (**a**,**b**). DAPI was used to stain DNA (blue), while α-tubulin was stained to allow the visualization of microtubules (green), and CREST (red) for kinetochores localization. Bar, 5 µm.

To determine the IC_{50} of Ispinesib, Barasertib, and Navitoclax along with their cytotoxicity both alone and in combination, the MTT assay was performed in the oral cancer cell lines SCC09 and SCC25 (Table 1) and the dose–response curves were obtained (Figure 3). We observed that the SCC25 cells were more sensitive to Ispinesib and Barasertib compared to the SCC09 cells, whereas both showed comparable sensitivity to Navitoclax.

Table 1. IC_{50} values of Navitoclax, Ispinesib, and Barasertib in SCC25 and SCC09 cell lines after 48 h incubation.

	IC_{50} (nM)	
**Drugs	Cell Line**	**SCC25**	**SCC09**
Navitoclax	5197.0 ± 364.0	3754.0 ± 237.0
Ispinesib	3.4 ± 0.5	58.9 ± 3.2
Barasertib	5580.0 ± 664.0	>64,000.0

The viability assay data are presented as two dual-drug concentration crosswise matrices for each combination. Each matrix cell presents the percentage of viable cells for the drugs alone or in combination (Figure 4a,c,e,g) or the combinatorial interaction effect score (Figure 4,b,d,f,h). The results demonstrated that both combinations exhibited synergistic effects in both cell lines. To perform the subsequent experiments, we selected the SCC25 cell line since it displays the most favorable phenotypic characteristics for conducting microscopy assays. Furthermore, the concentrations used in the experiments for both combinations were the lower concentrations that showed synergistic effects (1.875 nM Ispinesib + 1500 nM of Navitoclax and 1000 nM Barasertib + 3000 nM of Navitoclax).

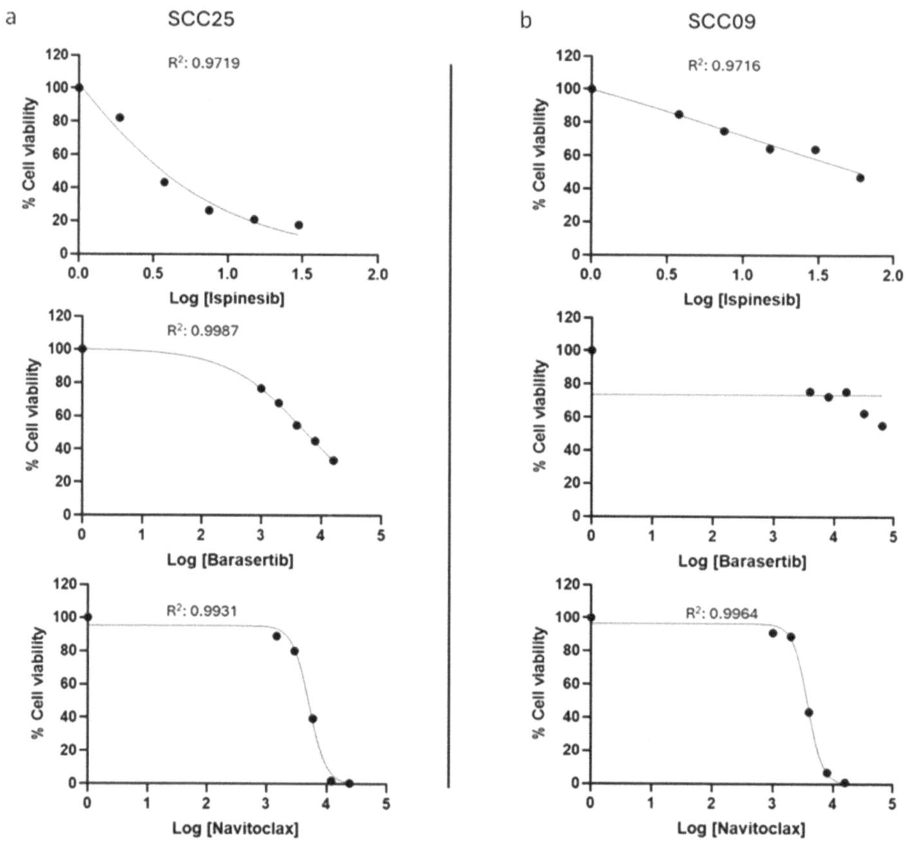

Figure 3. Dose−response curves of Ispinesib, Barasertib, and Navitoclax in SCC25 (**a**) and SCC09 (**b**) cell lines. The percentage of cell viability vs. the concentration of the different inhibitors (logarithmic scale) is shown. The R^2 values are shown for each curve indicating the fit of the model to the data.

Moreover, to further assess if the synergistic effects observed were exclusive to these inhibitors or if they were due to the combinatorial approaches, we also used Filanesib, (another KSP inhibitor), SP-96 (another Aurora B inhibitor), and ABT-737 (another BCL-2 and BCL-xL inhibitor) for some of the experiments performed in this study. Filanesib and SP-96 synergized with ABT-737 and behaved similarly to the combinations of Ispinesib with Navitoclax and Barasertib with Navitoclax, respectively (Figure S1 and Table S1).

To analyze the long-term effects of these combinations in the proliferation of oral cancer cells, a colony formation assay was performed and the addition of Ispinesib alone led to nearly a 40% reduction in colony formation capacity (61.42 ± 3.83 %), while Barasertib showed no difference in the untreated cells (101.41 ± 2.13%). However, the addition of Navitoclax to both Ispinesib and Barasertib led to significant decreases in the survival fraction compared to the drugs administered alone (13.85 ± 3.40% and 81.18 ± 2.44%, respectively) (Figure 4i,j,k). These results suggest that the combinatorial approaches exhibit an ability to maintain long-term cellular cytotoxicity, preventing the proliferation of cancer cells.

Our data showed that BH3-mimetics synergize with both KSP and Aurora B inhibitors. Thus, we proceeded with further analyses of these combinations in order to gather a deeper comprehension of the mechanisms underlying these synergistic effects. We first began by analyzing the mechanisms underlying the synergistic cytotoxicity of the KSP inhibition plus Navitoclax combination in the next subsection; then we analyzed that of the Aurora B inhibition plus Navitoclax combination in the subsequent subsection.

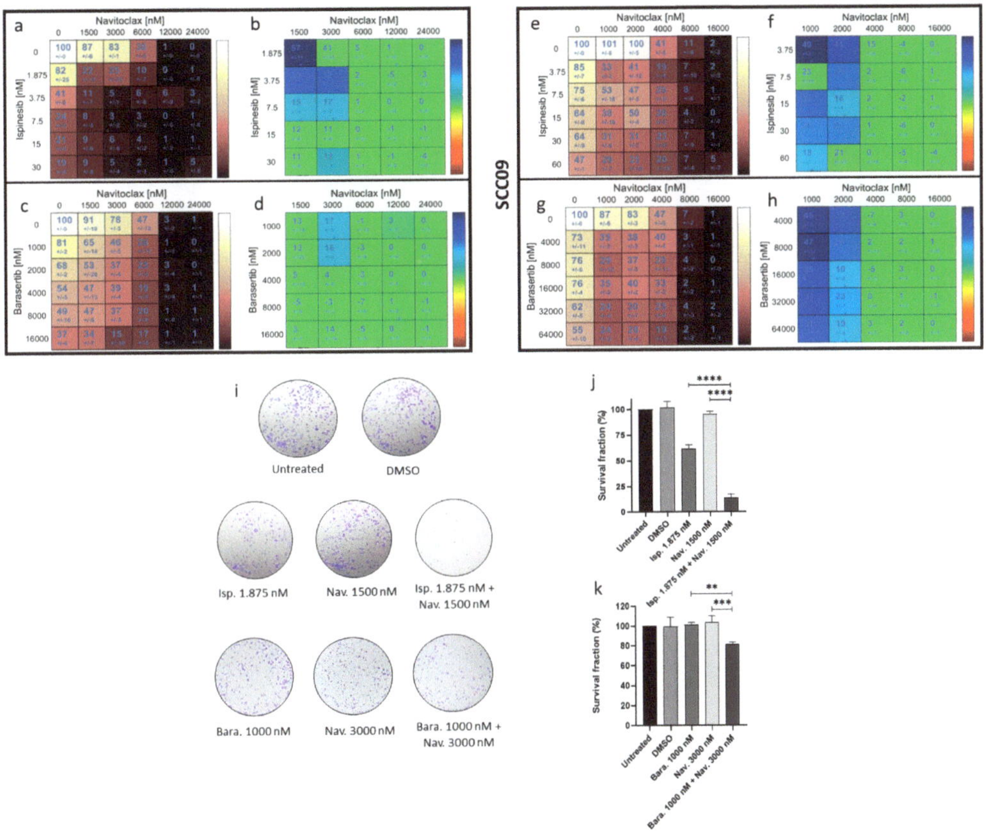

Figure 4. The combinatorial approaches Ispinesib + Navitoclax and Barasertib + Navitoclax enhance cytotoxicity in the SCC25 and SCC09 cell lines. Cell viability (%) following 48 h of drug exposure both alone or in combination (**a**,**c**,**e**,**g**), assessed by MTT assay with at least three independent experiments. The synergy scores were calculated using the Bliss model of the Combenefit software 2.021. Asterisks denote synergistic effects with statistical significance of * $p < 0.05$ and ** $p < 0.01$. (**b**,**d**,**f**,**h**). The representative images of colony formation assays following 6 days with SCC25 cells (**i**) are presented. The quantification of survival fraction (%) following treatment with drugs both alone and in combination is illustrated (**j**,**k**). The data presented are the average ± standard deviation of three separate experiments. Statistical analysis was performed using one-way ANOVA followed by Tukey's post hoc test for multiple comparisons. The significance levels were as follows: ** for $p < 0.01$; *** for $p < 0.001$; and **** for $p < 0.0001$.

3.3. *The Combined Treatment with Ispinesib and Navitoclax Enhances Death in Mitosis in Oral Cancer Cells*

When cells are arrested in mitosis, the two following outcomes can occur: death in mitosis or premature mitotic exit without undergoing cytokinesis, also known as mitotic slippage. Cell fate is decided according to the "competing networks-threshold model" where when cyclin B1 levels reach below the mitotic exit threshold first than apoptotic signaling reaches the apoptotic threshold, cells undergo mitotic slippage. On the other hand, if apoptotic signaling reaches the threshold first cell, death occurs [23]. Vorobjev et al. propose that when cells have a high concentration or high activity of BCL-xL, cyclin B1 degradation will reach the threshold for mitotic exit first before the apoptotic threshold is reached. However, post-slippage death (PSD) can occur if the level of BCL-xL is not high enough for cells to survive after mitotic exit. So, the level of the expression of BCL-xL at the time of slippage is the decisive factor between cell survival or PSD [24]. Therefore, with the purpose of promoting the apoptosis pathway, we analyzed the addition of Navitoclax to Ispinesib in oral cancer cells. To analyze the effect of this combination regarding mitotic index (MI) we used double the concentration of Ispinesib (3.75 nM) to ensure we would observe a clear outcome. Both the untreated cells (5.75 ± 0.46%) and the DMSO-treated (5.65 ± 0.42%) cells showed similar MIs showing no effect of the solvent at the concentration of 0.1%.

In addition, the MI of the cells treated with Navitoclax (5.67 ± 0.21%) showed no significant difference from the untreated ones. Nonetheless, the addition of Ispinesib both alone (28.31 ± 4.57%) and in combination with Navitoclax (28.82 ± 5.18%) led to a similar increase in MI, compared to the untreated SCC25 cells (Figure 5a,b).

To further assess the effects of Ispinesib alone and in combination with Navitoclax regarding cell fate and mitotic duration, time-lapse microscopy was conducted.

The untreated cells underwent mitosis on average for 46.11 ± 13.77 min and the addition of Navitoclax (58.33 ± 37.51 min), similarly to MI, did not significantly affect this duration. On the other hand, the cells treated with Ispinesib showed a significant increase in the mitotic duration (147.18 ± 127.50 min) when compared with the untreated cells (Figure 5c). Furthermore, a similar duration to Ispinesib alone was observed for the combination with Navitoclax (179.44 ± 150.21 min). Regarding the cell fate, our results showed that the Navitoclax-treated cells underwent mostly normal cell cycling (75.09 ± 29.99%) with 24.91% of the cells dying mostly by postmitotic death (PMD) (22.83 ± 26.17%) (Video S1). Ispinesib alone showed a similar percentage of cells undergoing normal cell division (90.63 ± 5.20%) to the untreated cells (97.06 ± 5.88%), which suggests that the cells delayed in mitosis under Ispinesib at 1.875 nM manage to form functional spindles and undergo normal cell division (Video S2). When we looked at the effects of the combination of Ispinesib and Navitoclax, a significant reduction in postmitotic survival was observed, with only 25.48 ± 25.98% undergoing normal cell cycling, when compared to the untreated cells and cells treated with the inhibitors alone (Figure 5d,e; Video S3). In addition, the combination showed a significant increase in cell death (68.90%) of which 87.3% corresponds to death in mitosis (DM). These results showcase that the addition of Navitoclax to Ispinesib enhances cell death mostly during mitosis.

Since the combination showed increased cell death, our next step was to assess if it was attributable to the promotion of apoptosis by the addition of Navitoclax using flow cytometry. Our results show that the addition of Navitoclax slightly increases the percentage of apoptotic cells (4.99 ± 0.60%) while Ispinesib (2.68 ± 0.48%) showed no difference when compared to the control (2.3 ± 0.79%). Nonetheless, the combination of Ispinesib and Navitoclax significantly enhanced the apoptotic signaling (7.4 ± 0.59%) (Figure 5f,g).

These results demonstrate that the addition of Navitoclax to Ispinesib increases the apoptotic signaling of the cells arrested in mitosis leading to increased cell death, making this combination a promising approach that needs to be further explored.

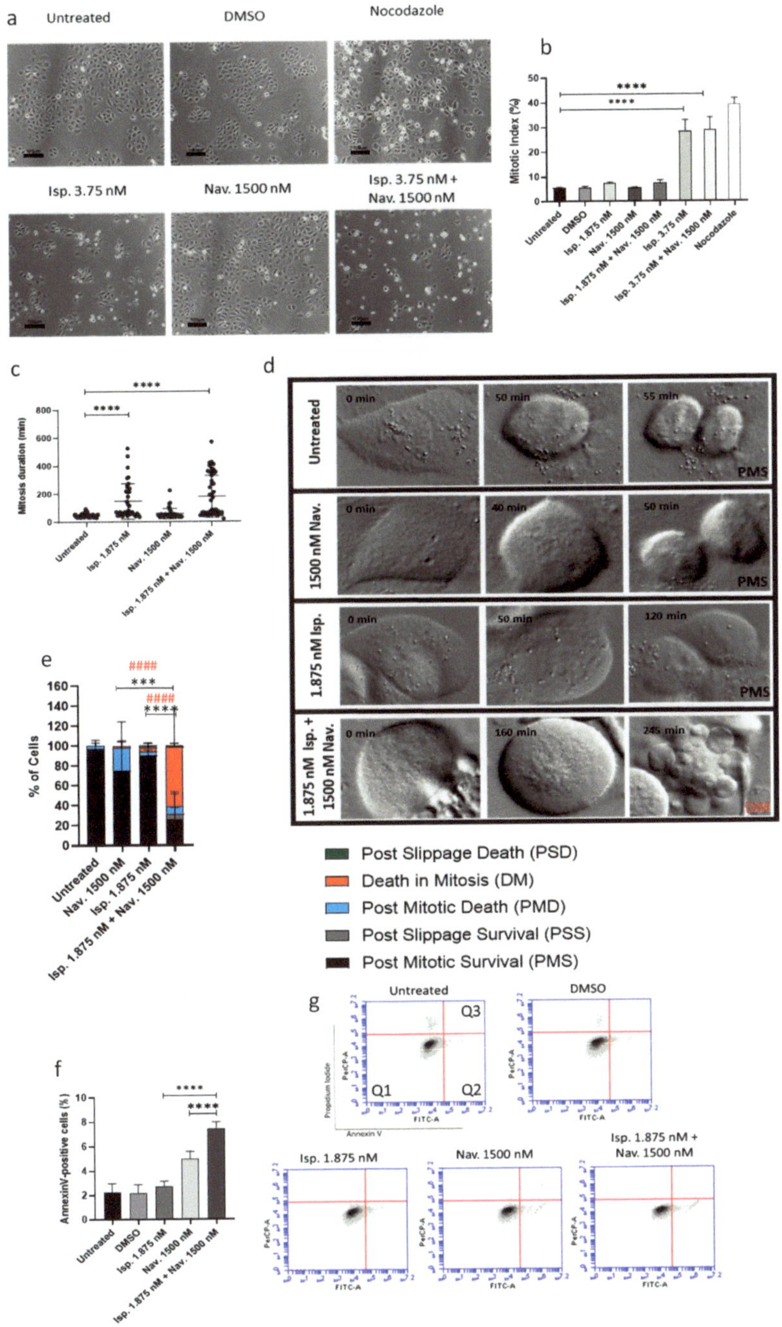

Figure 5. Addition of Navitoclax to Ispinesib increases cell death during mitosis in oral cancer cells. The representative images acquired by phase-contrast microscopy after drug exposure for 24 h for SCC25 (**a**). Mitotic index quantification for the SCC25 cell line (**b**); 0.2% of DMSO (drug solvent) was used as the negative control, while 1 μM of Nocodazole (mitotic blocker drug) was used as the positive control. The data presented are the average ± standard deviation of three separate experiments. Statistical analysis

was performed using one-way ANOVA followed by Tukey's post hoc test for multiple comparisons. **** $p < 0.0001$. The measurement of the duration of mitosis following the indicated drug treatments by time-lapse microscopy (**c**). The assessment of cell fate (%) over 48 h using indicated treatments (**f**). The representative time-lapse image sequences acquired during 48 h of exposure to drugs both alone and in combination (**d**). The assess-ment of cell fate (%) over 48 h using indicated treatments (**e**). The data presented are the average ± standard deviation of three separate experiments. Statistical analysis was performed using two-way ANOVA followed by Tukey's post hoc test for multiple comparisons. #### ($p < 0.0001$) statistically significant difference in the cells that underwent death in mitosis (%) between 1500 nM Navitoclax or 1.875 nM Ispinesib and 1.875 nM Ispinesib + 1500 nM Navitoclax. *** ($p < 0.001$) postmitotic survival cell (%) difference between 1500 nM Navitoclax and 1.875 nM Ispinesib + 1500 nM Navitoclax. **** ($p < 0.0001$) postmitotic survival cell (%) difference between 1.875 nM Ispinesib and 1.875 nM Ispinesib + 1500 nM Navitoclax. The combination of Ispinesib and Navitoclax enhances cell death in the SCC25 oral cancer cell line. The quantification of Annexin-V-positive cells (**f**). Cytograms demonstrative of the oral cancer cells double stained with Annexin V-FITC and propidium iodide (PI) (**g**). The quadrants Q are defined as Q1 = living cells (Annexin V- and PI-negative), Q2 = early-stage apoptosis (Annexin V-positive/PI-negative), and Q3 = late-stage apoptosis/secondary necrosis (Annexin V- and PI-positive). The data presented are the average ± standard deviation of three separate experiments. Statistical analysis was performed using one-way ANOVA followed by Tukey's post hoc test for multiple comparisons. The significance levels were as follows: **** for $p < 0.0001$.

3.4. *Combining Barasertib-Mediated Aurora B Inhibition with Navitoclax Shifts the Cancer Cell Fate from Post-Slippage Cell Survival to Post-Slippage Cell Death*

Aurora B plays a role in SAC activation by promoting mitotic checkpoint complex formation through the phosphorylation of Bub1 [17]. Consequently, inhibiting Aurora B suppresses sustained SAC activation [37]. In fact, the inhibition of Aurora B with Barasertib results in premature mitotic exit/mitotic slippage, ultimately leading to polyploidy [15,36]. According to Vorobjev et al.'s proposed model, the inhibition of BCL-xL and consequently increased apoptotic signaling should be enough to overcome mitotic slippage or lead to PSD. Thus, we proceeded to analyze the effects of the addition of Navitoclax to Barasertib.

Firstly, we analyzed the cell fate and mitotic duration of the cells that underwent mitosis by time-lapse microscopy, and, as referred above, the untreated cells had on average a mitotic duration of 46.11 ± 13.77 min, and the treatment with Navitoclax did not significantly affect this duration (53.60 ± 29.25 min). In the oral cancer cell line SCC25, Barasertib alone nearly doubled the mitotic duration when compared with the untreated cells (82.88 ± 33.21 min) (Figure 6a). This was expected since Aurora B inhibition leads to a transient arrest before the cells prematurely exit mitosis by satisfying the SAC [38,39]. The addition of Navitoclax to Barasertib led to a significant decrease in the mitotic duration when compared to Barasertib alone (59.40 ± 22.04 min).

When assessing the cell fate, the addition of Navitoclax led to 74.26 ± 1.04% of the cells completing normal cycling while Barasertib alone showed a 95.55% cell survivability. However, of those cells, 79.51% underwent post-slippage survival (PSS) while only 20.49% experienced normal cell division. Nonetheless, the addition of Navitoclax to Barasertib led to a decrease in cell survival (44.17%) with most cells undergoing PSS (25.83 ± 17.02%) (Figure 6b,c). In addition, the combination led to increased cell death (55.83%) when compared with the untreated (2.94 ± 5.88%) and both drugs alone (4.44% and 25.74% for Barasertib and Navitoclax, respectively) groups. The enhanced cell death observed for the combination was mostly due to the promotion of PSD (30.83 ± 13.77%). In this sense, the addition of Navitoclax to Barasertib does not seem to greatly reduce the mitotic slippage of cells (75.97 vs. 56.66%, for Barasertib alone and in combination with Navitoclax, respectively) but increases substantially cell death mainly post-slippage.

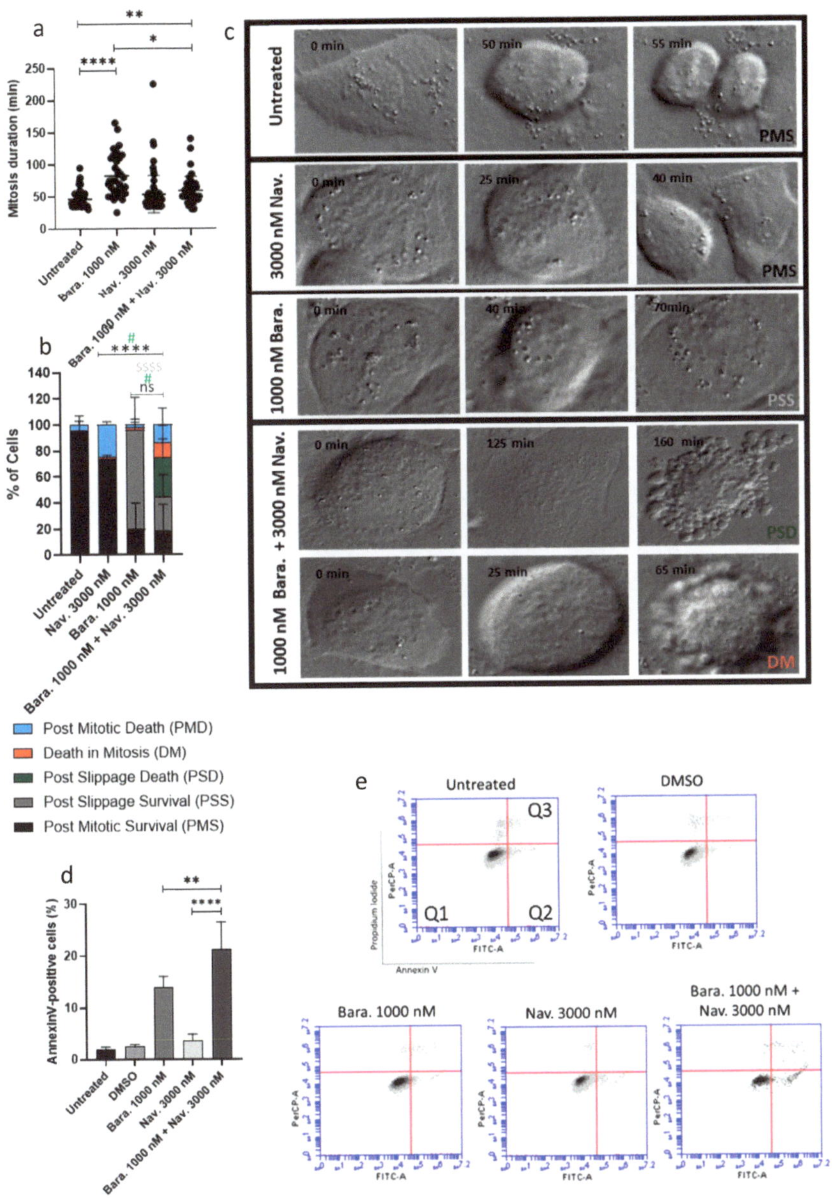

Figure 6. Addition of Navitoclax to Barasertib increases post-slippage death in oral cancer cells. The measurement of the duration of mitosis following the indicated drug treatments by time-lapse microscopy (**a**). The assessment of cell fate (%) over 48 h using indicated treatments (**b**). The representative time-lapse image sequences acquired during 48 h of exposure to drugs both alone and in combination (**c**). The data presented are the average ± standard deviation of three separate experiments. Statistical analysis was performed using two-way ANOVA followed by Tukey's post hoc test for multiple comparisons. # ($p < 0.05$) statistically significant difference in the cells that underwent post-slippage death (%) between 3000 nM Navitoclax or 1000 nM Barasertib and 1000 nM Barasertib + 3000 nM Navitoclax. **** ($p < 0.0001$) postmitotic survival cell (%) difference between 3000 nM Navitoclax and 1000 nM Barasertib + 3000 nM Navitoclax. $$$$ ($p < 0.0001$) post-slippage survival cell (%) difference between

1000 nM Barasertib and 1000 nM Barasertib + 3000 nM Navitoclax. The addition of Barasertib to Navitoclax enhances cell death in the oral cancer cell line SCC25. The quantification of Annexin-V-positive cells (**d**). Cytograms demonstrative of the oral cancer cells double stained with Annexin V-FITC and propidium iodide (PI) (**e**). The quadrants Q are defined as Q1 = living cells (Annexin V- and PI-negative), Q2 = early-stage apoptosis (Annexin V-positive/PI-negative), and Q3 = late-stage apoptosis/secondary necrosis (Annexin V- and PI-positive). The data presented are the average ± standard deviation of three separate experiments. Statistical analysis was performed using one-way ANOVA followed by Tukey's post hoc test for multiple comparisons. The significance levels were as follows: * for $p < 0.05$; ** for $p < 0.01$; and **** for $p < 0.0001$.

To assess if increased cell death was attributable to increased apoptosis, the annexin V/propidium iodide analysis by flow cytometry was performed after 24 h exposure for the combination of Barasertib with Navitoclax. The cells were only exposed for 24 h to guarantee no cell undergoing apoptosis would be lost in the analysis since it led to the killing of a high number of cells plated for cytometry analysis at this time point. Our results showed no significant increase in apoptotic cells with the addition of Navitoclax (3.68 ± 1.17%) when compared to the control (2.03 ± 0.41%). Barasertib alone (13.98 ± 2.05%) led to an increased percentage of cells undergoing apoptosis while the combination with Navitoclax (21.13 ± 5.32%) exacerbated even further this increase (Figure 6d,e; Videos S4 and S5).

The findings indicate that inhibiting Aurora B leads to cell slippage following a brief delay in mitosis. These slipped cells managed to survive, at least for the duration of the experiment. However, when combined with Navitoclax, the slipped cells underwent cell death, mainly through apoptosis, indicating a suppression of anti-apoptotic signals that would otherwise support the survival of these cells. This further emphasizes the clinical importance of combining antimitotics with BH3-mimetics to enhance cancer cell death.

4. Discussion

Cancers of the oral cavity are the most common types of HNSCC, and their treatment consists mostly of surgery with or without radiotherapy and/or chemotherapy [40]. Even though an improvement in overall survival has been observed in recent years with a 5-year survival rate between 60% and 65%, patients with regional and distant metastases show lower rates (between 40% and 50% and less than 10%, respectively) [6]. Therefore, new therapeutic strategies are urgently needed. MTAs are widely used for the treatment of oral cancer but show several disadvantages such as high toxicity and lack of specificity [8,9]. Thus, drugs targeting specific proteins involved in mitosis, known as the second generation of antimitotics (SGAs), were developed. However, in clinical trials such as monotherapy, SGAs showed disappointing results [18,20]. In this sense, combinatorial approaches with SGAs should be explored to give these drugs a second chance. Thus, targeting two distinct pathways crucial for cancer cell viability through the combination of SGA drugs with apoptotic inducers could be a great alternative for anticancer strategy. The possible synergistic effects, the ability to target multiple pathways, the potential to overcome drug resistance, and the broad applicability make this type of combination an attractive approach for improving treatment outcomes in cancer patients.

The aim of this study was to assess the effects of combining a KSP inhibitor or an Aurora B inhibitor with an inhibitor of BCL-2 family prosurvival members in OSCC cell lines. In our work, we showed that KSP and Aurora B are overexpressed in both SCC09 and SCC25 cell lines which is in accordance with prior studies that showed that both proteins are overexpressed in oral cancer cell lines, making them potential targets for the treatment of oral cancer [16,41,42].

Interestingly, the addition of Ispinesib and Barasertib led to a higher IC_{50} in the SCC09 cell line regardless of protein expression. This may have been due to the fact that SCC25 has a higher proliferation rate than SCC09 with a doubling time of 2–3 days vs. 5–7 days, respectively, and consequently, antimitotics have more opportunities to promote cell death in SCC25 [43,44]. Furthermore, the SCC09 cell line seems to be resistant to Barasertib treatment since the IC_{50} could not be reached, making this cell line potentially useful to understand and explore the mechanisms of resistance to this drug.

We then showed that the addition of Navitoclax to both Ispinesib and Barasertib led to synergistic effects in both cell lines used in this study at concentration levels lower than the IC_{50}. Since KSP inhibition leads to prolonged mitotic arrest, we expected the addition of Navitoclax to increase cell death during mitosis. In accordance, we showed here that, in fact, the addition of Navitoclax to Ispinesib exacerbated apoptotic signaling leading to cell death mainly during mitosis. Similarly, since Aurora B inhibition was shown to promote mitotic slippage, we were expecting that the addition of Navitoclax could increase cell death signaling enough to lead to cell death preventing premature mitotic exit. However, the addition of Navitoclax to Barasertib did not significantly affect the number of cells undergoing mitotic slippage but instead increased post-slippage death. Thus, and according to Vorobjev et al.'s model, SCC25 BCL-xL activity, at least after the addition of Navitoclax at the concentration of 3000 nM, should be high enough to still let mitotic slippage occur but not high enough to prevent PSD [24].

Additionally, we showed that the synergistic effects were not exclusive to these drugs but that the inhibition of the same targets with different drugs led to similar results (Figure S1). Furthermore, since one of the most common adverse reactions in clinical trials to the administration of Barasertib is neutropenia, SP-96 could be used as an alternative since it has been suggested that it is able to avoid these types of adverse events [45]. Nonetheless, no clinical trials have been conducted with this inhibitor, and thus, there is a need to further investigate these claims.

Several studies have shown that the inhibition of BCL-2 family members combined with antimitotics leads to increased cell death in several types of cancer [29–32]. Nonetheless, most have used antimicrotubules, such as Paclitaxel, that as previously stated, have low specificity to cancer cells. Furthermore, as far as we know, our study is the first to test these combinations and approaches in oral cancer cell lines. Moreover, the results presented here are in accordance with those our group has previously reported in non-small cell lung cancer lines with different antimitotics than the ones used in this study, which also showed synergistic effects [32,46]. This study thus contributes to increasing the scientific knowledge regarding this type of approach and further supports its potential for cancer treatment.

In summary, our results showcase the potential therapeutic benefits of concurrently inhibiting BCL-2 prosurvival family members with KSP or Aurora B proteins. Despite the encouraging outcomes observed in the investigated combinations, a constraint within the current study lies in the fact that the in vitro assays were conducted with only two cell lines and that no tests were conducted with these combinations in non-tumoral cell lines to assess if the combinations can improve the selective killing of oral cancer cells while minimizing harm to normal cells, as well as in models that can better mimic the tumor microenvironment such as heterotypic spheroids, and also in animal models. Nonetheless, we intend to perform these experiments in the foreseeable future since further investigations are imperative to gain a deeper comprehension of the underlying mechanisms driving the proposed combinations and to ascertain the in vivo pharmacodynamics and pharmacokinetics.

5. Conclusions

In conclusion, the addition of Navitoclax to both Ispinesib and Barasertib demonstrated synergistic effects in oral cancer cells, significantly increasing cell death primarily through enhanced apoptotic activity. Therefore, targeting apoptosis in combination with the inhibitors of KSP and Aurora B could be a more promising strategy to enhance cancer cell killing than using these inhibitors as monotherapy. The data point to a potential anticancer strategy that warrants further exploration.

Supplementary Materials: The following supporting information can be downloaded at: https://www.mdpi.com/article/10.3390/cancers16112014/s1, Table S1: IC50 values of ABT-737, Filanesib, and SP-96 in the SCC25 cell line, after 48 h incubation; Figure S1: The combinations of ABT-737 with Filanesib or SP-96 in SCC25 showed similar results to those of Navitoclax combined with Ispinesib or Barasertib enhancing cytotoxicity in SCC25. Video S1: Monitoring of an SCC25 cell treated with 1500 nM of Navitoclax that underwent normal cell cycling using timelapse microscopy (DIC). Time in the video is displayed in minutes; available online at https://youtu.be/WCpeu2xA0-0 (accessed on 14 April 2024). Video S2: Monitoring of an SCC25 cell treated with 1.875 nM of Ispinesib undergoing normal cell cycling using timelapse microscopy (DIC). Time in the video is displayed in minutes; available online at https://youtu.be/FTRhFMG3o8g (accessed on 14 April 2024). Video S3: Monitoring of an SCC25 cell treated with 1.875 nM of Ispinesib + 1500 nM of Navitoclax that died during mitosis using timelapse microscopy (DIC). Time in the video is displayed in minutes; available online at https://youtu.be/bJo7rPwBYrU (accessed on 14 April 2024). Video S4: Monitoring of an SCC25 cell treated with 1000 nM of Barasertib undergoing mitotic slippage using timelapse microscopy (DIC). Time in the video is displayed in minutes; available online at https://youtu.be/PjEc6NVpXNk (accessed on 14 April 2024). Video S5: Monitoring of an SCC25 cell treated with 1000 nM of Barasertib + 3000 nM of Navitoclax that died post-slippage using timelapse microscopy (DIC). Time in the video is displayed in minutes; available online at https://youtu.be/8Py7VXCONic (accessed on 14 April 2024). File S1: Original western blots.

Author Contributions: Conceptualization, H.B., P.M.A.S. and J.P.N.S.; methodology, J.P.N.S. and P.M.A.S.; formal analysis, J.P.N.S. and B.P.; investigation, J.P.N.S., B.P. and P.M.A.S.; resources, H.B. and P.M.A.S.; data curation, J.P.N.S., B.P. and P.M.A.S.; writing—original draft preparation, J.P.N.S.; writing—review and editing, J.P.N.S., B.P., L.M., P.M.A.S. and H.B.; supervision, L.M., P.M.A.S. and H.B.; project administration, H.B.; funding acquisition, P.M.A.S. and H.B. All authors have read and agreed to the published version of the manuscript.

Funding: This work was funded by CESPU—Cooperativa de Ensino Superior Politécnico e Universitário Crl (Grants Ref. AntiMitoSphere_APSFCT_IINFACTS_2021; Ref. Flav4Tumor-GI2-CESPU-2022; Ref. SGA4Cancer-GI2-CESPU-2022, and Ref. upPTXovcar-GI2-CESPU-2022) to H.B. and P.M.A.S. B.P. gratefully acknowledges CESPU (BD/CBAS/CESPU/01/2020) and Fundação para a Ciência e a Tecnologia (FCT) (2022.09451.BD) for financial support. J.P.N.S. gratefully acknowledges CESPU (BD/CBAS/CESPU/01/2021) for financial support.

Institutional Review Board Statement: Not applicable.

Informed Consent Statement: Not applicable.

Data Availability Statement: The data can be shared upon request.

Conflicts of Interest: The authors declare no conflicts of interest.

References

1. Sung, H.; Ferlay, J.; Siegel, R.L.; Laversanne, M.; Soerjomataram, I.; Jemal, A.; Bray, F. Global Cancer Statistics 2020: GLOBOCAN Estimates of Incidence and Mortality Worldwide for 36 Cancers in 185 Countries. CA. *Cancer J. Clin.* **2021**, *71*, 209–249. [CrossRef] [PubMed]
2. Melo, B.A.dC.; Vilar, L.G.; de Oliveira, N.R.; de Lima, P.O.; Pinheiro, M.d.B.; Domingueti, C.P.; Pereira, M.C. Human Papillomavirus Infection and Oral Squamous Cell Carcinoma—A Systematic Review. *Braz. J. Otorhinolaryngol.* **2021**, *87*, 346–352. [CrossRef] [PubMed]
3. Jiang, M.; Li, B. STAT3 and Its Targeting Inhibitors in Oral Squamous Cell Carcinoma. *Cells* **2022**, *11*, 3131. [CrossRef] [PubMed]
4. Nandini, D.B.; Rao, R.S.; Hosmani, J.; Khan, S.; Patil, S.; Awan, K.H. Novel Therapies in the Management of Oral Cancer: An Update. *Disease-a-Month* **2020**, *66*, 101036. [CrossRef] [PubMed]
5. Wang, D.; Lu, Y.; Nannapaneni, S.; Griffith, C.C.; Steuer, C.; Qian, G.; Wang, X.; Chen, Z.; Patel, M.; El-Deiry, M.; et al. Combinatorial Approaches Targeting the EGFR Family and C-Met in SCCHN. *Oral Oncol.* **2021**, *112*, 105074. [CrossRef] [PubMed]
6. Howard, A.; Agrawal, N.; Gooi, Z. Lip and Oral Cavity Squamous Cell Carcinoma. *Hematol. Oncol. Clin. N. Am.* **2021**, *35*, 895–911. [CrossRef] [PubMed]
7. Mokhtari, R.B.; Homayouni, T.S.; Baluch, N.; Morgatskaya, E.; Kumar, S.; Das, B.; Yeger, H. Combination Therapy in Combating Cancer. *Oncotarget* **2017**, *8*, 38022–38043. [CrossRef] [PubMed]
8. Guigay, J.; Tahara, M.; Licitra, L.; Keilholz, U.; Friesland, S.; Witzler, P.; Mesía, R. The Evolving Role of Taxanes in Combination With Cetuximab for the Treatment of Recurrent and/or Metastatic Squamous Cell Carcinoma of the Head and Neck: Evidence, Advantages, and Future Directions. *Front. Oncol.* **2019**, *9*, 668. [CrossRef] [PubMed]

9. Čermák, V.; Dostál, V.; Jelínek, M.; Libusová, L.; Kovář, J.; Rösel, D.; Brábek, J. Microtubule-Targeting Agents and Their Impact on Cancer Treatment. *Eur. J. Cell Biol.* **2020**, *99*, 151075. [CrossRef]
10. Novais, P.; Silva, P.M.A.; Amorim, I.; Bousbaa, H. Second-Generation Antimitotics in Cancer Clinical Trials. *Pharmaceutics* **2021**, *13*, 1011. [CrossRef]
11. Yu, W.-X.; Li, Y.-K.; Xu, M.-F.; Xu, C.-J.; Chen, J.; Wei, Y.-L.; She, Z.-Y. Kinesin-5 Eg5 Is Essential for Spindle Assembly, Chromosome Stability and Organogenesis in Development. *Cell Death Discov.* **2022**, *8*, 490. [CrossRef]
12. Bartoli, K.M.; Jakovljevic, J.; Woolford, J.L.; Saunders, W.S. Kinesin Molecular Motor Eg5 Functions during Polypeptide Synthesis. *Mol. Biol. Cell* **2011**, *22*, 3420–3430. [CrossRef] [PubMed]
13. Mann, B.J.; Wadsworth, P. Kinesin-5 Regulation and Function in Mitosis. *Trends Cell Biol.* **2019**, *29*, 66–79. [CrossRef]
14. Shao, Y.-Y.; Sun, N.-Y.; Jeng, Y.-M.; Wu, Y.-M.; Hsu, C.; Hsu, C.-H.; Hsu, H.-C.; Cheng, A.-L.; Lin, Z.-Z. Eg5 as a Prognostic Biomarker and Potential Therapeutic Target for Hepatocellular Carcinoma. *Cells* **2021**, *10*, 1698. [CrossRef]
15. Portella, G.; Passaro, C.; Chieffi, P. Aurora B: A New Prognostic Marker and Therapeutic Target in Cancer. *Curr. Med. Chem.* **2011**, *18*, 482–496. [CrossRef]
16. Qi, G.; Ogawa, I.; Kudo, Y.; Miyauchi, M.; Siriwardena, B.S.M.S.; Shimamoto, F.; Tatsuka, M.; Takata, T. Aurora-B Expression and Its Correlation with Cell Proliferation and Metastasis in Oral Cancer. *Virchows Arch.* **2007**, *450*, 297–302. [CrossRef]
17. Roy, B.; Han, S.J.Y.; Fontan, A.N.; Jema, S.; Joglekar, A.P. Aurora B Phosphorylates Bub1 to Promote Spindle Assembly Checkpoint Signaling. *Curr. Biol.* **2022**, *32*, 237–247. [CrossRef] [PubMed]
18. Tang, P.A.; Siu, L.L.; Chen, E.X.; Hotte, S.J.; Chia, S.; Schwarz, J.K.; Pond, G.R.; Johnson, C.; Colevas, A.D.; Synold, T.W.; et al. Phase II Study of Ispinesib in Recurrent or Metastatic Squamous Cell Carcinoma of the Head and Neck. *Investig. New Drugs* **2008**, *26*, 257–264. [CrossRef] [PubMed]
19. Lee, C.W.; Bélanger, K.; Rao, S.C.; Petrella, T.M.; Tozer, R.G.; Wood, L.; Savage, K.J.; Eisenhauer, E.A.; Synold, T.W.; Wainman, N.; et al. A Phase II Study of Ispinesib (SB-715992) in Patients with Metastatic or Recurrent Malignant Melanoma: A National Cancer Institute of Canada Clinical Trials Group Trial. *Investig. New Drugs* **2008**, *26*, 249–255. [CrossRef]
20. Boss, D.S.; Witteveen, P.O.; van der Sar, J.; Lolkema, M.P.; Voest, E.E.; Stockman, P.K.; Ataman, O.; Wilson, D.; Das, S.; Schellens, J.H. Clinical Evaluation of AZD1152, an i.v. Inhibitor of Aurora B Kinase, in Patients with Solid Malignant Tumors. *Ann. Oncol.* **2011**, *22*, 431–437. [CrossRef]
21. Helfrich, B.A.; Kim, J.; Gao, D.; Chan, D.C.; Zhang, Z.; Tan, A.-C.; Bunn, P.A. Barasertib (AZD1152), a Small Molecule Aurora B Inhibitor, Inhibits the Growth of SCLC Cell Lines In Vitro and In Vivo. *Mol. Cancer Ther.* **2016**, *15*, 2314–2322. [CrossRef]
22. Exertier, P.; Javerzat, S.; Wang, B.; Franco, M.; Herbert, J.; Platonova, N.; Winandy, M.; Pujol, N.; Nivelles, O.; Ormenese, S.; et al. Impaired Angiogenesis and Tumor Development by Inhibition of the Mitotic Kinesin Eg5. *Oncotarget* **2013**, *4*, 2302–2316. [CrossRef] [PubMed]
23. Sinha, D.; Duijf, P.H.G.; Khanna, K.K. Mitotic Slippage: An Old Tale with a New Twist. *Cell Cycle* **2019**, *18*, 7–15. [CrossRef] [PubMed]
24. Suleimenov, M.; Bekbayev, S.; Ten, M.; Suleimenova, N.; Tlegenova, M.; Nurmagambetova, A.; Kauanova, S.; Vorobjev, I. Bcl-XL Activity Influences Outcome of the Mitotic Arrest. *Front. Pharmacol.* **2022**, *13*, 933112. [CrossRef]
25. Alam, M.; Mishra, R. Bcl-XL Expression and Regulation in the Progression, Recurrence, and Cisplatin Resistance of Oral Cancer. *Life Sci.* **2021**, *280*, 119705. [CrossRef] [PubMed]
26. He, S.; Chakraborty, R.; Ranganathan, S. Proliferation and Apoptosis Pathways and Factors in Oral Squamous Cell Carcinoma. *Int. J. Mol. Sci.* **2022**, *23*, 1562. [CrossRef] [PubMed]
27. Chen, Y.; Kayano, T.; Takagi, M. Dysregulated Expression of Bcl-2 and Bax in Oral Carcinomas: Evidence of Post-Transcriptional Control. *J. Oral Pathol. Med.* **2000**, *29*, 63–69. [CrossRef]
28. Sharma, A.; Boise, L.; Shanmugam, M. Cancer Metabolism and the Evasion of Apoptotic Cell Death. *Cancers* **2019**, *11*, 1144. [CrossRef] [PubMed]
29. Shi, J.; Zhou, Y.; Huang, H.-C.; Mitchison, T.J. Navitoclax (ABT-263) Accelerates Apoptosis during Drug-Induced Mitotic Arrest by Antagonizing Bcl-XL. *Cancer Res.* **2011**, *71*, 4518–4526. [CrossRef]
30. Tan, N.; Malek, M.; Zha, J.; Yue, P.; Kassees, R.; Berry, L.; Fairbrother, W.J.; Sampath, D.; Belmont, L.D. Navitoclax Enhances the Efficacy of Taxanes in Non–Small Cell Lung Cancer Models. *Clin. Cancer Res.* **2011**, *17*, 1394–1404. [CrossRef]
31. Wang, C.; Huang, S.-B.; Yang, M.-C.; Lin, Y.-T.; Chu, I.-H.; Shen, Y.-N.; Chiu, Y.-H.; Hung, S.-H.; Kang, L.; Hong, Y.-R.; et al. Combining Paclitaxel with ABT-263 Has a Synergistic Effect on Paclitaxel Resistant Prostate Cancer Cells. *PLoS ONE* **2015**, *10*, e0120913. [CrossRef] [PubMed]
32. Pinto, B.; Novais, P.; Henriques, A.C.; Carvalho-Tavares, J.; Silva, P.M.A.; Bousbaa, H. Navitoclax Enhances the Therapeutic Effects of PLK1 Targeting on Lung Cancer Cells in 2D and 3D Culture Systems. *Pharmaceutics* **2022**, *14*, 1209. [CrossRef] [PubMed]
33. Silva, P.M.A.; Ribeiro, N.; Lima, R.T.; Andrade, C.; Diogo, V.; Teixeira, J.; Florindo, C.; Tavares, Á.; Vasconcelos, M.H.; Bousbaa, H. Suppression of Spindly Delays Mitotic Exit and Exacerbates Cell Death Response of Cancer Cells Treated with Low Doses of Paclitaxel. *Cancer Lett.* **2017**, *394*, 33–42. [CrossRef] [PubMed]
34. Pedro, M.; Ferreira, M.M.; Cidade, H.; Kijjoa, A.; Bronze-da-Rocha, E.; Nascimento, M.S.J. Artelastin Is a Cytotoxic Prenylated Flavone That Disturbs Microtubules and Interferes with DNA Replication in MCF-7 Human Breast Cancer Cells. *Life Sci.* **2005**, *77*, 293–311. [CrossRef]

35. Tsuda, Y.; Iimori, M.; Nakashima, Y.; Nakanishi, R.; Ando, K.; Ohgaki, K.; Kitao, H.; Saeki, H.; Oki, E.; Maehara, Y. Mitotic Slippage and the Subsequent Cell Fates after Inhibition of Aurora B during Tubulin-Binding Agent–Induced Mitotic Arrest. *Sci. Rep.* **2017**, *7*, 16762. [CrossRef]
36. Marxer, M.; Ma, H.T.; Man, W.Y.; Poon, R.Y.C. P53 Deficiency Enhances Mitotic Arrest and Slippage Induced by Pharmacological Inhibition of Aurora Kinases. *Oncogene* **2014**, *33*, 3550–3560. [CrossRef]
37. Gurden, M.D.; Anderhub, S.J.; Faisal, A.; Linardopoulos, S. Aurora B Prevents Premature Removal of Spindle Assembly Checkpoint Proteins from the Kinetochore: A Key Role for Aurora B in Mitosis. *Oncotarget* **2018**, *9*, 19525–19542. [CrossRef] [PubMed]
38. Salmela, A.-L.; Pouwels, J.; Mäki-Jouppila, J.; Kohonen, P.; Toivonen, P.; Kallio, L.; Kallio, M. Novel Pyrimidine-2,4-Diamine Derivative Suppresses the Cell Viability and Spindle Assembly Checkpoint Activity by Targeting Aurora Kinases. *Carcinogenesis* **2013**, *34*, 436–445. [CrossRef]
39. Li, J.; Yan, Z.; Li, H.; Shi, Q.; Ahire, V.; Zhang, S.; Nimishetti, N.; Yang, D.; Allen, T.D.; Zhang, J. The Phytochemical Scoulerine Inhibits Aurora Kinase Activity to Induce Mitotic and Cytokinetic Defects. *J. Nat. Prod.* **2021**, *84*, 2312–2320. [CrossRef]
40. Montero, P.H.; Patel, S.G. Cancer of the Oral Cavity. *Surg. Oncol. Clin. N. Am.* **2015**, *24*, 491–508. [CrossRef]
41. Pannone, G.; Hindi, S.A.H.; Santoro, A.; Sanguedolce, F.; Rubini, C.; Cincione, R.I.; De Maria, S.; Tortorella, S.; Rocchetti, R.; Cagiano, S.; et al. Aurora B Expression as a Prognostic Indicator and Possibile Therapeutic Target in Oral Squamous Cell Carcinoma. *Int. J. Immunopathol. Pharmacol.* **2011**, *24*, 79–88. [CrossRef] [PubMed]
42. Daigo, K.; Takano, A.; Manh, T.; Yoshitake, Y.; Shinohara, M.; Tohnai, I.; Murakami, Y.; Maegawa, J.; Daigo, Y. Characterization of KIF11 as a Novel Prognostic Biomarker and Therapeutic Target for Oral Cancer. *Int. J. Oncol.* **2018**, *52*, 155–165. [CrossRef] [PubMed]
43. Coon, J.; Kingsley, K. Assessment of MicroRNA (MiR)-365 Effects on Oral Squamous Carcinoma Cell Line Phenotypes. *Biomolecules* **2021**, *11*, 874. [CrossRef] [PubMed]
44. Mitchison, T.J. The Proliferation Rate Paradox in Antimitotic Chemotherapy. *Mol. Biol. Cell* **2012**, *23*, 1–6. [CrossRef] [PubMed]
45. Borah, N.A.; Reddy, M.M. Aurora Kinase B Inhibition: A Potential Therapeutic Strategy for Cancer. *Molecules* **2021**, *26*, 1981. [CrossRef]
46. Pinto, B.; Silva, J.P.N.; Silva, P.M.A.; Barbosa, D.J.; Sarmento, B.; Tavares, J.C.; Bousbaa, H. Maximizing Anticancer Response with MPS1 and CENPE Inhibition Alongside Apoptosis Induction. *Pharmaceutics* **2023**, *16*, 56. [CrossRef]

Disclaimer/Publisher's Note: The statements, opinions and data contained in all publications are solely those of the individual author(s) and contributor(s) and not of MDPI and/or the editor(s). MDPI and/or the editor(s) disclaim responsibility for any injury to people or property resulting from any ideas, methods, instructions or products referred to in the content.

Current Oncology

MDPI

Review

Antibody–Drug Conjugates: A Start of a New Era in Gynecological Cancers

Samir Fasih [1], Stephen Welch [1] and Ana Elisa Lohmann [1,2,*]

1 Department of Oncology, Division of Medical Oncology, University of Western Ontario, London, ON N6A 5W9, Canada; samir.fasih@lhsc.on.ca (S.F.); stephen.welch@lhsc.on.ca (S.W.)
2 Department of Epidemiology and Biostatistics, University of Western Ontario, London, ON N6A 5W9, Canada
* Correspondence: ana.lohmann@lhsc.on.ca; Tel.: +1-519-685-8640 (ext. 53292); Fax: +1-519-685-8808

Abstract: Antibody–drug conjugates (ADCs) are a new class of therapeutic agents designed to target specific antigens on tumor cells, combining the specificity of monoclonal antibodies with the cytotoxicity of chemotherapy agents. ADCs have been available for over a decade, but in gynecological cancers, these agents are relatively new with great promise ahead. More than 80% of ongoing trials in gynecological cancers are evaluating ADCs' safety and efficacy, of which 40% are early-phase trials. Around twenty ADCs are currently under investigation, either alone or in combination with chemotherapies or immune checkpoint inhibitors. Among them, mirvetuximab soravtansine has been recently approved by the Food and Drug Administration (FDA) in platinum-resistant ovarian cancer with high folate-α receptor expression, as a single agent or in combination. Tisotumab vedotin and trastuzumab deruxtecan are also now approved by the FDA in patients with pre-treated cervical and uterine cancers and further investigation is ongoing. Overall, the toxicity profiles of ADCs are acceptable. Ocular toxicity is one of the specific side effects of some ADCs, but most of the cases are manageable with the use of prophylactic steroids and dose adjustments. This review aims to provide an overview of the fundamental and operational features of ADCs and examine the latest and most promising data, with a particular focus on the Canadian viewpoint.

Keywords: antibody drug conjugates; gynecological cancers; ovarian cancer; cervical cancer

1. Introduction

Gynecological cancers are a group of neoplasms of female reproductive organs and genitals, including carcinomas of the vagina, vulva, cervix, uterus, ovaries, and fallopian tubes. Based on the statistics latest data available until the year 2022, cancer is the most common cause of death in Canada [1]. The most common gynecological cancer is uterine cancer (7.4%), followed by ovarian (2.7%) and cervical (1.4%), respectively [2]. The treatment of gynecological tumors depends on the cancer type and disease stage. Patients with distant metastasis or recurrences have a poor outcome with uterine and cervical cancer, having a 5-year survival rate of around 18% [3]. In ovarian cancer, the majority of patients present with advanced disease at initial diagnosis [4]. Despite excellent responses to surgery and chemotherapy, more than 80% [5] will relapse and eventually become platinum resistant. Recently, many immunotherapeutic treatments, including immune checkpoint inhibitors and monoclonal antibodies, have been used for treatment in gynecological malignancies, especially for uterine and cervical carcinomas, improving the therapeutic options of these diseases [6–8]. Antibody–drug conjugates (ADCs) have been in use for more than a decade in other cancers but in gynecological cancers they have recently come up, with a great promise for the future.

The first antibody–drug conjugate (ADC) utilized in clinical settings was gemtuzumab ozogamicin for acute myeloid leukemia, approved by the Food and Drug Administration (FDA) in 2001 [9]. Following that, brentuximab vedotin received approval for Hodgkin lymphoma [10]. Trastuzumab emtansine (T-DM1) was the first ADC approved by the FDA for solid tumors, used in the treatment of metastatic as well as early-stage breast cancer [11,12]. These ADCs feature a unique structure and design, employing monoclonal antibodies to selectively deliver potent cytotoxic agents directly to the tumor site. Theoretically, this design aims to target only the cancer cells while preserving healthy tissues. In the early 20th century, Paul Ehrlich coined the concept of "magic bullets", suggesting that certain compounds could reach specific cellular targets to treat diseases [13]. Since then, the field has advanced rapidly, with more than 100 different types of ADCs currently being investigated for use in both solid and hematological malignancies. To date, sixteen ADCs have been approved by the FDA, the European Medicines Agency (EMA), and other regulatory bodies, and have been launched in the market for the treatment of hematologic malignancies and solid tumors [14].

In this article, we discuss the use of new antibody drug conjugates for treating patients with various gynecologic cancers.

2. ADCs: Mechanism of Action

2.1. Structure

ADCs consist of three structural components that play a crucial role in determining the effectiveness and safety of the drug. The ADCs consist of a targeted antibody which is attached to a potent cytotoxic agent called the 'payload' via a chemical 'linker' [11]. The three structural components with their characteristics are shown in Figure 1 [12].

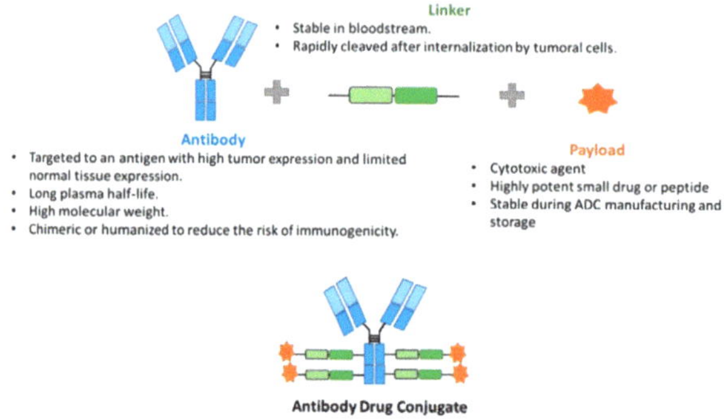

Figure 1. Scheme of the general structure of an ADC [12].

2.1.1. Antibody

The first component is a highly selective monoclonal antibody that specifically targets a tumor-associated antigen, with minimal expression on other tissues [13]. The latest ADCs are developed from fully humanized antibodies, typically of the IgG type. The utilization of fully humanized antibodies has been instrumental in reducing the immunogenicity of earlier ADCs, which were created using murine and chimeric components [14]. IgG1 antibodies are now more commonly used because of their overall stability in systemic circulation, with a long half-life of 2 to 3 weeks and a strong influence on innate immune cells, such as natural killer (NK) cells and macrophages, through interactions with Fcγ receptors [15].

2.1.2. Payload

The second component is the drug conjugate, also known as the payload, which typically consists of a conventional chemotherapy agent. Payloads refer to cytotoxic molecules that are very small and typically measure in the nanomolar or picomolar range. These molecules are attached to the structure of an antibody through a linker. Throughout the years, various classes of payloads have been created, with auristatins and maytansinoids being the most commonly used [16]. Auristatins are man-made compounds that mimic dolostatin, a natural substance that inhibits the assembly of tubulin [17]. The most commonly used auristatin is monomethyl auristatine E (MMAE), also known as vedotin. Another group of frequently used compounds are maytansinoids, which are synthetic versions of maytansine and function similarly to vinca alkaloids by inhibiting microtubule assembly. Maytansinoids, such as mertansine (DM1), emtansine, soravtansine, and ravtansine (DM4), are commonly used [18]. Calicheamicin, duocarmicins, and pyrrolobenzodiazepines are examples of additional payloads that have been developed for use in clinical practice. These payloads possess potent inhibitory properties against nucleic acid synthesis due to their unique capability to identify and attach to specific sequences within the minor groove of DNA. More recently, Topoisomerase I (TOP1) inhibitors constitute an emerging payload class to engineer antibody drug conjugates labelled as next-generation ADCs. These Exatecan-based linker–payload complexes are more potent and stable and can carry a higher concentration of drug to antibody ratio (DAR). One other factor is that hydrophobicity can determine the efficacy and toxicity of an ADC. Hydrophobic payloads can diffuse from the target expressing cells to adjacent normal cells, a phenomenon called the "bystander effect". This occurrence is very important, especially in regards to the heterogeneity of tumors, as the therapeutic effects are enhanced due to the bystander effect [19,20]. At the same time, the level of hydrophobicity can affect the penetration of the payload into the liver, causing liver toxicity if it is less hydrophobic, or the payload can be taken up by tissues, causing hematological and ocular toxicities [21–23]. The fine-tuning of payloads is necessary to maintain the bystander effect yet also maintain the efficacy by controlling the drug to antibody ratio (DAR) [24]. Other than the conventional payloads, immunomodulators [25] and protein-degrader-recruiting molecules [26] have recently emerged as novel payloads.

2.1.3. Linker

The final component is the linker, which joins the monoclonal antibody to the drug conjugate. It maintains the stability of the drug conjugate in the bloodstream while effectively releasing the payload inside the target cell [27]. Linkers are categorized into two types: cleavable and non-cleavable [27]. Cleavable linkers can be broken down by reactions involving proteases, acidic pH, endosomes, or lysosomes. This allows some of the cytotoxic payload to be released into the tumor microenvironment, impacting both antigen-expressing target cells and nearby non-antigen-expressing cells through the bystander effect [28]. Conversely, non-cleavable linkers rely on the lysosomal proteolytic activity of the antibody to release the payload. When non-cleavable linkers are cleaved, the payload remains attached to the linker, which can affect its electrical charge, hydrophobicity, or hydrophilicity. This may influence the payload's ability to cross the cell membrane. Moreover, the linker itself can be expelled from the cell by efflux pumps, leading to the removal of the linker–payload complex. This can decrease the intracellular concentration of the payload and potentially contribute to drug resistance [27].

2.1.4. Conjugation

Other than the structural details, conjugation is a crucial component for making an ADC more therapeutically effective. Most ADCs have traditionally been constructed using cysteine–maleimide alkylation or, less commonly, lysine–amide coupling. To lessen the chances of heterogeneity, different conjugation techniques are being used to improve payload delivery. The prime objective is to make homogenous conjugations which produce ADCs which are predictive in terms of their DAR. A few of the novel techniques of conjugation used are full alkylation of interchain disulfides used in T-DXd and sacituzumab govitecan, THIOMAB [28], incorporation of non-naturally occurring reactive amino acids [29,30], cysteine re-bridging [31,32], Fc-affinity tags [33], and site-specific conjugation using various enzymes (such as engineered glycosidases [34,35], transglutaminases [36,37], formyl glycine-generating enzymes [38,39], Fc-affinity peptides [40] (AJICAP-M) and sortases [41,42].

2.2. Mechanism of Action

When the antibody–drug conjugate (ADC) binds to its target using the fragment antigen binding (Fab) region, the entire ADC–antigen complex is internalized into the cell through receptor-mediated endocytosis [43]. The payload is then released within an endosome or lysosome, contingent on the linker type. Eventually, the drug conjugate makes its way to the nucleus, where it implements its cytotoxic action on DNA, RNA, or microtubules, resulting in cell death, as demonstrated in Figure 2 [44].

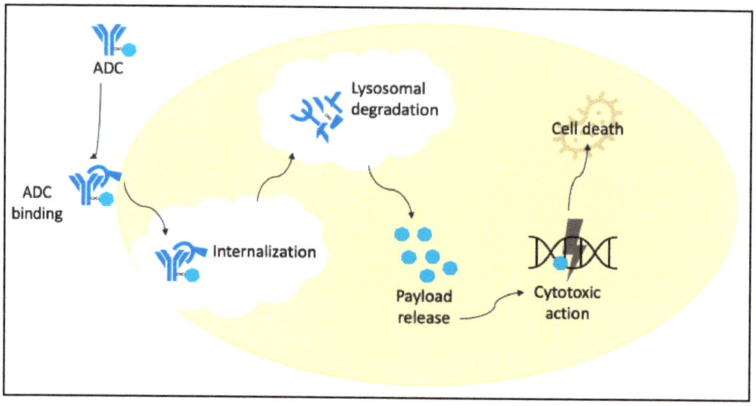

Figure 2. Mechanism of action of ADCs: Binding to the target, followed by internalization and release of cytotoxic payload, leading to cell death [44].

3. ADCs in Gynecological Malignancies

The objective of ADCs is to enhance effectiveness while reducing the overall toxicity by delivering targeted cytotoxic therapy specifically to cancer cells. However, there is a possibility of on-target, off-tumor toxicities occurring when ADCs bind to non-cancer cells that also express the target antigen [45]. In the field of gynecological tumors, there are currently three ADCs that have been approved by the FDA, namely tisotumab vedotin, mirvetuximab soravtansine, and Trastuzumab Deruxtecan (T-DXd) [46,47].

3.1. ADCs in Ovarian Cancer

In the first-line treatment of advanced stage III/IV ovarian cancer, the current recommended approach is to combine optimal cytoreductive surgery with platinum-based chemotherapy. Additionally, the use of maintenance therapy after front-line therapy involving the antiangiogenic medication bevacizumab, as seen in the ICON7 [48] and GOG218 [49] trials, and/or poly (ADP-ribose) polymerase (PARP) inhibitors, as observed in trial SOLO 1, particularly in patients with BRCA mutations, has shown notable improvements in patient outcomes (HR 0.66; 95% CI 0.50 to 0.87) based on a network meta-analysis [50]. Although patients initially exhibit a high response rate, eventually 80% of them will encounter disease recurrence and a gradual development of resistance to chemotherapy [51]. In particular, when platinum resistance is present, there are few treatment options available, and the outlook is not favorable. Conventional treatments currently in use have low rates of response (15–20%) and a limited progression-free survival (PFS) of 3–4 months, with an overall survival (OS) of only 12 months [52]. In the context of recurrent disease, treatment options are often restricted due to the residual toxicity from previous therapies. The use of ADCs presents a valuable opportunity to enhance the effectiveness of chemotherapy while reducing systemic toxicities.

3.1.1. Folate Receptor ADCs

Mirvetuximab soravtansine (MIRV) is an antibody–drug conjugate (ADC) that consists of a monoclonal antibody targeting the antifolate receptor α (FRα), a cleavable linker, and a potent antimitotic agent, DM4, which specifically targets tubulin [53]. The FRα receptor is a cell membrane protein responsible for binding and transporting folate into cells and is found in higher concentrations in epithelial tumors, especially high-grade serous ovarian and serous endometrial cancers, compared to its limited presence in normal adult tissues [54,55]. DM4 is electrically neutral and lipophilic, allowing it to penetrate cell membranes and generate the "bystander effect [56]". In a phase I trial, the recommended dose of MIRV for solid tumors, including previously treated epithelial ovarian cancer (EOC), was established at 6 mg/kg every 3 weeks, with initial signs of activity observed [57]. Dose-limiting toxicities included grade 3 hypophosphatemia and grade 3 ocular toxicity, such as punctate keratitis [57]. A follow-up study on an expansion cohort of 46 patients with platinum-resistant EOC and FRα positivity, assessed through immunohistochemistry, revealed an overall response rate of 26%, with one complete response and 11 partial responses. The median progression-free survival (mPFS) was 4.8 months, and the median duration of response (DOR) was 19.1 weeks [58]. A phase Ib study confirmed the correlation between FRα expression levels and MIRV efficacy, with no objective response in patients with low FRα expression and an mPFS of 2.8 months [59]. However, the phase III FORWARD I trial, which compared MIRV with standard chemotherapy in platinum-resistant ovarian cancer, did not achieve its primary endpoint of progression-free survival (HR 0.98; 95% CI 0.73 to 1.31) [60]. In a subset of patients with high FRα expression, MIRV demonstrated anti-tumor activity, but the results were not statistically significant. Despite this, the study suggested a favorable benefit/risk safety profile compared to standard chemotherapy [60]. Based on these findings, two subsequent studies, MIRASOL and SORAYA, were initiated to evaluate the efficacy of MIRV in patients with high FRα expression. The main objective of the SORAYA study was to determine the confirmed objective response rate, as assessed by the investigator [61]. One hundred and six patients were included in the study, with one hundred and five being evaluated for effectiveness. All patients had previously received bevacizumab, with 51% having undergone three previous lines of therapy and 48% having received a prior poly ADP-ribose polymerase inhibitor. The median follow-up period was 13.4 months. The overall response rate was determined to be 32.4% (95% CI 23.6 to 42.2), with five complete responses and 29 partial responses. The median duration of response was 6.9 months (95% CI 5.6 to 9.7). Among patients with one to two prior treatments, the determined by the investigator was 35.3% (95% CI 22.4 to 49.9), while in patients with three prior treatments, it was lower, at 30.2% (95% CI 18.3 to 44.3). The overall response rate determined by the investigator was 38.0% (95% CI 24.7 to 52.8) in patients with prior exposure to a poly ADP-ribose polymerase inhibitor and 27.5% (95% CI 15.9 to 41.7) in those without such exposure. The most common treatment-related adverse events, both overall and of grade 3–4 severity, were blurred vision (41% and 6%), keratopathy (29% and 9%), and nausea (29% and 0%). These adverse events led to dose delays, reductions, and discontinuations in 33%, 20%, and 9% of patients, respectively. Ocular toxicity with MIRV was off target, as there are no folate receptor alpha receptors on the cornea.

The MIRASOL investigators conducted a phase III clinical trial to assess the efficacy and safety of mirvetuximab soravtansine compared to chemotherapy in patients with platinum-resistant, high-grade serous ovarian cancer [62]. Participants in this study had previously received 1 to 3 lines of treatment and exhibited high FRα tumor expression. A total of 453 participants were randomly assigned to receive either mirvetuximab soravtansine or chemotherapy, with 227 in the MIRV group and 226 in the chemotherapy group. For those on mirvetuximab soravtansine, the median progression-free survival (PFS) was 5.62 months (95% CI 4.34 to 5.95), compared to 3.98 months (95% CI 2.86 to 4.47) for those on chemotherapy, showing an improvement with MIRV. The overall response rate was 42.3% for the mirvetuximab soravtansine group versus 15.9% for the chemotherapy group. Overall survival (OS) was significantly longer with MIRV, with a median of 16.46 months compared to 12.75 months for chemotherapy (HR 0.67; 95% CI 0.50 to 0.89). Grade 3 or higher adverse events occurred less frequently with mirvetuximab soravtansine at 41.7%, compared to 54.1% for chemotherapy. The most common adverse effects were mild gastrointestinal, neurosensory, and reversible ocular events. Serious adverse events of any grade (23.9% vs. 32.9%) and discontinuation events (9.2% vs. 15.9%) were also lower with mirvetuximab soravtansine.

The ocular side effects of MIRV are not related to folate receptor targeting, as there are no folate receptor alpha receptors on the cornea. Damage to the cornea starts at the outer edges after mirvetuximab soravtansine travels to the cornea through the limbal region, where stem cells that accumulate DM4 are located [55]. These damaged stem cells move inward and cause the formation of small cysts in the cornea. The use of ocular steroids can slow down the growth of these damaged stem cells at the outer edges, reducing their sensitivity to the harmful effects of DM4. The cornea can regenerate new cells within seven to 10 days, so ocular side effects usually resolve within a week.

Other studies with mirvetuximab, such as the PICCOLO study, are currently exploring the use of mirvetuximab soravtansine as a stand-alone treatment for patients with ovarian cancer that is sensitive to platinum [56]. In the GLORIOSA study, mirvetuximab soravtansine is being compared to bevacizumab alone, as well as a combination of mirvetuximab soravtansine and bevacizumab, for maintenance therapy after a positive response to platinum in ovarian cancer that is sensitive to platinum [57]. Additionally, the combination of mirvetuximab soravtansine and carboplatin is being investigated as a second-line treatment option for patients with epithelial ovarian cancer that are sensitive to platinum [58,59]. In one ongoing trial, MIRV is being studied as part of a front-line neoadjuvant therapy in combination with carboplatin in advanced ovarian cancer [61].

Luveltamab tazevibulin (STRO-002) is an ADC that also specifically targets the folate receptor alpha (FRα) in tumor cells. It is composed of the FRα-binding antibody SP8166, a cleavable protease linker, and a hemiasterlin-derivative payload called SC209 [63]. The ADC has a cathepsin-sensitive linker that, when cleaved in the tumor microenvironment or upon internalization into tumor cells, allows for a targeted delivery and cytotoxic effect in tumor cells. We expect that this antibody–drug conjugate will be more stable and have less toxicity, as it is more stable in blood, and SC209 demonstrates rapid clearance. In addition, SC209 is less likely to be pumped out of cells by the efflux pump P-glycoprotein, making STRO-002 a more potent treatment option for ovarian cancers that are resistant to other therapies like platinum or PARP inhibitors [63]. Another feature in favor of STRO-002 is its ability to produce bystander killing of neighboring tumor cells that do not express FRα, further enhancing its effectiveness in tumors with heterogeneous or low FRα expression. The hemiasterlin-derivative payload of STRO-002 not only inhibits tubulin, but also stimulates an immunogenic response upon cell death [63].

Preliminary data from a phase I dose escalation study in advanced ovarian cancer patients showed that a higher dose of STRO-002 resulted in a higher overall response rate (43.8%) compared to a lower dose with an overall response rate of 31.3%. The safety profile was also acceptable with most treatment-related adverse events being grades 1 or 2 and no ocular toxicity reported [64]. Most of the studies are ongoing and results are expected to be published in coming years. A phase I STRO-002-GM2 study (NCT05200364) is aimed at evaluating the combination of STRO-002 and bevacizumab in patients with advanced platinum-resistant ovarian cancer. The main goal of the STRO-002-GM2 study is to determine the recommended phase 2 dose (RP2D) of the STRO-002/bevacizumab combination and assess its safety. Secondary and exploratory objectives include investigating the pharmacokinetics (PK) and preliminary anti-tumor activity of the combination [65]. REFRaME-O1 (NCT05870748) is a two-part phase II trial evaluating the efficacy and safety of luveltamab tazevibulin in patients with relapsed platinum-resistant epithelial ovarian cancer expressing folate receptor alpha. In Part 1, it involves two dosing cohorts (Cohort A and Cohort B) with a 1:1 randomization, which aims to optimize the dosing in Part 1, and then Part 2 will further evaluate the efficacy and safety of the selected dosing regimen [66].

Another ADC targeting FRα is MORAb-202 (farletuzumab ecteribulin), which consists of a farletuzumab antibody aimed at FRα, combined with the cytotoxic agent eribulin mesylate through a cleavable linker. In a phase I dose-escalation study involving FRα-positive solid tumors, MORAb-202 achieved a disease control rate of 75%, with one complete response and two partial responses among nine ovarian cancer patients [67]. Additionally, a phase I/II trial is investigating MORAb-202 in various tumor types, including endometrial and platinum-resistant ovarian cancer. Eligible endometrial cancer patients must have experienced relapse or failure following at least one prior platinum-based chemotherapy or one immunotherapy regimen [67] (NCT04300556). Currently, MORAb-202 is undergoing a phase II trial to compare its efficacy with the investigator's choice of chemotherapy in patients with platinum-resistant high-grade serous ovarian, peritoneal, or fallopian tube cancer [68] (NCT05613088).

Another upcoming folate receptor alpha (FRα) ADC is AZD5335; its preliminary data were recently presented [69,70]. AZD5335 is a new ADC with an antibody portion targeting folate receptor alpha (FRα) and a conjugated topoisomerase 1 inhibitor (TOP1i) as a payload. It was reported that a single dose of AZD5335 at 2.5 mg/kg was sufficient to provide a solid and consistent anti-tumor response in FRα-expressing ovarian cancer cell line xenografts (CDX) with a tumor growth inhibition (TGI) of 75–94% and median best tumor volume reduction of >30% in 14/17 (82%) ovarian cancer patient-derived xenografts (PDX). An ongoing phase I/IIa study for AZD5335 as monotherapy and in combination with anti-cancer agents in participants with solid tumors (FONTANA) is recruiting patients. It will assess safety and tolerability along with response rate, duration of response, disease control rate, and progression-free and overall survival [71] (NCT05797168).

3.1.2. Other ADCs

MUC 16

Another drug, DMUC4064A, is a monoclonal antibody that targets MUC16, a protein overexpressed in most epithelial ovarian cancers. The antibody is conjugated to monomethyl auristatin E, a microtubule-disrupting agent. A phase I/II study was conducted to evaluate the safety, tolerability, pharmacokinetics, and preliminary activity of DMUC4064A in patients with platinum-resistant ovarian cancer (OC). A total of 65 patients with platinum-resistant OC were enrolled in the study. They received DMUC4064A once every 3 weeks in dose escalation cohorts. The patients received a median of 5 cycles of DMUC4064A. The maximum tolerated dose was not reached, and the recommended phase II dose (RP2D) was determined on the overall tolerability profile. The most common adverse events reported by patients included fatigue, nausea, abdominal pain, constipation, blurred vision, diarrhea, and anemia. The study did not report on the preliminary activity or efficacy of DMUC4064A in treating platinum-resistant OC. In conclusion, the study found that DMUC4064A was generally well-tolerated in patients with platinum-resistant OC, with the RP2D determined. Further studies are needed to evaluate the efficacy of DMUC4064A in treating platinum-resistant OC [72].

Mesothelin

Mesothelin is a cell membrane glycoprotein primarily present in the mesothelial cells lining the pleura, pericardium, and peritoneum. While its expression in normal tissues is limited, it is significantly overexpressed in various cancers, including up to 70% of ovarian cancer cases [73]. Its involvement in cell adhesion and metastasis makes mesothelin an appealing target for cancer-specific therapies [74]. Several anti-mesothelin antibody–drug conjugates (ADCs) are being explored, with anetumab ravtansine (BAY 94-9343) being a notable example. This ADC is composed of a fully humanized monoclonal antibody directed at mesothelin, a disulfide linker, and the cytotoxic agent DM4, a tubulin inhibitor [74]. In a study involving 65 patients with platinum-resistant epithelial ovarian cancer, anetumab ravtansine was administered with pegylated liposomal doxorubicin intravenously every three weeks. During the dose escalation phase, nine patients received two different doses of anetumab ravtansine without experiencing any dose-limiting toxicities. In the dose expansion phase, 56 patients were treated at the maximum tolerated dose. The most frequent side effects included nausea (47.7%), decreased appetite (43.1%), fatigue (38.5%), diarrhea (32.3%), and corneal disorder (29.2%). The overall objective response rate was 27.7%, with one complete response and 17 partial responses. The median duration of response was 7.6 months and the median progression-free survival was 5.0 months. Among patients with high mesothelin expression and three or fewer previous systemic therapies, the objective response rate was 42.1%, with a median response duration of 8.3 months and median progression-free survival of 8.5 months [75].

CDH6

Cadherin-6 (CDH6) is a transmembrane protein expressed in many cancers, including epithelial ovarian cancers [76]. A novel ADC, raludotatug deruxtecan (R-DXd) is a CDH6 protein-targeting antibody–drug conjugate [77]. A first-in-human phase I study recruited 42 patients with ovarian cancer; all were platinum resistant, 29 (69%) had received prior bevacizumab, and 26 (62%) had received prior PARP inhibitors. As per the latest update, half of the patients were still receiving the treatment. Treatment-emergent adverse events (TEAEs) were experienced by 37 patients (88%), and grade $\geq$ 3 TEAEs were observed in 21 (50%). The most common all-grade TEAEs were nausea (55%), fatigue (40%), vomiting (38%), and diarrhea (33%). Adverse effects led to R-DXd discontinuation in 14% of patients. In regards to efficacy, the overall response rate was 38%, with 1 CR, and 11 out of 21 patients were showing down-trending Ca-125 [78] (NCT04707248).

3.2. ADCs in Cervical Cancer

Cervical cancer has a 5-year survival rate of 67% [2,79]. Currently, the recommended initial treatment for patients with recurrent or metastatic cervical cancer is a combination therapy consisting of pembrolizumab, bevacizumab, and a chemotherapy doublet of paclitaxel and platinum, based on the PDL1 status [80]. In the second-line setting, there are limited options available. Available cytotoxic agents such gemcitabine, irinotecan, and pemetrexed have low levels of efficacy. Patients who are naïve to immune checkpoint inhibitor could be considered for pembrolizumab or cemiplimab in second-line treatment [80].

Tisotumab Vedotin

Many solid tumors, including cervical cancers, express high levels of Tissue Factor (TF), which can promote tumor growth, metastasis, and angiogenesis [46]. Tisotumab vedotin (TV) is an ADC targeting TF. GOG-3023/ENGOT-cx6/innovaTV204 evaluated the effectiveness and safety of TV in patients with previously treated recurrent or metastatic cervical cancer [46]. The phase 2 trial which led to its FDA approval enrolled 102 patients who had experienced disease progression after receiving doublet chemotherapy with or without bevacizumab. Eligible patients had received a maximum of two prior systemic treatment regimens for recurrent or metastatic cancer. During the trial, patients received TV intravenously at a dose of 2 mg/kg every 3 weeks until disease progression or unacceptable toxicity. The primary endpoint of the trial was the objective response rate based on the RECIST criteria. Secondary endpoints included safety analysis. The confirmed objective response rate was 24%, with 7% of patients achieving a complete response (CR) and 17% experiencing a partial response (PR). The median duration of response was 8.3 months. An exploratory analysis showed that patients responded to TV, regardless of the level of membrane tissue factor expression [46].

In InnovaTV 205/ENGOT-cx8/GOG-3024, tisotumab vedotin (TV) was found to be safe without any drug-related toxicities when combined with carboplatin, bevacizumab, and pembrolizumab. For TV given as first-line treatment, the objective response rate was 54.5% with carboplatin, 40.6% with pembrolizumab, and 35.3% with 2nd-line/3rd-line TV + pembrolizumab (arm F). The median duration of response was 8.6 months, not reached, and 14.1 months in arms D, E, and F, respectively. The grade $\geq$ 3 adverse events ($\geq$15%) observed were anemia, diarrhea, nausea, and thrombocytopenia in arm D and anemia in arm F (none $\geq$ 15% in arm E).

Further, a recently published phase III randomized trial, innovaTV 301/ENGOT-cx12/GOG-3057, reported that when used as a second- or third-line treatment for patients with recurrent or metastatic cervical cancer that has progressed on doublet chemotherapy, there was a 30% decrease in the risk of death compared to the investigators' choice of chemotherapy [81]. The findings revealed that after one year of follow up, the overall survival (OS) was 48.7% when using TV, compared to 35.3% with chemotherapy (HR, 0.70; 95% CI 0.54 to 0.89). In terms of progression-free survival (PFS), it was 30.4% with TV versus 18.9% with chemotherapy (HR, 0.67; 95% CI, 0.54 to 0.82). The disease control rate was 75.9 with TV compared to 58.2% with chemotherapy. The median duration of response (DOR) was 5.3 months for TV and 5.7 months for chemotherapy. The most common adverse events observed with TV included conjunctivitis, peripheral sensory neuropathy, alopecia, epistaxis, decreased appetite, diarrhea, and keratitis. Overall, the rates of these adverse events were significantly higher with TV compared to chemotherapy. Grade 1 to 3 adverse events were observed with TV, but no grade 4 adverse events were reported. Ocular events, peripheral neuropathy, and bleeding were the most common adverse events associated with TV. One patient with another tumor type treated with tisotumab vedotin at the recommended dose developed Guillain–Barre syndrome [82].

3.3. ADCs in Endometrial Cancer

In Canada, endometrial cancer is the second most prevalent and second most fatal gynecologic cancer [2]. The Cancer Genome Atlas has identified four molecular subtypes that have an impact on prognosis, leading to the recommendation of subtype-specific treatment considerations [83]. For previously treated cases with deficient mismatch repair/high microsatellite instability, pembrolizumab and dostarlimab have been approved by the FDA, while pembrolizumab/lenvatinib are approved for previously treated cases as a second-line treatment in cases with proficient mismatch repair/microsatellite stability [84]. However recently published data from RUBY and NRG-GY018 trials immunochemotherapy have shown promising results in dMMR, as well as pMMR subgroups, respectively [85,86]. Within this focused molecular landscape, there is ongoing research on ADCs.

Currently, there is a growing body of positive data on three sets of ADCs. Firstly, there are promising data on ADCs targeting HER2, particularly trastuzumab deruxtecan (T-DXd), which has shown positive results in terms of response rates, particularly in cases of serous subtype of endometrial cancer with HER2 expression. The activity of T-DXd will be discussed further in Section 3.4 below. Secondly, there are encouraging data on ADCs targeting Trop-2, specifically sacituzumab govitecan, which has shown positive results in terms of response and survival in endometrioid and serous subtypes of endometrial cancer where Trop2 is more commonly expressed [87].

Trop-2 is a tumor-associated calcium signal transducer found to be highly expressed in various types of endometrial cancer (EC), including grade 3 endometrioid adenocarcinoma (96%) and uterine serous carcinoma (65%). Its overexpression is associated with a poorer prognosis and increased likelihood of disease recurrence. Sacituzumab govitecan (IMMU-132) is an ADC that consists of a humanized anti-Trop-2 antibody linked to the active form of irinotecan, a topoisomerase-I inhibitor. In a phase 2 study in endometrial cancer, 21 patients were enrolled, including 48% with uterine serous carcinoma, 33% with endometrioid adenocarcinoma, 14% with carcinosarcoma, and one patient with mixed serous and clear cell histology. All patients had received at least one prior line of chemotherapy, with a median of three lines and a range of one to six. Among the 20 patients evaluated for response, 35% achieved an objective response. Eighteen patients were evaluated for durable disease control, with 39% achieving it. The median follow-up duration was 15.6 months. The median overall survival was 22.5 months and the median progression-free survival was 5.7 months. The treatment was well-tolerated, with no new or unexpected safety concerns reported [87].

Other Trop-2-targeting ADCs are under investigation. Datopotamab deruxtecan is an ADC made up of a highly effective topoisomerase I inhibitor payload chemically attached to a humanized anti-Trop-2 IgG1 monoclonal antibody using a tetra peptide-based cleavable linker that is stable and tumor-selective [88]. Dato-DXd is undergoing evaluation in a pan-tumor phase 2 trial which includes an endometrial cancer cohort (TROPION-PanTumor03, NCT05489211).

Another novel ADC targeting Trop-2 is SKB264. It utilizes the same monoclonal antibody as IMMU-132 and contains 7–8 molecules of a new toxic payload linked through disulfide bonds. The toxic payload, KL610023 (T030), is a belotecan derivative that inhibits topoisomerase I [73]. SKB264 has a longer half-life compared to IMMU-132 and exhibits stronger targeting and bystander toxicity [73]. Currently, there are ongoing phase I/II studies, such as (NCT04152499) and (NCT05642780), that are investigating dose escalation and combination approaches with immunotherapy [75,89].

Endometrial tumors also commonly exhibit an overexpression of FRα receptors, similar to ovarian cancer, with approximately 64% of endometrial tumors testing positive for FRα [74]. However, the clinical effectiveness of the anti-FRα ADC mirvetuximab soravtansine has not been as clear, despite promising preclinical data [90]. In a study examining multiple solid tumors, a positive response was observed in 2 out of 11 (18.2%) endometrial tumors when administered at a dose of 5 mg/kg once every 3 weeks [91]. Currently, a phase II trial is underway to assess the combination of mirvetuximab soravtansine and Pembrolizumab in microsatellite-stable endometrial cancer [92] (NCT03835819).

3.4. *HER2 ADCs in Gynecologic Cancers*

3.4.1. Trastuzumab Deruxtecan (T-DXd)

Trastuzumab deruxtecan is a HER2-specific antibody drug conjugate currently approved for the treatment of HER2-low metastatic breast cancer. The active payload, deruxtecan, is a potent DNA topoisomerase I inhibitor which is more potent than the irinotecan derivative SN-38. The interim findings from the DESTINY-PanTumor-02 study demonstrated activity of the ADC trastuzumab deruxtecan (T-DXd) in various tumor cohorts, including ovarian, endometrial, and cervical cancers. The study included 267 patients across six specific tumor cohorts, with an overall response rate of 37.1%. The median duration of response (DOR) was 11.3 months, median progression-free survival (PFS) was 6.9 months (95% CI, 5.6 to 8.0), and median overall survival (OS) was 13.4 months (95% CI, 11.9 to 15.5). In patients with central HER2 immunohistochemistry (IHC) 3+ expression, the objective response rate was 61.3%, with a median duration of response of 22.1 months, median PFS of 11.9 months, and median OS of 21.1 months. Grade $\geq$ 3 drug-related adverse events occurred in 40.8% of patients, with 10.5% experiencing drug-related interstitial lung disease (ILD) and three deaths related to ILD. The response rates were particularly high in patients with cervical, endometrial, and ovarian cancer, at 50.0%, 57.5%, and 45.0% respectively. In all cohorts, higher response rates were demonstrated in patients with HER2 3+ expression compared to those with HER2 2+ expression. This trial suggested T-DXd as a reasonable treatment option for all cancer types with HER2 overexpression. However, caution should be exercised due to the occurrence of ILD-related adverse events [93]. Recently, FDA granted accelerated approval to fam-trastuzumab deruxtecan for unresectable or metastatic HER2-positive solid tumors, agnostic to tumor type [94].

The results of the STATICE, a phase 2 trial, showed promising outcomes for T-DXd in the treatment of uterine carcinosarcoma with HER2 positivity. A total of 33 patients received T-DXd out of 84 screened patients. The objective response rate, as evaluated by central review, was 54.5% in the HER2-high group and 70.0% in the HER2-low group. The median progression-free survival (PFS) and overall survival (OS) in the HER2-high group were 6.2 and 13.3 months, respectively, while in the HER2-low group, the median PFS was 6.7 months and the OS was not reached. Grade $\geq$ 3 adverse events were observed in 20 patients (61%). Pneumonitis/interstitial lung disease of grades 1–2 and grade 3 occurred in eight (24%) and one (3%) patient(s), respectively [95].

3.4.2. Trastuzumab Duocarmazine

Trastuzumab duocarmazine (SYD985) is a combination of the monoclonal antibody trastuzumab, which targets HER2, and a duocarmycin derivative. The duocarmycin payload is attached to the antibody through a cleavable linker and includes a prodrug called seco-duocarmycin-hydroxybenzamide-azaindole (seco-DUBA) [96]. This payload acts by alkylating DNA, causing DNA damage and ultimately leading to cell death [96].

During a phase I clinical trial that aimed to expand the dose of trastuzumab duocarmazine in patients with HER2-positive breast, gastric, urothelial, or endometrial cancer, a total of 146 patients were included. Among these patients, 14 had endometrial cancer and received a dosage of 1.2 mg/kg of trastuzumab duocarmazine every 3 weeks. Out of the 14 patients with endometrial cancer, five (39%, 95% CI 13.9 to 68.4) showed partial disease responses [97]. The results of another study [98] (NCT04205630), which is a phase II trial, are currently being awaited. This study is an open-label, single-arm trial that includes patients with recurrent, advanced, or metastatic endometrial carcinoma expressing HER2. HER2 expression is determined by a score of 1+, 2+, or 3+ on immunohistochemistry or positive results on in situ hybridization. Patients eligible for this study must have experienced progression after first-line platinum-based chemotherapy, while those who have undergone two or more lines of chemotherapy for advanced or metastatic disease are not eligible. Eligible patients will be administered SYD985 until disease progression or unacceptable toxicity occurs. The results of this study are currently pending. Another phase 1 study involving 32 patients has been completed and is currently awaiting results. This study is a two-part phase 1 trial that aims to assess the safety, pharmacokinetics, and efficacy of the ADC SYD985 when combined with Niraparib in patients with locally advanced or metastatic solid tumors expressing HER2 [99].

3.5. Miscellaneous ADCs

Other than folate receptor alpha (FRα), NaPi2B, a protein involved in sodium-dependent phosphate transport, is found in approximately two thirds of high-grade serous ovarian cancer patients. Upifitamab rilsodotin (UpRi) is an ADC that specifically targets NaPi2B. However, the phase 1b/2 UPLIFT trial (NCT03319628) did not meet its primary endpoint of achieving a satisfactory objective response rate as assessed by investigators. Out of 141 NaPi2B-positive patients receiving UpRi, only 22 showed a response, resulting in an investigator-assessed objective response rate of 15.6% (95% CI, 10.0 to 22.7) [100–102]. Further investigations of UpRi are being conducted in combination with carboplatin in high-grade serous ovarian cancer patients in the phase 1 UPGRADE trial (NCT04907968), as well as in a phase 3 randomized UP-NEXT trial (NCT05329545) where it is being evaluated as a maintenance therapy compared to a placebo in patients with platinum-sensitive recurrent ovarian cancer. However, the FDA has placed a hold on patient enrollment for both the UP-NEXT and UPGRADE-A trials that are assessing UpRi [103], due to the higher-than-expected rates of bleeding observed.

3.6. Next Generation ADCs

Recently, newer techniques have been incorporated and next-generation ADCs have been created. Keeping tumor heterogeneity in consideration, bispecific antibodies have emerged as a way to enable simultaneous binding to two distinct target molecules or cells [104]. A few examples of biparatropic ADCs which target different epitopes of Her2 are under investigation, a notable example being MEDI4276, containing 4 antigen binding sites and targeting 2 epitopes [105,106]. Another anti-Her2 targeting biparatropic ADC is Zanidatamab Zovodotin [107]. ADCs often target known receptors which are not only expressed in tumor cells but also normal tissues. To overcome this cross-reactivity, probody–drug conjugates (PDCs) are under development. Praluzatamab Ravtansine (CX-2009) is a conditionally activated PDC, a CD166-targeting ADC that has recently been explored in epithelial ovarian epithelial cancer [108]. A few more examples of immune-stimulating ADCs, which carry immune stimulators as payloads, are under development. Degrader–Antibody Conjugates (DACs) are composed of an antibody that targets a specific protein on the surface of cancer cells and a small molecule degrader that binds to the targeted protein and induces its degradation; these have also been around and hold promise. Another example is ADCs which can deliver dual chemotherapeutic agents. We have summarized the completed as well as ongoing trials of selected ADCs in Table 1.

Table 1. Summary of selected ongoing clinical trials of ADCs in gynecological cancers.

ADC	Target	Payload	Mechanism of Action	Gynecologic Cancer Type	Phase	Clinical Trials Identifiers	Key Arms
Mirvetuximab Soravtansine (IMGN853)	FRα	DM4	Inhibition of tubulin polymerization	Ovarian	III	MIRASOL NCT04209855	MIRV vs. Investigator choice chemotherapy
					II	MIROVA (NCT04274426)	Carboplatin + MIRV -> MIRV maintenance vs. platinum-based chemotherapy
					II	PICCOLO (NCT05041257)	MIRV monotherapy
					III	GLORIOSA (NCT05445778)	MIRV + bevacizumab vs. bevacizumab monotherapy
Luveltamab tazide (STRO-002)	FRα	SC209	Inhibition of tubulin polymerization	Ovarian, Fallopian Tube, Primary Peritoneal, Endometrial	I/II	NCT03748186 NCT05870748	STRO-002 at escalating doses
					I	NCT05200364	STRO-002 at escalating doses + Bevacizumab
Farletuzumab Ecteribulinm (MORAb-202)	FRα	Eribulin	Inhibition of microtubules	Ovarian, Fallopian Tube, Primary Peritonel, Endometrial	I	NCT03386942	MORAb-202 at escalating doses
					I/II	NCT04300556	MORAb-202 at escalating doses
					II	NCT05613088	MORAb-202 at 2 different doses vs. Chemotherapy
Trastuzumab deruxtecan (DS-8201a)	HER2	Deruxtecan	Inhibition of topoisomerase I	Endometrial, Ovarian, Cervical	II	DESTINY-PanTumor02 NCT04482309	DS-8201a monotherapy
					I	NCT04585958	Trastuzumab Deruxtecan + olaparib
DB-1303	HER2	P1003	Inhibition of topoisomerase I	Endometrial	I/IIA	NCT05150691	DB-1303 dose monotherapy
Trastuzumab Duocarmazine (SYD985)	HER2	Duocarmycin	DNA alkylation	Endometrial, Ovarian	II	NCT04205630	SYD985 monotherapy
					I	NCT04235101	SYD985 + Niraparib at various doses
Tisotumab vedotin (HuMax-TF-ADC)	TF	MMAE (monomethyl auristatin E)	Inhibition of tubulin polymerization	Cervical	III	NCT04697628 (innovaTV 301)	Tisotumab Vedotin vs. another chemotherapy regimen

Table 1. *Cont.*

ADC	Target	Payload	Mechanism of Action	Gynecologic Cancer Type	Phase	Clinical Trials Identifiers	Key Arms
DMUC4064A	MUC16	MMAE (monomethyl auristatin E)	Inhibition of tubulin polymerization	Ovarian	I	NCT02146313	DMUC5754A at escalating doses
Anetumab ravtansine (BAY94-9343)	Mesothelin	DM4	Inhibition of microtubule polymerization	Ovarian, Fallopian Tube, Primary Peritoneal	I	NCT02751918	BAY94-9343 + Pegylated Liposomal Doxorubicin
					I	NCT01439152	BAY94-9343 at escalating doses
					II	NCT03587311	BAY94-9343 + Bevacizumab vs. Paclitaxel + Bevacizumab
Upifitamab Rilsodotin (XMT-1536) Discontinued	NaPi2b	Auristatin derivative	Inhibition of tubulin polymerization	Ovarian, Fallopian Tube, Primary Peritoneal	Ib/II	UPLIFT NCT03319628	UpRi at escalating doses
					I	UPGRADE-A NCT04907968	UpRi at escalatig doses +Carboplatin
					III	UP-NEXT NCT05329545	UpRi vs. Placebo
Sacituzumab govitecan (IMMU-132)	TROP2	SN-38 (irinotecan metabolite)	Inhibition of topoisomerase I	Endometrial	II	NCT04251416	IMMU-132 monotherapy
					II	NCT03964727	IMMU-132 monotherapy
SKB264	TROP2	Proprietary belotecan derivative	Inhibition of topoisomerase I	Ovarian, Endometrial, Cervical	I/II	NCT04152499	SKB264 at escalating doses
					II	NCT05642780	SKB264 + Pembrolizumab
Raludotatug Deruxtecan (R-DXd; DS-6000)	CDH6	Deruxtecan	Inhibition of topoisomerase I	Ovarian Cancer	I	NCT04707248	R-DXd, DS-6000 monotherapy

4. Beyond ADCs in Gynecological Cancers

At the moment there is no clear consensus how to treat recurrent/refractory gynecological cancers. Chemotherapy at this stage is usually not effective and can lead to unnecessary toxicities. Depending upon the molecular profile, certain targeted agents can be used. For example, Larotrectinib or Entrectinib can be used in NTRK fusion-positive tumors, and Selpercatinib is also an option for RET gene fusion-positive tumors.

5. Conclusions

ADCs, a novel and innovative approach, are being incorporated in the management of gynecologic cancers. Ongoing trials aim to identify effective agents for treating gynecologic cancers, particularly in cases where the cancer has spread or recurred and treatment options are limited. In general, ADCs have been shown to be more effective than traditional chemotherapy regimens, with less toxicity, especially in resistant cases. However, it is important to be cautious of the fact that ADCs can still cause specific side effects, such as ocular toxicity and neuropathy. Therefore, it is crucial to take preventive measures, closely monitor patients, and promptly address any issues that arise during treatment. While most agents have been studied as standalone treatments, researchers are considering combining them with other therapies to potentially achieve longer-lasting responses, although this may increase the risk of cumulative toxicity. ADCs have emerged as promising therapeutic options for gynecologic cancers, and ongoing and future research may help improve patient outcomes while minimizing treatment-related side effects.

Author Contributions: Conceptualization, S.F. and A.E.L.; writing—original draft preparation, and writing, S.F.; review and editing, A.E.L., S.W. and S.F.; supervision, A.E.L. and S.W. All authors have read and agreed to the published version of the manuscript.

Funding: This research received no external funding.

Conflicts of Interest: The authors declare no conflicts of interest.

References

1. Statistics Canada. *Leading Causes of Death, Total Population, by Age Group*; Statistics Canada: Ottawa, ON, USA, 2024. [CrossRef]
2. Canadian Cancer Society. *Canadian Cancer Statistics: A 2022 Special Report on Cancer Prevalence*; Canadian Cancer Society: Toronto, ON, Canada, 2022. Available online: https://cdn.cancer.ca/-/media/files/research/cancer-statistics/2022-statistics/2022-special-report/2022_prevalence_report_final_en.pdf?rev=7755f9f350e845d58e268a59e3be608e&hash=3F3F30CADD8CAF0049636B5A41EDBB13&_gl=1*1pf6nrr*_gcl_au*ODgwMjcwNTE2LjE2OTU4MjkyNjg.*_ga*Njg1NjY1MDEzLjE2OTU4MjkyNjg.*_ga_23YMKBE2C3*MTY5NTgyOTI2Ny4xLjEuMTY5NTgyOTYxOS4xNS4wLjA.#_ga=2.169392937.907078724.1695829268-685665013.1695829268 (accessed on 27 September 2023).
3. SEER*Explorer Application. Available online: https://seer.cancer.gov/statistics-network/explorer/application.html?site=58&data_type=4&graph_type=5&compareBy=stage&chk_stage_101=101&chk_stage_106=106&series=9&hdn_sex=3&race=1&age_range=1&advopt_precision=1&advopt_show_ci=on&hdn_view=0 (accessed on 27 September 2023).
4. SEER*Explorer Application. Available online: https://seer.cancer.gov/statistics-network/explorer/application.html?site=61&data_type=1&graph_type=4&compareBy=age_range&chk_age_range_1=1&hdn_sex=3&race=1&advopt_precision=1&hdn_view=0&advopt_show_apc=on&advopt_display=2#resultsRegion0 (accessed on 27 September 2023).
5. Salani, R.; Backes, F.J.; Fung, M.F.K.; Holschneider, C.H.; Parker, L.P.; Bristow, R.E.; Goff, B.A. Posttreatment Surveillance and Diagnosis of Recurrence in Women with Gynecologic Malignancies: Society of Gynecologic Oncologists Recommendations. *Am. J. Obstet. Gynecol.* **2011**, *204*, 466–478. [CrossRef] [PubMed]
6. Dyer, B.A.; Feng, C.H.; Eskander, R.; Sharabi, A.B.; Mell, L.K.; McHale, M.; Mayadev, J.S. Current Status of Clinical Trials for Cervical and Uterine Cancer Using Immunotherapy Combined with Radiation. *Int. J. Radiat. Oncol.* **2021**, *109*, 396–412. [CrossRef] [PubMed]
7. Kandalaft, L.E.; Odunsi, K.; Coukos, G. Immunotherapy in Ovarian Cancer: Are We There Yet? *J. Clin. Oncol.* **2019**, *37*, 2460–2471. [CrossRef] [PubMed]
8. Yang, C.; Xia, B.-R.; Zhang, Z.-C.; Zhang, Y.-J.; Lou, G.; Jin, W.-L. Immunotherapy for Ovarian Cancer: Adjuvant, Combination, and Neoadjuvant. *Front. Immunol.* **2020**, *11*, 577869. [CrossRef] [PubMed]
9. Sievers, E.L.; Larson, R.A.; Stadtmauer, E.A.; Estey, E.; Löwenberg, B.; Dombret, H.; Karanes, C.; Theobald, M.; Bennett, J.M.; Sherman, M.L.; et al. Efficacy and Safety of Gemtuzumab Ozogamicin in Patients with CD33-Positive Acute Myeloid Leukemia in First Relapse. *J. Clin. Oncol.* **2001**, *19*, 3244–3254. [CrossRef]

10. Younes, A.; Bartlett, N.L.; Leonard, J.P.; Kennedy, D.A.; Lynch, C.M.; Sievers, E.L.; Forero-Torres, A. Brentuximab Vedotin (SGN-35) for Relapsed CD30-Positive Lymphomas. *N. Engl. J. Med.* **2010**, *363*, 1812–1821. [CrossRef]
11. Fu, Z.; Li, S.; Han, S.; Shi, C.; Zhang, Y. Antibody Drug Conjugate: The "Biological Missile" for Targeted Cancer Therapy. *Signal Transduct. Target. Ther.* **2022**, *7*, 93. [CrossRef]
12. Martín-Sabroso, C.; Lozza, I.; Torres-Suárez, A.I.; Fraguas-Sánchez, A.I. Antibody-Antineoplastic Conjugates in Gynecological Malignancies: Current Status and Future Perspectives. *Pharmaceutics* **2021**, *13*, 1705. [CrossRef]
13. Damelin, M.; Zhong, W.; Myers, J.; Sapra, P. Evolving Strategies for Target Selection for Antibody-Drug Conjugates. *Pharm. Res.* **2015**, *32*, 3494–3507. [CrossRef]
14. Vankemmelbeke, M.; Durrant, L. Third-Generation Antibody Drug Conjugates for Cancer Therapy—A Balancing Act. *Ther. Deliv.* **2016**, *7*, 141–144. [CrossRef]
15. Yu, J.; Song, Y.; Tian, W. How to Select IgG Subclasses in Developing Anti-Tumor Therapeutic Antibodies. *J. Hematol. Oncol.* **2020**, *13*, 45. [CrossRef] [PubMed]
16. Wang, Z.; Li, H.; Gou, L.; Li, W.; Wang, Y. Antibody–Drug Conjugates: Recent Advances in Payloads. *Acta Pharm. Sin. B* **2023**, *13*, 4025–4059. [CrossRef] [PubMed]
17. Gutman, H.; Bazylevich, A.; Prasad, C.; Dorfman, O.; Hesin, A.; Marks, V.; Patsenker, L.; Gellerman, G. Discovery of Dolastatinol: A Synthetic Analog of Dolastatin 10 and Low Nanomolar Inhibitor of Tubulin Polymerization. *ACS Med. Chem. Lett.* **2021**, *12*, 1596–1604. [CrossRef] [PubMed]
18. Lopus, M.; Oroudjev, E.; Wilson, L.; Wilhelm, S.; Widdison, W.; Chari, R.; Jordan, M.A. Maytansine and Cellular Metabolites of Antibody-Maytansinoid Conjugates Strongly Suppress Microtubule Dynamics by Binding to Microtubules. *Mol. Cancer Ther.* **2010**, *9*, 2689–2699. [CrossRef] [PubMed]
19. Cellular-Resolution Imaging of Bystander Payload Tissue Penetration from Antibody-Drug Conjugates—PubMed. Available online: https://pubmed.ncbi.nlm.nih.gov/34911819/ (accessed on 25 October 2024).
20. Antibody Drug Conjugates and Bystander Killing: Is Antigen-Dependent Internalisation Required?—PubMed. Available online: https://pubmed.ncbi.nlm.nih.gov/29065110/ (accessed on 25 October 2024).
21. Modulation of Macropinocytosis-Mediated Internalization Decreases Ocular Toxicity of Antibody-Drug Conjugates—PubMed. Available online: https://pubmed.ncbi.nlm.nih.gov/29382707/ (accessed on 25 October 2024).
22. Zhao, H.; Gulesserian, S.; Ganesan, S.K.; Ou, J.; Morrison, K.; Zeng, Z.; Robles, V.; Snyder, J.; Do, L.; Aviña, H.; et al. Inhibition of Megakaryocyte Differentiation by Antibody–Drug Conjugates (ADCs) is Mediated by Macropinocytosis: Implications for ADC-induced Thrombocytopenia | Molecular Cancer Therapeutics. *Am. Assoc. Cancer Res.* **2017**, *16*, 1877–1886. Available online: https://aacrjournals.org/mct/article/16/9/1877/147253/Inhibition-of-Megakaryocyte-Differentiation-by (accessed on 25 October 2024).
23. Guffroy, M.; Falahatpisheh, H.; Biddle, K.; Kreeger, J.; Obert, L.; Walters, K.; Goldstein, R.; Boucher, G.; Coskran, T.; Reagan, W.; et al. Liver Microvascular Injury and Thrombocytopenia of Antibody-Calicheamicin Conjugates in Cynomolgus Monkeys-Mechanism and Monitoring. *Clin. Cancer Res.* **2017**, *23*, 1760–1770. [CrossRef]
24. Tsuchikama, K.; Anami, Y.; Ha, S.Y.Y. Exploring the Next Generation of Antibody—Drug Conjugates. *Nat. Rev. Clin. Oncol.* **2024**, *21*, 203–223. [CrossRef]
25. Immune-Stimulating Antibody Conjugates Elicit Robust Myeloid Activation and Durable Antitumor Immunity—PubMed. Available online: https://pubmed.ncbi.nlm.nih.gov/35121890/ (accessed on 25 October 2024).
26. Hong, K.B.; An, H. Degrader-Antibody Conjugates: Emerging New Modality. *J. Med. Chem.* **2023**, *66*, 140–148. [CrossRef]
27. Birrer, M.J.; Moore, K.N.; Betella, I.; Bates, R.C. Antibody-Drug Conjugate-Based Therapeutics: State of the Science. *J. Natl. Cancer Inst.* **2019**, *111*, 538–549. [CrossRef]
28. Adhikari, P.; Zacharias, N.; Ohri, R.; Sadowsky, J. Site-Specific Conjugation to Cys-Engineered THIOMAB^{TM} Antibodies. *Methods Mol. Biol.* **2020**, *2078*, 51–69. [CrossRef]
29. Zimmerman, E.S.; Heibeck, T.H.; Gill, A.; Li, X.; Murray, C.J.; Madlansacay, M.R.; Tran, C.; Uter, N.T.; Yin, G.; Rivers, P.J.; et al. Production of Site-Specific Antibody-Drug Conjugates Using Optimized Non-Natural Amino Acids in a Cell-Free Expression System. *Bioconjugate Chem.* **2014**, *25*, 351–361. [CrossRef] [PubMed]
30. Synthesis of Site-Specific Antibody-Drug Conjugates Using Unnatural Amino Acids—PubMed. Available online: https://pubmed.ncbi.nlm.nih.gov/22988081/ (accessed on 25 October 2024).
31. Schumacher, F.F.; Nunes, J.P.M.; Maruani, A.; Chudasama, V.; Smith, M.E.B.; Chester, K.A.; Baker, J.R.; Caddick, S. Next Generation Maleimides Enable the Controlled Assembly of Antibody-Drug Conjugates via Native Disulfide Bond Bridging. *Org. Biomol. Chem.* **2014**, *12*, 7261–7269. [CrossRef] [PubMed]
32. Homogeneous Antibody-Drug Conjugates via Site-Selective Disulfide Bridging—PubMed. Available online: https://pubmed.ncbi.nlm.nih.gov/30553515/ (accessed on 26 October 2024).
33. Fujii, T.; Matsuda, Y.; Seki, T.; Shikida, N.; Iwai, Y.; Ooba, Y.; Takahashi, K.; Isokawa, M.; Kawaguchi, S.; Hatada, N.; et al. AJICAP Second Generation: Improved Chemical Site-Specific Conjugation Technology for Antibody–Drug Conjugate Production. *Bioconjugate Chem.* **2023**, *34*, 728–738. [CrossRef] [PubMed]
34. Site-Specific Antibody-Drug Conjugation Through Glycoengineering—PubMed. Available online: https://pubmed.ncbi.nlm.nih.gov/24533768/ (accessed on 26 October 2024).

35. Manabe, S.; Yamaguchi, Y.; Matsumoto, K.; Fuchigami, H.; Kawase, T.; Hirose, K.; Mitani, A.; Sumiyoshi, W.; Kinoshita, T.; Abe, J.; et al. Characterization of Antibody Products Obtained through Enzymatic and Nonenzymatic Glycosylation Reactions with a Glycan Oxazoline and Preparation of a Homogeneous Antibody–Drug Conjugate via Fc N-Glycan. *Bioconjugate Chem.* **2019**, *30*, 1343–1355. [CrossRef] [PubMed]
36. Jeger, S.; Zimmermann, K.; Blanc, A.; Grünberg, J.; Honer, M.; Hunziker, P.; Struthers, H.; Schibli, R. Site-Specific and Stoichiometric Modification of Antibodies by Bacterial Transglutaminase. *Angew. Chem. Int. Ed. Engl.* **2010**, *49*, 9995–9997. [CrossRef]
37. Transglutaminase-Based Chemo-Enzymatic Conjugation Approach Yields Homogeneous Antibody-Drug Conjugates—PubMed. Available online: https://pubmed.ncbi.nlm.nih.gov/24483299/ (accessed on 26 October 2024).
38. Rabuka, D.; Rush, J.S.; de Hart, G.W.; Wu, P.; Bertozzi, C.R. Site-Specific Chemical Protein Conjugation Using Genetically Encoded Aldehyde Tags. *Nat. Protoc.* **2012**, *7*, 1052–1067. [CrossRef]
39. Drake, P.M.; Albers, A.E.; Baker, J.; Banas, S.; Barfield, R.M.; Bhat, A.S.; de Hart, G.W.; Garofalo, A.W.; Holder, P.; Jones, L.C.; et al. Aldehyde Tag Coupled with HIPS Chemistry Enables the Production of ADCs Conjugated Site-Specifically to Different Antibody Regions with Distinct in Vivo Efficacy and PK Outcomes. *Bioconjugate Chem.* **2014**, *25*, 1331–1341. [CrossRef]
40. Matsuda, Y.; Shikida, N.; Hatada, N.; Yamada, K.; Seki, T.; Nakahara, Y.; Endo, Y.; Shimbo, K.; Takahashi, K.; Nakayama, A.; et al. AJICAP-M: Traceless Affinity Peptide Mediated Conjugation Technology for Site-Selective Antibody-Drug Conjugate Synthesis. *Org. Lett.* **2024**, *26*, 5597–5601. [CrossRef]
41. Site-Specific Protein Labeling via Sortase-Mediated Transpeptidation—PubMed. Available online: https://pubmed.ncbi.nlm.nih.gov/28762490/ (accessed on 26 October 2024).
42. Sortase Enzyme-Mediated Generation of Site-Specifically Conjugated Antibody Drug Conjugates with High In Vitro and In Vivo Potency—PubMed. Available online: https://pubmed.ncbi.nlm.nih.gov/26132162/ (accessed on 26 October 2024).
43. Ritchie, M.; Tchistiakova, L.; Scott, N. Implications of Receptor-Mediated Endocytosis and Intracellular Trafficking Dynamics in the Development of Antibody Drug Conjugates. *mAbs* **2013**, *5*, 13–21. [CrossRef]
44. Verma, S.; Breadner, D.; Raphael, J. 'Targeting' Improved Outcomes with Antibody-Drug Conjugates in Non-Small Cell Lung Cancer—An Updated Review. *Curr. Oncol.* **2023**, *30*, 4329–4350. [CrossRef]
45. Chau, C.H.; Steeg, P.S.; Figg, W.D. Antibody–Drug Conjugates for Cancer. *Lancet* **2019**, *394*, 793–804. [CrossRef] [PubMed]
46. Coleman, R.L.; Lorusso, D.; Gennigens, C.; González-Martín, A.; Randall, L.; Cibula, D.; Lund, B.; Woelber, L.; Pignata, S.; Forget, F.; et al. Efficacy and Safety of Tisotumab Vedotin in Previously Treated Recurrent or Metastatic Cervical Cancer (innovaTV 204/GOG-3023/ENGOT-Cx6): A Multicentre, Open-Label, Single-Arm, Phase 2 Study. *Lancet Oncol.* **2021**, *22*, 609–619. [CrossRef] [PubMed]
47. Matulonis, U.A.; Lorusso, D.; Oaknin, A.; Pignata, S.; Dean, A.; Denys, H.; Colombo, N.; Van Gorp, T.; Konner, J.A.; Marin, M.R.; et al. Efficacy and Safety of Mirvetuximab Soravtansine in Patients with Platinum-Resistant Ovarian Cancer with High Folate Receptor Alpha Expression: Results From the SORAYA Study. *J. Clin. Oncol.* **2023**, *41*, 2436–2445. [CrossRef] [PubMed]
48. Oza, A.M.; Cook, A.D.; Pfisterer, J.; Embleton, A.; Ledermann, J.A.; Pujade-Lauraine, E.; Kristensen, G.; Carey, M.S.; Beale, P.; Cervantes, A.; et al. Standard Chemotherapy with or without Bevacizumab for Women with Newly Diagnosed Ovarian Cancer (ICON7): Overall Survival Results of a Phase 3 Randomised Trial. *Lancet Oncol.* **2015**, *16*, 928–936. [CrossRef]
49. Tewari, K.S.; Burger, R.A.; Enserro, D.; Norquist, B.M.; Swisher, E.M.; Brady, M.F.; Bookman, M.A.; Fleming, G.F.; Huang, H.; Homesley, H.D.; et al. Final Overall Survival of a Randomized Trial of Bevacizumab for Primary Treatment of Ovarian Cancer. *J. Clin. Oncol.* **2019**, *37*, 2317–2328. [CrossRef]
50. Suh, Y.J.; Lee, B.; Kim, K.; Jeong, Y.; Choi, H.Y.; Hwang, S.O.; Kim, Y.B. Bevacizumab versus PARP-Inhibitors in Women with Newly Diagnosed Ovarian Cancer: A Network Meta-Analysis. *BMC Cancer* **2022**, *22*, 346. [CrossRef]
51. Kemp, Z.; Ledermann, J. Update on First-Line Treatment of Advanced Ovarian Carcinoma. *Int. J. Women's Health* **2013**, *5*, 45–51. [CrossRef]
52. Matulonis, U.A. Ovarian Cancer. *Hematol. Oncol. Clin. N. Am.* **2018**, *32*, XIII–XIV. [CrossRef]
53. O'Malley, D.M.; Matulonis, U.A.; Birrer, M.J.; Castro, C.M.; Gilbert, L.; Vergote, I.; Martin, L.P.; Mantia-Smaldone, G.M.; Martin, A.G.; Bratos, R.; et al. Phase Ib Study of Mirvetuximab Soravtansine, a Folate Receptor Alpha (FRα)-Targeting Antibody-Drug Conjugate (ADC), in Combination with Bevacizumab in Patients with Platinum-Resistant Ovarian Cancer. *Gynecol. Oncol.* **2020**, *157*, 379–385. [CrossRef]
54. Moore, K.N.; Angelergues, A.; Konecny, G.E.; García, Y.; Banerjee, S.; Lorusso, D.; Lee, J.-Y.; Moroney, J.W.; Colombo, N.; Roszak, A.; et al. Mirvetuximab Soravtansine in FRα-Positive, Platinum-Resistant Ovarian Cancer. *N. Engl. J. Med.* **2023**, *389*, 2162–2174. [CrossRef]
55. Martin, J.; Zacholski, E.; O'Cearbhaill, R.; Matulonis, U.; Chen, L. Society of Gynecologic Oncology Journal Club: Controversial Conversations in Gynecologic Cancer—The ABCs of ADCs (Antibody Drug Conjugates). *Gynecol. Oncol. Rep.* **2023**, *45*, 101141. [CrossRef] [PubMed]
56. Secord, A.A.; Lewin, S.; Murphy, C.; Method, M. PICCOLO: An Open-Label, Single Arm, Phase 2 Study of Mirvetuximab Soravtansine in Recurrent Platinum Sensitive, High-Grade Epithelial Ovarian, Primary Peritoneal, or Fallopian Tube Cancers with High Folate-Alpha (FRα) Expression (300). *Gynecol. Oncol.* **2022**, *166*, S157–S158. [CrossRef]

57. O'Malley, D.M.; Myers, T.K.N.; Zamagni, C.; Diver, E.; Lorusso, D. GLORIOSA: A Randomized, Open-Label, Phase 3 Study of Mirvetuximab Soravtansine with Bevacizumab vs. Bevacizumab as Maintenance in Platinum-Sensitive Ovarian, Fallopian Tube, or Primary Peritoneal Cancer. *J. Clin. Oncol.* **2023**, *41* (Suppl. S16), TPS5622. [CrossRef]
58. Moore, K.; O'Malley, D.; Vergote, I.; Martin, L.; Gonzalez-Martin, A.; Wang, J.; Method, M.; Birrer, M. 18/#499 Mirvetuximab Soravtansine and Carboplatin for Treatment of Patients with Recurrent Folate Receptor Alpha-Positive Platinum-Sensitive Ovarian Cancer: A Final Analysis. *Int. J. Gynecol. Cancer* **2022**, *32* (Suppl. S3), A33–A34. [CrossRef]
59. Mirvetuximab Soravtansine (IMGN853), in Folate Receptor Alpha (FRα) High Recurrent Ovarian Cancer—Full Text View—ClinicalTrials.gov. Available online: https://clinicaltrials.gov/ct2/show/NCT04274426 (accessed on 20 December 2023).
60. Moore, K.N.; Oza, A.M.; Colombo, N.; Oaknin, A.; Scambia, G.; Lorusso, D.; Konecny, G.E.; Banerjee, S.; Murphy, C.G.; Tanyi, J.L.; et al. Phase III, Randomized Trial of Mirvetuximab Soravtansine versus Chemotherapy in Patients with Platinum-Resistant Ovarian Cancer: Primary Analysis of FORWARD I. *Ann. Oncol.* **2021**, *32*, 757–765. [CrossRef]
61. Study of Carboplatin and Mirvetuximab Soravtansine in First-Line Treatment of Patients Receiving Neoadjuvant Chemotherapy with Advanced-Stage Ovarian, Fallopian Tube Primary Peritoneal Cancer—Full Text View—ClinicalTrials.gov. Available online: https://classic.clinicaltrials.gov/ct2/show/NCT04606914 (accessed on 20 December 2023).
62. Angelergues, A.; Konecny, G.E.; Banerjee, S.N.; Pignata, S.; Colombo, N.; Moroney, J.W.; Cosgrove, C.; Lee, J.-Y.; Roszak, A.; Breuer, S.; et al. Phase III MIRASOL (GOG 3045/ENGOT-Ov55) Study: Initial Report of Mirvetuximab Soravtansine vs. Investigator's Choice of Chemotherapy in Platinum-Resistant, Advanced High-Grade Epithelial Ovarian, Primary Peritoneal, or Fallopian Tube Cancers with High Folate Receptor-Alpha Expression. *J. Clin. Oncol.* **2023**, *41*, LBA5507. [CrossRef]
63. Li, X.; Zhou, S.; Abrahams, C.L.; Krimm, S.; Smith, J.; Bajjuri, K.; Stephenson, H.T.; Henningsen, R.; Hanson, J.; Heibeck, T.H.; et al. Discovery of STRO-002, a Novel Homogeneous ADC Targeting Folate Receptor Alpha, for the Treatment of Ovarian and Endometrial Cancers. *Mol. Cancer Ther.* **2023**, *22*, 155–167. [CrossRef]
64. Sutro Biopharma, Inc. *Sutro Biopharma Announces Update from STRO-002, Luveltamab Tazevibulin (Luvelta), Phase 1 Dose-Expansion Study and Registrational Plans in Advanced Ovarian Cancer*; Sutro Biopharma, Inc.: South San Francisco, CA, USA, 2023. Available online: https://www.sutrobio.com/sutro-biopharma-announces-update-from-stro-002-luveltamab-tazevibulin-luvelta-phase-1-dose-expansion-study-and-registrational-plans-in-advanced-ovarian-cancer/ (accessed on 3 January 2024).
65. Naumann, R.W.; Martin, L.P.; Oaknin, A.; Spira, A.I.; Hamilton, E.P.; Schilder, R.J.; Lu, L.; Kuriakose, J.; Berman, C.J.; Molina, A. STRO-002-GM2: A phase 1, open-label, safety, pharmacokinetic, and preliminary efficacy study of STRO-002, an anti-folate receptor alpha (FolRα) antibody-drug conjugate (ADC), in combination with bevacizumab in patients with advanced epithelial ovarian cancer (EOC, including fallopian tube or primary peritoneal cancers). *J. Clin. Oncol.* **2022**, *40*, TPS5622. [CrossRef]
66. Sutro Biopharma, Inc. REFRaME-O1: A Phase 2 Open-Label Study Evaluating the Efficacy and Safety of Luveltamab Tazevibulin (STRO-002) in Women with Relapsed Platinum-Resistant Epithelial Ovarian Cancer (Including Fallopian Tube or Primary Peritoneal Cancers) Expressing Folate Receptor Alpha (FOLR1); Clinical Trial Registration NCT05870748; Clinicaltrials.gov. 2023. Available online: https://clinicaltrials.gov/study/NCT05870748 (accessed on 1 January 2024).
67. Shimizu, T.; Fujiwara, Y.; Yonemori, K.; Koyama, T.; Sato, J.; Tamura, K.; Shimomura, A.; Ikezawa, H.; Nomoto, M.; Furuuchi, K.; et al. First-in-Human Phase 1 Study of MORAb-202, an Antibody-Drug Conjugate Comprising Farletuzumab Linked to Eribulin Mesylate, in Patients with Folate Receptor-α-Positive Advanced Solid Tumors. *Clin. Cancer Res.* **2021**, *27*, 3905–3915. [CrossRef]
68. Bristol-Myers Squibb. A Phase 2 Open-Label Randomized Study of Farletuzumab Ecteribulin (MORAb-202), a Folate Receptor Alpha-Targeting Antibody-Drug Conjugate, Versus Investigator's Choice Chemotherapy in Women with Platinum-Resistant High-Grade Serous (HGS) Ovarian, Primary Peritoneal, or Fallopian Tube Cancer; Clinical Trial Registration NCT05613088; Clinicaltrials.gov. 2023. Available online: https://clinicaltrials.gov/study/NCT05613088 (accessed on 1 January 2024).
69. Meric-Bernstam, F.; Song, M.; Westin, S.N.; Au-Yeung, G.; Mitchell, P.; Myers, C.; Gymnopoulos, M.; Fraenkel, P.G.; Nawinne, M.; Brier, T.; et al. 819TiP FONTANA: A Phase I/IIa Study of AZD5335 as Monotherapy and in Combination with Anti-Cancer Agents in Patients with Solid Tumours. *Ann. Oncol.* **2023**, *34*, S541. [CrossRef]
70. Gymnopoulos, M.; Thomas, T.; Gasper, D.; Anderton, J.; Tammali, R.; Rosfjord, E.; Durham, N.; Ward, C.; Myers, C.; Wang, J.; et al. Abstract LB025: First Disclosure of AZD5335, a TOP1i-ADC Targeting Low and High FRα-Expressing Ovarian Cancer with Superior Preclinical Activity vs FRα-MTI ADC. *Cancer Res.* **2023**, *83* (Suppl. S8), LB025. [CrossRef]
71. Study Details | Phase I/IIa Study for AZD5335 as Monotherapy and in Combination with Anti-Cancer Agents in Participants with Solid Tumors | ClinicalTrials.gov. Available online: https://www.clinicaltrials.gov/study/NCT05797168?term=fontana&rank=1 (accessed on 21 May 2024).
72. Liu, J.; Burris, H.; Wang, J.S.; Barroilhet, L.; Gutierrez, M.; Wang, Y.; Vaze, A.; Commerford, R.; Royer-Joo, S.; Choeurng, V.; et al. An Open-Label Phase I Dose-Escalation Study of the Safety and Pharmacokinetics of DMUC4064A in Patients with Platinum-Resistant Ovarian Cancer. *Gynecol. Oncol.* **2021**, *163*, 473–480. [CrossRef] [PubMed]
73. Cheng, Y.; Yuan, X.; Tian, Q.; Huang, X.; Chen, Y.; Pu, Y.; Long, H.; Xu, M.; Ji, Y.; Xie, J.; et al. Preclinical Profiles of SKB264, a Novel Anti-TROP2 Antibody Conjugated to Topoisomerase Inhibitor, Demonstrated Promising Antitumor Efficacy Compared to IMMU-132. *Front. Oncol.* **2022**, *12*, 951589. [CrossRef]
74. Assaraf, Y.G.; Leamon, C.P.; Reddy, J.A. The Folate Receptor as a Rational Therapeutic Target for Personalized Cancer Treatment. *Drug Resist. Updates* **2014**, *17*, 89–95. [CrossRef]

75. Klus Pharma Inc. A Multicenter, Open-Label, Phase 2, Basket Study to Evaluate the Efficacy and Safety of SKB264 in Combination with Pembrolizumab in Subjects with Selected Solid Tumors; Clinical Trial Registration NCT05642780; Clinicaltrials.gov. 2023. Available online: https://clinicaltrials.gov/study/NCT05642780 (accessed on 1 January 2024).
76. Pang, L.; Ren, F.; Xu, X.; Fu, L.; Wang, T.; Guo, Z. Construction and Characterization of Cadherin 6 (CDH6)-Targeting Chimeric Antigen Receptor (CAR) Modified T Cells. *J. Environ. Pathol. Toxicol. Oncol.* **2022**, *41*, 55–71. [CrossRef]
77. Pommier, Y. Topoisomerase I Inhibitors: Camptothecins and Beyond. *Nat. Rev. Cancer* **2006**, *6*, 789–802. [CrossRef]
78. Moore, K.N.; Philipovskiy, A.; Harano, K.; Rini, B.I.; Sudo, K.; Kitano, S.; Spigel, D.R.; Lin, J.; Kundu, M.; Bensmaine, A.; et al. 745MO Raludotatug Deruxtecan (R-DXd; DS-6000) Monotherapy in Patients with Previously Treated Ovarian Cancer (OVC): Subgroup Analysis of a First-in-Human Phase I Study. *Ann. Oncol.* **2023**, *34*, S510. [CrossRef]
79. Cervical Cancer—Statistics. Cancer.Net. Available online: https://www.cancer.net/cancer-types/cervical-cancer/statistics (accessed on 3 January 2024).
80. Available online: https://www.nccn.org/professionals/physician_gls/pdf/cervical.pdf (accessed on 13 February 2024).
81. Fujiwara, K.; Slomovitz, B.M.; Martin, A.G.; Kalbacher, E.; Bagameri, A.; Ghamande, S.; Lee, J.-Y.; Banerjee, S.; Maluf, F.C.; Lorusso, D.; et al. 288MO InnovaTV 301/ENGOT-Cx12/GOG-3057: A Global, Randomized, Open-Label, Phase III Study of Tisotumab Vedotin vs Investigator's Choice of Chemotherapy in 2L or 3L Recurrent or Metastatic Cervical Cancer. *Ann. Oncol.* **2023**, *34*, S1586. [CrossRef]
82. Genmab and Seagen Announce That Tivdak® (Tisotumab Vedotin-Tftv) Met Its Primary Endpoint of Improved Overall Sur-Vival in Patients with Recurrent or Metastatic Cervical Cancer Compared to Chemotherapy—Genmab A/S. Available online: https://ir.genmab.com/news-releases/news-release-details/genmab-and-seagen-announce-tivdakr-tisotumab-vedotin-tftv-met/ (accessed on 4 January 2024).
83. Cancer Genome Atlas Research Network; Kandoth, C.; Schultz, N.; Cherniack, A.D.; Akbani, R.; Liu, Y.; Shen, H.; Robertson, A.G.; Pashtan, I.; Shen, R.; et al. Integrated Genomic Characterization of Endometrial Carcinoma. *Nature* **2013**, *497*, 67–73. [CrossRef]
84. Mitric, C.; Bernardini, M.Q. Endometrial Cancer: Transitioning from Histology to Genomics. *Curr. Oncol.* **2022**, *29*, 741–757. [CrossRef]
85. Mirza, M.R.; Chase, D.M.; Slomovitz, B.M.; dePont Christensen, R.; Novák, Z.; Black, D.; Gilbert, L.; Sharma, S.; Valabrega, G.; Landrum, L.M.; et al. Dostarlimab for Primary Advanced or Recurrent Endometrial Cancer. *N. Engl. J. Med.* **2023**, *388*, 2145–2158. [CrossRef] [PubMed]
86. Eskander, R.N.; Sill, M.W.; Beffa, L.; Moore, R.G.; Hope, J.M.; Musa, F.B.; Mannel, R.; Shahin, M.S.; Cantuaria, G.H.; Girda, E.; et al. Pembrolizumab plus Chemotherapy in Advanced Endometrial Cancer. *N. Engl. J. Med.* **2023**, *388*, 2159–2170. [CrossRef] [PubMed]
87. Santin, A.; McNamara, B.; Siegel, E.R.; Harold, J.; Mutlu, L.; Altwerger, G.; Huang, G.S.; Andikyan, V.; Clark, M.B.; Ratner, E.; et al. Preliminary results of a phase II trial with sacituzumab govitecan-hziy in patients with recurrent endometrial carcinoma overexpressing Trop-2. *J. Clin. Oncol.* **2023**, *41*, 5599. [CrossRef]
88. Study Details | Study of Dato-Dxd as Monotherapy and in Combination with Anti-Cancer Agents in Patients with Advanced Solid Tumours (Tropion-Pantumor03) | ClinicalTrials.gov. Available online: https://www.clinicaltrials.gov/study/NCT05489211 (accessed on 14 May 2024).
89. Klus Pharma Inc. A Phase I-II, First-in-Human Study of SKB264 in Patients with Locally Advanced Unresectable /Metastatic Solid Tumors Who Are Refractory to Available Standard Therapies; Clinical Trial Registration NCT04152499, Clinicaltrials.gov. 2022. Available online: https://clinicaltrials.gov/study/NCT04152499 (accessed on 1 January 2024).
90. Altwerger, G.; Bonazzoli, E.; Bellone, S.; Egawa-Takata, T.; Menderes, G.; Pettinella, F.; Bianchi, A.; Riccio, F.; Feinberg, J.; Zammataro, L.; et al. In Vitro and In Vivo Activity of IMGN853, an Antibody-Drug Conjugate Targeting Folate Receptor Alpha Linked to DM4, in Biologically Aggressive Endometrial Cancers. *Mol. Cancer Ther.* **2018**, *17*, 1003–1011. [CrossRef] [PubMed]
91. Moore, K.N.; Borghaei, H.; O'Malley, D.M.; Jeong, W.; Seward, S.M.; Bauer, T.M.; Perez, R.P.; Matulonis, U.A.; Running, K.L.; Zhang, X.; et al. Phase 1 Dose-Escalation Study of Mirvetuximab Soravtansine (IMGN853), a Folate Receptor α-Targeting Antibody-Drug Conjugate, in Patients with Solid Tumors. *Cancer* **2017**, *123*, 3080–3087. [CrossRef]
92. Konstantinopoulos, P. A Phase 2, Two-Stage, Study of Mirvetuximab Soravtansine (IMGN853) in Combination with Pembrolizumab in Patients with Microsatellite Stable (MSS) Recurrent or Persistent Endometrial Cancer (EC); Clinical Trial Registration NCT03835819, Clinicaltrials.gov. 2023. Available online: https://clinicaltrials.gov/study/NCT03835819 (accessed on 1 January 2024).
93. Meric-Bernstam, F.; Makker, V.; Oaknin, A.; Oh, D.-Y.; Banerjee, S.; González-Martín, A.; Jung, K.H.; Ługowska, I.; Manso, L.; Manzano, A.; et al. Efficacy and Safety of Trastuzumab Deruxtecan in Patients with HER2-Expressing Solid Tumors: Primary Results From the DESTINY-PanTumor02 Phase II Trial. *J. Clin. Oncol.* **2024**, *42*, 47–58. [CrossRef]
94. Center for Drug Evaluation and Research. *FDA Grants Accelerated Approval to Fam-Trastuzumab Deruxtecan-Nxki for Unresectable or Metastatic HER2-Positive Solid Tumors*; U.S. Food and Drug Administration: Silver Spring, MD, USA, 2024.
95. Nishikawa, T.; Hasegawa, K.; Matsumoto, K.; Mori, M.; Hirashima, Y.; Takehara, K.; Ariyoshi, K.; Kato, T.; Yagishita, S.; Hamada, A.; et al. Trastuzumab Deruxtecan for Human Epidermal Growth Factor Receptor 2–Expressing Advanced or Recurrent Uterine Carcinosarcoma (NCCH1615): The STATICE Trial. *J. Clin. Oncol.* **2023**, *41*, 2789–2799. [CrossRef]

96. Elgersma, R.C.; Coumans, R.G.E.; Huijbregts, T.; Menge, W.M.P.B.; Joosten, J.A.F.; Spijker, H.J.; de Groot, F.M.H.; van der Lee, M.M.C.; Ubink, R.; van den Dobbelsteen, D.J.; et al. Design, Synthesis, and Evaluation of Linker-Duocarmycin Payloads: Toward Selection of HER2-Targeting Antibody-Drug Conjugate SYD985. *Mol. Pharm.* **2015**, *12*, 1813–1835. [CrossRef]
97. Banerji, U.; van Herpen, C.M.L.; Saura, C.; Thistlethwaite, F.; Lord, S.; Moreno, V.; Macpherson, I.R.; Boni, V.; Rolfo, C.; de Vries, E.G.E.; et al. Trastuzumab Duocarmazine in Locally Advanced and Metastatic Solid Tumours and HER2-Expressing Breast Cancer: A Phase 1 Dose-Escalation and Dose-Expansion Study. *Lancet Oncol.* **2019**, *20*, 1124–1135. [CrossRef]
98. Byondis, B.V. A Single-Arm Phase II Trial to Evaluate the Safety and Efficacy of the Antibody-Drug Conjugate (ADC) SYD985 in Patients with Human Epidermal Growth Factor Receptor 2 (HER2)-Expressing Endometrial Carcinoma Who Previously Progressed on or After First Line Platinum-Based Chemotherapy; Clinical Trial Registration NCT04205630; Clinicaltrials.gov. 2023. Available online: https://clinicaltrials.gov/study/NCT04205630 (accessed on 1 January 2023).
99. Byondis, B.V. A Two-Part Phase I Study with the Antibody-Drug Conjugate SYD985 in Combination with Niraparib to Evaluate Safety, Pharmacokinetics and Efficacy in Patients with HER2-Expressing Locally Advanced or Metastatic Solid Tumors.; Clinical Trial Registration NCT04235101; Clinicaltrials.gov. 2024. Available online: https://clinicaltrials.gov/study/NCT04235101 (accessed on 1 January 2024).
100. Mersana Therapeutics. Upifitamab Rilsodotin (Xmt-1536). An Open-Label, Multicenter, Dose Escalation and Expansion Study of Upifitamab Rilsodotin in Combination with Carboplatin in Participants with High Grade Serous Ovarian Cancer (Upgrade-A); Clinical Trial Registration NCT04907968; Clinicaltrials.gov. 2023. Available online: https://clinicaltrials.gov/study/NCT04907968 (accessed on 31 December 2022).
101. Mersana Therapeutics. A Phase 3, Randomized, Double-Blind, Placebo-Controlled, Multicenter Study of Upifitamab Rilsodotin (XMT-1536) as Post-Platinum Maintenance Therapy for Participants with Recurrent, Platinum-Sensitive, Ovarian Cancer (UP-NEXT); Clinical Trial Registration NCT05329545; Clinicaltrials.gov. 2023. Available online: https://clinicaltrials.gov/study/NCT05329545 (accessed on 1 January 2023).
102. Mersana Therapeutics. A Phase 1b/2, First-in-Human, Dose Escalation and Expansion Study of XMT-1536 in Patients with Solid Tumors Likely to Express NaPi2b; Clinical Trial Registration NCT03319628; Clinicaltrials.gov. 2023. Available online: https://clinicaltrials.gov/study/NCT03319628 (accessed on 1 January 2023).
103. FDA Puts Mersana's Ovarian Cancer Trials on Partial Clinical Hold. BioSpace. Available online: https://www.biospace.com/fda-puts-mersana-s-ovarian-cancer-trials-on-partial-clinical-hold (accessed on 7 November 2024).
104. Beishenaliev, A.; Loke, Y.L.; Goh, S.J.; Geo, H.N.; Mugila, M.; Misran, M.; Chung, L.Y.; Kiew, L.V.; Roffler, S.; Teo, Y.Y. Bispecific Antibodies for Targeted Delivery of Anti-Cancer Therapeutic Agents: A Review. *J. Control. Release* **2023**, *359*, 268–286. [CrossRef]
105. A Biparatopic HER2-Targeting Antibody-Drug Conjugate Induces Tumor Regression in Primary Models Refractory to or Ineligible for HER2-Targeted Therapy. Available online: https://pubmed.ncbi.nlm.nih.gov/26766593/ (accessed on 26 October 2024).
106. First-in-Human, Phase 1 Dose-Escalation Study of Biparatopic Anti-HER2 Antibody–Drug Conjugate MEDI4276 in Patients with HER2-positive Advanced Breast or Gastric Cancer | Molecular Cancer Therapeutics | American Association for Cancer Research. Available online: https://aacrjournals.org/mct/article/20/8/1442/673290/First-in-Human-Phase-1-Dose-Escalation-Study-of (accessed on 26 October 2024).
107. Weisser, N.E.; Sanches, M.; Escobar-Cabrera, E.; O'Toole, J.; Whalen, E.; Chan, P.W.Y.; Wickman, G.; Abraham, L.; Choi, K.; Harbourne, B.; et al. An Anti-HER2 Biparatopic Antibody That Induces Unique HER2 Clustering and Complement-Dependent Cytotoxicity. *Nat. Commun.* **2023**, *14*, 1394. [CrossRef] [PubMed]
108. Boni, V.; Fidler, M.J.; Arkenau, H.T.; Spira, A.; Meric-Bernstam, F.; Uboha, N.; Sanborn, R.E.; Sweis, R.F.; LoRusso, P.; Nagasaka, M.; et al. Praluzatamab Ravtansine, a CD166-Targeting Antibody-Drug Conjugate, in Patients with Advanced Solid Tumors: An Open-Label Phase I/II Trial. *Clin. Cancer Res.* **2022**, *28*, 2020–2029. [CrossRef] [PubMed]

Disclaimer/Publisher's Note: The statements, opinions and data contained in all publications are solely those of the individual author(s) and contributor(s) and not of MDPI and/or the editor(s). MDPI and/or the editor(s) disclaim responsibility for any injury to people or property resulting from any ideas, methods, instructions or products referred to in the content.

pharmaceutics

MDPI

Article

Maximizing Anticancer Response with MPS1 and CENPE Inhibition Alongside Apoptosis Induction

Bárbara Pinto [1,2], João P. N. Silva [1], Patrícia M. A. Silva [1,3,*], Daniel José Barbosa [3,4], Bruno Sarmento [4,5], Juliana Carvalho Tavares [2] and Hassan Bousbaa [1,*]

1 UNIPRO—Oral Pathology and Rehabilitation Research Unit, University Institute of Health Sciences (IUCS), Cooperativa de Ensino Superior Politécnico e Universitário (CESPU), Rua Central de Gandra, 1317, 4585-116 Gandra, Portugal; barbara.fernandes.15@gmail.com (B.P.); a30242@alunos.cespu.pt (J.P.N.S.)

2 Department of Physiology and Biophysics, Institute of Biological Sciences, Federal University of Minas Gerais (UFMG), Av. Pres. Antônio Carlos, 6627, Belo Horizonte 31270-901, Brazil; julianact@ufmg.br

3 1H-TOXRUN—One Health Toxicology Research Unit, University Institute of Health Sciences, CESPU, CRL, 4585-116 Gandra, Portugal; daniel.barbosa@iucs.cespu.pt

4 i3S—Institute for Research and Innovation in Health, University of Porto, Rua Alfredo Allen 208, 4200-135 Porto, Portugal; bruno.sarmento@i3s.up.pt

5 INEB—Institute of Biomedical Engineering, University of Porto, Rua Alfredo Allen 208, 4200-393 Porto, Portugal

* Correspondence: patricia.silva@cespu.pt (P.M.A.S.); hassan.bousbaa@iucs.cespu.pt (H.B.); Tel.: +351-224157189 (P.M.A.S.); +351-224157186 (H.B.)

Abstract: Antimitotic compounds, targeting key spindle assembly checkpoint (SAC) components (e.g., MPS1, Aurora kinase B, PLK1, KLP1, CENPE), are potential alternatives to microtubule-targeting antimitotic agents (e.g., paclitaxel) to circumvent resistance and side effects associated with their use. They can be classified into mitotic blockers, causing SAC-induced mitotic arrest, or mitotic drivers, pushing cells through aberrant mitosis by overriding SAC. These drugs, although advancing to clinical trials, exhibit unsatisfactory cancer treatment outcomes as monotherapy, probably due to variable cell fate responses driven by cyclin B degradation and apoptosis signal accumulation networks. We investigated the impact of inhibiting anti-apoptotic signals with the BH3-mimetic navitoclax in lung cancer cells treated with the selective CENPE inhibitor GSK923295 (mitotic blocker) or the MPS1 inhibitor BAY1217389 (mitotic driver). Our aim was to steer treated cancer cells towards cell death. BH3-mimetics, in combination with both mitotic blockers and drivers, induced substantial cell death, mainly through apoptosis, in 2D and 3D cultures. Crucially, these synergistic concentrations were less toxic to non-tumor cells. This highlights the significance of combining BH3-mimetics with antimitotics, either blockers or drivers, which have reached the clinical trial phase, to enhance their effectiveness.

Keywords: CENPE inhibitor; MPS1 inhibitor; BCL-2 family inhibitor; antimitotics; antitumoral activity; combination therapy; cancer treatment

1. Introduction

Microtubule-targeting agents (MTAs) such as paclitaxel are widely adopted first-line chemotherapeutic agents in cancer clinical treatments, including for lung cancer. In fact, non-small cell lung cancer (NSCLC), the most prevalent form of lung cancer, is the leading cause of cancer death worldwide, resulting in one of the greatest public health challenges [1–3]. Approximately 350 people die each day from lung cancer and, in 2020, more than 2 million new lung cancer cases were reported [4,5]. By disrupting proper microtubule dynamics, MTAs lead to abnormal mitotic spindle assembly and compromise proper attachments of chromosomes to spindle microtubules, resulting in a chronic activation of the spindle assembly checkpoint (SAC), which eventually leads to cell death [6]. However, MTAs are associated with toxicity, as well as intrinsic and acquired resistance [7,8]. A plethora of second-generation antimitotic agents have thus been developed, including drugs targeting mitotic kinesins such as kinesin-like protein 1 (KLP1) and centromere protein E (CENPE), and mitotic kinases such as monopolar spindle 1 (MPS1), Aurora kinase B, and polo-like kinase 1 (PLK1), primarily involved in SAC signaling [9]. Unlike microtubules, which function in both mitosis and interphase, the role of these targets is primarily confined to mitosis. This limitation in function is expected to lead to lower toxicity compared to MTAs. Unfortunately, despite several of these antimitotic drugs advancing to clinical trials, they have shown unsatisfactory outcomes in cancer treatment, as monotherapy [9–11].

The effectiveness of antimitotic agents is hampered by the unpredictable outcomes of cancer cells during extended mitotic arrests [12,13]. Cancer cells arrested in mitosis may either die within this phase, or undergo slippage, wherein they exit mitosis without undergoing division. Slippage is primarily driven by the gradual degradation of cyclin B, even in the presence of an active SAC, which ultimately leads to mitotic exit. The determining factor between cell death in mitosis or slippage is the relative rates of cyclin B degradation and apoptotic signal accumulation [14–16]. According to these two competitive network models, in cases where cyclin B levels decline below the mitotic exit threshold before the accumulation of death signals reaches the necessary level for initiating apoptosis, slippage takes place. Conversely, if the death signals exceed the threshold required to trigger cell death before cyclin B levels diminish enough to prompt mitotic exit, the cells undergo cell death during mitosis [13,17]. Cells that have slipped into mitosis can proceed along one of three distinct routes: they might undergo post-slippage death, enter a state of senescence, or continue dividing, consequently contributing to tumor growth [12,13,18]. Therefore, slippage is recognized as a major resistance mechanism against antimitotic agents [14].

Cell death induced by antimitotic agents occurs through the activation of the intrinsic mitochondrial apoptotic pathway. This pathway is controlled by the anti-apoptotic proteins (BCL-2, BCL-W, BCL-XL, and MCL-1), pro-apoptotic proteins (BAX and BAK), and BH3-only proteins (e.g., BAD, BIK, BIM, BID, and NOXA) [19]. BH3-mimetics are a new class of pro-apoptotic anti-cancer drugs that target the intrinsic mitochondria-dependent apoptotic signaling pathway, showing promising clinical results, especially in patients with hematologic malignancies [20,21].

Hence, it becomes possible to exert deliberate control over the interplay between the two competitive pathways, namely, cyclin B degradation and apoptosis signal accumulation. For instance, combining BH3-mimetics with antimitotics should shift the balance from slippage to cell death in mitosis or post-mitosis, thereby enhancing the effectiveness of the antimitotic agents. This approach has recently undergone testing, yielding promising preclinical results [22–24].

In this study, we evaluated the effectiveness of this strategy by combining the BH3-mimetic navitoclax, known for its high affinity towards BCL-2 anti-apoptotic proteins such as BCL-2, BCL-W, and BCL-XL, along with two second-generation antimitotic agents: BAY1217389, a selective MPS1 inhibitor representing mitotic drivers, and GSK923295, a selective CENPE inhibitor representing mitotic blockers [25,26]. The approach was assessed using lung cancer cells cultured in both traditional 2D settings and a three-dimensional (3D) cancer model, serving as a preclinical system to mimic physiological drug responses. Additionally, we undertook a mechanistic study to understand how navitoclax promotes cancer cell death when combined with the antimitotic agents BAY1217389 or GSK923295. We found that the combination of the BH3-mimetic with both GSK923295 and BAY1217389 induced significant cell death, primarily through apoptosis, in both 2D and 3D cultures. Importantly, synergistic concentrations exhibited lower toxicity towards non-tumor cells. This underscores the relevance of combining BH3-mimetics with antimitotics, specifically CENPE and MPS-1 inhibitors, which have advanced to the clinical trial phase, to amplify their efficacy.

2. Materials and Methods

2.1. Small Molecule Inhibitors

Inhibitors of CENPE (GSK923295), BCL-2/BCL-XL (navitoclax), and MPS-1 (BAY1217389) were obtained from MedChem Express (Shanghai, China) and were reconstituted in sterile dimethyl sulfoxide (DMSO, Sigma-Aldrich Co., Ltd., St. Louis, MO, USA) to a stock concentration of 5 or 10 mM. Several aliquots were prepared and stored at −20 °C to avoid repeated cycles of freezing and thawing and, consequently, the loss of compounds' activity. For each independent experiment, a work solution was prepared in fresh culture medium to prepare the desired concentrations.

2.2. Cell Culture

A549 (Human Lung Adenocarcinoma; American Type Culture Collection) and NCI-H460 (Human large cell lung cancer; European Collection of Cell Culture) cancer cell lines were grown in RPMI-1640 (Roswell Park Memorial Institute, Biochrom, Buffalo, NY, USA) and DMEM (Dulbecco's Modified Eagle's, Biochrom) culture medium, respectively, and supplemented with 10% of heat-inactivated fetal bovine serum (FBS, Biochrom, Berlin, Germany) and 1% of Pen/Strep (Biochrom). In addition, DMEM was supplemented with 1% of non-essential amino acids (Sigma-Aldrich Co., Ltd.). The non-cancer cell line HPAEpiC (Human Pulmonary Alveolar Epithelial Cells; ScienCell Research Laboratories, San Diego, CA, USA) was grown in the same conditions as A549. All cell lines were maintained in a cell incubator at 37 °C with 5% CO_2 (Hera Cell, Heraeus, Hanau, Germany) with a humidified atmosphere.

2.3. RNA Extraction, cDNA Synthesis and Quantitative Real-Time PCR

Total RNA extraction and cDNA synthesis were performed as previously reported [18]. DNA was amplified using iQ™ SYBR Green Supermix Kit (Bio-Rad, Laboratories, Inc., Hercules, CA, USA) on an iQ Thermal Cycler (Bio-Rad), according to the following program: initial denaturing step at 95.0 °C for 3 min; 40 cycles at 94.0 °C for 20 s; 62.0 °C for 30 s and 72.0 °C for 30 s. The melt curve included temperatures from 65.0 to 95.0 °C, with increments of 0.5 °C for 5 s. The primers, at 10 µM, were as follows: MPS-1: forward 50-TCAAGGAACCTCTGGTGTCA-30 and reverse 50-GGTTACTCTCTGGAACCTCTGGT-30; CENPE: forward 50-GTCGGACCAGTTCAGCCTGATA-30 and reverse 50-CCAAGTGATT CTTCTCTGCTGTTC-30; GAPDH: forward 50-ACAGTCAGCCGCATCTTC-30 and reverse 50-GCCCAATACGACCAAATCC-30; Actin: forward 50-AATCTGGCACCACACCTTCTA-30 and reverse 50-ATAGCACAGCCTGGATAGCAA-30. The data were acquired using CFX ManagerTM Software (version 1.0, BioRad) and the results were analyzed according to CT and normalized against Actin and GAPDH expression levels, which were used as housekeeping genes.

2.4. Protein Extracts and Western Blotting

Protein extracts' pelleted cells were resuspended in lysis buffer (50 mM Tris pH 7.5; 150 mM NaCl; 1 mM EDTA; 1% Triton-100) containing a protease inhibitor cocktail (Sigma-Aldrich). A BCA™ Protein Assay Kit (Pierce Biotechnology, Rockford, IL, USA) was used for protein quantification according to the manufacturer's instructions. For MPS1 detection, a total of 20 µg of protein lysate was resuspended in SDS-sample buffer (375 mM Tris pH 6.8; 12% SDS; 60% Glycerol; 0.12% Bromophenol Blue; 600 nM DTT) and boiled for 3 min, and proteins were separated on a 7.5% SDS–PAGE gel. Following SDS-PAGE, proteins were transferred onto nitrocellulose membranes (Amersham) using the Trans-Blot Turbo Transfer System (Bio-Rad). For Cyclin B1 detection, the same procedure was followed, but using 10 µg of total protein lysate and a 10% SDS–PAGE gel. For CENPE detection, a total of 60 µg of protein lysate was also resuspended in SDS-sample buffer and boiled for 3 min, and was resolved on a 4–20% gradient gel (Bio-Rad). Then, proteins were transferred onto nitrocellulose membranes (Amersham) using wet-tank transfer via a Mini Trans-Blot Electrophoretic Transfer Cell (Bio-Rad). Then, membranes were blocked in 5% of non-fat dried milk (w/v) dissolved in TBST (50 mM Tris pH 7.5; 150 mM NaCl, 0.05% Tween-20), and were incubated overnight at 4 °C with the following primary antibodies diluted in TBST: mouse anti-α-tubulin (1:5000, T568 Clone B-5-1-2, Sigma-Aldrich), rabbit anti-cyclin B1 (1:500, C8831, Sigma-Aldrich), mouse anti-CENPE (1:250, (C-5): sc-376685, Santa Cruz Biotechnology, Heidelberg, Germany), and mouse anti-MPS-1 (1000, (N1): sc-56968, Santa Cruz Biotechnology, Heidelberg, Germany). The membranes were washed three times in TBST, and then incubated for 1 h with appropriate horseradish-peroxidase-conjugated secondary antibodies (1:1500 (anti-mouse) or 1:1000 (anti-rabbit), Vector). Proteins were detected using the Enhanced Chemiluminescence (ECL) method in a ChemiDOc (Bio-Rad). The protein signal intensity quantification was performed using Image Lab 6.1v software and normalized against α-tubulin expression levels.

2.5. Indirect Immunofluorescence

A total of 0.09×10^6 cells/mL were grown on poly-L-lysine-coated coverslips in complete culture medium for 24 h. Subsequently, cells underwent treatment with MPS-1 and CENPE inhibitors. After 24 h, they were fixed in methanol (Sigma-Aldrich, Co., Ltd., Gillingham, UK) at −20 °C for 10 min, followed by three washes with PBS for 5 min each. The cells were then blocked using 10% FBS in PBST (0.05% Tween-20 in PBS) for 30 min at room temperature. Then, cells were subjected to a 1 h incubation with primary antibodies (mouse anti-α-tubulin, 1:2500, Sigma-Aldrich Co., Ltd., Gillingham, UK; human anti-CREST, 1:3000, gifted by E. Bronze-da-Rocha, IBMC, Porto, Portugal) diluted in 5% FBS in PBST. After three washes in PBST, cells were exposed to Alexa Fluor 488-conjugated secondary antibody (1:1500, Molecular Probes, Eugene, OR, USA). To visualize the DNA, cells were stained with 2 μg/mL 4′,6-diamidino-2-phenylindole (DAPI, Sigma-Aldrich) diluted in Vectashield mounting medium (Vector, H-1000, Burlingame, CA, USA).

2.6. MTT Viability Assay

To measure cell viability, a tetrazolium salt 3-(4, 5-dimethylthiazol-2-yl)-2,5-diphenyltetrazolium bromide (MTT) assay was used. A total of 0.05×10^6 cells/mL of A549 or NCI-H460 cells and 0.065×10^6 cells/mL of HPAEpiC cells were seeded into a 96-well plate in complete media, allowing them to adhere overnight prior to drug exposure. After 24 h, the culture medium was replaced with fresh medium containing 2-fold serial dilutions of the inhibitors ranging from 62.5 nM to 1000 nM for GSK923295, 500 nM to 8000 nM for BAY1217389, and 1000 nM to 16,000 nM for Navitoclax. Forty-eight hours later, 20 μL of tetrazolium salt MTT (5 mg/mL PBS) was added to 200 μL of fresh medium for 4 h. The formazan crystals were dissolved in 100 μL of DMSO, and the optical density was retrieved at 570 nm using a microplate reader (Biotek Synergy 2, Winooski, VT, USA) coupled to Gen5 software (version 1.07.5, Biotek, Winooski, VT, USA). GraphPad Prism version 8 (GraphPad software Inc., San Diego, CA, USA) was used to calculate the mean 50% inhibition concentration (IC_{50}) values. Additionally, the combined treatment effects were evaluated using a dual-drug crosswise concentration via Combenefit Software (version 2.021, Cancer Research UK Cambridge Institute, Cambridge, UK).

2.7. Apoptosis Detection

2.7.1. TUNEL Assay

To detect apoptosis, the DeadEnd Fluorometric TUNEL System (Promega, Madison, WI, USA) was used following the manufacturer's guidelines. For DNA staining, 2 mg/mL of DAPI in Vectashield mounting medium was used. The extent of cell death was evaluated by counting TUNEL-positive cells among a total of 500 cells, from at least 10 random microscopic fields, for each experimental condition under a fluorescence microscope.

2.7.2. Annexin V/PI Staining

Apoptotic cell death was assessed using the Annexin V-FITC Apoptosis Detection Kit (eBioscience, Vienna, Austria) according to the manufacturer's instructions. Briefly,

0.09×10^6 cells/mL were seeded into 6-well plates, and 24 h later cells were treated with MPS1/CENPE inhibitors alone or in combination with navitoclax at the concentration of the respective synergistic points. After 48 h, both floating and adherent cells were gathered and pelleted by centrifugation at 1000 rpm for 5 min, then suspended in binding buffer 1×. Subsequently, Annexin V-FITC was added and allowed to incubate for 10 min, shielded from light. After washing, cells were once again resuspended in binding buffer 1×, and 20 µg/mL of Propidium iodide (PI) was added. Fluorescence analysis was performed using the BD Accuri™ C6 Plus Flow cytometer (BD Biosciences, Qume Drive, San Jose, CA, USA), and the data were processed using BD Accuri TM C6 Plus software, version 1.0.27.1. At least 20,000 events per sample were collected.

To evaluate apoptotic cell death in 3D cultures, after 48 h of treatment with MPS1/CENPE inhibitors alone or in combination with navitoclax at the concentration of the respective synergistic points, approximately 32 spheroids were collected from a 96-well ultra-low attachment plate and transferred to a 15 mL centrifuge tube. Once the spheroids precipitated, the supernatant was removed, and PBS was added to wash the spheroids. After, PBS was removed and 200 µL of trypsin (GIBCO, Invitrogen, Waltham, MA, USA) was added. The spheroids were then incubated at 37 °C for 25 min to guarantee their total dissociation into single cells. After addition of 500 µL of culture medium, the cells were centrifuged at 1000 rpm for 4 min and washed with PBS. The samples were treated with an "Annexin V-FITC Apoptosis Detection Kit" according to the manufacturer's instructions. At least 20,000 events per sample were collected.

2.8. Mitotic Index Determination

A total of 0.09×10^6 cells/mL were grown in six-well dishes and treated for 24 h with CENPE inhibitor alone or in combination with navitoclax at the concentration of the respective synergistic point. Cells treated with 1 µM of microtubule depolymerizing agent Nocodazole were used as the positive control for antimitotic activity. Untreated cells and cells treated with DMSO, to assess compound solvent-mediated cytotoxicity, were also included as controls. The mitotic index, the percentage of mitotic cells over a total cell population, was determined by cell rounding under phase-contrast microscopy. At least 3000 cells were counted from random microscope fields.

2.9. Time-Lapse Microscopy

For live-cell imaging, a total of 0.09×10^6 A549 cells were seeded into a LabTek II chambered cover glass (Nunc, Penfield, NY, USA) in complete RPMI culture medium. Sterile water was added to the remaining wells to guarantee a humidified atmosphere. The cells were incubated overnight at 37 °C under 5% CO_2. Then, the medium was replaced by fresh medium in the presence of MPS-1/CENPE inhibitors alone or in combination with navitoclax at the concentration of the respective synergistic points. Time-lapse images were taken every 5 min over a 48 h period using differential interference contrast (DIC) optics, and a 63× objective on an Axio Observer Z.1 SD inverted microscope (Carl Zeiss, Oberkochen, Germany). The microscope is equipped with an incubation chamber set to 37 °C and 5% CO_2. ImageJ software (version 1.47, Rasband, W.S., ImageJ, U. S. National Institutes of Health, Bethesda, MD, USA) was used to create movies from the time-lapse images.

2.10. Phase-Contrast and Fluorescence Microscopy Images

Phase-contrast microscopy images were obtained using a Nikon TE 2000-U microscope (Nikon, Amsterdam, The Netherlands) equipped with a 10× objective and connected to a DXM1200F digital camera running Nikon ACT-1 software version 2.63 (Melville, NY, USA). Fluorescence imaging was acquired using an Axio Observer Z.1 SD microscope, coupled with an AxioCam MR3 and the Plan Apochromatic 100×/NA 1.4 objective, and the images were processed using ImageJ.

2.11. Colony Formation Assay

A total of 500 A549 cells were seeded in six-well plates, allowed to attach for 24 h, and treated with drugs in monotherapy or in combination. Untreated and DMSO-treated cells were also included. Forty-eight hours later, cells were washed twice with PBS and incubated in a drug-free DMEM medium for 7 days. After this period, the colonies were fixed for 25 min using 100% methanol at −20 °C and then stained for 20 min with 0.05% (*w*/*v*) violet crystal (Merck, Rahway, NJ, USA) in distilled water. The count of colonies for each condition was derived from three independent experiments. Plating efficiency (PE) was calculated as the percentage of the number of colonies that grew compared to the number of cells seeded in the control. Additionally, the survival fraction for each condition was calculated as the number of colonies over the number of cells seeded $\times$ 1/PE.

2.12. Caspase Activity Assay

To evaluate caspase-9 activity, cells were seeded as described for immunofluorescence assay. Following a 24 h incubation with mitotic inhibitor, navitoclax, alone or in combination, the medium was aspirated, and cells were washed with PBS. Subsequently, 150 µL of Glo Lysis Buffer (Promega, Madison, WI, USA) was added to each well, and the cells were incubated for 5 min at room temperature. Caspase-9 activity was determined as previously described [27]. For caspase-9 detection, lysates (10 mL) were mixed with 200 mL of assay buffer (100 nM HEPES (pH 7.5), 20% (*v*/*v*) glycerol, 5 mM DTT, 0.5 mM EDTA) followed by incubation at 30 °C for 30 min. After incubation, the reaction was started by adding 10 mL of caspase-9 fluorogenic substrate N-acetyl-Leu-Glu-His-Asp 7-amido-4-trifluoromethylcoumarin (Sigma-Aldrich) at a final concentration of 180 mM. Fluorescence was determined using a microplate reader (Biotek Synergy 2) to 400 nm excitation and 500 nm emission, in a kinetic reaction for 5 min. The obtained results were normalized against the protein content. For each assay, normalization was also carried out against the value obtained in the untreated group, with a reference value set at 1.

2.13. Spheroid Formation, Drug Treatment and Viability Assay

The generation of A549 spheroids, drug treatment, and the assessment of spheroids viability were performed as previously reported [22]. Briefly, 4000 cells/well were seeded into 96-well ultra-low attachment plates and 4 days later treated with MPS1/CENPE inhibitors alone or in combination with navitoclax at the concentrations of 4000–16,000 nM. After 48 h, the spheroid viability was determined via CellTiter-Glo 3D cell viability assay (Promega) according to the manufacturer's instructions.

2.14. Statistical Analysis

All assays were performed in triplicate from at least three independent experiments. Data are expressed as mean ± standard deviation (SD), and statistical analysis was carried out in GraphPad Prism Software Inc. v8 using the unpaired *t*-test or two-way ANOVA with Tukey's multiple comparison test; values of * $p < 0.05$, ** $p < 0.01$, *** $p < 0.001$, and **** $p < 0.0001$ were considered statistically significant.

3. Results

3.1. CENPE and MPS1 Are Overexpressed in Lung Cancer Cells

CENPE is a microtubule-dependent plus-end-directed motor belonging to the kinesin-7 subfamily and is crucial for the congression of initially misaligned chromosomes [27]. Inhibitors of CENPE lead to chromosome misalignment, resulting in an extended mitotic arrest, acting as mitotic blockers, and ultimately leading to cell death in mitosis [28]. MPS-1 is a protein kinase and a crucial activator of the SAC [29]. Inhibitors of MPS1 override the SAC and induce premature mitotic exit, leading to massive chromosome missegregation and eventual cell death, acting as mitotic drivers [30,31]. Both MPS1 and CENPE have been reported to be overexpressed in cancer cells, making them potential targets for cancer therapy [32–35].

Thus, we first examined the expression of CENPE and MPS-1 in A549 and NCI-H460 non-small cell lung cancer (NSCLC) cell lines. The results demonstrated that CENPE and MPS1 mRNA levels, determined by qRT-PCR, were upregulated in both lung cancer cell lines when compared to the non-tumor cell line HPAEpiC (Figure 1a,c). Western blot analysis also evidenced an increase in protein levels for both targets (Figure 1b,d). The findings align with prior studies that have documented the increased expression of CENPE and MPS1 in lung cancer, underscoring the significance of targeting these proteins [33,36].

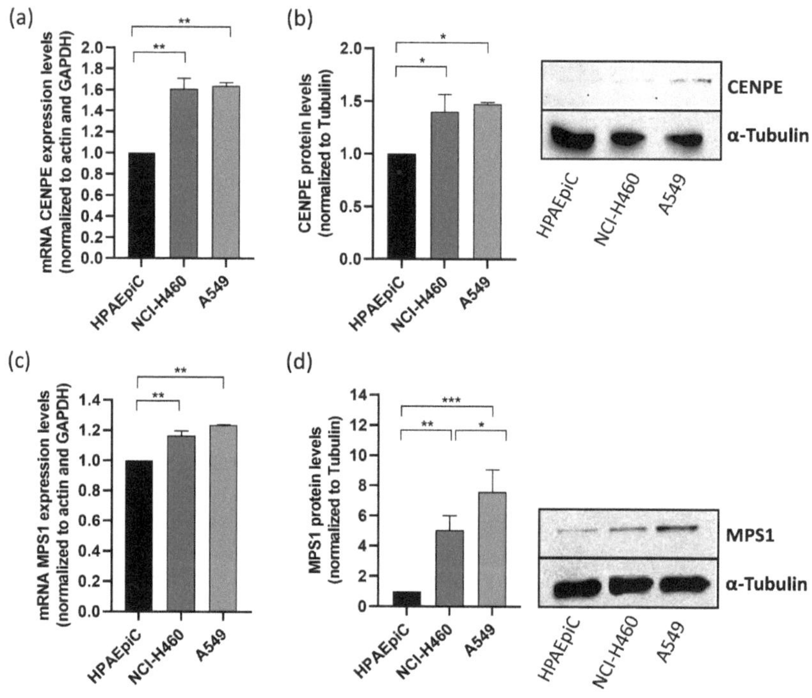

Figure 1. CENPE and MPS1 are overexpressed in NSCLC lung cancer cell lines. mRNA expression of CENPE (**a**) and MPS1 (**c**) was determined by qRT-PCR in A549 and NCI-H460 cancer cell lines, and was compared to that in non-tumor HPAEpiC cells. Protein levels of CENPE (**b**) and MPS1 (**d**) were quantified by Western blotting assay, using α-tubulin as control. Data represent the mean ± SD of three independent experiments, one-way ANOVA followed by Tukey's multiple comparisons test. * $p < 0.05$; ** $p < 0.01$; *** $p < 0.001$.

Due to the fact that A549 cells represent a model of NSCLC, the most common lung cancer type, and exhibit elevated protein expression of CENPE and MPS1 compared to the large cell lung cancer model NCI-H460 cells, we selected A549 cells for the subsequent experiments in this study [37].

3.2. Navitoclax Synergizes with the Mitotic Blocker GSK923295 and the Mitotic Driver BAY1217389 in Killing Lung Cancer Cells

To assess whether the BH3-mimetic navitoclax potentiates the antiproliferative activity of the CENPE inhibitor GSK923295 or the MPS1 inhibitor BAY1217389, we initially examined cellular cytotoxicity using the MTT assay, after exposure of A549 cells to these compounds, individually and in combination for 48 h. A dual-drug concentration crosswise matrix was performed for each combination, covering a concentration range from 0 to 16,000 nM for navitoclax, 0 to 1000 nM for GSK923295, and 0 to 8000 nM for BAY1217389.

Using the Combenefit Software, we assessed the percentage of viable cells (Figure 2a,b) and calculated the combinatorial interaction effect score (Figure 2c,d). This analysis allowed us to determine the IC_{50} of each compound (Tables 1 and 2).

Table 1. GSK923295 and navitoclax IC_{50} in 2D A549 cells.

Drugs	IC_{50} (nM)
GSK923295	150 ± 30
Navitoclax	13,050 ± 690

Table 2. BAY1217389 and Navitoclax IC_{50} in 2D A549 cells.

Drugs	IC_{50} (nM)
BAY1217389	4340 ± 60
Navitoclax	13,310 ± 910

The IC_{50} values of GSK923295 and BAY1217389 were 150.0 ± 30 nM and 4340.0 ± 60 nM, respectively, while that of navitoclax exceeded 13,000 nM, indicating its lower cytotoxicity. Interestingly, a synergistic effect was observed with both GSK923295 + navitoclax and BAY1217389 + navitoclax combinations (Figure 2c,d). The synergistic combination with the lowest concentrations (1000 nM of navitoclax with 125 nM of GSK923295, and 1000 nM of navitoclax with 500 nM of BAY1217389) were selected for subsequent experiments. It is noteworthy that the combination of 1000 nM of navitoclax with 125 nM of GSK923295 corresponds to 13- and 1.2-fold less than their respective IC_{50} values, while the combination of 1000 nM of navitoclax with 500 nM of BAY1217389 is approximately 13- and 8-fold less than their respective IC_{50} values. This is particularly relevant for minimizing toxicity and side effects reported in clinical trials for these drugs [9,38]. Interestingly, the selected concentrations of both GSK923295 + navitoclax and BAY1217389 + navitoclax did not significantly affect the viability of the non-cancer HPAEpiC cells (Figure S1). This suggests that cancer cells are more responsive to these treatments than non-cancer cells.

We also performed a colony formation assay in A549 cancer cells treated with the GSK923295 + navitoclax or BAY1217389 + navitoclax combinations. For this, after 48 h of drug exposure, the medium was replaced with fresh medium and A549 cells were maintained for 7 days in a cell culture incubator at 37 °C with 5% CO_2. On the 7th day, the colonies were counted. Our results showed that both combinations of GSK923295 + navitoclax and BAY1217389 + navitoclax were able to reduce colony formation when compared to single treatments (Figure 2e–g). Indeed, a reduction to 8.3 ± 4.2% of colony survival fraction after GSK923295 + navitoclax combination exposure was observed when compared to GSK923295 (30.0 ± 5.9%) and navitoclax (88.0 ± 7.1%) monotherapy, and a reduction to 4.4 ± 3.0% after BAY1217389 + navitoclax treatment compared to BAY1217389 (12.2 ± 3.6%) and navitoclax (86.7 ± 5.7%) drugs alone. These results suggest that the combinatorial approaches exhibit an ability to maintain long-term cellular cytotoxicity, preventing the proliferation of cancer cells.

Therefore, the BH3-mimetic synergizes with both the antimitotic agent that induces a SAC-mediated mitotic block and the antimitotic agent that drives cells through an aberrant mitosis by overriding the SAC. We next proceeded further with the selected combinations to obtain a deeper understanding of the cellular mechanism behind their synergistic cytotoxicity.

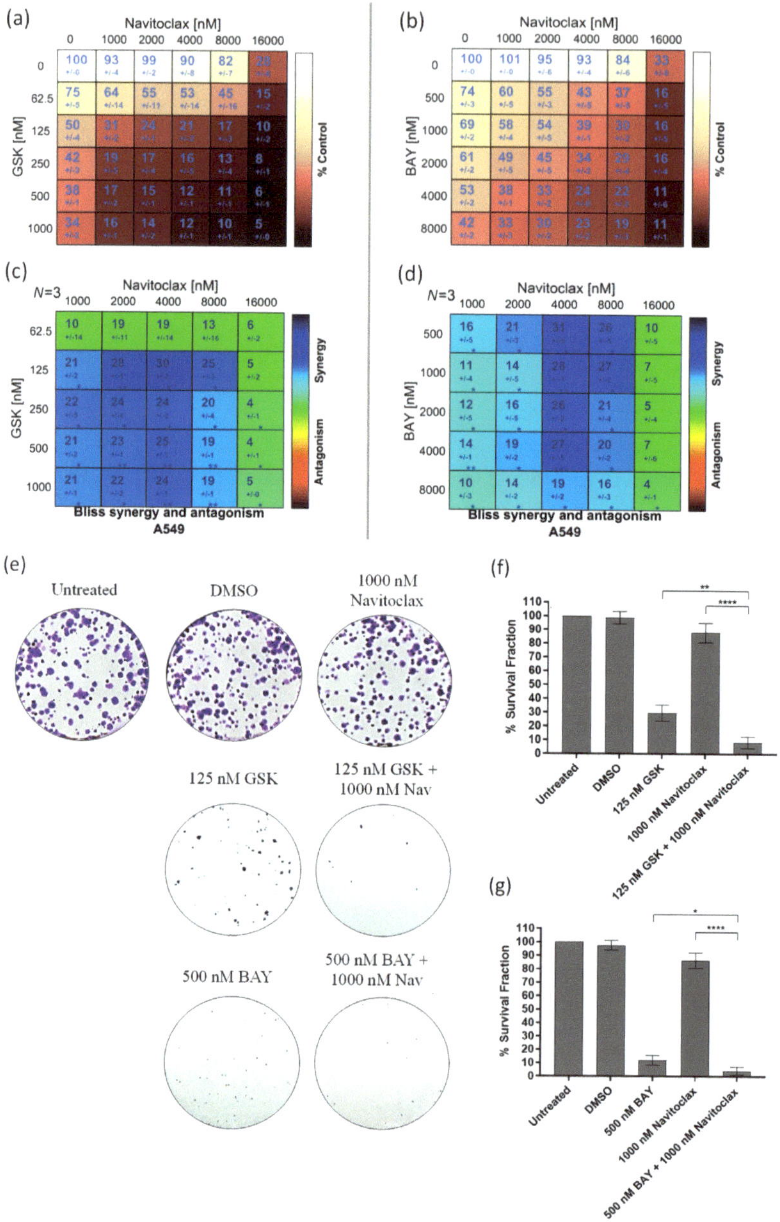

Figure 2. GSK923295 + navitoclax and BAY1217389 + navitoclax combinations potentiate cytotoxicity in 2D A549 lung cancer cell cultures. Cell viability (%) of single or combination therapies after 48 h of drug exposure (**a**,**b**), from three independent experiments as determined by MTT assay. Synergy scores calculated by the Bliss model of Combenefit software 2.021 with statistical relevance of * $p < 0.05$, ** $p < 0.01$, and *** $p < 0.001$. Asterisk indicates synergism effects (**c**,**d**). Colony formation assays were performed using A549 cells following 7 days (**e**). Quantification of survival fraction (%) after single or combination treatments as indicated (**f**,**g**). Data represent the mean ± SD of three independent experiments, one-way ANOVA followed by Tukey's multiple comparisons test. * $p < 0.05$; ** $p < 0.01$; **** $p < 0.0001$.

3.3. Navitoclax Prevents Mitotic Slippage Caused by GSK923295 Treatment by Accelerating Cell Death during Mitosis

To gain insights into the cellular mechanisms underlying the synergistic cytotoxicity of the GSK923295 + navitoclax combination, A549 cells were exposed to these combinations, single agents, or medium/DMSO (controls) for 48 h, and subsequently examined using phase-contrast microscopy. Upon treatment with GSK923295 alone, as expected, we observed an accumulation of mitotic cells, similar to the effect induced by Nocodazole, a well-known antimitotic agent used here as a positive control (Figure 3a,b). This observation was further confirmed by calculating the mitotic index, which was significantly higher in GSK923295-treated cell cultures (66.4 ± 6.6%) compared to untreated (8.7 + 0.5%) and DMSO-treated cells (6.6 + 1.8%) (Figure 3b). Treatment with navitoclax alone did not significantly impact normal cell cycling, except for a few instances of cell death. Interestingly, when GSK923295 was combined with navitoclax, the mitotic index decreased to 47.0 ± 2.4%, but it still remained higher compared to the controls. The complex formed by cyclin B1 and cyclin-dependent kinase 1 (CDK1) acts in the regulation of mitotic entry and progression. Cyclin B1 degradation is essential for mitotic exit [39]. Thus, high levels of cyclin B are indicative of a mitotic arrest. The results show an increase in cyclin B1 protein levels after GSK923295 exposure (Figure 3c), as expected, and are complementary to the mitotic index determination. Conversely, both the combinations of GSK923295 + navitoclax and BAY + navitoclax, as well as BAY and navitoclax alone, had no significant effect on cyclin B1 protein levels.

We then carried out time-lapse microscopy to track live cells treated with the GSK923295 + navitoclax combination, allowing us to monitor their spatiotemporal dynamics. Our objective was to unveil the fate of the cells arrested in mitosis due to GSK923295 or GSK923295 + navitoclax treatment. A549 tumor cells were treated with GSK923295 and navitoclax, alone or in combination, and each cell was followed over 48 h via live cell time-lapse microscopy.

Control cells completed mitosis within 28.2 ± 5.9 min, and the presence of navitoclax did not significantly affect this timing (26.8 ± 5.1 min) (Figure 3d). However, treatment with GSK923295 led to a substantial extension of mitosis duration, lasting an average of 952.1 ± 4165.0 min. Interestingly, when navitoclax was added to GSK923295, it significantly reduced the duration of mitotic arrest by more than 2.5-fold, suggesting that navitoclax accelerates cell death (Figure 3d). Regarding the cell fates, we observed that most of the navitoclax-treated cells underwent normal cell division, except for a few cells (2.9 + 4.0%) that experienced post-mitotic death (PMD). This suggests that navitoclax alone does not exhibit toxicity to tumor cells, at least at the given concentration (Figure 3e,f, and Video S1). For cells treated with GSK923295 alone, the majority (92.8%) of cells that arrested in mitosis managed to survive throughout the experiment, with only a small fraction (7.2 ± 8.8%) undergoing cell death in mitosis (DiM). Among the surviving cells, 54.0 ± 17.6% continued to survive after cell division (post-mitotic survival, PMS), and 38.8 ± 18.5% persisted after mitotic slippage (post-slippage survival, PSS) (Figure 3e,d, and Video S2). In contrast, in cells subjected to the GSK923295 + navitoclax combination treatment, a substantial portion (95%) of the cells arrested in mitosis died, with the majority (88.1 ± 17.2%) of these deaths occurring during mitosis (DiM), and the remainder (6.9 ± 13.6%) occurring after cell division (Figure 3e,d, and Video S3). Only a small fraction (5.0 ± 5.9%) managed to survive after completing mitosis (PMS). Notably, no cells underwent mitotic slippage. Therefore, when combined with GSK923295, navitoclax shifts cell fate from mitotic slippage to cell death in mitosis, thereby eliminating the possibility of cellular survival by slippage.

Apoptosis was the predominant mechanism of cell death in the GSK923295 + navitoclax combination, as evidenced by both flow cytometry analysis of Annexin V/PI-stained cells and immunostaining using the TUNEL assay (Figure 4a–d). In this context, to evaluate the possible apoptotic pathway associated with drug treatments, the activity of caspase-9 was assessed. Caspase-9, a critical initiator caspase essential for the intrinsic pathway of apoptosis, upon activation, cleaves and activates downstream effector caspases-3 and

-7. These effectors, in turn, target key regulatory and structural proteins for proteolysis, leading to cell death [40,41]. The results showed an increase in caspase-9 activity after GSK923295 + navitoclax combination treatment (4.6 ± 0.2), compared to GSK923295 (1.9 ± 0.2) and navitoclax (1.1 ± 0.3) drugs alone (Figure 4e), indicating that compounds target the intrinsic apoptosis pathway.

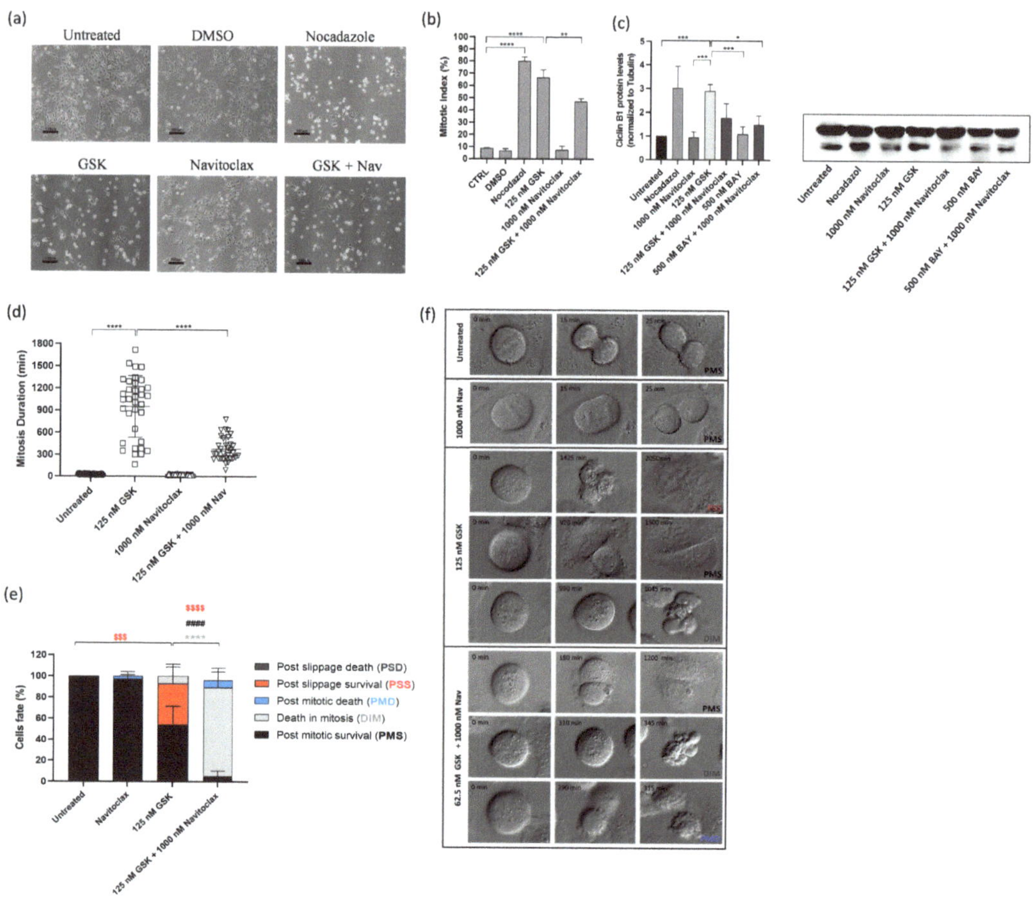

Figure 3. Combination of GSK923295 + navitoclax reduces mitotic arrest duration and prevents slippage by accelerating cell death in mitosis in lung cancer cells. Representative phase-contrate microscopy images after 24 h of drugs alone or in combination (**a**). Quantification of mitotic index; 0.25% DMSO (compound solvent) and 1 µM Nocodazole (mitotic blocker agent) were used as negative and positive controls, respectively (**b**). Quantification of mitosis duration after respective drug treatments via time-lapse microscopy (**c**). Cyclin B1 levels as determined by Western blotting assay. (**d**) Quantification of cell fate (%) for 48 h using different treatments as indicated (**e**). Representative time-lapse image sequences of A549 cells immediately after drug treatments (**f**). Data represent the mean ± SD of at least three independent experiments, one-way ANOVA followed by Tukey's multiple comparisons test. * $p < 0.05$, ** $p < 0.01$; *** $p < 0.001$; **** $p < 0.0001$. $$$ difference ($p < 0.001$) of post-slippage survival cells (%) between untreated and 125 nM GSK923295. $$$$ difference ($p < 0.0001$) of post-slippage survival cells (%) between 125 nM GSK923295 and 125 nM GSK923295 + 1000 nM navitoclax. * difference in death in mitosis cells (%) between 125 nM GSK923295 and 125 nM GSK923295 + 1000 nM navitoclax. #### difference ($p < 0.0001$) in post-mitotic survival cells (%) between 125 nM GSK923295 and 125 nM GSK923295 + 1000 nM navitoclax.

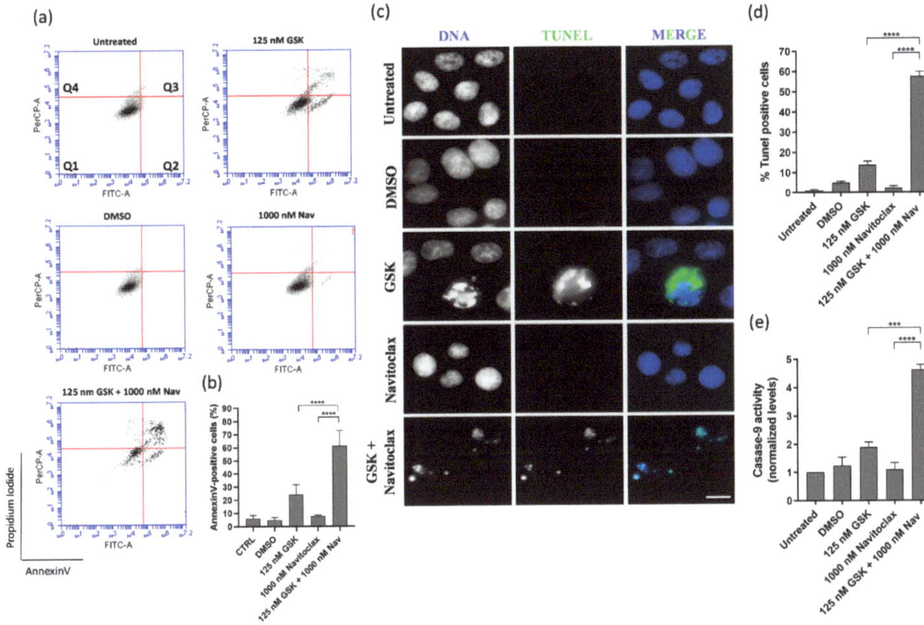

Figure 4. GSK923295 + navitoclax combination enhance A549 lung cancer cell death. Representative cytograms of A549 cell line double stained with Annexin V-FITC and propidium iodide (PI) (**a**). The quadrants Q are defined as Q1 = live (Annexin V- and PI-negative), Q2 = early stage of apoptosis (Annexin V-positive/PI-negative), Q3 = late stage of apoptosis (Annexin V- and PI-positive) and Q4 = necrosis (Annexin V-negative/PI-positive). Quantification of Annexin-V-positive cells (**b**). Representative images of A549 apoptotic cells after 48 h treatment, via TUNEL assay to detect DNA fragmentation (green). DNA (blue) was stained with DAPI. Bar, 5 μm (**c**). Quantification of A549 TUNEL-positive cells (**d**). Quantification of caspase-9 activity was normalized against the protein content of the extract. Additionally, normalization was performed against the value obtained in the untreated group, setting it as 1 for each assay (**e**). Data represent the mean ± SD of three independent experiments, one-way ANOVA followed by Tukey's multiple comparisons test. *** $p < 0.001$, **** $p < 0.0001$.

3.4. Navitoclax Prevents Post-Mitotic Survival Induced by BAY1217389 by Enhancing Post-Mitotic Death, but Only Partially

We also conducted time-lapse microscopy to monitor live cells treated with the combination of BAY1217389 and navitoclax, aiming to gain mechanistic insights into the cytotoxicity of this combination. Two-dimensional cultures of A549 cancer cells were subjected to treatment with BAY1217389 and navitoclax, either individually or in combination. Each cell was observed over 48 h using live cell time-lapse microscopy. The duration of mitosis in untreated cells was 28.2 ± 5.9 min, and navitoclax treatment did not significantly alter this duration (26.8 ± 5.1 min) (Figure 5a). In contrast, BAY1217389 treatment notably reduced mitosis duration to 17.7 ± 4.3 min, accelerating mitotic exit, as expected for a mitotic driver. Cotreatment with BAY1217389 and navitoclax did not significantly impact this phenotype, resulting in a mitosis duration of 15.5 ± 4.2 min. In terms of cell fate, we observed that the majority of navitoclax-treated cells underwent normal cell division, with only a few cells (2.9 ± 4.0%) experiencing PMD, again suggesting that, at least during the 48 h time course, navitoclax alone does not exhibit toxicity to cancer cells (Figure 5b,c). Treatment with BAY1217389 primarily induced PMS (75.1 ± 20.5%) and only a small percentage of PMD (6.0 ± 7.9%). Interestingly, cotreatment with BAY1217389 and navitoclax led to a significant increase in PMD (49.2 ± 11.3%, $p < 0.0001$), along with an almost 2-fold and significant decrease in PMS (39.1 ± 5.3%, $p < 0.0001$). However, the percentage of PMS cells is still significant and raises concerns about the efficient eradication of cancer cells. Therefore, navitoclax only partially sensitizes cancer cells to BAY1217389, as a significant fraction of cancer cells still escape cell death.

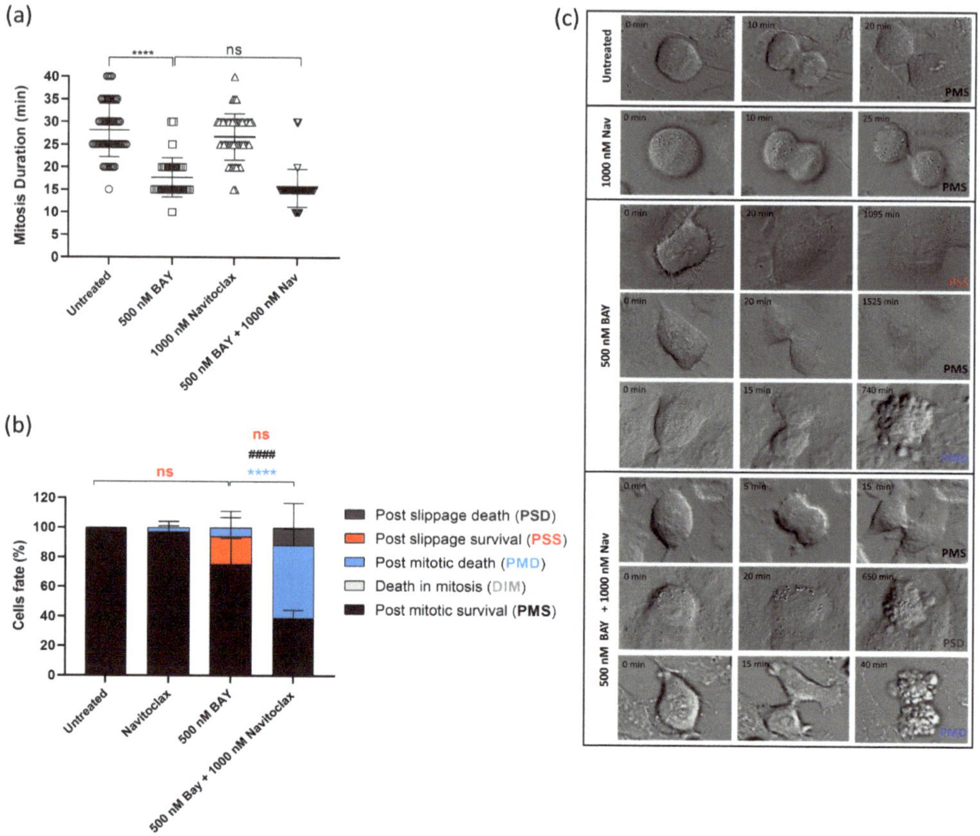

Figure 5. Combination of BAY1217389 + navitoclax induces post-mitotic death in 2D lung cancer cell cultures. Quantification of mitosis duration after respective drug treatments via time-lapse microscopy (**a**). Quantification of cell fate (%) for 48 h using different treatments as indicated (**b**). Representative time-lapse image sequences of A549 cells immediately after drug treatments (**c**). Data represent the mean ± SD of at least three independent experiments, one-way ANOVA followed by Tukey's multiple comparisons test. **** $p < 0.0001$. ns: not significant difference in mitosis duration between 500 nM BAY1217389 and 500 nM BAY1217389 + 1000 nM navitoclax, and in post-slippage survival cells (%) between untreated and 500 nM BAY1217389 and between 500 nM BAY1217389 and 500 nM BAY1217389 + 1000 nM navitoclax. **** difference in post-mitotic death cells (%) between 500 nM BAY1217389 and 500 nM BAY1217389 + 1000 nM navitoclax. #### difference ($p < 0.0001$) in post-mitotic survival cells (%) between 500 nM BAY1217389 and 500 nM BAY1217389 + 1000 nM navitoclax.

Cell death in the BAY1217389 + navitoclax combination was primarily attributed to apoptosis, as demonstrated by both flow cytometry analysis of Annexin V/PI-stained cells and immunostaining using the TUNEL assay (Figure 6a–d). The caspase-9 activity also was increased after BAY1217389 + navitoclax treatment (3.2 ± 0.4) when compared to

BAY1217389 (1.9 ± 0.5) and navitoclax (1.2 ± 0.1) drugs alone (Figure 6e), indicating an intrinsic apoptotic pathway participation.

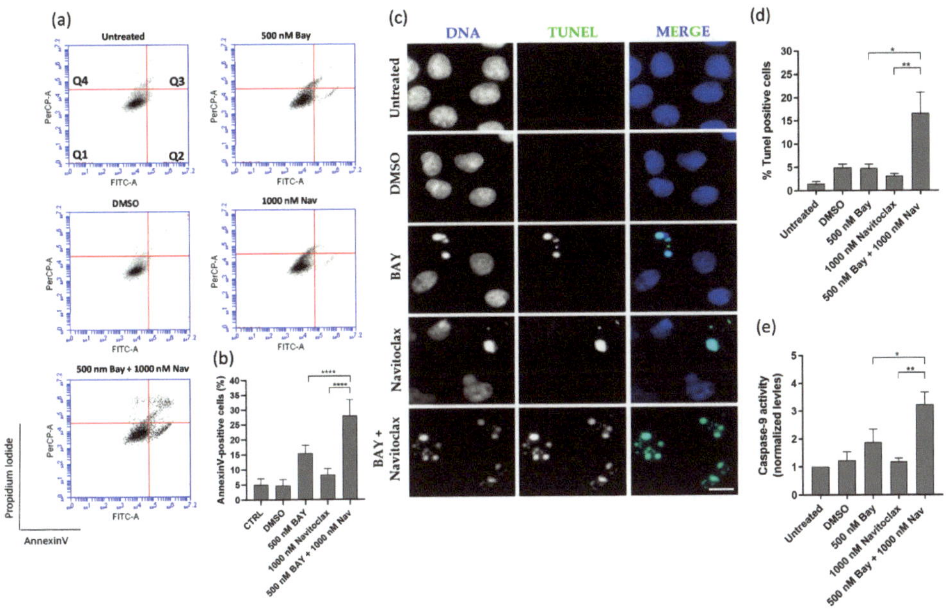

Figure 6. BAY1217389 + navitoclax combination enhances A549 lung cancer cell death by apoptosis. Representative cytograms of A549 cells double stained with Annexin V-FITC and propidium iodide (PI) (**a**). The quadrants Q are defined as Q1 = live (Annexin V- and PI-negative), Q2 = early stage of apoptosis (Annexin V-positive/PI-negative), Q3 = late stage of apoptosis (Annexin V- and PI-positive), and Q4 = necrosis (Annexin V-negative/PI-positive). Quantification of Annexin-V-positive cells (**b**). Representative images of A549 apoptotic cells after 48 h treatment, via TUNEL assay to detect DNA fragmentation (green). DNA (blue) was stained with DAPI. Bar, 5 µm (**c**). Quantification of A549 TUNEL-positive cells (**d**). Quantification of caspase-9 activity was normalized against the protein content of the extract. Additionally, normalization was performed against the value obtained in the untreated group, setting it as 1 for each assay (**e**). Data represent the mean ± SD of three independent experiments, one-way ANOVA followed by Tukey's multiple comparisons test. * $p < 0.05$; ** $p < 0.01$; **** $p < 0.0001$.

3.5. Navitoclax Sensitizes 3D Lung Cancer Spheroids to GSK923295 and BAY1217389 Treatment

Considering the substantial synergistic effect observed in a 2D system, we evaluated the effectiveness of the GSK923295 + navitoclax and BAY1217389 + navitoclax combinations in a 3D spheroid model. This model mimics tumor architecture and the microenvironment, making it a relevant in vitro preclinical model for cancer [42].

A dual-drug concentration crosswise matrix was made encompassing various different compound concentrations ranging from 0 to 16,000 nM. After 48 h of mono- or combination treatments, the spheroids' viability was determined by CellTiter-Glo assay and the IC_{50} values for the tested compounds were determined (Tables 3 and 4).

Table 3. GSK923295 and navitoclax IC_{50} in 3D A549 cells.

Drugs	IC_{50} (nM)
GSK923295	>16,000
navitoclax	6480 ± 1070

Table 4. BAY1217389 and navitoclax IC_{50} in 3D A549 cells.

Drugs	IC_{50} (nM)
BAY1217389	>16,000
navitoclax	6340 ± 930

The IC_{50} for both GSK923295 and BAY1217389 was >16,000 nM. In contrast, the IC_{50} for navitoclax was approximately 6400 nM in the spheroids, suggesting that lung cancer cells exhibit lower sensitivity to GSK923295 and BAY1217389 but higher sensitivity to navitoclax in a 3D cell culture system compared to a 2D system (Figure 7a,c,d,f). The combination of GSK923295 and BAY1217384 with navitoclax led to significantly greater cell death in A549 lung cancer cells compared to individual treatments, emphasizing the synergistic effect of the combinations (Figure 7b,e).

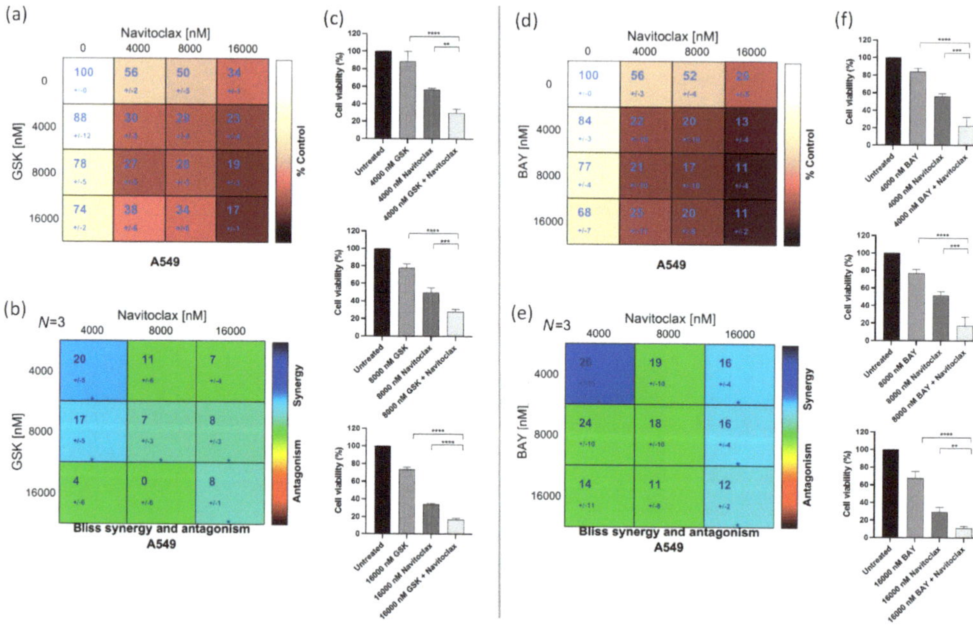

Figure 7. GSK923295 + navitoclax and BAY1217389 + navitoclax combinations enhance cytotoxicity in A549 3D spheroids. Cell viability (%) of single or combination therapies after 48 h of drug exposure (**a**,**d**) from three independent experiments as determined by MTT assay. Synergy scores calculated by the Bliss model of Combenefit software with statistical relevance of * $p < 0.05$. Asterisk indicates synergism effects (**b**,**e**). Three-dimensional spheroid viability (%) after 4000 nM, 8000 nM, and 16,000 nM drug concentration treatments (**c**,**f**). Data represent the mean ± SD of three independent experiments, one-way ANOVA followed by Tukey's multiple comparisons test. ** $p < 0.01$; *** $p < 0.001$; **** $p < 0.0001$.

Macroscopic examination of the spheroids treated with the lowest synergistic concentration of the GSK923295 + navitoclax and BAY1217389 + navitoclax combinations (4000 nM of navitoclax with 4000 nM of GSK923295 or BAY1217389) revealed a loosely compacted and partially fragmented structure (Figure 8a,d). Many cells had lost adhesion to the spheroid surface, indicating cytotoxic effects compared to the intact control spheroids. Additionally, cell death in both combinations was primarily attributed to apoptosis, as demonstrated by flow cytometry analysis of Annexin V/PI-stained cells (Figure 8b,c,e,f). Indeed, the combination of GSK923295 + navitoclax enhanced cell death by apoptosis (61.2 ± 11.7%) when compared to GSK923295 (40.7 ± 0.4%) and navitoclax (48.4 ± 1.2%)

alone treatments (Figure 8b,c). Similarly, BAY1217389 + navitoclax significantly increased the Annexin-V positive cells (62.5 ± 5.1%) compared to BAY1217389 (24.8 ± 6.7%) or navitoclax (42.8 ± 7.1%) (Figure 8e,f).

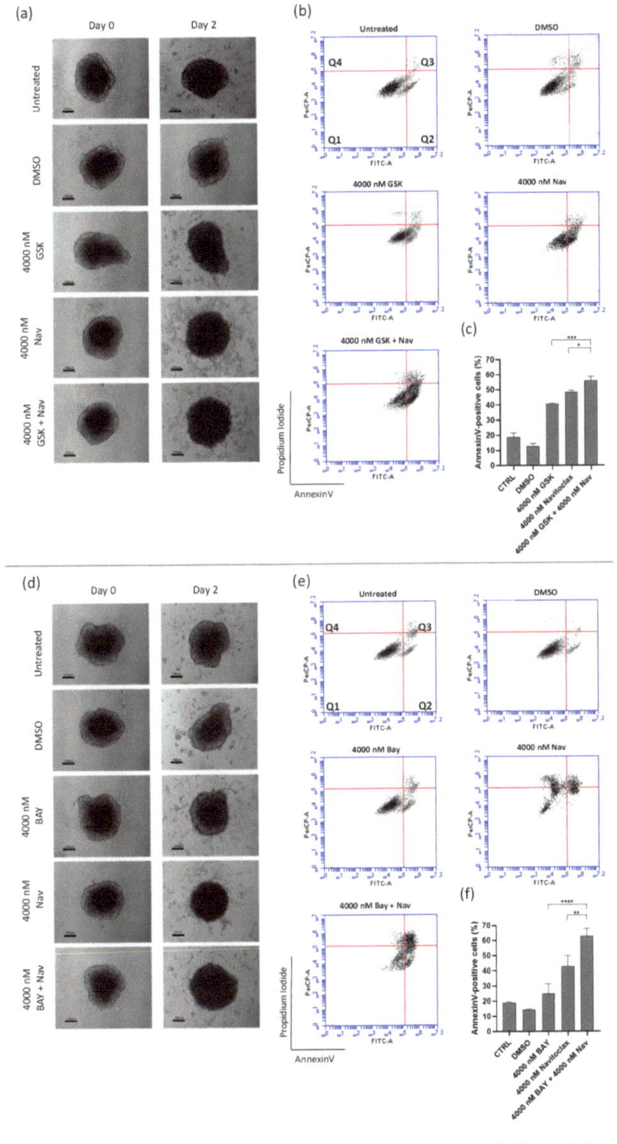

Figure 8. Combination of GSK923295 + navitoclax and BAY1217389 + navitoclax potentiates 3D lung cancer spheroid toxicity. Representative images of A549 3D spheroids at days 0 and 2 post-treatment with mono- or combination drugs (100 µm) (**a**,**d**). Representative cytograms (**b**,**e**) and quantification (**c**,**f**) of Annexin V−positive cells after 48 h of drug exposure. The quadrants Q are defined as Q1 = live (Annexin V− and PI−negative), Q2 = early stage of apoptosis (Annexin V−positive/PI−negative), Q3 = late stage of apoptosis (Annexin V− and PI−positive), and Q4 = necrosis (Annexin V−negative/PI−positive). Data represent the mean ± SD of three independent experiments, one-way ANOVA followed by Tukey's multiple comparisons test. * $p < 0.05$; ** $p < 0.01$; *** $p < 0.001$ **** $p < 0.0001$.

Overall, similar to the effect on 2D cancer cultures, the combination of the antimitotics GSK923295 and BAY1217389 with the anti-apoptotic inhibitor navitoclax enhances cancer cell death in a model that mimics a solid in vivo tumor. In contrast to the 2D results, where BAY1217389 + navitoclax combinations had only partial cytotoxic activity, we found that both GSK923295 + navitoclax and BAY1217389 + navitoclax combinations exhibited similar cytotoxic activity on spheroids derived from A549 lung cancer cells in the 3D model, although GSK923295 alone was more efficient in spheroid cell killing than BAY1217389.

4. Discussion

This study aimed to investigate the potential of combining the BH3-mimetic navitoclax with the mitotic blocker CENPE inhibitor GSK923295 or the mitotic driver MPS1 inhibitor BAY1217389 in 2D and 3D in vitro models of NSCLC. Our results demonstrate a synergistic cytotoxic activity against 2D cancer cell culture with both combinations, with significant degrees of cell death induced, mainly by apoptosis, which was more pronounced after GSK923295 + navitoclax than the BAY1217389 + navitoclax combinatorial treatment. Interestingly, the discrepancy between the two combinations was dissipated in the context of the 3D spheroid model, suggesting that the inhibition of CENPE or MPS1 in combination with BH3-mimetics is worth further investigation in the clinic as a potent therapeutic option.

The combination yielded increased cancer cell killing in both 2D and 3D culture systems, although establishing the IC_{50} of GSK923295 and BAY1217384 in 3D cultures proved challenging. This limitation may stem from the intricacies inherent in working with 3D spheroids. However, it also provides insight into why these drugs did not achieve success in clinical trials when used as monotherapy.

In the realm of drug testing, the divergence between 2D and 3D cellular models has yielded intriguing insights. It is commonly observed that the IC_{50} values of chemotherapeutic drugs are higher in 3D spheroids compared to their 2D counterparts. This phenomenon is expected due to the structural complexity of spheroids, mimicking the real tumor. Nonuniform growth and oxygen gradients with hypoxic cores and diffusion gradients similar to those in vivo can hinder the effective penetration of drugs into the cells, necessitating higher drug concentrations to elicit cell death [43–45]. Supporting the literature, our findings revealed that 3D spheroids require higher concentrations of GSK923295 and BAY1217389 to effectively inhibit cancer cells compared to the 2D system. On the contrary, we observed greater sensitivity to navitoclax in the 3D cell culture system when compared to the 2D system. This less common phenomenon could be attributed to distinct features of the drug, the cells, or the experimental design. Notably, in the presence of navitoclax, 3D spheroids exhibited a heightened synergistic response to both GSK923295 and BAY1217389, reaffirming the synergy observed in the 2D cell culture system. This underscores the potential for the 3D culture system's characteristics to facilitate synergistic interactions among the tested drugs.

Despite the observed differences between 2D and 3D systems, the study contributes to understanding the complexities of drug responses, and lays the groundwork for future investigations into the combination of navitoclax with GSK923295 and BAY1217389 in 3D and in vivo settings.

The BH3-mimetic navitoclax demonstrates synergistic effects with both GSK923295 and BAY1217389 in cancer cell killing. Our live-cell imaging analysis reveals distinct mechanisms for this synergy. Specifically, navitoclax seems to prevent mitotic slippage induced by GSK923295 by expediting cell death during mitosis. In contrast, it hinders post-mitotic survival prompted by BAY1217389 by intensifying post-mitotic cell death. In both scenarios, navitoclax tips the balance from cell survival towards cell death, effectively eliminating the opportunity for cellular escape, a phenomenon often observed when mitotic blockers and drivers are used as monotherapy [6,9,22].

These results align with our previously published work targeting polo-like kinase 1 (PLK1) [22]. The cytotoxic activity of PLK1 inhibitors, acting as mitotic blockers, was enhanced when combined with the BH3-mimetic navitoclax or ABT-737. This further reinforces the successful strategy of combining antimitotics with prosurvival inhibitors.

In conclusion, the results of the present study demonstrate the potential therapeutic advantages of co-inhibiting BCL-2 family proteins alongside CENPE or MPS1. These results warrant additional investigation, including long-term cellular assays and in vivo murine experiments, to assess the feasibility of translating these treatment approaches to clinical trials. Furthermore, the observed effects of these drug combinations, which include reduced viability and colony-forming capacity in cancer cells, as well as a significantly higher rate of cell death when compared to non-cancer cells, provide a robust basis for further clinical exploration.

Supplementary Materials: The following supporting information can be downloaded at: https://www.mdpi.com/article/10.3390/pharmaceutics16010056/s1, Figure S1: Non-cancer lung cells are less sensitive to GSK923295 + navitoclax and BAY1217389 + navitoclax combinations treatments than lung cancer cells. IC_{50} of all compounds in HPAEpiC cells (a,b). Cell viability (%) of single or combination treatments after 48 h of drug exposure in HPAEpiC cells (c,d), from three independent experiments determined by MTT assay. Synergy scores calculated by the Bliss model of Combenefit software with statistical relevance of * $p < 0.05$, and ** $p < 0.01$. Asterisk indicates synergism effects (e,f). Cell viability (%) of GSK923295 + navitoclax (g) and BAY1217389 + navitoclax (h) at the concentration of the respective synergistic points on A549 and HPAEpiC cells, with statistical relevance of ** $p < 0.01$ by unpaired t test. Figure S2: Inhibition of CENPE or MPS1 leads to mitosis abnormalities. Representative immunofluorescence images of A549 cells after 24 h treatment with 125 nM of GSK923295 or 500 nM of BAY1217389. Cells were immunostained for α-tubulin, to visualize microtubules (green), for CREST (red) to visualize centromeres, and the DNA (blue) was stained with DAPI. Bar, 5 μm. White arrows indicate the presence of multipolar spindles. Blue arrows indicate the presence of chromosome misalignment. Red arrows indicate the presence of monopolar spindles. Figure S3: GSK923295 + navitoclax and BAY1217389 + navitoclax combinations potentiate cytotoxicity in NCI-H460 lung cancer cells. IC_{50} of all compounds in NCI-H460 cells (a,b). Cell viability (%) of single or combination treatments after 48 h of drug exposure in NCI-H460 cells (c,d), from more than three independent experiments as determined by MTT assay. Synergy scores calculated by the Bliss model of Combenefit software 2.021 with statistical relevance of * $p < 0.05$, and ** $p < 0.01$ in NCI-H460 cells. Asterisk indicates synergism effects (e,f). Figure S4: GSK923295 + navitoclax and BAY1217389 + navitoclax combinations enhance NCI-H460 lung cancer cell death. Representative cytograms of NCI-H460 cell line double stained with Annexin V-FITC and propidium iodide (PI) (a,c). The quadrants Q are defined as Q1 = live (Annexin V- and PI-negative), Q2 = early stage of apoptosis (Annexin V-positive/PI-negative), Q3 = late stage of apoptosis (Annexin V- and PI-positive), and Q4 = necrosis (Annexin V-negative/PI-positive). Quantification of Annexin-V-positive cells (b,d). Data represent the mean ± SD of three independent experiments, one-way ANOVA followed by Tukey's multiple comparisons test. * $p < 0.05$; *** $p < 0.001$; **** $p < 0.0001$. Video S1: Time-lapse imaging (DIC microscopy) of a A549 cell treated with 1000 nM of navitoclax undergoing a normal mitosis; time is shown in minutes; available online at https://youtu.be/JsgMBkAczFc (accessed on 3 November 2023). Video S2: Time-lapse imaging (DIC microscopy) of a A549 cell treated with 125 nM of GSK923295 undergoing slippage and remaining alive; time is shown in minutes; available online at https://youtu.be/g4_5Okc5OYw (accessed on 3 November 2023). Video S3: Time-lapse imaging (DIC microscopy) of a A549 cell treated with 1000 nM of navitoclax + 125 nM of GSK923295 undergoing death in mitosis; time is shown in minutes; available online at https://youtu.be/xi9csADTsDI (accessed on 3 November 2023).

Author Contributions: Conceptualization, H.B., P.M.A.S. and B.P.; methodology, B.P., D.J.B. and P.M.A.S.; formal analysis, B.P. and J.P.N.S.; investigation, B.P., J.P.N.S. and P.M.A.S.; resources, H.B. and P.M.A.S.; data curation, B.P., J.P.N.S. and P.M.A.S.; writing—original draft preparation, B.P.; writing—review and editing, B.P., J.P.N.S., D.J.B., B.S., J.C.T., P.M.A.S. and H.B.; supervision, P.M.A.S. and H.B.; project administration, H.B.; funding acquisition, P.M.A.S. and H.B. All authors have read and agreed to the published version of the manuscript.

Funding: This research was funded by CESPU—Cooperativa de Ensino Superior Politécnico e Universitário Crl (Grants Ref. AntiMitoSphere_APSFCT_IINFACTS_2021; Ref. Flav4Tumor-GI2-CESPU-2022; Ref. SGA4Cancer-GI2-CESPU-2022, and Ref. upPTXovcar-GI2-CESPU-2022) to H.B.

and P.M.A.S., B.P. gratefully acknowledges CESPU (BD/CBAS/CESPU/01/2020) and Fundação para a Ciência e a Tecnologia (FCT) (2022.09451.BD) for financial support. J.P.N.S. gratefully acknowledges CESPU (BD/CBAS/CESPU/01/2021) for financial support. J.C.T. received financial support from Coordenação de Aperfeiçoamento de Pessoal de Nível Superior—Brasil (CAPES/Finance code 001-PRINT 88887.581726/2020-00).

Institutional Review Board Statement: Not applicable.

Informed Consent Statement: Not applicable.

Data Availability Statement: The data can be shared upon request.

Conflicts of Interest: The authors declare no conflict of interest.

References

1. Pilkington, G.; Boland, A.; Brown, T.; Oyee, J.; Bagust, A.; Dickson, R. A systematic review of the clinical effectiveness of first-line chemotherapy for adult patients with locally advanced or metastatic non-small cell lung cancer. *Thorax* **2015**, *70*, 359–367. [CrossRef]
2. Institute, N.C. SEER Cancer Statistics Review (CSR) 1975–2016. Available online: https://seer.cancer.gov/archive/csr/1975_2016/ (accessed on 19 October 2023).
3. Duma, N.; Santana-Davila, R.; Molina, J.R. Non-Small Cell Lung Cancer: Epidemiology, Screening, Diagnosis, and Treatment. *Mayo Clin. Proc.* **2019**, *94*, 1623–1640. [CrossRef] [PubMed]
4. Siegel, R.L.; Miller, K.D.; Wagle, N.S.; Jemal, A. Cancer statistics, 2023. *CA A Cancer J. Clin.* **2023**, *73*, 17–48. [CrossRef] [PubMed]
5. Luo, G.; Zhang, Y.; Etxeberria, J.; Arnold, M.; Cai, X.; Hao, Y.; Zou, H. Projections of Lung Cancer Incidence by 2035 in 40 Countries Worldwide: Population-Based Study. *JMIR Public Health Surveill.* **2023**, *9*, e43651. [CrossRef] [PubMed]
6. Henriques, A.C.; Ribeiro, D.; Pedrosa, J.; Sarmento, B.; Silva, P.M.A.; Bousbaa, H. Mitosis inhibitors in anticancer therapy: When blocking the exit becomes a solution. *Cancer Lett.* **2019**, *440–441*, 64–81. [CrossRef] [PubMed]
7. Sharma, A.; Broggini-Tenzer, A.; Vuong, V.; Messikommer, A.; Nytko, K.J.; Guckenberger, M.; Bachmann, F.; Lane, H.A.; Pruschy, M. The novel microtubule targeting agent BAL101553 in combination with radiotherapy in treatment-refractory tumor models. *Radiother. Oncol. J. Eur. Soc. Ther. Radiol. Oncol.* **2017**, *124*, 433–438. [CrossRef] [PubMed]
8. Kuo, T.C.; Li, L.W.; Pan, S.H.; Fang, J.M.; Liu, J.H.; Cheng, T.J.; Wang, C.J.; Hung, P.F.; Chen, H.Y.; Hong, T.M.; et al. Purine-Type Compounds Induce Microtubule Fragmentation and Lung Cancer Cell Death through Interaction with Katanin. *J. Med. Chem.* **2016**, *59*, 8521–8534. [CrossRef]
9. Novais, P.; Silva, P.M.A.; Amorim, I.; Bousbaa, H. Second-generation antimitotics in cancer clinical trials. *Pharmaceutics* **2021**, *13*, 1011. [CrossRef]
10. Schöffski, P.; Awada, A.; de la Bigne, A.M.; Felloussi, Z.; Burbridge, M.; Cantero, F.; Colombo, R.; Maruzzelli, S.; Ammattatelli, K.; de Jonge, M.; et al. First-in-man, first-in-class phase I study with the monopolar spindle 1 kinase inhibitor S81694 administered intravenously in adult patients with advanced, metastatic solid tumours. *Eur. J. Cancer* **2022**, *169*, 135–145. [CrossRef]
11. Chung, V.; Heath, E.I.; Schelman, W.R.; Johnson, B.M.; Kirby, L.C.; Lynch, K.M.; Botbyl, J.D.; Lampkin, T.A.; Holen, K.D. First-time-in-human study of GSK923295, a novel antimitotic inhibitor of centromere-associated protein E (CENP-E), in patients with refractory cancer. *Cancer Chemother. Pharmacol.* **2012**, *69*, 733–741. [CrossRef]
12. Raab, M.; Krämer, A.; Hehlgans, S.; Sanhaji, M.; Kurunci-Csacsko, E.; Dötsch, C.; Bug, G.; Ottmann, O.; Becker, S.; Pachl, F.; et al. Mitotic arrest and slippage induced by pharmacological inhibition of Polo-like kinase 1. *Mol. Oncol.* **2015**, *9*, 140–154. [CrossRef] [PubMed]
13. Gascoigne, K.E.; Taylor, S.S. Cancer Cells Display Profound Intra- and Interline Variation following Prolonged Exposure to Antimitotic Drugs. *Cancer Cell* **2008**, *14*, 111–122. [CrossRef] [PubMed]
14. Sinha, D.; Duijf, P.H.G.; Khanna, K.K. Mitotic slippage: An old tale with a new twist. *Cell Cycle* **2019**, *18*, 7–15. [CrossRef]
15. Serrano-del Valle, A.; Reina-Ortiz, C.; Benedi, A.; Anel, A.; Naval, J.; Marzo, I. Future prospects for mitosis-targeted antitumor therapies. *Biochem. Pharmacol.* **2021**, *190*, 114655. [CrossRef] [PubMed]
16. Partscht, P.; Simon, A.; Chen, N.P.; Erhardt, S.; Schiebel, E. The HIPK2/CDC14B-MeCP2 axis enhances the spindle assembly checkpoint block by promoting cyclin B translation. *Sci. Adv.* **2023**, *9*, eadd6982. [CrossRef] [PubMed]
17. Ghelli Luserna di Rorà, A.; Martinelli, G.; Simonetti, G. The balance between mitotic death and mitotic slippage in acute leukemia: A new therapeutic window? *J. Hematol. Oncol.* **2019**, *12*, 123. [CrossRef] [PubMed]
18. Silva, P.M.; Ribeiro, N.; Lima, R.T.; Andrade, C.; Diogo, V.; Teixeira, J.; Florindo, C.; Tavares, Á.; Vasconcelos, M.H.; Bousbaa, H. Suppression of spindly delays mitotic exit and exacerbates cell death response of cancer cells treated with low doses of paclitaxel. *Cancer Lett.* **2017**, *394*, 33–42. [CrossRef] [PubMed]
19. Czabotar, P.E.; Lessene, G.; Strasser, A.; Adams, J.M. Control of apoptosis by the BCL-2 protein family: Implications for physiology and therapy. *Nat. Rev. Mol. Cell Biol.* **2014**, *15*, 49–63. [CrossRef]
20. Klener, P.; Sovilj, D.; Renesova, N.; Andera, L. BH3 Mimetics in Hematologic Malignancies. *Int. J. Mol. Sci.* **2021**, *22*, 10157. [CrossRef]

21. Opydo-Chanek, M.; Gonzalo, O.; Marzo, I. Multifaceted anticancer activity of BH3 mimetics: Current evidence and future prospects. *Biochem. Pharmacol.* **2017**, *136*, 12–23. [CrossRef]
22. Pinto, B.; Novais, P.; Henriques, A.C.; Carvalho-Tavares, J.; Silva, P.M.A.; Bousbaa, H. Navitoclax Enhances the Therapeutic Effects of PLK1 Targeting on Lung Cancer Cells in 2D and 3D Culture Systems. *Pharmaceutics* **2022**, *14*, 1209. [CrossRef] [PubMed]
23. Bennett, A.; Sloss, O.; Topham, C.; Nelson, L.; Tighe, A.; Taylor, S.S. Inhibition of Bcl-xL sensitizes cells to mitotic blockers, but not mitotic drivers. *Open Biol.* **2016**, *6*, 160134. [CrossRef] [PubMed]
24. Henriques, A.C.; Silva, P.M.A.; Sarmento, B.; Bousbaa, H. Antagonizing the spindle assembly checkpoint silencing enhances paclitaxel and Navitoclax-mediated apoptosis with distinct mechanistic. *Sci. Rep.* **2021**, *11*, 4139. [CrossRef] [PubMed]
25. Wood, K.W.; Lad, L.; Luo, L.; Qian, X.; Knight, S.D.; Nevins, N.; Brejc, K.; Sutton, D.; Gilmartin, A.G.; Chua, P.R.; et al. Antitumor activity of an allosteric inhibitor of centromere-associated protein-E. *Proc. Natl. Acad. Sci. USA* **2010**, *107*, 5839–5844. [CrossRef] [PubMed]
26. Wengner, A.M.; Siemeister, G.; Koppitz, M.; Schulze, V.; Kosemund, D.; Klar, U.; Stoeckigt, D.; Neuhaus, R.; Lienau, P.; Bader, B.; et al. Novel Mps1 kinase inhibitors with potent antitumor activity. *Mol. Cancer Ther.* **2016**, *15*, 583–592. [CrossRef] [PubMed]
27. Kim, Y.; Heuser, J.E.; Waterman, C.M.; Cleveland, D.W. CENP-E combines a slow, processive motor and a flexible coiled coil to produce an essential motile kinetochore tether. *J. Cell Biol.* **2008**, *181*, 411–419. [CrossRef] [PubMed]
28. Bennett, A.; Bechi, B.; Tighe, A.; Thompson, S.; Procter, D.J.; Taylor, S.S. Cenp-E inhibitor GSK923295: Novel synthetic route and use as a tool to generate aneuploidy. *Oncotarget* **2015**, *6*, 20921–20932. [CrossRef]
29. Pachis, S.T.; Kops, G. Leader of the SAC: Molecular mechanisms of Mps1/TTK regulation in mitosis. *Open Biol.* **2018**, *8*, 180109. [CrossRef]
30. Tipton, A.R.; Ji, W.; Sturt-Gillespie, B.; Bekier, M.E., 2nd; Wang, K.; Taylor, W.R.; Liu, S.T. Monopolar spindle 1 (MPS1) kinase promotes production of closed MAD2 (C-MAD2) conformer and assembly of the mitotic checkpoint complex. *J. Biol. Chem.* **2013**, *288*, 35149–35158. [CrossRef]
31. Mason, J.M.; Wei, X.; Fletcher, G.C.; Kiarash, R.; Brokx, R.; Hodgson, R.; Beletskaya, I.; Bray, M.R.; Mak, T.W. Functional characterization of CFI-402257, a potent and selective Mps1/TTK kinase inhibitor, for the treatment of cancer. *Proc. Natl. Acad. Sci. USA* **2017**, *114*, 3127–3132. [CrossRef]
32. Ling, Y.; Zhang, X.; Bai, Y.; Li, P.; Wei, C.; Song, T.; Zheng, Z.; Guan, K.; Zhang, Y.; Zhang, B.; et al. Overexpression of Mps1 in colon cancer cells attenuates the spindle assembly checkpoint and increases aneuploidy. *Biochem. Biophys. Res. Commun.* **2014**, *450*, 1690–1695. [CrossRef] [PubMed]
33. Hao, X.; Qu, T. Expression of CENPE and its prognostic role in non-small cell lung cancer. *Open Med.* **2019**, *14*, 497–502. [CrossRef] [PubMed]
34. Zheng, L.; Chen, Z.; Kawakami, M.; Chen, Y.; Roszik, J.; Mustachio, L.M.; Kurie, J.M.; Villalobos, P.; Lu, W.; Behrens, C.; et al. Tyrosine threonine kinase inhibition eliminates lung cancers by augmenting apoptosis and polyploidy. *Mol. Cancer Ther.* **2019**, *18*, 1775–1784. [CrossRef] [PubMed]
35. Jiang, H.; Yuan, F.; Zhao, Z.; Xue, T.; Ge, N.; Ren, Z.; Zhang, L. Expression and Clinical Significance of MPS-1 in Hepatocellular Carcinoma. *Int. J. Gen. Med.* **2021**, *14*, 9145–9152. [CrossRef]
36. Landi, M.T.; Dracheva, T.; Rotunno, M.; Figueroa, J.D.; Liu, H.; Dasgupta, A.; Mann, F.E.; Fukuoka, J.; Hames, M.; Bergen, A.W.; et al. Gene expression signature of cigarette smoking and its role in lung adenocarcinoma development and survival. *PLoS ONE* **2008**, *3*, e1651. [CrossRef]
37. Naranjo, S.; Cabana, C.M.; LaFave, L.M.; Romero, R.; Shanahan, S.L.; Bhutkar, A.; Westcott, P.M.K.; Schenkel, J.M.; Ghosh, A.; Liao, L.Z.; et al. Modeling diverse genetic subtypes of lung adenocarcinoma with a next-generation alveolar type 2 organoid platform. *Genes Dev.* **2022**, *36*, 936–949. [CrossRef]
38. Mohamad Anuar, N.N.; Nor Hisam, N.S.; Liew, S.L.; Ugusman, A. Clinical Review: Navitoclax as a Pro-Apoptotic and Anti-Fibrotic Agent. *Front. Pharmacol.* **2020**, *11*, 564108. [CrossRef]
39. Nakayama, Y.; Yamaguchi, N. Role of cyclin B1 levels in DNA damage and DNA damage-induced senescence. *Int. Rev. Cell Mol. Biol.* **2013**, *305*, 303–337. [CrossRef]
40. Würstle, M.L.; Laussmann, M.A.; Rehm, M. The central role of initiator caspase-9 in apoptosis signal transduction and the regulation of its activation and activity on the apoptosome. *Exp. Cell Res.* **2012**, *318*, 1213–1220. [CrossRef]
41. Song, Z.; Chen, Y.; Chang, H.; Guo, Y.; Gao, Q.; Wei, Z.; Gong, L.; Zhang, G.; Zheng, Z. Rhein suppresses African swine fever virus replication in vitro via activating the caspase-dependent mitochondrial apoptosis pathway. *Virus Res.* **2023**, *338*, 199238. [CrossRef]
42. Pinto, B.; Henriques, A.C.; Silva, P.M.A.; Bousbaa, H. Three-Dimensional Spheroids as In Vitro Preclinical Models for Cancer Research. *Pharmaceutics* **2020**, *12*, 1186. [CrossRef] [PubMed]
43. Miranda, M.A.; Marcato, P.D.; Mondal, A.; Chowdhury, N.; Gebeyehu, A.; Surapaneni, S.K.; Bentley, M.; Amaral, R.; Pan, C.X.; Singh, M. Cytotoxic and chemosensitizing effects of glycoalkaloidic extract on 2D and 3D models using RT4 and patient derived xenografts bladder cancer cells. *Mater. Sci. Eng. C Mater. Biol. Appl.* **2021**, *119*, 111460. [CrossRef] [PubMed]

44. Samimi, H.; Sohi, A.N.; Irani, S.; Arefian, E.; Mahdiannasser, M.; Fallah, P.; Haghpanah, V. Alginate-based 3D cell culture technique to evaluate the half-maximal inhibitory concentration: An in vitro model of anticancer drug study for anaplastic thyroid carcinoma. *Thyroid Res.* **2021**, *14*, 27. [CrossRef] [PubMed]
45. Kerslake, R.; Belay, B.; Panfilov, S.; Hall, M.; Kyrou, I.; Randeva, H.S.; Hyttinen, J.; Karteris, E.; Sisu, C. Transcriptional Landscape of 3D vs. 2D Ovarian Cancer Cell Models. *Cancers* **2023**, *15*, 3350. [CrossRef]

Disclaimer/Publisher's Note: The statements, opinions and data contained in all publications are solely those of the individual author(s) and contributor(s) and not of MDPI and/or the editor(s). MDPI and/or the editor(s) disclaim responsibility for any injury to people or property resulting from any ideas, methods, instructions or products referred to in the content.

pharmaceutics

Review

Targeting Glucose Metabolism in Cancer Cells as an Approach to Overcoming Drug Resistance

Andrea Cunha [1], Patrícia M. A. Silva [1,2], Bruno Sarmento [1,3,4] and Odília Queirós [1,*]

1 UNIPRO—Oral Pathology and Rehabilitation Research Unit, University Institute of Health Sciences—CESPU (IUCS—CESPU), 4585-116 Gandra, Portugal; andrea.cunha@iucs.cespu.pt (A.C.); patricia.silva@cespu.pt (P.M.A.S.); bruno.sarmento@i3s.up.pt (B.S.)
2 1H—TOXRUN—One Health Toxicology Research Unit, University Institute of Health Sciences—CESPU (IUCS—CESPU), 3810-193 Gandra, Portugal
3 i3S—Instituto de Investigação e Inovação em Saúde, Universidade do Porto, 4200-135 Porto, Portugal
4 INEB—Instituto de Engenharia Biomédica, Universidade do Porto, 4200-135 Porto, Portugal
* Correspondence: odilia.queiros@iucs.cespu.pt

Abstract: The "Warburg effect" consists of a metabolic shift in energy production from oxidative phosphorylation to glycolysis. The continuous activation of glycolysis in cancer cells causes rapid energy production and an increase in lactate, leading to the acidification of the tumour microenvironment, chemo- and radioresistance, as well as poor patient survival. Nevertheless, the mitochondrial metabolism can be also involved in aggressive cancer characteristics. The metabolic differences between cancer and normal tissues can be considered the Achilles heel of cancer, offering a strategy for new therapies. One of the main causes of treatment resistance consists of the increased expression of efflux pumps, and multidrug resistance (MDR) proteins, which are able to export chemotherapeutics out of the cell. Cells expressing MDR proteins require ATP to mediate the efflux of their drug substrates. Thus, inhibition of the main energy-producing pathways in cancer cells, not only induces cancer cell death per se, but also overcomes multidrug resistance. Given that most anticancer drugs do not have the ability to distinguish normal cells from cancer cells, a number of drug delivery systems have been developed. These nanodrug delivery systems provide flexible and effective methods to overcome MDR by facilitating cellular uptake, increasing drug accumulation, reducing drug efflux, improving targeted drug delivery, co-administering synergistic agents, and increasing the half-life of drugs in circulation.

Keywords: tumor microenvironment; tumor metabolism; glycolysis; Warburg effect; resistance; nanoparticles

1. Introduction

The conversion of normal cells or benign tissue into neoplastic precursors usually corresponds to malignant transformation. Additional alterations bestow these cells with unlimited proliferative potential, dissemination and metastasis, resulting in tumor progression [1]. In order to sustain the acquired features, metabolic reprogramming is essential. Changes in cellular metabolism promote the fast production of adenosine triphosphate (ATP) and an increase in the synthesis of biomolecules, including nucleotides, lipids and amino acids. Several mechanisms are known to modulate cancer metabolism, which affect essential pathways for both energy production and carbon metabolism, such as glycolysis and the tricarboxylic acid (TCA) cycle. As a consequence of these alterations, there is an increased consumption of glucose and also of glutamine in tumor cells in order to maintain their metabolic requirements [2]. Metabolic reprogramming is one of the emerging characteristics of tumor progression and is crucial to support the energy needs of cells during their continuous growth and proliferation. This metabolic reprogramming is also a key factor in the development of cancer resistance to treatment [2,3]. Often, during these treatments, cancer cells adapt, altering their metabolic pathways and becoming less susceptible to therapies. Targeting and exploiting such metabolic changes can be a promising approach to improve the chance of curing cancer. For this, the development of metabolism-targeting nanoparticles, carrying multiple therapeutic agents, are increasingly being exploited, aiming to overcome drug resistance and thus constituting an appellative tool in future cancer therapies.

2. Glucose Metabolism

Most mammalian cells have glucose as their preferred metabolic substrate, which is used in the cytoplasm and/or mitochondria to provide energy for cell maintenance and proliferation [4] (Figure 1). Glycolysis, a metabolic pathway that does not require oxygen, partially oxidizes into two pyruvate molecules, producing two moles of ATP and two moles of nicotinamide adenine dinucleotide (NADH) per mole of consumed glucose [2,4]. In the presence of oxygen and active mitochondrial systems, healthy cells oxidize most of the pyruvate in the mitochondria, producing most of their ATP in this way (32 molecules of ATP from 1 single glucose molecule) [4,5]. When the anaerobic pathway is used, the pyruvate from glycolysis is reduced to lactate by the cytoplasmic enzyme lactate dehydrogenase (LDH), to regenerate the oxidized form NAD^+ for glycolysis, producing 16 times less ATP per consumed glucose. The monocarboxylate transporters (MCTs) will then transport the excess lactate produced out of the cell through a proton-symport mechanism [4,5].

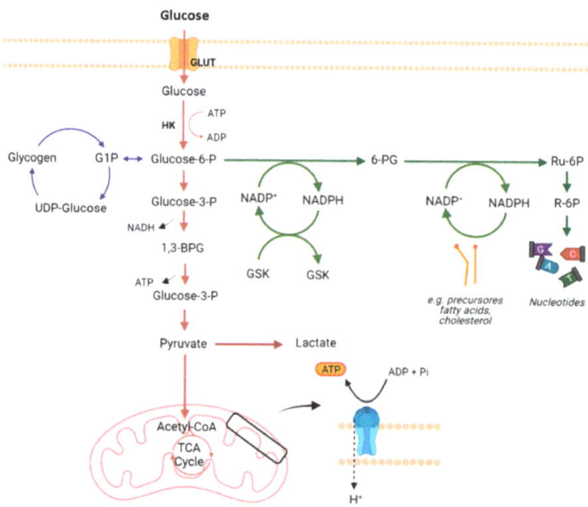

Figure 1. Glucose metabolism in mammalian cells. Illustrative scheme of glycolysis, TCA cycle, and the electron transport chain (red). Glucose from the blood stream is uptaken by the cells, converted into G6P by HK and posteriorly in pyruvate. In the absence of oxygen, pyruvate is converted into lactate, whereas in the presence of oxygen, the pyruvate is completely oxidized into Acetyl-CoA, which enters the mitochondrial TCA cycle. The generated NADH are then fed the OXPHOS-producing ATP (blue). The PPP (green) synthetizes the ribose-5-phosphate, which is needed for nucleic acid synthesis, and NADPH. The excess glucose is used to synthetize glycogen, via glycogenesis (purple). Created by the Authors with BioRender.com. ATP: adenosine triphosphate; G6P: glucose-6-phosphate; HK: hexokinase; NADH: nicotinamide adenine dinucleotide; NADPH: nicotinamide adenine dinucleotide phosphate; OXPHOS: oxidative phosphorylation; PPP: pentose phosphate pathway; TCA cycle: tricarboxylic acid cycle.

The first step in the glucose metabolism consists of its entrance into the cell. Glucose transporters (GLUTs) belong to the solute transporter (SLC2A) family of proteins and are present in many tissues/cells of the body, e.g., brain, erythrocytes, adipocytes, and liver, where they mediate glucose uptake [6]. The fourteen different isoforms of GLUTs are subdivided into three distinct protein classes, according to their sequence homology. Each GLUT isoform has a unique tissue distribution, substrate specificity, and a specific physiological function [7]. All GLUT proteins were originally assumed to catalyze the transport of hexoses into and out of cells. This is clearly the case for the class 1 GLUT proteins (GLUTs 1–4 and 14). However, class 2 (GLUTs 5, 7, 9 and 11) and class 3 (GLUTs 6, 8, 10, 12 and 13) GLUT proteins do not necessarily have a primary role in catalyzing glucose transport [8]. GLUT-1 is expressed in tissues with a high glycolytic rate, such as erythrocytes, which are responsible for glucose uptake in high-need cells [6,8]. However, this transporter also plays a central role in tumorigenesis, delivering glucose into hypoxic environments. In fact, GLUT-1, a target gene of hypoxia-inducible factor-1 (HIF-1), is highly expressed in hypoxic cancer cells, allowing for the maintenance of a high metabolic rate in these cells [6].

Although there are hundreds of types of cancer, they share some specific characteristics, namely the reprogramming of the energy metabolism. Many cancer cells predominantly rely on glycolysis, instead of oxidative phosphorylation (OXPHOS), to produce energy from glucose, even in the presence of O_2, with this metabolic shift being known as the "Warburg effect" or "aerobic glycolysis" [9]. Although OXPHOS is downregulated, cancer cells can still obtain the required ATP for cell survival and proliferation, increasing the glycolytic flux and metabolizing glucose at high rates, with lactate production [10]. This alteration in metabolism provides a selective advantage during tumor initiation and progression, sustaining the high proliferative rate of tumor cells and promoting resistance to cells. Nevertheless, in opposition to previous beliefs, this phenotype is not due to mitochondrial dysfunction and the whole ATP factory in cancer cells is important. In fact, not all tumor cell types completely restart glycolysis for the ATP supply, and some of them may equally or even predominantly use OXPHOS [11,12]. As TCA cycle intermediates are also required for amino acids, lipid and nucleotide biosynthesis, their functioning become as important as glycolysis for tumor cell metabolism. The TCA cycle is equally important for deoxyribonucleic acid (DNA) synthesis, since the synthesis of aspartate from oxaloacetate and glutamate is critical for nucleotide synthesis [2,13]. Malate, in turn, can be used separately to produce nicotinamide adenine dinucleotide phosphate (NADPH) through a distinct pathway [2,14].

Many TCA cycle intermediates are used in biosynthetic processes; thus, a new carbon supply is required to maintain the activity of the TCA cycle. Glutaminolysis, where glutamine is used to fuel the TCA cycle, is one of the most important anaplerotic pathways in cancer [2]. In fact, glutamine deserves special attention, as it is the second most consumed metabolite by proliferating cells [2,4]. Glutamine has been shown to be essential for the synthesis of proteins, fatty acids, and nucleotides. Once inside the cell, glutaminase (GLS) converts glutamine into glutamate. Glutamate, in turn, can be converted into α-ketoglutarate, which is an intermediate of the TCA cycle. As tumor cells proliferate at higher rates, they are more glutamine-dependent than their non-tumoral counterparts [2,15]. However, a number of other metabolites have also been described to activate the TCA cycle in tumor cells [2]. For instance, in addition to being important components of membranes, fatty acids are also important energy fuels that, when degraded, provide ATP through β-oxidation [2,15]. In addition, lactate, acetate, and branched-chain amino acids (BCAAs) can also supply carbons to the TCA cycle [16–18]. Of these, lactate deserves particular attention. In fact, lactate produced by glycolysis (and also by glutaminolysis) in cancer cells can be taken up by neighboring cells and converted into pyruvate, entering the mitochondria and producing ATP by OXPHOS. Both efflux and uptake of lactate mainly occur via the MCT1 and MCT4, and this transport mechanism is important in tumor growth and in the inhibition of cell death mechanisms. Furthermore, it was also reported that a symbiosis between glycolytic and oxidative cells can occur, mediated by these transporters [5,19]. In fact, under anaerobic conditions, even in healthy cells, pyruvate is reduced to lactate and secreted into the extracellular space, mainly via MCT4. On the other side, lactate can be taken up by the aerobic cancer cells or by the stromal cells, mainly by MCT1 (and sometimes by MCT2), and further converted into pyruvate that can be used in oxidative conditions by these cells, sparing glucose for the more hypoxic and glycolytic cancer cells. The heterogeneity of tumors may be a possible explanation for this symbiotic model [5]. Tumors are not metabolically homogeneous and different cancer cells preferentially use particular catabolites [20]. Cancer cells are continuously adapting their metabolism, depending on the metabolism of the specific type of cancer and also on its stage, being influenced both by genetics and by the microenvironment [21]. In this way, although sometimes some cancers rely more on aerobic glycolysis and others on OXPHOS, the type of metabolism is not always cancer-specific and it is very often possible to see both types of metabolism in a heterogeneous tumor. According to this, in certain cancer types, e.g., lung cancer, both glycolytic and oxidative metabolic phenotypes were observed in different regions within the same tumor [5]. Indeed, depending on their microenvironment, tumor cells from the same tumor can be divided into subgroups: highly glycolytic with a lower OXPHOS in hypoxic conditions with defective vasculature, where nutrients and oxygen are greatly reduced, and vice versa in normoxic regions, near functional blood vessels [5]. Also, in experimental models of breast, ovarian and prostate carcinomas and sarcomas, stromal cells have been shown to produce catabolites that can be oxidatively metabolized by cancer cells, thus revealing a metabolic coupling between stromal and cancer cells [20]. In this way, and although aerobic glycolysis is a phenotype associated with cancer, OXPHOS is not only often functional, but is also important to cancer proliferation and growth, depending on the cancer type and stage. Supporting this, recent data have demonstrated that certain cancers, such as breast cancer, pancreatic ductal adenocarcinoma, melanoma, and lymphomas, rely mostly on OXPHOS [22]. Furthermore, a Gepia analysis of a five gene signatures associated with OXPHOS (ATP6V0B, ATP6V1C1, ATP6V1E1, TIMM9, and UQCRH) also showed a higher expression of these genes in these cancer types, in addition endometrium, cervical, ovarium, thymus and liver cancers (http://gepia.cancer-pku.cn/index.html (accessed on 27 October 2023)). On the other hand, and also based on Gepia, the analysis of genes associated with a glycolytic phenotype (e.g., Glut1, LDHA, HK2, MCT4) mainly showed higher expression in the lung, esophagus, head and neck, glioblastoma, kidney or colon and rectum. This has been also shown in several reports using cancer cell lines. Such differences in the energetic profile can impact the way cancer cells respond to treatment. Table 1 summarizes the energy profile of different cancer cell lines, as well as the effect of antimetabolic agents, based on this. The basal levels of monocarboxylate transporters MCT1 and MCT4 in these cell lines, and the effect of these agents on their expression, when described, is also shown. In fact, MCT1 and MCT4 are main players in the metabolic pathway preferentially used by cancer cells. WMCT4 is mainly involved in the efflux of lactic acid, and is thus more expressed in glycolytic cancer cells and often downregulated when cancer cells shift their metabolism to OXPHOS; however, many cancer cells rely on MCT1 for the uptake of lactic acid that can be used in oxidative processes [23]. For instance, the leukemic cell line NB4 presents a more glycolytic phenotype and shows a good response to the anti-glycolytic agent 2-Deoxyglucose (2DG), a nonmetabolizable glucose analogue that inhibits glycolysis, whereas the more oxidative leukemic cell line, THP1, is resistant to this agent, and sensitive to oligomycin, which targets mitochondrial respiration [24]. In these cell lines, it a higher expression of MCT1 than MCT4 was observed in the oxidative cell line THP1, while in the glycolytic cell line NB4, the expression of both transporters was found, due to the dual role that MCT1 plays in both the influx and efflux of lactic acid, in contrast to MCT4, which is mainly involved only in its efflux. A little surprisingly, in THP1 cells, an upregulation of MCT4, but not of MCT1, was observed by the oxidative substrate lactate and by VEGF [25]. Breast cancer is other kind of cancer that can present different mechanisms of energy production, depending on the cancer type. The triple-negative breast cancers usually rely on OXPHOS as the energetic metabolic pathway. According to this, it has been shown that the OXPHOS inhibitor IACS-010759 induced cell death and inhibited oxygen consumption rate in the triple-negative breast cancer cell line MDA-MB-468 [26]. In another breast cancer cell line, MCF-7, which is estrogen and progesterone receptors (ER and PR)-positive, both kinds of metabolism were found, showing the plasticity of cancer cells to adapt to their microenvironment. MCF-7 cells are sensitive to the antiglycolytic agents 2DG, 3-bromopyruvate (3BP), dichloroacetate (DCA), Iodoacetate (IAA) and lonidamine, but also to the OXPHOS uncoupler Carbonyl Cyanide m-chlorophenyl Hydrazone (CCCP). All these agents induced cell death and potentiated MCF-7 cells for treatment with the conventional anticancer drugs paclitaxel (PTX) or doxorubicin (DOX). Again, in these cell lines, in the oxidative cells, only MCT1 is observed at the plasma membrane, while in MCF-7, both transporters were found [27–29]. In another example of oxidative cells versus glycolytic ones, it was found that the glioma glycolytic cells U251 are sensitive to the glycolytic inhibitors DCA, 2DG, resveratrol and 2-Cyano-3-(4-hydroxyphenyl)-2-propenoic acid (CHC) (an MCT1 and MCT4 inhibitor), while the more oxidative SW1088 cells are sensitive to phenformin, in addition to DCA and 2DG [23,30–34]. Again, a higher expression of plasma membrane MCT4 was found in the more glycolytic cells [35,36]. Thus, in general, it was observed that more glycolytic cancer cell lines are strongly affected by glycolytic inhibitors like 3BP, 2DG, DCA, IAA and lonidamine, as well as resveratrol, which was found to inhibit this metabolic pathway, and to the MCT1/4 inhibitor CHC [23,30–36]. These cell lines commonly presented a higher expression of MCT4, involved in lactic acid export. The more oxidative cells are more sensitive to OXPHOS inhibitors and more resistant to antiglycolytic agents. In these cells, a lower expression of MCT4 at the plasma membrane is usually found. Concerning MCT1, the expression of this transporter was found in both glycolytic and oxidative cells, demonstrating its dual role in the uptake and efflux of lactic acid. Although some of the glycolytic inhibitors, like 3BP and DCA, are monocarboxylate analogues, and thus presumably transported by MCTs, there are few works in the literature showing their influence on MCTs' expression and, in these cases, most of the time, no association between the treatment and the expression of the transporters was observed [27,37]. Thus, it can be assumed that their effect is usually independent of MCTs, although more studies in this area are needed. Furthermore, while some cell lines are identified as predominantly glycolytic and others as predominantly oxidative, different studies were found to attribute both of these characteristics to cell lines. These could be due to the previously mentioned fact that cancer cells present with high plasticity and can adapt their metabolism to the microenvironment characteristics, shifting from glycolysis to OXPHOS and vice-versa, what can lead to different results in the literature concerning MCTs' expression and antimetabolic drugs' effect. Nevertheless, some examples of cancer cell lines presenting a different effect regarding glycolytic or OXPHS inhibitors were found and are compiled in Table 1, as well as MCT1/4 expression and regulation (when the information was available), according to their energetic profile.

Table 1. Energy profile of different cancer cell lines, as well as the effect of antimetabolic agents and expression and regulation of MCTs based on this. Glycolytic Inhibitors—2-Cyano-3-(4-hydroxyphenyl)-2-propenoic acid (CHC), 2 Deoxyglucose (2DG), 3-bromopyruvate (3BP), Dichloroacetate (DCA) Iodoacetate (IAA), Lonidamine, Quercetin, Resveratrol, OXPHOS Inhibitors—Atovaquone, Uncoupler Carbonyl Cyanide m-chlorophenyl Hydrazone (CCCP), IACS-010759, Metformin, Olygomycin, Phenphormin.

Energetic Profile	Type of Cancer/ Cancer Cell Line	Antimetabolic Drug Effect	Expression and Regulation of MCTs	References
Mainly OXPHOS	Breast (MDA-MB-468)	IACS-010759 induced cell death and inhibited oxygen consumption rate	MCT1 expression at the plasma membrane. MCT4 is expressed on cytoplasm	[26,28]
	Cervical (HeLa)	Metformin and Rotenone promoted anoikis	MCT1 expression > MCT4 expression Hypoxia induced the expression of MCT4	[31,38,39]
	Cervical (siHa)	Rotenone decreased cell migration	2DG and rotenone increased the expression of MCT1 and CD147	[40,41]

Table 1. *Cont.*

Energetic Profile	Type of Cancer/ Cancer Cell Line	Antimetabolic Drug Effect	Expression and Regulation of MCTs	References
Mainly OXPHOS	Leukemia (THP-1)	Resistant to 2DG and sensitive to oligomycin	MCT4 expression Lactate and VEGF increased the expression of MCT4, but not of MCT1	[24,25]
	Lung (A549)	Resistant to 3BP, DCA and 2DG	No changes were observed in MCT1 and MCT4 upon treatment with 3BP, DCA and 2DG	[37]
	Melanoma (B16F10)	Metformin and Rotenone promoted anoikis	No data	[31]
	Ovarian (OVCAR-3)	Atovaquone slowed ovarian cancer growth	No data	[42]
Mainly Glycolytic	Bladder (5637)	Sensitive to 2DG. 2DG depleted cellular ATP and potentiated the toxicity of conventional drugs	High expression of MCT1, MCT4 and CD147 Knockdown of MCT4 inhibited 5637 cancer cell line proliferation and clonogenic activity	[43]
	Colon (SW480)	Sensitive to 3BP, 2DG and DCA	High expression of MCT1, MCT2 and MCT4 3BP decreased the expression of MCT1and MCT4, but not of MCT2	[35,44–47]
	Glioma (U251)	Sensitive to DCA, 2DG, resveratrol and CHC	High plasma-membrane expression of GLUT1, MCT1, CD147 Silencing of MCT1 decreased the glycolytic phenotype	[23,30,32–34,48]
	Leukemia (NB4)	Sensitive to 2DG and 3BP	High expression of MCT1 and MCT4	[24,49,50]
	Lung (NCI-H460)	Sensitive to 3BP, 2DG and DCA	No association was observed between MCT1 and MCT4 expression and treatment effect with 3BP, DCA and 2DG	[37]
	Melanoma (A375)	Sensitive to 3BP	High expression of MCT1	[51]
Both glycolytic and OXPHOS	Breast (MCF-7)	2DG, IAA, DCA and CCP and 3BP induced cell death Pre-treatment with 2DG, IAA, DCA and CCCP enhanced PTX and DOX toxicity Lonidamine potentiated the effect of PTX	High plasma-membrane expression of MCT1 and MCT4. 3BP did not alter the expression	[27,29,31,52,53]
	Glioma (SW1088)	Metformin and Rotenone promoted anoikis DCA, 2DG and phenformin led to a decrease in ATP content Resistent to CHC	Low plasma-membrane expression of MCT1, MCT4 and CD147	[23,32,36]
	Liver (HepG2)	2DG, 3BP and DCA induced cell death and potentiated the effect of DOX Phenphormin inhibited proliferation	High expression of MCT1 and MCT4 and lower expression of MCT2	[54–56]

3. The Warburg Effect

In 1920, Otto Warburg postulated that cancer cells are characterized by an increased glycolytic rate, with pyruvate mostly being converted to lactate, contrary to normal cells. This phenomenon became known as aerobic glycolysis or the "Warburg effect" [2,9,57]. This observation underlies the [18F]-fluorodeoxyglucose positron emission tomography (FDG-PET) of tumors, which is used in the diagnosis of cancer and in the detection of metastasis, due to the high consumption of the glucose analogue FDG by cancer cells [58].

Originally, Warburg postulated that the increased glycolytic activity observed in cancer cells should be due to impaired mitochondrial function. In fact, mutations in TCA cycle enzymes are present in several types of cancer, such as fumarate hydratase, succinate dehydrogenase, and isocitrate dehydrogenase [9,59,60]. However, even when mitochondrial function is normal, many cancer cells still prefer glycolysis, suggesting that glycolysis is associated with advantages to these cells [9]. As several glycolytic intermediates can be used in biosynthetic pathways, it is likely that the increase in the glycolytic rate supplies the biosynthetic needs of cancer cells [61]. In fact, the high consumption of glucose allows for the energy necessary for cell growth to be obtained and, under these conditions, the PPP pathway is also favored, generating NADPH and ribose-5-phosphate, which serve as a source for the formation of new nucleotides, lipids and proteins [10,11,62]. Furthermore, the use of glycolysis may prevent the production of ROS that occurs during OXPHOS and, in this way, protects the genome of cancer cells and inhibits anoikis, allowing for the cells to survive [6,63].

The overexpression of GLUTs is essential for cancer cells to meet their high demand for glucose, which is needed for their high glycolytic rates. In addition, cancer cells often present higher levels of MCTs, since they allow for the maintenance of intracellular pH and, consequently, the glycolytic way, as they are responsible for the export of lactate. Lactate secretion may help to create an acidic extracellular tumor microenvironment (TME) that favors tumor growth, promoting migration and invasion [2,5]. The low pH found in TME activates metalloproteinases released from the cancer cells, promoting the digestion of the surrounding matrix and leading to cells' detachment from the solid substrate [64,65]. Interestingly, cancer cells appear to be more dependent on specific isoforms of glycolytic enzymes. In fact, cancer cells may be more dependent on isoforms of hexokinase (HK2), pyruvate dehydrogenase kinase 1 (PDK1), phosphofructokinase 2 (PFK2), LDHA or pyruvate kinase isoform M2 (PKM2) [66–68]. In addition to these specific isoforms, to promote the glycolytic pathway, the overexpression of PDK1 inactivates the pyruvate dehydrogenase enzyme, preventing the mitochondrial conversion of pyruvate to acetyl-CoA. As a result, pyruvate remains in the cytosol and is converted to lactate [59]. The overexpression of these enzymes allows for cancer cells to easily adapt the glycolytic flux to sustain glycolytic rates and for the diversion of glycolytic intermediates to biosynthetic pathways [2]. At the same time, the excess of NADPH that is produced is closely linked to apoptosis escaping [69].

Thus, although ATP production through OXPHOS is more efficient, most cancer cells produce most of their ATP through glycolysis, even in the presence of oxygen [2,6,57] (Figure 2). In fact, 70–80% of human cancers present the Warburg phenotype, a metabolic alteration that results from the interaction between normoxic/hypoxic activation of the transcription factor HIF-1, oncogenes' activation, loss of tumor suppressors, altered signaling pathways and interactions with components of the TME, as well as being associated with epigenetic mechanisms [59].

As glycolysis less efficient in energetic terms than OXPHOS, cancer cells increase their glycolytic flux by about 15 times, leading to a drastic increase in the rate of ATP production, in order to compensate the energy yield [5]. In addition, and as previously discussed, the "Warburg effect" contributes to counteracting apoptosis and promotes macromolecule biosynthesis. However, high rates of OXPHOS are displayed by some cancer cells. In fact, some cancer cells, even in a glycolytic cancer, switch their metabolism to OXPHOS, as this metabolic pathway is the predominant supplier of ATP in these cases [21,69,70]. There is a significant emphasis on enzymes like isocitrate dehydrogenase (IDH) 1 and IDH2, which catalyze the first oxidative reaction of the TCA cycle, resulting in the generation of NADH, and thus have particular importance in mitochondrial respiration [71]. For example, in some models of breast cancer, mitochondrial respiration significantly increases [72]. Thus, a "two compartment" model, also called the "reverse Warburg effect", was proposed to reconsider a tumor metabolism where cancer cells and cells found in the TME, like cancer-associated fibroblasts (CAFs), become metabolically coupled [69,73]. In this model, cancer cells mainly use the oxidative pathway resulting from lactate obtained from aerobic glycolysis that occurs in tumor stromal fibroblasts [74]. As a result of this interaction, cancer cells induce oxidative stress by generating ROS in the form of H_2O_2 in CAFs, resulting in the increased production of energy-rich fuels (such as pyruvate, ketone bodies, fatty acids, and lactate) [69,75,76]. In turn, these molecules support OXPHOS in cancer cells, resulting in ATP production [69]. Even in a single tumor, OXPHOS and glycolysis contribute to different populations in different ways, since there is intratumoral heterogeneity, directing the metabolism of tumor tissue to different pathways depending on the conditions, as previously discussed [69,77]. In addition, substrates from different cancer cell populations can be shared and used, since these two different tumor cell populations may be metabolically linked [78]. For rapidly proliferating tumors, glycolysis may be more advantageous as, in addition to an abundant supply of energy, cancer cells need lipids, nucleic acids, and other glycolytic-derived intermediates for biosynthesis [69]. In fact, these types of cells need a high amount of metabolic intermediates for growth and division [79]. In differentiated tumors, which are more similar to normal tissues, with a slower growth and progression, OXPHOS may be more efficient in terms of their ATP production [69]. In addition to all the alterations inherent to glycolytic enzymes, the aberrant expression of transcription factors such as HIF-1, c-MYC and p53 also promotes metabolic reprogramming [59]. Such metabolic alterations are not only involved in cancer cells' adaptation to hostile environments, but are also mediators of mechanisms of resistance to several conventionally used chemotherapeutic drugs, a major problem in cancer treatment effectiveness [2].

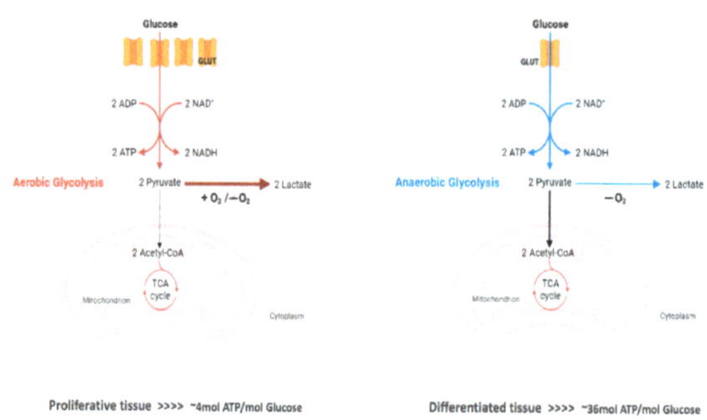

Figure 2. Schematic representation of the main differences between aerobic glycolysis ("Warburg effect") in proliferative tissue and OXPHOS and anaerobic glycolysis in differentiated tissues. In the presence of O_2, differentiated tissues (no proliferating) metabolize glucose to pyruvate via glycolysis and subsequently completely oxidize pyruvate to CO_2 in the mitochondria (OXPHOS). At low levels of O_2, pyruvate is partially oxidized by glycolysis, generating lactate (anaerobic glycolysis). The generation of lactate results in minimal ATP production when compared with OXPHOS. In contrast, cancer/proliferative cells predominantly produce energy through an increased rate of glycolysis, followed by a reduction of pyruvate into lactate in the cytosol, resulting in a high production of lactic acid. Created by the Authors with BioRender.com. ATP: adenosine triphosphate; OXPHOS: oxidative phosphorylation.

4. Mechanisms of Cancers' Drug Resistance

In the last few decades, cancer treatment has made great, promising advances. Nevertheless, despite these advances, tumors seem to always find a way to resist practically all types of anticancer therapy, hindering their treatment potential [2,80]. Cancer patients who are resistant to therapy often develop more metastases, which are the main cause of cancer-related deaths in these cases [81,82]. Thus, it is important to develop new therapeutic approaches to overcome resistance to therapy [80,81]. The growing knowledge of the molecular mechanisms of cancer has allowed for the discovery and improvement of new therapeutic compounds with a better progression-free survival. Unfortunately, this does not always translate into overall survival benefits, as resistance is one of the main problems to overcome. This resistance may be due to intrinsic mechanisms or to acquired mechanisms, which arise after the exposure of cancer cells to chemotherapeutic drugs [80] (Figure 3).

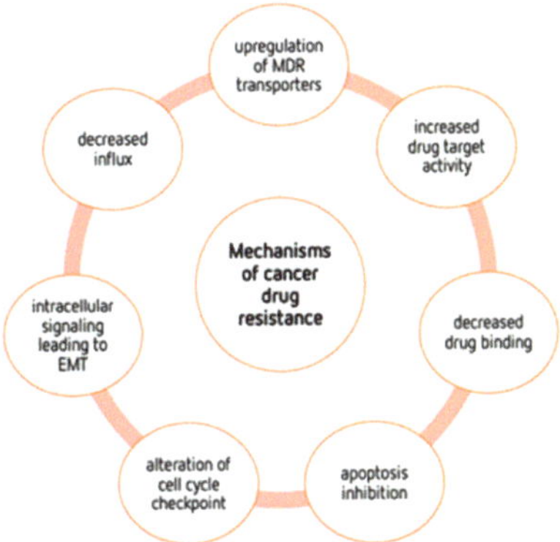

Figure 3. Mechanisms of chemotherapeutic drug resistance in cancer cells. This resistance may be due to intrinsic mechanisms or due to acquired mechanisms, such as the ones listed in the figure.

This acquired resistance may result from several factors, namely the acquisition of mutations that cause a decrease in drug binding, an increase in drug target activity, or an upregulation of multidrug resistance (MDR) transporters [83]. For example, mutations of the TP53 gene, a tumor suppressor responsible for genome stability, are frequently observed in cancer cells and involved in cancer resistance to therapy [84]. A genomic study carried out in patients with acute myeloid leukemia demonstrated that the presence of new genetic mutations in the genes WAC, SMC3, DIS3, DDX41, and DAXX was involved in tumor resistance [85]. Another example in ovarian cancer demonstrated that the presence of secondary somatic BRCA mutations induced high resistance, especially to platinum drugs [86–88]. Many more examples of genetic mutations associated with cancer resistance can be found in the literature, demonstrating the complexity of the phenomenon. Other factors, such as decreased influx, intracellular signaling leading to epithelial–mesenchymal transition (EMT), alterations in cell cycle checkpoints and apoptosis inhibition are also associated with drug resistance [89]. Adaptive resistance can either be achieved through attempts to improve drug efficacy or result from the heterogeneity and adaptability of cancer cells [90]. Therefore, an important contribution to improving cancer therapy is a more complete knowledge of the resistance mechanisms, and the metabolic reprogramming can be also a major player [2,3]. This metabolic reprogramming provides a mechanism through which cancer cells can adapt and evolve to counteract the effects of therapeutic interventions. Therefore, unravelling and targeting reprogramming mechanisms is a crucial aspect of developing effective cancer treatments and overcoming resistance.

EMT plays an important role in tumor progression, metastasis and therapy resistance and is often associated with metabolic alterations in cancer [81,91]. EMT is a highly conserved biological process that involves the transition of polarized, immobile epithelial cells into motile mesenchymal cells due to the loss of apicobasal polarity, loss of cell–cell contacts, reorganization of the actin cytoskeleton, and ability to invade the extracellular matrix as an individual cell [81]. Different studies using cancer cell lines demonstrated the responsibility of EMT in radio- or chemotherapy-driven resistance [81,92,93]. In fact, conventional anticancer drugs are mainly directed toward rapidly dividing cells, with EMT being associated with stem cell properties in cancer cells [94]. Furthermore, EMT can be involved in microenvironment modifications, causing the loss of cell–cell adherence and extracellular matrix remodeling, as well as in the interaction with the immune system, contributing to chemotherapy resistance [95–97]. A study demonstrated that highly proliferative non-EMT lung cells were sensitive to chemotherapy, and the emergence of EMT-derived metastases was observed after treatment [98]. Another study found that increased cellular metastasis in drug-resistant Non-Small Cell Lung Cancer (NSCLC) and, consequently, malignant progression is directly associated with the EMT phenotype [97]. EMT also promotes the heterogeneity of the tumor, and is intricately regulated by several factors, such as extracellular matrix components, diverse signal pathways, soluble growth factors or cytokines, and microRNAs [99–102]. Metabolic reprogramming is often associated with the resistance and is promoted by EMT. In fact, EMT can lead to a switch in the metabolism from OXPHOS to glycolysis, which is often associated with drug resistance [91]. Furthermore, EMT can give rise to metabolic heterogenous cancer cell populations, making treatment strategies more challenging [103].

A large number of studies on metabolism-mediated drug resistance have focused on glycolysis and the TCA cycle, including the roles of glucose and glutamine in such phenotypes [2,104–106]. Nevertheless, fatty acids and BCAAs may also be associated with both energy production and tumorigenesis. Concerning amino acids, their metabolism may also constitute a target for treating drug-resistant tumors. Cancer cells may be dependent on specific amino acids, like serine, glycine, proline, aspartate, and arginine. In fact, amino acid metabolism has been extensively studied and recognized as an important factor in both drug resistance and energy production. For example, Jones et al. demonstrated that increases in the level of amino acid metabolism are not related to the metabolic needs for protein synthesis, but rather to the TCA cycle, to allow for energy production. It has also been described that the overexpression of fatty acid (FA) synthase, or even the altered expression of anti-apoptotic proteins [81], induce resistance to antitumor drugs such as DOX and mitoxantrone in breast cancer cells [107].

Unfortunately, resistance to therapy not only includes resistance to conventional treatments, such as chemotherapy or radiation, but also immunological and targeted therapies [81], affecting the long-term therapeutic outcome of tumor patients [108]. Many scientific reports have shown that the MDR phenotype, which is characterized by a broad tumor's resistance to multiple drugs and can differ either in its structure or in its mechanism of action, often correlates with the expression of active transport mechanisms responsible for the efflux of a wide variety of drugs, leading to a reduction in the effect of the drug, as there is a reduction in its intracellular levels [82,108,109]. These transporters, which are frequently highly expressed in resistant cancer cells, belong to the ATP-binding cassette (ABC) family, with P-glycoprotein (Pgp) being the first-identified and best-studied ABC transporter [108,109]. In some normal human tissues, these proteins are responsible for endogenous and exogenous substrate transport across their membranes, avoiding toxic accumulation in the organism, but in cancer they are often associated with the MDR phenotype [110]. Furthermore, several findings showed the contribution of ABC transporters to some of the remaining hallmarks of cancer [82].

4.1. ABC Transporters

The ABC transporter family is composed of seven subfamilies (ABCA to ABCG), according to their genomic sequences and the core structure of transmembrane domains, but only a few of them transport drugs; therefore, they play an important role in their bioavailability [111–113]. In humans, the proteins of this ABC transporter superfamily comprise at least 48 genes with diverse functions [82,114]. Given their ability to extrude several conventional antitumor drugs, recent studies in cancer research focused on the members of this superfamily to understand the reasons for the failure of chemotherapy treatment (Figure 4) [82].

Three major subfamilies of ABC transporters have been associated with the MDR phenotype and extensively studied: ABCB, comprising ABCB1 (Pgp/MDR1), ABCC, comprising ABCC1 (Multidrug-Resistance Protein 1 (MRP1)) and ABCG, comprising ABCG2 (Breast Cancer-Resistance Protein (BCRP)) in their respective members. These three proteins are major players in both primary and acquired resistance to chemotherapeutic drugs [82,115,116]. A key factor in the clarification of the mechanisms behind MDR was the discovery of the MDR1 and MRP1 transporters, which allowed for the identification of a variety of proteins with similar structures and transport capabilities. In addition to their role in transport of drugs, several members of the ABCB subfamily are also involved in intracellular peptides' transport, including a key role in the presentation of major histocompatibility complex class I antigens [82]. MDR1, MRP1 and BCRP transporters can export an extensive range of chemotherapeutic compounds used in the treatment of cancer patients, making them attractive therapeutic targets [82]. In addition, cancer progression has been associated with the overexpression of some other ABC transporters, as in the case of melanoma, where a clinical correlation with ABCB5 expression was found [80,117]. To make the situation worse, several cancers overexpress more than one ABC transporter; this co-expression contributes to multiple-drug resistance [82,111]. Thus, to achieve a better clinical outcome, multi-carrier inhibitors are required [111]. For instance, the co-expression of MDR1, ABCB5 and ABCC2 was observed in a subpopulation of melanoma cells [80,117]. It has also been described that BCRP/MDR1 transporters are highly expressed in hematopoietic stem cells [80,118]. Furthermore, some studies demonstrated a possible relationship between ABC transporters and the in vivo formation of metastasis, although there is still no direct evidence of such an association [82,119].

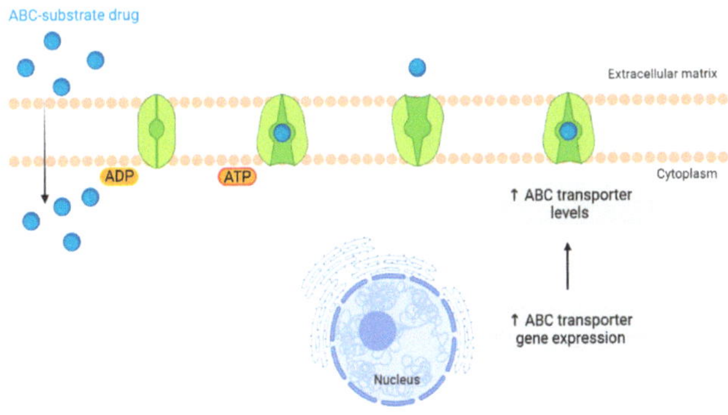

Figure 4. A simplified schematic diagram of ABC transporter overexpression leading to drug resistance in cancer cells. The ABC proteins (green) reduce intracellular drug concentration by actively transporting ABC substrate drugs (blue circles) out of the cancer cell, which leads to the MDR phenotype. Created by the Authors with BioRender.com. ABC: ATP-binding cassette; MDR: multidrug resistance.

4.1.1. MDR1 Transporter

The MDR1 transporter, or Pgp, was the first drug transporter to be identified and the most pharmacologically active and clinically important efflux pump; it is widely expressed and transports a large variety of chemical substrates [113,120,121]. Variations in the efficiency of its transport may result from single-nucleotide polymorphisms in its encoding gene [111,122]. It has been reported that MDR1 expression triggers a delay in apoptosis as the response to apoptotic stimuli, both in cancer and non-cancer cells. This process was reverted when Pgp inhibitors were used [82,123,124]. Pgp is believed to be responsible for the MDR phenotype in most cancers [109,111], as it is a protein capable of actively pumping various drugs (e.g., DOX, vinblastine and PTX) out of the cell, thus reducing their cytotoxic efficacy [108]. Yin et al. found that resistance to chemotherapy in liver cancer stem cells is due to the overexpression of MDR1 (but also BRCP), leading to DOX efflux [125]. Another example of DOX resistance occurs in osteosarcoma cell lines, where the increased MDR1 expression is associated with the degree of DOX resistance [126]. In MCF-7 cells, the overexpression of MDR1 causes resistance to tamoxifen [127]. PTX, also known as taxol, is another important clinical drug for the treatment of malignant breast, prostate and NSCLC tumors [128]. The mechanism by which PTX affects malignant cell division is believed to include microtubule hyperstabilization and the inhibition of cytoskeletal restructuring. These processes are considered crucial to cell division [129]. Nevertheless, PTX is also a Pgp substrate, and resistance to this drug is often associated with treatment failure [128,129]. Despite its physiological importance in protecting cells from xenobiotics, Pgp overexpression in clinical specimens in breast, kidney and lung cancer patients led to a poor response to chemotherapy, resulting in low survival rates [111].

4.1.2. MRP1 Transporter

MRP1 is a lipophilic anionic pump, which may increase resistance to antitumor drugs [130]. MRP1 has a wide variety of substrates, triggering it to confer resistance to anthracyclines, epipodophyllotoxins, vinca alkaloids and camptothecins [114]. Like other efflux pumps, MRP1 expression is associated with other processes, namely redox homeostasis, steroid, and lipid metabolism, and in the pathophysiology of different disorders [110]. It is also described that MRP1 is able to transport bioactive lipids and steroids, suggesting that the protein has additional functions during cancer growth and progression, besides the described resistance to chemotherapy drugs [131]. Although MRP1 and Pgp both belong to the ABC family of transporters, they present different levels of resistance to different families of drugs [114,132].

MRP1 overexpression is related to drug resistance in acute myeloblastic, glioma, lymphoblastic leukemia, head and neck cancer, NSCLC, neuroblastoma, melanoma, prostate, breast, kidney, and thyroid cancer [111]. In neuroblastoma, for example, MRP1 knockdown was found to reduce the mitotic index in a neuroblastoma cell line xenograft [82], and high levels of MRP1 have been used as predictors of a worse response to chemotherapy [133]. Indeed, it was discovered that the reduction in the tumor expression of MRP1 was enough to augment the antitumor effect of epirubicin in a xenograft model of NSCLC [134]. It is also important to identify specific factors that regulate ABC transporter expression in cancer contexts, specifically those of MRP1. For instance, some studies showed that p53 mutations promoted increased MRP1 expression and tumor immune-cell infiltration [135]. This correlation was verified by Zhou et al., in a study which MRP1 was correlated with the immunological infiltration of several cells of the immune system, namely B cells, CD8+ T cells, CD4+ T cells, macrophages, neutrophils and dendritic cells. The presence of these immune system cells contributes to heightened resistance to immunotherapies [136].

4.1.3. BCRP Transporter

BCRP is involved in the efflux of exogenous and endogenous substrates and drugs, being related to several types of multidrug-resistant cancers, such as acute lymphoblastic leukemia, liver metastases, gastric carcinoma, fibrosarcoma, NSCLC, glioblastoma and myeloma [111]. A mouse model of BRCA1-associated breast cancer demonstrated that, in the group of genetically modified animals (Brca1−/−p53−/− mice), BCRP overexpression resulted in acquired resistance to topotecan treatment, whereas its knockdown improved the survival rate of these animals [137]. It was also reported that BCRP and CD133 co-expression can identify tumor-initiating cells in melanomas [80,117]. However, while the BCRP mechanisms involved in MDR are clear, clinical trials for BCRP inhibitors have provided few satisfactory results [116]. The reasons for clinical failure are diverse. One of the primary factors is associated with the restrictions on the use of BCRP function inhibitors due to their potential to elevate the plasma concentration of drugs that are substrates of BCRP. This elevation in substrate concentration, particularly for drugs with a narrow therapeutic index, can result in severe side effects. [138]. Another reason is the fact that many drugs are transported not only by BCRP but also by Pgp and other ABC transporters [139]. In addition to these limitations, it has been noted that BCRP inhibitors may exhibit toxicity. An example of this is the fungal toxin fumitremorgin C (FTC), the first BCRP inhibitor to be described, which, because of its neurotoxicity, was not suitable for use [140–142]. Although, to date, the most promising candidate is Ko143, this inhibitor does not have a specific effect since, at high concentrations, it also inhibits Pgp [142–144].

Since ABC transporters are overexpressed in several types of cancer and they are related to chemotherapy treatment's ineffectiveness and a worse prognosis, their inhibition may be a way to prevent MDR and improve the prognosis [110]. Most inhibitors are designed to target MDR1, although there are also many cancer-related cell substrates that are exported by the ABCC subfamily [114]. However, the clinical use of ABC inhibitors was not very successful, making the discovery of a more effective strategy urgent. Moreover, when drugs are administered, they can also non-specifically target the ABC transporters of nontumor tissues, leading to side effects [111]. Furthermore, the high doses that are necessary to achieve this inhibition cause high toxicity in the brain and kidneys due to their possible accumulation [145]. The co-administration of inhibitors of these pumps and chemotherapeutic drugs can be one of the main strategies to improve the effectiveness of treatment, but more specific and precise delivery systems are still needed to avoid adverse side effects [114]. Another approach, which will be further detailed, could be the use of metabolic inhibitors, as these proteins, which are strongly associated with cancer therapy resistance, are ATP-dependent.

4.2. Metabolic Alterations Involved in Drug Resistance in Cancer

Recently, it has been shown that the response to first-line chemotherapy treatment largely depends on the metabolism of cancer cells, which can be reprogrammed during the treatment [5]. The development of tumor-cell-associated resistance due to drug-induced selective pressures demonstrates specific resistant metabolic characteristics [105]. Several conventional chemotherapeutics activate apoptosis, killing cancer cells. However, if cancer cells find mechanisms to avoid chemotherapy's cytotoxic effect, they will escape this programmed cell death and, as a consequence, the cancer will grow [106]. Several mechanisms are involved in the development of drug resistance in cancers, such as increased drug exportation, metabolic reprogramming and TME hypoxia [108,110]. The activation of different signaling pathways with the expression of signaling molecules is also involved in different mechanisms of drug resistance [108]. It is established that cells that express MDR proteins, such as Pgp or MRP, rely on ATP as their energy source to pump out drug substrates from within the cells. Consequently, the heightened expression of these proteins results in increased drug efflux due to the surplus production of cellular ATP, thereby inducing drug resistance [146]. Furthermore, as previously mentioned, TME plays an important role in the progression of cancers. Cancer cells have a greater need for nutrients to produce the necessary energy and sustain their anabolic needs. Thus, the availability of nutrients influences the proliferation rate of cancer cells. Despite this need, cancer cells have metabolic plasticity, which allows for them to adapt to conditions of reduced nutrient availability, and may, in turn, remodel the TME [147]. With changes in metabolism, the tumor microenvironment undergoes changes to ensure its survival, namely hypoxia, acidosis, and the formation of stroma cells. These changes, besides being particularly adverse to normal cells, are involved in the development of chemoresistance. Hypoxia can be caused by increased oxygen consumption, the rapid growth and proliferation of the tumor and also by the lack of a vascular system in certain tumor zones [10,147]. On the other hand, and as previously mentioned, hypoxia can lead to the greater use of glycolysis for the production of ATP in cancer cells, and this mechanism of obtaining energy leads to an accumulation of lactate in cells, facilitating the evasion of the immune system [148,149]. Lactate is transported to the outside of cells through the increased activity of pH regulators like ATPases, carbonic anhydrases and MCTs in order to maintain the intracellular acid-base balance. A study by Tavares-Valente shows that the inhibition of the pH regulator with concanamycin-A, cariporide, acetazolamide and cyano-4-hydroxycinnamate decreased the aggressiveness of the MDA-MB-231 cell line, a breast cancer line. A synergistic inhibitory effect was also verified in this study when these pH inhibitors were combined with DOX regarding the viability of the breast cancer cell line. These results support the interruption of proton dynamics as an antitumor strategy for breast cancer and the use of regular pH inhibitors to increase the activity of conventional therapy [149].

Several studies have shown that the specific therapeutic pressure induced by drugs and the adverse conditions found in the tumor environment, namely acidity and hypoxia, lead to treatment resistance, and such resistance is also promoted by a metabolic reprogramming [110,150]. Glycolysis upregulation is one of the major metabolic modifications and is associated with ABC transporter activity, reducing the sensitivity of cells to chemotherapeutic agents [110]. Pgp activity also depends on TME characteristics and it has been shown that its activity was doubly increased in prostate cancer cells exposed to acidic media (pH 6.6) [112]. This augmentation of activity leads to an increase in the efflux of Pgp substrates, such as PTX, and thus a decrease in drug cellular sensitivity. Furthermore, the acidification of the extracellular medium reduces the uptake of several therapeutic agents, such as DOX or PTX, thus contributing to drug inaction [110] (Figure 5).

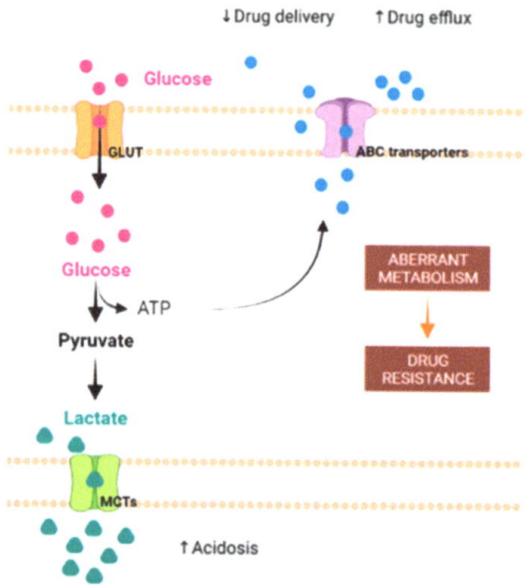

Figure 5. Metabolic alterations underlying the development of cancer cell drug resistance. Glycolysis upregulation is associated with ATP production and ABC transporter activity, leading to the reduced sensitivity of cells to chemotherapeutic agents. In addition, the low pH of TME, promoted by lactate accumulation and transported out of the cell by MCTs, reduces the therapeutic agent. Created by the Authors with BioRender.com. ABC: ATP-binding cassette; ATP: adenosine triphosphate; MCTs: monocarboxylate transporters; TME: tumor microenvironment.

At the mitochondrial level, mitochondrial DNA (mtDNA) depletion is related to tumor progression and metastasis, and may further act as a "progression signal" for chemoresistance [106,114]. Li et al. showed that mtDNA-depleted androgen-independent prostate carcinoma cells, despite growing slowly, are highly carcinogenic, revealing an overexpression of BCRP and extremely aggressive and radio- and chemoresistant characteristics [151]. In addition, the fact that these cancer cells present a slow growth may be an advantage in their resistance to chemotherapy treatments, since the cytotoxic agents used in conventional chemotherapy have a more direct impact on rapidly proliferative cells [106,116]. mtDNA depletion in hepatocarcinoma cells resulted in cisplatin, DOX, and SN-38 chemoresistance linked with the upregulation of the MDR1 gene and MRP1 and MRP2, which are particularly involved in MDR. In colon cancer cells that are mtDNA-depleted, the upregulation of MDR1 has also been observed [117,118].

4.3. Metabolic Modulation as an Approach to Overcome Drug Resistance

The metabolic reprogramming of cancer cells, besides its role in cancer proliferation and invasion, is also implicated in the acquisition of resistance to therapy in cancer patients. In this way, the recent increase in the knowledge of tumor cell metabolism and the subsequent exploration of metabolic alterations in these cells may offer an opportunity to discover new potential targets for therapeutic intervention and to overcome such resistance. This is particularly important in the different types of cancers that show resistance to drugs, to improve treatments and avoid adverse side effects. Disruption of the Warburg effect is the most often used means of sensitizing the cells to conventional antitumor drugs, exploiting cancer metabolic reprogramming [152]. Thus, glycolytic inhibitors can be used as a therapeutic strategy as they drastically decrease cellular ATP levels, which is necessary to maintain the activity of the drug efflux pumps [111] (Figure 6). This could be an effective strategy, as one of the best-described mechanisms of drug resistance is due to the increased level and/or activity of the efflux pumps that remove drugs from cells [110]. As previously described, the Warburg effect plays a significant role in therapy resistance mechanisms by contributing to metabolic reprogramming. Therefore, the use of glycolytic inhibitors alongside conventional chemotherapy may enhance the effectiveness of standard drugs by modulating metabolism. Some trials were carried out with the aim of targeting drugs in order to modulate the Warburg effect. AR-C155858, which targets MCTs 1 and 2, and AZD3965, an MCT1-specific inhibitor that partially inhibits MCT2, developed by the pharmaceutical company AstraZeneca, can have anti-cancer effects [153,154]. In a breast cancer cell xenograft model, AR-C155858 showed no significant effects on tumor growth [155]. AZD3965 has been demonstrated to inhibit the growth of several tumor cell lines, notably lymphoma [156,157]. A clinical trial in Phase I (NCT01791595) demonstrated that AZD3965 is tolerated at doses that allow for interaction with the target in advanced cancer [158]. A study demonstrated that phenformin and IAA induced a diminution in cancer cell proliferation and, when combined with conventional antitumor drugs, an increase in drug cytotoxicity was found [32]. Other drugs, such as 2DG, 3BP, DCA, lonidamine, resveratrol and apigenin, are known as inhibitors of glycolytic enzyme [159,160]. However, on the Clinical Trial website (https://clinicaltrials.gov (accessed on 20 October 2023)), most of them are under consideration in the preclinical phase.

Amino acid metabolism can be also related to MDR phenotype, as it provides cancer cells with specific adaptive characteristics to neutralize the mechanism of action of the antitumor drugs to which they are exposed [161]. In fact, amino acids play an important role both in most biosynthetic pathways, which are upregulated in cancer cells, and in maintaining the redox homeostasis balance [113]. Among these, glutamine plays a crucial role in cancer metabolism and in drug resistance in cancer cells, since glutaminolysis supports the biosynthesis of many essential molecules [105,162] (Figure 6). The importance of glutamine is also due to the fact that it is the amino acid with the largest carbon source for the TCA cycle. In the context of tumor cells, glutamine metabolism can provide essential building blocks for the excessive demands of both glycolysis and OXPHOS [163]. In addition to its role as an essential intermediary metabolite, glutamine regulates cell survival and proliferation via signal transduction pathways, specifically the mammalian target of the rapamycin (mTOR) pathway [164], as well as the extracellular signal-regulated protein kinase (ERK) signaling pathway [165]. Additionally, this metabolic pathway may induce resistance in tumor cells against chemotherapy drugs by perturbing the delicate balance of sugar, lipid, and protein metabolism [163]. Thus, the specific inhibition of enzymes involved in the cancer amino acid metabolism may emerge as a successful therapy strategy [161]. Figure 6 shows the use of metabolic modulation with different compounds as an approach to overcome drug resistance.

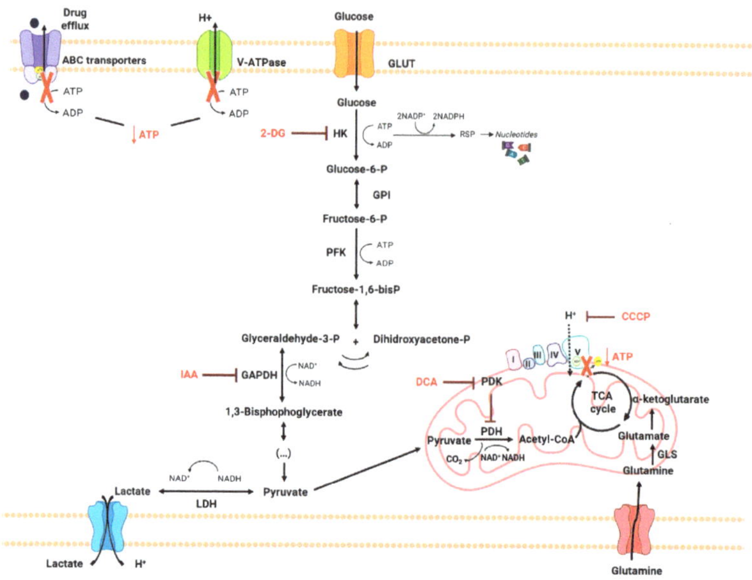

Figure 6. Metabolic modulation as an approach to overcome drug resistance. Glucose and glutamine metabolism, in tumor cells, supply vital components for the high requirements of both glycolysis and OXPHOS. The different compounds (IAA and 2DG) are glycolytic inhibitors. DCA inhibits PDK, reactivating PDH, and switching the metabolism from glycolysis towards OXPHOS. CCP is an uncoupler that inhibits ATP synthesis. The depletion of cancer cell energy probably leads to the inactivation of the pumps' ABC transporters. Created by the Authors with BioRender.com. 2DG: 2-deoxyglucose; ABC: ATP-binding transporter; ATP: adenosine triphosphate; CCP: Carbonyl Cyanide m-chlorophenyl Hydrazone; DCA: dichloroacetate; IAA: iodoacetate; OXPHOS: oxidative phosphorylation; PDH: pyruvate dehydrogenase.

For example, melanoma cells lacking argininosuccinate synthetase activity, and thus presenting with auxotrophy to arginine, were not able to proliferate under arginine deficiency in in vitro models [166]. In another example, the glutamine transporter SLC1A5 and the enzyme GLS were considerably upregulated in aromatase inhibitor (AI)-resistant breast cancer cells, and the inhibition of these proteins decreased cell proliferation [167]. PKM2 is another essential enzyme of the glycolysis pathway, an isoform that is a potential target in the search for anti-cancer drugs [153]. PKM2 is significantly upregulated in hepatocellular carcinoma, where it is associated with poor prognosis [66,168]. PKM2 inhibitors have been explored in cancer research because they have the potential to disrupt the abnormal metabolic processes in cancer cells, potentially slowing down their growth or even causing cell death. In other study, PKM2 knockdown inhibited hepatocellular carcinoma cell proliferation, migration, and invasion in vitro, as well as tumor growth in vivo. Also, in human melanoma cells, it was demonstrated that benserazide, an inhibitor of PKM2, in addition to being an aromatic L-amino acid used for the treatment of Parkinson's disease, inhibited cell proliferation [169]. Benserazide binds directly to the PKM2, blocking its activity, and thus leading to the inhibition of aerobic glycolysis and restoration of OXPHOS [170]. Hence, blocking the primary energy production pathways in cancer cells could lead to reduced drug efflux by depleting cellular ATP, potentially reducing drug resistance [37]. Various types of cancer, when treated with a variety of drugs, present a correlation between ABC transporters and resistance phenomena, since cells expressing MDR proteins such as Pgp require ATP to be used as an energy source to pump drug substrates. Thus, drug sensitivity in cancer cells can be re-established through glycolysis and/or OXPHOS inhibition, as this inhibition will lead to ATP depletion, with a negative and specific impact on ABC transporter activity. Nakano et al. demonstrated that the suppression of glycolysis by the glycolytic inhibitor 3BP preferentially occurs in cancer cells, causing an inhibition of ATP synthesis and, consequently, of the activity of the ABC transporter. In contrast to specific inhibitors targeting a single efflux pump, this ATP depletion simultaneously inactivates all ABC transporters expressed in cancer cells, preventing the efflux of antitumor drugs and potentiating their cytotoxic effect on the cell [171]. Resistant cell lines are often chosen to study the role of the glycolysis inhibition effect in drug resistance due to the aberrant ABC transporters' expression that expels drugs [159]. Ma et al. proposed that 2DG reversed the resistance of MCF-7 cells with an MDR phenotype and increased DOX-induced apoptosis by interfering with glucose metabolism. The process was related to the intracellular ATP depletion and, consequently, to drug efflux pump inactivation [172]. In cancer cell lines of multiple myeloma, and in leukemic cells, when treated with mitoxantrone and 3BP, a greater uptake of the chemotherapeutic agent mitoxantrone was verified. This suggested that the inhibition of glycolysis with 3BP simultaneously led to the inactivation of all types of ABC transporters in these cells, as these transporters were dependent on the ATP formed during increased glycolysis [37,159]. Other studies suggested that metformin and phenformin, antidiabetic drugs that also interfere with energetic metabolism in cancer cells, show promise in decreasing resistance through the inhibition of ABC transporters in breast cancer [32,80,173].

Metabolic adaptations in chemoresistant cells have a complex pattern involving further alterations in the reprogrammed metabolism, characteristic of cancer cells. Such modifications are mainly associated with the Warburg effect, but other players are also involved, such as amino acid and lipid metabolism, the redox state of the cell, mitochondrial reprogramming, or polyamine synthesis [3]. A profound knowledge of chemoresistant cells metabolomics is thus essential to identify metabolic targets that can be manipulated to circumvent such resistance.

4.4. Self-Delivery of Nanomedicine to Overcome Drug Resistance

Chemotherapy, radiation therapy and resection surgery remain the three "gold standard" anticancer therapies [174]. Whether radiotherapy and surgery can be indicated for localized cancers, chemotherapy is considered the most appropriate treatment for most patients with metastasis and advanced cancer, as chemotherapy drugs can be widely distributed in the organism through the bloodstream [175]. Nevertheless, the development of drug resistance and the low hydrosolubility of drugs are significant problems that restrict the clinical use of currently available chemotherapy drugs [175]. Major chemotherapeutic agents include compounds like platinum complexes, DOX, vinca alkaloids, and taxanes, and primarily affect nucleic acids and protein synthesis, interfering with cell cycle and triggering apoptosis [176,177]. However, most of the standard agents approved for clinical use do not have the capacity to differentiate normal cells from cancer cells. This leads to serious side effects, especially in rapidly growing cells, as these drugs generally compromise mitosis. These cells include hair follicles, bone marrow cells and the gastrointestinal system, leading to hair loss, immune system failure, and infections, respectively [178]. Thus, the decrease in the toxicity and side effects of the main chemotherapeutic agents is an urgent problem that needs to be overcome [176]. To overcome this problem, various compounds, such as 3BP, DCA and 2DG, that interfere with metabolism, have been tested and demonstrated their ability to decrease tumor cell metabolism [37]. However, there are disadvantages to a metabolism-based approach in cancer therapy, since the metabolic pathways required for cell survival are also present in normal cells. Thus, metabolism-based treatment can face the major hurdle of non-specific toxicity [5]. To decrease their toxic side effects and increase antitumor efficacy, a number of drug delivery systems have been developed, such as albumin-bound PTX (Abraxane®) or liposome-entrapped PTX and DOX, which have received clinical approval, as these formulations presented enhanced security but maintained their effectiveness [175,176,179]. Several countries, namely the EU, US and Japan, approved the use of Abraxane® combined with carboplatin as a first-line treatment in advanced NSCLC patients for whom curative surgery and/or radiation therapy was not an option [180]. Further investigations into the treatment of other solid tumors based on Abraxane® are ongoing. The use of Doxil® (liposomal DOX), with an improved safety profile in comparison to free DOX, has also been approved for clinical use in patients with multiple myeloma (NCT00103506) [179]. In other example, the combination of radiotherapy and Caelyx®, a pegylated liposomal DOX, led to a significant increase in the intratumoral concentration of DOX in the brain tissue of patients with glioblastoma [181]. These nanodrug delivery systems facilitate the drugs' entry into cancer cells and reduce their export, thus promoting intracellular drug accumulation and improving targeted drug delivery. In addition to this, they allow for the co-administration of synergistic agents, and increase the half-life of drug in circulation [181,182]. In fact, in a therapeutic context, the correct combination of drugs with different mechanisms of action is needed. As the doses and efficiency of these drugs are often limited due to their toxicity, is important to develop cancer-specific delivery systems, namely drug encapsulation in nanoparticles. These systems are able to transport both hydrophobic and hydrophilic drugs, ensuring the sustained release of the drug and increasing the half-life of the drug in the bloodstream. The half-life of temozolomide, for example, was increased to 13.4 h, compared to 1.8 h for the free drug, through encapsulation in chitosan-based nanoparticles (NPs) [181] (Figure 7). The hypoxic, hypoglycemic, and acidic conditions, characteristic of the TME, are important to trigger drug release, allowing for researchers to create a TME-responsive delivery system. Furthermore, the overexpression of surface receptors by cancer cells can be used to target these delivery systems toward cancer cells through antibodies with the aim of reducing side effects in normal tissues [183].

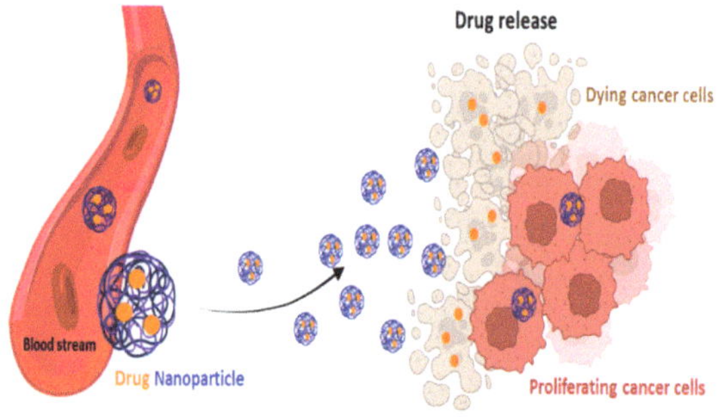

Figure 7. Schematic representation of nanoparticles as a drug delivery vehicle into cancer cells. The drug can be dissolved, entrapped, encapsulated, or attached to a nanoparticle matrix in order to promote therapeutic absorption, particularly in oncology. Once inside the cell, the nanoparticle is degraded through intracellular signals in order to release the drug. Created by the Authors with BioRender.com.

Nanotechnology-based cancer therapies aim to find new therapeutic methodologies correlated with disease mechanisms. The use of nanoparticles to encapsulate the drugs may increase the specificity of delivery to cancer cells and decrease the interaction with other non-cancer cells involved in tumor growth and spreading [174]. Poly(lactic-*co*-glycolic acid) (PLGA), a synthetic thermoplastic aliphatic biodegradable and biocompatible polyester, is widely studied and is one of the most characterized polymers [184]. PLGA is degraded in non-toxic products (H_2O and CO_2) that are easily excreted [176,184]. Its polymeric NPs are degraded in vivo into lactate and glycolate. D-lactate is not metabolized prior to excretion and L-lactate is transformed into CO_2, which is eliminated by pulmonary excretion, or converted to pyruvate, which fuels the TCA cycle. Glycolate can be directly excreted by the kidneys or can be oxidized to glyoxylate, which is, in turn, further metabolized producing glycine, serine, and pyruvate. Subsequently, pyruvate can re-enter the TCA cycle and follow the OXPHOS pathway [184]. The lactic acid (LA)/glycolic acid (GA) proportion is a good indicator not only when adjusting the degradation time, but also of the drug release rate [184,185]. Due to the absence of lateral methyl groups in GA, it has a higher hydrophilia, and thus, when higher amounts of GA are present, a higher degradation rate is observed [184,186]. Wu et al. showed that higher degradation rates of PLGA-based scaffolding were achieved when an LA:GA ratio of 75:25 was used, relative to a ratio of 85:15 [187]. Therefore, these polymeric features, as well as their size, prove to be important in adjusting the hydrophobicity, drug loading effectiveness, and pharmacokinetic profile of PLGA formulations [184,185]. The shape of the PLGA NPS appears to be another important feature, as it affects the outcome of cancer treatment. Needle-shaped PLGA NPs appear to cross endothelial cell membranes more efficiently compared to spherical forms [184]. In fact, needle-shaped PLGA NPs have been reported to significantly increase cytotoxicity. After being endocyted, these particles enter lysosomes, where they can activate apoptosis and induce cell death [184,188].

Some PLGA polymers are FDA-approved materials and various PLGA NPs formulations have been clinically introduced, such as a formulation targeting advanced prostate cancer, ELIGARD® [178]. PLGA NPs were also shown to be effective in increasing the accumulation of docetaxel in gastric tumors, thus causing an increase in anticancer activity [189]. Importantly, PLGA NPs are versatile systems as they can deliver hydrophobic or hydrophilic drugs [178]. Surface adjustment with, for example, PEGylation (PEG) increases the formulation's hydrophilicity, producing a particle with an improved blood circulation time and pharmacokinetics, preventing opsonization and absorption by the mononuclear phagocytic system [184].

Ongoing research underscores the significance of the TME in driving tumor proliferation, invasion, metastasis, and resistance to therapeutic interventions. As mentioned, the TME provides protection for cancer cells, enabling them to evade conventional treatments like surgery, radiotherapy, and chemotherapy. Furthermore, the constituents of the TME play a pivotal role in fostering therapy resistance in solid tumors. Consequently, directing interventions toward the TME presents a promising avenue for advancing the field of cancer nanomedicine. The combination of antitumor drugs with drugs that interfere with resistance mechanisms has largely been made possible by advancements in nanotechnology [190]. Hence, directing efforts toward the TME presents an innovative approach to advancing the field of cancer nanomedicine [37,191]. Nanoparticles developed in response to TME cues, such as a low pH, redox conditions, and hypoxia, enhance the pharmacokinetics and therapeutic effectiveness of nanomedicine, but also have glycolytic inhibitors [37,192–194]. Although not directly associated with this, and as has been shown for DCA in a lung cancer cell model, the use of nanoparticles improves the delivery of the compound, which can be important in cases of resistance. In fact, Cunha et al., with the aim of enhancing the cellular internalization of DCA, a glycolytic inhibitor, through lung cancer cells, and thereby increasing its anticancer activity, successfully achieved nanoencapsulation in PLGA [37]. In other study, the authors successfully encapsulated a glycolytic inhibitor, 2DG, in PLGA nanoparticles, and administered it to liver tumors in mice [193]. In addition to PLGA particles, 2DG was also encapsulated in liposome particles with the aim of achieving a synergistic effect with DOX. In vivo results show that this nanosystem has effective therapeutic characteristics, as well as reduced side effects [194]. Since cancer cells do not exclusively rely on ATP production through glycolysis, nanosystems loaded with mitochondrial inhibitors have also been developed. A nanoparticle designed to deplete copper specifically within the mitochondria (known as a mitochondria-targeted copper-depleting nanoparticle or CDN) was evaluated for its effectiveness against triple-negative breast cancer. The study revealed that CDNs effectively reduce oxygen consumption and OXPHOS, inducing a metabolic shift toward glycolysis and diminishing ATP production in these cells. This energy deficiency, coupled with compromised mitochondrial membrane potential and increased oxidative stress, ultimately leads to apoptosis [195]. On the other hand, some studies obtain a single nanoparticle, supplied with a glycolytic inhibitor and a mitochondrial inhibitor, with the aim of synergistically blocking both forms of energy production, such as the nanolipossoma [196,197]. In order to increase its effectiveness, NPs can be also coated with specific ligands directly targeted to cells in the TME, which promote tumor progression and aggressiveness [198,199]. Table 2 summarizes the metabolic-reprogramming-targeted, nanotechnology-based interference strategies for overcoming chemotherapy resistance.

Table 2. The metabolic-reprogramming-targeted, nanotechnology-based strategies.

Metabolism Pathway	Nanoparticle	Advantages	Disadvantages	Future Perspectives	References
Mitochondrial respiration	DCA NP PLGA	Control drug delivery system of small drug molecules	Increased DCA in normal cells could lead to serious side effects	Functionalize NPs to specific tissue receptors	[37]
	CDN polymersome NPs	Induce a metabolic shift toward glycolysis Low toxicity of CDNs in healthy mice	Not applicable to glycolytic cells	Apply to other types of cancer	[195]
Aerobic glycolysis	2DG-NPs-PLGA	Control drug-delivery system of small drug molecules	Extremely low loading rate of 2DG into the 2DG-PLGA-NPs	Combination therapy with 2DG-PLGA-NPs and other therapeutic agents	[193]
	Nanoenabled Energy Interrupter	Sensitive to an acidic TME	Preferential inhibition of NPs on melanoma cells	Increase specificity for other tumor types	[200]
Aerobic glycolysis and Mitochondrial respiration	Liposome NPs	Acidic TME favorable for the decomposition of NPs	No data	Combination therapy with nanolipossoma and antitumor agents	[196]

Using NPs to direct therapy to energy metabolism and the TME could be a promising approach to sensitizing cells to conventional chemotherapy. Although the use of nanotechnology is still a recent field in cancer therapy, there is already enough evidence of its potential for successful treatment, allowing for a more accurate and specific delivery of antitumor drugs into cancer cells and avoiding many adverse side effects. Many barriers still need to be overcome regarding the success of NPs in clinical trials. Some of these barriers include the size and timing of certain NP therapies. The majority of experimental tests of NPs are cell-based and use animal models, which may not lead to convincing results in human testing. Furthermore, as the presence of metastases is a significant property of cancer, more studies should be carried out with models of cancer metastasis [201].

5. Conclusions

Although conventional chemotherapy is particularly toxic to tumor cells, it is often non-specific, and is responsible for the significant side effects associated with cancer treatment. However, there are differences between cancer cells and healthy cells that can be explored to increase treatment specificity against cancer. One of these differences consists of the "Warburg effect", currently considered an emergent cancer hallmark, whereby the upregulation of the glycolytic rate in tumor cells is a key player in acid-resistant phenotypes through their adaptation to hypoxia and acidosis, as well as in tumor aggressiveness [2,9,159]. High glycolytic rates are widely reported to promote the chemoresistance of tumor cells to conventional therapy [2]. In fact, increased acidification of the extracellular space leads to lower drug stability and, consequently, lower drug efficacy. In parallel, the increased production of glycolytic intermediates promotes cell proliferation, since these are biosynthetic precursors, whereas ATP production sustains the activity of proteins involved in both drug efflux and cell division. Together, these effects underly multidrug resistance. Nevertheless, many cancer cells adapt to changes in TME, exhibiting metabolic plasticity and switching their metabolism from glycolysis to OXPHOS, and vice-versa. For example, OXPHOS could be the predominant metabolic pathway used by cancer stem cells, and is often involved in cancer resistance, metastasis, and tumor relapse [202]. Exploring specific characteristics of cancer cells, such as this change in metabolism, could be a promising strategy for the use of more effective and more specific drugs that primarily target cancer cells. In fact, metabolic changes in cancer cells can reveal specific vulnerabilities that could be targeted with precision therapies. However, the metabolic plasticity and interchange of glycolytic and oxidative cells, although occurring many times in the same cancer and being responsible for tumor heterogeneity, is not taken into account in cancer therapies. Thus, more integrated research is needed, investigating the main metabolic pathways used in different conditions and stages of each cancer type, and the influence of the TME characteristics (e.g., oxygen, pH, nutrients availability, immune components) on such metabolic adaptation and heterogeneity. An understanding of these metabolic switches, the identification of metabolic targets, and the use of combined therapies in a more targeted way through the use of nanoparticles could have a huge impact not only on the development of new drugs, but also on the ability to overcome drug resistance, one of the major problems that occurs during cancer treatment.

This review focuses on this integrated knowledge, with a triangle of three vertices, corresponding to metabolic reprogramming and plasticity, drug-resistance mechanisms, and drug-delivery systems, serving as a promising and hopeful strategy to effectively combat cancer.

Author Contributions: A.C. participated in the conception, design and writing of the manuscript; P.M.A.S. participated in the design of the manuscript; O.Q. and B.S. participated in the conception of the study, revision of the manuscript and work supervision. All authors have read and agreed to the published version of the manuscript.

Funding: This research was funded by CESPU through the projects MetabRes_CESPU_2017CESPU and Flav4Tumor_GI2-CESPU_2022.

Institutional Review Board Statement: Not applicable.

Informed Consent Statement: Not applicable.

Data Availability Statement: Not applicable.

Conflicts of Interest: The authors declare no conflict of interest.

References

1. Porporato, P.E.; Filigheddu, N.; Pedro, J.M.B.; Kroemer, G.; Galluzzi, L. Mitochondrial metabolism and cancer. *Cell Res.* **2018**, *28*, 265–280. [CrossRef] [PubMed]
2. Zaal, E.A.; Berkers, C.R. The Influence of Metabolism on Drug Response in Cancer. *Front. Oncol.* **2018**, *8*, 500. [CrossRef]
3. Chen, X.; Chen, S.; Yu, D. Metabolic Reprogramming of Chemoresistant Cancer Cells and the Potential Significance of Metabolic Regulation in the Reversal of Cancer Chemoresistance. *Metabolites* **2020**, *10*, 289. [CrossRef]
4. Ortega, A.D.; Sanchez-Arago, M.; Giner-Sanchez, D.; Sanchez-Cenizo, L.; Willers, I.; Cuezva, J.M. Glucose avidity of carcinomas. *Cancer Lett.* **2009**, *276*, 125–135. [CrossRef]
5. Vanhove, K.; Graulus, G.J.; Mesotten, L.; Thomeer, M.; Derveaux, E.; Noben, J.P.; Guedens, W.; Adriaensens, P. The Metabolic Landscape of Lung Cancer: New Insights in a Disturbed Glucose Metabolism. *Front. Oncol.* **2019**, *9*, 1215. [CrossRef]
6. Cameron, M.E.; Yakovenko, A.; Trevino, J.G. Glucose and Lactate Transport in Pancreatic Cancer: Glycolytic Metabolism Revisited. *J. Oncol.* **2018**, *2018*, 6214838. [CrossRef]
7. Reckzeh, E.S.; Waldmann, H. Small-Molecule Inhibition of Glucose Transporters GLUT-1-4. *Chembiochem* **2020**, *21*, 45–52. [CrossRef]
8. Holman, G.D. Structure, function and regulation of mammalian glucose transporters of the SLC2 family. *Pflug. Arch.* **2020**, *472*, 1155–1175. [CrossRef] [PubMed]
9. Warburg, O. On the origin of cancer cells. *Science* **1956**, *123*, 309–314. [CrossRef] [PubMed]
10. Liberti, M.V.; Locasale, J.W. The Warburg Effect: How Does it Benefit Cancer Cells? *Trends Biochem. Sci.* **2016**, *41*, 211–218. [CrossRef]
11. Moreno-Sanchez, R.; Rodriguez-Enriquez, S.; Marin-Hernandez, A.; Saavedra, E. Energy metabolism in tumor cells. *FEBS J.* **2007**, *274*, 1393–1418. [CrossRef] [PubMed]
12. Gillies, R.J.; Robey, I.; Gatenby, R.A. Causes and consequences of increased glucose metabolism of cancers. *J. Nucl. Med.* **2008**, *49* (Suppl. S2), 24S–42S. [CrossRef]
13. Sullivan, L.B.; Gui, D.Y.; Hosios, A.M.; Bush, L.N.; Freinkman, E.; Vander Heiden, M.G. Supporting Aspartate Biosynthesis Is an Essential Function of Respiration in Proliferating Cells. *Cell* **2015**, *162*, 552–563. [CrossRef]

14. DeBerardinis, R.J.; Mancuso, A.; Daikhin, E.; Nissim, I.; Yudkoff, M.; Wehrli, S.; Thompson, C.B. Beyond aerobic glycolysis: Transformed cells can engage in glutamine metabolism that exceeds the requirement for protein and nucleotide synthesis. *Proc. Natl. Acad. Sci. USA* **2007**, *104*, 19345–19350. [CrossRef]
15. Yoo, H.C.; Yu, Y.C.; Sung, Y.; Han, J.M. Glutamine reliance in cell metabolism. *Exp. Mol. Med.* **2020**, *52*, 1496–1516. [CrossRef] [PubMed]
16. Hui, S.; Ghergurovich, J.M.; Morscher, R.J.; Jang, C.; Teng, X.; Lu, W.; Esparza, L.A.; Reya, T.; Le, Z.; Yanxiang Guo, J.; et al. Glucose feeds the TCA cycle via circulating lactate. *Nature* **2017**, *551*, 115–118. [CrossRef] [PubMed]
17. Mashimo, T.; Pichumani, K.; Vemireddy, V.; Hatanpaa, K.J.; Singh, D.K.; Sirasanagandla, S.; Nannepaga, S.; Piccirillo, S.G.; Kovacs, Z.; Foong, C.; et al. Acetate is a bioenergetic substrate for human glioblastoma and brain metastases. *Cell* **2014**, *159*, 1603–1614. [CrossRef]
18. Green, C.R.; Wallace, M.; Divakaruni, A.S.; Phillips, S.A.; Murphy, A.N.; Ciaraldi, T.P.; Metallo, C.M. Branched-chain amino acid catabolism fuels adipocyte differentiation and lipogenesis. *Nat. Chem. Biol.* **2016**, *12*, 15–21. [CrossRef]
19. Amemiya, T.; Yamaguchi, T. Oscillations and Dynamic Symbiosis in Cellular Metabolism in Cancer. *Front. Oncol.* **2022**, *12*, 783908. [CrossRef]
20. Martinez-Outschoorn, U.E.; Peiris-Pages, M.; Pestell, R.G.; Sotgia, F.; Lisanti, M.P. Cancer metabolism: A therapeutic perspective. *Nat. Rev. Clin. Oncol.* **2017**, *14*, 11–31. [CrossRef]
21. Zheng, J. Energy metabolism of cancer: Glycolysis versus oxidative phosphorylation (Review). *Oncol. Lett.* **2012**, *4*, 1151–1157. [CrossRef] [PubMed]
22. Chen, W.; Yang, Z.; Chen, Y. A Novel Oxidative Phosphorylation-Associated Gene Signature for Prognosis Prediction in Patients with Hepatocellular Carcinoma. *Dis. Markers* **2022**, *2022*, 3594901. [CrossRef]
23. Miranda-Goncalves, V.; Honavar, M.; Pinheiro, C.; Martinho, O.; Pires, M.M.; Pinheiro, C.; Cordeiro, M.; Bebiano, G.; Costa, P.; Palmeirim, I.; et al. Monocarboxylate transporters (MCTs) in gliomas: Expression and exploitation as therapeutic targets. *Neuro Oncol.* **2013**, *15*, 172–188. [CrossRef] [PubMed]
24. Suganuma, K.; Miwa, H.; Imai, N.; Shikami, M.; Gotou, M.; Goto, M.; Mizuno, S.; Takahashi, M.; Yamamoto, H.; Hiramatsu, A.; et al. Energy metabolism of leukemia cells: Glycolysis versus oxidative phosphorylation. *Leuk. Lymphoma* **2010**, *51*, 2112–2119. [CrossRef] [PubMed]
25. Lopes-Coelho, F.; Nunes, C.; Gouveia-Fernandes, S.; Rosas, R.; Silva, F.; Gameiro, P.; Carvalho, T.; Gomes da Silva, M.; Cabecadas, J.; Dias, S.; et al. Monocarboxylate transporter 1 (MCT1), a tool to stratify acute myeloid leukemia (AML) patients and a vehicle to kill cancer cells. *Oncotarget* **2017**, *8*, 82803–82823. [CrossRef]
26. Evans, K.W.; Yuca, E.; Scott, S.S.; Zhao, M.; Paez Arango, N.; Cruz Pico, C.X.; Saridogan, T.; Shariati, M.; Class, C.A.; Bristow, C.A.; et al. Oxidative Phosphorylation Is a Metabolic Vulnerability in Chemotherapy-Resistant Triple-Negative Breast Cancer. *Cancer Res.* **2021**, *81*, 5572–5581. [CrossRef]
27. Queiros, O.; Preto, A.; Pacheco, A.; Pinheiro, C.; Azevedo-Silva, J.; Moreira, R.; Pedro, M.; Ko, Y.H.; Pedersen, P.L.; Baltazar, F.; et al. Butyrate activates the monocarboxylate transporter MCT4 expression in breast cancer cells and enhances the antitumor activity of 3-bromopyruvate. *J. Bioenerg. Biomembr.* **2012**, *44*, 141–153. [CrossRef]
28. Morais-Santos, F.; Granja, S.; Miranda-Goncalves, V.; Moreira, A.H.; Queiros, S.; Vilaca, J.L.; Schmitt, F.C.; Longatto-Filho, A.; Paredes, J.; Baltazar, F.; et al. Targeting lactate transport suppresses in vivo breast tumour growth. *Oncotarget* **2015**, *6*, 19177–19189. [CrossRef]
29. Chen, E.; Wang, T.; Zhang, J.; Zhou, X.; Niu, Y.; Liu, F.; Zhong, Y.; Huang, D.; Chen, W. Mitochondrial Targeting and pH-Responsive Nanogels for Co-Delivery of Lonidamine and Paclitaxel to Conquer Drug Resistance. *Front. Bioeng. Biotechnol.* **2021**, *9*, 787320. [CrossRef]
30. Jiang, H.; Zhang, L.; Kuo, J.; Kuo, K.; Gautam, S.C.; Groc, L.; Rodriguez, A.I.; Koubi, D.; Hunter, T.J.; Corcoran, G.B.; et al. Resveratrol-induced apoptotic death in human U251 glioma cells. *Mol. Cancer Ther.* **2005**, *4*, 554–561. [CrossRef]
31. Adeshakin, F.O.; Adeshakin, A.O.; Liu, Z.; Cheng, J.; Zhang, P.; Yan, D.; Zhang, G.; Wan, X. Targeting Oxidative Phosphorylation-Proteasome Activity in Extracellular Detached Cells Promotes Anoikis and Inhibits Metastasis. *Life* **2021**, *12*, 42. [CrossRef]
32. Tavares-Valente, D.; Granja, S.; Baltazar, F.; Queiros, O. Bioenergetic modulators hamper cancer cell viability and enhance response to chemotherapy. *J. Cell. Mol. Med.* **2018**, *22*, 3782–3794. [CrossRef]
33. Vorobyev, P.O.; Kochetkov, D.V.; Chumakov, P.M.; Zakirova, N.F.; Zotova-Nefedorova, S.I.; Vasilenko, K.V.; Alekseeva, O.N.; Kochetkov, S.N.; Bartosch, B.; Lipatova, A.V.; et al. 2-Deoxyglucose, an Inhibitor of Glycolysis, Enhances the Oncolytic Effect of Coxsackievirus. *Cancers* **2022**, *14*, 5611. [CrossRef] [PubMed]
34. Parczyk, J.; Ruhnau, J.; Pelz, C.; Schilling, M.; Wu, H.; Piaskowski, N.N.; Eickholt, B.; Kuhn, H.; Danker, K.; Klein, A. Dichloroacetate and PX-478 exhibit strong synergistic effects in a various number of cancer cell lines. *BMC Cancer* **2021**, *21*, 481. [CrossRef] [PubMed]
35. Sun, Y.; Liu, Z.; Zou, X.; Lan, Y.; Sun, X.; Wang, X.; Zhao, S.; Jiang, C.; Liu, H. Mechanisms underlying 3-bromopyruvate-induced cell death in colon cancer. *J. Bioenerg. Biomembr.* **2015**, *47*, 319–329. [CrossRef] [PubMed]
36. Miranda-Goncalves, V.; Granja, S.; Martinho, O.; Honavar, M.; Pojo, M.; Costa, B.M.; Pires, M.M.; Pinheiro, C.; Cordeiro, M.; Bebiano, G.; et al. Hypoxia-mediated upregulation of MCT1 expression supports the glycolytic phenotype of glioblastomas. *Oncotarget* **2016**, *7*, 46335–46353. [CrossRef]

37. Cunha, A.; Rocha, A.C.; Barbosa, F.; Baiao, A.; Silva, P.; Sarmento, B.; Queiros, O. Glycolytic Inhibitors Potentiated the Activity of Paclitaxel and Their Nanoencapsulation Increased Their Delivery in a Lung Cancer Model. *Pharmaceutics* **2022**, *14*, 2021. [CrossRef]
38. Herst, P.M.; Berridge, M.V. Cell surface oxygen consumption: A major contributor to cellular oxygen consumption in glycolytic cancer cell lines. *Biochim. Biophys. Acta* **2007**, *1767*, 170–177. [CrossRef]
39. Ullah, M.S.; Davies, A.J.; Halestrap, A.P. The plasma membrane lactate transporter MCT4, but not MCT1, is up-regulated by hypoxia through a HIF-1alpha-dependent mechanism. *J. Biol. Chem.* **2006**, *281*, 9030–9037. [CrossRef]
40. Porporato, P.E.; Payen, V.L.; Perez-Escuredo, J.; De Saedeleer, C.J.; Danhier, P.; Copetti, T.; Dhup, S.; Tardy, M.; Vazeille, T.; Bouzin, C.; et al. A mitochondrial switch promotes tumor metastasis. *Cell Rep.* **2014**, *8*, 754–766. [CrossRef]
41. De Saedeleer, C.J.; Porporato, P.E.; Copetti, T.; Perez-Escuredo, J.; Payen, V.L.; Brisson, L.; Feron, O.; Sonveaux, P. Glucose deprivation increases monocarboxylate transporter 1 (MCT1) expression and MCT1-dependent tumor cell migration. *Oncogene* **2014**, *33*, 4060–4068. [CrossRef] [PubMed]
42. Kapur, A.; Mehta, P.; Simmons, A.D.; Ericksen, S.S.; Mehta, G.; Palecek, S.P.; Felder, M.; Stenerson, Z.; Nayak, A.; Dominguez, J.M.A.; et al. Atovaquone: An Inhibitor of Oxidative Phosphorylation as Studied in Gynecologic Cancers. *Cancers* **2022**, *14*, 2297. [CrossRef] [PubMed]
43. Valera, V.F.M.; Prabharasuth, D.; Chaimowitz, M.; Choudhury, M.; Phillips, J.; Konno, S. Is targeting glycolysis with 2-deoxyglucose a viable therapeutic approach to bladder cancer? *Int. J. Cancer Ther. Oncol.* **2017**, *5*, 511.
44. Ho, N.; Morrison, J.; Silva, A.; Coomber, B.L. The effect of 3-bromopyruvate on human colorectal cancer cells is dependent on glucose concentration but not hexokinase II expression. *Biosci. Rep.* **2016**, *36*, e00299. [CrossRef]
45. Yu, H.; Zhang, H.; Dong, M.; Wu, Z.; Shen, Z.; Xie, Y.; Kong, Z.; Dai, X.; Xu, B. Metabolic reprogramming and AMPKalpha1 pathway activation by caulerpin in colorectal cancer cells. *Int. J. Oncol.* **2017**, *50*, 161–172. [CrossRef]
46. Madhok, B.M.; Yeluri, S.; Perry, S.L.; Hughes, T.A.; Jayne, D.G. Dichloroacetate induces apoptosis and cell-cycle arrest in colorectal cancer cells. *Br. J. Cancer* **2010**, *102*, 1746–1752. [CrossRef]
47. Olinger, A.M.P.; Tummala, H. Effect of 2-Deoxyglucose on Colorectal Cancer Cell Lines. *J. Undergrad. Res.* **2013**, *11*, 5.
48. Miranda-Goncalves, V.; Goncalves, C.S.; Granja, S.; Vieira de Castro, J.; Reis, R.M.; Costa, B.M.; Baltazar, F. MCT1 Is a New Prognostic Biomarker and Its Therapeutic Inhibition Boosts Response to Temozolomide in Human Glioblastoma. *Cancers* **2021**, *13*, 3468. [CrossRef]
49. Akers, L.J.; Fang, W.; Levy, A.G.; Franklin, A.R.; Huang, P.; Zweidler-McKay, P.A. Targeting glycolysis in leukemia: A novel inhibitor 3-BrOP in combination with rapamycin. *Leuk. Res.* **2011**, *35*, 814–820. [CrossRef]
50. Saulle, E.; Spinello, I.; Quaranta, M.T.; Pasquini, L.; Pelosi, E.; Iorio, E.; Castelli, G.; Chirico, M.; Pisanu, M.E.; Ottone, T.; et al. Targeting Lactate Metabolism by Inhibiting MCT1 or MCT4 Impairs Leukemic Cell Proliferation, Induces Two Different Related Death-Pathways and Increases Chemotherapeutic Sensitivity of Acute Myeloid Leukemia Cells. *Front. Oncol.* **2020**, *10*, 621458. [CrossRef]
51. Vital, P.D.S.; Bonatelli, M.; Dias, M.P.; de Salis, L.V.V.; Pinto, M.T.; Baltazar, F.; Maria-Engler, S.S.; Pinheiro, C. 3-Bromopyruvate Suppresses the Malignant Phenotype of Vemurafenib-Resistant Melanoma Cells. *Int. J. Mol. Sci.* **2022**, *23*, 15650. [CrossRef] [PubMed]
52. Rodriguez-Enriquez, S.; Carreno-Fuentes, L.; Gallardo-Perez, J.C.; Saavedra, E.; Quezada, H.; Vega, A.; Marin-Hernandez, A.; Olin-Sandoval, V.; Torres-Marquez, M.E.; Moreno-Sanchez, R. Oxidative phosphorylation is impaired by prolonged hypoxia in breast and possibly in cervix carcinoma. *Int. J. Biochem. Cell Biol.* **2010**, *42*, 1744–1751. [CrossRef] [PubMed]
53. Tavares-Valente, D.; Baltazar, F.; Moreira, R.; Queiros, O. Cancer cell bioenergetics and pH regulation influence breast cancer cell resistance to paclitaxel and doxorubicin. *J. Bioenerg. Biomembr.* **2013**, *45*, 467–475. [CrossRef] [PubMed]
54. Korga, A.; Ostrowska, M.; Iwan, M.; Herbet, M.; Dudka, J. Inhibition of glycolysis disrupts cellular antioxidant defense and sensitizes HepG2 cells to doxorubicin treatment. *FEBS Open Bio* **2019**, *9*, 959–972. [CrossRef] [PubMed]
55. Jardim-Messeder, D.; Moreira-Pacheco, F. 3-Bromopyruvic Acid Inhibits Tricarboxylic Acid Cycle and Glutaminolysis in HepG2 Cells. *Anticancer Res.* **2016**, *36*, 2233–2241.
56. Jeon, J.Y.; Lee, M.; Whang, S.H.; Kim, J.W.; Cho, A.; Yun, M. Regulation of Acetate Utilization by Monocarboxylate Transporter 1 (MCT1) in Hepatocellular Carcinoma (HCC). *Oncol. Res.* **2018**, *26*, 71–81. [CrossRef]
57. Sun, H.; Zhu, A.; Zhou, X.; Wang, F. Suppression of pyruvate dehydrogenase kinase-2 re-sensitizes paclitaxel-resistant human lung cancer cells to paclitaxel. *Oncotarget* **2017**, *8*, 52642–52650. [CrossRef]
58. Danhier, P.; Banski, P.; Payen, V.L.; Grasso, D.; Ippolito, L.; Sonveaux, P.; Porporato, P.E. Cancer metabolism in space and time: Beyond the Warburg effect. *Biochim. Biophys. Acta Bioenerg.* **2017**, *1858*, 556–572. [CrossRef]
59. Vaupel, P.; Multhoff, G. Revisiting the Warburg effect: Historical dogma versus current understanding. *J. Physiol.* **2021**, *599*, 1745–1757. [CrossRef]
60. Ghanbari Movahed, Z.; Rastegari-Pouyani, M.; Mohammadi, M.H.; Mansouri, K. Cancer cells change their glucose metabolism to overcome increased ROS: One step from cancer cell to cancer stem cell? *Biomed. Pharmacother.* **2019**, *112*, 108690. [CrossRef]
61. Nadzialek, S.; Vanparys, C.; Van der Heiden, E.; Michaux, C.; Brose, F.; Scippo, M.L.; De Coen, W.; Kestemont, P. Understanding the gap between the estrogenicity of an effluent and its real impact into the wild. *Sci. Total Environ.* **2010**, *408*, 812–821. [CrossRef] [PubMed]
62. Kroemer, G.; Pouyssegur, J. Tumor cell metabolism: Cancer's Achilles' heel. *Cancer Cell* **2008**, *13*, 472–482. [CrossRef] [PubMed]

63. Kamarajugadda, S.; Stemboroski, L.; Cai, Q.; Simpson, N.E.; Nayak, S.; Tan, M.; Lu, J. Glucose oxidation modulates anoikis and tumor metastasis. *Mol. Cell. Biol.* **2012**, *32*, 1893–1907. [CrossRef] [PubMed]
64. Jesser, E.A.; Brady, N.J.; Huggins, D.N.; Witschen, P.M.; O'Connor, C.H.; Schwertfeger, K.L. STAT5 is activated in macrophages by breast cancer cell-derived factors and regulates macrophage function in the tumor microenvironment. *Breast Cancer Res.* **2021**, *23*, 104. [CrossRef]
65. Putney, L.K.; Barber, D.L. Expression profile of genes regulated by activity of the Na-H exchanger NHE1. *BMC Genom.* **2004**, *5*, 46. [CrossRef]
66. Christofk, H.R.; Vander Heiden, M.G.; Harris, M.H.; Ramanathan, A.; Gerszten, R.E.; Wei, R.; Fleming, M.D.; Schreiber, S.L.; Cantley, L.C. The M2 splice isoform of pyruvate kinase is important for cancer metabolism and tumour growth. *Nature* **2008**, *452*, 230–233. [CrossRef]
67. Mazurek, S. Pyruvate kinase type M2: A key regulator of the metabolic budget system in tumor cells. *Int. J. Biochem. Cell Biol.* **2011**, *43*, 969–980. [CrossRef]
68. Murugan, A.K.; Alzahrani, A.S. Isocitrate Dehydrogenase IDH1 and IDH2 Mutations in Human Cancer: Prognostic Implications for Gliomas. *Br. J. Biomed. Sci.* **2022**, *79*, 10208. [CrossRef]
69. Fu, Y.; Liu, S.; Yin, S.; Niu, W.; Xiong, W.; Tan, M.; Li, G.; Zhou, M. The reverse Warburg effect is likely to be an Achilles' heel of cancer that can be exploited for cancer therapy. *Oncotarget* **2017**, *8*, 57813–57825. [CrossRef]
70. Fan, T.W.; Kucia, M.; Jankowski, K.; Higashi, R.M.; Ratajczak, J.; Ratajczak, M.Z.; Lane, A.N. Rhabdomyosarcoma cells show an energy producing anabolic metabolic phenotype compared with primary myocytes. *Mol. Cancer* **2008**, *7*, 79. [CrossRef]
71. Minemura, H.; Takagi, K.; Sato, A.; Yamaguchi, M.; Hayashi, C.; Miki, Y.; Harada-Shoji, N.; Miyashita, M.; Sasano, H.; Suzuki, T. Isoforms of IDH in breast carcinoma: IDH2 as a potent prognostic factor associated with proliferation in estrogen-receptor positive cases. *Breast Cancer* **2021**, *28*, 915–926. [CrossRef] [PubMed]
72. Lunetti, P.; Di Giacomo, M.; Vergara, D.; De Domenico, S.; Maffia, M.; Zara, V.; Capobianco, L.; Ferramosca, A. Metabolic reprogramming in breast cancer results in distinct mitochondrial bioenergetics between luminal and basal subtypes. *FEBS J.* **2019**, *286*, 688–709. [CrossRef] [PubMed]
73. Pertega-Gomes, N.; Vizcaino, J.R.; Attig, J.; Jurmeister, S.; Lopes, C.; Baltazar, F. A lactate shuttle system between tumour and stromal cells is associated with poor prognosis in prostate cancer. *BMC Cancer* **2014**, *14*, 352. [CrossRef] [PubMed]
74. Pavlides, S.; Whitaker-Menezes, D.; Castello-Cros, R.; Flomenberg, N.; Witkiewicz, A.K.; Frank, P.G.; Casimiro, M.C.; Wang, C.; Fortina, P.; Addya, S.; et al. The reverse Warburg effect: Aerobic glycolysis in cancer associated fibroblasts and the tumor stroma. *Cell Cycle* **2009**, *8*, 3984–4001. [CrossRef]
75. Arcucci, A.; Ruocco, M.R.; Granato, G.; Sacco, A.M.; Montagnani, S. Cancer: An Oxidative Crosstalk between Solid Tumor Cells and Cancer Associated Fibroblasts. *Biomed. Res. Int.* **2016**, *2016*, 4502846. [CrossRef]
76. Chan, J.S.; Tan, M.J.; Sng, M.K.; Teo, Z.; Phua, T.; Choo, C.C.; Li, L.; Zhu, P.; Tan, N.S. Cancer-associated fibroblasts enact field cancerization by promoting extratumoral oxidative stress. *Cell Death Dis.* **2017**, *8*, e2562. [CrossRef]
77. Faubert, B.; Li, K.Y.; Cai, L.; Hensley, C.T.; Kim, J.; Zacharias, L.G.; Yang, C.; Do, Q.N.; Doucette, S.; Burguete, D.; et al. Lactate Metabolism in Human Lung Tumors. *Cell* **2017**, *171*, 358–371.e359. [CrossRef]
78. Roy, S.; Kumaravel, S.; Sharma, A.; Duran, C.L.; Bayless, K.J.; Chakraborty, S. Hypoxic tumor microenvironment: Implications for cancer therapy. *Exp. Biol. Med.* **2020**, *245*, 1073–1086. [CrossRef]
79. Lunt, S.Y.; Vander Heiden, M.G. Aerobic glycolysis: Meeting the metabolic requirements of cell proliferation. *Annu. Rev. Cell Dev. Biol.* **2011**, *27*, 441–464. [CrossRef]
80. Rezayatmand, H.; Razmkhah, M.; Razeghian-Jahromi, I. Drug resistance in cancer therapy: The Pandora's Box of cancer stem cells. *Stem Cell Res. Ther.* **2022**, *13*, 181. [CrossRef]
81. De Las Rivas, J.; Brozovic, A.; Izraely, S.; Casas-Pais, A.; Witz, I.P.; Figueroa, A. Cancer drug resistance induced by EMT: Novel therapeutic strategies. *Arch. Toxicol.* **2021**, *95*, 2279–2297. [CrossRef] [PubMed]
82. Fletcher, J.I.; Haber, M.; Henderson, M.J.; Norris, M.D. ABC transporters in cancer: More than just drug efflux pumps. *Nat. Rev. Cancer* **2010**, *10*, 147–156. [CrossRef] [PubMed]
83. Vasan, N.; Baselga, J.; Hyman, D.M. A view on drug resistance in cancer. *Nature* **2019**, *575*, 299–309. [CrossRef]
84. Mantovani, F.; Collavin, L.; Del Sal, G. Mutant p53 as a guardian of the cancer cell. *Cell Death Differ.* **2019**, *26*, 199–212. [CrossRef] [PubMed]
85. Ding, L.; Ley, T.J.; Larson, D.E.; Miller, C.A.; Koboldt, D.C.; Welch, J.S.; Ritchey, J.K.; Young, M.A.; Lamprecht, T.; McLellan, M.D.; et al. Clonal evolution in relapsed acute myeloid leukaemia revealed by whole-genome sequencing. *Nature* **2012**, *481*, 506–510. [CrossRef] [PubMed]
86. Cancer Genome Atlas Research Network. Integrated genomic analyses of ovarian carcinoma. *Nature* **2011**, *474*, 609–615. [CrossRef]
87. Lord, C.J.; Ashworth, A. Mechanisms of resistance to therapies targeting BRCA-mutant cancers. *Nat. Med.* **2013**, *19*, 1381–1388. [CrossRef]
88. Kim, H.; Xu, H.; George, E.; Hallberg, D.; Kumar, S.; Jagannathan, V.; Medvedev, S.; Kinose, Y.; Devins, K.; Verma, P.; et al. Combining PARP with ATR inhibition overcomes PARP inhibitor and platinum resistance in ovarian cancer models. *Nat. Commun.* **2020**, *11*, 3726. [CrossRef]

89. Kaplon, J.; Zheng, L.; Meissl, K.; Chaneton, B.; Selivanov, V.A.; Mackay, G.; van der Burg, S.H.; Verdegaal, E.M.; Cascante, M.; Shlomi, T.; et al. A key role for mitochondrial gatekeeper pyruvate dehydrogenase in oncogene-induced senescence. *Nature* **2013**, *498*, 109–112. [CrossRef]
90. Swanton, C. Intratumor heterogeneity: Evolution through space and time. *Cancer Res.* **2012**, *72*, 4875–4882. [CrossRef]
91. Jia, D.; Park, J.H.; Kaur, H.; Jung, K.H.; Yang, S.; Tripathi, S.; Galbraith, M.; Deng, Y.; Jolly, M.K.; Kaipparettu, B.A.; et al. Towards decoding the coupled decision-making of metabolism and epithelial-to-mesenchymal transition in cancer. *Br. J. Cancer* **2021**, *124*, 1902–1911. [CrossRef] [PubMed]
92. Inoue, A.; Seidel, M.G.; Wu, W.; Kamizono, S.; Ferrando, A.A.; Bronson, R.T.; Iwasaki, H.; Akashi, K.; Morimoto, A.; Hitzler, J.K.; et al. Slug, a highly conserved zinc finger transcriptional repressor, protects hematopoietic progenitor cells from radiation-induced apoptosis in vivo. *Cancer Cell* **2002**, *2*, 279–288. [CrossRef] [PubMed]
93. Olmeda, D.; Moreno-Bueno, G.; Flores, J.M.; Fabra, A.; Portillo, F.; Cano, A. SNAI1 is required for tumor growth and lymph node metastasis of human breast carcinoma MDA-MB-231 cells. *Cancer Res.* **2007**, *67*, 11721–11731. [CrossRef] [PubMed]
94. Tavares-Valente, D.; Cannone, S.; Greco, M.R.; Carvalho, T.M.A.; Baltazar, F.; Queiros, O.; Agrimi, G.; Reshkin, S.J.; Cardone, R.A. Extracellular Matrix Collagen I Differentially Regulates the Metabolic Plasticity of Pancreatic Ductal Adenocarcinoma Parenchymal Cell and Cancer Stem Cell. *Cancers* **2023**, *15*, 3868. [CrossRef] [PubMed]
95. Jing, Y.; Han, Z.; Zhang, S.; Liu, Y.; Wei, L. Epithelial-Mesenchymal Transition in tumor microenvironment. *Cell Biosci.* **2011**, *1*, 29. [CrossRef]
96. Taki, M.; Abiko, K.; Ukita, M.; Murakami, R.; Yamanoi, K.; Yamaguchi, K.; Hamanishi, J.; Baba, T.; Matsumura, N.; Mandai, M. Tumor Immune Microenvironment during Epithelial-Mesenchymal Transition. *Clin. Cancer Res.* **2021**, *27*, 4669–4679. [CrossRef]
97. Wang, Q.; Wu, M.; Li, H.; Rao, X.; Ao, L.; Wang, H.; Yao, L.; Wang, X.; Hong, X.; Wang, J.; et al. Therapeutic targeting of glutamate dehydrogenase 1 that links metabolic reprogramming and Snail-mediated epithelial-mesenchymal transition in drug-resistant lung cancer. *Pharmacol. Res.* **2022**, *185*, 106490. [CrossRef]
98. Fischer, K.R.; Durrans, A.; Lee, S.; Sheng, J.; Li, F.; Wong, S.T.; Choi, H.; El Rayes, T.; Ryu, S.; Troeger, J.; et al. Epithelial-to-mesenchymal transition is not required for lung metastasis but contributes to chemoresistance. *Nature* **2015**, *527*, 472–476. [CrossRef]
99. Brown, M.S.; Abdollahi, B.; Wilkins, O.M.; Lu, H.; Chakraborty, P.; Ognjenovic, N.B.; Muller, K.E.; Jolly, M.K.; Christensen, B.C.; Hassanpour, S.; et al. Phenotypic heterogeneity driven by plasticity of the intermediate EMT state governs disease progression and metastasis in breast cancer. *Sci. Adv.* **2022**, *8*, eabj8002. [CrossRef]
100. Ochi, K.; Suzawa, K.; Tomida, S.; Shien, K.; Takano, J.; Miyauchi, S.; Takeda, T.; Miura, A.; Araki, K.; Nakata, K.; et al. Overcoming epithelial-mesenchymal transition-mediated drug resistance with monensin-based combined therapy in non-small cell lung cancer. *Biochem. Biophys. Res. Commun.* **2020**, *529*, 760–765. [CrossRef]
101. Du, B.; Shim, J.S. Targeting Epithelial-Mesenchymal Transition (EMT) to Overcome Drug Resistance in Cancer. *Molecules* **2016**, *21*, 965. [CrossRef] [PubMed]
102. Saitoh, M. Epithelial-mesenchymal transition is regulated at post-transcriptional levels by transforming growth factor-beta signaling during tumor progression. *Cancer Sci.* **2015**, *106*, 481–488. [CrossRef] [PubMed]
103. Jolly, M.K.; Celia-Terrassa, T. Dynamics of Phenotypic Heterogeneity Associated with EMT and Stemness during Cancer Progression. *J. Clin. Med.* **2019**, *8*, 1542. [CrossRef] [PubMed]
104. Yan, L.; Tu, B.; Yao, J.; Gong, J.; Carugo, A.; Bristow, C.A.; Wang, Q.; Zhu, C.; Dai, B.; Kang, Y.; et al. Targeting Glucose Metabolism Sensitizes Pancreatic Cancer to MEK Inhibition. *Cancer Res.* **2021**, *81*, 4054–4065. [CrossRef]
105. Guo, J.; Satoh, K.; Tabata, S.; Mori, M.; Tomita, M.; Soga, T. Reprogramming of glutamine metabolism via glutamine synthetase silencing induces cisplatin resistance in A2780 ovarian cancer cells. *BMC Cancer* **2021**, *21*, 174. [CrossRef]
106. Guo, J.; Yu, J.; Peng, F.; Li, J.; Tan, Z.; Chen, Y.; Rao, T.; Wang, Y.; Peng, J.; Zhou, H. In vitro and in vivo analysis of metabolites involved in the TCA cycle and glutamine metabolism associated with cisplatin resistance in human lung cancer. *Expert Rev. Proteom.* **2021**, *18*, 233–240. [CrossRef] [PubMed]
107. Li, J.; Eu, J.Q.; Kong, L.R.; Wang, L.; Lim, Y.C.; Goh, B.C.; Wong, A.L.A. Targeting Metabolism in Cancer Cells and the Tumour Microenvironment for Cancer Therapy. *Molecules* **2020**, *25*, 4831. [CrossRef]
108. Lotz, C.; Kelleher, D.K.; Gassner, B.; Gekle, M.; Vaupel, P.; Thews, O. Role of the tumor microenvironment in the activity and expression of the p-glycoprotein in human colon carcinoma cells. *Oncol. Rep.* **2007**, *17*, 239–244. [CrossRef]
109. Skeberdyte, A.; Sarapiniene, I.; Aleksander-Krasko, J.; Stankevicius, V.; Suziedelis, K.; Jarmalaite, S. Dichloroacetate and Salinomycin Exert a Synergistic Cytotoxic Effect in Colorectal Cancer Cell Lines. *Sci. Rep.* **2018**, *8*, 17744. [CrossRef]
110. Juan-Carlos, P.M.; Perla-Lidia, P.P.; Stephanie-Talia, M.M.; Monica-Griselda, A.M.; Luz-Maria, T.E. ABC transporter superfamily. An updated overview, relevance in cancer multidrug resistance and perspectives with personalized medicine. *Mol. Biol. Rep.* **2021**, *48*, 1883–1901. [CrossRef]
111. Xiao, H.; Zheng, Y.; Ma, L.; Tian, L.; Sun, Q. Clinically-Relevant ABC Transporter for Anti-Cancer Drug Resistance. *Front. Pharmacol.* **2021**, *12*, 648407. [CrossRef] [PubMed]
112. Robert, J.; Morvan, V.L.; Smith, D.; Pourquier, P.; Bonnet, J. Predicting drug response and toxicity based on gene polymorphisms. *Crit. Rev. Oncol. Hematol.* **2005**, *54*, 171–196. [CrossRef] [PubMed]
113. Aye, I.L.; Singh, A.T.; Keelan, J.A. Transport of lipids by ABC proteins: Interactions and implications for cellular toxicity, viability and function. *Chem. Biol. Interact.* **2009**, *180*, 327–339. [CrossRef]

114. Bugde, P.; Biswas, R.; Merien, F.; Lu, J.; Liu, D.X.; Chen, M.; Zhou, S.; Li, Y. The therapeutic potential of targeting ABC transporters to combat multi-drug resistance. *Expert Opin. Ther. Targets* **2017**, *21*, 511–530. [CrossRef] [PubMed]
115. Wang, S.A.; Young, M.J.; Wang, Y.C.; Chen, S.H.; Liu, C.Y.; Lo, Y.A.; Jen, H.H.; Hsu, K.C.; Hung, J.J. USP24 promotes drug resistance during cancer therapy. *Cell Death Differ.* **2021**, *28*, 2690–2707. [CrossRef]
116. Fletcher, J.I.; Williams, R.T.; Henderson, M.J.; Norris, M.D.; Haber, M. ABC transporters as mediators of drug resistance and contributors to cancer cell biology. *Drug Resist. Updates* **2016**, *26*, 1–9. [CrossRef]
117. Welte, Y.; Adjaye, J.; Lehrach, H.R.; Regenbrecht, C.R. Cancer stem cells in solid tumors: Elusive or illusive? *Cell Commun. Signal.* **2010**, *8*, 6. [CrossRef]
118. Scharenberg, C.W.; Harkey, M.A.; Torok-Storb, B. The ABCG2 transporter is an efficient Hoechst 33342 efflux pump and is preferentially expressed by immature human hematopoietic progenitors. *Blood* **2002**, *99*, 507–512. [CrossRef]
119. Zochbauer-Muller, S.; Filipits, M.; Rudas, M.; Brunner, R.; Krajnik, G.; Suchomel, R.; Schmid, K.; Pirker, R. P-glycoprotein and MRP1 expression in axillary lymph node metastases of breast cancer patients. *Anticancer Res.* **2001**, *21*, 119–124.
120. Ambudkar, S.V.; Kimchi-Sarfaty, C.; Sauna, Z.E.; Gottesman, M.M. P-glycoprotein: From genomics to mechanism. *Oncogene* **2003**, *22*, 7468–7485. [CrossRef]
121. Fung, K.L.; Gottesman, M.M. A synonymous polymorphism in a common MDR1 (ABCB1) haplotype shapes protein function. *Biochim. Biophys. Acta* **2009**, *1794*, 860–871. [CrossRef] [PubMed]
122. Dulucq, S.; Bouchet, S.; Turcq, B.; Lippert, E.; Etienne, G.; Reiffers, J.; Molimard, M.; Krajinovic, M.; Mahon, F.X. Multidrug resistance gene (MDR1) polymorphisms are associated with major molecular responses to standard-dose imatinib in chronic myeloid leukemia. *Blood* **2008**, *112*, 2024–2027. [CrossRef] [PubMed]
123. Robinson, L.J.; Roberts, W.K.; Ling, T.T.; Lamming, D.; Sternberg, S.S.; Roepe, P.D. Human MDR 1 protein overexpression delays the apoptotic cascade in Chinese hamster ovary fibroblasts. *Biochemistry* **1997**, *36*, 11169–11178. [CrossRef] [PubMed]
124. Smyth, M.J.; Krasovskis, E.; Sutton, V.R.; Johnstone, R.W. The drug efflux protein, P-glycoprotein, additionally protects drug-resistant tumor cells from multiple forms of caspase-dependent apoptosis. *Proc. Natl. Acad. Sci. USA* **1998**, *95*, 7024–7029. [CrossRef] [PubMed]
125. Yin, W.; Xiang, D.; Wang, T.; Zhang, Y.; Pham, C.V.; Zhou, S.; Jiang, G.; Hou, Y.; Zhu, Y.; Han, Y.; et al. The inhibition of ABCB1/MDR1 or ABCG2/BCRP enables doxorubicin to eliminate liver cancer stem cells. *Sci. Rep.* **2021**, *11*, 10791. [CrossRef]
126. Hattinger, C.M.; Stoico, G.; Michelacci, F.; Pasello, M.; Scionti, I.; Remondini, D.; Castellani, G.C.; Fanelli, M.; Scotlandi, K.; Picci, P.; et al. Mechanisms of gene amplification and evidence of coamplification in drug-resistant human osteosarcoma cell lines. *Genes Chromosomes Cancer* **2009**, *48*, 289–309. [CrossRef]
127. Liu, X.; Yuan, J.; Zhang, X.; Li, L.; Dai, X.; Chen, Q.; Wang, Y. ATF3 Modulates the Resistance of Breast Cancer Cells to Tamoxifen through an N(6)-Methyladenosine-Based Epitranscriptomic Mechanism. *Chem. Res. Toxicol.* **2021**, *34*, 1814–1821. [CrossRef]
128. Yusuf, R.Z.; Duan, Z.; Lamendola, D.E.; Penson, R.T.; Seiden, M.V. Paclitaxel resistance: Molecular mechanisms and pharmacologic manipulation. *Curr. Cancer Drug Targets* **2003**, *3*, 1–19. [CrossRef]
129. Hadzic, T.; Aykin-Burns, N.; Zhu, Y.; Coleman, M.C.; Leick, K.; Jacobson, G.M.; Spitz, D.R. Paclitaxel combined with inhibitors of glucose and hydroperoxide metabolism enhances breast cancer cell killing via H2O2-mediated oxidative stress. *Free Radic. Biol. Med.* **2010**, *48*, 1024–1033. [CrossRef]
130. Cole, S.P. Targeting multidrug resistance protein 1 (MRP1, ABCC1): Past, present, and future. *Annu. Rev. Pharmacol. Toxicol.* **2014**, *54*, 95–117. [CrossRef]
131. Emmanouilidi, A.; Casari, I.; Gokcen Akkaya, B.; Maffucci, T.; Furic, L.; Guffanti, F.; Broggini, M.; Chen, X.; Maxuitenko, Y.Y.; Keeton, A.B.; et al. Inhibition of the Lysophosphatidylinositol Transporter ABCC1 Reduces Prostate Cancer Cell Growth and Sensitizes to Chemotherapy. *Cancers* **2020**, *12*, 2022. [CrossRef] [PubMed]
132. Schinkel, A.H.; Jonker, J.W. Mammalian drug efflux transporters of the ATP binding cassette (ABC) family: An overview. *Adv. Drug Deliv. Rev.* **2003**, *55*, 3–29. [CrossRef] [PubMed]
133. Cole, S.P. Multidrug resistance protein 1 (MRP1, ABCC1), a "multitasking" ATP-binding cassette (ABC) transporter. *J. Biol. Chem.* **2014**, *289*, 30880–30888. [CrossRef] [PubMed]
134. Wu, Z.; Li, X.; Zeng, Y.; Zhuang, X.; Shen, H.; Zhu, H.; Liu, H.; Xiao, H. In vitro and in vivo inhibition of MRP gene expression and reversal of multidrug resistance by siRNA. *Basic Clin. Pharmacol. Toxicol.* **2011**, *108*, 177–184. [CrossRef]
135. Sullivan, G.F.; Yang, J.M.; Vassil, A.; Yang, J.; Bash-Babula, J.; Hait, W.N. Regulation of expression of the multidrug resistance protein MRP1 by p53 in human prostate cancer cells. *J. Clin. Investig.* **2000**, *105*, 1261–1267. [CrossRef]
136. Zhou, X.; Huang, J.M.; Li, T.M.; Liu, J.Q.; Wei, Z.L.; Lan, C.L.; Zhu, G.Z.; Liao, X.W.; Ye, X.P.; Peng, T. Clinical Significance and Potential Mechanisms of ATP Binding Cassette Subfamily C Genes in Hepatocellular Carcinoma. *Front. Genet.* **2022**, *13*, 805961. [CrossRef]
137. Zander, S.A.; Kersbergen, A.; van der Burg, E.; de Water, N.; van Tellingen, O.; Gunnarsdottir, S.; Jaspers, J.E.; Pajic, M.; Nygren, A.O.; Jonkers, J.; et al. Sensitivity and acquired resistance of BRCA1;p53-deficient mouse mammary tumors to the topoisomerase I inhibitor topotecan. *Cancer Res.* **2010**, *70*, 1700–1710. [CrossRef]
138. Deng, F.; Sjostedt, N.; Santo, M.; Neuvonen, M.; Niemi, M.; Kidron, H. Novel inhibitors of breast cancer resistance protein (BCRP, ABCG2) among marketed drugs. *Eur. J. Pharm. Sci.* **2023**, *181*, 106362. [CrossRef]
139. Robey, R.W.; Massey, P.R.; Amiri-Kordestani, L.; Bates, S.E. ABC transporters: Unvalidated therapeutic targets in cancer and the CNS. *Anticancer Agents Med. Chem.* **2010**, *10*, 625–633. [CrossRef]

140. Rabindran, S.K.; He, H.; Singh, M.; Brown, E.; Collins, K.I.; Annable, T.; Greenberger, L.M. Reversal of a novel multidrug resistance mechanism in human colon carcinoma cells by fumitremorgin C. *Cancer Res.* **1998**, *58*, 5850–5858.
141. Nishiyama, M.; Kuga, T. Central effects of the neurotropic mycotoxin fumitremorgin A in the rabbit (I). Effects on the spinal cord. *Jpn. J. Pharmacol.* **1989**, *50*, 167–173. [CrossRef] [PubMed]
142. Allen, J.D.; van Loevezijn, A.; Lakhai, J.M.; van der Valk, M.; van Tellingen, O.; Reid, G.; Schellens, J.H.; Koomen, G.J.; Schinkel, A.H. Potent and specific inhibition of the breast cancer resistance protein multidrug transporter in vitro and in mouse intestine by a novel analogue of fumitremorgin C. *Mol. Cancer Ther.* **2002**, *1*, 417–425. [PubMed]
143. Weidner, L.D.; Zoghbi, S.S.; Lu, S.; Shukla, S.; Ambudkar, S.V.; Pike, V.W.; Mulder, J.; Gottesman, M.M.; Innis, R.B.; Hall, M.D. The Inhibitor Ko143 Is Not Specific for ABCG2. *J. Pharmacol. Exp. Ther.* **2015**, *354*, 384–393. [CrossRef] [PubMed]
144. Kita, D.H.; Guragossian, N.; Zattoni, I.F.; Moure, V.R.; Rego, F.G.M.; Lusvarghi, S.; Moulenat, T.; Belhani, B.; Picheth, G.; Bouacida, S.; et al. Mechanistic basis of breast cancer resistance protein inhibition by new indeno[1,2-b]indoles. *Sci. Rep.* **2021**, *11*, 1788. [CrossRef]
145. Robey, R.W.; Pluchino, K.M.; Hall, M.D.; Fojo, A.T.; Bates, S.E.; Gottesman, M.M. Revisiting the role of ABC transporters in multidrug-resistant cancer. *Nat. Rev. Cancer* **2018**, *18*, 452–464. [CrossRef]
146. Maher, J.C.; Wangpaichitr, M.; Savaraj, N.; Kurtoglu, M.; Lampidis, T.J. Hypoxia-inducible factor-1 confers resistance to the glycolytic inhibitor 2-deoxy-D-glucose. *Mol. Cancer Ther.* **2007**, *6*, 732–741. [CrossRef]
147. Reina-Campos, M.; Moscat, J.; Diaz-Meco, M. Metabolism shapes the tumor microenvironment. *Curr. Opin. Cell Biol.* **2017**, *48*, 47–53. [CrossRef]
148. Liu, C.; Jin, Y.; Fan, Z. The Mechanism of Warburg Effect-Induced Chemoresistance in Cancer. *Front. Oncol.* **2021**, *11*, 698023. [CrossRef]
149. Tavares-Valente, D.; Sousa, B.; Schmitt, F.; Baltazar, F.; Queiros, O. Disruption of pH Dynamics Suppresses Proliferation and Potentiates Doxorubicin Cytotoxicity in Breast Cancer Cells. *Pharmaceutics* **2021**, *13*, 242. [CrossRef]
150. Kim, J.Y.; Lee, J.Y. Targeting Tumor Adaption to Chronic Hypoxia: Implications for Drug Resistance, and How It Can Be Overcome. *Int. J. Mol. Sci.* **2017**, *18*, 1854. [CrossRef]
151. Li, X.; Zhong, Y.; Lu, J.; Axcrona, K.; Eide, L.; Syljuasen, R.G.; Peng, Q.; Wang, J.; Zhang, H.; Goscinski, M.A.; et al. MtDNA depleted PC3 cells exhibit Warburg effect and cancer stem cell features. *Oncotarget* **2016**, *7*, 40297–40313. [CrossRef] [PubMed]
152. Schiliro, C.; Firestein, B.L. Mechanisms of Metabolic Reprogramming in Cancer Cells Supporting Enhanced Growth and Proliferation. *Cells* **2021**, *10*, 1056. [CrossRef] [PubMed]
153. Kozal, K.; Jozwiak, P.; Krzeslak, A. Contemporary Perspectives on the Warburg Effect Inhibition in Cancer Therapy. *Cancer Control* **2021**, *28*, 10732748211041243. [CrossRef]
154. Sonveaux, P.; Vegran, F.; Schroeder, T.; Wergin, M.C.; Verrax, J.; Rabbani, Z.N.; De Saedeleer, C.J.; Kennedy, K.M.; Diepart, C.; Jordan, B.F.; et al. Targeting lactate-fueled respiration selectively kills hypoxic tumor cells in mice. *J. Clin. Investig.* **2008**, *118*, 3930–3942. [CrossRef] [PubMed]
155. Guan, X.; Bryniarski, M.A.; Morris, M.E. In Vitro and In Vivo Efficacy of the Monocarboxylate Transporter 1 Inhibitor AR-C155858 in the Murine 4T1 Breast Cancer Tumor Model. *AAPS J.* **2018**, *21*, 3. [CrossRef]
156. Curtis, N.J.; Mooney, L.; Hopcroft, L.; Michopoulos, F.; Whalley, N.; Zhong, H.; Murray, C.; Logie, A.; Revill, M.; Byth, K.F.; et al. Pre-clinical pharmacology of AZD3965, a selective inhibitor of MCT1: DLBCL, NHL and Burkitt's lymphoma anti-tumor activity. *Oncotarget* **2017**, *8*, 69219–69236. [CrossRef]
157. Noble, R.A.; Bell, N.; Blair, H.; Sikka, A.; Thomas, H.; Phillips, N.; Nakjang, S.; Miwa, S.; Crossland, R.; Rand, V.; et al. Inhibition of monocarboxyate transporter 1 by AZD3965 as a novel therapeutic approach for diffuse large B-cell lymphoma and Burkitt lymphoma. *Haematologica* **2017**, *102*, 1247–1257. [CrossRef]
158. Halford, S.; Veal, G.J.; Wedge, S.R.; Payne, G.S.; Bacon, C.M.; Sloan, P.; Dragoni, I.; Heinzmann, K.; Potter, S.; Salisbury, B.M.; et al. A Phase I Dose-escalation Study of AZD3965, an Oral Monocarboxylate Transporter 1 Inhibitor, in Patients with Advanced Cancer. *Clin. Cancer Res.* **2023**, *29*, 1429–1439. [CrossRef]
159. Akins, N.S.; Nielson, T.C.; Le, H.V. Inhibition of Glycolysis and Glutaminolysis: An Emerging Drug Discovery Approach to Combat Cancer. *Curr. Top. Med. Chem.* **2018**, *18*, 494–504. [CrossRef]
160. Saunier, E.; Antonio, S.; Regazzetti, A.; Auzeil, N.; Laprevote, O.; Shay, J.W.; Coumoul, X.; Barouki, R.; Benelli, C.; Huc, L.; et al. Resveratrol reverses the Warburg effect by targeting the pyruvate dehydrogenase complex in colon cancer cells. *Sci. Rep.* **2017**, *7*, 6945. [CrossRef]
161. Pranzini, E.; Pardella, E.; Paoli, P.; Fendt, S.M.; Taddei, M.L. Metabolic Reprogramming in Anticancer Drug Resistance: A Focus on Amino Acids. *Trends Cancer* **2021**, *7*, 682–699. [CrossRef] [PubMed]
162. Li, T.; Copeland, C.; Le, A. Glutamine Metabolism in Cancer. *Adv. Exp. Med. Biol.* **2021**, *1311*, 17–38. [CrossRef] [PubMed]
163. Ma, W.W.; Jacene, H.; Song, D.; Vilardell, F.; Messersmith, W.A.; Laheru, D.; Wahl, R.; Endres, C.; Jimeno, A.; Pomper, M.G.; et al. [18F]fluorodeoxyglucose positron emission tomography correlates with Akt pathway activity but is not predictive of clinical outcome during mTOR inhibitor therapy. *J. Clin. Oncol.* **2009**, *27*, 2697–2704. [CrossRef] [PubMed]
164. Bhutia, Y.D.; Babu, E.; Ramachandran, S.; Ganapathy, V. Amino Acid transporters in cancer and their relevance to "glutamine addiction": Novel targets for the design of a new class of anticancer drugs. *Cancer Res.* **2015**, *75*, 1782–1788. [CrossRef]
165. Wise, D.R.; Thompson, C.B. Glutamine addiction: A new therapeutic target in cancer. *Trends Biochem. Sci.* **2010**, *35*, 427–433. [CrossRef]

166. Poillet-Perez, L.; Xie, X.; Zhan, L.; Yang, Y.; Sharp, D.W.; Hu, Z.S.; Su, X.; Maganti, A.; Jiang, C.; Lu, W.; et al. Autophagy maintains tumour growth through circulating arginine. *Nature* **2018**, *563*, 569–573. [CrossRef]
167. Gandhi, N.; Das, G.M. Metabolic Reprogramming in Breast Cancer and Its Therapeutic Implications. *Cells* **2019**, *8*, 89. [CrossRef]
168. Kurihara-Shimomura, M.; Sasahira, T.; Nakashima, C.; Kuniyasu, H.; Shimomura, H.; Kirita, T. The Multifarious Functions of Pyruvate Kinase M2 in Oral Cancer Cells. *Int. J. Mol. Sci.* **2018**, *19*, 2907. [CrossRef]
169. Li, T.E.; Wang, S.; Shen, X.T.; Zhang, Z.; Chen, M.; Wang, H.; Zhu, Y.; Xu, D.; Hu, B.Y.; Wei, R.; et al. PKM2 Drives Hepatocellular Carcinoma Progression by Inducing Immunosuppressive Microenvironment. *Front. Immunol.* **2020**, *11*, 589997. [CrossRef]
170. Zhou, Y.; Huang, Z.; Su, J.; Li, J.; Zhao, S.; Wu, L.; Zhang, J.; He, Y.; Zhang, G.; Tao, J.; et al. Benserazide is a novel inhibitor targeting PKM2 for melanoma treatment. *Int. J. Cancer* **2020**, *147*, 139–151. [CrossRef]
171. Nakano, A.; Tsuji, D.; Miki, H.; Cui, Q.; El Sayed, S.M.; Ikegame, A.; Oda, A.; Amou, H.; Nakamura, S.; Harada, T.; et al. Glycolysis inhibition inactivates ABC transporters to restore drug sensitivity in malignant cells. *PLoS ONE* **2011**, *6*, e27222. [CrossRef]
172. Ma, S.; Jia, R.; Li, D.; Shen, B. Targeting Cellular Metabolism Chemosensitizes the Doxorubicin-Resistant Human Breast Adenocarcinoma Cells. *Biomed. Res. Int.* **2015**, *2015*, 453986. [CrossRef]
173. Prieto-Vila, M.; Takahashi, R.U.; Usuba, W.; Kohama, I.; Ochiya, T. Drug Resistance Driven by Cancer Stem Cells and Their Niche. *Int. J. Mol. Sci.* **2017**, *18*, 2574. [CrossRef] [PubMed]
174. Martins, J.P.; das Neves, J.; de la Fuente, M.; Celia, C.; Florindo, H.; Gunday-Tureli, N.; Popat, A.; Santos, J.L.; Sousa, F.; Schmid, R.; et al. The solid progress of nanomedicine. *Drug Deliv. Transl. Res.* **2020**, *10*, 726–729. [CrossRef] [PubMed]
175. Yang, Y.; Zheng, X.; Chen, L.; Gong, X.; Yang, H.; Duan, X.; Zhu, Y. Multifunctional Gold Nanoparticles in Cancer Diagnosis and Treatment. *Int. J. Nanomed.* **2022**, *17*, 2041–2067. [CrossRef] [PubMed]
176. Yao, W.; Yao, J.; Qian, F.; Que, Z.; Yu, P.; Luo, T.; Zheng, D.; Zhang, Z.; Tian, J. Paclitaxel-loaded and folic acid-modified PLGA nanomedicine with glutathione response for the treatment of lung cancer. *Acta Biochim. Biophys. Sin.* **2021**, *53*, 1027–1036. [CrossRef]
177. van den Boogaard, W.M.C.; Komninos, D.S.J.; Vermeij, W.P. Chemotherapy Side-Effects: Not All DNA Damage Is Equal. *Cancers* **2022**, *14*, 627. [CrossRef]
178. Sousa, A.R.; Oliveira, M.J.; Sarmento, B. Impact of CEA-targeting Nanoparticles for Drug Delivery in Colorectal Cancer. *J. Pharmacol. Exp. Ther.* **2019**, *370*, 657–670. [CrossRef]
179. Barenholz, Y. Doxil(R)—The first FDA-approved nano-drug: Lessons learned. *J. Control. Release* **2012**, *160*, 117–134. [CrossRef]
180. Blair, H.A.; Deeks, E.D. Albumin-Bound Paclitaxel: A Review in Non-Small Cell Lung Cancer. *Drugs* **2015**, *75*, 2017–2024. [CrossRef]
181. Zhao, M.; van Straten, D.; Broekman, M.L.D.; Preat, V.; Schiffelers, R.M. Nanocarrier-based drug combination therapy for glioblastoma. *Theranostics* **2020**, *10*, 1355–1372. [CrossRef] [PubMed]
182. Zheng, R.R.; Zhao, L.P.; Liu, L.S.; Deng, F.A.; Chen, X.Y.; Jiang, X.Y.; Wang, C.; Yu, X.Y.; Cheng, H.; Li, S.Y. Self-delivery nanomedicine to overcome drug resistance for synergistic chemotherapy. *Biomater. Sci.* **2021**, *9*, 3445–3452. [CrossRef] [PubMed]
183. Niculescu, A.G.; Grumezescu, A.M. Novel Tumor-Targeting Nanoparticles for Cancer Treatment-A Review. *Int. J. Mol. Sci.* **2022**, *23*, 5253. [CrossRef]
184. Rezvantalab, S.; Drude, N.I.; Moraveji, M.K.; Guvener, N.; Koons, E.K.; Shi, Y.; Lammers, T.; Kiessling, F. PLGA-Based Nanoparticles in Cancer Treatment. *Front. Pharmacol.* **2018**, *9*, 1260. [CrossRef]
185. Lu, L.; Peter, S.J.; Lyman, M.D.; Lai, H.L.; Leite, S.M.; Tamada, J.A.; Uyama, S.; Vacanti, J.P.; Langer, R.; Mikos, A.G. In vitro and in vivo degradation of porous poly(DL-lactic-co-glycolic acid) foams. *Biomaterials* **2000**, *21*, 1837–1845. [CrossRef]
186. Luderer, F.; Lobler, M.; Rohm, H.W.; Gocke, C.; Kunna, K.; Kock, K.; Kroemer, H.K.; Weitschies, W.; Schmitz, K.P.; Sternberg, K. Biodegradable sirolimus-loaded poly(lactide) nanoparticles as drug delivery system for the prevention of in-stent restenosis in coronary stent application. *J. Biomater. Appl.* **2011**, *25*, 851–875. [CrossRef]
187. Wu, L.; Ding, J. In vitro degradation of three-dimensional porous poly(D,L-lactide-co-glycolide) scaffolds for tissue engineering. *Biomaterials* **2004**, *25*, 5821–5830. [CrossRef]
188. Zhang, B.; Sai Lung, P.; Zhao, S.; Chu, Z.; Chrzanowski, W.; Li, Q. Shape dependent cytotoxicity of PLGA-PEG nanoparticles on human cells. *Sci. Rep.* **2017**, *7*, 7315. [CrossRef]
189. Cai, J.; Qian, K.; Zuo, X.; Yue, W.; Bian, Y.; Yang, J.; Wei, J.; Zhao, W.; Qian, H.; Liu, B. PLGA nanoparticle-based docetaxel/LY294002 drug delivery system enhances antitumor activities against gastric cancer. *J. Biomater. Appl.* **2019**, *33*, 1394–1406. [CrossRef]
190. Zhang, L.; Zhai, B.Z.; Wu, Y.J.; Wang, Y. Recent progress in the development of nanomaterials targeting multiple cancer metabolic pathways: A review of mechanistic approaches for cancer treatment. *Drug Deliv.* **2023**, *30*, 1–18. [CrossRef]
191. Ren, M.; Zheng, X.; Gao, H.; Jiang, A.; Yao, Y.; He, W. Nanomedicines Targeting Metabolism in the Tumor Microenvironment. *Front. Bioeng. Biotechnol.* **2022**, *10*, 943906. [CrossRef] [PubMed]
192. Sa, P.; Sahoo, S.K.; Dilnawaz, F. Responsive Role of Nanomedicine in the Tumor Microenvironment and Cancer Drug Resistance. *Curr. Med. Chem.* **2023**, *30*, 3335–3355. [CrossRef] [PubMed]
193. Sasaki, K.; Nishina, S.; Yamauchi, A.; Fukuda, K.; Hara, Y.; Yamamura, M.; Egashira, K.; Hino, K. Nanoparticle-Mediated Delivery of 2-Deoxy-D-Glucose Induces Antitumor Immunity and Cytotoxicity in Liver Tumors in Mice. *Cell. Mol. Gastroenterol. Hepatol.* **2021**, *11*, 739–762. [CrossRef] [PubMed]

194. Yang, B.; Chen, Y.; Shi, J. Tumor-Specific Chemotherapy by Nanomedicine-Enabled Differential Stress Sensitization. *Angew. Chem. Int. Ed. Engl.* **2020**, *59*, 9693–9701. [CrossRef]
195. Cui, L.; Gouw, A.M.; LaGory, E.L.; Guo, S.; Attarwala, N.; Tang, Y.; Qi, J.; Chen, Y.S.; Gao, Z.; Casey, K.M.; et al. Mitochondrial copper depletion suppresses triple-negative breast cancer in mice. *Nat. Biotechnol.* **2021**, *39*, 357–367. [CrossRef]
196. Ding, X.L.; Liu, M.D.; Cheng, Q.; Guo, W.H.; Niu, M.T.; Huang, Q.X.; Zeng, X.; Zhang, X.Z. Multifunctional liquid metal-based nanoparticles with glycolysis and mitochondrial metabolism inhibition for tumor photothermal therapy. *Biomaterials* **2022**, *281*, 121369. [CrossRef]
197. Dong, F.; Jiang, Q.; Li, L.; Liu, T.; Zuo, S.; Gao, L.; Fang, M.; Gao, Y.; Sun, B.; Luo, C.; et al. Synergetic lethal energy depletion initiated by cancer cell membrane camouflaged nano-inhibitor for cancer therapy. *Nano Res.* **2022**, *15*, 3422–3433. [CrossRef]
198. Sung, H.; Ferlay, J.; Siegel, R.L.; Laversanne, M.; Soerjomataram, I.; Jemal, A.; Bray, F. Global Cancer Statistics 2020: GLOBOCAN Estimates of Incidence and Mortality Worldwide for 36 Cancers in 185 Countries. *CA Cancer J. Clin.* **2021**, *71*, 209–249. [CrossRef]
199. Wu, P.; Han, J.; Gong, Y.; Liu, C.; Yu, H.; Xie, N. Nanoparticle-Based Drug Delivery Systems Targeting Tumor Microenvironment for Cancer Immunotherapy Resistance: Current Advances and Applications. *Pharmaceutics* **2022**, *14*, 1990. [CrossRef]
200. Wu, S.; Zhang, K.; Liang, Y.; Wei, Y.; An, J.; Wang, Y.; Yang, J.; Zhang, H.; Zhang, Z.; Liu, J.; et al. Nano-enabled Tumor Systematic Energy Exhaustion via Zinc (II) Interference Mediated Glycolysis Inhibition and Specific GLUT1 Depletion. *Adv. Sci.* **2022**, *9*, e2103534. [CrossRef]
201. Guimaraes, P.P.G.; Gaglione, S.; Sewastianik, T.; Carrasco, R.D.; Langer, R.; Mitchell, M.J. Nanoparticles for Immune Cytokine TRAIL-Based Cancer Therapy. *ACS Nano* **2018**, *12*, 912–931. [CrossRef] [PubMed]
202. Liu, G.; Luo, Q.; Li, H.; Liu, Q.; Ju, Y.; Song, G. Increased Oxidative Phosphorylation Is Required for Stemness Maintenance in Liver Cancer Stem Cells from Hepatocellular Carcinoma Cell Line HCCLM3 Cells. *Int. J. Mol. Sci.* **2020**, *21*, 5276. [CrossRef] [PubMed]

Disclaimer/Publisher's Note: The statements, opinions and data contained in all publications are solely those of the individual author(s) and contributor(s) and not of MDPI and/or the editor(s). MDPI and/or the editor(s) disclaim responsibility for any injury to people or property resulting from any ideas, methods, instructions or products referred to in the content.

cancers

MDPI

Article

Targeting the EGFR and Spindle Assembly Checkpoint Pathways in Oral Cancer: A Plausible Alliance to Enhance Cell Death

Mafalda Calheiros-Lobo [1,†], João P. N. Silva [1,†], Leonor Delgado [1,2], Bárbara Pinto [1,3], Luís Monteiro [1,4], Carlos Lopes [1], Patrícia M. A. Silva [1,5,6,*] and Hassan Bousbaa [1,*]

1 UNIPRO—Oral Pathology and Rehabilitation Research Unit, University Institute of Health Sciences (IUCS), Cooperativa de Ensino Superior Politécnico e Universitário (CESPU), Rua Central de Gandra, 1317, 4585-116 Gandra, Portugal; mafalda.duarte@iucs.cespu.pt (M.C.-L.); joaosilva_06@hotmail.com (J.P.N.S.); mleonor.delgado@iucs.cespu.pt (L.D.); barbara.pinto@iucs.cespu.pt (B.P.); luis.monteiro@iucs.cespu.pt (L.M.); carlos.lopes@iucs.cespu.pt (C.L.)

2 Pathology Department, INNO Serviços Especializados em Veterinária, 4710-503 Braga, Portugal

3 Department of Physiology and Biophysics, Institute of Biological Sciences, Federal University of Minas Gerais (UFMG), Av. Pres. Antônio Carlos, 6627, Belo Horizonte 31270-901, Brazil

4 Medicine and Oral Surgery Department, University Institute of Health Sciences—CESPU (IUCS-CESPU), 4585-116 Gandra, Portugal

5 Associate Laboratory i4HB, Institute for Health and Bioeconomy, University Institute of Health Sciences—CESPU, 4585-116 Gandra, Portugal

6 UCIBIO—Applied Molecular Biosciences Unit, Translational Toxicology Research Laboratory, University Institute of Health Sciences (1H-TOXRUN, IUCS-CESPU), 4585-116 Gandra, Portugal

* Correspondence: patricia.silva@cespu.pt (P.M.A.S.); hassan.bousbaa@iucs.cespu.pt (H.B.); Tel.: +351-224157189 (P.M.A.S.); +351-224157186 (H.B.)

† These authors contributed equally to this work.

Simple Summary: Head and neck cancer (HNC), especially oral squamous cell carcinoma (OSCC), is a common and increasingly prevalent cancer worldwide. OSCC is challenging to treat due to its aggressive nature and resistance to standard therapies like surgery, radiation, and chemotherapy, particularly in advanced stages. Cetuximab, a drug targeting EGFR (a protein that supports cancer cell growth), is often used but has limitations in effectiveness. This study explores a new approach by combining Cetuximab with drugs that target proteins involved in cell division, specifically MPS-1, Aurora-B, and KSP. These proteins help cancer cells progress through the cell cycle and are crucial for tumor survival. By blocking both EGFR and these cell division proteins, the study aimed to increase the effectiveness of Cetuximab in killing OSCC cells. Results showed that targeting MPS-1, Aurora-B, or KSP alongside EGFR led to more cancer cell death, suggesting that this combined approach could reduce treatment resistance. Analysis of patient samples confirmed that these proteins are significant in OSCC. This combined therapy strategy shows promise for improving outcomes in OSCC and potentially other head and neck cancers.

Abstract: Background/Objectives: Head and neck cancer (HNC) is among the most common cancer types globally, with its incidence expected to increase significantly in the coming years. Oral squamous cell carcinoma (OSCC), the predominant subtype, exhibits significant heterogeneity and resistance to treatment. Current therapies, including surgery, radiation, and chemotherapy, often result in poor outcomes for advanced stages. Cetuximab, an EGFR inhibitor, is widely used but faces limitations. This study explores the combined inhibition of EGFR and mitotic proteins to enhance treatment efficacy. **Methods:** We analyzed the effects of co-treating OSCC cells with small molecules targeting MPS-1 (BAY1217389), Aurora-B (Barasertib), or KSP (Ispinesib), alongside Cetuximab. The rationale is based on targeting EGFR-mediated survival pathways and the mitotic checkpoint, addressing multiple cell cycle phases and reducing resistance. **Results:** Our findings indicate that inhibiting MPS-1, Aurora-B, or KSP enhances Cetuximab's therapeutic potential, promoting increased cancer cell death. Additionally, we examined EGFR, MPS-1, Aurora-B, and KSP expression in OSCC patient samples, revealing their clinicopathologic significance. **Conclusions:** This combinatorial approach suggests a promising strategy to improve treatment outcomes in OSCC.

Keywords: MPS-1 inhibitor; aurora-B inhibitor; KSP inhibitor; cetuximab; oral cancer; antimitotics; combination treatment; antitumor activity

1. Introduction

Head and neck cancer squamous cell carcinoma (HNSCC) ranks as the sixth most common cancer subtype globally, with over 870,000 new cases and 325,000 deaths reported annually [1]. The incidence of HNSCC is increasing, with projections suggesting a 30% rise in cases by 2030. HNSCCs can be classified into two groups according to human papillomavirus (HPV) status: HPV-negative and HPV-positive. HPV-positive HNSCCs are more commonly associated with the oropharynx, hypopharynx, and larynx and have a better prognosis [2]. Oral squamous cell carcinoma (OSCC), the predominant histological subtype of HNSCC, accounts for approximately 90% of all cases. OSCC originates from the epithelial cells lining the mucosal surfaces of the oral cavity, oropharynx, larynx, or hypopharynx [3]. OSCC is characterized by significant heterogeneity, exhibiting a variety of genetic and epigenetic alterations associated with distinct risk factors [4]. These alterations confer several advantages to cancer cells, including the ability to proliferate independently of growth factors, resist apoptosis, and effectively breach extracellular matrix barriers, facilitating invasion into adjacent or distant tissues. These characteristics contribute to the aggressive nature of OSCC and its frequent resistance to treatment [5].

The treatment strategy for OSCC typically involves a multimodal approach, and surgery is the primary treatment for both early and advanced OSCC. It is often supplemented with radiotherapy (RT) and/or chemotherapy (CT) for patients with pathological adverse features [6]. The overall survival rate for patients with advanced stages of OSCC cell carcinoma remains low, and thus, new treatment options need to be explored [7]. One of the most widely used drugs for OSCC treatment is Cetuximab, a monoclonal antibody that targets the epidermal growth factor receptor (EGFR). The EGFR, a receptor tyrosine kinase (RTK) within the HER/ErbB family (which also includes HER2-4), is overexpressed in 80–90% of HNC cases and is associated with poor prognosis and treatment outcomes [8]. The EGFR signaling network is complex, involving numerous components and intersecting with multiple other pathways [9]. In human cancers, the activation of RTK signaling pathways is driven by various mechanisms, including ligand or receptor overexpression, aberrant ligand binding, and gene rearrangements. These processes enhance tumor cell migration, survival, and proliferation, contributing to the malignancy's aggressive nature [10].

To counteract the development of aberrant cells, a network of quality control mechanisms, including checkpoints, operates throughout multiple phases of the cell cycle. Monopolar spindle 1 (MPS-1), alternatively known as threonine tyrosine kinase (TTK), serves as a vital component of the spindle assembly checkpoint (SAC). The SAC upholds the cell cycle at mitosis until all chromosomes have established stable bipolar attachments to the mitotic spindle and are aligned at the metaphase plate [11]. Deficient SAC activity leads to premature exit from mitosis, resulting in the generation of aneuploid cells due to chromosome mis-segregation. MPS-1 exhibits heightened expression levels across various cancer types, including breast cancer [12], hepatocellular carcinoma [13], pancreatic cancer [14], and gastric cancer [15], and its overexpression is mostly correlated with unfavorable patient prognosis. Notably, in breast cancer cell lines, downregulation of MPS-1 expression has been observed to diminish cell viability, highlighting its potential as a promising therapeutic target [16]. Importantly, Aurora-B, a member of the Aurora kinase family, including Aurora-A and Aurora-C, also plays a pivotal role in chromosome attachment and alignment, segregation, and cytokinesis. The inhibition of Aurora-B can induce polyploidy and subsequent cell death [17]. Overexpression of Aurora-B has been observed in metastatic and poorly differentiated OSCC, indicating its involvement in OSCC progression [18,19]. Kinesin spindle protein (KSP), also known as Eg5 or Kif11, is a member of the kinesin-5 family essential for the formation of bipolar mitotic spindles, the cross-linking of microtubules, and the proper chromosome alignment [20,21]. Its inhibition results in the formation of monopolar spindles, activation of the SAC, mitotic arrest, and subsequent cell death [22]. Overexpression of KSP is linked to poor prognoses in hepatocellular [23], breast [24] and laryngeal cancers [25].

Due to the critical role these proteins play in cell proliferation and their high expression levels in various types of cancer, which are linked with poor patient prognosis, several inhibitors have been developed. However, despite the promising results from preclinical trials, inhibitors of these proteins have shown disappointing outcomes as a monotherapy in clinical trials [26–30]. Several explanations were proposed for this lack of efficacy. One significant factor is that antimitotic agents act exclusively during mitosis, leading to low efficacy since only a small fraction of tumor cells undergo mitosis at any given time. Additionally, mitotic slippage, a phenomenon where cells exit mitosis without division, leading to aneuploidy and promoting cancer cell survival, has been identified as a major cause of resistance to antimitotic treatments [31].

The limitations of antimitotic agents as monotherapies highlight their reduced efficacy, which leads to cancer cell survival. Thus, alternative therapeutic strategies are needed. In this sense, we propose combining Cetuximab with antimitotic agents. The rationale for combining antimitotic inhibition with Cetuximab, an EGFR inhibitor, to enhance the death of oral cancer cells is based on the complementary roles these proteins play in cell proliferation and survival. By targeting both EGFR-mediated survival pathways and the mitotic checkpoint, this combination therapy aims to enhance the overall anti-cancer effect, leading to increased cancer cell death and improved treatment outcomes in oral cancer. Cetuximab primarily targets the G1 phase of the cell cycle, preventing cells from entering the S phase due to insufficient growth signals. In contrast, antimitotics target cells in the M phase. This combination ensures that cancer cells are targeted at multiple points in the cell cycle, reducing the likelihood of escape and resistance development and potentially leading to more effective and durable responses. Moreover, tumors often develop resistance to single-agent therapies through various mechanisms, such as compensatory signaling pathways or mutations.

The primary objective of this study was to comprehensively analyze the effects of co-treating oral cancer cells with small molecules targeting mitotic proteins, specifically an MPS-1 inhibitor (BAY1217389), an Aurora-B inhibitor (Barasertib), and a KSP inhibitor (Ispinesib), in combination with an EGFR inhibitor (Cetuximab). The EGFR, MPS-1, Aurora-B, and KSP expression patterns and the clinicopathologic significance in samples from OSCC patients were also meticulously analyzed.

2. Materials and Methods

2.1. Inhibitors

Inhibitors targeting EGFR (Cetuximab), MPS-1 (BAY1217389), Aurora-B (Barasertib), and KSP (Ispinesib) were obtained from MedChem Express (Shanghai, China) and reconstituted in sterile dimethyl sulfoxide (DMSO, Sigma-Aldrich Co., Ltd., St. Louis, MO, USA) to 10 mM or 5 mM stock concentrations. After reconstitution, aliquots were prepared from each inhibitor and promptly stored at −20 °C to mitigate the risk of compound degradation from repeated freeze–thaw cycles. Fresh working solutions were prepared in a culture medium on the day of the experiment to achieve the desired inhibitor concentrations.

2.2. Cell Lines and Culture Conditions

Two human oral cancer cell lines were used in this study: SCC-09 (Tongue Squamous Cell Carcinoma; The Global Bioresource Center-ATCC® CRL-1628) and SCC-25 (Tongue Squamous Cell Carcinoma; The Global Bioresource Center-ATCC® CRL-1629). The cells were maintained in a DMEM-F12 culture medium (Roswell Park Memorial Institute, Biochrom, Buffalo, NY, USA), supplemented with 10% fetal bovine serum (FBS, Biochrom, Berlin, Germany) and 40 ng/mL of hydrocortisone (Sigma-Aldrich). According to the manufacturer's instructions, human oral keratinocytes (HOK, ScienCell Research Laboratories, Carlsbad, CA, USA) were maintained in a specific HOK medium (Innoprot, Biscaia, Spain). All cell lines were cultured at 37 °C in a humidified atmosphere containing 5% CO_2 (Hera Cell, Heraeus, Hanau, Germany).

2.3. RNA Extraction, cDNA Synthesis, and Quantitative Real-Time PCR

Extraction of total RNA extraction and the subsequent synthesis of cDNA were carried out as previously described [31]. After, the iQ™ SYBR Green Supermix Kit (Bio-Rad Laboratories, Inc., Hercules, CA, USA) was used for DNA amplification on an iQ Thermal Cycler (Bio-Rad), with the following protocol: initial denaturation step at 95.0 °C for 3 min, followed by 40 cycles of denaturation at 94.0 °C for 20 s, annealing at 62.0 °C for 30 s, and extension at 72.0 °C for 30 s. The melt curve analysis encompassed temperatures ranging from 65.0 to 95.0 °C, incremented by 0.5 °C for 5 s. The sequences of the primers for the amplification of MPS-1 were as follows: forward 5′-CCGAGATTTGGTTGTGCCTGGA-3′ and reverse 5′-CATCTGACACCAGAGGTTCCTTG-3′. For the amplification of EGFR, they were as follows: forward 5′-AGGCACGAGTAACAAGCTCAC-3′ and reverse 5′-ATGAGGACATAACCAGCCACC-3′. For the amplification of actin, they were as follows: forward 5′-AATCTGGCACCACACCTTCTA-3′ and reverse 5′-ATAGCACAGCCTGGATA GCAA-3′. For the amplification of GAPDH, they were as follows: forward 5′-GTCTCCTCT GACTTCAACAGCG-3′ and reserve 5′-ACCACCCTGTTGCTGTAGCCAA-3′. Actin and GAPDH were used as a reference control to normalize the data. Each independent experiment (n = 3) was performed in triplicate, and the data was acquired using the CFX Manager™ Software (version 1.0, Bio-Rad). The relative quantification was calculated using the ΔΔCT method.

2.4. Protein Extracts and Western Blotting

The protein extracts retrieved from SCC-09, SCC-25, and HOK-cell pellets were suspended in lysis buffer composed of 50 mM Tris (pH 7.5), 150 mM NaCl, 1 mM EDTA, 1% Triton-100, and a protease inhibitor cocktail (Sigma-Aldrich). Following the manufacturer's guidelines, protein quantification was performed using the BCATM Protein Assay Kit (Pierce Biotechnology, Rockford, IL, USA). For MPS-1 and EGFR detection, 15 and 20 µg of protein lysate, respectively, were reconstituted in SDS-sample buffer (consisting of 375 mM Tris pH 6.8, 12% SDS, 60% Glycerol, 0.12% Bromophenol Blue, and 600 nM DTT) and boiled for 3 min.

Then, a 7.5% gradient gel (Bio-Rad) was used for protein separation. After SDS-PAGE, proteins were transferred onto nitrocellulose membranes (Amersham, UK) using the Trans-Blot Turbo Transfer System (Bio-Rad). Following the transfer, the membranes were blocked in a 5% non-fat dried milk (*w*/*v*) dissolved in TBST buffer (comprising 50 mM Tris pH 7.5, 150 mM NaCl, and 0.05% Tween-20) and incubated overnight at 4 °C with primary antibodies diluted in TBST. The primary antibodies used included mouse anti-α-tubulin (1:5000, 1:5000, T568 Clone B-5-1-2, Sigma-Aldrich), mouse anti-EGFR (1:250, HPA044700, Sigma-Aldrich), and mouse anti-MPS-1 (1:1000, (N1): sc-56968, Santa Cruz Biotechnology, Heidelberg, Germany). After three washes with TBST, the membranes were incubated with horseradish-peroxidase-conjugated secondary antibodies (1:1500 for anti-mouse and 1:1000 for anti-rabbit) for 1 h at room temperature.

A ChemiDOc system (Bio-Rad) was then used to visualize protein bands after exposure to the Enhanced Chemiluminescence (ECL) method. Image Lab 6.1v software or Image J (version 1.47, Rasband, W.S., ImageJ, U. S. National Institutes of Health, Bethesda, MD, USA)was used to quantify protein signal intensity with normalization against α-tubulin expression levels.

2.5. MTT Viability Assay

The cell viability was determined by tetrazolium salt 3-(4, 5-dimethylthiazol-2-yl)-2, 5-diphenyltetrazolium bromide (MTT) assay. In summary, SCC-09 and SCC-25 cells were seeded in 96-well plates at a density of 0.1×10^6 and 0.05×10^6 cells/mL, respectively. After 24 h, the culture medium was replaced with fresh medium containing 2-fold serial dilutions of Cetuximab ranging from 0 to 120 nM in combination with Barasertib (SCC-09 and SCC-25) and from 0 to 240 nM in combination with BAY1217389 and Ispinesib (SCC-09 and SCC-25), with BAY1217389 ranging from 0 to 6400 nM, Barasertib ranging from 0 to 16,000 nM (SCC-25) and from 0 to 64,000 nM (SCC-09), or Ispinesib ranging from 0 to 30 nM (SCC-25) and from 0 to 60 nM (SCC-09). After a 48 h incubation at 37 °C and 5% CO_2, the medium was removed and replaced with a combination of 200 µL of DMEM F12 only and 20 µL of tetrazolium salt MTT (5 mg/mL PBS). Afterward, the plates were placed in an incubator at 37 °C for 2–4 h, allowing formazan crystals to form. Then, the medium was extracted, and the formazan crystals were resuspended in 100 µL of DMSO. Next, the plates were placed in a microplate reader (Biotek Synergy 2, Winooski, VT, USA) coupled with Gen5 software (version 1.07.5, Biotek, Winooski, VT, USA) to measure the absorbance using a wavelength of 570 nm.

Cell viability was assessed as a percentage relative to the control group and presented as the mean ± standard deviation from three independent experiments, each performed in triplicate. IC_{50} values, representing the mean 50% inhibitory concentration, were determined using GraphPad Prism version 8 (GraphPad software Inc., San Diego, CA, USA). The combination treatment effects were analyzed using a dual-drug crosswise concentration matrix for each combination, applying the specified concentration ranges. The results were then analyzed using Combenefit Software (version 2.021, Cancer Research UK Cambridge Institute, Cambridge, UK).

2.6. Apoptosis Detection by Flow Cytometry

The assessment of apoptotic cell death was performed using the Annexin V-FITC Apoptosis Detection Kit (eBioscience, Vienna, Austria) in accordance with the manufacturer's protocol. Initially, cells were seeded at a 0.1×10^6 cells/mL density in 6-well plates. After 24 h of incubation, the cells were treated with EGFR, MPS-1, Aurora-B, and KSP inhibitors either individually or in combination, using concentrations corresponding to their respective synergistic points (30 nM of Cetuximab with 40 nM of BAY1217389, 15 nM of Cetuximab with 1000 nM of Barasertib, and 240 nM of Cetuximab with 1.875 nM of Ispinesib). Following a 24 h treatment with Ispinesib and Cetuximab and a 48 h incubation period for the other combinations, adherent and floating cells were harvested and pelleted by centrifugation at 1000 rpm for 5 min. The pelleted cells were then suspended in binding buffer 1×, followed by the addition of Annexin V-FITC, and incubated for 10 min in darkness. After washing, the cells were resuspended once again in binding buffer 1×, followed by the addition of Propidium iodide (PI) at a concentration of 20 µg/mL. A BD Accuri™ C6 Plus Flow cytometer (BD Biosciences, San Jose, CA, USA) was used for the fluorescence analysis. The acquired data was then processed using BD Accuri™ C6 Plus software, version 1.0.27.1.

For data analysis, 20,000 events were recorded per sample.

2.7. Colony Formation Assay

A total of 1000 SCC-25 cells were seeded into six-well plates and allowed to adhere for 24 h. Subsequently, the cells were exposed to drug treatments, administered either as monotherapies or in combination. Control groups consisted of untreated cells and DMSO-treated ones. The cells were incubated for 48 h with the respective treatments and then were rinsed twice with PBS. After the drug-free DMEM medium was added, the cells were maintained for 7 days in these conditions. Colonies fixation was performed by the addition of 100% methanol at −20 °C for 25 min, and then they were stained with a 0.05% (*w*/*v*) solution of crystal violet (Merck, Rahway, NJ, USA) in distilled water for 20 min. Three independent experiments were used to obtain the colony counts. The ratio of the number of colonies to the number of cells seeded in the control group was used to calculate the plating efficiency (PE), expressed as a percentage. The survival fraction for each condition was calculated by dividing the number of colonies by the number of cells seeded and then multiplying by the reciprocal of the PE.

2.8. Immunohistochemistry

2.8.1. Patients and Tissue Specimens

This study was approved by the institutional ethical board of the Hospital de Santo António (HSA), Centro Hospitalar do Porto, Portugal (Investigation, Formation, and Teaching Department—DEFI; 024/CES/03). Written informed consent was obtained from all participants. The research was conducted following the Declaration of Helsinki. Tissue samples from primary Oral Squamous Cell Carcinoma (OSCC) (ICD 10: C00-06) were retrospectively collected from 2000 to 2006 at the abovementioned hospital. Clinical characteristics of the OSCC patients are summarized in Supporting Information Table S1.

2.8.2. Processing and Evaluation

Immunohistochemistry on tissue microarray (TMA) sections was performed using the Novolink Polymer Detection System (Novocastra, Leica Biosystems Newcastle Ltd., Newcastle Upon Tyne, UK), following the protocol outlined by Monteiro et al. [32]. For TMA construction, two representative regions of OSCC from the invasive fronts of the tumors were chosen from hematoxylin and eosin-stained sections, deliberately excluding areas of keratin and necrosis. From each selected specimen, two tissue cores, each 2 mm in diameter, were extracted and embedded into a paraffin TMA block using the TMA Builder (Histopathology Ltd., Pécs, Hungary). Technical controls were represented by non-neoplastic tissue cores [33]. The primary antibodies utilized were mouse anti-human EGFR (1:500, HPA044700, Sigma-Aldrich), mouse anti-human MPS-1 (1:100, clone EPR5319(2), ab133699, Abcam, Cambridge, UK), rabbit anti-KSP (1:300, Abcam), and rabbit anti-Aurora-B (1:50, Sigma-Aldrich). Normal colon tissue was used as a positive control, while negative control sections were incubated without the primary antibody. Staining was measured semi-quantitatively independently by two authors blinded to clinicopathological data. For EGFR, we consider negative cases with a labeling index of $<10\%$ of tumor cells. We categorize cases with $\geq 10\%$ of tumor cells and weak intensity as a score of 1+, moderate intensity score of 2+, and strong intensity as 3+. For MPS-1, Aurora-B and KSP intensity scores were evaluated using a scale of 0 (negative), 1 (weak), 2 (moderate), and 3 (strong) intensity. Discordant cases were reviewed under a multihead microscope to reach consensus; unresolved discordant cases were excluded. For each patient, the highest score from the three cores was used in analyses if scores differed. Cutoffs were determined according to ROC curves. For EGFR, Aurora-B, and KSP, staining intensity was classified as low for scores ≤ 2 and high for scores 3. For MPS-1, staining intensity was classified as low for scores ≤ 1 and high for scores 2 and 3 [34].

2.9. Image Acquisition and Processing

Phase-contrast microscopy images were acquired using a Nikon TE 2000-U microscope (Nikon, Amsterdam, The Netherlands) with a 20× objective lens. The microscope was interfaced with a DXM1200F digital camera operated through Nikon ACT-1 software version 2.63 (Melville, NY, USA). Post-imaging processing and analysis were performed utilizing ImageJ software.

2.10. Bioinformatic Analysis

The UALCAN database (http://ualcan.path.uab.edu/ (accessed on 11 September 2024)) was used to analyze the expression of EGFR1, MPS-1, Aurora-B, and KSP in HNSCC and examine their association with the clinicopathologic characteristics of HNSCC patients. The screening parameters were set as follows: "Gene: EGFR, TTK (MPS-1), AURKB (Aurora-

B), or Kif11 (KSP)" and "Cancer Type: Head and Neck Squamous Cell Carcinoma". The analysis type was defined based on the target variable, such as "HNSCC vs. Normal Analysis". Transcriptomic data were sourced from The Cancer Genome Atlas (TCGA) via UALCAN, while proteomic data were retrieved from the Clinical Proteomic Tumor Analysis Consortium (CPTAC). Transcriptomic results were expressed as transcripts per million (TPM), and proteomic results were provided as Z-values, representing standard deviations from the median across HNSCC samples. Pearson correlation analysis was performed within UALCAN to calculate the Pearson correlation coefficient. For overall survival (OS) and disease-free survival (DFS) analysis, the GEPIA web tool (http://gepia.cancer-pku.cn/ (accessed on 11 September 2024)) was used, with the median as the group cutoff and a 95% confidence interval for statistical reliability. Data are presented as means ± standard deviation (SD), with statistical significance (p-values) provided by UALCAN or GEPIA.

2.11. Statistical Analysis

All experiments were performed in triplicate and repeated in at least three independent trials. Data are presented as mean values with standard deviation (SD). Statistical analyses were conducted using GraphPad Prism Software Inc. version 8, applying either an unpaired t-test or two-way analysis of variance (ANOVA) followed by Tukey's multiple comparisons test. Statistical significance was denoted as * $p < 0.05$, ** $p < 0.01$, *** $p < 0.001$, and **** $p < 0.0001$. Univariate survival analysis was carried out using Kaplan–Meier curves and the log-rank test, while the Cox regression model was employed to assess the independent significance variables identified in univariate analysis.

3. Results

3.1. EGFR, MPS-1, Aurora-B, and KSP Are Overexpressed in HNSCC and Are Correlated with Clinical Features

To investigate the expression and assess the potential as biomarkers and treatment targets of EGFR, MPS-1, Aurora-B, and KSP in HNSCC patients, we explored both the UALCAN and GEPIA databases. The analysis revealed that all four proteins are overexpressed at both the mRNA and protein levels compared to normal tissue samples (Figure 1a,b,d,e,g,h,j,k). Furthermore, when examining HPV status, we observed elevated mRNA levels of EGFR, MPS-1, Aurora-B, and KSP in both HPV-negative and HPV-positive samples (Figure 1c,f,i,l). Notably, HPV-positive samples exhibited higher mRNA expression levels for MPS-1, Aurora-B, and KSP, with EGFR showing a less pronounced but still significant increase.

After we explored the correlation of EGFR, MPS-1, Aurora-B, and KSP expression and clinicopathological features of patients with HNSCC, we observed that EGFR was overexpressed exclusively in male patients (Figure 2a), whereas MPS-1, Aurora-B, and KSP were overexpressed in both male and female patients compared to normal samples (Figure 2d,g,j). Additionally, even though not statistically significant, male patients demonstrated higher levels of protein expression than female patients.

Moreover, overexpression of MPS-1, Aurora-B, and KSP was observed across all tumor stages and grades, except for patients with stage 1 tumors, compared to normal samples (Figure 2e,f,h,i,k,l). In relation to tumor stages, EGFR showed overexpression in stages 3 and 4 compared to normal samples, with statistically significant differences noted between stage 1 and stages 3–4, as well as between stage 2 and stage 4 (Figure 2b). Regarding tumor grades, EGFR was overexpressed in grades 1 and 2, with a statistically significant difference observed between grade 2 and grade 3 (Figure 2c).

We subsequently explored the impact of overexpression of EGFR, MPS-1, Aurora-B, and KSP on the survivability of patients with HNSCC. Our analysis indicated that high expression levels of EGFR were associated with a trend toward worse overall survival (OS), while the opposite was observed for disease-free survival (DFS) (Figure 3a,b). Furthermore, MPS-1 overexpression appeared to correlate with poorer outcomes for both OS and DFS (Figure 3c,d). Although there was a trend suggesting that patients with high Aurora-B expression had lower DFS, this finding was not statistically significant. Additionally, the OS for patients with low and high Aurora-B expression was similar (Figure 3e,f). Notably, while not statistically significant, patients exhibiting high KSP expression demonstrated a tendency toward worse OS and DFS outcomes (Figure 3g,h).

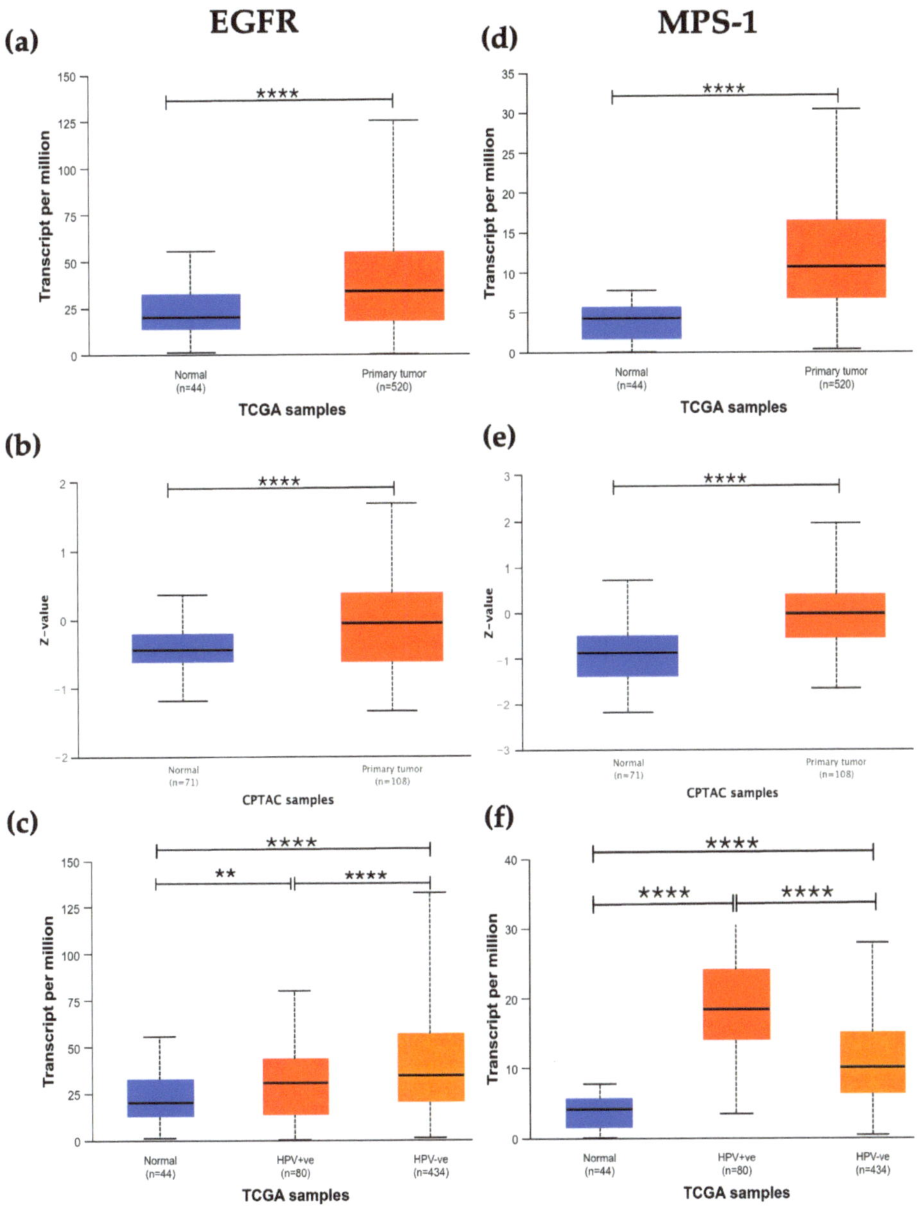

Figure 1. *Cont.*

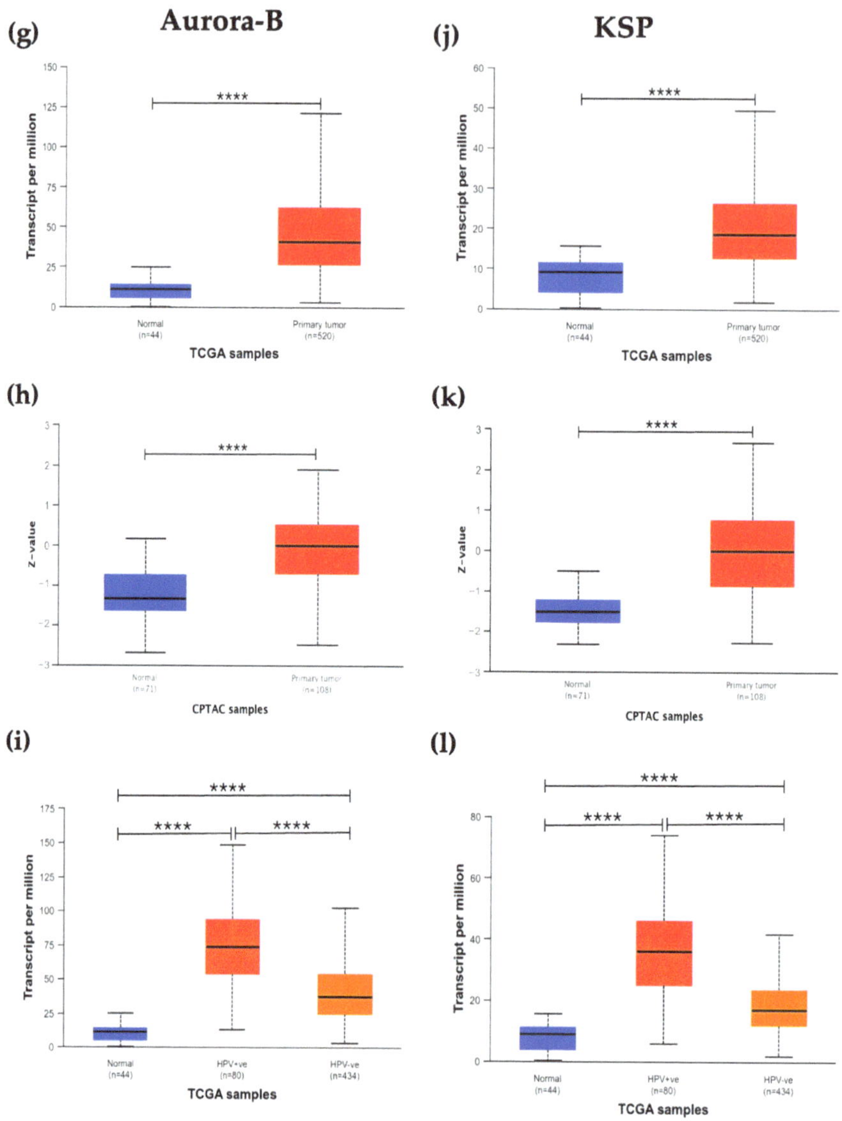

Figure 1. mRNA and protein expression of EGFR (**a**,**b**), MPS-1 (**d**,**e**), Aurora-B (**g**,**h**) and KSP (**j**,**k**) in HNSCC patients. mRNA expression of EGFR (**c**), MPS-1 (**f**), Aurora-B (**i**) and KSP (**l**) is increased in both HPV positive and negative patients. The significance levels were as follows: ** $p < 0.01$, **** $p < 0.0001$. Data were retrieved from UALCAN (http://ualcan.path.uab.edu/) on 11 September 2024. Abbreviations: CPTAC—Clinical Proteomic Tumor Analysis Consortium; TCGA—The Cancer Genome Atlas; HNSCC—Head and Neck Squamous Cell Carcinoma; EGFR—Epidermal Growth Factor Receptor; mRNA—messenger ribonucleic acid; UALCAN—University of Alabama at Birmingham Cancer data analysis Portal.

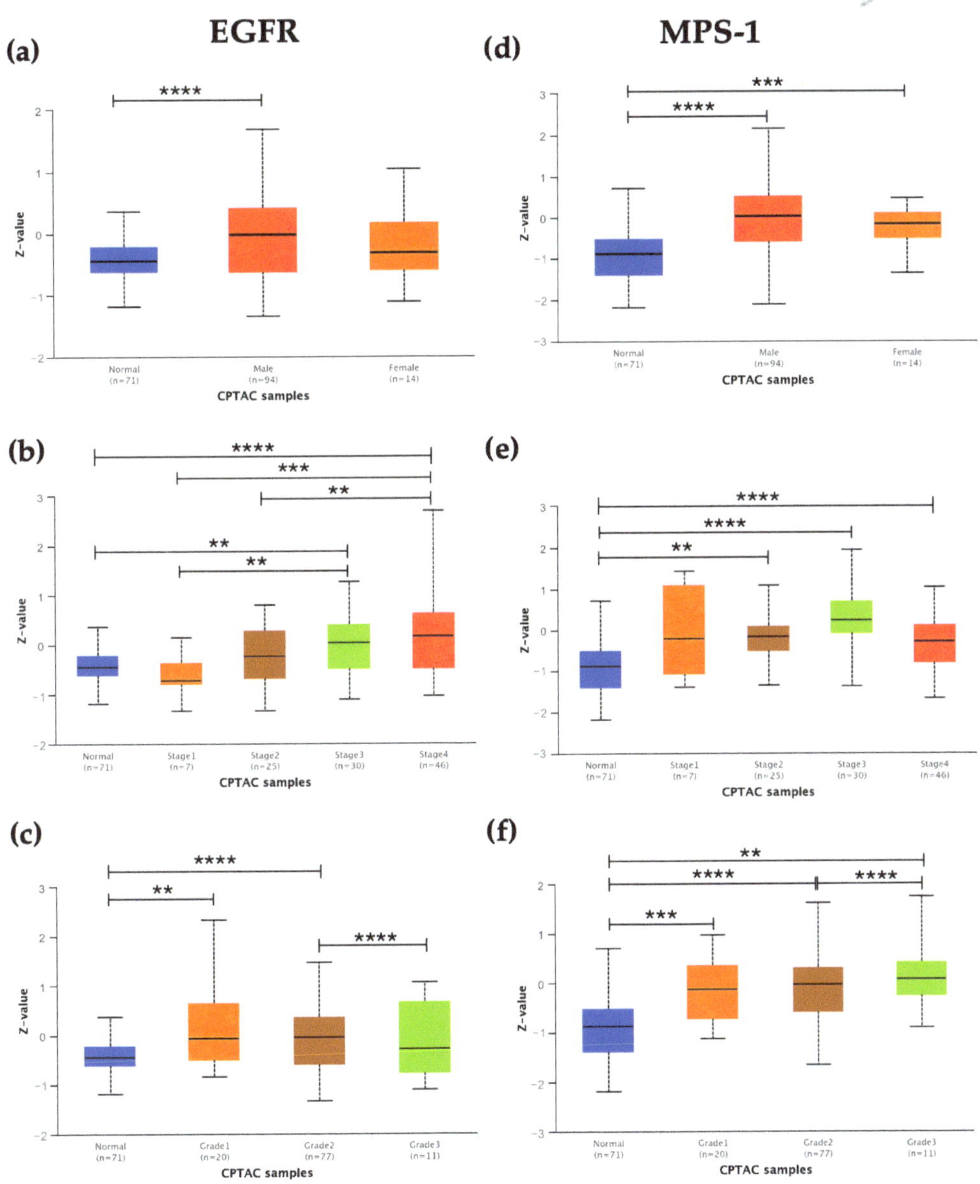

Figure 2. *Cont.*

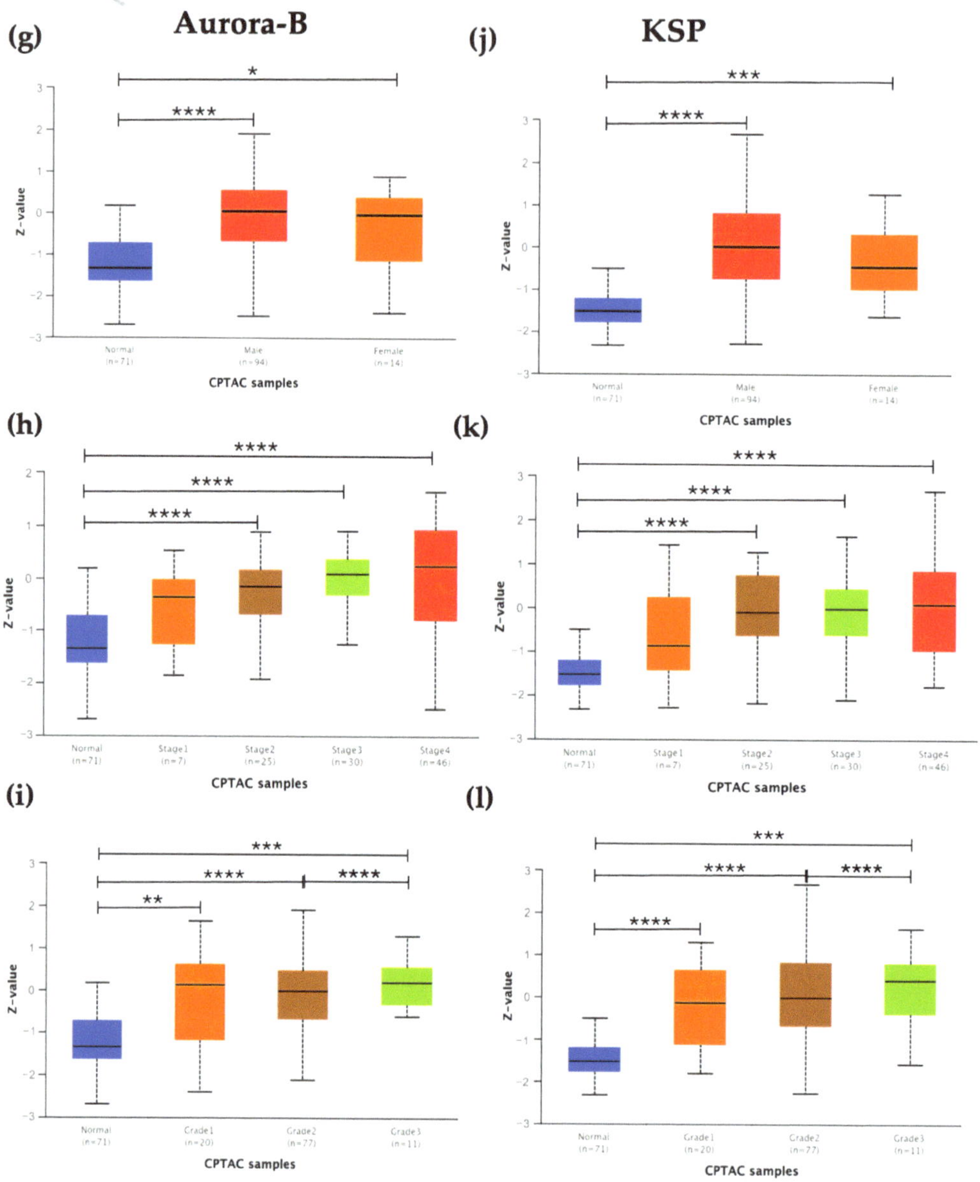

Figure 2. Association of HNSCC patients clinicopathological features with expression levels of EGFR, MPS-1, Aurora-B, and KSP. Correlation of EGFR, MPS-1, Aurora-B, and KSP expression with gender (**a**,**d**,**g**,**j**) tumor stage (**b**,**e**,**h**,**k**) and grade (**c**,**f**,**i**,**l**). The significance levels were as follows: * $p < 0.05$, ** $p < 0.01$, *** $p < 0.001$ and **** $p < 0.0001$. Data were retrieved from UALCAN (http://ualcan.path.uab.edu/) on 11 September 2024. Abbreviations: HNSCC—Head and Neck Squamous Cell Carcinoma; EGFR—Epidermal Growth Factor Receptor; KSP—Kinesin Spindle Protein; UALCAN—University of Alabama at Birmingham Cancer data analysis Portal.

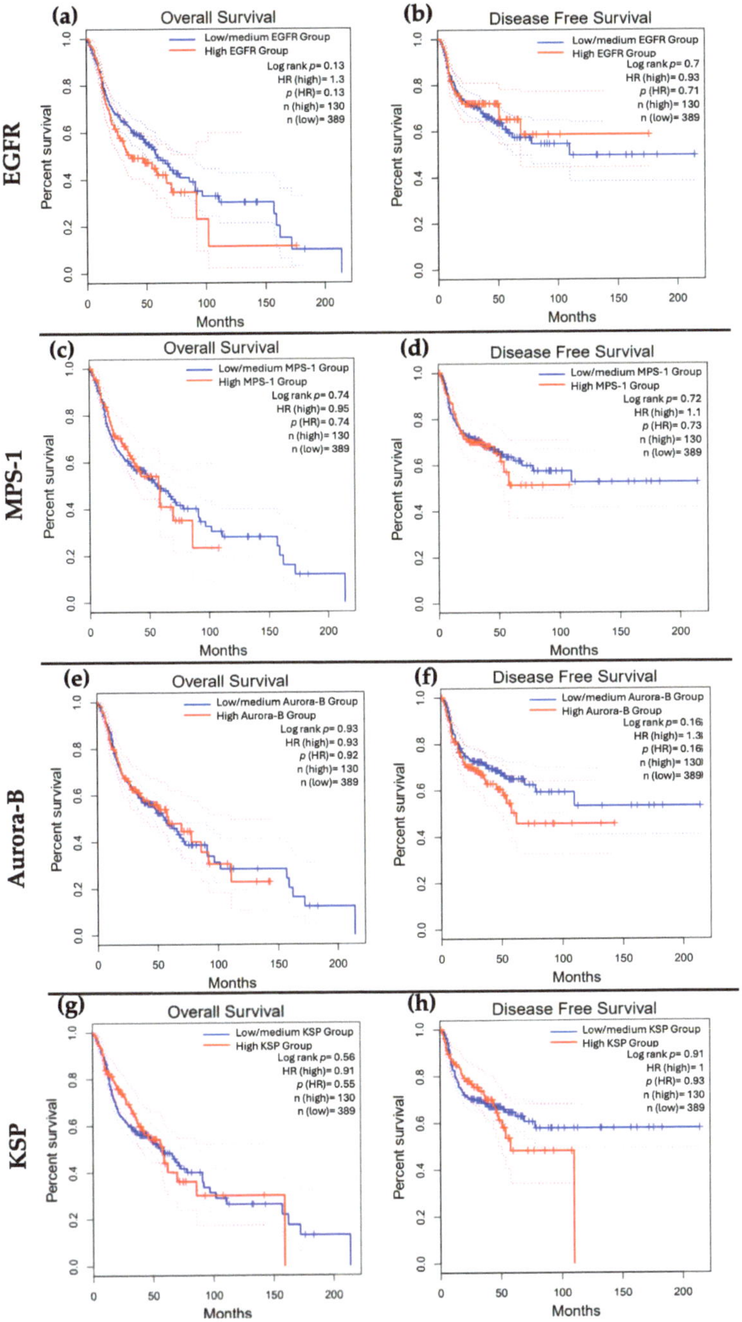

Figure 3. Effect of EGFR, MPS-1, Aurora-B, and expression on HNSCC patients' overall survival (OS) (**a**,**c**,**e**,**g**) and disease-free survival (DFS) (**b**,**d**,**f**,**h**). Data were retrieved from the GEPIA (http://gepia.cancer-pku.cn/) database on 11 September 2024. Abbreviations: AURKB—Aurora-B; EGFR—GEPIA—Gene Expression Profiling Interactive Analysis; KSP—Kinesin Spindle Protein; MPS-1—Monopolar spindle 1.

These results seem to suggest that the proteins explored in this study could have potential therapeutic targets in HNSCC, even though no clear association between their overexpression and survivability was observed. Nonetheless, their overexpression showed a tendency towards a worse OS; however, further research is warranted to establish statistical significance and to elucidate the precise nature of these associations.

3.2. EGFR, MPS-1, Aurora-B, and KSP Are Overexpressed in OSCC Patient Tissues

After the detailed UALCAN and GEPIA analysis, we proceeded to analyze samples from 30 patients with oral cancer to investigate their immunohistochemistry features and possible correlations with survivability. Firstly, EGFR, MPS-1, Aurora-B, and KSP staining intensity and the extent of Aurora-B and KSP were assessed for potential associations with the clinicopathological characteristics of OSCC patients. These features included gender, age, tumor location, stage, treatment modality, grade, margin status, vascular invasion, perineural permeation, lymphatic invasion, and muscular invasion. While no significant correlation was identified between protein expression and clinicopathological characteristics, a trend emerged that may become clinically significant with an increased sample size (N). As previously mentioned, only staining intensity was analyzed for EGFR and MPS-1 due to uniformly high-extent values across all cases (Table 1). In contrast, both staining intensity and extent were evaluated for Aurora-B and KSP (Tables 2 and 3).

Table 1. Clinicopathological characteristics of the OSCC patients and their association with EGFR and MPS-1 staining intensity.

		EGFR (N = 29)			MPS-1 (N = 25)		
		Staining Intensity			Staining Intensity		
		Low	High		Low	High	
Characteristic	*N* (%)	*N* (%)	*N* (%)	p^a	*N* (%)	*N* (%)	p^a
All cases	30						
Gender							
Female	7 (23.3)	3 (16.7)	4 (36.4)	0.229	2 (40)	4 (20)	0.349
Male	23 (76.7)	15 (83.3)	7 (63.6)		3 (60)	16 (80)	
Age							
<62 years	12 (40)	5 (27.8)	7 (63.6)	0.057	2 (40)	8 (40)	1.000
≥62 years	18 (60)	13 (72.2)	4 (36.4)		3 (60)	12 (60)	
Tumor location							
Lip	6 (20)	6 (33.3)	0 (0)	0.177	1 (20)	2 (10)	0.619
Floor of the mouth	4 (13.3)	2 (11.1)	2 (11.1)		1 (20)	3 (15)	
Tongue	10 (33.3)	5 (27.8)	4 (36.4)		3 (60)	5 (25)	
Buccal mucosa	2 (6.7)	1 (5.6)	1 (9.1)		0 (0)	2 (10)	
Retromolar trigone	2 (6.7)	2 (11.1)	0 (0)		0 (0)	2 (10)	
Hard palate	4 (13.3)	2 (11.1)	2 (11.1)		0 (0)	4 (20)	
Alveolar ridge	2 (6.7)	0 (0)	2 (11.1)		0 (0)	2 (10)	
Stage							
I + II	18 (60)	12 (66.7)	5 (45.5)	0.260	3 (60)	11 (55)	0.840
III + IV	12 (40)	6 (33.3)	6 (54.4)		2 (40)	9 (45)	
Treatment modality							
SG	17 (56.7)	11 (61.1)	5 (45.5)	0.411	3 (60)	11 (55)	0.840
SG + RT	13 (43.3)	7 (38.9)	6 (54.5)		2 (40)	9 (45)	
Tumor Grade							
G1	18 (60)	11 (61.1)	6 (54.5)	0.728	3 (60)	11 (55)	0.840
G2 + G3	12 (40)	7 (38.9)	5 (45.5)		2 (40)	9 (45)	
Margin status							
Free of tumor	19 (63.3)	12 (75)	6 (60)	0.420	3 (60)	13 (68.4)	0.722
Tumor proximity and with tumor	8 (26.7)	4 (25)	4 (40)		2 (40)	6 (31.6)	
Vascular invasion							
Absent	29 (96.7)	17 (94.4)	11 (100)	0.426	5 (100)	19 (95)	0.610
Present	1 (3.3)	1 (5.6)	0 (0)		0 (0)	1 (5)	

Table 1. *Cont.*

		EGFR (N = 29)			MPS-1 (N = 25)		
		Staining Intensity			Staining Intensity		
		Low	High		Low	High	
Perineural permeation							
Absent	26 (86.7)	16 (88.9)	9 (81.8)	0.592	4 (80)	17 (85)	0.785
Present	4 (13.3)	2 (11.1)	2 (18.2)		1 (20)	3 (15)	
Lymphatic invasion							
Absent	24 (80)	16 (88.9)	7 (63.6)	0.103	4 (80)	15 (75)	0.815
Present	6 (20)	2 (11.1)	4 (36.4)		1 (20)	5 (25)	
Muscular invasion							
Absent	25 (83.8)	14 (77.8)	10 (90.9)	0.364	4 (80)	16 (80)	1.000
Present	5 (16.7)	4 (22.2)	1 (9.1)		1 (20)	4 (20)	

[a] Chi-square test. p values with statistically significant differences highlighted in bold ($p < 0.05$).

Table 2. Clinicopathological characteristics of the OSCC patients and their association with Aurora-B extent and staining intensity.

	AurB (N = 20)					
	Extent			Staining Intensity		
	≤9%	≥10%		Low	High	
Characteristic	*N* (%)	*N* (%)	p [a]	*N* (%)	*N* (%)	p [a]
All cases						
Gender						
Female	4 (36.4)	2 (22.2)	0.492	4 (36.4)	2 (22.2)	0.492
Male	7 (63.6)	7 (77.8)		7 (63.6)	7 (77.8)	
Age						
<62 years	4 (36.4)	5 (55.6)	0.391	4 (36.4)	5 (55.6)	0.391
≥62 years	7 (63.6)	4 (44.4)		7 (63.6)	4 (44.4)	
Tumor location						
Lip	1 (9.1)	1 (11.1)	0.311	1 (9.1)	1 (11.1)	0.311
Floor of the mouth	1 (9.1)	2 (22.2)		1 (9.1)	2 (22.2)	
Tongue	6 (54.5)	1 (11.1)		6 (54.5)	1 (11.1)	
Buccal mucosa	1 (9.1)	1 (11.1)		1 (9.1)	1 (11.1)	
Retromolar trigone	0 (0)	1 (11.1)		0 (0)	1 (11.1)	
Hard palate	2 (18.2)	1 (11.1)		2 (18.2)	1 (11.1)	
Alveolar ridge	0 (0)	2 (22.2)		0 (0)	2 (22.2)	
Stage						
I + II	7 (63.6)	4 (44.4)	0.391	7 (63.6)	4 (44.4)	0.391
III + IV	4 (36.4)	5 (55.6)		4 (36.4)	5 (55.6)	
Treatment modality						
SG	6 (54.5)	5 (55.6)	0.964	6 (54.5)	5 (55.6)	0.964
SG + RT	5 (45.5)	4 (44.4)		5 (45.5)	4 (44.4)	
Tumor Grade						
G1	7 (63.6)	6 (66.7)	0.888	7 (63.6)	6 (66.7)	0.888
G2 + G3	4 (36.4)	3 (33.3)		4 (36.4)	3 (33.3)	
Margin status						
Free of tumor	6 (54.5)	7 (77.8)	0.279	6 (54.5)	7 (77.8)	0.279
Tumor proximity and with tumor	5 (45.5)	2 (22.2)		5 (45.5)	2 (22.2)	
Vascular invasion						
Absent	11 (100)	9 (100)	-	11 (100)	9 (100)	-
Present	0 (0)	0 (0)		0 (0)	0 (0)	
Perineural permeation						
Absent	9 (81.8)	8 (88.9)	0.660	9 (81.8)	8 (88.9)	0.660
Present	2 (18.2)	1 (11.1)		2 (18.2)	1 (11.1)	
Lymphatic invasion						
Absent	9 (81.8)	6 (66.7)	0.436	9 (81.8)	6 (66.7)	0.436
Present	2 (18.2)	3 (33.3)		2 (18.2)	3 (33.3)	

Table 2. *Cont.*

	AurB (N = 20)					
	Extent			Staining Intensity		
	≤9%	≥10%		Low	High	
Muscular invasion						
Absent	9 (81.8)	8 (88.9)	0.660	9 (81.8)	8 (88.9)	0.660
Present	2 (18.2)	1 (11.1)		2 (18.2)	1 (11.1)	

[a] Chi-square test. p values with statistically significant differences highlighted in bold ($p < 0.05$).

Table 3. Clinicopathological characteristics of the OSCC patients and their association with KSP extent and staining intensity.

	KSP (N = 20)					
	Extent			Staining Intensity		
	≤9%	≥10%		Low	High	
Characteristic	*N* (%)	*N* (%)	p [a]	*N* (%)	*N* (%)	p [a]
All cases						
Gender						
Female	1 (25)	5 (31.2)	0.807	4 (25)	2 (50)	0.329
Male	3 (75)	11 (68.8)		12 (75)	2 (50)	
Age						
<62 years	3 (75)	6 (37.5)	0.178	7 (43.8)	2 (50)	0.822
≥62 years	1 (25)	10 (62.5)		9 (56.2)	2 (50)	
Tumor location						
Lip	1 (25)	4 (25)	0.868	3 (18.8)	2 (50)	0.517
Floor of the mouth	1 (25)	1 (6.3)		1 (6.2)	1 (25)	
Tongue	1 (25)	5 (31.1)		6 (37.5)	0 (0)	
Buccal mucosa	0 (0)	2 (12.5)		2 (12.5)	0 (0)	
Retromolar trigone	0 (0)	1 (6.3)		1 (6.2)	0 (0)	
Hard palate	1 (25)	2 (12.5)		2 (12.5)	1 (25)	
Alveolar ridge	0 (0)	1 (6.3)		1 (6.2)	0 (0)	
Stage						
I + II	3 (75)	7 (43.8)	0.264	7 (43.8)	3 (75)	0.264
III + IV	1 (25)	9 (56.2)		9 (56.2)	1 (25)	
Treatment modality						
SG	2 (50)	8 (50)	1.000	8 (50)	2 (50)	1.000
SG + RT	2 (50)	8 (50)		8 (50)	2 (50)	
Tumor Grade						
G1	1 (25)	9 (56.2)	0.264	7 (43.8)	3 (75)	0.264
G2 + G3	3 (75)	7 (43.8)		9 (56.2)	1 (25)	
Margin status						
Free of tumor	2 (50)	9 (69.2)	0.482	9 (64.3)	2 (66.7)	0.938
Tumor proximity and with tumor	2 (50)	4 (30.8)		5 (35.7)	1 (33.3)	
Vascular invasion						
Absent	4 (100)	16 (100)	-	16 (100)	4 (100)	-
Present	0 (0)	0 (0)		0 (0)	0 (0)	
Perineural permeation						
Absent	3 (75)	15 (93.8)	0.264	14 (87.5)	4 (100)	0.456
Present	1 (25)	1 (6.2)		2 (12.5)	0 (0)	
Lymphatic invasion						
Absent	3 (75)	13 (81.2)	0.780	12 (75)	4 (100)	0.264
Present	1 (25)	3 (18.8)		4 (25)	0 (0)	
Muscular invasion						
Absent	4 (100)	16 (100)	-	16 (100)	4 (100)	-
Present	0 (0)	0 (0)		0 (0)	0 (0)	

[a] Chi-square test. p values with statistically significant differences highlighted in bold ($p < 0.05$).

Immunohistochemical analysis was performed to assess the localization and expression of EGFR, MPS-1, Aurora-B, and KSP in paraffin-embedded OSCC samples (Figure 4). EGFR expression was observed in all 30 (100%) OSCC tissue microarrays, primarily localized on the membrane of the tumor cells. The expression ranged from 50 to 74% in 3 cases (10%) and 75 to 100% in 27 cases (90%). For data analysis, EGFR staining intensity was categorized into two groups: low intensity in 18 cases (62%) and high intensity in 11 cases (38%). MPS-1 expression was found in 25 cases, predominantly localized in the cytoplasm of the tumor cells, with expression levels classified as 50–74% in 1 case (4%) and 75–100% in 24 cases (96%). For data analysis, MPS-1 staining intensity was divided into two groups: negative to medium intensity (0, 1+) in 5 cases (20%) and moderate to high intensity (2+, 3+) in 20 cases (80%). Due to the high expression levels in all cases, only intensity values were considered for those two biomarkers. Aurora-B expression was found in 20 cases, localized to the nucleus of tumor cells, and classified as 0–9% in 11 cases (55%), 10–24% in 5 cases (25%), 25–49% in 2 cases (10%), and 50–74% in 2 cases (10%). For data analysis, Aurora-B expression was grouped into ≤9% expression in 11 cases (55%) and ≥10% expression in 9 cases (45%). Intensity staining followed the same categorization. KSP was found in 20 cases, and it was also localized to the nucleus of tumor cells. Expression was categorized as 0-9% in 4 cases (20%), 10–24% in 2 cases (10%), 50–74% in 4 cases (20%), and 75–100% in 10 cases (50%). For data analysis, KSP expression was grouped into ≤9% expression in 4 cases (20%) and ≥10% expression in 16 cases (80%). Staining intensity was recorded into two groups: negative to moderate intensity (0, 1+, 2+) with 16 cases (80%) and strong intensity (3+) with 4 cases (20%). A statistically significant correlation was observed between MPS-1 and KSP expression ($p = 0.753$ **), with staining intensity being directly proportional.

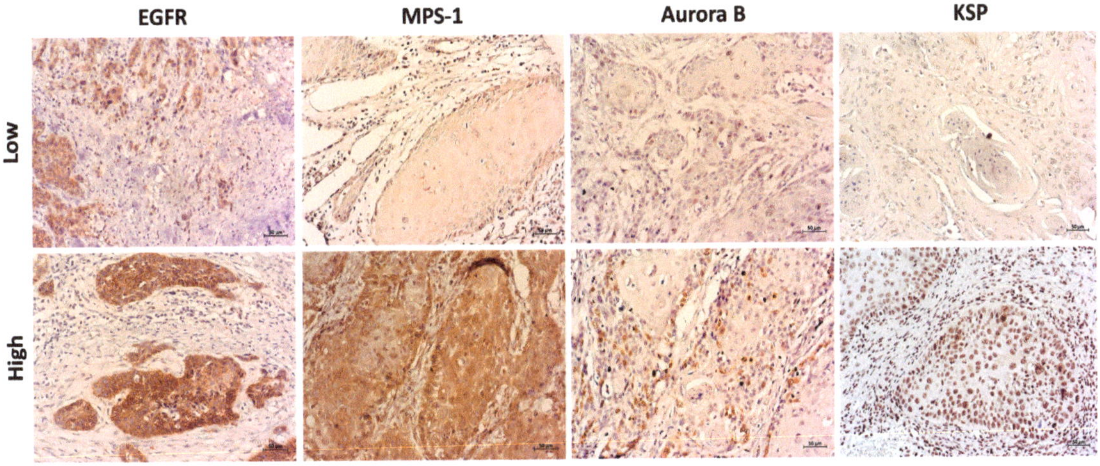

Figure 4. Immunohistochemical analysis of EGFR, MPS-1, Aurora-B, and KSP expression and localization in oral squamous cell carcinoma. Comparison between squamous cell carcinoma samples showing representative images in upper line correspondent to EGFR (75–100% and moderate intensity), MPS-1 (75–100% and weak intensity), Aurora-B (0–9% and weak intensity), and KSP (0–9% and weak intensity) low expression score. While the images in the lower line correspondent to EGFR (75–100% and strong intensity), MPS-1 (75–100% and strong intensity), Aurora-B (10–24% and strong intensity), and KSP (75–100% and strong intensity) high expression score. Cutoffs for the expression score were determined by ROC curves analysis. For EGFR, Aurora-B, and KSP, the staining intensity was classified as low for scores ≤ 2 and high for scores ≥ 3. While for MPS1, low intensity was considered for scores ≤ 1 and strong intensity for scores ≥ 2. Images at 200× magnification. Scale bar = 50 μm.

EGFR, MPS-1, Aurora-B, and KSP were also assessed for association with patient prognosis. The follow-up time for the 30 patients was 36 months. EGFR staining intensity is significantly associated with cancer-specific survival. Kaplan–Meier curves with univariate analyses showed that patients with the highest intensity of EGFR had reduced survival times compared to those with lower expression levels ($p = 0.023$). The stage of the tumor is also significantly associated with cancer-specific survival ($p = 0.020$), as is the treatment modality ($p = 0.027$) (Table 4 and Figure 5). No other variables were related to overall survival. These data highlight the significant prognostic value of tumor stage, treatment modality, and EGFR staining intensity in OSCC patients.

Table 4. Univariate analysis of cancer-specific survival (CSS) according to the clinicopathological characteristics and expression of EGFR, MPS-1, Aurora-B, and KSP.

Characteristic	N (%)	Dead	CSS [a]	p [b]
All cases	30			
Stage				
I	7 (23.3)	0	0	**0.020**
II	11 (36.7)	4	72.7	
III	5 (16.7)	1	80	
IV	7 (23.3)	5	28.6	
Treatment modality				
SG	17 (56.7)	3	87.5	**0.027**
SG + RT	13 (43.3)	7	44.9	
Tumor grade				
G1	18 (60)	5	75.5	0.346
G2 + G3	12 (40)	5	58.3	
Vascular invasion				
Absent	29 (96.7)	10	67.3	0.534
Present	1 (3.3)	0	0	
Perineural permeation				
Absent	26 (86.7)	8	71.4	0.231
Present	4 (13.3)	2	50	
Lymphatic invasion				
Absent	24 (80)	8	69.1	0.729
Present	6 (20)	2	66.7	
Muscular invasion				
Absent	25 (83.3)	9	65.9	0.482
Present	5 (16.7)	1	80	
EGFR staining intensity				
Low	19 (63.3)	4	76.4	**0.023**
High	11 (36.7)	7	43.6	
MPS-1 staining intensity				
Low	5 (20)	3	30	0.102
High	20 (80)	5	80	
AurB staining intensity				
Low	11 (55)	4	63.6	0.683
High	9 (45)	4	62.2	
KSP staining intensity				
Low	16 (80)	5	67	0.335
High	4 (20)	3	50	

[a] Percentage of cases without event at 3 years of follow-up. [b] Log-rank test. Information not available for every patient. p values with statistically significant differences are highlighted in bold ($p < 0.05$).

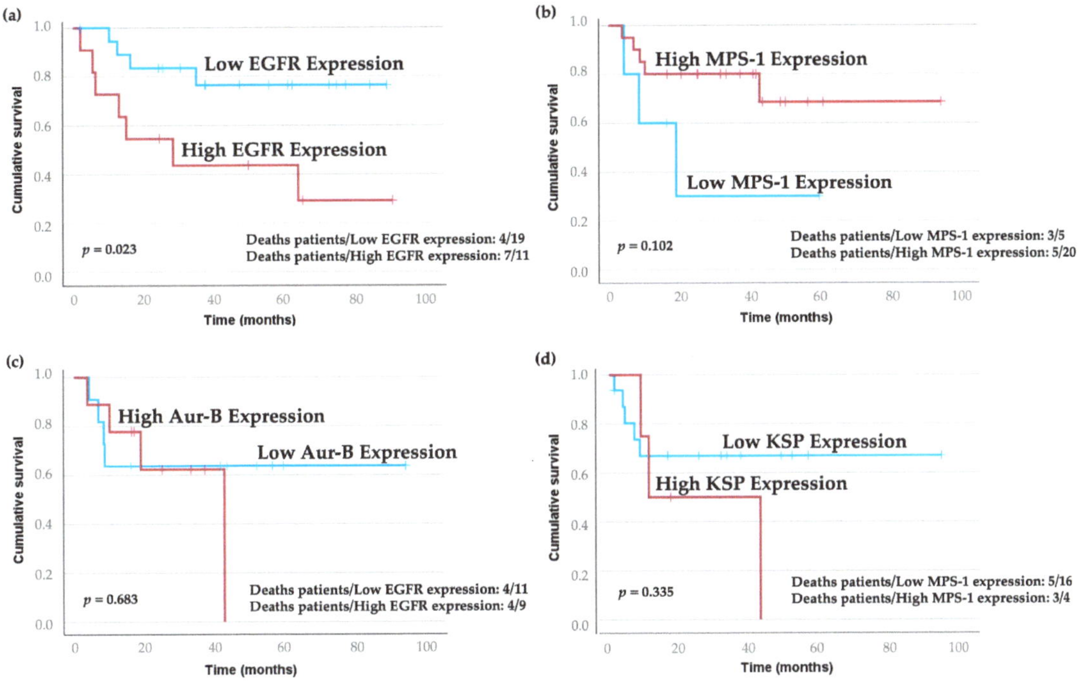

Figure 5. Kaplan–Meier curves illustrating overall patient survival based on expression levels of EGFR (**a**), MPS-1 (**b**), Aurora-B (**c**), and KSP (**d**). Blue lines correspond to cases with low expression, while red lines represent cases with high expression. Notably, higher EGFR staining intensity is significantly associated with reduced cancer-specific survival. Univariate analysis showed that patients with the highest EGFR expression had shorter survival times compared to those with lower expression levels ($p = 0.023$).

The variables evaluated with Kaplan–Meier curves, which demonstrated significant results in the Log-rank test, were subsequently incorporated into a multivariate analysis. This analysis showed that strong EGFR staining intensity is an independent prognostic factor associated with a significantly increased risk of reduced survival (HR = 4.745, $p = 0.029$) compared to individuals with low or moderate EGFR intensity. This finding suggests that high EGFR expression serves as a strong prognostic indicator in OSCC, consistent with previous studies linking EGFR overexpression to poor prognosis in various cancers, including OSCC. Furthermore, the type of treatment and tumor stage did not show significant associations with survival in this analysis. The lack of significant results for treatment modality could reflect the heterogeneity of grouped treatments or an insufficient sample size to detect a difference. Similarly, while advanced-stage disease typically correlates with poorer prognosis, the current sample may lack sufficient statistical power to confirm this relationship (Table 5).

In summary, we did not observe any correlation between the high expression levels of the proteins examined and the clinicopathological characteristics of OSCC patient samples, likely due to the limited sample size (low N). Notably, only high expression of EGFR exhibited statistical significance in relation to worse overall survival. Neither patient stage nor treatment modality demonstrated a significant correlation with patient survival. Furthermore, the multivariate analysis for the variables that showed significant results indicated that only EGFR intensity retained independent significance, highlighting an increased risk for a worse prognosis.

Table 5. Multivariate analysis of cancer-specific survival (CSS).

Variables		Exp (B)	p
Type of treatment	Surgery	1	
	Surgery + other treatments	2.066 (0.236–18.040)	0.512
EGFR intensity score	0/low/moderate	1	
	strong	4.745 (1.170–19.241)	**0.029**
Stage	I + II	1	
	III + IV	1.599 (0.602–4.244)	0.346

p values with statistically significant differences highare lighted in bold ($p < 0.05$).

3.3. EGFR, MPS-1, Aurora-B, and KSP Are Overexpressed in Oral Cancer Cells

EGFR is a transmembrane glycoprotein that belongs to the RTK family, and its primary function is to regulate cellular processes such as growth, proliferation, differentiation, and survival in various cell types, including epithelial, glial, and neuronal cells [35]. In HNC, EGFR is overexpressed in 80–90% of cases and is associated with poor prognosis and unfavorable treatment outcomes [4]. MPS-1 is a critical regulator of chromosome alignment during metaphase, ensuring proper kinetochore-microtubule attachments to prevent aneuploidy [36]. Inhibitors of MPS-1 circumvent the SAC, inducing premature mitotic exit that results in extensive chromosome mis-segregation and, ultimately, cell death, thereby acting as potent mitotic drivers [37]. Aurora-B, a member of the Aurora kinase family, is responsible for monitoring and correcting improper attachments of microtubules to kinetochores, as well as regulating the dissociation of cohesin, a protein essential for maintaining cohesion between sister chromatids during mitosis [38]. KSP plays a crucial role in establishing spindle bipolarity and ensuring the proper separation of spindle poles; inhibition of KSP leads to the collapse of mitotic spindles and the formation of mono-aster [39].

To explore the therapeutic potential of targeting these proteins, we first assessed their expression at both the mRNA and protein levels in two oral cancer cell lines (SCC-09 and SCC-25) using qRT-PCR and Western blot analysis, respectively (Figure 6). Our results indicated that both EGFR and MPS-1 mRNA levels were significantly overexpressed in the SCC-25 cell line compared to the non-tumor cell line HOK (25-fold increase and 1.5-fold increase for EGFR and MPS-1, respectively) (Figure 6a,b). Regarding protein expression, we observed elevated levels of EGFR in the SCC-25 cell line, while MPS-1 was overexpressed in both cell lines (Figure 6c,d).

Our group previously analyzed and reported the expression of Aurora-B and KSP using the same cell lines, demonstrating that both proteins were overexpressed at the mRNA and protein levels [40].

Globally, the overexpression of EGFR, MPS-1, Aurora-B, and KSP in oral cancer cell lines highlights the relevance of their targeting to potentiate current oral cancer treatments.

3.4. Co-Treatment of Cetuximab with MPS-1, Aurora-B, or KSP Inhibitors Showed Synergistic Effects in Oral Cancer Cells

We then evaluated the cytotoxic effects of MPS-1, Aurora-B, and KSP inhibitors in combination with the EGFR inhibitor Cetuximab on oral cancer cells.

Using the MTT assay, we determined the IC_{50} of BAY1217389 and Cetuximab in both SCC-09 and SCC-25 cell lines and evaluated the cytotoxic effects of BAY1217389, Barasertib, Ispinesib, and Cetuximab, both individually and in combination (Table 6). The IC_{50} of Cetuximab could not be established, even at a concentration of 800 nM; therefore, we employed lower concentrations in the MTT assay to identify potential synergistic points with reduced drug concentrations. Nonetheless, BAY1217389 exhibited comparable IC_{50} for both cell lines (402.95 ± 4.31 nM vs. 540.6 ± 2.12 nM for SCC-25 and SCC-09, respectively). The IC_{50} values of Barasertib and Ispinesib were previously determined, and as indicated in Table 1, the SCC-25 cell line demonstrated greater sensibility to these drugs compared to the SCC-09 cell line.

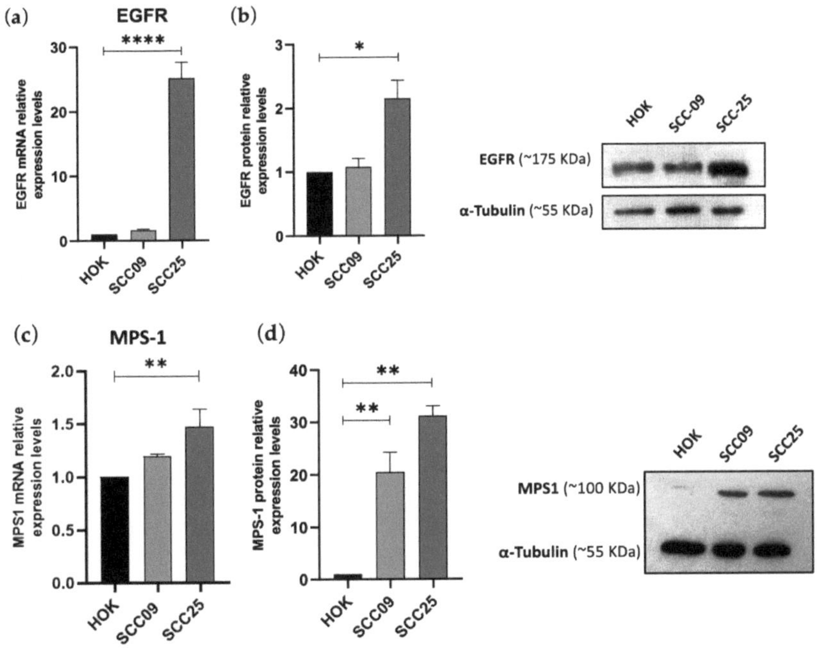

Figure 6. EGFR and MPS-1 are overexpressed in oral cancer cell lines. Relative expression of EGFR (**a**) and MPS-1 (**c**) mRNA as determined by qRT-PCR in SCC-09 and SCC-25 tumor cell lines, comparatively to non-tumor HOK. Representative Western Blots showing differential expression at protein levels of EGFR (**b**) and MPS-1 (**d**). α-tubulin was used as a loading control. The significance levels were as follows: * $p < 0.05$, ** $p < 0.01$ and **** $p < 0.0001$. Original western blots are presented in File S1.

Table 6. IC_{50} values of Cetuximab, BAY1217389, Barasertib, and Ispinesib in SCC-25 and SCC-09 cell lines after 48 h incubation.

	IC_{50} (nM)	
Drugs/Cell Line	**SCC-25**	**SCC-09**
Cetuximab	>800	>800
BAY1217389	402.95 ± 4.31	540.6 ± 2.12
Barasertib	5580.0 ± 664.0 [40]	>64,000.0 [40]
Ispinesib	3.4 ± 0.5 [40]	58.9 ± 3.2 [40]

Given that the SCC-25 cell line serves as a model of oral cancer and exhibits elevated protein expression levels of EGFR, MPS-1, Aurora-B, and KSP compared to SCC-09 cells, we selected SCC-25 cells for the subsequent experiments in this study. The results of the MTT assay for the SCC-09 cell lines can be found in the Supplementary Material (Figure S1). The effects of each drug combination were assessed, and the data are presented as two dual-drug concentration crosswise matrices: one depicting the percentage of cell viability and the other illustrating the effect score of the combinations (Figure 7). Notably, all combinations exhibited synergistic effects, and the synergistic combination with the lowest concentrations was selected for further experimentation (30 nM of Cetuximab with 40 nM of BAY1217389,

15 nM of Cetuximab with 1000 nM of Barasertib, and 240 nM of Cetuximab with 1.875 nM of Ispinesib).

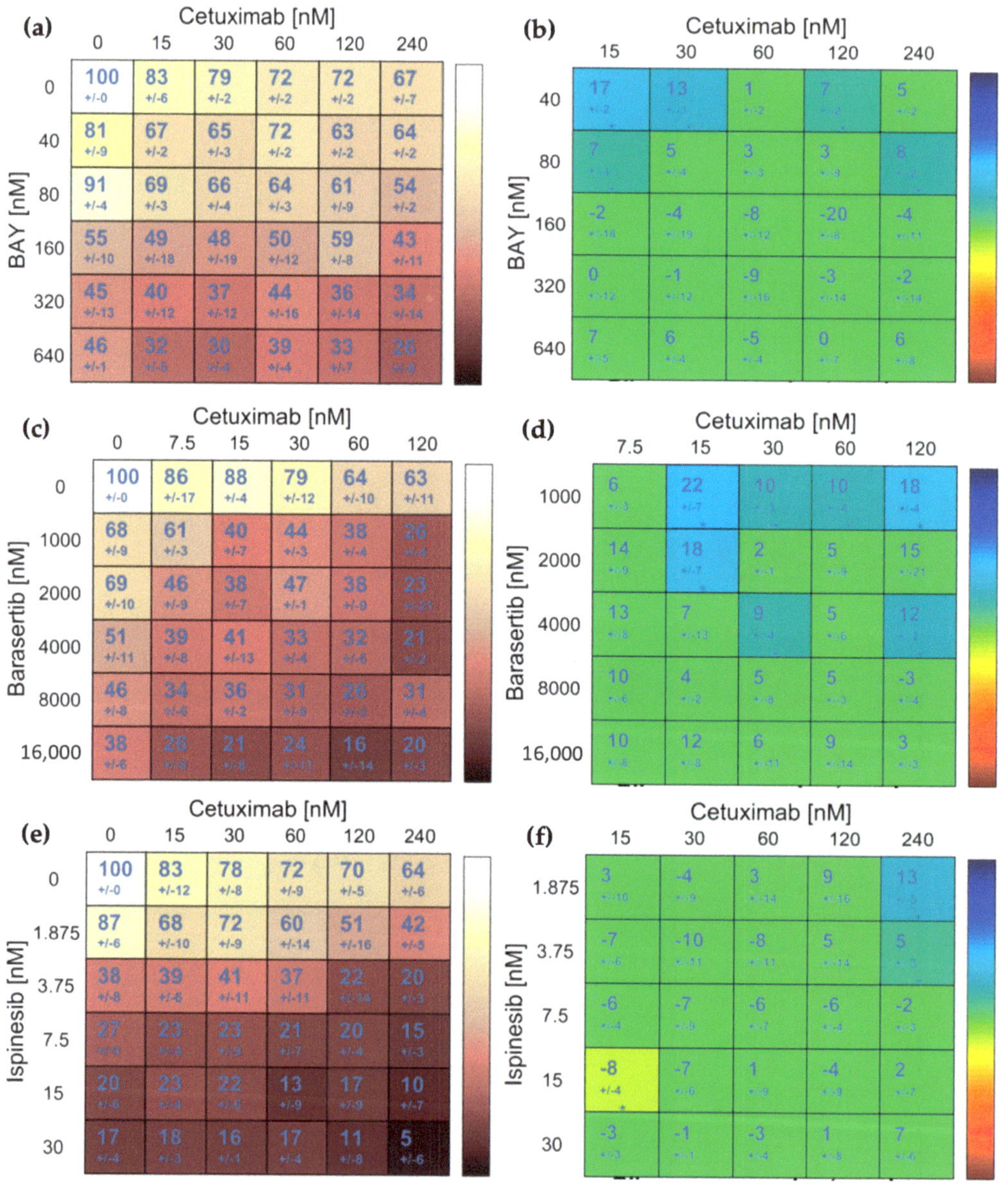

Figure 7. BAY1217389 + Cetuximab (**a**,**b**), Barasertib + Cetuximab (**c**,**d**), and Ispinesib + Cetuximab (**e**,**f**) combinations potentiate cytotoxicity in SCC-25 cell lines. Cell viability (%) after 48 h of exposure to single or combination therapies was determined by MTT assay (**a**,**c**,**e**) based on three independent experiments. Synergy scores (**b**,**d**,**f**) were calculated using the Bliss model in Combenefit software version 2.021, with asterisks denoting synergistic (cyan to blue) or antagonistic (yellow-green to red) effects. The statistical significance levels were the following: * $p < 0.05$.

Notably, the concentrations of BAY1217389, Barasertib, and Ispinesib used correspond to 10-, 5.6-, and 3-fold reductions, respectively, from their respective IC_{50} values. In contrast, the reduction in concentration for Cetuximab was even more pronounced, as the IC_{50} could not be achieved.

To evaluate whether drug combinations resulted in prolonged anticancer effects, we performed colony formation assays in SCC-25 cancer cells. The cells were exposed to the different combinations for 48 h, after which the medium was replaced with fresh medium. Colonies were counted after 7 days. Our results indicated that the combinations of Barasertib + Cetuximab and Ispinesib + Cetuximab significantly reduced colony formation compared to single treatments. In contrast, the combination of BAY1217389 + Cetuximab resulted in a reduction similar to that of BAY1217389 alone (Figure 8a–d). Specifically, a colony survival fraction of 53.69% ± 2.64 was observed following treatment with Barasertib + Cetuximab, compared to Barasertib (103.24% ± 3.02) and Cetuximab (84.22% ± 3.68) alone. Similarly, the Ispinesib + Cetuximab combination results in a colony survival fraction of 43% ± 1.18, compared to Ispinesib (57.82% ± 3.32) and Cetuximab (79.37% ± 2.12) drugs alone. In contrast, the combinatorial exposure to BAY1217389 + Cetuximab led to a colony survival fraction of 51.37% ± 3.16 compared to 52.64% ± 6.36 for BAY1217389 monotherapy and 78.25% ± 10.63 for Cetuximab monotherapy. These results suggest that the combinatorial approaches, at least for Barasertib + Cetuximab and Ispinesib + Cetuximab combinations, exhibit the ability to maintain long-term cellular cytotoxicity, preventing the proliferation of cancer cells, supporting the therapeutic promise of combining EGFR inhibition with Aurora-B or KSP inhibition, and to a lesser extent with MPS-1 inhibition, in oral cancer treatment. Thus, these combinations appear to be viable strategies to enhance therapeutic outcomes.

3.5. The Combined Treatment of Cetuximab with BAY1217389, Barasertib, or Ispinesib Enhances Mitotic Cell Death in Oral Cancer Cells

After observing increased cytotoxicity with the combination treatments, we further investigated whether this effect was mediated by Cetuximab promoting apoptosis, using flow cytometry for analysis. Cetuximab alone significantly increased the percentage of apoptotic cells compared to the control. BAY1217389 alone demonstrated a slight increase in apoptotic cells compared to the control (7.48 ± 1.60% vs. 2.3 ± 0.72%, respectively), while Barasertib alone resulted in a similar increase as Cetuximab alone (12.2 ± 2.47% vs. 11.63 ± 3.76%, respectively). For the combination of Cetuximab and Ispinesib, cells were exposed for 24 h to ensure the analysis captured all cells undergoing apoptosis, as this combination resulted in a high number of dead cells at this time, thereby minimizing the risk of loss. However, Ispinesib alone did not exhibit a statistically significant difference compared to the control (5.04 ± 1.77% vs. 2.3 ± 1%).

A significant increase in cell apoptosis was observed when Cetuximab was combined with BAY1217389 (21.62 ± 4.70%), Barasertib (42.37 ± 4.61%), or Ispinesib (22 ± 5.75%), compared to the effects of the individual drugs and the control (Figure 9). Additionally, the combinations of Cetuximab with Barasertib or Ispinesib were tested using SCC-09 cells. The combination of Cetuximab and Ispinesib demonstrated similar results, while Cetuximab and Barasertib showed a slight increase, although not statistically significant, in the percentage of apoptotic cells (Figure S2).

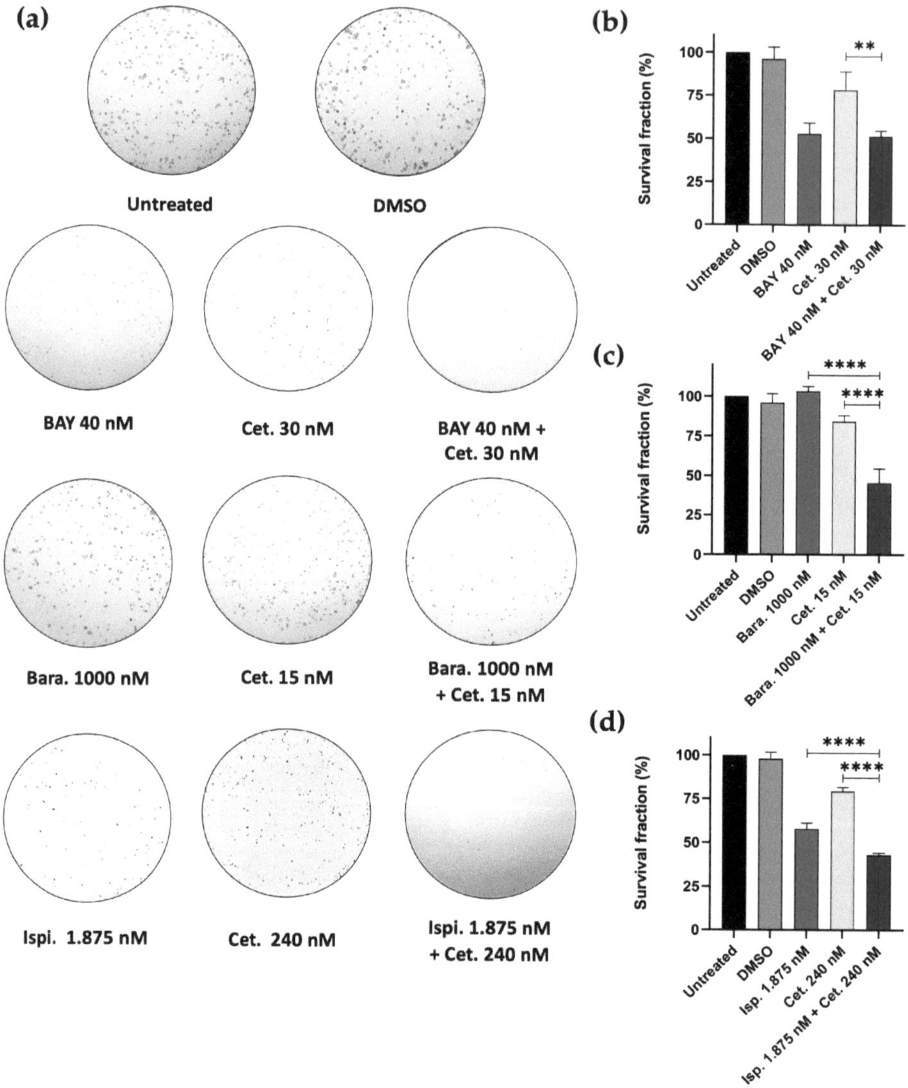

Figure 8. Colony formation assays were conducted using SCC-25 cells over a period of 7 days (**a**). The survival fraction (%) was quantified following single or combination treatments as specified (**b–d**). Data represent the mean ± SD of three independent experiments, analyzed using one-way ANOVA followed by Tukey's multiple comparisons test. Statistical significance is denoted as follows: ** $p < 0.01$; **** $p < 0.0001$.

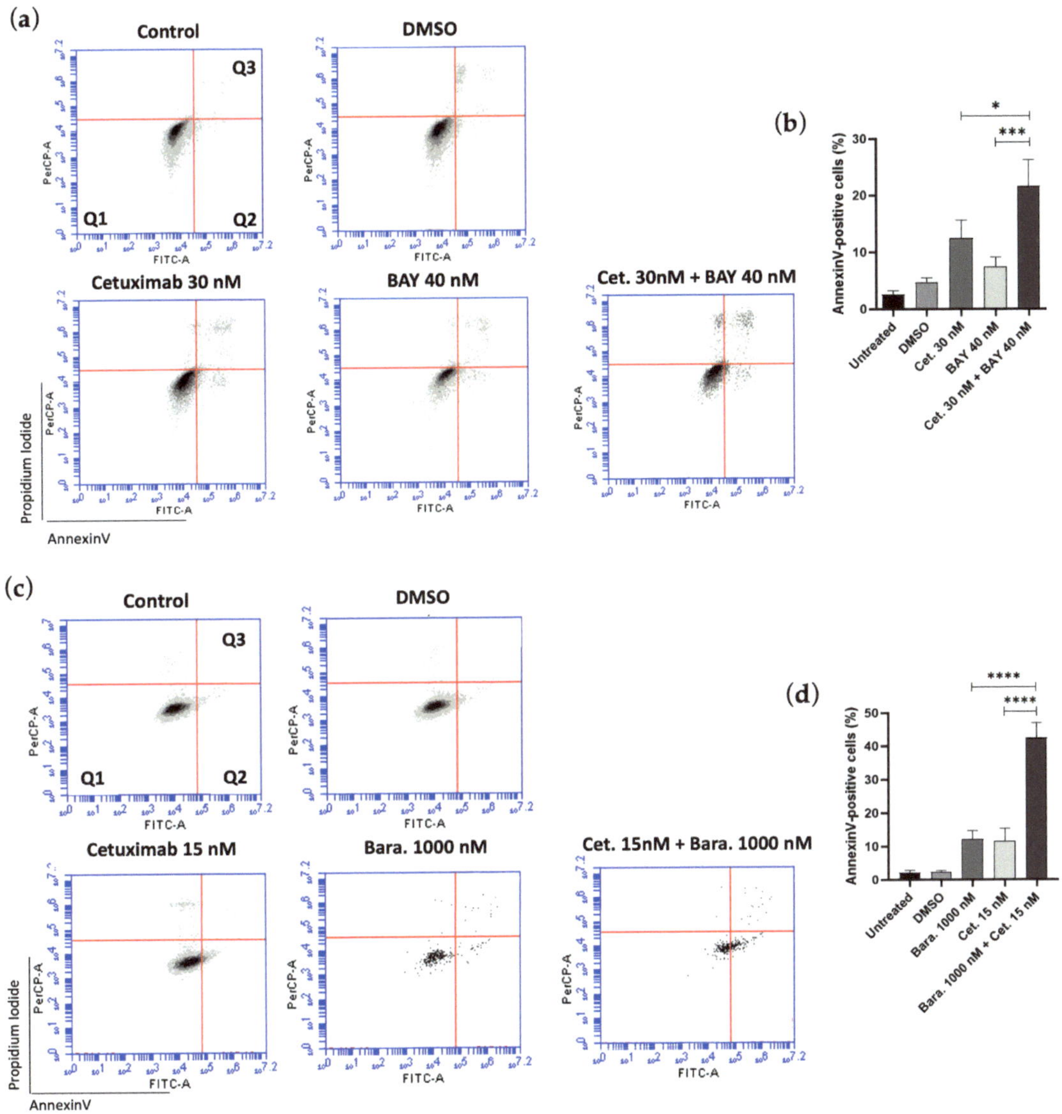

Figure 9. *Cont.*

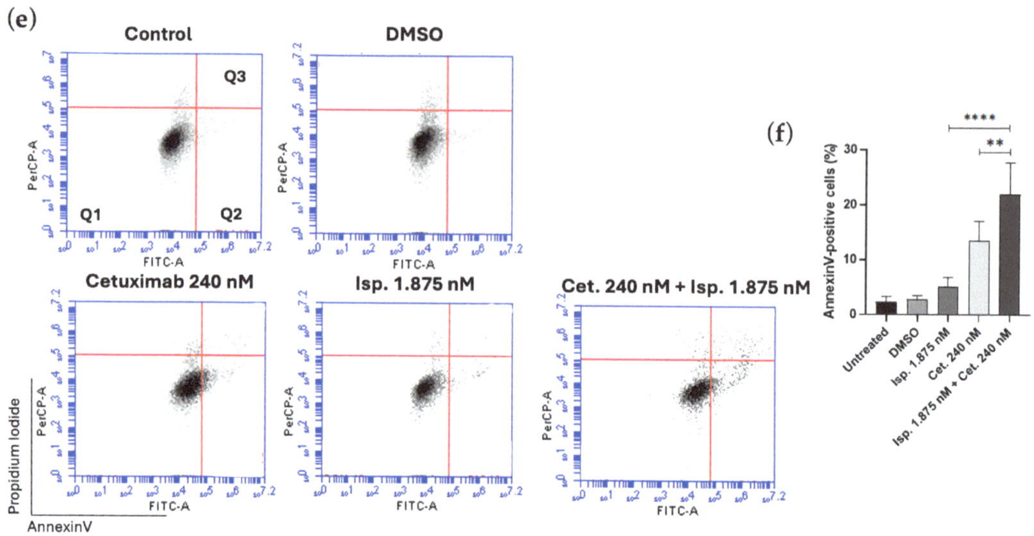

Figure 9. The combinations of BAY1217389 + Cetuximab, Barasertib + Cetuximab, and Ispinesib + Cetuximab promote increased cell death in SCC-25 oral cancer cells. Representative cytograms of SCC-25 cells double-stained with Annexin V-FITC and propidium iodide (PI) are displayed in panels (**a**,**c**,**e**). The quadrants are defined as follows: Q1 = live cells (Annexin V-negative, PI-negative), Q2 = early apoptosis (Annexin V-positive, PI-negative), and Q3 = late apoptosis (Annexin V-positive, PI-positive). Bar graphics (**b**,**d**,**f**) showing the percentage of Annexin V-positive cells. Data represent the mean ± SD from three independent experiments and were analyzed using one-way ANOVA with Tukey's multiple comparison test. Statistical significance is indicated as * $p < 0.05$, ** $p < 0.01$, *** $p < 0.001$, and **** $p < 0.0001$.

4. Discussion

EGFR, MPS-1, Aurora-B, and KSP are highly expressed in oral cancer cells and tissues from OSCC patients, which is in accordance with the data available in bioinformatic databases, such as UALCAN. Furthermore, EGFR, MPS-1, Aurora-B, and KSP expression levels have significant implications for the clinical outcomes of OSCC patients. High EGFR expression is associated with poorer prognosis and reduced survival, as indicated by the significant correlation with cancer-specific survival. This makes EGFR a valuable prognostic marker and a target for therapeutic intervention.

While the direct correlation of MPS-1, Aurora-B, and KSP with clinical outcomes, such as survival, was not statistically significant in the provided data, there is a notable trend.

Except for MPS-1, high expression levels of these proteins may correlate with more aggressive disease and poorer prognosis. However, a limitation of our study is the relatively small number of patient samples; a larger sample size might yield statistically significant results, thereby strengthening the validity of our results regarding the overexpression of MPS-1, Aurora-B, and KSP in clinical contexts.

To our knowledge, no studies have specifically assessed the correlation between MPS-1 expression and overall survival in OSCC patients. However, some studies conducted with triple-negative breast cancer (TNBC) patient samples have shown similar results to those observed in our study, wherein high expression of MPS-1 was correlated with better overall survival and disease-free survival [11,12]. One of these studies suggests that low expression of MPS-1 may be associated with reduced responsiveness to conventional chemotherapy, as these cells exhibit lower proliferative rates [11]. Conversely, other studies indicate that higher expression of MPS-1 in TNBC patients is linked to poor prognosis [41,42]. Thus, additional involving OSCC patients is required to fully elucidate the correlation between this protein and patient prognosis.

The trend observed for KSP appears to align with previously reported findings, which indicated that high expression of KSP is associated with worse prognosis in oral cancer patients [39]. Similar results have been reported for Aurora-B, although the correlation with poorer prognosis in OSCC patients was noted in relation to disease-free survival rather than overall survival, as indicated in our study [17].

Co-treatment with Cetuximab and inhibitors targeting MPS-1, Aurora-B, or KSP demonstrated synergistic effects in oral cancer cells. This synergy suggests that these proteins may be part of interconnected pathways that promote cancer cell survival and proliferation. By simultaneously targeting multiple nodes within these pathways, combination treatment may more effectively induce mitotic cell death.

Combining Cetuximab with BAY1217389 enhances mitotic cell death, indicating that inhibiting EGFR and MPS-1 disrupts critical signaling required for cell division and survival in oral cancer cells. Nonetheless, the results regarding the apoptosis evaluation had a more pronounced effect on the combination when compared to the long-term proliferation assay. This can be explained by the inherent differences between the methods used for the experiments, such as the duration of the assay (48 h vs. 7 days). Combining Cetuximab with Barasertib also amplifies mitotic cell death, suggesting that Aurora-B is a crucial mediator of cell cycle progression in these cells, and its inhibition, alongside EGFR blockade, leads to heightened cell death. Similarly to the other combinations, Cetuximab with Ispinesib increases mitotic cell death, indicating the essential role of KSP in mitotic spindle formation and function, which is critical for cell division. In addition to the body of work regarding the clinical relevance of these proteins, the results from our combinatorial treatment approaches suggest their potential as therapeutic targets.

Furthermore, the cell lines employed in this study were both HPV-negative SCCs from the tongue. HPV-negative oral cancers are generally associated with a poorer prognosis compared to their HPV-positive counterparts. Additionally, these two types exhibit distinct characteristics that must be considered when selecting treatment options. Therefore, our findings may not be extrapolated to HPV-positive cell lines, even though previous research has demonstrated similar responses to Cetuximab treatment regardless of HPV status [43]. Moreover, it is important to note that the incidence of HPV-positive oral cancers is on the rise, particularly in developed countries. This trend highlights the necessity for further research that includes HPV-positive cell lines to enhance our understanding of the effects of our combinatorial treatment approaches.

Our findings indicate that MPS-1, Aurora-B, or KSP are commonly expressed in OSCC, and inhibiting these proteins enhances the therapeutic potential of Cetuximab.

5. Conclusions

The overexpression of EGFR, MPS-1, Aurora-B, and KSP in OSCC underscores their critical roles in tumor progression. The synergistic effects of combined Cetuximab, and specific inhibitors highlight the potential for multi-targeted therapies. EGFR, with its significant association with poor prognosis, stands out as a key prognostic marker and therapeutic target. Future studies should aim to validate these findings in larger patient cohorts and further explore the interplay mechanism underlying the observed synergistic effects. This could pave the way for more effective, personalized treatment strategies for OSCC patients.

Supplementary Materials: The following supporting information can be downloaded at: https://www.mdpi.com/article/10.3390/cancers16223732/s1, Table S1: Clinicopathological characteristics of the OSCC patients; Figure S1: BAY1217389 + Cetuximab (a,b), Barasertib + Cetuximab (c,d) and Ispinesib + Cetuximab (e,f) combinations potentiate cytotoxicity in SCC-09 cell lines. Cell viability (%) of single or combination therapies after 48 h of drug exposure, from three independent experiments as determined by MTT assay (a,c,d). Synergy scores (b,d,f) calculated by the Bliss model of Combenefit software 2.021 with statistical relevance of * $p < 0.05$; Figure S2: The combination of Barasertib + Cetuximab (a,b) showed no cell death increase while Ispinesib + Cetuximab (c,d) enhanced cell death in SCC-09 oral cancer cells. Representative cytograms of the SCC-09 cell line, double-stained with Annexin V-FITC and propidium iodide (PI), are shown (a,c). The quadrants are defined as follows: Q1 = live cells (Annexin V-negative and PI-negative), Q2 = early stage of apoptosis (Annexin V-positive and PI-negative), and Q3 = late stage of apoptosis (Annexin V-positive and PI-positive). Quantification of Annexin V-positive cells is provided (b,d). Data represent the mean ± SD of three independent experiments and were analyzed using one-way ANOVA followed by Tukey's multiple comparisons test. Statistical significance is indicated as ** $p < 0.01$, and *** $p < 0.001$. File S1: Original western blots.

Author Contributions: Conceptualization, H.B., L.M., P.M.A.S., J.P.N.S. and M.C.-L.; data collection, M.C.-L., J.P.N.S., L.D. and P.M.A.S.; resources, C.L., H.B. and P.M.A.S.; writing—original draft preparation, M.C.-L.; writing—review and editing, J.P.N.S., L.M., B.P., P.M.A.S. and H.B.; supervision, H.B., L.M. and P.M.A.S.; funding acquisition and management, H.B. and P.M.A.S. All authors have read and agreed to the published version of the manuscript.

Funding: This work was funded by CESPU—Cooperativa de Ensino Superior Politécnico e Universitário Crl (Grants Ref. AntiMitoSphere_APSFCT_IINFACTS_2021; Ref. Flav4Tumor-GI2-CESPU-2022; Ref. SGA4Cancer-GI2-CESPU-2022, Ref. upPTXovcar-GI2-CESPU-2022 and Ref. BeatCancer-GI2-CESPU-2023) to H.B. and P.M.A.S. J.P.N.S. gratefully acknowledges CESPU (BD/CBAS/CESPU/01/2021) for financial support. B.P. gratefully acknowledges CESPU (BD/CBAS/CESPU/01/2020) and Fundação para a Ciência e a Tecnologia (FCT) (2022.09451.BD) for financial support.

Institutional Review Board Statement: Not applicable.

Informed Consent Statement: Not applicable.

Data Availability Statement: Data can be shared upon request.

Acknowledgments: We would like to thank the Pathology Department of Centro Hospitalar Universitário de Santo António for the support.

Conflicts of Interest: The authors declare no conflicts of interest.

References

1. Bray, F.; Laversanne, M.; Sung, H.; Ferlay, J.; Siegel, R.L.; Soerjomataram, I.; Jemal, A. Global Cancer Statistics 2022: GLOBOCAN Estimates of Incidence and Mortality Worldwide for 36 Cancers in 185 Countries. *CA Cancer J. Clin.* **2024**, *74*, 229–263. [CrossRef] [PubMed]
2. Li, Q.; Tie, Y.; Alu, A.; Ma, X.; Shi, H. Targeted Therapy for Head and Neck Cancer: Signaling Pathways and Clinical Studies. *Signal Transduct. Target. Ther.* **2023**, *8*, 31. [CrossRef] [PubMed]
3. Leemans, C.R.; Snijders, P.J.F.; Brakenhoff, R.H. The Molecular Landscape of Head and Neck Cancer. *Nat. Rev. Cancer* **2018**, *18*, 269–282. [CrossRef] [PubMed]
4. Hanahan, D.; Weinberg, R.A. Hallmarks of Cancer: The Next Generation. *Cell* **2011**, *144*, 646–674. [CrossRef]
5. Chamoli, A.; Gosavi, A.S.; Shirwadkar, U.P.; Wangdale, K.V.; Behera, S.K.; Kurrey, N.K.; Kalia, K.; Mandoli, A. Overview of Oral Cavity Squamous Cell Carcinoma: Risk Factors, Mechanisms, and Diagnostics. *Oral Oncol.* **2021**, *121*, 105451. [CrossRef]
6. Gharat, S.A.; Momin, M.; Bhavsar, C. Oral Squamous Cell Carcinoma: Current Treatment Strategies and Nanotechnology-Based Approaches for Prevention and Therapy. *Crit. Rev. Ther. Drug Carr. Syst.* **2016**, *33*, 363–400. [CrossRef]
7. Leemans, C.R.; Braakhuis, B.J.M.; Brakenhoff, R.H. The Molecular Biology of Head and Neck Cancer. *Nat. Rev. Cancer* **2011**, *11*, 9–22. [CrossRef]
8. Solomon, B.; Young, R.J.; Rischin, D. Head and Neck Squamous Cell Carcinoma: Genomics and Emerging Biomarkers for Immunomodulatory Cancer Treatments. *Semin. Cancer Biol.* **2018**, *52*, 228–240. [CrossRef]
9. Pai, S.I.; Westra, W.H. Molecular Pathology of Head and Neck Cancer: Implications for Diagnosis, Prognosis, and Treatment. *Annu. Rev. Pathol. Mech. Dis.* **2009**, *4*, 49–70. [CrossRef]
10. Lara-Gonzalez, P.; Westhorpe, F.G.; Taylor, S.S. The Spindle Assembly Checkpoint. *Curr. Biol.* **2012**, *22*, R966–R980. [CrossRef]
11. Xu, Q.; Xu, Y.; Pan, B.; Wu, L.; Ren, X.; Zhou, Y.; Mao, F.; Lin, Y.; Guan, J.; Shen, S.; et al. TTK Is a Favorable Prognostic Biomarker for Triple-Negative Breast Cancer Survival. *Oncotarget* **2016**, *7*, 81815–81829. [CrossRef] [PubMed]
12. Liu, X.; Liao, W.; Yuan, Q.; Ou, Y.; Huang, J. TTK Activates Akt and Promotes Proliferation and Migration of Hepatocellular Carcinoma Cells. *Oncotarget* **2015**, *6*, 34309–34320. [CrossRef]
13. Stratford, J.K.; Yan, F.; Hill, R.A.; Major, M.B.; Graves, L.M.; Der, C.J.; Yeh, J.J. Genetic and Pharmacological Inhibition of TTK Impairs Pancreatic Cancer Cell Line Growth by Inducing Lethal Chromosomal Instability. *PLoS ONE* **2017**, *12*, e0174863. [CrossRef] [PubMed]

14. Chen, X.; Zhang, D.; Jiang, F.; Shen, Y.; Li, X.; Hu, X.; Wei, P.; Shen, X. Prognostic Prediction Using a Stemness Index-Related Signature in a Cohort of Gastric Cancer. *Front. Mol. Biosci.* **2020**, *7*, 570702. [CrossRef]
15. Mason, J.M.; Wei, X.; Fletcher, G.C.; Kiarash, R.; Brokx, R.; Hodgson, R.; Beletskaya, I.; Bray, M.R.; Mak, T.W. Functional Characterization of CFI-402257, a Potent and Selective Mps1/TTK Kinase Inhibitor, for the Treatment of Cancer. *Proc. Natl. Acad. Sci. USA* **2017**, *114*, 3127–3132. [CrossRef]
16. Portella, G.; Passaro, C.; Chieffi, P. Aurora B: A New Prognostic Marker and Therapeutic Target in Cancer. *Curr. Med. Chem.* **2011**, *18*, 482–496. [CrossRef]
17. Qi, G.; Ogawa, I.; Kudo, Y.; Miyauchi, M.; Siriwardena, B.S.M.S.; Shimamoto, F.; Tatsuka, M.; Takata, T. Aurora-B Expression and Its Correlation with Cell Proliferation and Metastasis in Oral Cancer. *Virchows Arch.* **2007**, *450*, 297–302. [CrossRef] [PubMed]
18. Erpolat, O.P.; Gocun, P.U.; Akmansu, M.; Karakus, E.; Akyol, G. High Expression of Nuclear Survivin and Aurora B Predicts Poor Overall Survival in Patients with Head and Neck Squamous Cell Cancer. *Strahlenther. Onkol.* **2012**, *188*, 248–254. [CrossRef]
19. Mann, B.J.; Wadsworth, P. Kinesin-5 Regulation and Function in Mitosis. *Trends Cell Biol.* **2019**, *29*, 66–79. [CrossRef]
20. Yu, W.-X.; Li, Y.-K.; Xu, M.-F.; Xu, C.-J.; Chen, J.; Wei, Y.-L.; She, Z.-Y. Kinesin-5 Eg5 Is Essential for Spindle Assembly, Chromosome Stability and Organogenesis in Development. *Cell Death Discov.* **2022**, *8*, 490. [CrossRef]
21. Wang, Y.; Wu, X.; Du, M.; Chen, X.; Ning, X.; Chen, H.; Wang, S.; Liu, J.; Liu, Z.; Li, R.; et al. Eg5 Inhibitor YL001 Induces Mitotic Arrest and Inhibits Tumor Proliferation. *Oncotarget* **2017**, *8*, 42510–42524. [CrossRef] [PubMed]
22. Shao, Y.-Y.; Sun, N.-Y.; Jeng, Y.-M.; Wu, Y.-M.; Hsu, C.; Hsu, C.-H.; Hsu, H.-C.; Cheng, A.-L.; Lin, Z.-Z. Eg5 as a Prognostic Biomarker and Potential Therapeutic Target for Hepatocellular Carcinoma. *Cells* **2021**, *10*, 1698. [CrossRef] [PubMed]
23. Jin, Q.; Huang, F.; Wang, X.; Zhu, H.; Xian, Y.; Li, J.; Zhang, S.; Ni, Q. High Eg5 Expression Predicts Poor Prognosis in Breast Cancer. *Oncotarget* **2017**, *8*, 62208–62216. [CrossRef]
24. Lu, M.; Zhu, H.; Wang, X.; Zhang, D.; Xiong, L.; Xu, L.; You, Y. The Prognostic Role of Eg5 Expression in Laryngeal Squamous Cell Carcinoma. *Pathology* **2016**, *48*, 214–218. [CrossRef] [PubMed]
25. Tang, P.A.; Siu, L.L.; Chen, E.X.; Hotte, S.J.; Chia, S.; Schwarz, J.K.; Pond, G.R.; Johnson, C.; Colevas, A.D.; Synold, T.W.; et al. Phase II Study of Ispinesib in Recurrent or Metastatic Squamous Cell Carcinoma of the Head and Neck. *Investig. New Drugs* **2008**, *26*, 257–264. [CrossRef]
26. Lee, C.W.; Bélanger, K.; Rao, S.C.; Petrella, T.M.; Tozer, R.G.; Wood, L.; Savage, K.J.; Eisenhauer, E.A.; Synold, T.W.; Wainman, N.; et al. A Phase II Study of Ispinesib (SB-715992) in Patients with Metastatic or Recurrent Malignant Melanoma: A National Cancer Institute of Canada Clinical Trials Group Trial. *Investig. New Drugs* **2008**, *26*, 249–255. [CrossRef]
27. Boss, D.S.; Witteveen, P.O.; van der Sar, J.; Lolkema, M.P.; Voest, E.E.; Stockman, P.K.; Ataman, O.; Wilson, D.; Das, S.; Schellens, J.H. Clinical Evaluation of AZD1152, an i.v. Inhibitor of Aurora B Kinase, in Patients with Solid Malignant Tumors. *Ann. Oncol.* **2011**, *22*, 431–437. [CrossRef]
28. Helfrich, B.A.; Kim, J.; Gao, D.; Chan, D.C.; Zhang, Z.; Tan, A.-C.; Bunn, P.A. Barasertib (AZD1152), a Small Molecule Aurora B Inhibitor, Inhibits the Growth of SCLC Cell Lines In Vitro and In Vivo. *Mol. Cancer Ther.* **2016**, *15*, 2314–2322. [CrossRef]
29. Exertier, P.; Javerzat, S.; Wang, B.; Franco, M.; Herbert, J.; Platonova, N.; Winandy, M.; Pujol, N.; Nivelles, O.; Ormenese, S.; et al. Impaired Angiogenesis and Tumor Development by Inhibition of the Mitotic Kinesin Eg5. *Oncotarget* **2013**, *4*, 2302–2316. [CrossRef]
30. Lok, T.M.; Wang, Y.; Xu, W.K.; Xie, S.; Ma, H.T.; Poon, R.Y.C. Mitotic Slippage Is Determined by P31comet and the Weakening of the Spindle-Assembly Checkpoint. *Oncogene* **2020**, *39*, 2819–2834. [CrossRef]
31. Silva, P.M.A.; Ribeiro, N.; Lima, R.T.; Andrade, C.; Diogo, V.; Teixeira, J.; Florindo, C.; Tavares, Á.; Vasconcelos, M.H.; Bousbaa, H. Suppression of Spindly Delays Mitotic Exit and Exacerbates Cell Death Response of Cancer Cells Treated with Low Doses of Paclitaxel. *Cancer Lett.* **2017**, *394*, 33–42. [CrossRef] [PubMed]
32. Monteiro, L.S.; Diniz-Freitas, M.; Garcia-Caballero, T.; Forteza, J.; Fraga, M. EGFR and Ki-67 Expression in Oral Squamous Cell Carcinoma Using Tissue Microarray Technology. *J. Oral Pathol. Med.* **2010**, *39*, 571–578. [CrossRef] [PubMed]
33. Monteiro, L.S.; Delgado, M.L.; Ricardo, S.; Garcez, F.; Amaral, B.d.; Warnakulasuriya, S.; Lopes, C. Phosphorylated Mammalian Target of Rapamycin Is Associated with an Adverse Outcome in Oral Squamous Cell Carcinoma. *Oral Surg. Oral Med. Oral Pathol. Oral Radiol.* **2013**, *115*, 638–645. [CrossRef] [PubMed]
34. Sibilia, M.; Kroismayr, R.; Lichtenberger, B.M.; Natarajan, A.; Hecking, M.; Holcmann, M. The Epidermal Growth Factor Receptor: From Development to Tumorigenesis. *Differentiation* **2007**, *75*, 770–787. [CrossRef]
35. Hiruma, Y.; Koch, A.; Hazraty, N.; Tsakou, F.; Medema, R.H.; Joosten, R.P.; Perrakis, A. Understanding Inhibitor Resistance in Mps1 Kinase through Novel Biophysical Assays and Structures. *J. Biol. Chem.* **2017**, *292*, 14496–14504. [CrossRef]
36. Tipton, A.R.; Ji, W.; Sturt-Gillespie, B.; Bekier, M.E.; Wang, K.; Taylor, W.R.; Liu, S.-T. Monopolar Spindle 1 (MPS1) Kinase Promotes Production of Closed MAD2 (C-MAD2) Conformer and Assembly of the Mitotic Checkpoint Complex. *J. Biol. Chem.* **2013**, *288*, 35149–35158. [CrossRef]
37. Kovacs, A.H.; Zhao, D.; Hou, J. Aurora B Inhibitors as Cancer Therapeutics. *Molecules* **2023**, *28*, 3385. [CrossRef]
38. Garcia-Saez, I.; Skoufias, D.A. Eg5 Targeting Agents: From New Anti-Mitotic Based Inhibitor Discovery to Cancer Therapy and Resistance. *Biochem. Pharmacol.* **2021**, *184*, 114364. [CrossRef]
39. Silva, J.P.N.; Pinto, B.; Monteiro, L.; Silva, P.M.A.; Bousbaa, H. Coupling Kinesin Spindle Protein and Aurora B Inhibition with Apoptosis Induction Enhances Oral Cancer Cell Killing. *Cancers* **2024**, *16*, 2014. [CrossRef]

40. Daigo, K.; Takano, A.; Manh, T.; Yoshitake, Y.; Shinohara, M.; Tohnai, I.; Murakami, Y.; Maegawa, J.; Daigo, Y. Characterization of KIF11 as a Novel Prognostic Biomarker and Therapeutic Target for Oral Cancer. *Int. J. Oncol.* **2017**, *52*, 155–165. [CrossRef]
41. Thu, K.L.; Silvester, J.; Elliott, M.J.; Ba-Alawi, W.; Duncan, M.H.; Elia, A.C.; Mer, A.S.; Smirnov, P.; Safikhani, Z.; Haibe-Kains, B.; et al. Disruption of the anaphase-promoting complex confers resistance to TTK inhibitors in triple-negative breast cancer. *Proc. Natl. Acad. Sci. USA* **2018**, *115*, E1570–E1577. [CrossRef] [PubMed]
42. Anderhub, S.J.; Mak, G.W.-Y.; Gurden, M.D.; Faisal, A.; Drosopoulos, K.; Walsh, K.; Woodward, H.L.; Innocenti, P.; Westwood, I.M.; Naud, S.; et al. High proliferation rate and a compromised spindle assembly checkpoint confers sensitivity to the MPS1 inhibitor BOS172722 in triple-negative breast cancers. *Mol. Cancer Ther.* **2019**, *18*, 1696–1707. [CrossRef] [PubMed]
43. Pannone, G.; Hindi, S.A.H.; Santoro, A.; Sanguedolce, F.; Rubini, C.; Cincione, R.I.; De Maria, S.; Tortorella, S.; Rocchetti, R.; Cagiano, S.; et al. Aurora B Expression as a Prognostic Indicator and Possibile Therapeutic Target in Oral Squamous Cell Carcinoma. *Int. J. Immunopathol. Pharmacol.* **2011**, *24*, 79–88. [CrossRef] [PubMed]

Disclaimer/Publisher's Note: The statements, opinions and data contained in all publications are solely those of the individual author(s) and contributor(s) and not of MDPI and/or the editor(s). MDPI and/or the editor(s) disclaim responsibility for any injury to people or property resulting from any ideas, methods, instructions or products referred to in the content.

cancers

MDPI

Review

Design Principles and Applications of Fluorescent Kinase Inhibitors for Simultaneous Cancer Bioimaging and Therapy

Ab Majeed Ganai [1], Eirinaios I. Vrettos [1], Stavroula G. Kyrkou [1], Vasiliki Zoi [2], Tabasum Khan Pathan [1,3], Rajshekhar Karpoormath [3], Penelope Bouziotis [4], George A. Alexiou [2], George A. Kastis [4,5], Nicholas E. Protonotarios [4,5] and Andreas G. Tzakos [1,6,*]

1 Department of Chemistry, Section of Organic Chemistry and Biochemistry, University of Ioannina, 45110 Ioannina, Greece; ganaimajid66@gmail.com (A.M.G.); eirinaios.vrettos@stjude.org (E.I.V.); stavroylakyrkoy@gmail.com (S.G.K.); tabasumkp@gmail.com (T.K.P.)

2 Neurosurgical Institute, University of Ioannina, 45110 Ioannina, Greece; vasozoi95@gmail.com (V.Z.); galexiou@uoi.gr (G.A.A.)

3 Department of Pharmaceutical Chemistry, Discipline of Pharmaceutical Sciences, College of Health Sciences, University of KwaZulu-Natal (Westville), Durban 4000, South Africa; karpoormath@ukzn.ac.za

4 Institute of Nuclear and Radiological Science and Technology, Energy and Safety (INRASTES), National Center for Scientific Research "Demokritos", 15310 Athens, Greece; bouzioti@rrp.demokritos.gr (P.B.); gkastis@academyofathens.gr (G.A.K.); nprotonotarios@academyofathens.gr (N.E.P.)

5 Mathematics Research Center, Academy of Athens, 11527 Athens, Greece

6 Institute of Materials Science and Computing, University Research Center of Ioannina (URCI), Ioannina 45110, Greece

* Correspondence: atzakos@uoi.gr; Tel.: +30-2651008387

Simple Summary: This review highlights the recent advances in the development and application of dual function kinase inhibitors that also bear fluorescent properties (fluorescent kinase inhibitors), thus can be used as theranostics in the field of cancer. This is a rapidly growing field with significant potential for cancer therapy and diagnosis. This work mainly focuses on the key design principles that guide the development of these multifunctional compounds, emphasizing the integration of essential components such as the kinase cytotoxic warhead, the fluorophore, the linkers, and additional modular elements to enhance the efficacy of the final assembled compound. We anticipate this review to propel the advancement of this field by improving the understanding of the design principles and ultimately leading to the development of more effective tools for the concurrent diagnosis and treatment of cancer.

Abstract: Kinase inhibitors are potent therapeutic agents in cancer treatment, but their effectiveness is frequently restricted by the inability to image the tumor microenvironment. To address this constraint, kinase inhibitor–fluorophore conjugates have emerged as promising theranostic agents, allowing for simultaneous cancer diagnosis and treatment. These conjugates are gaining attention for their ability to visualize malignant tissues and concurrently enhance therapeutic interventions. This review explores the design principles governing the development of multimodal inhibitors, highlighting their potential as platforms for kinase tracking and inhibition via bioimaging. The structural aspects of constructing such theranostic agents are critically analyzed. This work could shed light on this intriguing field and provide adequate impetus for developing novel theranostic compounds based on small molecule inhibitors and fluorophores.

Keywords: bioimaging; conjugates; design principles; kinase inhibitors; theranostic agents

1. Introduction

Cancer is persistently one of the leading causes of death worldwide, responsible for nearly 20 million new cases in 2022 and almost 10 million deaths [1]. Unfortunately, these numbers are projected to rise to 30 million cases and more than 15 million deaths by 2040.

For the past 10 decades, chemotherapy, surgery, radiation, or a combination of these have been the major contenders in cancer therapy [2–5]. Although these methodologies have aided in reducing the tumor burden, they generally do not provide a comprehensive therapeutic approach with high predictability for achieving long-term remission. Furthermore, the combinatorial utilization of anticancer agents is often invoked during chemotherapy, but it leads mostly to poor cancer suppression and severe side effects, mainly due to nonspecific drug targeting. The type of drugs used, along with the dosage and treatment frequency, can influence how radiation therapy and chemotherapy impact the innate and acquired immunity of cancer patients—both of which are crucial for defending against pathogenic threats [6]. The major disadvantage of the current cancer treatments is their tendency to affect normal cells, thereby crippling the host's immune system. Thus, there is an unmet need for targeted therapeutic approaches, where the selective localization of the toxic warheads in malignant tumor sites can be boosted. Kinase inhibitors [7], small molecular weight compounds that target multiple receptors [8–12], are considered indispensable members of the targeted therapy approach [13].

Receptor tyrosine kinases (RTKs) are key targets for tyrosine kinase inhibitors due to their involvement in signal transduction and other cellular processes that drive cell proliferation and tumor growth. RTKs have been categorized into different families, including Type III RTKs (PDGFR, FLT3, and C-Kit), which are highly expressed in several cancer types, like breast or lung cancer [14,15]. All RTKs comprise three major parts: an intracellular tyrosine kinase domain, a transmembrane region, and an extracellular ligand binding domain [16]. RTKs' abnormal activation in cancer has been closely correlated to the upregulation of the signaling of the phosphoinositide 3-kinase (PI3K) pathway [17]. When an appropriate stimulus, including vascular endothelial growth factor (VEGF) or epidermal growth factor (EGF), binds to the extracellular domain of RTKs, dimerization and phosphorylation of the intracellular tyrosine kinase domain occurs, leading to the engagement of PI3K to the plasma membrane [18]. Following this event, the PI3K/Akt cascade is activated, starting with the phosphorylation of PIP2 to PIP3, resulting in the recruitment of protein kinase B (also known as Akt) and phosphoinositide-dependent protein kinase 1 (PDK1) to the plasma membrane. Phosphorylation of the Akt by another protein kinase, known as a mammalian target of rapamycin complex 2 (mTORC2), leads to its activation and consequently to the activation of important target proteins that control cell proliferation, survival, and resistance to therapy [16,19]. Since the PI3K/Akt pathway is one of the most frequently dysregulated pathways in cancer, and because hyperactivation of its major components has been at least partly attributed to RTKs' abnormal activation, research has nowadays shifted its focus to identifying novel tyrosine kinase inhibitors as potent medicines.

Tyrosine kinase inhibitors can inhibit protein phosphorylation, which is responsible for transferring the signals intracellularly to regulate cell proliferation, survival, migration metabolism, and growth response to stimuli, and therefore, it plays a crucial role in anticancer activity [20]. Kinase inhibitor-based targeted therapy selectively identifies and damages specific types of cancer cells or tissues, sparing normal cells. This type of cancer treatment has greatly improved the quality of tumor manipulation, lessened the unwanted side effects, and is generally well tolerated in patients with advanced cancer progression and/or poor prognosis [21]. Notably, 62 kinase inhibitors had been approved by the U.S. Food and Drug Administration by February 2024 [5] including dasatinib [22,23], dabrafenib [24,25], sorafenib [26,27], sunitinib [28,29], and many more [5].

Besides the traditional targeted anticancer therapies, including chemotherapeutic drugs and kinase inhibitors, multiple innovative therapeutic approaches have emerged over the past decades. Along these lines, targeted therapy using theranostic agents that promote the selective and concurrent diagnosis and therapy of malignant tumors is of high relevance. Targeted theranostic agents usually consist of a fluorophore, an anticancer drug, and a tumor-homing element, tethered via various linkages [30]. The classic fluorophores that were used heavily in the past years included coumarin, anilinonaphthalene-sulfonic acid derivatives, dansyl amine, 4-*N*,*N*-dimethylamino-1,8-naphthalimide, prodan derivatives, Nile red, BODIPY, fluorescein, and rhodamine. The new era of theranostic agents consists of NIR (near-infrared) dyes that can be categorized based on their emission wavelength as NIR-I (700–1000 nm) and NIR-II (1000–1700 nm). These include polymethine cyanine dyes, dicyanomethylene-based dyes, squaraines, etc. NIR dyes offer several advantages over traditional fluorophores, including higher spatiotemporal resolution, improved signal-to-background ratio for imaging, and greater tissue penetration depth.

Combining kinase inhibitors with diagnostic modalities into a single entity could offer a dual-functional approach, enabling simultaneous cancer treatment and diagnosis. This strategy relies on the covalent conjugation of small molecular weight inhibitors to fluorophores via various linkers, to produce fluorescent kinase inhibitors, able to selectively visualize and eliminate cancer cells in a concurrent manner (Figure 1). This review focuses on the principles governing the design of fluorescent kinase inhibitors which can be utilized against the menace of cancer. An extensive analysis of their constituents (fluorophore, inhibitor, linker, and additional elements) is presented, followed by several breakthroughs in this field, according to the current literature. Special focus is placed on the design principles that guide the development of fluorescent kinase inhibitors. The basic structural elements required to formulate the architecture of fluorescent kinase inhibitors that include the kinase inhibitor, the fluorophore and the linkers that will connect these elements are also elaborated., A thorough analysis is provided on the selection criteria for the linkers that will tether the kinase inhibitor warhead to the fluorophore as well as additional components that could enhance the pharmacokinetics (e.g., solubility-enhancing moieties).

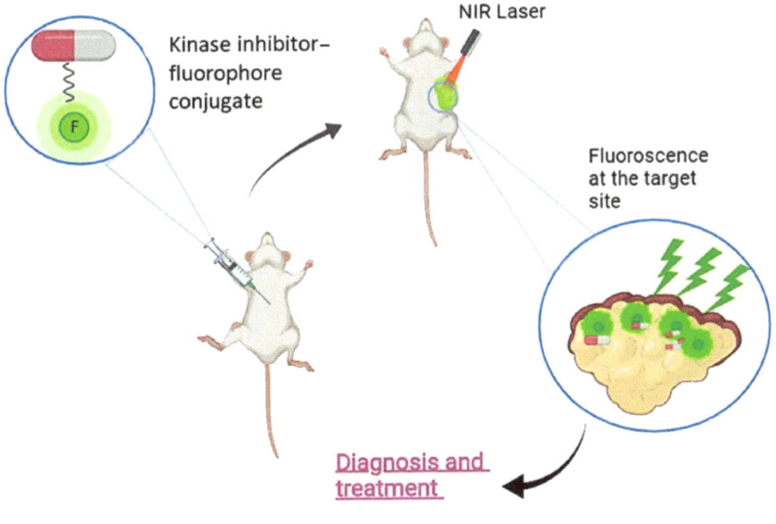

Figure 1. Example of fluorescence-guided diagnosis and therapy using fluorescent kinase inhibitors.

2. Design Principles and Analysis of Each Constituent

Fluorescent kinase inhibitors generally consist of a kinase inhibitor, a linker, and a fluorophore. However, some variants may also include additional components, such as moieties that enhance water solubility. The kinase inhibitor is used as the toxic warhead to eliminate the malignant tumor cells, the fluorophore (often a NIR dye) is used to enable the visualization of the tumor site, and the linker is used to tether the different elements and regulate the pharmacokinetic properties of the final conjugate.

However, additional elements can be introduced to address specific weaknesses, such as off-target toxicity and low aqueous solubility. The following section will emphasize each constituent and rationalize the criteria for selecting them, with a particular focus on their design principles.

2.1. The Chemical Space of the Kinase Inhibitors

Protein kinases are defined by their ability to catalyze the transfer of the terminal phosphate group of ATP to certain substrates, which usually contain a serine, threonine, or tyrosine residue. Kinases have different structures, but they all consist of an activation loop, which is important in monitoring the kinase activity. The activation loop has different conformations with catalytically competent sites, usually phosphorylated, and an 'inactive' conformer site where the activation loop blocks the substrate binding site. Kinase inhibitors are mostly ATP competitive and bind to the activation site of ATP, inhibiting the protein phosphorylation and thus preventing cell proliferation. Certain representative kinase inhibitors are listed in Table 1, categorized according to their target protein.

Table 1. Categorization of representative kinase inhibitors based on their targets.

FDA-Approved KINASE Inhibitors	Drug Target
Crizotinib, Ceritinib, Alectinib, Brigatinib, Lorlatinib	ALK
Bosutinib, Dasatinib, Imatinib, Nilotinib, Ponatinib	BCR–ABL
Vemurafenib, Dabrafenib, Encorafenib	B-Raf
Ibrutinib, Acalabrutinib, Zanubrutinib	BTK
Palbociclib, Sorafenib, Ribociclib Abemaciclib	CDK family
Crizotinib, Cabozantinib, Capmatinib	c-Met
Gefitinib, Erlotinib, Lapatinib, Vandetanib, Afatinib, Osimertinib, Dacomitinib	EGFR family
Neratinib, Tucatinib	ErbB2/HER2
Erdafitinib. Nintedanib, Pemigatinib	FGFR
Gilteritinib, Midostaurin	Flt3
Ruxolitinib, Tofacitinib, Baricitinib, Tofacitinib, Upadacitinib	JAK family
Trametinib, Binimetinib, Cobimetinib, Selumetinib	MEK1/2
Everolimus, Fedratinib, Sirolimus, Temsirolimus	Mtor
Axitinib, Gefitinib, Imatinib, Lenvatinib, Nintedanib, Pazopanib, Regorafenib, Sorafenib, Sunitinib, Avapritinib, Ripretinib	PDGFR α/β
Vandetanib, Cabozantinib, Pralsetinib, Selpercatinib	RET
Netarsudil	ROCK1/2
Entrectinib, Crizotinib	ROS1
Bosutinib, Dasatinib, Ponatinib, Vandetanib	Src family
Fostamatinib, R406	Syk
Larotrectinib	TRKA/B/C
Regorafenib, Pazopanib, Sorafenib, Axitinib, Lenvatinib, Nintedanib, Sunitinib, Cabozantinib, Vandetanib	VEGRF Family

In addition to other core moieties found in kinase inhibitors, special attention should be given to the quinazoline group. This group has been extensively utilized in several FDA-approved EGFR kinase inhibitors (Figure 2) [31,32].

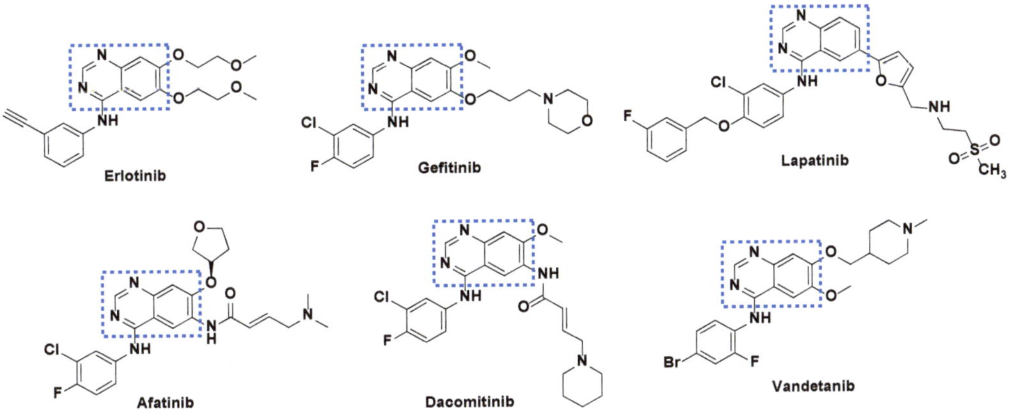

Figure 2. Quinazoline-based kinase inhibitors approved by the FDA for the treatment of different types of cancers. The quinazoline group is highlighted with a dotted blue line.

When designing a kinase inhibitor-based theranostic agent, the selection of the appropriate inhibitor should be guided by specific requirements. For instance, the inhibitor should bear the appropriate conjugation site (e.g., -COOH, -OH, $-NH_2$) that could be utilized for its conjugation with a fluorescent dye or a linker. If the inhibitor does not possess the desired conjugatable site, a relevant analog can be sculpted in certain cases, but it must undergo full validation in both in vitro and in vivo settings to ensure its efficacy. Such an example was described by Mubarak et al. [33], where a conjugatable site (-COOH) was incorporated within the structure of sunitinib after the replacement of the *N*,*N*-diethyl-moiety. The free -COOH could be potentially utilized to conjugate a hydroxyl- or amine-containing fluorescent dye. Along these lines, similar procedures could be employed to produce various kinase inhibitors bearing the preferred conjugatable groups, provided that they do not disturb the interactions of the kinase inhibitor with its target protein. Usually, scientists prefer to exploit an already known kinase inhibitor in order to avoid the laborious synthesis of new analogs and the consequent in vitro and in vivo validation experiments. For this purpose, the crystal structures of numerous kinase inhibitors and their related target domain exist in data banks, and they should be employed to predict the appropriate conjugation site prior to the syntheses. For example, the crystal structure of dasatinib (kinase inhibitor) bound to its target (ABL kinase domain) suggests that the hydroxyl group of dasatinib points out of the binding site of the target and, hence, it could be modified without mitigating its inhibition potency [34].

In addition, another aspect that should be taken into consideration when selecting the appropriate kinase inhibitor is the type of cancer to be targeted. Each kinase inhibitor exhibits optimal efficacy against certain cancer types, and thus, these data should guide the kinase inhibitor selection. For instance, osimertinib has shown significant activity against mutated non-small cell lung carcinomas (NSCLCs) and could be one of the leading focuses for such types of cancers [35]. However, osimertinib should not be overlooked for other types of cancers, as it may have significant potency that may have not been unveiled yet.

2.2. Selecting the Fluorophore

Selecting a fluorophore with excellent photophysical properties is essential when designing a fluorescent kinase inhibitor, and cyanine dyes represent a promising option due to their favorable characteristics [36–38]. The following section is meant to describe some current breakthroughs in cyanine dyes [39], as the majority of previously reported kinase conjugates bear a cyanine dye core. The cyanine molecule features a conjugated π-electronic system and a push–pull structural element, which both contribute to its strong fluorescence and tunable photophysical properties. Heteroatoms, such as oxygen or nitrogen, act as electron donors (push component), while electron-withdrawing groups, such as -NO_2, function as electron acceptors (pull component). This push–pull configuration enhances the molecule's electronic properties and fluorescence. It should be noted that nitrogen constitutes a better donor than oxygen because of its smaller electronegativity. If nitrogen has used its lone pair, it then behaves like an electron-withdrawing group [40]. In 2021, Syed Muhammad Usama and co-workers [41,42] summarized fluorescent heptamethine cyanine-7 (Cy-7) dyes, which have exceptional accumulation and persistence properties because of their in vivo covalent binding to albumin. The structures of such fluorescent cyanine dyes with their maximum emitted wavelengths are presented in Figure 3a. It was found that the meso-Cl group [41–43] is crucial for the dye to accumulate and reside longer in tumors, which is not the case with indocyanine green (ICG) because of the unavailability of the -Cl group. To confirm the importance of meso-Cl, dyes with different functionalities to a Cl group were tested, and it was evident that they did not produce a covalent adduct with albumin. The QuatCy dye derivative (Figure 3a), bearing a meso-Cl, formed covalent adducts with thiol-containing proteins other than albumin much faster than IR-808, because of the presence of a more electrophilic meso-carbon. However, dyes like IRDye 800CW and ZW800-1 (Figure 3b) are used in clinical trials as NIR contrast agents, although they do not contain a meso-Cl. Certain cyanine dyes can be used as treatment options in photothermal therapy (PTT) and photodynamic therapy (PDT) [44]. Along these lines, the Chunmeng Shi group [45] found a derivative of ICG (IR-DBI) with multimodal therapeutic activities including PDT and PTT (Figure 3c). The structural modification in IR-DBI seems to facilitate the binding to albumin, to form a dye–albumin complex that exerts a preferential accumulation and persistence at tumor sites via the enhanced permeability and retention effect. The released IR-DBI was taken up by the cancer cells via organic-anion-transporting polypeptide transporters and was selectively accumulated in the mitochondria, due to its lipophilic cationic nature. Apart from cyanines, other fluorescent chemotypes can also be used for conjugation with kinase inhibitors, including BODIPY, phthalocyanines, Alexa-532, and many more, depending on the specific requirements.

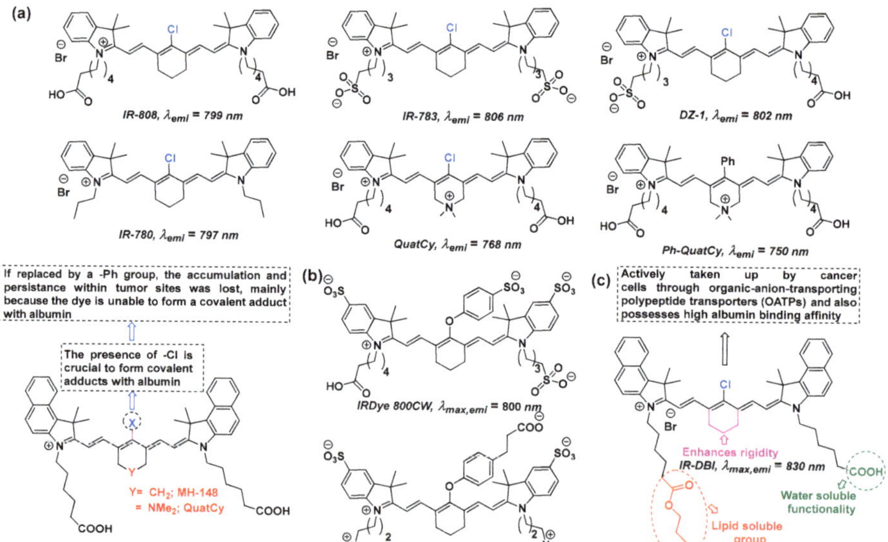

Figure 3. (**a**) Cyanine-based fluorescent dyes bearing either a meso-Cl (highlighted in blue) or a -Ph group. (**b**) Two cyanine derivatives used in clinical trials for fluorescence-guided surgery. (**c**) A multimodal therapeutic NIR dye containing a meso-Cl functionality [41].

In addition to the photophysical properties, the choice of a fluorophore can also depend on its available conjugation sites, as is similarly considered for kinase inhibitors. The literature provides a pool of fluorophores with a wide variety of conjugation sites that can be selected based on specific requirements. Furthermore, existing fluorophores can be modified to incorporate the desired functional groups, a process that is generally simpler than the modifications required for kinase inhibitors.

Additionally, the selection of a fluorophore can be guided by the intended application of the final kinase inhibitor–fluorophore conjugate [43]. For instance, if the final conjugate is expected to be used solely for in vitro assays, the selected fluorophore is usually relatively small in size, so as not to perturb the binding affinity/selectivity of the inhibitor. If the final conjugate is expected to be utilized within in vivo applications, specific aspects must be considered: A higher molecular weight dye can be utilized (e.g., a NIR-II emitting dye), which is usually associated with deeper tissue penetration, lower signal-to-noise ratio and lower toxicity [46].

2.3. Types and Selection Criteria for Linkers in Kinase Inhibitor–Fluorophores

Despite its relatively small size compared to the rest of the theranostic agent, the linker is crucial in determining the bioactivity profile of the final kinase inhibitor–fluorophore conjugate. The linker must be carefully selected to optimize the pharmacokinetics and augment the delivery capacity of the kinase inhibitor to the target site while preventing a premature release. Additionally, the linker should not interfere with the binding affinity and selectivity of the kinase inhibitor towards its protein target. An inappropriate linker choice can lead to reduced efficacy or complete abolishment of the binding.

Additionally, the linker should be chemically/enzymatically resilient within the blood circulation to allow the conjugate to reach its kinase target intact and afford a spatiotemporal drug release within the tumor site. An example is discussed in the succeeding section whereby the conjugate **C8a** can selectively release the drug in the tumor site via a glutathione-mediated disulfide bond cleavage, increasing the efficacy of the utilized parent anticancer drug. The linker also plays a key role in keeping the dye out of the primary kinase domain site, which otherwise may interfere and result in diminished potency of the drug [47].

The most common linkers used in kinase inhibitor–fluorophore conjugates include amides and esters. These linkers are specifically designed to be cleaved in the cancer microenvironment, where high levels of amidases and esterases are present [48]. Additionally, ethylene glycol linkers are frequently employed among classic linkers to enhance the pharmacokinetic properties of the inhibitor. Another class of linkers that is continuously gaining attention involves linkers that are rationally designed to become cleaved under specific stimuli overexpressed in the tumor environment. For instance, certain bonds can be hydrolyzed selectively in the presence of the slightly acidic pH of the tumor microenvironment to release the active drug, while they are stable in the blood circulation [49]. These include imine, oxime, hydrazone, orthoester, acetal, and vinyl ether. A prior rational design could result in a theranostic agent that shows enhanced fluorescence intensity (derived from the utilized dye) when the kinase inhibitor is released into the tumor microenvironment. Along these lines, self-immolative linkers are occasionally utilized, as they offer a controlled drug release, triggered by various tumor microenvironment stimuli [50]. The trigger group that is used to detonate the on-demand drug release can be attached to the donor moiety of the dye, resulting in the quenching of its fluorescence until the conjugate reaches the tumor site.

2.4. Additional Structural Elements: Refining the Architecture of Kinase Inhibitor–Fluorophores

Additional elements can be incorporated into the final conjugate to address various limitations, such as low water solubility, off-target toxicity, and insufficient chemical or enzymatic stability. Water solubility is a crucial parameter required to achieve the effective concentration of the drug in the target tumor area. The main issue of the majority of the drugs is their low aqueous solubility, which is closely associated with a low bioavailability. Various techniques are exploited to improve the water solubility of poorly soluble drugs, including physical and chemical modifications of the drugs. Specifically, this can be achieved through modification of their chemical structures with certain functionalities like -SO_3^-, -COOH, glycols, and morpholines. In addition, other techniques like particle size reduction, salt formation, solid dispersion, use of surfactant, encapsulation, nanoformulation, and complexation might also be employed. Along these lines, Juan Ouyang and co-workers developed an approach for the synthesis of various heptamethine cyanine-based NIR-II fluorophores with enhanced aqueous solubility and stability (Figure 4a) [51]. These were developed by introducing a pyridinium ring (on the top of the central cyclohexenyl group) and two PEG chains for solubility enhancement, and a tert-butyl group (on the central cyclohexenyl group) for stabilization. Recently, Usama and co-workers [52] reported a fluorogenic probe based on the heptamethine cyanine scaffold (Figure 4b). This probe bears two SO_3^- moieties aiming to enhance its water solubility. The protonation of the nitrogen in an acidic medium triggers the enhancement of the fluorescence intensity and, hence, this agent represents a turn-on probe for acidic organelles like lysosomes. This compound could be utilized via its conjugation with a kinase inhibitor to develop a kinase inhibitor–fluorophore.

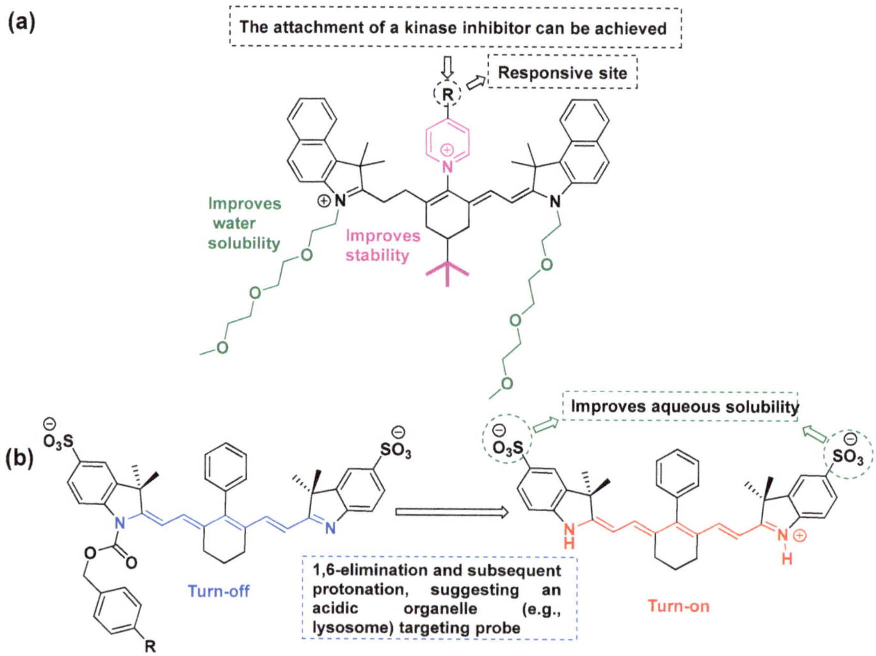

Figure 4. Water solubility enhancement by inserting different functional groups: (**a**) PEG and (**b**) SO_3^-.

In addition to water-soluble moieties, tumor-homing elements can also be incorporated to improve the selectivity of the final kinase inhibitor–fluorophore conjugate. These elements enhance targeted delivery while reducing off-target effects and increasing therapeutic efficacy and can also function as stability/solubility enhancers (Figure 5a). Certain receptors are overexpressed or uniquely expressed on the surface of malignant tumor cells, representing appealing candidates for tumor targeting [49,53–55]. Targeting these receptors with specific biomolecules could shape a methodology to target the cancer microenvironment and has been extensively exploited for several years. Recently, Song et al. took advantage of the polyamine uptake system (PUS) by developing a polyamine-targeting agent of gefitinib [56]. This agent consists of gefitinib (drug), disulfide bond (linker), BODIPY (fluorophore), and polyamine (tumor-targeting element) and is used to treat non-small cell lung carcinoma. The conjugate binds to the PUS by the polyamine ligand, thus leading to its accumulation within the solid tumor (Figure 5b).

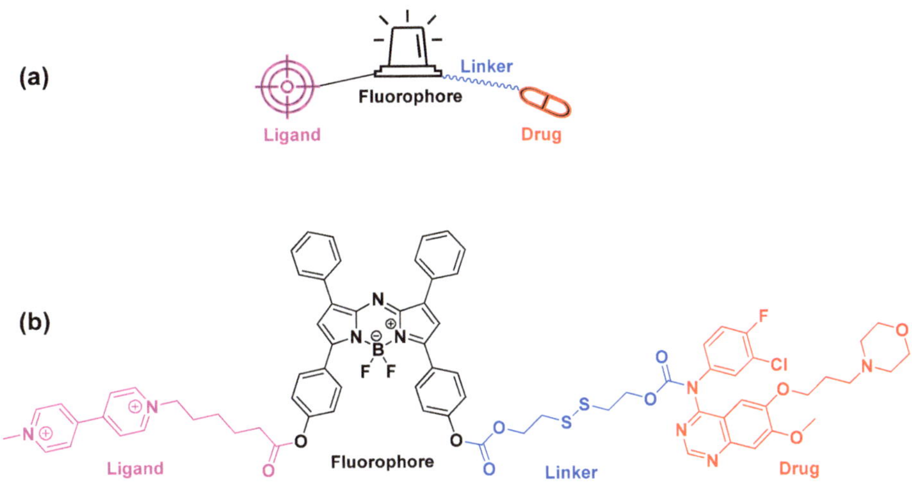

Figure 5. Incorporation of the tumor-homing polyamine to offer a selective accumulation of a theranostic BODIPY-gefitinib agent to the tumor site. (**a**) The general architecture of the fluorescent–drug conjugates with tumor-homing elements; (**b**) chemical structure of the BODIPY-gefitinib agent. The targeting element (polyamine) is colored purple, the fluorophore (BODIPY) black, the linker (disulfide bond) blue, and the cytotoxic and kinase targeting drug (gefitinib) red [56].

3. Representative Examples of the Architecture of Kinase Inhibitor–Fluorophores

The aforementioned structural components can be freely combined to create a single chemical entity consisting of a kinase inhibitor (toxic warhead), a fluorophore (visualization modality), necessary linkers (e.g., self-immolative linkers), and additional elements such as triggers or moieties that enhance solubility and stability. Representative examples of the current literature are presented in the following section and the design principles governing the selection of each constituent are extensively analyzed for each case.

3.1. Dasatinib-Based Conjugates

Dasatinib is a kinase inhibitor approved for the treatment of certain types of leukemia. In addition to its efficacy in leukemia, it has shown potent activity against other cancers, including glioblastoma, the most aggressive form of brain tumor. Based on computational studies, dasatinib is known to bind to multiple conformations of the ABL kinase [34], where the hydroxyl group projects towards solvent and could probably represent a site to tether an NIR dye (Figure 6a,b). Based on its binding mode and ongoing clinical trials against glioblastoma, Kevin Burgess's group [57] designed a cyanine-based dasatinib conjugate against glioblastoma and evaluated it in in vitro and in vivo settings. Based on the computational studies, the authors decided to conduct a direct conjugation with the cyanine dye **A** on the hydroxyl group of dasatinib, to develop the final conjugate named **C1**. The meso-Cl was not used due to its tumor-homing properties, as its binding to albumin could enhance its population within the tumor site. This was confirmed after comparing **C1** with ICG (Figure 6b) which does not bear the meso-Cl. Notably, the conjugation mode did not perturb the absorption and emission properties of the parent dye, as the conjugate **C1** absorbed (796 nm) and emitted (815 nm) within the same spectral region. The IC_{50} values of **C1** against Src and Lyn kinases were determined, and it was recorded that **C1** displayed higher IC_{50} values relative to the parent drug dasatinib (Figure 6b). Although the conjugate **C1** perturbed the affinity of the kinase inhibitor towards the studied kinases, significant binding was retained. After evaluating the in vitro cell viability of the synthesized conjugate, the authors aimed to determine its cellular uptake mechanism. Glioblastoma cells (U87) were treated with **C1**, and the results indicated that **C1** localized predominately in mitochondria due to its lipophilic and positively charged moieties. Finally, in vivo imaging in nude mice revealed the localization of **C1** in tumor sites for extended periods (~72 h). In a similar work, Kevin Burgess's group [58], used the same conjugate **C1** against liver cancer cells (HepG2). Similarly, it was observed that **C1** displayed higher IC_{50} values in comparison with the parent drug. **C1** efficiently suppressed the viability of the HepG2 cells in a more efficient manner than plain dasatinib at the same concentration and also prevented their regrowth. **C1** further proved to be cell permeable and also to localize in mitochondria.

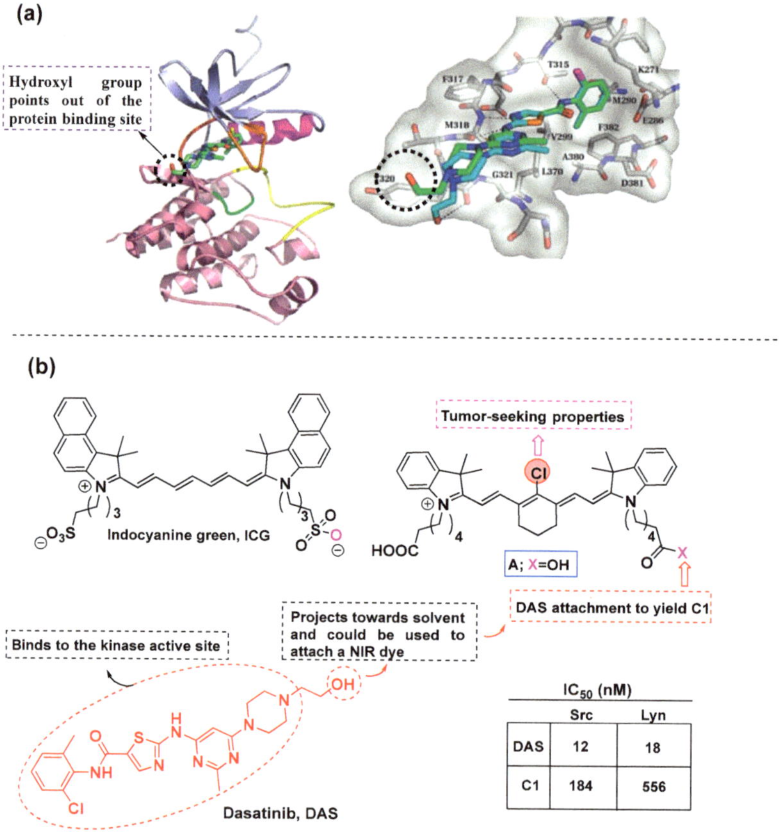

Figure 6. Dasatinib-based conjugates after rational design. (**a**) Crystal structure of dasatinib complex with ABL kinase, with the hydroxyl group pointing out of the kinase cavity [34]. (**b**) The structure of the fluorescent dasatinib-based analog **C1** utilized against glioblastoma and liver cancer [57,58].

It is known that gastrointestinal endoscopy is not able to effectively differentiate gastrointestinal stromal tumors (GISTs) from other subepithelial lesions. Therefore, the need for the development of pronounced treatments that could target a specific tumor tissue is critical. In the late 2020s, Fujimoto et al. [59] described a NIR-based conjugate of dasatinib, designated **C2a**, targeting GISTs. It was found that **C2a** visualizes both GIST-T1 and GIST-882M cells with moderate to good antitumor activity (Figure 7). Notably, the conjugate **C2a** displayed in vivo fluorescence signals in tumors with a high signal-to-noise ratio (SNR) ratio. Such a pattern of in vivo fluorescence imaging of GIST-T1 xenografted mice treated with **C2a** is shown in Figure 7b, in which **C2a** (10 mg/kg) was given intravenously and fluorescence images were acquired before and 12 h post-injection. The fluorescence images of various organs were acquired, as indicated in Figure 7c,d. In this study, fluorescence imaging was conducted in both subcutaneously xenografted mice and orthotopically xenografted rats to detect the accumulation of the conjugate in tumors. Therefore, this conjugate could operate as a useful architectural template when designing theranostic probes for GISTs.

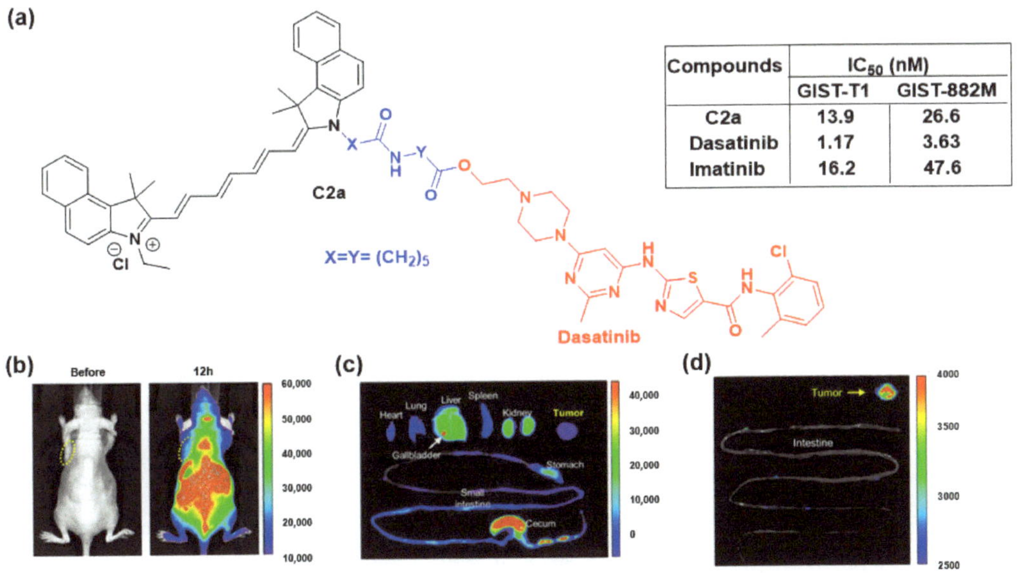

Compounds	IC_{50} (nM)	
	GIST-T1	GIST-882M
C2a	13.9	26.6
Dasatinib	1.17	3.63
Imatinib	16.2	47.6

Figure 7. Dasatinib-based conjugates. (**a**) Fluorescent dasatinib-based conjugate **C2a** utilized against GIST cancer; (**b**) In vivo fluorescence imaging pattern of GIST-T1 xenografted mice treated with conjugate **C2a** (10 mg/kg injected intravenously) and fluorescence images acquired before and 12 h post-injection. The yellow dashed circles correspond to the tumors; (**c**) The ex vivo fluorescence images of the heart, lung, liver, gallbladder, spleen, kidneys, stomach, small intestine, cecum, and tumor acquired 48 h after injection of **C2a** (10 mg/kg); (**d**) The ex vivo imaging pattern of the tumors and intestines after washing with saline. The tissues were collected from mice 48 h after injection with **C2a** (10 mg/kg) and images were acquired after washing [59]. The dye is colored black, the linker blue, and the inhibitor (dasatinib) red.

In another study, the radioactive conjugate of dasatinib **C2b** (Figure 8a) was synthesized and delivered to murine orthotopic glioma by convection-enhanced delivery (CED) [60]. The ^{18}F positron emission tomography (PET) and fluorescence imaging were used to track the entire drug delivery process. The localization of the fluorescence in the glioma cells was observed from the fluorescence imaging of mBSG co-incubated with **C2b** (15 min incubation) (Figure 8b). Apart from this, a similar distribution of **C2b** fluorescence (red) and DAPI (blue) nuclei was observed (Figure 8c). It was observed that the conjugate exhibited in vivo nanomolar potency in cell viability assays, albeit slightly less effectively than the parent drug dasatinib (Figure 8) [59]. Figure 8e presents two mice that were infused with [^{18}F]-1 by CED at time intervals of 15, 25, 40, 70, and 160 min. Glioma is indicated with blue arrows. Regarding the first mouse (symbolized by 'ii'), CED delivery to glioma was successful, unlike the second mouse (symbolized by 'iii'), where the delivery was unsuccessful. Importantly, PET imaging of [^{18}F]-1 allows for real-time monitoring of the drug delivery to the tumor area. Figure 8f visualizes an ex vivo fluorescence analysis of [^{18}F]-1 delivered by CED to the mouse (ii), followed by a PET scan.

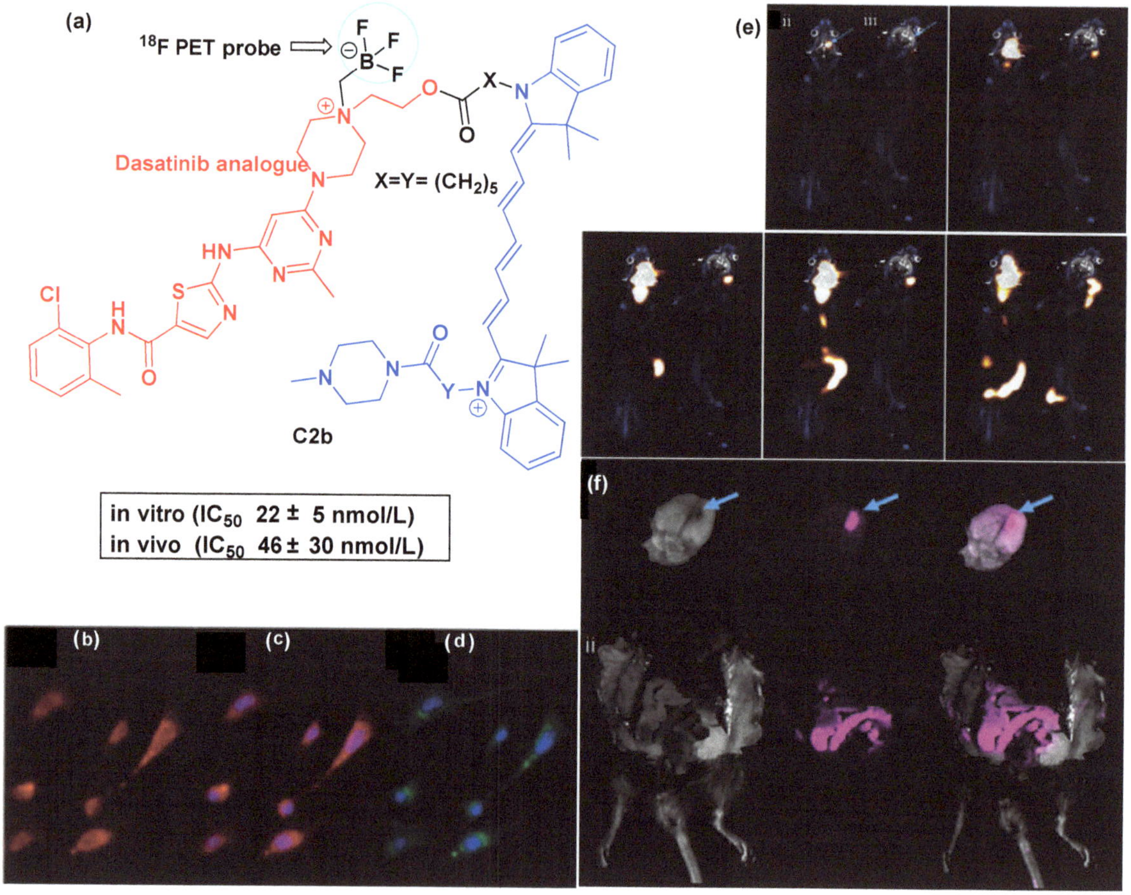

Figure 8. (**a**) The structure of the fluorescent dasatinib-based conjugate **C2b** utilized for PET imaging; (**b**) Fluorescence imaging of mBSG co-incubated with **C2b** shows fluorescence localization to glioma cells (15 min incubation); (**c**) similar distribution of staining in **C2b** fluorescence (red) and DAPI (blue) nuclei; (**d**) Cell mask plasma membrane stain (green)/DAPI(blue); (**e**) [^{18}F]-1 delivery by CED to glioma at 15, 25, 40, 70, and 160 min. Blue arrows indicate glioma location. Mouse (ii) indicates successful CED delivery. Mouse (iii) indicates unsuccessful CED delivery. The correspondence of the imaging technique with the colors is as follows: PET(red)/CT(blue)/MR(grey); (**f**) ex vivo fluorescence analysis of [^{18}F]-1 delivered by CED to the same mouse (ii). Fluorescence is represented in pink [60]. The dye is colored blue, the linker black, and the inhibitor (dasatinib) red.

3.2. Erlotinib-Based Conjugates

Erlotinib is an FDA-approved kinase inhibitor sold under the brand name Tarceva and is mainly used against NSCLC with mutations. It was observed that although the glycol part of erlotinib points out of the binding pocket, the modifications to the alkyne also retained the EGFR activity (Figure 9a). So, it is suggested that both parts of the erlotinib (glycol and alkyne) can be modified to achieve the desired results. Along these lines, in the year 2020, Xiaoguang Yang et al. [61] designed and synthesized several erlotinib derivatives conjugated with cyanine dyes (Figure 9b). The conjugation was achieved via the glycol moiety of erlotinib on the basis of computational studies. Molecular docking studies were also performed to confirm this hypothesis and revealed that the drug in the conjugate occupied the active site of the enzyme EGFR-TK (PDB: 1M17), whereas the NIR dye was found outside the protein cavity. The authors also performed structure–activity relationship (SAR) studies, and the key findings are illustrated in Figure 9b. Moreover, the cytotoxicity results revealed that most of the synthesized conjugates displayed better inhibition against A549, H460, H1299, and MDA-MB-231 cell lines in comparison with the parent drug erlotinib. It was observed that the conjugate **C3a** displayed higher EGFR-TK inhibition than erlotinib in the A549 cell line (Table 2) and also weaker cytotoxicity (38.6 μM) on human normal mammary epithelial MCF-10A cells. Therefore, the incorporation of a heptamethine cyanine dye into the glycol moiety of erlotinib could result in novel theranostic agents against NSCLC.

Table 2. The inhibition effect of **C3a** and **C3b** on EGFR activity in A549 cells.

Compounds	IC_{50} (μM)
C3a	0.124
C3b	0.205
Erlotinib	5.182

The current literature features numerous erlotinib conjugates formed through its alkyne moiety, which can be readily exploited in azide–alkyne click chemistry reactions. Using this type of click chemistry, Feng-Ling Zhang and co-workers [62] reported the design and synthesis of two erlotinib-based fluorescent conjugates (**C4a** and **C4b**) for simultaneous diagnosis and treatment via PTT (Figure 9c). The authors validated the selectivity of the conjugate for cancer cells overexpressing EGFR using confocal fluorescence microscopy. Both conjugates were evaluated for their subcellular localization and tested in vitro against HepG2 cancer cells, with IC_{50} values determined (Table 3). In vivo fluorescence imaging was performed in A431-bearing nude mice and revealed that the conjugate **C4a** accumulated in tumor tissues within 2.5 h.

Table 3. IC_{50} values for the erlotinib conjugates **C4a**, **C4b**, and phthalocyanine against HepG2 cancer cells with the light dose of 1.5 J/cm^2.

Compounds	IC_{50} (mM)
C4a	0.01
C4b	0.04
Phthalocyanine	0.03
Erlotinib	*N* [a]

[a] Non-cytotoxic up to 0.5 μM.

In another study, Ravindra K. Pandey's [63] group evaluated the iodinated erlotinib-dye conjugates as dual bioimaging and therapeutic agents (Figure 9d). The developed conjugates were utilized as multifunctional photosensitizers for bladder cancer imaging and photodynamic therapy (PDT). The conjugates that were synthesized were evaluated for their anticancer activity (in vitro and in vivo) and were compared with the relevant conjugates without erlotinib. The stable iodinated erlotinib conjugates **C5a** and **C5c** displayed high EGFR targeting specificity. The PDT efficacies of **C5a** and **C5c** were significantly influenced by the topology of the conjugation between erlotinib and the remaining part of the conjugate, as evidenced by the higher efficacy of **C5a** compared to **C5c**. It was also found that **C5c** produced significantly fewer singlet oxygen species as compared with **C5a** in a biological environment and could be a possible reason for the difference in efficacies. Interestingly, it was found that the radioactive isotope **C5b** of **C5a** demonstrated admirable

PET imaging ability. Therefore, this can be used uniquely in combination with **C5a** for the potential treatment of bladder cancers.

Another set of similar molecules was reported by Ravindra K. Pandey's group [47], consisting of erlotinib conjugated to tetrapyrroles. Various analogs of the conjugates were evaluated, including the effect of chirality, the length of the linker, and the point of tethering between erlotinib and the dye. They found that these alterations affected the in-tumor cell specificity and in vitro PDT efficacy (Figure 9e). Furthermore, it was observed that the uptake and accumulation were higher for the conjugate **C6b** than for **C6a**, suggesting an important role of the chiral center in the accumulation. In this research, **C6b** was found to be the most potent analog for accomplishing tumor cell-specific accumulation.

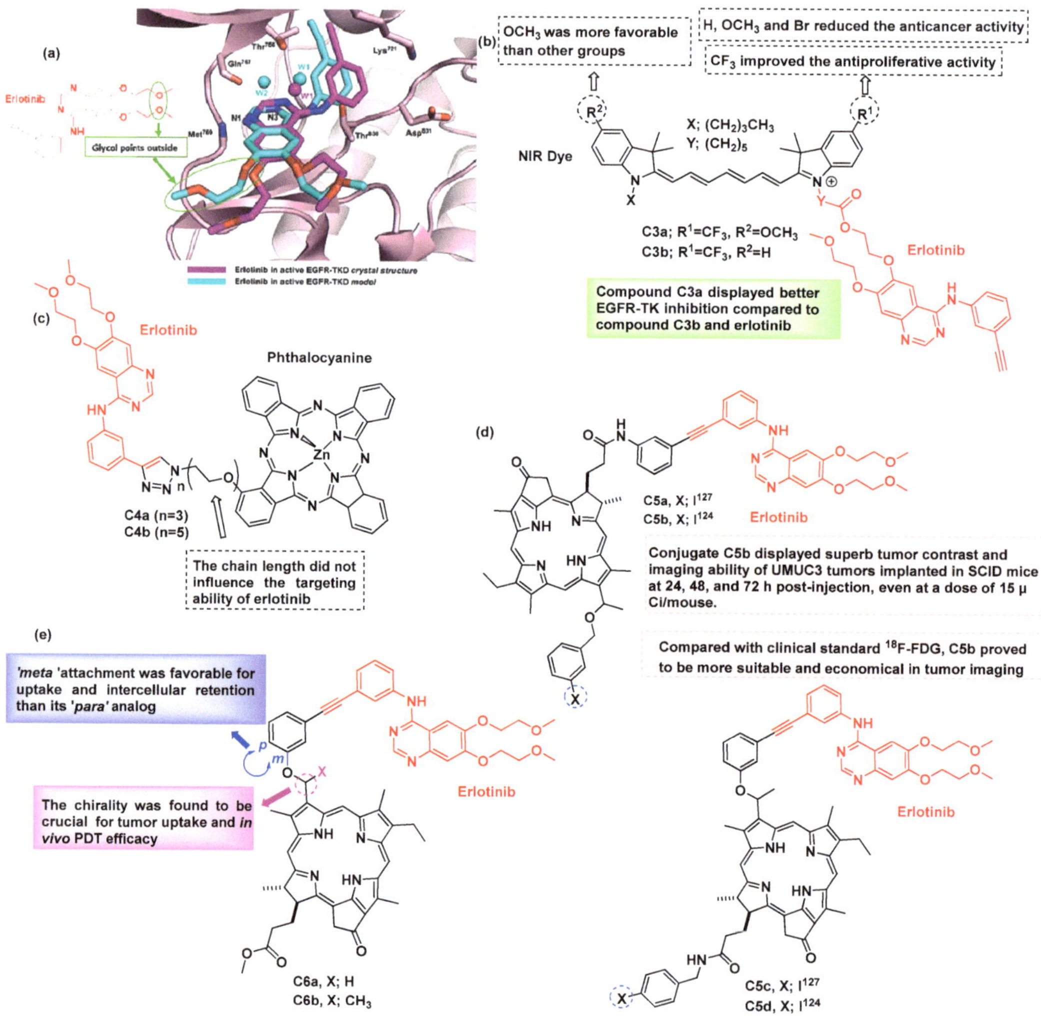

Figure 9. Erlotinib-based fluorescent inhibitors. (**a**) Erlotinib's binding to active EGFR-TKD in the crystal structure and model [64]; (**b**) SAR study of NIR-based erlotinib conjugates **C3a** and **C3b** [61]; (**c**) Phthalocyanine–erlotinib conjugates **C4a** and **C4b** [62]; (**d**) Erlotinib conjugate **C5a** to **C5d** [63]; (**e**) Erlotinib conjugates **C6a** and **C6b** [47]. Erlotinib is colored red in all cases.

3.3. Gefitinib-Based Conjugates

Gefitinib, sold under the brand name Iressa, is a medication used to treat various cancers, especially breast and lung cancers. It is an EGFR inhibitor that interrupts cellular signaling through the EGFR in target cells. The fluoro group of gefitinib is important for binding, so the reported molecules retain this group, and modifications are conducted in other parts of the core, like the -NH and -OCH_3 functional groups of the drug. Along these lines, Song et al. [56,65] reported various fluorescent or non-fluorescent conjugates of gefitinib that consisted of the kinase inhibitor (gefitinib), a fluorescent dye (BODIPY) in the case of the fluorescent conjugates, a cleavable linker (disulfide), and different targeting ligands. The conjugates were evaluated against NSCLC (Figure 10a(i)). The conjugate **C8a** efficiently delivered the drug to cancer tissues after a glutathione-mediated disulfide bond cleavage without resulting in off-target toxicity, therefore increasing the efficacy of the anticancer drug [56]. Glutathione (GSH) is a thiol that plays an important role in cellular processes, and its expression levels in cancer cells are higher compared to normal ones [66–70]. The disulfide linker was chosen during the design so as to enable its selective cleavage in the tumor environment, with the consequent drug release, where the levels of GSH are enhanced. Furthermore, it was observed that the synergistic effect between the drug and ligand played a vital role in the observed enhanced efficacy of the conjugate, suggesting apoptosis via ligand-mediated Akt inhibition. The advantage of **C8a** over gefitinib is that it was selectively localized in the tumor cells (both sensitive and resistant to gefitinib) and the strong fluorescence derived from the dye lasted around 24 h post-injection. This suggests that the activity of the conjugate is based both on BODIPY and the tumor-targeting ligand. Specifically, experiments were performed on gefitinib-sensitive cells (PC9 cells) and gefitinib-resistant cells (H1650 cells) and the results indicated that this compound was able to inhibit H1650 cell growth. In vivo experiments (Figure 10b–d) pinpointed that the conjugate leads to the detection of lung cancer tumors within 4 h. Therefore, the authors describe a prodrug that significantly improves the pharmacokinetic properties of gefitinib, through the attachment of the polyamine-targeting agent, minimizing potential side effects. The resulting agent also absorbs radiation in the NIR region leading to the detection of tumors and on-demand drug release in real-time. The conjugate **C8b** consists of a biotin moiety, a disulfide linker, a NIR fluorophore, and gefitinib [65]. As in the previous example, the anticancer drug gefitinib is modified with a biotin-recognizable binder resulting in the prodrug termed PBG. PBG possesses improved pharmacokinetic properties, while it can also acquire imaging properties when combined with the near-infrared azo-BODIPY, leading to the fluorophore-TBG conjugate. The fluorescence of the conjugate was attained in the presence of high concentrations of GSH and could not be achieved in the presence of other stimuli including various amino acids, peptides, anions, metal ions, reactive oxygen species, and reactive nitrogen species, thus confirming the high specificity of the conjugate towards GSH. The experiments were performed on the human lung adenocarcinoma PC9 cell line and corresponding cancer-bearing nude mice. Saline, gefitinib, PBG, and TBG were injected via the tail vein every second day, and the measurements were obtained every two days for 28 days. Compared with saline, reduced cell proliferation was observed in both PBG and TBG, as shown in Figure 10e. The targeting ability of TBG was also examined in vivo, giving satisfactory results in accumulation in the tumor area after the first 8 h after injection (Figure 10f,g). It was also observed that the drug release depends on both GSH concentration and the Sodium-Dependent Multivitamin Transporter (SDMT) expression level. It can be concluded that the critical challenges faced with the present cancer therapies could be surpassed by the newly emerging theranostics, which can deliver diagnostics and therapeutics with high accuracy.

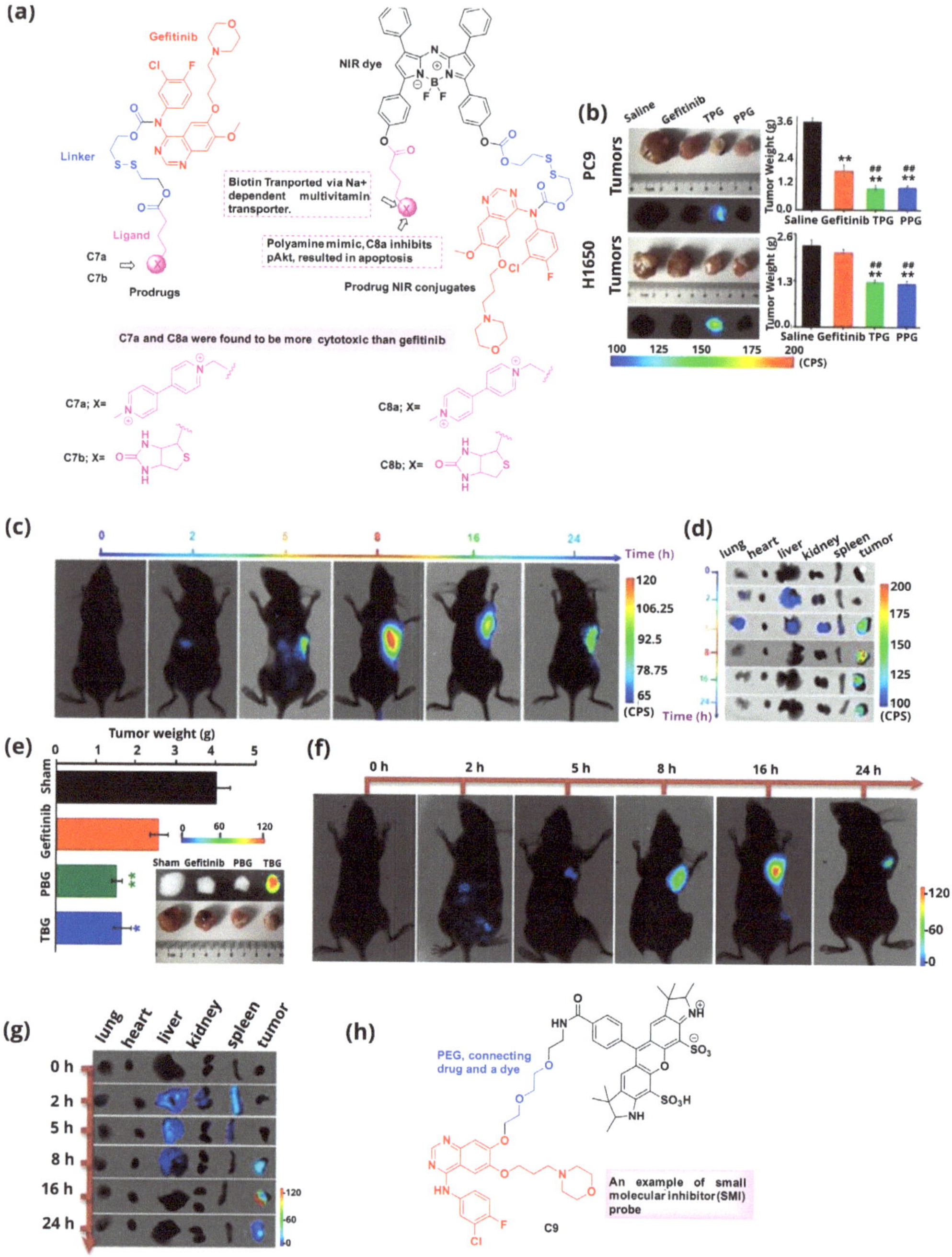

Figure 10. Gefitinib-based fluorescent inhibitors. (**a**) Structures of gefitinib-derived fluorescent conjugates **C8a** and **C8b**; (**b**) Tumor masses and fluorescence images of nude mice with PC9 cells and H1650 cells after treated with saline, Gefitinib, TPG-conjugate with the fluorophore, or PPG-conjugate without the fluorophore (0.5 mM in 0.2 mL, DMSO/saline, 1:1/*v*/*v*, qod. iv.) (n = 7 per group), ** $p < 0.01$ vs. control group. ## $p < 0.01$ vs. Gefitinib group; (**c**) Imaging of the subcutaneously implanted H1650 tumor xenografts of nude mice at 2, 5, 8, 16, and 24 h after tail vein injection of a

single dose of 0.2 mL of TPG (DMSO/saline 1:1/v/v) (n = 3 independent experiments), (**d**) Images of the excised organs (lung, heart, liver, kidney, spleen) and tumors of the mice (n = 3 independent experiments) [56]; (**e**) Tumor masses and fluorescent images of nude mice bearing PC9 cells subcutaneous cancer xenografts were established and treated with saline, gefitinib, TBG, PBG (0.5 mmol/L in 0.2 mL saline, DMSO/saline (1/1, v/v), qod. i.v.) (n = 5 per group) * $p < 0.05$, ** $p < 0.01$; (**f**) and their xenografts for 2, 5, 8, 16, and 24 h after tail vein injection of a single dose of 0.2 mL of TBG (DMSO/saline (1/1, v/v)) (n = 5); (**g**) Images of the excised organs (lung, heart, liver, kidney, spleen) and tumors of the mice (n = 5 independent experiments); (**h**) Structure of gefitinib-derived fluorescent conjugates **C9** [65].

Hongda Wang's group recently reported a small molecular inhibitor (SMI) probe (**C9**) for visualizing EGFR by utilizing gefitinib, a flexible linker, and a fluorescent dye (Figure 10h) [65]. The probe generated the highest labeling density and the smallest and most compact clusters, indicating its superiority toward accurate labeling of aggregated targets as compared to antibody and ligand probes. The conjugate demonstrated high specificity towards EGFR, suggesting that small molecule inhibitors (SMIs) can achieve significant target specificity. A key advantage of SMIs over antibodies is their ability to penetrate the cell membrane, allowing them to target intracellular compartments. This makes SMIs a straightforward method for fluorescence labeling of intracellular organelles without the need to disrupt the cell membrane. Additionally, dSTORM imaging revealed that SMIs provide a clearer spatial visualization of EGFR on the cell membrane compared to traditional total internal reflection fluorescence (TIRF) imaging. Additionally, multiple SMIs and especially kinase inhibitors possess high pharmacological activity [71]. The successful synthesis of such probes could be used to track the intracellular position of an SMI and unveil possible interactions between the SMI and related biomolecules. Thus, these findings might assist in revealing the exact mechanism of the interaction of drugs with their targets. With these advantages, SMI probes could serve as potential labeling agents in super-resolution fluorescence imaging.

3.4. Afatinib-Based Conjugates

Qingzhi Gao's group [72] reported small molecule fluorescent probes **C10a** and **C10b** consisting of a cyanine dye and a kinase inhibitor (afatinib) as efficient inhibitors for the detection of HER1/HER2 expression levels in cancer cells and in vivo tumor diagnostic imaging modality (Figure 11). Flow cytometry confirmed the reversible binding of the conjugate to kinases, as this was evident from the decreased signal intensity. The probes were unable to undergo receptor-mediated Michael additions, unlike the parent KI, because of the unavailability of the strategically positioned alkene. The synthesized conjugates **C10a** and **C10b** were evaluated through fluorescence imaging, flow cytometry, binding inhibitions, molecular docking, and in vivo tumor detection and demonstrated a high accumulation and cytotoxicity in xenografted tumors with a single dose. It was evident from ex vivo imaging that the fluorescence can be retained between 12-48 h post-injection in living mice, suggesting an efficient probe that could be further explored and tailored to achieve superior theranostic agents for HER1/HER2.

Evgueni Nesterov's group reported the development of the conjugate **C11** for sensing EGFR tyrosine kinase, an essential target in cancer treatment (Figure 11c) [73]. The conjugate **C11** was used as an example of a small molecule anchor and was supposed to target EGFR, which was later justified. The probe's turn-on mechanism was based on the aggregation/de-aggregation of phthalocyanine chromophores, which in turn depends on the selective binding of small molecules to their target biopolymer. Therefore, a turn-on fluorescence takes place with a high S/B ratio upon de-aggregation in a dark background of H-aggregated molecules without the need to remove unbound species. Thus, this approach makes it possible to design reliable turn-on NIR fluorescent sensors to detect specific protein targets present in the nanomolar concentration ranges (Figure 11d,e).

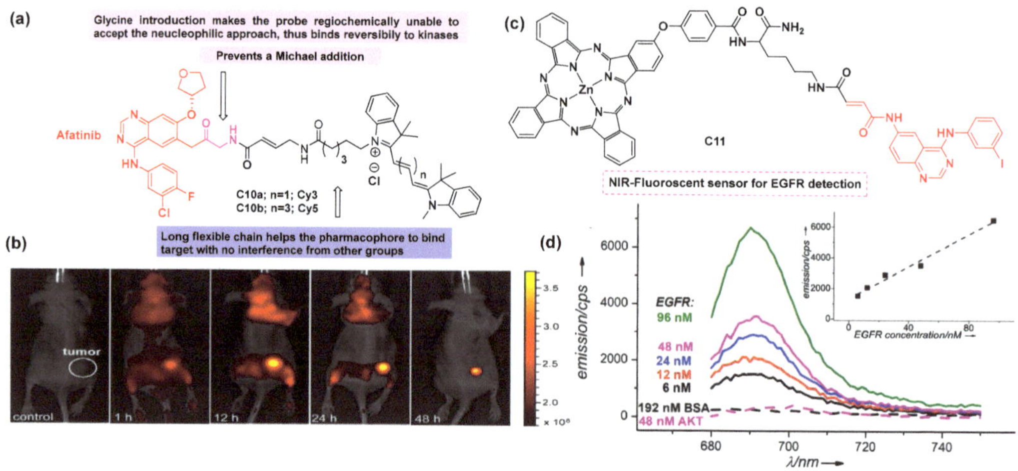

Figure 11. Afatinib-based fluorescent inhibitors. (**a**) Structures of afatinib-derived fluorescent conjugates **C10a** and **C10b**; (**b**) Fluorescence imaging obtained for **C10a**-treated xenografted mice for up to 48 h (λ_{ex} 540 ± 10 nm and λ_{em} 560 ± 20 nm) [72]; (**c**) Structure of the fluorescent conjugate **C11**; (**d**) Addition of increasing amounts of EGFR results in a turn-on fluorescent response of **C11** in aqueous conditions [73]. The inhibitor (afatinib) is colored red in both cases.

3.5. Additional Examples of Fluorescent Drug Conjugates

There is an array of different fluorescent conjugates based on other KIs, including palbociclib [74], crizotinib [75], vemurafenib [76], ibrutinib [77], 5-bromobenzofuran-2-carboxylic acid [78], and nilotinib [79], some of which are described in the following section. In 2021, Euphemia Leung et al. [74] synthesized a conjugate, designated as **C12** (Figure 12a), after the conjugation of palbociclib with MHI-148 (NIR dye). The conjugation occurred in the piperazine group of palbociclib since it is solvent-exposed, pointing out of the kinase cavity. **C12** showed enhanced potency in inhibiting cell growth and viability as compared to plain palbociclib in breast cancer cell lines, and also in non-cancerous cells (Table 4). Palbociclib-treated cells illustrated a significant difference in G1 cell cycle arrest compared to treatments with the conjugate **C12**, confirming a different mode of action for the conjugate **C12**. **C12** also showed increased cytotoxic effects and strong inhibitory effects on proliferation, growth, and viability compared to MH-148, which did not show any inhibitory effects.

Table 4. EC_{50} values of breast cancer cell lines and non-cancerous HEK293, 51D1, and 51D1.3 cell lines using WST-1 assay.

	EC_{50} (nM)				
	MCF-7	**MDA-MB-231**	**HEK293**	**51D1**	**51D1.3**
C12	718.8 ± 74.1	871.6 ± 98.9	543.8 ± 5.9	265.0 ± 20.3	471.3 ± 61.2
MH-148	>2500	>2500	>2500	>2500	>2500
Palbociclib	>2500	>2500	>2500	>2500	>2500

In 2019, Peter J. Choi and co-workers [75] described the synthesis and cytotoxic effects of a NIR-emitting crizotinib-based heptamethine cyanine dye conjugate **C13** (Figure 12b). The conjugate was evaluated in three different patient-derived glioblastoma cell lines and showed cytotoxicity in a nanomolar range of 50.9 nM (EC_{50}) and antiproliferative activity of 4.7 nM (IC_{50}) (Table 5). It was also found that the conjugate maintained the same mode of cellular uptake via organic-anion-transporting polypeptides (OATPs) as that of the parent heptamethine cyanine dye. The conjugate **C13** serves as an example of synthesizing a library of tyrosine kinase inhibitor-based NIR dye conjugates to afford potent fluorescent compounds to treat highly aggressive brain tumors.

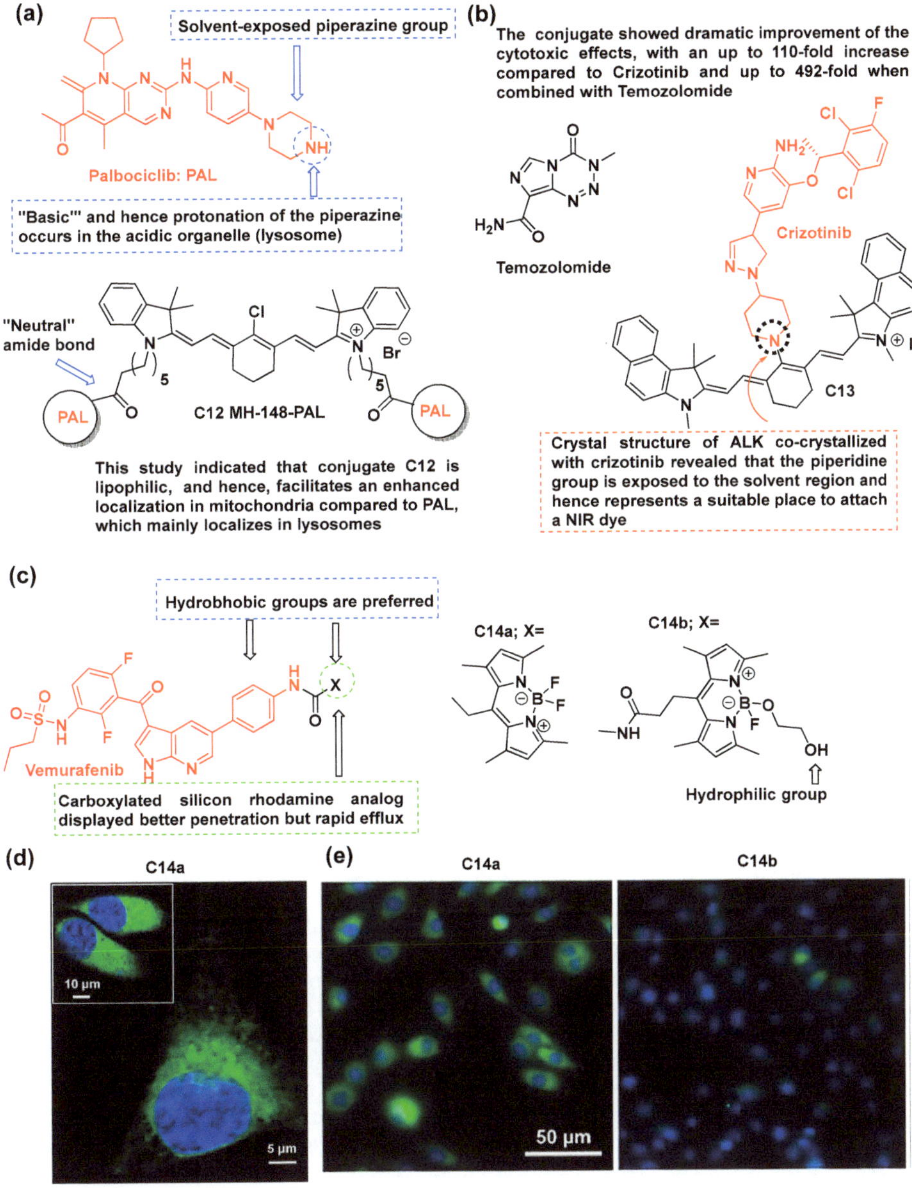

Figure 12. (**a**) The structure of MH-148-palbociclib conjugate **C12** [74]; (**b**) The structure of HMDA-based crizotinib conjugate **C13** [75]; (**c**) The structures of vemurafenib-based fluorescent conjugates **C14a** and **C14b** [76]; (**d**) High-resolution microscopy of **C14a** in A375 and SK-MEL-28 cells (inset); (**e**) In vitro imaging of **C14a** exhibiting prolonged cytoplasmic retention with minimal background fluorescence, in contrast to **C14b**, in SK-MEL-28 cells [blue: HOECHST 33342, green: BODIPY]. The fluorophores are colored black and the drugs in red all the examples [76].

Table 5. EC_{50} of the viability of the GBM cells and IC_{50} of the proliferation of the GBM cells.

	EC_{50} (nM)	IC_{50}(nM)
Crizotinib	5600 ± 460	540 ± 160
IR-786 iodide	1680 ± 110	280 ± 70
C13	50 ± 20	4.7 ± 3.3

In 2023, Zhu and colleagues developed a glutathione (GSH)-activatable theranostic agent based on crizotinib, a cancer treatment drug, designed for dual imaging and therapeutic purposes in tumor cells. The conjugate demonstrated high specificity, selectively activating in environments with elevated GSH levels, a hallmark of tumor cells. The study confirmed its effectiveness in both cellular models and zebrafish, highlighting its capability for precise tumor cell imaging [80]. Again in 2023, Chen and his group developed albumin-decorated nanoparticles, containing a cyanine–crizotinib conjugate, which can concurrently visualize and treat c-Met-positive colorectal tumor cells [81]. The developed nanoparticles were able to selectively visualize tumor cells and upon laser irradiation, the conjugate exhibited phototherapeutic properties.

The vemurafenib ($BRAF^{V600E}$ inhibitor) conjugate **C14a**, consisting of a NIR dye, was found in the cytoplasm of A375 and A375R tumor cells, indicating a potent cytosol localization and retention of the conjugate [76] (Figure 12c). The BODIPY-derived conjugate (**C14a**) possessed the most intriguing properties as compared to the MayaFluor and carboxylated silicon rhodamine analogs. The conjugate **C14a** showed efficient penetration into the cytoplasm of melanoma cells with extended retention as compared to the conjugate **C14b**, which comparatively showed poor penetration and retention. This could be attributed to the more hydrophilic nature of the MayaFluor-derived conjugate as compared to the BODIPY-derived one, which has a hydrophobic cleft. The high-resolution microscopy of **C14a** in A375 and SK-MEL-28 cells is illustrated in Figure 12d along with its in vitro imaging which displayed prolonged cytoplasmic retention with minimal background fluorescence (Figure 12e). Properties such as subcellular localization, target specificity, and slow dissociation kinetics make it crucial for effectively visualizing the targets of vemurafenib. Furthermore, in vivo imaging confirmed that conjugate **C14a** accumulated with preferential localization in tumors that responded to vemurafenib, and its fluorescence was retained even after 24 h post-injection. In 2023, Sabrina Taliani and colleagues developed a cy5-based NIR fluorescent vemurafenib analog to study $BRAF^{V600E}$ in cancer cells [82]. The scientists demonstrated that the specific conjugate could enter $BRAF^{V600E}$ mutant cells, bind to its target with high affinity, and then inhibit MEK phosphorylation and cell proliferation.

The conjugate **C15** was obtained by combining BODIPY with the Bruton tyrosine kinase inhibitor (ibrutinib) to generate a single-cell diagnostic imaging agent while preserving its irreversible target binding [77]. The conjugate demonstrated significantly reduced inhibition (approximately 100-fold) against the purified BTK enzyme compared to the parent kinase inhibitor, ibrutinib. However, it showed excellent in vivo target localization, with the capability to measure drug distribution and target inhibition. In vivo tumor imaging of a representative mouse with a BTK-positive HT1080 tumor provided key imaging insights before, and at 2, 5, and 24 h post-intravenous administration of **C15**. Extensive drug accumulation was noted in all cells, persisting even at the 24 h time The conjugate was also detectable for a longer period (>24 h) inside cancer cells, indicating that an efficient irreversible binding of the drug persisted. These longer hours of retention and persistence will help in examining the BTK-related cell environment, thus opening a new window for BTK inhibitors with the fluorescent tag.

Nilotinib, sold under the brand name Tasigna, is used to treat chronic myelogenous leukemia (CML). This medication suffers from some resistance, which is the main disadvantage of some kinase therapies. Along these lines, Suresh V. Ambudkar's group reported a nilotinib-based BODIPY conjugate as evidence for the transport of nilotinib and its fluorescent derivative **C16** by ATP-binding cassette (ABC) drug transporters (Figure 13b) [79]. ABC transporters are proteins that have been related to the detoxification of insecticides [83], multiple functions in reproductive tissues [84], transportation of photodynamic therapeutic agents by ABCG2 [85], and many more functions.

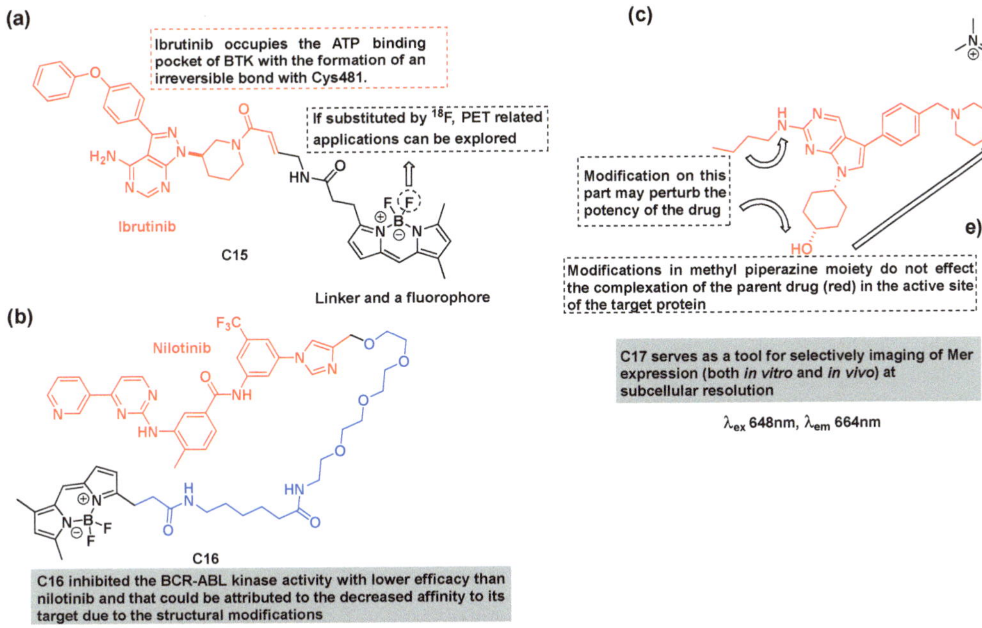

Figure 13. (**a**) The structure of ibrutinib-derived fluorescent conjugate **C15** [77]; (**b**) The structure of nilotinib-derived fluorescent conjugate **C16** [79]; (**c**) The structure of UNC2025-derived fluorescent conjugate **C17** [86]. The fluorophores are colored black and the drugs red in all the examples.

The development of drug resistance in CML has been associated with the efflux of tyrosine kinase inhibitors by ABC drug transporters, which actively pump the drugs out of the cells using ATP as an energy source. This study aimed to unveil the TKI-ABC drug transporter interactions with Pgp and ABCG2 using the fluorescent conjugate **C16** to confirm the possible route of drug uptake and related drug resistance. It was observed that the total intracellular levels of **C16** in Pgp- and ABCG2-expressing cells were lower as compared to the cells that do not express such transporters, signifying that it is actively pumped out of these cells. This efflux of the conjugate was inhibited by specific inhibitors of Pgp and ABCG2 in both in vitro and ex vivo assays. These observations collectively suggest that the conjugate is pumped out of the cell via Pgp or ABCG2. Furthermore, both nilotinib and the conjugate **C16** inhibit Pgp and ABCG2 and also bind at the substrate binding site, but not at the ATP-binding site, of these transporter proteins.

UNC2025 is an ATP-competitive and highly orally active **Mer/Flt3** inhibitor with IC_{50} values of 0.74 nM and 0.8 nM, respectively. UNC2025 is >45-fold selective for MERTK relative to Axl (IC_{50} = 122 nM; K_i = 13.3 nM). UNC2025 exhibits an excellent PK property and can be used for the investigation of acute leukemia. With this knowledge, an imidazopyrimidine-based conjugate **C17** (MERi-SiR) was designed, synthesized, and studied for imaging of tyrosine kinase Mer (MERTK) [86]. The conjugate consists of UNC2025, a preclinical inhibitor of tyrosine kinase Mer, and silicon rhodamine carboxylate, an NIR-emitting fluorescent agent. Crystallographic studies suggest that methyl piperazine serves as an efficient site for attaching an NIR dye without significantly affecting the overall complexation (Figure 13c). It also suggests that the fluorochrome gets exposed to the solvent, thus preserving the compound's interactions with the binding pocket of the Mer active site. Furthermore, the imaging results revealed that the conjugate **C17** accumulated in the cytoplasm on cells overexpressing Mer (SK-MEL-3 melanoma). The cytotoxicity results suggested that the conjugate showed reduced inhibition compared with the parent kinase inhibitor but co-localized with Mer in vivo. The conjugate demonstrated higher uptake and accumulation in Mer-expressing tumor-associated macrophages than in the tumor cells themselves, as revealed by the confocal microscopy of metastases in mice.

Pyrazolopyrimidine and quinazoline scaffolds are important in drug discovery and their analogs have been explored as various kinase inhibitors [87,88]. Recently, Joakim Andréasson's group reported pyrazolopyrimidine-derived prodan analogs (**C18a–C18e**) (Figure 14a) as fluorescent kinase inhibitors [89]. Polarity-based fluorescence probes such as prodan analogs have demonstrated excellent spectroscopic properties, including high fluorescence quantum yield and molar absorption coefficient, and excellent photostability [90]. It was observed that **C18a** and **C18c** displayed favorable fluorescent properties in aqueous solution and thus, they were evaluated for their ability to inhibit protein kinases. The two conjugates were initially tested against a panel of 65 kinases at 1 μM to screen their efficacy and selectivity. The conjugated analog **C18a** demonstrated strong inhibition against Aurora-A, Blk, and LCK, as compared to the non-conjugated **C18c**, where there was no apparent inhibition. Based on these encouraging results, **C18a** was further evaluated for cell-free IC_{50} assays against Aurora-A, Blk, and LCK and revealed moderate to good activity (IC_{50}: Aurora-A: 222 nM, Blk: 554 nM and LCK: 124 nM). Finally, **C18a** was subjected to multiphoton imaging experiments in live cells and demonstrated a favorable cross-section for two-photon microscopy (TPM) experiments. Thus, it is believed that **C18a** could operate as an interesting molecular tool for real-time intracellular studies of LCK signaling.

In 2021, Xinzeyu Yi and co-authors [91] developed a NIR-based drug conjugate **C19** (Figure 14b) to target osteosarcoma, the most common malignancy of the skeletal system, associated with the overexpression of PIM1 kinases. It was observed that **C19** displayed targeted imaging and anticancer activities (greater than the parent inhibitor) without much toxicity. NIRF images of the entire body, major organs, and tumors were acquired (Figure 14c–e). The NIR fluorescence imaging results of the organs and tumors were acquired at 48 h post-injection. There was a reduction in the fluorescence intensity within a few hours after injection, potentially indicating that OATPs may contribute to early cell entry of the compound. In addition, cyanine dyes without a meso-Cl group, as used in **C19**, do not remain in tumor tissues for a long period because they are unable to form covalent adducts with free thiol-containing biomolecules, like albumin. Furthermore, the conjugate **C19** accumulated in mitochondria, and thus, this approach may suggest a way to design conjugates for simultaneous NIR-guided surgery and chemotherapy.

Rashid Ilmi and co-workers [92] reported a quinazoline-based fluorescent conjugate, designated **C20**, consisting of a Ru(II)-Bipyridine complex, an ethylene glycol linker, and a kinase inhibitor (Figure 15a). The theranostic agent **C20** combines EGFR inhibition with fluorescence imaging properties, and it was found to localize in mitochondria, suggesting that it acts as an EGFR optical probe. Therefore, these organometallic conjugates hold potential for further exploration to develop more potent theranostic agents for EGFR-overexpressing cancers.

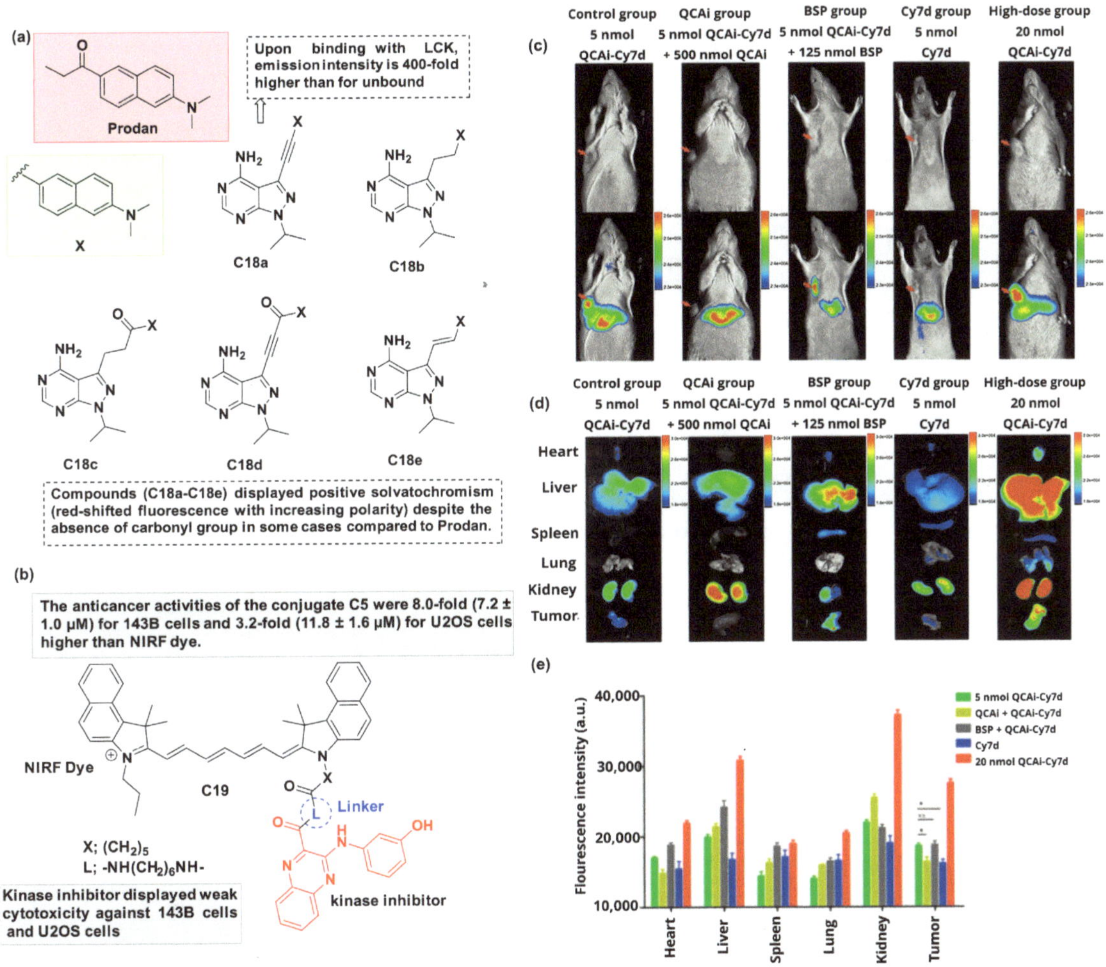

Figure 14. (**a**) The structures of prodan-derived fluorescent conjugates **C18a** and **C18e** [89]; (**b**) The structure of NIR dye-based PIM1 conjugate **C19** [91]. NIR fluorescence imaging and biodistribution of **C19** in vivo; (**c**) NIR imaging results of whole body at 48 h after the injection of the five different preparations (red arrow indicates tumors); (**d**) NIR fluorescence imaging results of organs and tumors at 48 h post-injection; (**e**) Graph presenting the fluorescence intensity of organs and tumors treated with different preparations (exposure time: 2 s). The drug is colored red, the linkers blue, and the fluorophores black.

Aranhikkal Shamsiya and Damodaran Bahulayan [93] reported several fluorescent derivatives of oxazolone–coumarin-based triazoles as anticancer agents (Figure 15b). Among the synthesized analogs, **C21** displayed the maximum calculated binding affinity with a binding score of 10.7 kcal/mol, suggesting that the nitro group enhances the binding affinity towards cyclin-dependent kinase-2 (CDK2). The experimental validation of the docking results was carried out using Western blot analysis using *b-actin* as an internal standard. The results indicated that the conjugate has a high potential to downregulate CDK2. This was supported by the fact that the active site of CDK2 comprises several amino acid residues that contain hydrophobic groups favorable to the formation of a tight 'hydrophobic pocket' in CDK2. The obtained binding energies suggest that the conjugate

C21 exhibits a strong hydrophobic interaction with the target CDK2. Consequently, down-regulation of CDK2 was observed using Western blot analysis. Furthermore, the conjugate **C21** was subjected to anticancer evaluation against human cervical cancer cells (HeLa). The results indicate that the conjugate exhibits promising cytotoxicity against HeLa cells with an IC50 value of 25 mg/mL. This highlights the need for further studies to investigate its optical properties and efficacy against CDK2. In 2020, research exploring the kinase polypharmacology landscape of clinical PARP inhibitors revealed that niraparib and rucaparib inhibit DYRK1s, CDK16, and PIM3 kinases at clinically achievable, submicromolar concentrations [94]. Peter J. Choi and co-workers [95] designed, synthesized, and evaluated in vitro the activity of the rucaparib-based NIR-emitting conjugate **C22** (Figure 15c). It was found that the conjugate **C22** had a strong cytotoxic activity (EC_{50}: 128 nM) against three different patient-derived glioblastoma cell lines. The synergistic effect of **C22** with the standard drug temozolomide (TMZ) for glioblastoma was observed, as evidenced by a two-fold reduction in the EC50 value, even in cell lines resistant to TMZ treatment (Table 6). Furthermore, the results suggest that **C22** has a high dependence on OATPs for their uptake into the tumor cells, similar to cyanine dye IR-786. The treatments based on cyanine conjugates of small molecules have a high effect on three different patient-derived glioblastoma cell lines and thus could be further explored to achieve the desired potent compound for various brain cancers. To further validate the conjugate against kinases, evaluations could be conducted with conjugates of rucaparib against various kinases such as DYRK1s, CDK16, and PIM3 kinases.

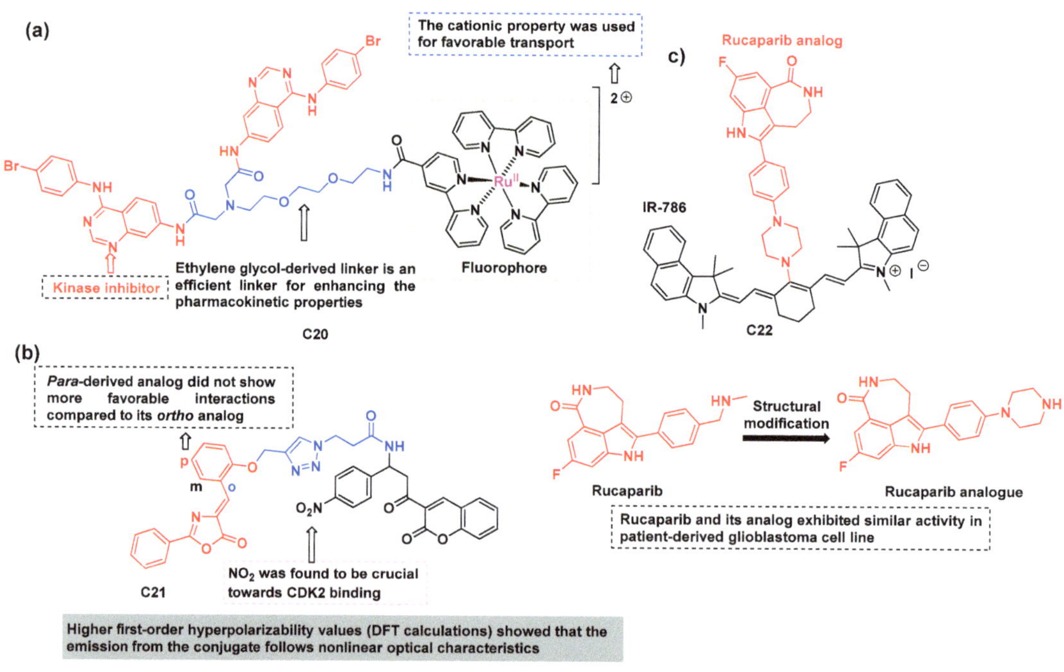

Figure 15. (**a**) The structure of the quinazoline-based Ru(II)-Bipyridine theranostic conjugate **C20** [92]; (**b**) The structure of the oxazolone–coumarin derived conjugate **C21** as a solid-state emitter [93]; (**c**) The structure of conjugate **C22** targeting three different patient-derived glioblastoma cell lines [95]. The drugs are colored red, the linkers blue, and the fluorophores black.

Table 6. IC_{50} and EC_{50} (GBM cells) values of dye, drug and conjugate **C22**. Data represent mean ± SEM. * = $p < 0.05$, *** = $p > 0.005$ relative to rucaparib.

	Compound		Compound with TMZ	
	EC_{50} (nM)	IC_{50} (nM)	EC_{50} (nM)	IC_{50} (nM)
IR-786	1735 ± 249	357 ± 39 ***	390 ± 45	120 ± 30 *
C22	128 ± 30	21 ± 4 ***	56 ± 6	20 ± 7 *
Rucaparib	>100,000	53,443 ± 473	>100,000	2262 ± 488

Besides the aforementioned examples, certain fluorescent inhibitors are not classified as conjugates because the fluorophore moiety is inherently part of their structure and not added post-conjugation. Notably, there are cases where the kinase inhibitor becomes fluorescent only upon binding to its respective target. James N. Wilson's group [96–98] developed certain quinazoline-based fluorescent kinase probes as theranostic agents. Molecule fluorescence tuning [98] was performed by changing the extent of π-conjugation and by modifying auxochrome substitution (Figure 16a). It was found that the quinazoline moiety exhibited a dual character, acting as both an electron-donating and electron-withdrawing component, depending on the substitution pattern and the potential movement of the π-electron current (**C23** and **C24**). Moreover, the strongest electron-donating (push) and withdrawing groups (e.g., -dimethylamino, -cyano, and -nitro) produced high on/off ratios, indicating that they are desirable candidates for designing future fluorescent probes. The presence of a fluorophore arm at the 6-position of quinazoline hardly affects the ability of the fluorescent probes to operate as ERBB inhibitors. The resulting probes possessed low aqueous solubility, and this could be resolved by attaching hydrophilic groups to the fluorophore, based on the design principles described in the introduction part.

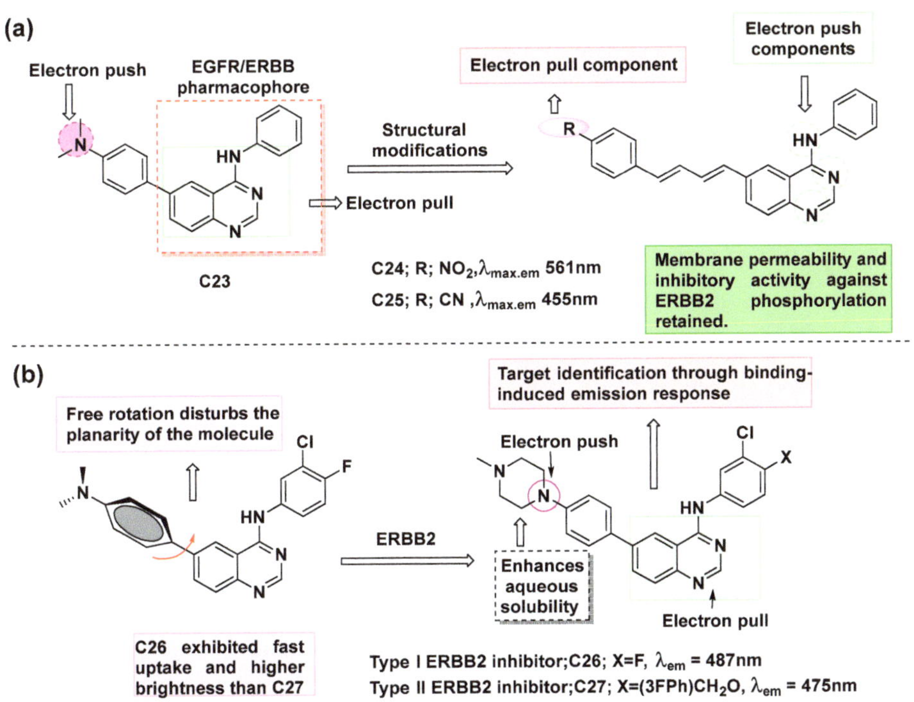

Figure 16. (**a**) The structure of fluorescent quinazoline-based analogs **C23–C25** [98]; (**b**) The structure of quinazoline-based fluorescent molecules **C26** and **C27** [97].

Similar types of molecules like **C26** were reported [97] and were found to 'turn on' when bound to kinases, suggesting a planner structure after binding the active site of the enzyme (Figure 16b). It was found that probe **C26** has a high affinity to identify ERBB2-overexpressing cells through a binding-induced emission response. The higher level of ERBB2 expression in BT474 cells permits improved binding of **C26**, which can be attributed to the higher emission intensity from BT474 cells compared to MCF7. These observations thus demonstrate that **C26** can stratify individual live cells by its dynamic response to activation.

In a continuation of earlier research, a 3-cyanoquinoline [96] core was investigated for its optical and biochemical properties (Figure 17a). It was found that the incorporation of this core improved the optical properties as compared to the previously reported molecules, suggesting the significance of the nitrile group in stabilizing the charge transfer excited state and red shift emission. Furthermore, **C28** demonstrated a moderate affinity for ERBB2 and was found to target the intracellular pool, permitting this fluorescent probe to operate as a reporter of the rapid dynamics of kinase internalization.

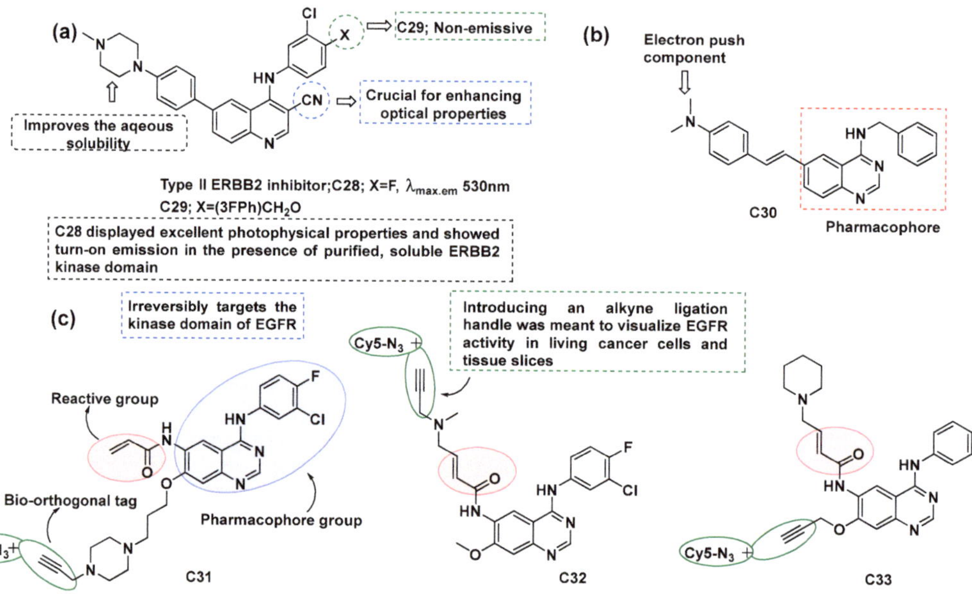

Figure 17. (**a**) The structure of cyanoquinazoline-derived fluorescent inhibitor **C28** [96]; (**b**) The structure of quinazoline-derived fluorescent inhibitor **C30** [99]; (**c**) The structure of quinazoline-derived fluorescent inhibitors **C31**, **C32** and **C33** [100].

Renaud Sicard et al. [99] reported **C30** as a fluorescent reporter to investigate ERBB populations and their state of activation (Figure 17b). It was found that the synthesized fluorescent 'turn-on' probe targeted the ATP binding pocket of ERBB and enhanced emission was observed while bound, which could be due to the restricted geometry of the ERBB2 kinase domain. In 2022, Weimin Li's group reported 4-anilinoquinazoline-derived molecules as clickable probes for the visualization of EGFR activity [100]. Three probes (**C31**, **C32**, and **C33**) were designed, synthesized, and evaluated against EGFR inhibition (Figure 17c). Probe **C31** was found to be the most potent analog, with the highest reactivity towards EGFR kinase with primary mutations: the IC_{50} values towards HCC827 and H1975 were 0.2 and 3.1 μM, respectively. Activity-based protein profiling (ABPP) was employed to visualize the protein activity and revealed that fluorescence labeling is specifically dependent on the clickable probes. Thus, probe **C31** may serve as a useful diagnostic tool and could improve the diagnosis of EGFR mutations and help in the EGFR-TKI therapeutic strategies. Jun Sheng's group reported a few gefitinib-derived molecular probes as turn-on fluorescent ligands to make the visualization of EGFR protein possible (**C34**, Figure 18a) [101]. The crystal structure of the EGFR kinase domain complexed with tyrosine kinase inhibitors (gefitinib) is illustrated in Figure 18b,c. The fluorescence imaging and in vivo xenograft tumor imaging suggest that probe **C34** particularly responded to tumor cells overexpressing EGFR. The EGFR inhibition of the probe was evaluated in A431 cells, demonstrating that it retains its function as an EGFR inhibitor. These results suggest that probe **C34** could be used for fluorescence imaging of cells overexpressing EGFR and thus adds a fluorescent tag to the present therapy, which may help to understand the tumor and its environment accurately.

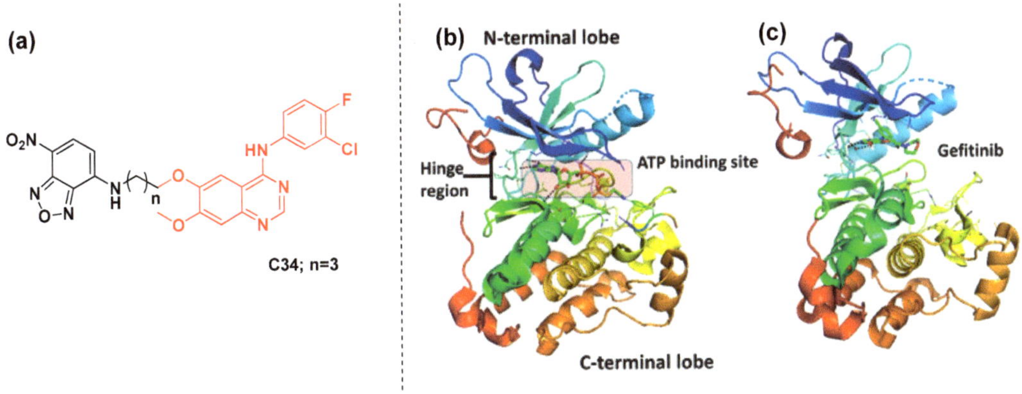

Figure 18. (**a**) The structure of quinazoline-derived fluorescent molecule; (**b**) Crystal structure of the kinase domain of EGFR with ATP binding site highlighted (PDB ID: 2GS6). TKIs of EGFR bind to EGFR in the ATP binding pocket, forming 1 to 3 hydrogen bonds to the hinge region; (**c**) EGFR kinase domain with gefitinib bound in the ATP binding pocket (PDB ID: 3UG2) [102]. The drug is colored red.

Other Examples of Kinase-Based Theranostic Targeting Gliomas

Miao Huang et. al. developed **C35**, aiming to discover if it can be used as an imaging agent for μPET/CT and NIR imaging to treat orthotopic glioblastoma brain tumors [103]. **C35** consists of the EphB4-binding peptide TNYL-RAW, the radiometal chelator DOTA (1,4,7,10-tetraazadodecane-N,N′,N″,N‴-tetraacetic acid), which was utilized to chelate ^{64}Cu, and the NIR dye Cy5.5. The authors initially utilized optical imaging (Figure 19a) and then μPET/CT (Figure 19b) to identify that U87-Luc and U251-Luc tumors can be efficiently visualized in mice. Therefore, it was supported that **C35** is capable of selectively binding to EphB4-expressing angiogenic blood vessels and EphB4-expressing tumor cells, rendering it an appealing bioimaging agent for both PET/CT and optical imaging of glioblastoma.

Chiara Vagaggini et. al. developed the theranostic prodrug **C36** (Figure 19c) to selectively target and eliminate glioblastoma tumors [104]. **C36** consists of SI306, a potent inhibitor of Src (non-receptor tyrosine kinase), a linker, and DOTA chelated with radioactive ^{68}Ga. First, the authors evaluated the ADME properties and the biological profile of the theranostic prodrug before the chelation of ^{68}Ga, showing appealing properties and effective reduction in the cell viability of GL261 and U87MG glioblastoma cell lines. Then, the authors validated the effective time-dependent cellular uptake of the radioactive prodrug **C36** (Figure 19d), unveiling the preliminary hints of a potentially important glioblastoma inhibitor that should be investigated further.

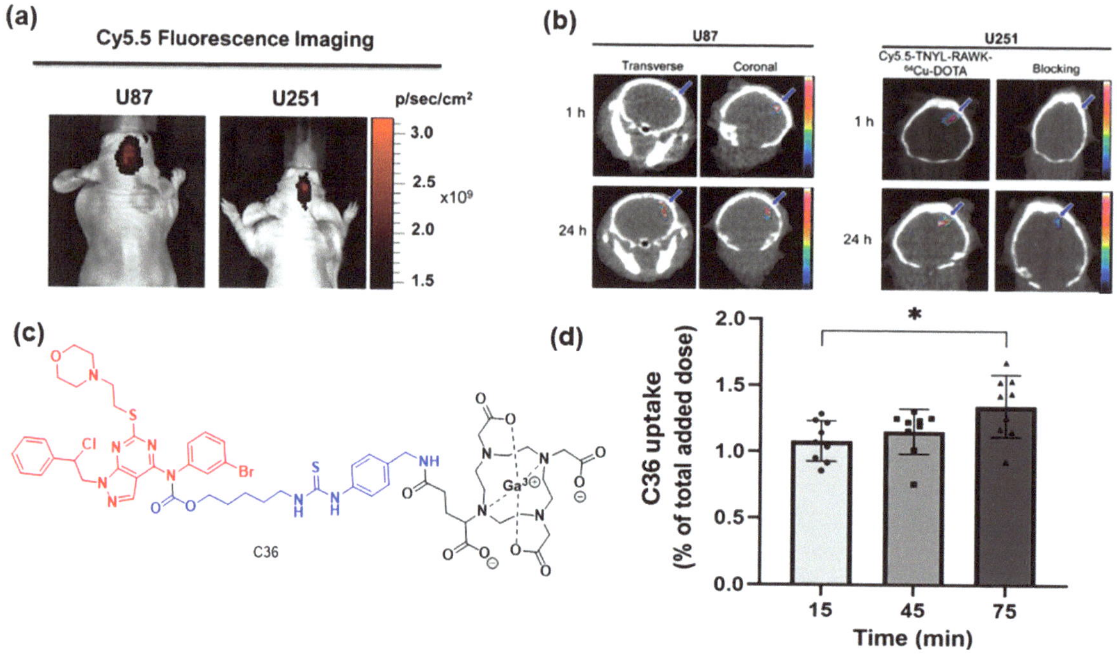

Figure 19. (**a**) Cy5.5 NIR optical imaging of U87-Luc and U251-Luc tumors 24 h after a tail vein injection of **C35**. (**b**) μPET/CT images of U87-Luc tumors (**left**) and U251-Luc tumors with **C35** and **C35** plus an excess of unlabeled **C35** (**right**) 1 h and 24 h post-injection [103]; (**c**) Structure of **C36**; (**d**) Cellular uptake of **C36** in U87MG glioblastoma cancer cells (experiments done in triplicate, * $p < 0.05$) [104].

4. Conclusions and Future Perspectives

In summary, this review highlights the key design principles behind the development of fluorescent kinase inhibitors and their use as anticancer theranostic agents. By conjugating various small molecule kinase inhibitors with different fluorophores, researchers have generated several fluorescent kinase inhibitors with promising therapeutic as also diagnostic applications (Figure 20).

Optimal efficacy requires careful consideration of all the components involved in the architecture of these compounds—drug, fluorophore, linker, and additional elements. Representative examples from the current literature have been discussed, paving the way for the development of new fluorescent inhibitors targeting the cancer microenvironment. Although this research area has grown in popularity in recent years, there is still a vast space to be explored. The limited number of reported conjugates emphasizes the need for further research to improve cancer theranostics. However, we anticipate that the continued advancements in NIR dyes and novel kinase inhibitors will provide the necessary tools to propel the field of fluorescent kinase inhibitors forward.

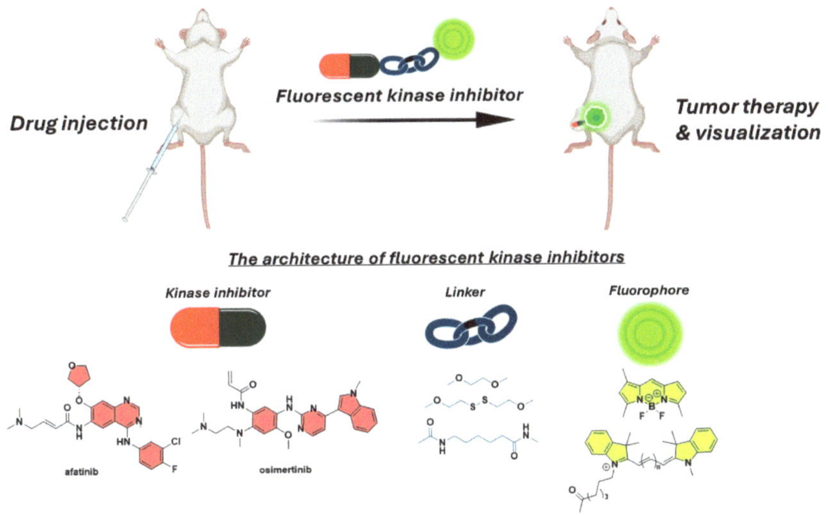

Figure 20. A schematic illustration highlighting the key components of a fluorescent drug conjugate: drug, linker, and fluorophore.

Author Contributions: Conceptualization, E.I.V., S.G.K., G.A.A. and A.G.T.; methodology, E.I.V., S.G.K., G.A.A. and A.G.T.; software, A.M.G., T.K.P., E.I.V., S.G.K. and V.Z.; validation E.I.V., S.G.K., G.A.A. and A.G.T.; formal analysis, E.I.V. and S.G.K.; investigation, E.I.V., S.G.K., R.K., V.Z., G.A.A., P.B., G.A.K., N.E.P. and A.G.T.; resources, E.I.V., S.G.K., R.K., V.Z., G.A.A., P.B., G.A.K., N.E.P. and A.G.T.; data curation, E.I.V., S.G.K., R.K., V.Z., G.A.A., P.B., G.A.K., N.E.P. and A.G.T.; writing—original draft preparation, E.I.V., S.G.K., V.Z. and A.G.T.; writing—review and editing, E.I.V., S.G.K., R.K., V.Z., G.A.A., P.B., G.A.K., N.E.P. and A.G.T.; visualization, A.M.G., E.I.V., S.G.K., T.K.P., R.K., V.Z., G.A.A., P.B., G.A.K., N.E.P. and A.G.T.; supervision, A.G.T.; project administration, A.G.T.; funding acquisition, A.G.T. All authors have read and agreed to the published version of the manuscript.

Funding: This research has been co-financed by the European Regional Development Fund of the European Union and Greek national funds through the Operational Program Competitiveness, Entrepreneurship and Innovation, under the call RESEARCH—CREATE—INNOVATE (project code: TAEDK-06189/ T2EDK-0326, Acronym: Glioblastoma).

Conflicts of Interest: The authors declare no conflict of interest.

References

1. Cancer Statistics. (n.d.). Cancer.gov. Available online: https://www.cancer.gov/about-cancer/understanding/statistics (accessed on 1 February 2023).
2. Shevtsov, M.; Sato, H.; Multhoff, G.; Shibata, A. Novel Approaches to Improve the Efficacy of Immuno-Radiotherapy. *Front. Oncol.* **2019**, *9*, 156. [CrossRef] [PubMed]
3. Gupta, S.; Howard, S.C.; Hunger, S.P.; Antillon, F.G.; Metzger, M.L.; Israels, T.; Harif, M.; Rodriguez-Galindo, C. Treating Childhood Cancer in Low- and Middle-Income Countries. In *Cancer: Disease Control Priorities*, 3rd ed.; Gelband, H., Jha, P., Sankaranarayanan, R., Horton, S., Eds.; The International Bank for Reconstruction and Development/The World Bank© 2015 International Bank for Reconstruction and Development the World Bank: Washington, DC, USA, 2015; Volume 3.
4. Schirrmacher, V. From chemotherapy to biological therapy: A review of novel concepts to reduce the side effects of systemic cancer treatment (Review). *Int. J. Oncol.* **2019**, *54*, 407–419. [CrossRef] [PubMed]
5. Roskoski, R., Jr. Properties of FDA-approved small molecule protein kinase inhibitors: A 2021 update. *Pharmacol. Res.* **2021**, *165*, 105463. [CrossRef] [PubMed]
6. Zembower, T.R. Epidemiology of infections in cancer patients. *Cancer Treat. Res.* **2014**, *161*, 43–89. [PubMed]
7. Roskoski, R., Jr. Properties of FDA-approved small molecule protein kinase inhibitors: A 2024 update. *Pharmacol. Res.* **2024**, *200*, 107059. [CrossRef]
8. Sun, X.; Xu, S.; Yang, Z.; Zheng, P.; Zhu, W. Epidermal growth factor receptor (EGFR) tyrosine kinase inhibitors for the treatment of non-small cell lung cancer: A patent review (2014–present). *Expert Opin. Ther. Pat.* **2021**, *31*, 223–238. [CrossRef]

9. Walz, L.; Cohen, A.J.; Rebaza, A.P.; Vanchieri, J.; Slade, M.D.; Cruz, C.S.D.; Sharma, L. JAK-inhibitor and type I interferon ability to produce favorable clinical outcomes in COVID-19 patients: A systematic review and meta-analysis. *BMC Infect. Dis.* **2021**, *21*, 47. [CrossRef]
10. Craig, E.; Wiltsie, L.M.; Beaupin, L.K.; Baig, A.; Kozielski, R.; Rothstein, D.H.; Li, V.; Twist, C.J.; Barth, M. Anaplastic lymphoma kinase inhibitor therapy in the treatment of inflammatory myofibroblastic tumors in pediatric patients: Case reports and literature review. *J. Pediatr. Surg.* **2021**, *56*, 2364–2371. [CrossRef]
11. Madkour, M.M.; Anbar, H.S.; El-Gamal, M.I. Current status and future prospects of p38α/MAPK14 kinase and its inhibitors. *Eur. J. Med. Chem.* **2021**, *213*, 113216. [CrossRef]
12. Song, Z.; Song, H.; Liu, D.; Yan, B.; Wang, D.; Zhang, Y.; Zhao, X.; Tian, X.; Yan, C.; Han, Y. Overexpression of MFN2 alleviates sorafenib-induced cardiomyocyte necroptosis via the MAM-CaMKIIδ pathway in vitro and in vivo. *Theranostics* **2022**, *12*, 1267–1285. [CrossRef]
13. Ganai, A.M.; Pathan, T.K.; Hampannavar, G.A.; Pawar, C.; Obakachi, V.A.; Kushwaha, B.; Kushwaha, N.D.; Karpoormath, R. Recent Advances on the s-Triazine Scaffold with Emphasis on Synthesis, Structure-Activity and Pharmacological Aspects: A Concise Review. *ChemistrySelect* **2021**, *6*, 1616–1660. [CrossRef]
14. Butti, R.; Das, S.; Gunasekaran, V.P.; Yadav, A.S.; Kumar, D.; Kundu, G.C. Receptor tyrosine kinases (RTKs) in breast cancer: Signaling, therapeutic implications and challenges. *Mol. Cancer* **2018**, *17*, 34. [CrossRef] [PubMed]
15. Mirshafiey, A.; Ghalamfarsa, G.; Asghari, B.; Azizi, G. Receptor Tyrosine Kinase and Tyrosine Kinase Inhibitors: New Hope for Success in Multiple Sclerosis Therapy. *Innov. Clin. Neurosci.* **2014**, *11*, 23–36. [PubMed]
16. Jiang, W.; Ji, M. Receptor tyrosine kinases in PI3K signaling: The therapeutic targets in cancer. *Semin. Cancer Biol.* **2019**, *59*, 3–22. [CrossRef] [PubMed]
17. Liu, P.; Cheng, H.; Roberts, T.M.; Zhao, J.J. Targeting the phosphoinositide 3-kinase pathway in cancer. *Nat. Rev. Drug Discov.* **2009**, *8*, 627–644. [CrossRef]
18. Miricescu, D.; Totan, A.; Stanescu, S., II; Badoiu, S.C.; Stefani, C.; Greabu, M. PI3K/AKT/mTOR Signaling Pathway in Breast Cancer: From Molecular Landscape to Clinical Aspects. *Int. J. Mol. Sci.* **2020**, *22*, 173. [CrossRef]
19. Yang, J.; Nie, J.; Ma, X.; Wei, Y.; Peng, Y.; Wei, X. Targeting PI3K in cancer: Mechanisms and advances in clinical trials. *Mol. Cancer* **2019**, *18*, 26. [CrossRef]
20. Pottier, C.; Fresnais, M.; Gilon, M.; Jérusalem, G.; Longuespée, R.; Sounni, N.E. Tyrosine Kinase Inhibitors in Cancer: Breakthrough and Challenges of Targeted Therapy. *Cancers* **2020**, *12*, 731. [CrossRef]
21. Grant, S.K. Therapeutic protein kinase inhibitors. *Cell Mol. Life Sci.* **2009**, *66*, 1163–1177. [CrossRef]
22. Harricharan, S.; Kee, A.; Grieve, S.L.; Brokars, J.; Forsythe, A.; Copher, R. CML-479: Systematic Literature Review of Treatment Patterns, Long-Term Efficacy, and Safety of Dasatinib Therapy for Patients with Chronic Myeloid Leukemia. *Clin. Lymphoma Myeloma Leuk.* **2021**, *21*, S337. [CrossRef]
23. Keating, G.M. Dasatinib: A Review in Chronic Myeloid Leukaemia and Ph+ Acute Lymphoblastic Leukaemia. *Drugs* **2017**, *77*, 85–96. [CrossRef] [PubMed]
24. Garzón-Orjuela, N.; Prieto-Pinto, L.; Lasalvia, P.; Herrera, D.; Castrillón, J.; González-Bravo, D.; Castañeda-Cardona, C.; Rosselli, D. Efficacy and safety of dabrafenib-trametinib in the treatment of unresectable advanced/metastatic melanoma with BRAF-V600 mutation: A systematic review and network meta-analysis. *Dermatol. Ther.* **2020**, *33*, e13145. [CrossRef] [PubMed]
25. Robert, C.; Grob, J.J.; Stroyakovskiy, D.; Karaszewska, B.; Hauschild, A.; Levchenko, E.; Chiarion Sileni, V.; Schachter, J.; Garbe, C.; Bondarenko, I.; et al. Five-Year Outcomes with Dabrafenib plus Trametinib in Metastatic Melanoma. *N. Engl. J. Med.* **2019**, *381*, 626–636. [CrossRef] [PubMed]
26. Fan, G.; Wei, X.; Xu, X. Is the era of sorafenib over? A review of the literature. *Ther. Adv. Med. Oncol.* **2020**, *12*, 1758835920927602. [CrossRef]
27. Elsadek, B.E.M.; Mansour, A.M.; Saleem, T.H.; Warnecke, A.; Kratz, F. The antitumor activity of a lactosaminated albumin conjugate of doxorubicin in a chemically induced hepatocellular carcinoma rat model compared to sorafenib. *Dig. Liver Dis. Off. J. Ital. Soc. Gastroenterol. Ital. Assoc. Study Liver* **2017**, *49*, 213–222. [CrossRef]
28. Moran, M.; Nickens, D.J.; Adcock, K.; Desscan, A.; Bennetts, M.; Charnley, N.; Fife, K. Sunitinib for metastatic renal cell carcinoma: A systematic review and meta-analysis of real world and clinical trials data. *J. Clin. Oncol.* **2019**, *37* (Suppl. 7), 650. [CrossRef]
29. Brown, T. Design thinking. *Harv. Bus. Rev.* **2008**, *86*, 84–92, 141.
30. Kyrkou, S.G.; Vrettos, E.I.; Gorpas, D.; Crook, T.; Syed, N.; Tzakos, A.G. Design Principles Governing the Development of Theranostic Anticancer Agents and Their Nanoformulations with Photoacoustic Properties. *Pharmaceutics* **2022**, *14*, 362. [CrossRef]
31. Bhatia, P.; Sharma, V.; Alam, O.; Manaithiya, A.; Alam, P.; Kahksha; Alam, M.T.; Imran, M. Novel quinazoline-based EGFR kinase inhibitors: A review focussing on SAR and molecular docking studies (2015–2019). *Eur. J. Med. Chem.* **2020**, *204*, 112640. [CrossRef]
32. Wdowiak, P.; Matysiak, J.; Kuszta, P.; Czarnek, K.; Niezabitowska, E.; Baj, T. Quinazoline Derivatives as Potential Therapeutic Agents in Urinary Bladder Cancer Therapy. *Front. Chem.* **2021**, *9*, 765552. [CrossRef]
33. El Mubarak, M.A.; Leontari, I.; Efstathia, G.; Vrettos, E.I.; Shaikh, A.K.; Konstantinos, S.E.; Danika, C.; Kalofonos, H.P.; Tzakos, A.G.; Sivolapenko, G.B. Development of a novel conjugatable sunitinib analogue validated through in vitro and in vivo preclinical settings. *J. Chromatogr. B* **2018**, *1092*, 515–523. [CrossRef]

34. Tokarski, J.S.; Newitt, J.A.; Chang, C.Y.; Cheng, J.D.; Wittekind, M.; Kiefer, S.E.; Kish, K.F.; Lee, F.Y.F.; Borzillerri, R.; Lombardo, L.J.; et al. The structure of Dasatinib (BMS-354825) bound to activated ABL kinase domain elucidates its inhibitory activity against imatinib-resistant ABL mutants. *Cancer Res.* **2006**, *66*, 5790–5797. [CrossRef]
35. Lee, C.S.; Milone, M.; Seetharamu, N. Osimertinib in EGFR-Mutated Lung Cancer: A Review of the Existing and Emerging Clinical Data. *Oncol. Targets Ther.* **2021**, *14*, 4579–4597. [CrossRef]
36. Singh, H.; Sareen, D.; George, J.; Bhardwaj, V.; Rha, S.; Lee, S.; Sharma, S.; Sharma, A.; Kim, J. Mitochondria targeted fluorogenic theranostic agents for cancer therapy. *Coord. Chem. Rev.* **2022**, *452*, 214283. [CrossRef]
37. Wang, L.; Xiong, Z.; Ran, X.; Tang, H.; Cao, D. Recent advances of NIR dyes of pyrrolopyrrole cyanine and pyrrolopyrrole aza-BODIPY: Synthesis and application. *Dye. Pigment.* **2021**, *198*, 110040. [CrossRef]
38. Fei, G.; Ma, S.; Wang, C.; Chen, T.; Li, Y.; Liu, Y.; Tang, B.; James, T.D.; Chen, G. Imaging strategies using cyanine probes and materials for biomedical visualization of live animals. *Coord. Chem. Rev.* **2021**, *447*, 214134. [CrossRef]
39. Li, Y.; Zhou, Y.; Yue, X.; Dai, Z. Cyanine conjugates in cancer theranostics. *Bioact. Mater.* **2021**, *6*, 794–809. [CrossRef]
40. Karton-Lifshin, N.; Albertazzi, L.; Bendikov, M.; Baran, P.S.; Shabat, D. "Donor–Two-Acceptor" Dye Design: A Distinct Gateway to NIR Fluorescence. *J. Am. Chem. Soc.* **2012**, *134*, 20412–20420. [CrossRef]
41. Usama, S.M.; Burgess, K. Hows and Whys of Tumor-Seeking Dyes. *ACC Chem. Res.* **2021**, *54*, 2121–2131. [CrossRef]
42. Usama, S.M.; Park, G.K.; Nomura, S.; Baek, Y.; Choi, H.S.; Burgess, K. Role of Albumin in Accumulation and Persistence of Tumor-Seeking Cyanine Dyes. *Bioconjugate Chem.* **2020**, *31*, 248–259. [CrossRef]
43. Usama, S.M.; Zhao, B.; Burgess, K. Fluorescent kinase inhibitors as probes in cancer. *Chem. Soc. Rev.* **2021**, *50*, 9794–9816. [CrossRef]
44. St. Lorenz, A.; Buabeng, E.R.; Taratula, O.; Taratula, O.; Henary, M. Near-Infrared Heptamethine Cyanine Dyes for Nanoparticle-Based Photoacoustic Imaging and Photothermal Therapy. *J. Med. Chem.* **2021**, *64*, 8798–8805. [CrossRef]
45. Tan, X.; Luo, S.; Long, L.; Wang, Y.; Wang, D.; Fang, S.; Ouyang, Q.; Su, Y.; Cheng, T.; Shi, C. Structure-Guided Design and Synthesis of a Mitochondria-Targeting Near-Infrared Fluorophore with Multimodal Therapeutic Activities. *Adv. Mater.* **2017**, *29*, 1704196. [CrossRef]
46. Cao, J.; Zhu, B.; Zheng, K.; He, S.; Meng, L.; Song, J.; Yang, H. Recent Progress in NIR-II Contrast Agent for Biological Imaging. *Front. Bioeng. Biotechnol.* **2020**, *7*, 487. [CrossRef]
47. Cheruku, R.R.; Cacaccio, J.; Durrani, F.A.; Tabaczynski, W.A.; Watson, R.; Siters, K.; Missert, J.R.; Tracy, E.C.; Dukh, M.; Guru, K.; et al. Synthesis, Tumor Specificity, and Photosensitizing Efficacy of Erlotinib-Conjugated Chlorins and Bacteriochlorins: Identification of a Highly Effective Candidate for Photodynamic Therapy of Cancer. *J. Med. Chem.* **2021**, *64*, 741–767. [CrossRef]
48. Vrettos, E.; Kyrkou, S.G.; Zoi, V.; Giannakopoulou, M.; Chatziathanasiadou, M.V.; Kanaki, Z.; Agalou, A.; Bistas, V.P.; Kougioumtzi, A.; Karampelas, T.; et al. A Novel Fluorescent Gemcitabine Prodrug That Follows a Nucleoside Transporter-Independent Internalization and Bears Enhanced Therapeutic Efficacy with Respect to Gemcitabine. *Chemistry* **2024**, *30*, e202401327. [CrossRef]
49. Vrettos, E.I.; Karampelas, T.; Sayyad, N.; Kougioumtzi, A.; Syed, N.; Crook, T.; Murphy, C.; Tamvakopoulos, C.; Tzakos, A.G. Development of programmable gemcitabine-GnRH pro-drugs bearing linker controllable "click" oxime bond tethers and preclinical evaluation against prostate cancer. *Eur. J. Med. Chem.* **2021**, *211*, 113018. [CrossRef]
50. Bhuniya, S.; Vrettos, E.I. Hypoxia-Activated Theragnostic Prodrugs (HATPs): Current State and Future Perspectives. *Pharmaceutics* **2024**, *16*, 557. [CrossRef]
51. Ouyang, J.; Sun, L.; Zeng, F.; Wu, S. Rational design of stable heptamethine cyanines and development of a biomarker-activatable probe for detecting acute lung/kidney injuries via NIR-II fluorescence imaging. *Analyst* **2022**, *147*, 410–416. [CrossRef]
52. Usama, S.M.; Inagaki, F.; Kobayashi, H.; Schnermann, M.J. Norcyanine-Carbamates Are Versatile Near-Infrared Fluorogenic Probes. *J. Am. Chem. Soc.* **2021**, *143*, 5674–5679. [CrossRef]
53. Kougioumtzi, A.; Chatziathanasiadou, M.V.; Vrettos, E.I.; Sayyad, N.; Sakka, M.; Stathopoulos, P.; Mantzaris, M.D.; Ganai, A.M.; Karpoormath, R.; Vartholomatos, G.; et al. Development of novel GnRH and Tat48–60 based luminescent probes with enhanced cellular uptake and bioimaging profile. *Dalton Trans.* **2021**, *50*, 9215–9224. [CrossRef] [PubMed]
54. Sayyad, N.; Vrettos, E.I.; Karampelas, T.; Chatzigiannis, C.M.; Spyridaki, K.; Liapakis, G.; Tamvakopoulos, C.; Tzakos, A.G. Development of bioactive gemcitabine-D-Lys6-GnRH prodrugs with linker-controllable drug release rate and enhanced biopharmaceutical profile. *Eur. J. Med. Chem.* **2019**, *166*, 256–266. [CrossRef]
55. Vrettos, E.I.; Mező, G.; Tzakos, A.G. On the design principles of peptide-drug conjugates for targeted drug delivery to the malignant tumor site. *Beilstein J. Org. Chem.* **2018**, *14*, 930–954. [CrossRef]
56. Song, X.; Han, X.; Yu, F.; Zhang, X.; Chen, L.; Lv, C. Polyamine-Targeting Gefitinib Prodrug and its Near-Infrared Fluorescent Theranostic Derivative for Monitoring Drug Delivery and Lung Cancer Therapy. *Theranostics* **2018**, *8*, 2217–2228. [CrossRef]
57. Usama, S.M.; Jiang, Z.; Pflug, K.; Sitcheran, R.; Burgess, K. Conjugation of Dasatinib with MHI-148 Has a Significant Advantageous Effect in Viability Assays for Glioblastoma Cells. *ChemMedChem* **2019**, *14*, 1575–1579. [CrossRef]
58. Usama, S.M.; Zhao, B.; Burgess, K. A Near-IR Fluorescent Dasatinib Derivative That Localizes in Cancer Cells. *Bioconjugate Chem.* **2019**, *30*, 1175–1181. [CrossRef]
59. Fujimoto, S.; Muguruma, N.; Nakao, M.; Ando, H.; Kashihara, T.; Miyamoto, Y.; Okamoto, K.; Sano, S.; Ishida, T.; Sato, Y.; et al. Indocyanine green-labeled dasatinib as a new fluorescent probe for molecular imaging of gastrointestinal stromal tumors. *J. Gastroenterol. Hepatol.* **2021**, *36*, 1253–1262. [CrossRef]

60. Wang, M.; Kommidi, H.; Tosi, U.; Guo, H.; Zhou, Z.; Schweitzer, M.E.; Wu, L.Y.; Singh, R.; Hou, S.; Law, B.; et al. A Murine Model for Quantitative, Real-Time Evaluation of Convection-Enhanced Delivery (RT-CED) Using an 18[F]-Positron Emitting, Fluorescent Derivative of Dasatinib. *Mol. Cancer Ther.* **2017**, *16*, 2902–2912. [CrossRef]
61. Yang, X.; Hou, Z.; Wang, D.; Mou, Y.; Guo, C. Design, synthesis and biological evaluation of novel heptamethine cyanine dye-erlotinib conjugates as antitumor agents. *Bioorganic Med. Chem. Lett.* **2020**, *30*, 127557. [CrossRef]
62. Zhang, F.-L.; Huang, Q.; Zheng, K.; Li, J.; Liu, J.-Y.; Xue, J.-P. A novel strategy for targeting photodynamic therapy. Molecular combo of photodynamic agent zinc(ii) phthalocyanine and small molecule target-based anticancer drug erlotinib. *Chem. Commun.* **2013**, *49*, 9570–9572. [CrossRef]
63. Cheruku, R.R.; Cacaccio, J.; Durrani, F.A.; Tabaczynski, W.A.; Watson, R.; Marko, A.; Kumar, R.; El-Khouly, M.E.; Fukuzumi, S.; Missert, J.R.; et al. Epidermal Growth Factor Receptor-Targeted Multifunctional Photosensitizers for Bladder Cancer Imaging and Photodynamic Therapy. *J. Med. Chem.* **2019**, *62*, 2598–2617. [CrossRef] [PubMed]
64. Park, J.H.; Liu, Y.; Lemmon, M.A.; Radhakrishnan, R. Erlotinib binds both inactive and active conformations of the EGFR tyrosine kinase domain. *Biochem. J.* **2012**, *448*, 417–423. [CrossRef]
65. Song, X.; Wang, R.; Gao, J.; Han, X.; Jin, J.; Lv, C.; Yu, F. Construction of a biotin-targeting drug delivery system and its near-infrared theranostic fluorescent probe for real-time image-guided therapy of lung cancer. *Chin. Chem. Lett.* **2022**, *33*, 1567–1571. [CrossRef]
66. Gamcsik, M.P.; Kasibhatla, M.S.; Teeter, S.D.; Colvin, O.M. Glutathione levels in human tumors. *Biomarkers* **2012**, *17*, 671–691. [CrossRef]
67. Le, T.-H.; Kim, J.-H.; Park, S.-J. "Turn on" Fluorescence Sensor of Glutathione Based on Inner Filter Effect of Co-Doped Carbon Dot/Gold Nanoparticle Composites. *Int. J. Mol. Sci.* **2022**, *23*, 190. [CrossRef]
68. Cheraghi, S.; Taher, M.A.; Karimi-Maleh, H.; Karimi, F.; Shabani-Nooshabadi, M.; Alizadeh, M.; Al-Othman, A.; Erk, N.; Yegya Raman, P.K.; Karaman, C. Novel enzymatic graphene oxide based biosensor for the detection of glutathione in biological body fluids. *Chemosphere* **2022**, *287*, 132187. [CrossRef]
69. Chen, Y.; Chen, M.; Zhai, T.; Zhou, H.; Zhou, Z.; Liu, X.; Yang, S.; Yang, H. Glutathione-Responsive Chemodynamic Therapy of Manganese(III/IV) Cluster Nanoparticles Enhanced by Electrochemical Stimulation via Oxidative Stress Pathway. *Bioconjugate Chem.* **2021**, *33*, 152–163. [CrossRef]
70. Fanyong, Y.; Yueyan, Z.; Yuyang, Z.; Xiang, L.; Ruijie, W.; Zhentong, L. The Fluorescent Probe for Detecting Glutathione. *Prog. Chem.* **2022**, *34*, 1136–1152. [CrossRef]
71. Zhang, J.; Yang, P.L.; Gray, N.S. Targeting cancer with small molecule kinase inhibitors. *Nat. Rev. Cancer* **2009**, *9*, 28–39. [CrossRef]
72. Liu, S.; Song, W.; Gao, X.; Su, Y.; Gao, E.; Gao, Q.; Liu, S.; Song, W.; Gao, X.; Su, Y.; et al. Discovery of Nonpeptide, Reversible HER1/HER2 Dual-Targeting Small-Molecule Inhibitors as Near-Infrared Fluorescent Probes for Efficient Tumor Detection, Diagnostic Imaging, and Drug Screening. *Anal. Chem.* **2018**, *91*, 1507–1515. [CrossRef]
73. Ducharme, G.T.; LaCasse, Z.; Sheth, T.; Nesterova, I.V.; Nesterov, E.E. Design of Turn-On Near-Infrared Fluorescent Probes for Highly Sensitive and Selective Monitoring of Biopolymers. *Angew. Chem. Int. Ed.* **2020**, *59*, 8440–8444. [CrossRef] [PubMed]
74. Choi, P.J.; Tomek, P.; Tercel, M.; Reynisson, J.; Park, T.I.H.; Cooper, E.A.; Denny, W.A.; Jose, J.; Leung, E. Conjugation of Palbociclib with MHI-148 Has an Increased Cytotoxic Effect for Breast Cancer Cells and an Altered Mechanism of Action. *Molecules* **2022**, *27*, 880. [CrossRef] [PubMed]
75. Choi, P.J.; Cooper, E.; Schweder, P.; Mee, E.; Faull, R.; Denny, W.A.; Dragunow, M.; Park, T.I.H.; Jose, J. The synthesis of a novel Crizotinib heptamethine cyanine dye conjugate that potentiates the cytostatic and cytotoxic effects of Crizotinib in patient-derived glioblastoma cell lines. *Bioorganic Med. Chem. Lett.* **2019**, *29*, 2617–2621. [CrossRef] [PubMed]
76. Mikula, H.; Stapleton, S.; Kohler, R.H.; Vinegoni, C.; Weissleder, R. Design and Development of Fluorescent Vemurafenib Analogs for In Vivo Imaging. *Theranostics* **2017**, *7*, 1257–1265. [CrossRef] [PubMed]
77. Turetsky, A.; Kim, E.; Kohler, R.H.; Miller, M.A.; Weissleder, R. Single cell imaging of Bruton's Tyrosine Kinase using an irreversible inhibitor. *Sci. Rep.* **2014**, *4*, 4782. [CrossRef]
78. Liu, C.; Wang, X.; Zhu, H.; Wang, K.; Yu, M.; Zhang, Y.; Su, M.; Rong, X.; Sheng, W.; Zhu, B. Multifunctional Theranostic Probe Based on the Pim-1 Kinase Inhibitor with the Function of Tracking pH Fluctuations during Treatment. *Anal. Chem.* **2023**, *95*, 11732–11740. [CrossRef]
79. Shukla, S.; Skoumbourdis, A.P.; Walsh, M.J.; Hartz, A.M.; Fung, K.L.; Wu, C.P.; Gottesman, M.M.; Bauer, B.; Thomas, C.J.; Ambudkar, S.V. Synthesis and characterization of a BODIPY conjugate of the BCR-ABL kinase inhibitor Tasigna (nilotinib): Evidence for transport of Tasigna and its fluorescent derivative by ABC drug transporters. *Mol. Pharm.* **2011**, *8*, 1292–1302. [CrossRef]
80. Liu, C.; Zhang, Y.; Sun, W.; Zhu, H.; Su, M.; Wang, X.; Rong, X.; Wang, K.; Yu, M.; Sheng, W.; et al. A novel GSH-activable theranostic probe containing kinase inhibitor for synergistic treatment and selective imaging of tumor cells. *Talanta* **2023**, *260*, 124567. [CrossRef]
81. Hu, Z.; Li, R.; Cui, X.; Chen, Z. Albumin-Based Cyanine Crizotinib Conjugate Nanoparticles for NIR-II Imaging-Guided Synergistic Chemophototherapy. *ACS Appl. Mater. Interfaces* **2023**, *15*, 33890–33902. [CrossRef]
82. Barresi, E.; Baldanzi, C.; Roncetti, M.; Roggia, M.; Baglini, E.; Lepori, I.; Vitiello, M.; Salerno, S.; Tedeschi, L.; Da Settimo, F.; et al. A cyanine-based NIR fluorescent Vemurafenib analog to probe BRAFV600E in cancer cells. *Eur. J. Med. Chem.* **2023**, *256*, 115446. [CrossRef]

83. Ju, D.; Dewer, Y.; Zhang, S.; Hu, C.; Li, P.; Yang, X. Genome-wide identification, characterization, and expression profiling of ATP-binding cassette (ABC) transporter genes potentially associated with abamectin detoxification in Cydia pomonella. *Ecotoxicol. Environ. Saf.* **2022**, *230*, 113152. [CrossRef] [PubMed]
84. Sales, A.D.; Duarte, A.B.G.; Rocha, R.M.P.; Brito, I.R.; Locatelli, Y.; Alves, B.G.; Alves, K.A.; Figueiredo, J.R.; Rodrigues, A.P.R. Transcriptional downregulation of ABC transporters is related to follicular degeneration after vitrification and in vitro culture of ovine ovarian tissue. *Theriogenology* **2022**, *177*, 127–132. [CrossRef] [PubMed]
85. Zattoni, I.F.; Kronenberger, T.; Kita, D.H.; Guanaes, L.D.; Guimarães, M.M.; de Oliveira Prado, L.; Ziasch, M.; Vesga, L.C.; Gomes de Moraes Rego, F.; Picheth, G.; et al. A new porphyrin as selective substrate-based inhibitor of breast cancer resistance protein (BCRP/ABCG2). *Chem.-Biol. Interact.* **2022**, *351*, 109718. [CrossRef] [PubMed]
86. Miller, M.A.; Kim, E.; Cuccarese, M.F.; Plotkin, A.L.; Prytyskach, M.; Kohler, R.H.; Pittet, M.J.; Weissleder, R. Near infrared imaging of Mer tyrosine kinase (MERTK) using MERi-SiR reveals tumor associated macrophage uptake in metastatic disease. *Chem. Commun.* **2017**, *54*, 42–45. [CrossRef]
87. Asati, V.; Anant, A.; Patel, P.; Kaur, K.; Gupta, G.D. Pyrazolopyrimidines as anticancer agents: A review on structural and target-based approaches. *Eur. J. Med. Chem.* **2021**, *225*, 113781. [CrossRef]
88. Shagufta; Ahmad, I. An insight into the therapeutic potential of quinazoline derivatives as anticancer agents. *MedChemComm* **2017**, *8*, 871–885. [CrossRef]
89. Fleming, C.L.; Sandoz, P.A.; Inghardt, T.; Önfelt, B.; Grøtli, M.; Andréasson, J. A Fluorescent Kinase Inhibitor that Exhibits Diagnostic Changes in Emission upon Binding. *Angew. Chem. Int. Ed.* **2019**, *58*, 15000–15004. [CrossRef]
90. Qin, X.; Yang, X.; Du, L.; Li, M. Polarity-based fluorescence probes: Properties and applications. *RSC Med. Chem.* **2021**, *12*, 1826–1838. [CrossRef]
91. Yi, X.; Cao, Z.; Yuan, Y.; Li, W.; Cui, X.; Chen, Z.; Hu, X.; Yu, A. Design and synthesis of a novel mitochondria-targeted osteosarcoma theranostic agent based on a PIM1 kinase inhibitor. *J. Control. Release* **2021**, *332*, 434–447. [CrossRef]
92. Ilmi, R.; Tseriotou, E.; Stylianou, P.; Christou, Y.A.; Ttofi, I.; Dietis, N.; Pitris, C.; Odysseos, A.D.; Georgiades, S.N. A Novel Conjugate of Bis[((4-bromophenyl)amino)quinazoline], a EGFR-TK Ligand, with a Fluorescent Ru(II)-Bipyridine Complex Exhibits Specific Subcellular Localization in Mitochondria. *Mol. Pharm.* **2019**, *16*, 4260–4273. [CrossRef]
93. Shamsiya, A.; Bahulayan, D. D–A systems based on oxazolone–coumarin triazoles as solid-state emitters and inhibitors of human cervical cancer cells (HeLa). *New J. Chem.* **2022**, *46*, 480–489. [CrossRef]
94. Antolin, A.A.; Ameratunga, M.; Banerji, U.; Clarke, P.A.; Workman, P.; Al-Lazikani, B. The kinase polypharmacology landscape of clinical PARP inhibitors. *Sci. Rep.* **2020**, *10*, 2585. [CrossRef] [PubMed]
95. Choi, P.J.; Cooper, E.; Schweder, P.; Mee, E.; Turner, C.; Faull, R.; Denny, W.A.; Dragunow, M.; Park, T.I.; Jose, J. PARP inhibitor cyanine dye conjugate with enhanced cytotoxic and antiproliferative activity in patient derived glioblastoma cell lines. *Bioorg. Med. Chem. Lett.* **2020**, *30*, 127252. [CrossRef]
96. Lee, H.; Landgraf, R.; Wilson, J.N. Synthesis and photophysical properties of a fluorescent cyanoquinoline probe for profiling ERBB2 kinase inhibitor response. *Bioorganic Med. Chem.* **2017**, *25*, 6016–6023. [CrossRef]
97. Lee, H.; Liu, W.; Brown, A.S.; Landgraf, R.; Wilson, J.N. Fluorescent Kinase Probes Enabling Identification and Dynamic Imaging of HER2(+) Cells. *Anal. Chem.* **2016**, *88*, 11310–11313. [CrossRef]
98. Dhuguru, J.; Liu, W.; Gonzalez, W.G.; Babinchak, W.M.; Miksovska, J.; Landgraf, R.; Wilson, J.N. Emission tuning of fluorescent kinase inhibitors: Conjugation length and substituent effects. *J. Org. Chem.* **2014**, *79*, 4940–4947. [CrossRef]
99. Sicard, R.; Dhuguru, J.; Liu, W.; Patel, N.; Landgraf, R.; Wilson, J.N. A fluorescent reporter of ATP binding-competent receptor kinases. *Bioorganic Med. Chem. Lett.* **2012**, *22*, 5532–5535. [CrossRef]
100. Deng, H.; Lei, Q.; Shang, W.; Li, Y.; Bi, L.; Yang, N.; Yu, Z.; Li, W. Potential applications of clickable probes in EGFR activity visualization and prediction of EGFR-TKI therapy response for NSCLC patients. *Eur. J. Med. Chem.* **2022**, *230*, 114100. [CrossRef]
101. Wang, L.-X.; Wang, Z.-H.; Sun, X.-L.; Zi, C.-T.; Wang, X.-J.; Sheng, J. Discovery of EGFR-Targeted Environment-Sensitive fluorescent probes for cell imaging and efficient tumor detection. *Bioorganic Chem.* **2022**, *121*, 105585. [CrossRef]
102. Kaufman, N.E.M.; Dhingra, S.; Jois, S.D.; Vicente, M. Molecular Targeting of Epidermal Growth Factor Receptor (EGFR) and Vascular Endothelial Growth Factor Receptor (VEGFR). *Molecules* **2021**, *26*, 1076. [CrossRef]
103. Huang, M.; Xiong, C.; Lu, W.; Zhang, R.; Zhou, M.; Huang, Q.; Weinberg, J.; Li, C. Dual-modality micro-positron emission tomography/computed tomography and near-infrared fluorescence imaging of EphB4 in orthotopic glioblastoma xenograft models. *Mol. Imaging Biol.* **2014**, *16*, 74–84. [CrossRef]
104. Vagaggini, C.; Petroni, D.; D'Agostino, I.; Poggialini, F.; Cavallini, C.; Cianciusi, A.; Salis, A.; D'Antona, L.; Francesconi, V.; Manetti, F.; et al. Early investigation of a novel SI306 theranostic prodrug for glioblastoma treatment. *Drug Dev. Res.* **2024**, *85*, e22158. [CrossRef]

Disclaimer/Publisher's Note: The statements, opinions and data contained in all publications are solely those of the individual author(s) and contributor(s) and not of MDPI and/or the editor(s). MDPI and/or the editor(s) disclaim responsibility for any injury to people or property resulting from any ideas, methods, instructions or products referred to in the content.

pharmaceutics

MDPI

Article

Glucose Metabolism as a Potential Therapeutic Target in Cytarabine-Resistant Acute Myeloid Leukemia

Joana Pereira-Vieira [1,2], Daniela D. Weber [3], Sâmia Silva [4], Catarina Barbosa-Matos [1,2], Sara Granja [1,2,5,6], Rui Manuel Reis [1,2,4], Odília Queirós [7], Young H. Ko [8], Barbara Kofler [3], Margarida Casal [9,*] and Fátima Baltazar [1,2,*]

[1] Life and Health Sciences Research Institute (ICVS), School of Medicine, University of Minho, Campus of Gualtar, 4710-057 Braga, Portugal; id8183@alunos.uminho.pt (J.P.-V.); id8801@alunos.uminho.pt (C.B.-M.); saragranja@med.uminho.pt (S.G.); rreis@med.uminho.pt (R.M.R.)
[2] ICVS/3B's—PT Government Associate Laboratory, Braga/Guimarães, Portugal
[3] Research Program for Receptor Biochemistry and Tumor Metabolism, Department of Pediatrics, University Hospital of the Paracelsus Medical University, 5020 Salzburg, Austria; d.weber@salk.at (D.D.W.); b.kofler@salk.at (B.K.)
[4] Molecular Oncology Research Center, Barretos Cancer Hospital, Barretos 14784-400, SP, Brazil; samiafrahia@hotmail.com
[5] Department of Pathological, Cytological and Thanatological Anatomy, ESS | P.PORTO, 4200-072 Porto, Portugal
[6] REQUIMTE/LAQV, Escola Superior de Saúde, Instituto Politécnico do Porto, Rua Dr. António Bernardino de Almeida, 4200-072 Porto, Portugal
[7] UNIPRO—Oral Pathology and Rehabilitation Research Unit, University Institute of Health Sciences, CESPU, CRL, 4585-116 Gandra, Portugal; odilia.queiros@iucs.cespu.pt
[8] KoDiscovery, LLC, Institute of Marine and Environmental Technology (IMET) Center, 701 East Pratt Street, Baltimore, MD 21202, USA; youngheeko@kodiscovery.org
[9] Center of Molecular and Environmental Biology (CBMA), University of Minho, 4710-057 Braga, Portugal
* Correspondence: mcasal@bio.uminho.pt (M.C.); fbaltazar@med.uminho.pt (F.B.)

Abstract: Altered glycolytic metabolism has been associated with chemoresistance in acute myeloid leukemia (AML). However, there are still aspects that need clarification, as well as how to explore these metabolic alterations in therapy. In the present study, we aimed to elucidate the role of glucose metabolism in the acquired resistance of AML cells to cytarabine (Ara-C) and to explore it as a therapeutic target. Resistance was induced by stepwise exposure of AML cells to increasing concentrations of Ara-C. Ara-C-resistant cells were characterized for their growth capacity, genetic alterations, metabolic profile, and sensitivity to different metabolic inhibitors. Ara-C-resistant AML cell lines, KG-1 Ara-R, and MOLM13 Ara-R presented different metabolic profiles. KG-1 Ara-R cells exhibited a more pronounced glycolytic phenotype than parental cells, with a weaker acute response to 3-bromopyruvate (3-BP) but higher sensitivity after 48 h. KG-1 Ara-R cells also display increased respiration rates and are more sensitive to phenformin than parental cells. On the other hand, MOLM13 Ara-R cells display a glucose metabolism profile similar to parental cells, as well as sensitivity to glycolytic inhibitors. These results indicate that acquired resistance to Ara-C in AML may involve metabolic adaptations, which can be explored therapeutically in the AML patient setting who developed resistance to therapy.

Keywords: chemoresistance; cytarabine; acute myeloid leukemia; metabolic inhibitors; seahorse; glucose metabolism; 3-bromopyruvate; phenformin

1. Introduction

Acute Myeloid Leukemia (AML) is an aggressive blood cancer that affects the myeloid cell lineage in the bone marrow, characterized by the rapid growth of immature white blood cells, myeloblasts, which compromise the production of normal blood cells [1,2]. The overall survival rates of AML patients are low, especially in patients above 60 years, who are at highest risk [3]. The standard treatment for AML is based on a 7 + 3 chemotherapy regimen, combining anthracyclines and antimetabolite drugs [4,5]. The efficacy of treatment depends on several factors, such as the overall patient health condition, patient age, and the presence of genetic mutations [5]. Targeted therapy has shown promising results in some AML subtypes that present specific gene mutations. AML patients with mutated fms-like tyrosine kinase 3 (*FLT3*) may be considered to receive intensive chemotherapy in combination with the FLT3 inhibitor midostaurin [6]. Patients harboring isocitrate dehydrogenase (*IDH*)*-1* or *IDH-2* mutations may be treated with ivosidenib and enasidenib [7], respectively. More recently, venetoclax, an inhibitor of the antiapoptotic BCL-2 protein, became available for AML patients above 75 years or for patients with other medical conditions that prohibit the use of intensive chemotherapy [8]. Even though targeted therapy is frequently used, conventional chemotherapy is still used in most AML patients.

Despite advances in AML treatment, relapse occurs in about 50% of patients who achieved remission after initial treatment and can occur from a few months to several years after treatment. Also, the survival of AML patients' post-relapse is dismal [9]. The 5-year overall survival (OS) of relapsed patients is around 10%, and factors such as age, cytogenetics at diagnosis, duration of first complete remission, and undergoing allogeneic transplantation are associated with OS from relapse [3]. Several mechanisms have been described as potential causes of relapse, including the existence of subclones that are present at diagnosis and survive treatment and clonal evolution from leukemic hematopoietic stem cells, as well as the pre-existence or acquisition of genetic mutations that result in drug insensitivity and, consequently, refractory response to treatment [10,11].

Metabolic reprogramming is a recognized hallmark of cancer [12]. Altered metabolism may induce resistance to chemotherapy in cancer cells by increasing energy production and drug efflux, decreasing drug-induced apoptosis, and/or activating proliferative signaling pathways [13]. *IDH-1* and *IDH-2* enzyme mutations lead to overproduction of the oncometabolite 2-hydroxyglutarate (2-HG), which interferes with cell metabolism and epigenetic regulation [14,15]. Additionally, AML cells present a strong dependency on glucose to maintain the increased activity of the pentose phosphate pathway (PPP) and nucleotide biosynthesis [16]. It has also been reported that enhanced glycolysis in AML cells contributes to reduced sensitivity to chemotherapy [17]. Moreover, a prognostic biomarker signature consisting of six glucose metabolism-associated metabolites, namely glycerol-3-phosphate, pyruvate, lactate, 2-oxoglutarate, citrate, and 2-HG, was identified in AML patients [17].

Otto Warburg's statement that tumor cells preferably use glycolysis even in the presence of oxygen due to mitochondrial dysfunction is outdated [18]. Current evidence suggests that oxidative phosphorylation (OXPHOS) co-exists with elevated glycolysis in cancer cells and is essential for cell bioenergetics, biosynthesis, signaling, and drug resistance [19–22]. There has been intensive research in the field of cancer metabolism, including AML, but there are still aspects related to metabolic flexibility, mitochondrial metabolism vs. glycolytic metabolism that need further investigation in the context of chemoresistance. Therefore, our aim was to understand the link between glucose metabolism and Ara-C resistance in AML and whether it could be translated into potential therapeutic strategies.

2. Materials and Methods

2.1. Cell Lines and Culture Conditions

Acute Myeloid Leukemia (AML) cell lines HL-60, NB-4, MOLM13, and KG-1 were acquired from the DSMZ-German Collection of Microorganisms and Cell Cultures GmbH. Cells were maintained and routinely subcultured in culture flasks at a cell density between 1×10^5 and 1×10^6 cells/mL. Cells were grown in a complete medium consisting of RPMI (PanBiotech, Aidenbach, Germany) supplemented with 10% Fetal Bovine Serum (FBS, PanBiotech) and 1% penicillin/streptomycin (PenStrep, PanBiotech). Cell cultures were maintained in a humidified incubator at 37 °C and a 5% CO_2 atmosphere. To induce resistance, cells were exposed to increasing concentrations of Cytarabine (Ara-C, C3350000, Sigma, Strasbourg, France) and Daunorubicin (DNR, D0125000, Sigma) for 3–6 months. To obtain enough biomass to perform the assays, cells were grown to high densities, but not exceeding 1×10^6 viable cells/mL and with cell viability up to 90%. Viable cell estimation was performed by adding 1:1 cell suspension to 0.2% trypan blue (sc-216028, Santa Cruz Biotechnology, Dallas, TX, USA), and cells were counted in a Neubauer chamber.

2.2. Mutational Profile Analysis

DNA was isolated from parental and resistant AML cell lines using the AllPrep® DNA/RNA/Protein Mini kit (Qiagen, Hilden, Germany), following the manufacturer's instructions. Next sequencing generation (NGS)-based mutation analysis was performed using the Archer Variant Plex® Core Myeloid gene panel (SK0121), which contains SNV/Indel, CNV and Internal tandem duplication (ITD) of 37 key genes with the customization of the genes Sterile Alpha Motif Domain Containing 9 (*SAMD9*) and Sterile Alpha Motif Domain Containing 9 Like (*SAMD9L*), at the Molecular Oncology Research Center, Barretos Cancer Hospital, Brazil. Sequencing data produced by this method was converted to de-multiplexed FASTQs and then processed using Archer Analysis (v6.0). For somatic variant interpretation, the AMP/ASCO/CAP consensus guidelines were used, along with other somatic mutations, to correctly classify these variants [23,24].

2.3. Cell Growth Rate Estimation

Growth rate (μ) and doubling time (Td) were determined as previously described [25]. AML-resistant and parental cell lines (2.5×10^4 cells/well) were seeded into 24-well plates in complete RPMI medium (11 mM glucose), as well as in RPMI medium without glucose, supplemented with different glucose concentrations (0, 2.5, 5, and 10 mM). Growth curves were generated using manual cell counting in the Neubauer chamber every 24 h for 4 days. The μ and Td were determined according to the growth curve and line equation determination.

2.4. Cell Viability Assay

1×10^5 cells/well were seeded in 24-well plates and exposed to a range of increasing Ara-C concentrations (0.05 to 200 μM), 3-Bromopyruvate (3-BP, 1 to 50 μM), 2-Deoxyglucose (2-DG, 1 to 200 mM) and phenformin (0.25 to 5 mM) for 48 h. Drug vehicles, 0.1% DMSO, and PBS were used as controls. Cells were counted using the Trypan blue assay, and cell viability and IC_{50} values for Ara-C, 3-BP, 2-DG, and phenformin were determined and normalized for control. Each treatment was performed in duplicate in at least three independent experiments.

2.5. Extracellular Lactate and Glucose Quantification

Cells were plated in 24-well plates at a density of 5×10^5 cells/well and incubated for 24 h. Cell culture supernatants were collected at 0, 4, 6, 12, and 24 h, and extracellular lactate and glucose were quantified as previously described [26], using the Lactate and Glucose-LQ Colorimetric Assays (Spinreact, Girona, Spain), according to the manufacturer's instructions. The obtained values were normalized for the total number of cells (determined by the Trypan blue assay) in three independent experiments. Glucose consumption was determined by the difference between glucose levels at timepoint 0 and the other timepoints. Data are expressed as mM/10^6 cells.

2.6. Bioenergetic Measurements (Seahorse Assays)

On the day of the assay, KG-1 and MOLM13 parental and Ara-R cells, respectively, were seeded in poly-L-lysine (0.1 mg/mL; Gibco™ A3890401) coated Seahorse XF96 plates at a density of 5×10^4 viable cells per well in 50 μL XF Assay Medium (Seahorse XF RPMI medium supplemented with 10 mM glucose, 1 mM sodium pyruvate and 2 mM L-glutamine, Seahorse Bioscience, Santa Clara, CA, USA). Cells were centrifuged for 1 min at $200\times g$ without brake for cell fixation and incubated at 37 °C in a CO_2-free incubator for 30 min. Once the cells were attached to the plate, an additional 130 μL XF Assay Medium was added, and cells were again incubated for 30 min at 37 °C without CO_2. To evaluate mitochondrial function by measuring oxygen consumption rate (OCR) in response to mitochondrial stressors and the glycolytic inhibitor 3-BP in parental as well as resistant cells, the Seahorse XF Cell Mito Stress Test was performed. Therefore, port A was loaded with either medium or 33 μM of 3-BP. Port B was loaded with 2.5 μM oligomycin to inhibit ATP-synthase in order to calculate ATP-linked oxygen consumption, port C with 0.5 μM fluoro-carbonyl cyanide phenylhydrazone (FCCP, uncoupler) to measure maximal respiration when cells are stressed, and port D with 0.5 μM rotenone combined with 0.5 μM antimycin A to completely inhibit mitochondrial respiration. To assess the glycolytic capacity of parental and resistant cells, the Glycolytic Rate Assay was performed; since this assay quantifies the glycolytic proton efflux rate (glycoPER), the rate of extracellular acidification due to glycolysis only. Therefore, port A was loaded with either medium or 33 μM of 3-BP, port B with 0.5 μM rotenone combined with 0.5 μM antimycin A to inhibit mitochondrial respiration and, in turn, to assess compensatory maximal glycolysis, followed by the injection of 50 mM 2-deoxy-glucose (2-DG) through port C to inhibit glycolysis. Each measurement was normalized for the number of cells (pmol/min/10^4 cells).

2.7. Western Blotting

Western analysis was performed in protein lysates as previously described [26]. Briefly, protein lysates were prepared from cultured cells using a lysis buffer (1% (*v*/*v*) Triton X-100 and 1% (*v*/*v*) NP-40 (Sigma) in ultrapure water; 1:7 protease inhibitors cocktail (Roche®, Basel, Switzerland) and 1:100 phosphatase inhibitor (Sigma). Cells were collected and washed with PBS and were allowed to lyse in 100μL of lysis buffer for 15 min at 4 °C. Lysates were then homogenized (vortex), centrifuged at high speed, and supernatants were collected. Protein concentration was determined using the Bradford assay (B6916, Sigma). Samples were then separated by 10% SDS/PAGE. Proteins were transferred on nitrocellulose membranes (Amersham Biosciences®, Amersham, UK) at 100 V for 90 min. For immunostaining, membranes were blocked with 5% (*w*/*v*) BSA in TBS containing 0.1% (*v*/*v*) Tween-20 (TBS-T). Membranes were incubated with GLUT1 (1:500, ab15309), HKII (1:2000, ab104836), MCT1 (1:500, sc-365501); MCT4 (1:500, sc-376465), LDHA (1:2000, sc-137243) and tubulin (1:20,000, ab6046 or 1:1000, sc-5286) primary antibodies, followed by two washing steps (15 min each) in TBS-Tween-20 and incubation with horseradish peroxidase-conjugated secondary antibodies (1:5000, sc-516102 and sc-2357). Proteins were detected using the ECL Chemiluminescence detection kit (ECL, Western Bright TM Sirius, Advansta, San Jose, CA, USA). Each immunoblot was performed at least three times, and the ones selected for figures are from representative experiments (Azure Biosystems, Dublin, CA, USA).

2.8. Statistical Analysis

Statistical analysis was performed using the GraphPad Prism 8.4.2 software. Data are presented as the mean ± standard deviation (SD) from 2 or 3 independent experiments. Differences between groups were considered statistically significant at $p \leq 0.05$, and a trend was considered at $0.05 < p \leq 0.10$.

3. Results

3.1. Development and Characterization of Cytarabine-Resistant KG-1 and MOLM13 Variants

Ara-C and DNR are the standard chemotherapeutic agents given to patients with AML. Thus, we tested the sensitivity of a panel of four AML cell lines (HL-60, NB-4, KG-1, and MOLM13) to Ara-C and DNR (Figure 1). Compared to HL-60 and NB-4, KG-1 and MOLM13 cell lines revealed lower sensitivity to Ara-C, presenting the highest IC_{50} values (>300 nM) (Figure 1A). This difference was not as evident for DNR. HL-60, NB-4, and MOLM13 cells showed IC_{50} values for DNR around 23 nM, while KG-1 displayed a higher IC_{50} value of 71 nM (Figure 1B). Both HL-60 and NB-4 are representative of the acute promyelocytic leukemia subtype, which presents a good prognosis and effective targeted therapy (e.g., all-trans retinoic acid-ATRA). Thus, we selected KG-1 and MOLM13, a myeloid and monocytic cell line, respectively, to induce resistance to Ara-C.

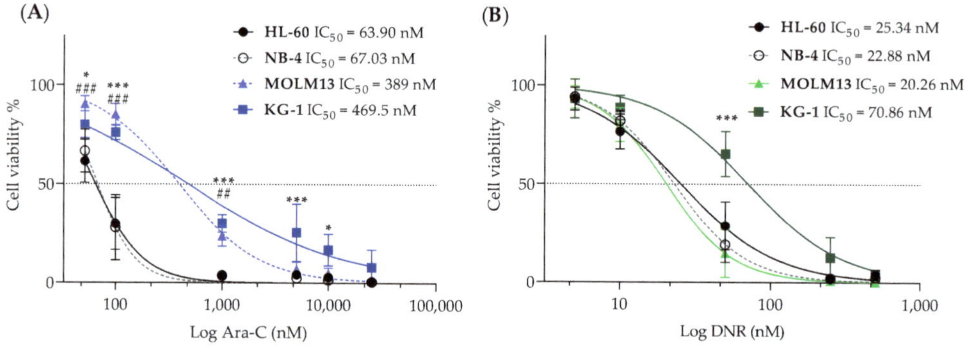

Figure 1. Viability of AML cell lines in response to chemotherapy. Dose-response curves and IC_{50} values for HL-60, NB-4, MOLM13, and KG-1 cell lines treated with (**A**) cytarabine (Ara-C) and (**B**) daunorubicin (DNR). Values are expressed as cell viability relative to vehicle-treated cells normalized to 100%. Values are given as mean ± SD. Two-way ANOVA followed by Sidak's Multiple Comparison Test: *, $p \leq 0.05$; ## $p \leq 0.01$; ***, ### $p \leq 0.001$. Comparing all cell lines with the KG-1 (*) or the MOLM13 (#) cell line. Results are from at least three independent experiments with two replicates each.

KG-1 and MOLM13 Ara-C-resistant variants were generated by stepwise exposure to Ara-C for 3–6 months (Figure S1). The two established AML-resistant cells were named KG-1 Ara-R and MOLM13 Ara-R. After the establishment of resistance, IC_{50} values were determined for the parental and resistant cell lines (Figure 2). The range of Ara-C concentrations used for KG-1 cells was not sufficient to determine the IC_{50} value for KG-1 Ara-R cells (for 200 μM Ara-C, about 75% of cells were still viable) (Figure 2A). On the other hand, the IC_{50} value for MOLM13 Ara-R cells was possible to determine, being about 10-fold higher than for MOLM13 parental cells (Figure 2B).

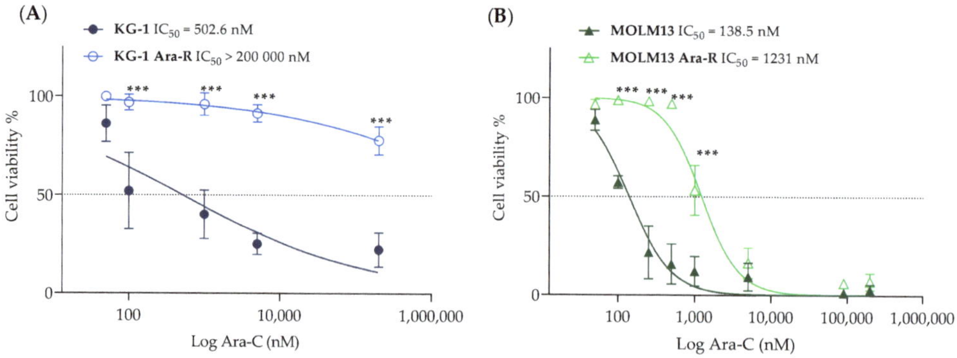

Figure 2. Dose–response curves and determination of the IC_{50} values of cytarabine (Ara-C) in (**A**) KG-1 and (**B**) MOLM13 parental and resistant cell lines. Values are expressed as cell viability relative to vehicle-treated cells normalized to 100%. Values are given as mean ± SD. Two-way ANOVA followed by Sidak's Multiple Comparison Test: *** $p \leq 0.001$. Results are from at least three independent experiments with two replicates each.

In addition to cell viability, growth rates and doubling times were determined for parental and Ara-C-resistant cells (Figure 3A–C and Figure S2). Comparing parental and Ara-C-resistant cells, no differences in growth rates were observed between KG-1 and KG-1 Ara-R cells (Figure 3A,C), while MOLM13 Ara-R cells grew at a slower rate than MOLM13 parental cells, with doubling times of about 24 h and 18 h, respectively (Figure 3B,C). We also evaluated the effect of the absence and the presence of different glucose concentrations (0, 2.5, 5, and 10 mM) on growth rate and doubling time. In general, the growth rates of both cell line pairs increased as glucose concentrations rose. No significant differences were observed in growth rates between parental and KG-1 Ara-R cells, but MOLM13 Ara-R grew faster than parental cells in the absence of glucose (Figure S3). To assess the capacity to maintain the resistance phenotype, we cultured Ara-C-resistant cells without Ara-C for 3 weeks, which did not result in the loss of Ara-C resistance (Figure S4). This indicates that Ara-C resistance was not reversible over time in these cell lines. Additionally, we assessed if Ara-C-resistant cells were also resistant to the DNR (Figure S5). KG-1 Ara-R cells were significantly less sensitive to DNR (higher IC_{50} values) when compared to parental cells. However, no differences were observed for MOLM13 cells, which suggests different mechanisms of resistance in the two cell lines.

(A) (B)

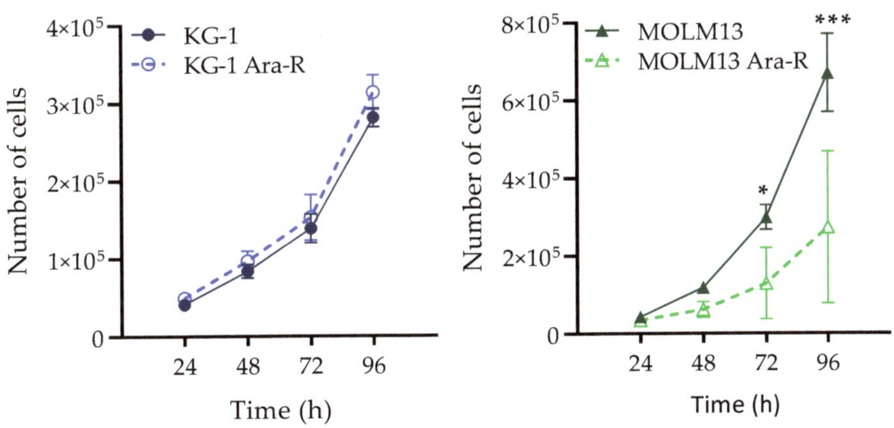

(C)

Cell line	KG-1	KG-1 Ara-R	MOLM13	MOLM13 Ara-R
μ ± SD (h^{-1})	0.027 ± 0.003	0.025 ± 0.002	0.038 ± 0.004	0.031 ± 0.004
Td ± SD (h)	26.1 ± 3.2	28.4 ± 2.8	18.2 ± 1.6	22.1 ± 4.6

μ; growth rate; Td, doubling time; h, hour; SD, standard deviation

Figure 3. Cell growth rates and doubling times of AML Ara-R resistant and parental cell lines. Cell growth curves of (**A**) KG-1 and KG-1 Ara-R and (**B**) MOLM13 and MOLM13 Ara-R were analyzed over multiple population doublings. 2.5×10^4 cells were plated, and cells were counted every 24 h using Trypan blue dye. (**C**) Values of growth rates (μ) and doubling times (*Td*) were calculated from the respective line equations (Figure S2). Statistical significance was determined by two-way ANOVA followed by Sidak's Multiple Comparison Test. * $p \leq 0.05$; *** $p \leq 0.001$. At least three independent experiments with three replicates were performed.

NGS-based mutation analysis of Ara-C resistant and parental cells identified a total of fourteen variants in ten genes frequently mutated in AML patients (Table 1) [27]. Five of the fourteen mutations found are described in the catalog of somatic mutations in cancer (COSMICs). According to the AMP/ASCO/CAP consensus guidelines [23,24], it was possible to classify one as Variants of Strong Clinical Significance (Tier I), one as Variants of Potential Clinical Significance (Tier II), four as Variants of Unknown Clinical Significance (Tier III) and eight as Benign or Likely Benign Variants (Tier IV). Comparing parental and Ara-C resistant cells, the differences found were loss of the *NRAS* mutation in KG-1 Ara-R cells, whereas MOLM13 Ara-R acquired an additional *CEBPA* variant mutation.

Table 1. Myeloid gene mutation panel in parental and Ara-R AML cell lines revealed by NGS analysis.

	KG-1	KG-1 Ara-R	COSMIC ID	Clinical Significance @	Consequence
Mutated genes	*BCOR* (c.4886G>A; p.(Trp1663*))	*BCOR* (c.4886G>A; p.(Trp1663*))		Tier III	Nonsense
	DDX41 (c.27+2_27+5dup)	*DDX41* (c.27+2_27+5dup)		Tier IV	Frameshift
	FLT3 (c.1669G>A; p.(Val557Ile))	*FLT3* (c.1669G>A; p.(Val557Ile))	COSM28043	Tier IV	Missense
	NRAS (c.360G>T; p.(Leu120Phe))	-		Tier III	Missense
	SAMD9 (c.223C>T; p.(Arg75Trp))	*SAMD9* (c.223C>T; p.(Arg75Trp))		Tier IV	Missense
	SAMD9L (c.1217G>A; p.(Arg406Gln))	*SAMD9L* (c.1217G>A; p.(Arg406Gln))		Tier IV	Missense
	TP53 (c.672+1G>A)	*TP53* (c.672+1G>A)	COSM2744696	Tier II	Splice donor
	MOLM13	**MOLM13 Ara-R**	**COSMIC ID**	**Clinical Significance @**	**Consequence**
Mutated genes	*ASXL1* (c.1954G>A; p.(Gly652Ser))	*ASXL1* (c.1954G>A; p.(Gly652Ser))	COSM1716555	Tier IV	Missense
	CBL (c.1227_1227+13del)	*CBL* (c.1227_1227+13del)		Tier IV	Frameshift
	CEBPA (c.584_589dup; p.(His195_Pro196dup))	*CEBPA* (c.584_589dup; p.(His195_Pro196dup))		Tier IV	Frameshift
	CEBPA (c.568T>C; p.(Ser190Pro))	*CEBPA* (c.568T>C; p.(Ser190Pro))		Tier III	Missense
	-	*CEBPA* (c.566C>A; p.(Pro189His))		Tier III	Missense
	FLT3 (c.1775_1795dup; p.(Glu598_Tyr599insPheAspPhe ArgGluTyrGlu) (FLT3-ITD, 21bp)	*FLT3* (c.1775_1795dup; p.(Glu598_Tyr599insPheAsp PheArgGluTyrGlu) (FLT3-ITD, 21bp)	COSM849	Tier I	Inframe insertion
	SAMD9L (c.866T>C; p.(Phe289Ser))	*SAMD9L* (c.866T>C; p.(Phe289Ser)))	COSM3982291	Tier IV	Missense

@ AMP/ASCO/CAP consensos [23,24].

3.2. *Characterization of the Glycolytic and Respiratory Profile of Parental and Ara-R AML Cell Lines*

The *FLT3*, *RAS*, and *TP53* genes are involved in cell metabolic regulation of glycolysis. As a first approach to identify metabolic alterations in glucose metabolism associated with Ara-C resistance, we assessed glucose consumption and lactate secretion to the medium of parental and resistant cells at different time points (Figure S6). However, no significant differences were observed between Ara-C resistant and parental cells for both cell lines. Nevertheless, at 4 h, KG-1 Ara-R cells showed a trend to increase in lactate secretion compared to KG-1 parental cells (Figure 4A), but no difference was observed in extracellular glucose levels (Figure 4B). When calculating glucose consumption, KG-1 Ara-R cells tended to consume glucose slower than KG-1 parental cells (Figure 4C). For MOLM13 cells, no significant differences were observed between parental and resistant cells either for lactate secretion (Figure 4A) or glucose consumption (Figure 4C).

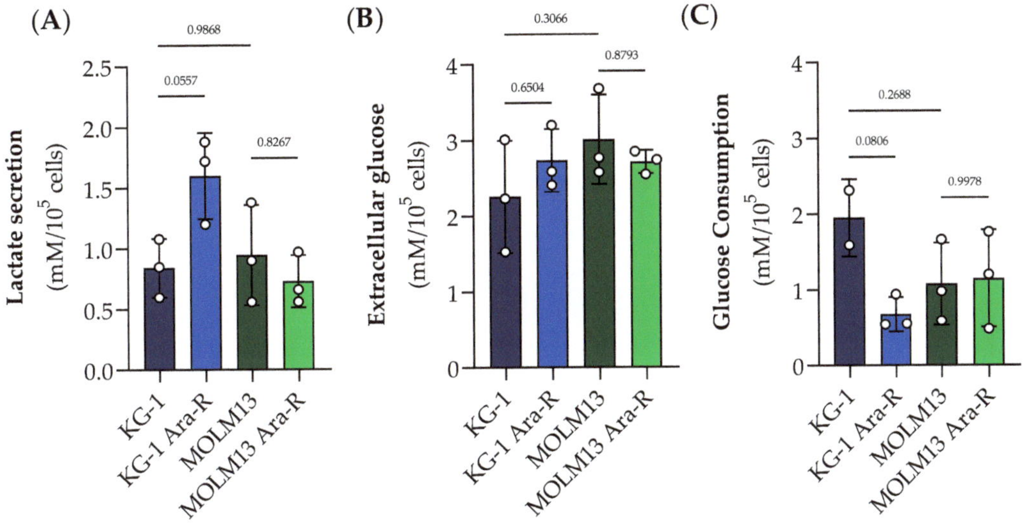

Figure 4. Lactate secretion and glucose consumption in parental and Ara-R cell lines. (**A**) Levels of lactate secretion and (**B**) extracellular glucose were evaluated at 4 h for KG-1, KG-1 Ara-R, MOLM13, and MOLM13 Ara-R cells. (**C**) Glucose consumption corresponds to the difference in glucose concentration between 0 h and 4 h of incubation (Figure S6). Results are presented as mean ± SD of at least three independent experiments. Statistical significance estimated by two-way ANOVA followed by Sidak's Multiple Comparison Test.

Next, we measured the glycolytic proton efflux rate (glycoPER) and oxygen consumption rate (OCR), indicators of glycolytic activity and mitochondrial function, respectively, to compare the glycolytic and respiratory profile between KG-1 and MOLM13 cells as well as between parental and Ara-C resistant cell lines (Figure 5).

Resistance to Ara-C increased basal glycolysis in KG-1 but not in MOLM13 cells. This result is in accordance with the observed increase in lactate secretion at 4 h in KG-1 Ara-R but not MOLM13 Ara-R cells compared to the respective parental cells. The comparison of both parental AML cell lines showed a trend to lower basal glycolysis in MOLM13 compared to KG-1 cells (Figure 5A,B). The ability of cells to compensate for energy production through glycolysis after inhibiting mitochondrial respiration (maximal glycolysis) was also increased by Ara-C resistance in the KG-1 but not in the MOLM13 cell line (Figure 5C). The glycolytic reserve (i.e., maximal/basal glycolysis), which indicates how close the glycolytic function is to the cell's theoretical maximum, did not differ between KG-1 parental and resistant cells but tended to be lower in MOLM13 Ara-R compared to MOLM13 cells. Moreover, MOLM13 cells showed a higher glycolytic reserve compared to KG-1 cells (Figure 5D).

In terms of respiration, Ara-C resistance increased basal as well as proton-leak-linked respiration and tended to increase ATP-linked respiration in KG-1 cells but not in MOLM13 cells (Figure 5E,F,J,K). However, resistance to Ara-C did not affect maximal respiration, spare respiratory capacity (i.e., maximal/basal respiration), and coupling efficiency (i.e., ATP-linked/basal respiration) (Figure 5G,H,L). Basal and maximal respiration, as well as ATP-linked respiration and coupling efficiency, were higher, whereas spare respiratory capacity tended to be higher in MOLM13 compared to KG-1 cells (Figure 5E–H,J,L).

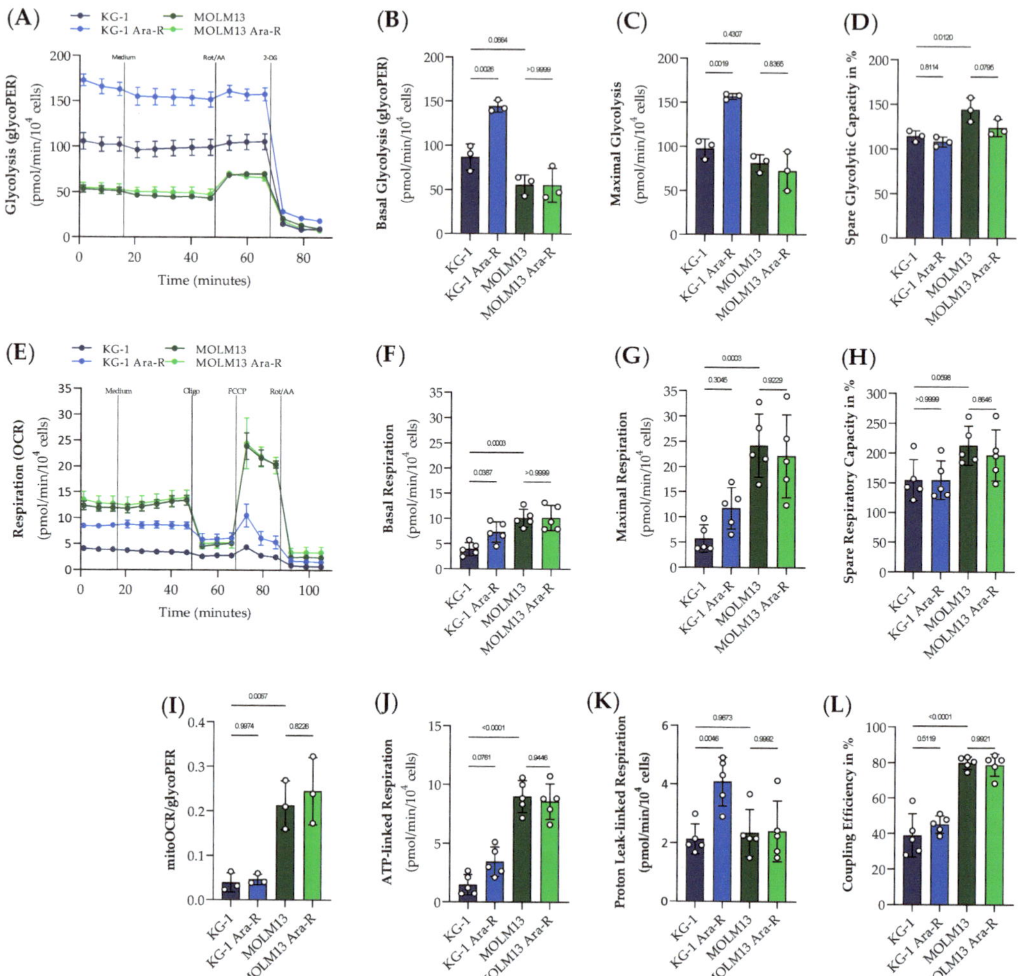

Figure 5. Characterization of the glycolytic and respiratory profile in parental and Ara-R cell lines. Results of the Glycolytic rate (**A**) and Mito Stress (**E**) test in KG-1, KG-1 Ara-R, MOLM13, and MOLM13 Ara-R cells are presented as real-time measurements of glycolytic proton efflux rate (glycoPER) and oxygen consumption rate (OCR) normalized to cell number, respectively. (**B**) Basal glycolysis, (**C**) maximal glycolysis, (**D**) glycolytic reverse in %, (**F**) basal respiration, (**G**) maximal respiration, (**H**) spare respiratory capacity in %, (**I**) ratio of respiration to glycolysis, (**J**) ATP-linked respiration, (**K**) proton leak-linked respiration, (**L**) coupling efficiency in %. Values are given as mean ± SD. One-way ANOVA followed by Sidak's Multiple Comparison Test. At least three independent measurements with 2 to 8 replicates were performed for each cell line. Treatments: 2.5 μM Oligomycin (Oligo.); 0.5 μM fluoro-carbonyl cyanide phenylhydrazone (FCCP); 0.5 μM Rotenone and Antimycin A (Rot/AA); 50 mM 2-Deoxy-d-glucose (2DG).

Since MOLM13 cells presented lower glycolysis and higher respiration rates compared to KG-1 cells, the ratio of respiration to glycolysis (mitoOCR/glycoPER) was also higher in MOLM13 compared to KG-1 cells (Figure 5I). However, the ratio of respiration to glycolysis remained unaffected by Ara-C resistance (Figure 5I) because glycolysis and respiration were both (a) increased by Ara-C resistance in KG-1 cells and (b) not affected by Ara-C resistance in MOLM13 cells.

To check if these metabolic alterations were translated into changes in protein expression, we evaluated the expression of metabolism-related key proteins by Western blot, namely glucose transporter 1 (GLUT1), monocarboxylate transporters 1 and 4 (MCT1/MCT4), as well as the hexokinase II (HKII) and lactate dehydrogenase A (LDHA) enzymes at different timepoints (6 and 24 h). The only difference observed was a significant decrease in LDHA at 24 h in KG-1 Ara-R compared to KG-1 parental cells (Figure S7). This could be explained by the fact that the levels of extracellular glucose were very low at 24 h (Figure S6), and the levels of secreted lactate did not increase after 12 h. Thus, the need for converting pyruvate into lactate might be lower.

3.3. *Effect of Metabolic Inhibitors on Cytarabine-Resistant Cells*

Aiming to target the increased glycolytic rate induced by Ara-C resistance in KG-1 cells, the effect of 3-BP, a glycolytic inhibitor, was evaluated in Ara-C-resistant and parental cells using the Seahorse XF Cell Mito Stress and Glycolytic Rate tests (Figure 6).

The acute treatment with 33 μM of 3-BP strongly reduced glycolysis in both KG-1 and KG-1 Ara-R cell lines. Although KG-1 Ara-R cells showed increased glycolysis compared to KG-1 cells, the acute response to 33 μM of 3-BP was relatively stronger in KG-1 compared to KG-1 Ara-R cells (Figure 6A,B). Moreover, 3-BP-treated cells were not able to increase glycolysis after Rot/AA treatment (Figure 6C), representing that 3-BP diminished the glycolytic reserve. As a response to reduced glycolysis induced by 33 μM 3-BP, both KG-1 and KG-1 Ara cells increased respiration (Figure 6E,F). Spare respiratory capacity was increased by 3-BP in KG-1 Ara-R cells compared to medium control treatment as well as between KG-1 Ara-R compared to KG-1 cells both treated with 3-BP (Figure 6G). Relative to the medium control, 3-BP induced a stronger increase in ATP-linked respiration in KG-1 compared to KG-1 Ara cells (Figure 6H). These results are also reflected in the stronger increase in the ratio of respiration to glycolysis in KG-1 cells compared to KG-1 Ara-R cells relative to the respective untreated control (Figure 6D).

3-BP also acutely inhibited glycolysis as well as the glycolytic reserve in MOLM13 and MOLM13 Ara-R cells (Figure 6I–K). However, MOLM13 parental as well as resistant cells were not able to compensate for the reduction in glycolysis by increased respiration, spare respiratory capacity, or ATP-linked respiration (Figure 6M–P). Also, the ratio of respiration to glycolysis remained unaffected by 3-BP treatment in MOLM13 parental and resistant cells (Figure 6L).

Next, we evaluated the effect of 3-BP on cell viability of both KG-1 and MOLM13 parental and Ara-R cells after 48 h, respectively (Figure 7). KG-1 Ara-R cells were more sensitive to 3-BP, with a significant decrease in cell viability compared to the KG-1 cells (Figure 7A), which is in line with the observed increased glycolytic activity induced by Ara-C resistance in KG-1 cells. For MOLM13 Ara-R and parental MOLM13 cells, no difference was observed in cell viability after 3-BP exposure (Figure 7B). Additionally, we tested another glycolytic inhibitor, 2-DG, and the respiration inhibitor, phenformin. 2-DG induced a similar effect to 3-BP in both KG-1 cell lines (higher sensitivity for Ara-C-resistant cells) and MOLM13 cell lines (no difference) (Figure S8). For phenformin treatment, KG-1 Ara-R cells exhibited higher sensitivity than parental KG-1 cells, while MOLM13 Ara-R were less sensitive to phenformin than MOLM13 cells (Figure 7C,D). Overall, KG-1 Ara-R cells displayed increased respiration levels (Figure 5), which might explain the increased sensitivity to phenformin in this cell line.

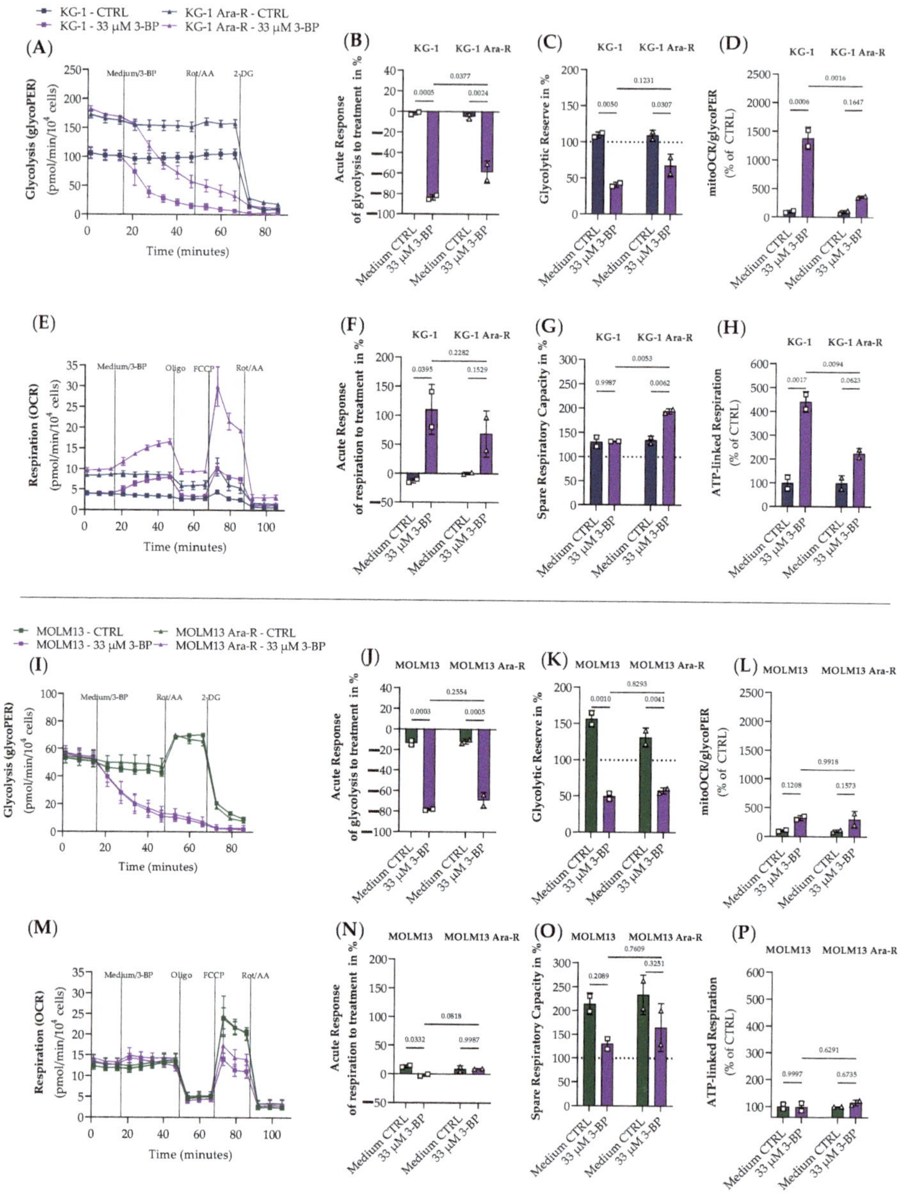

Figure 6. Effect of 3-bromopyruvate (3-BP) on glycolysis and respiration in parental and Ara-R cell lines. Results of the Glycolytic rate (**A**,**I**) and Mito Stress (**E**,**M**) test in (**A**–**H**)) KG-1, KG-1 Ara-R, (**I**–**P**) MOLM13, and MOLM13 Ara-R cells are presented as real-time measurements of glycolytic proton efflux rate (glycoPER) and oxygen consumption rate (OCR) normalized to cell number. (**B**,**J**) acute response of glycolysis to 3-BP, (**C**,**K**) glycolytic reserve in %, (**D**,**L**) ratio of respiration to glycolysis. (**F**,**N**) acute response of respiration to 3-BP, (**G**,**O**) spare respiratory capacity in %, (**H**,**P**) ATP-linked respiration. Values were given as mean ± SD. One-way ANOVA followed by Sidak's Multiple Comparison Test. Two independent measurements with 2 to 6 replicates were performed for each cell line. Treatments: 2.5 µM Oligomycin (Oligo.); 0.5 µM fluorocarbonyl cyanide phenylhydrazone (FCCP); 0.5 µM Rotenone and Antimycin A (Rot/AA); 50 mM 2-Deoxy-d-glucose (2DG).

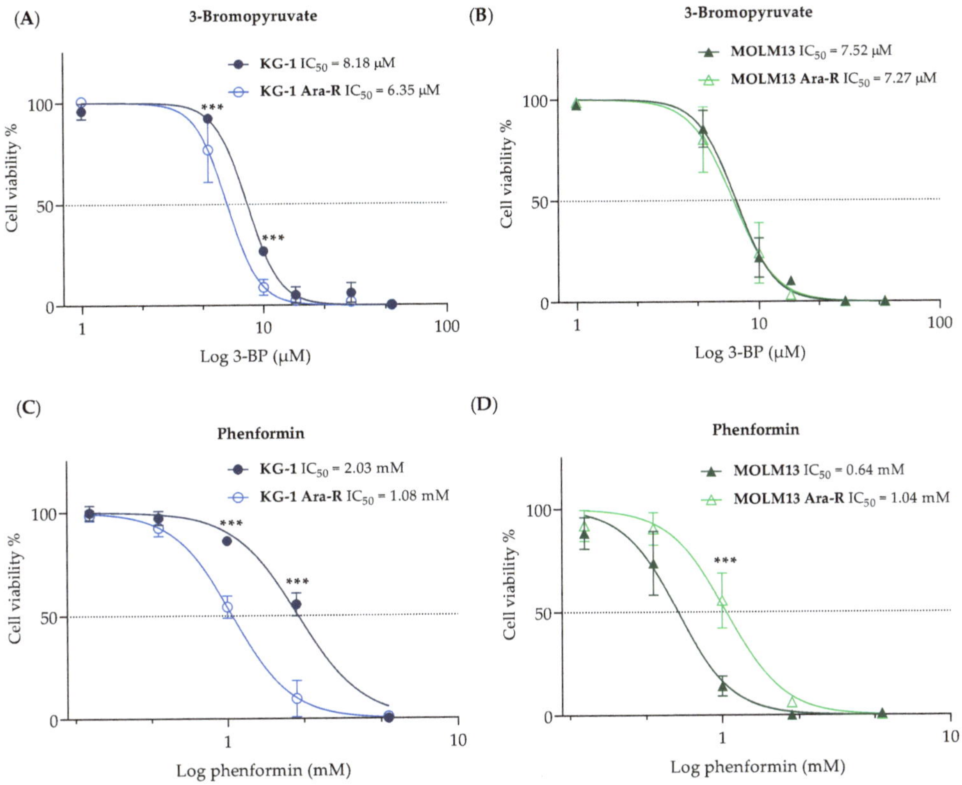

Figure 7. Effect of 3-bromopyruvate (3-BP) and phenformin on Ara-C-resistant and parental cell viability. Dose-response curve to generate IC_{50} values of (**A**,**C**) KG-1 and KG-1 Ara-R cell lines and (**B**,**D**) MOLM13 and MOLM13 Ara-R cell lines in response to (**A**,**B**) 3-BP, and (**C**,**D**) phenformin. Values are expressed as cell viability relative to vehicle-treated cells normalized to 100%. Values are given as mean ± SD. Two-way ANOVA followed by Sidak's Multiple Comparison Test. *** $p < 0.001$. At least three independent experiments with two replicates were performed.

4. Discussion

Different recurrent gene mutations have been identified in AML [28]. The established Ara-C-resistant cell lines showed similar mutation profiles as the parental cell lines, including mutations in *DDX41*, *CEBPA*, *ASXL1*, *SAMD9*, *SAMD9L*, *FLT3*, *NRAS*, and *TP53*. The diagnostic and prognostic value of those mutations was already reported in AML patients, as well as their involvement in cellular processes such as differentiation, proliferation, and cell death in AML [2,28,29]. CEBPA mutations are one the most frequent genetic alterations in AML patients. CEBPA is a transcription factor, controlling gene expressions responsible for cell proliferation and differentiation. Double-mutated CEBPA is associated with a favorable prognosis, while single-mutated CEBPA does not seem to improve prognosis [30]. Recent studies have shown that the biallelic CEBPA mutations in AML do not appear to modify prognostic, but the coexistence with other chromosomal abnormalities and gene mutations may influence prognostic [31]. Although the number of somatic mutations present at diagnosis appears to be present at relapse [32,33], our data show that KG-1 Ara-R cells lost *NRAS* mutation. According to the study of Farra et al. [34], most pediatric AML patients with mutated *NRAS* at first diagnosis lose this mutation at relapse [34]. Maybe this loss of *NRAS* mutation is a drug resistance-related alteration, which allows AML cells to survive after induction chemotherapy and make it a dominant clone and cause recurrence.

Moreover, *FLT3*, *TP53*, and *NRAS* mutations are classified as driver oncogenes in AML, and co-occurring mutations in those genes have been associated not only with resistance but also with metabolic adaptations [28,35–37]. Here, we observed that KG-1 Ara-R cells lost the *NRAS* mutation despite presenting higher levels of glycolysis and respiration compared to KG-1 cells. This issue deserves further investigation.

Our aim was to characterize glucose metabolism in Ara-C-resistant AML cell lines as a means of identifying potential metabolic targets for therapy. Otto Warburg described that even in the presence of oxygen, cancer cells prefer to ferment glucose to lactate rather than to oxidize glucose in the TCA cycle [18]. In AML, beyond the glycolytic phenotype, glucose metabolism has also been linked to pathways, including the pentose-phosphate, amino acid, glutamine, and fatty acid pathways [14,35,38]. Hence, glycolysis does not only generate energy but also serves the purpose of generating molecular building blocks to sustain cancer survival and proliferation [38].

The results of our established AML cells resistant to Ara-C suggest that different glycolytic and respiration profiles could influence the response to different stresses. MOLM13 cells are more dependent on respiration, whereas the corresponding resistant ones have less capacity to resort to glycolysis when exposed to respiratory inhibition (glycolytic reserve). On the other hand, KG-1 Ara-R cells are more glycolytic but also present higher levels of basal and ATP-linked respiration compared to KG-1 parental cells, indicating a higher ATP demand due to Ara-C resistance. The plasticity of cancer cells is frequently observed in terms of metabolic adaptations. For example, cancer cells are able to switch between glycolysis and respiration as well as to fuel these metabolic pathways with other substrates beyond glucose [39]. In AML, a highly diverse and flexible metabolism contributes to the aggressiveness of the disease, as well as drug resistance [40–42]. By using different sources of nutrients for energy and biomass supply, AML cells gain metabolic plasticity and outcompete normal hematopoietic cells [39].

Lastly, we explored glucose metabolism as a potential target in AML Ara-R cells. We tested a 3-BP, a derivative of pyruvate, which is an alkylating agent with anti-cancer effects in different in vitro and in vivo cancer models [42]. 3-BP is a substrate of the monocarboxylate transporters (MCTs), and once inside the cell, it blocks glycolysis by targeting HKII and thereby depleting cell energy. HKII inhibition leads to its dissociation from mitochondria and consequently promotes the release of the apoptosis-inducing factor (AIF) and cytochrome c, thus triggering apoptosis [43]. In this study, the acute treatment of cells with 3-BP inhibited glycolysis in KG-1 and MOLM13 parental and Ara-R cells. However, only KG-1 parental and Ara-C-resistant cells were able to compensate for this effect by switching from glycolysis to respiration. Treatment of cells with 3-BP for 48 h, however, reduced cell viability by 100%. The acute treatment with 3-BP may demonstrate that the first target is glycolysis, but given the alkylating nature of 3-BP, other intermediates involved in glucose metabolism may be targeted by 3-BP [42–45]. Additionally, we tested the effect of the mitochondrial inhibitor phenformin, which inhibits the complex I of the mitochondrial respiratory chain [46,47], and Ara-C resistance induced an increase in respiration in KG-1 Ara-R cells. On the other hand, KG-1 Ara-R cells also presented an increase in proton leakage that could indicate increased damage of mitochondrial membranes or complexes of the electron transport chain, supporting the observed higher sensitivity of KG-1 Ara-R cells to phenformin compared to KG-1 parental cells. In contrast, MOLM13 Ara-R cells were less sensitive to phenformin compared to MOLM13 parental cells. Still, the IC_{50} value for phenformin was about three times lower in MOLM13 compared to KG-1 cells, which corresponds to higher respiration levels observed in MOLM13 cells. In general, AML cells were more sensitive to treatment with 3-BP than phenformin (higher IC_{50} values), which could be explained by the fact that 3-BP may be acting by two mechanisms of action, being more potent than phenformin.

Hence, it is important to consider the remarkable metabolic adaptability of AML cells, which allows them to survive and thrive in toxic environments, such as when exposed to chemotherapy. This highlights the significance of incorporating a metabolic characterization of the malignant cells to guide the selection of therapeutic strategies. In our two Ara-C-resistant cell models, it became evident that the model that presented an enhanced glucose metabolism with a higher glycolytic profile (KG-1 Ara-R cells) was the one that responded better to the metabolic inhibitors. Thus, glycolytic inhibitors should be explored as a strategy to treat Ara-C-resistant AML with enhanced glucose metabolism.

5. Conclusions

In the present study, we report, by different methodologies, that MOLM13 and KG-1 parental cell lines have distinct metabolic profiles: MOLM13 cells are more oxidative, and KG-1 cells are more glycolytic. When inducing resistance to Ara-C, MOLM13 Ara-R cells did not change their metabolic profile, and their growth rate was lower than parental cells. This result suggests an arrest in the cell cycle that may be involved in the mechanism of resistance in MOLM13 Ara-R cells. On the other hand, Ara-R resistance in KG-1 cells induced a more pronounced glycolytic profile. KG-1 Ara-R cells display higher extracellular levels of lactate, glycoPER, and OCR. The response of KG-1 Ara-R cells to acute inhibition of glycolysis led to a shift towards respiration, but the treatment with 3-BP for 48 h significantly decreased cell viability, suggesting that the cells could not handle the induced stress at this time point. In summary, we established two AML cell line models of resistance to Ara-C, which involve metabolic adaptations and have different sensitivities to metabolic inhibitors. Thus, modulation of glucose metabolism has the potential to be explored in AML resistance.

Supplementary Materials: The following supporting information can be downloaded at https://www.mdpi.com/article/10.3390/pharmaceutics16040442/s1, Figure S1: Calculation of doubling time (Td) and growth rates (μ) in cytarabine (Ara-C)-resistant cell lines; Figure S2: Induction of Ara-C resistance in AML cell lines; Figure S3: Sensitivity of cytarabine (Ara-C)-resistant cells in the absence of Ara-C; Figure S4: Extracellular lactate and glucose, glucose consumption in parental and Ara-C resistant cell lines; Figure S5: Effect of 2-deoxy-glucose (2-DG) on Ara-C-resistant and parental AML cell viability; Figure S6: Extracellular lactate and glucose, glucose consumption in parental and Ara-C resistant cell lines; Figure S7: Characterization of glycolytic phenotype-associated protein expression in cytarabine (Ara-C)-resistant cell lines; Figure S8: Effect of 2-deoxy-glucose (2-DG) on Ara-C-resistant and parental AML cell viability

Author Contributions: Conceptualization, J.P.-V., O.Q., M.C. and F.B.; methodology, J.P.-V., C.B.-M., D.D.W. and S.S.; analysis, J.P.-V., C.B.-M., D.D.W., B.K.; S.S., R.M.R. and F.B.; investigation, J.P.-V., Y.H.K., M.C. and F.B., writing—original draft preparation, J.P.-V.; writing—review and editing, J.P.-V., D.D.W., C.B.-M., S.G., B.K., S.S., R.M.R., O.Q., Y.H.K., M.C. and F.B.; supervision, M.C. and F.B.; project administration, F.B.; Funding acquisition, Y.H.K. and F.B. All authors have read and agreed to the published version of the manuscript.

Funding: The work presented herein was performed at the Life and Health Sciences Research Institute (ICVS), University of Minho. Financial support was provided by National funds through the Foundation for Science and Technology (FCT)—projects UIDB/50026/2020 and UIDP/50026/2020, and by the projects NORTE-01-0145-FEDER-000039 and NORTE-01-0145-FEDER-000055, supported by Norte Portugal Regional Operational Programme (NORTE 2020), under the PORTUGAL 2020 Partnership Agreement, through the European Regional Development Fund (ERDF). This work was also supported by the Strategic Programme UID/BIA/ 04050/2020 and the project LA/P/0069/2020 granted to the Associate Laboratory ARNET, both funded by Portuguese funds through the FCT-IP. Additional financial support also provided by the NewG Lab Pharma and the Children Cancer Foundation Salzburg, Austria. J. P-V and C. B-M were supported by FCT fellowship grants (SFRH/BD/146065/2019 and SFRH/BD/145955/2019 and COVID/BD/153456/2023).

Institutional Review Board Statement: Not applicable.

Informed Consent Statement: Not applicable.

Data Availability Statement: Data is available on request due to restrictions.

Acknowledgments: We thank Paula Ludovico (Life and Health Sciences Research Institute (ICVS)/School of Health Sciences/University of Minho, Braga, Portugal) for sharing the HL-60, NB-4, and KG-1 cell lines.

Conflicts of Interest: Y.H.K. was co-founder of the company NewG Lab Pharma and KoDiscovery. The remaining authors declare that the research was conducted in the absence of any commercial or financial relationships that could be construed as a potential conflict of interest.

References

1. Khoury, J.D.; Solary, E.; Abla, O.; Alaggio, R.; Apperley, J.F.; Bejar, R.; Hochhaus, A. The 5th edition of the World Health Organization Classification of Haematolymphoid Tumours: Myeloid and Histiocytic/Dendritic Neoplasms. *Leukemia* **2022**, *36*, 1703–1719. [CrossRef]
2. Arber, D.A.; Orazi, A.; Hasserjian, R.; Thiele, J.; Borowitz, M.J.; Le Beau, M.M.; Bloomfield, C.D.; Cazzola, M.; Vardiman, J.W. The 2016 revision to the World Health Organization classification of myeloid neoplasms and acute leukemia. *Blood* **2016**, *127*, 2391–2405. [CrossRef]
3. Ganzel, C.; Sun, Z.; Cripe, L.D.; Fernandez, H.F.; Douer, D.; Rowe, J.M.; Paietta, E.M.; Ketterling, R.; O'Connell, M.J.; Wiernik, P.H.; et al. Very poor long-term survival in past and more recent studies for relapsed AML patients: The ECOG-ACRIN experience. *Am. J. Hematol.* **2018**, *93*, 1074–1081. [CrossRef]
4. Cancer.Net. Leukemia-Acute Myeloid-AML. Available online: https://www.cancer.net/cancer-types/leukemia-acute-myeloid-aml/statistics,%202023 (accessed on 5 August 2023).
5. Döhner, H.; Estey, E.; Grimwade, D.; Amadori, S.; Appelbaum, F.R.; Büchner, T.; Dombret, H.; Ebert, B.L.; Fenaux, P.; Larson, R.A.; et al. Diagnosis and management of AML in adults: 2017 ELN recommendations from an international expert panel. *Blood* **2017**, *129*, 424–447. [CrossRef] [PubMed]
6. Abbas, H.A.; Alfayez, M.; Kadia, T.; Ravandi-Kashani, F.; Daver, N. Midostaurin In Acute Myeloid Leukemia: An Evidence-Based Review And Patient Selection. *Cancer Manag. Res.* **2019**, *11*, 8817–8828. [CrossRef]
7. Wouters, B.J. Targeting IDH1 and IDH2 Mutations in Acute Myeloid Leukemia: Emerging Options and Pending Questions. *HemaSphere* **2021**, *5*, e583. [CrossRef]
8. Campos, E.D.V.; Pinto, R. Targeted therapy with a selective BCL-2 inhibitor in older patients with acute myeloid leukemia. *Hematol. Transfus. Cell Ther.* **2019**, *41*, 169–177. [CrossRef] [PubMed]
9. Thol, F.; Ganser, A. Treatment of Relapsed Acute Myeloid Leukemia. *Curr. Treat. Options Oncol.* **2020**, *21*, 66. [CrossRef] [PubMed]
10. Shlush, L.I.; Mitchell, A.; Heisler, L.; Abelson, S.; Ng, S.W.K.; Trotman-Grant, A.; Medeiros, J.J.F.; Rao-Bhatia, A.; Jaciw-Zurakowsky, I.; Marke, R.; et al. Tracing the origins of relapse in acute myeloid leukaemia to stem cells. *Nature* **2017**, *547*, 104–108. [CrossRef]
11. Zhang, J.; Gu, Y.; Chen, B. Mechanisms of drug resistance in acute myeloid leukemia. *OncoTargets Ther.* **2019**, *12*, 1937–1945. [CrossRef]
12. Hanahan, D. Hallmarks of Cancer: New Dimensions. *Cancer Discov.* **2022**, *12*, 31–46. [CrossRef] [PubMed]
13. Devendran, R.; Ramesh, V.; Gnanasekaran, P. CHAPTER 8-Fundamentals of cell metabolism and cancer. In *Understanding Cancer*; Jain, B., Pandey, S., Eds.; Academic Press: Cambridge, MA, USA, 2022; pp. 117–132. ISBN 978-0-323-99883-3.
14. Grassian, A.R.; Parker, S.J.; Davidson, S.M.; Divakarun, A.S.; Green, C.R.; Zhang, X.; Slocum, K.L.; Pu, M.; Lin, F.; Vickers, C.; et al. IDH1 Mutations Alter Citric Acid Cycle Metabolism and Increase Dependence on Oxidative Mitochondrial Metabolism. *Cancer Res.* **2016**, *74*, 3317–3331. [CrossRef] [PubMed]
15. Raffel, S.; Falcone, M.; Kneisel, N.; Hansson, J.; Wang, W.; Lutz, C.; Bullinger, L.; Poschet, G.; Nonnenmacher, Y.; Barnert, A.; et al. BCAT1 restricts αKG levels in AML stem cells leading to IDHmut-like DNA hypermethylation. *Nature* **2017**, *551*, 384–388. [CrossRef]
16. Poulain, L.; Sujobert, P.; Zylbersztejn, F.; Barreau, S.; Stuani, L.; Lambert, M.; Palama, T.L.; Chesnais, V.; Birsen, R.; Vergez, F.; et al. High mTORC1 activity drives glycolysis addiction and sensitivity to G6PD inhibition in acute myeloid leukemia cells. *Leukemia* **2017**, *31*, 2326–2335. [CrossRef]
17. Chen, W.-L.; Wang, J.-H.; Zhao, A.-H.; Xu, X.; Wang, Y.-H.; Chen, T.-L.; Li, J.-M.; Mi, J.-Q.; Zhu, Y.-M.; Liu, Y.-F.; et al. A distinct glucose metabolism signature of acute myeloid leukemia with prognostic value. *Blood* **2014**, *124*, 1645–1654. [CrossRef]
18. Warburg, O. On the Origin of Cancer Cells. *Science* **1956**, *123*, 309–314. [CrossRef]
19. Ma, L.; Zong, X. Metabolic Symbiosis in Chemoresistance: Refocusing the Role of Aerobic Glycolysis. *Front. Oncol.* **2020**, *10*, 5. [CrossRef]
20. Herst, P.M.; Hesketh, E.L.; Ritchie, D.S.; Berridge, M.V. Glycolytic metabolism confers resistance to combined all-trans retinoic acid and arsenic trioxide-induced apoptosis in HL60ρ0 cells. *Leuk. Res.* **2008**, *32*, 327–333. [CrossRef]
21. Herst, P.M.; Howman, R.A.; Neeson, P.J.; Berridge, M.V.; Ritchie, D.S. The level of glycolytic metabolism in acute myeloid leukemia blasts at diagnosis is prognostic for clinical outcome. *J. Leukoc. Biol.* **2011**, *89*, 51–55. [CrossRef]
22. Song, K.; Li, M.; Xu, X.; Xuan, L.; Huang, G.; Liu, Q. Resistance to chemotherapy is associated with altered glucose metabolism in acute myeloid leukemia. *Oncol. Lett.* **2016**, *12*, 334–342. [CrossRef]

23. Li, M.M.; Datto, M.; Duncavage, E.J.; Kulkarni, S.; Lindeman, N.I.; Roy, S.; Tsimberidou, A.M.; Vnencak-Jones, C.L.; Wolff, D.J.; Younes, A.; et al. Standards and Guidelines for the Interpretation and Reporting of Sequence Variants in Cancer. *J. Mol. Diagn.* **2017**, *19*, 4–23. [CrossRef]
24. Horak, P.; Griffith, M.; Danos, A.M.; Pitel, B.A.; Madhavan, S.; Liu, X.; Chow, C.; Williams, H.; Carmody, L.; Barrow-Laing, L.; et al. Standards for the classification of pathogenicity of somatic variants in cancer (oncogenicity): Joint recommendations of Clinical Genome Resource (ClinGen), Cancer Genomics Consortium (CGC), and Variant Interpretation for Cancer Consortium (VICC). *Genet. Med.* **2022**, *24*, 986–998. [CrossRef]
25. Lindström, H.J.G.; Friedman, R. Inferring time-dependent population growth rates in cell cultures undergoing adaptation. *BMC Bioinform.* **2020**, *21*, 583. [CrossRef]
26. Pereira-Nunes, A.; Ferreira, H.; Abreu, S.; Guedes, M.; Neves, N.M.; Baltazar, F.; Granja, S. Combination Therapy with CD147-Targeted Nanopartic.pdf. *Adv. Biol.* **2023**, *7*, 2300080. [CrossRef] [PubMed]
27. Klco, J.M.; Mullighan, C.G. Advances in germline predisposition to acute leukaemias and myeloid neoplasms. *Nat. Rev. Cancer* **2021**, *21*, 122–137. [CrossRef]
28. Kishtagari, A.; Levine, R.L. The Role of Somatic Mutations in Acute Myeloid Leukemia Pathogenesis. *Cold Spring Harb. Perspect. Med.* **2021**, *11*, a034975. [CrossRef] [PubMed]
29. KEGG PATHWAY: Acute Myeloid Leukemia-Homo Sapiens (Human). Available online: https://www.genome.jp/kegg-bin/show_pathway?hsa05221 (accessed on 29 November 2023).
30. Wakita, S.; Sakaguchi, M.; Oh, I.; Kako, S.; Toya, T.; Najima, Y.; Doki, N.; Kanda, J.; Kuroda, J.; Mori, S.; et al. Prognostic impact of *CEBPA* bZIP domain mutation in acute myeloid leukemia. *Blood Adv.* **2022**, *6*, 238–247. [CrossRef] [PubMed]
31. Wang, H.; Chu, T.-T.; Han, S.-Y.; Qi, J.-Q.; Tang, Y.-Q.; Qiu, H.-Y.; Fu, C.-C.; Tang, X.-W.; Ruan, C.-G.; Wu, D.-P.; et al. FLT3-ITD and CEBPA Mutations Predict Prognosis in Acute Myelogenous Leukemia Irrespective of Hematopoietic Stem Cell Transplantation. *Biol. Blood Marrow Transplant.* **2019**, *25*, 941–948. [CrossRef] [PubMed]
32. Stieglitz, E.; Taylor-Weiner, A.N.; Chang, T.Y.; Gelston, L.C.; Wang, Y.-D.; Mazor, T.; Esquivel, E.; Yu, A.; Seepo, S.; Olsen, S.R.; et al. The genomic landscape of juvenile myelomonocytic leukemia. *Nat. Genet.* **2015**, *47*, 1326–1333. [CrossRef]
33. Gui, P.; Bivona, T.G. Stepwise evolution of therapy resistance in AML. *Cancer Cell* **2021**, *39*, 904–906. [CrossRef]
34. Farrar, J.E.; Schuback, H.L.; Ries, R.E.; Wai, D.; Hampton, O.A.; Trevino, L.R.; Alonzo, T.A.; Guidry Auvil, J.M.; Davidsen, T.M.; Gesuwan, P.; et al. Genomic Profiling of Pediatric Acute Myeloid Leukemia Reveals a Changing Mutational Landscape from Disease Diagnosis to Relapse. *Cancer Res.* **2016**, *76*, 2197–2205. [CrossRef] [PubMed]
35. Mesbahi, Y.; Trahair, T.N.; Lock, R.B.; Connerty, P. Exploring the Metabolic Landscape of AML: From Haematopoietic Stem Cells to Myeloblasts and Leukaemic Stem Cells. *Front. Oncol.* **2022**, *12*, 807266. [CrossRef] [PubMed]
36. Decroocq, J.; Birsen, R.; Montersino, C.; Chaskar, P.; Mano, J.; Poulain, L.; Friedrich, C.; Alary, A.-S.; Guermouche, H.; Sahal, A.; et al. RAS activation induces synthetic lethality of MEK inhibition with mitochondrial oxidative metabolism in acute myeloid leukemia. *Leukemia* **2022**, *36*, 1237–1252. [CrossRef] [PubMed]
37. Sabatier, M.; Birsen, R.; Lauture, L.; Mouche, S.; Angelino, P.; Dehairs, J.; Goupille, L.; Boussaid, I.; Heiblig, M.; Boet, E.; et al. C/EBPα Confers Dependence to Fatty Acid Anabolic Pathways and Vulnerability to Lipid Oxidative Stress–Induced Ferroptosis in FLT3-Mutant Leukemia. *Cancer Discov.* **2023**, *13*, 1720–1747. [CrossRef] [PubMed]
38. Ediriweera, M.K.; Jayasena, S. The Role of Reprogrammed Glucose Metabolism in Cancer. *Metabolites* **2023**, *13*, 345. [CrossRef] [PubMed]
39. Kreitz, J.; Schönfeld, C.; Seibert, M.; Stolp, V.; Alshamleh, I.; Oellerich, T.; Steffen, B.; Schwalbe, H.; Schnütgen, F.; Kurrle, N.; et al. Metabolic Plasticity of Acute Myeloid Leukemia. *Cells* **2019**, *8*, 805. [CrossRef]
40. Tabe, Y.; Konopleva, M.; Andreeff, M. Fatty Acid Metabolism, Bone Marrow Adipocytes, and AML. *Front. Oncol.* **2020**, *10*, 155. [CrossRef] [PubMed]
41. Farge, T.; Saland, E.; De Toni, F.; Aroua, N.; Hosseini, M.; Perry, R.; Bosc, C.; Sugita, M.; Stuani, L.; Fraisse, M.; et al. Chemotherapy-Resistant Human Acute Myeloid Leukemia Cells Are Not Enriched for Leukemic Stem Cells but Require Oxidative Metabolism. *Cancer Discov.* **2017**, *7*, 716–735. [CrossRef]
42. Azevedo-Silva, J.; Queirós, O.; Baltazar, F.; Ułaszewski, S.; Goffeau, A.; Ko, Y.H.; Pedersen, P.L.; Preto, A.; Casal, M. The anticancer agent 3-bromopyruvate: A simple but powerful molecule taken from the lab to the bedside. *J. Bioenerg. Biomembr.* **2016**, *48*, 349–362. [CrossRef]
43. Chen, Z.; Zhang, H.; Lu, W.; Huang, P. Role of mitochondria-associated hexokinase II in cancer cell death induced by 3-bromopyruvate. *Biochim. Biophys. Acta Bioenerg.* **2009**, *1787*, 553–560. [CrossRef]
44. Li, J.; Pan, J.; Liu, Y.; Luo, X.; Yang, C.; Xiao, W.; Li, Q.; Yang, L.; Zhang, X. 3-Bromopyruvic acid regulates glucose metabolism by targeting the c-Myc/TXNIP axis and induces mitochondria-mediated apoptosis in TNBC cells. *Exp. Ther. Med.* **2022**, *24*, 1–11. [CrossRef] [PubMed]
45. Jardim-Messeder, D.; Moreira-Pacheco, F. 3-Bromopyruvic Acid Inhibits Tricarboxylic Acid Cycle and Glutaminolysis in HepG2 Cells. *Anticancer Res.* **2016**, *36*, 2233–2241. [PubMed]

46. García Rubiño, M.E.; Carrillo, E.; Ruiz Alcalá, G.; Domínguez-Martín, A.; Marchal, J.A.; Boulaiz, H. Phenformin as an Anticancer Agent: Challenges and Prospects. *Int. J. Mol. Sci.* **2019**, *20*, 3316. [CrossRef] [PubMed]
47. Veiga, S.R.; Ge, X.; Mercer, C.A.; Hernández-Álvarez, M.I.; Thomas, H.E.; Hernandez-Losa, J.; Ramón Y Cajal, S.; Zorzano, A.; Thomas, G.; Kozma, S.C. Phenformin-Induced Mitochondrial Dysfunction Sensitizes Hepatocellular Carcinoma for Dual Inhibition of mTOR. *Clin. Cancer Res.* **2018**, *24*, 3767–3780. [CrossRef]

Disclaimer/Publisher's Note: The statements, opinions and data contained in all publications are solely those of the individual author(s) and contributor(s) and not of MDPI and/or the editor(s). MDPI and/or the editor(s) disclaim responsibility for any injury to people or property resulting from any ideas, methods, instructions or products referred to in the content.

cancers MDPI

Article

IGF1 and Insulin Receptor Single Nucleotide Variants Associated with Response in HER2-Negative Breast Cancer Patients Treated with Neoadjuvant Chemotherapy with or without a Fasting Mimicking Diet (BOOG 2013-04 DIRECT Trial)

Nadia de Gruil [1,*], Stefan Böhringer [2], Stefanie de Groot [1], Hanno Pijl [3], Judith R. Kroep [1,*] and Jesse J. Swen [4]

1 Department of Medical Oncology, Leiden University Medical Center, 2333 ZA Leiden, The Netherlands; s.de_groot.int@lumc.nl
2 Department of Medical Statistics and Bioinformatics, Leiden University Medical Center, 2333 ZA Leiden, The Netherlands; s.boehringer@lumc.nl
3 Department of Endocrinology, Leiden University Medical Center, 2333 ZA Leiden, The Netherlands; h.pijl@lumc.nl
4 Department of Clinical Pharmacy and Toxicology, Leiden University Medical Center, 2333 ZA Leiden, The Netherlands; j.j.swen@lumc.nl
* Correspondence: n.de_gruil@lumc.nl (N.d.G.); j.r.kroep@lumc.nl (J.R.K.)

Simple Summary: Insulin and insulin-like growth factor 1 (IGF1) are metabolic hormones, which are often upregulated to stimulate proliferation in breast cancer. A fasting mimicking diet (FMD) targets insulin signaling pathway downregulation to hamper tumor growth. Genes encoding for the insulin receptors on the cell's surface contain genetic variation between patients, which can affect insulin receptor function and cellular response. Therefore, a group of 113 patients with HER2-negative breast cancer receiving neoadjuvant chemotherapy with or without a fasting mimicking diet were investigated. We found that two IGF1 receptor variants were associated with worse pathological response compared to the reference alleles, out of the 17 interrogated common variants. Additionally, two IGF1 receptor variants could interact negatively within the FMD group regarding radiological response. These results emphasize that genetic variation harbors predictive clinical relevance to optimize and personalize cancer therapy.

Abstract: Aim: We aimed to investigate associations between *IGF1R* and *INSR* single nucleotide variants (SNVs) and clinical response in patients with breast cancer treated with neoadjuvant chemotherapy with or without a fasting mimicking diet (FMD) from the DIRECT trial (NCT02126449), since insulin-like growth factor 1 (IGF1) and the insulin pathway are heavily involved in tumor growth and progression. Methods: Germline DNA from 113 patients was tested for 17 systematically selected candidate SNVs in *IGF1R* and *INSR* with pathological and radiological response. Results: *IGF1R* variants A > G (rs3743259) and G > A (rs3743258) are associated with worse pathological response compared to reference alleles $p = 0.002$, OR = 0.42 (95%CI: 0.24; 0.73); $p = 0.0016$; OR = 0.40 (95%CI: 0.23; 0.70). *INSR* T > C (rs1051690) may be associated with worse radiological response $p = 0.02$, OR = 2.92 (95%CI: 1.16; 7.36), although not significant after Bonferroni correction. Exploratory interaction analysis suggests that *IGF1R* SNVs rs2684787 and rs2654980 interact negatively with the FMD group regarding radiological response $p = 0.036$, OR = 5.13 (95%CI: 1.12; 23.63); $p = 0.024$, OR = 5.71 (95%CI: 1.26; 25.85). Conclusions: The *IGF1R* variants rs3743259 and rs3743258 are negatively associated with pathological response in this cohort, suggesting potential relevance as a predictive biomarker. Further research is needed to validate these findings and elucidate the underlying mechanisms and interaction with FMD.

Keywords: breast cancer; *IGF1R*; insulin pathway; biomarkers; neoadjuvant chemotherapy; fasting mimicking diet

1. Introduction

The insulin-like growth factor 1 (IGF1) and insulin pathway are both involved in tumor proliferation and progression [1,2]. Elevated IGF1 levels are specifically associated with increased risk of breast cancer [3], and high IGF1 levels are associated with increased breast cancer mortality, with a hazard ratio of 3.1. Increased IGF1 receptor (IGF1R) expression is found in 50% of breast cancers. Therefore, it is hypothesized that genetic variation affecting the IGF1/insulin axis may also influence cancer risk, progression and therapy response [4].

De Groot et al. previously showed that the *IGF1R* SNV G > T rs2016347 is associated with pathological response after neoadjuvant chemotherapy in patients with human epidermal growth factor receptor 2 (HER2)-negative breast cancer, emphasizing that genetic variation could impact treatment response in these patients [5]. The insulin receptor (*INSR*) gene has been studied less extensively in cancer, even though its protein can bind the same ligands as the IGF1R.

Moreover, *IGF1R* and *INSR* SNVs may influence the effects of short-term fasting or a fasting mimicking diet (FMD), since the FMD is suggested to operate at least partially through the IGF1 and insulin pathways [6]. Fasting has repeatedly been shown to have anti-cancer effects in preclinical research by sensitizing tumor cells for chemotherapy [7–9]. The underlying mechanism of FMD on the anti-cancer effect is that a decrease in the blood concentration of glucose, insulin and IGF1 causes IGF1R- protein kinase B(Akt)-mammalian target of rapamycin (mTOR) pathway downregulation [10,11], which leads to gene expression profile alterations that ultimately promote autophagy and cell death in cancer cells [12]. Subsequently, our phase 2 DIRECT study (NCT02126449) suggested a positive effect of the FMD compared to regular diet in addition to neoadjuvant chemotherapy on pathological and radiological response, in patients with early-stage HER2-negative breast cancer [13].

Therefore, we hypothesize that genetic variation affecting the IGF1/insulin axis may influence chemotherapy response and interact with FMD therapy, such as reported in the DIRECT study (NCT02126449). Here, we investigated *IGF1R* and *INSR* SNVs and, subsequently, IGF1R expression for association with pathological and radiological response.

2. Materials and Methods

The 131 patients who participated from February 2014 to January 2018 in the phase II randomized DIRECT trial (NCT02126449) were randomized to receive standard neoadjuvant chemotherapy with or without FMD [13]. Patient characteristics are shown in Table 1, and the study inclusion and exclusion criteria were described previously [13]. Further, 2 patients were excluded from analysis due to informed consent withdrawal and metastasis at inclusion.

Pathological response was evaluated by the Miller–Payne (MP) score on a 1 to 5 scale [14]. Radiological response was assessed after chemotherapy and scored according to the RECIST1.1 criteria [15]. MP score was also grouped, with responders defined as score 4–5, less than 10% tumor cells, and the non-responders as score 1–3, as shown in Table 1. Radiological response is grouped as responders comprising complete response (CR) and partial response (PR) and the non-responders of stable disease (SD) and progressive disease (PD). The response data are primarily analyzed as intention-to-treat (ITT) and secondary in per protocol (PP) analysis with FMD-compliant versus control group, since 22 (33.8%) out of 65 FMD patients were able to comply with at least half of the planned FMD cycles. All patients provided written informed consent at the start of the study participation. The study was conducted in accordance with the Declaration of Helsinki (2008) and approved by the Medical Ethics Committee of the Leiden University Medical Center in agreement with the Dutch law for medical research involving humans.

Table 1. Patient characteristics.

Characteristics	Label	*n* Cases (Median)	%	Missing Cases	Total Cases
Median Age	(range) years	50 (27–71)		0	129
Median BMI	(range) kg/m^2	25.8 (19.7–41.2)		0	129
Randomization	chemo + FMD chemo	65 64	50.4% 49.6%	0	129
Per-protocol *	chemo + FMD compliant chemo + FMD non-compliant chemo	22 43 59	17.1% 34.7% 47.6%	0	124
HR status	ER−/Progesterone− ER+/Progesterone− ER+/Progesterone+	21 18 89	16.3% 14.0% 69.8%	1 (0.8%)	128
Tumor Type	Other Lobular Ductal/Carcinoma	5 22 102	3.5% 20.2% 76.3%	0	129
Tumor status **	cT1 cT2 cT3 cT4	11 83 32 3	8.4% 64.9% 24.4% 2.3%	0	129
Lymph node status **	cN0 cN1 cN2 cN3	63 55 11 2	48.1% 42.0% 8.4% 1.5%	0	129
Miller&Payne score	grade 1 no reduction grade 2 < 30% tumor reduction grade 3 30–90% tumor reduction grade 4 > 90% tumor reduction grade 5 no tumor	35 26 33 20 14	27.1% 20.9% 25.6% 15.5% 10.9%	1 (0.8%)	128
Miller&Payne pooled	grade 1–3 non-responders grade 4–5 responders	94 34	73.3% 26.4%	2 (1.5%)	128
Radiological response	CR PR SD PD	16 69 22 1	14.8% 63.9% 20.4% 0.9%	23 (17.6%)	108
Radiological response pooled	CR or PR responders SD or PD non-responders	85 23	78.7% 21.3%	23 (17.6%)	108

* Per protocol groups consisted of chemo + FMD compliant (≥half of the planned FMD cycles), chemo + FMD non-compliant (≤half of the planned FMD cycles) and the control group chemo. ** Tumor and lymph node status according to TNM classification. BMI body mass index (kg/m^2). HR-status hormone receptor status. ER estrogen receptor. Progesterone progesterone receptor. CR complete response. PR partial response. SD stable disease. PD progression of disease.

The 1000 Genomes database [16,17], version GRCh37p13, provided all SNVs for *IGF1R* (n = 1364) and *INSR* (n = 1244) genes. Selection criteria for SNV selection included (1) localization in exon positions, (2) minor allele frequency ≥0.2 in the sub-population with Northern and Western European ancestry (CEU) and (3) non-duplicates. These selection criteria resulted in a total of 24 SNVs, 15 for *IGF1R* and 9 for *INSR*. Due to technical limitations in primer design of the custom Open Array chip, 6 SNVs had to be replaced with proxy SNVs. Haploview software (version 4.1) identified 4 SNVs in high linkage disequilibrium $r^2 > 0.9$, namely *IGF1R* rs1815009 for rs66745311, rs2684788 for rs3051367, rs2654980 for rs9282714 and *INSR* rs2252673 for rs2352955 (Table S1). INSR rs34045095 and rs2352954 had to be excluded due to lack of proxy SNV and internal quality control. Ultimately, 17 candidate SNVs were selected, 11 in *IGF1R* and 6 in *INSR* (Table S2).

DNA was isolated from baseline blood samples ($n = 113$) collected in Ethylene diamine tetra acetic acid tubes stored at from −80 °C. Isolated DNA samples were stored at −20 °C until genotyping for the 17 candidate *IGF1R* and *INSR* SNVs. Genotyping was performed using a PCR-based fixed-format OpenArray™ Panel (Thermo Fisher Scientific, Waltham, MA, USA) to detect SNVs using specific probes for the genes *IGF1R* and *INSR*. Reactions were run on the QuantStudio™ 12 K Flex OpenArray Genotyping system (Thermo Fisher Scientific, Waltham, MA, USA) and analyzed with the TaqMan Genotyper Software® (version 1.3). The predefined minimum call rate was >85%.

Formalin-fixed paraffin-embedded blocks of the diagnostic biopsies and resection material were sectioned (4 μm) and immunohistochemically stained for membranous IGF-1R expression, as described elsewhere more extensively [5]. For positive controls, placenta tissue with previously confirmed IGF1R expression was used, while negative control sections underwent the same IHC procedure without the primary antibody. Scoring the membranous IGF1R expression was performed by two assessors (SdG, NdG) simultaneously and, if necessary, sections were checked by a pathologist to reach consensus. The scoring method, as described elsewhere in more detail [5], was, in short, carried out on a scale from 0 to 3+. A score 0 was given if <10% of the tumor cells were incompletely stained, 1 if >10% of tumor cells showed incomplete staining, 2 if weak to moderate staining in >10% of the tumor cells was observed and 3+ if strong complete staining was observed in >10% of tumor cells. A score of 0 and 1+ was considered negative and 2+ and 3+ as positive [5]. Statistical analysis was performed in Statistical Package for Social Sciences (IBM SPSS, version 24.0 and 25.0, Armonk, NY, USA: IBM Corp). Genotype distribution in 1000 Genomes and the DIRECT cohort were compared and tested for deviation from Hardy–Weinberg equilibrium (HWE) using a goodness-of-fit test with p-value of <0.05 as significance threshold. Ordinal and binary logistic regression using univariate and multivariate models was used for pathological and radiological response and IGF1R expression. The proportional odds assumption was not violated for the significant SNVs, as assessed by comparing regression coefficients to a separate multinomial regression analysis (Table S3). For the primary analysis, the ITT population was used. First, model selection was performed with univariate regressions performed on potential confounders and influential variables. Variables with p-values < 0.1 were carried forward into the primary multivariate analysis. In the genetic association models, genotypes were used with additive coding. Coding of genotypes was performed according to the variant allele, i.e., the genotype represents how often the variant allele is present, and associations are interpreted in terms of the variant allele. In secondary analyses, the PP population was considered. Further analyses were conducted in an explorative way to investigate possible interactions between SNV and treatment group. For the primary analysis, Bonferroni correction was applied to account for multiple testing of 17 SNVs, with a significance threshold of 0.05/17 = 0.003.

3. Results

3.1. IGF1R and INSR SNV Distribution

Baseline blood samples from 113 out of 131 patients were available for analysis. The SNV distribution among the study cohort shown in Table 2 is comparable to the frequencies observed in the publicly available databases of PubMed and 1000 Genomes GRCh37p13 (Table S4). Furthermore, all the SNVs followed HWE at the 0.05 threshold. The predetermined minimum call rate of >85% was achieved with a minimum of 92% (Table S4).

3.2. IGF1 Receptor SNVs Are Associated with Worsened Pathological Response and INSR SNV Is Potentially Associated with Worse Radiological Response

In the model selection step, tumor and lymph node status, age, randomization and hormone receptor (HR) status were selected as covariates for the primary analysis (Table S5). Tumor type and HR status are biologically similar factors; therefore, only HR status was entered into the final ordinal regression model to optimize the noise-to-signal ratio.

Table 2. SNV distribution.

SNV	Reference Genotype	Heterozygous Genotype	Homozygous Genotype	MAF Ref Allele	N	HWE	*p*-Value *
IGF1R rs2016347	32	56	25	53%	113	0.003	0.957
IGF1R rs2229765	35	60	17	58%	112	1.116	0.291
IGF1R rs1815009	5	49	59	26%	113	1.735	0.188
INSR rs1051651	78	28	6	82%	112	2.447	0.118
INSR rs3745551	12	50	50	33%	112	0.009	0.924
IGF1R rs3743259	58	41	12	71%	111	1.297	0.255
IGF1R rs2684787	60	42	10	72%	112	0.449	0.503
IGF1R rs2654981	25	55	33	46%	113	0.053	0.818
IGF1R rs2654980	61	42	10	73%	113	0.499	0.480
IGF1R rs2684788	27	55	31	48%	113	0.072	0.788
IGF1R rs3743249	59	47	7	73%	113	0.346	0.556
IGF1R rs45484096	51	46	16	65%	113	1.118	0.290
INSR rs3833238	77	30	6	81%	113	1.700	0.192
INSR rs1051690	2	29	82	15%	113	0.095	0.757
INSR rs1799817	85	24	4	86%	113	1.802	0.179
INSR rs2252673	3	23	82	13%	108	0.760	0.383
IGF1R rs3743258	57	35	12	72%	104	3.072	0.080

SNV single nucleotide variant, *INSR* insulin receptor gene, *IGF1R* insulin like growth factor 1 receptor gene, MAF mean allele frequency, HWE Hardy–Weinberg equation. * if <0.05—not consistent with HWE. Call rate minimum is 92%.

IGF1R rs3743259 and rs3743258 SNVs were associated with worse pathological response compared to the reference genotype in the ITT analysis with an additive model, $p = 0.002$, OR = 0.42 (95%CI: 0.24; 0.73); $p = 0.0016$; OR = 0.40 (95%CI: 0.23; 0.70), respectively, as shown in Table 3.

Table 3. Primary multivariate ordinal regression model intention to treat.

	Miller & Payne							Radiological Response						
SNVs	**N**	**OR**	**95%CI Lower-Upper**			***p*-Value**	**N**	**OR**	**95%CI Lower-Upper**			***p*-Value**
IGF1R rs2016347	112	1.52	0.94	-	2.46	0.09	92	0.89	0.48	-	1.67	0.72
IGF1R rs2229765	111	1.03	0.61	-	1.73	0.91	91	1.14	0.58	-	2.25	0.70
IGF1R rs1815009	112	0.83	0.46	-	1.50	0.53	92	0.92	0.43	-	1.98	0.84
INSR rs1051651	111	1.46	0.82	-	2.62	0.20	91	1.69	0.80	-	3.59	0.17
INSR rs3745551	111	0.99	0.60	-	1.66	0.98	91	1.88	0.93	-	3.77	0.08
IGF1R rs3743259	110	0.42	0.24	-	0.73	**0.002**	91	1.10	0.56	-	2.16	0.79
IGF1R rs2684787	111	1.23	0.73	-	2.07	0.44	91	0.92	0.47	-	1.80	0.80
IGF1R rs2654981	112	1.23	0.77	-	1.98	0.39	92	0.98	0.54	-	1.78	0.96
IGF1R rs2654980	112	1.25	0.75	-	2.11	0.39	92	0.88	0.45	-	1.72	0.71
IGF1R rs2684788	112	1.54	0.96	-	2.49	0.08	92	1.00	0.54	-	1.83	0.99
IGF1R rs3743249	112	1.39	0.79	-	2.45	0.25	92	0.95	0.47	-	1.94	0.89
IGF1R rs45484096	112	1.03	0.64	-	1.65	0.91	92	1.04	0.56	-	1.94	0.89
INSR rs3833238	112	1.32	0.75	-	2.35	0.34	92	1.75	0.83	-	3.67	0.14
INSR rs1051690	112	0.53	0.27	-	1.06	0.07	92	2.92	1.16	-	7.36	**0.02**
INSR rs1799817	112	0.78	0.40	-	1.49	0.45	92	1.89	0.74	-	4.81	0.18
INSR rs2252673	107	0.87	0.42	-	1.78	0.70	88	2.37	0.89	-	6.34	0.09
IGF1R rs3743258	103	0.40	0.23	-	0.70	**0.002**	86	1.12	0.57	-	2.20	0.75

Cut off value Bonferroni correction for multiple testing is 0.05/17 = 0.0029. OR odds ratio, CI confidence interval, SNV single nucleotide variant, *INSR* insulin receptor, *IGF1R* insulin like growth factor 1 receptor. Bold: statistically significant.

Multivariate analysis in a PP fashion yielded associations with the same SNVs and similar effect sizes, though these were not statistically significant after Bonferroni correction for multiple testing (See Table 4).

Table 4. Primary multivariate ordinal regression model per protocol.

SNVs	Miller & Payne						Radiological Response					
	N	OR	95%CI			p-Value	N	OR	95%CI			p-Value
IGF1R rs2016347	72	1.40	0.74	-	2.63	0.30	61	0.76	0.34	-	1.74	0.52
IGF1R rs2229765	72	1.21	0.63	-	2.33	0.57	61	0.93	0.41	-	2.13	0.87
IGF1R rs1815009	72	1.07	0.52	-	2.19	0.86	61	0.56	0.22	-	1.41	0.22
INSR rs1051651	72	1.11	0.56	-	2.21	0.77	61	1.67	0.71	-	3.94	0.24
INSR rs3745551	72	1.49	0.79	-	2.80	0.22	61	1.72	0.77	-	3.87	0.19
IGF1R rs3743259	72	0.49	0.25	-	0.94	0.03	61	1.24	0.56	-	2.72	0.59
IGF1R rs2684787	71	1.29	0.66	-	2.52	0.46	60	0.45	0.18	-	1.12	0.09
IGF1R rs2654981	72	0.98	0.51	-	1.88	0.94	61	0.91	0.42	-	2.00	0.82
IGF1R rs2654980	72	1.36	0.70	-	2.64	0.37	61	0.43	0.17	-	1.05	0.06
IGF1R rs2684788	72	1.33	0.71	-	2.50	0.37	61	0.85	0.38	-	1.87	0.68
IGF1R rs3743249	72	1.10	0.54	-	2.21	0.80	61	1.37	0.57	-	3.30	0.49
IGF1R rs45484096	72	1.07	0.59	-	1.94	0.83	61	0.68	0.31	-	1.49	0.33
INSR rs3833238	72	1.01	0.51	-	2.02	0.97	61	1.58	0.67	-	3.73	0.29
INSR rs1051690	72	0.41	0.16	-	1.04	0.061	61	3.41	1.09	-	10.63	0.035
INSR rs1799817	72	0.51	0.21	-	1.28	0.15	61	1.55	0.46	-	5.31	0.48
INSR rs2252673	69	1.30	0.56	-	3.04	0.54	59	1.68	0.56	-	5.02	0.35
IGF1R rs3743258	68	0.46	0.24	-	0.91	0.03	59	1.23	0.56	-	2.70	0.61

Cut off value Bonferroni correction for multiple testing is 0.05/17 = 0.0029. OR odds ratio, CI confidence interval, SNV single nucleotide variant, *INSR* insulin receptor, *IGF1R* insulin-like growth factor 1 receptor.

Furthermore, *INSR* rs1051690 presence suggested association with worse radiological response compared to patients with the reference genotype (Table 3: OR = 2.92 (95%CI: 1.16; 7.36); $p = 0.02$), although this association was not significant after Bonferroni correction. The logistic regression model with responders vs. non-responders for radiological and pathological response showed no significant correlation after correction for multiple testing for ITT, which suggests that the ordinal regression analysis best retains information on the association (Table S6).

3.3. IGF1R SNVs and FMD Interaction

Further ordinal regression analyses were conducted to analyze potential interaction between SNVs and FMD. This analysis suggested that the presence of *IGF1R* SNVs rs2684787 and rs2654980 might interact with the ITT FMD group differently compared to the control group, affecting radiological response negatively, $p = 0.036$, OR = 5.13 (95%CI: 1.12–23.63); $p = 0.024$, OR = 5.71 (95%CI: 1.26–25.85), respectively (Table S7), but not in PP. For pathological response, there was no indication of interaction in the ITT or PP.

Secondary models included responders vs. non-responders, which revealed that there were no indications for interaction between SNVs and treatment group affecting radiological response and pathological responders vs. non-responders after correction for multiple comparison (Table S8).

3.4. IGF1R Expression Score Is Not Associated with Clinical Response

We found that 58 of the total 104 biopsies (55.8%) were IGF1R-positive at baseline; 28 positive IGF1R biopsies at baseline became negative (48.3% of positive biopsies; 26.9% of total), while 30 remained IGF1R positive (51.7% of positive biopsies; 28.8% of total) at resection, as seen in Figure 1. Further, 44 of 46 (42.3% of total) biopsies remained IGF1R negative at resection (95.7% negative biopsies; 42.3% of total), while 2 became positive (4.3% of negative biopsies; 1.9% of total) (see Figure 1). Multivariate regression analysis uncovered no association between IGF1R biopsy or resection score and pathological or radiological response in both the ITT and PP multivariate model.

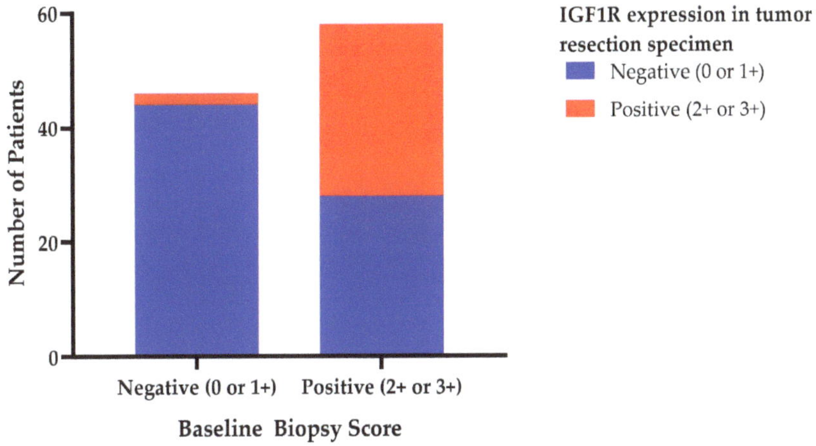

Figure 1. IGF1R expression in baseline tumor biopsy and tumor resection specimen.

4. Discussion

This study shows that the presence of *IGF1R* SNVs rs3743259 and rs3743258 is associated with worse pathological response compared to the reference genotype in this cohort of patients with breast cancer treated with neoadjuvant chemotherapy (see Table 3). Additionally, our results suggest that *INSR* rs1051690 may be associated with worse radiological response compared to patients with the reference genotype in this study, although this association was not significant after Bonferroni correction. These findings indicate that patients with rs3743259 and rs3743258 may respond less to chemotherapy, which could imply treatment consequences, for example, to consider an alternative systemic therapy regimen. The association between rs3743259 and rs3743258 was not significant in the PP analysis, most likely due to the smaller sample size of 72 compared to 112 in the ITT analysis. Furthermore, there might be an interaction between FMD and the presence of SNVs, as shown by the exploratory analysis, and *IGF1R* SNVs rs2684787 and rs2654980 might interact with the FMD group differently compared to the control group regarding radiological response (Table S7).

To assess whether the observed associations could be attributed to other genes as indicated by SNVs exhibiting high linkage disequilibrium (LD), online tools LDlink and Haploreg (version 4.1) were used [18,19]. Firstly, *IGF1R* rs3743259 shows high LD with six other SNVs ($r^2 > 0.8$), including *IGF1R* rs3743258 ($r^2 = 0.9$). All six SNVs have not been associated with disease or pathologic processes according to PubMed. Furthermore, LDlink reports that *IGF1R* rs3743258 is in LD with five SNVs with an $r^2 > 0.8$, whereas HaploReg only reports rs3743259. Nevertheless, all associated SNVs hail from the *IGF1R* gene, and it is, therefore, unlikely that the observed effect is originating from another gene or SNV.

Biong et al. found that rs3743259 was associated with increased mammographic density [20], which is a known risk factor for breast cancer development [21]. Together with our findings on rs3743259, this study supports the hypothesis that there could be a biological mechanism to drive breast cancer. Nevertheless, the structural and functional consequences of these SNVs on IGF1 receptor signaling have yet to be investigated.

The limitations of this study are the relatively small sample size for a genetic association study. In order to decrease the risk of reporting false-positive results, we applied a strict Bonferroni correction. The statistical limitation of this study is illustrated by the exploratory generalized linear models used to investigate the interaction between SNVs and FMD versus SNVs and control group. These results should be interpreted carefully, since analyzing the cohort in smaller groups or more complex models decreases statistical power. Therefore, the interaction between the *IGF1R/INSR* SNVs and FMD is important to investigate in future studies. Furthermore, radiological response data were missing for 21/129 patients (16.3%), although separate regression analysis confirmed that these missing data did not arise due to other variables.

Lastly, future research could focus on the structural effect of these *IGF1R* SNVs on the protein in silico, for example. Subsequently, the functional consequences, in terms of receptor affinity for ligands, should be investigated as well. In parallel, the findings of this study need validation in another, preferably larger, breast cancer cohort or a genetic databank cohort. Moreover, future studies, such as the ongoing phase III DIRECT2 (NCT05503108) study, are necessary to validate the currently reported associations. In conclusion, more translational research is needed to reveal the underlying mechanisms between the genetic variation in *IGF1R* and *INSR* in the context of fasting and clinical response in cancer.

5. Conclusions

This study identified *IGF1R* SNVs rs3743259 and rs3743258 as potential predictive markers for worse pathological response on neoadjuvant chemotherapy in patients with HER2-negative breast cancer. Validation and further research are essential before any clinical recommendations can be made.

Supplementary Materials: The following supporting information can be downloaded at: https://www.mdpi.com/article/10.3390/cancers15245872/s1, Table S1: Haploview; Table S2: SNV information; Table S3: Proportional odds assumption; Table S4: SNV information; Table S5: Univariate model for covariates; Table S6: Logistic regression models responders versus non-responders; Table S7: Generalized linear model SNVs and treatment interaction; Table S8: Generalized linear model SNVs and treatment interaction responders versus non-responders.

Author Contributions: Conceptualization, N.d.G., S.d.G., H.P., J.R.K. and J.J.S.; methodology, S.B. and J.J.S.; software, N.d.G. and S.B.; formal analysis, N.d.G., S.B., J.R.K. and J.J.S.; investigation, N.d.G., S.B., J.R.K. and J.J.S.; resources, S.B., J.R.K. and J.J.S.; data curation, N.d.G., S.d.G. and J.R.K.; writing—original draft preparation, N.d.G.; writing—review and editing, S.B., S.d.G., H.P., J.R.K. and J.J.S.; visualization, N.d.G. and J.J.S.; supervision, H.P., J.R.K. and J.J.S.; project administration, N.d.G. and S.d.G.; funding acquisition, S.d.G., H.P. and J.R.K. All authors have read and agreed to the published version of the manuscript.

Funding: This research was funded by Pink ribbon (grant number 2012.WO31.C155) and Amgen (20139098). The Dutch Breast Cancer Research Group (BOOG), Utrecht, the Netherlands is sponsor of this study. The APC was funded by the Leiden University Medical Center.

Institutional Review Board Statement: The study was conducted in accordance with the Declaration of Helsinki (October 2013) and approved by the Ethics Committee of Leiden University Medical Center (P13.135, date of approval 12 September 2013).

Informed Consent Statement: Informed consent was obtained from all subjects involved in the study.

Data Availability Statement: The data that support the findings of this study are available from the corresponding author, J.R.K., upon reasonable request.

Acknowledgments: The authors sincerely thank all the patients participating in this trial as well as all the participating centers, not to mention the LUMC clinical research center for trial coordination and data collection.

Conflicts of Interest: The authors declare no conflict of interest. The funders had no role in the design of the study; in the collection, analyses, or interpretation of data; in the writing of the manuscript; or in the decision to publish the results.

References

1. Pollak, M. Insulin and insulin-like growth factor signalling in neoplasia. *Nat. Rev. Cancer* **2008**, *8*, 915–928. [CrossRef] [PubMed]
2. Hanahan, D.; Weinberg, R.A. Hallmarks of Cancer: The Next Generation. *Cell* **2011**, *144*, 646–674. [CrossRef] [PubMed]

3. Endogenous Hormones and Breast Cancer Collaborative Group; Key, T.J.; Appleby, P.N.; Reeves, G.K.; Roddam, A.W. Insulin-like growth factor 1 (IGF1), IGF binding protein 3 (IGFBP3), and breast cancer risk: Pooled individual data analysis of 17 prospective studies. *Lancet Oncol.* **2010**, *11*, 530–542. [PubMed]
4. Key, T.J. Diet, insulin-like growth factor-1 and cancer risk. *Proc. Nutr. Soc.* **2011**, *70*, 385–388. [CrossRef] [PubMed]
5. de Groot, S.; Charehbili, A.; van Laarhoven, H.W.; Mooyaart, A.L.; Dekker-Ensink, N.G.; van de Ven, S.; Janssen, L.G.M.; Swen, J.J.; Smit, V.T.H.B.M.; Heijns, J.B.; et al. Insulin-like growth factor 1 receptor expression and IGF1R 3129G > T polymorphism are associated with response to neoadjuvant chemotherapy in breast cancer patients: Results from the NEOZOTAC trial (BOOG 2010-01). *Breast Cancer Res BCR.* **2016**, *18*, 3. [CrossRef] [PubMed]
6. Nencioni, A.; Caffa, I.; Cortellino, S.; Longo, V.D. Fasting and cancer: Molecular mechanisms and clinical application. *Nat. Rev. Cancer* **2018**, *18*, 707–719. [CrossRef] [PubMed]
7. Raffaghello, L.; Lee, C.; Safdie, F.M.; Wei, M.; Madia, F.; Bianchi, G.; Longo, V.D. Starvation-dependent differential stress resistance protects normal but not cancer cells against high-dose chemotherapy. *Proc. Natl. Acad. Sci. USA* **2008**, *105*, 8215–8220. [CrossRef] [PubMed]
8. Lee, C.; Safdie, F.M.; Raffaghello, L.; Wei, M.; Madia, F.; Parrella, E.; Hwang, D.; Cohen, P.; Bianchi, G.; Longo, V.D. Reduced levels of IGF-I mediate differential protection of normal and cancer cells in response to fasting and improve chemotherapeutic index. *Cancer Res.* **2010**, *70*, 1564–1572. [CrossRef]
9. Longo, V.D.; Mattson, M.P. Fasting: Molecular mechanisms and clinical applications. *Cell Metab.* **2014**, *19*, 181–192. [CrossRef]
10. Brandhorst, S.; Choi, I.Y.; Wei, M.; Cheng, C.W.; Sedrakyan, S.; Navarrete, G.; Dubeau, L.; Yap, L.P.; Park, R.; Vinciguerra, M.; et al. A Periodic Diet that Mimics Fasting Promotes Multi-System Regeneration, Enhanced Cognitive Performance, and Healthspan. *Cell Metab.* **2015**, *22*, 86–99. [CrossRef]
11. Merimee, T.J.; Zapf, J.; Froesch, E.R. Insulin-like growth factors in the fed and fasted states. *J. Clin. Endocrinol. Metab.* **1982**, *55*, 999–1002. [CrossRef] [PubMed]
12. Vernieri, C.; Fuca, G.; Ligorio, F.; Huber, V.; Vingiani, A.; Iannelli, F.; Raimondi, A.; Rinchai, D.; Frigè, G.; Belfiore, A.; et al. Fasting-mimicking diet is safe and reshapes metabolism and antitumor immunity in cancer patients. *Cancer Discov.* **2021**, *12*, 90–107. [CrossRef] [PubMed]
13. de Groot, S.; Lugtenberg, R.T.; Cohen, D.; Welters, M.J.P.; Ehsan, I.; Vreeswijk, M.P.G.; Smit, V.T.; de Graaf, H.; Heijns, J.B.; Portielje, J.E.; et al. Fasting mimicking diet as an adjunct to neoadjuvant chemotherapy for breast cancer in the multicentre randomized phase 2 DIRECT trial. *Nat. Commun.* **2020**, *11*, 3083. [CrossRef] [PubMed]
14. Ogston, K.N.; Miller, I.D.; Payne, S.; Hutcheon, A.W.; Sarkar, T.K.; Smith, I.; Schofield, A.; Heys, S.D. A new histological grading system to assess response of breast cancers to primary chemotherapy: Prognostic significance and survival. *Breast* **2003**, *12*, 320–327. [CrossRef]
15. Schwartz, L.H.; Litière, S.; de Vries, E.; Ford, R.; Gwyther, S.; Mandrekar, S.; Shankar, L.; Bogaerts, J.; Chen, A.; Dancey, J.; et al. RECIST 1.1—Update and Clarification: From the RECIST Committee. *Eur. J. Cancer* **2016**, *62*, 132–137. [CrossRef] [PubMed]
16. Kent, W.J.; Sugnet, C.W.; Furey, T.S.; Roskin, K.M.; Pringle, T.H.; Zahler, A.M.; Haussler, D. The human genome browser at UCSC. *Genome Res.* **2002**, *12*, 996–1006. [CrossRef] [PubMed]
17. Nassar, L.R.; Barber, G.P.; Benet-Pagès, A.; Casper, J.; Clawson, H.; Diekhans, M.; Fischer, C.; Gonzalez, J.N.; Hinrichs, A.S.; Lee, B.T.; et al. The UCSC Genome Browser database: 2023 update. *Nucleic Acids Res.* **2023**, *51*, D1188–D1195. [CrossRef]
18. Ward, L.D.; Kellis, M. HaploReg: A resource for exploring chromatin states, conservation, and regulatory motif alterations within sets of genetically linked variants. *Nucleic Acids Res.* **2012**, *40*, D930–D934. [CrossRef]
19. Machiela, M.J.; Chanock, S.J. LDlink: A web-based application for exploring population-specific haplotype structure and linking correlated alleles of possible functional variants. *Bioinformatics* **2015**, *31*, 3555–3557. [CrossRef]
20. Biong, M.; Gram, I.T.; Brill, I.; Johansen, F.; Solvang, H.K.; Alnaes, G.I.; Fagerheim, T.; Bremnes, Y.; Chanock, S.J.; Burdett, L.; et al. Genotypes and haplotypes in the insulin-like growth factors, their receptors and binding proteins in relation to plasma metabolic levels and mammographic density. *BMC Med. Genom.* **2010**, *3*, 9. [CrossRef]
21. Tice, J.A.; Cummings, S.R.; Smith-Bindman, R.; Ichikawa, L.; Barlow, W.E.; Kerlikowske, K. Using clinical factors and mammographic breast density to estimate breast cancer risk: Development and validation of a new predictive model. *Ann. Intern. Med.* **2008**, *148*, 337–347. [CrossRef] [PubMed]

Disclaimer/Publisher's Note: The statements, opinions and data contained in all publications are solely those of the individual author(s) and contributor(s) and not of MDPI and/or the editor(s). MDPI and/or the editor(s) disclaim responsibility for any injury to people or property resulting from any ideas, methods, instructions or products referred to in the content.

biomedicines

MDPI

Article

Identifying Key Genes as Progression Indicators of Prostate Cancer with Castration Resistance Based on Dynamic Network Biomarker Algorithm and Weighted Gene Correlation Network Analysis

Siyuan Liu [1], Yi Hu [1], Fei Liu [2], Yizheng Jiang [1], Hongrui Wang [1], Xusheng Wu [2,*] and Dehua Hu [1,*]

[1] School of Life Sciences, Central South University, Changsha 410013, China; 212501030@csu.edu.cn (S.L.); 15243664769@163.com (Y.H.); jyzgenetic@outlook.com (Y.J.); 223254@csu.edu.cn (H.W.)

[2] Shenzhen Health Development Research and Data Management Center, Shenzhen 518028, China; liufei_csu@163.com

* Correspondence: jysgwuxusheng@163.com (X.W.); hudehua@csu.edu.cn (D.H.)

Abstract: Background: Androgen deprivation therapy (ADT) is the mainstay of treatment for prostate cancer, yet dynamic molecular changes from hormone-sensitive to castration-resistant states in patients treated with ADT remain unclear. **Methods:** In this study, we combined the dynamic network biomarker (DNB) method and the weighted gene co-expression network analysis (WGCNA) to identify key genes associated with the progression to a castration-resistant state in prostate cancer via the integration of single-cell and bulk RNA sequencing data. Based on the gene expression profiles of CRPC in the GEO dataset, the DNB method was used to clarify the condition of epithelial cells and find out the most significant transition signal DNB modules and genes included. Then, we calculated gene modules associated with the clinical phenotype stage based on the WGCNA. IHC was conducted to validate the expression of the key genes in CRPC and primary PCa patients Results:Nomograms, calibration plots, and ROC curves were applied to evaluate the good prognostic accuracy of the risk prediction model. **Results:** By combining single-cell RNA sequence data and bulk RNA sequence data, we identified a set of DNBs, whose roles involved in androgen-associated activities indicated the signals of a prostate cancer cell transition from an androgen-dependent state to a castration-resistant state. In addition, a risk prediction model including the risk score of four key genes (SCD, NARS2, ALDH1A1, and NFXL1) and other clinical–pathological characteristics was constructed and verified to be able to reasonably predict the prognosis of patients receiving ADT. **Conclusions:** In summary, four key genes from DNBs were identified as potential diagnostic markers for patients treated with ADT and a risk score-based nomogram will facilitate precise prognosis prediction and individualized therapeutic interventions of CRPC.

Keywords: castrate-resistant prostate cancer; dynamic network biomarker; risk prediction model; bulk RNA sequence; single-cell RNA sequence

1. Introduction

Prostate cancer (PCa) is the most prevalent cancer for men in the USA and a leading cause of oncological death in men worldwide, with an estimated 35,000 deaths and more than 299,000 new cases in the US in 2024 [1]. For most PCa patients, castration-resistant prostate cancer (CRPC), whether metastatic (mCRPC) or nonmetastatic (nmCRPC), generally occurs in response to therapeutic pressure, specifically the use of androgen deprivation therapy (ADT) [2]. Worse still, almost all patients treated with ADT eventually develop castration-resistant prostate cancer (CRPC), as evidenced by imaging progression or an increased prostate-specific antigen (PSA) despite castration levels of testosterone [3]. CRPC has a poor prognosis with an average survival time of only 16–18 months from progression [4], while the overall survival of patients with metastatic CRPC is only 9–13 months [5].

Currently, the prognosis and treatment of CRPC remain major challenges and the exact mechanism of the transition from a hormone-sensitive to a castration-resistant state is still not fully understood [6,7], Thus, there is a critical need to explore the molecular markers between hormone-naive prostate cancer and CRPC to better understand the mechanism by which primary prostate cancer transforms to CRPC and provide new targets for treating CRPC.

There have been a range of studies concerning progression indicators and drug resistance biomarkers of CRPC. For instance, glutamate decarboxylase 1 (GAD1) was found to promote prostate cancer progression and decrease the therapeutic effect of docetaxel or enzalutamide [8]. B7-H3 (also known as CD276), a B7 family immune checkpoint, can be a promising target for PCa immunotherapy, particularly in the early weeks post-ADT before PCa enters dormancy [9]. Recently, active Stat5 signaling, a known promoter of prostate cancer growth and clinical progression, was unexpectedly found to be a potent inducer of AR gene transcription in PCa, which indicates that pharmacological Stat5 inhibitors may represent a new strategy for suppressing ARs and CRPC growth [10].

With the development of DNA microarrays and high-throughput sequencing, it is both efficient and effective to explore key gene modules related to tumor progression via the use of bioinformatics techniques and big data integration. The weighted correlation network analysis (WGCNA) is an efficient and accurate bioinformatics method for analyzing microarray data that can be used to systematically investigate highly synergistically altered gene modules [11]. The WGCNA divides genes into several modules based on the similarity of gene expression profiles and can be used to identify the relationship between gene sets and clinical characteristics. WGCNA methods have been successfully applied to identify key gene modules in many cancers, including bladder cancer [12], ovarian cancer [13], and breast cancer [14]. However, the primary objective of WGCNA aims to tell the difference between the "disease state" and "normal state" and may fail to accurately predict the early onset of disease before its development. To overcome this bottleneck, the dynamic network biomarker (DNB) theory, based on the dynamic features of molecules within the biological system, was proposed [15]. The DNB theory is a kind of nonlinear dynamics theory which aims to find a group with high correlation and strong collective fluctuations that affect the dramatic changes in diseases. DNBs reveal early warning signals of critical transitions before the deterioration of complex diseases. The DNB method has been applied to real disease datasets and has been used to identify the pre-disease states of several cancers, such as hepatocellular carcinoma [16], colon and rectal cancer [17], and liver cancer [18]. These studies provide us with a reliable and robust technical basis for identifying critical signals, as well as prognostic indicators, in CRPC.

In this study, we combined the methods of DNBs and the WGCNA to explore novel biomarkers in androgen deprivation therapy resistance and the prognosis of prostate cancer. The flowchart of this study is shown in Figure 1. By analyzing the dynamic changes in key modules involved in androgen-associated activities in CRPC and identifying stage-related gene modules combined in the weighted gene co-expression network, we identified four genes, including *SCD*, *NARS2*, *ALDH1A1*, and *NFXL1*, as core members of DNBs, which can serve as biomarkers involved in the transition of prostate cancer cells from an androgen-dependent state to a castration-resistant state. This study is expected to provide novel diagnostic and therapeutic targets for prostate cancer patients treated with androgen deprivation therapy and offer new insights into the molecular pathology of CRPC progression from dynamic network perspectives.

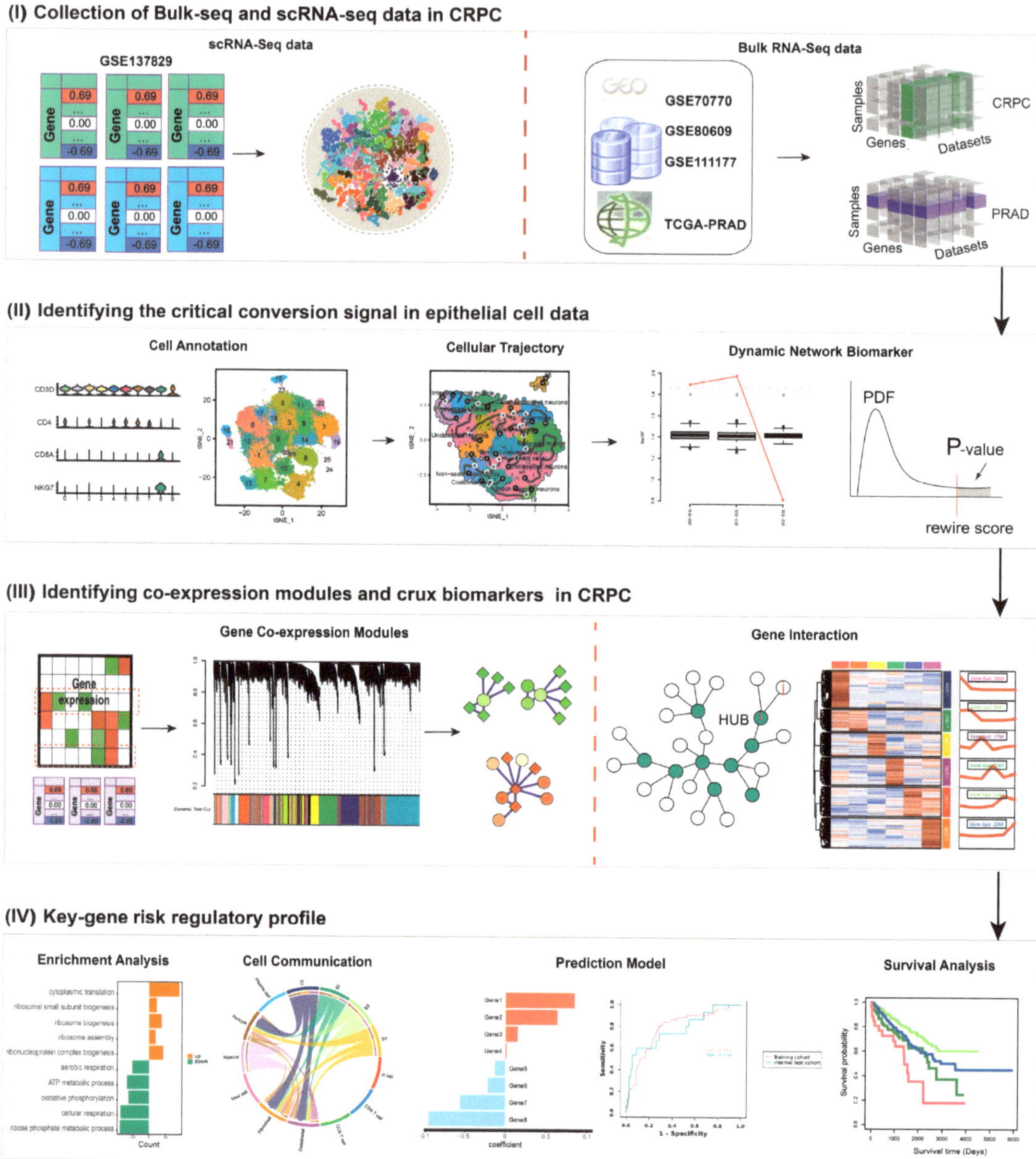

Figure 1. Flowchart of this study.

2. Materials and Methods

2.1. Data Acquisition and Preprocessing

The RNA sequencing data and corresponding clinical data of prostate cancer samples were acquired from The Cancer Genome Atlas (TCGA) (http://cancergenome.nih.gov/ accessed on 15 February 2024). The single-cell RNA sequencing (scRNA-seq) information of GSE137829 was obtained via the Gene Expression Omnibus (GEO) database (https://www.ncbi.nlm.nih.gov/ accessed on 9 December 2023). CRPC bulk RNA-seq data were obtained from 3 GEO datasets (GSE700770, GSE80609, and GSE111177). TCGA-PRAD data were downloaded from the UCSC Xena database (https://xenabrowser.net/datapages/ accessed on 12 March 2024).

Based on the description in the article, a total of 14 CRPC patients were selected from the CRPC cohort according to their clinical information, and the corresponding single-cell RNA matrix data of 13 CRPC patients were found and downloaded from the GSE70770 dataset. In GSE80609, 12 CRPC patients were identified from the NGS cohort based on their clinical characteristics and the corresponding raw matrix data were downloaded. In GSE111177, we screened and selected 20 CRPC patients who underwent ADT based on their clinical information provided by the original article.

On the basis of the 2021 Canadian Urological Association (CUA)–Canadian Uro-Oncology Group (CUOG) guideline, for the management of castration-resistant prostate cancer (CRPC), we defined the "disease progression" of CRPC as "Deterioration occurred in the patient after receiving treatment, including disease worsening despite castrate levels of testosterone, the occurrence of new lesions, the progression of pre-existing disease, and/or the appearance of new metastases" in this study.

We applied the R package "Seurat (V4.0)" to process scRNA-seq data and conduct cell type annotation. We excluded cells with fewer than 200 or more than 6000 detected expressed genes (where each gene had to have at least one unique molecular identifier aligned in at least three cells). Cells with more than 10% expression of mitochondrial genes were excluded to remove low-activity cells.

We performed logarithmic normalization separately on the data from 6 samples. The "FindVariableFeatures" function was used to identify highly variable genes (based on variance stabilizing transformation, "vst"), followed by the removal of batch effects from the samples using the "FindIntegrationAnchors" function of the canonical correlation analysis (CCA) method. Additionally, we integrated the data using the IntegrateData function and scaled all genes using the ScaleData function. Principal component analysis (PCA) was employed to conduct dimensionality reduction and identify anchors. We selected dim = 30 and clustered cells using the "FindNeighbors" and "FindClusters" functions (resolution = 0.5), resulting in 21 clusters. Furthermore, we downloaded marker genes and related data for human cells from CellMarker (http://bio-bigdata.hrbmu.edu.cn/CellMarker1.0/, 17 September 2024) and manually annotated the cells [19].

2.2. Bulk RNA-Seq Data Processing

We downloaded the series matrix files and their platform annotation information and eliminated more than half of the sample values or probes that detected multiple genes for analysis. Due to the differences in gene symbols across different microarray platforms, the probes were assigned to their Entrez identifiers according to each platform's annotation file. The R package "limma" was employed to identify differentially expressed genes (DEGs). We used the arithmetic mean and integrated groups to interpret the gene expression level if multiple probe groups corresponded to the same Entrez ID. Then, the differentially expressed genes (DEGs) were normalized by the number of reads per sample, and the ensemble IDs were converted to gene IDs by the R package "biomartr" [20]. We selected 13 CRPC patient samples from the GSE70770 dataset, 12 from the GSE80609 dataset, and 20 from the GSE111177 dataset from patients who received androgen deprivation therapy (ADT). For the TCGA dataset, genes with an expression level of 0 (not detected) in more than 10% of patients were excluded from further analysis. We combined clinical information from the TCGA database to identify patient samples that underwent ADT.

2.3. Pseudotime Trajectory Analysis

The "Monocle2" R package (version 2.20.0) was employed to elucidate the epithelial cell developmental trajectory and characterize the functional change processes and identify potential lineage differentiation between clusters. Based on the machine learning method of "reversed graph embedding", it can automatically infer the trajectory from high-dimensional RNA-seq data. In this study, we constructed the developmental trajectory based on the following steps. First, the core genes in each cluster were identified by the "Differential Gene Test" function. Then, the expression spectrum was simplified by the "reduceDimension" function and the "DDRTree" method (max_components = 2) to construct a minimum spanning tree (MST), which represents the potential path of cell differentiation. Then, the "orderCells" function was used to sort cells and assign pseudotime values. After this, branch expression analysis modeling (BEAM) was employed to detect and analyze specific branch points and identify genes with branch-dependent expression based on the pseudotime value.

2.4. Dynamic Network Biomarker (DNB)

The transition process of disease can be roughly divided into three states, the before-transition state, critical state, and after-transition state. The genes that only appear in the critical state and play key roles in the critical state can be identified as DNBs. In this work, we applied the R package "BioTIP" to identify dynamic network biomolecules and predict the differentiation trajectory of the prostate epithelium [21]. Dynamic network biomarkers (DNBs) are used for biological tipping-point characterization and focus on the detection and assessment of different stages of disease. It is a time-dependent method [22] which studies the location changes in the markers over time and the relationships among network markers over time. The DNB method follows three major criteria: (1) the standard deviation of the DNB molecule group increases dramatically in the critical state; (2) the correlation between any two molecules in the DNB molecule group increases significantly in the critical state; (3) the correlation between the DNB molecule group and the other group decreases steeply in the critical state.

In this study, we performed a DNB analysis according to the following steps: (1) data preparation and preprocessing: we extracted the expression data of different development trajectory states and removed genes with mean cell expression values less than 0.01; (2) estimating the random IC scores by permuting the expression values of genes: we applied the "Simulation_Ic" function to calculate a random index of critical transition and randomly filtered 300 genes and ran it 1000 times to calculate IC scores for each state of every cell subset; (3) filtering a multi-state dataset based on a cutoff value for standard deviation per state and optimization: we used the "optimize.sd_selection" function to select the top 1% transcripts and randomly selected 80% of samples and calculated it 100 times to select the filtered expression dataset matrix with the highest standard deviation; and (4) building node networks: We applied the "getNetwork" function to construct a correlation network for each trajectory state. Pearson's coefficient analysis was used to identify significantly correlated genes ($p < 0.1$) in the co-expression network. Then, we used the "getCluster_methods" function to extract genes from each subnetwork (module). (5) We identified critical transition signals (CTSs) used in the DNB module. We calculated the module key index (MCI) for each trajectory state in the dataset using the "getMCI" function and used the "getMaxMCImember" function to filter out the top 3 modules in each trajectory state. (6) Finding the tipping point and evaluating the CTS: We first recorded the maximum MCI of candidate modules at different trajectory states, and then extracted the top 2 modules according to the MCI scores. After this, we estimated the correlation matrix using the "cor.shrink" function, followed by a recalculation of the critical transition random index (IC) using the "simulation_Ic" function for each module gene; (7) verifying using the IC score: We estimated the random IC scores by permutating the expression values of genes and returned to the observed IC (red) and simulated IC scores (gray) for a given state. Then, we estimated the random IC scores by randomly shuffling the cell labels. We evaluated the random score from the shuffling sample labels and excluded natural sample correlations within phenotypic states (cell subsets) and returned the score to the IC of observed (red) and simulated IC scores (gray) for a given state.

2.5. Gene Set Variation Analysis (GSVA)

Gene set variation analysis (GSVA) is a nonparametric and unsupervised method for estimating the enrichment of gene sets in transcriptomic data [23]. By performing comprehensive scoring on the gene sets of interest, GSVA converts changes at the gene level to those at the pathway level, subsequently determining the biological functions of the sample. In this study, we employed the GSVA algorithm to score the identified DNB module gene sets and to evaluate the potential biological function changes across different modules.

2.6. CellChat Analysis

We employed the "CellChat" R package (v1.6.1) for the cell interaction analysis [24]. We analyzed the possible interactions among epithelial subgroups based on the data of ligand–receptor pair data in the CellChatDB.

2.7. Weighted Correlation Network Analysis (WGCNA)

We applied the "WGCNA" R package to perform WGCNA according to the following steps [25]. (1) Define the similarity matrix. (2) Select the weight coefficient $\beta = 12$ and convert the similarity matrix into an adjacency matrix. (3) Convert the adjacency matrix into a topological overlap matrix (TOM). (4) Perform hierarchical clustering of data based on the TOM to obtain a hierarchical clustering tree. (5) Use the dynamic tree-cutting method to identify modules from the hierarchical clustering tree. (6) Calculate the module eigengenes (MEs) for each module, where MEs represent the overall expression level of the module. We calculated the Pearson correlation coefficient between the MEs of each module, and the Pearson correlation coefficient was defined as the average distance between MEs of each module. We applied the average linkage hierarchical clustering method to cluster all MEs of the modules, with a minimum value (genome) set to 100 and combined modules with high similarity to obtain a co-expression network.

2.8. Gene Enrichment Analysis

We downloaded a dataset related to the cancer hallmark and gene oncology (GO) pathway from the MisgDB website (https://www.gsea-msigdb.org/gsea/msigdb, access on 23 February 2024) [26]. The "clusterProfiler" R package [27] was used to perform the gene pathway enrichment analysis.

2.9. PPI and Fuzzy Clustering

To assess the strength of the correlations between genes in the DNB module, we downloaded protein–protein interaction pairs from Homo sapiens from the STRING database and filtered them for those with combined scores greater than 400, constructing a DNB module-based interaction network. We then selected all the interacting genes from the network. Considering the difficulty in separating gene expression trends, we used a noise-robust soft clustering method [28]. We applied a fuzzy c-means clustering method (FCM) based on the time trend to classify genes with similar expression patterns into clusters. The R package "Mfuzz" was employed to conduct analysis. The clustering parameter was set to 6.

2.10. Construction of the Risk Prediction Model and Nomogram

We used the following formula to calculate the risk score for each patient. "RiskScore = gene Exp1 $\times$ β1 + gene Exp2 $\times$ β2 + gene Exp3 $\times$ β3 + . . . + gene Expi $\times$ βi".

In the formula, "gene Expi" refers to the gene expression level, while β refers to the correlation coefficient of ligand–receptor pairs in the multivariable Cox regression analysis. We applied the "surv_cutpoint" function to evaluate thresholds and divided patients into "high-risk" and "low-risk" groups and used the Kaplan–Meier method to plot survival curves for prognostic analysis. The log-rank test was performed to determine the significance of the differences. Patient survival curves and risk maps were visualized by the R packages "survminer" and "ggrisk" [29,30]. The ROC curves were plotted using the "survROC" R package.

To further evaluate the robustness of the risk prediction model, we combined patient information with detailed clinical and pathological outcomes including age, Gleason score, and pathological tumor stage from the TCGA dataset to construct a nomogram evaluation model [31]. The serum PSA level was excluded, as there were few patients whose preoperative PSA level was high (PSA > 10 ng/mL). All clinical and pathological characteristics were considered as categorical variables for evaluation via the nomogram analysis.

2.11. Immunohistochemistry (IHC)

IHC staining was performed on the samples from 20 hormone-sensitive PC patients and 10 CRPC patients. The study was approved by the Institutional Review Board of the School of Life Sciences, Central South University (approval number: IRB 2024-1-43), and compliant with recommendations from the Declaration of Helsinki for biomedical research involving human subjects. The samples were fixed in 4% neutral buffered paraformaldehyde, embedded in paraffin, and cut into 5 μm slices. After deparaffinization, hydration, and antigen retrieval, these sections were incubated with a corresponding primary antibody, followed by incubation with a biotinylated secondary antibody. Sample tissues were probed with antibodies against SCD, ALDH1A1, NARS2, and NFXL1 at a 1:100 dilution following standard IHC protocol. The primary antibodies were anti-SCD (, dilution 1:100, Abcam, Cambridge, MA, USA), anti-ALDH1A1 (dilution 1:100, Proteintech, Wuhan China), anti-NARS2 (dilution 1:100, Abcam, Cambridge, MA, USA), and anti-NFXL1 (dilution 1:100, Abcam, Cambridge, MA, USA). For cell visualization and imaging, the KF-PRO-400-HI high-throughput digital pathology slide scanner (KFBio Inc., Ningbo, Zhejiang, China) was used. For the immunoreactive score of each gene, a staining index (values, 0–12) was determined by multiplying the score for staining intensity with the score for positive area. The intensity of staining was scored as follows: 0, negative; 1, weak; 2, moderate; and 3, strong. The frequency of positive cells was defined as follows: 0, less than 5%; 1, 5% to 25%; 2, 26% to 50%; 3, 51% to 75%; and 4, greater than 75%. When the staining was heterogeneous, each component was scored independently and summed for the results. For example, a specimen containing 80% tumor cells with moderate intensity ($4 \times 2 = 8$) and another 20% tumor cells with weak intensity ($1 \times 1 = 1$) received a final score of $8 + 1 = 9$. For statistical analysis, scores of 0 to 7 were considered low expression and scores of 8 to 12 were considered high expression. The protein expression was scored by two independent pathologists who lacked prior knowledge of the patients' clinicopathological characteristics (double-blinded). In cases of discrepant results, the values were discussed until an agreement was reached.

2.12. Statistical Analysis

All data analyses were conducted on the R platform (version 4.3.0). Student's t-test or the Wilcoxon rank-sum test were used to compare continuous variables between two subgroups. One-way ANOVA or the Kruskal–Wallis test was used to compare differences among the three groups. Pearson correlation was used to assess the correlation between normally distributed variables, while Spearman correlation was used to analyze nonnormally distributed variables. The Benjamini and Hochberg (BH) method was applied to estimate the false discovery rate of multiple tests. The "survminer" R package [32] was used to perform Kaplan–Meier analysis and log-rank tests to evaluate survival differences among groups.

3. Results

3.1. Segmentation and Trajectory Inference of CRPC Epithelial Cells

Epithelial cells play vital roles in cancer tissues, and changes in epithelial cells in tumor tissues often suggest the occurrence and progression of cancer. To study the features of the epithelial cell group of patients with castration-resistant prostate cancer (CRPC), scRNA-seq profiles of 23,987 cells were collected. The samples of six CRPC patients from the

GSE137829 dataset were merged. The R package "Seurat(V4.0)" was employed to process scRNA-seq data and annotate the cell type. Furthermore, we applied the "FindCluster" function to select an optimal cell resolution of 0.5 for clustering, and obtained a total of 21 clusters (Figure 2A,B). Then, 21 clusters were manually annotated into 10 types of cells by different cell markers (CD4 T cells, CD8T cells, B cells, plasma cells, myeloid cells, mast cells, epithelial cells, endothelial cells, fibroblasts, and pericytes) (Figure 2D). The expression of cell marker genes is shown in Figure 2C. We found that the percentage of each type of cell subtype among the sample of each patient was roughly the same in the dataset, and the most prominent subtype is epithelial cells. Endothelial cells and fibroblasts accounted for a greater proportion of cells in some patients (Figure 2E).

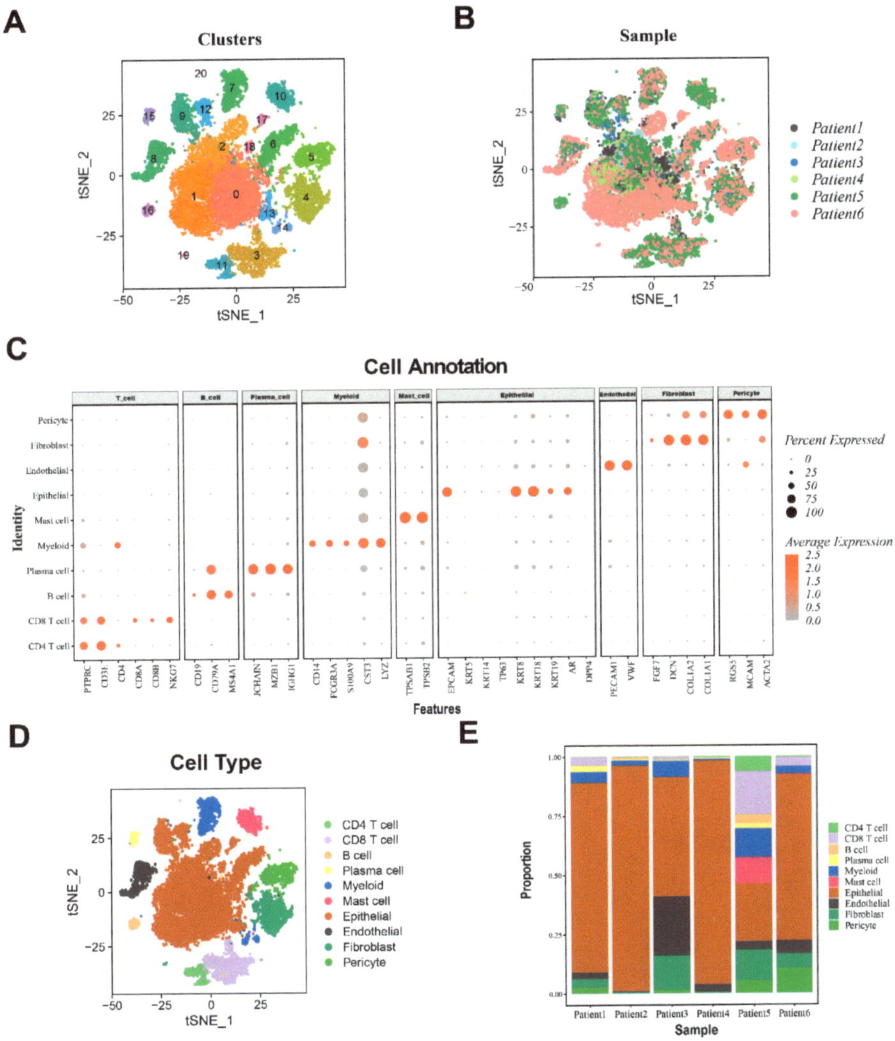

Figure 2. Ten cell clusters with different annotations based on CRPC scRNA-seq data, revealing cellular heterogeneity in CRPC. (**A**,**B**) Dimensionality reduction based on t-SNE algorithm and the distribution of 6 CRPC samples from GSE137829 dataset and 21 clusters were acquired; (**C**) expression level of marker genes in each cell cluster; (**D**) cell cluster annotation based on the composition of marker genes; and (**E**) proportion of different cell types in each sample.

To analyze the cytodifferentiation characteristics of epithelial cells in patients with CRPC, the "subset" function was applied to select 11,143 epithelial cells and reclusters. The "Findcluster" function with resolution set to 1.2 was used for clustering, resulting in 15 clusters (Figure S1A). The epithelial cells were reannotated into four cell types by epithelial cell subgroup markers (Figure 3A) (basal cells, luminal cells, neuroendocrine cells, and other cells), in which clusters 0, 1, 2, 3, 5, 7, 9, 10, 11, 12, 13, and 14 were labeled as luminal cells, while cluster 4 was labeled as other cells. Cluster 6 was labeled as neuroendocrine cells and cluster 8 was labeled as basal cells. The cell marker gene expression levels are shown in Figure 3C. The proportions of epithelial cell subgroups were similar across different samples, with the most significant proportion being the luminal subgroup (Figure 3B). Luminal cells have been identified as the primary cell type associated with prostate carcinogenesis and development [33].

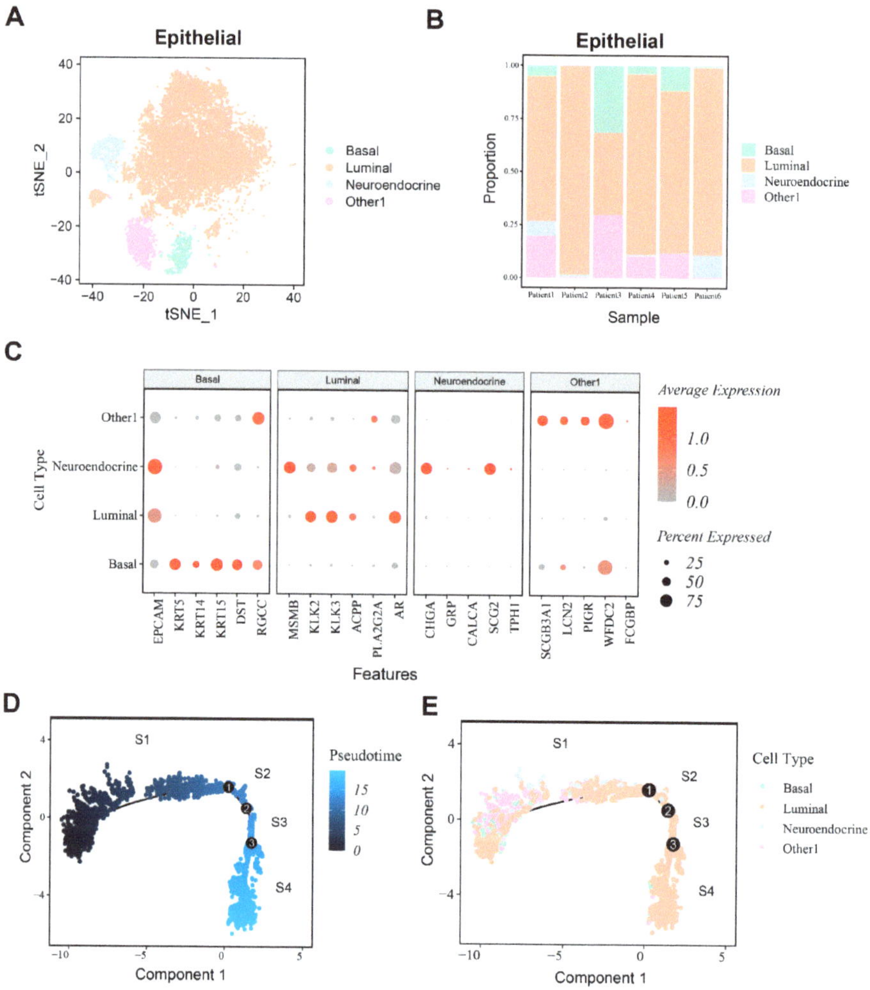

Figure 3. Cell annotation and construction of differentiation trajectories in epithelial cells based on single cell sequence data. (**A**) Annotating epithelial cells according to marker genes; (**B**) proportion of epithelial cell subgroups in different samples; (**C**) marker gene expression level of each epithelial cell subgroup; (**D**) pseudotime differentiation trajectories of epithelial cells; and (**E**) differentiation trajectory states of different subgroups.

To better understand the molecular mechanism underlying the occurrence of castration resistance, we applied the R package "Monocle2" to construct a developmental trajectory of CRPC epithelial cells. The trajectory demonstrates a continuous transition process of cellular differentiation states in epithelial cells, revealing the dynamic process of epithelial cell development. The results showed the state of cellular pseudotime development, differentiation states, and the sample distribution among different epithelial subtypes (Figures 3D,E and S1B). The trajectory was divided into four parts (S1, S2, S3, and S4) based on the trajectory nodes. According to a previous study [33], three important gene markers (TACSTD2, KRT4, and PSCA) originating from luminal cells were expressed in deteriorating trajectories (Figure S1C) and can be recognized as the beginning of pseudotime development. The level of androgen receptors (ARs), an important marker of castration-resistant prostate cancer, gradually increases with the continuous differentiation of epithelial cells (Figure S1D), suggesting that the differentiated cells of tumor epithelial cells gradually develop into castration-resistant cells [34].

3.2. *Prediction of Key Transition Subgroups and Gene Modules in Epithelial Cells*

The function of epithelial cells at different stages may change with the cellular differentiation of epithelial cells. We applied dynamic network biomarker (DNB) methods to clarify the status of epithelial cells in prostate cancer patients who develop castration resistance after androgen deprivation therapy (ADT). The "BioTIP" package was used to perform the DNB analysis. First, we identified critical tipping points of cellular differentiation states in different epithelial cells, calculated the corresponding critical transition random index (IC scores), and filtered the expression spectral matrix. Through the correlation analysis, we constructed a gene co-expression network module across various differentiated cellular states and identified the hypothesized critical transition signals (CTSs) in CRPC epithelial cells (Figure 4A). Next, we estimated the gene correlation matrix for each module and recalculated the critical transition random index by randomly perturbing the gene tags (Figure 4B,C) and sample tags (Figure 4D,E). Finally, the significance of different modules was calculated. The most significant transition signal conversion DNB module was identified in the cellular differentiation state S2. The DNB module consists of 32 genes, and through gene expression analysis, it was discovered that all genes in the module have a greater expression level than genes in other epithelial cell subgroups (Figure 4F).

To clarify the functional differences in the DNB module across different epithelial cell differentiation states, we applied the GSVA (gene set variation analysis) method to calculate the enrichment matrix for the GO terms and the cancer hallmark pathways. The results showed that the DNB module gene sets were mainly enriched in androgen-related GO pathways, including the androgen metabolic signaling pathway, the androgen receptor signaling pathway, and the androgen biosynthetic process (Figure 4G). Similarly, the DNB module showed significantly greater gene expression in the androgen response, protein secretion, and mTORC1 signaling pathways of the cancer hallmark (Figure 4H,I), which revealed that the DNB module may play a crucial role in transition signals during the development and occurrence of CRPC in patients. Therefore, it is likely that this epithelial cell subgroup possesses a dynamic gene expression module with key transitional state functions and unique expression patterns.

3.3. *Cellular Communication in Key Subgroups of Epithelial Cells*

We explored differences in the functions of epithelial cells in critical transition states based on CRPC scRNA-seq data. First, based on the results of epithelial cell differentiation, the "CellChat" R package was applied to conduct a cellular communication analysis in epithelial cells in both the S2 and S1 stages. The total number and strength of epithelial cells in S2 were slightly greater than those in S1 (Figures 5A and S2A). Further analysis was conducted to clarify the communication patterns between epithelial cells and other cell subsets. The results revealed that the number and strength of pericyte cells and epithelial and fibroblast cells that communicated with epithelial cells were increased in the S2 subgroup (Figures 5B and S2B).

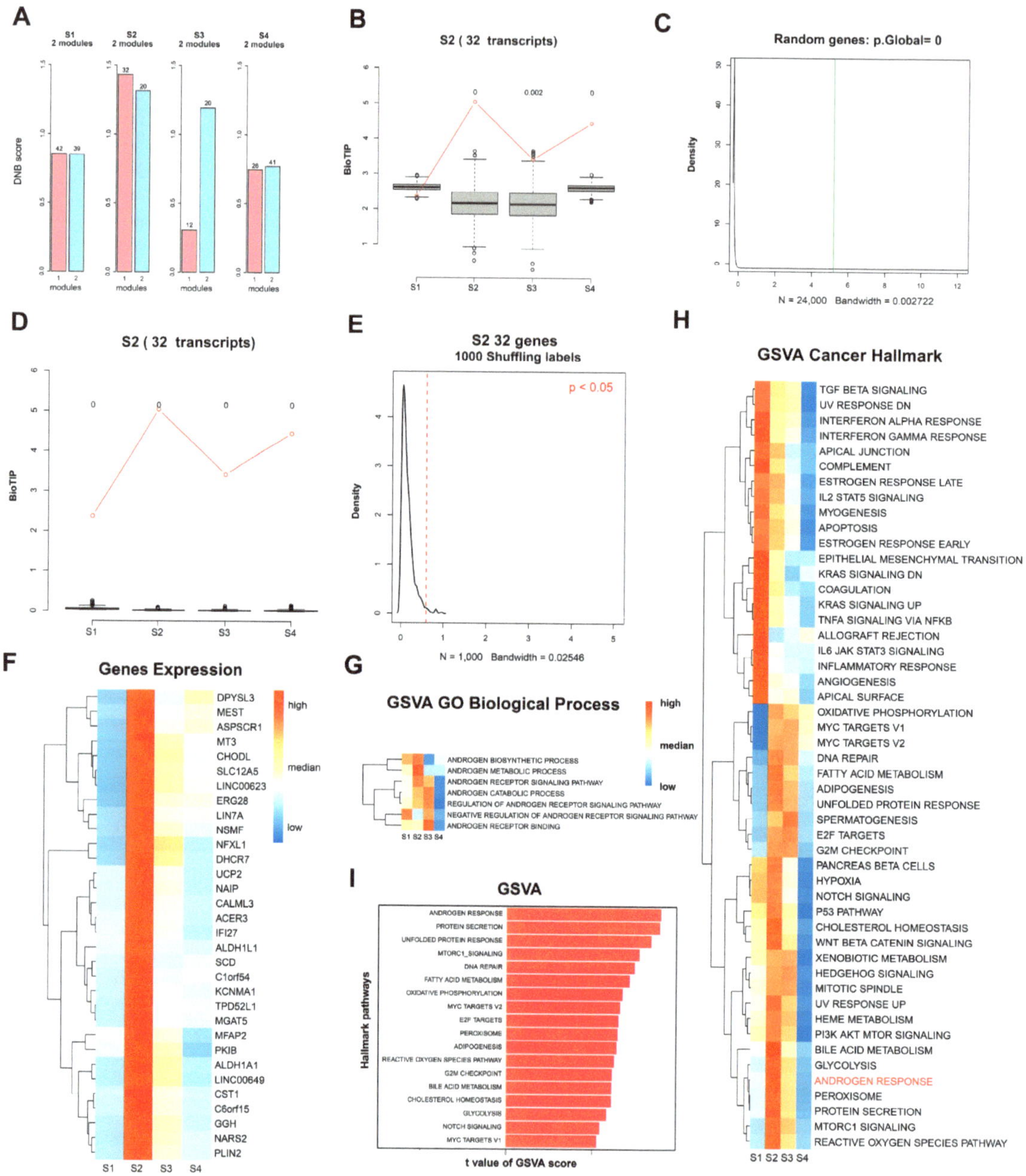

Figure 4. Key transformed cell subgroups and gene modules of epithelial cells. (**A**) Assumed key transforming signal in different cellular differentiation states in epithelial cells. (**B**,**C**) Random score of key transforming signals after shuffling gene labels; (**D**,**E**) random score of key transforming signals after shuffling sample labels; (**F**) expression of key transforming module genes in different epithelial cell states; (**G**) GO BP enrichment state of key transforming module genes in different epithelial cell states; and (**H**,**I**) cancer hallmark enrichment and significance of key transforming module genes in different subgroups of epithelial cells.

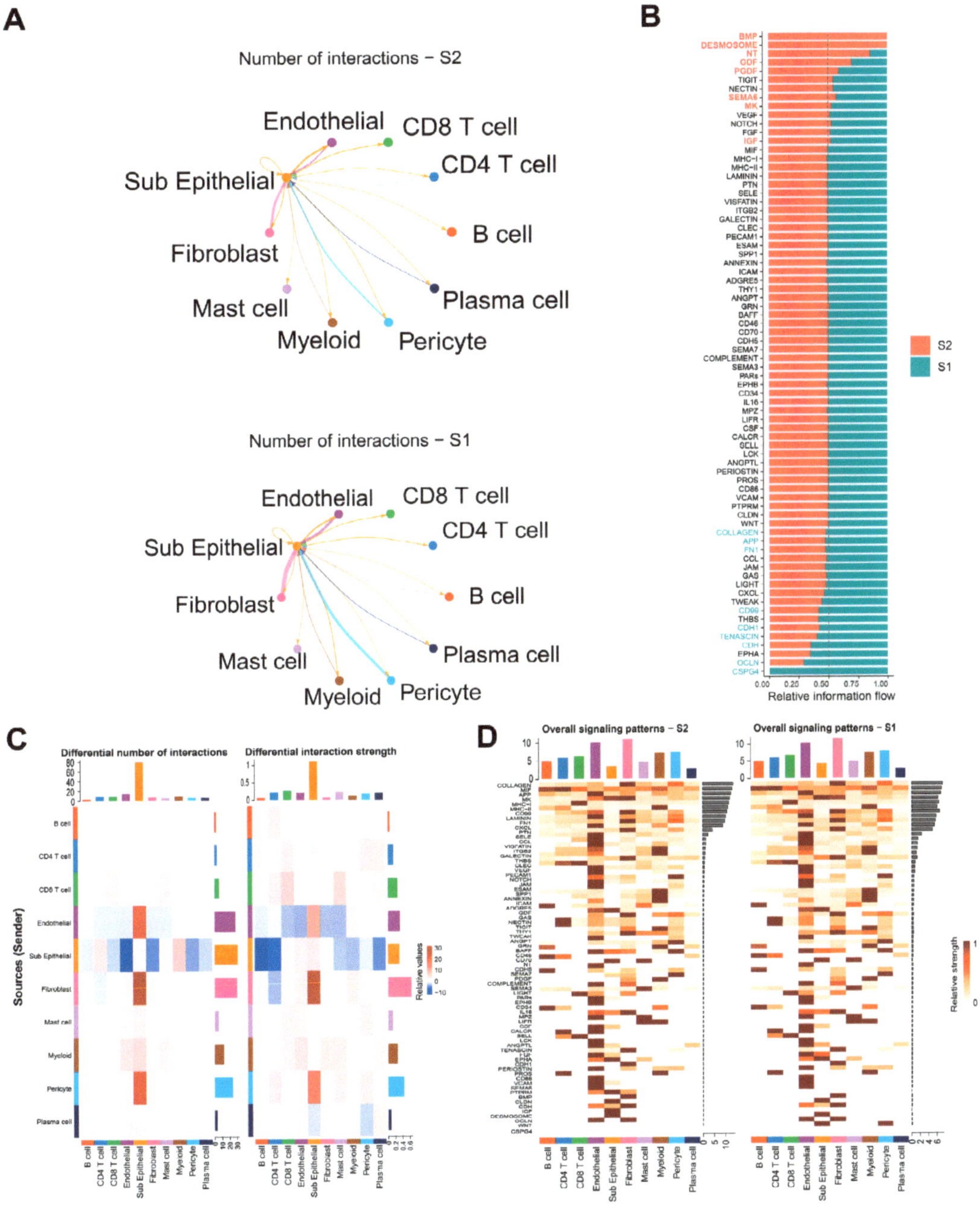

Figure 5. Heterogeneity in cell communication of S1 and S2 epithelial cells in CRPC. (**A**) Cell communication network of S1 and S2 epithelial cells with other cell types (the S2 group is at the top and the S1 group is at the bottom. The size of the spot indicates the number of cells). (**B**) Comparison of the communication strength in different signaling pathways in S1 and S2 epithelial cells. The color "red" on the vertical axis indicates that cell communication was more active in S2 and the color "blue" indicates cell communication was more active in S1. The color "black" indicates that there was no

significance between the two groups. (**C**) Cell communication number and strength among different cell types. The color indicates the difference. The color "red" indicates cell communication was more active in S2 and the color "blue" indicates that cell communication was more active in S1. The bar chart on the right indicates that the outgoing signal and the bar chart on the top indicates the incoming signal. (**D**) Heatmap of signaling pathway strength in epithelial cells in the S1 and S2 groups.

Subsequently, we examined the cellular communication pathways of S2 and S1 epithelial cells. After performing dimensionality reduction based on functional similarity among different signaling pathways, we discovered that pathways such as EPHA1, SEMA6, and others exhibited the most significant functional differences between the two groups (Figure S2C,D). SEMA6 can promote angiogenesis [35]. The EPHA pathway contributes to the stimulation of ARs through inducing expression of proto-oncogenes [36], and could increase the invasion of CRPC [37,38].

Moreover, we compared the differences in cell communication between the S2 epithelial cell subgroups and other cell types and found that the increased signal intensity occurred mainly in signaling pathways such as BMP, DESMOSOME, GDF, and PGDF (Figure 5C). To further explore differences in these signaling pathways, we investigated pathway alterations between the two groups. The BMP signaling pathway mainly involved the transduction of signals from fibroblasts in the S2 subgroup to epithelial cells, whereas the DESMOSOME signaling pathway mainly changed in the internal signaling within the epithelial cells in the S2 subgroup. Changes in the GDF signaling pathway were mainly related to intercellular signaling between S2 epithelial cells, fibroblasts, and endothelial cells. Changes in the PGDF signaling pathway primarily occurred in the signal transmission from epithelial cells to fibroblasts and pericytes within the S2 subgroup (Figures 5D and S2E,F). The BMP signaling pathway can be involved in various developmental processes, including cell proliferation, cellular differentiation, apoptosis, and angiogenesis [39], and the DESMOSOME signaling pathway can stimulate and enhance cell adhesion [40]. Finally, we observed specific differential ligand–receptor interactions between the two groups, where 75-fold greater numbers of ligand–receptor interactions were found in ligands between epithelial cells from group 1 (S1) and group 2 (S2), which act on other cells. The expression of MDK- and APP-related ligand–receptors in the S2 subgroups significantly increased in epithelial cells and most of the other cells, whereas the expression of MIF and other ligand–receptors significantly decreased in epithelial cells and most of the other cells (Figure 6A,B). The MDK signaling pathway plays a role in driving castration resistance and has been previously identified in CTCs [41]. The APP signaling pathway participates in the regulation of androgen and is related to the binding of the AR gene [42]. However, the MIF signaling pathway can inhibit prostate cell growth, invasion, and the inflammatory response [43]. Cell communication of COL1A1 and other ligand-receptors discovered in other cell subgroups significantly increasd in ligand–receptors in the lower score group, while MDK ligand–receptors significantly decreased (Figure 6C,D).

To further explore the significance of S2 epithelial cells in cellular communication, we applied "CellChat" analysis to the subgroups of epithelial cells from S1 to S4. We found that the subset of S2 epithelial cells had relatively stronger interactions with pericytes and fibroblasts in the PGDF signaling pathway than with the other subsets of epithelial cells (Figure S2F), whereas the FGF signaling pathway was mediated by fibroblasts on S2 epithelial cells (Figure S2G). The PGDF signaling pathway is primarily composed of platelet-derived growth factor-related genes and is a crucial regulatory factor for mesenchymal cells. These genes are often expressed in relation to aggressiveness, tumor size, chemotherapy resistance, and the clinical recurrence of prostate cancer [44,45]. The fibroblast growth factor signaling pathway is mainly composed of genes related to fibroblast growth factors, which can influence the progression of prostate cancer through the interactions between epithelial and stromal components [46]. By identifying the unique communication within the subgroup of S2 epithelial cells, our results suggested changes in related signaling pathways and their potential impact on tumor progression and recurrence.

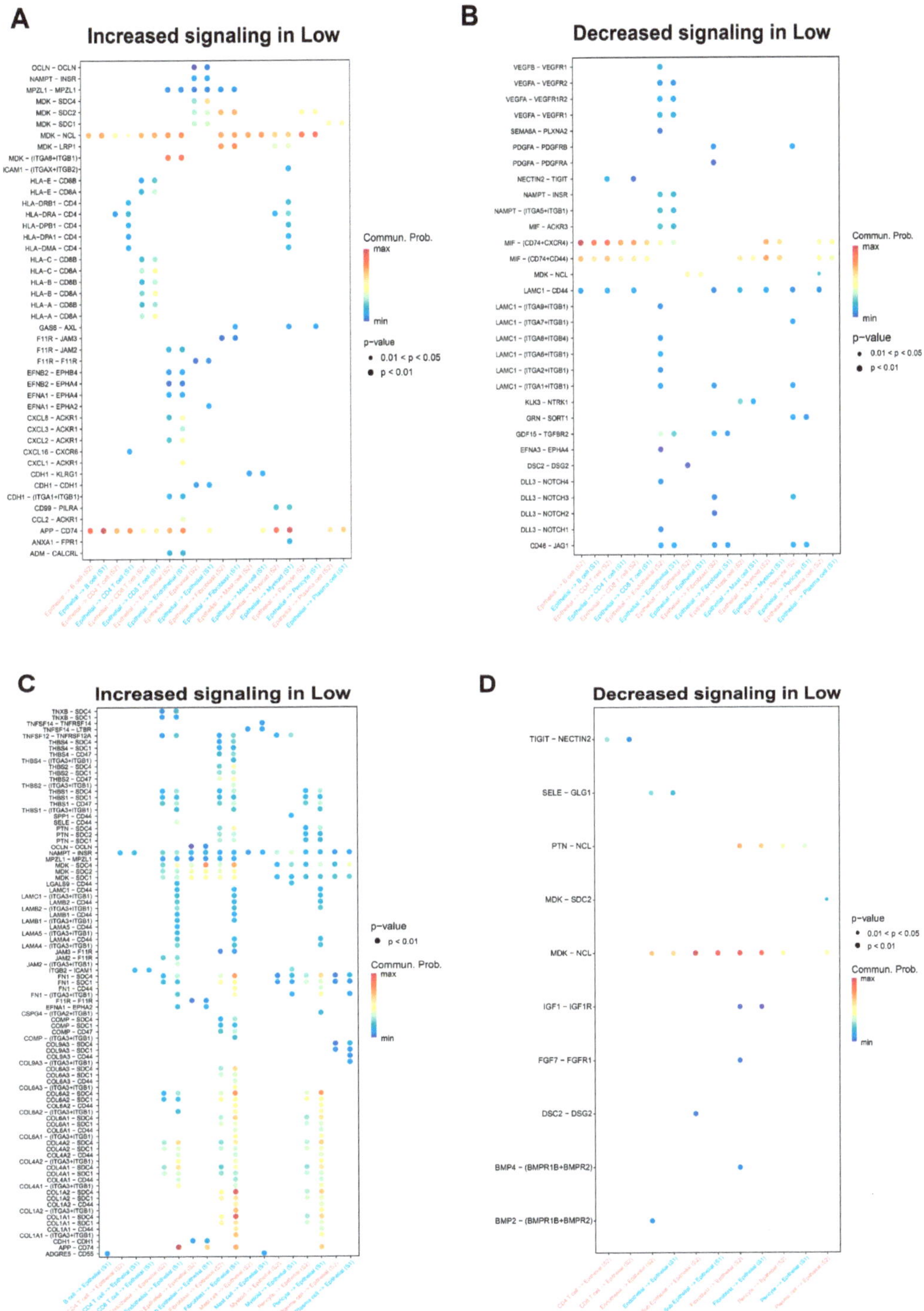

Figure 6. Ligand–receptor differences between S1 and S2 epithelial cells in CRPC. (**A**,**B**) Differences in functional ligand–receptor interactions in epithelial cells in S1 and S2 groups to other cell subgroups.

The color "red" on the horizontal axis indicates communication of epithelial cells in the S2 group and the color "cyan" indicates communication of epithelial cells in the S1 group. The color of the spot indicates the cellular communication probability and the size of the spot indicates the significance of the p value. (**C**,**D**) Differences in functional ligand–receptors of other cell subgroups to epithelial cells in the S1 and S2 groups. The color "red" on the horizontal axis indicates communication of epithelial cells in the S2 group and color "cyan" indicates communication of epithelial cells in the S1 group. The color of the spot indicates the cellular communication probability and the size of the spot indicates the significance of the p value.

3.4. Construction of the Co-Expressed Gene Module Associated with Androgen Regulation via Bulk RNA-Seq of CRPC Cells

The interactions between genes resemble cellular interactions. To explore the potential associations between gene expression patterns in CRPC patients, we applied the WGCNA method to further analyze the gene co-expression profiles in CRPC patients. First, we obtained two gene expression datasets of prostate cancer patients, GSE70770 and GSE80609, from the GEO database. After performing data preprocessing based on clinical information labels, the gene expression profiles of CRPC patients were extracted from two datasets. Next, we performed the weighted gene co-expression network analysis (WGCNA) on the two datasets. In this study, the co-expression network was classified as an unstructured network, and we calculated the optimal soft threshold for near neighbors. The expression matrix was converted into a neighbor matrix, and then the neighbor matrix was transformed into a topological matrix. Based on this topological matrix, the averaging linkage clustering method was used to cluster genes. Following the standard of the hybrid dynamic shear tree, the number of genes in the module was set to 100 as the minimum number in each module. We performed a clustering analysis on the modules and merged modules with close distances into new modules. Finally, 15 module clusters were identified in GSE70770 (Figures 7A and S3A) and 13 module clusters were identified in GSE80609 (Figures 7B and S3D–F). Each module consisted of genes with similar expression patterns.

After performing a cancer hallmark pathway enrichment analysis on the two datasets, we discovered that the "midnightblue" module in the GSE70770 dataset and the "blue" module in the GSE80609 dataset were significantly enriched in the androgen response hallmark signaling pathway and protein secretion hallmark signaling pathway (Figure 7C,D). It will stimulate the secretion of androgen and proteins in cancer tissues in the corresponding cancerous tissue at the same time. This may increase the probability of immune evasion of the epithelial cells, which suggests that these two modules may be potentially associated with tumorigenesis and tumor development in CRPC [47].

3.5. Identification of Key Biomarkers for Castration Resistance in PCa

To explore the interactions among DNB module genes and their effects on various biological processes, we combined protein interaction information in STRING and constructed a PPI network of the DNB module, where 30 genes in the DNB module have interacted with other genes. Then, we extracted genes from the protein interaction network and applied the soft clustering algorithm to classify the gene sets according to the expression trend in the DNB module and its neighboring gene classification (Figure 8A). The results showed that cluster 2 and cluster 4 gene sets had greater expression changes in the S2 epithelial cell subgroup. Subsequently, we combined the enrichment analysis outcomes of the two cluster gene sets; the cluster 2 gene set was more likely to be enriched in cancer-related pathways such as DNA repairment and oxidative phosphorylation (Figure S4A). The cluster 4 gene set was more likely to be enriched in cancer-related pathways such as androgen response pathways (Figure 8B). Moreover, the GO enrichment analysis showed that the cluster 4 gene set was significantly correlated with numerous metabolic and biosynthetic processes (Figure S4B). The results revealed that the cluster 4 gene set plays an important role in the process of castration resistance in prostate cancer (Figure 8C).

Combining our findings from the WGCNA of bulk RNA-seq datasets, we identified a set of gene modules associated with androgen-responsive pathways. In parallel, we applied the DNB method to clarify the condition of epithelial cell subgroups in scRNA-seq datasets and found the cellular differentiation state S2 as the most significant transition signal conversion DNB module, which consists of 32 genes. We then explored the co-expression modules of the key transformations in the DNB module and the WGCNA module using the soft clustering analysis (R package "Mfuzz"), and finally identified four genes (*SCD*, *NARS2*, *ALDH1A1*, and *NFXL1*) that may be related to castration resistance development in PCa patients. On the one hand, studies have shown that the expression of *SCD* (stearoyl-CoA desaturase) has significantly increased, indicating *SCD* can be considered as a potential treatment target [48,49]. On the other hand, SCD can promote the proliferation of androgen receptor-positive LNCaP cells, enhance the transcriptional activity of ARs induced by dihydrotestosterone (DHT), and result in the increased expression of prostate-specific antigens (PSAs) and kallikrein-related peptidase 2 (*KLK2*) [50]. Aldehyde dehydrogenase 1 family member A1 (*ALDH1A1*) is not only a marker for malignant prostate stem cells but can also serve as a predictor of prognosis in PCa patients [51]. Its high expression is associated with the development of prostate cancer [52], suggesting that this gene may play a role in the progression of prostate cancer.

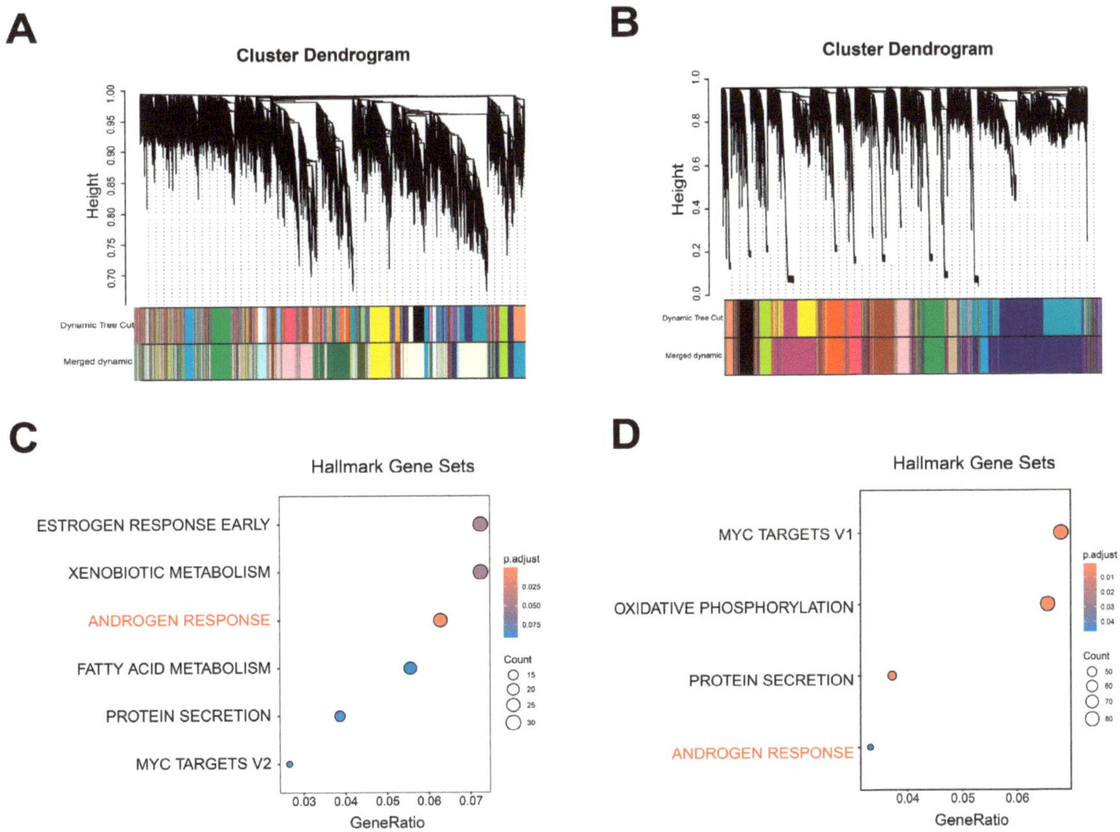

Figure 7. Identification of co-expression modules of androgen-related key genes based on CRPC bulk seq. data. (**A**,**B**) Cluster dendrogram of co-expression network modules in GSE70770 and GSE80609 (1-TOM). (**C**) GO analysis of "midnightblue" co-expressed gene modules in GSE70770. (**D**) GO analysis of "blue" co-expressed gene modules in GSE80609.

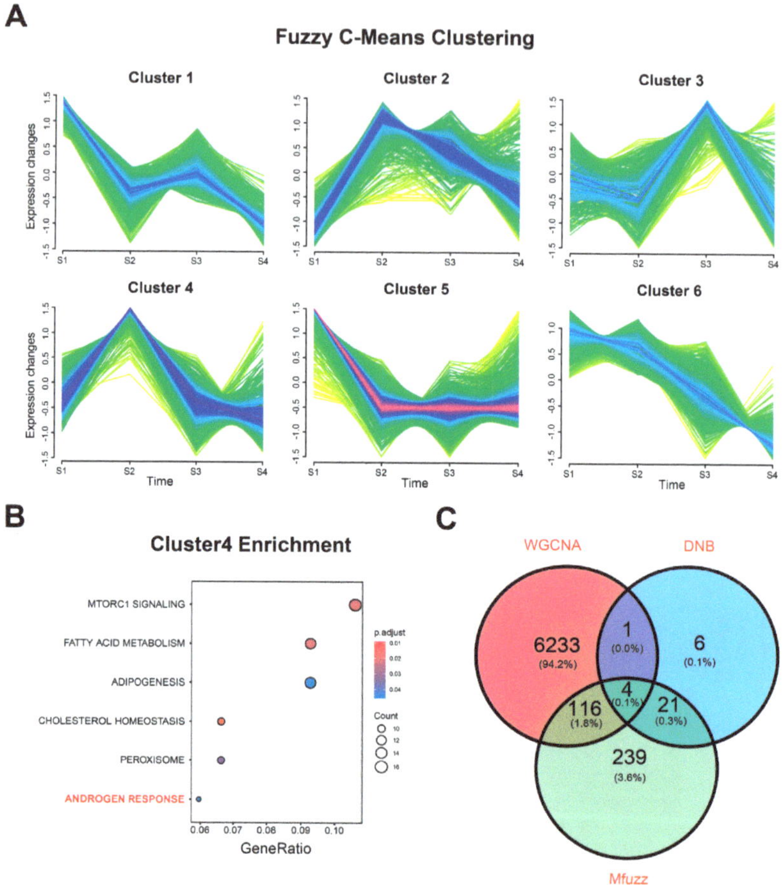

Figure 8. Fuzzy clustering and evaluation of key biomarkers in the key transformation subgroups of epithelial cells. (**A**) Using Mfuzz to clarify the dynamic change in neighboring genes in the key transforming signaling modules in different states of cytodifferentiation in epithelial cells. (**B**) Hallmark enrichment analysis of the cluster 4 gene set. (**C**) Intersection Venn plot of genes in the WGCNA, DNB, and soft clustering analysis.

3.6. Construction and Evaluation of the Prognostic Risk Model

To verify the progression-free interval (PFI) evaluation of gene status in the context of androgen deprivation therapy (ADT) for PCa patients, we performed a multivariable Cox regression analysis to fit the four genes (*SCD*, *NARS2*, *ALDH1A1*, and *NFXL1*) into an initial model. For each patient, the risk score (Figure 9A) was calculated by multiplying the gene expression level by the corresponding regression coefficients derived from the multivariable Cox regression model. The risk score in this case is = (0.3111 × *ALDH1A1* expression level) + (0.0087 × *SCD* expression level) and (−0.10137 × *NARS2* expression level) + (−0.4833 × *NFXL1* expression level). In the TCGA training cohort, a best-fitting threshold was applied to group patients into low- and high-risk groups. The Kaplan–Meier analysis results showed that patients in the low-risk group had significantly longer progression-free intervals (PFIs) than those in the high-risk group (Figure 9B). In the GSE111177 validation cohort, we used the same risk score model to grade 20 patients on progression risk with the best cutoff value. By grouping patients into low- and high-risk groups, the Kaplan–Meier analysis indicated that the high-risk group had shorter recurrence times (Figure 9C).

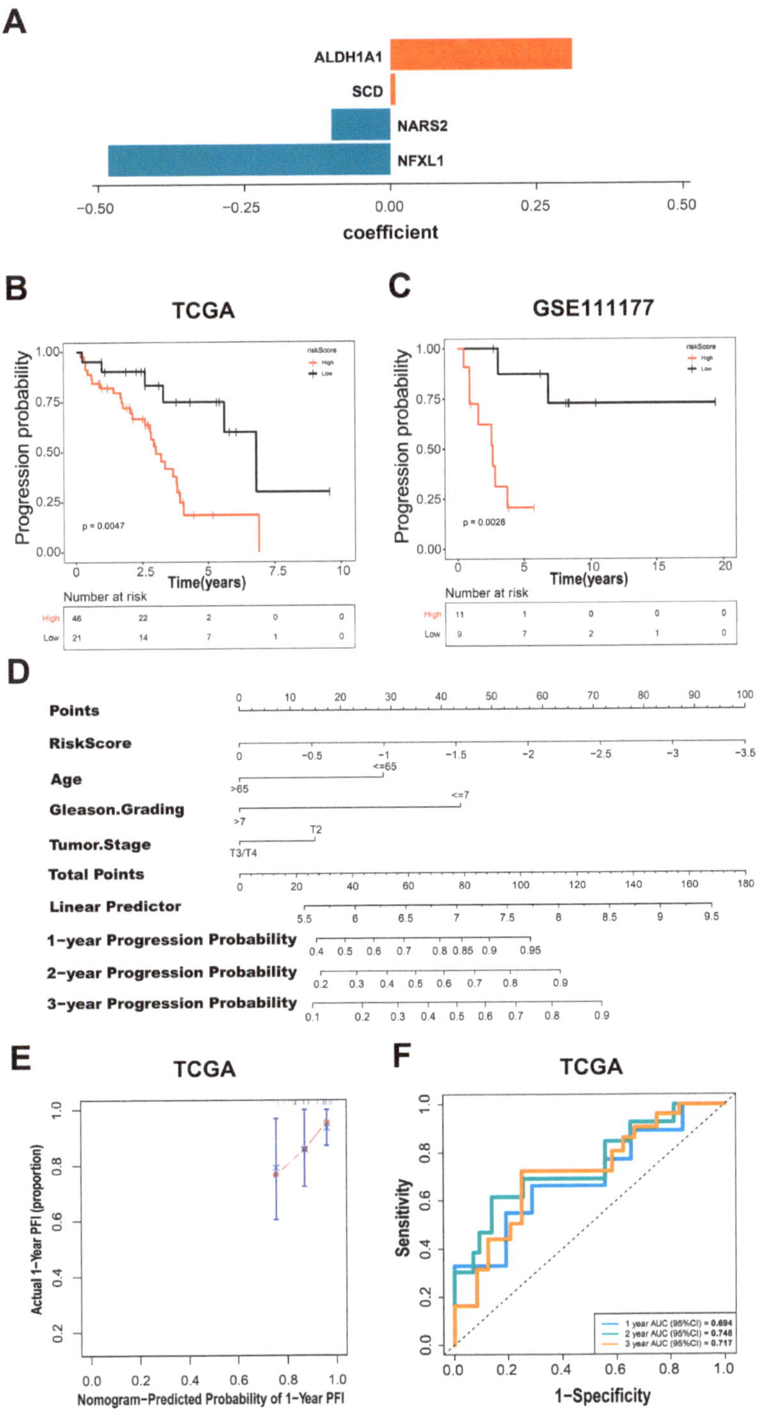

Figure 9. Key transformed cell subgroups and gene modules of epithelial cells. (**A**) Risk score of the 4 key biomarkers. (**B**) Kaplan–Meier curve of the TCGA training cohort. (**C**) Kaplan–Meier curve of the

GSE111177 validation cohort. (**D**) A nomogram combining the risk score, age, Gleason grade, and tumor stage was developed to predict the 1-, 2-, and 3-year PFIs of patients who underwent ADT in the TCGA cohort. (**E**) A 1-year calibration analysis of the TCGA cohort nomogram. (**F**) ROC curves of multiple time points (1 year, 2 years, 3 years) of the PFI in the TCGA cohort.

To develop a quantitative method for predicting the progression-free interval (PFI), we combined the progression risk score with other clinicopathological characteristics, including the age at diagnosis, Gleason score, and tumor stage at biopsy, in the TCGA training cohort. For each factor, we calculated a point and then obtained the total points for all factors to create the nomogram of the TCGA training cohort to evaluate the overall PFI rate. Additionally, we created receiver operating characteristic (ROC) curves and calibration curves to evaluate the reliability of the nomogram, which showed the relationship between clinical sensitivity and specificity across different cutoff points. We performed a Cox multivariate regression analysis on the clinical data and the risk score. The results showed that the risk score was an independent prognostic factor for the PFI in the TCGA dataset (hazard ratio (HR) = 2.71, 95% CI = 1.39 to 5.28, * $p < 0.05$). Based on the results of univariate and multivariate analyses, we constructed a nomogram model combining clinical characteristics and the risk score (Figure 9D). In the model, the risk score-based features had the greatest impact on survival prediction. As depicted in Figures 9E and S4C,D, the 1-, 2-, and 3-year survival nomogram calibration curves were in good agreement with the standard curve. Furthermore, the areas under the ROC curves (AUCs) for the 1-year, 2-year, and 3-year PFI predictions were 0.694, 0.748, and 0.717, respectively (Figure 9F). In summary, this risk model can reasonably predict the prognosis of prostate cancer patients treated with androgen deprivation therapy (ADT).

3.7. IHC Analysis

The IHC analysis showed that compared to HSPC samples, ALDH1A1 and SCD protein expression levels were significantly higher in CRPC patients, but the protein expression level of NARS2 was relatively lower Figure 10A,B. These data further validated the risk score of the genes in the nomogram and suggested that both ALDH1A1 and SCD can be risk factors, while NARS2 may be a protective factor in CRPC progression.

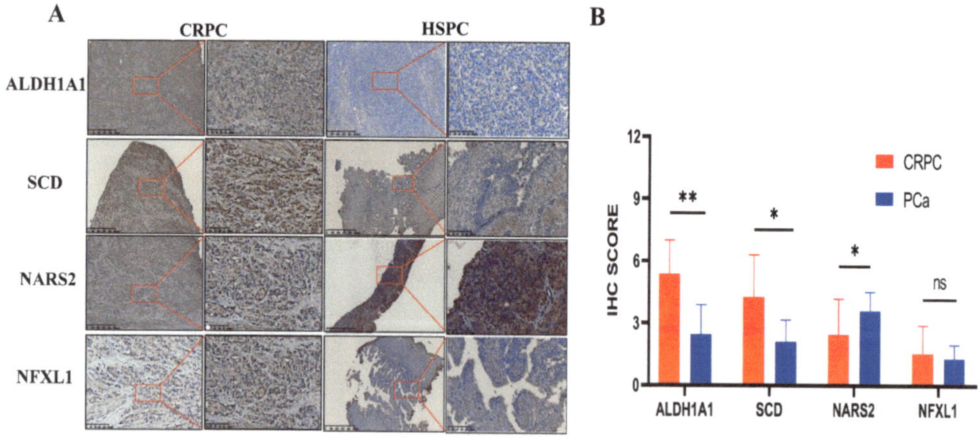

Figure 10. Representative photo images and histograms of ALDH1A1, SCD, NARS2, or NFXL1 protein expression levels in CRPC or HSPC sample tissues. (**A**) Representative IHC images showing high ALDH1A1 and SCD expression in CRPC tissue and high NARS2 expression in HSPC tissue. (**B**) Histograms of ALDH1A1, SCD, NARS2, and NFXL1 expression levels. Scale bars, 625 µm and 100 µm. * $p < 0.05$, ** $p < 0.01$; ns, not significant.

4. Discussion

This study comprehensively analyzed key gene modules in CRPC cells through the integration of single-cell and bulk RNA sequencing data combined with the methods of DNBs, a WGCNA, and noise-robust soft clustering. By combining our findings from the DNB method in the scRNA-seq dataset and the WGCNA in bulk RNA-seq datasets, we identified a set of key biomarkers associated with androgen-related pathways, including four key genes (SCD, NARS2, ALDH1A1, and NFXL1). Finally, we developed a risk prediction model combining the risk scores of the four key genes and other clinicopathological characteristics to assess the prognosis of patients treated with androgen deprivation therapy (ADT). The TCGA training cohort demonstrated that this risk score model reliably evaluated the PFI of prostate cancer patients treated with androgen deprivation therapy (ADT). The external GEO cohort (GSE111177) also validated the high performance of this risk prediction model. An IHC analysis was conducted to compare the protein expression level of the genes in CRPC and HSPC patient tissues. Overall, our findings show that SCD, NARS2, ALDH1A1, and NFXL1 are key biomarkers associated with androgen-related signaling pathways in CRPC.

Nomograms have been widely used by oncologists to generate prognostic information for individual patients due to their numerical probability and user-friendly interface [53–55]. In this study, a novel nomogram was established by integrating the risk score of four genes (SCD, ALDH1A1, NARS2, and NFXL1), age, Gleason score, and tumor stage, each of which was an independent prognostic factor according to the multivariate Cox regression analysis. This risk score model showed the ability to predict the prognosis of prostate cancer patients treated with androgen deprivation therapy (ADT). This risk score model is superior to traditional clinical factors for prognosis evaluation. First, it can quantify the risk score of PCa patients treated with ADT; a higher risk score represents a higher chance of tumor progression. Second, the predictive ability of the risk score was also better than that of other clinical variables, as exemplified by the highest AUC of 0.748 in the ROC curves. Third, the genes in the risk score model were identified by DNBs and the WGCNA and further filtered by univariate Cox and multivariate Cox regression analyses. This prognostic model relied on fewer genes but retained good performance for predicting patient prognosis. Fourth, the reliability of the risk score model was validated in the GSE111177 validation cohort. Overall, the proposed risk score model may be useful for the prognostic evaluation of prostate cancer patients treated with ADT.

With respect to the genes in the risk score model, we found that SCD and ALDH1A1 may be potential risk genes, while NARS2 and NFXL1 can be favorable prognostic genes. Stearoyl-CoA desaturase (SCD) is an enzyme that controls the synthesis of unsaturated fatty acids and is essential in breast and prostate cancer cells. SCD has been shown to promote proliferation and disease progression in prostate cancer by affecting cellular signaling cascades and modulating androgen receptor transactivation [56]. A functional genomics analysis showed that SCD inhibition altered the cellular lipid composition and impeded cell viability in the absence of exogenous lipids in prostate cancer cells. SCD inhibition also altered the cardiolipin composition, leading to the release of cytochrome C and the induction of apoptosis [57,58]. This is in line with our findings from the CellChat analysis that signaling pathways which are associated with apoptosis were more active in the subpopulation of S2 epithelial cells than in other cells. The aldehyde dehydrogenase 1A1 (ALDH1A1) isoform, which can positively regulate tumor cell survival in circulation, extravasation, and metastatic dissemination, is correlated with Aldefluor activity in PCa patients' tissue specimens [52]. PCa cells with high ALDH activity were previously characterized as a population with high metastasis-initiating properties [59]. ALDH1A isoform members have generated considerable interest, as ALDH1A1 has frequently been shown to be expressed in prostate cancer stem cell populations and may contribute to malignancy [60]. Recently, in vivo models confirmed that ALDH1A1 plays as a positive regulator of metastatic dissemination in the regulation of PCa metastases [52]. Higher ALDH1A1 and SCD expression was found in CRPC patients compared with HSPC groups in our IHC analysis, which was consistent with previous studies implying that higher SCD and ALDH1A1 expression levels were closely associated with CRPC progression [60,61].

NARS2 (asparaginyl-tRNA synthetase 2, also known as asnRS) is a nuclear gene encoding AsnRS that functions in mitochondria [62]. Biallelic mutations in NARS2 have been recently identified in patients with hearing impairment, intellectual disability, seizures, hypotonia, delayed neurodevelopment, renal dysfunction, and/or liver involvement [63]. NARS2 variants can disrupt the integrity of the mitochondrial protein synthesis, which is essential and fundamental for the mitochondrial oxidative phosphorylation complex, thus influencing cellular energy production [64]. Recently, research has shown that NARS2 has an important impact on immune resistance and drug resistance in melanoma [65]. Yet, few studies have demonstrated the role of NARS2 in prostate cancer. The IHC analysis in our study suggested that the protein expression level of NARS2 might decrease with the progression of CRPC. This may be one of the few studies to provide some evidence about the role of NARS2 in prostate cancer progression and yet, more in vivo analysis is needed to clarify the role of such a gene. The NFXL1 gene encodes an NFX-1-type nuclear zinc finger transcriptional repressor that is expressed in the cytoplasm [66]. NFXL1 is socalled because it is a paralog of the NF-X1 transcription factor which binds the X-box sequence of class II MHC genes [67]. This feature may be relevant according to a study that revealed an association between human leukocyte antigen (HLA) loci and specific language impairments [68]. However, until now, little is known about the function of the NFXL1 protein, nor have disorders been identified that arise from the mutation of this gene; additionally, no animal knockouts have been described.

At present, the prognostic value of these genes in the risk core model has been evaluated in PCa patients treated with ADT, which will hopefully provide novel biomarkers for future studies on molecular insights into PCa. Based on the risk score and clinical factors, including age, Gleason grade, and tumor stage, we constructed a nomogram for precisely evaluating the patients' 1-, 2-, and 3-year PFIs. A higher score calculated from this nomogram represents a greater chance of deterioration. Integrating the risk score with clinicopathological factors will improve the accuracy of PFI prediction. This may provide crucial information for the individual management of PCa patients treated with ADT. In general, this risk score model and nomogram will be helpful for evaluating the prognosis of PCa patients treated with ADT.

While general biomarkers usually treat patients on the basis that the disease has already occurred, DNBs are a group of biomolecules with strong dynamic correlation, and their molecular concentrations undergo dynamic changes rather than maintaining a constant value for the critical state [15]. DNBs reveal early warning signals of critical transitions before the disease deteriorates. Taking advantage of this technique, pathophysiological changes at different stages and periods can be dynamically displayed in a time series through DNBs, and stage-specific and severity-specific biomarkers of prostate cancer patients can be identified [69]. Thus, patients can be treated by adjusting the role of DNBs in disease through gene targeting therapy and other methods before the cancer progresses further. The key modules in DNBs may play an important role in the diagnosis and treatment of the disease. However, the specific application of DNBs still needs to be repeatedly validated by a series of both in vitro and in vivo experiments, and the development of such scientific tools and clinical practices still needs time to be explored and clarified. Our study found that DNBs and four genes (SCD, NARS2, ALDH1A1, and NFXL1), as relevant factors associated with androgen-related signaling pathways in prostate cancer cells, can be further used as indicators of PCa progression after androgen deprivation therapy. Although the prediction of related gene expression is not currently feasible, we anticipate that with the advancement of artificial intelligence and technological convergence, expression prediction can be achieved at an early stage with a combination of microarray chip technology.

5. Conclusions

In summary, we applied the DNB method to identify a set of biomarkers that change dramatically in the early stages of CRPC and can serve as indicators of the transition of prostate cancer cells from an androgen-dependent state to a castration-resistant state. In addition, the WGCNA method was used to identify core genes, and when combined with DNBs, four genes including SCD, NARS2, ALDH1A1, and NFXL1 were found to be associated with androgen-related signaling pathways in prostate cancer cells. A nomogram model was established by integrating the risk score of the four genes and other clinical characteristics and was verified to reasonably predict the progression-free interval (PFI) of prostate cancer patients treated with androgen deprivation therapy (ADT). High ALDH1A1 and SCD expression were significantly correlated with prostate cancer's transition from the hormone-sensitive to castration-resistant state. However, since the relevant analyses are based on public data sources (TCGA and GEO), limitations still exist. The expression level of each gene needs to be further validated in different prostate cancer cells. Animal models and more in vivo experiments will be designed to further explore the mechanisms of the biomarkers' mediation role in CRPC in our future research.

Supplementary Materials: The following supporting information can be downloaded at: https://www.mdpi.com/article/10.3390/biomedicines12092157/s1, Figure S1: Dimensionality reduction, cluster and differentiation trajectories of epithelial cells (A) Distribution of 21 clusters after reducing dimensionality of epithelial cells. (B) Trajectories of cytodifferentiation in epithelial cells in each sample. (C) Expression level of marker genes in differentiation trajectories luminal initial cells. (D) Expression level of AR gene in cellular differentiation trajectories (S1–S4 refer to different states of cellular differentiation in epithelial cells); Figure S2: Differences in cellular communication between epithelial cells and other cells in subgroup S1 and S2. (A) Total number (left) and strength (right) of cell communication between epithelial cells and other cells in subgroup S1, S2, including both incoming and outgoing signals. (B) Scattergram of signal strength in different types of cells in epithelial cells of S1 and S2 subgroups. (C) Pathway functional distance comparison of epithelial cells and other cells in S1 and S2 subgroups. (D) Heatmap of outgoing signaling patterns in different communication pathways of epithelial cells in S2 (left) and S1 subgroups (right). (E) Heatmap of incoming signaling patterns in different communication pathways of epithelial cells in S2 (left) and S1 subgroups (right). (F,G) Unique cell communication network between epithelial cells and other cells in S2 subgroups; Figure S3: Co-expression gene modules of CRPC Bulk-seq. (A) Co-expression gene modules in GSE70770 dataset. (B) Cluster of 14 samples from GSE70770 dataset. (C) Correlation analysis of gene modules in GSE70770 dataset. (D) Co-expression gene modules in GSE80609 dataset. (E) Cluster of 11 samples from GSE80609 dataset. (F) Correlation analysis of gene modules in GSE80609 dataset; Figure S4: Enrichment analysis results and calibration curve of PFI. (A) Hallmark enrichment analysis of gene sets in Cluster2. (B) GO analysis of gene sets in Cluster4. (C) Nomogram-Predicted Probability of 2-year PFI. (D) Nomogram-Predicted Probability of 3-year PFI.

Author Contributions: Conceptualization, D.H., X.W. and S.L.; methodology, D.H. and Y.H.; software, F.L. and X.W.; data curation, Y.H., H.W. and S.L.; formal analysis, Y.H., Y.J., F.L. and H.W.; validation, Y.H. and S.L.; investigation, S.L.; funding acquisition, D.H. and X.W.; visualization, Y.H., Y.J. and F.L.; writing—original draft, S.L.; writing—review and editing, D.H., Y.H. and S.L.; supervision and project administration, D.H. and X.W.; funding acquisition, D.H. All authors have read and agreed to the published version of the manuscript.

Funding: This research was supported by the Key Research and Development Program of Hunan Province (International Scientific and Technological Cooperation Category) (No. 2021WK2003) and the Application of AI in Medical Scientific Research and Technology Evaluation Project by the Shenzhen Health Development Research and Data Management Center (sz20230404).

Institutional Review Board Statement: Not applicable. Ethical review and approval for this analysis of public data were previously described in the original articles referenced.

Informed Consent Statement: Not applicable.

Data Availability Statement: Publicly available datasets were analyzed in this study. These data can be found here: https://www.ncbi.nlm.nih.gov/geo/query/acc.cgi?acc=GSE137829, accessed on 1 September 2020; https://www.ncbi.nlm.nih.gov/geo/query/acc.cgi?acc=GSE70770, accessed on 30 July 2015; https://www.ncbi.nlm.nih.gov/geo/query/acc.cgi?acc=GSE80609, accessed on 22 April 2018; https://www.ncbi.nlm.nih.gov/geo/query/acc.cgi?acc=GSE111177, accessed on 11 October 2018; https://portal.gdc.cancer.gov/projects/TCGA-PRAD, accessed on 16 December 2019.

Acknowledgments: We thank the investigators of the TCGA project and the GEO database for sharing data.

Conflicts of Interest: The authors declare no conflicts of interest. The funders had no role in the design of the study; in the collection, analyses, or interpretation of data; in the writing of the manuscript; or in the decision to publish the results.

References

1. Siegel, R.L.; Giaquinto, A.N.; Jemal, A. Cancer statistics, 2024. *CA Cancer J. Clin.* **2024**, *74*, 12–49. [CrossRef] [PubMed]
2. Lowrance, W.; Dreicer, R.; Jarrard, D.F.; Scarpato, K.R.; Kim, S.K.; Kirkby, E.; Buckley, D.I.; Griffin, J.C.; Cookson, M.S. Updates to Advanced Prostate Cancer: AUA/SUO Guideline. *J. Urol.* **2023**, *209*, 1082–1090. [CrossRef] [PubMed]
3. Davies, A.; Conteduca, V.; Zoubeidi, A.; Beltran, H. Biological Evolution of Castration-resistant Prostate Cancer. *Eur. Urol. Focus.* **2019**, *5*, 147–154. [CrossRef] [PubMed]
4. Gorlov, I.P.; Sircar, K.; Zhao, H.; Maity, S.N.; Navone, N.M.; Gorlova, O.Y.; Troncoso, P.; Pettaway, C.A.; Byun, J.Y.; Logothetis, C.J. Prioritizing genes associated with prostate cancer development. *BMC Cancer* **2010**, *10*, 599. [CrossRef]
5. Antonarakis, E.S.; Eisenberger, M.A. Expanding treatment options for metastatic prostate cancer. *N. Engl. J. Med.* **2011**, *364*, 2055–2058. [CrossRef]
6. Watson, P.A.; Arora, V.K.; Sawyers, C.L. Emerging mechanisms of resistance to androgen receptor inhibitors in prostate cancer. *Nat. Rev. Cancer* **2015**, *15*, 701–711. [CrossRef]
7. Li, X.; Xiong, H.; Mou, X.; Huang, C.; Thomas, E.R.; Yu, W.; Jiang, Y.; Chen, Y. Androgen receptor cofactors: A potential role in understanding prostate cancer. *Biomed. Pharmacother.* **2024**, *15*, 116338. [CrossRef]
8. Wan, L.; Liu, Y.; Liu, R.; Mao, W. GAD1 contributes to the progression and drug resistance in castration resistant prostate cancer. *Cancer Cell Int.* **2023**, *23*, 255. [CrossRef]
9. Kang, N.; Xue, H.; Lin, Y.Y.; Dong, X.; Classen, A.; Wu, R.; Jin, Y.; Lin, D.; Volik, S.; Ong, C.; et al. Influence of ADT on B7-H3 expression during CRPC progression from hormone-naïve prostate cancer. *Cancer Gene Ther.* **2023**, *30*, 1382–1389. [CrossRef]
10. Maranto, C.; Sabharwal, L.; Udhane, V.; Pitzen, S.P.; McCluskey, B.; Qi, S.; O'Connor, C.; Dev, I.S.; Johnson, S.; Jacobsohn, K.; et al. Stat5 induces androgen receptor (AR) gene transcription in prostate cancer and offers a druggable pathway to target AR signaling. *Sci. Adv.* **2024**, *10*, eadi2742. [CrossRef]
11. Zhang, B.; Horvath, S. A general framework for weighted gene co-expression network analysis. *Stat. Appl. Genet. Mol. Biol.* **2005**, *4*, 17. [CrossRef] [PubMed]
12. Xue, Y.; Zhao, G.; Pu, X.; Jiao, F. Construction of T cell exhaustion model for predicting survival and immunotherapy effect of bladder cancer based on WGCNA. *Front. Oncol.* **2023**, *13*, 1196802. [CrossRef] [PubMed]
13. He, X.; He, X.; Feng, W. Identification and Validation of NK Marker Genes in Ovarian Cancer by scRNA-seq Combined with WGCNA Algorithm. *Mediat. Inflamm.* **2023**, *2023*, 6845701. [CrossRef] [PubMed]
14. Chen, W.; Kang, Y.; Sheng, W.; Huang, Q.; Cheng, J.; Pei, S.; Meng, Y. A new 4-gene-based prognostic model accurately predicts breast cancer prognosis and immunotherapy response by integrating WGCNA and bioinformatics analysis. *Front. Immunol.* **2024**, *15*, 1331841. [CrossRef]
15. Chen, L.; Liu, R.; Liu, Z.P.; Li, M.; Aihara, K. Detecting early-warning signals for sudden deterioration of complex diseases by dynamical network biomarkers. *Sci. Rep.* **2012**, *2*, 342. [CrossRef]
16. Yang, B.; Li, M.; Tang, W.; Liu, W.; Zhang, S.; Chen, L.; Xia, J. Dynamic network biomarker indicates pulmonary metastasis at the tipping point of hepatocellular carcinoma. *Nat. Commun.* **2018**, *9*, 678. [CrossRef]
17. Tong, Y.; Song, Y.; Xia, C.; Deng, S. Theoretical and in silico Analyses Reveal MYC as a Dynamic Network Biomarker in Colon and Rectal Cancer. *Front. Genet.* **2020**, *11*, 555540. [CrossRef]
18. Han, Y.; Akhtar, J.; Liu, G.; Li, C.; Wang, G. Early warning and diagnosis of liver cancer based on dynamic network biomarker and deep learning. *Comput. Struct. Biotechnol. J.* **2023**, *21*, 3478–3489. [CrossRef]
19. Zhang, X.; Lan, Y.; Xu, J.; Quan, F.; Zhao, E.; Deng, C.; Luo, T.; Xu, L.; Liao, G.; Yan, M.; et al. CellMarker: A manually curated resource of cell markers in human and mouse. *Nucleic Acids Res.* **2019**, *47*, D721–D728. [CrossRef]
20. Drost, H.G.; Paszkowski, J. Biomartr: Genomic data retrieval with R. *Bioinformatics* **2017**, *33*, 1216–1217. [CrossRef]
21. Yang, X.H.; Goldstein, A.; Sun, Y.; Wang, Z.; Wei, M.; Moskowitz, I.P.; Cunningham, J.M. Detecting critical transition signals from single-cell transcriptomes to infer lineage-determining transcription factors. *Nucleic Acids Res.* **2022**, *50*, e91. [CrossRef] [PubMed]
22. Yan, J.; Li, P.; Gao, R.; Li, Y.; Chen, L. Identifying critical states of complex diseases by single-sample Jensen-Shannon divergence. *Front. Oncol.* **2021**, *11*, 684781. [CrossRef] [PubMed]

23. Hänzelmann, S.; Castelo, R.; Guinney, J. GSVA: Gene set variation analysis for microarray and RNA-seq data. *BMC Bioinform.* **2013**, *14*, 7. [CrossRef] [PubMed]
24. Jin, S.; Guerrero, J.C.F.; Zhang, L.; Chang, I.; Ramos, R.; Kuan, C.H.; Myung, P.; Plikus, M.V.; Nie, Q. Inference and analysis of cell-cell communication using CellChat. *Nat. Commun.* **2021**, *12*, 1088. [CrossRef]
25. Langfelder, P.; Horvath, S. WGCNA: An R package for weighted correlation network analysis. *BMC Bioinform.* **2008**, *29*, 559. [CrossRef]
26. Liberzon, A.; Subramanian, A.; Pinchback, R.; Thorvaldsdóttir, H.; Tamayo, P.; Mesirov, J.P. Molecular signatures database (MSigDB) 3.0. *Bioinformatics* **2011**, *27*, 1739–1740. [CrossRef]
27. Wu, T.; Hu, E.; Xu, S.; Chen, M.; Guo, P.; Dai, Z.; Feng, T.; Zhou, L.; Tang, W.; Zhan, L.; et al. clusterProfiler 4.0: A universal enrichment tool for interpreting omics data. *Innovation* **2021**, *3*, 100141. [CrossRef]
28. Kumar, L.; Futschik, E.M. Mfuzz: A software package for soft clustering of microarray data. *Bioinformation* **2007**, *2*, 5–7. [CrossRef]
29. Zhang, Z. Semi-parametric regression model for survival data: Graphical visualization with R. *Ann. Transl. Med.* **2016**, *4*, 461. [CrossRef]
30. Hebert, P.D.; Cywinska, A.; Ball, S.L.; de Waard, J.R. Biological identifications through DNA barcodes. *Proc. Biol. Sci.* **2003**, *270*, 313–321. [CrossRef]
31. Zhang, Z.; Kattan, M.W. Drawing Nomograms with R: Applications to categorical outcome and survival data. *Ann. Transl. Med.* **2017**, *5*, 211. [CrossRef] [PubMed]
32. Benjamini, Y.; Hochberg, Y. Controlling the false discovery rate: A practical and powerful approach to multiple testing. *J. R. Stat. Soc. Ser. B* **1995**, *57*, 289–300. [CrossRef]
33. Guo, W.; Li, L.; He, J.; Liu, Z.; Han, M.; Li, F.; Xia, X.; Zhang, X.; Zhu, Y.; Wei, Y.; et al. Single-cell transcriptomics identifies a distinct luminal progenitor cell type in distal prostate invagination tips. *Nat. Genet.* **2020**, *52*, 908–918. [CrossRef] [PubMed]
34. Fujita, K.; Nonomura, N. Role of Androgen Receptor in Prostate Cancer: A Review. *World J. Mens. Health* **2019**, *37*, 288–295. [CrossRef]
35. Ohnuki, H.; Tosato, G. Characterization of Semaphorin 6A-Mediated Effects on Angiogenesis Through Regulation of VEGF Signaling. *Methods Mol. Biol.* **2017**, *1493*, 345–361.
36. Hood, G.; Laufer-Amorim, R.; Fonseca-Alves, C.E.; Palmieri, C. Overexpression of Ephrin A3 Receptor in Canine Prostatic Carcinoma. *J. Comp. Pathol.* **2016**, *154*, 180–185. [CrossRef]
37. Chen, J.; Li, L.; Yang, Z.; Luo, J.; Yeh, S.; Chang, C. Androgen-deprivation therapy with enzalutamide enhances prostate cancer metastasis via decreasing the EPHB6 suppressor expression. *Cancer Lett.* **2017**, *408*, 155–163. [CrossRef]
38. Li, C.; Lanman, N.A.; Kong, Y.; He, D.; Mao, F.; Farah, E.; Zhang, Y.; Liu, J.; Wang, C.; Wei, Q.; et al. Inhibition of the erythropoietin-producing receptor EPHB4 antagonizes androgen receptor overexpression and reduces enzalutamide resistance. *J. Biol. Chem.* **2020**, *295*, 5470–5483. [CrossRef]
39. Nordstrand, A.; Bovinder, Y.E.; Thysell, E.; Jernberg, E.; Crnalic, S.; Widmark, A.; Bergh, A.; Lerner, U.H.; Wikström, P. Bone Cell Activity in Clinical Prostate Cancer Bone Metastasis and Its Inverse Relation to Tumor Cell Androgen Receptor Activity. *Int. J. Mol. Sci.* **2018**, *19*, 1223. [CrossRef]
40. Ballangrud, A.M.; Yang, W.H.; Dnistrian, A.; Lampen, N.M.; Sgouros, G. Growth and characterization of LNCaP prostate cancer cell spheroids. *Clin. Cancer Res.* **1999**, *5*, 3171–3176.
41. Josefsson, A.; Larsson, K.; Freyhult, E.; Damber, J.E.; Welén, K. Gene Expression Alterations during Development of Castration-Resistant Prostate Cancer Are Detected in Circulating Tumor Cells. *Cancers* **2019**, *12*, 39. [CrossRef] [PubMed]
42. Takayama, K.; Tsutsumi, S.; Suzuki, T.; Horie, I.K.; Ikeda, K.; Kaneshiro, K.; Fujimura, T.; Kumagai, J.; Urano, T.; Sakaki, Y.; et al. Amyloid precursor protein is a primary androgen target gene that promotes prostate cancer growth. *Cancer Res.* **2009**, *69*, 137–142. [CrossRef] [PubMed]
43. Twu, O.; Dessí, D.; Vu, A.; Mercer, F.; Stevens, G.C.; de Miguel, N.; Rappelli, P.; Cocco, A.R.; Clubb, R.T.; Fiori, P.L.; et al. Trichomonas vaginalis homolog of macrophage migration inhibitory factor induces prostate cell growth, invasiveness, and inflammatory responses. *Proc. Natl. Acad. Sci. USA* **2014**, *111*, 8179–8184. [CrossRef] [PubMed]
44. Pandey, P.; Khan, F.; Upadhyay, T.K.; Seungjoon, M.; Park, M.N.; Kim, B. New insights about the PDGF/PDGFR signaling pathway as a promising target to develop cancer therapeutic strategies. *Biomed. Pharmacother.* **2023**, *161*, 114491. [CrossRef]
45. Nordby, Y.; Richardsen, E.; Rakaee, M.; Ness, N.; Donnem, T.; Patel, H.R.; Busund, L.T.; Bremnes, R.M.; Andersen, S. High expression of PDGFR-β in prostate cancer stroma is independently associated with clinical and biochemical prostate cancer recurrence. *Sci. Rep.* **2017**, *7*, 43378. [CrossRef]
46. Teishima, J.; Hayashi, T.; Nagamatsu, H.; Shoji, K.; Shikuma, H.; Yamanaka, R.; Sekino, Y.; Goto, K.; Inoue, S.; Matsubara, A. Fibroblast Growth Factor Family in the Progression of Prostate Cancer. *J. Clin. Med.* **2019**, *8*, 183. [CrossRef]
47. Zhang, N.; Hao, J.; Cai, Y.; Wang, M. Research advances of secretory proteins in malignant tumors. *Chin. J. Cancer Res.* **2021**, *33*, 115–132. [CrossRef]
48. Yan, Y.; Mao, X.; Zhang, Q.; Ye, Y.; Dai, Y.; Bao, M.; Zeng, Y.; Huang, R.; Mo, Z. Molecular mechanisms, immune cell infiltration, and potential drugs for prostate cancer. *Cancer Biomark.* **2021**, *31*, 87–96. [CrossRef]
49. Yi, J.; Zhu, J.; Wu, J.; Thompson, C.B.; Jiang, X. Oncogenic activation of PI3K-AKT-mTOR signaling suppresses ferroptosis via SREBP-mediated lipogenesis. *Proc. Natl. Acad. Sci. USA* **2020**, *117*, 31189–31197. [CrossRef]

50. Kim, S.J.; Choi, H.; Park, S.S.; Chang, C.; Kim, E. Stearoyl CoA desaturase (SCD) facilitates proliferation of prostate cancer cells through enhancement of androgen receptor transactivation. *Mol. Cells* **2011**, *31*, 371–377. [CrossRef]
51. Li, T.; Su, Y.; Mei, Y.; Leng, Q.; Leng, B.; Liu, Z.; Stass, S.A.; Jiang, F. ALDH1A1 is a marker for malignant prostate stem cells and predictor of prostate cancer patients' outcome. *Lab. Investig.* **2010**, *90*, 234–244. [CrossRef] [PubMed]
52. Gorodetska, I.; Offermann, A.; Püschel, J.; Lukiyanchuk, V.; Gaete, D.; Kurzyukova, A.; Freytag, V.; Haider, M.T.; Fjeldbo, C.S.; Di Gaetano, S.; et al. ALDH1A1 drives prostate cancer metastases and radioresistance by interplay with AR- and RAR-dependent transcription. *Theranostics* **2024**, *14*, 714–737. [CrossRef] [PubMed]
53. Iasonos, A.; Schrag, D.; Raj, G.V.; Panageas, K.S. How to build and interpret a nomogram for cancer prognosis. *J. Clin. Oncol.* **2008**, *26*, 1364–1370. [CrossRef] [PubMed]
54. Zhang, T.; Wei, Y.; Hong, B.H.; Sumiyoshi, T.; Ong, E.H.W.; Zeng, H.; Li, Y.; Ng, C.F.; Pan, J.; Fang, B.; et al. Development and validation of a nomogram (APGRC) to predict the presence of germline DNA damage repair pathogenic variants in Asian patients with prostate cancer. *Clin. Transl. Med.* **2023**, *13*, e1411. [CrossRef] [PubMed]
55. Xu, C.; Pei, D.; Liu, Y.; Guo, J.; Liu, N.; Wang, Q.; Yu, Y.; Kang, Z. Clinical characteristics and prostate-cancer-specific mortality of competitive risk nomogram in the second primary prostate cancer. *Front. Oncol.* **2023**, *13*, 918324. [CrossRef]
56. Fritz, V.; Benfodda, Z.; Rodier, G.; Henriquet, C.; Iborra, F.; Avancès, C.; Allory, Y.; de la Taille, A.; Culine, S.; Blancou, H.; et al. Abrogation of de novo lipogenesis by stearoyl-CoA desaturase 1 inhibition interferes with oncogenic signaling and blocks prostate cancer progression in mice. *Mol. Cancer Ther.* **2010**, *9*, 1740–1754. [CrossRef]
57. Peck, B.; Schug, Z.T.; Zhang, Q.; Dankworth, B.; Jones, D.T.; Smethurst, E.; Patel, R.; Mason, S.; Jiang, M.; Saunders, R.; et al. Inhibition of fatty acid desaturation is detrimental to cancer cell survival in metabolically compromised environments. *Cancer metab.* **2016**, *4*, 6. [CrossRef]
58. Contreras, L.E.F.; Cruz-Hernández, C.D.; Cortés, S.A.; Ramírez, H.A.; Peña, M.C.; Rodríguez, D.M.; Oliart-Ros, R.M. Inhibition of Stearoyl-CoA Desaturase by Sterculic Oil Reduces Proliferation and Induces Apoptosis in Prostate Cancer Cell Lines. *Nutr. Cancer* **2022**, *74*, 1308–1321. [CrossRef]
59. Van den Hoogen, C.; van der Horst, G.; Cheung, H.; Buijs, J.T.; Lippitt, J.M.; Guzmán, R.N.; Hamd, F.C.; Eaton, C.L.; Thalmann, G.N.; Cecchini, M.G.; et al. High aldehyde dehydrogenase activity identifies tumor-initiating and metastasis-initiating cells in human prostate cancer. *Cancer Res.* **2010**, *70*, 5163–5173. [CrossRef]
60. Le Magnen, C.; Bubendorf, L.; Rentsch, C.A.; Mengus, C.; Gsponer, J.; Zellweger, T.; Rieken, M.; Thalmann, G.N.; Cecchini, M.G.; Germann, M.; et al. Characterization and clinical relevance of ALDHbright populations in prostate cancer. *Clin. Cancer Res.* **2013**, *19*, 5361–5371. [CrossRef]
61. Lounis, M.A.; Péant, B.; Leclerc-Desaulniers, K.; Ganguli, D.; Daneault, C.; Ruiz, M.; Zoubeidi, A.; Mes-Masson, A.M.; Saad, F. Modulation of de Novo Lipogenesis Improves Response to Enzalutamide Treatment in Prostate Cancer. *Cancers* **2020**, *12*, 3339. [CrossRef]
62. Simon, M.; Richard, E.M.; Wang, X.; Shahzad, M.; Huang, V.H.; Qaiser, T.A.; Potluri, P.; Mahl, S.E.; Davila, A.; Nazli, S.; et al. Mutations of human NARS2, encoding the mitochondrial asparaginyl-tRNA synthetase, cause nonsyndromic deafness and Leigh syndrome. *PLoS Genet.* **2015**, *11*, e1005097. [CrossRef] [PubMed]
63. Vafaee, S.M.; Farhadi, M.; Razmara, E.; Morovvati, S.; Ghasemi, S.; Abedini, S.S.; Bagher, Z.; Alizadeh, R.; Falah, M. Novel phenotype and genotype spectrum of NARS2 and literature review of previous mutations. *Ir. J. Med. Sci.* **2022**, *191*, 1877–1890. [CrossRef] [PubMed]
64. Moulinier, L.; Ripp, R.; Castillo, G.; Poch, O.; Sissler, M. MiSynPat: An integrated knowledge base linking clinical, genetic, and structural data for disease-causing mutations in human mitochondrial aminoacyl-tRNA synthetases. *Hum. Mutat.* **2017**, *38*, 1316–1324. [CrossRef] [PubMed]
65. Zhang, W.; Kong, Y.; Li, Y.; Shi, F.; Lyu, J.; Sheng, C.; Wang, S.; Wang, Q. Novel Molecular Determinants of Response or Resistance to Immune Checkpoint Inhibitor Therapies in Melanoma. *Front. Immunol.* **2022**, *12*, 798474. [CrossRef]
66. Tang, W.; Yuan, J.; Chen, X.; Shan, Y.; Luo, K.; Guo, Z.; Zhang, Y.; Wan, B.; Yu, L. Cloning and characterization of the CDZFP gene which encodes a putative zinc finger protein. *DNA Seq.* **2005**, *16*, 391–396. [CrossRef]
67. Song, Z.; Krishna, S.; Thanos, D.; Strominger, J.L.; Ono, S.J. A novel cysteine-rich sequence-specific DNA-binding protein interacts with the conserved X-box motif of the human major histocompatibility complex class II genes via a repeated Cys-His domain and functions as a transcriptional repressor. *J. Exp. Med.* **1994**, *180*, 1763–1774. [CrossRef]
68. Nudel, R.; Simpson, N.H.; Baird, G.; O'Hare, A.; Conti, R.G.; Bolton, P.F.; Hennessy, E.R.; Consortium, T.S.L.; Monaco, A.P.; Knight, J.C.; et al. Associations of HLA alleles with specific language impairment. *J. Neurodev. Disord.* **2014**, *6*, 1. [CrossRef]
69. Wang, X. Role of clinical bioinformatics in the development of network-based Biomarkers. *J. Clin. Bioinform.* **2011**, *1*, 28. [CrossRef]

Disclaimer/Publisher's Note: The statements, opinions and data contained in all publications are solely those of the individual author(s) and contributor(s) and not of MDPI and/or the editor(s). MDPI and/or the editor(s) disclaim responsibility for any injury to people or property resulting from any ideas, methods, instructions or products referred to in the content.

cancers

MDPI

Review

The Neurodevelopmental and Molecular Landscape of Medulloblastoma Subgroups: Current Targets and the Potential for Combined Therapies

Hasan Slika [1,2], Paolo Alimonti [3], Divyaansh Raj [2], Chad Caraway [2], Safwan Alomari [2], Eric M. Jackson [2] and Betty Tyler [2,*]

1 Faculty of Medicine, American University of Beirut, Beirut P.O. Box 11-0236, Lebanon; hgs09@mail.aub.edu
2 Department of Neurosurgery, Johns Hopkins University School of Medicine, Baltimore, MD 21287, USA; draj3@jhmi.edu (D.R.); ccarawa2@jhu.edu (C.C.); salomar1@jhmi.edu (S.A.); ejackson@jhmi.edu (E.M.J.)
3 School of Medicine, Vita-Salute San Raffaele University, 20132 Milan, Italy; p.alimonti@studenti.unisr.it
* Correspondence: btyler@jhmi.edu

Simple Summary: Medulloblastoma is the most common malignant brain tumor in the pediatric population. Despite the utilization of aggressive treatment modalities, including surgery, chemotherapy, and radiation therapy, patients with medulloblastoma still have a poor prognosis. Moreover, these modalities are associated with dramatic life-long complications. Hence, this calls for the development of novel therapeutic agents that can more effectively and safely target this tumor and improve the survival and quality of life for patients. The molecular-based classification of medulloblastoma into WNT activated, SHH activated, group 3, and group 4 opened the door for research endeavors that aim to study the specific cellular, molecular, and neurodevelopmental characteristics of each subtype. This review aims to summarize the literature on the different profiles of these subtypes, elaborate on the pharmacologic therapies that have been investigated to target each, and suggest potential combination therapies that can offer superior outcomes.

Abstract: Medulloblastoma is the most common malignant pediatric brain tumor and is associated with significant morbidity and mortality in the pediatric population. Despite the use of multiple therapeutic approaches consisting of surgical resection, craniospinal irradiation, and multiagent chemotherapy, the prognosis of many patients with medulloblastoma remains dismal. Additionally, the high doses of radiation and the chemotherapeutic agents used are associated with significant short- and long-term complications and adverse effects, most notably neurocognitive delay. Hence, there is an urgent need for the development and clinical integration of targeted treatment regimens with greater efficacy and superior safety profiles. Since the adoption of the molecular-based classification of medulloblastoma into wingless (WNT) activated, sonic hedgehog (SHH) activated, group 3, and group 4, research efforts have been directed towards unraveling the genetic, epigenetic, transcriptomic, and proteomic profiles of each subtype. This review aims to delineate the progress that has been made in characterizing the neurodevelopmental and molecular features of each medulloblastoma subtype. It further delves into the implications that these characteristics have on the development of subgroup-specific targeted therapeutic agents. Furthermore, it highlights potential future avenues for combining multiple agents or strategies in order to obtain augmented effects and evade the development of treatment resistance in tumors.

Keywords: medulloblastoma subgroups; molecular pathways; targeted therapy; combination therapy; neurodevelopmental origin; pediatric brain tumors

1. Introduction

Medulloblastoma is defined as a WHO grade IV embryonal tumor that arises in the cerebellum or brain stem. It accounts for approximately 63.3% of intracranial embryonal tumors and approximately 20% of all pediatric brain tumors. It has a peak incidence between ages 0 and 9 years and exhibits a male predominance with a 1.7:1 male to female ratio [1]. The current mainstay of therapy for medulloblastoma is maximal safe surgical resection followed by risk-adapted craniospinal irradiation, a radiation boost to the primary tumor bed, and adjuvant multi-agent chemotherapy [2]. However, treatment with radiation therapy may be deferred in infants and toddlers less than 3 years of age due to the debilitating long-term neurocognitive effects of early exposure to radiation [3]. Unfortunately, despite this aggressive combination of treatment modalities, the 10-year survival rate of medulloblastoma remains less than 65% [1]. Nevertheless, these statistics and prognostic information differ among the different subgroups of medulloblastoma. In fact, a radical paradigm shift has been observed in medulloblastoma research since the 2016 WHO Classification of Tumors of the Central Nervous System, which divided medulloblastomas into four molecularly stratified subgroups: wingless (WNT) activated, sonic hedgehog (SHH) activated, group 3, and group 4 [4] (Table 1). This stratification was reiterated in the 2021 classification with further molecular-based subclassifications [5]. The unveiling of the vast differences in the genomes, epigenomes, transcriptomes, and proteomes of these subgroups ignited the search for subgroup-specific targeted therapies that can offer superior clinical outcomes with less devastating systemic side effects.

Table 1. Clinical characteristics and the neurodevelopmental, genetic, and epigenetic profiles of the four molecular subgroups of medulloblastoma.

	WNT-Activated	SHH-Activated	Group 3	Group 4
Prevalence	10%	30%	25%	35%
5-year survival	>90%	70%	50%	75%
Neurodevelopmental origin	Pontine mossy fibers of the lower rhombic lip	Granule neuron precursor cells of the upper rhombic lip	Unipolar brush cells and glutamatergic cerebellar nuclei of the upper rhombic lip	
Commonly mutated genes	*CTNNB1, DDX3X, CREBBP, SMARC4*	*TP53, TERT, PTCH1, GLI2, SMO, SUFU*	*MYC, SOX11, PVT1, OTX2, GFI1/GFI1B*	*MYCN, SNCAIP, GFI1/GFI1B*
Important epigenetic players	ARID1, ARID2, SMARC4, promoter methylation of CDH1	MLL2/KMT2D, MLL3/KMT2C, NCOR2, LDB1	LSD1, PRC2, EZH2, BRD	KDM6A/UTX, LSD1

BRD, bromodomain; CREBBP, CREB binding protein; GFI, growth factor independent protein; GLI, glioma-associated oncogene; EZH, enhancer of zeste homolog; PRC, polycomb repressor complex; PTCH, patched; SHH, sonic hedgehog; SMO, smoothened; WNT, wingless. References for table [6–8].

This paper aims to provide a summary of the neurodevelopmental and molecular profiles of medulloblastoma subtypes. Moreover, it builds on this characterization to further elaborate on the targeted therapeutic options that have been investigated in each subgroup, and it explores the promising potential of combination therapies as the future of medulloblastoma research and clinical practice.

2. Neurodevelopmental and Molecular Underpinnings of Medulloblastoma Subgroups

Several efforts of transcriptional profiling of medulloblastomas have demonstrated how these tumors closely recapitulate their physiological cellular counterparts in the developing cerebellum [9–12]. Even more importantly, the putative cells of origin of each medulloblastoma type seem to arise in specific spatiotemporal niches of the developing cerebellum, each giving rise to different cerebellar cellular lineages [9–12]. Therefore, the combination of timing, location of the initiating mutations, and the cell type affected by these mutations dictates the resulting medulloblastoma subgroup (Figure 1).

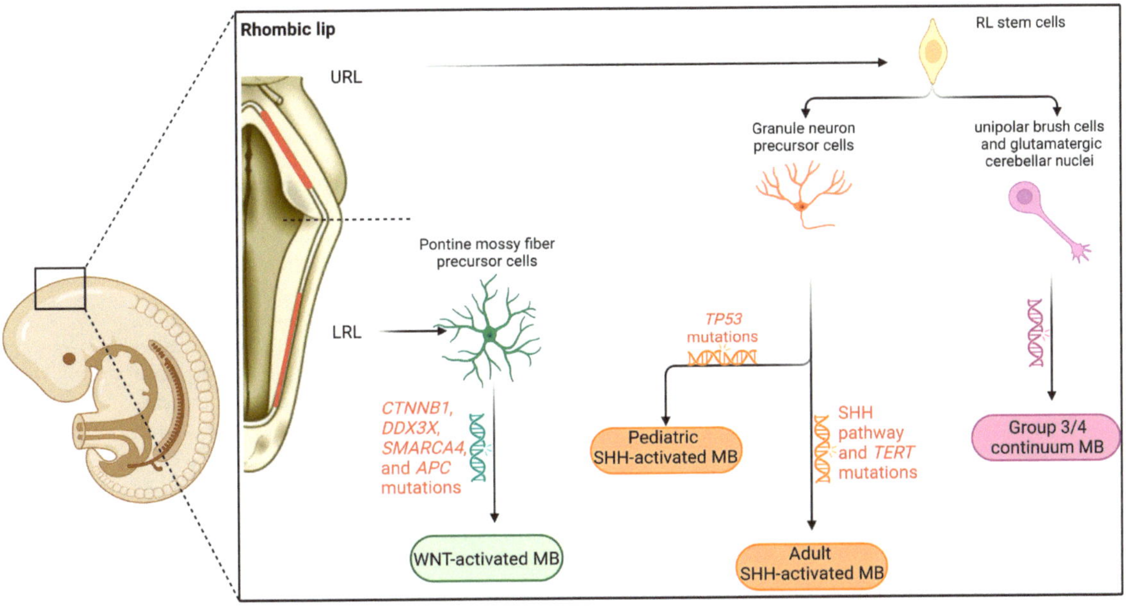

Figure 1. The neurodevelopmental origin of the four subgroups of medulloblastoma. WNT-activated tumors derive from the pontine mossy fiber precursor cell of the LRL and are characterized by mutations that involve the *CTNNB1*, *DDX3X*, SMARCA4, and *APC* genes. SHH-activated tumors derive from the granule neuron precursor cells of the URL, with the adult subtype commonly having mutations in the genes of the SHH pathway and TERT promoter and the pediatric subtype commonly possessing mutations in the TP53 gene. Finally, the unipolar brush cells and glutamatergic cerebellar nuclei give rise to the group 3/group 4 continuum of medulloblastoma tumors with a differential of transcriptional and DNA methylation profiles. LRL, lower rhombic lip; MB, medulloblastoma; RL, rhombic lip; SHH, sonic hedgehog; URL, upper rhombic lip; WNT, wingless.

2.1. Cerebellar Embryonal Development

Given the strong developmental footprint of medulloblastomas, understanding the basic processes of cerebellar development is essential to uncover the embryonal origins of the different medulloblastoma subgroups. In the developing cerebellum, two main germinal epithelia can be identified: the ventricular zone (VZ), which is marked by the PTF1A marker and will generate the whole GABAergic cell lineage (including Purkinje cells) [13], and the rhombic lip (RL), the dorsal-most portion of the hindbrain proliferative neuroepithelium [14]. The RL is identified by the MATH1 marker and can be divided craniocaudally into the upper rhombic lip (URL) and the lower rhombic lip (LRL) [15].

On a purely morphological basis, this anatomical division relates to the segmentation of the hindbrain into rhombomeres (r1–r7) along the craniocaudal axis, with the URL developing from the dorsal pole or r1 and the LRL deriving from r2 to r7 segments [16]. On the other hand, from a gene expression standpoint, the URL is defined by the MATH1 marker gene as well as NEUROD1 [16]. In comparison, the LRL expresses PTF1a, WNT1 in its dorsoventral portion, and MATH1 in its dorsal portion [17], and it will partake in generating mostly extracerebellar neurons [18] including those forming the cochlear and pre-cerebellar nuclei [17]. The MATH1-expressing URL and dorsal LRL generate the cells of the glutamatergic lineage, including cerebellar nuclei neurons, granule cell progenitors (GCPs), and unipolar brush cells (UBCs) [13,17,19]. Overall, all cerebellar neurons are generated by both the PTF1a+ VZ and the MATH1+ portions of the RL [20].

Starting from post-conception week 10, the RL splits in two substructures: the RL ventricular zone (RLvz) and the RL subventricular zone (RLsvz). They are divided by a vascularized bed which is evident by post conception week 11 in humans [21]. The RLvz is characterized by Ki67-rich Sox2+ cells, while the RLsvz has Ki67-rich Sox2-sparse cells [21]. Additional markers include Wntless (WLS), CRYAB, SOX2, and PAX6 for the RLvz and TBR2 and EOMES for the RLsvz, while a common marker for all RL cells is LMX1A [21].

2.2. WNT-Activated Medulloblastoma

The WNT-activated subgroup constitutes approximately 10% of all medulloblastoma cases [2]. The median age at diagnosis is 11 years, with an almost equal male-to-female ratio [22]. This tumor group is believed to arise from the pontine mossy fiber precursor cells [9,23] of the extracerebellar LRL [9,10,12] that harbor somatic mutations in β-catenin (encoded by the gene *CTNNB1*), DDX3X, and SMARCA4 or germline APC mutations responsible for constitutive WNT signaling [22,24,25] (Figure 1). Using a Similarity Network Fusion approach on 763 primary medulloblastoma samples, Cavalli et al. identified two subtypes of WNT-activated medulloblastoma: WNT-α, typical of younger patients and characterized by monosomy at chromosome 6, and WNT-β, characteristic of adult patients and devoid of monosomy 6 [26]. The latter group featured a worse prognosis compared to the pediatric group.

Hovestadt et al. [9] conducted a single-cell transcriptomics analysis of medulloblastoma to highlight the peculiar cellular states of malignant cells in each subgroup. They found that WNT-amplified medulloblastoma cells exist in a differentiated neuronal-like state and display four transcriptional metaprograms with distinctive cellular signatures: WNT-A, associated with cell cycle activity; WNT-B, related to protein biosynthesis and metabolism; WNT-C, mirroring neuronal differentiation; and WNT-D, featuring the expression of early response and WNT pathway genes. Further scoring of transcriptional metaprograms outlined a developmental hierarchy within the WNT subgroup of medulloblastoma, in which tumor cells with high WNT-B and low WNT-C/WNT-D signatures possess proliferative capacity and drive tumor growth.

From the epigenetic perspective, the WNT subgroup of medulloblastoma features mutations in the epigenetic regulators of a sparse set of genes. Most of these mutations are shared with other subgroups, including those in *ARID1A*, *ARID2*, *CREBBP*, *MLL2/KMT2D*, and *SMARCA4*, a gene belonging to the SWI/SNF family of ATP-dependent chromatin remodeling complexes [8,27,28]. Promoter methylation of the tumor suppressor CDH1 is instead restricted to this MB type, a finding supported by studies showing the importance of CDH1 in regulating the WNT signaling in the LRL [8,27,29].

2.3. SHH-Activated Medulloblastoma

This subgroup is the most common group of medulloblastoma in kids less than three years of age and in adults (>18 years of age), with an approximately 2:1 male-to-female ratio [14,15]. It is thought to arise from GCPs and granule cells in the URL, presumably from the portion giving rise to the external granular layer [10,12,22]. The clinical outcome in this type is heterogeneous and strongly dictated by the underlying transcriptional and cellular activity [30]. Cavalli et al. [26] identified four main subtypes of SHH-activated medulloblastoma, along with their main mutations and age groups: SHH-α, typical of 3–16-year-old patients, has the worst prognosis among this group and harbors TP53 mutations in one-third of the cases; SHH-β and SHH-γ groups are more prevalent in infants (1.3 and 1.9 years of age, respectively), with SHH-β displaying a poorer prognosis compared to SHH-γ due to increased rate of metastatic dissemination. Finally, SHH-δ group occurs mainly in adults, features TERT promoter mutations, and has an overall good prognosis.

Hovestadt et al. [9] demonstrated three transcriptional metaprograms in SHH-amplified medulloblastoma cells. These metaprograms are related to cell cycle activity, undifferentiated progenitors, and neuronal differentiation (SHH-A, SHH-B, and SHH-C, respectively). In accordance with epidemiologic findings, this work also showed that the cellular origin of SHH medulloblastoma is dichotomic according to age: pediatric tumors feature cells in granule neuron-like states expressing high levels of NEUROD1, while adult tumors express higher levels of MATH1 and feature cells in either granule neuron progenitor-like state or in a mixed state between UBCs and granule neurons (Figure 1). These genes are prototypical markers of the URL during cerebellar development [16].

Adult SHH-activated medulloblastomas display a higher mutation burden compared to their pediatric counterparts, particularly with mutations associated with the SHH pathway, mainly Patched1 (PTCH1) and Smoothened (SMO), as well as mutations in CREB binding protein (CREBBP), BRPF1, and TERT promoter [22]. Additionally, adult tumors display higher proportions of cells in the undifferentiated granule neuron progenitor-like state compared to pediatric tumors [31]. Overall, these findings may help explain the differences in therapeutic outcomes in SHH-activated medulloblastomas and their susceptibility to targeted therapies. Moreover, Hovestadt et al. [9] noted that the SHH-B metaprogram was the only proliferating compartment associated with the expression of SHH pathway genes, but they did not explore which age groups had the highest score for SHH-B and how this expression affects response to therapy. Future studies should aim to characterize the effects of targeted therapy on the different transcriptional metaprograms of SHH-activated medulloblastoma and stratify those results according to age.

Recurrent epigenetic alterations in SHH-activated medulloblastoma have been described in MLL2/KMT2D and MLL3/KMT2C, two lysine methyltransferases associated with an active chromatin state and the H3K4me2/3 status [8,32,33]. These mutations have also been reported for group 3 and group 4 tumors. Alternatively, subtype-specific mutations have been reported in NCOR2 and LDB1, two chromatin remodelers belonging to the nuclear co-repressor (N-CoR) complex [33]. Importantly, N-CoR dysregulation has been described as a crucial driver for SHH medulloblastoma onset [33].

2.4. *Group 3 Medulloblastoma*

Group 3 medulloblastomas bear the worst prognosis among all subtypes. Approximately 50% of group 3 tumors feature dissemination along the neuroaxis at diagnosis [34]. Cavalli et al. [26] classified group 3 tumors into three discrete subcategories: Group 3α, present in infants with metastatic dissemination but associated with better outcomes; Group 3β, occurring in an older age group and having a reduced metastatic rate; and Group 3γ, which has the worst prognosis among all subgroups. This last subgroup has been identified as originating from the earlier RLvz [10].

Luo et al. demonstrated that group 3 medulloblastoma cells resemble transitional cerebellar progenitor (TCP) cells, a transient-amplifying proliferating compartment physiologically more present in the RLvz, RL transitional zone (RLtz), and to a lesser extent in the RLsvz [11] during neurodevelopment. TCPs may be the cells of origin of group 3 medulloblastoma and can be identified by two signature markers, HNRNPH1 and SOX11. At the molecular level, the juxtaposition of HNRNPH1 and SOX11 super-enhancers to MYC cis-regulatory elements, through a mechanism of distance looping, appears to be responsible for MYC overexpression and the abnormal proliferation of group 3 tumor cells [11]. The proportion of TCP-like tumor cells in group tumors correlated with the rate of dissemination to the spinal cord and leptomeninges [11]. Therefore, sampling HNRNPH1 and SOX11 in tumor specimens and correlating their expression with the risk of metastasis may represent a future prognostic strategy in this group of medulloblastoma.

The study by Northcott et al. [25] employed the Cis Expression Structural Alteration Mapping (CESAM) technique to demonstrate that enhancer hijacking of growth factor independent 1 (GFI1) or GFI1B proto-oncogenes potentiate the effects of MYC amplification and further promotes tumor proliferation in group 3 medulloblastomas. The action of GFI1 is also mediated by LSD1, a histone lysine demethylase that is a potential treatment target for both group 3 and group 4 tumors [22].

Hovestadt et al. [9] demonstrated that prototypic group 3 tumors displayed cells in an undifferentiated progenitor-like metaprogram, characterized by ribosomal and translational initiation/elongation and MYC target gene expression. They also showed that group

3 tumor cells appear stalled in an undifferentiated neural progenitor cell state, hinting to mutations inducing a block of neural differentiation. In support of this evidence, another study [35] showed that OTX2 amplification reduces the expression of downstream regulators of neuronal differentiation including PAX3 and PAX6, serving as a differentiation blocker for group 3 medulloblastoma cells and inducing downstream mammalian target of rapamycin 1 (mTOR1) activation for protein synthesis and translation/elongation factor genes, consistent with the findings by Hovestadt et al. [9].

It appears that multiple structural variants confer selective growth advantages to group 3 medulloblastoma cells. Amplification of OTX2 halts the process of differentiation in the undifferentiated progenitor cell compartment present in the early RL [35]. MYC oncogene amplification and upregulation of pathways involved in protein synthesis further promote cellular proliferation [11]. Finally, GFI1/GFI1B activation by enhancer hijacking increases the action of MYC [25]. Driver mutations have been shown to differ according to the DNA methylation subtype of each group 3 tumor [22,26] and may help explain the intratumoral heterogeneity of this group of medulloblastomas.

Finally, group 3 medulloblastomas are characterized by an array of epigenetic dysregulations, some of which include distance looping and enhancer hijacking to block differentiation and boost tumor cell proliferation. At the histone level instead, group 3 tumors harbor mutations in genes belonging to the lysine demethylase family (KDM), sharing several of these mutations with group 4 medulloblastomas [8]. Bromodomain (BRD) and extra C-terminal (BET)-containing proteins bind acetylated histones and recruit the transcriptional machinery to control MYC levels, which is crucial in group 3 onset [36–38].

Peculiar alterations in histone regulators can help explain the biology of group 3 tumor cells. In fact, group 3 medulloblastomas display mutations in the polycomb repressor complex 2 (PRC2) gene set, which is a crucial regulator of differentiation, proliferation, and cell identity [8]. Among the components of PRC2 lies the enhancer of zeste homolog 2 (EZH2), the catalytic partner of PRC2 that causes the addition of methyl groups to histone 3 to promote the H3K27me3 status, with consequent chromatin compaction and transcriptional repression [39]. EZH2 overexpression in group 3 medulloblastoma increases H3K27me3 and impairs H3K4 methylation, thereby keeping cells in a stem-like/progenitor state [40]. This finding may promote the maintenance of group 3 cells in an undifferentiated state and further boost their malignant potential.

2.5. Group 4 Medulloblastoma

Group 4 medulloblastomas are the overall most common type [2], spanning across all age groups and having a 2:1 male-to-female ratio [22]. They are believed to originate from cells of the glutamatergic lineage, particularly from UBCs and glutamatergic cerebellar nuclei (Glu-CN) neurons arising in the URL [9,41,42]. In the developing cerebellum, these cells are marked by glutamatergic and RLsvz-specific transcription factors including EOMES, LMX1A, and TBR2 [9,10,21]. Cavalli et al. [26] identified three main subgroups of group 4 medulloblastoma: group 4α, featuring MYCN amplification; group 4β, characterized by SNCAIP duplication; and group 4γ, displaying cyclin-dependent kinase 6 (CDK6) amplification.

In the analysis by Hovestadt et al., prototypic group 4 tumors expressed a differentiated neuronal-like metaprogram (Group 3/4-C), including genes associated with the neuronal lineage [9]. Hendrikse et al. [10] showed that mutations in the CBFA gene complex (most notably alterations in KDM6A and enhancer hijacking of PRDM6 and GFI1/GFI1B) in UBCs, the last cells to develop from the RLsvz, are responsible for group 4 medulloblastoma development. Herein, GFI1 and GFI1B oncogenes are abnormally expressed in both group 3 and group 4 tumors in a mutually exclusive fashion [25]. In fact, local enhancer hijacking of GFI1 and distal enhancer hijacking of GFI1B drive medulloblastoma growth, either by cooperating with MYC to drive group 3 tumors or with other drivers to promote group 4 medulloblastoma development [43].

The PRDM6 gene encodes for a transcriptional repressor that uses histone 4 lysine 20 (H4K20) methyltransferase to induce gene silencing [22]. It is the most frequent somatically altered gene in group 4, being present in 17% of patients with this subtype of medulloblastoma [22] and featuring a more than 20-fold upregulation in group 4 tumors [25]. Moreover, it is located 600 kb downstream of the SNCAIP locus, a hotspot for tandem duplications that are unique to group 4 medulloblastoma [44]. By utilizing the CESAM technique, Northcott et al. [25] revealed the presence of structural variants bringing the SNCAIP super-enhancers closer to PRDM6, inducing its activation and overexpression.

Like group 3 tumors, group 4 medulloblastomas also display epigenetic alterations at multiple levels. In fact, both enhancer hijacking and histone alteration mechanisms are found in this subtype. From the histone mutation standpoint, group 4 tumors feature a prototypical inactivation of KDM6A/UTX, a member of the lysine demethylase family [27,36]. The interesting point lies in the fact that KDM6A/UTX mutations, which are more common in this group, have the opposite effect of EZH2 amplifications typical of group 3 tumors. In particular, while the former promotes transcription by removing methyl groups and acetylating histones, the latter causes histone demethylation and chromatin compaction. Further, these two mutations are mutually exclusive in group 3 and group 4 medulloblastomas [40]. This finding may help shed light on the differences between these subtypes.

2.6. Intermediate Group 3/Group 4 Medulloblastoma

There is an ongoing debate about the cellular and transcriptional nature of intermediate group 3/group 4 tumors. Luo et al. [11] have reported the presence of distinct group 3 and group 4 subpopulations in intermediate tumors by single-cell clustering. This finding is in direct contrast with those of Williamson et al. [45], showing that group 3 and group 4 tumor cells exist along a common transcriptional continuum that reflects the glutamatergic lineage of cerebellar development. In this last model, group 3 cells resemble more primitive cells in the rhombic lip while group 4 cells are closer to the more differentiated excitatory UBC cohort. Moreover, the DNA methylation subtypes of group 3/4 tumor cells also lie along this same continuum. The distribution of single-medulloblastoma tumors along this spectrum is influenced by both transcriptional status and methylation subtype and appears to have prognostic significance, particularly in the first five years post-diagnosis.

In the analysis by Hovestadt et al., intermediate group 3/group 4 tumors consisted of an admixture of both DNA methylation subtypes and metaprograms from the two extremes. The authors interpreted these findings as reflecting a cell state continuum rather than a combination of distinct cellular populations [9]. Similarly, a recent work by Smith et al. [41] identified a common developmental origin for both group 3 and group 4 medulloblastomas in the RLsvz. The whole spectrum of group 3, group 4, and intermediate group 3/group 4 tumors lies along the differentiation axis of cells arising from the RLsvz, with early cells that bear a photoreceptor gene signature developing into group 3 medulloblastomas and late cells with a UBC signature giving rise to group 4 medulloblastomas. In this context, intermediate group 3/4 tumors featured a mixed photoreceptor-like and UBC-like expression profile, and a specific gene signature still lining along the RL-UBC developmental axis (DDX31-GFI1B, OTX2, and MYCN) (Figure 1).

In this emerging perspective, group 3 and group 4 medulloblastomas may share a developmental origin in the RL, supporting the idea of a transcriptional and DNA methylation gradient encompassing group 3, group 4, and intermediate group 3/4 tumors. The proportion of differentiated cell states may reveal the precise biology of each individual tumor and determine its position along this axis. In fact, while group 3 tumors are comprised only up to 10% differentiated neuronal-like cells, group 4 tumors may almost entirely be composed of differentiated UBC-like and Glu-CN-like cells [31]. On the other hand, intermediate group 3/4 medulloblastomas feature a mixture of undifferentiated and mature neuron-like cells [9,31]. Finally, differences in epigenetic alterations, which were discussed previously, may provide another way to distinguish group 3 and group 4 tumors along the group 3/4 tumor spectrum.

3. Subgroup-Specific Targeted Therapies in Medulloblastoma

3.1. WNT-Activated Medulloblastoma

This subgroup of medulloblastomas is known for its excellent prognosis and high survival rates. Indeed, it has been reported by multiple studies that the 5-year survival rate of patients less than 16 years of age with WNT-activated medulloblastomas is greater than 90% following standard treatment with surgery, chemotherapy, and radiation therapy [34,46,47]. The favorable prognosis of this subtype is attributed to the greater penetration of chemotherapeutic agents due to the aberrant vasculature and disrupted blood–brain barrier function in the vicinity of these tumors [48]. In this context, when compared to other subtypes, WNT medulloblastomas were found to have more dense and tortuous vessels with fenestrated endothelial lining and disrupted tight junctions. This leaky phenotype is due to the suppression of the WNT pathway, which is crucial for proper angiogenesis, in the endothelial cells by paracrine signaling from neighboring WNT-activated tumors. In specific, these tumors secrete WNT inhibitors, such as WNT Inhibitor Factor 1 (WIF1) and Dickkopf 1 (DKK1), potentially as part of a negative feedback loop. These WNT inhibitors diffuse and execute their angiogenesis-disrupting effects on the nearby vasculature, thus producing the leaky phenotype [48].

Despite the excellent prognosis achieved with the current treatment regimen, the used modalities are not without risks and complications. One of the major concerns for using the high doses of craniospinal irradiation that are used in cases of medulloblastoma in the pediatric population is the association with long-term neurocognitive impairment [49]. Therefore, research on WNT-activated medulloblastomas has shifted towards de-escalation trails that aim at reducing the unnecessarily high doses of radiation and chemotherapy in this well-responding group. The importance of these dose de-escalation efforts is supported by evidence on the reduced intellectual burden in WNT medulloblastoma survivors who received lower radiation doses [50]. Investigating the possibility of de-escalated therapies in WNT-activated medulloblastoma gained great traction after the results of the Children's Oncology Group (COG) trial, ACNS0331 (NCT00085735), were published. This trial showed that reducing the dose of craniospinal irradiation resulted in lower survival rates for patients with medulloblastoma; however, a subgroup analysis of patients with WNT-activated medulloblastomas showed favorable outcomes for dose de-escalation in this subgroup only [51]. Based on that, another trial by COG (NCT02724579) was initiated and is currently ongoing to assess the outcomes of reduced dose radiotherapy (18 Gy craniospinal irradiation and 36 Gy to the tumor bed) and reduced chemotherapy (eliminating vincristine during radiotherapy and using a reduced maintenance dose) in WNT-activated medulloblastoma (clinicaltrials.gov (accessed on 24 July 2023)). Similarly, the FOR-WNT2 clinical trial (NCT04474964) is also currently recruiting and investigates the impact of the same reduced dose of radiation therapy on clinical outcomes in this subgroup of medulloblastoma. However, it is worth mentioning that previous attempts to avoid radiation therapy altogether or use focal radiation therapy only instead of craniospinal irradiation were aborted due to the high relapse rates [52].

Although the de-escalation trials provide a promising route for attenuating the deleterious side effects of radiation and chemotherapy, new targeted agents are still needed to replace these traditional therapies or at least help in further reducing the needed doses. In this context, targeting the WNT pathway might present itself as a rational option in this subgroup (Figure 2); however, there are several challenges that arise when attempting to target this pathway. First, the WNT pathway plays a pivotal role in bone formation, hematopoiesis, tissue repair and regeneration, and homeostatic balance in several organs, and thus multiple deleterious effects and interruption of developmental processes can be anticipated if this pathway is disrupted [53]. Second, there is valid concern that targeting the WNT pathway might jeopardize the favorable features seen in WNT-activated medulloblastomas, such as their leaky vasculature and excellent response to chemotherapy. Finally, the complexity of this signaling pathway makes it difficult to determine which players in the cascade are the ideal targets for pharmacotherapeutic approaches [53].

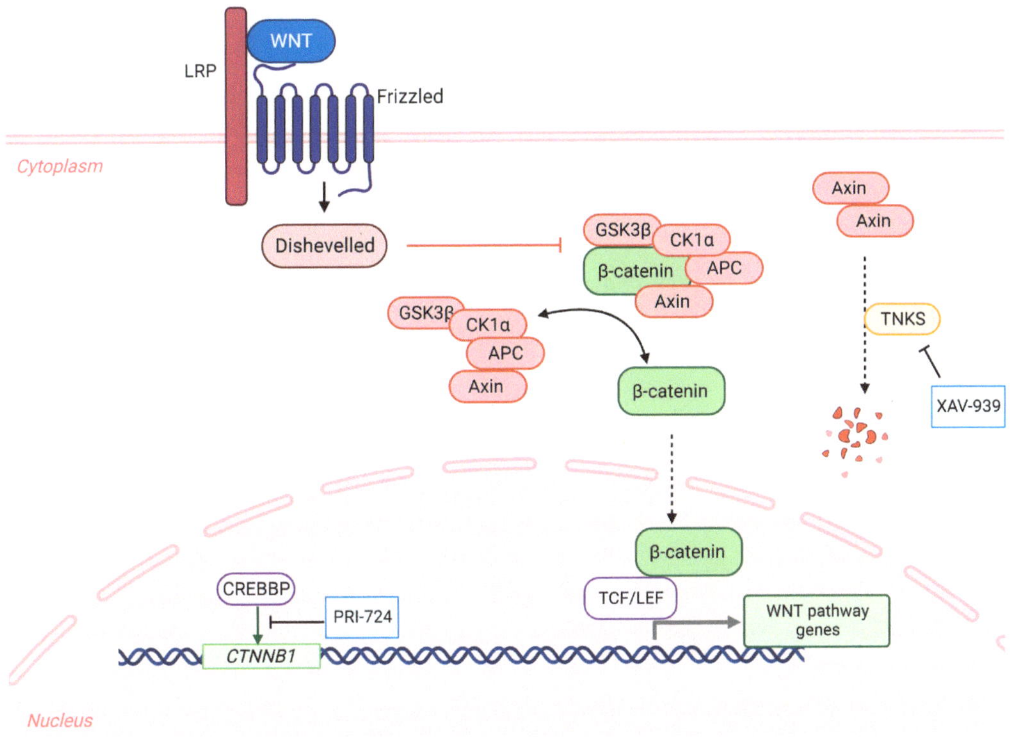

Figure 2. The activated canonical WNT pathway and potential pharmacotherapeutic options to target it. Canonical WNT signaling begins with the binding of the WNT ligand to the dimeric cell surface receptor composed of the Frizzled transmembrane protein and LRP. This causes the activation of the downstream Disheveled protein, which in its turn leads to the dissociation of β-catenin from the complex (Axin, APC, GSK3β, and CK1α) that tags it for degradation. The freed β-catenin can now translocate into the nucleus to cooperate with TCF/LEF in inducing the expression of the effector WNT pathway genes. Pharmacotherapeutic interventions that can target this pathway include PRI-724, which disrupts the CREBBP-mediated expression of the *CTNNB1* gene, which encodes β-catenin. Another drug is the TNKS inhibitor XAV-939, which can prevent the TNKS-mediated destruction of Axin, hence, leaving more Axin available to hinder the actions of β-catenin. APC, adenomatous polyposis coli; CK1α, Casein kinase 1 alpha; CREBBP, CREB binding protein; GSK3β, glycogen synthase kinase 3 beta; LRP, lipoprotein receptor-related protein; TCF/LEF, T-cell factor/lymphoid enhancer factor; TNKS, tankyrase; WNT, wingless.

Despite these challenges, there are several molecular targets that are worth being explored in this subtype. Mutant DDX3, an RNA helicase, has been shown to augment the activity mutant β-catenin, and the two molecules synergistically increased the proliferation of medulloblastoma cell lines [54]. Interestingly, using RK-33, a small-molecule inhibitor of DDX3, resulted in inhibition of the WNT pathway and G1 arrest in the medulloblastoma cells in vitro [55]. Not only that, but RK-33 was also associated with increased radiosensitivity of in vitro DAOY and UW228 cell cultures and of DAOY flank tumors in nude mice [55]. Another molecule that has been investigated as a potential target for interfering with the WNT pathway is tankyrase (TNKS), which is implicated in the regulation of this pathway. TNKS inhibitors induce the accumulation of Axin, thus further stabilizing the complex (Axin, APC, GSK3β, and CKIα) that tags β-catenin for destruction [56] (Figure 2). Herein, XAV-939, one of the earliest TKNS inhibitors, was shown to inhibit WNT signaling in DAOY and ONS-76 cell lines. Furthermore, XAV-939 treatment disrupts the DNA repair abilities of these cell lines and increases their sensitivity to ionizing radiation [57]. However, it is important to mention that XAV-939 can also inhibit the poly-ADP-ribose polymerase 1 (PARP1). So, it is not clear whether the XAV-939-induced radiosensitivity is mainly due to its TNKS or PARP1 inhibitory effects. Nevertheless, TNKS inhibitors are worth being considered as promising agents in WNT-activated medulloblastomas especially with the advent of newer and more effective agents in this class [58]. Additionally, fenretinide, which is a synthetic analogue of all-trans retinoic acid, has shown that it possesses anti-WNT properties. In specific, the expression of WNT3A and its downstream effectors was reduced in DAOY and ONS-76 cells after treatment with fenretinide [59]. Moreover, fenretinide was able to inhibit the proliferation of these cell lines in vitro [59]. However, further studies are warranted to confirm whether fenretinide's anti-cancer effects are reproducible in animal models and whether they are solely due to WNT inhibition or to its other effects on cellular oxidative balance [60].

On top of the aforementioned approaches, there are multiple tractable targets that can be exploited to hinder WNT signaling and that have shown promising results in other types of cancer with WNT upregulation. However, these targets have not been well-studied in the context of medulloblastoma yet. For instance, the interaction between CREBBP and *CTNNB1* is crucial for the transcriptional activation of this gene, and thus for WNT signaling (Figure 2). Here, it is worth mentioning that PRI-724, which inhibits the CREBBP: *CTNNB1* interaction, has shown promising results as a combination therapy in a phase 1 trial against advanced pancreatic adenocarcinoma (NCT01764477) [61]. In addition to inhibiting the WNT pathway itself, other pathways that are commonly overactivated in the WNT subgroup of medulloblastomas can serve as potential targets. In specific, the ALK pathway has been proven to be a commonly overexpressed pathway in WNT-activated medulloblastomas and was even suggested as a novel biomarker for the diagnosis of this subgroup [62,63]. Therefore, ALK inhibitors might be appealing pharmacologic agents that deserve to be investigated in these tumors.

Furthermore, the emergence of epigenetic profiling and targeting techniques created novel routes for molecular-based therapeutics in medulloblastoma. Herein, the role of histone deacetylation was explored in these tumors, and it was found to contribute to the downregulation of the WNT inhibitor DKK1 in medulloblastoma. In fact, the use of the histone deacetylase inhibitor trichostatin A resulted in rescuing the expression of DKK1 and a subsequent increase in the apoptotic cell death of medulloblastoma cells [64]. Such epigenetic interventions are worth being further studied to confirm their applicability and efficacy.

3.2. SHH-Activated Medulloblastoma

The SHH-activated subgroup has the most adequately characterized molecular and genetic profile offering a wide array of appealing targets. Subsequently, a myriad of therapeutic agents has been investigated to modulate the SHH pathway or other oncogenic pathways that interact with it (Figure 3). In a nutshell, the SHH signaling cascade is initiated with the binding of the SHH ligand to the PTCH transmembrane receptor, thus removing the blockade of the latter on SMO, which is a G protein-coupled receptor. In its turn, SMO translocates to the primary cilium where it causes the activation of proteins belonging to the glioma-associated oncogene (GLI) family by triggering their dissociation from their repressor SUFU. Upon that, GLI proteins translocate to the nucleus and orchestrate the transcription of effector genes involved in the actions of the SHH pathway. In addition to this canonical pathway, multiple alternative non-canonical pathways have been shown to activate SHH signaling downstream of SMO [65].

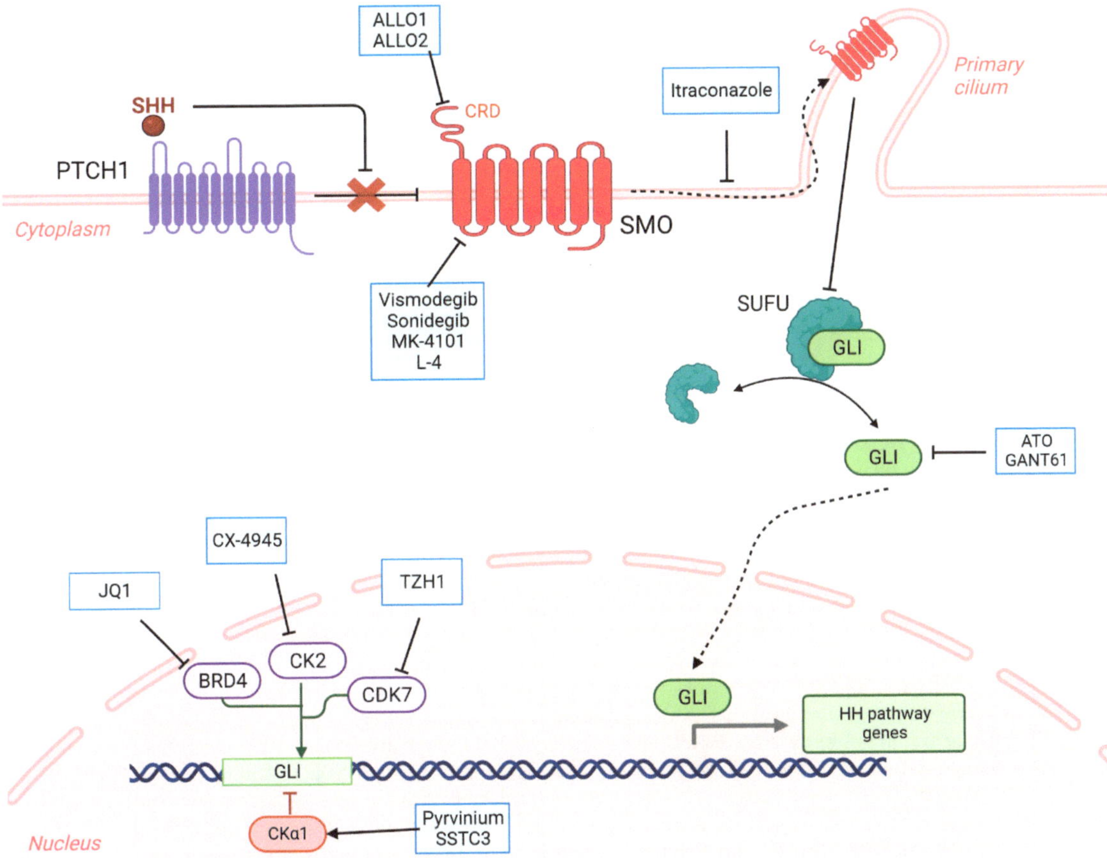

Figure 3. The activated SHH pathway and potential pharmacotherapeutic options to target it. SHH pathway signaling commences with the binding of the SHH ligand to the PTCH1 receptor. This binding lifts the PTCH1-mediated inhibition SMO. SMO is now able to translocate to the primary cilium where it can activate downstream signaling, mainly causing the dissociation of GLI from it repressor SUFU. The freed GLI protein translocates to the nucleus to induce the expression of effector SHH pathway genes. The expression of GLI itself is under the control of certain mediators, with BRD4, CK2, and CDK7 positively regulating the gene's transcription and CKα1 negatively regulating it. Several pharmacotherapeutic agents can target the SHH pathway at different levels. Vismodegib, sonidegib, MK-4101, and L-4 can all inhibit SMO by binding to its transmembrane domain, while ALLO1 and ALLO2 can inhibit this receptor by binding to its CRD. On the other hand, itraconazole can block the actions of SMO by hindering its translocation to the primary cilium. Inhibiting the GLI protein can be achieved by directly targeting it via antagonists such as ATO and GANT61 or through targeting its expression. The latter process can be achieved by either inhibiting the GLI gene's positive transcriptional regulators (BRD4, CK2, and CDK7) or activating its negative transcriptional regulator CK α1. ATO, arsenic trioxide; BRD4, bromodomain 4; CDK7, cyclin-dependent kinase 7; CKα1, casein kinase alpha 1; CK2, casein kinase 2; CRD, cysteine-rich domain; GANT61, GLI antagonist 61; GLI, glioma-associated oncogene; PTCH1, patched 1; SHH, sonic hedgehog; SMO, smoothened.

The road towards developing targeted therapies that can disrupt SHH signaling started with SMO inhibitors. In specific, SMO is composed of two extracellular domains called the cysteine-rich domain and the linker domain, a transmembrane domain consisting of seven membrane-spanning subunits, and an intracellular domain responsible for downstream signaling. Herein, cyclopamine is the earliest SMO inhibitor investigated in the context of SHH-activated medulloblastoma, and it acts by binding to the transmembrane portion of the receptor (Figure 3). However, several concerns regarding the safety of this drug have arisen and led to the abortion of further clinical investigations regarding its utility in medulloblastoma [66]. Nevertheless, cyclopamine ignited the search for other small molecules that can suppress the activity of SMO with comparable efficacy and more acceptable safety profiles. The most popular among these are vismodegib (GDC-0449) and sonidegib (LDE-225), which have shown promising effects in preclinical models [67,68] and made it to clinical trials. Interestingly, both drugs have already been FDA-approved for use in locally advanced basal cell carcinoma [69]. In the context of medulloblastoma, the Pediatric Brain Tumor Consortium (PBTC) conducted a phase I clinical trial (PBTC-025, NCT00822458) that confirmed the tolerability of vismodegib [70], and then followed this trial with two phase II trials involving adult patients (PBTC-025B, NCT00939484) and pediatric patients (PBTC-032, NCT01239316) with recurrent or refractory medulloblastomas. The results of these phase II trials showed an increased progression-free survival in adult patients with SHH medulloblastoma compared to those with non-SHH medulloblastoma, suggesting an effective role for vismodegib in the former subgroup [71]. Currently, an ongoing phase II clinical trial (NCT01878617) by St. Jude's Children's Research Hospital that assigns different interventions based on molecular subgroup and risk stratification investigates the efficacy of vismodegib in skeletally mature patients belonging to both standard-risk and high-risk SHH subgroups. In a similar fashion, sonidegib has shown good safety and efficacy in pediatric and adult patients with progressive or refractory SHH-activated medulloblastomas during a phase I/II trial (NCT01125800) [72]. In addition, an actively recruiting randomized controlled phase II trial (PersoMed-I, NCT04402073) by the European Organisation for Research and Treatment of Cancer aims to assess the efficacy of sonidegib with reduced-dose radiotherapy in post-pubertal patients with SHH-activated medulloblastomas. Although vismodegib and sonidegib are the most popular agents that target the transmembrane domain of SMO, there are several other drugs that have a similar mechanism and that have also shown promising results in animal models of medulloblastoma, such as MK-4101, L-4, and nilotinib; however, these agents have not entered clinical trials yet [66]. Additionally, the agents ALLO1 and ALLO2 have been found to inhibit SMO through a different mechanism involving the cysteine-rich domain and have shown anti-proliferative effects in medulloblastoma cells [66] (Figure 3).

Although the results of the mentioned trials involving vismodegib and sonidegib were encouraging in the SHH-activated subgroups, the development of resistance to these agents was reported clinically. One identified mutation that causes this resistance is the D473H mutation of the SMO protein. Herein, a relatively newer agent, taladegib (ENV-101, LY2940680), has been shown to overcome this resistance method and suppress SMO in its wild-type and mutated forms [73]. Taladegib is currently being investigated in a phase II clinical trial (NCT05199584) involving patients with solid tumors and PTCH1 loss of function mutations, which is a common mutation in SHH-activated medulloblastomas. Recently, Ji et al. synthesized a taladegib-based compound that elicits a more potent inhibition of SMO and a more significant attenuation of DAOY cells proliferation [74]. On the other hand, the antifungal itraconazole inhibits the activity of SMO through halting its translocation to the cilium (Figure 3), and it appears to be effective against D477G-mutant medulloblastoma mouse models that are resistant to other SMO antagonists [75,76]. In a similar fashion, the repurposing of the antiparasitic drug mebendazole has gained wide attention for its promising potential as an anti-cancer drug [77]. In specific, mebendazole was also found to inhibit SHH signaling by hindering the formation of the primary cilium, and thus resulted in decreased proliferation of DAOY cells in vitro and extended the survival of SHH medulloblastoma orthotopic models [78,79]. Importantly, the inhibitory effect of mebendazole was also present when used on vismodegib-resistant models. A phase 1 clinical trial of mebendazole in progressive/refractory pediatric brain tumors, including medulloblastoma, was conducted at the Sidney Kimmel Comprehensive Cancer Center at Johns Hopkins (NCT02644291), but the results are yet to be published.

In addition to resistance at the level of SMO itself, other genetic alterations were commonly found in non-responders to vismodegib and sonidegib. As expected, these genetic alterations consist of mutations involving members of the SHH pathway downstream of SMO, such as SUFU and GLI1 [71,80,81]. Not only that, but also the crosstalk between SHH and other oncogenic pathways that are commonly overactivated in medulloblastoma, such as PI3K/mTOR and RAS/REF/MEK, can play a significant role in evading SMO inhibition [6].

The aforementioned challenges have geared the research efforts towards targeting the SHH pathway at points that are further downstream of SMO. In specific, disrupting the production and action of GLI proteins at different levels has gained significant attention (Figure 3). For instance, BET proteins have been recognized as tractable epigenetic targets in several cancer types, including medulloblastoma. In specific, BRD4 interacts with the promoter regions of GLI1 and GLI2 and enhances their transcription. Notably, JQ1, a BRD4 inhibitor, was shown to inhibit the SHH-mediated proliferation of several tumors, including medulloblastomas, and to overcome their resistance to SMO antagonists [82]. A phase I clinical trial (NCT03936465) is currently recruiting pediatric patients with solid tumors or lymphoma, with a separate arm for refractory or metastatic CNS tumors, to assess the safety of the BRD inhibitors BMS-986378 and BMS-986158. Another avenue for modulating the transcription of GLI proteins is targeting the casein kinases alpha 1 and 2 (CKα1 and CK2). CKα1 is a negative regulator of GLI transcription factors, while CK2 is a positive one. Expectedly, both CKα1 agonists (pyrvinium and SSTC3) and CK2 antagonists (CX-4945) have shown significant efficacy in SHH-activated medulloblastoma mouse models, even in the presence of the TP53 mutation which, as previously mentioned, imparts a worse prognosis [66]. In fact, an actively recruiting clinical trial (NCT03904862) investigates the safety and tolerability of CX-4945 in skeletally immature patients with refractory/recurrent SHH-activated medulloblastoma (phase I) and its efficacy in skeletally mature patients with refractory/recurrent SHH-activated medulloblastoma (phase II). Moreover, the CDK7 is implicated in the transcriptional regulation of GLI and has been investigated as a potential target to disrupt SHH signaling. The CDK7 inhibitor, TZH1, has shown significant potency in suppressing the SHH-mediated proliferation of medulloblastoma cells, including those that are resistant to SMO inhibitors [83]. In addition to targeting GLI proteins at the transcriptional level, direct inhibitors of the protein have been discovered and evaluated (Figure 3). In this context, the GLI antagonist 61 (GANT61) and arsenic trioxide (ATO) have both shown promising results as direct inhibitors of GLI proteins in medulloblastoma. Specifically, GANT61 was able to attenuate the proliferation and migration of DAOY cells, induce their apoptosis, augment their response to cisplatin, and sensitize them to particle radiation (protons and carbon ions) [84,85]. ATO inhibited the proliferation of SHH-activated medulloblastoma cell lines both in vitro and in vivo [86,87]. Moreover, it increased the sensitivity of TP53-mutated SHH-activated medulloblastoma cells to radiation [87]. It is worth mentioning that ATO has already entered phase I and phase II clinical trials for other pediatric brain tumors and has shown encouraging results [88,89].

Apart from targeting the SHH pathway itself at different levels, several groups have investigated the utility of targeting other pathways or effectors that are commonly overactivated in this subgroup of medulloblastomas. For instance, the Mesenchymal–Epithelial Transition factor (cMET) was found to be upregulated in SHH-activated medulloblastoma and to correlate with worse prognosis [90]. Hence, the cMET inhibitor foretinib was investigated for the treatment of this subgroup of medulloblastoma, and it showed acceptable penetration of the blood–brain barrier and significant suppression of the proliferation and migration of SHH-activated medulloblastomas in xenograft mouse models [90]. Another molecule that has been found to possess interesting interactions with the SHH pathway is the AMP-activated protein kinase (AMPK). In this context, AMPK is a cellular sensor of a low energy state that regulates energy-demanding function and shuts them down when needed, and among these functions is the activation of the SHH pathway. Indeed, activated AMPK has been proven to negatively regulate GLI1 in a direct manner by triple phosphorylating it, undermining its stability, and promoting its degradation [91]. In addition, AMPK has been suggested to regulate GLI1 in an indirect manner also, mainly through its suppression of the activity of the mTOR/S6K pathway, which upregulates GLI1 expression [91]. Hence, these inhibitory effects that AMPK exerts on the SHH pathway downstream of SMO are worth being explored for their potential therapeutic benefits. In fact, the antidiabetic drug metformin has been investigated as an anti-cancer agent due to its ability to promote the activity of AMPK, suppress the action of mTOR, and subsequently attenuate SHH/GLI signaling. Promising effects of the drug have been documented in the context of prostate cancer, gastric cancer, and hepatocellular carcinoma [92–94], and it is, therefore, worth being further investigated in the setting of SHH-activated medulloblastoma. On another note, with the increased interest in epigenetics and their utility in cancer therapeutics, epigenetic profiling of SHH-driven medulloblastomas exhibited an increased expression of the miR17~92 polycitron in this subgroup and a synergistic effect between this overexpression and the SHH pathway to augment the growth of cancer cells [95]. Herein, the use of locked nucleic acid (LNA) antisense oligonucleotides (anti-miRs) to inhibit miRNAs has been explored. Specifically, anti-miR17 and anti-miR19, which inhibit miRNAs 17 and 19-a that belong to the miR17~92 complex, were able to suppress the proliferation of SHH-activated medulloblastoma cells in vitro and hinder the progression of tumors belonging to this subgroup in vivo [96]. Not only that, but differences in the immune profiles of medulloblastoma subgroups have been exploited to derive subgroup-specific immunomodulators. In this context, Tumor-associated macrophages (TAMs) were noticed to play a cancer-promoting role in medulloblastomas belonging to the SHH subgroup with SMO mutations [97]. Hence, the treatment of mice harboring SMO-mutated SHH-activated medulloblastomas with PLX5622, an inhibitor of the colony-stimulating factor 1 receptor (CSF1R), resulted in a reduced proportion of TAMs in the tumor microenvironment, shrinkage in tumor sizes, and prolonged survival of the mice [97].

A field that is attracting significant interest is the identification and targeting of cancer stem cells in brain tumors. This is because these cells are suggested to be major contributors to recurrence and resistance to conventional therapies [98]. Therefore, the identification of biomarkers that are characteristic of cancer stem cells in medulloblastoma has been crucial for deriving modalities to target these cells more effectively. For instance, CD15-positive cells were identified as tumor progenitor cells in an SHH medulloblastoma mouse model, and a large proportion of these cells was found to be in the G2/M phase of the cell cycle. Hence, targeting players that are specific to this phase was hypothesized as an effective method to abolish the proliferative potential of these cells. Indeed, inhibiting polo-like kinase (PLK) and Aurora kinase (AURK), which are pivotal for the G2/M transition of the cell cycle, using BI-2536 and VX-680 (tozasertib), respectively, resulted in increased apoptosis of SHH-driven medulloblastoma cells in vitro and in vivo [99]. Additionally, single-cell transcriptomics revealed that the OLIG2/SOX2 axis is especially overactivated in actively cycling progenitor cells in SHH-driven medulloblastomas and is a significant contributor to their self-renewal capacity. In fact, OLIG2 expression was also observed to be prominent in recurrent tumors, suggesting a role for this molecule in resistance to treatment [100]. Since OLIG2 is a nuclear transcriptional factor that is difficult to target directly, Zhang et al. identified other targetable effectors that mediate the actions of OLIG2 in these progenitor cells. Herein, the HIPPO-YAP/TAZ and the AURK/MYCN pathways are major mediators of OLIG2 actions. Notably, the combination of CD532, which disrupts the interaction between AURK and MYCN, and verteporfin, a YAP inhibitor, was associated with a dramatic suppression of tumor growth both in vitro and in vivo and an increased survival of SHH-activated medulloblastoma-bearing mice [100].

At any rate, with the discovery of novel agents that can disrupt the SHH pathway at multiple layers or target other oncogenic pathways that synergize with it, the potential for combination therapies that can achieve more efficacious results and reduce resistance to treatment is reinforced. For instance, in order to avoid the non-canonical activation of the SHH pathway by the oncogenic PI3k pathway, the concomitant use of PI3K inhibitors with sonidegib was attempted. Indeed, this combination impeded the development of resistance in SHH-driven medulloblastoma cells [101]. Similarly, the combination of an SMO inhibitor with the PLK inhibitor BI-2536 exhibited superior responses as compared to the use of the former agent alone [99]. Not only that, but evidence suggests that combination therapies can also be utilized against populations of tumor progenitor cells in medulloblastoma. In specific, the chemokine receptor CXCR4 was found to be frequently expressed with CD15, indicating a role for the former in progenitor cells [102]. Intriguingly, the co-inhibition of CXCR4 and SMO using AMD3100 and vismodegib, respectively, attenuated the proliferation of SHH-driven medulloblastoma flank and intracerebellar xenografts [102]. Finally, it is worth noting that an active phase I trial by the St. Jude Children's research hospital (NCT03434262, SJDAWN) compares multiple combinations of molecularly driven therapies in pediatric patients with medulloblastoma, and it includes an arm that evaluates the combination of sonidegib with ribociclib, a CDK4/6 inhibitor, in refractory/recurrent cases of SHH-activated medulloblastoma.

3.3. Group 3 Medulloblastoma

This subtype of medulloblastomas has the greatest potential for invasion and metastasis and carries the most dismal prognosis. Consequently, it shows minimal response to conventional therapies. Hence, novel targeted therapies that are effective against this subgroup are greatly needed and have been a topic of interest for several laboratories worldwide. One of the factors that have been associated with a worse prognosis in this subgroup is the presence of MYC amplification. In this context, a relationship was discovered between BRD inhibitors and MYC activity. Specifically, the BRD4 inhibitor, JQ1, was shown to reduce the proliferation of group 3 medulloblastoma cells with MYC amplification and to prolong the survival of mouse models with tumors having these characteristics [103,104] (Figure 4). In a similar fashion, a novel in silico drug screening method, named DiSCoVER, predicted a potential role for CDK inhibitors in MYC-activated group 3 medulloblastomas [105]. Indeed, the CDK4/6 inhibitor, palbociclib, was proven to elicit anti-proliferative and pro-apoptotic effects against in vivo and in vitro models of this subgroup [105,106]. Likewise, the CDK1/5 inhibitor, alsterpaullone, has also shown significant inhibition of the MYC-dependent proliferation of against group 3 medulloblastoma cells [107]. Notably, the safety of palbociclib in pediatric patients has been confirmed in a phase I clinical trial (NCT02255461) involving pediatric patients with progressive or refractory brain tumors [108]. Further, a phase II trial (SJDAWN, NCT03434262) is currently active and evaluates the efficacy of ribociclib, another CDK4/6 inhibitor, combined with gemcitabine in recurrent/refractory group 3/4 medulloblastoma. In a surveillance of the phosphor-proteomic footprint of medulloblastoma, the DNA-dependent protein kinase PRKDC was predicted to play an important role in group 3 medulloblastomas [109]. Indeed, it was found that the levels of this kinase were elevated in this subgroup, and other experiments have uncovered its contribution to MYC stability. Additionally, PRKDC is known to play a role in non-homologous end joining during repair of DNA damage. Consequently, PRKDC inhibitors were investigated for their potential role in therapy, and they were found to elicit radiosensitizing effects in the D458 cell line, which resembles group 3 medulloblastoma with MYC amplification. However, PRKDC inhibitors did not show cytotoxic effects on their own [109]. In a parallel fashion, a large genomic analysis of MYC-driven group 3 medulloblastoma revealed an elevated expression of the inhibitory GABA-A receptor subunit alpha 5 (α5-GABAA). Therefore, an increased susceptibility of these cells to GABA agonists was hypothesized. Indeed, the α5-GABAA-specific agonist, QHii066, was able to induce apoptosis and cell cycle arrest of MYC-amplified medulloblastoma cells and to sensitize mice harboring D425 tumors, which mimic group 3 medulloblastoma with MYC amplification, to radiation therapy and cisplatin [110]. The anti-proliferative effects of this agonism were dependent on the activation of HOX5 and its related genes, which has already been implicated as an anti-cancer player in several cancers [110]. Based on these encouraging results, Jonas et al. tested the efficacy of several GABA agonists delivered to a model of intracranial group 3 medulloblastoma with MYC amplification, and they concluded that the benzodiazepine derivative KRM-II-08 is more potent that other agonists, including QHii066, and can offer a greater pro-apoptotic effect in these tumors [111]. Furthermore, targeting PLK1, SETD8, and facilitator of chromatin transcription (FACT) with their respective inhibitors onvasertib, UNC0379, and CBL0137 has also shown preclinical activity against MYC-amplified medulloblastoma [112–114]. It is also worth mentioning that the FDA-approved antiviral ribavirin, whose repurposing is currently being investigated in clinical trials for several cancer types [115], elicited anti-proliferative effects in D425 cells and showed a survival advantage in mice with intracranially implanted D425 tumors [116]. These effects of ribavirin were attributed to its ability to inhibit eukaryotic initiation factor 4E (eIF4E) and EZH2, both of which have been associated with MYC overexpression and group 3 medulloblastoma tumorigenesis [116]. Another FDA-approved drug that has shown good potential for repurposing is disulfiram, known as Antabuse. This drug, when combined with copper gluconate, induced apoptosis of group 3 and SHH-activated cell lines in vivo and prolonged the survival of mice with implanted cells from these lines [117]. Specifically, the effects of this combination were found to be mediated by the accumulation of nuclear protein localization protein-4 (NPL4) and the subsequent induction of cell death. Moreover, disulfiram plus copper treatment was shown to suppress DNA repair mechanisms, thus contributing to its lethal effect and suggesting a potential role as a sensitizer to radiotherapy or certain chemotherapies [117].

Based on the aforementioned therapeutic approaches, one can safely say that targeting MYC-amplified group 3 medulloblastoma has attracted a great majority of the research in this subtype. This overrepresentation of MYC-amplified group 3 medulloblastomas in the literature is, in fact, a reflection of the overabundance of cell lines that mimic this specific molecular profile [26]. Although MYC-activation is one of the hallmarks of this subgroup and inflicts a worse prognosis, it is only present in approximately 17% of group 3 tumors. Hence, several groups explored the utility of targeting other overactivated pathways that this subgroup might be dependent on. In particular, GFI1/GFI1B overexpression was found to be a present in 15–20% of group 3 medulloblastoma and to play a significant role at the different stages of tumorigenesis [118]. A downstream effector that was implicated in the GIF1/GIF1B-driven growth is LSD1. As expected, the use of LSD1 inhibitors, GSK-LSD1 and ORY-1001, attenuated the proliferation GIF1/GIF1B-driven medulloblastoma cells both in vitro and in mouse models with flank-implanted tumors, however, not those with intracranially implanted tumors (Figure 4). This indicates that these agents have inadequate brain–blood barrier penetration, which calls for evaluating other agents with better pharmacologic properties or alternative drug delivery methods [118]. Additionally, gene set enrichment analysis revealed an especially elevated activity of the folate metabolism pathway in group 3 medulloblastomas. Subsequently, the utility of the combination of the folate pathway inhibitor pemetrexed and the chemotherapeutic agent gemcitabine was investigated, and it showed significant inhibition of the growth of both in vitro and in vivo models of group 3 medulloblastoma. This combination is currently being investigated as part of a phase II clinical trial (NCT01878617) in the arms involving intermediate- and high-risk patients with non-WNT non-SHH medulloblastoma. Another pattern that was identified in group 3 medulloblastoma cells is the abundance of CD47 on their surface. CD47 is a cell membrane protein that helps cells evade being phagocytosed by cells of the innate immunity, and it achieves this effect by downstream activation of the signal regulatory protein alpha (SIRPα). In this framework, systemic treatment with Hu5F9-G4, which disrupts the interaction between CD47 and SIRPα, resulted in shrinkage of primary tumors and leptomeningeal metastasis in mouse models with implanted patient-derived group 3 medulloblastoma xenografts and mouse cell lines of this subgroup. On the other hand, intraventricular delivery of Hu5F9-G4 provided a more effective route in combating leptomeningeal and spinal metastases; however, it did not show significant impact at the primary tumor site [119]. This suggests that if this therapeutic agent reaches clinical application, the preferred mode of delivery might be dependent on the stage of the disease and the extent of resection of the primary tumor during surgery. Importantly, Hu5F9-G4 was determined to have minimal cytotoxic side effects on normal central nervous system cells, implying a favorable safety profile and a greater potential for clinical use [119]. In addition to targeting metastatic sites themselves, other experiments focused on hindering the initiation of metastasis altogether. Herein, the NOTCH1 pathway was implicated as an important contributor to the invasion and migration abilities of group 3 medulloblastoma cells. As a result, the intrathecal administration of anti-NOTCH1 Negative Regulatory Region antibody (anti-NRR1) in mice bearing group 3 medulloblastomas resulted in an attenuation of the metastatic potential of these tumors and a survival advantage for the treated mice [120]. Due to the lower response of group 3 medulloblastomas to conventional chemotherapeutic regimens, research has also focused on underscoring the mechanisms that mediate its chemoresistance and exploring druggable targets. In particular, the interleukin-6 (IL6)/gp130/Janus kinase (JAK)/signal transducer and activator of transcription 3 (STAT3) signaling pathway has been implicated in the development of chemoresistance to vincristine in group 3 medulloblastomas [121,122]. As a result, gp130 inhibitors (SC144 or bazedoxifene) and a JAK inhibitor (ruxolitinib) were individually investigated at non-cytotoxic doses and resulted in overcoming the acquired IL6-mediated resistance to vincristine in group 3 medulloblastomas [122].

The use of non-coding RNAs in the treatment of this subgroup has been widely studied with the hopes of finding alternative more effective therapies. Contextually, RNA-seq and miRNA profiling showed that medulloblastoma cells, especially those belonging to group 3, are enriched in miR-217 expression, which is known to promote proliferation and survival. As expected, interfering with miR-217 using anti-miR significantly reduced the proliferative, invasive, and migratory capacity of the group 3 medulloblastoma cell line HDMB03 [123]. Another miRNA that comprises a potential target is the pro-tumorigenic and pro-metastatic miR-183~96~182 complex, which was found to be upregulated in MYC-amplified medulloblastomas and to be an upstream inducer of PI3k/mTOR signaling [124]. On the other hand, several miRNAs were found to be downregulated in this subgroup, and their introduction can serve as a promising therapeutic avenue. In fact, the good prognostic role of two miRNAs, miR-148a and miR-193a, was discovered when group 3 medulloblastoma were compared to WNT medulloblastomas, which are known to carry the most favorable prognosis. In particular, restoration of miR-193a expression in group 3 medulloblastoma cells through treatment with 5-aza-deoxycytidine, a DNA methylation inhibitor, resulted in reduced proliferation and increased apoptosis and radiosensitivity of these cells [125]. In a similar fashion, miR-148a was found to be overexpressed in WNT medulloblastomas compared to the other subgroups, and rescuing its expression in D425 cells hindered their proliferative and invasive potential through downregulation of neuropillin1 (NRP1) [126]. In addition, two other miRNAs, miR-211 and miR-212-3p, were proven to elicit anti-oncogenic effects in in vitro models of group 3 medulloblastoma [127,128]. In addition to miRNAs, long non-coding RNAs (lncRNAs) also attracted the interest of researchers, and their expression profiles and implications in oncogenesis were investigated [129]. Herein, lnc-HLX-2-7 exhibited a differential overexpression in group 3 medulloblastomas, and its depletion resulted in attenuated proliferation and survival of cells belonging to this subgroup [130]. In fact, regulation of this lnRNA might be a major mechanism that mediates the previously discussed actions of the BRD4 inhibitor, JQ1, in this subgroup [130].

It important to note that the use of combination therapies has also emerged as an appealing route in the fight against group 3 medulloblastoma due to the aggressiveness and resistance of this subgroup. For instance, it has been shown that the combination of JQ1 with a CDK2 inhibitor (Milciclib), an mTOR inhibitor (BEZ235), or a pan-HDAC inhibitor (Panobinostat) resulted in synergistic anti-cancer effects in MYC-driven group 3 medulloblastoma and amplified the potential of each of the combined agents [131–133].

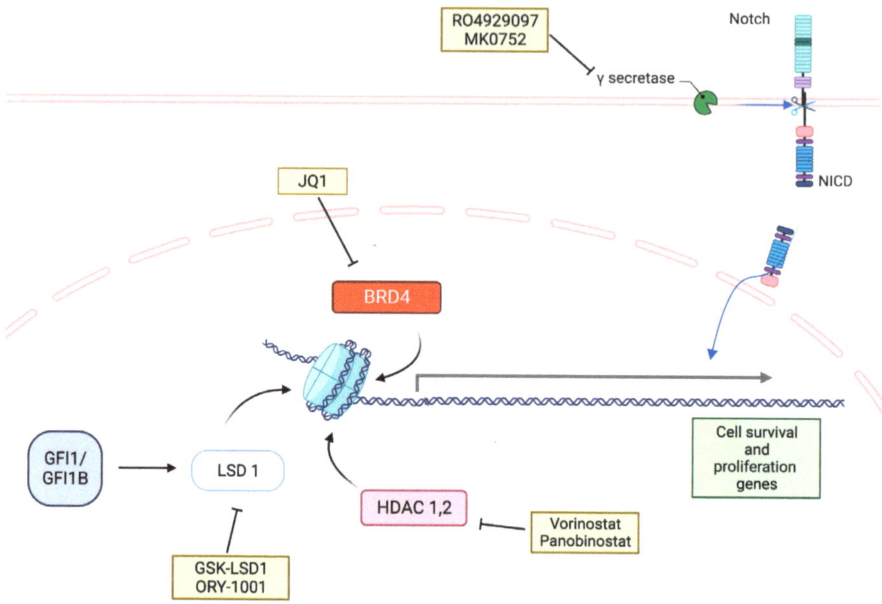

Figure 4. Molecular pathways implicated in tumoregenesis of non-WNT non-SHH medulloblastomas and potential pharmacotherapeutic options to target them. The NOTCH1 pathway is overactivated in group 3 and group 4 meduloblastoma. The activity of the pathway is dependent on the Gamma secretase cleavage of the NOTCH receptor, which results in the dissociation of NICD. Subsequently, NICD translocates to the nucleus and promotes the expression of downstream genes. In addition, the epigenetic modifiers HDACs 1/2, BRD4, and GFI1/GFI1B/LSD1 have been shown to play major roles in promoting the expression of pro-oncogenic genes (such as *MYC* in group 3 medulloblastoma). These epigenetic modifiers can be targeted using vorinostat and panobinostat for HDACs 1/2, JQ1 for BRD4, and GSK-LSD1 and ORY-1001 for LSD1. BRD4, Bromodomain 4; GFI, growth factor independent protein; HDAC, histone deacytylase; NICD, NOTCH intracellular domain.

3.4. Group 4 Medulloblastoma

Despite its prevalence, this subtype has the poorest characterization when it comes to genetic and molecular profiles. It also lacks representative preclinical models that allow for better profiling of this group and the development of targeted therapies. In specific, the only currently available cell lines that are used for group 4 research are CHLA-01-MED and CHLA-01R-MED, which were derived from the same patient [134]. This lack of representative cell lines and the ambiguity of this group's biology is reflected in the scarcity of selective therapies that target it. In fact, group 4 is frequently lumped with group 3 when it comes to the development of targeted therapies, even in emerging clinical trials. For instance, in the SJDAWN phase 1 clinical trial (NCT03434262) both group 3 and group 4 tumors belong to the same arm receiving ribociclib combined with gemcitabine although the efficacy of CDK4/6 inhibitors has only been proven in preclinical models of group 3 medulloblastoma. Nevertheless, tumors that belong to group 4 are also expected to respond to these inhibitors due to the high activity of CDK6 in this subgroup. In addition, it was suggested that LSD1 inhibitors have promising anti-proliferative effects against GFI1/GFI1B-driven group 3/4 medulloblastomas [118].

In light of the aforementioned findings, it is obvious that the development of adequate preclinical models for group 4 and the testing of novel agents that target it are crucial steps. Notably, some groups attempted to identify molecular targets that are overexpressed in this subtype using the two available cell lines. In particular, it was shown that the RNA-binding protein Musashi1 (MSI1) is specifically overexpressed in group 4 medulloblastoma, and it correlates with worse prognosis. Consequently, the use of an Msi1 inhibitor, luteolin, showed significant reduction in the proliferation of CHLA-01-MED and CHLA-01R-MED cells in vitro and augmented the effect of vincristine treatment [135]. Another effector that has been proven to be overexpressed in group 4 tumors and to be associated with more aggressive phenotypes is EZH2 [136]. In fact, using DZNep, an inhibitor of EZH2, was able to attenuate the proliferation of medulloblastoma cells in vitro [136]. This suggests that EZH2 inhibition can be of great potential in this subgroup; however, this needs to be further investigated using in vitro and in vivo models that specifically mimic group 4 medulloblastomas. Finally, a genome-wide gene enrichment analysis revealed several pathways that can provide tractable therapeutic targets in this subgroup. Herein, the NOTCH pathway was found to be overexpressed and to be closely related to prognosis [137]. In addition, the expression of NOTCH was also found to be associated with that of several immune-related effectors [137], hence suggesting a central role for this pathway in the survival of these tumors and their interaction with the immune system. In fact, several previous studies have highlighted the role of NOTCH signaling in regulating TAMs and mediating the immune resistance of other cancer types [138–141]. Interestingly, the gamma-secretase inhibitors (MK-0751, RO4929097), which hinder the cleavage of NOTCH intracellular domain (NICD) and its translocation to the nucleus to promote downstream effects, have entered clinical trials as potential therapeutic agents for refractory pediatric central nervous system tumors [142] (Figure 4). However, there are no dedicated studies that investigate the efficacy of NOTCH inhibition in preclinical models of group 4 medulloblastoma yet. In addition, other pharmacologic interventions that were predicted to be effective in this subgroup of medulloblastoma based on gene enrichment analyses are those that inhibit the estrogen-related receptor gamma (ESRRG), the JAK-STAT pathway, and members of the nucleotide biosynthesis pathway, such as dihydrofolate reductase [137]. At any rate, the efficacy of these modalities is also yet to be backed up by evidence from in vitro and in vivo experiments.

Despite the relatively low research interest in this subgroup, some attempts were made at characterizing the expression and roles of non-coding RNAs. In this context, the lnRNA SPRIGHTLY was found to be overexpressed in this subgroup. Additionally, the knockdown of SPRIGHTLY attenuated the proliferation of group 4 medulloblastoma cell lines and patient-derived xenografts both in vitro and in vivo [143]. This suggests that targeting this lnRNA might provide a compelling treatment avenue in group 4 medulloblastoma. Moreover, miR-592 was shown to play an oncogenic role in this subgroup through promoting mTOR and MAPK signaling [144]. However, it remains unclear if targeting this miRNA will produce favorable effects and whether it might offer a novel therapeutic approach.

4. Other Non-Specific Combination Therapies in Medulloblastoma

The concomitant deployment of therapeutic strategies could potentially offer a groundbreaking approach to treating medulloblastoma more effectively and aggressively, especially in the pediatric population. Indeed, combination therapy has yielded sustained and effective therapeutic solutions for other challenging cancer types. Here, we detail possible empiric combination regimens that may yield novel therapeutic strategies for medulloblastoma.

4.1. Targeting the PI3K/mTOR Pathway

Medulloblastomas and other malignant brain tumors are often associated with genetic mutations and epigenetic modifications that activate the PI3K/AKT/mTOR signaling pathway [145]. Activation of this pathway induces cell proliferation, migration, survival, metabolism, growth, and angiogenesis, thus making it a potential target for novel medulloblastoma combination therapeutics [146,147]. Several papers in the literature have investigated combination therapy involving this pathway as a pharmacologic target. The aberrant activation of the Hedgehog (HH) pathway along with the PI3K/mTOR pathway is frequently implicated in high-risk medulloblastoma. The roles of both HH and PI3K-mTOR signaling pathways have been linked to cancer "stem" cells, which can contribute to drug resistance in medulloblastoma. In this context it has been shown that vismodegib synergized well with BEZ235, a PI3K/mTOR dual inhibitor, to delay tumor growth both in vivo and in vitro [147]. Furthermore, this combination therapy sensitized cells to cisplatin, the current standard of care for patients diagnosed with medulloblastoma.

Moreover, some researchers investigated the combination of ribociclib with PI3K/mTOR inhibitors to investigate in vivo and in vitro efficacy [148]. However, their findings indicated that while molecular analysis displayed increased activity in vitro, this therapeutic strategy struggled to show in vivo enhanced survival or delay in tumor growth. Further investigations could show promising results on how CDK 4/6 inhibitors can be coupled with PI3K inhibitors to significantly improve the survival of medulloblastoma-bearing mice.

HDAC inhibitors are another potential therapeutic option for medulloblastomas and are particularly effective against established MYC-driven medulloblastoma cell lines and patient-derived xenografts [4]. HDAC inhibitors have been shown to upregulate expression of the FOXO1 tumor suppressor and they also work synergistically with PI3K/mTOR inhibitors to reduce tumor growth [149]. Activation of the PI3K/AKT/mTOR pathway results in phosphorylation of FOXO1 and prevents it from entering the nucleus [150], providing a mechanistic explanation for the enhanced anti-tumor effect of HDAC inhibitor and PI3K/mTOR inhibitor combination therapy [149,151].

4.2. Targeting Tyrosine Kinases

The receptor tyrosine kinase (RTK) family plays a crucial role in the development of medulloblastoma. Inappropriate activation of proteins such as EGFR, PDGFR, and cMET have been linked to the development and growth of medulloblastoma. Targeting RTK pathways has emerged as a promising approach for developing novel therapeutics against this type of tumor.

One unique therapeutic strategy aimed to leverage the role of epigenetics in medulloblastoma to develop a combination approach involving RTK inhibitors and HDAC/DNA methyltransferase (DNMT) inhibitors [152]. Specifically, epigenetic modifiers may enhance the expression of genes involved in tumor suppression and may synergistically work with RTK inhibitors that promote tumor growth. HDAC inhibitors such as 4-phenylbutyrate (4PB), suberoylanilide hydroxamic acid (SAHA), trichostatin A (TSA), and valproic acid (VPA) and DNMT inhibitors such as 5-azacytidine (5-AZA) and 5-aza-2′-deoxycytidine (5-AZA-CdR) were investigated [152]. These were combined with imatinib, a multi-kinase inhibitor. The study found that combining certain RTK inhibitors with certain epigenetic modifiers, such as SAHA and 5-AZA-CdR, resulted in a significant reduction in medulloblastoma cell growth compared to treatment with either agent alone. The combination of small-molecule inhibitors of RTKs and epigenetic modifiers may be a promising therapeutic approach for medulloblastoma. The potential of this therapeutic strategy was corroborated by the combination of 4PB with gefitinib/vandetanib and showed similar in vitro efficacy [153]. The researchers also observed changes in the expression of genes involved in cell proliferation and DNA damage response, suggesting that the combination of 4-PB and RTK inhibitors may have multiple targets in brain tumor cells [153]. Further research is needed to determine the optimal combination of agents and to assess the safety and efficacy of this approach in vivo [152,153].

The previously mentioned cMET is an RTK that is overexpressed in many human cancers, including medulloblastoma, while focal adhesion kinase (FAK) family members are involved in the regulation of cell adhesion, migration, and invasion. Previous literature has identified that cMET and FAK potentially cooperate in medulloblastoma. When co-overexpressed in medulloblastoma cells, the two proteins formed a complex and cooperated to promote cell proliferation, migration, and invasion [148,154]. RNA interference knockdown of cMET or FAK family members individually resulted in a partial reduction in medulloblastoma cell growth, while knockdown of both cMET and FAK family members resulted in a significant reduction in cell growth. A combination of cMET and FAK inhibitors resulted in a synergistic reduction in cell growth compared to treatment with either agent alone in vitro. However, since an oral FAK inhibitor was not pharmaceutically available, in vivo work utilizing this combination approach remains to be completed [148]. A recent study investigating glioblastoma showed that temozolomide and radiation treatment resulted in the cleavage of FAK, which was found to be mediated by caspase 3 [155]. Cleavage of FAK disrupted its activity and prevented its ability to promote cell invasion. Future work combining temozolomide/radiation with cMET inhibitors could be an interesting therapeutic strategy that could translate these in vitro findings to in vivo models.

4.3. Targeting Vascular Endothelial Growth Factor

Tumor cells commonly overexpress vascular endothelial growth factor (VEGF), which promotes angiogenesis and is associated with enhanced tumor invasiveness, metastasis, and growth [156]. Gao et al. reported that miRNA-210, which has previously been shown to regulate VEGF expression in other tumor environments [157], is also elevated in medulloblastomas and may influence metastasis via regulation of VEGF expression [158].

The SHH pathway plays a critical role in the development of the cerebellum and is frequently dysregulated in medulloblastoma [159]. A recent study published by Krushanov et al. conducted an integrated molecular analysis of adult SHH-activated medulloblastomas and identified two clinically relevant tumor subsets with distinct molecular features and prognoses. The authors found that VEGFA expression was significantly upregulated in one of the subsets and that high VEGFA expression was associated with poor clinical outcomes. These findings suggest that VEGFA may serve as a potent prognostic indicator and a potential therapeutic target for SHH-activated medulloblastomas [97]. In addition to VEGFA, emerging evidence suggests that hypoxia-inducible factor 1 alpha (HIF-1α) may also play a critical role in medulloblastoma pathogenesis. HIF-1α is a transcription factor that regulates various cellular processes in response to hypoxic conditions and is frequently overexpressed in solid tumors [160].

Since HIF-1α activates the expression of genes that promote angiogenesis (formation of new blood vessels), metabolic adaptation, and cell survival under hypoxic conditions. Inhibition of HIF-1α can disrupt these adaptive responses and can potentially induce cell death or sensitize cancer cells to other treatments. Combination of VEGFA and HIF-1α inhibitors could provide a synergistic combination therapy against medulloblastoma. While both targets have been individually investigated, very little research has explored the combination of these therapeutic strategies in medulloblastoma. Further research is necessary to evaluate the efficacy of this combination therapy in clinical trials and to identify biomarkers that can predict response to treatment.

4.4. Immunotherapy

Immunotherapy has been shown to be a promising approach for treating medulloblastoma, as it can induce long-lasting anti-tumor immune responses. Adoptive immunotherapy using chimeric antigen receptor (CAR) T-cells has shown encouraging results in treating medulloblastoma and other brain tumors.

Recent studies have explored the potential of combining chemotherapy with immunotherapy to enhance the anti-tumor effects of both modalities [161]. Gemcitabine has been shown to decrease the proliferation and viability of DAOY cells and also decreased the expression of stem-cell-related genes in these cells. Next, this therapy was combined with generated anti-tumor T-cells that had been exposed to DAOY medulloblastoma cell lines. The combination treatment resulted in a significant reduction in tumor growth compared to either treatment alone in a subcutaneous xenograft model.

Another strategy developed CAR T-cells that were pre-targeted to the EPHA2, HER2, and IL 13-α2 receptors that are uniquely expressed in medulloblastoma. This strategy was coupled with the methylation inhibitor azacytidine to understand the potential for chemo-immunotherapy in targeting medulloblastoma [162]. These therapies were delivered intrathecally into mouse models of group 3 medulloblastoma. This study not only showed evidence for the repeat local delivery of CAR-T cells into CSF spaces but also showed that the combination of chemo-immunotherapy with trivalent CAR T-cells exhibited the highest clinical efficacy in this murine model. Future work demonstrating how azacytidine synergizes with CAR T-cells to promote an anti-tumor effect could help optimize therapy and improve future combination regimens.

In addition to CAR T-cell therapy, the use of immunomodulating agents has attracted wide interest in oncology research. This interest has been ignited by the discovery that cancer cells induce the overexpression of immune checkpoint proteins, which attenuate the immune response, on tumor infiltrating lymphocytes. Hence, immune checkpoint inhibitors were investigated as anti-cancer agents, and they have shown considerable efficacy against various solid tumors. This inspired testing their efficacy in the context of CNS tumors, including medulloblastoma [163]. Specifically, preclinical experiments on immune checkpoint blockade in SHH and group 3 medulloblastoma mouse models showed a differential response between the two subgroups. Indeed, mice with group 3 medulloblastoma showed a significant survival benefit after treatment with anti-programmed death 1 (anti-PD1) antibodies compared to untreated mice, whereas mice with SHH-activated medulloblastoma did not show a significant response to the same therapy. This differential response to immune-modulatory agents can be attributed to the distinct baseline characteristics of the tumor microenvironment and immune infiltration profile of the two subtypes [164]. In particular, the high expression of PD-1 on the lymphocytes of group 3 tumor suggests a greater reliance on the immunosuppressive function of immune checkpoint proteins, and thus a greater susceptibility to agents blocking the actions of these proteins [164]. Nevertheless, when it comes to clinical outcomes, conflicting results have been reported by observational studies regarding the response of pediatric medulloblastoma to immune checkpoint blockade [165,166]. Hence, the results of the currently ongoing phase II clinical trials (NCT03585465, NCT03173950) evaluating the efficacy of nivolumab in recurrent CNS tumors should help resolve this debate and provide valuable insights regarding the translational reproducibility of preclinical findings. Moreover, the new generation of immune-modulating agents involves antibodies that are agonists to the costimulatory pathways of immune cells [163]. For instance, APX005M, which is a monoclonal antibody that activates the costimulatory surface protein CD40, is also being investigated as part of a phase I clinical trial including pediatric patients with recurrent or refractory CNS malignancies (NCT03389802).

5. Conclusions and Future Directions

This review highlighted how the development of medulloblastoma subtypes can be tracked back to neuronal progenitors in the developing cerebellum. It also elaborated on the unique genetic, epigenetic, transcriptional, and translational profiles of each group, which have been excessively investigated and utilized for the design of efficacious targeted therapies. Indeed, the development of such therapies has shown great promise for the future of medulloblastoma treatment, and several agents have already entered clinical trials and are in advanced stages of testing. Table 2 offers a summary of all registered clinical trials that investigate molecular-targeted therapies in medulloblastoma. However, despite the intriguing preclinical results that the studied agents have shown, treatment resistance is not uncommon. Therefore, with the rapid emergence of such resistance to the currently available targeted therapies and due to the long periods required for developing and testing novel agents, the future of medulloblastoma therapeutics should focus more on the upfront use of combination therapies. As shown in this review, combination therapies can hinder the development and progression of medulloblastoma at different stages, thus eliciting synergistic effects in tumor control and regression. At any rate, the current status quo in studying and testing combination therapies in medulloblastoma is still suboptimal, and further future efforts should be channeled into this avenue.

Table 2. Summary of concluded and ongoing clinical trials investigating molecular-targeted agents in medulloblastoma.

Group	Agent	Mechanism of Action	Trials	Type/Design	Population	Intervention	Status
SMO inhibitors	Sonidegib (LDE-225)	Binds to the transmembrane portion of the SMO protein and inhibits downstream signaling	NCT04402073 (PersoMed-I)	Phase II Comparative Randomized	Adult and post-pubertal patients with SHH-activated medulloblastoma	Sonidegib and reduced dose radiotherapy	Recruiting
			NCT01708174	Phase II Single arm	Pediatric and adult patients with relapsed SHH-activated medulloblastoma	Sonidegib	Completed. Results available on ClinicalTrials.gov (accessed on 24 July 2023)
			NCT01208831	Phase I Dose escalation	Adult patients with advanced solid tumors (including medulloblastoma)	Sonidegib	Completed. Results available on Novartis website
			NCT01125800	Phase I/II Dose escalation	Pediatric and adult patients with recurrent or refractory SHH-activated medulloblastoma	Sonidegib	Completed. Results published [72]
			NCT00880308	Phase I Dose escalation	Adult patients with advanced solid tumors (including medulloblastoma)	Sonidegib	Completed. Results published [167]

Table 2. *Cont.*

Group	Agent	Mechanism of Action	Trials	Type/Design	Population	Intervention	Status
SMO inhibitors	Vismodegib (GDC-0449)	Binds to the transmembrane portion of the SMO protein and inhibits downstream signaling	NCT01878617	Phase II Parallel assignment Non-randomized	Skeletally mature patients with newly diagnosed standard and high-risk SHH-activated medulloblastoma	Standard chemoradiotherapy with vesmodegib added to maintenance therapy	Active, not recruiting
			NCT01601184	Phase I/II Parallel assignment Randomized	Adult patients with recurrent or refractory SHH-activated medulloblastomas	Vismodegib plus temozolomide versus temozolomide alone	Terminated (number of successes not reached)
			NCT01208831 PBTC-032	Phase II Single group	Pediatric patients with recurrent or refractory medulloblastoma without (stratum A) or with (Stratum B) SHH activation	Vismodegib	Completed. Published results [71]
			NCT00939484 PBTC-025B	Phase II Single group	Adult patients with recurrent or refractory medulloblastoma without (stratum A) or with (Stratum B) SHH activation	Vismodegib	Completed. Published results [71]
			NCT00822458 PBTC-025	Phase I Dose finding	Young patients with recurrent or refractory medulloblastoma	Vismodegib	Completed. Published results [70]

Table 2. *Cont.*

Group	Agent	Mechanism of Action	Trials	Type/Design	Population	Intervention	Status
SMO inhibitors	Taladegib (ENV-101)	Binds to the transmembrane portion of the SMO protein and inhibits downstream signaling	NCT05199584	Phase II Parallel assignment Randomized	Adult patients with refractory advanced solid tumors (including medulloblastoma) with loss of function mutations in the *PTCH1* gene	Taladegib	Recruiting
			NCT01697514	Phase I Single group	Pediatric patients with recurrent or refractory medulloblastoma or rhabdomyosarcoma	Taladegib	Withdrawn (poor recruitment)
	ZSP1602	SMO antagonist (specific mechanism not known)	NCT03734913	Phase I Parallel assignment Non-randomized	Adult patients with advanced solid tumors	ZSP1602	Unknown (last update in July 2020 was recruiting)
	LEQ506	Second generation SMO antagonist (specific mechanism not known) [168]	NCT01106508	Phase I Dose finding	Adult patients with advanced solid tumors	LEQ506	Completed. Results available on Novartis website
GLI inhibitors	ATO	Direct inhibitor of GLI	NCT00024258	Phase II Single group	Pediatric and adult patients with neuroblastoma and other pediatric solid tumors (nonmyeloid and nonlymphoid)	ATO	Completed. Results available on ClinicalTraial.gov (accessed on 24 July 2023)
	Silmitasertib (CX-4945)	CK2 antagonist that reduces the transcription of *GLI* genes	NCT03904862	Phase I/II Parallel assignment Non-randomized	Skeletally immature (phase I) and skeletally mature (phase II) patients with recurrent SHH-activated medulloblastomas	Silmitasertib with or without surgical resection	Recruiting

Table 2. *Cont.*

Group	Agent	Mechanism of Action	Trials	Type/Design	Population	Intervention	Status
HDAC inhibitors	Vorinostat	Inhibitor of class I and II HDACs	NCT01076530	Phase I Single group	Young patients with relapsed or refractory primary CNS tumors	Vorinostat plus temozolomide	Completed. Published results [169]
			NCT00994500	Phase I Single group	Young patients with refractory or recurrent solid tumors (including medulloblastoma)	Vorinostat and Bortezomib (ubiquitin-proteosome pathway inhibitor)	Completed. Published results [170]
			NCT00867178	Phase I Single group	Younger patients with newly diagnosed CNS embryonal tumors	Adding vorinostat and isotretinoin to induction chemotherapy (cisplatin, etoposide, vincristine, cyclophosphamide)	Completed. Published results [171]
			NCT00217412	Phase I Parallel assignment Non-randomized	Young patients with recurrent or refractory solid tumors (including medulloblastoma), lymphoma, or leukemia	Vorinostat plus isotretinoin	Completed. Published results [172]
	Panobinostat (MTX110)	Pan-HDAC inhibitor	NCT04315064	Phase I Single group	Pediatric and adult patients with recurrent medulloblastoma	Infusions of Panobinostat into the fourth ventricle of the brain or tumor resection cavity	Recruiting

Table 2. *Cont.*

Group	Agent	Mechanism of Action	Trials	Type/Design	Population	Intervention	Status
HDAC inhibitors	Fimepinostat	Pan-HDAC and PI3K inhibitor	NCT03893487 PNOC016	Phase I Single group	Pediatric and adult patients with newly diagnosed DIPG, recurrent medulloblastoma (any subtype), or recurrent high-grade glioma	Fimepinostat 2 days preoperatively followed by surgical resection, then maintenance with fimepinostat	Active, not recruiting
	Romidepsin (FR901228)	HDAC inhibitor	NCT00053963	Phase I Single group	Pediatric patients with refractory or recurrent solid tumors	Romidepsin	Completed. Results not available
Cell cycle-disrupting agents	Prexasertib (LY2606368)	Checkpoint kinases 1 and 2 (CHK1/2) inhibitor	NCT04023669 (St. Jude ELIOT)	Phase I Parallel assignment Non-randomized	Pediatric and adult (up to 24 years old) patients with refractory or recurrent SHH-activated, group 3, or group 4 medulloblastoma	Prexasertib in combination with cyclophosphamide (all three subtypes) or gemcitabine (only groups 3 and 4)	Active, not recruiting
	Palbociclib	CDK4/6 inhibitor	NCT03709680	Phase I-Dose escalation Phase II-Randomized	Pediatric patients with refractory or recurrent solid tumors (including medulloblastoma)	Palboociclib combined with chemotherapy (temozolomide plus irinotecan or topotecan plus cyclophosphamide)	Recruiting

Table 2. *Cont.*

Group	Agent	Mechanism of Action	Trials	Type/Design	Population	Intervention	Status
Cell cycle-disrupting agents	Palbociclib	CDK4/6 inhibitor	NCT03526250 (Subprotocol of the NCI-COG Pediatric MATCH trial)	Phase II Single group	Pediatric patients with relapsed or refractory Rb-positive solid tumors non-Hodgkin lymphoma, or histiocytic disorders with activating alterations in cell cycle genes	Palbociclib	Active, not recruiting
			NCT02255461 (PBTC-042)	Phase I Single group	Pediatric patients with Rb-positive recurrent, progressive, or refractory primary CNS tumors.	Palbociclib	Completed. Published results [108]
	Ribociclib (LEE011)	CDK4/6 inhibitor	NCT05429502	Phase I/II Parallel assignment Randomized	Pediatric patients with relapsed or refractory solid tumors	Ribociclib combined with topotecan and temozolomide	Recruiting

Table 2. *Cont.*

Group	Agent	Mechanism of Action	Trials	Type/Design	Population	Intervention	Status
Cell cycle-disrupting agents	Ribociclib (LEE011)	CDK4/6 inhibitor	NCT03434262 (SJDAWN)	Phase I Parallel assignment Non-randomized	Pediatric and adult patients with refractory or recurrent brain tumors	Stratum A: ribociclib and gemcitabine for patients with recurrent/refractory group 3/4 medulloblastoma or ependymoma Stratum B: ribociclib and trametinib for recurrent/refractory WNT-activated or SHH-activated medulloblastoma and other CNS tumors Stratum C: ribociclib and sonidegib for skeletally mature patients with recurrent/refractory SHH-activated medulloblastoma	Active, not recruiting
			NCT03387020	Phase I Single group	Pediatric patients with recurrent, progressive, or refractory CNS tumors	Ribociclib and everolimus (mTOR inhibitor)	Completed. Published results [173]
	Abemaciclib	CDK4/6 inhibitor	NCT04238819	Phase I Dose escalation	Pediatric patients with recurrent or refractory solid tumors	Abemaciclib combined with temozolomide alone or with irinotecan and temozolomide	Recruiting

Table 2. *Cont.*

Group	Agent	Mechanism of Action	Trials	Type/Design	Population	Intervention	Status
Tyrosine kinase inhibitors (TKIs)	Apatinib	TKI that blocks the activity of vascular endothelial growth factor receptor 2 (VEGFR2)	NCT04501718	Phase II Single group	Pediatric patients with recurrent medulloblastoma	Apatinib combined with temozolomide and etoposide	Recruiting
	Volitinib	TKI that blocks cMET signaling	NCT03598244	Phase I Single group	Pediatric patients with refractory, progressive, or recurrent primary CNS tumors	Volitinib	Recruiting
	Erdafitinib	TKI that blocks fibroblast growth factor receptor	NCT03210714 (Subprotocol of the NCI-COG Pediatric MATCH trial)	Phase II Single group	Pediatric patients with relapsed or refractory solid tumors non-Hodgkin lymphoma, or histiocytic disorders with FGFR mutations	Erdafitinib	Active, not recruiting
	Entrectinib (Rxdx-101)	TKI that blocks the activity of tropomyosin receptor kinases, ROS1, and ALK	NCT02650401	Phase I/II Single group	Pediatric patients with locally advanced, metastatic, or refractory solid or primary CNS tumors	Entrectinib	Active, not recruiting
	Adavosertib (MK-1775)	TKI that block the activity of WEE1	NCT02095132	Phase I/II Single group	Pediatric patients with relapsed or refractory solid tumors	Adavosertib combined with irinotecan	Active, not recruiting
	Cediranib (AZD-2171)	TKI that blocks the activity of VEGF	NCT00326664	Phase I Single group	Pediatric patients with recurrent, progressive, or refractory primary CNS tumors	Cediranib	Completed. Published results [174]

Table 2. *Cont.*

Group	Agent	Mechanism of Action	Trials	Type/Design	Population	Intervention	Status
Tyrosine kinase inhibitors (TKIs)	Lapatinib	Dual TKI that blocks epidermal growth factor receptor and HER2 signaling	NCT00095940	Phase I/II Single group	Pediatric patients with recurrent or refractory CNS tumors	Lapatinib	Completed. Results available on ClinicalTrials.gov (accessed on 24 July 2023)
Antiangiogenic factors	Pomalidomide	Decreases the concentrations of VEGF and HIF1α. Increases the production of immune-stimulatory cytokines	NCT03257631	Phase II Single group	Pediatric patients with recurrent or progressive primary brain tumors	Pomalidomide	Completed. Published results [175]
	Bevacizumab and other drugs (multidrug)	Bevacizumab is a monoclonal antibody that binds VEGF. Thalidomide, celecoxib, and fenofibrate also have antiangiogenic effects [176]	NCT01356290	Phase II Single group	Pediatric patients with recurrent or progressive medulloblastoma, ependymoma, or ATRT.	Bevacizumab in combination with 5 oral drugs (thalidomide, celecoxib, fenofibrate, etoposide, and cyclophosphamide)	Recruiting
	PTC-299	Targets VEGF mRNA and inhibits their translation	NCT01158300	Phase I Single group	Pediatric patients with recurrent or refractory primary CNS tumors	PTC-299	Completed. Published results [177]
	Cilengitide	Integrin antagonist that disrupts endothelial interactions	NCT00063973 PBTC-012	Phase I Single group	Pediatric patients with refractory primary brain tumors	Cilengitide	Completed. Published results [178]

Table 2. *Cont.*

Group	Agent	Mechanism of Action	Trials	Type/Design	Population	Intervention	Status
Immunomodulatory agents	Nivolumab	Monoclonal antibody against the immune checkpoint protein programmed death 1 (PD1)	NCT03585465	Phase I/II Parallel assignment Randomized	Pediatric patients with relapsed or refractory solid tumors	Nivolumab combined with cyclophosphamide and vinblastine (Arm A), capecitabine (Arm B), or metronomic chemotherapy (Metronomic+ Nivolumab arm)	Recruiting
			NCT03173950	Phase II Parallel assignment Non-randomized	Adult patients with recurrent select rare CNS cancers (including medulloblastoma)	Nivolumab	Recruiting
	Pembrolizamab	Monoclonal antibody against the immune checkpoint protein PD1	NCT02359565	Phase I Single group	Pediatric patients with recurrent, progressive, or refractory high-grade gliomas, DIPGs, hypermutated brain tumors, ependymoma, or medulloblastoma	Pembrolizumab	Recruiting
	Cemiplimab (REGN2810)	Monoclonal antibody against the immune checkpoint protein PD1	NCT03690869	Phase I	Pediatric patients with relapsed or refractory solid or CNS tumors	Cemiplimab	Recruiting

Table 2. *Cont.*

Group	Agent	Mechanism of Action	Trials	Type/Design	Population	Intervention	Status
Immunomodulatory agents	Indoximod	Inhibitor of the immune-suppressive enzyme Indoleamine-2,3-dioxygenase (IDO)	NCT05106296	Phase I Single group	Patients aged 12–25 years with pediatric brain tumors	Indoximod combined with ibrutinib (Bruton's tyrosine kisase inhibitor, and chemoradiotherapy	Recruiting
			NCT04049669	Phase II Crossover Non-randomized	Pediatric patients with relapsed brain tumors or newly diagnosed DIPG	Indoximod administered during chemotherapy and/or radiation therapy	Recruiting
			NCT02502708	Phase I Parallel assignment Non-randomized	Pediatric patients with progressive primary brain tumors	Indoximod in combination with temozolomide-based chemotherapy	Completed. No results available
	Sotigalimab (APX005M)	CD40 agonist that activates antigen-presenting cells	NCT03389802	Phase I Sequential Non-randomized	Pediatric patients with recurrent, progressive, or refractory primary malignant CNS tumor	Sotigalimab	Active, not recruiting
EZH2 inhibitors	Tazemostat	EZH2 inhibitor	NCT03213665 (Subprotocol of the NCI-COG Pediatric MATCH trial)	Phase II Single group	Pediatric patients with relapsed or refractory solid tumors, non-Hodgkin lymphoma, or histiocytic disorders with gain of function mutations in EZH2 or loss of function mutations in SMARCB1 or SMARCA4	Tazemostat	Active, not recruiting

Table 2. *Cont.*

Group	Agent	Mechanism of Action	Trials	Type/Design	Population	Intervention	Status
PI3K/mTOR inhibitors	Samotolisib (LY3023414)	Dual PI3K and mTOR inhibitor	NCT03213678 (Subprotocol of the NCI-COG Pediatric MATCH trial)	Phase II Single group	Pediatric patients with relapsed or refractory solid tumors, non-Hodgkin lymphoma, or histiocytic disorders with TSC loss of function mutations, and/or other PI3K/mTOR activating mutations	Samotolisib	Recruiting
	Sirolimus	mTOR inhibitor	NCT02574728	Phase II Single group	Pediatric patients with relapsed or refractory solid or CNS tumors	Sirolimus in combination with metronomic chemotherapy	Recruiting
BRD inhibitors	BMS-986158 and BMS-986378	BRD inhibitors that prevent the interaction between BET proteins and histones	NCT03936465	Phase I Parallel assignment Non-randomized	Pediatric patients with relapsed or progressive solid or CNS tumors	BMS-986158 or BMS-986378 as monotherapies	Recruiting
Gamma secretase inhibitors	RO492909 7	Blocks the cleavage of Notch intracellular domain (NICD) and its translocation to the nucleus to induce the expression of Notch pathway effector genes	NCT01088763	Phase I/II Single group	Pediatric patients with relapsed or refractory solid tumors, CNS tumors, lymphoma, or T-cell leukemia	RO4929097	Terminated

Table 2. *Cont.*

Group	Agent	Mechanism of Action	Trials	Type/Design	Population	Intervention	Status
Gamma secretase inhibitors	MK0752	Blocks the cleavage of Notch intracellular domain (NICD) and its translocation to the nucleus to induce the expression of Notch pathway effector genes	NCT00572182	Phase I Single group	Pediatric patients with recurrent or refractory CNS tumors	MK0752	Terminated due to discontinued financial support
JAK/STAT inhibitors	WP1066	JAK2/STAT3 pathway inhibitor	NCT04334863	Phase I Single group	Pediatric patients with recurrent or progressive malignant brain tumors	WP1066	Completed. No results available
Others	TB-403	Monoclonal antibody against placental growth factor (PIGF)	NCT02748135	Phase I Single group	Pediatric patients with relapsed or refractory medulloblastoma, neuroblastoma, Ewing sarcoma, and alveolar rhabdomyosarcoma	TB-403	Completed. Published results [179]
	Mebendazole	Antiparasitic drug that has been shown to have anti-proliferative and proapoptotic roles in several cancer types via its ability to modulate several oncogenic pathways (including SHH, MEK/ERK, and STAT1/2)	NCT02644291	Phase I Single group	Pediatric patients with recurrent or progressive brain tumors	Mebendazole	Completed. No results available

Author Contributions: Conceptualization, B.T.; methodology, H.S., P.A., D.R. and S.A.; software, H.S.; investigation, H.S., P.A., D.R. and C.C.; resources, B.T.; data curation, H.S., P.A., D.R. and C.C.; writing—original draft preparation, H.S., P.A., D.R. and C.C.; writing—review and editing, S.A., E.M.J. and B.T.; visualization, H.S.; supervision, B.T.; project administration, B.T. All authors have read and agreed to the published version of the manuscript.

Funding: This research received no external funding.

Acknowledgments: Figures 1–4 were created with BioRender.com, accessed on 24 July 2023.

Conflicts of Interest: The authors declare no conflict of interest.

References

1. Ostrom, Q.T.; Gittleman, H.; Truitt, G.; Boscia, A.; Kruchko, C.; Barnholtz-Sloan, J.S. CBTRUS Statistical Report: Primary Brain and Other Central Nervous System Tumors Diagnosed in the United States in 2011–2015. *Neuro. Oncol.* **2018**, *20*, iv1–iv86. [CrossRef] [PubMed]
2. Cohen, A.R. Brain Tumors in Children. *N. Engl. J. Med.* **2022**, *386*, 1922–1931. [CrossRef] [PubMed]
3. Northcott, P.A.; Robinson, G.W.; Kratz, C.P.; Mabbott, D.J.; Pomeroy, S.L.; Clifford, S.C.; Rutkowski, S.; Ellison, D.W.; Malkin, D.; Taylor, M.D.; et al. Medulloblastoma. *Nat. Rev. Dis. Primers* **2019**, *5*, 11. [CrossRef]
4. Louis, D.N.; Perry, A.; Reifenberger, G.; von Deimling, A.; Figarella-Branger, D.; Cavenee, W.K.; Ohgaki, H.; Wiestler, O.D.; Kleihues, P.; Ellison, D.W. The 2016 World Health Organization Classification of Tumors of the Central Nervous System: A summary. *Acta Neuropathol.* **2016**, *131*, 803–820. [CrossRef] [PubMed]
5. Louis, D.N.; Perry, A.; Wesseling, P.; Brat, D.J.; Cree, I.A.; Figarella-Branger, D.; Hawkins, C.; Ng, H.K.; Pfister, S.M.; Reifenberger, G.; et al. The 2021 WHO Classification of Tumors of the Central Nervous System: A summary. *Neuro-Oncology* **2021**, *23*, 1231–1251. [CrossRef] [PubMed]
6. Wang, J.; Garancher, A.; Ramaswamy, V.; Wechsler-Reya, R.J. Medulloblastoma: From Molecular Subgroups to Molecular Targeted Therapies. *Annu. Rev. Neurosci.* **2018**, *41*, 207–232. [CrossRef] [PubMed]
7. Luzzi, S.; Giotta Lucifero, A.; Brambilla, I.; Semeria Mantelli, S.; Mosconi, M.; Foiadelli, T.; Savasta, S. Targeting the medulloblastoma: A molecular-based approach. *Acta Biomed.* **2020**, *91*, 79–100. [CrossRef] [PubMed]
8. Roussel, M.F.; Stripay, J.L. Epigenetic Drivers in Pediatric Medulloblastoma. *Cerebellum* **2018**, *17*, 28–36. [CrossRef]
9. Hovestadt, V.; Smith, K.S.; Bihannic, L.; Filbin, M.G.; Shaw, M.L.; Baumgartner, A.; De Witt, J.C.; Groves, A.; Mayr, L.; Weisman, H.R.; et al. Resolving medulloblastoma cellular architecture by single-cell genomics. *Nature* **2019**, *572*, 74–79. [CrossRef]
10. Hendrikse, L.D.; Haldipur, P.; Saulnier, O.; Millman, J.; Sjoboen, A.H.; Erickson, A.W.; Ong, W.; Gordon, V.; Coudiere-Morrison, L.; Mercier, A.L.; et al. Failure of human rhombic lip differentiation underlies medulloblastoma formation. *Nature* **2022**, *609*, 1021–1028. [CrossRef]
11. Luo, Z.; Xia, M.; Shi, W.; Zhao, C.; Wang, J.; Xin, D.; Dong, X.; Xiong, Y.; Zhang, F.; Berry, K.; et al. Human fetal cerebellar cell atlas informs medulloblastoma origin and oncogenesis. *Nature* **2022**, *612*, 787–794. [CrossRef] [PubMed]
12. Vladoiu, M.C.; El-Hamamy, I.; Donovan, L.K.; Farooq, H.; Holgado, B.L.; Sundaravadanam, Y.; Ramaswamy, V.; Hendrikse, L.D.; Kumar, S.; Mack, S.C.; et al. Childhood cerebellar tumours mirror conserved fetal transcriptional programs. *Nature* **2019**, *572*, 67–73. [CrossRef] [PubMed]
13. Leto, K.; Arancillo, M.; Becker, E.B.; Buffo, A.; Chiang, C.; Ding, B.; Dobyns, W.B.; Dusart, I.; Haldipur, P.; Hatten, M.E.; et al. Consensus Paper: Cerebellar Development. *Cerebellum* **2016**, *15*, 789–828. [CrossRef] [PubMed]
14. Wingate, R.J. The rhombic lip and early cerebellar development. *Curr. Opin. Neurobiol.* **2001**, *11*, 82–88. [CrossRef]
15. Wang, V.Y.; Rose, M.F.; Zoghbi, H.Y. Math1 expression redefines the rhombic lip derivatives and reveals novel lineages within the brainstem and cerebellum. *Neuron* **2005**, *48*, 31–43. [CrossRef]
16. Belzunce, I.; Belmonte-Mateos, C.; Pujades, C. The interplay of atoh1 genes in the lower rhombic lip during hindbrain morphogenesis. *PLoS ONE* **2020**, *15*, e0228225. [CrossRef]
17. Wullimann, M.F.; Mueller, T.; Distel, M.; Babaryka, A.; Grothe, B.; Koster, R.W. The long adventurous journey of rhombic lip cells in jawed vertebrates: A comparative developmental analysis. *Front. Neuroanat.* **2011**, *5*, 27. [CrossRef]
18. Gibson, P.; Tong, Y.; Robinson, G.; Thompson, M.C.; Currle, D.S.; Eden, C.; Kranenburg, T.A.; Hogg, T.; Poppleton, H.; Martin, J.; et al. Subtypes of medulloblastoma have distinct developmental origins. *Nature* **2010**, *468*, 1095–1099. [CrossRef] [PubMed]
19. Yeung, J.; Ha, T.J.; Swanson, D.J.; Choi, K.; Tong, Y.; Goldowitz, D. Wls provides a new compartmental view of the rhombic lip in mouse cerebellar development. *J. Neurosci.* **2014**, *34*, 12527–12537. [CrossRef]
20. Consalez, G.G.; Goldowitz, D.; Casoni, F.; Hawkes, R. Origins, Development, and Compartmentation of the Granule Cells of the Cerebellum. *Front. Neural Circuits* **2020**, *14*, 611841. [CrossRef]
21. Haldipur, P.; Aldinger, K.A.; Bernardo, S.; Deng, M.; Timms, A.E.; Overman, L.M.; Winter, C.; Lisgo, S.N.; Razavi, F.; Silvestri, E.; et al. Spatiotemporal expansion of primary progenitor zones in the developing human cerebellum. *Science* **2019**, *366*, 454–460. [CrossRef] [PubMed]
22. Hovestadt, V.; Ayrault, O.; Swartling, F.J.; Robinson, G.W.; Pfister, S.M.; Northcott, P.A. Medulloblastomics revisited: Biological and clinical insights from thousands of patients. *Nat. Rev. Cancer* **2020**, *20*, 42–56. [CrossRef] [PubMed]

23. Jessa, S.; Blanchet-Cohen, A.; Krug, B.; Vladoiu, M.; Coutelier, M.; Faury, D.; Poreau, B.; De Jay, N.; Hebert, S.; Monlong, J.; et al. Stalled developmental programs at the root of pediatric brain tumors. *Nat. Genet.* **2019**, *51*, 1702–1713. [CrossRef]
24. Waszak, S.M.; Northcott, P.A.; Buchhalter, I.; Robinson, G.W.; Sutter, C.; Groebner, S.; Grund, K.B.; Brugieres, L.; Jones, D.T.W.; Pajtler, K.W.; et al. Spectrum and prevalence of genetic predisposition in medulloblastoma: A retrospective genetic study and prospective validation in a clinical trial cohort. *Lancet Oncol.* **2018**, *19*, 785–798. [CrossRef]
25. Northcott, P.A.; Buchhalter, I.; Morrissy, A.S.; Hovestadt, V.; Weischenfeldt, J.; Ehrenberger, T.; Grobner, S.; Segura-Wang, M.; Zichner, T.; Rudneva, V.A.; et al. The whole-genome landscape of medulloblastoma subtypes. *Nature* **2017**, *547*, 311–317. [CrossRef]
26. Cavalli, F.M.G.; Remke, M.; Rampasek, L.; Peacock, J.; Shih, D.J.H.; Luu, B.; Garzia, L.; Torchia, J.; Nor, C.; Morrissy, A.S.; et al. Intertumoral Heterogeneity within Medulloblastoma Subgroups. *Cancer Cell* **2017**, *31*, 737–754.e736. [CrossRef]
27. Robinson, G.; Parker, M.; Kranenburg, T.A.; Lu, C.; Chen, X.; Ding, L.; Phoenix, T.N.; Hedlund, E.; Wei, L.; Zhu, X.; et al. Novel mutations target distinct subgroups of medulloblastoma. *Nature* **2012**, *488*, 43–48. [CrossRef]
28. Parsons, D.W.; Li, M.; Zhang, X.; Jones, S.; Leary, R.J.; Lin, J.C.; Boca, S.M.; Carter, H.; Samayoa, J.; Bettegowda, C.; et al. The genetic landscape of the childhood cancer medulloblastoma. *Science* **2011**, *331*, 435–439. [CrossRef]
29. Sexton-Oates, A.; MacGregor, D.; Dodgshun, A.; Saffery, R. The potential for epigenetic analysis of paediatric CNS tumours to improve diagnosis, treatment and prognosis. *Ann. Oncol.* **2015**, *26*, 1314–1324. [CrossRef]
30. Shih, D.J.; Northcott, P.A.; Remke, M.; Korshunov, A.; Ramaswamy, V.; Kool, M.; Luu, B.; Yao, Y.; Wang, X.; Dubuc, A.M.; et al. Cytogenetic prognostication within medulloblastoma subgroups. *J. Clin. Oncol.* **2014**, *32*, 886–896. [CrossRef]
31. Gonzalez Castro, L.N.; Liu, I.; Filbin, M. Characterizing the biology of primary brain tumors and their microenvironment via single-cell profiling methods. *Neuro. Oncol.* **2023**, *25*, 234–247. [CrossRef]
32. Kaderali, Z.; Lamberti-Pasculli, M.; Rutka, J.T. The changing epidemiology of paediatric brain tumours: A review from the Hospital for Sick Children. *Childs Nerv. Syst.* **2009**, *25*, 787–793. [CrossRef]
33. Paugh, B.S.; Qu, C.; Jones, C.; Liu, Z.; Adamowicz-Brice, M.; Zhang, J.; Bax, D.A.; Coyle, B.; Barrow, J.; Hargrave, D.; et al. Integrated molecular genetic profiling of pediatric high-grade gliomas reveals key differences with the adult disease. *J. Clin. Oncol.* **2010**, *28*, 3061–3068. [CrossRef]
34. Ramaswamy, V.; Remke, M.; Bouffet, E.; Bailey, S.; Clifford, S.C.; Doz, F.; Kool, M.; Dufour, C.; Vassal, G.; Milde, T.; et al. Risk stratification of childhood medulloblastoma in the molecular era: The current consensus. *Acta Neuropathol.* **2016**, *131*, 821–831. [CrossRef]
35. Zagozewski, J.; Shahriary, G.M.; Morrison, L.C.; Saulnier, O.; Stromecki, M.; Fresnoza, A.; Palidwor, G.; Porter, C.J.; Forget, A.; Ayrault, O.; et al. An OTX2-PAX3 signaling axis regulates Group 3 medulloblastoma cell fate. *Nat. Commun.* **2020**, *11*, 3627. [CrossRef]
36. Lund, L.W.; Schmiegelow, K.; Rechnitzer, C.; Johansen, C. A systematic review of studies on psychosocial late effects of childhood cancer: StructuRes. of society and methodological pitfalls may challenge the conclusions. *Pediatr. Blood Cancer* **2011**, *56*, 532–543. [CrossRef]
37. Rousseau, A.; Idbaih, A.; Ducray, F.; Criniere, E.; Fevre-Montange, M.; Jouvet, A.; Delattre, J.Y. Specific chromosomal imbalances as detected by array CGH in ependymomas in association with tumor location, histological subtype and grade. *J. Neurooncol.* **2010**, *97*, 353–364. [CrossRef] [PubMed]
38. Korshunov, A.; Witt, H.; Hielscher, T.; Benner, A.; Remke, M.; Ryzhova, M.; Milde, T.; Bender, S.; Wittmann, A.; Schottler, A.; et al. Molecular staging of intracranial ependymoma in children and adults. *J. Clin. Oncol.* **2010**, *28*, 3182–3190. [CrossRef] [PubMed]
39. Rickert, C.H.; Strater, R.; Kaatsch, P.; Wassmann, H.; Jurgens, H.; Dockhorn-Dworniczak, B.; Paulus, W. Pediatric high-grade astrocytomas show chromosomal imbalances distinct from adult cases. *Am. J. Pathol.* **2001**, *158*, 1525–1532. [CrossRef]
40. Dubuc, A.M.; Remke, M.; Korshunov, A.; Northcott, P.A.; Zhan, S.H.; Mendez-Lago, M.; Kool, M.; Jones, D.T.; Unterberger, A.; Morrissy, A.S.; et al. Aberrant patterns of H3K4 and H3K27 histone lysine methylation occur across subgroups in medulloblastoma. *Acta Neuropathol.* **2013**, *125*, 373–384. [CrossRef]
41. Smith, K.S.; Bihannic, L.; Gudenas, B.L.; Haldipur, P.; Tao, R.; Gao, Q.; Li, Y.; Aldinger, K.A.; Iskusnykh, I.Y.; Chizhikov, V.V.; et al. Unified rhombic lip origins of group 3 and group 4 medulloblastoma. *Nature* **2022**, *609*, 1012–1020. [CrossRef] [PubMed]
42. Lin, C.Y.; Erkek, S.; Tong, Y.; Yin, L.; Federation, A.J.; Zapatka, M.; Haldipur, P.; Kawauchi, D.; Risch, T.; Warnatz, H.J.; et al. Active medulloblastoma enhancers reveal subgroup-specific cellular origins. *Nature* **2016**, *530*, 57–62. [CrossRef] [PubMed]
43. Northcott, P.A.; Lee, C.; Zichner, T.; Stutz, A.M.; Erkek, S.; Kawauchi, D.; Shih, D.J.; Hovestadt, V.; Zapatka, M.; Sturm, D.; et al. Enhancer hijacking activates GFI1 family oncogenes in medulloblastoma. *Nature* **2014**, *511*, 428–434. [CrossRef] [PubMed]
44. Northcott, P.A.; Shih, D.J.; Peacock, J.; Garzia, L.; Morrissy, A.S.; Zichner, T.; Stutz, A.M.; Korshunov, A.; Reimand, J.; Schumacher, S.E.; et al. Subgroup-specific structural variation across 1000 medulloblastoma genomes. *Nature* **2012**, *488*, 49–56. [CrossRef] [PubMed]
45. Williamson, D.; Schwalbe, E.C.; Hicks, D.; Aldinger, K.A.; Lindsey, J.C.; Crosier, S.; Richardson, S.; Goddard, J.; Hill, R.M.; Castle, J.; et al. Medulloblastoma group 3 and 4 tumors comprise a clinically and biologically significant expression continuum reflecting human cerebellar development. *Cell Rep.* **2022**, *40*, 111162. [CrossRef]

46. Ellison, D.W.; Onilude, O.E.; Lindsey, J.C.; Lusher, M.E.; Weston, C.L.; Taylor, R.E.; Pearson, A.D.; Clifford, S.C.; United Kingdom Children's Cancer Study Group Brain Tumour Committee. beta-Catenin status predicts a favorable outcome in childhood medulloblastoma: The United Kingdom Children's Cancer Study Group Brain Tumour Committee. *J. Clin. Oncol.* **2005**, *23*, 7951–7957. [CrossRef]
47. Clifford, S.C.; Lannering, B.; Schwalbe, E.C.; Hicks, D.; O'Toole, K.; Nicholson, S.L.; Goschzik, T.; Zur Muhlen, A.; Figarella-Branger, D.; Doz, F.; et al. Biomarker-driven stratification of disease-risk in non-metastatic medulloblastoma: Results from the multi-center HIT-SIOP-PNET4 clinical trial. *Oncotarget* **2015**, *6*, 38827–38839. [CrossRef]
48. Phoenix, T.N.; Patmore, D.M.; Boop, S.; Boulos, N.; Jacus, M.O.; Patel, Y.T.; Roussel, M.F.; Finkelstein, D.; Goumnerova, L.; Perreault, S.; et al. Medulloblastoma Genotype Dictates Blood Brain Barrier Phenotype. *Cancer Cell* **2016**, *29*, 508–522. [CrossRef]
49. Ris, M.D.; Packer, R.; Goldwein, J.; Jones-Wallace, D.; Boyett, J.M. Intellectual outcome after reduced-dose radiation therapy plus adjuvant chemotherapy for medulloblastoma: A Children's Cancer Group study. *J. Clin. Oncol.* **2001**, *19*, 3470–3476. [CrossRef]
50. Moxon-Emre, I.; Taylor, M.D.; Bouffet, E.; Hardy, K.; Campen, C.J.; Malkin, D.; Hawkins, C.; Laperriere, N.; Ramaswamy, V.; Bartels, U.; et al. Intellectual Outcome in Molecular Subgroups of Medulloblastoma. *J. Clin. Oncol.* **2016**, *34*, 4161–4170. [CrossRef]
51. Michalski, J.M.; Janss, A.J.; Vezina, L.G.; Smith, K.S.; Billups, C.A.; Burger, P.C.; Embry, L.M.; Cullen, P.L.; Hardy, K.K.; Pomeroy, S.L.; et al. Children's Oncology Group Phase III Trial of Reduced-Dose and Reduced-Volume Radiotherapy with Chemotherapy for Newly Diagnosed Average-Risk Medulloblastoma. *J. Clin. Oncol.* **2021**, *39*, 2685–2697. [CrossRef] [PubMed]
52. Cooney, T.; Lindsay, H.; Leary, S.; Wechsler-Reya, R. Current studies and future directions for medulloblastoma: A review from the pacific pediatric neuro-oncology consortium (PNOC) disease working group. *Neoplasia* **2023**, *35*, 100861. [CrossRef] [PubMed]
53. Kahn, M. Can we safely target the WNT pathway? *Nat. Rev. Drug Discov.* **2014**, *13*, 513–532. [CrossRef] [PubMed]
54. Pugh, T.J.; Weeraratne, S.D.; Archer, T.C.; Pomeranz Krummel, D.A.; Auclair, D.; Bochicchio, J.; Carneiro, M.O.; Carter, S.L.; Cibulskis, K.; Erlich, R.L.; et al. Medulloblastoma exome sequencing uncovers subtype-specific somatic mutations. *Nature* **2012**, *488*, 106–110. [CrossRef] [PubMed]
55. Tantravedi, S.; Vesuna, F.; Winnard, P.T., Jr.; Martin, A.; Lim, M.; Eberhart, C.G.; Berlinicke, C.; Raabe, E.; van Diest, P.J.; Raman, V. Targeting DDX3 in Medulloblastoma Using the Small Molecule Inhibitor RK-33. *Transl. Oncol.* **2019**, *12*, 96–105. [CrossRef]
56. Huang, S.M.; Mishina, Y.M.; Liu, S.; Cheung, A.; Stegmeier, F.; Michaud, G.A.; Charlat, O.; Wiellette, E.; Zhang, Y.; Wiessner, S.; et al. Tankyrase inhibition stabilizes axin and antagonizes Wnt signalling. *Nature* **2009**, *461*, 614–620. [CrossRef]
57. Renna, C.; Salaroli, R.; Cocchi, C.; Cenacchi, G. XAV939-mediated ARTD activity inhibition in human MB cell lines. *PLoS ONE* **2015**, *10*, e0124149. [CrossRef]
58. Ferri, M.; Liscio, P.; Carotti, A.; Asciutti, S.; Sardella, R.; Macchiarulo, A.; Camaioni, E. Targeting Wnt-driven cancers: Discovery of novel tankyrase inhibitors. *Eur. J. Med. Chem.* **2017**, *142*, 506–522. [CrossRef]
59. Bassani, B.; Bartolini, D.; Pagani, A.; Principi, E.; Zollo, M.; Noonan, D.M.; Albini, A.; Bruno, A. Fenretinide (4-HPR) Targets Caspase-9, ERK 1/2 and the Wnt3a/beta-Catenin Pathway in Medulloblastoma Cells and Medulloblastoma Cell Spheroids. *PLoS ONE* **2016**, *11*, e0154111. [CrossRef]
60. Wen, J.; Hadden, M.K. Medulloblastoma drugs in development: Current leads, trials and drawbacks. *Eur. J. Med. Chem.* **2021**, *215*, 113268. [CrossRef]
61. Ko, A.H.; Chiorean, E.G.; Kwak, E.L.; Lenz, H.-J.; Nadler, P.I.; Wood, D.L.; Fujimori, M.; Inada, T.; Kouji, H.; McWilliams, R.R. Final results of a phase Ib dose-escalation study of PRI-724, a CBP/beta-catenin modulator, plus gemcitabine (GEM) in patients with advanced pancreatic adenocarcinoma (APC) as second-line therapy after FOLFIRINOX or FOLFOX. *J. Clin. Oncol.* **2016**, *34*, e15721. [CrossRef]
62. Lastowska, M.; Trubicka, J.; Niemira, M.; Paczkowska-Abdulsalam, M.; Karkucinska-Wieckowska, A.; Kaleta, M.; Drogosiewicz, M.; Tarasinska, M.; Perek-Polnik, M.; Kretowski, A.; et al. ALK Expression Is a Novel Marker for the WNT-activated Type of Pediatric Medulloblastoma and an Indicator of Good Prognosis for Patients. *Am. J. Surg. Pathol.* **2017**, *41*, 781–787. [CrossRef] [PubMed]
63. Lastowska, M.; Trubicka, J.; Karkucinska-Wieckowska, A.; Kaleta, M.; Tarasinska, M.; Perek-Polnik, M.; Sobocinska, A.A.; Dembowska-Baginska, B.; Grajkowska, W.; Matyja, E. Immunohistochemical detection of ALK protein identifies APC mutated medulloblastoma and differentiates the WNT-activated medulloblastoma from other types of posterior fossa childhood tumors. *Brain Tumor Pathol.* **2019**, *36*, 1–6. [CrossRef]
64. Vibhakar, R.; Foltz, G.; Yoon, J.G.; Field, L.; Lee, H.; Ryu, G.Y.; Pierson, J.; Davidson, B.; Madan, A. Dickkopf-1 is an epigenetically silenced candidate tumor suppressor gene in medulloblastoma. *Neuro. Oncol.* **2007**, *9*, 135–144. [CrossRef]
65. Skoda, A.M.; Simovic, D.; Karin, V.; Kardum, V.; Vranic, S.; Serman, L. The role of the Hedgehog signaling pathway in cancer: A comprehensive review. *Bosn J. Basic Med. Sci.* **2018**, *18*, 8–20. [CrossRef]
66. Lospinoso Severini, L.; Ghirga, F.; Bufalieri, F.; Quaglio, D.; Infante, P.; Di Marcotullio, L. The SHH/GLI signaling pathway: A therapeutic target for medulloblastoma. *Expert Opin. Ther. Targets* **2020**, *24*, 1159–1181. [CrossRef]
67. Robarge, K.D.; Brunton, S.A.; Castanedo, G.M.; Cui, Y.; Dina, M.S.; Goldsmith, R.; Gould, S.E.; Guichert, O.; Gunzner, J.L.; Halladay, J.; et al. GDC-0449-a potent inhibitor of the hedgehog pathway. *Bioorg. Med. Chem. Lett.* **2009**, *19*, 5576–5581. [CrossRef] [PubMed]
68. Pan, S.; Wu, X.; Jiang, J.; Gao, W.; Wan, Y.; Cheng, D.; Han, D.; Liu, J.; Englund, N.P.; Wang, Y.; et al. Discovery of NVP-LDE225, a Potent and Selective Smoothened Antagonist. *ACS Med. Chem. Lett.* **2010**, *1*, 130–134. [CrossRef]

69. Sekulic, A.; Migden, M.R.; Oro, A.E.; Dirix, L.; Lewis, K.D.; Hainsworth, J.D.; Solomon, J.A.; Yoo, S.; Arron, S.T.; Friedlander, P.A.; et al. Efficacy and safety of vismodegib in advanced basal-cell carcinoma. *N. Engl. J. Med.* **2012**, *366*, 2171–2179. [CrossRef]
70. Gajjar, A.; Stewart, C.F.; Ellison, D.W.; Kaste, S.; Kun, L.E.; Packer, R.J.; Goldman, S.; Chintagumpala, M.; Wallace, D.; Takebe, N.; et al. Phase I study of vismodegib in children with recurrent or refractory medulloblastoma: A pediatric brain tumor consortium study. *Clin. Cancer Res.* **2013**, *19*, 6305–6312. [CrossRef]
71. Robinson, G.W.; Orr, B.A.; Wu, G.; Gururangan, S.; Lin, T.; Qaddoumi, I.; Packer, R.J.; Goldman, S.; Prados, M.D.; Desjardins, A.; et al. Vismodegib Exerts Targeted Efficacy Against Recurrent Sonic Hedgehog-Subgroup Medulloblastoma: Results From Phase II Pediatric Brain Tumor Consortium Studies PBTC-025B and PBTC-032. *J. Clin. Oncol.* **2015**, *33*, 2646–2654. [CrossRef] [PubMed]
72. Kieran, M.W.; Chisholm, J.; Casanova, M.; Brandes, A.A.; Aerts, I.; Bouffet, E.; Bailey, S.; Leary, S.; MacDonald, T.J.; Mechinaud, F.; et al. Phase I study of oral sonidegib (LDE225) in pediatric brain and solid tumors and a phase II study in children and adults with relapsed medulloblastoma. *Neuro. Oncol.* **2017**, *19*, 1542–1552. [CrossRef] [PubMed]
73. Xin, M.; Ji, X.; De La Cruz, L.K.; Thareja, S.; Wang, B. Strategies to target the Hedgehog signaling pathway for cancer therapy. *Med. Res. Rev.* **2018**, *38*, 870–913. [CrossRef] [PubMed]
74. Ji, D.; Zhang, W.; Xu, Y.; Zhang, J.J. Design, synthesis and biological evaluation of anthranilamide derivatives as potent SMO inhibitors. *Bioorg. Med. Chem.* **2020**, *28*, 115354. [CrossRef] [PubMed]
75. Kim, J.; Tang, J.Y.; Gong, R.; Kim, J.; Lee, J.J.; Clemons, K.V.; Chong, C.R.; Chang, K.S.; Fereshteh, M.; Gardner, D.; et al. Itraconazole, a commonly used antifungal that inhibits Hedgehog pathway activity and cancer growth. *Cancer Cell* **2010**, *17*, 388–399. [CrossRef]
76. Kim, J.; Aftab, B.T.; Tang, J.Y.; Kim, D.; Lee, A.H.; Rezaee, M.; Kim, J.; Chen, B.; King, E.M.; Borodovsky, A.; et al. Itraconazole and arsenic trioxide inhibit Hedgehog pathway activation and tumor growth associated with acquired resistance to smoothened antagonists. *Cancer Cell* **2013**, *23*, 23–34. [CrossRef]
77. Meco, D.; Attina, G.; Mastrangelo, S.; Navarra, P.; Ruggiero, A. Emerging Perspectives on the Antiparasitic Mebendazole as a Repurposed Drug for the Treatment of Brain Cancers. *Int. J. Mol. Sci.* **2023**, *24*, 1334. [CrossRef]
78. Larsen, A.R.; Bai, R.Y.; Chung, J.H.; Borodovsky, A.; Rudin, C.M.; Riggins, G.J.; Bunz, F. Repurposing the antihelmintic mebendazole as a hedgehog inhibitor. *Mol. Cancer Ther.* **2015**, *14*, 3–13. [CrossRef]
79. Bodhinayake, I.; Symons, M.; Boockvar, J.A. Repurposing mebendazole for the treatment of medulloblastoma. *Neurosurgery* **2015**, *76*, N15–N16. [CrossRef]
80. Lou, E.; Nelson, A.C.; Kool, M. Differential response of SHH-expressing adult medulloblastomas to the sonic hedgehog inhibitor vismodegib: Whole-genome analysis. *Cancer Biol. Ther.* **2019**, *20*, 1398–1402. [CrossRef]
81. Kool, M.; Jones, D.T.; Jager, N.; Northcott, P.A.; Pugh, T.J.; Hovestadt, V.; Piro, R.M.; Esparza, L.A.; Markant, S.L.; Remke, M.; et al. Genome sequencing of SHH medulloblastoma predicts genotype-related response to smoothened inhibition. *Cancer Cell* **2014**, *25*, 393–405. [CrossRef]
82. Tang, Y.; Gholamin, S.; Schubert, S.; Willardson, M.I.; Lee, A.; Bandopadhayay, P.; Bergthold, G.; Masoud, S.; Nguyen, B.; Vue, N.; et al. Epigenetic targeting of Hedgehog pathway transcriptional output through BET bromodomain inhibition. *Nat. Med.* **2014**, *20*, 732–740. [CrossRef] [PubMed]
83. Liu, F.; Jiang, W.; Sui, Y.; Meng, W.; Hou, L.; Li, T.; Li, M.; Zhang, L.; Mo, J.; Wang, J.; et al. CDK7 inhibition suppresses aberrant hedgehog pathway and overcomes resistance to smoothened antagonists. *Proc. Natl. Acad. Sci. USA* **2019**, *116*, 12986–12995. [CrossRef] [PubMed]
84. Lin, Z.; Li, S.; Sheng, H.; Cai, M.; Ma, L.Y.; Hu, L.; Xu, S.; Yu, L.S.; Zhang, N. Suppression of GLI sensitizes medulloblastoma cells to mitochondria-mediated apoptosis. *J. Cancer Res. Clin. Oncol.* **2016**, *142*, 2469–2478. [CrossRef] [PubMed]
85. Konings, K.; Vandevoorde, C.; Belmans, N.; Vermeesen, R.; Baselet, B.; Walleghem, M.V.; Janssen, A.; Isebaert, S.; Baatout, S.; Haustermans, K.; et al. The Combination of Particle Irradiation With the Hedgehog Inhibitor GANT61 Differently Modulates the Radiosensitivity and Migration of Cancer Cells Compared to X-ray Irradiation. *Front. Oncol.* **2019**, *9*, 391. [CrossRef]
86. Kim, J.; Lee, J.J.; Kim, J.; Gardner, D.; Beachy, P.A. Arsenic antagonizes the Hedgehog pathway by preventing ciliary accumulation and reducing stability of the Gli2 transcriptional effector. *Proc. Natl. Acad. Sci. USA* **2010**, *107*, 13432–13437. [CrossRef]
87. Dos Santos Klinger, P.H.; Delsin, L.E.A.; Cruzeiro, G.A.V.; Andrade, A.F.; Lira, R.C.P.; de Andrade, P.V.; das Chagas, P.F.; de Paula Queiroz, R.G.; Trevisan, F.A.; de Oliveira, R.S.; et al. Arsenic Trioxide exerts cytotoxic and radiosensitizing effects in pediatric Medulloblastoma cell lines of SHH Subgroup. *Sci. Rep.* **2020**, *10*, 6836. [CrossRef]
88. Cohen, K.J.; Gibbs, I.C.; Fisher, P.G.; Hayashi, R.J.; Macy, M.E.; Gore, L. A phase I trial of arsenic trioxide chemoradiotherapy for infiltrating astrocytomas of childhood. *Neuro. Oncol.* **2013**, *15*, 783–787. [CrossRef]
89. Li, C.; Peng, X.; Feng, C.; Xiong, X.; Li, J.; Liao, N.; Yang, Z.; Liu, A.; Wu, P.; Liang, X.; et al. Excellent Early Outcomes of Combined Chemotherapy with Arsenic Trioxide for Stage 4/M Neuroblastoma in Children: A Multicenter Nonrandomized Controlled Trial. *Oncol. Res.* **2021**, *28*, 791–800. [CrossRef]
90. Faria, C.C.; Golbourn, B.J.; Dubuc, A.M.; Remke, M.; Diaz, R.J.; Agnihotri, S.; Luck, A.; Sabha, N.; Olsen, S.; Wu, X.; et al. Foretinib is effective therapy for metastatic sonic hedgehog medulloblastoma. *Cancer Res.* **2015**, *75*, 134–146. [CrossRef]

91. Li, Y.H.; Luo, J.; Mosley, Y.Y.; Hedrick, V.E.; Paul, L.N.; Chang, J.; Zhang, G.; Wang, Y.K.; Banko, M.R.; Brunet, A.; et al. AMP-Activated Protein Kinase Directly Phosphorylates and Destabilizes Hedgehog Pathway Transcription Factor GLI1 in Medulloblastoma. *Cell Rep.* **2015**, *12*, 599–609. [CrossRef] [PubMed]
92. Gonnissen, A.; Isebaert, S.; McKee, C.M.; Muschel, R.J.; Haustermans, K. The Effect of Metformin and GANT61 Combinations on the Radiosensitivity of Prostate Cancer Cells. *Int. J. Mol. Sci.* **2017**, *18*, 399. [CrossRef] [PubMed]
93. Song, Z.; Wei, B.; Lu, C.; Huang, X.; Li, P.; Chen, L. Metformin suppresses the expression of Sonic hedgehog in gastric cancer cells. *Mol. Med. Rep.* **2017**, *15*, 1909–1915. [CrossRef]
94. Hu, A.; Hu, Z.; Ye, J.; Liu, Y.; Lai, Z.; Zhang, M.; Ji, W.; Huang, L.; Zou, H.; Chen, B.; et al. Metformin exerts anti-tumor effects via Sonic hedgehog signaling pathway by targeting AMPK in HepG2 cells. *Biochem. Cell Biol.* **2022**, *100*, 142–151. [CrossRef]
95. Northcott, P.A.; Fernandez, L.A.; Hagan, J.P.; Ellison, D.W.; Grajkowska, W.; Gillespie, Y.; Grundy, R.; Van Meter, T.; Rutka, J.T.; Croce, C.M.; et al. The miR-17/92 polycistron is up-regulated in sonic hedgehog-driven medulloblastomas and induced by N-myc in sonic hedgehog-treated cerebellar neural precursors. *Cancer Res.* **2009**, *69*, 3249–3255. [CrossRef]
96. Murphy, B.L.; Obad, S.; Bihannic, L.; Ayrault, O.; Zindy, F.; Kauppinen, S.; Roussel, M.F. Silencing of the miR-17~92 cluster family inhibits medulloblastoma progression. *Cancer Res.* **2013**, *73*, 7068–7078. [CrossRef]
97. Tan, I.L.; Arifa, R.D.N.; Rallapalli, H.; Kana, V.; Lao, Z.; Sanghrajka, R.M.; Sumru Bayin, N.; Tanne, A.; Wojcinski, A.; Korshunov, A.; et al. CSF1R inhibition depletes tumor-associated macrophages and attenuates tumor progression in a mouse sonic Hedgehog-Medulloblastoma model. *Oncogene* **2021**, *40*, 396–407. [CrossRef]
98. Read, T.A.; Fogarty, M.P.; Markant, S.L.; McLendon, R.E.; Wei, Z.; Ellison, D.W.; Febbo, P.G.; Wechsler-Reya, R.J. Identification of CD15 as a marker for tumor-propagating cells in a mouse model of medulloblastoma. *Cancer Cell* **2009**, *15*, 135–147. [CrossRef] [PubMed]
99. Markant, S.L.; Esparza, L.A.; Sun, J.; Barton, K.L.; McCoig, L.M.; Grant, G.A.; Crawford, J.R.; Levy, M.L.; Northcott, P.A.; Shih, D.; et al. Targeting sonic hedgehog-associated medulloblastoma through inhibition of Aurora and Polo-like kinases. *Cancer Res.* **2013**, *73*, 6310–6322. [CrossRef] [PubMed]
100. Zhang, L.; He, X.; Liu, X.; Zhang, F.; Huang, L.F.; Potter, A.S.; Xu, L.; Zhou, W.; Zheng, T.; Luo, Z.; et al. Single-Cell Transcriptomics in Medulloblastoma Reveals Tumor-Initiating Progenitors and Oncogenic Cascades during Tumorigenesis and Relapse. *Cancer Cell* **2019**, *36*, 302–318.e307. [CrossRef]
101. Buonamici, S.; Williams, J.; Morrissey, M.; Wang, A.; Guo, R.; Vattay, A.; Hsiao, K.; Yuan, J.; Green, J.; Ospina, B.; et al. Interfering with resistance to smoothened antagonists by inhibition of the PI3K pathway in medulloblastoma. *Sci. Transl. Med.* **2010**, *2*, 51ra70. [CrossRef] [PubMed]
102. Ward, S.A.; Warrington, N.M.; Taylor, S.; Kfoury, N.; Luo, J.; Rubin, J.B. Reprogramming Medulloblastoma-Propagating Cells by a Combined Antagonism of Sonic Hedgehog and CXCR4. *Cancer Res.* **2017**, *77*, 1416–1426. [CrossRef] [PubMed]
103. Bandopadhayay, P.; Bergthold, G.; Nguyen, B.; Schubert, S.; Gholamin, S.; Tang, Y.; Bolin, S.; Schumacher, S.E.; Zeid, R.; Masoud, S.; et al. BET bromodomain inhibition of MYC-amplified medulloblastoma. *Clin. Cancer Res.* **2014**, *20*, 912–925. [CrossRef] [PubMed]
104. Venkataraman, S.; Alimova, I.; Balakrishnan, I.; Harris, P.; Birks, D.K.; Griesinger, A.; Amani, V.; Cristiano, B.; Remke, M.; Taylor, M.D.; et al. Inhibition of BRD4 attenuates tumor cell self-renewal and suppresses stem cell signaling in MYC driven medulloblastoma. *Oncotarget* **2014**, *5*, 2355–2371. [CrossRef]
105. Hanaford, A.R.; Archer, T.C.; Price, A.; Kahlert, U.D.; Maciaczyk, J.; Nikkhah, G.; Kim, J.W.; Ehrenberger, T.; Clemons, P.A.; Dancik, V.; et al. DiSCoVERing Innovative Therapies for Rare Tumors: Combining Genetically Accurate Disease Models with In Silico Analysis to Identify Novel Therapeutic Targets. *Clin. Cancer Res.* **2016**, *22*, 3903–3914. [CrossRef]
106. Cook Sangar, M.L.; Genovesi, L.A.; Nakamoto, M.W.; Davis, M.J.; Knobluagh, S.E.; Ji, P.; Millar, A.; Wainwright, B.J.; Olson, J.M. Inhibition of CDK4/6 by Palbociclib Significantly Extends Survival in Medulloblastoma Patient-Derived Xenograft Mouse Models. *Clin. Cancer Res.* **2017**, *23*, 5802–5813. [CrossRef]
107. Faria, C.C.; Agnihotri, S.; Mack, S.C.; Golbourn, B.J.; Diaz, R.J.; Olsen, S.; Bryant, M.; Bebenek, M.; Wang, X.; Bertrand, K.C.; et al. Identification of alsterpaullone as a novel small molecule inhibitor to target group 3 medulloblastoma. *Oncotarget* **2015**, *6*, 21718–21729. [CrossRef]
108. Van Mater, D.; Gururangan, S.; Becher, O.; Campagne, O.; Leary, S.; Phillips, J.J.; Huang, J.; Lin, T.; Poussaint, T.Y.; Goldman, S.; et al. A phase I trial of the CDK 4/6 inhibitor palbociclib in pediatric patients with progressive brain tumors: A Pediatric Brain Tumor Consortium study (PBTC-042). *Pediatr. Blood Cancer* **2021**, *68*, e28879. [CrossRef]
109. Archer, T.C.; Ehrenberger, T.; Mundt, F.; Gold, M.P.; Krug, K.; Mah, C.K.; Mahoney, E.L.; Daniel, C.J.; LeNail, A.; Ramamoorthy, D.; et al. Proteomics, Post-translational Modifications, and Integrative Analyses Reveal Molecular Heterogeneity within Medulloblastoma Subgroups. *Cancer Cell* **2018**, *34*, 396–410.e398. [CrossRef]
110. Sengupta, S.; Weeraratne, S.D.; Sun, H.; Phallen, J.; Rallapalli, S.K.; Teider, N.; Kosaras, B.; Amani, V.; Pierre-Francois, J.; Tang, Y.; et al. alpha5-GABAA receptors negatively regulate MYC-amplified medulloblastoma growth. *Acta Neuropathol.* **2014**, *127*, 593–603. [CrossRef]
111. Jonas, O.; Calligaris, D.; Methuku, K.R.; Poe, M.M.; Francois, J.P.; Tranghese, F.; Changelian, A.; Sieghart, W.; Ernst, M.; Krummel, D.A.; et al. First In Vivo Testing of Compounds Targeting Group 3 Medulloblastomas Using an Implantable Microdevice as a New Paradigm for Drug Development. *J. Biomed. Nanotechnol.* **2016**, *12*, 1297–1302. [CrossRef] [PubMed]

112. Wang, D.; Veo, B.; Pierce, A.; Fosmire, S.; Madhavan, K.; Balakrishnan, I.; Donson, A.; Alimova, I.; Sullivan, K.D.; Joshi, M.; et al. A novel PLK1 inhibitor onvansertib effectively sensitizes MYC-driven medulloblastoma to radiotherapy. *Neuro. Oncol.* **2022**, *24*, 414–426. [CrossRef] [PubMed]
113. Veo, B.; Danis, E.; Pierce, A.; Sola, I.; Wang, D.; Foreman, N.K.; Jin, J.; Ma, A.; Serkova, N.; Venkataraman, S.; et al. Combined functional genomic and chemical screens identify SETD8 as a therapeutic target in MYC-driven medulloblastoma. *JCI Insight* **2019**, *4*, e122933. [CrossRef] [PubMed]
114. Wang, J.; Sui, Y.; Li, Q.; Zhao, Y.; Dong, X.; Yang, J.; Liang, Z.; Han, Y.; Tang, Y.; Ma, J. Effective inhibition of MYC-amplified group 3 medulloblastoma by FACT-targeted curaxin drug CBL0137. *Cell Death Dis.* **2020**, *11*, 1029. [CrossRef] [PubMed]
115. Casaos, J.; Gorelick, N.L.; Huq, S.; Choi, J.; Xia, Y.; Serra, R.; Felder, R.; Lott, T.; Kast, R.E.; Suk, I.; et al. The Use of Ribavirin as an Anticancer Therapeutic: Will It Go Viral? *Mol. Cancer Ther.* **2019**, *18*, 1185–1194. [CrossRef]
116. Huq, S.; Kannapadi, N.V.; Casaos, J.; Lott, T.; Felder, R.; Serra, R.; Gorelick, N.L.; Ruiz-Cardozo, M.A.; Ding, A.S.; Cecia, A.; et al. Preclinical efficacy of ribavirin in SHH and group 3 medulloblastoma. *J. Neurosurg. Pediatr.* **2021**, *27*, 482–488. [CrossRef]
117. Serra, R.; Zhao, T.; Huq, S.; Gorelick, N.L.; Casaos, J.; Cecia, A.; Mangraviti, A.; Eberhart, C.; Bai, R.; Olivi, A.; et al. DisulfirAm. and copper combination therapy targets NPL4, cancer stem cells and extends survival in a medulloblastoma model. *PLoS ONE* **2021**, *16*, e0251957. [CrossRef]
118. Lee, C.; Rudneva, V.A.; Erkek, S.; Zapatka, M.; Chau, L.Q.; Tacheva-Grigorova, S.K.; Garancher, A.; Rusert, J.M.; Aksoy, O.; Lea, R.; et al. Lsd1 as a therapeutic target in Gfi1-activated medulloblastoma. *Nat. Commun.* **2019**, *10*, 332. [CrossRef]
119. Gholamin, S.; Mitra, S.S.; Feroze, A.H.; Liu, J.; Kahn, S.A.; Zhang, M.; Esparza, R.; Richard, C.; Ramaswamy, V.; Remke, M.; et al. Disrupting the CD47-SIRPalpha anti-phagocytic axis by a humanized anti-CD47 antibody is an efficacious treatment for malignant pediatric brain tumors. *Sci. Transl. Med.* **2017**, *9*, eaaf2968. [CrossRef]
120. Kahn, S.A.; Wang, X.; Nitta, R.T.; Gholamin, S.; Theruvath, J.; Hutter, G.; Azad, T.D.; Wadi, L.; Bolin, S.; Ramaswamy, V.; et al. Notch1 regulates the initiation of metastasis and self-renewal of Group 3 medulloblastoma. *Nat. Commun.* **2018**, *9*, 4121. [CrossRef]
121. Sreenivasan, L.; Wang, H.; Yap, S.Q.; Leclair, P.; Tam, A.; Lim, C.J. Autocrine IL-6/STAT3 signaling aids development of acquired drug resistance in Group 3 medulloblastoma. *Cell Death Dis.* **2020**, *11*, 1035. [CrossRef] [PubMed]
122. Sreenivasan, L.; Li, L.V.; Leclair, P.; Lim, C.J. Targeting the gp130/STAT3 Axis Attenuates Tumor Microenvironment Mediated Chemoresistance in Group 3 Medulloblastoma Cells. *Cells* **2022**, *11*, 381. [CrossRef] [PubMed]
123. Kumar, V.; Kumar, V.; Chaudhary, A.K.; Coulter, D.W.; McGuire, T.; Mahato, R.I. Impact of miRNA-mRNA Profiling and Their Correlation on Medulloblastoma Tumorigenesis. *Mol. Ther. Nucleic Acids* **2018**, *12*, 490–503. [CrossRef] [PubMed]
124. Weeraratne, S.D.; Amani, V.; Teider, N.; Pierre-Francois, J.; Winter, D.; Kye, M.J.; Sengupta, S.; Archer, T.; Remke, M.; Bai, A.H.; et al. Pleiotropic effects of miR-183~96~182 converge to regulate cell survival, proliferation and migration in medulloblastoma. *Acta Neuropathol.* **2012**, *123*, 539–552. [CrossRef]
125. Bharambe, H.S.; Joshi, A.; Yogi, K.; Kazi, S.; Shirsat, N.V. Restoration of miR-193a expression is tumor-suppressive in MYC amplified Group 3 medulloblastoma. *Acta Neuropathol. Commun.* **2020**, *8*, 70. [CrossRef]
126. Yogi, K.; Sridhar, E.; Goel, N.; Jalali, R.; Goel, A.; Moiyadi, A.; Thorat, R.; Panwalkar, P.; Khire, A.; Dasgupta, A.; et al. MiR-148a, a microRNA upregulated in the WNT subgroup tumors, inhibits invasion and tumorigenic potential of medulloblastoma cells by targeting Neuropilin 1. *Oncoscience* **2015**, *2*, 334–348. [CrossRef]
127. Katsushima, K.; Lee, B.; Yuan, M.; Kunhiraman, H.; Stapleton, S.; Jallo, G.; Raabe, E.; Eberhart, C.; Perera, R. CSIG-32. microRNA 211, A POTENTIAL THERAPEUTIC AGENT FOR GROUP 3 MEDULLOBLASTOMA IN CHILDREN. *Neuro-Oncology* **2021**, *23*, vi40. [CrossRef]
128. Perumal, N.; Kanchan, R.K.; Doss, D.; Bastola, N.; Atri, P.; Chirravuri-Venkata, R.; Thapa, I.; Vengoji, R.; Maurya, S.K.; Klinkebiel, D.; et al. MiR-212-3p functions as a tumor suppressor gene in group 3 medulloblastoma via targeting nuclear factor I/B (NFIB). *Acta Neuropathol. Commun.* **2021**, *9*, 195. [CrossRef]
129. Rea, J.; Carissimo, A.; Trisciuoglio, D.; Illi, B.; Picard, D.; Remke, M.; Laneve, P.; Caffarelli, E. Identification and Functional Characterization of Novel MYC-Regulated Long Noncoding RNAs in Group 3 Medulloblastoma. *Cancers* **2021**, *13*, 3853. [CrossRef]
130. Katsushima, K.; Lee, B.; Kunhiraman, H.; Zhong, C.; Murad, R.; Yin, J.; Liu, B.; Garancher, A.; Gonzalez-Gomez, I.; Monforte, H.L.; et al. The long noncoding RNA lnc-HLX-2-7 is oncogenic in Group 3 medulloblastomas. *Neuro. Oncol.* **2021**, *23*, 572–585. [CrossRef]
131. Bolin, S.; Borgenvik, A.; Persson, C.U.; Sundstrom, A.; Qi, J.; Bradner, J.E.; Weiss, W.A.; Cho, Y.J.; Weishaupt, H.; Swartling, F.J. Combined BET bromodomain and CDK2 inhibition in MYC-driven medulloblastoma. *Oncogene* **2018**, *37*, 2850–2862. [CrossRef] [PubMed]
132. Chaturvedi, N.K.; Kling, M.J.; Griggs, C.N.; Kesherwani, V.; Shukla, M.; McIntyre, E.M.; Ray, S.; Liu, Y.; McGuire, T.R.; Sharp, J.G.; et al. A Novel Combination Approach Targeting an Enhanced Protein Synthesis Pathway in MYC-driven (Group 3) Medulloblastoma. *Mol. Cancer Ther.* **2020**, *19*, 1351–1362. [CrossRef] [PubMed]
133. Kling, M.J.; Kesherwani, V.; Mishra, N.K.; Alexander, G.; McIntyre, E.M.; Ray, S.; Challagundla, K.B.; Joshi, S.S.; Coulter, D.W.; Chaturvedi, N.K. A novel dual epigenetic approach targeting BET proteins and HDACs in Group 3 (MYC-driven) Medulloblastoma. *J. Exp. Clin. Cancer Res.* **2022**, *41*, 321. [CrossRef] [PubMed]

134. Menyhart, O.; Giangaspero, F.; Gyorffy, B. Molecular markers and potential therapeutic targets in non-WNT/non-SHH (group 3 and group 4) medulloblastomas. *J. Hematol. Oncol.* **2019**, *12*, 29. [CrossRef] [PubMed]
135. Baroni, M.; Guardia, G.D.A.; Lei, X.; Kosti, A.; Qiao, M.; Landry, T.; Mau, K.; Galante, P.A.F.; Penalva, L.O.F. The RNA-Binding Protein Musashi1 Regulates a Network of Cell Cycle Genes in Group 4 Medulloblastoma. *Cells* **2021**, *11*, 56. [CrossRef]
136. Alimova, I.; Venkataraman, S.; Harris, P.; Marquez, V.E.; Northcott, P.A.; Dubuc, A.; Taylor, M.D.; Foreman, N.K.; Vibhakar, R. Targeting the enhancer of zeste homologue 2 in medulloblastoma. *Int. J. Cancer* **2012**, *131*, 1800–1809. [CrossRef]
137. Park, A.K.; Lee, J.Y.; Cheong, H.; Ramaswamy, V.; Park, S.H.; Kool, M.; Phi, J.H.; Choi, S.A.; Cavalli, F.; Taylor, M.D.; et al. Subgroup-specific prognostic signaling and metabolic pathways in pediatric medulloblastoma. *BMC Cancer* **2019**, *19*, 571. [CrossRef]
138. Liu, H.; Wang, J.; Zhang, M.; Xuan, Q.; Wang, Z.; Lian, X.; Zhang, Q. Jagged1 promotes aromatase inhibitor resistance by modulating tumor-associated macrophage differentiation in breast cancer patients. *Breast Cancer Res. Treat* **2017**, *166*, 95–107. [CrossRef]
139. Shen, Q.; Cohen, B.; Zheng, W.; Rahbar, R.; Martin, B.; Murakami, K.; Lamorte, S.; Thompson, P.; Berman, H.; Zuniga-Pflucker, J.C.; et al. Notch Shapes the Innate Immunophenotype in Breast Cancer. *Cancer Discov.* **2017**, *7*, 1320–1335. [CrossRef]
140. Sierra, R.A.; Trillo-Tinoco, J.; Mohamed, E.; Yu, L.; Achyut, B.R.; Arbab, A.; Bradford, J.W.; Osborne, B.A.; Miele, L.; Rodriguez, P.C. Anti-Jagged Immunotherapy Inhibits MDSCs and Overcomes Tumor-Induced Tolerance. *Cancer Res.* **2017**, *77*, 5628–5638. [CrossRef]
141. Meurette, O.; Mehlen, P. Notch Signaling in the Tumor Microenvironment. *Cancer Cell* **2018**, *34*, 536–548. [CrossRef] [PubMed]
142. Hoffman, L.M.; Fouladi, M.; Olson, J.; Daryani, V.M.; Stewart, C.F.; Wetmore, C.; Kocak, M.; Onar-Thomas, A.; Wagner, L.; Gururangan, S.; et al. Phase I trial of weekly MK-0752 in children with refractory central nervous system malignancies: A pediatric brain tumor consortium study. *Childs Nerv. Syst.* **2015**, *31*, 1283–1289. [CrossRef]
143. Lee, B.; Katsushima, K.; Pokhrel, R.; Yuan, M.; Stapleton, S.; Jallo, G.; Wechsler-Reya, R.J.; Eberhart, C.G.; Ray, A.; Perera, R.J. The long non-coding RNA SPRIGHTLY and its binding partner PTBP1 regulate exon 5 skipping of SMYD3 transcripts in group 4 medulloblastomas. *Neurooncol. Adv.* **2022**, *4*, vdac120. [CrossRef]
144. Paul, R.; Bapat, P.; Deogharkar, A.; Kazi, S.; Singh, S.K.V.; Gupta, T.; Jalali, R.; Sridhar, E.; Moiyadi, A.; Shetty, P.; et al. MiR-592 activates the mTOR kinase, ERK1/ERK2 kinase signaling and imparts neuronal differentiation signature characteristic of Group 4 medulloblastoma. *Hum. Mol. Genet.* **2021**, *30*, 2416–2428. [CrossRef]
145. Dimitrova, V.; Arcaro, A. Targeting the PI3K/AKT/mTOR signaling pathway in medulloblastoma. *Curr. Mol. Med.* **2015**, *15*, 82–93. [CrossRef] [PubMed]
146. Ersahin, T.; Tuncbag, N.; Cetin-Atalay, R. The PI3K/AKT/mTOR interactive pathway. *Mol. Biosyst.* **2015**, *11*, 1946–1954. [CrossRef] [PubMed]
147. Chaturvedi, N.K.; Kling, M.J.; Coulter, D.W.; McGuire, T.R.; Ray, S.; Kesherwani, V.; Joshi, S.S.; Sharp, J.G. Improved therapy for medulloblastoma: Targeting hedgehog and PI3K-mTOR signaling pathways in combination with chemotherapy. *Oncotarget* **2018**, *9*, 16619–16633. [CrossRef]
148. Jonchere, B.; Williams, J.; Zindy, F.; Liu, J.; Robinson, S.; Farmer, D.M.; Min, J.; Yang, L.; Stripay, J.L.; Wang, Y.; et al. Combination of Ribociclib with BET-Bromodomain and PI3K/mTOR Inhibitors for Medulloblastoma Treatment In Vitro and In Vivo. *Mol. Cancer Ther.* **2023**, *22*, 37–51. [CrossRef]
149. Pei, Y.; Liu, K.W.; Wang, J.; Garancher, A.; Tao, R.; Esparza, L.A.; Maier, D.L.; Udaka, Y.T.; Murad, N.; Morrissy, S.; et al. HDAC and PI3K Antagonists Cooperate to Inhibit Growth of MYC-Driven Medulloblastoma. *Cancer Cell* **2016**, *29*, 311–323. [CrossRef]
150. Calnan, D.R.; Brunet, A. The FoxO code. *Oncogene* **2008**, *27*, 2276–2288. [CrossRef]
151. Pei, Y.; Moore, C.E.; Wang, J.; Tewari, A.K.; Eroshkin, A.; Cho, Y.J.; Witt, H.; Korshunov, A.; Read, T.A.; Sun, J.L.; et al. An animal model of MYC-driven medulloblastoma. *Cancer Cell* **2012**, *21*, 155–167. [CrossRef]
152. Marino, A.M.; Frijhoff, J.; Calero, R.; Baryawno, N.; Ostman, A.; Johnsen, J.I. Effects of epigenetic modificators in combination with small molecule inhibitors of receptor tyrosine kinases on medulloblastoma growth. *Biochem. Biophys. Res. Commun.* **2014**, *450*, 1600–1605. [CrossRef]
153. Marino, A.M.; Sofiadis, A.; Baryawno, N.; Johnsen, J.I.; Larsson, C.; Vukojevic, V.; Ekstrom, T.J. Enhanced effects by 4-phenylbutyrate in combination with RTK inhibitors on proliferation in brain tumor cell models. *Biochem. Biophys. Res. Commun.* **2011**, *411*, 208–212. [CrossRef]
154. Guessous, F.; Yang, Y.; Johnson, E.; Marcinkiewicz, L.; Smith, M.; Zhang, Y.; Kofman, A.; Schiff, D.; Christensen, J.; Abounader, R. Cooperation between c-Met and focal adhesion kinase family members in medulloblastoma and implications for therapy. *Mol. Cancer Ther.* **2012**, *11*, 288–297. [CrossRef] [PubMed]
155. Wick, W.; Wick, A.; Schulz, J.B.; Dichgans, J.; Rodemann, H.P.; Weller, M. Prevention of irradiation-induced glioma cell invasion by temozolomide involves caspase 3 activity and cleavage of focal adhesion kinase. *Cancer Res.* **2002**, *62*, 1915–1919.
156. Roberts, E.; Cossigny, D.A.; Quan, G.M. The role of vascular endothelial growth factor in metastatic prostate cancer to the skeleton. *Prostate Cancer* **2013**, *2013*, 418340. [CrossRef] [PubMed]
157. Quero, L.; Dubois, L.; Lieuwes, N.G.; Hennequin, C.; Lambin, P. miR-210 as a marker of chronic hypoxia, but not a therapeutic target in prostate cancer. *Radiother Oncol.* **2011**, *101*, 203–208. [CrossRef]

158. Zhang, L.; Cheng, X.; Gao, Y.; Zheng, J.; Xu, Q.; Sun, Y.; Guan, H.; Yu, H.; Sun, Z. Apigenin induces autophagic cell death in human papillary thyroid carcinoma BCPAP cells. *Food Funct.* **2015**, *6*, 3464–3472. [CrossRef] [PubMed]
159. Insel, P.A.; Murray, F.; Yokoyama, U.; Romano, S.; Yun, H.; Brown, L.; Snead, A.; Lu, D.; Aroonsakool, N. cAMP and Epac in the regulation of tissue fibrosis. *Br. J. Pharmacol.* **2012**, *166*, 447–456. [CrossRef]
160. Valencia-Cervantes, J.; Huerta-Yepez, S.; Aquino-Jarquin, G.; Rodriguez-Enriquez, S.; Martinez-Fong, D.; Arias-Montano, J.A.; Davila-Borja, V.M. Hypoxia increases chemoresistance in human medulloblastoma DAOY cells via hypoxia-inducible factor 1alpha-mediated downregulation of the CYP2B6, CYP3A4 and CYP3A5 enzymes and inhibition of cell proliferation. *Oncol. Rep.* **2019**, *41*, 178–190. [CrossRef]
161. Lasky, J.L., 3rd; Bradford, K.L.; Wang, Y.; Pak, Y.; Panosyan, E.H. Chemotherapy Can Synergize With Adoptive Immunotherapy to Inhibit Medulloblastoma Growth. *Anticancer Res.* **2022**, *42*, 1697–1706. [CrossRef]
162. Donovan, L.K.; Delaidelli, A.; Joseph, S.K.; Bielamowicz, K.; Fousek, K.; Holgado, B.L.; Manno, A.; Srikanthan, D.; Gad, A.Z.; Van Ommeren, R.; et al. Locoregional delivery of CAR T cells to the cerebrospinal fluid for treatment of metastatic medulloblastoma and ependymoma. *Nat. Med.* **2020**, *26*, 720–731. [CrossRef] [PubMed]
163. Menyhart, O.; Gyorffy, B. Molecular stratifications, biomarker candidates and new therapeutic options in current medulloblastoma treatment approaches. *Cancer Metastasis Rev.* **2020**, *39*, 211–233. [CrossRef] [PubMed]
164. Pham, C.D.; Flores, C.; Yang, C.; Pinheiro, E.M.; Yearley, J.H.; Sayour, E.J.; Pei, Y.; Moore, C.; McLendon, R.E.; Huang, J.; et al. Differential Immune Microenvironments and Response to Immune Checkpoint Blockade among Molecular Subtypes of Murine Medulloblastoma. *Clin. Cancer Res.* **2016**, *22*, 582–595. [CrossRef] [PubMed]
165. Blumenthal, D.T.; Yalon, M.; Vainer, G.W.; Lossos, A.; Yust, S.; Tzach, L.; Cagnano, E.; Limon, D.; Bokstein, F. Pembrolizumab: First experience with recurrent primary central nervous system (CNS) tumors. *J. Neurooncol.* **2016**, *129*, 453–460. [CrossRef]
166. Gorsi, H.S.; Malicki, D.M.; Barsan, V.; Tumblin, M.; Yeh-Nayre, L.; Milburn, M.; Elster, J.D.; Crawford, J.R. Nivolumab in the Treatment of Recurrent or Refractory Pediatric Brain Tumors: A Single Institutional Experience. *J. Pediatr. Hematol. Oncol.* **2019**, *41*, e235–e241. [CrossRef]
167. Rodon, J.; Tawbi, H.A.; Thomas, A.L.; Stoller, R.G.; Turtschi, C.P.; Baselga, J.; Sarantopoulos, J.; Mahalingam, D.; Shou, Y.; Moles, M.A.; et al. A phase I, multicenter, open-label, first-in-human, dose-escalation study of the oral smoothened inhibitor Sonidegib (LDE225) in patients with advanced solid tumors. *Clin. Cancer Res.* **2014**, *20*, 1900–1909. [CrossRef]
168. Peukert, S.; He, F.; Dai, M.; Zhang, R.; Sun, Y.; Miller-Moslin, K.; McEwan, M.; Lagu, B.; Wang, K.; Yusuff, N.; et al. Discovery of NVP-LEQ506, a second-generation inhibitor of smoothened. *ChemMedChem* **2013**, *8*, 1261–1265. [CrossRef]
169. Hummel, T.R.; Wagner, L.; Ahern, C.; Fouladi, M.; Reid, J.M.; McGovern, R.M.; Ames, M.M.; Gilbertson, R.J.; Horton, T.; Ingle, A.M.; et al. A pediatric phase 1 trial of vorinostat and temozolomide in relapsed or refractory primary brain or spinal cord tumors: A Children's Oncology Group phase 1 consortium study. *Pediatr. Blood Cancer* **2013**, *60*, 1452–1457. [CrossRef]
170. Muscal, J.A.; Thompson, P.A.; Horton, T.M.; Ingle, A.M.; Ahern, C.H.; McGovern, R.M.; Reid, J.M.; Ames, M.M.; Espinoza-Delgado, I.; Weigel, B.J.; et al. A phase I trial of vorinostat and bortezomib in children with refractory or recurrent solid tumors: A Children's Oncology Group phase I consortium study (ADVL0916). *Pediatr. Blood Cancer* **2013**, *60*, 390–395. [CrossRef]
171. Leary, S.E.S.; Kilburn, L.; Geyer, J.R.; Kocak, M.; Huang, J.; Smith, K.S.; Hadley, J.; Ermoian, R.; MacDonald, T.J.; Goldman, S.; et al. Vorinostat and isotretinoin with chemotherapy in young children with embryonal brain tumors: A report from the Pediatric Brain Tumor Consortium (PBTC-026). *Neuro. Oncol.* **2022**, *24*, 1178–1190. [CrossRef] [PubMed]
172. Fouladi, M.; Park, J.R.; Stewart, C.F.; Gilbertson, R.J.; Schaiquevich, P.; Sun, J.; Reid, J.M.; Ames, M.M.; Speights, R.; Ingle, A.M.; et al. Pediatric phase I trial and pharmacokinetic study of vorinostat: A Children's Oncology Group phase I consortium report. *J. Clin. Oncol.* **2010**, *28*, 3623–3629. [CrossRef] [PubMed]
173. DeWire, M.D.; Fuller, C.; Campagne, O.; Lin, T.; Pan, H.; Young Poussaint, T.; Baxter, P.A.; Hwang, E.I.; Bukowinski, A.; Dorris, K.; et al. A Phase I and Surgical Study of Ribociclib and Everolimus in Children with Recurrent or Refractory Malignant Brain Tumors: A Pediatric Brain Tumor Consortium Study. *Clin. Cancer Res.* **2021**, *27*, 2442–2451. [CrossRef]
174. Kieran, M.W.; Chi, S.; Goldman, S.; Onar-Thomas, A.; Poussaint, T.Y.; Vajapeyam, S.; Fahey, F.; Wu, S.; Turner, D.C.; Stewart, C.F.; et al. A phase I trial and PK study of cediranib (AZD2171), an orally bioavailable pan-VEGFR inhibitor, in children with recurrent or refractory primary CNS tumors. *Childs Nerv. Syst.* **2015**, *31*, 1433–1445. [CrossRef] [PubMed]
175. Fangusaro, J.; Cefalo, M.G.; Garre, M.L.; Marshall, L.V.; Massimino, M.; Benettaib, B.; Biserna, N.; Poon, J.; Quan, J.; Conlin, E.; et al. Phase 2 Study of Pomalidomide (CC-4047) Monotherapy for Children and Young Adults With Recurrent or Progressive Primary Brain Tumors. *Front. Oncol.* **2021**, *11*, 660892. [CrossRef]
176. Slavc, I.; Mayr, L.; Stepien, N.; Gojo, J.; Aliotti Lippolis, M.; Azizi, A.A.; Chocholous, M.; Baumgartner, A.; Hedrich, C.S.; Holm, S.; et al. Improved Long-Term Survival of Patients with Recurrent Medulloblastoma Treated with a "MEMMAT-like" Metronomic Antiangiogenic Approach. *Cancers* **2022**, *14*, 5128. [CrossRef] [PubMed]
177. Packer, R.J.; Rood, B.R.; Turner, D.C.; Stewart, C.F.; Fisher, M.; Smith, C.; Young-Pouissant, T.; Goldman, S.; Lulla, R.; Banerjee, A.; et al. Phase I and pharmacokinetic trial of PTC299 in pediatric patients with refractory or recurrent central nervous system tumors: A PBTC study. *J. Neurooncol.* **2015**, *121*, 217–224. [CrossRef]

178. MacDonald, T.J.; Stewart, C.F.; Kocak, M.; Goldman, S.; Ellenbogen, R.G.; Phillips, P.; Lafond, D.; Poussaint, T.Y.; Kieran, M.W.; Boyett, J.M.; et al. Phase I clinical trial of cilengitide in children with refractory brain tumors: Pediatric Brain Tumor Consortium Study PBTC-012. *J. Clin. Oncol.* **2008**, *26*, 919–924. [CrossRef]
179. Saulnier-Sholler, G.; Duda, D.G.; Bergendahl, G.; Ebb, D.; Snuderl, M.; Laetsch, T.W.; Michlitsch, J.; Hanson, D.; Isakoff, M.S.; Bielamowicz, K.; et al. A Phase I Trial of TB-403 in Relapsed Medulloblastoma, Neuroblastoma, Ewing Sarcoma, and Alveolar Rhabdomyosarcoma. *Clin. Cancer Res.* **2022**, *28*, 3950–3957. [CrossRef]

Disclaimer/Publisher's Note: The statements, opinions and data contained in all publications are solely those of the individual author(s) and contributor(s) and not of MDPI and/or the editor(s). MDPI and/or the editor(s) disclaim responsibility for any injury to people or property resulting from any ideas, methods, instructions or products referred to in the content.

cancers

MDPI

Review

DNA Damage Responses in Tumors Are Not Proliferative Stimuli, but Rather They Are DNA Repair Actions Requiring Supportive Medical Care

Zsuzsanna Suba

Department of Molecular Pathology, National Institute of Oncology, Ráth György Str. 7-9, H-1122 Budapest, Hungary; subazdr@gmail.com; Tel.: +36-00-36-1-224-86-00; Fax: +36-00-36-1-224-86-20

Simple Summary: This work challenges the traditional principles of cancer therapy: simply targeting and blocking the regulatory pathways of rapidly proliferating tumors is a serious mistake. Since tumor initiation and growth may be attributed to a patient's genomic instability and damage, genotoxic medications are inappropriate as they cause additional genomic damage in both patients and their cancers. Tumor cells are not enemies to be killed, but rather they are ill human cells which have the remnants of same genome stabilizer pathways like healthy cells. Within tumors, there is a combat for the improvement of their genomic defects. Moreover, tumors ask for help in their kamikaze action by recruiting immune competent cells into their environment. We should learn by watching the genome repairing activities within tumors, in the peritumoral region and in the whole body, and may follow them with supportive care. Successful cancer therapy does not remain a dream to be realized in the far future, but we should set about a cancer cure without delay.

Abstract: Background: In tumors, somatic mutagenesis presumably drives the DNA damage response (DDR) via altered regulatory pathways, increasing genomic instability and proliferative activity. These considerations led to the standard therapeutic strategy against cancer: the disruption of mutation-activated DNA repair pathways of tumors.Purpose: Justifying that cancer cells are not enemies to be killed, but rather that they are ill human cells which have the remnants of physiologic regulatory pathways. Results: 1. Genomic instability and cancer development may be originated from a flaw in estrogen signaling rather than excessive estrogen signaling; 2. Healthy cells with genomic instability exhibit somatic mutations, helping DNA restitution; 3. Somatic mutations in tumor cells aim for the restoration of DNA damage, rather than further genomic derangement; 4. In tumors, estrogen signaling drives the pathways of DNA stabilization, leading to apoptotic death; 5. In peritumoral cellular infiltration, the genomic damage of the tumor induces inflammatory cytokine secretion and increased estrogen synthesis. In the inflammatory cells, an increased growth factor receptor (GFR) signaling confers the unliganded activation of estrogen receptors (ERs); 6. In breast cancer cells responsive to genotoxic therapy, constitutive mutations help the upregulation of estrogen signaling and consequential apoptosis. In breast tumors non-responsive to genotoxic therapy, the possibilities for ER activation via either liganded or unliganded pathways are exhausted, leading to farther genomic instability and unrestrained proliferation. Conclusions: Understanding the real character and behavior of human tumors at the molecular level suggests that we should learn the genome repairing methods of tumors and follow them by supportive therapy, rather than provoking additional genomic damages.

Keywords: anti-estrogen; cancer therapy; estrogen; DNA damage; DNA damage response; DNA repair; endocrine disruptor; estrogen receptor; growth factor receptor; mutation

1. Introduction

Cancer is a complex disease, presumably originating from mutations in genes, promoting genomic instability, and initiating cancer development [1]. In cancers, mutagenesis drives the DNA damage response (DDR) via altered regulatory pathways, increasing genomic instability and helping proliferative activity [2]. Altered DNA damage responses in tumors serve the maintenance of survival and unrestrained proliferative activity of cells. These considerations led to the standard therapeutic strategy against cancer: the disruption of mutation-activated DNA repair pathways of tumors, which should lead to the clinical recovery of cancer patients [3]. However, the derangement of the mutation-driven DNA repair techniques of tumors could not bridge the gap between basic research and clinical practice.

In tumors, the accumulation of somatic mutations yields so-called cancer driver genes, and their altered regulatory protein products may manage aggressive expansion [4]. Catalogues of genes known to be involved in cancer development were prepared by whole-exome and later, whole-genome sequencing of numerous tumor samples. Analyses of thousands of cancer genomes return a remarkably similar catalogue of around 300 genes that are mutated in at least one cancer type. Yet, many features of these mutated genes and their exact role in cancer development remain unclear. The accumulation of certain mutated genes in tumors is not enough to justify their pro-oncogenic nature.

There is a close collaboration between the activity of the immune system and cancer driver mutations. The immune system has a strong impact on determining the expression of certain cancer driver genes [5]. At the same time, the appearance of certain cancer driver mutations shows correlations with the density and composition of immune competent cells in the tumor microenvironment [6]. The connection of the immune system with the appearance of cancer driver mutations is probably mediated by the fact that all somatic mutations can create neoantigens. These unknown peptides may trigger an immune response, eliminating the cell that carries them; this process is known as immune-editing [5].

Cancer driver mutations influence the quantity and composition of immune cell infiltration in the tumor microenvironment [6]. Somatic mutations in cancer driver genes with well-known roles in immune signaling, such as *CASP8* or *HLA*, generally recruit higher concentrations of immune cells into the tumor microenvironment. These pro-oncogenic mutations most likely result in immune-evading mechanisms. In contrast, colorectal tumors, with accumulated *KRAS* mutation, show weaker immune cell infiltration than those without this mutation, and the tumors are resistant to the immune-checkpoint blockade [7].

Surprisingly, cancer driver genes are exposed, even in various healthy cells exhibiting the same somatic mutations as tumors. Two studies examined somatic mutations in the entire human body [8,9]. In some individuals, cancer driver somatic mutations were found in virtually all tissues, although none of them had been diagnosed with cancer. The most interesting recent finding is the presence of somatic *PTEN*, *KMT2D*, and *ARID1A* mutations in healthy liver cells [10]. Hepatocytes showing these well-known cancer driver mutations exhibited conspicuously increased fitness, faster expansion, and regeneration under stress or other injury as compared to their counterparts without mutation.

The study on liver cells showing high fitness and regenerative capacity despite their cancer driving mutation justifies the positive impact of somatic mutations on genomic stability rather than tumor promotion. There is a plausible explanation; the concentration of genome driver somatic mutations in tumors may not be pro-oncogenic stimuli, but may rather be DNA stabilizer actions via genomic plasticity. Somatic mutations in clinically cancer-free patients may derive from the earlier occurrence of accidental genomic instability or subclinical cancer in an organ, which were repaired or eliminated via activated mutations.

Molecular cancer therapies targeting the altered DNA damage response pathways lead to continuous failures. This problem evokes the idea that some modern cancer therapies might cause more harm than benefit, as we do not exactly understand the molecular events in the background of diseases [11]. The analysis of therapeutic failures urges a complete turn in our anti-cancer strategy rather than farther developing and improving the families of moderately effective or even genotoxic drugs.

The aim of this study is to justify that tumor cells are not enemies to be killed, butrather that they are ill human cells which have the remnants of the same regulatory pathways like patients' healthy cells [12]. Understanding the real character and behavior of human tumors at the molecular level suggests that we should learn by watching the genome repairing methods of tumors instead of provoking additional genomic damages.

2. Endocrine Disruptor Synthetic Estrogens Increase the Risk for Certain Cancers and Cardiovascular Complications

In the early 1940s, synthetic estrogens were developed for medical purposes; for the treatment of miscarriage and menopausal complaints and later, for oral contraception. Diethylstilbestrol (DES) was a non-steroidal hormone; ethinylestradiol (EE) was a steroidal product; while conjugated equine estrogens (CEEs) were extracted from biological samples [13].

Increased breast cancer risk in DES-treated patients mistakenly suggested that synthetic estrogens activate the same subcellular pathways that a high endogenous estradiol level does, leading to alterations in all cellular functions including interactions with DNA [14]. In reality, malformations and increased breast cancer risk induced by prenatal exposure to DES may be attributed to the deregulation of estrogen signaling pathways. In animal experiments, DES and EE treatment provoked histone modification and further genomic damages via ER deregulation, justifying their endocrine disruptor character [15].

The development of synthetic estrogens, including both DES and EE, may be regarded as a pharmaceutical mistake as they are endocrine disruptors. Endocrine disruptors exhibit a special toxicological mechanism; higher doses induce more genomic damages as compared to lower doses; however, there are no safety low levels of these chemicals [16]. Low doses of synthetic estrogens exert an inhibitory effect on the ligand independent, ancient AF1 domain of ERs, while inducing compensatory estrogen-like activation on the ligand-dependent AF2 domain. Conversely, high doses of synthetic estrogens provoke a serious imbalance between the liganded and unliganded activation of ERs, resulting in uncompensated damages in the whole genomic machinery [17].

2.1. Controversial Correlations between Menopausal Hormone Therapy (MHT) and Women's Health

For menopausal hormone therapy (MHT), both synthetic EE and CEE extracted from biological samples were prescribed [13]. From the 1940s, MHT became widely used among postmenopausal women for the treatment of menopausal symptoms and for the prevention of chronic illnesses, such as cardiovascular and thromboembolic complications and osteoporosis. In menopausal women, both natural and synthetic estrogens were applied alone or in combination with synthetic progestins as exogenous hormone therapies. Among HRT-using women, ambiguous clinical results were experienced; either increased or decreased risks for arterial and venous thromboembolism and for breast cancer was experienced. The guidance from the Food and Drug Administration (FDA) established that the benefits of MHT use surpass their risks [18]. Nevertheless, no comparative information was available on the efficacy and toxicity of synthetic versus natural hormone products.

In the early 2000s, two great Women's Health Initiative (WHI) studies reported quite controversial results in women who underwent MHT. In 2002, increased risks for breast cancer, thromboembolism, and cardiovascular diseases were reported in menopausal women treated with conjugated equine estrogen (CEE) plus medroxyprogesterone acetate (MPA) [19]. Conversely, in 2004, another great WHI study reported on a striking reduction of breast cancer risk in women treated with CEE (Premarin, Pfizer) alone [20]. In the latter study, the protective effect of Premarin, with its natural origin, may be explained by the omission of the highly toxic progestin, MPA [21].

In 2019, a great meta-analysis study reported worldwide epidemiological evidence of the breast cancer-inducing capacity of MHT independent of the used hormone formuli and the timing of treatment [22]. All MHT studies reporting the breast cancer preventive effect of

Premarin alone were omitted from this analysis. The concept of "estrogen-induced cancer" was both the starting point and the goal of investigation, creating a circular reasoning.

In 2020, the earlier WHI study was repeated on the surviving women eighteen years following the MHT, and the results reflected the long-lasting breast cancer preventive effect of Premarin. Both morbidity and breast cancer-associated mortality were significantly decreased among estrogen treated women [23]. These results justified the long term genome stabilizer power of natural estrogen treatment without synthetic progestin use [17].

In 2021, Premarin treatment of women with ER positive, PR negative breast cancers (N = 10,739) resulted in a significant reduction in tumors and breast cancer-related deaths. The authors established that here is the time for change in their breast cancer risk reduction strategies in clinical practice [24].

An analysis of the results of MHT studies using different hormone schedules justified that horse urine-derived Premarin without synthetic progestin is a highly beneficial formula against breast cancer, coronary heart disease, thromboembolism, and bone loss [21]. Although only synthetic hormones may be blamed for increased breast cancer risk and further complications in MHT-using women, the "estrogen-induced cancer" remained evidence-based fact.

2.2. Oral Contraceptives Are Endocrine Disruptors Inducing either Increased or Decreased Cancer Risk in Different Organs

Oral contraceptives (OCs) comprising synthetic EE were developed in the 1960s. OCs may induce serious toxic side effects, such as venous thromboembolism, stroke, and cardiovascular diseases [13]. OC use induced the deregulation of ER signaling and led to an increased risk for insulin resistance and metabolic diseases [25].

Wide spread use of OC use among premenopausal women caused highly ambiguous correlations with cancer risk at different sites. Among OC user women, a slightly increased risk for overall breast cancer was observed [26], while strongly increased risks for ER/PR negative and triple-negative breast cancer (TNBC) were registered [27,28]. Conversely, OC use significantly reduced the risk of endometrial [29], ovarian [30], and colon cancer [31]. The controversial correlations between OC use and reduced or enhanced cancer risk at different sites strongly justified that ethinylestradiol is an endocrine disruptor compound rather than a bioidentical estrogen [17].

In *BRCA* gene mutation carriers, long term OC use significantly increases the risk for overall breast cancer as compared to non-carriers [32]. Long term OC use in *BRCA* mutation carriers may exert an additional inhibition on the non-liganded ER activation aggravating mutation associated weakness of ERs. Conversely, in women, with *BRCA1/2* gene mutations, the risk for ovarian cancer is strongly reduced by OC use [33] via exerting an advantageous estrogen-like effect by the indirect activation of the AF2 domain [17].

Despite the known metabolic, thrombotic, and carcinogenic complications of OCs, they are widely used in medical practice. Clinicians do not believe, or do not want to believe, in the endocrine-disrupting nature of OCs. In addition, OC use strengthened the misbelief that endogenous estrogens in higher concentrations may induce increased breast cancer risk.

3. In *BRCA* Gene Mutation Carriers, the Defect of Liganded ER Activation Is the Initiator of DNA Damage and Cancer Development

Patients with the germline *BRCA* gene mutation are pathological models for genomic instability and have an increased predisposition for breast and ovarian cancer development. The first breast cancer gene (*BRCA1*) was identified in 1994, showing close correlation with breast cancer development when becoming mutated [34], while the second breast cancer gene (*BRCA2*) was announced in 1995 [35]. *BRCA1* and *BRCA2* genes may be regarded as safeguards of the genome. Their BRCA protein products control DNA replication, transcriptional processes, DNA recombination, and the repair of DNA damages [36].

Although functional BRCA proteins have crucial role in the health of all cell types in both men and women, germline *BRCA* gene mutations are preferentially associated with tumor development in female breasts and ovaries [37,38].

The tissue specificity of *BRCA1* mutation-associated tumors suggested a potential relationship between *BRCA1*-loss and excessive estrogen signaling in breast cancer development. However, *BRCA1* mutation-linked tumors are typically ER-alpha negative, poorly differentiated, and show rapid growth and poor prognosis [39]. Receptor expression profiling of *BRCA1* mutant tumors showed that their vast majority proved to be ER-alpha negative and ER/PR/HER2 negative, nominated as triple negative breast cancer (TNBC) [40]. In addition, the development of ER-alpha negative breast cancer has been reported to be a predictor of *BRCA1* mutation status in patients [41]. In sporadic ER-alpha negative breast cancers, reduced BRCA1 protein expression and a decreased level of ER-alpha mRNA were parallel observed, while estrogen treatment increased BRCA1/2 mRNA levels [42]. These results suggest that *BRCA* gene mutation deteriorates the regulatory interplay with ERs, leading to decreased ER expression and consequential decreased estrogen signaling [43].

Since the regulation of healthy female breast requires a strict balance between liganded and unliganded ER activation, the weakness in ER expression and estrogen activation results in a preferential susceptibility to genomic damage in the breasts of *BRCA* mutation carrier women [43]. In diabetes and obesity, weak estrogen signaling-associated defects in the hormonal and metabolic equilibrium are directly associated with an increased TNBC risk.

Molecular studies on the interactions between BRCA1 protein and ER alpha yielded highly controversial results supporting either the upregulating or downregulating effect of BRCA1 on ER alpha transactivation.

Wild type *BRCA1* gene was demonstrated to inhibit ER alpha transcriptional activity under the control of its estrogen responsive elements [44]. *BRCA1* could suppress the expression of near all estrogen-regulated genes [45]. In addition, *BRCA1* was able to inhibit p300 mediated ER acetylation, which is essential for the transactivation of ERs [46]. In contrast, it was reported that *BRCA1* may induce an increased transcriptional activity of ER alpha by the upregulation of p300 expression, a co-activator of ER alpha [47]. Similarly, BRCA1 ensured co-activator Cyclin D binding to ER alpha so as to facilitate the transcriptional activity [48].

These controversial findings reflect the complexity of regulatory processes, including both the activation and repression of ERs. In conclusion, estrogen-liganded ER alpha may choose momentarily appropriate cofactors, promoter regions, and transcriptional pathways in harmony with optimal BRCA1 expression and activation [49].

In genome stabilization, BRCA and ER proteins are in mutual interaction by direct binding regulating each other's activation [50]. The amino-terminus of BRCA1 increases the activation of ER alpha, while the carboxyl-terminus of BRCA1 may function as a transcriptional repressor on the ER alpha protein. ER alpha and BRCA1 are crucial components of the regulatory circuit of DNA stabilization as well [49]. Defective expression or activation of either BRCA1 or ER alpha protein disturbs their interaction, endangering both estrogen signaling and genomic stability.

In women with the *BRCA* gene mutation, anovulatory infertility frequently occurs [51], reflecting the defects of the liganded estrogen signal. In addition, early menopause associated with ovarian failure is also a characteristic finding in *BRCA* mutation carriers [52]. In 85% of *BRCA1* mutation carriers, loss of functional BRCA1 protein correlated with elevated aromatase levels and increased estrogen synthesis [53] suggesting compensatory actions against decreased ER expression.

In *BRCA* mutation carrier breast cells, decreased BRCA1 protein synthesis is associated with the down-regulation of ER alpha mRNA expression and low ER alpha expression [54]. In *BRCA* gene mutation carrier tumor cells, a consequently decreased liganded activation of ERs was observed [44]. In *BRCA* gene mutation carrier breast cancer cells, a decreased expression of ER alpha was experienced [55].

The defect of liganded ER activation in *BRCA* mutation carriers is a crucial finding, as it explains the increased inclination for cancers, the ER negativity of developing tumors, and the ovulatory disorders of female patients.

Both Healthy Cells and Tumor Cells with BRCA Mutation Show Compensatory Molecular Changes, Improving Genomic Stability

In BRCA mutation carriers, the defect in estrogen signaling endangers the genome stability in healthy cells, and means a risk for further genomic deregulation in tumor cells. In healthy cells with BRCA mutation, a compensatory upregulation of estrogen signaling may preserve genomic stability, while in BRCA mutation carrier tumor cells, increased estrogen signaling may protect from further genomic damage and increasing proliferative activity. Tumor cells possess the remnants of the same genome stabilizer pathways like healthy cells have. In the emergency situation of a weakening estrogen signal, tumor cells may show various activating mutations, increasing both liganded and unliganded ER activation [56].

Healthy cells: In mammary epithelial cells, the loss of the *BRCA1* gene leads to increased epidermal growth factor receptor expression [57], which means an unliganded activation of ERs instead of a pro-oncogenic impact. In *BRCA1* mutation carrier women, BRCA1 protein activity confers the selection of an appropriate *CYP19* aromatase promoter region for the compensatory intensifying of estrogen synthesis [58]. In mammary fibrous adipose cells, the downregulation of the *BRCA1* gene increased the specific activation of the PII promoter on *Cyp19* aromatase gene, leading to increased estrogen synthesis. The mutation of the *BRCA1* gene may be counteracted by the unliganded activation of ERs via the upregulation of growth factor receptors and P13K/Akt pathways interacting with BRCA1 protein [59].

Tumor cells: In *BRCA1*-deficient human ovarian cancer cells, ER alpha exhibited increased ligand independent transcriptional activity that was not observed in *BRCA1* proficient cells [60]. Authors suggested that the loss of *BRCA1* increased unliganded ER activation increasing cancer risk; however, it was a compensatory activation attributed to the defective liganded activation.

In the tumor cell line with *BRCA* mutation, increased estrogen signaling was observed via enhanced activation of p300, a transcriptional coactivator of ERs [47]. In familiar breast cancers with *BRCA* mutation, a further transcriptional activator of ERs—Cyclin D1—was highly accumulated [61]. Nuclear factor kappaB (NF-κB), an important ER coactivator, was persistently activated in a subset of *BRCA1*-deficient mammary luminal progenitor cells [62].

In *BRCA1/2* gene mutation carriers, the most frequently co-mutated gene was *TP53* (38.1%). Patients with both *BRCA1/2* and *TP53* gene mutations were more likely to have hormone receptor negative cancers, high Ki-67 values, and increased genetic mutations, especially of hormone receptor-related genes. Survival benefits were observed in the *BRCA2* mutation carrier patients with *TP53* co-mutation, compared to those with *TP53* wild types [63]. This valuable observation supports the increased genome stabilizer impact of mutated *TP53*, providing compensatory genome stabilization in tumors with *BRCA2* gene mutation.

In sporadic breast cancer cells, the wild *BRCA* gene is capable of increasing the expression of the coding gene of ER alpha—*ESR1*—mediated by the activator Oct-1 [55]. Moreover, *BRCA* could transcriptionally increase the expression of ER alpha mRNA.

Studies on *BRCA* mutation carriers teach us crucial new aspects for cancer research: 1. Genomic instability is linked to the weakness of liganded ER activation rather than excessive estrogen signaling; 2. *BRCA* gene mutation carrier healthy cells are working on the improvement of endangered DNA, via the upregulation of both liganded and unliganded ER activation; 3. In *BRCA* mutant tumor cells, the upregulation of estrogen synthesis and unliganded ER activation are efforts to protect DNA from further damage; 4. Both healthy and tumor cells with *BRCA* gene mutation exhibit gene amplification and activate gene mutations so as to increase estrogen synthesis and improve ER activation; 5. In *BRCA* mutation carriers, the whole body works on genome stabilization via increased ovarian and peripheral estrogen synthesis.

4. Estrogens Are the Principal Regulators of Genomic Machinery in Mammalian Cells

At the cellular level, estrogen-activated ERs (ER alpha and ER beta) are the hubs of genomic machinery, orchestrating all cellular functions affecting both somatic and reproductive health [64]. Molecular factors of all cellular processes are working in regulatory circuits. They receive the regulatory commands from estrogen-activated ERs directly or indirectly and, at the same time, send their signals back to the ERs closing the circuit.

ER-alpha-regulated DNA stabilizer circuit. ER-alphas activated by the estrogen hormone are the initiators and drivers of the regulatory circuit of DNA stabilization. ERs, genome safeguarding proteins, such as BRCA1, and estrogen synthesizing aromatase enzyme (A450) create a triangular partnership. The appropriate expression of ER-alpha, BRCA1 protein, and aromatase enzyme is harmonized by firm interplay among ESR1, BRCA1, and CYP19 genes and their transcriptional activity in the promoter regions [49]. The upregulation of estrogen signaling ensures DNA stability in all phases of cell proliferation.

Liganded ER-alpha as a transcriptional factor induces *ESR1* gene expression, driving protein coding ER-alpha-mRNA and ER-alpha protein expression. Liganded ER-alphas are capable of occupying the *BRCA1* gene promoter region as well, facilitating the expression of BRCA1 mRNA transcripts and increased BRCA1 protein synthesis [37].

The BRCA1 protein, as a transcriptional factor, drives the expression of the *BRCA1* gene and amplifies BRCA1 protein expression. The BRCA1 protein activates *ESR1* gene expression and increases ER-alpha protein synthesis [55]. Moreover, the BRCA1 protein is capable of occupying the promoter region of the *CYP19A* gene, conferring the augmented expression of the aromatase enzyme. The BRCA1 protein ensures safety equilibrium between the ER-alpha protein and aromatase enzyme expression [56]. Abundant BRCA1 proteins may induce epigenetic modification and activate mutations on *ESR1*, *BRCA1*, and *CYP19* aromatase genes via increasing the appropriate lncRNA expression and resulting in increased production of the three regulatory proteins: ER, BRCA1, and aromatase [56]. In addition, abundant BRCA1 proteins are capable of increasing the transcriptional activity of ER-alpha mediated by either Cyclin D1 [48] or p300 coactivator protein [47]. Increased *BRCA1* activity confers a decreased unliganded activation of ERs [60], while increasing liganded ER activation and strengthening DNA stability [17]. Some lncRNA transcripts of *BRCA1* may induce transcription on the *CYP19* aromatase promoter, facilitating A450 aromatase enzyme expression and estrogen concentration [58]. A high estrogen concentration helps in the binding and activation of abundant ER-alphas, further stimulating the DNA stabilizer circuit [49].

The process of estrogen-induced genome stabilization through the ER-BRCA-aromatase circuit may take many hours as protein synthesis is a time consuming procedure. In emergency situations, 17beta-estradiol can rapidly enhance aromatase enzyme activity and estrogen synthesis in both healthy and tumor cells. The non-receptor tyrosine kinase c-Src shows direct involvement in E2 stimulated quick aromatase activation via a short nongenomic autocrine loop [65].

ER-alpha and BRCA1 proteins can directly bind with each other as transcriptional factors. Certain binding sites facilitate upregulative processes, while others may quench each other's transcriptional activity [50]. Mutagenic defects or the decreased expression of ER-alpha may dangerously repress the expression of BRCA1 mRNA transcripts and BRCA1-protein synthesis; endangering DNA-safeguarding [42]. Similarly, decreased synthesis or mutagenic alteration of BRCA1-protein results in the downregulation of the expression of the ER-alpha mRNA and ER-alpha protein [54]. If either the ER-alpha or BRCA1 protein function suffers damage, the result will be genomic instability and increased cancer risk [49].

ER-alpha-regulated circuit of cell proliferation. The principal regulator of cell proliferation is the ligand-activated ER-alpha in strong interactions with membrane-bound tyrosine kinase growth factor receptors; insulin-like growth factor receptor 1 (IGF-1R) and epidermal growth factor receptor (EGFR) [12]. The equilibrium between liganded and unliganded ER-alpha activation provides an accurate control over DNA replication in both high and low phases of cell proliferation. The interplay between ER and GFR receptor families is the prerequisite of the regulation of cell growth and proliferation and it may be more or less preserved even in malignant tumors [17].

IGF-1R shows a bidirectional signaling pathway with ligand-activated ERs [66]. IGF-I expression is influenced by both insulin and growth hormone (GH) stimulating the IGF-I synthesis in the liver [67]. IGF-1 binding to its receptor, IGF-1R may upregulate two chief signaling pathways: the phosphatidyloinositol 3-kinase (PI3K-AKT) and the Ras-mitogen-activated protein kinase (MAPK) pathways. These kinase cascades drive the unliganded transcriptional activity of ER-alpha by the phosphorylation of serine residues [68].

ERs are driving many protein components in the insulin-IGF-1 system, such as the IGF-1R and insulin receptor substrate 1 (IRS-1) [69]. ER-alpha is capable of binding and phosphorylating IGF-1R and taking care of its signaling pathways. In IGF-1 KO mice, estradiol-activated uterine growth is missing [70]. Conversely, in vivo IGF-1 activation of uterine cell proliferation is strongly dependent on ER-alpha activation [71].

Estrogen stimulates the EGF synthesis in uterine epithelial cells through ER activation, resulting in a proliferative effect [72]. In estrogen-free milieu, EGFR signaling may be activated through unliganded ER activation [73]. In turn, in the uterus of ER-alpha KO mice, EGF could not induce DNA synthesis and transcriptional activity [74]. In ovariectomized mice, estradiol treatment resulted in a rapid increase in uterine EGFR mRNA and protein expression and increased the binding sites on EGF through ER activation [75].

In the nucleus, the EGFR signal induces phosphorylation and activation on ER-alpha at serine 118 location conferred by the growth factor receptor-activated MAPK pathway [76,77]. Phosphorylation at serine 118 increases the ER-associated transactivation of several genes that are activated by EGFR. The growth factor receptor signal is capable of increasing the transcriptional activity of nuclear ERs through the phosphorylation of their coactivator proteins, such as steroid receptor coactivator 1, p300 protein, and cyclin D1 [78,79].

In the cytoplasm, estrogen-activated ERs induce EGFR activation and EGFR conferred upregulation of the PI3K signaling pathway [80]. In endothelial cells, estrogen treatment induced PI3K activation resulted in the rapid upregulation of 250 estrogen-regulated genes within 40 min [81]. The ER/EGFR interplay at the membrane promotes the activation of numerous signaling pathways that further increases the wide-ranging transcriptional activity of ERs [66].

In human breast cancer, an inverse correlation may be observed between ER and EGFR expression [82,83]. In breast cancer cell lines responsive to tamoxifen, a counteractive increased expression of ERs may be experienced, improving estrogen signaling. In tumors non-responsive to tamoxifen, an additional increased expression of growth factor receptors may be experienced [84], conferring the unliganded activation of ERs. Abundant GFRs highly increase ER activation via unliganded pathway; however, they cannot compensate the tamoxifen blockade of AF2 domain [17].

ER-alpha-regulated fuel supply circuit. Liganded ER-alpha drives a regulatory circuit to maintain glucose homeostasis and to stimulate all the phases of cellular glucose uptake providing fuel for all cellular functions [49]. Defects in the estrogen signal results in serious alterations in cellular glucose uptake designated as insulin resistance and leads to serious chronic diseases including cancer [85]. In conclusion, insulin resistance is the linkage between a weak estrogen signal and increased cancer risk.

Estrogen-regulated genes activate insulin synthesis and secretion, as well as the expression and activation of insulin receptor [86]. When insulin binds to its receptor, autophosphorylations of multiple tyrosines induce the activation of insulin signal transduction [87]. Liganded ERs upregulate the expression and functional activity of intracellular glucose transporter-4 (GLUT4), promoting insulin-assisted glucose uptake [88]. Liganded ER-alpha drives the insulin receptor substrate 1 (IRS1) conferred activation of PI3K/mTOR signaling pathway which ensures the hormone free activation of nuclear ERs [89].

Estrogen signal activates glucose uptake even in cancer cells supplying energy for the self-directed improvement of DNA stability. In the MCF-7 breast cancer cell line, estradiol enhances the expression of the insulin receptor substrate-1 (IRS-1), activating insulin signaling [90]. In ZR-75-1 breast cancer cells, estrogen/progesterone treatment increased glucose transporter 1 (GLUT1) expression [91]. In MCF-7 cell lines, estradiol treatment activated ERs via the PI3K/Akt signaling pathway and, at the same time, increased the translocation of glucose transporter 4 (GLUT4) vesicles to the plasma membrane [92]. A defective or blocked estrogen signal results in the failure of glucose uptake even in cancer cells, declining the activity of genome stabilizer pathways.

5. Estrogens Are Master Regulators of Metabolism and Energy Homeostasis via Orchestrating Adipose Tissue Functions

Adipose tissue, deposited all over the body, provides energy and epigenetic regulatory commands for all tissues and organs via its estrogen-activated ER network. In healthy adipose tissue, estrogen signaling regulates the glucose homeostasis and the balance of lipolysis/lipogenesis [93,94]. In adipose tissue, damaged estrogen signaling leads to defects in all regulatory functions, and serious diseases may develop in the fat-regulated visceral organs, cardiovascular structures, and hemopoietic bone marrow [95].

The subcutaneously located adipose tissue provides energy and estrogen regulation for the skin and the skeletal muscles. Centrally positioned fatty tissue within the trunk and abdomen closely surrounds the visceral organs and cardiovascular structures [96]. Visceral fat is largely located in the omental and mesenteric adipose tissue in the vicinity of stomach, intestines, liver and pancreas. Kidneys, and the attached adrenal glands, are embedded into abundant fatty tissue capsule. Adipose tissue deposition within the visceral pericardium surrounds the myocardium and coronary arteries providing estrogen signaling and energy for the moving heart. Perivascular adipose tissue nurses most blood vessels, with the exception of the pulmonary and cerebral arteries [97]. A further depot of adipose tissue is gonadal fat (GAT) surrounding the ovaries and testes having specific regulatory functions [98].

Female breasts enjoy an exceptional nursing level as mammary lobules are intimately intermingled with the estrogen and ER rich fatty tissue pad [99]. This close connection between the adipocytes and mammary cells is associated with the extreme demand of breasts for strict regulatory control and abundant energy supply. The high claim of breasts for regulatory commands may explain their unique vulnerability to estrogen loss or defects in ER activation.

The third largest fat depot is the bone marrow fat, following subcutaneous and visceral fatty tissue. Adipocytes are active components of the bone marrow microenvironment, regulating hemopoietic and immune cell proliferation and function via their estrogen signal and secretome [100].

Interestingly, the central nervous system does not enjoy the estrogen driven adipose tissue safeguard, while the brain shows an extreme claim for estrogen regulation. Recently, microbial sequences were found in healthy human brain samples [101] suggesting that they may provide important support for cerebral functions. Microbiom in the gut has great role in increasing unbound, free estrogen levels via their β-glucuronidase activity [102,103]. It is a plausible possibility that gut microbiom colonized in the brain increases the level of accessible free estrogen.

Adipose tissue is an essential source of estrogen production in extragonadal sites in both women and men [104]. The functional activity of adipose tissue is regulated by circulating and locally synthesized estrogens. In the fatty tissue, estrogens are acting in an autocrine manner, while in the adjacent organs; they increase ER activation in a paracrine manner [105]. Estrogens are the chief regulators of the health of adipose tissue through metabolic and epigenetic pathways [106]. Estrogen exerts its special effects on estrogen responsive adipocytes by estrogen receptors (E-alpha, ER-beta and GPR30) [107].

In the gonads, the essential precursors of estrogen synthesis are C19 steroids, while extragonadal sites are unable to synthesize estrogens directly from these factors. With ageing, increasing estrogen synthesis in peripheral tissues requires a precursor supply from external sources, for example, dehydroepiandrosterone (DHEA) intake is important [108].

The remarkable volume of ubiquitous fatty tissue and its noteworthy estrogen synthesis justify that fat cells have crucial roles in safeguarding and regulating the signaling network of neighboring tissues, organs, and the whole body.

Secretory Activities of Visceral Adipose Tissue in Healthy Lean and Obese Cases

Abdominal fatty tissue has crucial secretory functions [109]. Estrogen-regulated genes orchestrate adipokine, cytokine, and growth factor secretion, which are important signaling molecules and their estrogen-regulated activation controls the health of the whole body.

Sexual steroids: In adipose tissue, estrogens are the crucial sexual steroids. Appropriate estrogen signaling controls the expression of numerous genes and the coordinated synthesis of signaling molecules [106].

Adipokines: Leptin controls the equilibrium of energy in the hypothalamus, conferring anorexinogenic and lipolytic signals. Estrogen treatment results in the increased expression of leptin receptors in various cells, sensitizing them to leptin [110]. In aromatase knock out (ARKO) mice with estrogen loss, visceral fat deposition develops and leptin levels are highly elevated [111]. Adiponectin signaling protects against insulin resistance by quenching various inflammatory reactions and improving endothelial functions. In adult mice, oophorectomy increases adiponectin levels, while it may be reduced by estradiol substitution [112]. Obesity increases the level of resistin, which may be a compensatory response. In subcutaneous fat cells, an estradiol benzoate treatment decreases resistin levels [113].

Proinflammatory cytokines and low-grade inflammation: Proinflammatory cytokines are regulatory proteins which have a great role in the maintenance of genomic and metabolic stability. In obese fatty tissue, low-grade inflammatory reactions and abundantly expressed cytokines are counteractions to genomic deregulation via increasing estrogen synthesis [114]. The insulin resistance of obese estrogen deficient adipose tissue leads to further regulatory disorders in the adjacent organs, resulting in serious co-morbidities, such as fatty degeneration and malignancies [115,116].

In the low-grade inflammation of obese adipose tissue, increased levels of inflammatory cytokines and immune cell infiltration comprising macrophages and T cells may be found [117]. Proinflammatory cytokines, including tumor necrosis factor alpha (TNF-α) and interleukin-6 (IL-6) generate an increased expression and activation of the aromatase enzyme, resulting in increased estrogen synthesis [118]. Proinflammatory cytokines have beneficial effects against obesity and obesity-related metabolic disorders via increasing the aromatase activity and estrogen synthesis. Estrogen treatment of obese ovariectomized mice decreased the expression of inflammatory cytokines, including TNFα and upregulated estrogen signaling, which improved the insulin sensitivity in both adipose tissue and liver [119].

Insulin-IGF system. The insulin-like growth factor (IGF) system has a great role in the regulation and control of growth and differentiation. The receptors of insulin and insulin-like growth factors work as ligand-specific modulators, regulating various genes on similar pathway [120]. In the early stage of insulin resistance, an increased IGF-1 level confers increased insulin synthesis, leading to compensatory hyperinsulinemia.

Harmonized crosstalk and interaction among signaling pathways of ERs and growth factor receptors (IGF-1R, EGFR, VGFR) are identified in both health and disease [121,122]. In health, growth factor-activated ERs may either facilitate or silence cell growth and proliferation. In tumors with regulatory defects, abundant growth factor receptors activate

ERs via unliganded pathway so as to initiate DNA stabilization and apoptotic death rather than providing excessive proliferative stimulus.

In adipocytes, estrogens control the synthesis of insulin-like growth factor 1 (IGF-1) and the expression of its receptor (IGF-1R). In turn, the upregulation of IGF-1 synthesis and its receptor expression increases the unliganded activation of ERs via the AKT and MAPK regulatory pathways [123]. In an estrogen deficient milieu, increased IGF-1 receptor signaling stimulates the unliganded activation of ERs, which may momentarily ensure the genome wide expression of estrogen-regulated genes [64]. In conclusion, in insulin resistance and obesity, the increased activation and expression of IGF-1 receptors do not exert pro-oncogenic effects, but rather facilitate unliganded ER activation.

Interaction between adipocytes and immune cells. Adipocytes are in signaling crosstalk with immune cells in both healthy and obese adipose tissue. In lean adipose tissue, IL-4 secreted by eosinophil granulocytes and regulatory T (Treg) cells activate M2 type macrophages, which express arginase and anti-inflammatory cytokines such as IL-10. In contrast, in obese adipose tissue, a high number of M1 type macrophages and increased secretion of pro-inflammatory cytokines, such as TNFα and IL-6, are coupled with a decrease in anti-inflammatory immune cells [117]. In animal experiments, estrogen is capable of improving metabolic disorders and, at the same time, exerts anti-inflammatory effects. In female mice, estrogen protects from adipocyte hypertrophy, obesity, and prevents adipose tissue oxidative stress and inflammation [124].

In obesity, the upregulation of estrogen signaling restores insulin sensitivity, reduces lipid deposition, decreases pro-inflammatory cytokine synthesis and quenches inflammatory infiltration. Estrogen treatment provides quite new ways for the prevention and cure of obesity and obesity-related complications.

6. The Tumor Cell Itself Is the Frontline of Anticancer Combat

According to global medical concepts, tumor cells are enemies to be killed as they presumably fight for their survival, similar to how pathogenic bacteria fight against antibiotics. Seemingly, tumor cells express cancer driver genes via somatic mutation, and their altered protein products defeat both the immune defense of body and the therapeutic effect of pharmaceutical agents.

In reality, the recognition of DNA damage means an emergency state even for tumor cells. The upregulation of estrogen signaling via the liganded and/or unliganded pathway is the appropriate means for the restoration of DNA stability. However, in tumors, the possibility for DNA repair is questionable, attributed to the genomic damage. The more differentiated a tumor, the stronger its capacity for the compensatory upregulation of estrogen signaling, coupled with DNA restorative efforts [125].

The spontaneous healing of early breast tumors is a well-known finding justifying the capacity of initial cancers for self-directed remission. A systematic review and meta-analysis study evaluated a high prevalence of incidental breast cancer and precursor lesions in autopsy studies on clinically tumor-free cases. The estimated mean prevalence of incidental cancer and precursor lesions were surprisingly high: 19.5% and 0.85% [126].

Breast cancer is regarded as a multifactorial and very heterogeneous disease that refers to the abnormal proliferation of the lobular and ductal epithelium of the breast, resulting in tumor formation [127]. The classifications of breast cancers follow the recommendations of the World Health Organization (WHO), which are regularly revised in accordance with the scientific progress [128].

The most important parameter for the classification of breast cancers is their molecular profile as it was described in 2000 [129]. The heterogeneity of breast cancers at a molecular level was revealed through the various expression of a panel of genes. Breast cancers were divided into four main groups: 1. Luminal A (60% of cases); 2. Luminal B (10% of cases); 3. The overexpression of human epidermal growth factor receptor2 (HER2) (20% of cases); and 4. Basal-like triple-negative breast cancers (TNBCs) (about 10% of breast cancers). Another subgroup has also been described as a normal breast-like subcategory which resembles the luminal A group but shows a worse prognosis.

In clinical practice, these tumor groups are identified by immunohistochemical markers, such as ER-alpha, progesterone (PR), and human epidermal growth factor receptor (HER2) expression [127]. In breast cancers, the overexpression of certain receptor families is mistakenly regarded as an aggressive survival technique and their targeted inhibition is the principle of current therapeutic measures. In reality, missing or decreased expression of certain receptors in tumor cells highlights the points of genomic defects requiring repair. Conversely, the overexpression of certain receptors and regulators, as well as the activating mutation of their genes indicate the efforts for self-directed genomic repair of tumors rather than developing survival techniques [12,56]. In reality, the loss of certain receptors indicates the genomic damage, while the overexpression of others represents the genome repairing effort.

Immunohistochemical markers of breast cancers show the alterations in their gene and receptor protein expression as compared to healthy breast epithelium. Molecular alterations reflecting the grade of DNA damage and the concomitant DNA repairing actions in different breast cancer subtypes are shown in Table 1.

Table 1. Receptor pattern in breast cancer subtypes reflecting the grade of DNA damage and the concomitant actions for DNA repair.

Subtype of Breast Cancer	Receptor Status	Signs of DNA Damage	Sigs of DNA Repair	Proliferative Activity Endocrine	Response to Therapy
Luminal A type (50–60%)	ER overexpression PR positive	no	ER overexpression	low	good in 50%
Luminal B type (10%)	ER positive PR pos/neg HER2 pos/neg	PR negative PR positive HER2 positive	ER positive	increased	moderate/inverse
HER2 enriched (20%)	ER negative PR negative HER2 rich	ER negative PR negative	HER2 rich	high	no
Triple negative (10%)	ER negative PR negative HER2 negative	ER negative PR negative HER2 negative	no	high	no

Luminal type A cancers are the least aggressive tumors with the expression of ER alpha, and PR. Increased ER expression in breast tumors is traditionally regarded as a crucial inducer and promoter of tumor growth [127]. This concept derives from confusing the constellation with causation. Increased ER expression is not a causal factor for tumor growth, but rather it is an effort for improving estrogen signaling and DNA stabilization in an estrogen deficient milieu [43].

Estrogen receptor expression was shown to be parallel with DNA repair capacity in breast cancer cells [130]. This correlation justifies that the high ER expression of untreated tumors is the key to self-directed DNA repair, rather than a fuel for tumor growth. The strong belief in estrogen induced cancer does not allow consideration of opposite alternatives.

Luminal A breast cancer may exhibit a transiently good response in 50% of tumors to adjuvant endocrine therapy; however, near all patients previously showing good tumor responses later become non-responders [131]. Patients with early luminal ER-positive breast cancer are at a continuous risk of relapse even after more than 10 years of tamoxifen treatment [132]. These experiences underline that endocrine disruptor therapy is not appropriate method even for early ER-positive breast cancer care.

Luminal B tumors are more aggressive than luminal A types. They express lower ER alpha and lower PR expression or may be PR-negative, in correlation with the weakening estrogen signal [133]. Luminal B tumors are associated with an increased rate of p53 mutations and in certain B type tumors, HER2 may also be expressed [134]. Activating p53 mutations are not oncogenic changes, but rather they mean stronger DNA protection in tumors with weakening genome stability. In luminal B type tumors, the appearance of HER2 expression works on the compensatory unliganded activation of ERs [17].

After tamoxifen therapy, patients with ER-positive, PR-negative, and HER2-positive tumors exhibited higher rates of tumor recurrence and mortality as compared to those who did not receive the agent [135]. This observation suggests that in type B tumors, the weakening ER signal is further worsened by endocrine disruptor treatment. In contrast, Premarin treatment of ER-positive, PR-negative breast cancer cases resulted in a significant reduction in tumor size and improved patients' survival [24].

HER2-enriched breast cancer is ER- and PR-negative and HER2-positive. HER-2-enriched cancers tend to grow faster than luminal cancers and can have a worse prognosis. ER- and PR-negativity in HER-2 enriched breast cancers reflects a loss of estrogen signaling and strong defects in all genomic processes. HER2 overexpression in hormone receptor negative tumors is mistakenly regarded as a trigger for tumor proliferation, similarly to all other growth factors [127]. In contrast, in the emergency situation of DNA damage, HER-2 overexpression is a compensatory effort for the unliganded activation of ERs occurring scarcely in this tumor type [17]. HER-2 protein-targeted therapies against HER-2-enriched tumors show similarly ambiguous results, like ER-inhibitor anti-estrogens against ER-positive tumors [12].

Triple-negative or basal-like breast cancer is ER-negative, progesterone receptor-negative, and HER-2-negative. Triple-negative breast cancer is more common in people with BRCA1 gene mutation, younger women, and black women. Triple-negative breast cancers are more aggressive than either luminal A or luminal B breast cancers and they are not responsive to endocrine therapy [127].

In triple negative breast cancers (TNBCs), the lack of ER, PR, and HER-2 receptors indicate the serious deregulation of the whole genomic machinery. These tumors are poorly differentiated and clinically show rapid growth and spread. In TNBC type tumors, there is no possibility for self-directed DNA repair as ERs seem to be absent or hidden and the regulatory pathways for both liganded and non-liganded ER activations are unnoticeable [43]. The increased risk for TNBC-type tumors in African American women may be attributed to their excessive pigmentation in a relatively light-deficient geographical region. Poor light exposure leads to metabolic and hormonal alterations, conferring an increased cancer risk [136].

The molecular classification of breast cancer types reflects the fact that in women, stronger estrogen signaling may suppress, while a defective estrogen signal liberates breast cancer initiation and growth [43]. In tumor cells, the higher the ER expression, the stronger is the apoptotic effect of therapeutic estrogen exposure. In contrast, endocrine disruptor therapies may achieve only transient tumor responses in appropriately ER-positive breast cancers. Poorly differentiated ER/PR-negative and TNBC-type tumors are refractory to anti-estrogen therapy, attributed to their serious genomic deregulation.

In conclusion, breast cancers are not multifaceted tumors with quite different etiology and pathogenesis. Consequently, they do not need quite different therapies depending on their receptor status. The levels of regulatory defects create a line of variously differentiated tumors between strongly ER-positive, highly differentiated, and poorly differentiated TNBC-type ones. In breast cancer therapy, natural estrogen is a risk-free available option for ER-positive tumors [24]. Against ER-negative and TNBC-type poorly differentiated tumors, Maloney's mRNA technology would be a promising therapy to be introduced in the near future [125].

7. Peritumoral Microenvironment: The Second Line of the Antitumor Battle

In the early 2000s, the role of the tumor microenvironment emerged as being an important player in cancer development, tumor invasion, and metastatic spread [137]. Today, cancer is regarded as a complex disease built up from the neoplastic lump and its altered cellular and stromal microenvironment [138,139]. There is a strengthening belief that tumors insidiously influence all players in their microenvironment via dynamic intercellular communication. Tumors presumably ensure their invasive growth via escape from defensive immune reactions and anti-cancer treatment.

The supposed conspiration between tumors and their microenvironment is based on the belief that all signaling molecules and regulatory proteins are taken for pro-oncogenic factors when their expression is highly elevated in tumors and in the adjacent cellular infiltration [139–141]. In addition, when important regulatory genes, such as *ESR1*, are accumulated or mutated in tumors, they are regarded as pro-oncogenic alterations, rather than self-regulated efforts in the repair of genomic damages [142–146]. According to the reigning preconception, in tumor cells, the upregulation of estrogen signaling and its activator pathways are regarded as the keys to tumor growth.

In reality, in tumors, the upregulation of certain signaling pathways and activating mutations are not pro-oncogenic factors, but rather they are efforts for metabolic improvement and genomic stabilization [56]. Unfortunately, advanced tumors have weakened capacities for self-directed genomic repair and they ask for help via sending messages to their microenvironment. In turn, peritumoral-activated cells send signals and regulatory molecules, helping the tumor to achieve DNA repair and to commit apoptosis as a kamikaze action.

The re-evaluation of studies on the biochemical and genomic communication between tumors and activated microenvironmental cells revealed that all signal messages and transported exosomes aim for the upregulation of each other's estrogen signaling and the improvement of all genomic functions. These activating processes serve the elimination of the tumor rather than helping its proliferation and invasion. In conclusion, the dynamic communication between the tumor and its microenvironment is a marvelous collaboration among molecular players fighting for the genomic repair and apoptosis of tumor by means of their genomic plasticity.

Cancer-associated fibroblasts (CAFs) are major components emerging in the tumor microenvironment. Their assembly and activation may be attributed to signals deriving from cancer cells [138]. CAFs are in continuous signal communication with cancer cells and all other cell types in the tumor microenvironment [139]. Distant intercellular communication occurs by spherical extracellular vesicles (EVs) comprising exosomes carrying different molecules, such as proteins, DNAs, non-coding RNAs, miRNAs, and mRNAs. Biochemical and genetic cross-talk between cancer cells and CAFs are important observations; however, the presumed cooperation for tumor invasion and metastatic spread is not justified, it is a biased labeling.

Activation of growth factor signaling cascades. In CAFs, the expression of growth factors, such as the insulin-like growth factor (IGF-1), fibroblast growth factor FGF-7, FGF-10, HGF, and TGF-beta 2 are regarded as pro-tumorigenic factors [147]. In reality, estrogen receptors and growth factor receptors are common regulators of crucial cellular functions including cell growth and apoptosis, as well as metabolic processes even in tumors [66].

Transforming the growth factor beta (TGF-beta) superfamily is the main inducer of CAF activation and in turn, CAFs secrete large amount of TGF-beta isoforms for improving tumor cell regulation [148]. Tumor cell-derived extracellular vesicles (EVs) may frequently contain growth factor TGF-beta, which is regarded as a typical mitogen factor of tumors [149]. Considering the ER-activating role of growth factors, tumors send them to CAFs for the activation of their estrogen signal. Tumor-derived EVs, containing certain miRNAs, contribute to the enhanced TGF-beta expression in CAFs through the phosphoinositide 3-kinase (PI3K)/protein kinase B (AKT)/mammalian target of rapamycin (mTOR) signaling pathway [150]. PI3K and AKT/mTOR pathways upregulate ER activation and improve glucose uptake, which are not pro-tumorigenic processes, but rather increase anti-tumor activity. Cancer cell-derived EVs, containing mRNA coding for CXCR-4 and IGF-1R, provoke CAFs for growth factor secretion in acute myeloid leukemia [151].

Cytokines secreted by CAFs, macrophages and immune cells are important regulators of inflammatory processes and immune reactions in the tumor microenvironment [152]. Estrogen signaling orchestrates the secretion of both pro-inflammatory and anti-inflammatory cytokines according to the momentary requirements. Pro-inflammatory cytokines stimulate aromatase activity, estrogen synthesis and ER expression in the estrogen responsive peritumoral cellular infiltration. When estrogen concentration reaches an appropriately high concentration, the accumulation of anti-inflammatory cytokines will quench the inflammatory reaction parallel with the decreasing estrogen level [114].

IL-1β accumulation in hyperplastic lesions activates CAF formation from fibroblasts via the NF-κB pathway [153], which is a coactivator of ERs, promoting genome stabilization. Proinflammatory cytokines, IL-6 and TNF-α, are capable of aromatase activation, leading to increased estrogen concentration and the upregulation of estrogen signaling [154]. In gastric cancer, tumors send miRNA containing vesicles to CAFs so as to induce inflammatory cytokine/chemokine secretion through the Janus kinase (JAK)/STAT and NF-κB signaling pathways [155]. In colorectal cancers, the constitutive mutation of KRAS increases the activation of EGFR kinase cascades PI3K-Akt and RAS-RAF-MAPK, whereas increases RAS-GEF signaling pathway, which is related to abundant cytokine production [156]. In Hodgkin lymphoma, CAFs exposed to tumor cell-derived EVs show increased proinflammatory cytokine secretion [157]. CAFs activated by tumor EVs, may in turn shed additional EVs that will transfer signaling and regulatory molecules to tumor cells.

Various tumors promote aromatase activity and estradiol synthesis in the peritumoral stroma via the promotion of proinflammatory cytokine secretion [158]. In breast cancers, aromatase is abundantly expressed in tumor cells, intratumoral fibrous cells, and neighboring adipocytes, justifying their collaboration in promotion of excessive estrogen synthesis [159]. These observations mistakenly support the role of increased estrogen concentration in tumor growth and invasion.

In contrast, a combined genetic and clinical investigation justified the anti-cancer capacity of increased local estrogen synthesis in tumors and their stroma. In a large prospective study, the examination of the surgical breast tumor samples revealed a significant correlation between a low aromatase level and an increased loco-regional recurrence rate of tumors [160]. This study suggests that missing estrogen synthesis in tumors is associated with worse prognosis in breast cancer cases.

Circulating estradiol may be systemic modulator of CAF secretome as CAFs express steroid receptors [161]. Estradiol regulates the expression of several microRNAs in CAFs deriving from breast cancer [162]. In gastric cancer, estrogens stimulate IL-6 secretion of CAFs, promoting the signal transducer and activator of transcription (STAT-3) expression [163]. The increased expression of STAT3 in CAFs secretome confers an effort for genome stabilization, as STAT3 is a transcription factor which has an important role in DNA replication.

Few studies evaluated growth factors and cytokines as positive regulators of the genome rather than pro-tumorigenic factors. TGF-beta was considered as a tumor suppressor factor due to its cytostatic effect on cancer cells [164]. IL-11 was known for its capacity to stimulate platelet production in cancer patients with thrombocytopenia [165].

Immune cells in the tumor microenvironment show intense interactions with tumor cells. The interaction between immune cells and other cell types are regulated by cell surface immune checkpoints [138].Mast cells are recruited near tumors during tumorgenesis and release a variety of cytokines and chemokines [166]. Cytokines and chemokines are crucial regulators of both genomic and immunologic processes and their accumulation is an anti-cancer effort. Natural killer cells (NK) are cytotoxic and secrete tumor necrosis factor so as to kill tumor cells [167].

Tumor-associated macrophages (TAMs) infiltrate the microenvironment of tumors and are mainly divided into two categories: classically activated macrophages (M1 type) and alternatively activated macrophages (M2 type). The activated M2 type macrophages are blamed for managing the immune escape of tumors. The abundance of TAM infiltration in tumors is mechanically linked with poor disease prognosis [168]. TAM activation and accumulation in tumors is not a pro-oncogenic feature, but rather their intensive cytokine secretion is helping aromatase activity and increasing estrogen concentration.

Myeloid-derived suppressor cells (MDSC) have apparently immunosuppressive effects; they may block immunotherapy and may play a role in tumor maintenance and progression [169]. MDSCs also accumulate in response to the chronic inflammation and lipid deposition in obesity and contribute to the more rapid progression of cancers in obese individuals. In reality, the accumulation of MDSCs is not a causal factor of rapid tumor progression and obesity associated inflammation, but rather it seems to be an intense immune defense against metabolic disorder associated tumors.

Tumor-infiltrating lymphocytes (TILs) are important participants of the tumor microenvironment [152]. Immune cell infiltrates may exhibit ambiguous properties, either promoting or inhibiting tumor progression depending on the features of the primary tumor [170]. $CD4^+$ T cell polarization has been identified as a mediator of tumor immune surveillance. T helper 1 (Th1) cell functions are associated with tumor suppression and the upregulation of IFNγ and IL-12. T helper 2 (Th2) responses are reliant on IL-4 production and presumably exhibit tumor-promoting activity [171,172]. Murine and human studies reported that increased E2 concentration induces increased Th2 responses and upregulates IL-4 secretion [173,174].

A remarkable fact is that constellation of strong estrogen signal and increasing tumor growth does not justify causal correlation. A recent study reported increased immune cell infiltrate comprising Th1 T cells, B cells, and cytotoxic T lymphocytes (CTLs) in ER-negative breast tumors as compared to ER-positive cancers [175]. The correlation between ER-negative breast tumors and more intensive immune cell infiltration strongly suggests that poorly differentiated tumors with a loss of estrogen signaling need stronger immune support for their DNA repair than highly differentiated ER-positive ones.

Gene expression analysis in ER-positive breast cancer patients showed that blocking the liganded ER activation with aromatase inhibitor (letrozole) continuously increased the tumor infiltration with B cell and T helper lymphocyte subsets following treatment initiation [158]. This result justified that letrozole inhibition of estrogen signal in ER-positive tumors induced an emergency state, promptly recruiting strong immune cell infiltration.

In conclusion, tumors and their microenvironment are allies in the fight against worsening genomic defects and consequential tumor invasion. The more serious the genomic damage of a tumor, the denser is the peritumoral immune cell infiltration attributed to the emergency state. Invasive tumor spread, coupled with intensive peritumoral cellular infiltration, may be regarded as a common failure of tumor and peritumoral cells rather than the victory of presumably conspirator partners.

8. Molecular Changes in Tumors Responsive and Non-Responsive to Endocrine Therapy

The traditional belief of estrogen-induced breast cancer required the introduction of inhibitors of estrogen signaling for breast cancer care. The pharmaceutical industry developed two kinds of anti-estrogens for therapeutic purposes: a selective estrogen receptor modulator—tamoxifen—and an aromatase inhibitor (AI)—letrozole [176]. Since the early 1970s, anti-estrogens are commonly used compounds for breast cancer care as adjuvant therapy.

In breast cancer cases, anti-estrogen therapy caused many difficulties from the onset because of the development of so-called endocrine resistance in tumors. Results of anti-estrogen use could not surpass the "magic" 30% of tumor response rate, showing similar weaknesses to other endocrine therapies like oophorectomy or high dose synthetic estrogen [177]. About 70% of overall breast cancers could not respond to anti-estrogen therapy, showing stagnation or an even faster growth. Moreover, about half of the targeted ER-positive breast cancers exhibited primary resistance to anti-estrogen treatment [131]. Moreover, near all patients showing earlier good tumor responses to endocrine treatment later experienced secondary resistance, leading to metastatic disease and a fatal outcome [178].

In the past decades, great efforts were exerted for revealing the mechanism of presumed endocrine resistance of ER-positive breast cancers so as to predict responses to adjuvant endocrine therapy in patients. Researchers mistakenly supposed that both responsive and non-responsive tumor cells are aggressive enemies, developing various techniques in fighting for their survival [12].

8.1. Successful Fight of Anti-estrogen Responsive Tumors against the Endocrine Disruptor Treatment

In tumors responsive to anti-estrogen, the chief action against AF2 blockade is the restoration and amplification of the estrogen activation of ERs [56]:

1. Tamoxifen treatment provokes compensatory unliganded ER activation without delay by ER-alpha translocation from the nucleus to the membrane-bound EGFRs [179] (Figure 1); 2. The long term "therapeutic" ER blockade amplifies the expression of the ER-alpha coactivator; AIB1 (amplified in breast cancer 1) [180]. Under tamoxifen treatment, another coactivator of ERs, cyclin D1 amplifies the activation of both STAT3 and ERs [181]; 3. Tamoxifen treatment highly activates the transcription factor NFκB and its upregulative interaction with ER-alpha [182,183]; 4. Tamoxifen induces the increasing expression of certain microRNAs that bind to ER mRNAs, activating the translational processes [184]; 5. Tamoxifen provokes the amplification of the *ESR1* gene associated with the increased expression and activation of ERs [185,186] (Figure 2); 6. Aromatase inhibitor treatment provokes an acquired amplification of the *CYP19A1* gene, increasing both aromatase expression and estrogen synthesis [187]; 7. In tumor cells treated with tamoxifen, abundant lncRNA transcripts of ERs mediate the activating mutations for crucial genes of the genome stabilizer circuit; such as *ESR1*, *BRCA1*, and *CYP19A* [56].

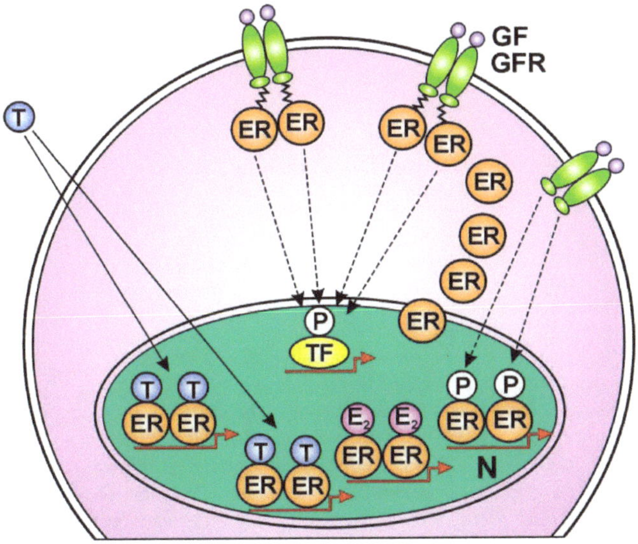

Figure 1. Rapid response to Tamoxifen (T) induced ER blockade in cancer cells.The rapid translocation of unbound estrogen receptors (ERs) out of the nucleus helps their interactions with membrane-associated growth factor receptors; GFRs (IGF1-R, EGFR). Cytoplasmic ERs activated by growth factor receptors initiate rapid transcriptional processes in the nucleus via transcriptional factors (TFs). Growth factor (GF)-activated GFRs may also induce unliganded activation on nuclear unbound ERs, driving their transcriptional activity. E: estrogen, P: phosphorylation, N: nucleus, Dotted arrow: activation, black solid arrow: inhibition, red arrow: schematic DNA segment.

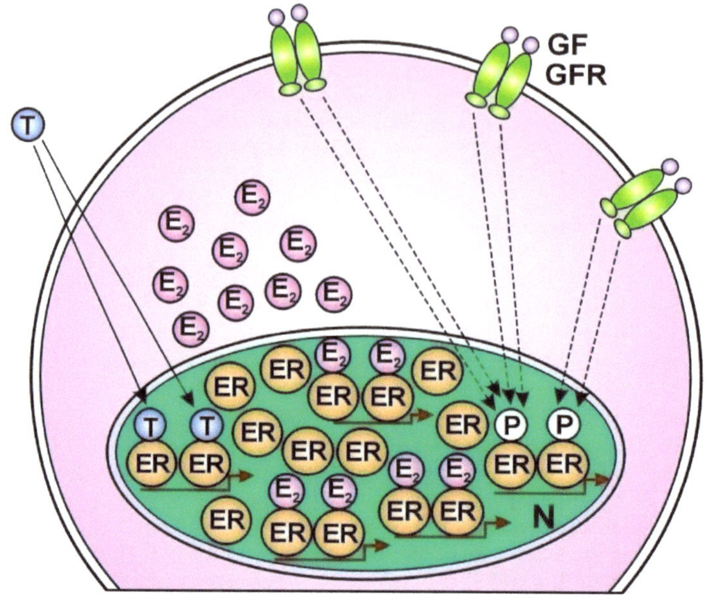

Figure 2. Molecular mechanism of tumor response in Tamoxifen (T) treated cancer cells. Increased estradiol (E_2) concentration activates newly expressed abundant estrogen receptors (ERs) increasing the expression of estrogen-regulated genes. In the meantime, growth factors (GFs) activate growth factor receptors (GFRs) conferring unliganded activation for free nuclear ERs. The predominance of estradiol (E_2) bound ERs over T bound ones leads to DNA repair, apoptotic death and clinical tumor response. P: phosphorylation, N: nucleus, Dotted arrow: activation, black solid arrow: inhibition, red arrow: schematic DNA segment.

8.2. Unsuccessful Fight of Tumors Non Responsive to Endocrine Disruptor Treatment

In anti-estrogen responsive breast cancers, the increased regulatory processes promote the compensatory improvement of estrogen activation of ERs and may achieve a successful tumor response [188]. Earlier anti-estrogen responsive breast cancers become non-responsive as the possibilities for liganded ER activation are exhausted. In non-responsive tumors, increased growth factor receptor signaling remains an ultimate refuge for unliganded ER activation and DNA stabilization [17]. However, when the liganded ER activation is completely blocked, the increased unliganded activation of ERs is incapable of restoring ER signaling (Figure 3).

In anti-estrogen resistant breast cancers, physiological regulatory pathways are working so as to increase unliganded ER activation. In tamoxifen-resistant cancers, the ER coactivator HOXB7 exhibits an increased expression and may activate kinase phosphorylation of both EGFR [189] and HER2 [190], promoting unliganded ER activation. Further ER coactivators—AIB1 and HER2/neu—stimulate hormone-free ER activation [191]. In tumor xenografts, both ER and HER2 activations were coupled with the compensatory activation of MUCIN4 [192]. In anti-estrogen resistant tumors, the increased expressions of plasma membrane-bound EGFRs [193] and IGF-1Rs [194,195] amplify unliganded ER activation. In endocrine-resistant cancers, acquired somatic mutations may strongly increase the compensatory hormone-free ER activation.

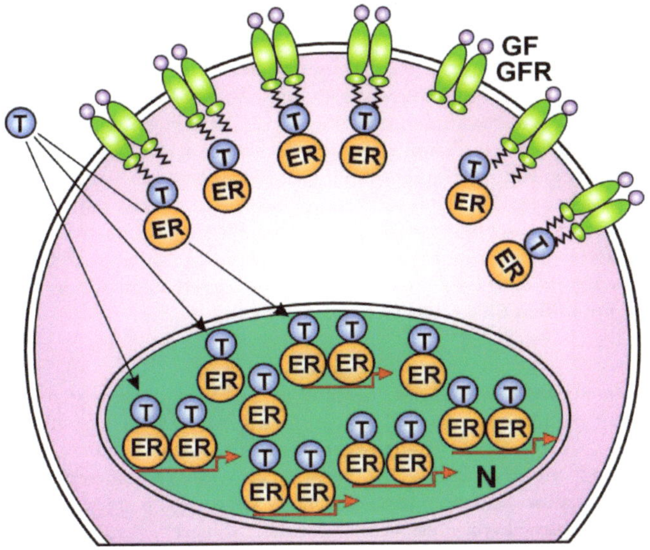

Figure 3. Molecular mechanism of tumor resistance in Tamoxifen (T)-treated cancer cells. The liganded activation of abundant nuclear estrogen receptors (ERs) is completely blocked by T-binding. The compensatory abundant expression of membrane-associated growth factor receptors (GFRs) struggles for the unliganded activation of T-bound ERs. However, the T blockade inhibits the restoration of ER signaling resulting in unrestrained proliferation. GF: growth factor, N: nucleus, black solid arrow: inhibition, spiral: unsuccessful activation, red arrow: schematic DNA segment.

In tumors resistant to endocrine therapy, acquired somatic mutations may strongly increase the compensatory hormone-free activation of ERs:

1. Estrogen conferred somatic mutation of *ERBB2* gene amplifies the expression and activity of growth factor receptors, conferring estrogen-free ER activation [191]; 2. In endocrine refractory ER-positive breast tumors, the *PIK3CA* gene is frequently mutated, upregulating the components of the PI3K-AKT-mTOR pathway and increasing hormone free ER activation [196]; 3. In AI-resistant breast cancers, acquired point mutations in the ligand binding domain (LBD) of *ESR1* gene confer hormone-independent activation of ERs [142]; 4. In anti-estrogen resistant tumors, chromosomal rearrangement on the *ESR1* gene leads to somatic mutations driving an increased unliganded activation of ERs [144]; 5. In tamoxifen-resistant tumor cells, the activation of the PI3K/AKT pathway led to a significant increase in BARD1 and BRCA1 protein expressions via increased estrogen independent activation of ERs [197].

9. Estrogen Induced Apoptosis Is Promising in Both the Prevention and Therapy of Cancer

Estrogen treatment of breast cancers resistant to either long term estrogen deprivation (LTED-R) or tamoxifen (TAM-R) triggers an apoptotic death in tumors [198].

In clinical practice, estrogen dramatically decreased the mortality of advanced breast cancer cases after stopping the long term tamoxifen therapy [199]. Following long term estrogen deprivation, estrogen reduced metastatic tumors and prolonged the survival of patients [200]. The biology of estrogen-induced apoptosis in breast and prostatic cancers seem to be promising in both the prevention and therapy of tumors [201].

Breast cancers unresponsive to anti-estrogen treatment exhibit extreme upregulation of both ER and GFR expressions. Estrogen may exert intensive anti-cancer capacity via balanced liganded and unliganded activation of abundant ERs. In reality, estrogen treatment does not return non-responsive tumors to anti-estrogen sensitivity. Conversely, estrogen helps tumor cells to defeat the genotoxic drug as they are highly sensitized to estrogen signal.

Important lessons may be drawn from the 50 years of breast cancer therapy with anti-estrogens: 1. In tumors, there is no endocrine therapy resistance, but rather the possibilities for compensatory ER activation are exhausted; 2. In tumors responsive to anti-estrogen therapy, increased ER expression and activation is not a survival technique, but rather it is an effort for increasing estrogen signaling; 3. In tumors non-responsive to anti-estrogen therapy, increased growth factor receptor expression and activation is not a survival technique, but rather it is an effort for compensatory unliganded ER activation; 4. Tumors exhaustively treated by aromatase inhibitors, show genomic plasticity, exhibiting acquired mutations on the ligand binding domain of *ESR1* gene conferring new, hormone-independent activation of modified ERs in the absence of estrogen.

10. Conclusions

Compared to various organs, female breasts exhibit unique sensitivity to genomic instability caused by either germline or acquired gene mutations. This fact may partially explain why breast cancer has become the flagship of cancer research. Although the preconception of "estrogen-induced" breast cancer has led breast cancer care to a quite erroneous pathway, a thorough examination of the controversies between estrogen signaling and cancer development yielded valuable progress in overall cancer research.

The correlation between genomic instability and conspicuously increased breast cancer risk in germline *BRCA* gene mutation carriers revealed that the defect in the genome stabilizer circuit is the origin of cancer initiation, rather than excessive estrogen signaling. Defects in ER, BRCA, or the aromatase enzyme upsets the triangular partnership of these regulatory proteins, leading to weaknesses in estrogen signaling and genomic instability. *BRCA* mutation carrier healthy and tumor cells similarly show efforts for increasing the liganded and unliganded ER activation and for compensatory upregulation of another genome safeguarding protein, p53.

Understanding the fight of cancer cells for the activation of estrogen signaling, together with genome stabilization, reveals the secret of various receptor landscapes of breast cancer subtypes. In tumors, the increased expression of hormone receptors reflects efforts for increasing liganded ER activation, while the overexpression of HER2 represents trying to increase unliganded ER activation. The blockade of either ERs or HER2s seems to be an erroneous therapeutic concept. Breast cancers are not resistant to genotoxic therapies, but rather they exhausted all possibilities for defending the remnants of genomic stability. Progressive genomic instability leads to unrestrained proliferative activity.

The cellular infiltration of the tumor microenvironment is not an organic part of tumors. Inflammatory cells are recruited by the tumor itself and the intercellular communication by messages and extracellular vesicles confer in asking for help. The stronger the genomic deregulation in the tumor, the denser is the adjacent infiltration of activated mesenchymal and immune competent cells. Immune competent cells do not need therapeutic genomic machination as they know exactly their task in the anti-cancer fight. When tumor invasion is coupled with dense peritumoral infiltration, supportive genome repairing therapy is necessary, rather than the disruption of mutation-activated DNA repair pathways of tumors.

In conclusion, the improvement of genomic stability may be the new strategy in cancer therapy. The upregulation of estrogen signaling leads to strengthened immune response, whilst inducing the apoptotic death of tumors in a Janus-faced manner.

Funding: This research received no external funding.

Conflicts of Interest: The author declares no conflicts of interest.

References

1. Hanahan, D.; Weinberg, R.A. Hallmarks of cancer: The next generation. *Cell* **2011**, *144*, 646–674. [CrossRef] [PubMed]
2. Klapp, V.; Álvarez-Abril, B.; Leuzzi, G.; Kroemer, G.; Ciccia, A.; Galluzzi, L. The DNA Damage Response and Inflammation in Cancer. *Cancer Discov.* **2023**, *13*, 1521–1545. [CrossRef] [PubMed]
3. Sinkala, M. Mutational landscape of cancer-driver genes across human cancers. *Sci. Rep.* **2023**, *13*, 12742. [CrossRef] [PubMed]
4. Porta-Pardo, E.; Valencia, A.; Godzik, A. Understanding oncogenicity of cancer driver genes and mutations in the cancer genomics era. *FEBS Lett.* **2020**, *594*, 4233–4246. [CrossRef] [PubMed]
5. Marty, R.; Kaabinejadian, S.; Rossell, D.; Slifker, M.J.; van de Haar, J.; Engin, H.B.; de Prisco, N.; Ideker, T.; Hildebrand, W.H.; Font-Burgada, J.; et al. MHC-I genotype restricts the oncogenic mutational landscape. *Cell* **2017**, *171*, 1272–1283.e15. [CrossRef] [PubMed]
6. Thorsson, V.; Gibbs, D.L.; Brown, S.D.; Wolf, D.; Bortone, D.S.; Ou Yang, T.H.; Porta-Pardo, E.; Gao, G.F.; Plaisier, C.L.; Eddy, J.A.; et al. The immune landscape of cancer. *Immunity* **2018**, *48*, 812–830.e14. [CrossRef] [PubMed]
7. Liao, W.; Overman, M.J.; Boutin, A.T.; Shang, X.; Zhao, D.; Dey, P.; Li, J.; Wang, G.; Lan, Z.; Li, J.; et al. KRAS IRF2 axis drives immune suppression and immune therapy resistance in colorectal cancer. *Cancer Cell* **2019**, *35*, 559–572.e7. [CrossRef] [PubMed]
8. García-Nieto, P.E.; Morrison, A.J.; Fraser, H.B. The somatic mutation landscape of the human body. *Genome Biol.* **2019**, *20*, 298. [CrossRef] [PubMed]
9. Yizhak, K.; Aguet, F.; Kim, J.; Hess, J.M.; Kübler, K.; Grimsby, J.; Frazer, R.; Zhang, H.; Haradhvala, N.J.; Rosebrock, D.; et al. RNA sequence analysis reveals macroscopic somatic clonal expansion across normal tissues. *Science* **2019**, *364*, eaaw0726. [CrossRef]
10. Zhu, M.; Lu, T.; Jia, Y.; Luo, X.; Gopal, P.; Li, L.; Odewole, M.; Renteria, V.; Singal, A.G.; Jang, Y.; et al. Somatic mutations increase hepatic clonal fitness and regeneration in chronic liver disease. *Cell* **2019**, *177*, 608–621.e12. [CrossRef]
11. Mirzayans, R.; Murray, D. What Are the Reasons for Continuing Failures in Cancer Therapy? Are Misleading/Inappropriate Preclinical Assays to Be Blamed? Might Some Modern Therapies Cause More Harm than Benefit? *Int. J. Mol. Sci.* **2022**, *23*, 13217. [CrossRef] [PubMed]
12. Suba, Z. Compensatory estrogen signal is capable of DNA repair in antiestrogen-responsive cancer cells via activating mutations. *J. Oncol.* **2020**, *2020*, 5418365. [CrossRef] [PubMed]
13. Coelingh-Bennink, H.J.; Verhoeven, C.; Dutman, A.E.; Thijssen, J. The use of high-dose estrogens for the treatment of breast cancer. *Maturitas* **2017**, *95*, 11–23. [CrossRef] [PubMed]
14. Saeed, M.; Rogan, E.; Cavalieri, E. Mechanism of metabolic activation and DNA adduct formation by the human carcinogen diethylstilbestrol: The defining link to natural estrogens. *Int. J. Cancer* **2009**, *124*, 1276–1284. [CrossRef] [PubMed]
15. Hilakivi-Clarke, L.; de Assis, S.; Warri, A. Exposures to Synthetic Estrogens at Different Times during the Life, and Their Effect on Breast Cancer Risk. *J. Mammary Gland. Biol. Neoplasia* **2013**, *18*, 25–42. [CrossRef] [PubMed]
16. Gray, J.M.; Rasanayagam, S.; Engel, C.; Rizzo, J. State of the evidence 2017: An update on the connection between breast cancer and the environment. *Environ. Health* **2017**, *16*, 94. [PubMed]
17. Suba, Z. Amplified crosstalk between estrogen binding and GFR signaling mediated pathways of ER activation drives responses in tumors treated with endocrine disruptors. *Recent Pat. Anticancer Drug Discov.* **2018**, *13*, 428–444. [CrossRef]
18. Stefanick, M.L. Estrogens and progestins: Background and history, trends in use, and guidelines and regimens approved by the US Food and Drug Administration. *Am. J. Med.* **2005**, *118*, 64–73. [CrossRef]
19. Rossouw, J.E.; Anderson, G.L.; Prentice, R.L.; LaCroix, A.Z.; Kooperberg, C.; Stefanick, M.L.; Jackson, R.D.; Beresford, S.A.; Howard, B.V.; Johnson, K.C.; et al. Risks and benefits of estrogen plus progestin in healthy postmenopausal women: Principal results from the Women's Health Initiative randomized controlled trial. *JAMA* **2002**, *288*, 321–333.
20. Anderson, G.L.; Limacher, M.; Assaf, A.R. Effects of conjugated equine estrogen in postmenopausal women with hysterectomy: The Women's Health Initiative randomized controlled trial. *JAMA* **2004**, *291*, 1701–1712.
21. Suba, Z. Synthetic Estrogens Deregulate Estrogen Receptors Inducing Thromboembolic Complications and Cancer. In *Topics in Anti-Cancer Research*; Rahman, A., Zaman, K., Eds.; Bentham Science Publishers: Sharjah, United Arab Emirates, 2019; Volume 8, Chapter 2; pp. 44–73. [CrossRef]
22. Collaborative Group on Hormonal Factors in Breast Cancer. Type and timing of menopausal hormone therapy and breast cancer risk: Individual participant meta-analysis of the worldwide epidemiological evidence. *Lancet* **2019**, *394*, 1159–1168. [CrossRef] [PubMed]
23. Chlebowski, R.T.; Anderson, G.L.; Aragaki, A.K.; Manson, J.E.; Stefanick, M.L.; Pan, K.; Barrington, W.; Kuller, L.H.; Simon, M.S.; Lane, D.; et al. Association of Menopausal Hormone Therapy with Breast Cancer Incidence and Mortality during Long Term Follow-up of Women's Health Initiative Randomized Clinical Trials. *JAMA* **2020**, *324*, 369–380. [CrossRef] [PubMed]
24. Chlebowski, R.T.; Aragaki, A.K.; Pan, K. Breast Cancer Prevention: Time for Change. *JCO Oncol. Pract.* **2021**, *17*, 709–716. [CrossRef] [PubMed]
25. Cortés, M.E.; Alfaro, A.A. The effects of hormonal contraceptives on glycemic regulation. *Linacre Q.* **2014**, *81*, 209–218. [CrossRef] [PubMed]
26. Mørch, L.S.; Skovlund, C.W.; Hannaford, P.C.; Iversen, L.; Fielding, S.; Lidegaard, Ø. Contemporary Hormonal Contraception and the Risk of Breast Cancer. *N. Engl. J. Med.* **2017**, *377*, 2228–2239. [CrossRef] [PubMed]

27. Rosenberg, L.; Boggs, D.A.; Wise, L.A.; Adams-Campbell, L.L.; Palmer, J.R. Oral contraceptive use and estrogen/progesterone receptor-negative breast cancer among African American women. *Cancer Epidemiol. Biomark. Prev.* **2010**, *19*, 2073–2079. [CrossRef] [PubMed]
28. Ma, H.; Wang, Y.; Sullivan-Halley, J.; Weiss, L.; Marchbanks, P.A.; Spirtas, R.; Ursin, G.; Burkman, R.T.; Simon, M.S.; Malone, K.E.; et al. Use of four biomarkers to evaluate the risk of breast cancer subtypes in the women's contraceptive and reproductive experiences study. *Cancer Res.* **2010**, *70*, 575–587. [CrossRef] [PubMed]
29. Collaborative Group on Epidemiological Studies on Endometrial Cancer. Endometrial cancer and oral contraceptives: An individual participant meta-analysis of 27,276 women with endometrial cancer from 36 epidemiological studies. *Lancet Oncol.* **2015**, *16*, 1061–1070. [CrossRef]
30. Collaborative Group on Epidemiological Studies of Ovarian Cancer. Ovarian cancer and oral contraceptives: Collaborative reanalysis of data from 45 epidemiological studies including 23,257 women with ovarian cancer and 87,303 controls. *Lancet* **2008**, *371*, 303–314. [CrossRef]
31. Bosetti, C.; Bravi, F.; Negri, E.; La Vecchia, C. Oral contraceptives and colorectal cancer risk: A systematic review and meta-analysis. *Hum. Reprod. Update* **2009**, *15*, 489–498. [CrossRef]
32. Peng, H.; Qi, X.; Wang, Q. Long term use of oral contraceptives comprising synthetic estrogens induces an excessive breast cancer risk in BRCA mutation carrier women: A meta-analysis. *Clin. Exp. Obstet. Gynecol.* **2022**, *49*, 1. [CrossRef]
33. Huber, D.; Seitz, S.; Kast, K.; Emons, G.; Ortmann, O. Use of oral contraceptives in BRCA mutation carriers and risk for ovarian and breast cancer: A systematic review. *Arch. Gyn. Obst.* **2020**, *301*, 875–884. [CrossRef] [PubMed]
34. Miki, Y.; Swensen, J.; Shattuck-Eidens, D.; Futreal, P.A.; Harshman, K.; Tavtigian, S.; Liu, Q.; Cochran, C.; Bennett, L.M.; Ding, W.; et al. A strong candidate for the breast and ovarian cancer susceptibility gene BRCA1. *Science* **1994**, *266*, 66–71. [CrossRef] [PubMed]
35. Wooster, R.; Bignell, G.; Lancaster, J.; Swift, S.; Seal, S.; Mangion, J.; Collins, N.; Gregory, S.; Gumbs, C.; Micklem, G.; et al. Identification of the breast cancer susceptibility gene BRCA2. *Nature* **1995**, *378*, 789–792. [CrossRef] [PubMed]
36. Venkitaraman, A.R. Cancer susceptibility and the functions of BRCA1 and BRCA2. *Cell* **2002**, *108*, 171–182. [CrossRef] [PubMed]
37. Gorski, J.J.; Kennedy, R.D.; Hosey, A.M.; Harkin, D.P. The complex relationship between BRCA1 and ERalpha in hereditary breast cancer. *Clin. Cancer Res.* **2009**, *15*, 1514–1518. [CrossRef] [PubMed]
38. Wang, L.; Di, L.J. BRCA1 and estrogen/estrogen receptor in breast cancer: Where they interact? *Int. J. Biol. Sci.* **2014**, *10*, 566–575. [CrossRef] [PubMed]
39. Lakhani, S.R.; Van De Vijver, M.J.; Jacquemier, J.; Anderson, T.J.; Osin, P.P.; McGuffog, L.; Easton, D.F. The pathology of familial breast cancer: Predictive value of immunohistochemical markers estrogen receptor, progesterone receptor, HER-2, and p53 in patients with mutations in BRCA1 and BRCA2. *J. Clin. Oncol.* **2002**, *20*, 2310–2318. [CrossRef] [PubMed]
40. Sorlie, T.; Perou, C.M.; Tibshirani, R.; Aas, T.; Geisler, S.; Johnsen, H.; Hastie, T.; Eisen, M.B.; van de Rijn, M.; Jeffrey, S.S.; et al. Gene expression patterns of breast carcinomas distinguish tumor subclasses with clinical implications. *Proc. Natl. Acad. Sci. USA* **2001**, *98*, 10869–10874. [CrossRef]
41. Foulkes, W.D.; Stefansson, I.M.; Chappuis, P.O.; Bégin, L.R.; Goffin, J.R.; Wong, N.; Trudel, M.; Akslen, L.A. Germline BRCA1 mutations and a basal epithelial phenotype in breast cancer. *J. Natl. Cancer Inst.* **2003**, *95*, 1482–1485. [CrossRef]
42. Spillman, M.A.; Bowcock, A.M. BRCA1 and BRCA2 mRNA levels are coordinately elevated in human breast cancer cells in response to estrogen. *Oncogene* **1996**, *13*, 1639–1645.
43. Suba, Z. Triple-negative breast cancer risk in women is defined by the defect of estrogen signaling: Preventive and therapeutic implications. *OncoTargets Ther.* **2014**, *7*, 147–164. [CrossRef] [PubMed]
44. Fan, S.; Wang, J.; Yuan, R.; Ma, Y.; Meng, Q.; Erdos, M.R.; Pestell, R.G.; Yuan, F.; Auborn, K.J.; Goldberg, I.D.; et al. BRCA1 inhibition of estrogen receptor signaling in transfected cells. *Science* **1999**, *284*, 1354–1356. [CrossRef] [PubMed]
45. Xu, J.; Fan, S.; Rosen, E.M. Regulation of the estrogen-inducible gene expression profile by the breast cancer susceptibility gene BRCA1. *Endocrinology* **2005**, *146*, 2031–2047. [CrossRef] [PubMed]
46. Ma, Y.; Fan, S.; Hu, C.; Meng, Q.; Fuqua, S.A.; Pestell, R.G.; Tomita, Y.A.; Rosen, E.M. BRCA1 regulates acetylation and ubiquitination of estrogen receptor-alpha. *Mol. Endocrinol.* **2010**, *24*, 76–90. [CrossRef] [PubMed]
47. Fan, S.; Ma, Y.X.; Wang, C.; Yuan, R.-Q.; Meng, Q.; Wang, J.-A.; Erdos, M.; Goldberg, I.D.; Webb, P.; Kushner, P.J.; et al. p300 Modulates the BRCA1 inhibition of estrogen receptor activity. *Cancer Res.* **2002**, *62*, 141–151. [PubMed]
48. Wang, C.; Fan, S.; Li, Z.; Fu, M.; Rao, M.; Ma, Y.; Lisanti, M.P.; Albanese, C.; Katzenellenbogen, B.S.; Kushner, P.J.; et al. Cyclin D1 antagonizes BRCA1 repression of estrogen receptor alpha activity. *Cancer Res.* **2005**, *65*, 6557–6567. [CrossRef] [PubMed]
49. Suba, Z. DNA stabilization by the upregulation of estrogen signaling in BRCA gene mutation carriers. *Drug Des. Dev. Ther.* **2015**, *9*, 2663–2675. [CrossRef] [PubMed]
50. Fan, S.; Ma, Y.X.; Wang, C.; Yuan, R.Q.; Meng, Q.; Wang, J.A.; Erdos, M.; Goldberg, I.D.; Webb, P.; Kushner, P.J.; et al. Role of direct interaction in BRCA1 inhibition of estrogen receptor activity. *Oncogene* **2001**, *20*, 77–87. [CrossRef]
51. Oktay, K.; Kim, J.Y.; Barad, D.; Babayev, S.N. Association of BRCA1 mutations with occult primary ovarian insufficiency: A possible explanation for the link between infertility and breast/ovarian cancer risks. *J. Clin. Oncol.* **2010**, *28*, 240–244. [CrossRef]
52. Lin, W.T.; Beattie, M.; Chen, L.M.; Oktay, K.; Crawford, S.L.; Gold, E.B.; Cedars, M.; Rosen, M. Comparison of age at natural menopause in BRCA1/2 mutation carriers with a non-clinic-based sample of women in northern California. *Cancer* **2013**, *119*, 1652–1659. [CrossRef] [PubMed]

53. Chand, A.L.; Simpson, E.R.; Clyne, C.D. Aromataseexpression is increased in BRCA1mutationcarriers. *BMC Cancer* **2009**, *9*, 148. [CrossRef]
54. Russo, J.; Russo, I.H. *Toward a Unified Concept of Mammary Carcinogenesis*; Aldaz, M.C., Gould, M.N., McLachlan, J., Slaga, T.J., Eds.; Progress in Clinical and Biological Research; Wiley-Liss: New York, NY, USA, 1997; pp. 1–16.
55. Hosey, A.M.; Gorski, J.J.; Murray, M.M.; Quinn, J.E.; Chung, W.Y.; Stewart, G.E.; James, C.R.; Farragher, S.M.; Mulligan, J.M.; Scott, A.N.; et al. Molecular basis for estrogen receptor alpha deficiency in BRCA1-linked breast cancer. *J. Natl. Cancer Inst.* **2007**, *99*, 1683–1694. [CrossRef]
56. Suba, Z. Activating mutations of ESR1, BRCA1 and CYP19 aromatase genes confer tumor response in breast cancers treated with antiestrogens. *Recent Pat. Anticancer Drug Discov.* **2017**, *12*, 136–147. [CrossRef]
57. Burga, L.N.; Hu, H.; Juvekar, A.; Tung, N.M.; Troyan, S.L.; Hofstatter, E.W.; Wulf, G.M. Loss of *BRCA1* leads to an increase in epidermal growth factor receptor expression in mammary epithelial cells, and epidermal growth factor receptor inhibition prevents estrogen receptor-negative cancers in *BRCA1*-mutant mice. *Breast Cancer Res.* **2011**, *13*, R30. [CrossRef] [PubMed]
58. Ghosh, S.; Lu, Y.; Katz, A.; Hu, Y.; Li, R. Tumor suppressor BRCA1 inhibits a breast cancer-associated promoter of the aromatase gene (CYP19) in human adipose stromal cells. *Am. J. Physiol. Endocrinol. Metab.* **2007**, *292*, 246–252. [CrossRef] [PubMed]
59. Ma, Y.; Hu, C.; Riegel, A.T.; Fan, S.; Rosen, E.M. Growth factor signaling pathways modulate BRCA1 repression of estrogen receptor-alpha activity. *Mol. Endocrinol.* **2007**, *21*, 1905–1923. [CrossRef]
60. Zheng, L.; Annab, L.A.; Afshari, C.A.; Lee, W.H.; Boyer, T.G. BRCA1 mediates ligand-independent transcriptional repression of the estrogen receptor. *Proc. Natl. Acad. Sci. USA* **2001**, *98*, 9587–9592. [CrossRef]
61. Arnold, A.; Papanikolaou, A. Cyclin D1 in Breast Cancer Pathogenesis. *J. Clin. Oncol.* **2005**, *23*, 4215–4224. [CrossRef]
62. Sau, A.; Lau, R.; Cabrita, M.A.; Nolan, E.; Crooks, P.A.; Visvader, J.E.; Pratt, M.C. Persistent Activation of NF-κB in BRCA1-Deficient Mammary Progenitors Drives Aberrant Proliferation and Accumulation of DNA damage. *Cell Stem Cell* **2016**, *19*, 52–65. [CrossRef]
63. Kim, J.; Jeong, K.; Jun, H.; Kim, K.; Bae, J.M.; Song, M.G.; Yi, H.; Park, S.; Woo, G.U.; Lee, D.W.; et al. Mutations of TP53 and genes related to homologous recombination repair in breast cancer with germline BRCA1/2 mutations. *Hum. Genom.* **2023**, *17*, 2. [CrossRef]
64. Maggi, A. Liganded and unliganded activation of estrogen receptor and hormone replacement therapies. *Biochim. Biophys Acta* **2011**, *1812*, 1054–1060. [CrossRef]
65. Charlier, T.D.; Cornil, C.A.; Patte-Mensah, C.; Meyer, L.; Mensah-Nyagan, A.G.; Balthazart, J. Local modulation of steroid action: Rapid control of enzymatic activity. *Front. Neurosci.* **2015**, *9*, 83. [CrossRef]
66. Levin, E.R. Bidirectional Signaling between the Estrogen Receptor and the Epidermal Growth Factor Receptor. *Mol. Endocrinol.* **2003**, *17*, 309–317. [CrossRef]
67. Ohlsson, C.; Mohan, S.; Sjögren, K.; Tivesten, A.; Isgaard, J.; Isaksson, O.; Jansson, J.-O.; Svensson, J. The role of liver-derived insulin-like growth factor-I. *Endocr. Rev.* **2009**, *30*, 494–535. [CrossRef] [PubMed]
68. Martin, M.B.; Franke, T.F.; Stoica, G.E.; Chambon, F.; Katzenellenbogen, B.S.; Stoica, B.A.; McLemore, M.S.; Olivo, S.E.; Stoica, A. A role for Akt in mediating the estrogenic functions of epidermal growth factor and insulin-like growth factor I. *Endocrinology* **2000**, *141*, 4503–4511. [CrossRef]
69. Chan, T.W.; Pollak, M.; Huynh, H. Inhibition of insulin-like growth factor signaling pathways in mammary gland by pure antiestrogen ICI 182,780. *Clin. Cancer Res.* **2001**, *7*, 2545–2554. [PubMed]
70. Sato, T.; Wang, G.; Hardy, M.P.; Kurita, T.; Cuncha, G.R.; Cooke, P.S. Role of systemic and local IGF-I in the effects of estrogen on growth and epithelial proliferation of mouse uterus. *Endocrinology* **2002**, *143*, 2673–2679. [CrossRef] [PubMed]
71. Klotz, D.M.; Hewitt, S.C.; Ciana, P.; Raviscioni, M.; Lindzey, J.K.; Foley, J.; Maggi, A.; DiAugustine, R.P.; Korach, K.S. Requirement of estrogen receptor-α in insulin-like growth factor-1 (IGF-1)-induced uterine responses and in vivo evidence for IGF-1/estrogen receptor cross talk. *J. Biol. Chem.* **2002**, *277*, 8531–8537. [CrossRef]
72. DiAugustine, R.P.; Petrusz, P.; Bell, G.I.; Brown, C.F.; Korach, K.S.; McLachlan, J.A.; Teng, C.T. Influence of estrogens on mouse uterine epidermal growth factor precursor protein and messenger ribonucleic acid. *Endocrinology* **1988**, *122*, 2355–2363. [CrossRef]
73. Vignon, F.; Bouton, M.M.; Rochefort, H. Antiestrogens inhibit the mitogenic effect of growth factors on breast cancer cells in the total absence of estrogens. *Biochem. Biophys Res. Commun.* **1987**, *146*, 1502–1508. [CrossRef] [PubMed]
74. Curtis, S.W.; Washburn, T.; Sewall, C.; DiAugustine, R.; Lindzey, J.; Couse, J.F.; Korach, K.S. Physiological coupling of growth factor and steroid receptor signaling pathways: Estrogen receptor knockout mice lack estrogen-like response to epidermal growth factor. *Proc. Natl. Acad. Sci. USA* **1996**, *93*, 12626–12630. [CrossRef] [PubMed]
75. Das, S.K.; Tsukamura, H.; Paria, B.C.; Andrews, G.K.; Dey, S.K. Differential expression of epidermal growth factor receptor (EGF-R) gene and regulation of EGF-R bioactivity by progesterone and estrogen in the adult mouse uterus. *Endocrinology* **1994**, *134*, 971–981. [CrossRef] [PubMed]
76. Kato, S.; Endoh, H.; Masuhiro, Y.; Kitamoto, T.; Uchiyama, S.; Sasaki, H.; Masushige, S.; Gotoh, Y.; Nishida, E.; Kawashima, H.; et al. Activation of the estrogen receptor through phosphorylation by mitogen-activated protein kinase. *Science* **1995**, *270*, 1491–1494. [CrossRef] [PubMed]
77. Bunone, G.; Briand, P.A.; Miksicek, R.J.; Picard, D. Activation of the unliganded estrogen receptor by EGF involves the MAP kinase pathway and direct phosphorylation. *EMBO J.* **1996**, *15*, 2174–2183. [CrossRef] [PubMed]

78. Zwijsen, R.M.; Buckle, R.S.; Hijmans, E.M.; Loomans, C.J.; Bernards, R. Ligand-independent recruitment of steroid receptor coactivators to estrogen receptor by cyclin D1. *Genes Dev.* **1998**, *12*, 3488–3498. [CrossRef] [PubMed]
79. McMahon, C.; Suthiphongchai, T.; DiRenzo, J.; Ewen, M.E. P/CAF associates with cyclin D1 and potentiates its activation of the estrogen receptor. *Proc. Natl. Acad. Sci. USA* **1999**, *96*, 5382–5387. [CrossRef]
80. Razandi, M.; Pedram, A.; Parks, S.; Levin, E.R. Proximal events in signaling by plasma membrane estrogen receptors. *J. Biol. Chem.* **2003**, *278*, 2701–2712. [CrossRef]
81. Pedram, A.; Razandi, M.; Aitkenhead, M.; Hughes, C.C.W.; Levin, E.R. Integration of the non-genomic and genomic actions of estrogen. Membrane-initiated signaling by steroid to transcription and cell biology. *J. Biol. Chem.* **2002**, *277*, 50768–50775. [CrossRef]
82. Wilson, M.A.; Chrysogelos, S.A. Identification and characterization of a negative regulatory element within the epidermal growth factor receptor gene first intron in hormone-dependent breast cancer cells. *J. Cell Biochem.* **2002**, *85*, 601–614. [CrossRef]
83. de Fazio, A.; Chiew, Y.E.; Sini, R.L.; Janes, P.W.; Sutherland, R.L. Expression of c-erbB receptors, heregulin and oestrogen receptor in human breast cell lines. *Int. J. Cancer* **2000**, *87*, 487–498. [CrossRef]
84. Massarweh, S.; Osborne, C.K.; Creighton, C.J.; Qin, L.; Tsimelzon, A.; Huang, S.; Weiss, H.; Rimawi, M.; Schiff, R. Tamoxifen resistance in breast tumors is driven by growth factor receptor signaling with repression of classic estrogen receptor genomic function. *Cancer Res.* **2008**, *68*, 826–833. [CrossRef] [PubMed]
85. Suba, Z. Interplay between insulin resistance and estrogen deficiency as co-activators in carcinogenesis. *Pathol. Oncol. Res.* **2012**, *18*, 123–133. [CrossRef] [PubMed]
86. Choi, S.B.; Jang, J.S.; Park, S. Estrogen and exercise may enhance beta-cell function and mass via insulin receptor substrate-2 induction in ovariectomized diabetic rats. *Endocrinology* **2005**, *146*, 4786–4794. [CrossRef] [PubMed]
87. Kasuga, M.; Hedo, J.A.; Yamada, K.M.; Kahn, C.R. The structure of insulin receptor and its subunits. Evidence for multiple non reduced forms and a 210,000 possible proreceptor. *J. Biol. Chem.* **1982**, *257*, 10392–10399. [CrossRef]
88. Campello, R.S.; Fátima, L.A.; Barreto-Andrade, J.N.; Lucas, T.F.; Mori, R.C.; Porto, C.S.; Machado, U.F. Estradiol-induced regulation of GLUT4 in 3T3-L1 cells: Involvement of ESR1 and AKT activation. *J. Mol. Endocrinol.* **2017**, *59*, 257–268. [CrossRef]
89. Richards, R.G.; DiAugustine, R.P.; Petrusz, P.; Clark, G.C.; Sebastian, J. Estradiol stimulates tyrosine phosphorylation of the insulin-like growth factor-1 receptor and insulin receptor substrate-1 in the uterus. *Proc. Natl. Acad. Sci. USA* **1996**, *93*, 12002–12007. [CrossRef] [PubMed]
90. Mauro, L.; Salerno, M.; Panno, M.L.; Bellizzi, D.; Sisci, D.; Miglietta, A.; Surmacz, E.; Andò, S. Estradiol increases IRS-1 gene expression and insulin signaling in breast cancer cells. *Biochem. Biophys. Res. Commun.* **2001**, *288*, 685–689. [CrossRef]
91. Medina, R.A.; Meneses, A.M.; Vera, J.C.; Guzman, C.; Nualart, F.; Astuya, A.; García, M.d.L.A.; Kato, S.; Carvajal, A.; Pinto, M.; et al. Estrogen and progesterone up-regulate glucose transporter expression in ZR-75-1 human breast cancer cells. *Endocrinology* **2003**, *144*, 4527–4535. [CrossRef]
92. Garrido, P.; Morán, J.; Alonso, A.; González, S.; González, C. 17β-estradiol activates glucose uptake via GLUT4 translocation and PI3K/Akt signaling pathway in MCF-7 cells. *Endocrinology* **2013**, *154*, 1979–1989. [CrossRef]
93. Saltiel, A.R.; Kahn, C.R. Insulin signaling and the regulation of glucose and lipid metabolism. *Nature* **2001**, *414*, 799–806. [CrossRef] [PubMed]
94. Mahboobifard, F.; Pourgholami, M.H.; Jorjani, M.; Dargahi, L.; Amiri, M.; Sadeghi, S.; Tehrani, F.R. Estrogen as a key regulator of energy homeostasis and metabolic health. *Biomed. Pharmacother.* **2022**, *156*, 113808. [CrossRef] [PubMed]
95. Suba, Z. Low estrogen exposure and/or defective estrogen signaling induces disturbances in glucose uptake and energy expenditure. *J. Diabet. Metab.* **2013**, *4*, 272–281. [CrossRef]
96. Donohoe, C.L.; Doyle, S.L.; Reynolds, J.V. Visceral adiposity, insulin resistance and cancer risk. *Diabetol. Metab. Syndr.* **2011**, *3*, 12. [CrossRef] [PubMed]
97. Rajsheker, S.; Manka, D.; Blomkalns, A.L.; Chatterjee, T.K.; Stoll, L.L.; Weintraub, N. Crosstalk between perivascular adipose tissue and blood vessels. *Curr. Opin. Pharmacol.* **2010**, *10*, 191–196. [CrossRef] [PubMed]
98. Roca-Rivada, A.; Alonso, J.; Al-Massadi, O.; Castelao, C.; Peinado, J.R.; Seoane, L.M.; Casanueva, F.F.; Pardo, M. Secretome analysis of rat adipose tissues shows location-specific roles for each depot type. *J. Proteom.* **2011**, *74*, 1068–1079. [CrossRef]
99. Pelekanou, V.; Leclercq, G. Recent insights into the effect of natural and environmental estrogens on mammary development and carcinogenesis. *Int. J. Dev. Biol.* **2011**, *55*, 869–878. [CrossRef] [PubMed]
100. Wang, H.; Leng, Y.; Gong, Y. Bone Marrow Fat and Hematopoiesis. *Front. Endocrinol.* **2018**, *9*, 694. [CrossRef] [PubMed]
101. Link, C.D. Is There a Brain Microbiome? *Neurosci. Insights* **2021**, *16*, 26331055211018709. [CrossRef] [PubMed]
102. Ervin, S.M.; Li, H.; Lim, L.; Roberts, L.R.; Liang, X.; Mani, S.; Redinbo, M.R. Gut microbial β-glucuronidases reactivate estrogens as components of the estrobolome that reactivate estrogens. *J. Biol. Chem.* **2019**, *294*, 18586–18599. [CrossRef]
103. Baker, J.M.; Al-Nakkash, L.; Herbst-Kralovetz, M.M. Estrogen-gut microbiome axis: Physiological and clinical implications. *Maturitas* **2017**, *103*, 45–53. [CrossRef] [PubMed]
104. Barakat, R.; Oakley, O.; Kim, H.; Jin, J.; Ko, C.J. Extra-gonadalsites of estrogenbiosynthesis and function. *BMB Rep.* **2016**, *49*, 488–496. [CrossRef] [PubMed]
105. Labrie, F.; Bélanger, A.; Luu-The, V.; Labrie, C.; Simard, J.; Cusan, L.; Gomez, J.-L.; Candas, B. DHEA and the intracrine formation of androgens and estrogens in peripheral target tissues: Its role during aging. *Steroids* **1998**, *63*, 322–328. [CrossRef] [PubMed]

106. Bjune, J.-I.; Strømland, P.P.; Jersin, R.Å.; Mellgren, G.; Dankel, S.N. Metabolic and Epigenetic Regulation by Estrogen in Adipocytes. *Front. Endocrinol.* **2022**, *13*, 828780. [CrossRef] [PubMed]
107. Dieudonné, M.N.; Leneveu, M.C.; Giudicelli, Y.; Pecquery, R. Evidence for functional estrogen receptors α and β in human adipose cells: Regional specificities and regulation by estrogens. *Am. J. Physiol. Cell Physiol.* **2004**, *286*, C655–C661. [CrossRef] [PubMed]
108. Nelson, L.R.; Bulun, S.E. Estrogen production and action. *J. Am. Acad. Dermatol.* **2001**, *45*, S116–S124. [CrossRef] [PubMed]
109. Wang, P.; Mariman, E.; Renes, J.; Keijer, J. The Secretory Function of Adipocytes in the Physiology of White Adipose Tissue. *J. Cell Physiol.* **2008**, *216*, 3–13. [CrossRef] [PubMed]
110. Clegg, D.J.; Brown, L.M.; Woods, S.C.; Benoit, S.C. Gonadal hormones determine sensitivity to central leptin and insulin. *Diabetes* **2006**, *55*, 978–987. [CrossRef] [PubMed]
111. Simpson, E.R.; Misso, M.; Hewitt, K.N.; Hill, R.A.; Boon, W.C.; Jones, M.E.; Kovacic, A.; Zhou, J.; Clyne, C.D. Estrogen—The good, the bad, and the unexpected. *Endocr. Rev.* **2005**, *26*, 322–330. [CrossRef]
112. Combs, T.P.; Pajvani, U.B.; Berg, A.H.; Lin, Y.; Jelicks, L.A.; Laplante, M.; Nawrocki, A.R.; Rajala, M.W.; Parlow, A.F.; Cheeseboro, L.; et al. A transgenic mouse with a deletion in the collagenous domain of adiponectin displays elevated circulating adiponectin and improved insulin sensitivity. *Endocrinology* **2004**, *145*, 367–383. [CrossRef]
113. Steppan, C.M.; Bailey, S.T.; Bhat, S.; Brown, E.J.; Banerjee, R.R.; Wright, C.M.; Patel, H.R.; Ahima, R.S.; Lazar, M.A. The hormone resistin links obesity to diabetes. *Nature* **2001**, *409*, 307–312. [CrossRef] [PubMed]
114. Suba, Z. Crossroad between obesity and cancer: A defective signaling function of heavily lipid laden adipocytes. In *Crosstalk in Biological Processes*; El-Esawi, M.A., Ed.; InTechOpen: London, UK, 2019. [CrossRef]
115. Armani, A.; Berry, A.; Cirulli, F.; Caprio, M. Molecular mechanisms underlying metabolic syndrome: The expanding role of the adipocyte. *FASEB J.* **2017**, *31*, 4240–4255. [CrossRef]
116. De Pergola, G.; Silvestris, F. Obesity as a major risk factor for cancer. *J. Obes.* **2013**, *2013*, 291546. [CrossRef] [PubMed]
117. Huh, J.Y.; Park, Y.J.; Ham, M.; Kim, J.B. Crosstalk between Adipocytes and Immune Cells in Adipose Tissue Inflammation and Metabolic Dysregulation in Obesity. *Mol. Cells* **2014**, *37*, 365–371. [CrossRef]
118. Purohit, A.; Newman, S.P.; Reed, M.J. The role of cytokines in regulating estrogen synthesis: Implications for the etiology of breast cancer. *Breast Cancer Res.* **2002**, *4*, 65. [CrossRef]
119. Ye, J.; McGuinness, O.P. Inflammation during obesity is not all bad: Evidence from animal and human studies. *Am. J. Physiol. Endocrinol. Metab.* **2013**, *304*, E466–E477. [CrossRef] [PubMed]
120. Boucher, J.; Tseng, J.-H.; Kahn, C.R. Insulin and insulin-like growth factor receptors act as ligand-specific amplitude modulators of a common pathway regulating gene. *J. Biol. Chem.* **2010**, *285*, 17235–17245. [CrossRef]
121. Smith, C.L. Cross-talk between peptide growth factor and estrogen receptor signaling pathways. *Biol. Reprod.* **1998**, *58*, 627–632. [CrossRef]
122. Xu, J.; Xiang, Q.; Lin, G.; Fu, X.; Zhou, K.; Jiang, P.; Zheng, S.; Wang, T. Estrogen improved metabolic syndrome through down-regulation of VEGF and HIF-1α to inhibit hypoxia of periaortic and intra-abdominal fat in ovariectomized female rats. *Mol. Biol. Rep.* **2012**, *39*, 8177–8185. [CrossRef]
123. Caizzi, L.; Ferrero, G.; Cutrupi, S.; Cordero, F.; Ballaré, C.; Miano, V.; Reineri, S.; Ricci, L.; Friard, O.; Testori, A.; et al. Genome-wide activity of unliganded estrogen receptor-α in breast cancer cells. *Proc. Natl. Acad. Sci. USA* **2014**, *111*, 4892–4897. [CrossRef]
124. Stubbins, R.E.; Najjar, K.; Holcomb, V.B.; Hong, J.; Núñez, N.P. Oestrogen alters adipocyte biology and protects female mice from adipocyte inflammation and insulin resistance. *Diabetes Obes. Metab.* **2012**, *14*, 58–66. [CrossRef]
125. Suba, Z. Rosetta Stone for Cancer Cure: Comparison of the Anticancer Capacity of Endogenous Estrogens, Synthetic Estrogens and Antiestrogens. *Oncol. Rev.* **2023**, *17*, 10708. [CrossRef]
126. Thomas, E.T.; Mar, C.D.; Glasziou, P.; Wright, G.; Barratt, A.; Bell, K.J.L. Prevalence of incidental breast cancer and precursor lesions in autopsy studies: A systematic review and meta-analysis. *BMC Cancer* **2017**, *17*, 808. [CrossRef]
127. Clusan, L.; Ferrière, F.; Flouriot, G.; Pakdel, F. A Basic Review on Estrogen Receptor Signaling Pathways in Breast Cancer. *Int. J. Mol. Sci.* **2023**, *24*, 6834. [CrossRef]
128. Tan, P.H.; Ellis, I.; Allison, K.; Brogi, E.; Fox, S.B.; Lakhani, S.; Lazar, A.J.; Morris, E.A.; Sahin, A.; Salgado, R.; et al. The 2019 World Health Organization Classification of Tumours of the Breast. *Histopathology* **2020**, *77*, 181–185. [CrossRef]
129. Perou, C.M.; Sørlie, T.; Eisen, M.B.; van de Rijn, M.; Jeffrey, S.S.; Rees, C.A.; Pollack, J.R.; Ross, D.T.; Johnsen, H.; Akslen, L.A.; et al. Molecular Portraits of Human Breast Tumours. *Nature* **2000**, *406*, 747–752. [CrossRef]
130. Matta, J.; Morales, L.; Ortiz, C.; Adams, D.; Vargas, W.; Casbas, P.; Dutil, J.; Echenique, M.; Suárez, E. Estrogen Receptor Expression Is Associated with DNA Repair Capacity in Breast Cancer. *PLoS ONE* **2016**, *11*, e0152422. [CrossRef]
131. Hayes, D.F. Tamoxifen: Dr. Jekyll and Mr. Hyde? *J. Natl. Cancer Inst.* **2004**, *96*, 895–897. [CrossRef]
132. Munzone, E.; Colleoni, M. Optimal management of luminal breast cancer: How much endocrine therapy is long enough? *Ther. Adv. Med. Oncol.* **2018**, *10*, 1758835918777437. [CrossRef]
133. Arpino, G.; Weiss, H.; Lee, A.V.; Schiff, R.; De Placido, S.; Osborne, C.K.; Elledge, R.M. Estrogen receptor-positive, progesterone receptor-negative breast cancer: Association with growth factor receptor expression and tamoxifen resistance. *J. Natl. Cancer Inst.* **2005**, *97*, 1254–1261. [CrossRef]

134. Parker, J.S.; Mullins, M.; Cheang, M.C.U.; Leung, S.; Voduc, D.; Vickery, T.; Davies, S.; Fauron, C.; He, X.; Hu, Z.; et al. Supervised Risk Predictor of Breast Cancer Based on Intrinsic Subtypes. *J. Clin. Oncol. Off. J. Am. Soc. Clin. Oncol.* **2009**, *27*, 1160–1167. [CrossRef]
135. Rouanet, P.; Roger, P.; Rousseau, E.; Thibault, S.; Romieu, G.; Mathieu, A.; Cretin, J.; Barneon, G.; Granier, M.; Maran-Gonzalez, A.; et al. HER2 overexpression a major risk factor for recurrence in pT1a-bN0M0 breast cancer: Results from a French regional cohort. *Cancer Med.* **2014**, *3*, 134–142. [CrossRef]
136. Suba, Z. Light deficiency confers breast cancer risk by endocrine disorders. *Recent Pat. Anticancer Discov.* **2012**, *7*, 337–344. [CrossRef]
137. Chew, V.; Toh, H.; Abastado, J. Immune Microenvironment in Tumor Progression: Characteristics and Challenges for Therapy. *J. Oncol.* **2012**, *2012*, 2312956. [CrossRef]
138. Wang, Q.; Shao, X.; Zhang, Y.; Zhu, M.; Wang, F.X.C.; Mu, J.; Li, J.; Yao, H.; Chen, K. Role of tumor microenvironment in cancer progression and therapeutic strategy. *Cancer Med.* **2023**, *12*, 11149–11165. [CrossRef]
139. Linares, J.; Marín-Jiménez, J.A.; Badia-Ramentol, J.; Calon, A. Determinants and Functions of CAFs Secretome during Cancer progression and Therapy. *Front. Cell Dev. Biol.* **2021**, *8*, 621070. [CrossRef]
140. Mantovani, A.; Allavena, P.; Marchesi, F.; Garlanda, C. Macrophages as tools and targets in cancer therapy. *Nat. Rev. Drug Discov.* **2022**, *21*, 799–820. [CrossRef]
141. Chen, Y.; McAndrews, K.M.; Kalluri, R. Clinical and therapeutic relevance of cancer-associated fibroblasts. *Nat. Rev. Clin. Oncol.* **2021**, *18*, 792–804. [CrossRef]
142. Pejerrey, S.M.; Dustin, D.; Kim, J.A.; Gu, G.; Rechoum, Y.; Fuqua, S.A.W. The impact of ESR1 mutations on the treatment of metastatic breast cancer. *Horm. Cancer* **2018**, *9*, 215–228. [CrossRef]
143. Miano, V.; Ferrero, G.; Reineri, S.; Caizzi, L.; Annaratone, L.; Ricci, L.; Cutrupi, S.; Castellano, I.; Cordero, F.; De Bortoli, M. Luminal long non-coding RNAs regulated by estrogen receptor alpha in a ligand-independent manner show functional roles in breast cancer. *Oncotarget* **2016**, *7*, 3201–3216. [CrossRef]
144. Lei, J.T.; Gou, X.; Seker, S.; Seker, S.; Ellis, M.J. *ESR1* alterations and metastasis in estrogen receptor positive breast cancer. *J. Cancer Metastasis Treat.* **2019**, *5*, 38. [CrossRef]
145. Stellato, C.; Porreca, I.; Cuomo, D.; Tarallo, R.; Nassa, G.; Ambrosino, C. The "busy life" of unliganded estrogen receptors. *Proteomics* **2016**, *16*, 288–300. [CrossRef]
146. Fan, P.; Jordan, V.C. New insights into acquired endocrine resistance of breast cancer. *Cancer Drug Resist.* **2019**, *2*, 198–209. [CrossRef]
147. Yu, B.; Wu, K.; Wang, X.; Zhang, J.; Wang, L.; Jiang, Y.; Zhu, X.; Chen, W.; Yan, M. Periostin secreted by cancer-associated fibroblasts promotes cancer stemness in head and neck cancer by activating protein tyrosine kinase 7. *Cell Death Dis.* **2018**, *9*, 1082. [CrossRef]
148. Kalluri, R. The biology and function of fibroblasts in cancer. *Nat. Rev. Cancer* **2016**, *16*, 582–598. [CrossRef]
149. Giusti, I.; Francesco, M.; Di D'Ascenzo, S.; Palmerini, M.G.; Macchiarelli, G.; Carta, G.; Dolo, V. Ovarian cancer-derived extracellular vesicles affect normal human fibroblast behavior. *Cancer Biol. Ther.* **2018**, *19*, 722. [CrossRef]
150. Dai, G.; Yao, X.; Zhang, Y.; Gu, J.; Geng, Y.; Xue, F.; Zhang, J. Colorectal cancer cell–derived exosomes containing miR-10b regulate fibroblast cells via the PI3K/Akt pathway. *Bull. Cancer* **2018**, *105*, 336–349. [CrossRef]
151. Huan, J.; Hornick, N.I.; Shurtleff, M.J.; Skinner, A.M.; Goloviznina, N.A.; Roberts, C.T.; Kurre, P. RNA trafficking by acute myelogenous leukemia exosomes. *Cancer Res.* **2013**, *73*, 918–929. [CrossRef]
152. Rothenberger, N.J.; Somasundaram, A.; Stabile, L.P. The Role of the Estrogen Pathway in the Tumor Microenvironment. *Int. J. Mol. Sci.* **2018**, *19*, 611. [CrossRef]
153. Erez, N.; Truitt, M.; Olson, P.; Hanahan, D. Cancer-associated fibroblasts are activated in incipient neoplasia to orchestrate tumor-promoting inflammation in an NF-κB-dependent manner. *Cancer Cell* **2010**, *17*, 135–147. [CrossRef]
154. Reed, M.J.; Purohit, A. Breast Cancer and the Role of Cytokines in Regulating Estrogen Synthesis: An Emerging Hypothesis. *Endocr. Rev.* **1997**, *18*, 701–715. [CrossRef]
155. Naito, Y.; Yamamoto, Y.; Sakamoto, N.; Shimomura, I.; Kogure, A.; Kumazaki, M.; Yokoi, A.; Yashiro, M.; Kiyono, T.; Yanagihara, K.; et al. Cancer extracellular vesicles contribute to stromal heterogeneity by inducing chemokines in cancer-associated fibroblasts. *Oncogene* **2019**, *38*, 5566–5579. [CrossRef]
156. Meng, M.; Zhong, K.; Jiang, T.; Liu, Z.; Kwan, H.Y.; Su, T. The current understanding on the impact of KRAS on colorectal cancer. *Biomed. Pharmacother.* **2021**, *140*, 111717. [CrossRef]
157. Dörsam, B.; Bösl, T.; Reiners, K.S.; Barnert, S.; Schubert, R.; Shatnyeva, O.; Zigrino, P.; Engert, A.; Hansen, H.P.; Von Strandmann, E.P. Hodgkin lymphoma-derived extracellular vesicles change the secretome of fibroblasts toward a CAF phenotype. *Front. Immunol.* **2018**, *9*, 1358. [CrossRef]
158. Dannenfelser, R.; Nome, M.; Tahiri, A.; Ursini-Siegel, J.; Vollan, H.K.M.; Haakensen, V.D.; Helland, A.; Naume, B.; Caldas, C.; Borresen-Dale, A.L.; et al. Data-driven analysis of immune infiltrate in a large cohort of breast cancer and its association with disease progression, er activity, and genomic complexity. *Oncotarget* **2017**, *8*, 57121–57133. [CrossRef]
159. Suzuki, T.; Miki, Y.; Akahira, J.I.; Moriya, T.; Ohuchi, N.; Sasano, H. Review: Aromatase in human breast carcinoma as a key regulator of intratumoral sex steroid concentrations. *Endocr. J.* **2008**, *55*, 455–463. [CrossRef]

160. Bollet, M.A.; Savignoni, A.; De Koning, L.; Tran-Perennou, C.; Barbaroux, C.; Degeorges, A.; Sigal-Zafrani, B.; Almouzni, G.; Cottu, P.; Salmon, R.; et al. Tumor aromatase expression as a prognostic factor for local control in young breast cancer patients after breast-conserving treatment. *Breast Cancer Res.* **2009**, *11*, R54. [CrossRef]
161. Clocchiatti, A.; Ghosh, S.; Procopio, M.G.; Mazzeo, L.; Bordignon, P.; Ostano, P.; Goruppi, S.; Bottoni, G.; Katarkar, A.; Levesque, M.; et al. Androgen receptor functions as transcriptional repressor of cancer-associated fibroblast activation. *J. Clin. Investig.* **2018**, *128*, 5465–5478. [CrossRef]
162. Vivacqua, A.; Muoio, M.G.; Miglietta, A.M.; Maggiolini, M. Differential microRNA landscape triggered by estrogens in cancer associated fibroblasts (CAFs) of primary and metastatic breast tumors. *Cancers* **2019**, *11*, 412. [CrossRef]
163. Zhang, Y.; Cong, X.; Li, Z.; Xue, Y. Estrogen facilitates gastric cancer cell proliferation and invasion through promoting the secretion of interleukin-6 by cancer-associated fibroblasts. *Int. Immunopharmacol.* **2020**, *78*, 105937. [CrossRef]
164. Akhurst, R.J.; Hata, A. Targeting the TGFbetasignalling pathway in disease. *Nat. Rev. Drug Discov.* **2012**, *11*, 790–811. [CrossRef]
165. Wu, S.; Zhang, Y.; Xu, L.; Dai, Y.; Teng, Y.; Ma, S.; Ho, S.-H.; Kim, J.-M.; Yu, S.S.; Kim, S.; et al. Multicenter, randomized study of genetically modified recombinant human interleukin-11 to prevent chemotherapy-induced thrombocytopenia in cancer patients receiving chemotherapy. *Support. Care Cancer* **2012**, *20*, 1875–1884. [CrossRef]
166. da Silva, E.Z.; Jamur, M.C.; Oliver, C. Mast cell function: A new vision of an old cell. *J. Histochem. Cytochem.* **2014**, *62*, 698–738. [CrossRef]
167. Shimasaki, N.; Jain, A.; Campana, D. NK cells for cancer immunotherapy. *Nat. Rev. Drug Discov.* **2020**, *19*, 200–218. [CrossRef]
168. Ngambenjawong, C.; Gustafson, H.H.; Pun, S.H. Progress in tumor-associated macrophage (TAM)-targeted therapeutics. *Adv. Drug Deliv. Rev.* **2017**, *114*, 206–221. [CrossRef]
169. Ostrand-Rosenberg, S. Myeloid-derived suppressor cells: Facilitators of cancer and obesity-induced cancer. *Annu. Rev. Cancer Biol.* **2021**, *5*, 17–38. [CrossRef]
170. Fridman, W.H.; Pages, F.; Sautes-Fridman, C.; Galon, J. The immune contexture in human tumours: Impact on clinical outcome. *Nat. Rev. Cancer* **2012**, *12*, 298–306. [CrossRef]
171. Haabeth, O.A.; Lorvik, K.B.; Hammarstrom, C.; Donaldson, I.M.; Haraldsen, G.; Bogen, B.; Corthay, A. Inflammation driven by tumour-specific th1 cells protects against b-cell cancer. *Nat. Commun.* **2011**, *2*, 240. [CrossRef]
172. DeNardo, D.G.; Barreto, J.B.; Andreu, P.; Vasquez, L.; Tawfik, D.; Kolhatkar, N.; Coussens, L.M. Cd4(+) t cells regulate pulmonary metastasis of mammary carcinomas by enhancing protumor properties of macrophages. *Cancer Cell* **2009**, *16*, 91–102. [CrossRef]
173. Fish, E.N. The x-files in immunity: Sex-based differences predispose immune responses. *Nat. Rev. Immunol.* **2008**, *8*, 737–744. [CrossRef]
174. Khan, D.; Ansar Ahmed, S. The immune system is a natural target for estrogen action: Opposing effects of estrogen in two prototypical autoimmune diseases. *Front. Immunol.* **2015**, *6*, 635. [CrossRef]
175. Ali, H.R.; Provenzano, E.; Dawson, S.J.; Blows, F.M.; Liu, B.; Shah, M.; Earl, H.M.; Poole, C.J.; Hiller, L.; Dunn, J.A.; et al. Association between cd8+ t-cell infiltration and breast cancer survival in 12,439 patients. *Ann. Oncol.* **2014**, *25*, 1536–1543. [CrossRef]
176. Bentrem, D.J.; Jordan, V.C. Role of antiestrogens and aromatase inhibitors in breast cancer treatment. *Curr. Opin. Obstet. Gynecol.* **2002**, *14*, 5–12. [CrossRef]
177. Jordan, V.C.; Lewis-Wambi, J.S.; Patel, R.R.; Kim, H.; Ariazi, E.A. New hypotheses and opportunities in endocrine therapy: Amplification of oestrogen-induced apoptosis. *Breast.* **2009**, *18* (Suppl. S3), S10–S17. [CrossRef]
178. Osborne, C.K. Tamoxifen in the treatment of breast cancer. *N. Engl. J. Med.* **1998**, *339*, 1609–1618. [CrossRef]
179. Fan, P.; Agboke, F.A.; Cunliffe, H.E.; Ramos, P.; Jordan, V.C. A molecular model for the mechanism of acquired tamoxifen resistance in breast cancer. *Eur. J. Cancer* **2014**, *50*, 2866–2876. [CrossRef]
180. Tilghman, S.L.; Sabnis, G.; Brodie, A.M.H. Upregulation of AIB1, aromatase and ERα provides long-term estrogen-deprived human breast cancer cells with a mechanistic growth advantage for survival. *Horm. Mol. Biol. Clin. Investig.* **2011**, *3*, 357–366. [CrossRef]
181. Ishii, Y.; Waxman, S.; Germain, D. Tamoxifen Stimulates the Growth of Cyclin D1–Overexpressing Breast Cancer Cells by Promoting the Activation of Signal Transducer and Activator of Transcription 3. *Cancer Res.* **2008**, *68*, 852–860. [CrossRef]
182. Zhou, Y.; Yau, C.; Joe, W.; Gray, J.W.; Chew, K.; Dairkee, S.H.; Moore, D.H.; Eppenberger, U.; Eppenberger-Castori, S.; Benz, C.C. Enhanced NFκB and AP-1 transcriptional activity associated with antiestrogen resistant breast cancer. *BMC Cancer* **2007**, *7*, 59. [CrossRef]
183. Frasor, J.; El-Shennawy, L.; Stender, J.D.; Kastrati, I. NFκB Affects Estrogen Receptor Expression and Activity in Breast Cancer through Multiple Mechanisms. *Mol. Cell Endocrinol.* **2015**, *418*, 235–239. [CrossRef]
184. Hayes, E.L.; Lewis-Wambi, J.S. Mechanisms of endocrine resistance in breast cancer: An overview of the proposed roles of noncoding RNA. *Breast Cancer Res.* **2015**, *17*, 40. [CrossRef]
185. Holst, F.; Stahl, P.R.; Ruiz, C.; Hellwinkel, O.; Jehan, Z.; Wendland, M.; Lebeau, A.; Terracciano, L.; Al-Kuraya, K.; Jänicke, F.; et al. Estrogen receptor alpha (ESR1) gene amplification is frequent in breast cancer. *Nat. Genet.* **2007**, *39*, 655–660. [CrossRef]
186. Tomita, S.; Zhang, Z.; Nakano, M.; Ibusuki, M.; Kawazoe, T.; Yamamoto, Y.; Iwase, H. Estrogen receptor alpha gene ESR1 amplification may predict endocrine therapy responsiveness in breast cancer patients. *Cancer Sci.* **2009**, *100*, 1012–1017. [CrossRef]

187. Magnani, L.; Frige, G.; Gadaleta, R.M.; Corleone, G.; Fabris, S.; Kempe, H.; Verschure, P.J.; Barozzi, I.; Vircillo, V.; Hong, S.P.; et al. Acquired CYP19A1 amplification is an early specific mechanism of aromatase inhibitor resistance in ER alpha metastatic breast cancer. *Nat. Genet.* **2017**, *49*, 444–450. [CrossRef]
188. Suba, Z. The pitfall of the transient, inconsistent anticancer capacity of antiestrogens and the mechanism of apparent antiestrogen resistance. *Drug Des. Dev. Ther.* **2015**, *9*, 4341–4353. [CrossRef]
189. Jin, K.; Kong, X.; Shah, T.; Penet, M.-F.; Wildes, F.; Sgroi, D.C.; Ma, X.J.; Huang, Y.; Kallioniemi, A.; Landberg, G.; et al. The HOXB7 protein renders breast cancer cells resistant to tamoxifen through activation of the egfr pathway. *Proc. Natl. Acad. Sci. USA* **2012**, *109*, 2736–2741. [CrossRef]
190. Jin, K.; Park, S.; Teo, W.W.; Korangath, P.; Cho, S.S.; Yoshida, T.; Győrffy, B.; Goswami, C.P.; Nakshatri, H.; Cruz, L.A.; et al. HOXB7 is an ERA cofactor in the activation of HER2 and multiple er target genes leading to endocrine resistance. *Cancer Discov.* **2015**, *5*, 944–959. [CrossRef]
191. Osborne, C.K.; Bardou, V.; Hopp, T.A.; Chamness, G.C.; Hilsenbeck, S.G.; Fuqua, S.A.; Wong, J.; Allred, D.C.; Clark, G.M.; Schiff, R. Role of the estrogen receptor coactivator AIB1 (SRC-3) and HER-2/neu in tamoxifen resistance in breast cancer. *J. Natl. Cancer Inst.* **2003**, *95*, 353–361. [CrossRef]
192. Chen, A.C.; Migliaccio, I.; Rimawi, M.; Lopez-Tarruella, S.; Creighton, C.J.; Massarweh, S.; Huang, C.; Wang, Y.-C.; Batra, S.K.; Gutierrez, M.C.; et al. Upregulation of MUCIN4 in ER-positive/HER2-overexpressing breast cancer xenografts with acquired resistance to endocrine and HER2-targeted therapies. *Breast Cancer Res. Treat.* **2012**, *134*, 583–593. [CrossRef]
193. Fan, P.; Wang, J.; Santen, R.J.; Yue, W. Long-term treatment with tamoxifen facilitates translocation of estrogen receptor alpha out of the nucleus and enhances its interaction with EGFR in MCF-7 breast cancer cells. *Cancer Res.* **2007**, *67*, 1352–1360. [CrossRef]
194. Song, R.X.; Barnes, C.J.; Zhang, Z.; Bao, Y.; Kumar, R.; Santen, R.J. The role of Shc and insulin-like growth factor 1 receptor in mediating the translocation of estrogen receptor alpha to the plasma membrane. *Proc. Natl. Acad. Sci. USA* **2004**, *101*, 2076–2081. [CrossRef] [PubMed]
195. Zhang, Y.; Moerkens, M.; Ramaiahgari, S.; de Bont, H.; Price, L.; Meerman, J.; van de Water, B. Elevated insulin-like growth factor-1 receptor signaling induces antiestrogen resistance through the MAPK/ERK and PI3K/Akt signaling routes. *Breast Cancer Res.* **2011**, *13*, R52. [CrossRef] [PubMed]
196. Ellis, M.J.; Perou, C.M. The genomic landscape of breast cancer as a therapeutic roadmap. *Cancer Discov.* **2013**, *3*, 27–34. [CrossRef] [PubMed]
197. Zhu, Y.; Liu, Y.; Zhang, C.; Chu, J.; Wu, Y.; Li, Y.; Liu, J.; Li, Q.; Li, S.; Shi, Q.; et al. Tamoxifen-resistant breast cancer cells are resistant to DNA-damaging chemotherapy because of upregulated BARD1 and BRCA1. *Nat. Commun.* **2018**, *9*, 1595. [CrossRef] [PubMed]
198. Mansouri, S.; Farahmand, L.; Hosseinzade, A.; Eslami-S, Z.; Majidzadeh-A, K. Estrogen can restore Tamoxifen sensitivity in breast cancer cells amidst the complex network of resistance. *Biomed. Pharmacother.* **2017**, *93*, 1320–1325. [CrossRef] [PubMed]
199. Jordan, V.C. Linking estrogen induced apoptosis with decreases in mortality following long term adjuvant tamoxifen therapy. 2014, 106, dju296.
200. Jordan, V.C. The new biology of estrogen induced apoptosis applied to treat and prevent breast cancer. *Endocr. Relat. Cancer* **2015**, *22*, R1–R31. [CrossRef]
201. Jordan, V.C.; Fan, P.; Abderrahman, B.; Maximov, P.Y.; Hawsawi, Y.M.; Bhattacharya, P.; Pokharel, N. Sex steroid induced apoptosis as a rational strategy to treat anti-hormone resistant breast and prostate cancer. *Discov. Med.* **2016**, *21*, 411–427.

Disclaimer/Publisher's Note: The statements, opinions and data contained in all publications are solely those of the individual author(s) and contributor(s) and not of MDPI and/or the editor(s). MDPI and/or the editor(s) disclaim responsibility for any injury to people or property resulting from any ideas, methods, instructions or products referred to in the content.

pharmaceutics

MDPI

Review

The Value of Microbes in Cancer Neoantigen Immunotherapy

Junrui Tian [1,2,3] and Jian Ma [1,2,3,*]

1 NHC Key Laboratory of Carcinogenesis and Hunan Key Laboratory of Cancer Metabolism, Hunan Cancer Hospital and the Affiliated Cancer Hospital of Xiangya School of Medicine, Central South University, Changsha 410013, China; 226511035@csu.edu.cn
2 Cancer Research Institute and School of Basic Medical Science, Central South University, Changsha 410078, China
3 Key Laboratory of Carcinogenesis and Cancer Invasion of the Chinese Ministry of Education, Hunan Key Laboratory of Nonresolving Inflammation and Cancer, Changsha 410078, China
* Correspondence: majian@csu.edu.cn

Abstract: Tumor neoantigens are widely used in cancer immunotherapy, and a growing body of research suggests that microbes play an important role in these neoantigen-based immunotherapeutic processes. The human body and its surrounding environment are filled with a large number of microbes that are in long-term interaction with the organism. The microbiota can modulate our immune system, help activate neoantigen-reactive T cells, and play a great role in the process of targeting tumor neoantigens for therapy. Recent studies have revealed the interconnection between microbes and neoantigens, which can cross-react with each other through molecular mimicry, providing theoretical guidance for more relevant studies. The current applications of microbes in immunotherapy against tumor neoantigens are mainly focused on cancer vaccine development and immunotherapy with immune checkpoint inhibitors. This article summarizes the related fields and suggests the importance of microbes in immunotherapy against neoantigens.

Keywords: tumor neoantigen; cancer immunotherapy; microbes; cancer vaccines; immune checkpoint inhibitors

1. Introduction

Tumor neoantigens can be summarized as substances with immunogenic properties that are specifically expressed by tumor cells. Due to their specific presence on tumor cells and the fact that the T-cells recognizing these antigens are not affected by central T-cell tolerance [1], neoantigens are considered ideal targets for cancer therapy [2,3]. The content about tumor neoantigens has been evolving, and with continuous research, many types of neoantigens have been identified. Tumor neoantigens can be divided into two categories: classical neoantigens and noncanonical neoepitopes [4]. Among these, classical neoantigens are derived from cancer-specific genetically hardwired alterations, including oncogenic missense mutations, frameshift mutations, splice sites, gene fusions, and long noncoding RNA-derived neoantigens. Noncanonical neoepitopes are not derived from genetic alterations, encompassing neoepitopes originating from alternative splicing, post-translational modifications, RNA editing, and aberrant mRNA translation [4,5]. Cancer immunotherapies developed against neoantigens have developed rapidly in recent decades [6]. The main therapeutic strategies are neoantigen vaccines [7,8], adoptive cell transfer (ACT) therapy [9,10], and immune checkpoint blockade therapy [11].

Microbes have been found to play an important role in cancer immunotherapies. Immunotherapy aims to trigger a specific anti-tumor response in cancer patients. The availability of specific neoepitopes in tumor cells, as well as the ability of these neoepitopes to effectively activate immune cells targeting such epitopes, are necessary for successful immunotherapy [2,12]. Numerous studies have shown that microbes play a regulatory role in the host immune system. They can modulate the host immune system by virtue of their immunogenic peptides or metabolites, activate the relevant immune cells, and enhance the effect of immunotherapy [13–15]. In addition, because microbes are small in size and simple in structure, researchers can achieve the modification of microbes more easily via genetic engineering and use them as tools in the development of neoantigen immunotherapy [16,17]. Using these modified microbes or their components, it is possible to design suitable delivery vehicles for neoantigen vaccines or drugs targeting neoantigens [18]. The judicious use of microbes has great potential in immunotherapy against tumor neoantigens.

Here, we reviewed the current research on tumor neoantigens and microbes and summarized the development of neoantigen identification. We discussed how microbes influence the mechanisms of neoantigen immunotherapy and hope to provide a better guideline for the application of microbes in neoantigen immunotherapy. We also summarized the importance and application results of microbes in cancer neoantigen vaccines and immune checkpoint blockade therapy in recent years. We hope this review can draw attention to the importance of microbes in neoantigen immunotherapy, advancing the development of therapeutic approaches.

2. The Development History of Neoantigen Identification

Since the discovery and isolation of the first tumor neoantigen, P91A, in a mouse tumor model by De Plaen's team in 1988 [19], there has been continuous development regarding the identification of neoantigens. Due to technical limitations at the time, early neoantigen identification [20–22] was usually low-throughput and labor-intensive. For nearly twenty years, most neoantigens were identified by constructing cDNA libraries, overexpressing the selected neoantigen cDNAs and major histocompatibility complex (MHC) molecules in cell lines, co-culturing them with T cells, and finally determining the immunogenicity of the screened neoantigens by measuring the differentiation status of the T cells. At the same time, mass spectrometry is also being applied to the identification of neoantigens [23]. Human leukocyte antigen (HLA) molecules on the surface of tumor cells are first isolated, and then these peptides are analyzed by mass spectrometry to identify tumor neoantigens.

The period of rapid development of tumor neoantigen identification technology came with the birth of next-generation sequencing (NGS). In 2012, Hirokazu Matsushita et al. identified neoantigens in mouse sarcoma cells for the first time with the help of NGS approaches [24]. This technique identified mutant proteins expressed in patients' tumor cells by whole exome sequencing analysis and then predicted candidate mutant T-cell epitopes [25]. Theoretically, by continuously optimizing the MHC prediction model, a large number of mutant neoantigens can be rapidly identified. On the basis of this theory, many prediction pipelines were subsequently developed. Examples include p-VAC-seq [26], which integrates tumor mutation and expression data and automates multiple antigen screening steps; PSSMHCpan [27], which can effectively predict the affinity of peptide binding to HLA class I alleles; DBTpred [28], which focuses on single amino acid residue mutations resulting in altered peptide-MHC binding affinity; and RBM-MHC [29], which improved predictions for rare alleles. In addition to these algorithms based on peptide affinity, there are also prediction methods that assess the prediction of immunogenicity based on the stability of the peptide-MHC complex [30,31].

Most of these algorithms predict neoantigens arising from genetic mutations while ignoring neoantigens produced by other possibilities. Recently, identification methods for neoantigens arising from these non-mutational alterations have been gradually developed. For instance, identification of neoantigens arising from alterations in extracellular regions of membrane proteins [32], gene fusions [33], single nucleotide variations (SNVs), Indels, and gene fusions by analysis of original sequencing data [34,35]. The computer prediction of MHC class-II binding epitopes is more complex compared to the prediction of MHC class-I binding epitopes because the binding properties of the peptide-binding groove of these molecules are less stringent [36]. In recent years, a series of prediction pipelines for predicting MHC-II binding epitopes have been developed—for example, MAPTAC [37] and FIONA [38]. With the continuous maturation of tumor neoantigen identification technology, a large number of neoantigens have been identified. Researchers have also built more complete neoantigen databases on this basis [39–41], and these abundant neoantigen resources have, in turn, contributed to the accuracy of neoantigen prediction [42].

In addition to computerized prediction models, mass spectrometry (MS) to identify neoantigens has been widely used with the advent of NGS technology [43]. With high mass resolving power, MS can identify typical and non-typical antigens from the MHC-binding peptides, reducing the false–positive rate [44]. For example, with the help of gene sequencing and MS analysis, researchers identified new epitopes of tumor antigens in the mouse tumor model [45,46]. Specific neoantigens have also been identified in human tumor tissue samples by MS technology [47]. The coupling of liquid chromatography (LC) with MS, such as LC–tandem MS (LC–MS/MS) [48] and nano-ultra-performance LC coupled to high-resolution MS (nUPLC–MS/MS) [49], has expanded the coverage of the MHC peptidome and improved the sensitivity of MS, which has more advantages in neoantigen identification. In recent years, there has been continuous research combining mass spectrometry techniques with computerized prediction models to develop efficient and accurate prediction channels. For example, NetMHCpan-4.0 [50], which is commonly used in neoantigen identification, can integrate the MHC-peptide binding affinity (BA) datasets and MS-eluting ligand (EL) datasets into a single framework to train machine learning models and obtain superior prediction performance. Training prediction models using MS data greatly improves the specificity of HLA-peptide binding prediction algorithms [51,52].

Based on the evolving neoantigen prediction methods described above, many neoantigens have been identified. However, not all predicted neoantigens are immunogenic [53]. Only a small fraction of the mutated peptides identified by bioinformatics are immunogenic [54]. Some studies show that the quality rather than the quantity of neoantigens expressed by tumor cells could better predict clinical outcomes [55,56]. Neoantigens with homology to infectious disease-derived epitopes would be more immunogenic [55], which provides inspiration for subsequent identification of neoantigens.

With the in-depth study of neoantigens, many previously unnoticed neoantigens have been discovered [4], such as neoantigens arising from post-translational modifications and RNA editing. These neoantigens do not result from alterations at the gene level and cannot be identified by relying on sequencing technology or MS-based analysis. It is important to develop new identification methods with the help of new technologies. Recently, Naoki Hosen's team identified a specific antigen for multiple myeloma through extensive screening of primary human tumor specimens and found that the specificity of this antigen is due to altered protein glycosylation [57]. This provides a new dimension for neoantigen identification. In recent years, with the maturation of glycoproteomics [58,59], some researchers have pointed out that glycoproteomics has great potential for future applications in the identification of cancer-specific antigenic epitopes formed by post-translational modifications of proteins [60–62]. Many studies have revealed that tumor cells exhibit unique glycoproteins on their surfaces [63,64]. Therefore, the integration of glycomics and glycoproteomics into neoantigen discovery platforms is of great significance for neoantigen identification [60]. To better identify immunogenic neoantigens, researchers have recently introduced tumor organoids into neoantigen identification. Organoids can better mimic the structure and function of in situ tumor cells in vitro [65,66]. Using this method, researchers characterized the HLA-class-I neoantigen landscape in hepatobiliary tumors, providing a practical strategy with a tumor organoid model for neoantigen peptide identification in personalized immunotherapy [67]. In conclusion, during the three decades of the development of tumor neoantigen identification, many prediction methods for neoantigens have been developed based on the continuous development of two major technologies—NGS and MS (Figure 1). Nowadays, the superficial neoantigen-based library has been basically tapped, so we need to use new means and methods to tap the potential neoantigen library.

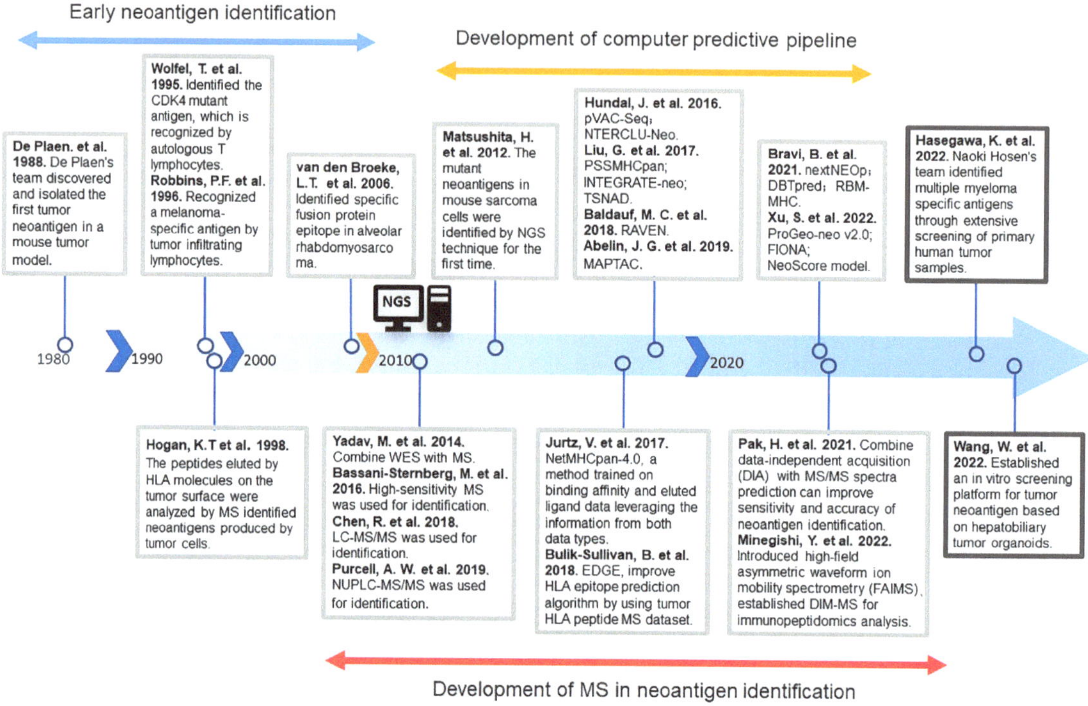

Figure 1. The history of the development of neoantigen identification [19–21,23,24,26,27,29,37,38,45,47–51,57,67–71].

3. Microbial and Tumor Neoantigens

3.1. Homology of Microbes and Tumor Neoantigens

Individuals are exposed to an environment full of various microbes, and tumors are not independent of the environment. Tumorigenesis is closely related to the contribution of pathogens in the environment—for instance, the common human papillomavirus (HPV) [72], the hepatitis B/C virus (HBV, HCV) [73], the Epstein–Barr virus (EBV) [74], and some cancer-inducing pathogenic bacteria such as *Helicobacter pylori* [75]. Meanwhile, some microbes have also been closely associated with cancer therapies [76]. In recent years, microbial relevance has been increasingly found in the study of tumor neoantigens [56,77–79]. Here, we describe the significance of microbes in tumor neoantigens. After nearly three decades of research, many neoantigens have been identified. However, not all of them are highly immunogenic. Searching for tumor neoantigens that are immunogenic and can activate T-cell responses is the key to targeted tumor therapy. Several reports have indicated that many neoantigens have been found to be homologous to microbial-derived peptides [56,77,78,80] (see Table 1). And such derived peptides usually have the same epitope core as the tumor neoantigen [81]. Furthermore, some studies have shown that neoantigens homologous to pathogenic antigens are more likely to be immunogenic than non-homologous neoantigens [82,83], which makes microbes very attractive in the field of tumor neoantigen research.

Table 1. Tumor neoantigens that share homologs with microbial peptides.

Neoantigen Peptide	Microbial Peptide	Tumor Type/Species	Microbial Species	Reference
NLLGRNSFK	LLGRNSFEV	Pancreatic ductal adenocarcinoma/Human	*Homo sapiens*	[56]
QEFENIKSY	QRFHNIRGR	Pancreatic ductal adenocarcinoma/Human	*Human papillomavirus*	[56]
GIICLDYKL	TMGVLCLAIL	Pancreatic ductal adenocarcinoma/Human	*Dengue virus*	[56]
LLLMSTLGI	LLMGTLGIV	Pancreatic ductal adenocarcinoma/Human	*Human papillomavirus*	[56]
QTYQHMWNY	AFWAKHMWNF	Pancreatic ductal adenocarcinoma/Human	*Hepatitis C virus*	[56]
LPRQYWEAL	KLLPEGYWV	Pancreatic ductal adenocarcinoma/Human	*Francisella tularensis*	[56]
RPQGQRPAL	SPRGSRPSW	Pancreatic ductal adenocarcinoma/Human	*Hepatitis C virus*	[56]
RVWDIVPTL	KPWDVVPTV	Pancreatic ductal adenocarcinoma/Human	*Dengue virus*	[56]
SIYRYYGL	SVYRYYGL	Melanomas/Mouse	*Bifidobacterium breve*	[77]
GSLARFRNI	TSLARFANI	MCA205 sarcomas and TC1 lung cancers)/Mouse	*Siphoviridae phages*	[78]
TLAGFWARL	RLAGFFPRL	CT26 M12/Mouse	*Ruminococcaceae*	[80]
PGPWRSGRLL	LGPWRSGGVL	CT26 M19/Mouse	*Bacteroidales/Prevotella/ Muribaculacee*	[80]
SMPGPWRSG	SLPGSWRSL	CT26 M19/Mouse	*Bacteria*	[80]
YIALVDKNI	YIALFDGFI	CT26 M39/Mouse	*Duncaniella/Bacteroides/ Bacteroidales*	[80]

A major source of tumor neoantigens is the peptides encoded by viral genes [4]. These oncogenic viral-encoded molecules can be used to distinguish tumor cells from normal cells, exhibiting unique characteristics of tumor cells and being a major target for early neoantigen identification [84]. Viruses enter cells and use host cells to encode their own proteins. These peptides are presented on the surface of tumor cells and can be judged as non-self peptides by the host immune system, triggering an immune effect that specifically kills tumor cells. With the continuous enrichment of the Antigen Peptide Library, Ragone C. et al. recently screened all tumor-associated antigens (TAAs) in the literature and compared them with proteins from viral sequences in a homology search. They found 82 viral sequences homologous to TAAs, showing a high homology of sequence and structure between TAAs and viral sequences [85]. In some cases, this homology is striking, and this high-homology epitope does not resemble a random event. Researchers previously performed neoantigen prediction in patients with HCV-induced hepatocellular carcinoma (HCC) and found that mutated neoantigens showed >50% sequence similarity to pathogen-associated antigens (PaAs) [55]. Bioinformatics tools have also been developed to identify tumor peptides with high similarity to viral epitopes. This could help us better recognize tumor neoantigens that are homologous to pathogens [86].

In addition to the presence of neoantigen homologous sequences in pathogenic viruses, the bacterial community, especially the gut microbiota, is also considered a potential source for neoantigens. Most of the immune system's exposure to the external environment occurs in the gastrointestinal tissue. The gut microbiome encodes more than 3 million genes in total, while the individual human genome has about 23,000 genes [87], so there is a high probability of homology between the two. The resident gut microbiota induces multiple reactions within the human body and is a great source of variant antigens [88]. A research team recently compared the homology of TAAs with the peptides from species of the *Firmicutes* and *Bacteroidetes phyla*, which together account for 90% of gut microbiota. They found a high degree of homology [89], which demonstrates the interactions between the microbiota colonizing the organism and tumor tissue. For instance, an epitope SVYRYYGL (SVY) was identified in the genome of the commensal bacterium *Bifidobacterium breve* (*B. breve*), which is homologous to the neoepitope antigen SIYRYYGL (SIY) expressed in B16 tumor models [77].

These studies suggest that homology between microbes and tumor neoantigens does not exist by chance (see Table 1). Additionally, the studies revealed that these highly similar sequences may harbor great potential for cancer therapy.

3.2. Immune Response Induced by Microbial Neoantigen Mimicry

These microbial-derived peptides that resemble tumor neoantigens are molecular mimicry, which is a concept that is widely used in the field of autoimmunity [90,91]. Molecular mimicry is the sharing of sequence or structural similarity between foreign antigens and self-antigens; thus, T cell receptors (TCRs) that recognize pathogenic antigens can also recognize self-antigens. In recent years, with the continued discovery of microbial-derived peptides, this molecular mimicry theory has been extended to the field of cancer [92–94]. This theory holds that neoantigens that share structural features with microbial antigens are more likely to be immunogenic and recognized by TCR libraries. Some researchers have further indicated how this molecular mimicry affects the immune response. Exposure of the body to microbes produces memory T cells, which further recognize tumor surface antigens homologous to microbial antigens. This recognition results in cross-reactivity, ultimately killing tumor cells (Figure 2) [82]. This theory was confirmed in several studies. For instance, one study found that the phage-encoded TMP peptide expressed in *Enterococcus hirae* (*E. hirae*) has the MHC1-binding epitope TSLARFANI and carries this prophage-containing *E. hirae*-induced T-cell anticancer responses in mice and humans. In patients with kidney cancer and lung adenocarcinoma, another *E. hirae* TMP-derived peptide, KLAKFASVV, was found to potentially elicit an anticancer immune response to the non-mutated tumor antigen KLQKFASTV contained in the GPD1-L protein [78]. This finding demonstrates cross-reactivity between commensal microbial antigens and tumor antigens. It has also been found that SVYRYYGL (SVY), which is expressed in *B. breve* in the intestinal commensal bacteria, is homologous to the neoantigen SIYRYYGL (SIY) expressed in the B16 tumor model. Moreover, mice lacking *B. breve* were found to have reduced SVY-reactive T cells and faster tumor growth compared to mice colonized with *B. breve*. This shows that the neoantigen mimicry of commensal bacteria can stimulate anti-tumor immune responses through T-cell cross-reactivity [77]. Furthermore, the possible role of "molecular mimicry" in anticancer immunity is supported by the identification of sequences highly homologous to immunogenic neoepitopes of CT26 cells in the proteome of specific intestinal flora (the abundance of which directly correlates with tumor regression) of a BALB/c-CT26 cancer mouse model treated with oral *Bifidobacterium* [80]. To evaluate the molecular mimicry theory, a research team engineered *Escherichia coli Nissle* to take on the SIINFEKL epitope (OVA-*E. coli Nissle*). They then orally administered this engineered *E. coli* to C57BL/6 mice. Compared to controls, OVA-*E. coli Nissle* induced OVA-specific CD8^{+} T cells and inhibited the growth of OVA-expressing B16F10 melanoma cells. Next, researchers took a shotgun sequencing of the microbiome. They sequenced the TCR of T cells and demonstrated that the main reason for tumor suppression was mediated by cross-reactive T cells triggered at the intestinal site [95]. These findings confirmed that the microbes can trigger T cell cross-reactivity through their own expression of peptides that are highly similar to tumor antigens and thus affect tumor development.

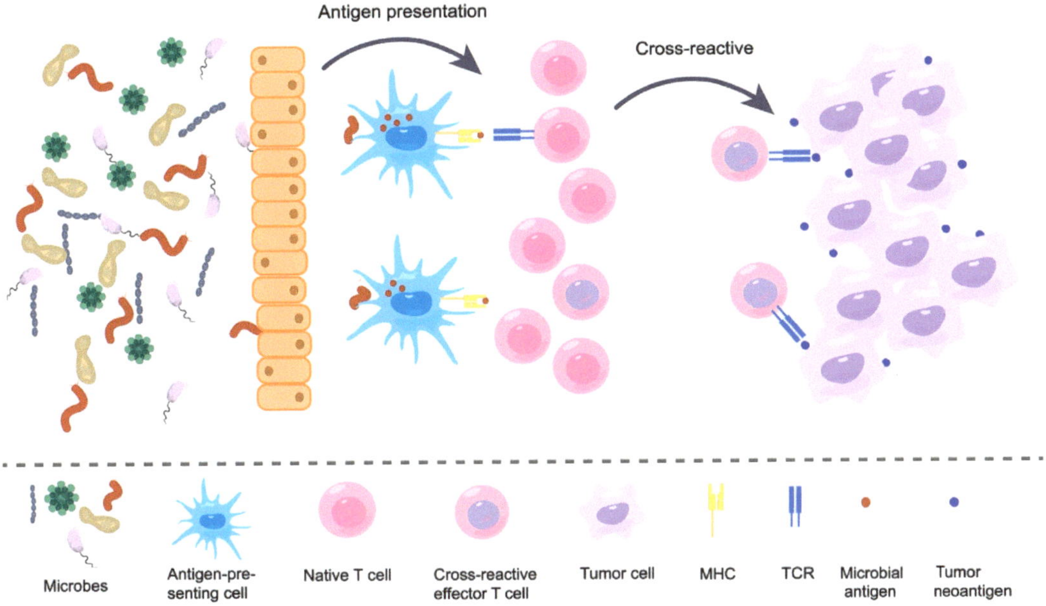

Figure 2. Microbes induce T-cell cross-reactivity by mimicking tumor neoantigens.

Although these studies have confirmed that microbial molecular mimicry can inhibit tumor growth through T-cell cross-reactivity, there is still a lack of evidence and studies on whether their presence is universal and whether they have an effective stimulation effect on T cells. It has been shown that tumors are flooded with anti-microbial T cells, such as tumor-infiltrating cytotoxic T lymphocytes (TIL). Moreover, CD8$^+$ TILs present in human lung and colorectal cancer are not only specific for tumor antigens but also recognize viral epitopes [96]. Researchers used bioinformatics techniques to compare tumor antigen libraries with intestinal bacteria and viral sequences and found substantial sequence homology between them [85,89]. Furthermore, some investigators have identified peptides from intracellular bacteria in melanoma tumors with the help of HLA peptidomics and 16S rRNA sequencing. They demonstrate that the bacteria that colonize melanoma tumors can enter melanoma cells and that their peptides can be presented on the surface of tumor cells [97]. In a recent study, researchers injected persistently infected cytomegalovirus mouse (MCMV)-derived T cell epitopes into tumors. They found that CMV-specific T-cell responses could be redirected into tumors to stimulate anti-tumor immune responses [98]. It is suggested that viral-derived peptide epitopes can effectively activate anti-tumor T-cell responses.

Individuals are exposed to an environment full of various microbes. These microbes enter the body through a barrier and are recognized by patrolling immune cells, such as antigen-presenting cells. Subsequently, they are presented on MHC. These presented microbial antigens are recognized by T cells and cause T cells to activate and show killing effects. As the picture on the right shows, neoantigens presented on the surface of tumor cells are sometimes highly similar to these microbial antigens. Thus, T cells that recognize microbial antigens can also recognize similar tumor neoantigens, causing T cell cross-reactivity and eventually killing tumor cells.

4. Applications of Microbes in the Treatment of Tumor Neoantigens

4.1. Application of Microbes in Tumor Neoantigen Vaccines

Tumor neoantigens, with their highly specific expression, have long been considered ideal targets for tumor therapy [99]. In 2017, two articles published in the journal Nature simultaneously reported on the therapeutic role of individualized tumor neoantigen vaccines in human melanoma. One was a 15–30 amino acid peptide mixture vaccine using poly-ICLC (a TLR3 stimulator) as an adjuvant [100], and the other was an mRNA vaccine encoding multiple tumor neoantigen epitopes [101]. Vaccination of melanoma patients had a good therapeutic effect on patients, demonstrating the great potential of personalized neoantigen vaccines in tumor therapy. However, less than 1% of mutant neoantigens in cancer cells can be spontaneously presented to the immune system to elicit an immune response [102]. Therefore, neoantigen vaccines need to be developed with the help of suitable vectors. Efficient tumor vaccines usually require the assistance of immune adjuvants and delivery vectors [103]. Microbes and their components, as natural foreign substances that can enter the host immune system and synergistically promote the immune response, have been widely used as vaccine-delivery vehicles and adjuvants [104]. They have also been explored in the delivery of tumor antigens [16,17]. Several recent studies have found that these microbial components also achieve good outcomes in the delivery of neoantigen vaccines. There is a study in which a tumor neoantigen was incorporated into the vaccine vector of attenuated *Listeria* monocytogenes (Lm). It was found that the vaccine effectively induced activation of specific $CD8^+$ T cells and prevented tumor growth [105]. These vaccine delivery vectors derived from microbial components are diverse [106,107]. Here, we focus on neoantigen delivery platforms based on bacterial outer membrane vesicles (OMV) and phages. They have recently achieved good therapeutic outcomes in the application of neoantigen vaccines and are considered to be efficient vaccine vectors [18].

4.1.1. Bacterial Outer Membrane Vesicles and Delivery of Neoantigen Vaccines

OMVs are spherical particles derived from Gram-negative bacteria [108]. These vesicles contain many immunogenic substances from parental bacteria and have the ability to activate the innate immune system. Furthermore, they can be genetically engineered to express selected antigens, thus having great potential for vaccine production [109]. Recently, researchers have used a "plug-and-display" strategy to fuse foreign tumor neoantigens with Cly-A, a protein commonly found on the surface of OMVs, using recombinant gene technology to present exogenous antigens on the surface of OMVs. It was demonstrated that this tumor antigen displayed on the surface of OMVs could induce T cell-mediated specific anti-tumor immunity. They also developed a bioengineered tumor antigen display system for OMVs capable of displaying multiple antigens simultaneously, which provides great value for the development of individualized tumor vaccines [110]. There is also an mRNA vaccine platform based on the same "plug-and-display" strategy. By genetic engineering, the archaeal RNA-binding protein L7Ae was fused to the C-terminus of the OMV surface protein ClyA. Then, the mRNA was modified in vitro, ultimately designing an OMV that can effectively display mRNA antigens. Moreover, pathogen-associated molecular patterns (PAMPs) in OMVs also enhance the activation effect of antigen-specific T cells and suppress tumor development [111]. Meanwhile, an in situ vaccine study of OMVs has shown an alternative treatment option. Photothermal therapy (PTT) can activate tumor-specific T cells by releasing tumor antigens. Here, researchers constructed an OMV in situ vaccine, OMV-Mal, that captured these tumor antigens. They demonstrated that this vaccine could effectively deliver tumor antigens to dendritic cells and ultimately activate anti-tumor immune responses with the help of OMVs [17]. OMVs can integrate vectors and adjuvants in tumor vaccines to activate multiple immune signaling pathways to their own advantage [112], providing a significant role in tumor neoantigen vaccine therapy value.

4.1.2. Phage and Neoantigen Vaccine Delivery

In addition to these bacterial-derived components, phages are also considered an ideal vehicle for neoantigen vaccines due to their characteristics [113]. The phage display technique was first introduced by Smith et al. in 1985 [114], which allows the expression of a variety of exogenous peptides on the surface of phages, targeting a variety of molecules [115,116]. Phage particles can also act as a foreign substance recognized by the body's immune system and presented by antigen-presenting cells to MHC I or MHC II molecules, inducing specific humoral or cellular immunity. This makes phages attractive vaccine carriers [117]. In recent years, the display of antigen peptides on the surface of phages with the help of this technique has become increasingly considered an effective cancer vaccine delivery strategy [118]. Many researchers have successfully constructed vaccines expressing tumor antigens with the help of phages. For example, a recombinant T7 phage vaccine expressing a new epitope of the B16-F10 melanoma cell mutant protein was constructed. And it was found that vaccination with these vaccines induced B-lymphocyte responses in mice and the effective production of specific antibodies [119]. Another study constructed a λ-phage vaccine displaying the HER2/neu-derived peptide GP2, which was vaccinated in a BALB/c mouse transplantation tumor model, showing that this fusion peptide-expressing phage nanoparticles induced a robust cytotoxic T lymphocyte (CTL) response [120]. These achievements demonstrate the great progress of phage display technology in the development of neoantigen vaccines, yet the development of efficient vaccine platforms remains a great challenge. Recently, some researchers have developed several efficient neoantigenic vaccine presentation platforms using phage display technology. Li W. et al. designed an antigen peptide vaccine delivery system based on P22 virus-like particles (VLPs). They prepared two types of vaccine particles (VLP-OVAB and VLP-OVAT) by presenting the B-epitope and the T-epitope of ovalbumin (OVA) in VLPs that were selected from the P22 phage. In their experiments, VLP-OVAB induced high titer antibody levels (5.0×10^5) and effectively activated CTL responses by cross-presentation, while VLP-OVAT induced strong immune activation and immune memory and remarkably inhibited tumor growth [121]. Another study developed a vaccine delivery platform (HMP@Ag) that can deliver personal tumor antigens by M13 phage using a chemical approach to adsorb various antigen substances onto M13 phages by electrostatic. When the mice were vaccinated subcutaneously, such a hybrid M13 phage carrier could effectively promote antigen delivery and cross-presentation and activate cytotoxic $CD8^+$ T cells. Furthermore, combining the HMP@Ag vaccine with immune checkpoint blockade (ICB) treatment can trigger a robust and specific anti-tumor immune response in several tumor models [122].

This microbial-derived biological nanoparticle material has demonstrated great application in the development and delivery of neoantigen vaccines due to its ability to carry naturally occurring PAMPs and the ease of genetic engineering modifications.

4.2. Microbes Improve Treatment of Immune Checkpoint Inhibitors (ICIs) by Influencing Neoantigens

4.2.1. Gut Microbes Play a Role in the Treatment of ICIs

With the rise of tumor immunotherapy, ICB therapy has become a major weapon in the fight against cancer over the past decades [123]. ICIs activate T cells and promote their anti-tumor function by targeting and blocking PD-1, PD-L1, CTLA-4, LAG3, and other immunosuppressive targets [124,125]. Immunotherapy with the help of ICIs has led to breakthroughs in the treatment of a variety of malignancies [123,126–128]. Additionally, a number of ICIs have been approved for clinical cancer treatment [129]. However, ICB therapies still have limitations, as they show low response rates (10–30%) in most cancer treatments (10–30%) [123] and present drug resistance [130,131], and only a small proportion of patients benefit from ICB. Therefore, it is necessary to further investigate the mechanism of ICB and find ways to improve the effectiveness of immune checkpoint blockade therapy.

Studies in recent years have found that the gut microbiota that interacts with the organism plays an important role in the treatment of ICIs. This influence has been confirmed in many cancer models. Two studies in 2015 in mouse models of melanoma first showed that gut microbiome composition can modulate the host immune system and influence the efficacy of anti-PD-L1 and anti-CTLA-4 treatments [132,133]. Influencing the host microbiota by administering antibiotics demonstrated that the intestinal microbiome significantly influenced the outcome of PD-1 blockade in mice and patients with non-small cell lung cancer (NSCLC) and kidney cell carcinoma (RCC) [134]. Analyzing the fecal microbiome of patients with hepatocellular carcinoma (HCC) during anti-PD-1 immunotherapy by macrogenomic sequencing revealed microbiome-specific changes and suggested an association between the gut microbiome and anti-PD-1 immunotherapy [135]. Immunotherapy with anti-PD-1 in an antibiotic-treated colorectal cancer (CRC) mouse model revealed that antibiotic injection counteracted the efficacy of the PD-1 antibody. Additionally, it was demonstrated that gut microbiome changes affected the tumor's immune microenvironment [136]. All these studies illustrate the critical role of microbes in ICB therapy. Most of these microbes are gut microbes because the gastrointestinal tract involves the entire digestive system and has an abundance of microbes [137]. Moreover, the gastrointestinal tract is relatively easy to study, allowing interventions by simple means [138,139]. Gut microbes not only inhibit tumor growth but also promote tumorigenesis and progression. Currently known oncogenic gut bacteria include *Salmonella typhi* [140] and *Helicobacter* spp. [141]. It has been found that certain microbes can also block the body's anti-tumor immune function and form a pro-inflammatory microenvironment that contributes to cancer progression. It is commonly believed that dysregulation of gut microbiota homeostasis is associated with cancer development and progression [142]. This dual role of gut microbes is due to the complexity of gut microbial species, with different species causing different consequences. For example, the antigenic peptide produced by the microbes described earlier causes T-cell cross-reactivity, and whether the immune response provoked by this antigenic peptide is pro- or anticancer depends on the specific peptide. Suppose it so happens that this antigenic peptide has similarities to tumor antigens. In that case, it may kill tumor cells, while other microbial peptides may cause host immune suppression or disruption of the immune system, with the disease progressing in a worsening direction [143]. Here, we focus on those microbes that may have a positive effect on cancer therapy.

Comprehensive analysis of 16S rRNA and shotgun metagenome sequencing of the gut microbiome revealed a significantly higher (2.5-fold) ratio of *Prevotella/Bacteroides* in the gut microbiome of gastrointestinal cancer patients who showed a better response to ICIs treatment [144]. In addition to these, a correlation between the abundance of *Akkermansia muciniphila* and the response to treatment with ICIs was found in the intestinal bacteria of patients with NSCLC and RCC [134]. In the analysis of the bacteria in melanoma patients, symbiotic *bifidobacteria* were found to play an important role in the anti-tumor process [133]. In patients with metastatic melanoma treated with anti-CTLA-4 checkpoint inhibitors, it was observed that patients enriched with *Faecalibacterium* and other *Firmicutes* had a better therapeutic effect [145]. In addition to the gut microbiome, microbiota at other sites, such as the skin and liver, showed a correlation with ICB therapy [146]. In conclusion, tumor-related microbes play an encouraging role in ICB therapy.

4.2.2. Microbes Enhance the Therapeutic Effect of ICIs by Molecular Mimicry

How exactly do these microbes affect ICB therapy? Why are they performing well in the treatment of ICIs? There is no conclusive answer yet. We know that a successful anti-tumor response in ICB therapy relies on the activation and proliferation of specific T cells. It is crucial to effectively activate tumor-specific T cells that target tumors during the whole treatment process [147]. The reasons for the poor therapeutic effect of ICIs can be briefly summarized into three categories: insufficient anti-tumor T cell production, insufficient tumor-specific T cell function, and memory T cell formation [148]. Microbial modulation of ICB therapy is ultimately achieved by affecting these immune cells and thus affecting tumor therapy. In 2016, Laurence et al. synthesized the findings at that time and proposed two microbial mechanism hypotheses for tumor immune surveillance that helped us better understand the role of microbes in ICB therapy. One mechanism is the antigen pathway, in which microbial antigens that are highly similar to tumor antigens activate specific anti-tumor T cells by affecting the immune system and generating T cell cross-reactivity. Another mechanism is the non-antigen pathway, in which these microbes regulate immune tonus through their own PAMPs, producing a series of metabolites such as interferons and cytokines to modulate T cell anti-tumor activity [92, 149]. In the treatment of ICIs, microbes can influence tumor therapeutic effects through both of these pathways.

In recent years, an increasing number of studies have provided evidence for the first antigen mimicry mechanism. Here, we focus on how microbes can influence immune checkpoint blockade therapy through tumor antigen mimicry. Tumor neoantigens, recognized by the immune system as external peptides, possess distinct specificity and immunogenicity. These neoantigens can be selectively engaged by T cells, which holds significance in the context of ICI treatment. The absence of these neoantigens can lead to therapy resistance [131]. ICB therapy can effectively activate tumor neoantigen-specific T cells for better anti-tumor effects [11,150]. At the same time, microbes can help activate specific T cells through antigen mimicry, enhancing the therapeutic effect of ICIs. In 2020, researchers found that the commensal bacterium *Bifidobacterium breve* (*B. breve*) contains a peptide (SVY) that is highly similar to a melanoma-specific epitope. They also found that mice lacking *B. breve* had fewer SVY-reactive T cells and faster tumor growth. They further demonstrated that *B. breve* can specifically kill tumor cells by causing T-cell cross-reactivity through antigen mimicry [77]. In addition, previous studies found that *B. breve* from gut microbes plays an important role in the anti-tumor process in melanoma patients and can combine with PD-L1 antibodies to produce a good therapeutic effect in mice [133]. These two studies provide us with a thought that perhaps *B. breve* enhances the anti-PD-L1 therapeutic effect of melanoma by T-cell activation through molecular mimicry. In addition, another study identified a tail length tape measure protein (TMP) of prophage in the bacteriophage *Enterococcus hirae* genome that could bind MHC I epitopes and induce memory $CD8^+$ T-cell responses, which in turn cross-react with cancer antigens. Immunotherapy with anti-PD-1 induced TMP-specific $CD8^+$ T cell responses and showed that the presence of the bacteriophage *Enterococcus hirae* and expression of TMP cross-reactive antigens correlated with the long-term efficacy of PD-1 blockade therapy in patients with kidney and lung cancer [78]. These examples suggest that microbial-associated peptides can activate anti-tumor T cells through cross-reactivity to target tumor cells with neoepitopes in ICB therapy.

4.2.3. Use of Microbes to Enhance the Treatment of ICIs

The hypothesis about the effect of microbes through antigen mimicry has gradually become convincing in recent years [149,151]. High tumor mutation burden (TMB) significantly improves the ICI's therapeutic effect, as demonstrated in many studies [152,153]. Although tumor-specific antigens are mechanistically thought to promote ICB therapy, they lack further therapeutic potential. In contrast, the microbiome can be more dynamically regulated to influence T-cell responses against tumor-specific epitopes and thus improve the efficacy of ICIs [81]. And interventions such as probiotic supplementation and increased microbial diversity could be considered rational therapeutic approaches for clinical investigation [13].

Fecal microbiota transplantation (FMT) therapy has shown promising effects in recent studies. FMT therapy allows the transfer of the entire gut microbiota from one host to another, usually transferring the gut microbiota from patients who have responded to ICI therapy to immune-tolerant patients [154]. Recently, researchers have achieved positive outcomes in phase I clinical trials by using FMT treatment. It was shown that after treatment with FMT and anti-PD-1 re-induction, three out of ten patients with melanoma lacking responsiveness to anti-PD-1 therapy had a decrease in tumor volume. Notably, two of these had complete remission and one had partial remission [155]. Another clinical trial evaluated the safety and efficacy of FMT in combination with anti-PD-1 therapy in patients with PD-1 refractory melanoma. In this trial, six of fifteen patients demonstrated a beneficial response, with three patients achieving remission and three patients having stable disease [156]. In both trials, a good safety profile was demonstrated, showing great value in clinical treatment. In addition to this, there are also many clinical trials of combined treatment with FMT and ICIs currently underway [157].

Furthermore, modifying microbes via genetic engineering or using their own characteristics and then delivering them back into the body to work is also a convenient and feasible treatment modality [158]. Through genetic engineering, these microbes can carry various target genes to improve the therapeutic effect of ICIs. Among them, the combination therapy of oncolytic viruses (OVs) and ICIs has shown good promise. OVs have good properties that cause the lysis of tumor cells to release tumor neoantigens and activate specific T cells, and they are widely used in immunotherapy [159]. In parallel, clinical trials using OVs in cancer therapy have highlighted the importance of combining them with checkpoint inhibitors [160,161]. For example, local infection with OVs in tumor models with resistance to ICIs therapy revealed that OV infection triggered activation of T cells targeting tumor neoepitopes, significantly eliminating systemic resistance to PD-1 immunotherapy and improving the elimination of disseminated lung tumors [162]. In addition to those, OV can be designed to express various immunomodulatory genes [163]. Many combination therapies have been developed, such as when researchers engineered a new oncolytic herpes simplex virus (oHSV) expressing a single-chain antibody against PD-1 (scFvPD-1) and evaluated its efficacy against glioblastoma (GBM). This confirms that it induced durable anti-tumor responses in a preclinical mouse model of GBM [164]. Also, researchers generated an engineered OV co-expressing PD-L1 inhibitor and a genetically modified granulocyte-macrophage colony-stimulating factor (GM-CSF). When these engineered OVs were injected into tumors, they overcame PD-L1-mediated immunosuppression during both the priming and effector phases, activated a systemic T-cell response, and led to an effective rejection of both virus-injected and distant tumors [165].

5. Conclusions and Perspectives

Immunotherapy targeting tumor neoantigens has attracted many researchers in recent years and is considered to have great promise in cancer immunotherapy [166]. However, neoantigen-driven immunotherapies still face great challenges in clinical application [167], such as an insufficient number of neoantigens with immunogenicity and inadequate activation of specific T cells targeting neoepitopes. In the early days of neoantigen identification, researchers mainly targeted single nucleotide-producing mutations due to technical limitations. After decades of development, the content of neoantigens has been continuously expanded, and more and more previously unnoticed neoepitope types have been classified as tumor neoantigens [4]. The exploitation of potential neoantigen pools, especially those with high immunogenicity, has been a constant research direction in related fields. Abnormalities can occur during gene expression, transcription, translation, and post-translational modifications, which can lead to the formation of neoepitopes. Although some studies have shown that some classes of neoantigens are more protective, there are no comprehensive studies to determine which are the most effective neoantigens [8]. In recent years, neoepitopes that are highly similar to microbial-derived peptides have been found to exhibit good immunogenicity in studies [56,77]. Some researchers have introduced the concept of homology with pathogenic peptides in the comprehensive assessment models constructed for the immunogenicity of neoantigens [168]. Homology comparison with foreign microbial peptides may be a feasible approach for the identification of neoantigens.

We are exposed to an environment populated by microbes. These microbes not only regulate the health of the body but also influence the onset and development of disease. Recent advances in oncology have listed the polymorphic microbiome among the fourteen features of malignancy [169]. Several studies have shown that the flora in the body plays an important role in immunity [13]. For example, in the microbiome-enriched gastrointestinal tract, it has been found that the efficacy of ICB therapy for malignant tumors is closely linked to intestinal flora. And some specific microbial species are highly correlated with the effectiveness of therapies such as anti-PD-1/PD-L1 [132,133]. In addition, probiotic supplementation or the use of FMT therapy during cancer immunotherapy can also help treatment [154–156]. Although the exact mechanism of microbial influence on immunotherapy remains unclear, recent studies have found that microbes, through their own peptides that are highly similar to tumor antigens, may be able to influence the immune system. This generates a T-cell cross-reaction, activating specific anti-tumor T cells. Meanwhile, some studies have found that these microbial antigenic peptides, which are similar to tumor neoantigens, play an important role in immune checkpoint therapy [77,78]. These examples remind us that perhaps the combination of immune checkpoint inhibitors with HLA that mimic tumor antigen-like peptides will improve therapeutic and prognostic outcomes.

Currently, many researchers are working on the development of new antigenic vaccines for cancer. Additionally, many vaccines are being evaluated in early clinical trials, such as synthetic long peptide (SLP) vaccines, dendritic cell (DC) vaccines, and nucleic acid vaccines [7]. The success of cancer vaccines is influenced by many factors, among which the superiority of the vaccine platform is an important reason [170], and the development of a simple and efficient cancer vaccine platform is necessary. As described above, microbes such as bacteria and phages are structurally simple. They can be modified by genetic engineering and have exogenous immunogenicity, which plays a significant role in cancer vaccine development and is a good delivery vehicle [18,106,111,120]. They have great potential for neoantigen vaccine development.

Regardless of which therapeutic technique is used, the fundamental aim of cancer immunotherapy is to regulate the patient's own immune system, causing immune cells to attack the tumor [2,12]. In practical research and applications, neoantigens with high immunogenicity and efficient and convenient therapeutic approaches are worth continuously exploring. The microbes that fill our lives are closely linked to the development of cancer. As mentioned above, microbes play an important role in the therapeutic process against tumor neoantigens [16,17,104]. There is evidence that tumor neoantigens homologous to peptides from microbes could better activate anti-tumor immune responses during therapy [77,78]. However, the evidence is currently scarce, and more studies are needed to reveal confirmation in the future. It is also important to consider how to use this property to treat tumors. The good results triggered by FMT in the treatment of ICIs may be related to this effect. Some specific microbial species have been identified to play a role in this process [133,145,154,155], and whether these microbes can be better used in the treatment of ICIs still needs to be explored. In addition, developing more microbial tools, such as vaccine delivery vectors, adjuvants, etc., will also facilitate immunotherapy against neoantigens in tumors.

Funding: This work was supported by the National Natural Science Foundation of China (82073261), the China 111 Project (111-2-12), the Natural Science Foundation of Changsha (kq2202125), and the Hunan Province Science and Technology Project (2021SK2021).

Institutional Review Board Statement: Not applicable.

Informed Consent Statement: Not applicable.

Data Availability Statement: Not applicable.

Conflicts of Interest: The authors declare no conflict of interest.

References

1. Gilboa, E. The makings of a tumor rejection antigen. *Immunity* **1999**, *11*, 263–270. [CrossRef] [PubMed]
2. Schumacher, T.N.; Schreiber, R.D. Neoantigens in cancer immunotherapy. *Science* **2015**, *348*, 69–74. [CrossRef] [PubMed]
3. Tran, E.; Turcotte, S.; Gros, A.; Robbins, P.F.; Lu, Y.C.; Dudley, M.E.; Wunderlich, J.R.; Somerville, R.P.; Hogan, K.; Hinrichs, C.S.; et al. Cancer immunotherapy based on mutation-specific CD4+ T cells in a patient with epithelial cancer. *Science* **2014**, *344*, 641–645. [CrossRef]
4. Nagel, R.; Pataskar, A.; Champagne, J.; Agami, R. Boosting Antitumor Immunity with an Expanded Neoepitope Landscape. *Cancer Res.* **2022**, *82*, 3637–3649. [CrossRef] [PubMed]
5. Lang, F.; Schrors, B.; Lower, M.; Tureci, O.; Sahin, U. Identification of neoantigens for individualized therapeutic cancer vaccines. *Nat. Rev. Drug Discov.* **2022**, *21*, 261–282. [CrossRef]
6. Lu, Y.C.; Robbins, P.F. Cancer immunotherapy targeting neoantigens. *Semin. Immunol.* **2016**, *28*, 22–27. [CrossRef]
7. Supabphol, S.; Li, L.; Goedegebuure, S.P.; Gillanders, W.E. Neoantigen vaccine platforms in clinical development: Understanding the future of personalized immunotherapy. *Expert Opin. Investig. Drugs* **2021**, *30*, 529–541. [CrossRef]
8. Redwood, A.J.; Dick, I.M.; Creaney, J.; Robinson, B.W.S. What's next in cancer immunotherapy?—The promise and challenges of neoantigen vaccination. *OncoImmunology* **2022**, *11*, 2038403. [CrossRef]
9. Sun, C.; Xu, S. Advances in personalized neoantigen vaccines for cancer immunotherapy. *Biosci. Trends* **2020**, *14*, 349–353. [CrossRef]
10. Arnaud, M.; Bobisse, S.; Chiffelle, J.; Harari, A. The Promise of Personalized TCR-Based Cellular Immunotherapy for Cancer Patients. *Front. Immunol.* **2021**, *12*, 701636. [CrossRef]
11. Gubin, M.M.; Zhang, X.; Schuster, H.; Caron, E.; Ward, J.P.; Noguchi, T.; Ivanova, Y.; Hundal, J.; Arthur, C.D.; Krebber, W.J.; et al. Checkpoint blockade cancer immunotherapy targets tumour-specific mutant antigens. *Nature* **2014**, *515*, 577–581. [CrossRef] [PubMed]
12. Abbott, M.; Ustoyev, Y. Cancer and the Immune System: The History and Background of Immunotherapy. *Semin. Oncol. Nurs.* **2019**, *35*, 150923. [CrossRef] [PubMed]
13. Finlay, B.B.; Goldszmid, R.; Honda, K.; Trinchieri, G.; Wargo, J.; Zitvogel, L. Can we harness the microbiota to enhance the efficacy of cancer immunotherapy? *Nat. Rev. Immunol.* **2020**, *20*, 522–528. [CrossRef] [PubMed]
14. Luu, M.; Riester, Z.; Baldrich, A.; Reichardt, N.; Yuille, S.; Busetti, A.; Klein, M.; Wempe, A.; Leister, H.; Raifer, H.; et al. Microbial short-chain fatty acids modulate CD8+ T cell responses and improve adoptive immunotherapy for cancer. *Nat. Commun.* **2021**, *12*, 4077. [CrossRef]
15. Derosa, L.; Routy, B.; Desilets, A.; Daillère, R.; Terrisse, S.; Kroemer, G.; Zitvogel, L. Microbiota-Centered Interventions: The Next Breakthrough in Immuno-Oncology? *Cancer Discov.* **2021**, *11*, 2396–2412. [CrossRef]
16. Chen, L.; Qin, H.; Zhao, R.; Zhao, X.; Lin, L.; Chen, Y.; Lin, Y.; Li, Y.; Qin, Y.; Li, Y.; et al. Bacterial cytoplasmic membranes synergistically enhance the antitumor activity of autologous cancer vaccines. *Sci. Transl. Med.* **2021**, *13*, eabc2816. [CrossRef]
17. Li, Y.; Zhang, K.; Wu, Y.; Yue, Y.; Cheng, K.; Feng, Q.; Ma, X.; Liang, J.; Ma, N.; Liu, G.; et al. Antigen Capture and Immune Modulation by Bacterial Outer Membrane Vesicles as In Situ Vaccine for Cancer Immunotherapy Post-Photothermal Therapy. *Small* **2022**, *18*, e2107461. [CrossRef]
18. Xie, J.; Li, Q.; Haesebrouck, F.; Van Hoecke, L.; Vandenbroucke, R.E. The tremendous biomedical potential of bacterial extracellular vesicles. *Trends Biotechnol.* **2022**, *40*, 1173–1194. [CrossRef]
19. De Plaen, E.; Lurquin, C.; Van Pel, A.; Mariame, B.; Szikora, J.P.; Wolfel, T.; Sibille, C.; Chomez, P.; Boon, T. Immunogenic (tum-) variants of mouse tumor P815: Cloning of the gene of tum- antigen P91A and identification of the tum- mutation. *Proc. Natl. Acad. Sci. USA* **1988**, *85*, 2274–2278. [CrossRef]
20. Wolfel, T.; Hauer, M.; Schneider, J.; Serrano, M.; Wolfel, C.; Klehmann-Hieb, E.; De Plaen, E.; Hankeln, T.; Meyer zum Buschenfelde, K.H.; Beach, D. A p16INK4a-insensitive CDK4 mutant targeted by cytolytic T lymphocytes in a human melanoma. *Science* **1995**, *269*, 1281–1284. [CrossRef]
21. Robbins, P.F.; El-Gamil, M.; Li, Y.F.; Kawakami, Y.; Loftus, D.; Appella, E.; Rosenberg, S.A. A mutated beta-catenin gene encodes a melanoma-specific antigen recognized by tumor infiltrating lymphocytes. *J. Exp. Med.* **1996**, *183*, 1185–1192. [CrossRef] [PubMed]
22. Zhou, J.; Dudley, M.E.; Rosenberg, S.A.; Robbins, P.F. Persistence of multiple tumor-specific T-cell clones is associated with complete tumor regression in a melanoma patient receiving adoptive cell transfer therapy. *J. Immunother.* **2005**, *28*, 53–62. [CrossRef] [PubMed]
23. Hogan, K.T.; Eisinger, D.P.; Cupp, S.B., 3rd; Lekstrom, K.J.; Deacon, D.D.; Shabanowitz, J.; Hunt, D.F.; Engelhard, V.H.; Slingluff, C.L., Jr.; Ross, M.M. The peptide recognized by HLA-A68.2-restricted, squamous cell carcinoma of the lung-specific cytotoxic T lymphocytes is derived from a mutated elongation factor 2 gene. *Cancer Res.* **1998**, *58*, 5144–5150. [PubMed]
24. Matsushita, H.; Vesely, M.D.; Koboldt, D.C.; Rickert, C.G.; Uppaluri, R.; Magrini, V.J.; Arthur, C.D.; White, J.M.; Chen, Y.S.; Shea, L.K.; et al. Cancer exome analysis reveals a T-cell-dependent mechanism of cancer immunoediting. *Nature* **2012**, *482*, 400–404. [CrossRef]
25. Robbins, P.F.; Lu, Y.C.; El-Gamil, M.; Li, Y.F.; Gross, C.; Gartner, J.; Lin, J.C.; Teer, J.K.; Cliften, P.; Tycksen, E.; et al. Mining exomic sequencing data to identify mutated antigens recognized by adoptively transferred tumor-reactive T cells. *Nat. Med.* **2013**, *19*, 747–752. [CrossRef]

26. Hundal, J.; Carreno, B.M.; Petti, A.A.; Linette, G.P.; Griffith, O.L.; Mardis, E.R.; Griffith, M. pVAC-Seq: A genome-guided in silico approach to identifying tumor neoantigens. *Genome Med.* **2016**, *8*, 11. [CrossRef]
27. Liu, G.; Li, D.; Li, Z.; Qiu, S.; Li, W.; Chao, C.C.; Yang, N.; Li, H.; Cheng, Z.; Song, X.; et al. PSSMHCpan: A novel PSSM-based software for predicting class I peptide-HLA binding affinity. *Gigascience* **2017**, *6*, 1–11. [CrossRef]
28. Feng, P.; Zeng, J.; Ma, J. Predicting MHC-peptide binding affinity by differential boundary tree. *Bioinformatics* **2021**, *37*, i254–i261. [CrossRef]
29. Bravi, B.; Tubiana, J.; Cocco, S.; Monasson, R.; Mora, T.; Walczak, A.M. RBM-MHC: A Semi-Supervised Machine-Learning Method for Sample-Specific Prediction of Antigen Presentation by HLA-I Alleles. *Cell Syst.* **2021**, *12*, 195–202.e199. [CrossRef]
30. Rasmussen, M.; Fenoy, E.; Harndahl, M.; Kristensen, A.B.; Nielsen, I.K.; Nielsen, M.; Buus, S. Pan-Specific Prediction of Peptide-MHC Class I Complex Stability, a Correlate of T Cell Immunogenicity. *J. Immunol.* **2016**, *197*, 1517–1524. [CrossRef]
31. Blaha, D.T.; Anderson, S.D.; Yoakum, D.M.; Hager, M.V.; Zha, Y.; Gajewski, T.F.; Kranz, D.M. High-Throughput Stability Screening of Neoantigen/HLA Complexes Improves Immunogenicity Predictions. *Cancer Immunol. Res.* **2019**, *7*, 50–61. [CrossRef]
32. Zhou, Z.; Lyu, X.; Wu, J.; Yang, X.; Wu, S.; Zhou, J.; Gu, X.; Su, Z.; Chen, S. TSNAD: An integrated software for cancer somatic mutation and tumour-specific neoantigen detection. *R. Soc. Open Sci.* **2017**, *4*, 170050. [CrossRef] [PubMed]
33. Zhang, J.; Mardis, E.R.; Maher, C.A. INTEGRATE-neo: A pipeline for personalized gene fusion neoantigen discovery. *Bioinformatics* **2017**, *33*, 555–557. [CrossRef] [PubMed]
34. Rieder, D.; Fotakis, G.; Ausserhofer, M.; Rene, G.; Paster, W.; Trajanoski, Z.; Finotello, F. nextNEOpi: A comprehensive pipeline for computational neoantigen prediction. *Bioinformatics* **2021**, *38*, 1131–1132. [CrossRef] [PubMed]
35. Liu, C.; Zhang, Y.; Jian, X.; Tan, X.; Lu, M.; Ouyang, J.; Liu, Z.; Li, Y.; Xu, L.; Chen, L.; et al. ProGeo-Neo v2.0: A One-Stop Software for Neoantigen Prediction and Filtering Based on the Proteogenomics Strategy. *Genes* **2022**, *13*, 783. [CrossRef]
36. Schumacher, T.N.; Scheper, W.; Kvistborg, P. Cancer Neoantigens. *Annu. Rev. Immunol.* **2019**, *37*, 173–200. [CrossRef] [PubMed]
37. Abelin, J.G.; Harjanto, D.; Malloy, M.; Suri, P.; Colson, T.; Goulding, S.P.; Creech, A.L.; Serrano, L.R.; Nasir, G.; Nasrullah, Y.; et al. Defining HLA-II Ligand Processing and Binding Rules with Mass Spectrometry Enhances Cancer Epitope Prediction. *Immunity* **2019**, *51*, 766–779.e717. [CrossRef] [PubMed]
38. Xu, S.; Wang, X.; Fei, C. A Highly Effective System for Predicting MHC-II Epitopes with Immunogenicity. *Front. Oncol.* **2022**, *12*, 888556. [CrossRef]
39. Wu, J.; Chen, W.; Zhou, Y.; Chi, Y.; Hua, X.; Wu, J.; Gu, X.; Chen, S.; Zhou, Z. TSNAdb v2.0: The Updated Version of Tumor-specific Neoantigen Database. *Genom. Proteom. Bioinform.* **2022**. [CrossRef]
40. Li, W.; Sun, T.; Li, M.; He, Y.; Li, L.; Wang, L.; Wang, H.; Li, J.; Wen, H.; Liu, Y.; et al. GNIFdb: A neoantigen intrinsic feature database for glioma. *Database* **2022**, *2022*, baac004. [CrossRef]
41. Lu, M.; Xu, L.; Jian, X.; Tan, X.; Zhao, J.; Liu, Z.; Zhang, Y.; Liu, C.; Chen, L.; Lin, Y.; et al. dbPepNeo2.0: A Database for Human Tumor Neoantigen Peptides from Mass Spectrometry and TCR Recognition. *Front. Immunol.* **2022**, *13*, 855976. [CrossRef]
42. Chen, F.; Zou, Z.; Du, J.; Su, S.; Shao, J.; Meng, F.; Yang, J.; Xu, Q.; Ding, N.; Yang, Y.; et al. Neoantigen identification strategies enable personalized immunotherapy in refractory solid tumors. *J. Clin. Investig.* **2019**, *129*, 2056–2070. [CrossRef]
43. Polyakova, A.; Kuznetsova, K.; Moshkovskii, S. Proteogenomics meets cancer immunology: Mass spectrometric discovery and analysis of neoantigens. *Expert Rev. Proteom.* **2015**, *12*, 533–541. [CrossRef]
44. Zhang, X.; Qi, Y.; Zhang, Q.; Liu, W. Application of mass spectrometry-based MHC immunopeptidome profiling in neoantigen identification for tumor immunotherapy. *Biomed. Pharmacother.* **2019**, *120*, 109542. [CrossRef]
45. Yadav, M.; Jhunjhunwala, S.; Phung, Q.T.; Lupardus, P.; Tanguay, J.; Bumbaca, S.; Franci, C.; Cheung, T.K.; Fritsche, J.; Weinschenk, T.; et al. Predicting immunogenic tumour mutations by combining mass spectrometry and exome sequencing. *Nature* **2014**, *515*, 572–576. [CrossRef] [PubMed]
46. Kalaora, S.; Barnea, E.; Merhavi-Shoham, E.; Qutob, N.; Teer, J.K.; Shimony, N.; Schachter, J.; Rosenberg, S.A.; Besser, M.J.; Admon, A.; et al. Use of HLA peptidomics and whole exome sequencing to identify human immunogenic neo-antigens. *Oncotarget* **2016**, *7*, 5110–5117. [CrossRef] [PubMed]
47. Bassani-Sternberg, M.; Braunlein, E.; Klar, R.; Engleitner, T.; Sinitcyn, P.; Audehm, S.; Straub, M.; Weber, J.; Slotta-Huspenina, J.; Specht, K.; et al. Direct identification of clinically relevant neoepitopes presented on native human melanoma tissue by mass spectrometry. *Nat. Commun.* **2016**, *7*, 13404. [CrossRef] [PubMed]
48. Chen, R.; Fauteux, F.; Foote, S.; Stupak, J.; Tremblay, T.L.; Gurnani, K.; Fulton, K.M.; Weeratna, R.D.; Twine, S.M.; Li, J. Chemical Derivatization Strategy for Extending the Identification of MHC Class I Immunopeptides. *Anal. Chem.* **2018**, *90*, 11409–11416. [CrossRef]
49. Purcell, A.W.; Ramarathinam, S.H.; Ternette, N. Mass spectrometry-based identification of MHC-bound peptides for immunopeptidomics. *Nat. Protoc.* **2019**, *14*, 1687–1707. [CrossRef]
50. Jurtz, V.; Paul, S.; Andreatta, M.; Marcatili, P.; Peters, B.; Nielsen, M. NetMHCpan-4.0: Improved Peptide-MHC Class I Interaction Predictions Integrating Eluted Ligand and Peptide Binding Affinity Data. *J. Immunol.* **2017**, *199*, 3360–3368. [CrossRef]
51. Bulik-Sullivan, B.; Busby, J.; Palmer, C.D.; Davis, M.J.; Murphy, T.; Clark, A.; Busby, M.; Duke, F.; Yang, A.; Young, L.; et al. Deep learning using tumor HLA peptide mass spectrometry datasets improves neoantigen identification. *Nat. Biotechnol.* **2019**, *37*, 55–63. [CrossRef]
52. Zhou, L.Y.; Zou, F.; Sun, W. Prioritizing candidate peptides for cancer vaccines through predicting peptide presentation by HLA-I proteins. *Biometrics* **2022**. [CrossRef]

53. Chen, I.; Chen, M.Y.; Goedegebuure, S.P.; Gillanders, W.E. Challenges targeting cancer neoantigens in 2021: A systematic literature review. *Expert Rev. Vaccines* **2021**, *20*, 827–837. [CrossRef]
54. Strønen, E.; Toebes, M.; Kelderman, S.; van Buuren, M.M.; Yang, W.; van Rooij, N.; Donia, M.; Böschen, M.-L.; Lund-Johansen, F.; Olweus, J.; et al. Targeting of cancer neoantigens with donor-derived T cell receptor repertoires. *Science* **2016**, *352*, 1337–1341. [CrossRef] [PubMed]
55. Petrizzo, A.; Tagliamonte, M.; Mauriello, A.; Costa, V.; Aprile, M.; Esposito, R.; Caporale, A.; Luciano, A.; Arra, C.; Tornesello, M.L.; et al. Unique true predicted neoantigens (TPNAs) correlates with anti-tumor immune control in HCC patients. *J. Transl. Med.* **2018**, *16*, 286. [CrossRef] [PubMed]
56. Balachandran, V.P.; Łuksza, M.; Zhao, J.N.; Makarov, V.; Moral, J.A.; Remark, R.; Herbst, B.; Askan, G.; Bhanot, U.; Senbabaoglu, Y.; et al. Identification of unique neoantigen qualities in long-term survivors of pancreatic cancer. *Nature* **2017**, *551*, 512–516. [CrossRef] [PubMed]
57. Hasegawa, K.; Ikeda, S.; Yaga, M.; Watanabe, K.; Urakawa, R.; Iehara, A.; Iwai, M.; Hashiguchi, S.; Morimoto, S.; Fujiki, F.; et al. Selective targeting of multiple myeloma cells with a monoclonal antibody recognizing the ubiquitous protein CD98 heavy chain. *Sci. Transl. Med.* **2022**, *14*, eaax7706. [CrossRef] [PubMed]
58. Chernykh, A.; Kawahara, R.; Thaysen-Andersen, M. Towards structure-focused glycoproteomics. *Biochem. Soc. Trans.* **2021**, *49*, 161–186. [CrossRef]
59. Thomas, D.R.; Scott, N.E. Glycoproteomics: Growing up fast. *Curr. Opin. Struct. Biol.* **2021**, *68*, 18–25. [CrossRef]
60. Ferreira, J.A.; Relvas-Santos, M.; Peixoto, A.; Silva, A.M.; Lara Santos, L. Glycoproteogenomics: Setting the Course for Next-generation Cancer Neoantigen Discovery for Cancer Vaccines. *Genom. Proteom. Bioinform.* **2021**, *19*, 25–43. [CrossRef]
61. Rolland, D.C.M.; Basrur, V.; Jeon, Y.-K.; McNeil-Schwalm, C.; Fermin, D.; Conlon, K.P.; Zhou, Y.; Ng, S.Y.; Tsou, C.-C.; Brown, N.A.; et al. Functional proteogenomics reveals biomarkers and therapeutic targets in lymphomas. *Proc. Natl. Acad. Sci. USA* **2017**, *114*, 6581–6586. [CrossRef] [PubMed]
62. Mun, D.G.; Bhin, J.; Kim, S.; Kim, H.; Jung, J.H.; Jung, Y.; Jang, Y.E.; Park, J.M.; Kim, H.; Jung, Y.; et al. Proteogenomic Characterization of Human Early-Onset Gastric Cancer. *Cancer Cell* **2019**, *35*, 111–124.e110. [CrossRef] [PubMed]
63. Fernandes, E.; Sores, J.; Cotton, S.; Peixoto, A.; Ferreira, D.; Freitas, R.; Reis, C.A.; Santos, L.L.; Ferreira, J.A. Esophageal, gastric and colorectal cancers: Looking beyond classical serological biomarkers towards glycoproteomics-assisted precision oncology. *Theranostics* **2020**, *10*, 4903–4928. [CrossRef] [PubMed]
64. Azevedo, R.; Peixoto, A.; Gaiteiro, C.; Fernandes, E.; Neves, M.; Lima, L.; Santos, L.L.; Ferreira, J.A. Over forty years of bladder cancer glycobiology: Where do glycans stand facing precision oncology? *Oncotarget* **2017**, *8*, 91734–91764. [CrossRef] [PubMed]
65. Grönholm, M.; Feodoroff, M.; Antignani, G.; Martins, B.; Hamdan, F.; Cerullo, V. Patient-Derived Organoids for Precision Cancer Immunotherapy. *Cancer Res.* **2021**, *81*, 3149–3155. [CrossRef]
66. Dao, V.; Yuki, K.; Lo, Y.H.; Nakano, M.; Kuo, C.J. Immune organoids: From tumor modeling to precision oncology. *Trends Cancer* **2022**, *8*, 870–880. [CrossRef]
67. Wang, W.; Yuan, T.; Ma, L.; Zhu, Y.; Bao, J.; Zhao, X.; Zhao, Y.; Zong, Y.; Zhang, Y.; Yang, S.; et al. Hepatobiliary Tumor Organoids Reveal HLA Class I Neoantigen Landscape and Antitumoral Activity of Neoantigen Peptide Enhanced with Immune Checkpoint Inhibitors. *Adv. Sci.* **2022**, *9*, e2105810. [CrossRef]
68. van den Broeke, L.T.; Pendleton, C.D.; Mackall, C.; Helman, L.J.; Berzofsky, J.A. Identification and epitope enhancement of a PAX-FKHR fusion protein breakpoint epitope in alveolar rhabdomyosarcoma cells created by a tumorigenic chromosomal translocation inducing CTL capable of lysing human tumors. *Cancer Res.* **2006**, *66*, 1818–1823. [CrossRef]
69. Baldauf, M.C.; Gerke, J.S.; Kirschner, A.; Blaeschke, F.; Effenberger, M.; Schober, K.; Rubio, R.A.; Kanaseki, T.; Kiran, M.M.; Dallmayer, M.; et al. Systematic identification of cancer-specific MHC-binding peptides with RAVEN. *Oncoimmunology* **2018**, *7*, e1481558. [CrossRef]
70. Pak, H.; Michaux, J.; Huber, F.; Chong, C.; Stevenson, B.J.; Müller, M.; Coukos, G.; Bassani-Sternberg, M. Sensitive Immunopeptidomics by Leveraging Available Large-Scale Multi-HLA Spectral Libraries, Data-Independent Acquisition, and MS/MS Prediction. *Mol. Cell. Proteom. MCP* **2021**, *20*, 100080. [CrossRef]
71. Minegishi, Y.; Kiyotani, K.; Nemoto, K.; Inoue, Y.; Haga, Y.; Fujii, R.; Saichi, N.; Nagayama, S.; Ueda, K. Differential ion mobility mass spectrometry in immunopeptidomics identifies neoantigens carrying colorectal cancer driver mutations. *Commun. Biol.* **2022**, *5*, 831. [CrossRef]
72. Dunne, E.F.; Park, I.U. HPV and HPV-associated diseases. *Infect. Dis. Clin. N. Am.* **2013**, *27*, 765–778. [CrossRef] [PubMed]
73. D'Souza, S.; Lau, K.C.; Coffin, C.S.; Patel, T.R. Molecular mechanisms of viral hepatitis induced hepatocellular carcinoma. *World J. Gastroenterol.* **2020**, *26*, 5759–5783. [CrossRef]
74. Farrell, P.J. Epstein-Barr Virus and Cancer. *Annu. Rev. Pathol.* **2019**, *14*, 29–53. [CrossRef] [PubMed]
75. Wang, F.; Meng, W.; Wang, B.; Qiao, L. Helicobacter pylori-induced gastric inflammation and gastric cancer. *Cancer Lett.* **2014**, *345*, 196–202. [CrossRef] [PubMed]
76. Roy, S.; Trinchieri, G. Microbiota: A key orchestrator of cancer therapy. *Nat. Rev. Cancer* **2017**, *17*, 271–285. [CrossRef]
77. Bessell, C.A.; Isser, A.; Havel, J.J.; Lee, S.; Bell, D.R.; Hickey, J.W.; Chaisawangwong, W.; Glick Bieler, J.; Srivastava, R.; Kuo, F.; et al. Commensal bacteria stimulate antitumor responses via T cell cross-reactivity. *JCI Insight* **2020**, *5*, e135597. [CrossRef]
78. Fluckiger, A.; Daillere, R.; Sassi, M.; Sixt, B.S.; Liu, P.; Loos, F.; Richard, C.; Rabu, C.; Alou, M.T.; Goubet, A.G.; et al. Cross-reactivity between tumor MHC class I-restricted antigens and an enterococcal bacteriophage. *Science* **2020**, *369*, 936–942. [CrossRef]

79. Snyder, A.; Makarov, V.; Merghoub, T.; Yuan, J.; Zaretsky, J.M.; Desrichard, A.; Walsh, L.A.; Postow, M.A.; Wong, P.; Ho, T.S.; et al. Genetic Basis for Clinical Response to CTLA-4 Blockade in Melanoma. *N. Engl. J. Med.* **2014**, *371*, 2189–2199. [CrossRef]
80. Tomasi, M.; Dalsass, M.; Beghini, F.; Zanella, I.; Caproni, E.; Fantappie, L.; Gagliardi, A.; Irene, C.; Konig, E.; Frattini, L.; et al. Commensal Bifidobacterium Strains Enhance the Efficacy of Neo-Epitope Based Cancer Vaccines. *Vaccines* **2021**, *9*, 1356. [CrossRef]
81. Boesch, M.; Baty, F.; Rothschild, S.I.; Tamm, M.; Joerger, M.; Fruh, M.; Brutsche, M.H. Tumour neoantigen mimicry by microbial species in cancer immunotherapy. *Br. J. Cancer* **2021**, *125*, 313–323. [CrossRef] [PubMed]
82. Leng, Q.; Tarbe, M.; Long, Q.; Wang, F. Pre-existing heterologous T-cell immunity and neoantigen immunogenicity. *Clin. Transl. Immunol.* **2020**, *9*, e01111. [CrossRef] [PubMed]
83. Luksza, M.; Riaz, N.; Makarov, V.; Balachandran, V.P.; Hellmann, M.D.; Solovyov, A.; Rizvi, N.A.; Merghoub, T.; Levine, A.J.; Chan, T.A.; et al. A neoantigen fitness model predicts tumour response to checkpoint blockade immunotherapy. *Nature* **2017**, *551*, 517–520. [CrossRef] [PubMed]
84. Finn, O.J.; Rammensee, H.G. Is It Possible to Develop Cancer Vaccines to Neoantigens, What Are the Major Challenges, and How Can These Be Overcome? Neoantigens: Nothing New in Spite of the Name. *Cold Spring Harb. Perspect. Biol.* **2018**, *10*, a028829. [CrossRef]
85. Ragone, C.; Manolio, C.; Cavalluzzo, B.; Mauriello, A.; Tornesello, M.L.; Buonaguro, F.M.; Castiglione, F.; Vitagliano, L.; Iaccarino, E.; Ruvo, M.; et al. Identification and validation of viral antigens sharing sequence and structural homology with tumor-associated antigens (TAAs). *J. Immunother. Cancer* **2021**, *9*, e002694. [CrossRef]
86. Chiaro, J.; Kasanen, H.H.E.; Whalley, T.; Capasso, C.; Gronholm, M.; Feola, S.; Peltonen, K.; Hamdan, F.; Hernberg, M.; Makela, S.; et al. Viral Molecular Mimicry Influences the Antitumor Immune Response in Murine and Human Melanoma. *Cancer Immunol. Res.* **2021**, *9*, 981–993. [CrossRef]
87. Rinninella, E.; Raoul, P.; Cintoni, M.; Franceschi, F.; Miggiano, G.A.D.; Gasbarrini, A.; Mele, M.C. What is the Healthy Gut Microbiota Composition? A Changing Ecosystem across Age, Environment, Diet, and Diseases. *Microorganisms* **2019**, *7*, 14. [CrossRef]
88. Brown, E.M.; Kenny, D.J.; Xavier, R.J. Gut Microbiota Regulation of T Cells During Inflammation and Autoimmunity. *Annu. Rev. Immunol.* **2019**, *37*, 599–624. [CrossRef]
89. Ragone, C.; Manolio, C.; Mauriello, A.; Cavalluzzo, B.; Buonaguro, F.M.; Tornesello, M.L.; Tagliamonte, M.; Buonaguro, L. Molecular mimicry between tumor associated antigens and microbiota-derived epitopes. *J. Transl. Med.* **2022**, *20*, 316. [CrossRef]
90. Cusick, M.F.; Libbey, J.E.; Fujinami, R.S. Molecular mimicry as a mechanism of autoimmune disease. *Clin. Rev. Allergy Immunol.* **2012**, *42*, 102–111. [CrossRef]
91. Rojas, M.; Restrepo-Jimenez, P.; Monsalve, D.M.; Pacheco, Y.; Acosta-Ampudia, Y.; Ramirez-Santana, C.; Leung, P.S.C.; Ansari, A.A.; Gershwin, M.E.; Anaya, J.M. Molecular mimicry and autoimmunity. *J. Autoimmun.* **2018**, *95*, 100–123. [CrossRef]
92. Zitvogel, L.; Ayyoub, M.; Routy, B.; Kroemer, G. Microbiome and Anticancer Immunosurveillance. *Cell* **2016**, *165*, 276–287. [CrossRef] [PubMed]
93. Sioud, M. T-cell cross-reactivity may explain the large variation in how cancer patients respond to checkpoint inhibitors. *Scand. J. Immunol.* **2018**, *87*, e12643. [CrossRef] [PubMed]
94. Sahin, U.; Tureci, O. Personalized vaccines for cancer immunotherapy. *Science* **2018**, *359*, 1355–1360. [CrossRef] [PubMed]
95. Tomasi, M.; Caproni, E.; Benedet, M.; Zanella, I.; Giorgetta, S.; Dalsass, M.; Konig, E.; Gagliardi, A.; Fantappie, L.; Berti, A.; et al. Outer Membrane Vesicles From The Gut Microbiome Contribute to Tumor Immunity by Eliciting Cross-Reactive T Cells. *Front. Oncol.* **2022**, *12*, 912639. [CrossRef] [PubMed]
96. Simoni, Y.; Becht, E.; Fehlings, M.; Loh, C.Y.; Koo, S.L.; Teng, K.W.W.; Yeong, J.P.S.; Nahar, R.; Zhang, T.; Kared, H.; et al. Bystander CD8(+) T cells are abundant and phenotypically distinct in human tumour infiltrates. *Nature* **2018**, *557*, 575–579. [CrossRef]
97. Kalaora, S.; Nagler, A.; Nejman, D.; Alon, M.; Barbolin, C.; Barnea, E.; Ketelaars, S.L.C.; Cheng, K.; Vervier, K.; Shental, N.; et al. Identification of bacteria-derived HLA-bound peptides in melanoma. *Nature* **2021**, *592*, 138–143. [CrossRef]
98. Cuburu, N.; Bialkowski, L.; Pontejo, S.M.; Sethi, S.K.; Bell, A.T.F.; Kim, R.; Thompson, C.D.; Lowy, D.R.; Schiller, J.T. Harnessing anti-cytomegalovirus immunity for local immunotherapy against solid tumors. *Proc. Natl. Acad. Sci. USA* **2022**, *119*, e2116738119. [CrossRef]
99. Hacohen, N.; Fritsch, E.F.; Carter, T.A.; Lander, E.S.; Wu, C.J. Getting personal with neoantigen-based therapeutic cancer vaccines. *Cancer Immunol. Res.* **2013**, *1*, 11–15. [CrossRef]
100. Ott, P.A.; Hu, Z.; Keskin, D.B.; Shukla, S.A.; Sun, J.; Bozym, D.J.; Zhang, W.; Luoma, A.; Giobbie-Hurder, A.; Peter, L.; et al. An immunogenic personal neoantigen vaccine for patients with melanoma. *Nature* **2017**, *547*, 217–221. [CrossRef]
101. Sahin, U.; Derhovanessian, E.; Miller, M.; Kloke, B.P.; Simon, P.; Lower, M.; Bukur, V.; Tadmor, A.D.; Luxemburger, U.; Schrors, B.; et al. Personalized RNA mutanome vaccines mobilize poly-specific therapeutic immunity against cancer. *Nature* **2017**, *547*, 222–226. [CrossRef] [PubMed]
102. Tran, E.; Ahmadzadeh, M.; Lu, Y.C.; Gros, A.; Turcotte, S.; Robbins, P.F.; Gartner, J.J.; Zheng, Z.; Li, Y.F.; Ray, S.; et al. Immunogenicity of somatic mutations in human gastrointestinal cancers. *Science* **2015**, *350*, 1387–1390. [CrossRef] [PubMed]
103. Hu, Z.; Ott, P.A.; Wu, C.J. Towards personalized, tumour-specific, therapeutic vaccines for cancer. *Nat. Rev. Immunol.* **2018**, *18*, 168–182. [CrossRef]
104. Toussaint, B.; Chauchet, X.; Wang, Y.; Polack, B.; Le Gouellec, A. Live-attenuated bacteria as a cancer vaccine vector. *Expert. Rev. Vaccines* **2013**, *12*, 1139–1154. [CrossRef] [PubMed]

105. Zebertavage, L.; Bambina, S.; Shugart, J.; Alice, A.; Zens, K.D.; Lauer, P.; Hanson, B.; Gough, M.J.; Crittenden, M.R.; Bahjat, K.S. A microbial-based cancer vaccine for induction of EGFRvIII-specific CD8+ T cells and anti-tumor immunity. *PLoS ONE* **2019**, *14*, e0209153. [CrossRef]
106. Bommareddy, P.K.; Shettigar, M.; Kaufman, H.L. Integrating oncolytic viruses in combination cancer immunotherapy. *Nat. Rev. Immunol.* **2018**, *18*, 498–513. [CrossRef]
107. Singer, J.; Manzano-Szalai, K.; Fazekas, J.; Thell, K.; Bentley-Lukschal, A.; Stremnitzer, C.; Roth-Walter, F.; Weghofer, M.; Ritter, M.; Pino Tossi, K.; et al. Proof of concept study with an HER-2 mimotope anticancer vaccine deduced from a novel AAV-mimotope library platform. *Oncoimmunology* **2016**, *5*, e1171446. [CrossRef]
108. Toyofuku, M.; Nomura, N.; Eberl, L. Types and origins of bacterial membrane vesicles. *Nat. Rev. Microbiol.* **2019**, *17*, 13–24. [CrossRef]
109. Kaparakis-Liaskos, M.; Ferrero, R.L. Immune modulation by bacterial outer membrane vesicles. *Nat. Rev. Immunol.* **2015**, *15*, 375–387. [CrossRef]
110. Cheng, K.; Zhao, R.; Li, Y.; Qi, Y.; Wang, Y.; Zhang, Y.; Qin, H.; Qin, Y.; Chen, L.; Li, C.; et al. Bioengineered bacteria-derived outer membrane vesicles as a versatile antigen display platform for tumor vaccination via Plug-and-Display technology. *Nat. Commun.* **2021**, *12*, 2041. [CrossRef]
111. Li, Y.; Ma, X.; Yue, Y.; Zhang, K.; Cheng, K.; Feng, Q.; Ma, N.; Liang, J.; Zhang, T.; Zhang, L.; et al. Rapid Surface Display of mRNA Antigens by Bacteria-Derived Outer Membrane Vesicles for a Personalized Tumor Vaccine. *Adv. Mater.* **2022**, *34*, e2109984. [CrossRef]
112. Gao, X.; Feng, Q.; Wang, J.; Zhao, X. Bacterial outer membrane vesicle-based cancer nanovaccines. *Cancer Biol. Med.* **2022**, *19*, 1290–1300. [CrossRef] [PubMed]
113. Goracci, M.; Pignochino, Y.; Marchio, S. Phage Display-Based Nanotechnology Applications in Cancer Immunotherapy. *Molecules* **2020**, *25*, 843. [CrossRef] [PubMed]
114. Smith, G.P. Filamentous fusion phage: Novel expression vectors that display cloned antigens on the virion surface. *Science* **1985**, *228*, 1315–1317. [CrossRef] [PubMed]
115. Pande, J.; Szewczyk, M.M.; Grover, A.K. Phage display: Concept, innovations, applications and future. *Biotechnol. Adv.* **2010**, *28*, 849–858. [CrossRef]
116. Lai, Y.D.; Wu, Y.Y.; Tsai, Y.J.; Tsai, Y.S.; Lin, Y.Y.; Lai, S.L.; Huang, C.Y.; Lok, Y.Y.; Hu, C.Y.; Lai, J.S. Generation of Potent Anti-Vascular Endothelial Growth Factor Neutralizing Antibodies from Mouse Phage Display Library for Cancer Therapy. *Int. J. Mol. Sci.* **2016**, *17*, 214. [CrossRef]
117. Hess, K.L.; Jewell, C.M. Phage display as a tool for vaccine and immunotherapy development. *Bioeng. Transl. Med.* **2020**, *5*, e10142. [CrossRef]
118. Arab, A.; Behravan, N.; Razazn, A.; Barati, N.; Mosaffa, F.; Nicastro, J.; Slavcev, R.; Behravan, J. The viral approach to breast cancer immunotherapy. *J. Cell. Physiol.* **2018**, *234*, 1257–1267. [CrossRef]
119. Shukla, G.S.; Sun, Y.J.; Pero, S.C.; Sholler, G.S.; Krag, D.N. Immunization with tumor neoantigens displayed on T7 phage nanoparticles elicits plasma antibody and vaccine-draining lymph node B cell responses. *J. Immunol. Methods* **2018**, *460*, 51–62. [CrossRef]
120. Razazan, A.; Nicastro, J.; Slavcev, R.; Barati, N.; Arab, A.; Mosaffa, F.; Jaafari, M.R.; Behravan, J. Lambda bacteriophage nanoparticles displaying GP2, a HER2/neu derived peptide, induce prophylactic and therapeutic activities against TUBO tumor model in mice. *Sci. Rep.* **2019**, *9*, 2221. [CrossRef]
121. Li, W.; Jing, Z.; Wang, S.; Li, Q.; Xing, Y.; Shi, H.; Li, S.; Hong, Z. P22 virus-like particles as an effective antigen delivery nanoplatform for cancer immunotherapy. *Biomaterials* **2021**, *271*, 120726. [CrossRef] [PubMed]
122. Dong, X.; Pan, P.; Ye, J.J.; Zhang, Q.L.; Zhang, X.Z. Hybrid M13 bacteriophage-based vaccine platform for personalized cancer immunotherapy. *Biomaterials* **2022**, *289*, 121763. [CrossRef] [PubMed]
123. He, X.; Xu, C. Immune checkpoint signaling and cancer immunotherapy. *Cell Res.* **2020**, *30*, 660–669. [CrossRef] [PubMed]
124. Wei, S.C.; Duffy, C.R.; Allison, J.P. Fundamental Mechanisms of Immune Checkpoint Blockade Therapy. *Cancer Discov.* **2018**, *8*, 1069–1086. [CrossRef] [PubMed]
125. Wang, M.; Du, Q.; Jin, J.; Wei, Y.; Lu, Y.; Li, Q. LAG3 and its emerging role in cancer immunotherapy. *Clin. Transl. Med.* **2021**, *11*, e365. [CrossRef] [PubMed]
126. Zhou, F.; Qiao, M.; Zhou, C. The cutting-edge progress of immune-checkpoint blockade in lung cancer. *Cell Mol. Immunol.* **2021**, *18*, 279–293. [CrossRef]
127. Nathan, P.; Hassel, J.C.; Rutkowski, P.; Baurain, J.F.; Butler, M.O.; Schlaak, M.; Sullivan, R.J.; Ochsenreither, S.; Dummer, R.; Kirkwood, J.M.; et al. Overall Survival Benefit with Tebentafusp in Metastatic Uveal Melanoma. *N. Engl. J. Med.* **2021**, *385*, 1196–1206. [CrossRef]
128. Goldberg, S.B.; Schalper, K.A.; Gettinger, S.N.; Mahajan, A.; Herbst, R.S.; Chiang, A.C.; Lilenbaum, R.; Wilson, F.H.; Omay, S.B.; Yu, J.B.; et al. Pembrolizumab for management of patients with NSCLC and brain metastases: Long-term results and biomarker analysis from a non-randomised, open-label, phase 2 trial. *Lancet Oncol.* **2020**, *21*, 655–663. [CrossRef]
129. Ribas, A.; Wolchok, J.D. Cancer immunotherapy using checkpoint blockade. *Science* **2018**, *359*, 1350–1355. [CrossRef]

130. Schadendorf, D.; Hodi, F.S.; Robert, C.; Weber, J.S.; Margolin, K.; Hamid, O.; Patt, D.; Chen, T.T.; Berman, D.M.; Wolchok, J.D. Pooled Analysis of Long-Term Survival Data From Phase II and Phase III Trials of Ipilimumab in Unresectable or Metastatic Melanoma. *J. Clin. Oncol.* **2015**, *33*, 1889–1894. [CrossRef]
131. Anagnostou, V.; Smith, K.N.; Forde, P.M.; Niknafs, N.; Bhattacharya, R.; White, J.; Zhang, T.; Adleff, V.; Phallen, J.; Wali, N.; et al. Evolution of Neoantigen Landscape during Immune Checkpoint Blockade in Non-Small Cell Lung Cancer. *Cancer Discov.* **2017**, *7*, 264–276. [CrossRef]
132. Vetizou, M.; Pitt, J.M.; Daillere, R.; Lepage, P.; Waldschmitt, N.; Flament, C.; Rusakiewicz, S.; Routy, B.; Roberti, M.P.; Duong, C.P.; et al. Anticancer immunotherapy by CTLA-4 blockade relies on the gut microbiota. *Science* **2015**, *350*, 1079–1084. [CrossRef]
133. Sivan, A.; Corrales, L.; Hubert, N.; Williams, J.B.; Aquino-Michaels, K.; Earley, Z.M.; Benyamin, F.W.; Lei, Y.M.; Jabri, B.; Alegre, M.L.; et al. Commensal Bifidobacterium promotes antitumor immunity and facilitates anti-PD-L1 efficacy. *Science* **2015**, *350*, 1084–1089. [CrossRef] [PubMed]
134. Routy, B.; Le Chatelier, E.; Derosa, L.; Duong, C.P.M.; Alou, M.T.; Daillere, R.; Fluckiger, A.; Messaoudene, M.; Rauber, C.; Roberti, M.P.; et al. Gut microbiome influences efficacy of PD-1-based immunotherapy against epithelial tumors. *Science* **2018**, *359*, 91–97. [CrossRef] [PubMed]
135. Zheng, Y.; Wang, T.; Tu, X.; Huang, Y.; Zhang, H.; Tan, D.; Jiang, W.; Cai, S.; Zhao, P.; Song, R.; et al. Gut microbiome affects the response to anti-PD-1 immunotherapy in patients with hepatocellular carcinoma. *J. Immunother. Cancer* **2019**, *7*, 193. [CrossRef] [PubMed]
136. Xu, X.; Lv, J.; Guo, F.; Li, J.; Jia, Y.; Jiang, D.; Wang, N.; Zhang, C.; Kong, L.; Liu, Y.; et al. Gut Microbiome Influences the Efficacy of PD-1 Antibody Immunotherapy on MSS-Type Colorectal Cancer via Metabolic Pathway. *Front. Microbiol.* **2020**, *11*, 814. [CrossRef]
137. Qin, J.; Li, R.; Raes, J.; Arumugam, M.; Burgdorf, K.S.; Manichanh, C.; Nielsen, T.; Pons, N.; Levenez, F.; Yamada, T.; et al. A human gut microbial gene catalogue established by metagenomic sequencing. *Nature* **2010**, *464*, 59–65. [CrossRef]
138. Wastyk, H.C.; Fragiadakis, G.K.; Perelman, D.; Dahan, D.; Merrill, B.D.; Yu, F.B.; Topf, M.; Gonzalez, C.G.; Van Treuren, W.; Han, S.; et al. Gut-microbiota-targeted diets modulate human immune status. *Cell* **2021**, *184*, 4137–4153.e4114. [CrossRef]
139. Fong, W.; Li, Q.; Yu, J. Gut microbiota modulation: A novel strategy for prevention and treatment of colorectal cancer. *Oncogene* **2020**, *39*, 4925–4943. [CrossRef]
140. Di Domenico, E.G.; Cavallo, I.; Pontone, M.; Toma, L.; Ensoli, F. Biofilm Producing Salmonella Typhi: Chronic Colonization and Development of Gallbladder Cancer. *Int. J. Mol. Sci.* **2017**, *18*, 1887. [CrossRef]
141. Huang, Y.; Fan, X.G.; Wang, Z.M.; Zhou, J.H.; Tian, X.F.; Li, N. Identification of helicobacter species in human liver samples from patients with primary hepatocellular carcinoma. *J. Clin. Pathol.* **2004**, *57*, 1273–1277. [CrossRef]
142. Helmink, B.A.; Khan, M.A.W.; Hermann, A.; Gopalakrishnan, V.; Wargo, J.A. The microbiome, cancer, and cancer therapy. *Nat. Med.* **2019**, *25*, 377–388. [CrossRef] [PubMed]
143. Sepich-Poore, G.D.; Zitvogel, L.; Straussman, R.; Hasty, J.; Wargo, J.A.; Knight, R. The microbiome and human cancer. *Science* **2021**, *371*, eabc4552. [CrossRef] [PubMed]
144. Peng, Z.; Cheng, S.; Kou, Y.; Wang, Z.; Jin, R.; Hu, H.; Zhang, X.; Gong, J.F.; Li, J.; Lu, M.; et al. The Gut Microbiome Is Associated with Clinical Response to Anti-PD-1/PD-L1 Immunotherapy in Gastrointestinal Cancer. *Cancer Immunol. Res.* **2020**, *8*, 1251–1261. [CrossRef] [PubMed]
145. Chaput, N.; Lepage, P.; Coutzac, C.; Soularue, E.; Le Roux, K.; Monot, C.; Boselli, L.; Routier, E.; Cassard, L.; Collins, M.; et al. Baseline gut microbiota predicts clinical response and colitis in metastatic melanoma patients treated with ipilimumab. *Ann. Oncol.* **2017**, *28*, 1368–1379. [CrossRef] [PubMed]
146. Boesch, M.; Horvath, L.; Baty, F.; Pircher, A.; Wolf, D.; Spahn, S.; Straussman, R.; Tilg, H.; Brutsche, M.H. Compartmentalization of the host microbiome: How tumor microbiota shapes checkpoint immunotherapy outcome and offers therapeutic prospects. *J. Immunother. Cancer* **2022**, *10*, e005401. [CrossRef]
147. Sharma, P.; Hu-Lieskovan, S.; Wargo, J.A.; Ribas, A. Primary, Adaptive, and Acquired Resistance to Cancer Immunotherapy. *Cell* **2017**, *168*, 707–723. [CrossRef] [PubMed]
148. Jenkins, R.W.; Barbie, D.A.; Flaherty, K.T. Mechanisms of resistance to immune checkpoint inhibitors. *Br. J. Cancer* **2018**, *118*, 9–16. [CrossRef] [PubMed]
149. Hayase, E.; Jenq, R.R. Role of the intestinal microbiome and microbial-derived metabolites in immune checkpoint blockade immunotherapy of cancer. *Genome Med.* **2021**, *13*, 107. [CrossRef]
150. Gros, A.; Parkhurst, M.R.; Tran, E.; Pasetto, A.; Robbins, P.F.; Ilyas, S.; Prickett, T.D.; Gartner, J.J.; Crystal, J.S.; Roberts, I.M.; et al. Prospective identification of neoantigen-specific lymphocytes in the peripheral blood of melanoma patients. *Nat. Med.* **2016**, *22*, 433–438. [CrossRef]
151. Mishra, S.; Amatya, S.B.; Salmi, S.; Koivukangas, V.; Karihtala, P.; Reunanen, J. Microbiota and Extracellular Vesicles in Anti-PD-1/PD-L1 Therapy. *Cancers* **2022**, *14*, 5121. [CrossRef] [PubMed]
152. Eroglu, Z.; Zaretsky, J.M.; Hu-Lieskovan, S.; Kim, D.W.; Algazi, A.; Johnson, D.B.; Liniker, E.; Ben, K.; Munhoz, R.; Rapisuwon, S.; et al. High response rate to PD-1 blockade in desmoplastic melanomas. *Nature* **2018**, *553*, 347–350. [CrossRef] [PubMed]

153. Samstein, R.M.; Lee, C.H.; Shoushtari, A.N.; Hellmann, M.D.; Shen, R.; Janjigian, Y.Y.; Barron, D.A.; Zehir, A.; Jordan, E.J.; Omuro, A.; et al. Tumor mutational load predicts survival after immunotherapy across multiple cancer types. *Nat. Genet.* **2019**, *51*, 202–206. [CrossRef]
154. Lu, Y.; Yuan, X.; Wang, M.; He, Z.; Li, H.; Wang, J.; Li, Q. Gut microbiota influence immunotherapy responses: Mechanisms and therapeutic strategies. *J. Hematol. Oncol.* **2022**, *15*, 47. [CrossRef] [PubMed]
155. Baruch, E.N.; Youngster, I.; Ben-Betzalel, G.; Ortenberg, R.; Lahat, A.; Katz, L.; Adler, K.; Dick-Necula, D.; Raskin, S.; Bloch, N.; et al. Fecal microbiota transplant promotes response in immunotherapy-refractory melanoma patients. *Science* **2021**, *371*, 602–609. [CrossRef]
156. Davar, D.; Dzutsev, A.K.; McCulloch, J.A.; Rodrigues, R.R.; Chauvin, J.M.; Morrison, R.M.; Deblasio, R.N.; Menna, C.; Ding, Q.; Pagliano, O.; et al. Fecal microbiota transplant overcomes resistance to anti-PD-1 therapy in melanoma patients. *Science* **2021**, *371*, 595–602. [CrossRef]
157. Xu, H.; Cao, C.; Ren, Y.; Weng, S.; Liu, L.; Guo, C.; Wang, L.; Han, X.; Ren, J.; Liu, Z. Antitumor effects of fecal microbiota transplantation: Implications for microbiome modulation in cancer treatment. *Front. Immunol.* **2022**, *13*, 949490. [CrossRef]
158. Mondal, M.; Guo, J.; He, P.; Zhou, D. Recent advances of oncolytic virus in cancer therapy. *Hum. Vaccin. Immunother.* **2020**, *16*, 2389–2402. [CrossRef]
159. Malogolovkin, A.; Gasanov, N.; Egorov, A.; Weener, M.; Ivanov, R.; Karabelsky, A. Combinatorial Approaches for Cancer Treatment Using Oncolytic Viruses: Projecting the Perspectives through Clinical Trials Outcomes. *Viruses* **2021**, *13*, 1271. [CrossRef]
160. Chaurasiya, S.; Chen, N.G.; Fong, Y. Oncolytic viruses and immunity. *Curr. Opin. Immunol.* **2018**, *51*, 83–90. [CrossRef]
161. Chiu, M.; Armstrong, E.J.L.; Jennings, V.; Foo, S.; Crespo-Rodriguez, E.; Bozhanova, G.; Patin, E.C.; McLaughlin, M.; Mansfield, D.; Baker, G.; et al. Combination therapy with oncolytic viruses and immune checkpoint inhibitors. *Expert Opin. Biol. Ther.* **2020**, *20*, 635–652. [CrossRef] [PubMed]
162. Woller, N.; Gurlevik, E.; Fleischmann-Mundt, B.; Schumacher, A.; Knocke, S.; Kloos, A.M.; Saborowski, M.; Geffers, R.; Manns, M.P.; Wirth, T.C.; et al. Viral Infection of Tumors Overcomes Resistance to PD-1-immunotherapy by Broadening Neoantigenome-directed T-cell Responses. *Mol. Ther.* **2015**, *23*, 1630–1640. [CrossRef] [PubMed]
163. Russell, L.; Peng, K.W.; Russell, S.J.; Diaz, R.M. Oncolytic Viruses: Priming Time for Cancer Immunotherapy. *BioDrugs* **2019**, *33*, 485–501. [CrossRef]
164. Passaro, C.; Alayo, Q.; De Laura, I.; McNulty, J.; Grauwet, K.; Ito, H.; Bhaskaran, V.; Mineo, M.; Lawler, S.E.; Shah, K.; et al. Arming an Oncolytic Herpes Simplex Virus Type 1 with a Single-chain Fragment Variable Antibody against PD-1 for Experimental Glioblastoma Therapy. *Clin. Cancer Res.* **2019**, *25*, 290–299. [CrossRef] [PubMed]
165. Wang, G.; Kang, X.; Chen, K.S.; Jehng, T.; Jones, L.; Chen, J.; Huang, X.F.; Chen, S.Y. An engineered oncolytic virus expressing PD-L1 inhibitors activates tumor neoantigen-specific T cell responses. *Nat. Commun.* **2020**, *11*, 1395. [CrossRef]
166. Zhang, Z.; Lu, M.; Qin, Y.; Gao, W.; Tao, L.; Su, W.; Zhong, J. Neoantigen: A New Breakthrough in Tumor Immunotherapy. *Front. Immunol.* **2021**, *12*, 672356. [CrossRef]
167. Lybaert, L.; Lefever, S.; Fant, B.; Smits, E.; De Geest, B.; Breckpot, K.; Dirix, L.; Feldman, S.A.; van Criekinge, W.; Thielemans, K.; et al. Challenges in neoantigen-directed therapeutics. *Cancer Cell* **2023**, *41*, 15–40. [CrossRef]
168. Wells, D.K.; van Buuren, M.M.; Dang, K.K.; Hubbard-Lucey, V.M.; Sheehan, K.C.F.; Campbell, K.M.; Lamb, A.; Ward, J.P.; Sidney, J.; Blazquez, A.B.; et al. Key Parameters of Tumor Epitope Immunogenicity Revealed Through a Consortium Approach Improve Neoantigen Prediction. *Cell* **2020**, *183*, 818–834.e813. [CrossRef]
169. Hanahan, D. Hallmarks of Cancer: New Dimensions. *Cancer Discov.* **2022**, *12*, 31–46. [CrossRef]
170. Saxena, M.; van der Burg, S.H.; Melief, C.J.M.; Bhardwaj, N. Therapeutic cancer vaccines. *Nat. Rev. Cancer* **2021**, *21*, 360–378. [CrossRef]

Disclaimer/Publisher's Note: The statements, opinions and data contained in all publications are solely those of the individual author(s) and contributor(s) and not of MDPI and/or the editor(s). MDPI and/or the editor(s) disclaim responsibility for any injury to people or property resulting from any ideas, methods, instructions or products referred to in the content.

cancers

Review

Navigating the Immune Maze: Pioneering Strategies for Unshackling Cancer Immunotherapy Resistance

Liqin Yao [1,*], Qingqing Wang [2] and Wenxue Ma [3,*]

1 Key Laboratory for Translational Medicine, The First Affiliated Hospital, Huzhou University, Huzhou 313000, China
2 Institute of Immunology, Zhejiang University School of Medicine, Hangzhou 310058, China; wqq@zju.edu.cn
3 Department of Medicine, Moores Cancer Center, Sanford Stem Cell Institute, University of California San Diego, La Jolla, CA 92093, USA
* Correspondence: ningmeng2914@sina.com (L.Y.); wma@health.ucsd.edu (W.M.); Tel.: +1-858-2461477 (W.M.)

Simple Summary: Cancer treatments have made remarkable advances with the introduction of immunotherapy, which recruits the body's immune system to fight cancer. Despite these advancements, cancer can sometimes develop resistance to such treatments, diminishing their effectiveness. Our research is focused on the early detection of signs that indicate a cancer's resistance to immunotherapy, enabling physicians to swiftly alter treatment approaches and improve the chances of patient recovery. We are particularly keen on identifying distinct markers in tumors that indicate this resistance. To achieve a deeper understanding, we utilized scaled-down models of patient tumors, including organoids and xenografts, in laboratory studies. Our goal was to discover innovative methods to combat treatment resistance, potentially enhancing patient care and providing valuable insights for ongoing cancer research.

Abstract: Cancer immunotherapy has ushered in a transformative era in oncology, offering unprecedented promise and opportunities. Despite its remarkable breakthroughs, the field continues to grapple with the persistent challenge of treatment resistance. This resistance not only undermines the widespread efficacy of these pioneering treatments, but also underscores the pressing need for further research. Our exploration into the intricate realm of cancer immunotherapy resistance reveals various mechanisms at play, from primary and secondary resistance to the significant impact of genetic and epigenetic factors, as well as the crucial role of the tumor microenvironment (TME). Furthermore, we stress the importance of devising innovative strategies to counteract this resistance, such as employing combination therapies, tailoring immune checkpoints, and implementing real-time monitoring. By championing these state-of-the-art methods, we anticipate a paradigm that blends personalized healthcare with improved treatment options and is firmly committed to patient welfare. Through a comprehensive and multifaceted approach, we strive to tackle the challenges of resistance, aspiring to elevate cancer immunotherapy as a beacon of hope for patients around the world.

Keywords: cancer immunotherapy; resistance; tumor microenvironment; combination therapies; immune checkpoint targets; adoptive cell therapies; cancer vaccines; personalized medicine

1. Introduction

Cancer immunotherapy heralds a promising revolution in the realm of oncological treatments. This groundbreaking approach, rooted in historical milestones like "Coley's toxins" [1] and, later, the identification of cytotoxic T-lymphocyte-associated antigen 4 (CTLA-4), has consistently showcased the potential to redefine cancer treatment paradigms [2–4]. As we deepened our understanding of tumor antigens and immune–tumor interactions in the latter half of the 20th century, the emergence of agents targeting CTLA-4, programmed cell death protein 1 (PD-1), and programmed death-ligand 1 (PD-L1) pathways marked significant successes in treating a range of malignancies [5–7]. Additionally, personalized strategies, such as chimeric antigen receptor (CAR) T-cell therapies, offer compelling efficacy, particularly in hematological malignancies [8–10]. The scope of cancer immunotherapy has since broadened, delving into influencing factors like the tumor microenvironment (TME) and even the gut microbiome to amplify therapeutic impact [11,12].

Despite these advances, resistance to immunotherapy presents a formidable barrier, emerging from innate tumor characteristics and adaptive changes in the genetic and proteomic landscape [13]. At the heart of this challenge lies the TME, which harbors elements like regulatory T cells (Tregs) and certain cytokines that shield tumor cells, allowing them to cleverly sidestep immune detection [14–16].

Our objectives are to dissect the complexity of immunotherapy resistance, evaluate both primary and secondary mechanisms, and consider the profound influence of genetic, epigenetic, and environmental factors [17]. We spotlight emerging strategies to overcome resistance and highlight the necessity of an integrated approach involving real-time monitoring, precision analytics, and patient-centered care [18]. By addressing these challenges head-on, we aim to advance the efficacy of cancer immunotherapy, reinforcing its position as a cornerstone of modern cancer care.

Through navigating the intricate landscape of resistance, we present insights into both established and novel strategies to outmaneuver the adaptive nature of tumors [19]. This review encapsulates the critical need for adaptability in treatment approaches, the ongoing quest for data-driven precision in patient-focused care, and the overarching potential of immunotherapy to redefine the future of cancer treatment [20–22].

2. The Immune Maze: Understanding the Complex Landscape

At the heart of the challenges presented by immunotherapy lies a deep-rooted, intricate interplay between the immune system and cancerous tumors. Grasping this landscape is pivotal to addressing the ever-evolving complexities of immunotherapy resistance [23,24]. To embark on this journey, it is crucial to recognize the distinctions between primary and secondary resistance and the multifarious mechanisms that underlie them [25].

Primary resistance: Innate to certain tumors, primary resistance emerges due to various factors that hinder the immune system's capability to detect and counteract tumor cells. Some tumors are devoid of the critical antigens essential for immune recognition, rendering them less amenable to immunotherapeutic strategies [26,27]. Another dominant culprit is the immunosuppressive TME, characterized by a plethora of inhibitory factors and cells that dampen immune responses [28,29].

Consequently, secondary resistance develops as a backlash to therapeutic interventions. This form of resistance revitalizes tumor growth even after an initial successful response to immunotherapy including nivolumab (a PD-1 inhibitor) and ipilimumab (a CTLA-4 inhibitor) [30]. The driving forces behind this resistance span a spectrum from the genetic evolution of the tumor, which can lead to the modification or loss of previously identifiable antigens, to dynamic modifications to the TME, such as the amplification of immunosuppressive molecules or the influx of inhibitory cells [26,31,32].

Building on this, recent discoveries in the field have shed light on crucial aspects of immunotherapy resistance. Cutting-edge research has delved into the genetic and epigenetic blueprints of tumors. It has been shown that genetic modifications can recalibrate a tumor's antigenic composition, impeding its visibility to immune cells [27,33–35]. Moreover, epigenetic shifts can mute genes vital for immune detection without altering the DNA structure or can modify how the tumor communicates with the surrounding immune framework [36–38].

Simultaneously, within the TME are distinct cellular entities that have gained prominence. These include Tregs, myeloid-derived suppressor cells (MDSCs), and tumor-associated macrophages (TAMs), which play cardinal roles in dampening immune activity and forming a protective bulwark around tumors [39–41]. Current research endeavors are evaluating their potential as resistance biomarkers, offering a glimpse into therapeutic trajectories [42,43].

Another pivotal aspect is the TME hypoxia [44,45]. Rapid tumor growth often surpasses its vascular supply, instigating hypoxia, which in turn sparks resistance pathways [44,46,47]. This oxygen deficiency is correlated with elevated PD-L1 expression, which mutes T-cell responses, facilitating tumor evasion [48,49].

Furthermore, the interplay between tumors and major histocompatibility complex (MHC) molecules is gaining traction [9,50]. MHCs are paramount in displaying tumor-specific peptides on the tumor surface for the T-cell detection [27,51,52]. Tumors have been found to employ evasion techniques, such as downregulating MHC expression or tweaking antigen-processing systems [27,53].

On a related note, immune checkpoints continue to be a focal point in the resistance discourse [54,55]. Often regulators in the immune system, these checkpoints are manipulated by tumors to serve as barriers against immune onslaughts [56,57]. Contemporary treatments, especially checkpoint disruptors, aspire to dismantle these barriers, amplifying immune responses against malignancies [7,58,59]. The latest clinical trials are unraveling the effectiveness of and obstacles to bypassing checkpoint-triggered resistance [60–63].

In summary, a profound understanding of the intricacies of immunotherapy resistance, its genesis, current revelations, and the TME's role is fundamental in forging ahead with innovative strategies to subvert these hurdles. Subsequent sections provide a deeper exploration of these tactics.

3. Frontline Foes: Decoding the Architects of Immunotherapy Resistance

The TME serves as a dynamic milieu, evolving continuously and influencing the efficacy of cancer immunotherapies [64]. Key cytokines, notably transforming growth factor beta (TGF-β) and IL-10, are pivotal in modulating the TME, orchestrating immunosuppressive signals that underpin tumor resilience against therapeutic strategies.

Tregs are essential players within the TME, possessing the capability to subdue robust immune responses, particularly from formidable cells like cytotoxic T cells (CTLs) [65–67]. This suppression presents formidable challenges for immunotherapies, with Tregs secreting TGF-β and IL-10 to augment their inhibitory functions [68,69].

MDSCs further complicate the TME dynamics. These immune cells exacerbate the suppressive atmosphere, inhibiting CTLs and natural killer (NK) cells, thus limiting their tumor-fighting abilities [43,70]. They excel in restraining CTLs and NK cells, thus curtailing the NK cells' tumor-eradicating capabilities [43,71,72]. Additionally, the MDSCs foster Treg proliferation, intensifying the suppressive milieu [73,74].

TAMs, with their versatile roles, are noteworthy contributors to the TME. Their ability to transition between M1-like (TAM1) and M2-like (TAM2) states plays a significant role in the balance between tumor defense and progression [75,76]. While TAM1 cells act aggressively against cancer cells, TAM2 cells encourage a suppressive environment, promoting tissue repair and angiogenesis, as well as safeguarding tumors from immune attacks [77–79].

Tumor-associated neutrophils (TAN) also differentiate into two major phenotypes within the TME. While TAN1 cells inhibit cancer progression, TAN2 cells support tumor growth, underscoring the multifaceted interactions within the TME [80,81].

Other factors, like rapid tumor growth leading to hypoxic conditions, activate various resistance mechanisms [82,83]. This includes the upregulation of immune checkpoint molecules such as PD-L1 on tumor surfaces, hindering T-cell functionality [84,85]. Hypoxia-triggered signaling pathways further deepen the TME's suppressive nature [45,86].

Cancer cells also deploy evasion strategies, manipulating MHC molecules to reduce their visibility to the immune system [87,88]. Despite the promise of immune checkpoint inhibitors (ICIs), challenges remain in terms of assuring sustained outcomes and managing emergent resistance [7,89,90].

In closing, a profound grasp of these pivotal agents within the TME is paramount for charting successful strategies against the immunotherapy resistance [91]. As the research community continues its quest, the hope is to modulate these elements, enhancing the potency of the cancer immunotherapy [91–93]. By appreciating the TME's intricacies, we inch closer to reshaping therapeutic outcomes and offering renewed hope to countless patients.

Figure 1 below provides a schematic representation of the intricate cellular interactions within the hypoxic TME, highlighting the key players involved in immunotherapy resistance.

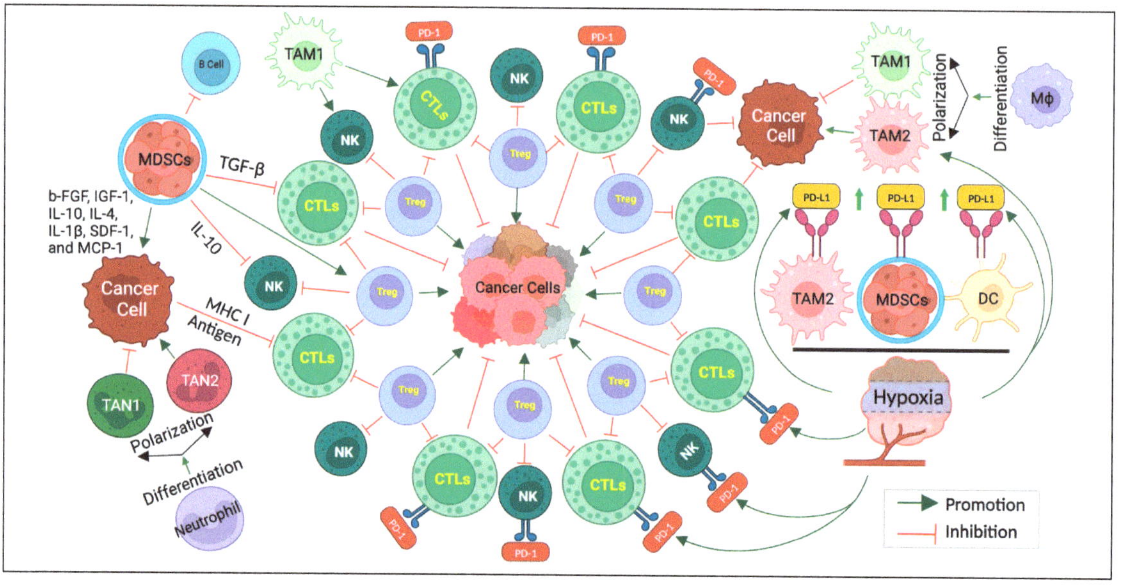

Figure 1. The keys to overcoming immunotherapy resistance. Schematic representation of cellular interactions within the hypoxic TME. Cancer cells are surrounded by various cells, including Treg, CTLs, NK cells, TAM, TAN, MDSCs, etc. CTLs and NK cells exhibit PD-1 receptors that interact with PD-L1 expressed by TAM2, MDSCs, and DCs in the hypoxic TME. TAMs can undergo polarization and differentiation influenced via the hypoxic TME. TAM1 exhibits antitumor, while TAM2 promotes tumors. MDSCs release a series of cytokines (b-FGF, IGF-1, IL-10, IL-4, IL-1β, SDF-1, and MCP-1) affecting cancer cell behavior. TGF-β and IL-10 act as regulatory molecules inhibiting CTLs and NK cells, respectively. While the MHC I molecule and tumor antigen facilitate the interaction between cancer cells and CTLs, TAN1, and TAN2, differentiated from TAN, play the roles of inhibiting and promoting cancer cells, respectively. This figure illustrates the complex network of cellular interactions within the hypoxic TME.

4. Pioneering Strategies to Overcome Resistance

Cancer immunotherapy, while promising, is often hindered by the development of resistance. Several innovative strategies have been developed to address this, each designed to improve patient outcomes and enhance treatment efficacy.

4.1. Combination Therapies

Combination therapies represent a multi-pronged attack against cancer, targeting different aspects of tumor biology. These therapies may combine agents that halt tumor growth with those that boost the immune response. Despite the potential for increased toxicity, the benefits often outweigh the risks, necessitating careful patient management [94–96].

4.2. Tumor Microenvironment (TME)

Strategies that modify the TME aim to disrupt the supportive network of the tumor, including alterations in blood flow and stromal cell inhibition. Such interventions highlight the TME's critical role in cancer therapy [97–102].

4.3. Emerging Immune Checkpoints

New research is focused on uncovering and targeting novel immune checkpoints that tumors exploit to evade immune detection. Agents targeting the ITIM domain (TIGIT), T cell immunoglobulin and mucin-domain-containing-3 (TIM-3), and lymphocyte activation gene-3 (LAG-3) are under investigation for their therapeutic potential [103,104].

4.4. Enhancing Immunotherapy with Oncolytic Viruses

Oncolytic viruses are emerging as a novel countermeasure to immunotherapy resistance. These viruses are engineered to selectively infect and destroy cancer cells while also modulating the immune environment to reverse resistance mechanisms. For example, the oncolytic virus VSV-GP, when combined with PD-1 inhibitors, has been found to effectively kill tumor cells. It also encourages the maturation of DCs and the influx of T-cells into the tumor milieu, which are crucial steps in reigniting the immune system's attack on the cancer [105].

Furthermore, clinical trials, such as one led by Chesney et al., have revealed that T-VEC, an oncolytic virus derived from the herpes simplex virus, can significantly enhance treatment outcomes for melanoma patients, especially when administered in conjunction with ICIs [106]. This dual approach not only targets the tumor directly, but also reactivates the patient's immune response against the tumor, providing a two-pronged attack against cancer resistance.

These developments signify a stride forward in integrating oncolytic virotherapy into the arsenal of immunotherapeutic strategies. By continuing to leverage these biological agents, researchers aim to unlock new pathways to overcome resistance and maximize the therapeutic potential of cancer immunotherapy.

4.5. Cell Therapy (ACT)

ACT personalizes treatment by using the patient's immune cells, like TILs or chimeric antigen receptor (CAR)-T cells, to combat cancer. While effective in blood cancers, its application in solid tumors is an active area of research [107–110].

4.6. Cancer Vaccines

Cancer vaccines aim to prime the immune system to recognize and attack tumors, with DC and viral vector vaccines leading the way. This strategy is part of a broader effort to induce durable immune responses against cancer [111–114].

4.7. Navigating Medication-Induced Resistance in Immunotherapy

The interplay between certain medications and cancer immunotherapy is complex and can inadvertently contribute to treatment resistance. Corticosteroids, which are commonly prescribed to alleviate the side effects of immunotherapy, may inadvertently suppress the immune response, reducing the efficacy of treatments like ICIs [115,116]. Additionally, chemotherapeutic agents, while targeting cancer cells, may also inadvertently modify the immune environment in a way that fosters resistance [117,118]. This alteration in the immune landscape can hinder the immune system's ability to effectively recognize and attack tumor cells.

Moreover, the use of antibiotics has been linked to disruptions in the gut microbiome, an emerging factor in the modulation of immunotherapy responses [119]. The gut microbiome plays a crucial role in maintaining a balanced immune system, and its disturbance may impact the success of immunotherapeutic strategies.

Furthermore, kinase inhibitors, used in targeted therapies, might alter critical signaling pathways that are essential for the activation and function of immune cells, contributing to a resistance scenario [120,121]. Such unintended effects underscore the necessity for clinicians to carefully consider the full spectrum of a patient's medication regimen when administering immunotherapy.

By comprehensively understanding these drug interactions and their implications, medical professionals can devise strategies to avoid or counteract the resistance-inducing effects of these drugs. This may involve adjusting dosages, sequencing treatments, or selecting alternative therapeutic agents to maintain the robustness of the immune response [122].

Integrating advanced strategies that account for drug-induced resistance with conventional cancer therapies represents a significant step toward a new era in cancer treatment. This multifaceted approach emphasizes the need for continuous research and adaptation to refine immunotherapy regimens, ensuring they remain potent against cancer while respecting the patient's overall well-being and minimizing unintended resistance [17,123].

Figure 2 below provides a visual representation of the different immunotherapeutic agents and their specific targets within the tumor microenvironment, illustrating the mechanisms by which they exert their effects.

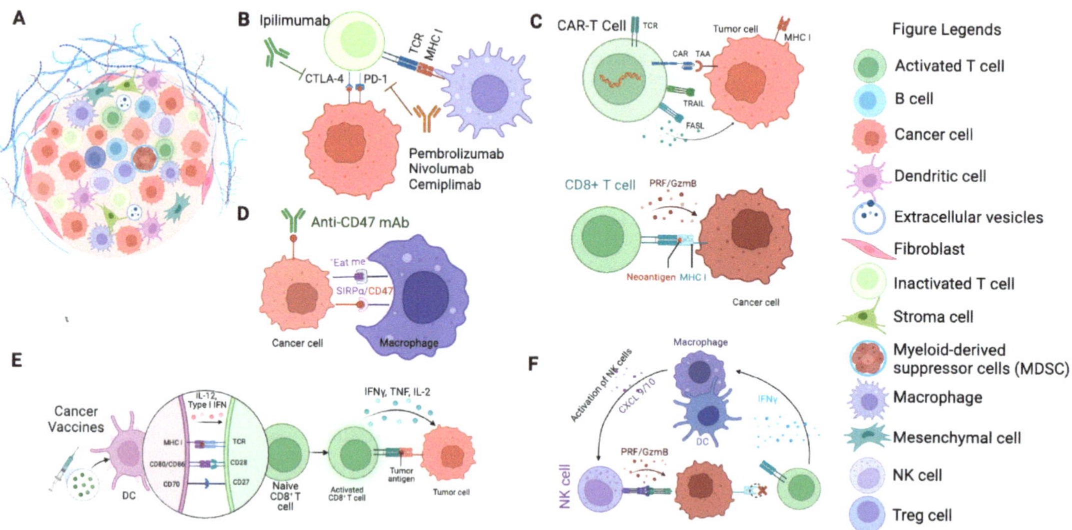

Figure 2. Targets of immunotherapeutic agents in cancer therapy. (**A**) Illustration of the TME featuring cancer cells surrounded by various immune cells and extracellular matrix components. (**B**) Depiction of immune checkpoint inhibitors (ICIs) such as CTLA-4 and PD-1 (e.g., ipilimumab, pembrolizumab, nivolumab, cemiplimab) binding to their respective receptors on T cells, preventing immune evasion by cancer cells. (**C**) Representation of CAR T-cells targeting tumor-associated antigens (TAAs) on cancer cells, triggering cytotoxic responses. (**D**) Macrophage checkpoint inhibition: anti-CD47 mAb blocks the "don't eat me" signal on cancer cells, promoting their phagocytosis by macrophages. (**E**) Depiction of dendritic cells (DCs) presenting tumor antigens to naïve T cells, leading to their activation and the initiation of an adaptive immune response against cancer cells. (**F**) Illustration of activated NK cells targeting cancer cells, mediated by cytokine signaling (e.g., IFNγ production), which enhances the innate immune response against tumors.

4.8. Integrated Strategies for Overcoming Resistance

To surmount the challenges presented by resistance to immunotherapy, an integrated approach is necessary. This involves not only the combination of therapeutic modalities but also the development of new agents that can tackle the evolved defense mechanisms of tumors. Precision medicine plays a crucial role in this, with targeted therapies designed to counteract specific pathways of resistance identified in a patient's tumor profile [17]. Adopting personalized treatment regimens based on molecular diagnostics and patient-derived models, such as organoids and xenografts, is showing promise in enhancing treatment efficacy and reducing toxicity [123]. Furthermore, the implementation of real-time monitoring systems and predictive biomarkers facilitates a more responsive approach to immunotherapy adjustments [124,125]. The future of overcoming immunotherapy resistance lies in the synergy of these innovative strategies, each contributing a piece to the complex puzzle of cancer treatment [126].

In the following section, we provide an overview of pioneering strategies in cancer immunotherapy. Table 1 summarizes these strategies, including their approaches, key components, benefits, drug examples, and supporting references.

Table 1. Overview of pioneering strategies in cancer immunotherapy.

Strategies	Description	Key Components and Benefits	Representative Drugs/Cells/Vaccines	References
Combination Therapies	Integration of several therapeutic modalities to optimize oncological outcomes.	Synergistic modalities enhance response. Versatility against varying tumor behaviors. Potential for prolonged patient benefits.	Anti-NKG2A: Monalizumab, Anti-PD-1: Nivolumab, Pembrolizumab Anti-PD-L1: Atezolizumab, Avelumab, Anti-CTLA-4: Ipilimumab, Durvalumab	[94–96,110]
TME	Considers the composite of stromal and immune cells intertwined with signaling pathways. Affects tumor progression and anti-tumor immunity.	Stroma including ECM and fibroblasts; mesenchymal stromal cells; and immune cells such as TAMs, TANs, and Tregs, signaling pathways that influence tumor progression.	Anti-LOXL2: Simtuzumab, anti-hyaluronic acid: PEGPH20, anti-CTGF: Pamrevlumab, anti-Integrin: Cilengitide, ATN-161, MEDI-522, anti-TGF-β: Fresolimumab, etc.	[97,98,127]
Immune Checkpoints (ICIs)	Novel checkpoints open up promising therapeutic possibilities. They modulate immune functions.	Potential checkpoints like TIGIT, TIM-3, and LAG-3 receptors, expanding therapeutic avenues.	Anti-LAG-3 mAbs: Relatlimab, Favezelimab, REGN3767, GSK2831781, LAG525, TSR-033, Relatlimab + Nivolumab, etc. Anti-TIM3: Sabatolimab, spartalizumab.	[127,128]
Adoptive Cell Therapy (ACT)	Capitalizes on an individual's immune cells. Offers a tailored therapeutic approach.	Precision with techniques like TIL extraction; potential of CAR-T cells provide a tailored therapeutic approach. Enhanced therapeutic results when combined with other modalities.	Tumor-infiltrating lymphocytes (TILs), T cell-receptor-engineered T (TCR-T) cells, natural killer T (NKT) cells	[107–109]
Cancer Vaccines	Utilization of neoantigens to boost immune responses targeting tumors.	Innovation with DC vaccines and viral vector vaccines; enhances immune response.	Peptide vaccines: Gardasil®, gp96, OSE2101, DSP-7888, etc.; DNA vaccines: HER2, VGX-3100, WT1, P, MA, hTERT, etc. mRNA vaccines: BNT112, BNT113, MAGE-A3, KRAS, etc.; virus-based vaccines: PROSTVAC-V/F, TG4010, BT-001; cell-based vaccines: DC vaccines; GVAX, etc.	[111–114]

To wrap up this exploration, the integration of these advanced strategies with traditional therapies offers a multifaceted approach to overcoming immunotherapy resistance, signaling a new era of hope for cancer treatment [129,130].

5. Recent Insights and Developments in Overcoming Immunotherapy Resistance

The endeavor to unravel and overcome resistance in cancer immunotherapy has uncovered significant genetic and epigenetic influences that affect patient outcomes [91,131–133].

5.1. Genetic Alterations and Immunotherapy Resistance

The emergence of resistance to immunotherapy due to genetic alterations within cancer cells is a major concern that complicates treatment outcomes. These mutations can significantly alter the immune system's ability to recognize and destroy cancer cells. One of the key genetic changes involves mutations in the beta-2-microglobulin (B2M) gene, a critical component of the major histocompatibility complex (MHC) class I molecules. The MHC class I molecule presents tumor antigens to T cells, and any disruption in this pathway, as caused by B2M mutations, can lead to ineffective T cell-mediated tumor cell lysis [134,135].

Moreover, the Janus kinase (JAK) pathway, which includes the genes JAK1 and JAK2, plays a pivotal role in immune response signaling [136]. Mutations in these genes can have profound effects on the efficacy of immunotherapies. Shen et al.'s investigation into JAK1/JAK2 alterations revealed that such mutations can result in resistance to PD-1 blockade therapies by impairing the interferon signaling pathway, which is vital for the activation of the immune response against tumor cells [137].

Additionally, research indicates that alterations in the neoantigen landscape of cancer cells, due to genetic mutations, can influence the responsiveness to immunotherapy. The mutational burden and the quality of the neoantigens presented can either enhance or diminish the therapeutic efficacy, as the immune system may or may not recognize these neoantigens as targets [138,139].

These genetic alterations underscore the need for comprehensive genomic profiling of tumors to anticipate and overcome resistance mechanisms. By understanding and mapping these genetic changes, clinicians can personalize immunotherapy approaches, potentially restoring the sensitivity of cancer cells to treatment and improving patient prognosis.

5.2. Epigenetic Dynamics and Their Role in Resistance

The regulatory landscape of epigenetic modifications is significant in immunotherapy resistance, profoundly affecting gene expression and the immune detection of tumors. DNA methylation, which adds a methyl group to DNA and often leads to gene silencing, has been implicated in immune evasion. Mehdi et al. [140] have identified that hypermethylation of the promoter regions of Th1-type cytokine genes can result in the suppression of crucial immune signaling pathways. This hypermethylation effectively reduces the expression of cytokines necessary for a robust anti-tumor immune response, thus facilitating tumor cells' escape from immune surveillance [141].

Histone modifications, another crucial aspect of epigenetics, involve changes to the proteins around which DNA is wound. Histone acetylation and deacetylation, controlled by histone acetyltransferases (HATs) and histone deacetylases (HDACs), can alter the accessibility of DNA to transcription machinery. Aberrations in HDAC activity have been linked to the repression of tumor suppressor genes. For example, overactivity of HDACs can lead to the tight winding of DNA around histones, effectively "hiding" tumor antigens from immune cells and contributing to resistance to immunotherapies such as checkpoint inhibitors [141,142].

Specific treatments, like the DNA methyltransferase inhibitors azacitidine and decitabine, have been shown to induce these epigenetic changes. They can enhance the effectiveness of immunotherapy by altering the expression of cancer/testis antigens and MHC molecules, heightening tumor immunogenicity [34,143]. However, they can also trigger immune evasion, necessitating a nuanced approach to their use in conjunction with immunotherapies [144].

Histone deacetylase inhibitors, such as vorinostat and romidepsin, have dual roles. While they can increase antigen presentation, they have also been implicated in promoting regulatory T-cell functions, which could dampen the immune response [145,146]. This highlights the delicate balance required when integrating epigenetic therapies with immunotherapy and underscores the need for further research to optimize these combinations.

5.3. The Microbiome's Influence on Immunotherapy Efficacy

The interplay between the gut microbiome and the efficacy of cancer immunotherapy is a an intensively researched topic. The diverse community of microbes residing in the gastrointestinal tract exerts a substantial influence on the body's immune responses, with significant implications for the effectiveness of immunotherapeutic agents.

In a landmark study by Derosa et al., researchers identified that the presence of specific gut bacteria, such as Akkermansia muciniphila, significantly improved the efficacy of PD-1 inhibitors. This microbe appeared to bolster the host immune system's capacity for tumor surveillance, potentially by maintaining mucosal integrity or enhancing immune cell activation, thus increasing the effectiveness of immunotherapies [147]. Such findings have led to the proposal that the gut microbiome could serve as a predictive biomarker for immunotherapy responses, and through interventions such as diet or probiotics, could be adjusted to improve clinical outcomes.

Conversely, antibiotic use can disrupt the delicate balance of the gut microbiome, with studies like those conducted by Patel et al. demonstrating negative impacts on the efficacy of immunotherapies. Antibiotics may diminish beneficial bacteria, impair immune function, and lessen the host's response to PD-1 inhibitors, highlighting the need for careful consideration of antibiotic use during immunotherapy [148].

This emerging research area has spurred interest in probiotics and fecal microbiota transplantation (FMT) as methods to modulate the gut microbiome favorably. Ongoing clinical trials are exploring the potential of these interventions to modulate the gut microbiome in order to improve the patient response rate to cancer immunotherapy [149,150].

Overall, a growing body of evidence supports the notion that therapeutic modulation of the microbiome could serve as an adjunct to enhance the efficacy of immunotherapy and reduce resistance. Ongoing research into microbiome-based adjuvants holds promise for refining the management of cancer through these novel interventions.

6. Clinical Implications and Translational Approaches

The recognition and early identification of biomarkers indicative of resistance is pivotal in optimizing cancer treatment protocols. Biomarkers, such as high PD-L1 expression or a significant tumor mutational burden (TMB), as well as genetic alterations like JAK1/2 mutations, are at the forefront of predicting and countering immunotherapy resistance [151]. These biomarkers not only facilitate diagnosis, but are also vital for the creation of targeted strategies that preemptively confront specific resistance pathways [152].

Translational research tools like patient-derived organoids (PDOs) and xenograft models (PDX) are instrumental in applying preclinical findings to clinical treatment design. For instance, PDOs derived from colorectal cancer patients have been utilized to evaluate the efficacy of novel drugs, replicating the complex cellular environment of the originating tumor [153,154]. These studies have led directly to clinical trials and adjustments to treatment regimens, exemplifying how PDOs can significantly influence therapeutic planning and patient management.

In the vanguard of translational research, PDX models stand out for their direct impact on clinical decision-making. By engrafting human tumor tissues into immunodeficient mice, PDX models maintain the tumor's intrinsic heterogeneity, providing insights into the tumor's response to new treatments. These models have significantly advanced our understanding of resistance mechanisms, guiding the design of clinical trials aimed at targeted resistance pathways.

For instance, PDX research has led to the discovery of alternative immune checkpoints and changes in antigen presentation, shaping the development of combination therapies and influencing clinical treatment modifications. Such studies have also identified biomarkers predictive of treatment response, allowing for the adaptation of clinical protocols [155].

A key example of the impact of PDX models is their use in pinpointing specific genetic mutations that confer resistance to standard therapies. Insights gained from PDX studies have informed the enrollment of patients in trials for new targeted agents, leading to improved outcomes. These translational models are thus integral to the evolution of personalized medicine, enhancing the specificity and adaptability of cancer therapies [155].

PDX models, together with PDOs, enhance therapeutic planning by replicating the complex tumor environment, thereby offering a dynamic platform for drug evaluation and the development of personalized treatment regimens [153,154].

The synergy between clinical acumen and advanced translational models is reshaping cancer therapy, increasing the precision of the current treatments, and paving the way for innovative strategies to navigate the complexities of immunotherapy resistance. This integrated approach is set to refine patient care, promising a future where cancer treatment is as personalized as it is effective.

7. Future Perspectives in Immunotherapy

The future of immunotherapy is illuminated by advancements across varied disciplines, seamlessly integrating cutting-edge technologies poised to redefine oncological breakthroughs.

At the vanguard of these advancements, the integration of artificial intelligence (AI) and machine learning offers the capability to decipher vast genetic and proteomic datasets [156–158]. While this technological leap revolutionizes personalized immunotherapy by predicting tumor behavior and resistance mechanisms, as well as enabling real-time patient monitoring, it also brings forth challenges. For instance, ensuring the privacy and security of patient data processed by AI becomes paramount. Moreover, the algorithms' decision-making processes require transparency, especially when used to make clinical recommendations. Ethical considerations arise, questioning the extent of reliance on AI for treatment decisions and potential biases embedded within the algorithms.

Nanotechnology, emphasizing nanoparticles, holds significant potential to enhance the immunotherapy [8,50,52,159–161]. Its ability to deliver drugs precisely to tumor sites and fine-tune immune responses charts the path for groundbreaking strategies. These include modifying the TME to impede tumor growth, optimizing nutrient dynamics within the TME, and propelling the development of neoantigen vaccines. However, the use of nanoparticles raises concerns regarding long-term safety, potential off-target effects, and their interactions with the body's natural systems. Ethical discussions also surround the equitable distribution of such advanced treatments and the potential high costs associated with them.

Tumor epigenetics is a rising domain, with research directed toward harnessing epigenetic modulators to manipulate gene expression patterns. This tactic could potentially combat immunotherapeutic resistance, thus diversifying treatment avenues.

Simultaneously, telemedicine platforms are bridging geographical chasms, ensuring that specialized care becomes universally accessible [162]. Such platforms empower individuals in regions with constrained specialty resources to receive optimal treatment recommendations. The prevailing transformative phase in immunotherapy flourishes with interdisciplinary collaboration. Disciplines like genetics, immunology, bioengineering, and sociology coalesce, exemplified by the amalgamation of genomic sequencing, microfluidic technologies, and 3D tumor modeling to sharpen therapeutic strategies.

In summation, the dynamic realm of immunotherapy intertwines an array of disciplines, pioneering technologies, and global partnerships. The forthcoming epoch promises unmatched precision and flexibility, as well as a rejuvenated wave of oncological innovations, albeit not without its challenges and ethical dilemmas.

8. Conclusions

Throughout our journey into the complex landscape of immunotherapy, we confronted a myriad of challenges and opportunities. The foremost among these was the issue of immunotherapy resistance. While such challenges might seem daunting, they also serve as gateways to novel innovations. Our increasingly profound comprehension, bolstered by advancements in AI, nanotechnology, and epigenetics, is propelling us toward solutions that were once considered beyond reach.

Immunotherapy heralds a paradigm shift in oncological treatments, emphasizing the body's intrinsic defenses against malignancies. Yet, the ever-present shadow of resistance reminds us of the continuous need for exploration, adaptation, and innovation. It is the collective endeavors of researchers, clinicians, and pioneers across disciplines that underpin the remarkable breakthroughs we witness today. These efforts inch us closer to the overarching goal: to overcome cancer resistance and elevate patient outcomes.

However, like all scientific pursuits, our research has its confines. Future studies might focus on deeper dives into molecular mechanisms, patient-specific factors, or even socio-economic considerations that could influence resistance. Expanding on these areas would undeniably enrich our understanding.

In summary, our journey through the complexities of immunotherapy resistance is continuous, but the advancements made signal a hopeful future. Here, cancer treatments are envisioned to be not only more personalized and powerful, but also characterized by fewer adverse effects. The crux of this progress lies in persistent research, international cooperation, and a steadfast commitment to revolutionizing the story of cancer treatment.

Author Contributions: L.Y. and W.M. conceptualized the article and prepared figures. L.Y., Q.W., and W.M. wrote and edited the manuscript. W.M. finalized the figures and manuscript. All authors have read and agreed to the published version of the manuscript.

Funding: This research received no external funding.

Institutional Review Board Statement: Not applicable.

Informed Consent Statement: Not applicable.

Data Availability Statement: No new data were created or analyzed in this study. Data sharing does not apply to this article.

Conflicts of Interest: The authors confirm that the research was undertaken without any commercial or financial affiliations that might be perceived as potential conflicts of interest.

Abbreviations

ACT	adoptive cell therapy
AI	artificial intelligence
CAR	chimeric antigen receptor
CTLs	cytotoxic T cells
CTLA-4	cytotoxic T-lymphocyte-associated antigen 4
cfDNA	cell-free DNA
CTCs	circulating tumor cells
EGFR	epidermal growth factor receptor
LAG-3	lymphocyte activation gene-3
MDSCs	myeloid-derived suppressor cells
MHC	major histocompatibility complex
NK	natural killer
NSCLC	non-small-cell lung cancer
PBMC	peripheral blood mononuclear cells

PD-1	programmed cell death protein 1
PD-L1	programmed death-ligand 1
PDO	patient-derived organoids
PDX	patient-derived xenograft
TAMs	tumor-associated macrophages
TAM1	type-1 TAM
TAM2	type-2 TAM
TAN1	type-1 TAN
TAN2	type-2 TAN
TANs	tumor-associated neutrophils
TIGIT	T cell immunoreceptor with immunoglobulin and ITIM domain
TIM-3	T cell immunoglobulin and mucin-domain-containing-3
TGF	transforming growth factor
Tregs	regulatory T cells
TMB	tumor mutational burden
TME	tumor microenvironment

References

1. Shin, Y.H.; Bang, S.; Park, S.M.; Ma, X.; Cassilly, C.; Graham, D.; Xavier, R.; Clardy, J. Revisiting Coley's Toxins: Immunogenic Cardiolipins from Streptococcus pyogenes. *J. Am. Chem. Soc.* **2023**, *145*, 21183–21188. [CrossRef]
2. McCarthy, E.F. The toxins of William B. Coley and the treatment of bone and soft-tissue sarcomas. *Iowa Orthop. J.* **2006**, *26*, 154–158.
3. Coley, W.B. The treatment of malignant tumors by repeated inoculations of erysipelas; with a report of ten original cases. *Am. J. Med. Sci.* **1893**, *105*, 487–511. [CrossRef]
4. Brunet, J.F.; Denizot, F.; Luciani, M.F.; Roux-Dosseto, M.; Suzan, M.; Mattei, M.G.; Golstein, P. A new member of the immunoglobulin superfamily—CTLA-4. *Nature* **1987**, *328*, 267–270. [CrossRef]
5. Zahavi, D.; Weiner, L. Monoclonal Antibodies in Cancer Therapy. *Antibodies* **2020**, *9*, 34. [CrossRef] [PubMed]
6. Lee, H.T.; Lee, S.H.; Heo, Y.S. Molecular Interactions of Antibody Drugs Targeting PD-1, PD-L1, and CTLA-4 in Immuno-Oncology. *Molecules* **2019**, *24*, 1190. [CrossRef]
7. Yao, L.; Jia, G.; Lu, L.; Bao, Y.; Ma, W. Factors affecting tumor responders and predictive biomarkers of toxicities in cancer patients treated with immune checkpoint inhibitors. *Int. Immunopharmacol.* **2020**, *85*, 106628. [CrossRef]
8. Bae, J.; Parayath, N.; Ma, W.; Amiji, M.; Munshi, N.; Anderson, K.C. BCMA peptide-engineered nanoparticles enhance induction and function of antigen-specific CD8(+) cytotoxic T lymphocytes against multiple myeloma: Clinical applications. *Leukemia* **2020**, *34*, 210–223. [CrossRef] [PubMed]
9. Chen, Q.; Lu, L.; Ma, W. Efficacy, Safety, and Challenges of CAR T-Cells in the Treatment of Solid Tumors. *Cancers* **2022**, *14*, 5983. [CrossRef] [PubMed]
10. Jogalekar, M.P.; Rajendran, R.L.; Khan, F.; Dmello, C.; Gangadaran, P.; Ahn, B.C. CAR T-Cell-Based gene therapy for cancers: New perspectives, challenges, and clinical developments. *Front. Immunol.* **2022**, *13*, 925985. [CrossRef] [PubMed]
11. Murciano-Goroff, Y.R.; Warner, A.B.; Wolchok, J.D. The future of cancer immunotherapy: Microenvironment-targeting combinations. *Cell Res.* **2020**, *30*, 507–519. [CrossRef]
12. Li, X.; Zhang, S.; Guo, G.; Han, J.; Yu, J. Gut microbiome in modulating immune checkpoint inhibitors. *EBioMedicine* **2022**, *82*, 104163. [CrossRef] [PubMed]
13. Jackson, C.M.; Choi, J.; Lim, M. Mechanisms of immunotherapy resistance: Lessons from glioblastoma. *Nat. Immunol.* **2019**, *20*, 1100–1109. [CrossRef] [PubMed]
14. Khalaf, K.; Hana, D.; Chou, J.T.; Singh, C.; Mackiewicz, A.; Kaczmarek, M. Aspects of the Tumor Microenvironment Involved in Immune Resistance and Drug Resistance. *Front. Immunol.* **2021**, *12*, 656364. [CrossRef] [PubMed]
15. Haist, M.; Stege, H.; Grabbe, S.; Bros, M. The Functional Crosstalk between Myeloid-Derived Suppressor Cells and Regulatory T Cells within the Immunosuppressive Tumor Microenvironment. *Cancers* **2021**, *13*, 210. [CrossRef] [PubMed]
16. Iliadi, C.; Verset, L.; Bouchart, C.; Martinive, P.; Van Gestel, D.; Krayem, M. The current understanding of the immune landscape relative to radiotherapy across tumor types. *Front. Immunol.* **2023**, *14*, 1148692. [CrossRef]
17. Piper, M.; Kluger, H.; Ruppin, E.; Hu-Lieskovan, S. Immune Resistance Mechanisms and the Road to Personalized Immunotherapy. *Am. Soc. Clin. Oncol. Educ. Book* **2023**, *43*, e390290. [CrossRef]
18. Fountzilas, E.; Tsimberidou, A.M.; Vo, H.H.; Kurzrock, R. Clinical trial design in the era of precision medicine. *Genome Med.* **2022**, *14*, 101. [CrossRef]
19. Zhang, C.; Liu, X.; Jin, S.; Chen, Y.; Guo, R. Ferroptosis in cancer therapy: A novel approach to reversing drug resistance. *Mol. Cancer* **2022**, *21*, 47. [CrossRef]
20. Liao, J.; Li, X.; Gan, Y.; Han, S.; Rong, P.; Wang, W.; Li, W.; Zhou, L. Artificial intelligence assists precision medicine in cancer treatment. *Front. Oncol.* **2022**, *12*, 998222. [CrossRef]

21. Brown, C.E.; Bucktrout, S.; Butterfield, L.H.; Futer, O.; Galanis, E.; Hormigo, A.; Lim, M.; Okada, H.; Prins, R.; Marr, S.S.; et al. The future of cancer immunotherapy for brain tumors: A collaborative workshop. *J. Transl. Med.* **2022**, *20*, 236. [CrossRef]
22. Luo, J.; Li, X.; Wei, K.L.; Chen, G.; Xiong, D.D. Advances in the application of computational pathology in diagnosis, immunomicroenvironment recognition, and immunotherapy evaluation of breast cancer: A narrative review. *J. Cancer Res. Clin. Oncol.* **2023**, *149*, 12535–12542. [CrossRef] [PubMed]
23. Abaza, A.; Sid Idris, F.; Anis Shaikh, H.; Vahora, I.; Moparthi, K.P.; Al Rushaidi, M.T.; Muddam, M.R.; Obajeun, O.A.; Jaramillo, A.P.; Khan, S. Programmed Cell Death Protein 1 (PD-1) and Programmed Cell Death Ligand 1 (PD-L1) Immunotherapy: A Promising Breakthrough in Cancer Therapeutics. *Cureus* **2023**, *15*, e44582. [CrossRef] [PubMed]
24. Yu, J.; Guo, Z.; Wang, L. Progress and Challenges of Immunotherapy Predictive Biomarkers for Triple Negative Breast Cancer in the Era of Single-Cell Multi-Omics. *Life* **2023**, *13*, 1189. [CrossRef] [PubMed]
25. Lei, Z.N.; Tian, Q.; Teng, Q.X.; Wurpel, J.N.D.; Zeng, L.; Pan, Y.; Chen, Z.S. Understanding and targeting resistance mechanisms in cancer. *MedComm (2020)* **2023**, *4*, e265. [CrossRef]
26. Kim, S.K.; Cho, S.W. The Evasion Mechanisms of Cancer Immunity and Drug Intervention in the Tumor Microenvironment. *Front. Pharmacol.* **2022**, *13*, 868695. [CrossRef] [PubMed]
27. Dhatchinamoorthy, K.; Colbert, J.D.; Rock, K.L. Cancer Immune Evasion Through Loss of MHC Class I Antigen Presentation. *Front. Immunol.* **2021**, *12*, 636568. [CrossRef] [PubMed]
28. Liu, Z.; Zhou, Z.; Dang, Q.; Xu, H.; Lv, J.; Li, H.; Han, X. Immunosuppression in tumor immune microenvironment and its optimization from CAR-T cell therapy. *Theranostics* **2022**, *12*, 6273–6290. [CrossRef]
29. Tie, Y.; Tang, F.; Wei, Y.Q.; Wei, X.W. Immunosuppressive cells in cancer: Mechanisms and potential therapeutic targets. *J. Hematol. Oncol.* **2022**, *15*, 61. [CrossRef]
30. Trujillo, J.A.; Luke, J.J.; Zha, Y.; Segal, J.P.; Ritterhouse, L.L.; Spranger, S.; Matijevich, K.; Gajewski, T.F. Secondary resistance to immunotherapy associated with beta-catenin pathway activation or PTEN loss in metastatic melanoma. *J. Immunother. Cancer* **2019**, *7*, 295. [CrossRef]
31. Cendrowicz, E.; Sas, Z.; Bremer, E.; Rygiel, T.P. The Role of Macrophages in Cancer Development and Therapy. *Cancers* **2021**, *13*, 1946. [CrossRef] [PubMed]
32. Baghban, R.; Roshangar, L.; Jahanban-Esfahlan, R.; Seidi, K.; Ebrahimi-Kalan, A.; Jaymand, M.; Kolahian, S.; Javaheri, T.; Zare, P. Tumor microenvironment complexity and therapeutic implications at a glance. *Cell Commun. Signal.* **2020**, *18*, 59. [CrossRef] [PubMed]
33. Chakravarthi, B.V.; Nepal, S.; Varambally, S. Genomic and Epigenomic Alterations in Cancer. *Am. J. Pathol.* **2016**, *186*, 1724–1735. [CrossRef] [PubMed]
34. Dai, E.; Zhu, Z.; Wahed, S.; Qu, Z.; Storkus, W.J.; Guo, Z.S. Epigenetic modulation of antitumor immunity for improved cancer immunotherapy. *Mol. Cancer* **2021**, *20*, 171. [CrossRef]
35. Martinez-Jimenez, F.; Priestley, P.; Shale, C.; Baber, J.; Rozemuller, E.; Cuppen, E. Genetic immune escape landscape in primary and metastatic cancer. *Nat. Genet.* **2023**, *55*, 820–831. [CrossRef]
36. Cao, J.; Yan, Q. Cancer Epigenetics, Tumor Immunity, and Immunotherapy. *Trends Cancer* **2020**, *6*, 580–592. [CrossRef] [PubMed]
37. Liang, Y.; Turcan, S. Epigenetic Drugs and Their Immune Modulating Potential in Cancers. *Biomedicines* **2022**, *10*, 211. [CrossRef]
38. Yang, J.; Xu, J.; Wang, W.; Zhang, B.; Yu, X.; Shi, S. Epigenetic regulation in the tumor microenvironment: Molecular mechanisms and therapeutic targets. *Signal Transduct. Target. Ther.* **2023**, *8*, 210. [CrossRef]
39. Lindau, D.; Gielen, P.; Kroesen, M.; Wesseling, P.; Adema, G.J. The immunosuppressive tumour network: Myeloid-derived suppressor cells, regulatory T cells and natural killer T cells. *Immunology* **2013**, *138*, 105–115. [CrossRef]
40. Ma, T.; Renz, B.W.; Ilmer, M.; Koch, D.; Yang, Y.; Werner, J.; Bazhin, A.V. Myeloid-Derived Suppressor Cells in Solid Tumors. *Cells* **2022**, *11*, 310. [CrossRef]
41. Sun, R.; Zhao, H.; Gao, D.S.; Ni, A.; Li, H.; Chen, L.; Lu, X.; Chen, K.; Lu, B. Amphiregulin couples IL1RL1(+) regulatory T cells and cancer-associated fibroblasts to impede antitumor immunity. *Sci. Adv.* **2023**, *9*, eadd7399. [CrossRef]
42. Shi, H.; Li, K.; Ni, Y.; Liang, X.; Zhao, X. Myeloid-Derived Suppressor Cells: Implications in the Resistance of Malignant Tumors to T Cell-Based Immunotherapy. *Front. Cell Dev. Biol.* **2021**, *9*, 707198. [CrossRef]
43. Li, K.; Shi, H.; Zhang, B.; Ou, X.; Ma, Q.; Chen, Y.; Shu, P.; Li, D.; Wang, Y. Myeloid-derived suppressor cells as immunosuppressive regulators and therapeutic targets in cancer. *Signal Transduct. Target. Ther.* **2021**, *6*, 362. [CrossRef]
44. Kopecka, J.; Salaroglio, I.C.; Perez-Ruiz, E.; Sarmento-Ribeiro, A.B.; Saponara, S.; De Las Rivas, J.; Riganti, C. Hypoxia as a driver of resistance to immunotherapy. *Drug Resist. Updat.* **2021**, *59*, 100787. [CrossRef] [PubMed]
45. Wang, B.; Zhao, Q.; Zhang, Y.; Liu, Z.; Zheng, Z.; Liu, S.; Meng, L.; Xin, Y.; Jiang, X. Targeting hypoxia in the tumor microenvironment: A potential strategy to improve cancer immunotherapy. *J. Exp. Clin. Cancer Res.* **2021**, *40*, 24. [CrossRef] [PubMed]
46. Shi, T.; Zhu, J.; Zhang, X.; Mao, X. The Role of Hypoxia and Cancer Stem Cells in Development of Glioblastoma. *Cancers* **2023**, *15*, 2613. [CrossRef] [PubMed]
47. Bhattacharya, S.; Calar, K.; de la Puente, P. Mimicking tumor hypoxia and tumor-immune interactions employing three-dimensional in vitro models. *J. Exp. Clin. Cancer Res.* **2020**, *39*, 75. [CrossRef] [PubMed]
48. Shurin, M.R.; Umansky, V. Cross-talk between HIF and PD-1/PD-L1 pathways in carcinogenesis and therapy. *J. Clin. Investig.* **2022**, *132*, e159473. [CrossRef] [PubMed]

49. Wu, Q.; You, L.; Nepovimova, E.; Heger, Z.; Wu, W.; Kuca, K.; Adam, V. Hypoxia-inducible factors: Master regulators of hypoxic tumor immune escape. *J. Hematol. Oncol.* **2022**, *15*, 77. [CrossRef]
50. Li, H.; Shao, S.; Cai, J.; Burner, D.; Lu, L.; Chen, Q.; Minev, B.; Ma, W. Artificial human antigen-presenting cells are superior to dendritic cells at inducing cytotoxic T-cell responses. *Immunology* **2017**, *152*, 462–471. [CrossRef] [PubMed]
51. Lu, L.; Ma, W.; Johnson, C.H.; Khan, S.A.; Irwin, M.L.; Pusztai, L. In silico designed mRNA vaccines targeting CA-125 neoantigen in breast and ovarian cancer. *Vaccine* **2023**, *41*, 2073–2083. [CrossRef]
52. Ma, W.; Smith, T.; Bogin, V.; Zhang, Y.; Ozkan, C.; Ozkan, M.; Hayden, M.; Schroter, S.; Carrier, E.; Messmer, D.; et al. Enhanced presentation of MHC class Ia, Ib and class II-restricted peptides encapsulated in biodegradable nanoparticles: A promising strategy for tumor immunotherapy. *J. Transl. Med.* **2011**, *9*, 34. [CrossRef] [PubMed]
53. Kallingal, A.; Olszewski, M.; Maciejewska, N.; Brankiewicz, W.; Baginski, M. Cancer immune escape: The role of antigen presentation machinery. *J. Cancer Res. Clin. Oncol.* **2023**, *149*, 8131–8141. [CrossRef] [PubMed]
54. Haddad, A.F.; Young, J.S.; Gill, S.; Aghi, M.K. Resistance to immune checkpoint blockade: Mechanisms, counter-acting approaches, and future directions. *Semin. Cancer Biol.* **2022**, *86*, 532–541. [CrossRef] [PubMed]
55. Wang, B.; Han, Y.; Zhang, Y.; Zhao, Q.; Wang, H.; Wei, J.; Meng, L.; Xin, Y.; Jiang, X. Overcoming acquired resistance to cancer immune checkpoint therapy: Potential strategies based on molecular mechanisms. *Cell Biosci.* **2023**, *13*, 120. [CrossRef] [PubMed]
56. Gonzalez, H.; Hagerling, C.; Werb, Z. Roles of the immune system in cancer: From tumor initiation to metastatic progression. *Genes Dev.* **2018**, *32*, 1267–1284. [CrossRef] [PubMed]
57. Marin-Acevedo, J.A.; Dholaria, B.; Soyano, A.E.; Knutson, K.L.; Chumsri, S.; Lou, Y. Next generation of immune checkpoint therapy in cancer: New developments and challenges. *J. Hematol. Oncol.* **2018**, *11*, 39. [CrossRef]
58. Naimi, A.; Mohammed, R.N.; Raji, A.; Chupradit, S.; Yumashev, A.V.; Suksatan, W.; Shalaby, M.N.; Thangavelu, L.; Kamrava, S.; Shomali, N.; et al. Tumor immunotherapies by immune checkpoint inhibitors (ICIs); the pros and cons. *Cell Commun. Signal.* **2022**, *20*, 44. [CrossRef]
59. Webb, E.S.; Liu, P.; Baleeiro, R.; Lemoine, N.R.; Yuan, M.; Wang, Y.H. Immune checkpoint inhibitors in cancer therapy. *J. Biomed. Res.* **2018**, *32*, 317–326. [CrossRef]
60. Xie, Q.; Zhang, P.; Wang, Y.; Mei, W.; Zeng, C. Overcoming resistance to immune checkpoint inhibitors in hepatocellular carcinoma: Challenges and opportunities. *Front. Oncol.* **2022**, *12*, 958720. [CrossRef]
61. Fares, C.M.; Van Allen, E.M.; Drake, C.G.; Allison, J.P.; Hu-Lieskovan, S. Mechanisms of Resistance to Immune Checkpoint Blockade: Why Does Checkpoint Inhibitor Immunotherapy Not Work for All Patients? *Am. Soc. Clin. Oncol. Educ. Book* **2019**, *39*, 147–164. [CrossRef]
62. Passaro, A.; Brahmer, J.; Antonia, S.; Mok, T.; Peters, S. Managing Resistance to Immune Checkpoint Inhibitors in Lung Cancer: Treatment and Novel Strategies. *J. Clin. Oncol.* **2022**, *40*, 598–610. [CrossRef] [PubMed]
63. Metropulos, A.E.; Munshi, H.G.; Principe, D.R. The difficulty in translating the preclinical success of combined TGFbeta and immune checkpoint inhibition to clinical trial. *EBioMedicine* **2022**, *86*, 104380. [CrossRef]
64. Tiwari, A.; Trivedi, R.; Lin, S.Y. Tumor microenvironment: Barrier or opportunity towards effective cancer therapy. *J. Biomed. Sci.* **2022**, *29*, 83. [CrossRef]
65. Chen, M.L.; Pittet, M.J.; Gorelik, L.; Flavell, R.A.; Weissleder, R.; von Boehmer, H.; Khazaie, K. Regulatory T cells suppress tumor-specific CD8 T cell cytotoxicity through TGF-beta signals in vivo. *Proc. Natl. Acad. Sci. USA* **2005**, *102*, 419–424. [CrossRef] [PubMed]
66. Huang, L.; Guo, Y.; Liu, S.; Wang, H.; Zhu, J.; Ou, L.; Xu, X. Targeting regulatory T cells for immunotherapy in melanoma. *Mol. Biomed.* **2021**, *2*, 11. [CrossRef] [PubMed]
67. Itahashi, K.; Irie, T.; Nishikawa, H. Regulatory T-cell development in the tumor microenvironment. *Eur. J. Immunol.* **2022**, *52*, 1216–1227. [CrossRef]
68. Nishikawa, H.; Koyama, S. Mechanisms of regulatory T cell infiltration in tumors: Implications for innovative immune precision therapies. *J. Immunother. Cancer* **2021**, *9*, e002591. [CrossRef]
69. Zhao, H.; Wu, L.; Yan, G.; Chen, Y.; Zhou, M.; Wu, Y.; Li, Y. Inflammation and tumor progression: Signaling pathways and targeted intervention. *Signal Transduct. Target. Ther.* **2021**, *6*, 263. [CrossRef]
70. Wang, S.; Zhao, X.; Wu, S.; Cui, D.; Xu, Z. Myeloid-derived suppressor cells: Key immunosuppressive regulators and therapeutic targets in hematological malignancies. *Biomark. Res.* **2023**, *11*, 34. [CrossRef]
71. Zalfa, C.; Paust, S. Natural Killer Cell Interactions with Myeloid Derived Suppressor Cells in the Tumor Microenvironment and Implications for Cancer Immunotherapy. *Front. Immunol.* **2021**, *12*, 633205. [CrossRef]
72. Jakos, T.; Pislar, A.; Jewett, A.; Kos, J. Myeloid-Derived Suppressor Cells Hamper Natural Killer Cell Activity in Cancer: Role of Peptidases. *Crit. Rev. Immunol.* **2021**, *41*, 77–99. [CrossRef] [PubMed]
73. Li, Y.; He, H.; Jihu, R.; Zhou, J.; Zeng, R.; Yan, H. Novel Characterization of Myeloid-Derived Suppressor Cells in Tumor Microenvironment. *Front. Cell Dev. Biol.* **2021**, *9*, 698532. [CrossRef] [PubMed]
74. Mehdizadeh, R.; Shariatpanahi, S.P.; Goliaei, B.; Ruegg, C. Targeting myeloid-derived suppressor cells in combination with tumor cell vaccination predicts anti-tumor immunity and breast cancer dormancy: An in silico experiment. *Sci. Rep.* **2023**, *13*, 5875. [CrossRef] [PubMed]
75. He, Z.; Zhang, S. Tumor-Associated Macrophages and Their Functional Transformation in the Hypoxic Tumor Microenvironment. *Front. Immunol.* **2021**, *12*, 741305. [CrossRef] [PubMed]

76. Chen, S.; Saeed, A.; Liu, Q.; Jiang, Q.; Xu, H.; Xiao, G.G.; Rao, L.; Duo, Y. Macrophages in immunoregulation and therapeutics. *Signal Transduct. Target. Ther.* **2023**, *8*, 207. [CrossRef]
77. Li, M.; He, L.; Zhu, J.; Zhang, P.; Liang, S. Targeting tumor-associated macrophages for cancer treatment. *Cell Biosci.* **2022**, *12*, 85. [CrossRef] [PubMed]
78. Mehta, A.K.; Kadel, S.; Townsend, M.G.; Oliwa, M.; Guerriero, J.L. Macrophage Biology and Mechanisms of Immune Suppression in Breast Cancer. *Front. Immunol.* **2021**, *12*, 643771. [CrossRef]
79. Feng, Y.; Ye, Z.; Song, F.; He, Y.; Liu, J. The Role of TAMs in Tumor Microenvironment and New Research Progress. *Stem Cells Int.* **2022**, *2022*, 5775696. [CrossRef]
80. Yan, M.; Zheng, M.; Niu, R.; Yang, X.; Tian, S.; Fan, L.; Li, Y.; Zhang, S. Roles of tumor-associated neutrophils in tumor metastasis and its clinical applications. *Front. Cell Dev. Biol.* **2022**, *10*, 938289. [CrossRef]
81. Que, H.; Fu, Q.; Lan, T.; Tian, X.; Wei, X. Tumor-associated neutrophils and neutrophil-targeted cancer therapies. *Biochim. Biophys. Acta Rev. Cancer* **2022**, *1877*, 188762. [CrossRef] [PubMed]
82. Wicks, E.E.; Semenza, G.L. Hypoxia-inducible factors: Cancer progression and clinical translation. *J. Clin. Investig.* **2022**, *132*, e159839. [CrossRef] [PubMed]
83. Li, Y.; Zhao, L.; Li, X.F. Hypoxia and the Tumor Microenvironment. *Technol. Cancer Res. Treat.* **2021**, *20*, 15330338211036304. [CrossRef]
84. Patsoukis, N.; Wang, Q.; Strauss, L.; Boussiotis, V.A. Revisiting the PD-1 pathway. *Sci. Adv.* **2020**, *6*, eabd2712. [CrossRef]
85. Yi, M.; Jiao, D.; Xu, H.; Liu, Q.; Zhao, W.; Han, X.; Wu, K. Biomarkers for predicting efficacy of PD-1/PD-L1 inhibitors. *Mol. Cancer* **2018**, *17*, 129. [CrossRef]
86. Zhang, Y.; Coleman, M.; Brekken, R.A. Perspectives on Hypoxia Signaling in Tumor Stroma. *Cancers* **2021**, *13*, 3070. [CrossRef] [PubMed]
87. Shklovskaya, E.; Rizos, H. MHC Class I Deficiency in Solid Tumors and Therapeutic Strategies to Overcome It. *Int. J. Mol. Sci.* **2021**, *22*, 6741. [CrossRef]
88. Wen, M.; Li, Y.; Qin, X.; Qin, B.; Wang, Q. Insight into Cancer Immunity: MHCs, Immune Cells and Commensal Microbiota. *Cells* **2023**, *12*, 1882. [CrossRef]
89. Zhou, J.; Bashey, A.; Zhong, R.; Corringham, S.; Messer, K.; Pu, M.; Ma, W.; Chut, T.; Soiffer, R.; Mitrovich, R.C.; et al. CTLA-4 blockade following relapse of malignancy after allogeneic stem cell transplantation is associated with T cell activation but not with increased levels of T regulatory cells. *Biol. Blood Marrow Transplant.* **2011**, *17*, 682–692. [CrossRef]
90. Chen, X.; Zhang, W.; Yang, W.; Zhou, M.; Liu, F. Acquired resistance for immune checkpoint inhibitors in cancer immunotherapy: Challenges and prospects. *Aging* **2022**, *14*, 1048–1064. [CrossRef]
91. Said, S.S.; Ibrahim, W.N. Cancer Resistance to Immunotherapy: Comprehensive Insights with Future Perspectives. *Pharmaceutics* **2023**, *15*, 1143. [CrossRef]
92. Lao, Y.; Shen, D.; Zhang, W.; He, R.; Jiang, M. Immune Checkpoint Inhibitors in Cancer Therapy—How to Overcome Drug Resistance? *Cancers* **2022**, *14*, 3575. [CrossRef]
93. Baxter, M.A.; Middleton, F.; Cagney, H.P.; Petty, R.D. Resistance to immune checkpoint inhibitors in advanced gastro-oesophageal cancers. *Br. J. Cancer* **2021**, *125*, 1068–1079. [CrossRef]
94. Dutta, S.; Ganguly, A.; Chatterjee, K.; Spada, S.; Mukherjee, S. Targets of Immune Escape Mechanisms in Cancer: Basis for Development and Evolution of Cancer Immune Checkpoint Inhibitors. *Biology* **2023**, *12*, 218. [CrossRef] [PubMed]
95. Vanneman, M.; Dranoff, G. Combining immunotherapy and targeted therapies in cancer treatment. *Nat. Rev. Cancer* **2012**, *12*, 237–251. [CrossRef] [PubMed]
96. Emran, T.B.; Shahriar, A.; Mahmud, A.R.; Rahman, T.; Abir, M.H.; Siddiquee, M.F.; Ahmed, H.; Rahman, N.; Nainu, F.; Wahyudin, E.; et al. Multidrug Resistance in Cancer: Understanding Molecular Mechanisms, Immunoprevention and Therapeutic Approaches. *Front. Oncol.* **2022**, *12*, 891652. [CrossRef] [PubMed]
97. Flies, D.B.; Langermann, S.; Jensen, C.; Karsdal, M.A.; Willumsen, N. Regulation of tumor immunity and immunotherapy by the tumor collagen extracellular matrix. *Front. Immunol.* **2023**, *14*, 1199513. [CrossRef] [PubMed]
98. Chen, C.; Liu, X.; Chang, C.Y.; Wang, H.Y.; Wang, R.F. The Interplay between T Cells and Cancer: The Basis of Immunotherapy. *Genes* **2023**, *14*, 1008. [CrossRef]
99. Mantovani, A.; Allavena, P.; Marchesi, F.; Garlanda, C. Macrophages as tools and targets in cancer therapy. *Nat. Rev. Drug Discov.* **2022**, *21*, 799–820. [CrossRef]
100. Park, K.; Veena, M.S.; Shin, D.S. Key Players of the Immunosuppressive Tumor Microenvironment and Emerging Therapeutic Strategies. *Front. Cell Dev. Biol.* **2022**, *10*, 830208. [CrossRef]
101. Wang, Y.; Huang, T.; Gu, J.; Lu, L. Targeting the metabolism of tumor-infiltrating regulatory T cells. *Trends Immunol.* **2023**, *44*, 598–612. [CrossRef]
102. Bejarano, L.; Jordao, M.J.C.; Joyce, J.A. Therapeutic Targeting of the Tumor Microenvironment. *Cancer Discov.* **2021**, *11*, 933–959. [CrossRef]
103. Lee, J.B.; Ha, S.J.; Kim, H.R. Clinical Insights into Novel Immune Checkpoint Inhibitors. *Front. Pharmacol.* **2021**, *12*, 681320. [CrossRef]
104. Dulal, D.; Boring, A.; Terrero, D.; Johnson, T.; Tiwari, A.K.; Raman, D. Tackling of Immunorefractory Tumors by Targeting Alternative Immune Checkpoints. *Cancers* **2023**, *15*, 2774. [CrossRef]

105. Zhu, X.; Fan, C.; Xiong, Z.; Chen, M.; Li, Z.; Tao, T.; Liu, X. Development and application of oncolytic viruses as the nemesis of tumor cells. *Front. Microbiol.* **2023**, *14*, 1188526. [CrossRef]
106. Chesney, J.A.; Ribas, A.; Long, G.V.; Kirkwood, J.M.; Dummer, R.; Puzanov, I.; Hoeller, C.; Gajewski, T.F.; Gutzmer, R.; Rutkowski, P.; et al. Randomized, Double-Blind, Placebo-Controlled, Global Phase III Trial of Talimogene Laherparepvec Combined with Pembrolizumab for Advanced Melanoma. *J. Clin. Oncol.* **2023**, *41*, 528–540. [CrossRef] [PubMed]
107. Feldman, S.A.; Assadipour, Y.; Kriley, I.; Goff, S.L.; Rosenberg, S.A. Adoptive Cell Therapy—Tumor-Infiltrating Lymphocytes, T-Cell Receptors, and Chimeric Antigen Receptors. *Semin. Oncol.* **2015**, *42*, 626–639. [CrossRef]
108. Li, J.; Xiao, Z.; Wang, D.; Jia, L.; Nie, S.; Zeng, X.; Hu, W. The screening, identification, design and clinical application of tumor-specific neoantigens for TCR-T cells. *Mol. Cancer* **2023**, *22*, 141. [CrossRef] [PubMed]
109. Ingram, Z.; Madan, S.; Merchant, J.; Carter, Z.; Gordon, Z.; Carey, G.; Webb, T.J. Targeting Natural Killer T Cells in Solid Malignancies. *Cells* **2021**, *10*, 1329. [CrossRef] [PubMed]
110. Zhu, S.; Zhang, T.; Zheng, L.; Liu, H.; Song, W.; Liu, D.; Li, Z.; Pan, C.X. Combination strategies to maximize the benefits of cancer immunotherapy. *J. Hematol. Oncol.* **2021**, *14*, 156. [CrossRef] [PubMed]
111. Liu, J.; Fu, M.; Wang, M.; Wan, D.; Wei, Y.; Wei, X. Cancer vaccines as promising immuno-therapeutics: Platforms and current progress. *J. Hematol. Oncol.* **2022**, *15*, 28. [CrossRef] [PubMed]
112. Kaczmarek, M.; Poznanska, J.; Fechner, F.; Michalska, N.; Paszkowska, S.; Napierala, A.; Mackiewicz, A. Cancer Vaccine Therapeutics: Limitations and Effectiveness—A Literature Review. *Cells* **2023**, *12*, 2159. [CrossRef] [PubMed]
113. Lee, K.W.; Yam, J.W.P.; Mao, X. Dendritic Cell Vaccines: A Shift from Conventional Approach to New Generations. *Cells* **2023**, *12*, 2147. [CrossRef] [PubMed]
114. Gupta, M.; Wahi, A.; Sharma, P.; Nagpal, R.; Raina, N.; Kaurav, M.; Bhattacharya, J.; Rodrigues Oliveira, S.M.; Dolma, K.G.; Paul, A.K.; et al. Recent Advances in Cancer Vaccines: Challenges, Achievements, and Futuristic Prospects. *Vaccines* **2022**, *10*, 2011. [CrossRef] [PubMed]
115. Goodman, R.S.; Johnson, D.B.; Balko, J.M. Corticosteroids and Cancer Immunotherapy. *Clin. Cancer Res.* **2023**, *29*, 2580–2587. [CrossRef] [PubMed]
116. Kalfeist, L.; Galland, L.; Ledys, F.; Ghiringhelli, F.; Limagne, E.; Ladoire, S. Impact of Glucocorticoid Use in Oncology in the Immunotherapy Era. *Cells* **2022**, *11*, 770. [CrossRef]
117. Meng, L.; Wei, Y.; Xiao, Y. Chemo-immunoablation of solid tumors: A new concept in tumor ablation. *Front. Immunol.* **2022**, *13*, 1057535. [CrossRef]
118. Li, J.Y.; Chen, Y.P.; Li, Y.Q.; Liu, N.; Ma, J. Chemotherapeutic and targeted agents can modulate the tumor microenvironment and increase the efficacy of immune checkpoint blockades. *Mol. Cancer* **2021**, *20*, 27. [CrossRef]
119. Eng, L.; Sutradhar, R.; Niu, Y.; Liu, N.; Liu, Y.; Kaliwal, Y.; Powis, M.L.; Liu, G.; Peppercorn, J.M.; Bedard, P.L.; et al. Impact of Antibiotic Exposure before Immune Checkpoint Inhibitor Treatment on Overall Survival in Older Adults with Cancer: A Population-Based Study. *J. Clin. Oncol.* **2023**, *41*, 3122–3134. [CrossRef]
120. Peng, C.; Rabold, K.; Mulder, W.J.M.; Jaeger, M.; Netea-Maier, R.T. Kinase Inhibitors' Effects on Innate Immunity in Solid Cancers. *Cancers* **2021**, *13*, 5695. [CrossRef]
121. Castelo-Soccio, L.; Kim, H.; Gadina, M.; Schwartzberg, P.L.; Laurence, A.; O'Shea, J.J. Protein kinases: Drug targets for immunological disorders. *Nat. Rev. Immunol.* **2023**, *23*, 787–806. [CrossRef]
122. Fogli, L.K.; Aurigemma, R.; Sommers, C.L.; Singh, A.; Bourcier, K.; Ernstoff, M.S.; NCI Cell Therapy Workshop Committee. Challenges and next steps in the advancement of immunotherapy: Summary of the 2018 and 2020 National Cancer Institute workshops on cell-based immunotherapy for solid tumors. *J. Immuno Ther. Cancer* **2021**, *9*, e003048. [CrossRef]
123. Xu, S.; Tan, S.; Guo, L. Patient-Derived Organoids as a Promising Tool for Multimodal Management of Sarcomas. *Cancers* **2023**, *15*, 4339. [CrossRef] [PubMed]
124. Seyhan, A.A.; Carini, C. Insights and Strategies of Melanoma Immunotherapy: Predictive Biomarkers of Response and Resistance and Strategies to Improve Response Rates. *Int. J. Mol. Sci.* **2022**, *24*, 41. [CrossRef] [PubMed]
125. Bai, R.; Lv, Z.; Xu, D.; Cui, J. Predictive biomarkers for cancer immunotherapy with immune checkpoint inhibitors. *Biomark. Res.* **2020**, *8*, 34. [CrossRef]
126. Shao, J.; Jin, Y.; Jin, C. A new approach to overcoming resistance to immunotherapy: Nanotechnology. *Front. Oncol.* **2023**, *13*, 1210245. [CrossRef] [PubMed]
127. Xu, M.; Zhang, T.; Xia, R.; Wei, Y.; Wei, X. Targeting the tumor stroma for cancer therapy. *Mol. Cancer* **2022**, *21*, 208. [CrossRef]
128. Curigliano, G.; Gelderblom, H.; Mach, N.; Doi, T.; Tai, D.; Forde, P.M.; Sarantopoulos, J.; Bedard, P.L.; Lin, C.C.; Hodi, F.S.; et al. Phase I/Ib Clinical Trial of Sabatolimab, an Anti-TIM-3 Antibody, Alone and in Combination with Spartalizumab, an Anti-PD-1 Antibody, in Advanced Solid Tumors. *Clin. Cancer Res.* **2021**, *27*, 3620–3629. [CrossRef]
129. Finck, A.V.; Blanchard, T.; Roselle, C.P.; Golinelli, G.; June, C.H. Engineered cellular immunotherapies in cancer and beyond. *Nat. Med.* **2022**, *28*, 678–689. [CrossRef]
130. Kiaie, S.H.; Salehi-Shadkami, H.; Sanaei, M.J.; Azizi, M.; Shokrollahi Barough, M.; Nasr, M.S.; Sheibani, M. Nano-immunotherapy: Overcoming delivery challenge of immune checkpoint therapy. *J. Nanobiotechnol.* **2023**, *21*, 339. [CrossRef]
131. Bai, R.; Chen, N.; Li, L.; Du, N.; Bai, L.; Lv, Z.; Tian, H.; Cui, J. Mechanisms of Cancer Resistance to Immunotherapy. *Front. Oncol.* **2020**, *10*, 1290. [CrossRef] [PubMed]
132. Audia, J.E.; Campbell, R.M. Histone Modifications and Cancer. *Cold Spring Harb. Perspect. Biol.* **2016**, *8*, a019521. [CrossRef]

133. Xu, J.; Xu, H.M.; Yang, M.F.; Liang, Y.J.; Peng, Q.Z.; Zhang, Y.; Tian, C.M.; Wang, L.S.; Yao, J.; Nie, Y.Q.; et al. New Insights Into the Epigenetic Regulation of Inflammatory Bowel Disease. *Front. Pharmacol.* **2022**, *13*, 813659. [CrossRef]
134. Wang, C.; Wang, Z.; Yao, T.; Zhou, J.; Wang, Z. The immune-related role of beta-2-microglobulin in melanoma. *Front. Oncol.* **2022**, *12*, 944722. [CrossRef] [PubMed]
135. Liu, F.; Zhong, F.; Wu, H.; Che, K.; Shi, J.; Wu, N.; Fu, Y.; Wang, Y.; Hu, J.; Qian, X.; et al. Prevalence and Associations of Beta2-Microglobulin Mutations in MSI-H/dMMR Cancers. *Oncologist* **2023**, *28*, e136–e144. [CrossRef]
136. Hu, Q.; Bian, Q.; Rong, D.; Wang, L.; Song, J.; Huang, H.S.; Zeng, J.; Mei, J.; Wang, P.Y. JAK/STAT pathway: Extracellular signals, diseases, immunity, and therapeutic regimens. *Front. Bioeng. Biotechnol.* **2023**, *11*, 1110765. [CrossRef]
137. Shen, H.; Huang, F.; Zhang, X.; Ojo, O.A.; Li, Y.; Trummell, H.Q.; Anderson, J.C.; Fiveash, J.; Bredel, M.; Yang, E.S.; et al. Selective suppression of melanoma lacking IFN-gamma pathway by JAK inhibition depends on T cells and host TNF signaling. *Nat. Commun.* **2022**, *13*, 5013. [CrossRef]
138. Xie, N.; Shen, G.; Gao, W.; Huang, Z.; Huang, C.; Fu, L. Neoantigens: Promising targets for cancer therapy. *Signal Transduct. Target. Ther.* **2023**, *8*, 9. [CrossRef]
139. Blass, E.; Ott, P.A. Advances in the development of personalized neoantigen-based therapeutic cancer vaccines. *Nat. Rev. Clin. Oncol.* **2021**, *18*, 215–229. [CrossRef]
140. Mehdi, A.; Rabbani, S.A. Role of Methylation in Pro- and Anti-Cancer Immunity. *Cancers* **2021**, *13*, 545. [CrossRef]
141. Desaulniers, D.; Vasseur, P.; Jacobs, A.; Aguila, M.C.; Ertych, N.; Jacobs, M.N. Integration of Epigenetic Mechanisms into Non-Genotoxic Carcinogenicity Hazard Assessment: Focus on DNA Methylation and Histone Modifications. *Int. J. Mol. Sci.* **2021**, *22*, 10969. [CrossRef]
142. Markouli, M.; Strepkos, D.; Basdra, E.K.; Papavassiliou, A.G.; Piperi, C. Prominent Role of Histone Modifications in the Regulation of Tumor Metastasis. *Int. J. Mol. Sci.* **2021**, *22*, 2778. [CrossRef]
143. Xiong, D.; Zhang, L.; Sun, Z.J. Targeting the epigenome to reinvigorate T cells for cancer immunotherapy. *Mil. Med. Res.* **2023**, *10*, 59. [CrossRef]
144. Hu, C.; Liu, X.; Zeng, Y.; Liu, J.; Wu, F. DNA methyltransferase inhibitors combination therapy for the treatment of solid tumor: Mechanism and clinical application. *Clin. Epigenet.* **2021**, *13*, 166. [CrossRef]
145. Shen, C.; Li, M.; Duan, Y.; Jiang, X.; Hou, X.; Xue, F.; Zhang, Y.; Luo, Y. HDAC inhibitors enhance the anti-tumor effect of immunotherapies in hepatocellular carcinoma. *Front. Immunol.* **2023**, *14*, 1170207. [CrossRef]
146. Lu, G.; Jin, S.; Lin, S.; Gong, Y.; Zhang, L.; Yang, J.; Mou, W.; Du, J. Update on histone deacetylase inhibitors in peripheral T-cell lymphoma (PTCL). *Clin. Epigenet.* **2023**, *15*, 124. [CrossRef]
147. Derosa, L.; Routy, B.; Thomas, A.M.; Iebba, V.; Zalcman, G.; Friard, S.; Mazieres, J.; Audigier-Valette, C.; Moro-Sibilot, D.; Goldwasser, F.; et al. Intestinal Akkermansia muciniphila predicts clinical response to PD-1 blockade in patients with advanced non-small-cell lung cancer. *Nat. Med.* **2022**, *28*, 315–324. [CrossRef]
148. Patel, P.; Poudel, A.; Kafle, S.; Thapa Magar, M.; Cancarevic, I. Influence of Microbiome and Antibiotics on the Efficacy of Immune Checkpoint Inhibitors. *Cureus* **2021**, *13*, e16829. [CrossRef]
149. Najmi, M.; Tran, T.; Witt, R.G.; Nelson, K.C. Modulation of the Gut Microbiome to Enhance Immunotherapy Response in Metastatic Melanoma Patients: A Clinical Review. *Dermatol. Ther.* **2022**, *12*, 2489–2497. [CrossRef]
150. Villemin, C.; Six, A.; Neville, B.A.; Lawley, T.D.; Robinson, M.J.; Bakdash, G. The heightened importance of the microbiome in cancer immunotherapy. *Trends Immunol.* **2023**, *44*, 44–59. [CrossRef]
151. Sarhadi, V.K.; Armengol, G. Molecular Biomarkers in Cancer. *Biomolecules* **2022**, *12*, 1021. [CrossRef]
152. Seyhan, A.A.; Carini, C. Are innovation and new technologies in precision medicine paving a new era in patients centric care? *J. Transl. Med.* **2019**, *17*, 114. [CrossRef]
153. Wang, W.; Li, Y.; Lin, K.; Wang, X.; Tu, Y.; Zhuo, Z. Progress in building clinically relevant patient-derived tumor xenograft models for cancer research. *Anim. Model. Exp. Med.* **2023**, *6*, 381–398. [CrossRef]
154. Chen, K.; Li, Y.; Wang, B.; Yan, X.; Tao, Y.; Song, W.; Xi, Z.; He, K.; Xia, Q. Patient-derived models facilitate precision medicine in liver cancer by remodeling cell-matrix interaction. *Front. Immunol.* **2023**, *14*, 1101324. [CrossRef]
155. Chitrangi, S.; Vaity, P.; Jamdar, A.; Bhatt, S. Patient-derived organoids for precision oncology: A platform to facilitate clinical decision making. *BMC Cancer* **2023**, *23*, 689. [CrossRef]
156. Singh, S.; Kumar, R.; Payra, S.; Singh, S.K. Artificial Intelligence and Machine Learning in Pharmacological Research: Bridging the Gap Between Data and Drug Discovery. *Cureus* **2023**, *15*, e44359. [CrossRef]
157. Dlamini, Z.; Francies, F.Z.; Hull, R.; Marima, R. Artificial intelligence (AI) and big data in cancer and precision oncology. *Comput. Struct. Biotechnol. J.* **2020**, *18*, 2300–2311. [CrossRef]
158. Subbiah, V. The next generation of evidence-based medicine. *Nat. Med.* **2023**, *29*, 49–58. [CrossRef]
159. Chen, Q.; Jia, G.; Zhao, X.; Bao, Y.; Zhang, Y.; Ozkan, C.; Minev, B.; Ma, W. Novel Survivin Peptides Screened with Computer Algorithm Induce Cytotoxic T Lymphocytes with Higher Cytotoxic Efficiency to Cancer Cells. *Front. Mol. Biosci.* **2020**, *7*, 570003. [CrossRef]
160. Chen, Q.; Bao, Y.; Burner, D.; Kaushal, S.; Zhang, Y.; Mendoza, T.; Bouvet, M.; Ozkan, C.; Minev, B.; Ma, W. Tumor growth inhibition by mSTEAP peptide nanovaccine inducing augmented CD8(+) T cell immune responses. *Drug Deliv. Transl. Res.* **2019**, *9*, 1095–1105. [CrossRef]

161. Ma, W.; Chen, M.; Kaushal, S.; McElroy, M.; Zhang, Y.; Ozkan, C.; Bouvet, M.; Kruse, C.; Grotjahn, D.; Ichim, T.; et al. PLGA nanoparticle-mediated delivery of tumor antigenic peptides elicits effective immune responses. *Int. J. Nanomed.* **2012**, *7*, 1475–1487. [CrossRef] [PubMed]
162. Haimi, M. The tragic paradoxical effect of telemedicine on healthcare disparities—A time for redemption: A narrative review. *BMC Med. Inform. Decis. Mak.* **2023**, *23*, 95. [CrossRef] [PubMed]

Disclaimer/Publisher's Note: The statements, opinions and data contained in all publications are solely those of the individual author(s) and contributor(s) and not of MDPI and/or the editor(s). MDPI and/or the editor(s) disclaim responsibility for any injury to people or property resulting from any ideas, methods, instructions or products referred to in the content.

pharmaceutics

MDPI

Article

New MoS_2/Tegafur-Containing Pharmaceutical Formulations for Selective LED-Based Skin Cancer Photo-Chemotherapy

Miguel T. Campos [1,2,3,4], Filipa A. L. S. Silva [1,2,3,4], José Ramiro Fernandes [5,6], Susana G. Santos [3,4], Fernão D. Magalhães [1,2], Maria J. Oliveira [3,4] and Artur M. Pinto [1,2,3,4,*]

1 LEPABE, Faculdade de Engenharia, Universidade do Porto, 4200-465 Porto, Portugal; migueltcampos1234@gmail.com (M.T.C.); fdmagalh@fe.up.pt (F.D.M.)
2 ALICE—Associate Laboratory in Chemical Engineering, Faculdade de Engenharia, Universidade do Porto, 4200-465 Porto, Portugal
3 i3S—Instituto de Investigação e Inovação em Saúde, Universidade do Porto, 4200-135 Porto, Portugal
4 INEB—Instituto de Engenharia Biomédica, Universidade do Porto, 4200-135 Porto, Portugal
5 CQVR—Centro de Química Vila Real, University of Trás-os-Montes and Alto Douro, 5000-801 Vila Real, Portugal; jraf@utad.pt
6 Physical Department, University of Trás-os-Montes and Alto Douro, 5000-801 Vila Real, Portugal
* Correspondence: arturp@fe.up.pt

Abstract: Non-melanoma skin cancer (NMSC) is one of the most common types of cancer worldwide. Despite the low mortality rate, rising incidence and recurrence rates are a burden on healthcare systems. Standard treatments such as chemotherapy, radiotherapy, and surgery are either invasive or toxic to healthy tissues; therefore, new, alternative, selective treatments are needed. In this work, a combined photothermal and chemotherapeutic approach is proposed. MoS_2 was used as photothermal agent. It was prepared by a liquid-phase exfoliation and intercalation method using polyvinylpyrrolidone (PVP), followed by recirculation through a custom-built high-power ultrasonication probe. After 6 h of ultrasonication treatment, the average particle size was 165 ± 170 nm. Near-infrared (NIR) irradiation assays (810 nm, 0.1 W/cm^2, 30 min, 180 J/cm^2) confirmed that MoS_2 nanosheets can efficiently convert NIR light into heat and reach 52 °C. The therapeutic doses of MoS_2 (125 µg/mL) and Tegafur (50 µg/mL) were optimized and both were simultaneously incorporated into a Carbopol hydrogel. The cells were brought into contact with the hydrogel and irradiated with a custom-built NIR LED system. In HFF-1 cells (normal human fibroblasts), the metabolic activity was 78% (above the 70% toxicity limit—ISO 10993-5:2009(E)), while in A-431 skin cancer cells, it was 28%. In addition, the MoS_2 + Tegafur hydrogels led to a 1.9-fold decrease in A-431 cancer cell metabolic activity, 72 h after irradiation, in comparison to MoS_2 hydrogels, indicating a combined effect of photothermal and chemotherapy.

Keywords: photothermal therapy; 2D nanomaterials; transition metal dichalcogenides (TMDs; TMDCs); biocompatibility; targeted selective therapy; anticancer drugs

1. Introduction

Skin cancer is one of the most common types of cancer worldwide [1,2]. Non-melanoma skin cancer (NMSC) is the most common form of skin cancer and is increasingly common in patients under the age of 40, with basal cell carcinoma accounting for 80% of all NMSC cases [3,4]. The treatments used to cure NMSC are based on the risk that each case poses to the patient's health [5,6]. The most important therapies include surgery, chemotherapy, and radiotherapy [7]. Despite their frequent use, all of these therapies also have disadvantages [8]. Surgery consists of removing the tumor tissue, although sometimes, complete removal is not achieved, leading to recurrence; also, surgical trauma causes high inflammation and reduces the anticancer immune response [9,10]. Often, the aesthetic results are not ideal, considering that NMSC is more common on the face and neck [11,12].

Chemotherapy can lead to cancer cell resistance to the drugs and local and systemic toxicity to normal cells and tissues [8,13,14]. Radiotherapy can lead to systemic symptoms such as malaise, hair loss, loss of fertility, and indiscriminate cell destruction [8]. Photothermal therapy (PTT) has been investigated as a new therapeutic approach for cancer treatment as it is a non-invasive, cost-effective, and specific therapeutic approach. PTT is based on the irradiation of nanomaterials with light, usually in the NIR range [15,16]. During treatment, the radiation that hits the surface of the photothermal agents is converted into heat, leading to an increase in temperature to a point that can initiate cellular apoptosis or lead to tumor cell necrosis [17–19]. Necrosis is considered the most probable primary cause of cell death through PTT. Especially when extremely high temperatures are achieved, this pathway corresponds to an early cell death caused exclusively by external factors [20,21]. The downside of necrosis lies in the fact that, as cell functions and structures abruptly break down, the cellular contents leak into the extracellular space, inducing inflammation. Also, in the later stages of necrosis, the remaining cells release pro-inflammatory factors, exacerbating the inflammatory response [20]. The following inflammation may lead to tumor recurrence and increased resistance to further therapies [22,23].

To perform PTT more effectively and adjust doses to avoid necrosis, photothermal agents with strong NIR absorption are necessary. Transition metal dichalcogenides (TMDCs) and other 2D nanomaterials have a high surface-to-volume ratio and great optical properties, namely strong NIR absorption and high photothermal conversion efficiency [24–26]. The optical and electronic properties of TMDCs are related to a band gap that increases as the lateral size and the number of layers decrease [27]. In addition, the absence of dangling surface bonds is responsible for their high stability in liquids [24]. The structure of TMDCs consists of a layer of transition metal atoms sandwiched between two layers of chalcogen atoms [28,29]. Usually, TMDCs for biomedical applications are prepared by top-down methods, which are also used for photoelectric devices and catalysis [30]. Molybdenum disulfide (MoS_2)-based nanomaterials have great potential to be utilized as a platform for numerous biomedical applications and therapeutic approaches, such as photothermal and photodynamic therapy, imaging, drug delivery, and biosensing [31–34]. The crystal structure of MoS_2 takes the form of a hexagonal plane of S atoms on both sides of a plane of Mo atoms [31]. These triple planes stack on top of each other, with strong covalent bonds between the Mo and S atoms but weak van der Waals forces holding the layers together [31,35]. As a result, they can be easily exfoliated using top-down methods based on mechanical and chemical approaches [31,36,37]. Single-layered or few-layered MoS_2 nanosheets exhibit high absorption of near-infrared radiation (NIR) and high photothermal conversion efficiency [38]. In addition, this nanomaterial exhibits crystal-dependent fluorescence or fluorescence-quenching properties [31]. MoS_2 nanostructures, especially MoS_2 nanosheets, have also shown high stability, biocompatibility, high binding affinity to biomolecules, a large surface area, and remarkable magnetic and electronic properties [39,40]. Nanomaterials with a smaller lateral size than 100–200 nm and low-to-single-layer thickness are the gold standard for numerous biomedical applications, as the mentioned size and thickness promote biological interactions, the penetration of tissue and cell membranes, an improved permeability and retention effect (EPR), and rapid biodegradation and elimination [41,42]. Compared with other commonly studied photothermal therapy agents, such as metals, MoS_2 presents relevant advantages, since metals are toxic in high concentrations and lack water stability. Furthermore, MoS_2's lateral size and layer number can be reduced to maximize its photothermal conversion to values above those achieved by metals [24,43].

Two-dimensional nanomaterial (2DnMat) conjugates provide excellent nanoplatforms for various synergistic therapeutic approaches, including the combination of PTT and chemotherapy. The best results in terms of treatment efficacy have been achieved with combined therapies [24]. Numerous papers have been published that confirm that the conjugation of 2DnMats with anticancer drugs significantly increase the efficiency of the treatments [44–61]. An example of a drug never tested for combined therapy, but that has great potential, is Tegafur ($C_8H_9FN_2O_3$), an FDA- and EMA-approved anticancer drug used to treat gastric and colorectal cancer [62–64]. Other tumors treated with this drug include skin, breast, and pancreatic cancer [65]. Tegafur is an inactive oral prodrug that is metabolized to 5-FU [66,67]. Its mechanism of action is the inhibition of the enzyme thymidylate synthetase, which leads to a definitive alteration of the DNA replication pathway [68]. A practical way to combine 2DnMats and drugs such as Tegafur is by incorporating them into pharmaceutical formulations. Hydrogel delivery systems can provide a controlled release of various therapeutic agents without significant toxicity [69,70]. Carbopol hydrogels are made of an acrylic polymer approved by the FDA, being an ingredient in various pharmaceutical formulations, used for topical administration through the skin. They enable controlled release, improve skin permeability, and exhibit high biocompatibility and thermal stability [71,72].

Here, a new pharmaceutical formulation of a Carbopol hydrogel containing MoS_2 nanosheets and Tegafur was developed for combined phototherapy and chemotherapy of skin cancer. All conditions that are important for an effective and selective treatment are optimized, starting with the reduction in the MoS_2 particle size to below 200 nm, through the ideal MoS_2 and Tegafur concentration and irradiation time, which we determined using our custom-built NIR LED systems.

2. Materials and Methods

2.1. MoS_2 Nanosheet Production

Molybdenum disulfide (MoS_2) nanosheets were prepared by MoS_2 90 nm nanopowder (Merk, Darmstadt Germany) liquid-phase exfoliation and intercalation using polyvinylpyrrolidone (PVP) [73]. First, 2.5 g of PVP was dispersed in 1000 mL of deionized water; then, the dispersion was magnetically stirred for 1 h and mechanically stirred for 20 h (ATM40-3LCD, Ovan, Barcelona, Spain). The resulting dispersion was processed for 6 h in a custom-built recirculation system using a peristaltic pump (Watson Marlow 323 Peristaltic Pump, Falmouth, UK) and an industrial ultrasonic probe (Hielscher Ultrasonics GmbH, Teltow, Germany). The temperature was kept below 40 °C by a cooling bath (Julabo F12, Julabo GmbH, Seelbach, Germany). Finally, the washing process was completed by centrifuging three times at 8000 rpm [74].

2.2. MoS_2 Nanosheets Characterization

2.2.1. Transmission Electron Microscopy

The morphology and lateral dimensions of the aqueous MoS_2 dispersions were analyzed by transmission electron microscopy (TEM, JEOL JEM 1400 TEM, Tokyo, Japan) at a concentration of 30 μg/mL. Samples were sonicated and a volume of 10 μL was applied to a carbon-coated TEM grid, where it was allowed to settle for 30 min. The lateral dimensions of MoS_2 were measured using the ImageJ 1.53a software, with 80–588 counts per sample.

2.2.2. Zeta Potential Measurements

MoS_2 particles at a concentration of 10 μg/mL were analyzed using a Zetasizer Nano-NS (Malvern Instruments, Malvern, UK) in a disposable Zetasizer cuvette. Four measurements were performed at neutral pH and room temperature.

2.2.3. Thermogravimetric Analysis

A thermogravimetric analysis (TGA) of the dehydrated MoS_2 samples was performed using a Netzsch STA 449 F3 Jupiter instrument (Selb, Germany). The sample mass was between 6 and 8 mg. The thermograms were recorded between 30 and 1000 °C at a heating rate of 10 °C min^{-1} under nitrogen flow.

2.2.4. Energy-Dispersive X-ray Spectrometry

MoS_2 dispersions (30 μg/mL) were sonicated for 30 min, and a volume of 10 μL was applied to the surface of an aluminum-coated sample holder and allowed to dry overnight.

EDS data were obtained using the EDAX Genesis X4M software (Oxford Instruments, Oxford, UK) after acquisition using a QUANTA 400 FEG-SEM (FEI, Hillsboro, OR, USA) with an accelerating voltage of 3 kV.

2.2.5. UV–Visible Spectroscopy

Absorbance spectra of aqueous MoS_2 dispersions with a concentration of 12.5 μg/mL were recorded with a Lambda 35 UV/vis spectrometer (Perkin-Elmer, Waltham, USA). The samples were placed in a 50 μL quartz cuvette (Hellma Analytics, Müllheim, Germany) with a light path length of 10 mm, and their spectra were recorded between 200 and 850 nm. Measurements were performed in triplicate at room temperature with a baseline correction based on water as a blank control.

2.2.6. Photothermal Properties

To evaluate the light-to-heat conversion ability of MoS_2 water dispersions and hydrogels, a volume of 600 μL was added to 48-well plates in both cases. All wells were irradiated with a custom-built LED-based system with NIR emission (810 nm) and an irradiance of 0.1 W/cm^2 [75], measured using a Delta Ohm HD 2102.2 radiometer. In total, 24 LEDs (Model: WL-5P5050EP120IR-810 Lumixtar, Shenzhen, Guangdong, China) were used in a matrix configuration of 6 × 4, and each LED only directly illuminated one well. All of them were soldered to an individual aluminum star base of 16 mm and were dispersed in the top of an aluminum heatsink with 100 mm × 120 mm × 2 mm. Each LED had an epoxy resin lens creating a beam angle (2θ1/2) of 120°. An additional PMMA Lens was used on top of the LED lens to reduce the effective beam angle to 9°. The LEDs and LED parts were obtained directly from the mentioned manufacturer according to the author's specifications.

The light-induced temperature rise of the samples was recorded for 30 min by placing a K-type thermocouple in the center and halfway up the suspension and connecting it to a TC-08 thermocouple data logger (Pico Technology, Eaton Socon, UK). Nine replicates per condition were performed, and the results are reported as the mean and standard deviation. Prior to irradiation, samples were pre-warmed to 37 °C in an incubator to replicate the conditions of the biological tests.

2.3. *Hydrogel Production*

Hydrogels (HGs) were prepared by dispersing Carbopol 974 NF (0.5% *w/v*) at a concentration of 5 mg/mL in water, MoS_2, Tegafur, or MoS_2 + Tegafur dispersions. The selected concentration of MoS_2 was 125 μg/mL and that of Tegafur was 50 μg/mL. The dispersions were sonicated for 10 min, 1 h after preparation. Gelification was carried out by adding NaOH dropwise at an initial concentration of 0.5 M. Concentrations of 12.5 mM of NaOH were used for the dispersions of Carbopol and Tegafur, MoS_2, and MoS_2 + Tegafur.

2.4. *In Vitro Studies*

2.4.1. Cell Culture

Biological studies were performed with A-431 human epidermoid carcinoma cells (ATCC, CRL-1555, Manassas, VA, USA) and HFF-1 human foreskin fibroblasts (ATCC, SCRC-1041, Manassas, VA, USA). Cells were cultured in Dulbecco's Modified Eagle's Medium (DMEM, Thermo Fisher Scientific, Waltham, MA, USA) supplemented with 10% (*v/v*) fetal bovine serum (Alfagene, Carcavelos, Portugal) and 1% (*v/v*) penicillin/streptomycin (Biowest, Pays De La Loire, France). Cells were maintained in a humidified atmosphere with 5% CO_2 and 95% air at 37 °C. The medium was replaced every 2–3 days and the cells were detached when 80% confluency was reached. In biological experiments, the effect of Tegafur, MoS_2 alone, and MoS_2/Tegafur-loaded hydrogels was investigated with both healthy and cancer cells in the presence or absence of NIR irradiation, as described in detail below.

2.4.2. Cytotoxicity Assays of Tegafur and MoS_2 Nanosheets

A-431 or HFF-1 cells were seeded in 48-well plates at a density of 10,000 cells/well and 40,000 cells/well, respectively. After 24 h, the culture medium was replaced with MoS_2 (125–500 µg/mL) or Tegafur dispersions (0.1–500 µg/mL) in complete DMEM and incubated for additional 24, 48, or 72 h. In brief, material dispersions were removed and cells were incubated in a 10% (*v*/*v*) resazurin reagent (Sigma-Aldrich, St. Louis, MO, USA) in complete DMEM at 37 °C and 5% CO_2 for 2 h. The fluorescence of the supernatant ($\lambda_{ex/em}$ = 530/590 nm) was measured using a microplate reader spectrophotometer (Synergy Mx, Bio-Tek Instruments, Winooski, VT, USA). Negative and positive controls for cell viability decreases were performed by incubating the cells in complete DMEM or with 10% (*v*/*v*) dimethyl sulfoxide (DMSO) in complete DMEM, respectively. Data for each sample were normalized to the negative control for cell viability decrease and the results are expressed as the mean percentage of the control and standard deviation. All assays were performed in triplicate with six replicates for each condition tested. These tests yielded the appropriate concentrations of Tegafur and MoS_2 to be added to the HG for the next biological assays.

2.4.3. Cytocompatibility of MoS_2/Tegafur Hydrogels and Photothermal Therapy

A-431 or HFF-1 cells were incubated with HGs at a final concentration of 125 µg/mL of MoS_2 and 50 µg/mL of Tegafur in DMEM for 24–72 h. Resazurin assays were then performed as described above. Live/dead staining was performed after 72 h, as described below. After incubating the cells with HG for 30 min, irradiation was performed using our custom-made NIR LED systems as described above (Section 2.2.6). After 24, 48, and 72 h, the medium was removed and the resazurin assay was performed, as described above.

Live/Dead Assays

The live/dead assay with fluorescent labeling was performed to assess the viability of cells after treatment with irradiated or non-irradiated Carbopol/MoS_2/Tegafur. Live cells were identified with Calcein AM (Invitrogen, ThermoFisher Scientific, Waltham, MA, USA), which penetrates the cell membrane and labels both the nucleus and the cytoplasm. Dead cells were stained with propidium iodide (PI; ThermoFisher Scientific, Waltham, MA, USA), which penetrates only the damaged cell membranes and stains the nucleus. Cells were seeded in 48-well plates. After the different treatments (24, 48, and 72 h), cells were washed with PBS and incubated for 20 min at 37 °C in the dark with a solution of PI and of Calcein AM in PBS at 2.0 µg/mL. Then, a PI solution of 1.0 µg/mL in PBS was added to each well. Images were acquired using the Operetta CLS High-Content Imager (Perkin Elmer, Waltham, MA, USA) and data were processed using the Harmony software 5.2.

2.4.4. Statistical Analysis

A statistical analysis was performed using the GraphPad Prism software (version 8.4.2, San Diego, CA, USA). For parametric data, a one-way analysis of variance (ANOVA) with Tukey's tests for multiple comparisons was performed. Differences between the experimental groups are considered significant if $p < 0.05$.

3. Results and Discussion

3.1. *MoS_2 Dispersions' Physico-Chemical Characterization*

Transmission electron microscopy (TEM) was used to investigate the particle size and morphology of the MoS_2 nanosheets after fabrication and after ultrasonic treatment for different lengths of time in a custom-built recirculating system. The average size of the MoS_2 nanosheets decreased from 901 ± 633 nm, before sonication, to 450 ± 372 nm, 405 ± 362 nm, and 165 ± 170 nm after 2, 4, and 6 h of sonication, respectively. The effectiveness of the ultrasonication method is shown by the fact that the lateral size of MoS_2 decreases with the duration of sonication, while the degree of exfoliation increases. After 6 h of ultrasonication treatment, well-dispersed MoS_2 layers were obtained without visible agglomeration, with good exfoliation and an average lateral size of 165 ± 170 nm (Figure 1). There is a substantial size heterogeneity in the samples, with the standard deviation decreasing as ultrasonication time increases (Figure 1B). After 6 h, we reach a size distribution ideal for the desired bioapplications in topical skin cancer phototherapy, since most particles present sizes in the range of 10–200 nm. Note that the particles present a few layers of thickness in the nanometric range at around 1–10 nm. This favors potential biological interactions, the penetration of tissue and cell membranes, improved permeability and retention effects (EPRs), and rapid biodegradation and elimination [41,42]. The zeta potential of the MoS_2 nanosheets was determined by electrophoretic light scattering (ELS) using a Zetasizer device (1.C). The values were −39.7 ± 1.3 mV, −40.8 ± 1.3 mV, −41.8 ± 0.5 mV, and −32.7 ± 1.0 mV after 0, 2, 4, and 6 h of ultrasonication treatment, respectively. Particles with a surface charge below −30 mV are considered very stable and well dispersible in water [76]. This is consistent with the good stability and dispersibility of MoS_2 nanosheets.

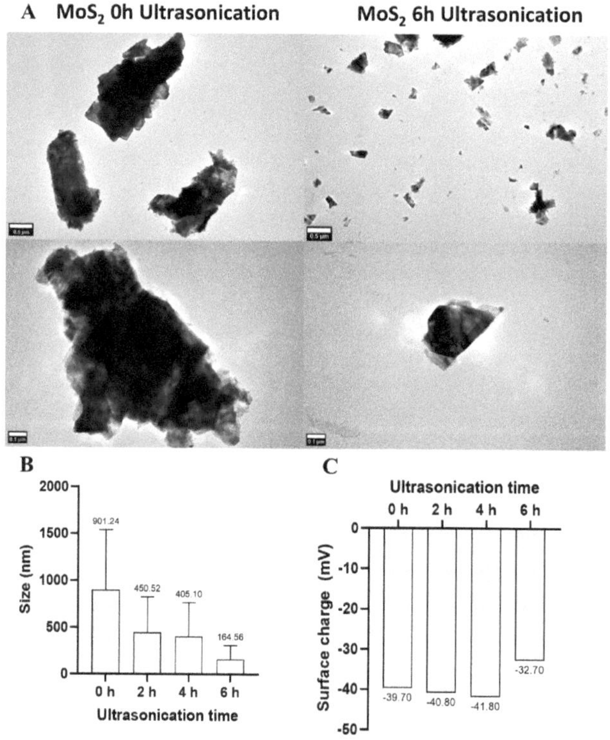

Figure 1. MoS_2 particle size and morphology and surface charge at 0, 2, 4, and 6 h after ultrasonication. (**A**) Transmission electron microscopy (TEM) images of MoS2 aqueous dispersions at 0 and 6 h of ultrasonication (30 µg/mL). (**B**) MoS_2 particle size after different ultrasonication periods, determined by TEM image analysis. (**C**) Surface charge of MoS_2 particles (0, 2, 4, and 6 h of ultrasonication) determined by electrophoretic light scattering (ELS). (**A**) Scale bars represent 0.5 µm (**top images**) and 0.1 µm (**bottom images**).

Thermogravimetric analysis (TGA) was used to evaluate the thermal stability of the MoS_2 nanosheets after 0–6 h of ultrasonication. Figure 2A shows a gradual weight loss of about 7% in the tested temperature range. Other authors have observed similar behavior in thermogravimetric experiments with MoS_2 under inert conditions, but no clear thermal degradation mechanism is suggested, aside from loss of chemisorbed water [77–79]. It was not possible to establish a correlation between the duration of ultrasonication treatment and the loss of thermal stability, as all samples showed only small weight losses, preserving more than 90% of the initial mass, indicating that the nanosheets produced have high thermal stability, even when the particle size decreases.

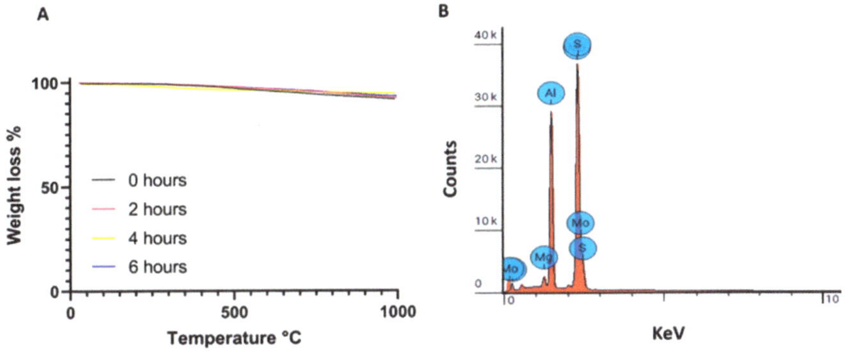

Figure 2. (**A**) Thermogravimetric analysis of MoS_2 ultrasonicated for 0, 2, 4, and 6 h, performed under nitrogen atmosphere. (**B**) Energy-dispersive X-ray spectroscopy (EDS) analysis of MoS_2 samples ultrasonicated for 6 h.

Energy-dispersive X-ray spectroscopy (EDS) was performed to determine the composition of MoS_2 samples ultrasonicated for 6 h. Figure 2B and Table 1 reveal the presence of Mo, S, C, and Al and a vestigial presence of Mg. The presence of aluminum can be attributed to the sample holder in which the MoS_2 samples were placed for analysis. The carbon comes from the PVP used in MoS_2 production. Table 1 shows that the atomic ratio between S and Mo is about 1.8, which corresponds approximately to the expected theoretical ratio of two, as there must be two sulfur atoms to one Mo atom in each MoS_2 molecule. Similar ratios have also been found in the literature [80].

Table 1. Energy-dispersive X-ray spectroscopy analysis of MoS_2 nanosheets after 6 h of ultrasonication.

Element Number	Element Symbol	Element Name	Atomic %	Weight %
6	C	Carbon	24.7	8.5
12	Mg	Magnesium	1.3	0.9
13	Al	Aluminum	32.1	24.8
16	S	Sulfur	27.0	24.8
42	Mo	Molybdenum	14.9	41.0

The optical properties of MoS_2 treated with ultrasound by ultrasonication for 0, 2, 4, and 6 h were investigated by UV-VIS spectroscopy (Figure 3A). The maximum absorption peaks for all samples are at 200 nm, which can be associated with the presence of PVP on the nanosheets, resultant from the production process [81]. Other peaks appear at 620 and 680 nm for all samples; according to the literature, these peaks can be accredited to the excitonic transitions from the K point to the Brillouin zone [82]. MoS_2 sonicated for 6 h shows a 1.2-fold increase in NIR absorbance (810 nm) compared to the sample without ultrasonication. An increase in optical absorption with decreasing particle size and exfoliation is frequently observed in the literature for 2D nanomaterials [83,84]. Due to its smaller particle size and water stability, MoS_2 ultrasonicated for 6 h was selected for the following assays.

To determine the potential of the six-hour-ultrasonicated MoS_2 nanosheets as photothermal agents, aqueous dispersions of MoS_2 (100 to 500 μg/mL) were irradiated with a custom-made LED-NIR device (810 nm, 0.1 W/cm^2) for 30 min. The temperatures were registered at various time points, as illustrated in Figure 3B. After 30 min, 49, 51, and 54 °C were reached for MoS_2 dispersions with the following concentrations: 125, 175, and 500 μg/mL.

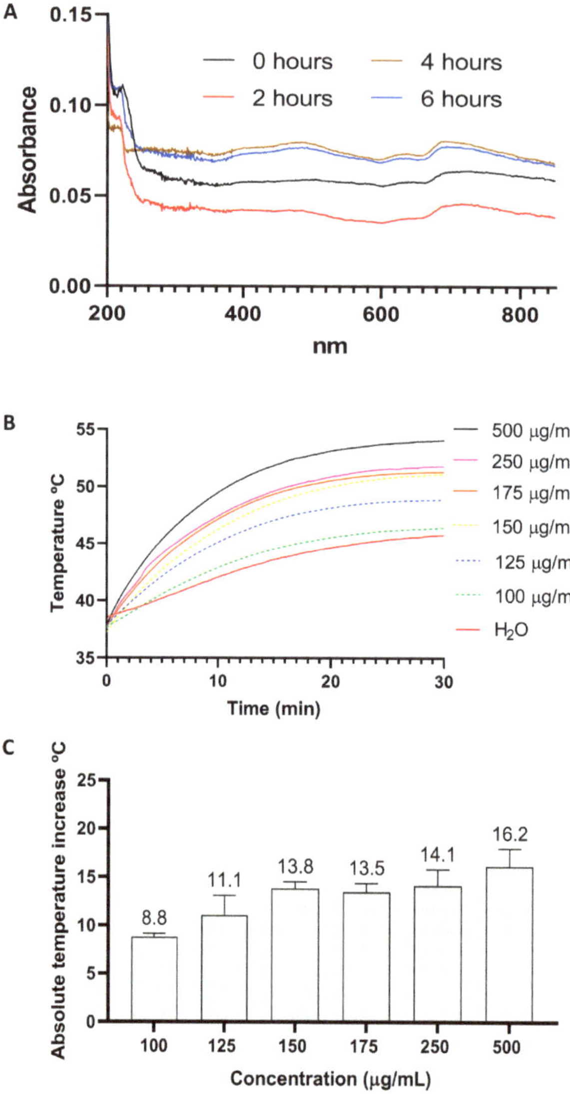

Figure 3. (**A**) UV–visible absorption spectra (200–850 nm) of MoS_2 ultrasonicated for 0 h, 2 h, 4 h, and 6 h. (**B**) NIR light-to-heat conversion assays. Photothermal heating curves of MoS_2 (6 h sonication) water dispersions (100–500 μg/mL) irradiated with a custom-built NIR LED system (810 nm, 0.1 W/cm^2) for 30 min. Water was used as a control. (**C**) Absolute temperature increases of MoS_2 (6 h sonication) water dispersions (100–500 μg/mL) irradiated with a custom-built NIR LED system (810 nm, 0.1 W/cm^2) for 30 min.

3.2. MoS_2 Cytocompatibility Optimization

Since MoS_2 nanosheets have the potential to be used in various biomedical applications, including photothermal therapy, it is important to confirm that these nanoparticles are not toxic to healthy tissues [31,44,85]. For this reason, HFF-1 human fibroblasts were incubated with MoS_2 (125–500 µg/mL) for 24, 48, and 72 h, as shown in Figure 4. At each time point, the cells' metabolic activity was determined using the resazurin assay. Controls were performed with DMEM (cell-death-negative control, referred as "control") and 10% DMSO (cell-death-positive control) only.

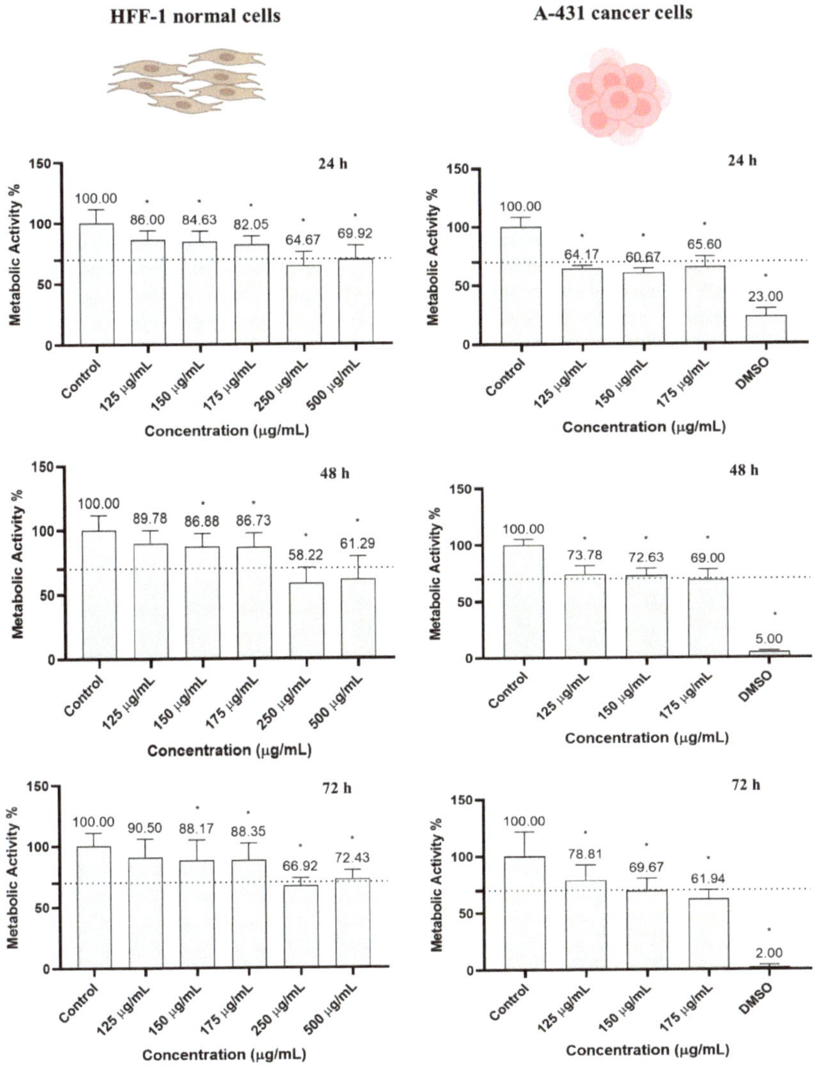

Figure 4. Metabolic activity of HFF-1 and A-431 cells incubated with MoS_2 (125–500 µg/mL), determined using the resazurin assay after 24, 48, and 72 h. Results are normalized to values obtained for the control (complete DMEM). Results are presented as average and standard deviation (n = 6). Statistically significant differences against the control (complete DMEM) are represented as * $p < 0.05$. DMSO; dimethyl sulfoxide 10% (was used as positive control of cell death). The dashed line marks the toxicity limit (ISO 10993-5:2009 [86]).

Cells incubated with the two highest concentrations (250 and 500 µg/mL) showed a metabolic activity, already at the first time point (24 h), below the toxicity limit of 70% defined by ISO 10993-5:2009. Concentrations of 150 and 175 µg/mL led to a slight but significant decrease in metabolic activity of approximately 12% after 72 h. In contrast, no significant changes in metabolic activity were observed in cells incubated with 125 μg/mL after 72 h, as their metabolic activity was 90%. In view of the results described, concentrations below 175 μg/mL were considered safe for normal cells and, thus, this range was selected for further studies.

Next, to investigate the cytotoxic effect of the nanomaterial, MoS_2 nanosheets were tested in A-431, a skin cancer cell line. Even without NIR irradiation, MoS_2 was demonstrated to be cytotoxic. After 24 h, the cancer cell metabolic activity decreased to below 70%, but no cumulative cytotoxic effect was observed, as this activity remained at a similar level after 48 h and 72 h of incubation.

3.3. MoS_2 Cytotoxicity under NIR Irradiation

To investigate the phototherapeutic effect of MoS_2 nanoparticles under NIR irradiation, and to confirm that this effect is sufficient to kill A-431 skin carcinoma cells, they were incubated with different nanoparticle concentrations (125–175 μg/mL) and then irradiated for 30 min with a custom-built NIR LED system (810 nm, 0.1 W/cm^2, 180 J/cm^2). After 72 h, the metabolic activity of A-431 was approximately 20% at 125 μg/mL, 20% at a concentration of 150 μg/mL, and 30% at 175 μg/mL, proving that all tested concentrations had a significant photothermal effect on cancer cells after 30 min of irradiation (Figure 5). However, no significant differences in metabolic activity were observed between the groups of cells incubated at 125, 150, or 175 μg/mL, indicating that higher concentrations were not directly associated with a greater decrease in metabolic activity or a higher photothermal effect.

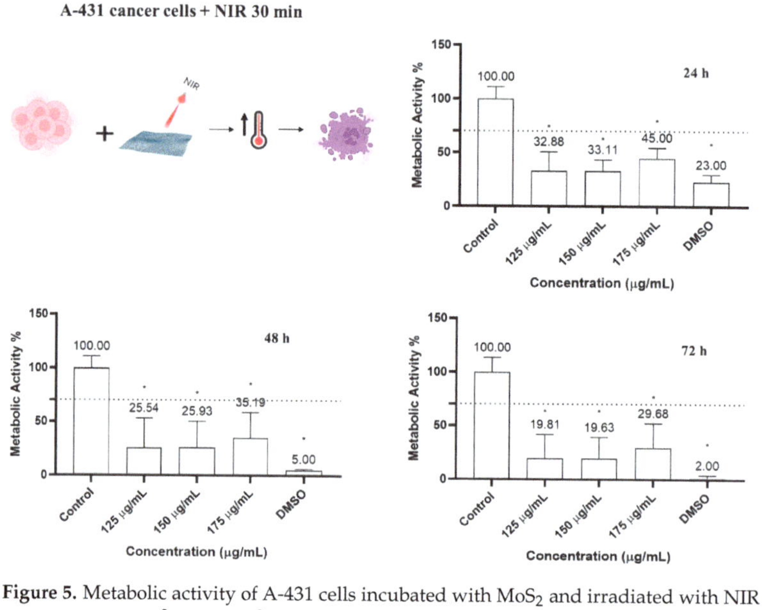

Figure 5. Metabolic activity of A-431 cells incubated with MoS_2 and irradiated with NIR for 30 min (810 nm, 0.1 W/cm^2, 180 J/cm^2), determined using the resazurin assay after 24, 48, and 72 h. Results are normalized to values obtained for the control (complete DMEM). Results are presented as average and standard deviation (n = 6). Statistically significant differences against the control (complete DMEM) are represented as * $p < 0.05$. DMSO; dimethyl sulfoxide 10% (control of cell death). The dashed line marks the toxicity limit (ISO 10993-5:2009(E)).

A concentration of 125 μg/mL was selected as the optimal concentration to be incorporated in the pharmaceutical formulations (Carbopol hydrogels) for further tests, as it reduced the metabolic activity of A-431 skin carcinoma cells, without affecting HFF-1 normal skin fibroblasts.

3.4. *Tegafur Cytotoxicity/Cytocompatibility Optimization*

The cytotoxicity of Tegafur on human skin fibroblasts (HFF-1) and human skin carcinoma cells (A-431) was investigated to determine the minimum concentration that leads to cancer cell death without damaging healthy tissue. Both cell lines were incubated for 24, 48, and 72 h with different concentrations of Tegafur between 0.1 and 500 µg/mL. At each time point, the viability of the cells was tested using the resazurin assay (Figure 6). Controls were performed using cell culture media (DMEM, negative control) and DMSO 10% (cell-death-positive control) only.

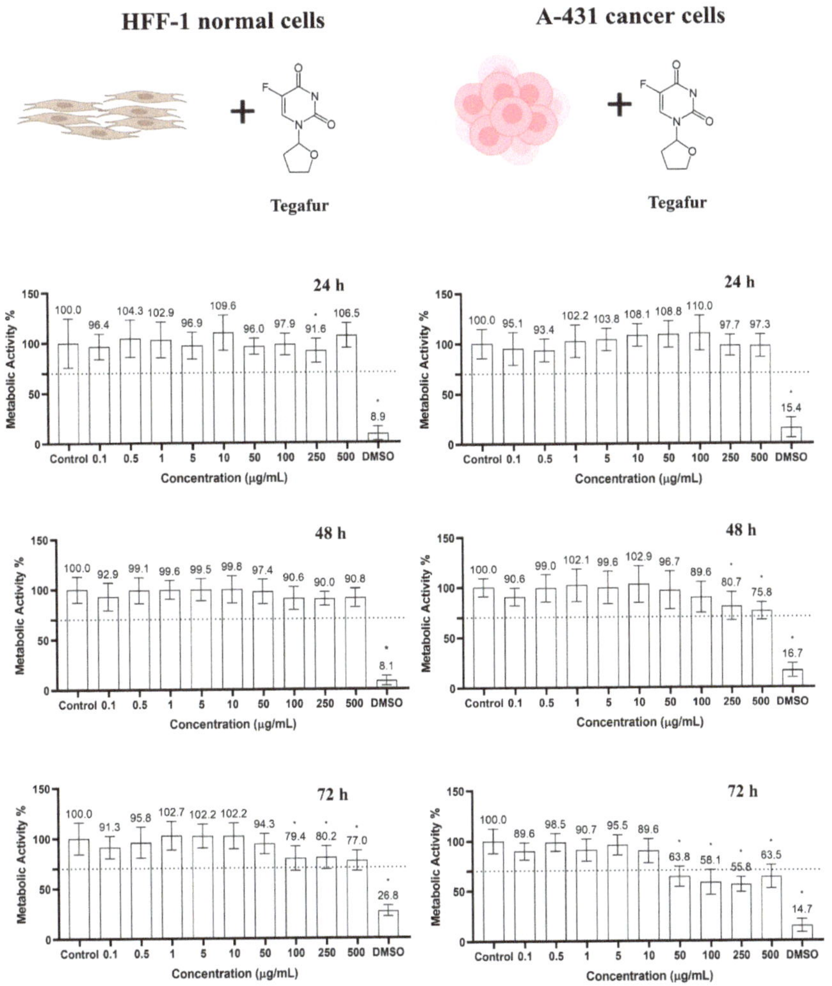

Figure 6. Metabolic activity of HFF-1 and A-431 cells incubated with Tegafur, determined using the resazurin assay after 24, 48, and 72 h. Results are normalized to the control (complete DMEM). Results are presented as average and standard deviation (n = 6). Statistically significant differences against the control (complete DMEM, negative control) are represented as * $p < 0.05$. DMSO; dimethyl sulfoxide 10% (positive control of cell death). The dashed line marks the toxicity limit (ISO 10993-5:2009(E)).

At all tested concentrations and time points (24, 48, 72 h), HFF-1 showed a cell metabolic activity of more than 70% and was therefore considered as not cytotoxic, according to the ISO 10993-5:2009(E) norm. However, at concentrations of more than 50 μg/mL, the metabolic activity significantly decreased after 72 h of incubation.

In A-431 human skin carcinoma cells, metabolic activities below 70% were observed after 72 h at concentrations of Tegafur above 50 μg/mL. The metabolic activity values were 63.8, 58.1, 55.8, and 63.5% for 50, 100, 250, and 500 μg/mL, respectively. These results can be explained by the mechanism of action of Tegafur, which is metabolized into 5-FU, an anticancer drug that directly interferes with DNA replication. Since the mechanism depends on the metabolic activity of the cancer cells, it is expected that it takes some time for a sufficient concentration to accumulate in the cells, which eventually leads to a decrease in cell viability [66,68]. Since 50 μg/mL of Tegafur was biocompatible with HFF-1 human skin fibroblasts and toxic to A-431 human skin cancer cells, this concentration was chosen as the optimal amount for the pharmaceutical formulation with Carbopol, as described below.

4. Hydrogels' Characterization

Carbopol hydrogels (HGs) were prepared by dispersing Carbopol 974 NF (0.5% *w/v*) at a concentration of 5 mg/mL in water, MoS_2, Tegafur, or MoS_2 + Tegafur water dispersions. The final concentration of MoS_2 was 125 μg/mL and the final concentration of Tegafur was 50 μg/mL (based on previously described biological tests). Sodium hydroxide (NaOH) was then added to the solutions to allow gelification. The HGs containing MoS_2 were black in color, while the HGs without MoS_2 were completely transparent (Figure 7A).

Figure 7B shows the UV–visible absorbance spectra of MoS_2 nanosheets in water dispersion, the MoS_2 HG, the Teg HG, and the MoS_2 + Teg HG. The maximum absorption peaks at 200 nm in all samples are due to the presence of PVP on the surface of the nanosheets [81]. Samples containing Tegafur show a typical absorption peak at 270 nm [87,88]. The NIR absorbance of the MoS_2 + Teg HG and MoS_2 HG (810 nm) increased 1.6-fold compared to the MoS_2 6 h ultrasonication water dispersions. To investigate the photothermal effect of the MoS_2 nanosheets in the HG, NIR irradiation tests were performed. After 30 min of irradiation with a custom-made LED NIR device (810 nm, 0.1 W/cm^2, 180 J/cm^2), the HG containing MoS_2 (125 μg/mL) reached approximately 49 °C. This temperature is within the range required for effective photothermal therapy of cancer (Figure 7C). Since Tegafur does not exhibit significant NIR absorption, the Carbopol/Teg HG was not tested.

4.1. MoS_2/Tegafur Hydrogels' Cytocompatibility

HFF-1 skin fibroblasts were incubated for 24 and 48 h with the Carbopol HG dispersed in DMEM, the Carbopol/MoS_2 HG (125 μg/mL), and with the HG containing both MoS_2 (125 μg/mL) and Tegafur (50 μg/mL)—Carbopol/MoS_2 + Teg. Controls were performed with cell culture media (DMEM) and DMSO 10% (cell death control) only. At each time point, the metabolic activity of the cells was determined using resazurin assays (Figure 8). At both time points, the metabolic activity was always above the toxicity limit of 70% specified in ISO 10993-5:2009(E). Therefore, neither MoS_2 nor Tegafur caused toxicity to normal skin cells.

Live/dead staining of HFF-1 cells was performed to investigate the cytocompatibility of the HGs after 72 h of incubation. The number of cells/area was 22,039, 22,563, 24,995, and 20,166 for HFF-1 cells incubated with DMEM, Carbopol HGs, Carbopol/MoS_2 HGs and Carbopol/MoS_2/Teg HGs, respectively (Figure 8). Interestingly, no statistically significant differences in the number of cells were observed. Figure 9 also shows that the HFF-1 cells exhibited a normal spindle-shaped fibroblast morphology, metabolized calcein, and excluded propidium iodide under all conditions tested, confirming the cytocompatibility of the pharmaceutical formulation components.

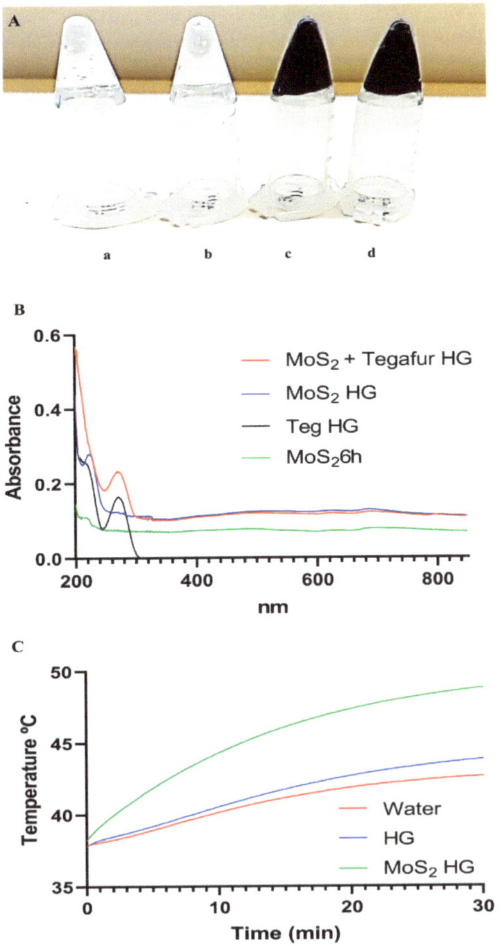

Figure 7. Hydrogels' morphological and photothermal potential characterization. (**A**) Images of hydrogels right after being prepared in inverted Eppendorfs: (**a**) Carbopol hydrogel (0.5% w/v); (**b**) Carbopol/Teg hydrogel (0.050 µg/mL Tegafur); (**c**) Carbopol/MoS_2 hydrogel (125 µg/mL MoS_2); (**d**) Carbopol/MoS_2/Teg hydrogel (125 µg/mL MoS_2 + 50 µg/mL Tegafur). (**B**) UV-VIS absorption spectra (200–850 nm) of MoS_2 + Tegafur HG, MoS_2 HG, Tegafur HG, and a MoS_2 dispersion ultrasonicated for 6 h. (**C**) Photothermal heating curves for Carbopol/MoS_2 hydrogels. Water and Carbopol hydrogel were used as non-heating controls.

4.2. MoS_2/Tegafur Hydrogels' Selective PTT Effect Optimization

Different irradiation times (15, 20, 25, and 30 min) were tested to determine the optimal condition to maximize the efficiency of the phototherapeutic effect. Tegafur is an inactive oral prodrug which is metabolized to 5-FU [66]. This inhibits the enzyme thymidylate synthetase, which will lead to a definitive change in the DNA replication mechanisms [68]. Tegafur should possess high targetability, since its activation requires a complex metabolic pathway that is more common in cancer cells [89].

Mild PTT strategies include a temperature increase to 39–45 °C, as cancer cells are less tolerant to heat stress; this therapeutic approach should present selectivity. The increase in temperature drastically reduces DNA and RNA synthesis, as well as DNA repair, and increases the permeability of tumor cells, leading to an increase in drug and nanomaterial intake [90,91]. The optimization of this effect should destroy the A-431 skin carcinoma cells without killing the normal HFF-1 skin fibroblasts. Therefore, both cell lines were incubated with the Carbopol HG containing MoS_2 (125 μg/mL) and Tegafur (50 μg/mL). The cells were then irradiated with custom-made NIR LED systems (810 nm, 0.1 W/cm^2) for 15, 20, 25, and 30 min. These irradiation conditions correspond to doses of 90, 120, 150, and 180 J/cm^2.

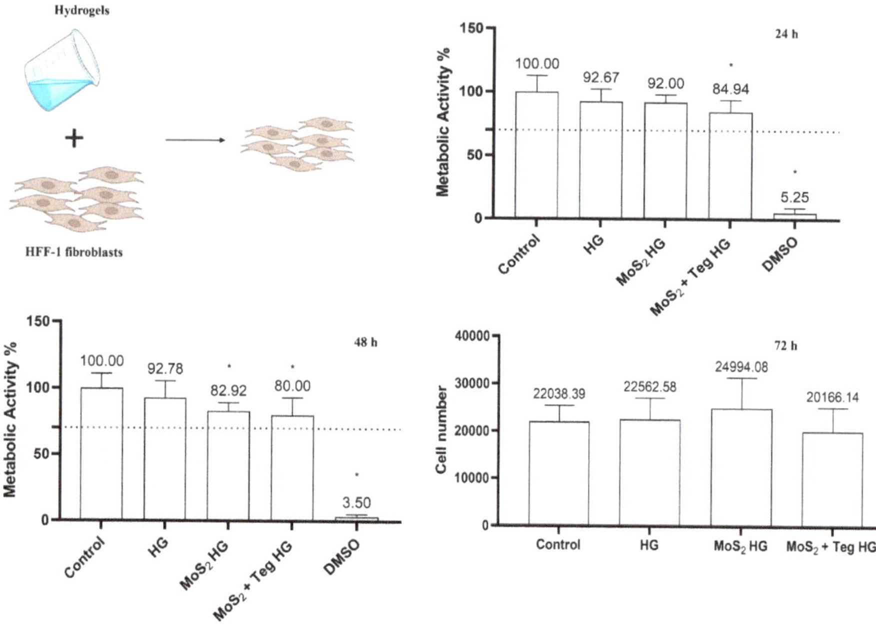

Figure 8. Metabolic activity of HFF-1 cells incubated with HG, HG containing MoS_2, or MoS_2 + Tegafur (Teg), determined using the resazurin assay after 24 h, 48 h, and 72 h. Results are normalized to values obtained for the control (complete DMEM). Results are presented as average and standard deviation (n = 6). Statistically significant differences against the control (complete DMEM, negative control) are presented as * $p < 0.05$. DMSO; dimethyl sulfoxide 10% (positive cell death control). The dashed line marks the toxicity limit (ISO 10993-5:2009(E)). Number of cells counted on the live/dead staining of HFF-1 cells incubated with HG or HG with MoS_2 with and without Tegafur for 72 h. For all conditions tested, MoS_2 was at a concentration of 125 μg/mL and Tegafur was at a concentration of 50 μg/mL. No statistically significant differences in the number of cells were found between all conditions tested.

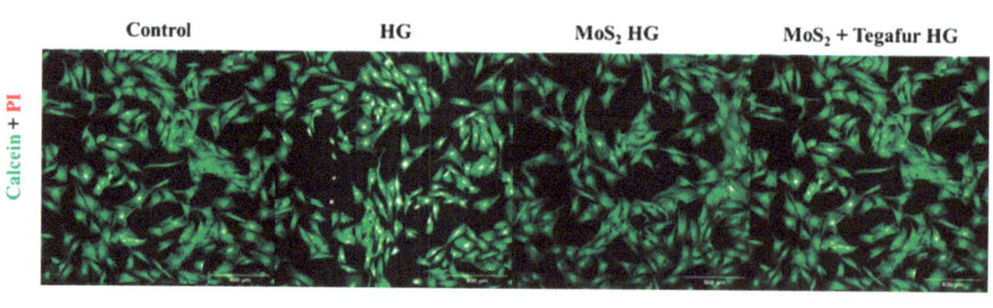

Figure 9. Live/dead staining of HFF-1 cells incubated with HG, MoS2 HG, and MoS_2 + Tegafur HG for 72 h. MoS2 was at a concentration of 125 μg/mL and Tegafur was at a concentration of 50 μg/mL. The control corresponds to cells incubated with cell culture media (DMEM, negative control) only. Live cells metabolize calcein (green), and dead/dying cells are stained by propidium iodide (PI) (red), which penetrates their membrane. The scale bar represents 500 μm.

Resazurin assays were performed to determine the effects of the treatment on the metabolic activity of the two cell lines after 24, 48, and 72 h.

First, both cell lines were incubated with the MoS_2 + Teg HG and irradiated for 30 min (Figure 10). The resazurin tests show that the above conditions were highly cytotoxic for both cell lines at both tested time points (24 and 72 h). This is undesirable, as the treatment should be specific for skin cancer cells. Shorter irradiation times were therefore tested.

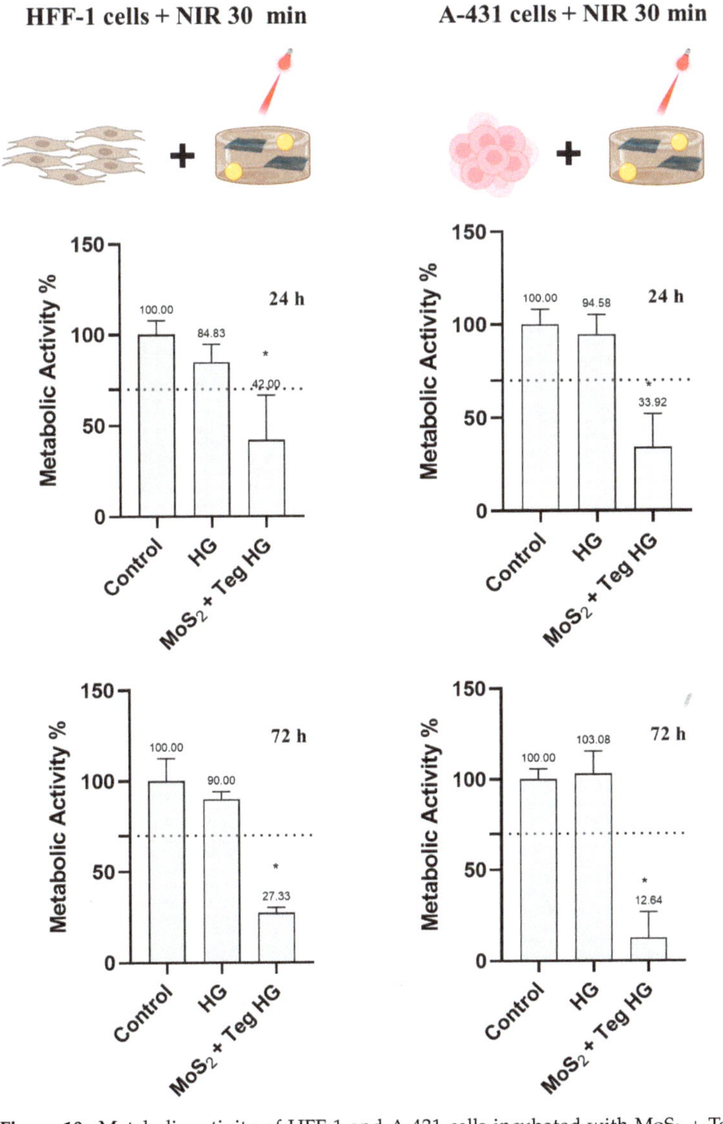

Figure 10. Metabolic activity of HFF-1 and A-431 cells incubated with MoS_2 + Tegafur HG and irradiated for 30 min with NIR LED devices (810 nm, 0.1 W/cm^2, 180 J/cm^2), determined using the resazurin assay after 24 and 72 h. Results are normalized to values obtained for the negative control (complete DMEM). Results are presented as average and standard deviations (n = 6). Statistically significant differences against the control (complete DMEM) are presented as * $p < 0.05$. The dashed line marks the toxicity limit (ISO 10993-5:2009(E)). MoS2 was at a concentration of 125 μg/mL and Tegafur was at a concentration of 50 μg/mL.

HFF-1 cells irradiated with NIR for 15 and 20 min evidenced no cytotoxicity after 24 h and a metabolic activity of about 92%. After 25 min, the NIR irradiation decreased to 84%, which is still within the toxicity limit of 70% (ISO 10993-5:2009(E)) (Figure 11). In contrast, toxicity was observed in the A-431 skin carcinoma cells at all irradiation times tested, with metabolic activity values below 52% in all cases. No significant metabolic activity differences were found between the distinct irradiation times. For this reason, 15 min was chosen, as shorter irradiation times are most likely ensure cytocompatibility with the normal HFF-1 skin cells.

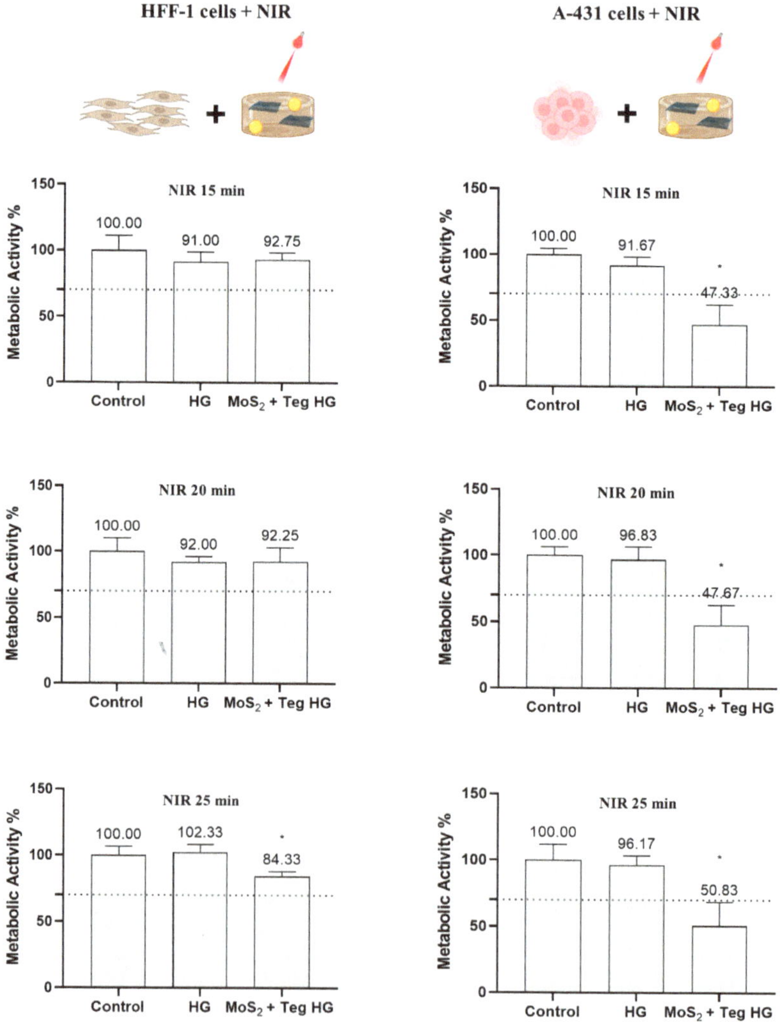

Figure 11. Metabolic activity of HFF-1 and A-431 cells incubated with MoS_2 + Tegafur HG and irradiated for 15, 20, or 25 min with NIR LED devices (810 nm, 0.1 W/cm^2), corresponding to doses of 90, 120, or 150 J/cm^2, respectively, determined using the resazurin assay after 24 h. Results are normalized to values obtained for the negative control (complete DMEM). Results are presented as average and standard deviation (n = 6). Statistically significant differences against the negative control (complete DMEM) are presented as * $p < 0.05$. The dashed line marks the toxicity limit (ISO 10993-5:2009(E)). MoS_2 was at a concentration of 125 μg/mL and Tegafur was at a concentration of 50 μg/mL.

Finally, both cell lines were treated with the pharmaceutical formulations and subjected to 15 min of NIR irradiation. Their metabolic activity was examined after 24 and 72 h (Figure 12). After the last time point (72 h), no cytotoxicity was observed for MoS_2 or the MoS_2 + Teg HG against normal HFF-1 skin cells, as the metabolic activity was about 78% in both cases. This value is above the cytotoxicity limit of 70% specified in ISO 10993-5:2009(E). In contrast, in the A-431 cells, the MoS_2 + Teg HG clearly led to significant cytotoxicity after 72 h, as the metabolic activity was reduced to 28%. Moreover, this effect increased with time and was more pronounced in the presence of Tegafur than with the MoS_2 HG alone, clearly indicating a combined effect between the anticancer drug and the nanomaterial.

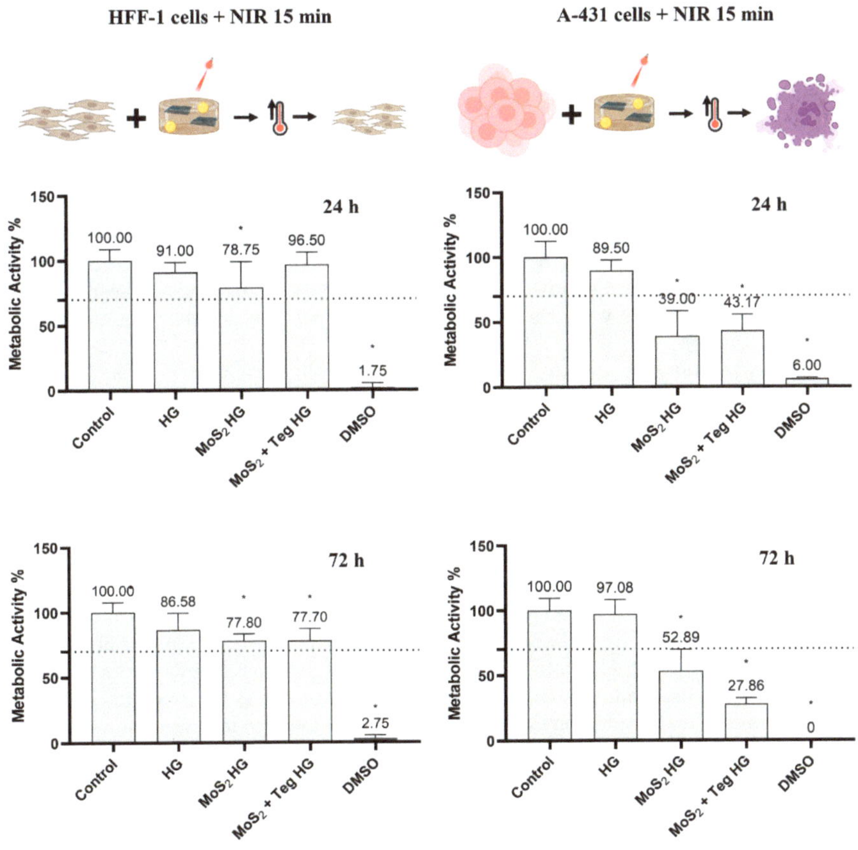

Figure 12. Metabolic activity of HFF-1 and A-431 cells incubated with MoS_2 + Tegafur HG and irradiated for 15 min with NIR LED devices (810 nm, 0.1 W/cm^2, 90 J/cm^2), determined using the resazurin assay after 24 and 72 h. Results are normalized to values obtained for the negative control (complete DMEM). Results are presented as average and standard deviation (n = 6). Statistically significant differences against the negative control (complete DMEM) are presented as * $p < 0.05$. The dashed line marks the toxicity limit (ISO 10993-5:2009(E)). MoS_2 was at a concentration of 125 µg/mL and Tegafur was at a concentration of 50 µg/mL.

Liu et al. demonstrated the selective photothermal effect of MnO_2 functionalized with Au by incubating a human epithelial cell line (BEAS-2B) and a human lung adenocarcinoma cell line (A549) with the nanomaterial. After 24 h of incubation, both cell lines were irradiated with an 808 nm laser (1.5 W/cm^2) for 10 min. A concentration of 50 µg/mL was able to reduce the viability of the A549 cancer cells to 13%, while the viability of the

BEAS-2B normal cells was 75% [92]. Sahu et al. produced nano graphene oxide (nanoGO) non-covalently functionalized with Pluronic complexed with methylene blue (MB). HeLa cells and NIH/3T3 fibroblasts were incubated with the nanocomplex at a concentration of 10 μg/mL for 24 h. Subsequently, cells were irradiated with an 808 nm laser (2 W/cm^2) for 3 min. The cell viabilities were approximately 70% and 40% for the NIH/3T3 fibroblasts and Hela cancer cells. The results revealed that the treatments achieved a selective effect [93]. Tegafur is an inactive oral prodrug which is metabolized to 5-FU [66]. 5-FU is also used for topical treatments of skin cancer and its mechanism is based on the inhibition of the enzyme thymidylate synthetase; the successful inhibition of this enzyme will lead to a definitive change in the DNA replication mechanisms [68]. Tegafur presents high selectivity since its activation requires a complex metabolic pathway, which includes steps that are 10 times more efficient in cancer cells than in normal cells [89]. Engel et al. studied the selectivity of Tegafur on normal astrocyte cells and human glioblastoma cells (U251). The cells were incubated with the anticancer drug for 72 h. The final half-maximal inhibitory concentrations (IC_{50}) were 4295 and 384 μM for normal astrocytes and human glioblastoma cells, respectively. The results proved the high selectivity of this anticancer drug, as reported in our study (Figure 6) [94].

Mild PTT strategies involve increasing the temperature to between 39 and 45 °C, affecting mainly tumor cells, because they are less tolerant to heat stress. It inhibits DNA and RNA synthesis, as well as DNA repair, while tumor cell membranes become more permeable, improving drug and nanomaterial intake [90,91]. This strategy has been used to enhance chemotherapy effects. Above 60 °C, cell necrosis occurs through thermal ablation [90,91,95].

So far, authors have mostly used lasers that kill both normal and cancer cells. The use of LEDs presents several significant benefits when compared to laser sources, especially in applications requiring light irradiation. One of the foremost advantages is the cost-effectiveness of LEDs. On average, a high-powered NIR LED can be purchased for approximately EUR 20, a stark contrast to the cost of a similarly powered laser, which can range from several hundred to even thousands of euros. This makes LEDs an economically viable option for a wide range of applications. Moreover, the coherence of the light emitted by these two sources are fundamentally different and have practical implications. Laser light is highly coherent, meaning that it maintains a consistent phase across the beam, leading to a uniform wavefront. While this property is beneficial for certain applications, it poses challenges when irradiating heterogeneous semi-transparent materials, such as biological tissues. The high spatial coherence of laser light can result in the formation of interference patterns, leading to uneven energy distribution across the irradiated area. This unevenness can create high-intensity spots, which, in turn, can induce second-order effects (such as nonlinear optical phenomena) and localized thermal effects. These effects have the potential to cause localized damage to the material or sample being studied, which is particularly concerning in sensitive applications like medical treatments or biological research. In contrast, the light emitted by LEDs is inherently incoherent. This means that the phase of the light varies randomly across the beam, resulting in a more uniform irradiation pattern when the light interacts with these heterogeneous materials. The lack of coherence in LED light effectively mitigates the risk of forming high-intensity spots and the subsequent undesirable effects. Therefore, LEDs offer a safer and more controllable option for applications requiring gentle and uniform illumination, such as phototherapy [96,97].

To date, MoS_2 selective LED-based phototherapy, together with combined chemotherapy, has never been shown in the literature. Zhang et al. irradiated MoS_2 nanosheets functionalized with doxorubicin (DOX) with an NIR laser (808 nm, 1 W/cm^2) for 15 min. After treatment, the viability of MDA-MB-231 breast cancer cells decreased to less than 20%, while the viability of L929, as normal mouse fibroblasts, decreased to less than 40% under the same conditions [48]. Yang et al. functionalized a MoS_2 nanoparticle with melanin, hyaluronic acid, and DOX to perform combined chemo- and photothermal therapies. L929 cells and MCF-9 cancer cells were treated with 24 μg/mL of the nanocomplex and irradiated with an NIR laser (808 nm, 1 W/cm^2) for 10 min. After treatment, the viability of MCF-7 breast cancer cells was reduced to about 20%. However, the viability of the L929 cells decreased to less than 40%, indicating high toxicity to healthy cells [47]. Therefore, the selectivity achieved in our study using MoS_2 + Tegafur + LED NIR irradiation constitutes a novelty.

5. Conclusions

In this study, a new pharmaceutical formulation composed of a Carbopol hydrogel containing MoS_2 nanosheets was proposed as an alternative innovative treatment to overcome the limitation of currently available therapies for skin cancer, such as invasiveness or a lack of selectivity.

After concentration versus cytotoxicity optimization, Carbopol pharmaceutical formulations were prepared containing 125 μg/mL of MoS_2 and 50 μg/mL of Tegafur. An LED-based system emitting at 810 nm with an irradiance of 0.1 W/cm^2 was shown to reduce skin cancer A-431 cells' viability to 28%, after a treatment time of 15 min, corresponding to a dose of 90 J/cm^2. Furthermore, a combined anticancer effect was identified when using MoS_2 together with Tegafur. Also, no toxicity was found towards HFF-1 human skin fibroblasts.

In conclusion, this study demonstrated that MoS_2 can be incorporated, together with Tegafur, in pharmaceutical hydrogel formulations, which, upon safe, LED-based NIR irradiation, leads to a combined destruction of skin cancer cells. This represents an innovative treatment strategy that enables safe and selective combined phototherapy and chemotherapy for skin cancer, constituting a possible alternative to currently offered therapeutic options.

Author Contributions: Conceptualization, M.T.C., F.A.L.S.S., F.D.M. and A.M.P.; methodology, M.T.C., F.A.L.S.S., J.R.F., S.G.S., M.J.O., F.D.M. and A.M.P.; validation, M.T.C., S.G.S., M.J.O., F.D.M. and A.M.P.; formal analysis, M.T.C., S.G.S., M.J.O., F.D.M. and A.M.P.; investigation M.T.C. and F.A.L.S.S.; resources, S.G.S., M.J.O., J.R.F., F.D.M. and A.M.P.; data curation, M.T.C. and A.M.P.; writing—original draft preparation, M.T.C. and A.M.P.; writing—review and editing, M.T.C., S.G.S., M.J.O., F.D.M. and A.M.P.; supervision, S.G.S., M.J.O., F.D.M. and A.M.P.; project administration, F.D.M. and A.M.P.; funding acquisition, S.G.S., M.J.O., F.D.M. and A.M.P. All authors have read and agreed to the published version of the manuscript.

Funding: This work was financially supported by ALiCE, LA/P/0045/2020 (DOI: http://doi.org/10.54499/LA/P/0045/2020); LEPABE UIDB/00511/2020 (DOI: http://doi.org/10.54499/UIDB/00511/2020); UIDP/00511/2020 (DOI: http://doi.org/10.54499/UIDP/00511/2020); and UIDB/QUI/00616/2020 (CQVR), funded by national funds through FCT/MCTES (PIDDAC), base UIDB/04293/2020: Funding of the Institute for Research and Innovation in Health—i3S. This work was financially supported by national funds through the FCT/MCTES (PIDDAC), under the UT Austin PT Program, under the project UTAP-EXPL/NPN/0044/2021—2D-Therapy (DOI: http://doi.org/10.54499/UTAP-EXPL/NPN/0044/2021), as well as under the FCT project 2022.04494.PTDC—PhotoRect. Project 2SMART—engineered Smart materials for Smart citizens, with reference NORTE-01-0145-FEDER-000054, supported by the Norte Portugal Regional Operational Programme (NORTE 2020), under the PORTUGAL 2020 Partnership Agreement, through the European Regional Development Fund (ERDF) and through the project Cancer Challenge 2022 supported by IPATIMUP—Institute of Pathology and Immunology of the University of Porto. Artur Pinto thanks the Portuguese Foundation for Science and Technology (FCT) for the financial support of his work contract through the Scientific Employment Stimulus—Individual Call—CEECIND/03908/2017 (DOI: https://doi.org/10.54499/CEECIND/03908/2017/CP1399/CT0008). Filipa Silva (2021.05897.BD) would like to thank FCT and the European Social Fund (ESF) for financial support.

Data Availability Statement: The data presented in this study are available in this article.

Acknowledgments: The authors would like to thank Rui Fernandes and Ana Rita Malheiro from the Histology and Electron Microscopy Service (HEMS) of i3S, Porto, for their assistance with TEM studies; André Maia from the BioSciences Screening of i3S, Porto, for assistance with the LIVE/DEAD studies; the Biointerfaces and Nanotechnology (BN) Laboratory for assistance with laboratory issues; and Inês Pedro for the training on cell culture procedures.

Conflicts of Interest: The authors declare no conflicts of interest.

References

1. Pacheco, A.G.; Krohling, R.A. The impact of patient clinical information on automated skin cancer detection. *Comput. Biol. Med.* **2020**, *116*, 103545. [CrossRef]
2. Salehiniya, H.; Soltani, S.; Enayatrad, M.; Fathali-Loy-Dizaji, M.; Razi, S.; Mohammadian-Hafshejani, A. The epidemiology of skin cancer and its trend in Iran. *Int. J. Prev. Med.* **2015**, *6*, 64. [CrossRef]
3. Siegel, R.L.; Miller, K.D.; Wagle, N.S.; Jemal, A. Cancer statistics. *Ca Cancer J. Clin.* **2023**, *73*, 17–48. [CrossRef]
4. Rubin, A.I.; Chen, E.H.; Ratner, D. Basal-cell carcinoma. *N. Engl. J. Med.* **2005**, *353*, 2262–2269. [CrossRef]
5. Kauvar, A.N.; Cronin, T., Jr.; Roenigk, R.; Hruza, G.; Bennett, R. Consensus for nonmelanoma skin cancer treatment: Basal cell carcinoma, including a cost analysis of treatment methods. *Dermatol. Surg.* **2015**, *41*, 550–571. [CrossRef]
6. Ermertcan, A.T.; Hellings, P.W.; Cingi, C. Nonmelanoma Skin Cancer of the Head and Neck Nonsurgical Treatment. *Facial Plast. Surg. Clin. N. Am.* **2012**, *20*, 445–454. [CrossRef] [PubMed]
7. Newlands, C.; Currie, R.; Memon, A.; Whitaker, S.; Woolford, T. Non-melanoma skin cancer: United Kingdom National Multidisciplinary Guidelines. *J. Laryngol. Otol.* **2016**, *130*, S125–S132. [CrossRef]
8. Simões, M.C.F.; Sousa, J.J.S.; Pais, A.A.C.C. Skin cancer and new treatment perspectives: A review. *Cancer Lett.* **2015**, *357*, 8–42. [CrossRef] [PubMed]
9. Tohme, S.; Simmons, R.L.; Tsung, A. Surgery for cancer: A trigger for metastases. *Cancer Res.* **2017**, *77*, 1548–1552. [CrossRef] [PubMed]
10. Grewal, S.; Oosterling, S.J.; van Egmond, M. Surgery for Colorectal Cancer: A Trigger for Liver Metastases Development? New Insights into the Underlying Mechanisms. *Biomedicines* **2021**, *9*, 177. [CrossRef] [PubMed]
11. Lin, A.; Schmalbach, C.E. Surgery in the Era of Immunotherapy for Advanced Head and Neck Non-melanoma Skin Cancer. *Curr. Oncol. Rep.* **2023**, *25*, 735–742. [CrossRef] [PubMed]
12. Kansara, S.; Bell, D.; Weber, R. Surgical management of non melanoma skin cancer of the head and neck. *Oral Oncol.* **2020**, *100*, 104485. [CrossRef]
13. Sabir, F.; Barani, M.; Rahdar, A.; Bilal, M.; Nadeem, M. How to face skin cancer with nanomaterials: A review. *Biointerface Res. Appl. Chem.* **2021**, *11*, 11931–11955.
14. Hasan, N.; Nadaf, A.; Imran, M.; Jiba, U.; Sheikh, A.; Almalki, W.H.; Almujri, S.S.; Mohammed, Y.H.; Kesharwani, P.; Ahmad, F.J. Skin cancer: Understanding the journey of transformation from conventional to advanced treatment approaches. *Mol. Cancer* **2023**, *22*, 168. [CrossRef]
15. Caro, C.; Gámez, F.; Quaresma, P.; Páez-Muñoz, J.; Domínguez, A.; Pearson, J.; Leal, M.P.; Beltrán, A.; Fernandez-Afonso, Y.; De la Fuente, J.; et al. Fe_3O_4-Au Core-Shell Nanoparticles as a Multimodal Platform for In Vivo Imaging and Focused Photothermal Therapy. *Pharmaceutics* **2021**, *13*, 416. [CrossRef] [PubMed]
16. Zhou, S.; Li, D.; Lee, C.; Xie, J. Nanoparticle Phototherapy in the Era of Cancer Immunotherapy. *Trends Chem.* **2020**, *2*, 1082–1095. [CrossRef] [PubMed]
17. Castro, F.; Sarmento, B. *Targeted Photodynamic Immunotherapy, in Systemic Drug Delivery Strategies*; Elsevier: Amsterdam, The Netherlands, 2022; pp. 463–481.
18. Deng, X.; Shao, Z.; Zhao, Y. Solutions to the Drawbacks of Photothermal and Photodynamic Cancer Therapy. *Adv. Sci.* **2021**, *8*, 2002504. [CrossRef]
19. Zou, L.; Wang, H.; He, B.; Zeng, L.; Tan, T.; Cao, H.; He, X.; Zhang, Z.; Guo, S.; Li, Y. Current Approaches of Photothermal Therapy in Treating Cancer Metastasis with Nanotherapeutics. *Theranostics* **2016**, *6*, 762–772. [CrossRef]
20. Pattani, V.P.; Shah, J.; Atalis, A.; Sharma, A.; Tunnell, J.W. Role of apoptosis and necrosis in cell death induced by nanoparticle-mediated photothermal therapy. *J. Nanoparticle Res.* **2015**, *17*, 20. [CrossRef]
21. Zhang, Y.; Zhan, X.; Xiong, J.; Peng, S.; Huang, W.; Joshi, R.; Cai, Y.; Liu, Y.; Li, R.; Yuan, K.; et al. Temperature-dependent cell death patterns induced by functionalized gold nanoparticle photothermal therapy in melanoma cells. *Sci. Rep.* **2018**, *8*, 8720. [CrossRef]
22. Wang, D.; Wang, Y.; Zhang, X.; Lv, Q.; Ma, G.; Gao, Y.; Liu, S.; Wang, C.; Li, C.; Sun, X.; et al. A Polyoxometalate-Encapsulated Metal–Organic Framework Nanoplatform for Synergistic Photothermal–Chemotherapy and Anti-Inflammation of Ovarian Cancer. *Molecules* **2022**, *27*, 8350. [CrossRef] [PubMed]
23. Li, L.; Liang, X.; He, T.; Li, X.; Huang, X.; Wang, N.; Shen, M.; Shu, Y.; Wu, R.; Zhang, M.; et al. Multifunctional light-activatable nanocomplex conducting temperate-heat photothermal therapy to avert excessive inflammation and trigger augmented immunotherapy. *Biomaterials* **2022**, *290*, 121815. [CrossRef] [PubMed]
24. Silva, F.A.L.S.; Chang, H.; Incorvia, J.A.C.; Oliveira, M.J.; Sarmento, B.; Santos, S.G.; Magalhães, F.D.; Pinto, A.M. 2D Nanomaterials and Their Drug Conjugates for Phototherapy and Magnetic Hyperthermia Therapy of Cancer and Infections. *Small* **2023**, *20*, e2306137. [CrossRef] [PubMed]
25. Sen, R.K.; Prabhakar, P.; Bisht, N.; Patel, M.; Mishra, S.; Yadav, A.K.; Venu, D.V.; Gupta, G.K.; Solanki, P.R.; Ramakrishnan, S.; et al. 2D Materials-Based Aptamer Biosensors: Present Status and Way Forward. *Curr. Med. Chem.* **2022**, *29*, 5815–5849. [CrossRef]
26. Zhang, A.; Li, A.; Zhao, W.; Liu, J. Recent Advances in Functional Polymer Decorated Two-Dimensional Transition-Metal Dichalcogenides Nanomaterials for Chemo-Photothermal Therapy. *Chem.—A Eur. J.* **2018**, *24*, 4215–4227. [CrossRef]

27. Liu, Y.; Zhu, S.; Gu, Z.; Zhao, Y. A bibliometric analysis: Research progress and prospects on transition metal dichalcogenides in the biomedical field. *Chin. Chem. Lett.* **2021**, *32*, 3762–3770. [CrossRef]
28. Singh, A.K.; Kumar, P.; Late, D.; Kumar, A.; Patel, S.; Singh, J. 2D layered transition metal dichalcogenides (MoS2): Synthesis, applications and theoretical aspects. *Appl. Mater. Today* **2018**, *13*, 242–270. [CrossRef]
29. Kolobov, A.V.; Tominaga, J. *Two-Dimensional Transition-Metal Dichalcogenides*; Springer: Berlin/Heidelberg, Germany, 2016; Volume 239.
30. Zhou, X.; Sun, H.; Bai, X. Two-Dimensional Transition Metal Dichalcogenides: Synthesis, Biomedical Applications and Biosafety Evaluation. *Front. Bioeng. Biotechnol.* **2020**, *8*, 236. [CrossRef]
31. Liu, T.; Liu, Z. 2D MoS_2 Nanostructures for Biomedical Applications. *Adv. Health Mater.* **2017**, *7*, e1701158. [CrossRef]
32. Yadav, V.; Roy, S.; Singh, P.; Khan, Z.; Jaiswal, A. 2D MoS2-based nanomaterials for therapeutic, bioimaging, and biosensing applications. *Small* **2019**, *15*, 1803706. [CrossRef]
33. Bazaka, K.; Levchenko, I.; Lim, J.W.M.; Baranov, O.; Corbella, C.; Xu, S.; Keidar, M. MoS_2-based nanostructures: Synthesis and applications in medicine. *J. Phys. D Appl. Phys.* **2019**, *52*, 183001. [CrossRef]
34. Shi, J.; Li, J.; Wang, Y.; Cheng, J.; Zhang, C.Y. Recent advances in MoS_2-based photothermal therapy for cancer and infectious disease treatment. *J. Mater. Chem. B* **2020**, *8*, 5793–5807. [CrossRef] [PubMed]
35. Zhao, W.; Pan, J.; Fang, Y.; Che, X.; Wang, D.; Bu, K.; Huang, F. Metastable MoS_2: Crystal structure, electronic band structure, synthetic approach and intriguing physical properties. *Chem.—A Eur. J.* **2018**, *24*, 15942–15954. [CrossRef] [PubMed]
36. Liu, M.; Zhu, H.; Wang, Y.; Sevencan, C.; Li, B.L. Functionalized MoS_2-Based Nanomaterials for Cancer Phototherapy and Other Biomedical Applications. *ACS Mater. Lett.* **2021**, *3*, 462–496. [CrossRef]
37. Radisavljevic, B.; Radenovic, A.; Brivio, J.; Giacometti, V.; Kis, A. Single-layer MoS_2 transistors. *Nat. Nanotechnol.* **2011**, *6*, 147–150. [CrossRef] [PubMed]
38. Chen, J.; Liu, C.; Hu, D.; Wang, F.; Wu, H.; Gong, X.; Liu, X.; Song, L.; Sheng, Z.; Zheng, H. Single-Layer MoS_2 Nanosheets with Amplified Photoacoustic Effect for Highly Sensitive Photoacoustic Imaging of Orthotopic Brain Tumors. *Adv. Funct. Mater.* **2016**, *26*, 8715–8725. [CrossRef]
39. Bharti, S.; Tripathi, S.; Singh, K. Recent progress in MoS_2 nanostructures for biomedical applications: Experimental and computational approach. *Anal. Biochem.* **2023**, *685*, 115404. [CrossRef]
40. Xu, Z.; Lu, J.; Zheng, X.; Chen, B.; Luo, Y.; Tahir, M.N.; Huang, B.; Xia, X.; Pan, X. A critical review on the applications and potential risks of emerging MoS_2 nanomaterials. *J. Hazard. Mater.* **2020**, *399*, 123057. [CrossRef]
41. Caro, C.; Avasthi, A.; Paez-Muñoz, J.M.; Pernia Leal, M.; García-Martín, M.L. Passive targeting of high-grade gliomas via the EPR effect: A closed path for metallic nanoparticles? *Biomater. Sci.* **2021**, *9*, 7984–7995. [CrossRef]
42. Nichols, J.W.; Bae, Y.H. EPR: Evidence and fallacy. *J. Control. Release* **2014**, *190*, 451–464. [CrossRef]
43. Silva, F.A.L.S.; Costa-Almeida, R.; Timochenco, L.; Amaral, S.I.; Pinto, S.; Gonçalves, I.C.; Fernandes, J.R.; Magalhães, F.D.; Sarmento, B.; Pinto, A.M. Graphene Oxide Topical Administration: Skin Permeability Studies. *Materials* **2021**, *14*, 2810. [CrossRef]
44. Liu, T.; Wang, C.; Gu, X.; Gong, H.; Cheng, L.; Shi, X.; Feng, L.; Sun, B.; Liu, Z. Drug Delivery with PEGylated MoS_2 Nano-sheets for Combined Photothermal and Chemotherapy of Cancer. *Adv. Mater.* **2014**, *26*, 3433–3440. [CrossRef]
45. Liu, Y.; Ji, X.; Liu, J.; Tong, W.W.L.; Askhatova, D.; Shi, J. Tantalum Sulfide Nanosheets as a Theranostic Nanoplatform for Computed Tomography Imaging-Guided Combinatorial Chemo-Photothermal Therapy. *Adv. Funct. Mater.* **2017**, *27*, 1703261. [CrossRef]
46. Meng, X.; Liu, Z.; Cao, Y.; Dai, W.; Zhang, K.; Dong, H.; Feng, X.; Zhang, X. Fabricating Aptamer-Conjugated PEGylated-MoS2/Cu1. 8S Theranostic Nanoplatform for Multiplexed Imaging Diagnosis and Chemo-Photothermal Therapy of Cancer. *Adv. Funct. Mater.* **2017**, *27*, 1605592. [CrossRef]
47. Yang, Y.; Wu, J.; Bremner, D.H.; Niu, S.; Li, Y.; Zhang, X.; Xie, X.; Zhu, L.-M. A multifunctional nanoplatform based on MoS2-nanosheets for targeted drug delivery and chemo-photothermal therapy. *Colloids Surfaces B Biointerfaces* **2020**, *185*, 110585. [CrossRef]
48. Zhang, X.; Wu, J.; Williams, G.R.; Niu, S.; Qian, Q.; Zhu, L.-M. Functionalized MoS2-nanosheets for targeted drug delivery and chemo-photothermal therapy. *Colloids Surfaces B Biointerfaces* **2019**, *173*, 101–108. [CrossRef]
49. Yin, W.; Yan, L.; Yu, J.; Tian, G.; Zhou, L.; Zheng, X.; Zhang, X.; Yong, Y.; Li, J.; Gu, Z.; et al. High-Throughput Synthesis of Single-Layer MoS_2 Nanosheets as a Near-Infrared Photothermal-Triggered Drug Delivery for Effective Cancer Therapy. *ACS Nano* **2014**, *8*, 6922–6933. [CrossRef]
50. Liu, J.; Zheng, J.; Nie, H.; Chen, H.; Li, B.; Jia, L. Co-delivery of erlotinib and doxorubicin by MoS2 nanosheets for synergetic photothermal chemotherapy of cancer. *Chem. Eng. J.* **2020**, *381*, 122541. [CrossRef]
51. Xie, M.; Yang, N.; Cheng, J.; Yang, M.; Deng, T.; Li, Y.; Feng, C. Layered MoS_2 nanosheets modified by biomimetic phospholipids: Enhanced stability and its synergistic treatment of cancer with chemo-photothermal therapy. *Colloids Surfaces B Biointerfaces* **2020**, *187*, 110631. [CrossRef] [PubMed]
52. Ma, N.; Zhang, M.; Wang, X.; Zhang, L.; Feng, J.; Zhang, X. NIR Light-Triggered Degradable $MoTe_2$ Nanosheets for Combined Photothermal and Chemotherapy of Cancer. *Adv. Funct. Mater.* **2018**, *28*, 1801139. [CrossRef]
53. Xu, M.; Zhang, K.; Liu, Y.; Wang, J.; Wang, K.; Zhang, Y. Multifunctional MoS_2 nanosheets with Au NPs grown in situ for synergistic chemo-photothermal therapy. *Colloids Surfaces B Biointerfaces* **2019**, *184*, 110551. [CrossRef] [PubMed]

54. Chai, S.; Kan, S.; Sun, R.; Zhou, R.; Sun, Y.; Chen, W.; Yu, B. Fabricating polydopamine-coated $MoSe_2$-wrapped hollow mesoporous silica nanoplatform for controlled drug release and chemo-photothermal therapy. *Int. J. Nanomed.* **2018**, *13*, 7607–7621. [CrossRef] [PubMed]
55. Wang, Y.; Zhang, F.; Wang, Q.; Yang, P.; Lin, H.; Qu, F. Hierarchical $MoSe_2$ nanoflowers as novel nanocarriers for NIR-light-mediated synergistic photo-thermal/dynamic and chemo-therapy. *Nanoscale* **2018**, *10*, 14534–14545. [CrossRef] [PubMed]
56. Wang, C.; Bai, J.; Liu, Y.; Jia, X.; Jiang, X. Polydopamine Coated Selenide Molybdenum: A New Photothermal Nanocarrier for Highly Effective Chemo-Photothermal Synergistic Therapy. *ACS Biomater. Sci. Eng.* **2016**, *2*, 2011–2017. [CrossRef] [PubMed]
57. Wang, Y.; Zhang, F.; Lin, H.; Qu, F. Biodegradable hollow $MoSe_2/Fe_3O_4$ nanospheres as the photodynamic therapy-enhanced agent for multimode CT/MR/IR imaging and synergistic antitumor therapy. *ACS Appl. Mater. Interfaces* **2019**, *11*, 43964–43975. [CrossRef]
58. Xie, M.; Ye, P.; Zhao, R.; Yang, M. Magnetic WS2 nanosheets functionalized by biomimetic lipids with enhanced dispersibility for combined photothermal and chemotherapy therapy. *J. Drug Deliv. Sci. Technol.* **2023**, *86*, 104744. [CrossRef]
59. Long, Y.; Wu, X.; Li, Z.; Fan, J.; Hu, X.; Liu, B. PEGylated WS_2 nanodrug system with erythrocyte membrane coating for chemo/photothermal therapy of cervical cancer. *Biomater. Sci.* **2020**, *8*, 5088–5105. [CrossRef]
60. Li, J.; Qi, X.; Ye, P.; Yang, M.; Xie, M. Construction of WS_2/Au-lipid drug delivery system for multiple combined therapy of tumor. *J. Drug Deliv. Sci. Technol.* **2022**, *76*, 103747. [CrossRef]
61. Deng, R.; Yi, H.; Fan, F.; Fu, L.; Zeng, Y.; Wang, Y.; Li, Y.; Liu, Y.; Ji, S.; Su, Y. Facile exfoliation of MoS_2 nanosheets by protein as a photothermal-triggered drug delivery system for synergistic tumor therapy. *RSC Adv.* **2016**, *6*, 77083–77092. [CrossRef]
62. Aronson, J.K. *Meyler's Side Effects of Drugs 15E The International Encyclopedia of Adverse Drug Reactions and Interactions*; Newnes: Waltham, MA, USA, 2016.
63. E Ward, S.; Kaltenthaler, E.; Cowan, J.; Marples, M.; Orr, B.; Seymour, M.T. The clinical and economic benefits of capecitabine and tegafur with uracil in metastatic colorectal cancer. *Br. J. Cancer* **2006**, *95*, 27–34. [CrossRef] [PubMed]
64. Kobayakawa, M.; Kojima, Y. Tegafur/gimeracil/oteracil (S-1) approved for the treatment of advanced gastric cancer in adults when given in combination with cisplatin: A review comparing it with other fluoropyrimidine-based therapies. *OncoTargets Ther.* **2011**, *4*, 193–201. [CrossRef]
65. Saif, M.W.; Elfiky, A.A. Identifying and treating fluoropyrimidine-associated hand-and-foot syndrome in white and non-white patients. *J. Support. Oncol.* **2007**, *5*, 337–343. [PubMed]
66. Rifai, N.; Horvath, A.R.; Wittwer, C.T. *Principles and Applications of Molecular Diagnostics*; Elsevier: Amsterdam, The Netherlands, 2018.
67. Hashimoto, Y.; Yoshida, Y.; Yamada, T.; Aisu, N.; Yoshimatsu, G.; Yoshimura, F.; Hasegawa, S. Current Status of Therapeutic Drug Monitoring of 5-Fluorouracil Prodrugs. *Anticancer. Res.* **2020**, *40*, 4655–4661. [CrossRef] [PubMed]
68. Taveira, S.F.; Lopez, R.V. Topical Administration of Anticancer Drugs for Skin Cancer Treatment. In *Skin Cancers-Risk Factors, Prevention and Therapy*; Porta, C.A.L., Ed.; IntechOpen: Rijeka, Croatia, 2011; pp. 247–272.
69. Li, J.; Mooney, D.J. Designing hydrogels for controlled drug delivery. *Nat. Rev. Mater.* **2016**, *1*, 16071. [CrossRef] [PubMed]
70. Sun, Z.; Song, C.; Wang, C.; Hu, Y.; Wu, J. Hydrogel-Based Controlled Drug Delivery for Cancer Treatment: A Review. *Mol. Pharm.* **2019**, *17*, 373–391. [CrossRef]
71. Safitri, F.I.; Nawangsari, D.; Febrina, D. Overview: Application of carbopol 940 in gel. In *International Conference on Health and Medical Sciences (AHMS 2020)*; Atlantis Press: Paris, France, 2021.
72. Wang, J.; Yuan, Y.; Liu, C.; Zhu, D.; Shen, X.; Yang, B. Preparation and pharmaceutical/pharmacodynamic evaluation of topical brucine-loaded liposomal hydrogel. *J. Mater. Sci. Mater. Med.* **2009**, *20*, 2075–2084. [CrossRef] [PubMed]
73. Zhang, S.; Li, J.; Wang, E. Ultrafine transition metal dichalcogenide nanodots prepared by polyvinylpyrrolidone-assisted liquid phase exfoliation. *J. Mater. Chem. B* **2017**, *5*, 2609–2615. [CrossRef] [PubMed]
74. Timochenco, L.; Costa-Almeida, R.; Bogas, D.; Silva, F.A.L.S.; Silva, J.; Pereira, A.; Magalhães, F.D.; Pinto, A.M. High-Yield Production of Nano-Lateral Size Graphene Oxide by High-Power Ultrasonication. *Materials* **2021**, *14*, 1916. [CrossRef]
75. Silva, F.A.; Timochenco, L.; Costa-Almeida, R.; Fernandes, J.R.; Santos, S.G.; Magalhães, F.D.; Pinto, A.M. UV-C driven reduction of nanographene oxide opens path for new applications in phototherapy. *Colloids Surfaces B Biointerfaces* **2024**, *233*, 113594. [CrossRef]
76. Das, P.; Das, M.K. *Production and Physicochemical Characterization of Nanocosmeceuticals, in Nanocosmeceuticals*; Elsevier: Amsterdam, The Netherlands, 2022; pp. 95–138.
77. Thangappan, R.; Kalaiselvam, S.; Elayaperumal, A.; Jayavel, R.; Arivanandhan, M.; Karthikeyan, R.; Hayakawa, Y. Graphene decorated with MoS_2 nanosheets: A synergetic energy storage composite electrode for supercapacitor applications. *Dalton Trans.* **2016**, *45*, 2637–2646. [CrossRef]
78. Jiang, Y.; Wang, J.; Wu, J.; Zhang, Y. Preparation of high-performance natural rubber/carbon black/molybdenum disulfide composite by using the premixture of epoxidized natural rubber and cysteine-modified molybdenum disulfide. *Polym. Bull.* **2021**, *78*, 1213–1230. [CrossRef]
79. Lin, C.-H.; Tsai, C.-H.; Tseng, F.-G.; Yu, Y.-Y.; Wu, H.-C.; Hsieh, C.-K. Low-Temperature Thermally Reduced Molybdenum Disulfide as a Pt-Free Counter Electrode for Dye-Sensitized Solar Cells. *Nanoscale Res. Lett.* **2015**, *10*, 446. [CrossRef]
80. Yan, H.; Song, P.; Zhang, S.; Yang, Z.; Wang, Q. Facile synthesis, characterization and gas sensing performance of ZnO nanoparticles-coated MoS2 nanosheets. *J. Alloy. Compd.* **2016**, *662*, 118–125. [CrossRef]

81. Wang, J.; Tsuzuki, T.; Tang, B.; Cizek, P.; Sun, L.; Wang, X. Synthesis of silica-coated ZnO nanocomposite: The resonance structure of polyvinyl pyrrolidone (PVP) as a coupling agent. *Colloid Polym. Sci.* **2010**, *288*, 1705–1711. [CrossRef]
82. Wang, J.; Zhang, W.; Wang, Y.; Zhu, W.; Zhang, D.; Li, Z.; Wang, J. Enhanced Exfoliation Effect of Solid Auxiliary Agent On the Synthesis of Biofunctionalized MoS_2 Using Grindstone Chemistry. *Part. Part. Syst. Charact.* **2016**, *33*, 825–832. [CrossRef]
83. Robinson, J.T.; Tabakman, S.M.; Liang, Y.; Wang, H.; Casalongue, H.S.; Vinh, D.; Dai, H. Ultrasmall Reduced Graphene Oxide with High Near-Infrared Absorbance for Photothermal Therapy. *J. Am. Chem. Soc.* **2011**, *133*, 6825–6831. [CrossRef] [PubMed]
84. Dumcenco, D.; Ovchinnikov, D.; Marinov, K.; Lazic, P.; Gibertini, M.; Marzari, N.; Sanchez, O.L.; Kung, Y.C.; Krasnozhon, D.; Chen, M.W. Large-area epitaxial monolayer MoS_2. *ACS Nano* **2015**, *9*, 4611–4620. [CrossRef] [PubMed]
85. Ramana, L.N.; Mudakavi, R.J.; Raichur, A.M. Self-assembled albumin decorated MoS_2 aggregates and photo-stimuli induced geometrical switching for enhanced theranostics applications. *Mater. Adv.* **2020**, *1*, 3000–3008. [CrossRef]
86. *ISO 10993-5:2009*; Biological Evaluation of Medical Devices. Part 5: Tests for In Vitro Cytotoxicity. International Organization for Standardization: Geneva, Switzerland, 2009.
87. Hu, Q.-D.; Fan, H.; Lou, W.-J.; Wang, Q.-Q.; Tang, G.-P. Polyethylenimine-cyclodextrin-tegafur conjugate shows anti-cancer activity and a potential for gene delivery. *J. Zhejiang Univ. B* **2011**, *12*, 720–729. [CrossRef] [PubMed]
88. Badea, I.; Moja, D.; Tudose, A.; Stoicescu, D. Determination of the 5-fluorouracil and N1(2′-furanidyl)uracil in the presence of tegafur by zero-crossing first derivative spectrometry. *J. Pharm. Biomed. Anal.* **2002**, *30*, 1371–1378. [CrossRef] [PubMed]
89. Avendaäno, C.; Menâendez, J.C. *Medicinal Chemistry of Anticancer Drugs*; Elsevier: Amsterdam, The Netherlands, 2008.
90. Zhang, B.; Wang, Y.; Liu, J.; Zhai, G. Recent Developments of Phototherapy Based on Graphene Family Nanomaterials. *Curr. Med. Chem.* **2017**, *24*, 268–291. [CrossRef]
91. Amaral, S.I.; Silva, F.A.L.S.; Costa-Almeida, R.; Timochenco, L.; Fernandes, J.R.; Sarmento, B.; Gonçalves, I.C.; Magalhães, F.D.; Pinto, A.M. Pharmaceutical Formulations Containing Graphene and 5-Fluorouracil for Light-Emitting Diode-Based Photochemotherapy of Skin Cancer. *ACS Appl. Mater. Interfaces* **2024**, *16*, 4333–4347. [CrossRef]
92. Liu, J.; Cui, H.; Yan, S.; Jing, X.; Wang, D.; Meng, L. Gold nanostars decorated MnO_2 nanosheets for magnetic resonance imaging and photothermal erasion of lung cancer cell. *Mater. Today Commun.* **2018**, *16*, 97–104. [CrossRef]
93. Sahu, A.; Choi, W.I.; Lee, J.H.; Tae, G. Graphene oxide mediated delivery of methylene blue for combined photodynamic and photothermal therapy. *Biomater.* **2013**, *34*, 6239–6248. [CrossRef] [PubMed]
94. Engel, D.; Nudelman, A.; Tarasenko, N.; Levovich, I.; Makarovsky, I.; Sochotnikov, S.; Tarasenko, I.; Rephaeli, A. Novel Prodrugs of Tegafur that Display Improved Anticancer Activity and Antiangiogenic Properties. *J. Med. Chem.* **2008**, *51*, 314–323. [CrossRef] [PubMed]
95. Costa-Almeida, R.; Bogas, D.; Fernandes, J.R.; Timochenco, L.; Silva, F.A.L.S.; Meneses, J.; Gonçalves, I.C.; Magalhães, F.D.; Pinto, A.M. Near-Infrared Radiation-Based Mild Photohyperthermia Therapy of Non-Melanoma Skin Cancer with PEGylated Reduced Nanographene Oxide. *Polymers* **2020**, *12*, 1840. [CrossRef]
96. Hadis, M.A.; Cooper, P.R.; Milward, M.R.; Gorecki, P.C.; Tarte, E.; Churm, J.; Palin, W.M. Development and application of LED arrays for use in phototherapy research. *J. Biophotonics* **2017**, *10*, 1514–1525. [CrossRef]
97. Yeh, N.G.; Wu, C.-H.; Cheng, T.C. Light-emitting diodes—Their potential in biomedical applications. *Renew. Sustain. Energy Rev.* **2010**, *14*, 2161–2166. [CrossRef]

Disclaimer/Publisher's Note: The statements, opinions and data contained in all publications are solely those of the individual author(s) and contributor(s) and not of MDPI and/or the editor(s). MDPI and/or the editor(s) disclaim responsibility for any injury to people or property resulting from any ideas, methods, instructions or products referred to in the content.

cancers

MDPI

Systematic Review

Systematic Review and Meta-Analysis of Laparoscopic versus Robotic-Assisted Surgery for Colon Cancer: Efficacy, Safety, and Outcomes—A Focus on Studies from 2020–2024

Roxana Loriana Negrut [1,2], Adrian Cote [3,*], Vasile Aurel Caus [4] and Adrian Marius Maghiar [1,3]

1 Department of Medicine, Faculty of Medicine and Pharmacy, Doctoral School of Biomedical Sciences, University of Oradea, 410087 Oradea, Romania; popa.roxanaloriana@student.uoradea.ro (R.L.N.)
2 County Clinical Emergency Hospital Bihor, 410087 Oradea, Romania
3 Department of Surgical Disciplines, Faculty of Medicine and Pharmacy, University of Oradea, 410073 Oradea, Romania
4 Department of Mathematics and Computer Science, University of Oradea, 410087 Oradea, Romania
* Correspondence: adrian.cote@didactic.uoradea.ro; Tel.: +40-722881440

Simple Summary: In this research, we explored the latest advancements in minimally invasive surgery for colon cancer, by comparing laparoscopic surgery to the robotic approach. Our goal was to determine which method has better outcomes in terms of length of surgery, hospital stay, the likelihood of conversion, rate of complications, anastomotic leaks, and the effectiveness of tumor removal by evaluating the number of lymphatic nodes harvested. The findings could help surgeons and patients make more informed decisions related to the surgical options, considering the benefits of each technique. This summary aims to give a straightforward overview of the importance of this research and how it could impact the surgical approach.

Abstract: Background: Minimally invasive surgery in the treatment of colon cancer has significantly advanced over the years. This systematic review and meta-analysis aimed to compare the operative outcomes of robotic and laparoscopic surgery in the treatment of colon cancer, focusing on operative time, hospital stay, conversion rates, anastomotic leak rates, and total number lymph node harvested. Methods: Following PRISMA guidelines, we conducted a systematic search across four databases up to January 2024, registering our protocol with PROSPERO (CRD42024513326). We included studies comparing robotic and laparoscopic surgeries for colon cancer, assessing operative time, hospital length of stay, and other perioperative outcomes. Risk of bias was evaluated using the JBI Critical Appraisal Checklist. Statistical analysis utilized a mix of fixed and random-effects models based on heterogeneity. Results: A total of 21 studies met the inclusion criteria, encompassing 50,771 patients, with 21.75% undergoing robotic surgery and 78.25% laparoscopic surgery. Robotic surgery was associated with longer operative times (SMD = −1.27, $p < 0.00001$) but shorter hospital stays (MD = 0.42, $p = 0.003$) compared to laparoscopic surgery. Conversion rates were significantly higher in laparoscopic procedures (OR = 2.02, $p < 0.00001$). No significant differences were found in anastomotic leak rates. A higher number of lymph nodes was harvested by robotic approach (MD = −0.65, $p = 0.04$). Publication bias was addressed through funnel plot analysis and Egger's test, indicating the presence of asymmetry ($p = 0.006$). Conclusions: The choice of surgical method should be individualized, considering factors such as surgeon expertise, medical facilities, and patient-specific considerations. Future research should aim to elucidate long-term outcomes to further guide the clinical decision-making.

Keywords: colon cancer; surgery; laparoscopic surgery; robotic surgery; outcomes

1. Introduction

Colon cancer is a well-known pathology in the medical field, being one of the most prevalent malignancies and a leading cause of cancer-related mortality globally. Surgical intervention remains a cornerstone of colon cancer treatment, with minimally invasive techniques such as laparoscopic and robotic surgery becoming increasingly adopted due to the reduced postoperative pain, shorter hospital stays, and faster recovery. Continuous research and advancements in the surgical and oncological treatments are necessary to improve patient outcomes [1]. Minimally invasive surgery, including laparoscopic and robotic approaches, has played a significant role in the treatment of colon cancer, offering benefits such as reduced postoperative pain, shorter hospital stays, and fast recovery. While laparoscopic surgery has been widely used, robotic surgery has emerged as a promising alternative, claiming to enhance the accuracy of minimally invasive procedures with advanced maneuverability and other patient benefits, such as reduced complications [2–4].

Initial reports of laparoscopic colon resection appeared in early 1990s, and over three decades, the use of laparoscopy has increased to 40–50% of all colorectal resections for both benign and malignant conditions [5–10]. Robotic surgery received Food and Drug Administration (FDA) approval in July 2020 for various specialties, including general surgery. The first series of robotic colorectal surgery was documented in 2002 focusing on benign conditions, and it was followed by numerous studies comparing the laparoscopic and robotic approaches [11–13].

This study sought to answer the following question: What are the comparative effects of laparoscopic and robotic surgery on the outcomes of colon cancer treatment in terms of operative time, hospital stay, conversion rates, anastomotic leak rated, and oncological outcomes? To address this research question, we aimed to determine the outcomes by evaluating the objectives for each surgical approach and evaluate which method was more efficient.

In this study, we aimed to compare the operative outcomes of laparoscopic and robotic surgery for colon cancer, with a focus on operative time, hospital stay, conversion rates, anastomotic leak rates, and the total number of lymph nodes harvested. By evaluating and analyzing the latest studies published between 2020–2024, we aimed to provide insights into the benefits and drawbacks of each surgical approach, aiding surgeons and patients in making informed decisions regarding the most suitable surgical technique for colon cancer treatment.

2. Materials and Methods

A systematic review was conducted in accordance with the PRISMA (Preferred Reporting Items for Systematic Reviews and Meta-Analysis) guidelines [14]. The protocol was registered in PROSPERO database CRD42024513326, ensuring a structured and transparent review process. The study was designed to provide a comprehensive comparison of laparoscopic versus robotic surgery for colon cancer.

Inclusion criteria:

1. Study types: peer-reviewed randomized controlled trials and cohort studies;
2. Population: adult patients (aged 18 and older) diagnosed with colon cancer at any stage;
3. Interventions: studies comparing laparoscopic and robotic surgical techniques used specifically for colon cancer resections;
4. Outcomes: Studies must report at least one of the following outcomes: operative time, hospital stay, conversion rates, anastomotic leak rates, or harvested lymph nodes.

Exclusion criteria:

1. Non-comparative studies;
2. Cadaveric or animal studies;
3. Irrelevant conditions (other types of cancer or non-oncological surgeries);
4. Language restrictions;

5. Incomplete data (missing outcome data relevant to the primary endpoints of this review).

2.1. Search Strategy

The literature search was performed in January 2024, using four databases: Web of Science, SCOPUS, Science Direct, and PubMed. The search was made using the MeSH-term for greater precision [15]. The following terms were used: colonic neoplasm, colorectal neoplasms, colorectal tumor, colorectal tumors, minimal invasive surgical procedures, laparoscopic surgery, minimally invasive surgery, robotics, robotic surgery. The search included Boolean operators (AND, OR), using round and square brackets for the grouping of the search terms. The timeframe was filtered for articles published from January 2020 until the present (January 2024) to provide a contemporary analysis, considering the newest research and developments in the surgical field for colon cancer. Only the publication type "articles" was selected using the website filters, excluding any other type of publication (review article, proceeding papers, editorial material, early access, correction, letter, book chapters, etc.). The detailed search strategy can be found in Supplementary File S1.

2.2. Study Selection

The records were introduced on the Rayyan platform (Qatar Computing Research Institute) [16] for duplicate removal and a blind screening process by the two authors (N.R., C.A.). First evaluation of the records included a blind selection based on the title, keywords, and abstract. Any disagreement of the records screened was solved by discussion and by consulting the third reviewer (M.A.). The second screening included in-depth record evaluation. Any concerns of difference of opinion were solved by a group debate including the third reviewer.

The studies were included for assessment if they evaluated robotic and laparoscopic surgical approaches for colon cancer, including any stage 0/I/II/III/IV, and any location (caecum, ascending, transverse, descending, and sigmoid). If the paper reviewed in the same group colon and rectal cancer, it was excluded. If an article presented colon and rectal cancer, it was included only if the two groups were analyzed individually and data related to colon cancer could be extracted.

The studies were omitted following specific exclusion criteria:

1. Wrong publication type (review, meta-analysis);
2. Focusing on other diseases (rectal cancer, hepatic pathology, urologic-gynecologic pathology, gastric cancer, NOSES—natural orifice specimen extraction site, endometriosis, etc.);
3. Restricted access;
4. Animal or cadaveric study;
5. Foreign language;
6. No relevant data;
7. Missing data.

2.3. Data Extraction

Data extraction was performed by the researchers for the following study details: author names, publication year, research design, country where the study was conducted, and the timeframe for each study. Primary outcomes were operative time, length of hospital stay, conversion rate, anastomotic leak, and number of harvested lymph nodes. The secondary outcomes included overall complications, Clavien-Dindo classification I–IV, specimen size, distance from tumor to distal margin and proximal margin, margin rate positivity, 30-day mortality and 30-day readmission, and overall survival. Demographic data included age, number of male cases, BMI, ASA score, UICC (Union for International Cancer Control) stage, tumor location, and type of surgical procedure. Discrepancies in data extraction were resolved through discussion.

2.4. Assessment

Each of the studies included was independently assessed for the risk of bias and relevance by three authors (N.R., C.A., M.A.) using the Joanna Briggs Institute (JBI) Critical Appraisal Checklist [17]. The checklist consists in 11 questions that evaluate different study areas that might identify possible bias risk. Discrepancies among reviewers were solved by discussion and through agreement. The bias risk in individual studies was categorized based on specific thresholds: low risk of bias if there were 70% or more answers with "yes", moderate risk for those with 50–69%, and high risk for studies with less than 50% affirmative responses [17].

2.5. Statistical Analysis

The statistical analysis was made in RevMan 5.4 provided by the Cochrane Collaboration [18]. For continuous variables, we calculated the mean difference (MD) or standardized mean difference (SMD) with 95% confidence intervals (CI), based on the scales used for measurements across the studies. For dichotomous variables, we calculated odds ratios (OR) or 95%CI to estimate effect size. Both fixed-effects and random-effects models were employed, depending on the detected heterogeneity among studies results. The heterogeneity across studies was calculated using I square statistics, chi-square tests, and Z tests for the overall effect. Tests were also performed to determine the presence of heterogeneity. As the *Cochrane Handbook for Systematic Reviews and Interventions* describes, the I square test was interpreted as follows: 0–40% might not be important, 30–60% may represent moderate heterogeneity, 50–90% may represent substantial heterogeneity, and 75–100% considerable heterogeneity [19].

Continuous variables that were initially reported as medians and ranges have been transformed into means and standard deviations, following the methodology proposed by Hozo et al. [20] and transformation methods by Wan et al. [21]. This conversion facilitates the application of parametric statistical analysis, which requires data to be presented as mean and standard deviation.

A fixed-effects model was used in studies with heterogeneity under 50%, while a random-effects model was used for studies with high heterogeneity.

Regarding the p-value, this was considered statistically significant if p was under 0.05. To mitigate the risk of publication bias, funnel plots were employed.

For the publication bias assessment, we used funnel plots for asymmetry and applied Egger's regression rest.

All statistical analyses were conducted using RevMan 5.4 [18] and JASP Team (2024, version 0.18.3) software for additional analyses such as the Egger's regression rest and Bayesian analysis.

3. Results

3.1. Study Selection

The process of selected studies is synthetized in Figure 1, accordingly to PRISMA guidelines. At the beginning, after the systematic literature search, 4104 records were retrieved. After duplicate removal, 1949 studies were screened for title, keywords, and abstract. After the first screening, 61 studies were assessed for eligibility for the second screening process that meant complete text analysis. After that, the articles were assessed for data extraction. Following this, 21 articles were selected for inclusion in the quantitative analysis [22–42]. The identification of studies via databases and the inclusion and exclusion of the studies is presented in Figure 1.

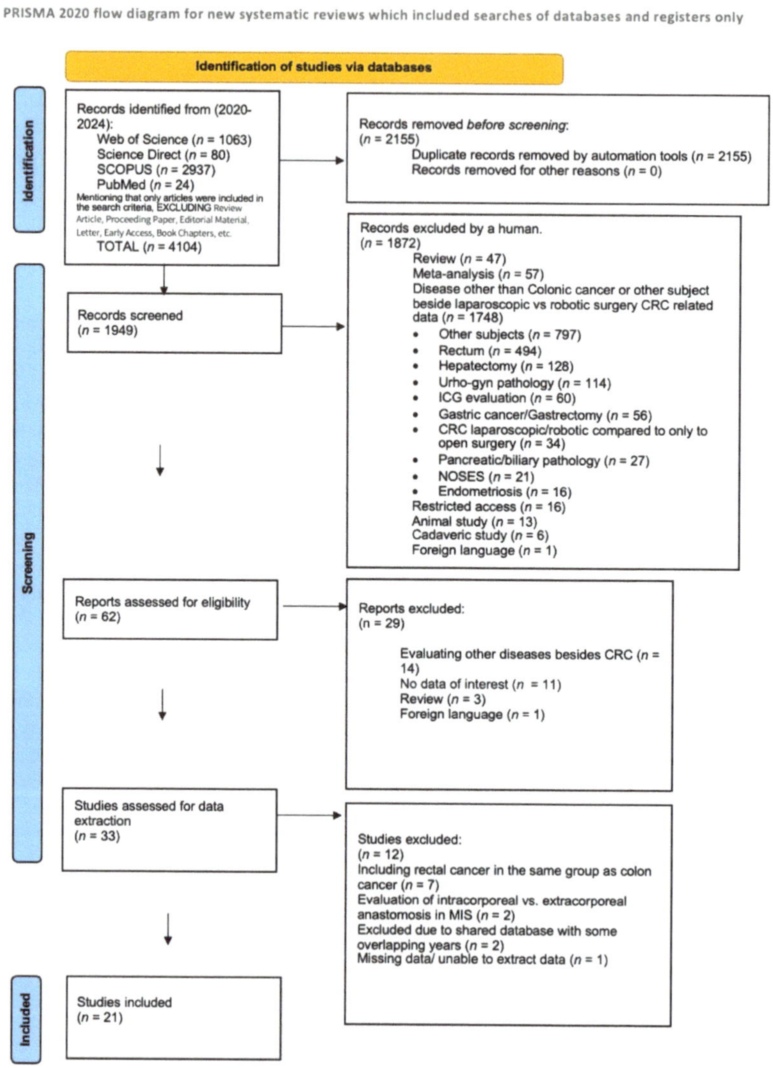

Figure 1. PRISMA flow diagram of studies selection.

3.2. Risk of Bias

Six studies were assessed as having moderate risk of bias, while the others were classified as having a low risk of bias according to the JBI Critical Appraisal Checklist (Table 1). The checklist can be found in Supplementary File S2.

3.3. Studies Characteristics

The characteristics of each study are shown in Table 2. A total of 50,771 patients were included from all studies; 11,059 of them were treated by robot-assisted surgery, and 39,712 were treated by the laparoscopic approach. Of the studies, six were from China, four from Italy, two from the United Kingdom, two from the United States, two from Korea, one from Slovenia, one from Denmark, one from Netherland, one from Spain, and one from Turkey.

Table 1. Risk of bias.

Study	Q1	Q2	Q3	Q4	Q5	Q6	Q7	Q8	Q9	Q10	Q11	% YES	RISK	RISK
Jan Grosek et al., Slovenia, 2021 [22]	Y	Y	Y	Y	Y	Y	Y	U	U	U	Y	73%	☺	LOW
Niclas Dohrn et al. Denmark 2021 [23]	Y	Y	Y	Y	Y	Y	Y	U	U	U	Y	73%	☺	LOW
Yaqi Zhang et al., China 2022 [24]	Y	Y	Y	Y	Y	Y	Y	Y	U	U	Y	82%	☺	LOW
J. S. Khan et al., UK 2021 [25]	Y	Y	Y	Y	Y	Y	Y	Y	U	U	Y	82%	☺	LOW
Yue Tian et al., China 2023 [26]	Y	U	U	Y	Y	Y	Y	Y	Y	U	Y	73%	☺	LOW
Nadia Sorgato et al., Italy 2022 [27]	Y	U	U	Y	Y	Y	Y	Y	Y	U	Y	73%	☺	LOW
Alessandra Di Lascia et al., Italy 2020 [28]	Y	Y	Y	U	U	Y	Y	U	U	U	Y	55%	☺	MODERATE
Zhixiang Huang et al., China 2022 [29]	Y	Y	Y	Y	Y	Y	Y	Y	U	U	Y	82%	☺	LOW
Valentina Ferri et al., Spain 2020 [30]	Y	U	U	Y	Y	Y	Y	Y	Y	U	Y	73%	☺	LOW
Fulvio Tagliabue et al., Italy 2020 [31]	Y	U	U	Y	Y	Y	Y	Y	U	U	Y	64%	☺	MODERATE
V. Ozben et al., Turkey 2020 [32]	Y	U	U	Y	Y	Y	Y	Y	Y	U	Y	73%	☺	LOW
Filipe Pacheco et al., USA 2023 [33]	Y	U	U	Y	Y	Y	Y	Y	U	U	Y	64%	☺	MODERATE
Huichao Zeng et al., China 2023 [34]	Y	Y	Y	Y	Y	Y	Y	Y	Y	Y	Y	100%	☺	LOW
Maolin Xu et al., China 2020 [35]	Y	Y	Y	Y	Y	Y	Y	Y	U	U	Y	82%	☺	LOW
Tung-Cheng Chang et al., China 2021 [36]	Y	Y	Y	Y	Y	Y	Y	U	U	U	Y	73%	☺	LOW
Ho Segun Kim et al., Korea 2021 [37]	Y	Y	Y	Y	Y	Y	Y	U	U	U	Y	73%	☺	LOW
V. Maertens et al., UK 2022 [38]	Y	Y	Y	U	Y	Y	Y	Y	U	U	Y	73%	☺	LOW
Marlou F. M. Sterk et al., Netherland 2023 [39]	Y	Y	Y	U	Y	Y	Y	U	U	U	Y	64%	☺	MODERATE
Emile Farah et al., USA 2023 [40]	Y	Y	Y	Y	Y	Y	Y	Y	U	U	Y	82%	☺	LOW
Sung Uk Bae et al., Korea 2022 [41]	Y	U	U	Y	Y	Y	Y	Y	U	U	Y	64%	☺	MODERATE
Graziano Ceccarelli et al., Italy 2020 [42]	Y	Y	Y	Y	Y	Y	Y	U	U	U	Y	55%	☺	MODERATE

Green color for yes answers. Q1–Q11 refer to the JBI questions numerated from 1 to 11. Y means yes, U means uncertain.

Table 2. Study characteristics.

Author, Country, Year of Publication, Ref. Nr.	Nr	Study Type, Period of Study	Cases Number Lap/Rob	Propensity Score Matching	Sex Male Lap/Rob	Age Lap/Rob	BMI Lap/Rob
Jan Grosek et al., Slovenia 2021 [22]	1	Retrospective single center 2019–2020	37 LAP 46 ROB	-	23/26	67.5 ± 10.1/66.8 ± 11	27.2 (25.1–29.4)/27.5 (25.7–31.3)
Niclas Dohrn et al., Denmark 2021 [23]	2	Retrospective National Cancer Database 2015–2018	3621 LAP 381 ROB	-	1621/185	73 ± 8.89/73 ± 8.89	25.7 (22.9–29.04)/25.6 (23.2–28.8)
Yaqi Zhang et al., China 2022 [24]	3	Retrospective single center 2016–2018	100 LAP 45 ROB	1:3	41/19	-	-
J. S. Khan et al., UK 2021 [25]	4	Prospective single center 2007–2017, 2014–2017	80 LAP 40 ROB	2:1	37/19	71 ± 33.3/69 ± 34.07	28 (19–47)/26 (20–37)
Yue Tian et al., China 2023 [26]	5	Retrospective multicenter 2016–2021	142 LAP 142 ROB	1:1	79/74	63.4 ± 11.3/63.2 ± 2.4	22.5 (3.24)/22.5 (3.2)
Nadia Sorgato et al., Italy 2022 [27]	6	Prospective multicenter 2018–2019	40 LAP 48 ROB	-	28/27	68 ± 10/71 ± 12.2	26.6 (17.9–36.3)/25.6 (17.5–47.3)
Alessandra Di Lascia et al., Italy 2020 [28]	7	Retrospective single center 2014–2017	15 LAP 7 ROB	-	8/4	75 ± 3/75.7 ± 2.56	25 (19–41)/26 (21–38)
Zhixiang Huang et al., China 2022 [29]	8	Retrospective single center 2012–2017	92 LAP 70 ROB	-	-	-	-
Valentina Ferri et al., Spain 2020 [30]	9	Prospective single center 2013–2017, 2014–2018	35 LAP 35 ROB	1:1	20/23	68.2 ± 8.67/69.6 ± 7	25 (20–34)/23 (19–31)
Fulvio Tagliabue et al., Italy 2020 [31]	10	Retrospective single center 2014–2019	68 LAP 55 ROB	-	40/32	-	24.81 (23.10–28.45)/24.31 (22.11–27.56)
V. Ozben et al., Turkey 2020 [32]	11	Retrospective multicenter 2011–2018	80 LAP 38 ROB	-	47/27	64.1 ± 15.5/62.3 ± 15.7	26.7 (7.7)/25.3 (6.1)

Table 2. *Cont.*

Author, Country, Year of Publication, Ref. Nr.	Nr	Study Type, Period of Study	Cases Number Lap/Rob	Propensity Score Matching	Sex Male Lap/Rob	Age Lap/Rob	BMI Lap/Rob
Filipe Pacheco et al., USA 2023 [33]	12	Retrospective National Cancer Database 2010–2018	9343 LAP 3116ROB	3:1	3957/1314	-	-
Huichao Zeng et al., China 2023 [34]	13	Retrospective multicenter 2014–2022	102 LAP 102 ROB	1:1	66/71	59 ± 12.5/61 ± 16.25	23.5 (4.86)/23.7 (4.46)
Maolin Xu et al., China 2020 [35]	14	Retrospective single center 2012–2018	255 LAP 205 ROB	-	170/123	60.26 ± 11.04/60.36 ± 11.33	24.78 (4.27)/24.8 (4.51)
Tung-Cheng Chang et al., China 2021 [36]	15	Retrospective multicenter 2013–2019	84 LAP 21 ROB	1:4	43/9	65.6 ± 13.6/62.1 ± 11.9	24.6 (4.19)/24.7 (5.27)
Ho Segun Kim et al., Korea 2021 [37]	16	Retrospective single center 2019–2022	97 LAP 43 ROB	-	63/12	70.6 ± 7.7/58.8 ± 7.7	24.3 (10.4)/23.4 (4.05)
V. Maertens et al., UK 2022 [38]	17	Retrospective single center 2005–2021	137 LAP 38 ROB	-	82/20	71 ± 9.17/65 ± 8.17	27 (18–40)/26.5 (20–33)
Marlou F. M. Sterk et al., Netherland 2023 [39]	18/1; 18/2; 18/3	Retrospective Dutch colorectal audit 2018–2020	14353 LAP 1096 ROB	-	Gr1:3557/136 Gr2:913/70 Gr3: 2886/405	Gr1: 73 ± 9.63/73 ± 9.63 Gr2:70 ± 10.37/71 ± 11.11 Gr3:69 ± 12.59/69 ± 11.85	Gr1:26.0 (23.4–29.1)/25.7 (23.4–28.9) Gr2: 26.2 (23.5–29.4)/26.7 (24.4–29.6) Gr3: 26.1 (23.6–29.1)/26.0 (23.7–28.7)
Emile Farah et al., USA 2023 [40]	19/1; 19/2	Retrospective ACS-NSQIP Database 2015–2020	10950 LAP 5475 ROB	2:1	Gr1:2187/1106 Gr2: 3266/1633	-	-
Sung Uk Bae et al., Korea, 2022 [41]	20	Retrospective single center 2014–2016	61 LAP 36 ROB	-	38/17	67 ± 10.37/62 ± 10.37	24.0 (21.0–27.0)/24.6 (21.0–27.0)
Graziano Ceccarelli et al., Italy, 2020 [42]	1	Retrospective single center 2014–2019	20 LAP 20 ROB	1:1	13/14	74.6 (± 13.8)/70.6 (± 9.9)	24.1 (22.14–26.06)/23 (21.38–24.62)

Values are expressed as mean-SD for age and median [IQR] for BMI. Lap—laparoscopic surgery, Rob—robotic-assisted surgery. Nr 1–22 refers to the numeration of each article in the meta-analysis.

3.4. Meta-Analysis

In the meta-analysis, we included 21 studies [22–42] out of 33 from the systematic literature search (see Figure 1). Of the total of 50.771 cases, 11.059 (21.75%) of them were treated by robot-assisted surgery, and 39.712 (78.25%) by the laparoscopic approach. For the meta-analysis, article 18 [38] had three subgroups, the first for right colectomy, the second for left colectomy, and the third for sigmoid resection, while article 19 [39] had two subgroups, the first for right colectomy, and the second for left colectomy, due to data distribution in the original research.

Analysis of the data related to patient demographics is presented in Table 3.

Table 3. Patient demographics.

Outcome	Nr. of Studies	Lap	Rob	OR/MD (95%CI Interval)	I^2 (%)	*p*-Value
Age mean(SD)	18	69.065 ± 10.577	67.96 ± 12.697	0.98 [0.01–1.95]	80%	0.05
Sex male	20	19,085 (48.16%)	5366 (48.81%)	0.96 [0.85, 1.08]	70%	0.48
ASA score > 3	18	12,863 (42.64%)	4033 (51.75%)	1.04 [0.98, 1.10]	33%	0.18
UICC stage III–IV	17	4737 (33.11%)	1443 (32.44%)	1.01 [0.94–1.09]	0%	0.80

OR—odds ratio, MD—mean difference, CI—confidence interval, I^2—heterogeneity, Lap—laparoscopic surgery, Rob—robotic surgery, UICC Stage—Union for International Cancer Control Staging.

The statistical analysis is shown in Supplementary File S3.

Primary outcomes:

For surgery duration, 18 studies were analyzed. The standardized mean difference (SMD) was −1.27 [−1.79, −0.75], indicating that laparoscopic surgery took significantly less time than robotic surgery. This difference was statistically significant, with a $p < 0.00001$ (Figure 2).

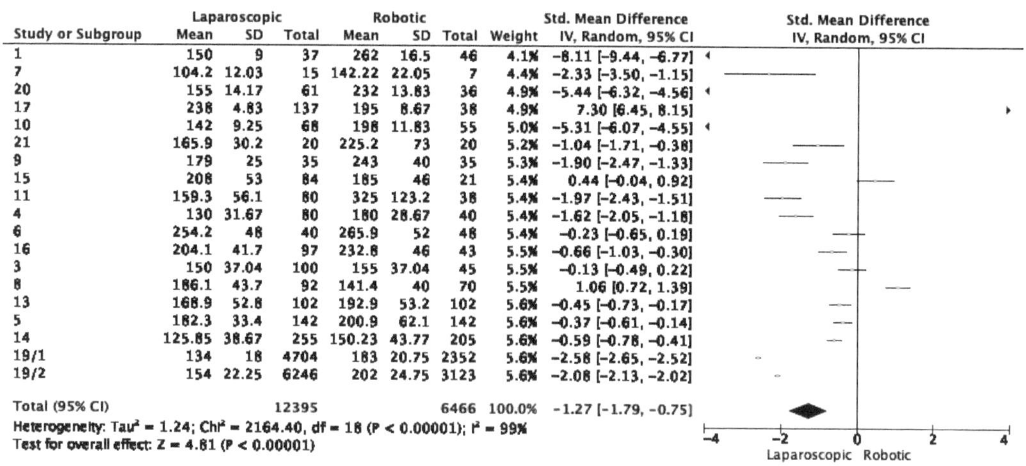

Figure 2. Forest plot for surgery time. Green dots represent point estimates of the mean difference between laparoscopic and robotic groups.

Length of hospital stay (days) was reported in 20 studies, shown in Figure 3. The pooled data indicated a total mean difference of 0.42, meaning shorter hospitalization for robotic surgery, with a p value of 0.003 (Figure 3).

Study or Subgroup	Laparoscopic Mean	Laparoscopic SD	Laparoscopic Total	Robotic Mean	Robotic SD	Robotic Total	Weight	Mean Difference IV, Random, 95% CI
1	7	1.48	37	6	1.48	46	5.2%	1.00 [0.36, 1.64]
10	7	3.33	68	6	1.48	55	4.2%	1.00 [0.12, 1.88]
11	7.9	4	80	7.2	3.1	38	2.7%	0.70 [−0.62, 2.02]
12	6.4	5.1	9343	5.9	6	3116	6.9%	0.50 [0.27, 0.73]
13	8.7	3	102	8.7	4.4	102	3.6%	0.00 [−1.03, 1.03]
14	9.14	3.08	255	9.23	3.37	205	5.4%	−0.09 [−0.69, 0.51]
15	9.3	6.5	84	8.3	1.7	21	2.2%	1.00 [−0.57, 2.57]
16	8.6	3.5	97	7.7	2	43	4.0%	0.90 [−0.02, 1.82]
17	9	2.96	137	7	4.44	38	2.3%	2.00 [0.50, 3.50]
18/1	4	2.96	7821	4	2.22	281	6.8%	0.00 [−0.27, 0.27]
18/2	4	2.96	1663	5	2.96	130	5.7%	−1.00 [−1.53, −0.47]
18/3	4	1.48	4869	4	1.48	685	7.2%	0.00 [−0.12, 0.12]
19/1	4.7	3.8	4704	4	3.4	2352	7.1%	0.70 [0.52, 0.88]
19/2	4.6	3.8	6246	3	3.5	3123	7.1%	1.60 [1.45, 1.75]
20	9	2.22	61	9	2.22	36	4.0%	0.00 [−0.91, 0.91]
21	7.8	3	20	7.2	1.6	20	2.3%	0.60 [−0.89, 2.09]
3	8	5.93	100	7	5.19	45	1.6%	1.00 [−0.91, 2.91]
4	5	3.71	100	6	4.45	40	2.2%	−1.00 [−2.56, 0.56]
5	9	4.7	142	8.7	3.4	142	3.9%	0.30 [−0.65, 1.25]
6	7.4	3.17	40	7.8	2.67	48	2.9%	−0.40 [−1.64, 0.84]
7	7.67	1.23	15	7.71	1.79	7	2.4%	−0.04 [−1.50, 1.42]
8	8.7	4.8	92	7.7	3.1	70	3.0%	1.00 [−0.22, 2.22]
9	8.7	0.1	25	8.3	0.1	25	7.2%	0.40 [0.34, 0.46]
Total (95% CI)			36101			10668	100.0%	0.42 [0.14, 0.69]

Heterogeneity: Tau² = 0.27; Chi² = 340.09, df = 22 (P < 0.00001); I² = 94%
Test for overall effect: Z = 2.97 (P = 0.003)

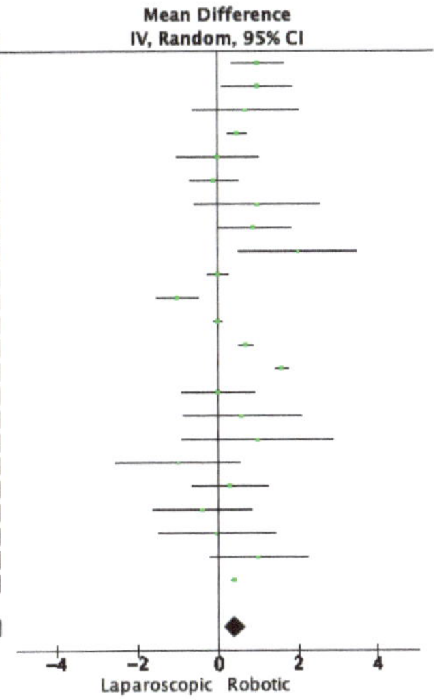

Figure 3. Forest plot for hospital stay. Green dots represent point estimates of the mean difference between laparoscopic and robotic groups.

The analysis for conversion rates (Figure 4) when comparing laparoscopic to robotic surgery showed a total odds ratio of 2.02 (95%CI, [1.79, 2.28], which suggests the likelihood of surgery conversion was significantly higher for laparoscopic methods. The heterogeneity was low ($I^2 = 26\%$) and the overall effect was highly significant ($Z = 11.41$, $p < 0.00001$).

Study or Subgroup	Laparoscopic Events	Laparoscopic Total	Robotic Events	Robotic Total	Weight	Odds Ratio M-H, Fixed, 95% CI
1	5	37	0	46	0.1%	15.74 [0.84, 294.61]
10	3	68	5	55	1.2%	0.46 [0.11, 2.02]
11	6	80	0	38	0.1%	6.72 [0.37, 122.42]
13	4	102	1	102	0.2%	4.12 [0.45, 37.54]
15	1	84	0	21	0.2%	0.77 [0.03, 19.64]
16	2	97	0	43	0.2%	2.28 [0.11, 48.45]
17	5	137	0	38	0.2%	3.20 [0.17, 59.10]
18/1	868	7821	14	281	5.5%	2.38 [1.38, 4.09]
18/2	229	1663	11	130	4.0%	1.73 [0.92, 3.25]
18/3	398	4869	16	685	5.8%	3.72 [2.24, 6.18]
19/1	399	4704	97	2352	26.8%	2.15 [1.72, 2.71]
19/2	551	6246	161	3123	44.4%	1.78 [1.49, 2.13]
2	373	3621	26	381	9.6%	1.57 [1.04, 2.37]
20	0	61	1	36	0.4%	0.19 [0.01, 4.85]
3	0	100	0	45		Not estimable
4	4	80	0	40	0.1%	4.76 [0.25, 90.71]
5	6	142	0	142	0.1%	13.57 [0.76, 243.22]
6	0	40	0	48		Not estimable
7	0	15	0	7		Not estimable
8	0	92	0	70		Not estimable
9	29	35	28	35	1.1%	1.21 [0.36, 4.04]
Total (95% CI)		30094		7718	100.0%	2.02 [1.79, 2.28]
Total events	2883		360			

Heterogeneity: Chi² = 21.76, df = 16 (P = 0.15); I² = 26%
Test for overall effect: Z = 11.41 (P < 0.00001)

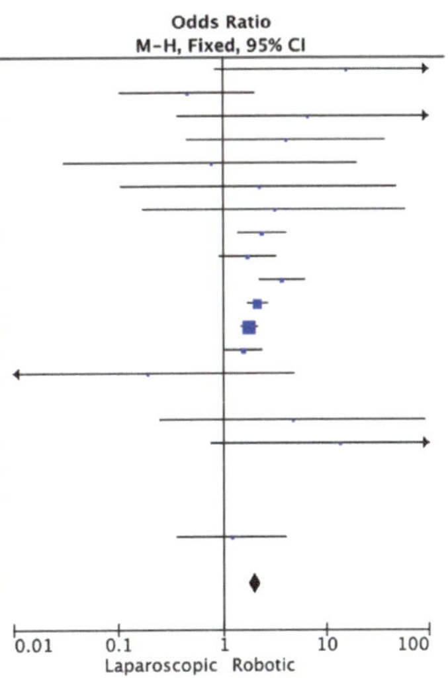

Figure 4. Forest plot for surgery conversion. Blue squares represent point estimate of odds ratio.

The pooled results for anastomotic leak between laparoscopic and robotic surgery showed no significant difference between the two methods, with a risk difference of −0.00 (95% CI [−0.00, 0.00]). The heterogeneity was non-existent, meaning no variation between studies, with an overall effect of −0.34 and a p value of 0.73, suggesting no statistically significant difference between the two surgical techniques. The results are shown in Figure 5.

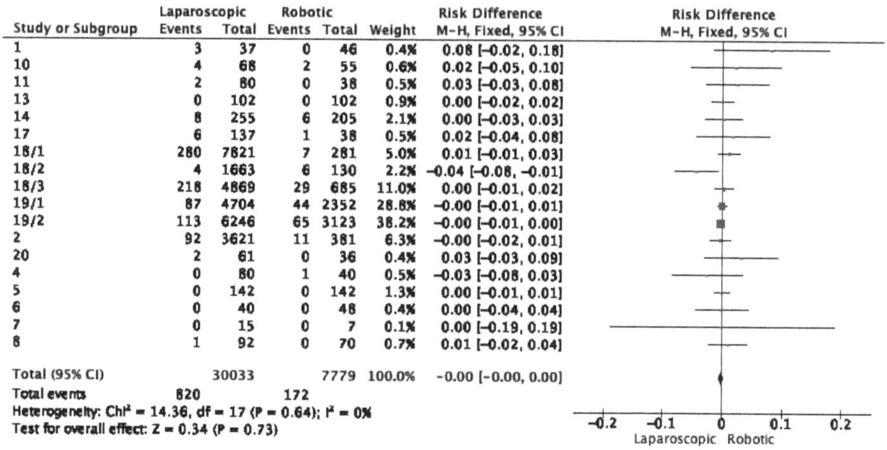

Figure 5. Risk difference for anastomotic leak between laparoscopic and robotic surgery. Blue squares represent point estimates of Risk Difference.

Analyzing the mean number of harvested lymph nodes, the total mean difference was −0.65, indicating that on average, laparoscopic surgery resulted in 0.65 fewer lymph nodes harvested compared to robotic surgery. The heterogeneity was high (72%), suggesting substantial variation in outcomes across studies, a significant overall effect with a Z score of −2.03 and a p-value of 0.04. This indicates that robotic surgery was associated with a higher number of harvested lymphatic nodes. Results are shown in Figure 6.

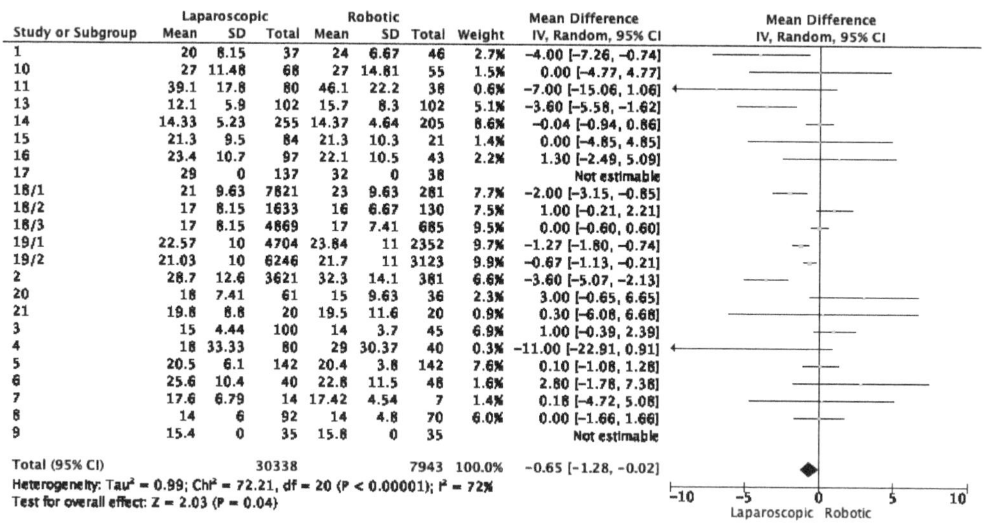

Figure 6. Lymphatic nodes harvested by laparoscopic and robotic-assisted approach. Green dots represent point estimates of the mean difference between laparoscopic and robotic groups.

Secondary outcomes:

Table 4 summarizes secondary outcomes from the meta-analysis, showing that none of the reported outcomes (specimen size, positive resection margins, distance from tumor to distal or proximal margin, complications, and major complications, 30-day mortality) showed a statistically significant difference between the two surgical techniques, as indicated by the *p*-values that were above the conventional threshold for significance of 0.05.

Table 4. Secondary outcomes meta-analysis results for laparoscopic vs. robotic surgery.

Laparoscopic vs. Robotic Surgery	Number of Studies	*p*-Value	I^2	OR/MD (95%CI)	Chi^2	Z
Specimen size	4	0.43	69%	−1.64 [−5.69, 2.42]	12.72	0.79
Positive resection margins	12	0.81	0%	−0.00 [−0.02, 0.01]	2.14	0.24
Distance from tumor to distal margin	4	0.79	0%	0.15 [−0.96, 1.26]	2.04	0.27
Distance from tumor to proximal margin	6	0.30	92%	1.52 [−1.35, 4.38]	66.61	1.04
Complications	18	0.44	0%	1.03 [0.95, 1.12]	17.01	0.78
Major complications Clavien-Dindo III–IV	17	0.98	0%	1.00 [0.89, 1.13]	7.18	0.03
30-day mortality	14	0.21	31%	0.00 [−0.00, 0.01]	20.38	1.26

Publication Bias

We used a funnel plot of surgery conversion to estimate the presence of publication bias. The funnel plot displays a degree of asymmetry, with more studies being on the right side of the mean effect size line, suggesting potential publication bias (Figure 7).

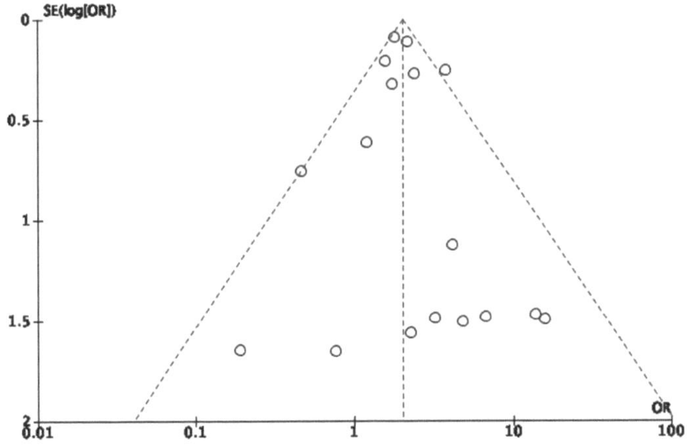

Figure 7. Funnel plot for conversion rates, used to ases publication bias.

Therefore, due to the asymmetry of the funnel plot, further analyses were conducted. For assessment of publication bias, JASP software [43] was used. Egger's test was applied, showing a *p*-value of 0.006, which was below the 0.05 threshold, indicating significant funnel plot asymmetry, as shown in Table 5. The results for the precision-effect test—precision effect estimate are shown in Table 6. The results suggest that after adjusting for publication bias, there was no statistically significant effect detected by the PET-PEESE analysis.

Table 5. Egger's test.

Regression Test for Funnel Plot Asymmetry ("Egger's Test")		
	Z	*p*
sei	2.733	0.006

Table 6. PET-PEESE analysis.

	Mean Estimates (μ)						
						95% Confidence Interval	
	Estimate	Standard Error	t	df	p	Lower	Upper
PET	−0.076	0.061	−1.242	19	0.229	−0.196	0.044
PEESE	0.038	0.069	0.555	19	0.585	−0.097	0.173

A robust Bayesian analysis was conducted, and its results are shown in Table 7. The Bayesian approach revealed evidence of both heterogeneity and publication bias, with effect sizes uncertain and wide credibility intervals, suggesting there may have been an effect, but not one estimated with precision.

Table 7. Robust Bayesian meta-analysis.

	Summary			
	Models	P(M)	P(M I Data)	Inclusion BF
Effect	18/36	0.500	0.533	1.140
Heterogeneity	18/36	0.500	1.000	$1.503 \times 10^{+125}$
Publication bias	32/36	0.500	0.977	41.566

Publication bias represents a notable concern in the research field arising when studies with positive or statistically significant results are preferentially published over those with non-significant findings. This is also compounded by the small studies that report large effect sizes, which can distort the perceived efficacy of interventions. While comprehensive literature searches and statistical adjustments are employed to minimize this bias, it is challenging to fully correct due to various factors. Therefore, publication bias is a limitation that is acknowledged in interpreting the results of the meta-analysis.

4. Discussion

The findings of this systematic review and meta-analysis shed light on the comparative outcomes of robotic and laparoscopic surgery for colon cancer. Our analysis revealed that robotic surgery was associated with longer operative times compared to laparoscopic surgery, indicating a distinct operative time disadvantage. However, it is important to note that robotic surgery offered benefits in terms of reduced hospital stay and higher lymph node harvest. These findings suggest that while laparoscopic surgery may require more time in the operating room, it can contribute to shorter hospital stays and potentially improved oncological outcomes through a higher number of lymph nodes harvested.

The analysis of conversion rates indicated that laparoscopic surgery had a higher likelihood of conversion to open surgery compared to robotic methods, with an odds ratio of 2.02 (95%CT, [1.79, 2.28]). This suggests a statistically significant difference, supported by low heterogeneity ($Z = 11.41$, $p < 0.00001$). However, it is crucial to consider this information within a broader spectrum of surgical practice. Conversion from laparoscopic to an open approach should not be viewed as a shortfall of the laparoscopic method. Instead, it is often a reflection of prudent surgical judgment in which the primary concern is patient safety and optimal outcomes. Conversions are typically associated with intraoperative challenges such as unexpected anatomical complexities, technical difficulties or other patient factors that may not and cannot be fully appreciated preoperatively. By choosing to convert to an open procedure, when necessary, surgeons demonstrate adaptability and commitment to the best outcomes for the patient. Even though our study highlights a numerical difference in conversion rates, this should not be interpreted as a failure of the laparoscopic approach.

The operative time for laparoscopic surgery was significantly shorter than that for robotic surgery, due to subjective factors that might implicate the learning curve, the experience of the surgeon, but also the complexity of the case and because of the time needed for each instrument change [44,45]. This finding corroborates the work of previous meta-analyses that suggested efficiency in operative time as a key advantage of laparoscopic surgery [46]. It is pertinent to consider that extended operative times associated with robotic surgery may not reflect inefficiency but also encompass the learning curve for surgeons less experienced with robotic techniques. In this context, the robotic reduced-port approach has been recognized for its feasibility and safety across a spectrum of surgeons' expertise, even among those with limited case volumes in single or reduced port surgeries [47].

In terms of anastomotic integrity, our meta-analysis focused on the critical comparison of anastomotic leak rates between the two surgical approaches. The results from pooled studies revealed a risk difference of −0.00 (95%CI [−0.00, 0.00]), indicating no significant discrepancy in the incidence of anastomotic leak. This finding underscores a consistent similarity in outcomes between the two minimal invasive surgical approaches, having a non-existent heterogeneity. While the incidence of anastomotic leaks did not differ between the two approaches, it remains mandatory for surgeons to continue to refine their techniques and decision-making to minimize this complication. Anastomotic healing is influenced by numerous factors, including tissue perfusion, surgical technique, and patient-related factors; the equivalent rates of anastomotic leaks suggest that both laparoscopic and robotic techniques are capable of achieving the standards of care necessary for optimal outcomes.

The lymphatic nodes harvest is a critical metric in oncologic surgery, serving as a marker for the thoroughness of the oncologic resection and impacting the staging accuracy. Our meta-analysis observed a total mean difference of −0.65, with laparoscopic surgery having on average 0.65 fewer lymph nodes retrieved, suggesting a slight advantage of robotic surgery. The heterogeneity of this result is high, indicating a considerable variability in the number of nodes harvested across different studies. This high heterogeneity could be due to multiple factors such as differences in surgical technique, the extent of the mesocolic excision, patient characteristics, tumor location, and even the interpretation of the examiner from the department of pathological anatomy. However, the difference of less than one lymph node on average may not translate into a clinically significant advantage.

Our review did not reveal any statistically significant oncological differences between laparoscopic and robotic surgery in terms of specimen size, positive resection margins, or distance from tumor to distal or proximal margin. These results suggest a parity between the two surgical approaches. The lack of statistically significant difference, with p values exceeding the conventional threshold of 0.05, indicates that both methods perform comparably across this metrics.

Similarly, the comparable rates of postoperative complications, major complications, and the 30-day mortality reflect the safety of both approaches. While the meta-analysis did not detect a difference in mortality between the two surgical techniques, it is important to mention and acknowledge that mortality is a multifaceted endpoint, that is influenced by many factors beyond surgical procedure itself.

The absence of significant differences further underscores the necessity for decision-making to be guided by surgeon expertise, resource availability, and patient factors. Future research with larger, more homogeneous study populations and long-term follow-up data is mandatory to validate this findings.

While this systematic review and meta-analysis was extensive, it has several limitations that must be considered when interpreting the findings:

1. Study design variability.

When both randomized control trials and cohort studies are included, heterogeneity is induced. Observational studies, in particular, may provide higher levels of bias compared to randomized trials.

2. Confounding factors

Unmeasured confounding factors such as surgeon expertise, patient selection, and hospital resources could influence the outcomes.

3. Geographical representation.

The studies included in the analysis do not cover all geographical regions.

4. Outcomes measured.

This review focused on short-term surgical outcomes.

5. Publication bias.

One limitation of our study is the presence of publication bias, as indicated by the funnel plot and Egger's test. This suggests that there may be an overrepresentation of studies with positive results, which could potentially influence the overall findings and conclusions. Future research should aim to address this bias and include a more comprehensive range of studies to ensure a balanced and unbiased analysis.

The limitations of this review must be acknowledged. The inclusion of studies with various designs and quality, the conversion of medians to means for continuous variables, and the presence of publication bias may impact the validity of the conclusions. It emphasizes the necessity for more high-quality, randomized controlled trials with transparent reporting to better understand the comparative effectiveness of these surgical approaches.

Furthermore, it is important to acknowledge that the choice of surgical method should be individualized, considering factors such as surgeon expertise and patient-specific considerations. The decision-making process should weigh the advantages of reduced hospital stay and potentially improved oncological outcomes with the disadvantage of longer operative times.

The practical implications of this study extend beyond the data to inform clinical decision-making in the treatment of colon cancer. Our analysis suggests that robotic surgery, despite longer operative times, may confer the benefit of shorter hospital stays, which are critical considerations in surgical planning and resource allocation. The findings also highlight the importance of surgical expertise in both laparoscopic and robotic techniques. Training programs should continue to expand skill development in both modalities. Our study supports a tailored approach where surgical method selection is based on surgeon comfort and experience, as well as patient-specific factors. Patient selection for each surgical approach should be individualized, considering factors such as the patient's overall health, tumor characteristics, and the potential for faster postoperative mobilization with robotic surgery, which could be particularly beneficial for patients with comorbidities that may be exacerbated by prolonged hospitalization.

Future research should be conducted, including more randomized trials and prospective cohort studies with standardized outcome measures to provide a clearer comparison between these surgical modalities. Additionally, further investigation into the long-term outcomes and cost-effectiveness of robotic versus laparoscopic surgery is warranted to inform practice guidelines. Further research could also benefit from including detailed subgroup analyses based on patient demographics, tumor characteristics, and surgeon experience. By expanding the research to include more diverse geographical areas, surgeons could gain insights into how regional differences in healthcare practices and infrastructure impact the surgical outcomes.

5. Conclusions

This systematic review and meta-analysis add to the existing literature by providing a contemporary analysis that includes recent advances in surgical techniques. While both robotic and laparoscopic surgeries are viable options for the treatment of colon cancer, the decision on which to choose should be guided by a multidisciplinary team to optimize patient outcomes. With the surgical field being in continuous development with technological advancements, ongoing evaluation and comparison of operative approaches remain essential.

The findings highlight that robotic surgery is associated with longer operative times but tends to result in shorter hospital stays.

The nuanced outcome of conversion rates further explains the complexity of surgical decision-making, reinforcing that conversion should not be deemed a failure of the laparoscopic technique but rather a strategic move towards ensuring patient safety and optimal surgical outcomes.

The equivalence observed in the outcomes such as specimen size, margin positivity, and the insignificant difference in the number of lymph nodes harvested, emphasizes that both laparoscopic and robotic surgeries meet the high standards required for oncological resection in colon cancer treatment.

The presence of publication bias, as indicated by the funnel plot asymmetry and Egger's regression test, is a limitation of this study and the field at large, which can influence the generalizability of our findings.

This analysis calls for a more individualized approach to surgical method selection and underscores the imperative for ongoing, high-quality research to refine the comparative understanding of these surgical modalities. Future research should include more randomized trials and prospective cohort studies with standardized outcome measures and long follow-up periods to better compare long-term outcomes.

In summary, both surgical approaches are competent, showing no substantial differences in outcomes that would distinctly favor one technique over the other.

As we advance, it is crucial that we continue to critically assess and integrate new evidence to refine our surgical choices and enhance patient care.

Supplementary Materials: The following supporting information can be downloaded at: https://www.mdpi.com/article/10.3390/cancers16081552/s1, Supplementary File S1: Search Strategy. Supplementary File S2: JBI Critical Appraisal Checklist. Supplementary File S3: Statistical Analysis. References [22–42] are cited in the Supplementary Materials.

Author Contributions: Conceptualization, R.L.N., A.C., V.A.C. and A.M.M.; methodology, R.L.N. and A.C.; software, R.L.N. and V.A.C.; validation, R.L.N., A.C., V.A.C. and A.M.M.; formal analysis, R.L.N. and V.A.C.; investigation, R.L.N.; resources, R.L.N.; data curation, R.L.N. and A.C.; writing—original draft preparation, R.L.N.; writing—review and editing, R.L.N., A.C. and V.A.C.; visualization, R.L.N.; supervision, A.M.M. and V.A.C.; project administration, R.L.N. All authors have read and agreed to the published version of the manuscript.

Funding: The APC was funded by University of Oradea.

Institutional Review Board Statement: Not applicable.

Informed Consent Statement: Not applicable.

Data Availability Statement: Data are contained within the article and the Supplementary Materials.

Conflicts of Interest: The authors declare no conflicts of interest.

References

1. World Health Organization. Colorectal Cancer. WHO. Available online: https://www.who.int/news-room/fact-sheets/detail/colorectal-cancer (accessed on 10 February 2024).
2. Reddy, K.; Gharde, P.; Tayade, H.; Patil, M.; Reddy, L.S.; Surya, D.; Srivani Reddy, L.; Surya, D., Jr. Advancements in Robotic Surgery: A Comprehensive Overview of Current Utilizations and Upcoming Frontiers. *Cureus* **2023**, *15*, e50415. [CrossRef] [PubMed]
3. Sheetz, K.H.; Claflin, J.; Dimick, J.B. Trends in the adoption of robotic surgery for common surgical procedures. *JAMA Netw. Open* **2020**, *3*, e1918911. [CrossRef] [PubMed]
4. Grimsley, E.A.; Barry, T.M.; Janjua, H.; Eguia, E.; DuCoin, C.; Kuo, P.C. Exploring the paradigm of robotic surgery and its contribution to the growth of surgical volume. *Surg. Open Sci.* **2022**, *10*, 36–42. [CrossRef] [PubMed]
5. Jacobs, M.; Verdeja, J.C.; Goldstein, H.S. Minimally invasive colon resection (laparoscopic colectomy). *Surg. Laparosc. Endosc.* **1991**, *1*, 144–150. [PubMed]
6. Monson, J.R.; Darzi, A.; Carey, P.D.; Guillou, P.J. Prospective evaluation of laparoscopic-assisted colectomy in an unselected group of patients. *Lancet* **1992**, *340*, 831–833. [CrossRef] [PubMed]
7. Falk, P.M.; Beart, R.W., Jr.; Wexner, S.D.; Thorson, A.G.; Jagelman, D.G.; Lavery, I.C.; Johansen, O.B.; Fitzgibbons, R.J. Laparoscopic colectomy: A critical appraisal. *Dis. Colon Rectum* **1993**, *36*, 28–34. [CrossRef] [PubMed]
8. Simorov, A.; Shaligram, A.; Shostrom, V.; Boilesen, E.; Thompson, J.; Oleynikov, D. Laparoscopic colon resection trends in utilization and rate of conversion to open procedure: A national database review of academic medical centers. *Ann. Surg.* **2012**, *256*, 462–468. [CrossRef]

9. Fox, J.; Gross, C.P.; Longo, W.; Reddy, V.M. Laparoscopic colectomy for the treatment of cancer has been widely adopted in the United States. *Dis. Colon Rectum* **2012**, *55*, 501–508. [CrossRef] [PubMed]
10. Wright, J.P.; Albert, M.R. A current review of robotic colorectal surgery. *Ann. Laparosc. Endosc. Surg.* **2020**, *5*, 9. [CrossRef]
11. Administration USFaD. 510(k) Premarket Notification. Available online: https://www.accessdata.fda.gov/scripts/cdrh/cfdocs/cfpmn/pmn.cfm?ID=K990144 (accessed on 28 February 2024).
12. Weber, P.A.; Merola, S.; Wasielewski, A.; Ballantyne, G.H. Telerobotic-assisted laparoscopic right and sigmoid colectomies for benign disease. *Dis. Colon Rectum* **2002**, *45*, 1689–1694; discussion 1695–1786. [CrossRef]
13. Hashizume, M.; Shimada, M.; Tomikawa, M.; Ikeda, Y.; Takahashi, I.; Abe, R.; Koga, F.; Gotoh, N.; Konishi, K.; Maehara, S.; et al. Early experiences of endoscopic procedures in general surgery assisted by a computer-enhanced surgical system. *Surg. Endosc.* **2002**, *16*, 1187–1191. [CrossRef]
14. Page, M.J.; McKenzie, J.E.; Bossuyt, P.M.; Boutron, I.; Hoffmann, T.C.; Mulrow, C.D.; Shamseer, L.; Tetzlaff, J.M.; Akl, E.A.; Brennan, S.E.; et al. The PRISMA 2020 statement: An updated guideline for reporting systematic reviews. *BMJ* **2021**, *372*, n71. [CrossRef] [PubMed]
15. DeMars, M.M.; Perruso, C. MeSH and text-word search strategies: Precision, recall, and their implications for library instruction. *J. Med. Libr. Assoc.* **2022**, *110*, 23–33. [CrossRef]
16. Ouzzani, M.; Hammady, H.; Fedorowicz, Z.; Elmagarmid, A. Rayyan—A Web and Mobile App for Systematic Reviews. *Syst. Rev.* **2016**, *5*, 210. [CrossRef]
17. Peters, M.D.; Godfrey, C.M.; McInerney, P.; Soares, C.B.; Khalil, H.; Parker, D. *The Joanna Briggs Institute Reviewers' Manual 2015: Methodology for JBI Scoping Reviews*; The Joanna Briggs Institute: Adelaide, Australia, 2015.
18. *Review Manager (RevMan) [Computer Program]*, version 5.4; The Cochrane Collaboration: London, UK, 2020.
19. Higgins, J.P.T.; Thomas, J.; Chandler, J.; Cumpston, M.; Li, T.; Page, M.J.; Welch, V.A. (Eds.) *Cochrane Handbook for Systematic Reviews of Interventions*; Version 6.4 (Updated August 2023); Cochrane: London, UK, 2023. Available online: www.training.cochrane.org/handbook (accessed on 28 February 2024).
20. Hozo, S.P.; Djulbegovic, B.; Hozo, I. Estimating the mean and variance from the median, range, and the size of a sample. *BMC Med. Res. Methodol.* **2005**, *5*, 13. [CrossRef]
21. Wan, X.; Wang, W.; Liu, J.; Tong, T. Estimating the sample mean and standard deviation from the sample size, median, range and/or interquartile range. *BMC Med. Res. Methodol.* **2014**, *14*, 135. [CrossRef]
22. Grosek, J.; Ales Kosir, J.; Sever, P.; Erculj, V.; Tomazic, A. Robotic versus laparoscopic surgery for colorectal cancer: A case-control study. *Radiol. Oncol.* **2021**, *55*, 433–438. [CrossRef] [PubMed]
23. Dohrn, N.; Klein, M.F.; Gögenur, I. Robotic versus laparoscopic right colectomy for colon cancer: A nationwide cohort study. *Int. J. Colorectal. Dis.* **2021**, *36*, 2147–2158. [CrossRef]
24. Zhang, Y.; Feng, H.; Wang, S.; Gu, Y.; Shi, Y.; Song, Z.; Deng, Y.; Ji, X.; Cheng, X.; Zhang, T.; et al. Short- and long-term outcomes of robotic- versus laparoscopic-assisted right hemicolectomy: A propensity score-matched retrospective cohort study. *Int. J. Surg.* **2022**, *105*, 106855. [CrossRef]
25. Khan, J.S.; Ahmad, A.; Odermatt, M.; Jayne, D.G.; Ahmad, N.Z.; Kandala, N.; West, N.P. Robotic complete mesocolic excision with central vascular ligation for right colonic tumours—A propensity score-matching study comparing with standard laparoscopy. *BJS Open* **2021**, *5*, zrab016. [CrossRef]
26. Tian, Y.; Xiong, D.; Xu, M.; Fan, Q.; Zheng, H.; Shen, H.; Huang, B.; Wang, L.; Li, C.; Zhang, A.; et al. Robotic versus laparoscopic right hemicolectomy with complete mesocolic excision: A retrospective multicenter study with propensity score matching. *Front. Oncol.* **2023**, *13*, 1187476. [CrossRef]
27. Sorgato, N.; Mammano, E.; Contardo, T.; Vittadello, F.; Sarzo, G.; Morpurgo, E. Right colectomy with intracorporeal anastomosis for cancer: A prospective comparison between robotics and laparoscopy. *J. Robot. Surg.* **2022**, *16*, 655–663. [CrossRef] [PubMed]
28. Di Lascia, A.; Tartaglia, N.; Petruzzelli, F.; Pacilli, M.; Maddalena, F.; Fersini, A.; Pavone, G.; Vovola, F.; Ambrosi, A. Right hemicolectomy: Laparoscopic versus robotic approach. *Ann. Ital. Chir.* **2020**, *91*, 478–485. [PubMed]
29. Huang, Z.; Li, T.; Zhang, G.; Zhou, Z.; Shi, H.; Tang, C.; Yang, L.; Lei, X. Comparison of open, laparoscopic, and robotic left colectomy for radical treatment of colon cancer: A retrospective analysis in a consecutive series of 211 patients. *World J. Surg. Oncol.* **2022**, *20*, 345. [CrossRef] [PubMed]
30. Ferri, V.; Quijano, Y.; Nuñez, J.; Caruso, R.; Duran, H.; Diaz, E.; Fabra, I.; Malave, L.; Isernia, R.; d'Ovidio, A.; et al. Robotic-assisted right colectomy versus laparoscopic approach: Case-matched study and cost-effectiveness analysis. *J. Robot. Surg.* **2021**, *15*, 115–123. [CrossRef]
31. Tagliabue, F.; Burati, M.; Chiarelli, M.; Fumagalli, L.; Guttadauro, A.; Arborio, E.; De Simone, M.; Cioffi, U. Robotic vs. laparoscopic right colectomy—The burden of age and comorbidity in perioperative outcomes: An observational study. *World J. Gastrointest. Surg.* **2020**, *12*, 287–297. [CrossRef]
32. Ozben, V.; de Muijnck, C.; Sengun, B.; Zenger, S.; Agcaoglu, O.; Balik, E.; Aytac, E.; Bilgin, I.A.; Baca, B.; Hamzaoglu, I.; et al. Robotic complete mesocolic excision for transverse colon cancer can be performed with a morbidity profile similar to that of conventional laparoscopic colectomy. *Tech. Coloproctol.* **2020**, *24*, 1035–1042. [CrossRef]
33. Pacheco, F.; Harris-Gendron, S.; Luciano, E.; Zreik, J.; Kamel, M.K.; Solh, W.A. Robotic versus laparoscopic colectomy outcomes in colon adenocarcinoma in the elderly population: A propensity-score matched analysis of the National Cancer Database. *Int. J. Colorectal. Dis.* **2023**, *38*, 183, Erratum in *Int. J. Colorectal. Dis.* **2023**, *39*, 9. [CrossRef]

34. Zheng, H.; Wang, Q.; Fu, T.; Wei, Z.; Ye, J.; Huang, B.; Li, C.; Liu, B.; Zhang, A.; Li, F.; et al. Robotic versus laparoscopic left colectomy with complete mesocolic excision for left-sided colon cancer: A multicentre study with propensity score matching analysis. *Tech. Coloproctol.* **2023**, *27*, 569–578. [CrossRef]
35. Xu, M.; Zhao, Z.; Jia, B.; Liu, R.; Liu, H. Perioperative and long-term outcomes of robot-assisted versus laparoscopy-assisted hemicolectomy for left-sided colon cancers: A retrospective study. *Updates Surg.* **2021**, *73*, 1049–1056. [CrossRef]
36. Chang, T.C.; Lin, E.K.; Lu, Y.J.; Huang, M.T.; Chen, C.H. Single-incision robotic colectomy versus single-incision laparoscopic colectomy: A matched case control study. *Asian J. Surg.* **2021**, *44*, 749–754. [CrossRef] [PubMed]
37. Kim, H.S.; Oh, B.Y.; Chung, S.S.; Lee, R.A.; Noh, G.T. Short-term outcomes of single-incision robotic colectomy versus conventional multiport laparoscopic colectomy for colon cancer. *J. Robot. Surg.* **2023**, *17*, 2351–2359. [CrossRef]
38. Maertens, V.; Stefan, S.; Rutgers, M.; Siddiqi, N.; Khan, J.S. Oncological outcomes of open, laparoscopic and robotic colectomy in patients with transverse colon cancer. *Tech. Coloproctol.* **2022**, *26*, 821–830. [CrossRef] [PubMed]
39. Sterk, M.F.M.; Crolla, R.M.P.H.; Verseveld, M.; Dekker, J.W.T.; van der Schelling, G.P.; Verhoef, C.; Olthof, P.B. Uptake of robot-assisted colon cancer surgery in the Netherlands. *Surg. Endosc.* **2023**, *37*, 8196–8203. [CrossRef]
40. Farah, E.; Abreu, A.A.; Rail, B.; Salgado, J.; Karagkounis, G.; Zeh, H.J., 3rd; Polanco, P.M. Perioperative outcomes of robotic and laparoscopic surgery for colorectal cancer: A propensity score-matched analysis. *World J. Surg. Oncol.* **2023**, *21*, 272. [CrossRef] [PubMed]
41. Bae, S.U.; Jegon, W.K.; Baek, S.K. Single plus one-port robotic surgery using the da Vinci Single-Site Platform versus conventional multi-port laparoscopic surgery for left-sided colon cancer. *Wideochir Inne Tech. Maloinwazyjne* **2022**, *17*, 179–187. [CrossRef]
42. Ceccarelli, G.; Costa, G.; Ferraro, V.; De Rosa, M.; Rondelli, F.; Bugiantella, W. Robotic or three-dimensional (3D) laparoscopy for right colectomy with complete mesocolic excision (CME) and intracorporeal anastomosis? A propensity score-matching study comparison. *Surg. Endosc.* **2021**, *35*, 2039–2048. [CrossRef]
43. JASP Team. *JASP*, version 0.18.3; Computer software; JASP Team: Amsterdam, The Netherlands, 2024.
44. Köckerling, F. Robotic vs. Standard Laparoscopic Technique—What is Better? *Front. Surg.* **2014**, *1*, 15. [CrossRef]
45. Liu, H.; Kinoshita, T.; Tonouchi, A.; Kaito, A.; Tokunaga, M. What are the reasons for a longer operation time in robotic gastrectomy than in laparoscopic gastrectomy for stomach cancer? *Surg. Endosc.* **2019**, *33*, 192–198. [CrossRef]
46. Zheng, J.C.; Zhao, S.; Chen, W.; Wu, J.X. Robotic versus laparoscopic right colectomy for colon cancer: A systematic review and meta-analysis. *Wideochir Inne Tech. Maloinwazyjne* **2023**, *18*, 20–30. [CrossRef]
47. Wei, P.-L.; Huang, Y.-J.; Wang, W.; Huang, Y.-M. Comparison of robotic reduced-port and laparoscopic approaches for left sided colorectal cancer surgery. *Asian J. Surg.* **2023**, *46*, 698–704. [CrossRef]

Disclaimer/Publisher's Note: The statements, opinions and data contained in all publications are solely those of the individual author(s) and contributor(s) and not of MDPI and/or the editor(s). MDPI and/or the editor(s) disclaim responsibility for any injury to people or property resulting from any ideas, methods, instructions or products referred to in the content.

pharmaceutics

MDPI

Review

Prospect of Gold Nanoparticles in Pancreatic Cancer

Tianyi Yin [1,2], Jingrun Han [1,2], Yuying Cui [2], Dong Shang [1,2,3,*] and Hong Xiang [2,*]

1 Department of General Surgery, The First Affiliated Hospital of Dalian Medical University, Dalian 116011, China; ytydmu@163.com (T.Y.); wslhjr1999@163.com (J.H.)
2 Clinical Laboratory of Integrative Medicine, The First Affiliated Hospital of Dalian Medical University, Dalian 116011, China; cuiyuying0220@163.com
3 Institute of Integrative Medicine, Dalian Medical University, Dalian 116044, China
* Correspondence: shangdong@dmu.edu.cn (D.S.); xianghong@dmu.edu.cn (H.X.)

Abstract: Pancreatic cancer (PC) is characterized by its notably poor prognosis and high mortality rate, underscoring the critical need for advancements in its diagnosis and therapy. Gold nanoparticles (AuNPs), with their distinctive physicochemical characteristics, demonstrate significant application potential in cancer therapy. For example, upon exposure to lasers of certain wavelengths, they facilitate localized heating, rendering them extremely effective in photothermal therapy. Additionally, their extensive surface area enables the conjugation of therapeutic agents or targeting molecules, increasing the accuracy of drug delivery systems. Moreover, AuNPs can serve as radiosensitizers, enhancing the efficacy of radiotherapy by boosting the radiation absorption in tumor cells. Here, we systematically reviewed the application and future directions of AuNPs in the diagnosis and treatment of PC. Although AuNPs have advantages in improving diagnostic and therapeutic efficacy, as well as minimizing damage to normal tissues, concerns about their potential toxicity and safety need to be comprehensively evaluated.

Keywords: gold nanoparticles; pancreatic cancer; diagnosis; therapy; safety

1. Introduction

Pancreatic cancer (PC) represents a malignancy characterized by poor prognosis and high mortality. In 2020, it was responsible for an estimated 460,000 deaths globally, making it the seventh most deadly malignant tumor [1]. The absence of effective screening approaches for PC and its presentation with mild and nonspecific symptoms, such as abdominal pain, weight loss, jaundice, and digestive problems, leads to the majority of patients being diagnosed in the advanced stages. The delay in discovery complicates treatment and markedly impacts the prognosis [2]. According to 2023 cancer statistics, the 5-year survival rate for PC patients in the United States is less than 12% [3]. Post-operative outcomes indicate that the 5-year survival rate for PC is only 20% [4]. Currently, research on PC is experiencing a critical impasse. On the one hand, PC is challenging to diagnose early due to the lack of early-stage biomarkers and distinct clinical symptoms. Computed tomography (CT) and magnetic resonance imaging (MRI) are frequently used in clinical imaging diagnosis of PC. Research indicates endoscopic ultrasound (EUS) to be more sensitive than CT, particularly for tumors under 3 cm in diameter, and has seen increased application in PC diagnosis in recent years [5]. Nevertheless, the majority of PC cases have metastasized by the time of initial diagnosis, with only 9.7% in a localized stage [2,6]. Therefore, identifying improved diagnostic methods is vital to enhance the prognosis of PC. On the other hand, PC theory depends on the stage of the tumor. Standard treatment for resectable tumors involves adjuvant chemotherapy post-surgery. FOLFIRINOX and nab-paclitaxel-gemcitabine are recommended for patients with metastatic PC [7]. For patients with locally advanced tumors at the borderline of surgical treatment, neoadjuvant chemotherapy or chemoradiotherapy followed by surgical resection is applicable [8].

Targeted therapy and immunotherapy are viewed as promising methods in the ongoing development and trials for PC [4]. In conclusion, the effectiveness of current diagnosis and treatment protocols of PC still require enhancement, necessitating the development of novel diagnostic and therapeutic approaches.

The application of gold nanoparticles (AuNPs) in medicine has attracted significant attention due to their distinctive physicochemical characteristics. AuNPs have made significant strides in fields including photothermal therapy, drug delivery, radiation sensitization, and assisting in the diagnosis of malignant tumors, especially in diagnosing and treating breast and gastrointestinal cancers [9–12]. Furthermore, AuNPs provide advantages including cost-effectiveness, eco-friendliness, and high biocompatibility. Recently, the exploration of using AuNPs for diagnosing and treating PC has seen a surge in interest. This article aims to deliver a comprehensive review of the advances in AuNPs for the diagnosis and treatment of PC, along with its clinical challenges. In comparison to prior reviews [13,14], this article additionally covers the characteristics, preparation techniques, diagnostic applications in PC, and the safety aspects of AuNPs. Moreover, it amalgamates recent research findings, providing a systematic review of the use of AuNPs in diagnosing, drug delivery, and phototherapy in PC, as depicted in Figure 1.

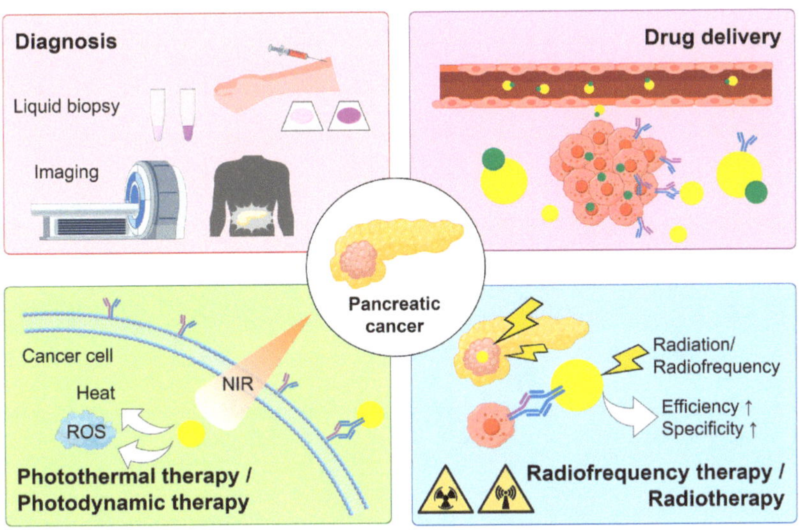

Figure 1. Schematic illustration of the application of AuNPs in the diagnosis and treatment of PC. NIR: near infrared; ROS: reactive oxygen species; "↑" signifies that AuNPs can improve the specificity and efficiency of radiofrequency therapy and radiotherapy in PC. By figdraw.

2. Characteristics of AuNPs

AuNPs display a variety of remarkable characteristics, making them highly promising for applications in cancer therapy. Localized Surface Plasmon Resonance (LSPR) constitutes a key feature of AuNPs, characterized by the interaction of conduction electrons with incident radiation, leading to light scattering and absorption [15]. Utilizing the LSPR effect enables AuNPs to efficiently absorb light energy and convert it into thermal energy. This capability is extensively utilized in cancer photothermal therapy for inducing localized hyperthermia and tumor ablation [16,17], while simultaneously enhancing the tumor's immune response [18]. Adjusting the size of AuNPs enables researchers to optimize their absorption of near infrared (NIR), which is safe and penetrates deep tissues, thereby enhancing therapeutic effectiveness [16].

The enhanced permeability and retention (EPR) effect, proposed by Maeda et al. in 1986, is recognized as a fundamental aspect of nanoparticle-tumor interactions [19]. The

EPR effect elucidates why nanoparticles of a certain size tend to accumulate in tumor vessels, attributable to the rapid growth of tumor cells compared to normal tissues, gaps between tumor vascular endothelial cells, and deficiencies in the lymphatic system [20]. Subsequent research into the passive targeting of tumors by nanoparticles has thoroughly incorporated the EPR effect, yielding numerous positive findings. The widely adopted PEGylation process for nanoparticles prolongs their systemic circulation, further enhancing their ability to passively target tumor tissues through the EPR effect [21]. The first commercialized nanodrug, Doxil® (PEGylated liposomal doxorubicin), capitalizes on the EPR effect for passive tumor targeting [22]. Despite its validation in preclinical trials, most clinical treatments that utilize the EPR effect have not met expectations [23]. Many clinical studies have found that nanoparticles only reduce toxicity and have limited improvement in therapeutic efficacy. The EPR effect exhibits significant heterogeneity across different patients, tumor types, tumor sizes, and tumor locations, termed as the heterogeneity of EPR. For example, the EPR effect varies between different solid tumors and even different regions within the same tumor. The EPR effect performs poorly in PC due to the dense extracellular matrix (ECM) and abnormal vascular structures within the tumor microenvironment (TME). This variability in the EPR effect is further exemplified by significant differences between a patient's primary and metastatic tumors [24]. Typically, the EPR effect is predominantly observed in larger and mature tumors, while it is less effective in newly formed, smaller tumors [25]. Moreover, events such as thrombosis, which decrease blood perfusion, can further modify the EPR effect [26]. In addition to this heterogeneity, design deficiencies in nanoparticles can lead to ineffective EPR outcomes. According to Dr. Maeda, unlike passive targeting, the EPR effect's tumor targeting is distinct, as evidenced by differing accumulation times within tumor tissues [27]. The half-life of nanoparticles also plays a crucial role. A short half-life means that after conversion to free low molecular weight drugs, they are unable to target and accumulate in tumors for prolonged periods using the EPR effect. Conversely, a long half-life can result in slow drug release, which may consequently lead to poor therapeutic outcomes. Moreover, factors such as the size, shape, surface charge, and surface modifications of nanoparticles significantly influence the efficacy of the EPR effect.

In light of these findings, many studies have devised strategies to augment the EPR effect. These strategies encompass nanoparticle modification and both physical and pharmacological treatments to modify the TME [24,28]. Appropriate design regarding size, shape, half-life, charge, surface characteristics, and biocompatibility of nanoparticles can enhance their EPR effect [29]. Generally, nanoparticles ranging from a few to approximately 100 nanometers in size are seen as more effective at utilizing the EPR effect to target tumors, with effectiveness varying by the tumor type and nanoparticle variety [28]. This size range is crucial for optimizing the EPR effect in targeting tumors, although the ideal size may differ based on the type of tumor and nanoparticle [28]. For the design of nanoparticle half-lives, it is critical that they release drugs at the optimal moment since releasing too early or too late can compromise therapeutic efficacy. Furthermore, designs that leverage hydrophobicity, pH, and hypoxic conditions of the TME ensure nanoparticles release drugs at the proper time [30]. Enhancement of the EPR effect in nanoparticles through physical therapies, such as hyperthermia (HT), photodynamic therapy (PDT), boron neutron capture therapy (BNCT), sonodynamic therapy (SDT), and radiation therapy (RT) is also recognized [27,28,30]. Specifically, PDT leads to the disassembly of endothelial cell microtubules and induces the formation of actin stress fibers, thus increasing gaps within the tumor vascular endothelium and enhancing vascular permeability [30,31]. To combat abnormal tumor blood flow, enhancing the EPR effect can be achieved by increasing vascular permeability, improving blood flow within the tumor, or vascular normalization, such as using vasodilators and vascular active cytokines [27,32]. Moreover, apart from altering nanoparticles and the TME, direct infusion of nanoparticles into tumor arteries allows for enhanced drug targeting and reduces the dosage and side effects of systemic medications, showing promising clinical effectiveness [27].

For nearly forty years, the EPR effect has been considered the mechanism by which nanoparticles penetrate solid tumors. Recently, another mechanism for the accumulation of nanoparticles in tumors has been suggested. Sindhwani and colleagues have concluded from extensive experimental analysis that more nanoparticles likely penetrate tumor tissues through transendothelial routes, with fewer nanoparticles extravasating through inter-endothelial gaps [33,34]. Although this finding presents a different perspective on how nanoparticles enter solid tumors, further experimental validation is needed due to the diverse characteristics of different nanoparticles, which may yield different observations [35]. In conclusion, whether optimizing the EPR effect or exploring new mechanisms, the pathways and mechanisms by which nanoparticles enter solid tumors remain worthy of research and discussion.

3. Synthesis of AuNPs

The prevalent fabrication methods for AuNPs are classified into 'top-down' and 'bottom-up' categories, representing the synthesis from bulk materials and the atomic level, respectively [36]. While top-down synthesis is suitable for mass production, it requires significant investment. In contrast, bottom-up synthesis is distinguished by its low cost, operational simplicity, and excellent scalability [37]. Predominantly, bottom-up synthesis involves techniques such as chemical reduction and biosynthesis. The Turkevich method for synthesizing AuNPs holds a milestone significance in the chemical synthesis of AuNPs. Briefly, the method entails dissolving chloroauric acid ($HAuCl_4$) in deionized water, heating it to boiling, and then adding sodium citrate as the reducing agent. By varying temperature, pressure, pH, and sodium citrate concentration, AuNPs with different diameters, parameters, and features can be produced [38]. Later studies have modified the Turkevich method to attain lower variability, enhanced uniformity, and repeatability [39–44]. The use of certain reducing agents or stabilizers in the chemical synthesis process, such as sodium borohydride, could potentially be toxic to both individuals and the environment [37,45]. Compared to other methods, the biosynthesis of AuNPs offers environmentally friendly, cost-effective, non-toxic, and highly biocompatible solutions. Several green biosynthesis approaches for synthesizing AuNPs in PC diagnosis and treatment employ plants such as *Borassus flabellifer* L., *Scutellaria barbata*, *Panax notoginseng* leaves, Acai berry, and Elderberry [46–49]. Extracts from these plants are added to $HAuCl_4$ or $NaAuCl_4$ solutions and thoroughly mixed. A visible color change occurs during this process, and after adjusting temperature and other parameters, an initial aqueous solution of AuNPs is produced. The AuNPs synthesized via this green method using plants are not only non-toxic and cost-effective but also demonstrate remarkable results in the diagnosis and treatment of PC.

4. Applications of AuNPs in the Diagnosis of PC

Accurate staging of PC at the time of diagnosis is crucial for guiding patients toward the most effective treatment strategies [50]. CT angiography, as well as chest and pelvic CT, are utilized for evaluating vascular anatomy and staging the disease. MRI and cholangiography aid in ascertaining if uncertain liver lesions might indicate metastasis and in identifying cancers that CT imaging may not adequately characterize [2]. However, these diagnostic techniques are reliant on the physician's image-reading skills and experience, potentially resulting in missed diagnoses. Currently, numerous studies are employing nanoparticle-assisted imaging to increase diagnostic sensitivity. Conjugates of AuNPs with F19 monoclonal antibodies significantly aid in the MRI detection of human PC tissues [51]. Darkfield microscopic imaging of PC tissues treated with AuNPs near their maximum resonance scattering (approximately 560 nm) shows distinct positive images in the tumor interstitium, whereas healthy tissues display only sparse isolated nanoparticles. This research offers a promising direction for enhancing the sensitivity of laparoscopic examinations in identifying tumor metastatic sites. In comparison to conventional contrast agents, Gd(III) contrast agents derived from AuNPs enhance the low contrast typically seen in pancreatic imaging. The experiments showed a marked enhancement in pancreatic contrast, enabling clear delineation of the pancreas with a contrast-to-noise ratio over 35:1 [52]. $HAuCl_4$ is combined with the MRI contrast agent dotarem and then formed into a contrast agent–AuNPs conjugate using a lactose-modified chitosan polymer. In vivo experiments demonstrate that the conjugate possesses an effective T1 high signal and features a reduced clearance time [53]. 5B1 is a fully humanized monoclonal antibody that targets the CA19-9 antigen, commonly overexpressed in PDAC [54]. Researchers utilized AuNPs integrated with the 5B1 antibody, clodronate liposomes, and 89Zr for innovative PET/CT imaging in in vivo PDAC models. AuNPs labeled with 5B1 demonstrated an accumulation in subcutaneous and orthotopic PDAC that was 4–7 times greater than that in the IgG control group [55]. AuNPs notably increase the sensitivity of radiographic diagnosis, surpassing the constraints of conventional CT and MRI, thus providing a promising approach for more precise diagnosis and staging of PC.

Fluid-based research biomarkers, such as free DNA, exosomes, and circulating tumor cells, are also applicable in tumor auxiliary diagnosis, treatment response monitoring, and assessing resistance to treatments [56–59]. Many researchers utilize PC-specific antibodies in conjunction with AuNPs to create antibody–AuNPs conjugates (Ab-AuNPs), thereby increasing detection sensitivity. Microfluidic technology, frequently used in detecting circulating tumor cells, is known for its high sensitivity and specificity. A novel lateral filter array, equipped with AuNPs carrying anti-EpCAM antibodies, is capable of capturing circulating tumor cells. In both in vitro PC cell line and clinical sample experiments, this array notably enhances the capture efficiency of CTCs [60]. The new tyrosine kinase PEAK1 is found to be overexpressed in PDAC and pancreatic intraepithelial neoplasia [61]. A paper-based immunosensor exploits the catalytic properties of AuNPs in dye degradation to colorimetrically detect the PC biomarker PEAK1 [62]. The sensitivity of this detection approach is ten times higher than that of non-signal amplified AuNPs immunochromatography. AuNPs, when conjugated with anti-CA19-9 antibodies, are capable of detecting the PC biomarker CA19-9 in plasma efficiently [63]. This technique is not just highly sensitive, but it is also anticipated to quantitatively assess CA19-9 levels for future treatment monitoring. Lin et al. developed an amplified time-resolved lock nucleic acid sensor with AuNPs for the selective electrochemical detection of K-ras mutations in PC. The sensor shows high specificity and sensitivity, distinguishing between wild-type and mutation-type K-ras DNA, with an estimated detection limit of 0.5 fM, providing a novel diagnostic perspective for K-ras point mutations in PC [64]. Research indicates that the lncRNA HOXA distal transcript antisense RNA (HOTTIP) is aberrantly elevated in PC [65], making it an effective circulating biomarker for PDAC diagnosis. Lou et al. devised a colorimetric technique that combines reverse transcription coupled with loop-mediated isothermal amplification and the aggregation of positively charged AuNPs for detecting HOTTIP [66]. Leveraging the characteristics of AuNPs, the researchers developed a sensitive, stable, and portable platform for mRNA detection. Using catalytic hairpin assembly and an Au enhancer buffer ($HAuCl_4/NH_2OH \cdot HCl$) to boost gold deposition, they doubled the amplification of the PC mRNA GPC1 signal, effectively identifying the PC cell line AsPC-1 [67]. AuNPs, when conjugated with specific antibodies, substantially enhance the detection efficiency of circulating tumor cells, PEAK1, CA19-9, and HOTTIP, paving the way for new opportunities in early detection and treatment monitoring of PC.

5. Applications of AuNPs in the Treatment of PC

5.1. Drug Delivery

Systemic chemotherapy regimens such as FOLFIRINOX (5-fluorouracil, folinic acid, irinotecan, and oxaliplatin) and gemcitabine plus nab-paclitaxel continue to be the main treatments for patients with advanced PC [4]. Numerous studies have confirmed the clinical effectiveness of chemotherapy in treating PC [68]. The dense connective tissue proliferation and immunosuppressive traits within the TME in PC contribute to the less-than-optimal outcomes of chemotherapy [69–71]. Furthermore, standard chemotherapy regimens for PC are known to have substantial side effects. In an effort to bypass the drawbacks of traditional chemotherapy, the synthesis of chemotherapy drugs with nanoparticles into polymers for targeted delivery to PC is gaining traction as a novel area of interest.

The pathways for drug delivery to PC by AuNPs can be divided into passive and active targeting. The EPR effect is the key mechanism behind AuNPs' passive targeting. Many experiments have successfully improved the EPR effect of AuNPs by modifying their diameter, shape, and surface chemical properties, thus achieving substantial passive targeting outcomes [72]. A common method involves the PEGylation of AuNPs to prolong their systemic circulation time [21]. AuNPs with smaller diameters are found to exhibit greater accumulation in tumors [72]. However, the dense extracellular matrix (ECM) and complex TME of PC can significantly reduce the EPR effect [73,74]. In response to this challenge, many researchers use phototherapy to modify the TME of PC, facilitating easier passage of AuNPs through the ECM and enhancing drug accumulation.

Furthermore, distinct from passive targeting, AuNPs can actively target tumor cells through conjugation with antibodies, proteins, peptides, nucleic acid aptamers, carbohydrates, and small molecules, and be selectively uptaken by tumors via receptor-mediated endocytosis [75,76]. Chitta and colleagues pioneered the use of cetuximab to actively target GEM-loaded AuNPs to PC, marking the first study of antibody-mediated active targeting of AuNPs [76,77]. Zoë et al.'s review thoroughly summarizes studies related to the active targeting of AuNPs [76]. In active targeting therapy for PC, nanoparticles are directed towards targets such as EGFR, urokinase plasminogen activator receptor (uPAR), transferrin, ERBB2, CA125, and stem cell markers like epithelial cell adhesion molecule (EpCAM), CD44, and CD133 [78]. After reaching the tumor tissue through either passive or active targeting, drug-loaded AuNPs release their drugs via pH alterations, enzyme-triggered reactions, or by utilizing the LSPR effect in photothermal and ultrasound applications [79]. Figure 2 shows the mechanism of action of AuNPs in the drug delivery for PC.

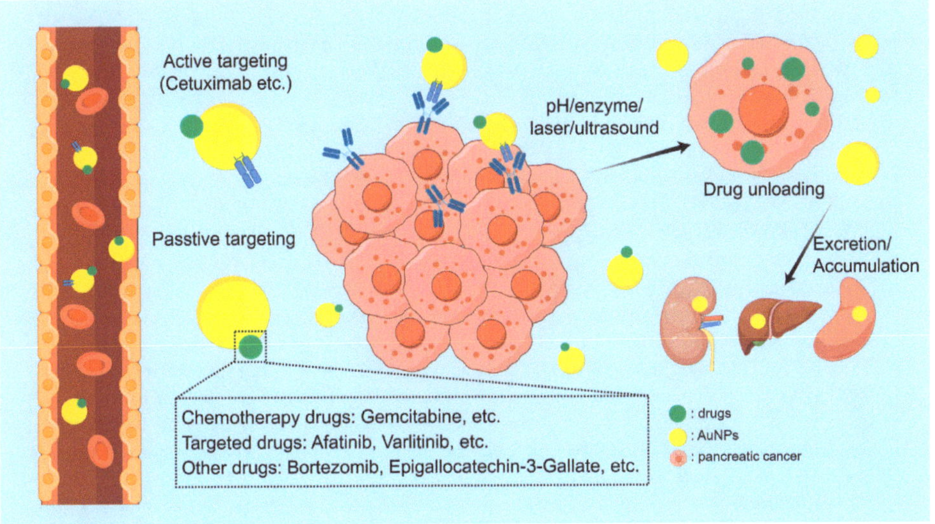

Figure 2. Schematic illustration of the mechanism of drug delivery by AuNPs in PC. AuNPs target tumor tissues through active and passive targeting mechanisms. Drugs are released from AuNPs via alterations in pH, enzymatic reactions, laser irradiation, or ultrasound. Post-drug release, AuNPs are excreted or may accumulate in organs such as the kidneys, liver, and spleen. By figdraw.

GEM serves as a primary chemotherapy agent in treating advanced PC and is deemed the gold standard for single-agent therapy in this cancer [80]. However, the therapeutic efficacy of GEM in the treatment of PC falls short of expectations [81]. To improve its therapeutic efficacy, numerous nanodelivery systems such as liposomes, polymeric nanoparticles (albumin and chitosan), etc., have been explored for GEM-based treatment of PC [82]. Lizhou et al. developed a scheme for ultrasound-targeted microbubble destruction (UTMD)-assisted targeted delivery of GEM using AuNPs for treating PC. UTMD enhances the permeability of cancer cells, facilitating the uptake of drugs [83]. During in vitro experiments, under UTMD assistance, AuNPs release GEM slowly, yet cytotoxicity increases over time, leading to a higher rate of cell apoptosis. In vivo experiments revealed that the conjugate group also attained more notable tumor suppression outcomes [84]. A drug delivery system that includes polyethylene glycol (PEG), cetuximab, and AuNPs carrying GEM yielded favorable outcomes in in vitro experiments. With a 10 μM concentration of AuNPs conjugates, the cell survival rate for PC cells Panc-1 and AsPC-1, and stellate cells CAF-19, was 30%, showing lesser toxicity to healthy human pancreatic cells [85]. The targeted delivery of GEM via AuNPs, along with glutathione, notably reduces the viability of PC cells. After treatment of Panc-1 cells with the conjugate, their viability dropped to approximately 25% [86]. By combining GEM with AuNPs, researchers have enhanced the drug's cellular uptake and the apoptosis rate of tumor cells in the nanodelivery system. The experiments demonstrate that AuNPs hold substantial potential in boosting the chemotherapeutic impact of GEM on PC.

The use of AuNPs in conjunction with targeted drugs also yields affirmative outcomes in PC treatment. Afatinib irreversibly binds to the intracellular tyrosine kinase domains of the ErbB receptor family [87]. Research has shown that the combination of afatinib and GEM possesses significant potential in the treatment of PC [88]. In the PC cell line S2-013, combining PEGAuNPs with afatinib was five times more efficacious in suppression than afatinib alone (with half maximal inhibitory concentration [IC50] values being 0.103 ± 0.001 vs. 0.50 ± 0.02, respectively) [89]. Varlitinib, a reversible small-molecule pan-HER inhibitor, targets EGFR, HER2, and HER4 [90]. Experiments involving targeted drug delivery to the PC cell line MIA PaCa-2 using AuNPs conjugated with varlitinib yielded significant outcomes. The IC50 was 2.5 times lower with AuNPs conjugates compared to using varlitinib alone. With equivalent concentrations of varlitinib, AuNPs conjugates demonstrated increased cytotoxicity towards MIA PaCa-2 cells [91]. In vitro, the release of doxorubicin and varlitinib linked with PEGAuNPs was more prolonged in 48 h than free drugs, augmenting the inhibition of PC cell lines S2-013 and MIA PaCa-2 by 2–4 times. The conjugates also diminished the drug's toxicity towards bystander cells hTERT-HPNE [92].

AuNPs are also capable of delivering various drugs for PC treatment. Bortezomib (BTZ), a boronic acid-based proteasome inhibitor, is typically used to treat multiple myeloma [93]. Research indicates that BTZ causes apoptosis in PC cells, potentially linked to ceramide production in primary and transformed PC cells [94]. The combination of BTZ and PEGAuNPs in treating PC cells leads to increased mass transfer across cell membranes, facilitated by augmented cellular uptake and endosome formation, thereby enhancing the cytotoxic effect of BTZ at extremely low concentrations (0.1–1.0 nM) [95]. The free BTZ requires a 63-fold higher concentration than PEGAuNPs-BTZ conjugate to attain comparable cytotoxicity [96]. Epigallocatechin-3-Gallate (EGCG), a major polyphenolic component of green tea, suppresses PC cell growth, invasion, and migration by inhibiting the Akt pathway and the epithelial-mesenchymal transition [97]. Conjugates of AuNPs with EGCG not only inhibit the growth of BxPC3 cells, but also preserve the antioxidant properties of EGCG [98].

In addition to drug delivery, AuNPs also increase drug sensitivity in PC cells through mechanisms such as inhibiting epithelial–mesenchymal transition, stemness, and mitogen-activated protein kinase signaling, and reducing tumor fibroblast proliferation, thus boosting chemotherapy effectiveness [99,100]. Targeting the dense stroma surrounding PC, nanoparticles equipped with collagenase are capable of degrading the collagen components of the PC matrix, thus enhancing the efficacy of tumor-targeted therapies [101]. In vitro studies show that AuNPs reduce the tumorigenic potential of Panc-2 and MIA PaCa-2 cells. In combination therapy with GEM, AuNPs suppress epithelial–mesenchymal transition, stemness, and mitogen-activated protein kinase signaling in PC cells, resulting in a marked decrease in cell colony formation [100].

5.2. Phototherapy

Phototherapy comprises both photothermal therapy (PTT) and PDT. PDT relies on the interaction between photosensitizers, light, and oxygen to generate cytotoxic reactive oxygen species (ROS), which lead to the death of cancer cells. Conversely, PTT employs NIR to elevate tissue temperature, thus directly annihilating cancer cells via thermal effects [102]. Within the realm of nanomedicine, phototherapy presents a vast potential, as it has shown notable antitumor activity when combined with chemotherapy, immunotherapy, and radiotherapy. The characteristic of LSPR is an optical phenomenon, specifically, the interaction between surface electrons in the conduction band and incident light [103]. AuNPs exploit their LSPR effect to absorb specific wavelengths of light and convert this energy into heat. This process selectively increases the temperature of certain tissues, leading to protein denaturation and swift cell death [102,104]. Irreversible cell damage occurs when tissues are subjected to thermotherapy temperatures (above 42 °C) [105]. Table 1 presents the research parameters and results of AuNPs in phototherapy.

In the initial research on the phototherapy of AuNPs, Guo et al. treated Panc-1 cells with nanoparticles that had an iron oxide core and a gold shell, subsequently exposing them to laser irradiation at 7.9 W/cm^2. The application of cellular MRI techniques revealed a notable decrease in tumor cell proliferation, which varied in a dose-dependent manner with nanoparticle concentration [106]. Kim and colleagues then developed branched AuNPs, synthesized from deoxycholic bile acids, enabling these nanoparticles to absorb higher energy NIR for effective photothermal treatment [107]. Subsequent in vitro experiments employing NIR irradiation on BxPC3 human PC cells resulted in temperatures swiftly rising to 50 °C, achieving a cell mortality rate as high as 90% within three minutes. Further in vivo research showed that photothermal therapy using branched AuNPs was able to elevate the temperature of tumor tissues to 60 °C in 6 min, leading to the dissolution of nuclei in PC cells without evidence of tumor recurrence. Subsequently, Hui and his team developed AuNPs carrying the U11 peptide for actively targeting pancreatic tumors and the PDT agent CRQAGFSL-5-ALA, facilitating combined PTT/PDT treatment of PC under confocal laser endomicroscopy [108]. This active targeting strategy enhanced the concentration of AuNPs in PC, minimizing harm to healthy tissues. Moreover, the combination of PTT/PDT treatments was found to demonstrate significant synergistic effects, with the treated mice exhibiting higher survival rates, lower cell viability, and increased reactive oxygen species (ROS) production compared to controls. Additionally, the NFL-TBS.40-63 peptide (BIOT-NFL) has been shown to be capable of destroying the microtubule network in targeted glioma cancer cells. By leveraging the properties of BIOT-NFL, Spadavecchia's group utilized AuNPs equipped with BIOT-NFL for the treatment of PC. In this context, MIA PaCa-2 cells treated with BIOT-NFL-PEG-AuNPs demonstrated a higher internal concentration of AuNPs and a more significant decrease in cell vitality post-phototherapy than those treated with PEG-AuNPs [109]. Furthermore, BIOT-NFL-PEG-AuNPs significantly raised the levels of serum IL-6, IFN-γ, and TNF-α, thereby bolstering the immune system's capacity to suppress PC [109].

The limited depth penetration of NIR in PTT has led to the emergence of interventional photothermal therapy (IPTT) as a novel strategy for the treatment of deep-seated tumors. Hu et al. developed AuNPs that specifically target PC with anti-urokinase plasminogen activator receptor (uPAR) antibodies, thus employing IPTT to treat deeper layers of PC. IPTT offers a more precise eradication of deep-seated PC compared to Iodine-125 (125I) interstitial brachytherapy, resulting in reduced damage to healthy tissues and lower overall toxicity [110]. Honeycomb-like AuNPs (HGNs)-mediated interventional photothermal-near-field radiation therapy (IPT-BT) demonstrates superior synergistic antitumor properties. The in vitro studies on SW1990 and Panc-1 cell lines have shown that HGNs-treated cells exhibited fewer active cell colonies post X-ray exposure compared to untreated ones; cells in the HGNs + PT-RT group exhibited significantly higher late apoptosis rates than controls [111]. Furthermore, in vivo research has indicated that synergistic treatment with HGNs-based IPT-BT aids in eradicating deep-seated tumors and alleviating hypoxia-associated BT resistance, with hemoglobin levels rising in the HGNs + IPTT group upon laser exposure.

The wavelength of NIR plays a critical role in determining penetration and therapeutic efficacy. The NIR wavelengths most frequently studied and applied are NIR-I (750–900 nm) and NIR-II (1000–1700 nm). NIR wavelengths at the longer end of the spectrum possess deeper tissue penetration capabilities, higher radiation thresholds, and increased tissue tolerance [112]. One study compared the impact of two distinct wavelengths on the photothermal treatment of pancreatic tissues. This research revealed that, under identical conditions, the temperature generated by AuNPs at 808 nm was 200% higher than at 1064 nm, resulting in less damage to adjacent normal tissues [113]. Zhang et al. utilized perfluorocarbon (PFC) as an oxygen carrier, aiming to replenish oxygen in the hypoxic environment of PC for PDT [114]. Gold nanorods carrying PFC and DOX were directed towards PC, initially irradiated with the deeper penetrating NIR-II (980 nm) to emit oxygen, leading to engorgement, followed by the release of silicon phthalocyanine (SiPc) with an extinction peak at 680 nm and DOX into PC tissues, and culminating in a PDT treatment using 680 nm NIR. This sequential application of the two NIR types nearly entirely eradicated the mouse tumors, contrasting with less effective outcomes when the sequence was reversed or when only one type of NIR was used. This demonstrates the crucial importance of the NIR wavelength, with the stronger penetration of NIR-II suggesting a new research direction.

Table 1. Studies and results of AuNPs in phototherapy for PC.

Nanoparticles	Radiate Time (Min)	Laser Power Density (W/cm^2)	The Wavelength of Laser (nm)	Outcome	Cell Lines	Ref
Iron-oxide core/gold-shell nanoparticles	5	7.9	808	Photothermal ablation of Panc-1 cells demonstrated an effective treatment response	Panc-1	[99]
cRGD-branched GNPs	5	1.4	808	Tumors were effectively ablated, without any observation of tumor recurrence	BxPC3	[100]
AuS-U11	5	2	750	Provided better synergistic therapeutic effects against pancreatic tumors	Panc-1	[101]
BIOT-NFL-PEG-AuNPs	15	0.5	808	The vitality of tumor cells significantly decreased	MIA PaCa-2	[102]
gold nanoshells	6	2	808	IPTT offers a more precise eradication of deep-seated PC compared to 125I interstitial brachytherapy	SW1990	[104]
honeycomb-like GNPs	5	2	808	Helpful for eliminating the deep tumors and improving hypoxia-associated BT resistance	Panc-1	[105]
gold nanorods	1	2–5	808/1064	Under 808 nm laser irradiation, tissue heats up slowly, demonstrating selective tissue heating capability	–	[107]
PSPP-Au980-D	5/5	0.1/0.05	980/680	The sequential application of the two NIR types nearly entirely eradicated the mouse tu-mors	MIA PaCa-2	[108]
GEM–polymer conjugate NPs	1	1.4	640	The polymer-bound GEM and the GNPs exhibit a synergistic effect	MIA PaCa-2	[109]
GNPs-pD-PTX-PLGA-MS	3	2	808	Enhanced apoptosis and downregulation of antioxidant enzymes	Panc-1	[111]
gold nanoshells	3	4	808	Demonstrated the synergistic effect of photothermal therapy and chemotherapy	MIA PaCa-2/ Panc-1	[112]
Tf-GNRs	3	0.5	808	Laser irradiation obviously induced the blood perfusion and extravasation in tumor areas	MIA PaCa-2	[113]
gold nanocages	5	1	808	NO improves the effectiveness of GEM chemotherapy through vasodilation in tumor tissues	SW1990	[114]

Combining phototherapy with chemotherapy significantly enhances cytotoxic effects against PC cells [115]. A contributing factor to the dense extracellular matrix of PC, which impedes chemotherapeutic drug delivery to tumor tissues, is identified as a key factor in the poor response to chemotherapy. Utilizing NIR, AuNPs are able to accurately release drugs and modify the cancer cell membrane's permeability, thus enhancing chemotherapeutic drug absorption, improving treatment efficiency, reducing dosage, and lessening chemotherapy's side effects [17,116]. This combined approach of AuNPs-based phototherapy with chemotherapy for PC demonstrates their synergistic impact. Specifically, for MiaPaCa-2 PC cell lines, the IC50 was almost two times lower when treated with GEM-loaded AuNPs following NIR irradiation, compared to direct drug delivery via AuNPs [115]. Moreover, PTX-carrying AuNPs, post-NIR irradiation, exhibited triple the cytotoxicity against a control group without NIR, along with increased ROS generation and reduced expression of antioxidant enzymes [117]. Innovatively, Poudel et al. created gold nanoshells combining BTZ and GEM chemotherapy with photothermal therapy, using low-power NIR for accurate drug release and high-power lasers for direct tumor cell destruction via photothermal effects. In comparison, compared to control groups treated with either photothermal therapy alone or drug delivery alone, the combination therapy led to a significantly higher rate of cell apoptosis [118]. Exploiting PTT, Zhao et al. leveraged its capacity to boost blood flow and microvascular permeability in tumor cells, thereby enhancing the chemotherapeutic effectiveness of GEM when combined. The Transferrin-coated rod-like mesoporous silica gold nanoshell NPs (Tf-GNRS) actively target PC. Following NIR exposure, increased tumor blood perfusion significantly enhances chemotherapeutic drug accumulation in PC, effectively suppressing the tumor [119]. Furthermore, Zhang et al. utilized nitrogen oxide (NO) for its ability to induce tumor vasodilation and normalize tumor vessels, in synergy with PTT, to boost the efficacy of GEM treatment for PC. The Au nanocages carrying L-arginine (L-Arg) generate NO due to increased ROS levels within the TME. After NIR irradiation, there's a notable increase in tumor permeability and deep-layer drug accumulation, leading to significant tumor suppression [120].

To conclude, AuNPs have extensive applications in the PTT treatment of PC. By utilizing passive/active targeting by AuNPs, the precise heating of tumor tissues effectively leads to the destruction of tumor cells. Specifically designed for deep-seated tumors beyond the reach of NIR, IPTT has proven to yield favorable therapeutic results. By leveraging PTT's capacity to enhance tumor blood perfusion and improve the TME, along with AuNPs that are loaded with chemotherapeutic drugs aiming at targeting tumor cells to increase drug concentration in tumor tissues, the combination of PTT and chemotherapy has been shown to achieve notable effectiveness. Photothermal-immunotherapy is gaining increasing attention recently. After undergoing PTT, thermal injury to tumors significantly alters the TME and releases tumor antigens, thereby boosting tumor immunogenicity. The synergy between this approach and immunotherapy yields optimal treatment outcomes [121,122]. Looking ahead, the future of PTT research is expected to focus on the integration of active targeting, chemotherapy, and immunotherapy.

5.3. Radiofrequency Therapy

The use of radiofrequency ablation for treating inoperable PC is on the rise [123]. Nonetheless, the non-selective and invasive characteristics of current radiofrequency therapy may lead to patient discomfort. Nanoparticles can serve as a substitute for radiofrequency probes, selectively targeting tumor sites and reducing patient discomfort. Radio waves, unlike NIR-mediated PTT, can travel through objects with minimal absorption, hence they have enhanced biosafety [124]. The combination of AuNPs with radiofrequency fields in cancer treatment creates intense heat within the cells, leading to necrosis or cell death, with little to no harm to surrounding cells or tissues [125].

Treating Panc-1 cells with cetuximab-conjugated AuNPs and subjecting them to a 200 W, 13.56 MHz radiofrequency field for 5 min resulted in Panc-1 cell viability dropping to $39.4 \pm 8.3\%$, with no harm to neighboring Cama-1 cells [126]. Christopher's team applied a 13.56 MHz external radiofrequency field on Hep3B and Panc-1 cell lines treated with AuNPs at a concentration of 67 μM/L. The death rate in these cells was significantly higher at all points compared to the control, unlike cells that only received the same frequency of external radiofrequency irradiation, which showed no notable cytotoxicity [127]. In another research, in vivo tests were performed to ascertain the anti-PC efficacy of AuNPs. Researchers treated mice implanted subcutaneously with Panc-1 and Capan-1 using AuNPs conjugated with cetuximab and PAM4 antibodies. Post-radiofrequency irradiation, the xenografted pancreatic tumors were notably damaged. Even though AuNPs concentrations rose in the mice's liver and spleen, no apparent signs of treatment toxicity were observed throughout the study [128]. Table 2 shows the study parameters and outcomes of AuNPs in radiofrequency therapy for PC.

Table 2. Studies and results of AuNPs in radiofrequency therapy for PC.

Nanoparticles	Operating Frequency (MHz)	Operating Power (W)	Particle Diameter (nm)	Outcome	Cell Lines	Ref
AuNP-C225-AF647	13.56	200	20	Radiofrequency fields show selective cytotoxic effects on Panc-1 without damaging bystander Cama-1	Panc-1/Cama-1	[126]
AuNP	13.56	200–1000	5	AuNP inflict fatal harm on panc-1 in radiofrequency field	Panc-1	[127]
C225-AuNP	13.56	600	32.6 ± 0.7	Heterologous PC grafts were notably disrupted without evident treatment toxicity	Panc-1/Capan-1	[126]

5.4. Radiotherapy

In cases of inoperable PC, chemotherapy is often used in conjunction with traditional fractionated external beam radiotherapy [129]. Traditional radiation therapy tends to heavily damage normal tissues around the tumor. Radiation therapy guided by AuNPs as radiosensitizers focuses the treatment on tumor tissues and enhances the efficacy of radiation therapy. During radiation therapy, AuNPs exhibit characteristics like producing ROS and locally heating the tumor tissues [130]. A study demonstrated that AuNP-molecularly imprinted polymer microgels (Au-MIP microgels), used as radiosensitizers for PC, significantly inhibited tumor growth in mice injected with these microgels compared to control mice injected with phosphate-buffered saline during X-ray irradiation [131]. Abdulaziz et al. employed AuNPs to enhance radiation therapy in a 3D in vitro tumor model comprising tumor-associated fibroblasts and MIA PaCa-3 PC cells. The combined use of AuNPs and radiation therapy resulted in a significant reduction in tumor size and cell proliferation, with increased DNA double-strand breaks in both co-culture and single-culture groups, showing AuNPs' effective radiosensitizing capability [132].

Using docetaxel (DTX) and a lipid nanoparticle-encapsulated DTX prodrug (LNPDTX-P), the authors found that the treated tumor samples exhibited twice the AuNP uptake as control samples in both in vivo and in vitro settings [133]. The combination of ultrasmall AuNPs (USNPs) with a cisplatin precursor enhances the efficacy of radiation therapy. When exposed to ionizing radiation, the combined application of USNPs and a cisplatin precursor delays the DNA damage response induced by ionizing radiation, leading to apoptosis in PC cells [134]. There is growing interest in targeted alpha particle radiation therapy for cancer, with research demonstrating its significant impact on both the diagnosis and treatment of PC [135,136]. An experiment using AuNPs for targeted delivery of 211At in adjunct radiation therapy showed prolonged retention of 211At in PC tissues, indicating substantial anti-PC activity [137]. Table 3 shows the study outcomes of AuNPs in radiotherapy for PC.

Table 3. Studies and results of AuNPs in radiotherapy for PC.

Nanoparticles	Outcome	Cell Lines	Ref
Au-MIP microgels	Tumor growth in mice was effectively inhibited	MIAPaCa-2	[131]
AuNP	The size of tumors and cellular proliferation significantly decreased	MIAPaCa-2	[132]
LNPDTX-P	The intake of AuNPs significantly increased	MIAPaCa-2	[133]
gold ultra-small nanoparticles	Enhanced DNA damage and cell apoptosis led to delayed tumor growth	MIAPaCa-2/SUIT2-028	[134]
211At-AuNPs@mPEG	The prolonged retention of 211At in PC tissues results in notable antitumor activity	Panc-1	[137]

6. Safety of AuNPs in the Treatment of PC

While AuNPs show substantial potential in medicine, their potential toxicity and safety concerns deserve careful consideration. The article previously referenced experiments assessing AuNPs toxicity, including the addition of bystander cells in vitro and monitoring AuNPs accumulation or reactions in other organs in vivo. Across these studies, no marked toxic effects of AuNPs were detected. Other research has identified potential safety concerns with AuNPs in normal tissues or cells in both in vitro and in vivo settings. Lopez-Chaves' experiments revealed that AuNPs damage DNA, lipids, and proteins, with smaller-sized AuNPs causing more severe damage [138]. For example, 13 nm diameter PEG-AuNPs have been shown to induce acute inflammation and apoptosis in mouse livers. Post-injection, AuNPs remain for an extended period in the liver, spleen, and bloodstream [139]. In contrast to those measuring 20 nm and 50 nm, 5 nm AuNPs inflict dose-dependent DNA damage and generate ROS. In vivo, 5 nm AuNPs demonstrated considerable embryotoxic damage [140]. The female ovulation cycle must be considered when utilizing nanoparticles. The application of nanoparticles during mice ovulation results in nanoparticle accumulation in the ovaries and uterus being double that of non-ovulatory periods [141]. The excessive buildup of nanoparticles in the ovaries and uterus could potentially impact the reproductive system. Nanoparticles could selectively stimulate tumor cell growth. Nanoparticles with a small diameter are capable of activating the protein kinase B (AKT) and extracellular signal-regulated kinase (ERK) pathways, enhancing cell growth through coupling with EGFR [142]. The research indicates that despite AuNPs' optimistic application prospects, a comprehensive evaluation of their toxicity and safety is crucial prior to further clinical use. As Khlebtsov and colleagues noted in their paper, AuNPs may present potential risks to humans, yet this does not imply all AuNPs are hazardous, and each new variety should undergo stringent safety testing [143].

7. Conclusions and Perspectives

This review emphasizes the diverse applications of gold nanoparticles (AuNPs) in overcoming the challenges of diagnosing and treating pancreatic cancer (PC). PC remains a significant obstacle in oncology, attributed to its delayed diagnosis and limited treatment outcomes. Nanotechnology has shown great promise in enhancing the diagnosis of PC, delivering chemotherapy drugs, and utilizing phototherapy, among other applications. The increasing focus on AuNPs in the treatment of PC is attributed to their advantages such as high biocompatibility, the potential for green synthesis, stability, and low toxicity. By utilizing passive or active targeting methods combined with specific receptors, AuNPs enable the precise delivery of chemotherapy drugs while also mitigating their side effects. Moreover, the combination of drug delivery and phototherapy can significantly improve blood flow and drug permeability in PC, thus boosting the efficacy of chemotherapy. The LSPR characteristics of AuNPs play a critical role in their application in phototherapy for PC. Recent studies have explored the issue of phototherapy's limited impact on deep-seated tumors through interventional techniques or by adjusting NIR wavelengths. Furthermore, AuNPs have a marked impact on radiosensitization and radiotherapy in PC, reducing the discomfort, harm to adjacent healthy tissues, and systemic adverse effects associated with invasive therapies.

Despite this, the potential toxicity and safety issues related to AuNPs warrant further investigation. The long-term consequences of AuNPs excessively accumulating in organs like the liver and kidneys are still not fully understood. Across different studies, the size and surface modifications of AuNPs vary, which may lead to side effects of differing severities. Addressing this issue requires comprehensive preclinical and clinical studies to establish the safety profiles of various kinds of AuNPs. In using AuNPs for the treatment of PC with diverse modifications and structures, it is essential to conduct a thorough examination of side effects and to perform a careful assessment of the overall benefits relative to these side effects.

Integrating different AuNPs therapeutic methods could represent a promising future research pathway. For example, synergies have been observed in the conjoint use of AuNPs for chemotherapy drug delivery and phototherapy. Phototherapy has been shown to modify the dense ECM of PC, thereby improving its blood flow. AuNPs not only enable precise delivery of chemotherapy drugs but also enhance the drug's permeation into the tumor. Additionally, to address the challenge of PC's depth beneath the skin, the exploration of NIR-II, known for its superior tissue penetration, is steadily growing. Presently, research into utilizing AuNPs for supplementary immunotherapy in PC is still emerging. However, PTT/PDT not only modifies the TME of PC but also increases tumor immunogenicity and enhances immune cell infiltration. Combining this approach with immunotherapy could lead to significant therapeutic outcomes. In conclusion, despite the challenges ahead, AuNPs have significant potential to revolutionize the diagnosis and treatment of PC. Building on the existing foundation and addressing future challenges with innovative approaches, the prospects for diagnosing and treating PC appear promising, offering hope for improved patient outcomes and quality of life.

Author Contributions: Conceptualization, D.S. and H.X.; writing—original draft preparation, T.Y. and J.H.; writing—review and editing, H.X.; visualization, Y.C.; supervision, D.S. All authors have read and agreed to the published version of the manuscript.

Funding: This work was financially supported by grants from the National Natural Science Foundation of China (Grant Numbers: 82374248).

Institutional Review Board Statement: Not applicable.

Informed Consent Statement: Not applicable.

Data Availability Statement: Not applicable.

Conflicts of Interest: The authors declare no conflicts of interest.

References

1. Cai, J.; Chen, H.; Lu, M.; Zhang, Y.; Lu, B.; You, L.; Zhang, T.; Dai, M.; Zhao, Y. Advances in the epidemiology of pancreatic cancer: Trends, risk factors, screening, and prognosis. *Cancer Lett.* **2021**, *520*, 1–11. [CrossRef] [PubMed]
2. Park, W.; Chawla, A.; O'Reilly, E.M. Pancreatic Cancer: A Review. *JAMA* **2021**, *326*, 851–862. [CrossRef] [PubMed]
3. Siegel, R.L.; Miller, K.D.; Wagle, N.S.; Jemal, A. Cancer statistics, 2023. *CA Cancer J. Clin.* **2023**, *73*, 17–48. [CrossRef] [PubMed]
4. Mizrahi, J.D.; Surana, R.; Valle, J.W.; Shroff, R.T. Pancreatic cancer. *Lancet* **2020**, *395*, 2008–2020. [CrossRef] [PubMed]
5. Dewitt, J.; Devereaux, B.M.; Lehman, G.A.; Sherman, S.; Imperiale, T.F. Comparison of endoscopic ultrasound and computed tomography for the preoperative evaluation of pancreatic cancer: A systematic review. *Clin. Gastroenterol. Hepatol. Off. Clin. Pract. J. Am. Gastroenterol. Assoc.* **2006**, *4*, 717–725. [CrossRef] [PubMed]
6. Zhang, L.; Sanagapalli, S.; Stoita, A. Challenges in diagnosis of pancreatic cancer. *World J. Gastroenterol.* **2018**, *24*, 2047–2060. [CrossRef] [PubMed]
7. Neoptolemos, J.P.; Kleeff, J.; Michl, P.; Costello, E.; Greenhalf, W.; Palmer, D.H. Therapeutic developments in pancreatic cancer: Current and future perspectives. *Nat. Rev. Gastroenterol. Hepatol.* **2018**, *15*, 333–348. [CrossRef] [PubMed]
8. Kolbeinsson, H.M.; Chandana, S.; Wright, G.P.; Chung, M. Pancreatic Cancer: A Review of Current Treatment and Novel Therapies. *J. Investig. Surg.* **2023**, *36*, 2129884. [CrossRef] [PubMed]
9. Aldahhan, R.; Almohazey, D.; Khan, F.A. Emerging trends in the application of gold nanoformulations in colon cancer diagnosis and treatment. *Semin. Cancer Biol.* **2022**, *86*, 1056–1065. [CrossRef] [PubMed]
10. Zhou, J.; Chen, L.; Chen, L.; Zhang, Y.; Yuan, Y. Emerging role of nanoparticles in the diagnostic imaging of gastrointestinal cancer. *Semin. Cancer Biol.* **2022**, *86*, 580–594. [CrossRef]
11. Kesharwani, P.; Ma, R.; Sang, L.; Fatima, M.; Sheikh, A.; Abourehab, M.A.S.; Gupta, N.; Chen, Z.-S.; Zhou, Y. Gold nanoparticles and gold nanorods in the landscape of cancer therapy. *Mol. Cancer* **2023**, *22*, 98. [CrossRef] [PubMed]
12. Gerosa, C.; Crisponi, G.; Nurchi, V.M.; Saba, L.; Cappai, R.; Cau, F.; Faa, G.; Van Eyken, P.; Scartozzi, M.; Floris, G.; et al. Gold Nanoparticles: A New Golden Era in Oncology? *Pharmaceuticals* **2020**, *13*, 192. [CrossRef] [PubMed]
13. Tomşa, A.M.; Răchişan, A.L.; Aldea, A.A.; Ciumărnean, L. Perspectives of gold nanoparticles and their applications in pancreatic cancer (Review). *Exp. Ther. Med.* **2021**, *21*, 258. [CrossRef] [PubMed]
14. Patra, C.R.; Bhattacharya, R.; Mukhopadhyay, D.; Mukherjee, P. Fabrication of gold nanoparticles for targeted therapy in pancreatic cancer. *Adv. Drug Del. Rev.* **2010**, *62*, 346–361. [CrossRef] [PubMed]
15. Hou, X.; Tao, Y.; Pang, Y.; Li, X.; Jiang, G.; Liu, Y. Nanoparticle-based photothermal and photodynamic immunotherapy for tumor treatment. *Int. J. Cancer* **2018**, *143*, 3050–3060. [CrossRef] [PubMed]
16. Riley, R.S.; Day, E.S. Gold nanoparticle-mediated photothermal therapy: Applications and opportunities for multimodal cancer treatment. *Wiley Interdiscip. Rev. Nanomed. Nanobiotechnol.* **2017**, *9*, e1449. [CrossRef] [PubMed]
17. Gupta, N.; Malviya, R. Understanding and advancement in gold nanoparticle targeted photothermal therapy of cancer. *Biochim. Biophys. Acta Rev. Cancer* **2021**, *1875*, 188532. [CrossRef] [PubMed]
18. Hou, Y.-J.; Yang, X.-X.; Liu, R.-Q.; Zhao, D.; Guo, C.-X.; Zhu, A.-C.; Wen, M.-N.; Liu, Z.; Qu, G.-F.; Meng, H.-X. Pathological Mechanism of Photodynamic Therapy and Photothermal Therapy Based on Nanoparticles. *Int. J. Nanomed.* **2020**, *15*, 6827–6838. [CrossRef] [PubMed]
19. Matsumura, Y.; Maeda, H. A new concept for macromolecular therapeutics in cancer chemotherapy: Mechanism of tumoritropic accumulation of proteins and the antitumor agent smancs. *Cancer Res.* **1986**, *46*, 6387–6392.

20. Kalyane, D.; Raval, N.; Maheshwari, R.; Tambe, V.; Kalia, K.; Tekade, R.K. Employment of enhanced permeability and retention effect (EPR): Nanoparticle-based precision tools for targeting of therapeutic and diagnostic agent in cancer. *Mater. Sci. Eng. C Mater. Biol. Appl.* **2019**, *98*, 1252–1276. [CrossRef]
21. Suk, J.S.; Xu, Q.; Kim, N.; Hanes, J.; Ensign, L.M. PEGylation as a strategy for improving nanoparticle-based drug and gene delivery. *Adv. Drug Deliv. Rev.* **2016**, *99*, 28–51. [CrossRef] [PubMed]
22. Barenholz, Y. Doxil®--the first FDA-approved nano-drug: Lessons learned. *J. Control. Release* **2012**, *160*, 117–134. [CrossRef] [PubMed]
23. Youn, Y.S.; Bae, Y.H. Perspectives on the past, present, and future of cancer nanomedicine. *Adv. Drug Deliv. Rev.* **2018**, *130*, 3–11. [CrossRef] [PubMed]
24. Sun, R.; Xiang, J.; Zhou, Q.; Piao, Y.; Tang, J.; Shao, S.; Zhou, Z.; Bae, Y.H.; Shen, Y. The tumor EPR effect for cancer drug delivery: Current status, limitations, and alternatives. *Adv. Drug Deliv. Rev.* **2022**, *191*, 114614. [CrossRef] [PubMed]
25. Tee, J.K.; Yip, L.X.; Tan, E.S.; Santitewagun, S.; Prasath, A.; Ke, P.C.; Ho, H.K.; Leong, D.T. Nanoparticles' interactions with vasculature in diseases. *Chem. Soc. Rev.* **2019**, *48*, 5381–5407. [CrossRef] [PubMed]
26. Subhan, M.A.; Parveen, F.; Filipczak, N.; Yalamarty, S.S.K.; Torchilin, V.P. Approaches to Improve EPR-Based Drug Delivery for Cancer Therapy and Diagnosis. *J. Pers. Med.* **2023**, *13*, 389. [CrossRef] [PubMed]
27. Maeda, H. The 35th Anniversary of the Discovery of EPR Effect: A New Wave of Nanomedicines for Tumor-Targeted Drug Delivery-Personal Remarks and Future Prospects. *J. Pers. Med.* **2021**, *11*, 229. [CrossRef] [PubMed]
28. Ikeda-Imafuku, M.; Wang, L.L.; Rodrigues, D.; Shaha, S.; Zhao, Z.; Mitragotri, S. Strategies to improve the EPR effect: A mechanistic perspective and clinical translation. *J. Control. Release* **2022**, *345*, 512–536. [CrossRef] [PubMed]
29. Fang, J.; Islam, W.; Maeda, H. Exploiting the dynamics of the EPR effect and strategies to improve the therapeutic effects of nanomedicines by using EPR effect enhancers. *Adv. Drug Deliv. Rev.* **2020**, *157*, 142–160. [CrossRef]
30. Park, J.; Choi, Y.; Chang, H.; Um, W.; Ryu, J.H.; Kwon, I.C. Alliance with EPR Effect: Combined Strategies to Improve the EPR Effect in the Tumor Microenvironment. *Theranostics* **2019**, *9*, 8073–8090. [CrossRef]
31. Chen, B.; Pogue, B.W.; Luna, J.M.; Hardman, R.L.; Hoopes, P.J.; Hasan, T. Tumor vascular permeabilization by vascular-targeting photosensitization: Effects, mechanism, and therapeutic implications. *Clin. Cancer Res.* **2006**, *12*, 917–923. [CrossRef] [PubMed]
32. Lahooti, B.; Akwii, R.G.; Zahra, F.T.; Sajib, M.S.; Lamprou, M.; Alobaida, A.; Lionakis, M.S.; Mattheolabakis, G.; Mikelis, C.M. Targeting endothelial permeability in the EPR effect. *J. Control. Release* **2023**, *361*, 212–235. [CrossRef] [PubMed]
33. Sindhwani, S.; Syed, A.M.; Ngai, J.; Kingston, B.R.; Maiorino, L.; Rothschild, J.; MacMillan, P.; Zhang, Y.; Rajesh, N.U.; Hoang, T.; et al. The entry of nanoparticles into solid tumours. *Nat. Mater.* **2020**, *19*, 566–575. [CrossRef] [PubMed]
34. Pandit, S.; Dutta, D.; Nie, S. Active transcytosis and new opportunities for cancer nanomedicine. *Nat. Mater.* **2020**, *19*, 478–480. [CrossRef] [PubMed]
35. de Lázaro, I.; Mooney, D.J. A nanoparticle's pathway into tumours. *Nat. Mater.* **2020**, *19*, 486–487. [CrossRef] [PubMed]
36. Amina, S.J.; Guo, B. A Review on the Synthesis and Functionalization of Gold Nanoparticles as a Drug Delivery Vehicle. *Int. J. Nanomed.* **2020**, *15*, 9823–9857. [CrossRef] [PubMed]
37. Cai, F.; Li, S.; Huang, H.; Iqbal, J.; Wang, C.; Jiang, X. Green synthesis of gold nanoparticles for immune response regulation: Mechanisms, applications, and perspectives. *J. Biomed. Mater. Res. A* **2022**, *110*, 424–442. [CrossRef] [PubMed]
38. Vijayaram, S.; Razafindralambo, H.; Sun, Y.-Z.; Vasantharaj, S.; Ghafarifarsani, H.; Hoseinifar, S.H.; Raeeszadeh, M. Applications of Green Synthesized Metal Nanoparticles—A Review. *Biol. Trace Elem. Res.* **2023**, *202*, 360–386. [CrossRef] [PubMed]
39. Schulz, F.; Homolka, T.; Bastús, N.G.; Puntes, V.; Weller, H.; Vossmeyer, T. Little adjustments significantly improve the Turkevich synthesis of gold nanoparticles. *Langmuir* **2014**, *30*, 10779–10784. [CrossRef]
40. Herizchi, R.; Abbasi, E.; Milani, M.; Akbarzadeh, A. Current methods for synthesis of gold nanoparticles. *Artif. Cells Nanomed. Biotechnol.* **2016**, *44*, 596–602. [CrossRef]
41. Dong, J.; Carpinone, P.L.; Pyrgiotakis, G.; Demokritou, P.; Moudgil, B.M. Synthesis of Precision Gold Nanoparticles Using Turkevich Method. *Kona* **2020**, *37*, 224–232. [CrossRef] [PubMed]
42. Dzhagan, V.; Kapush, O.; Plokhovska, S.; Buziashvili, A.; Pirko, Y.; Yeshchenko, O.; Yukhymchuk, V.; Yemets, A.; Zahn, D.R.T. Plasmonic colloidal Au nanoparticles in DMSO: A facile synthesis and characterisation. *RSC Adv.* **2022**, *12*, 21591–21599. [CrossRef] [PubMed]
43. Figat, A.M.; Bartosewicz, B.; Liszewska, M.; Budner, B.; Norek, M.; Jankiewicz, B.J. α-Amino Acids as Reducing and Capping Agents in Gold Nanoparticles Synthesis Using the Turkevich Method. *Langmuir* **2023**, *39*, 8646–8657. [CrossRef]
44. Karmakar, S.; Sankhla, A.; Katiyar, V. Reversible and biocompatible AuNP-decorated [Zn^{2+}]:[Insulin] condensed assembly for potential therapeutic applications. *Eur. J. Pharm. Sci.* **2022**, *173*, 106168. [CrossRef]
45. Chen, Y.-S.; Hung, Y.-C.; Liau, I.; Huang, G.S. Assessment of the In Vivo Toxicity of Gold Nanoparticles. *Nanoscale Res. Lett.* **2009**, *4*, 858–864. [CrossRef]
46. Chinnaiyan, S.K.; Soloman, A.M.; Perumal, R.K.; Gopinath, A.; Balaraman, M. 5 Fluorouracil-loaded biosynthesised gold nanoparticles for the in vitro treatment of human pancreatic cancer cell. *IET Nanobiotechnol.* **2019**, *13*, 824–828. [CrossRef] [PubMed]
47. Wang, L.; Xu, J.; Yan, Y.; Liu, H.; Karunakaran, T.; Li, F. Green synthesis of gold nanoparticles from Scutellaria barbata and its anticancer activity in pancreatic cancer cell (PANC-1). *Artif. Cells Nanomed. Biotechnol.* **2019**, *47*, 1617–1627. [CrossRef]

48. Sibuyi, N.R.S.; Thipe, V.C.; Panjtan-Amiri, K.; Meyer, M.; Katti, K.V. Green synthesis of gold nanoparticles using Acai berry and Elderberry extracts and investigation of their effect on prostate and pancreatic cancer cells. *Nanobiomedicine* **2021**, *8*, 1849543521995310. [CrossRef]
49. Wang, L.; Xu, J.; Yan, Y.; Liu, H.; Li, F. Synthesis of gold nanoparticles from leaf Panax notoginseng and its anticancer activity in pancreatic cancer PANC-1 cell lines. *Artif. Cells Nanomed. Biotechnol.* **2019**, *47*, 1216–1223. [CrossRef]
50. Al-Hawary, M.M.; Francis, I.R.; Chari, S.T.; Fishman, E.K.; Hough, D.M.; Lu, D.S.; Macari, M.; Megibow, A.J.; Miller, F.H.; Mortele, K.J.; et al. Pancreatic ductal adenocarcinoma radiology reporting template: Consensus statement of the Society of Abdominal Radiology and the American Pancreatic Association. *Radiology* **2014**, *270*, 248–260. [CrossRef]
51. Eck, W.; Craig, G.; Sigdel, A.; Ritter, G.; Old, L.J.; Tang, L.; Brennan, M.F.; Allen, P.J.; Mason, M.D. PEGylated gold nanoparticles conjugated to monoclonal F19 antibodies as targeted labeling agents for human pancreatic carcinoma tissue. *ACS Nano.* **2008**, *2*, 2263–2272. [CrossRef] [PubMed]
52. Holbrook, R.J.; Rammohan, N.; Rotz, M.W.; MacRenaris, K.W.; Preslar, A.T.; Meade, T.J. Gd(III)-Dithiolane Gold Nanoparticles for T1-Weighted Magnetic Resonance Imaging of the Pancreas. *Nano Lett.* **2016**, *16*, 3202–3209. [CrossRef]
53. Khan, M.; Liu, H.; Sacco, P.; Marsich, E.; Li, X.; Djaker, N.; Spadavecchia, J. DOTAREM (DOTA)-Gold-Nanoparticles: Design, Spectroscopic Evaluation to Build Hybrid Contrast Agents to Applications in Nanomedecine. *Int. J. Nanomed.* **2022**, *17*, 4105–4118. [CrossRef] [PubMed]
54. Sawada, R.; Sun, S.-M.; Wu, X.; Hong, F.; Ragupathi, G.; Livingston, P.O.; Scholz, W.W. Human monoclonal antibodies to sialyl-Lewis (CA19.9) with potent CDC, ADCC, and antitumor activity. *Clin. Cancer Res.* **2011**, *17*, 1024–1032. [CrossRef]
55. Sobol, N.B.; Korsen, J.A.; Younes, A.; Edwards, K.J.; Lewis, J.S. ImmunoPET Imaging of Pancreatic Tumors with (89)Zr-Labeled Gold Nanoparticle-Antibody Conjugates. *Mol. Imaging Biol.* **2021**, *23*, 84–94. [CrossRef]
56. Lee, J.-S.; Park, S.S.; Lee, Y.K.; Norton, J.A.; Jeffrey, S.S. Liquid biopsy in pancreatic ductal adenocarcinoma: Current status of circulating tumor cells and circulating tumor DNA. *Mol. Oncol.* **2019**, *13*, 1623–1650. [CrossRef]
57. Sun, Z.-F.; Chang, Y.; Xia, N. Recent Development of Nanomaterials-Based Cytosensors for the Detection of Circulating Tumor Cells. *Biosensors* **2021**, *11*, 281. [CrossRef]
58. Nikanjam, M.; Kato, S.; Kurzrock, R. Liquid biopsy: Current technology and clinical applications. *J. Hematol. Oncol.* **2022**, *15*, 131. [CrossRef] [PubMed]
59. Yang, J.; Xu, R.; Wang, C.; Qiu, J.; Ren, B.; You, L. Early screening and diagnosis strategies of pancreatic cancer: A comprehensive review. *Cancer Commun.* **2021**, *41*, 1257–1274. [CrossRef]
60. Pedrosa, V.A.; Chen, K.; George, T.J.; Fan, Z.H. Gold Nanoparticle-Based Microfluidic Chips for Capture and Detection of Circulating Tumor Cells. *Biosensors* **2023**, *13*, 706. [CrossRef]
61. Kelber, J.A.; Reno, T.; Kaushal, S.; Metildi, C.; Wright, T.; Stoletov, K.; Weems, J.M.; Park, F.D.; Mose, E.; Wang, Y.; et al. KRas induces a Src/PEAK1/ErbB2 kinase amplification loop that drives metastatic growth and therapy resistance in pancreatic cancer. *Cancer Res.* **2012**, *72*, 2554–2564. [CrossRef] [PubMed]
62. Prasad, K.S.; Abugalyon, Y.; Li, C.; Xu, F.; Li, X. A new method to amplify colorimetric signals of paper-based nanobiosensors for simple and sensitive pancreatic cancer biomarker detection. *Analyst* **2020**, *145*, 5113–5117. [CrossRef] [PubMed]
63. Soares, J.C.; Iwaki, L.E.O.; Soares, A.C.; Rodrigues, V.C.; Melendez, M.E.; Fregnani, J.; Reis, R.M.; Carvalho, A.L.; Corrêa, D.S.; Oliveira, O.N., Jr. Immunosensor for Pancreatic Cancer Based on Electrospun Nanofibers Coated with Carbon Nanotubes or Gold Nanoparticles. *ACS Omega* **2017**, *2*, 6975–6983. [CrossRef] [PubMed]
64. Lin, L.; Liu, A.; Zhao, C.; Weng, S.; Lei, Y.; Liu, Q.; Lin, X.; Chen, Y. A chronocoulometric LNA sensor for amplified detection of K-ras mutation based on site-specific DNA cleavage of restriction endonuclease. *Biosens. Bioelectron.* **2013**, *42*, 409–414. [CrossRef] [PubMed]
65. Wang, Y.; Li, Z.; Zheng, S.; Zhou, Y.; Zhao, L.; Ye, H.; Zhao, X.; Gao, W.; Fu, Z.; Zhou, Q.; et al. Expression profile of long non-coding RNAs in pancreatic cancer and their clinical significance as biomarkers. *Oncotarget* **2015**, *6*, 35684–35698. [CrossRef]
66. Lou, U.K.; Wong, C.H.; Chen, Y. A simple and rapid colorimetric detection of serum lncRNA biomarkers for diagnosis of pancreatic cancer. *RSC Adv.* **2020**, *10*, 8087–8092. [CrossRef] [PubMed]
67. Li, H.; Warden, A.R.; Su, W.; He, J.; Zhi, X.; Wang, K.; Zhu, L.; Shen, G.; Ding, X. Highly sensitive and portable mRNA detection platform for early cancer detection. *J. Nanobiotechnol.* **2021**, *19*, 287. [CrossRef] [PubMed]
68. Suker, M.; Beumer, B.R.; Sadot, E.; Marthey, L.; Faris, J.E.; Mellon, E.A.; El-Rayes, B.F.; Wang-Gillam, A.; Lacy, J.; Hosein, P.J.; et al. FOLFIRINOX for locally advanced pancreatic cancer: A systematic review and patient-level meta-analysis. *Lancet Oncol.* **2016**, *17*, 801–810. [CrossRef] [PubMed]
69. Neesse, A.; Algül, H.; Tuveson, D.A.; Gress, T.M. Stromal biology and therapy in pancreatic cancer: A changing paradigm. *Gut* **2015**, *64*, 1476–1484. [CrossRef] [PubMed]
70. Liang, C.; Shi, S.; Meng, Q.; Liang, D.; Ji, S.; Zhang, B.; Qin, Y.; Xu, J.; Ni, Q.; Yu, X. Complex roles of the stroma in the intrinsic resistance to gemcitabine in pancreatic cancer: Where we are and where we are going. *Exp. Mol. Med.* **2017**, *49*, e406. [CrossRef]
71. Sherman, M.H.; Beatty, G.L. Tumor Microenvironment in Pancreatic Cancer Pathogenesis and Therapeutic Resistance. *Annu. Rev. Pathol.* **2023**, *18*, 123–148. [CrossRef] [PubMed]
72. Li, B.; Lane, L.A. Probing the biological obstacles of nanomedicine with gold nanoparticles. *Wiley Interdiscip. Rev.: Nanomed. Nanobiotechnol.* **2019**, *11*, e1542. [CrossRef] [PubMed]

73. Erkan, M.; Hausmann, S.; Michalski, C.W.; Fingerle, A.A.; Dobritz, M.; Kleeff, J.; Friess, H. The role of stroma in pancreatic cancer: Diagnostic and therapeutic implications. *Nat. Rev. Gastroenterol. Hepatol.* **2012**, *9*, 454–467. [CrossRef] [PubMed]
74. Tanaka, H.Y.; Kano, M.R. Stromal barriers to nanomedicine penetration in the pancreatic tumor microenvironment. *Cancer Sci.* **2018**, *109*, 2085–2092. [CrossRef] [PubMed]
75. Daraee, H.; Eatemadi, A.; Abbasi, E.; Fekri Aval, S.; Kouhi, M.; Akbarzadeh, A. Application of gold nanoparticles in biomedical and drug delivery. *Artif. Cells Nanomed. Biotechnol.* **2016**, *44*, 410–422. [CrossRef] [PubMed]
76. Goddard, Z.R.; Marín, M.J.; Russell, D.A.; Searcey, M. Active targeting of gold nanoparticles as cancer therapeutics. *Chem. Soc. Rev.* **2020**, *49*, 8774–8789. [CrossRef]
77. Patra, C.R.; Bhattacharya, R.; Wang, E.; Katarya, A.; Lau, J.S.; Dutta, S.; Muders, M.; Wang, S.; Buhrow, S.A.; Safgren, S.L.; et al. Targeted delivery of gemcitabine to pancreatic adenocarcinoma using cetuximab as a targeting agent. *Cancer Res.* **2008**, *68*, 1970–1978. [CrossRef] [PubMed]
78. Yu, X.; Zhang, Y.; Chen, C.; Yao, Q.; Li, M. Targeted drug delivery in pancreatic cancer. *Biochim. Biophys. Acta* **2010**, *1805*, 97–104. [CrossRef] [PubMed]
79. Huang, H.; Liu, R.; Yang, J.; Dai, J.; Fan, S.; Pi, J.; Wei, Y.; Guo, X. Gold Nanoparticles: Construction for Drug Delivery and Application in Cancer Immunotherapy. *Pharmaceutics* **2023**, *15*, 1868. [CrossRef]
80. Tempero, M.; Oh, D.Y.; Tabernero, J.; Reni, M.; Van Cutsem, E.; Hendifar, A.; Waldschmidt, D.T.; Starling, N.; Bachet, J.B.; Chang, H.M.; et al. Ibrutinib in combination with nab-paclitaxel and gemcitabine for first-line treatment of patients with metastatic pancreatic adenocarcinoma: Phase III RESOLVE study. *Ann. Oncol.* **2021**, *32*, 600–608. [CrossRef]
81. Aspe, J.R.; Diaz Osterman, C.J.; Jutzy, J.M.S.; Deshields, S.; Whang, S.; Wall, N.R. Enhancement of Gemcitabine sensitivity in pancreatic adenocarcinoma by novel exosome-mediated delivery of the Survivin-T34A mutant. *J. Extracell. Vesicles* **2014**, *3*, 23244. [CrossRef] [PubMed]
82. Birhanu, G.; Javar, H.A.; Seyedjafari, E.; Zandi-Karimi, A. Nanotechnology for delivery of gemcitabine to treat pancreatic cancer. *Biomed. Pharmacother.* **2017**, *88*, 635–643. [CrossRef] [PubMed]
83. Miller, D.L.; Dou, C. Induction of apoptosis in sonoporation and ultrasonic gene transfer. *Ultrasound Med. Biol.* **2009**, *35*, 144–154. [CrossRef] [PubMed]
84. Lin, L.; Fan, Y.; Gao, F.; Jin, L.; Li, D.; Sun, W.; Li, F.; Qin, P.; Shi, Q.; Shi, X.; et al. UTMD-Promoted Co-Delivery of Gemcitabine and miR-21 Inhibitor by Dendrimer-Entrapped Gold Nanoparticles for Pancreatic Cancer Therapy. *Theranostics* **2018**, *8*, 1923–1939. [CrossRef] [PubMed]
85. Elechalawar, C.K.; Hossen, M.N.; Shankarappa, P.; Peer, C.J.; Figg, W.D.; Robertson, J.D.; Bhattacharya, R.; Mukherjee, P. Targeting Pancreatic Cancer Cells and Stellate Cells Using Designer Nanotherapeutics in vitro. *Int. J. Nanomed.* **2020**, *15*, 991–1003. [CrossRef] [PubMed]
86. Steckiewicz, K.P.; Barcinska, E.; Sobczak, K.; Tomczyk, E.; Wojcik, M.; Inkielewicz-Stepniak, I. Assessment of Anti-Tumor potential and safety of application of Glutathione stabilized Gold Nanoparticles conjugated with Chemotherapeutics. *Int. J. Med. Sci.* **2020**, *17*, 824–833. [CrossRef] [PubMed]
87. Tsai, Y.-C.; Yeh, C.-H.; Tzen, K.-Y.; Ho, P.-Y.; Tuan, T.-F.; Pu, Y.-S.; Cheng, A.-L.; Cheng, J.C.-H. Targeting epidermal growth factor receptor/human epidermal growth factor receptor 2 signalling pathway by a dual receptor tyrosine kinase inhibitor afatinib for radiosensitisation in murine bladder carcinoma. *Eur. J. Cancer* **2013**, *49*, 1458–1466. [CrossRef] [PubMed]
88. Ioannou, N.; Dalgleish, A.G.; Seddon, A.M.; Mackintosh, D.; Guertler, U.; Solca, F.; Modjtahedi, H. Anti-tumour activity of afatinib, an irreversible ErbB family blocker, in human pancreatic tumour cells. *Br. J. Cancer* **2011**, *105*, 1554–1562. [CrossRef] [PubMed]
89. Coelho, S.C.; Almeida, G.M.; Pereira, M.C.; Santos-Silva, F.; Coelho, M.A.N. Functionalized gold nanoparticles improve afatinib delivery into cancer cells. *Expert Opin. Drug Deliv.* **2016**, *13*, 133–141. [CrossRef]
90. Javle, M.M.; Oh, D.Y.; Ikeda, M.; Yong, W.P.; Hsu, K.; Lindmark, B.; McIntyre, N.; Firth, C. Varlitinib plus capecitabine in second-line advanced biliary tract cancer: A randomized, phase II study (TreeTopp). *ESMO Open* **2022**, *7*, 100314. [CrossRef]
91. Coelho, S.C.; Reis, D.P.; Pereira, M.C.; Coelho, M.A.N. Gold Nanoparticles for Targeting Varlitinib to Human Pancreatic Cancer Cells. *Pharmaceutics* **2018**, *10*, 91. [CrossRef] [PubMed]
92. Coelho, S.C.; Reis, D.P.; Pereira, M.C.; Coelho, M.A.N. Doxorubicin and Varlitinib Delivery by Functionalized Gold Nanoparticles Against Human Pancreatic Adenocarcinoma. *Pharmaceutics* **2019**, *11*, 551. [CrossRef] [PubMed]
93. Deshantri, A.K.; Metselaar, J.M.; Zagkou, S.; Storm, G.; Mandhane, S.N.; Fens, M.H.A.M.; Schiffelers, R.M. Development and characterization of liposomal formulation of bortezomib. *Int. J. Pharm. X* **2019**, *1*, 100011. [CrossRef] [PubMed]
94. Gong, L.; Yang, B.; Xu, M.; Cheng, B.; Tang, X.; Zheng, P.; Jing, Y.; Wu, G.-j. Bortezomib-induced apoptosis in cultured pancreatic cancer cells is associated with ceramide production. *Cancer Chemother. Pharmacol.* **2014**, *73*, 69–77. [CrossRef] [PubMed]
95. Coelho, S.C.; Rocha, S.; Juzenas, P.; Sampaio, P.; Almeida, G.M.; Silva, F.S.; Pereira, M.C.; Coelho, M.A.N. Gold nanoparticle delivery-enhanced proteasome inhibitor effect in adenocarcinoma cells. *Expert. Opin. Drug Deliv.* **2013**, *10*, 1345–1352. [CrossRef] [PubMed]
96. Coelho, S.C.; Almeida, G.M.; Santos-Silva, F.; Pereira, M.C.; Coelho, M.A. Enhancing the efficiency of bortezomib conjugated to pegylated gold nanoparticles: An in vitro study on human pancreatic cancer cells and adenocarcinoma human lung alveolar basal epithelial cells. *Expert. Opin. Drug Deliv.* **2016**, *13*, 1075–1081. [CrossRef]

97. Wei, R.; Penso, N.E.C.; Hackman, R.M.; Wang, Y.; Mackenzie, G.G. Epigallocatechin-3-Gallate (EGCG) Suppresses Pancreatic Cancer Cell Growth, Invasion, and Migration partly through the Inhibition of Akt Pathway and Epithelial-Mesenchymal Transition: Enhanced Efficacy when Combined with Gemcitabine. *Nutrients* **2019**, *11*, 1856. [CrossRef]
98. Cunha, L.; Coelho, S.C.; Pereira, M.D.C.; Coelho, M.A.N. Nanocarriers Based on Gold Nanoparticles for Epigallocatechin Gallate Delivery in Cancer Cells. *Pharmaceutics* **2022**, *14*, 491. [CrossRef] [PubMed]
99. Saha, S.; Xiong, X.; Chakraborty, P.K.; Shameer, K.; Arvizo, R.R.; Kudgus, R.A.; Dwivedi, S.K.D.; Hossen, M.N.; Gillies, E.M.; Robertson, J.D.; et al. Gold Nanoparticle Reprograms Pancreatic Tumor Microenvironment and Inhibits Tumor Growth. *ACS Nano.* **2016**, *10*, 10636–10651. [CrossRef]
100. Huai, Y.; Zhang, Y.; Xiong, X.; Das, S.; Bhattacharya, R.; Mukherjee, P. Gold Nanoparticles sensitize pancreatic cancer cells to gemcitabine. *Cell Stress* **2019**, *3*, 267–279. [CrossRef]
101. Zinger, A.; Koren, L.; Adir, O.; Poley, M.; Alyan, M.; Yaari, Z.; Noor, N.; Krinsky, N.; Simon, A.; Gibori, H.; et al. Collagenase Nanoparticles Enhance the Penetration of Drugs into Pancreatic Tumors. *ACS Nano.* **2019**, *13*, 11008–11021. [CrossRef]
102. Overchuk, M.; Weersink, R.A.; Wilson, B.C.; Zheng, G. Photodynamic and Photothermal Therapies: Synergy Opportunities for Nanomedicine. *ACS Nano* **2023**, *17*, 7979–8003. [CrossRef]
103. Petryayeva, E.; Krull, U.J. Localized surface plasmon resonance: Nanostructures, bioassays and biosensing—A review. *Anal. Chim. Acta* **2011**, *706*, 8–24. [CrossRef]
104. Cui, X.; Ruan, Q.; Zhuo, X.; Xia, X.; Hu, J.; Fu, R.; Li, Y.; Wang, J.; Xu, H. Photothermal Nanomaterials: A Powerful Light-to-Heat Converter. *Chem. Rev.* **2023**, *123*, 6891–6952. [CrossRef] [PubMed]
105. Cobley, C.M.; Au, L.; Chen, J.; Xia, Y. Targeting gold nanocages to cancer cells for photothermal destruction and drug delivery. *Expert. Opin. Drug Deliv.* **2010**, *7*, 577–587. [CrossRef]
106. Guo, Y.; Zhang, Z.; Kim, D.H.; Li, W.; Nicolai, J.; Procissi, D.; Huan, Y.; Han, G.; Omary, R.A.; Larson, A.C. Photothermal ablation of pancreatic cancer cells with hybrid iron-oxide core gold-shell nanoparticles. *Int. J. Nanomed.* **2013**, *8*, 3437–3446. [CrossRef] [PubMed]
107. Kim, D.H.; Larson, A.C. Deoxycholate bile acid directed synthesis of branched Au nanostructures for near infrared photothermal ablation. *Biomaterials* **2015**, *56*, 154–164. [CrossRef] [PubMed]
108. Li, H.; Wang, P.; Deng, Y.; Zeng, M.; Tang, Y.; Zhu, W.H.; Cheng, Y. Combination of active targeting, enzyme-triggered release and fluorescent dye into gold nanoclusters for endomicroscopy-guided photothermal/photodynamic therapy to pancreatic ductal adenocarcinoma. *Biomaterials* **2017**, *139*, 30–38. [CrossRef]
109. Liu, Q.; Liu, H.; Griveau, A.; Li, X.; Eyer, J.; Arib, C.; Spadavecchia, J. NFL-TBS.40-63 Peptide Gold Complex Nanovector: A Novel Therapeutic Approach to Increase Anticancer Activity by Breakdown of Microtubules in Pancreatic Adenocarcinoma (PDAC). *ACS Pharmacol. Transl. Sci.* **2022**, *5*, 1267–1278. [CrossRef]
110. Hu, Y.; Chi, C.; Wang, S.; Wang, L.; Liang, P.; Liu, F.; Shang, W.; Wang, W.; Zhang, F.; Li, S.; et al. A Comparative Study of Clinical Intervention and Interventional Photothermal Therapy for Pancreatic Cancer. *Adv. Mater.* **2017**, *29*, 1700448. [CrossRef]
111. Zhang, F.; Han, X.; Hu, Y.; Wang, S.; Liu, S.; Pan, X.; Wang, H.; Ma, J.; Wang, W.; Li, S.; et al. Interventional Photothermal Therapy Enhanced Brachytherapy: A New Strategy to Fight Deep Pancreatic Cancer. *Adv. Sci.* **2019**, *6*, 1801507. [CrossRef] [PubMed]
112. Zhang, Y.; Zhang, S.; Zhang, Z.; Ji, L.; Zhang, J.; Wang, Q.; Guo, T.; Ni, S.; Cai, R.; Mu, X.; et al. Recent Progress on NIR-II Photothermal Therapy. *Front. Chem.* **2021**, *9*, 728066. [CrossRef] [PubMed]
113. Akhter, F.; Manrique-Bedoya, S.; Moreau, C.; Smith, A.L.; Feng, Y.; Mayer, K.M.; Hood, R.L. Assessment and Modeling of Plasmonic Photothermal Therapy Delivered via a Fiberoptic Microneedle Device Ex Vivo. *Pharmaceutics* **2021**, *13*, 2133. [CrossRef] [PubMed]
114. Zhang, S.; Li, Z.; Wang, Q.; Liu, Q.; Yuan, W.; Feng, W.; Li, F. An NIR-II Photothermally Triggered "Oxygen Bomb" for Hypoxic Tumor Programmed Cascade Therapy. *Adv. Mater.* **2022**, *34*, e2201978. [CrossRef] [PubMed]
115. Joubert, F.; Pasparakis, G. Hierarchically designed hybrid nanoparticles for combinational photochemotherapy against a pancreatic cancer cell line. *J. Mater. Chem. B* **2018**, *6*, 1095–1104. [CrossRef] [PubMed]
116. Chen, Y.; Li, H.; Deng, Y.; Sun, H.; Ke, X.; Ci, T. Near-infrared light triggered drug delivery system for higher efficacy of combined chemo-photothermal treatment. *Acta Biomater.* **2017**, *51*, 374–392. [CrossRef] [PubMed]
117. Banstola, A.; Pham, T.T.; Jeong, J.H.; Yook, S. Polydopamine-tailored paclitaxel-loaded polymeric microspheres with adhered NIR-controllable gold nanoparticles for chemo-phototherapy of pancreatic cancer. *Drug Deliv.* **2019**, *26*, 629–640. [CrossRef]
118. Poudel, B.K.; Gupta, B.; Ramasamy, T.; Thapa, R.K.; Pathak, S.; Oh, K.T.; Jeong, J.-H.; Choi, H.-G.; Yong, C.S.; Kim, J.O. PEGylated thermosensitive lipid-coated hollow gold nanoshells for effective combinational chemo-photothermal therapy of pancreatic cancer. *Colloids and Surfaces. B, Biointerfaces* **2017**, *160*, 73–83. [CrossRef] [PubMed]
119. Zhao, R.; Han, X.; Li, Y.; Wang, H.; Ji, T.; Zhao, Y.; Nie, G. Photothermal Effect Enhanced Cascade-Targeting Strategy for Improved Pancreatic Cancer Therapy by Gold Nanoshell@Mesoporous Silica Nanorod. *ACS Nano.* **2017**, *11*, 8103–8113. [CrossRef]
120. Zhang, F.; Hu, Q.; Li, B.; Huang, Y.; Wang, M.; Shao, S.; Tang, H.; Yao, Z.; Ping, Y.; Liang, T. A biomimetic nanodrug for enhanced chemotherapy of pancreatic tumors. *J. Control. Release* **2023**, *354*, 835–850. [CrossRef]
121. Yang, Q.; Peng, J.; Shi, K.; Xiao, Y.; Liu, Q.; Han, R.; Wei, X.; Qian, Z. Rationally designed peptide-conjugated gold/platinum nanosystem with active tumor-targeting for enhancing tumor photothermal-immunotherapy. *J. Control. Release* **2019**, *308*, 29–43. [CrossRef]

122. Odion, R.A.; Liu, Y.; Vo-Dinh, T. Plasmonic Gold Nanostar-Mediated Photothermal Immunotherapy. *IEEE J. Sel. Top. Quantum Electron.* **2021**, *27*, 4800109. [CrossRef] [PubMed]
123. Yousaf, M.N.; Ehsan, H.; Muneeb, A.; Wahab, A.; Sana, M.K.; Neupane, K.; Chaudhary, F.S. Role of Radiofrequency Ablation in the Management of Unresectable Pancreatic Cancer. *Front. Med.* **2020**, *7*, 624997. [CrossRef]
124. Li, D.; Jung, Y.S.; Tan, S.; Kim, H.K.; Chory, E.; Geller, D.A. Negligible absorption of radiofrequency radiation by colloidal gold nanoparticles. *J. Colloid. Interface Sci.* **2011**, *358*, 47–53. [CrossRef] [PubMed]
125. Rejinold, N.S.; Jayakumar, R.; Kim, Y.-C. Radio frequency responsive nano-biomaterials for cancer therapy. *J. Nanobiotechnol.* **2015**, *204*, 85–97. [CrossRef] [PubMed]
126. Glazer, E.S.; Curley, S.A. Radiofrequency field-induced thermal cytotoxicity in cancer cells treated with fluorescent nanoparticles. *Cancer* **2010**, *116*, 3285–3293. [CrossRef]
127. Gannon, C.J.; Patra, C.R.; Bhattacharya, R.; Mukherjee, P.; Curley, S.A. Intracellular gold nanoparticles enhance non-invasive radiofrequency thermal destruction of human gastrointestinal cancer cells. *J. Nanobiotechnol.* **2008**, *6*, 2. [CrossRef]
128. Glazer, E.S.; Zhu, C.; Massey, K.L.; Thompson, C.S.; Kaluarachchi, W.D.; Hamir, A.N.; Curley, S.A. Noninvasive radiofrequency field destruction of pancreatic adenocarcinoma xenografts treated with targeted gold nanoparticles. *Clin. Cancer Res.* **2010**, *16*, 5712–5721. [CrossRef]
129. Tempero, M.A.; Malafa, M.P.; Behrman, S.W.; Benson, A.B.; Casper, E.S.; Chiorean, E.G.; Chung, V.; Cohen, S.J.; Czito, B.; Engebretson, A.; et al. Pancreatic adenocarcinoma, version 2.2014: Featured updates to the NCCN guidelines. *J. Natl. Compr. Cancer Network* **2014**, *12*, 1083–1093. [CrossRef]
130. Geng, F.; Song, K.; Xing, J.Z.; Yuan, C.; Yan, S.; Yang, Q.; Chen, J.; Kong, B. Thio-glucose bound gold nanoparticles enhance radio-cytotoxic targeting of ovarian cancer. *Nanotechnology* **2011**, *22*, 285101. [CrossRef]
131. Yoshida, A.; Kitayama, Y.; Kiguchi, K.; Yamada, T.; Akasaka, H.; Sasaki, R.; Takeuchi, T. Gold Nanoparticle-Incorporated Molecularly Imprinted Microgels as Radiation Sensitizers in Pancreatic Cancer. *ACS Appl. Bio Mater.* **2019**, *2*, 1177–1183. [CrossRef] [PubMed]
132. Alhussan, A.; Jackson, N.; Calisin, R.; Morgan, J.; Beckham, W.; Chithrani, D.B. Utilizing Gold Nanoparticles as Prospective Radiosensitizers in 3D Radioresistant Pancreatic Co-Culture Model. *Int. J. Mol. Sci.* **2023**, *24*, 12523. [CrossRef] [PubMed]
133. Alhussan, A.; Jackson, N.; Eaton, S.; Santos, N.D.; Barta, I.; Zaifman, J.; Chen, S.; Tam, Y.Y.C.; Krishnan, S.; Chithrani, D.B. Lipid-Nanoparticle-Mediated Delivery of Docetaxel Prodrug for Exploiting Full Potential of Gold Nanoparticles in the Treatment of Pancreatic Cancer. *Cancers* **2022**, *14*, 6137. [CrossRef] [PubMed]
134. Che, P.P.; Mapanao, A.K.; Gregori, A.; Ermini, M.L.; Zamborlin, A.; Capula, M.; Ngadimin, D.; Slotman, B.J.; Voliani, V.; Sminia, P.; et al. Biodegradable Ultrasmall-in-Nano Architectures Loaded with Cisplatin Prodrug in Combination with Ionizing Radiation Induces DNA Damage and Apoptosis in Pancreatic Ductal Adenocarcinoma. *Cancers* **2022**, *14*, 3034. [CrossRef] [PubMed]
135. Guerra Liberal, F.D.C.; O'Sullivan, J.M.; McMahon, S.J.; Prise, K.M. Targeted Alpha Therapy: Current Clinical Applications. *Cancer Biother. Radiopharm.* **2020**, *35*, 404–417. [CrossRef] [PubMed]
136. Watabe, T.; Liu, Y.; Kaneda-Nakashima, K.; Shirakami, Y.; Lindner, T.; Ooe, K.; Toyoshima, A.; Nagata, K.; Shimosegawa, E.; Haberkorn, U.; et al. Theranostics Targeting Fibroblast Activation Protein in the Tumor Stroma: 64Cu- and 225Ac-Labeled FAPI-04 in Pancreatic Cancer Xenograft Mouse Models. *J. Nucl. Med. Off. Publ. Soc. Nucl. Med.* **2020**, *61*, 563–569. [CrossRef] [PubMed]
137. Huang, X.; Kaneda-Nakashima, K.; Kadonaga, Y.; Kabayama, K.; Shimoyama, A.; Ooe, K.; Kato, H.; Toyoshima, A.; Shinohara, A.; Haba, H.; et al. Astatine-211-Labeled Gold Nanoparticles for Targeted Alpha-Particle Therapy via Intravenous Injection. *Pharmaceutics* **2022**, *14*, 2705. [CrossRef] [PubMed]
138. Lopez-Chaves, C.; Soto-Alvaredo, J.; Montes-Bayon, M.; Bettmer, J.; Llopis, J.; Sanchez-Gonzalez, C. Gold nanoparticles: Distribution, bioaccumulation and toxicity. In vitro and in vivo studies. *Nanomed. Nanotechnol. Biol. Med.* **2018**, *14*, 1–12. [CrossRef]
139. Cho, W.-S.; Cho, M.; Jeong, J.; Choi, M.; Cho, H.-Y.; Han, B.S.; Kim, S.H.; Kim, H.O.; Lim, Y.T.; Chung, B.H.; et al. Acute toxicity and pharmacokinetics of 13 nm-sized PEG-coated gold nanoparticles. *Toxicol. Appl. Pharmacol.* **2009**, *236*, 16–24. [CrossRef]
140. Xia, Q.; Li, H.; Liu, Y.; Zhang, S.; Feng, Q.; Xiao, K. The effect of particle size on the genotoxicity of gold nanoparticles. *J. Biomed. Mater. Res. Part A* **2017**, *105*, 710–719. [CrossRef]
141. Poley, M.; Mora-Raimundo, P.; Shammai, Y.; Kaduri, M.; Koren, L.; Adir, O.; Shklover, J.; Shainsky-Roitman, J.; Ramishetti, S.; Man, F.; et al. Nanoparticles Accumulate in the Female Reproductive System during Ovulation Affecting Cancer Treatment and Fertility. *ACS Nano.* **2022**, *16*, 5246–5257. [CrossRef] [PubMed]
142. Semashko, V.V.; Pudovkin, M.S.; Cefalas, A.-C.; Zelenikhin, P.V.; Gavriil, V.E.; Nizamutdinov, A.S.; Kollia, Z.; Ferraro, A.; Sarantopoulou, E. Tiny Rare-Earth Fluoride Nanoparticles Activate Tumour Cell Growth via Electrical Polar Interactions. *Nanoscale Res. Lett.* **2018**, *13*, 370. [CrossRef] [PubMed]
143. Khlebtsov, N.; Dykman, L. Biodistribution and toxicity of engineered gold nanoparticles: A review of in vitro and in vivo studies. *Chem. Soc. Rev.* **2011**, *40*, 1647–1671. [CrossRef] [PubMed]

Disclaimer/Publisher's Note: The statements, opinions and data contained in all publications are solely those of the individual author(s) and contributor(s) and not of MDPI and/or the editor(s). MDPI and/or the editor(s) disclaim responsibility for any injury to people or property resulting from any ideas, methods, instructions or products referred to in the content.

pharmaceutics

MDPI

Article

Curcumin and Baicalin Co-Loaded Nanoliposomes for Synergistic Treatment of Non-Small Cell Lung Cancer

Qijun Su †, Junqian Pan †, Chunxin Wang, Meng Zhang, Haixin Cui and Xiang Zhao *

Institute of Environment and Sustainable Development in Agriculture, Chinese Academy of Agricultural Sciences, Beijing 100081, China; 82101215249@caas.cn (Q.S.); panjunqian@caas.cn (J.P.); wangchunxin@caas.cn (C.W.); 82101225293@caas.cn (M.Z.); cuihaixin@caas.cn (H.C.)

* Correspondence: zhaoxiang@caas.cn

† These authors contributed equally to this work.

Abstract: Currently, the treatment of patients with advanced non-small cell lung cancer (NSCLC) mainly relies on traditional chemotherapeutic drugs; however, most of them have limited therapeutic effects and high toxicity. Some natural products with good therapeutic efficacy and low toxicity and side effects are limited in clinical application due to their low solubility and bioavailability. In this study, a nanoliposome drug-carrying system (Lip-Cur/Ba) was developed for the co-delivery of curcumin (Cur) and baicalin (Ba) using the thin-film hydration method. In vitro experiments demonstrated that Lip-Cur/Ba had a strong killing effect on A549 cells, and the inhibitory effect of Lip-Cur/Ba on A549 cells was enhanced by 67.8% and 51.9% relative to that of the single-carrier system, which could reduce the use of a single-drug dose (Lip-Cur and Lip-Ba), delay the release rate of the drug and improve the bioavailability. In vivo experiments demonstrated the antitumor activity of Lip-Cur/Ba by intravitreal injection in BALB/c mice, and there were no obvious toxic side effects. This study provides a new idea for curcumin and baicalin to be used in the co-treatment of NSCLC by constructing a new vector.

Keywords: nanoliposomes; curcumin; baicalin; non-small cell lung cancer; nano-delivery system

1. Introduction

Lung cancer is a common type of cancer that has become the number one contributor to malignancy deaths worldwide [1]. Non-small cell lung cancer (NSCLC) is a common classification of lung cancer, accounting for approximately 80% of cases [2]. In addition, about 35% of patients suffering from NSCLC are already in intermediate to advanced stages at the initial diagnosis, while the 5-year survival rate of patients with stage IV is only 5.8% [3]. The current standard of care for early-stage NSCLC patients is surgical resection, which can achieve some therapeutic effect [4]. However, most of the patients in the middle and late stages of NSCLC are unable to reach the standard of surgical resection due to poor health and other factors, and they can only improve their condition and maintain their survival through chemotherapy and radiation therapy [5]. Nevertheless, due to the high toxicity and side effects of traditional treatments, such as nausea and vomiting, liver function damage, decreased immunity and other symptoms [6], as well as the limited therapeutic effect, it is necessary to research and develop more new therapeutic methods to deal with NSCLC.

Curcumin (Cur) and baicalin (Ba) are both extracted from natural sources, and several studies have confirmed the beneficial effects of these two substances on the human body [7]. Cur is a polyphenol compound mainly extracted from the Curcuma root, which is widely used for its anticancer, antibacterial and antioxidant properties. In recent years, the anticancer activity of curcumin has been focused on lung cancer, liver cancer, cervical cancer and so on [8–10]. For example, it has been proved that the Cur anticancer effect on NSCLC is to inhibit the miR-21 signaling pathway to promote the elevation of the

PTEN gene, thus inhibiting cell proliferation and promoting cancer cell apoptosis [11]. In addition, Cur inhibits the proliferation of lung cancer cell lines and induces apoptosis in A549 cells by affecting the Wnt/β protein signaling pathway [12]. Ba is a flavonoid extracted from the root of *Scutellaria baicalensis*, which has significant biological activities such as antibacterial, anti-inflammatory and anticancer effects [13–15]. Ba has been shown to inhibit liver cancer, breast cancer and lung cancer [16–18]. For example, Ba inhibits the growth of NSCLC cells by inhibiting PBK/TOPK and downstream signaling molecules histone H3 and ERK2 in vitro [19]. In addition, it has been demonstrated that Cur and Ba can be co-administered for the treatment of hepatitis in rats, and that their joint inhibition of the TSC1/eIF-2α/ATF4 pathway synergizes in lung diseases [20]. There have also been studies on the co-encapsulation of Cur and Ba by nano-micelles as carriers for the treatment of NSCLC [21]. Therefore, the potential synergistic effect of Cur and Ba and their combination therapy has become an interesting research direction, but there are no studies on the co-encapsulation of Cur and Ba using nano-liposomes as a carrier, which may be due to the immature technology of the preparation of the liposomes, and the low solubility, bioavailability and poor stability of the drug.

Liposomes are lipid delivery systems made by encapsulating or embedding active ingredients in lipid-like nuclei as a closed vesicular substance similar to the structure of biological membranes, formed by encapsulating and using phospholipids and cholesterol as membrane materials [22]. Nanoliposome is a new type of lipid nanocarrier developed on the basis of liposomes, with particle sizes between 10 and 1000 nm. Nanoliposomes can improve the solubility and bioavailability of difficult-to-solve drugs and enhance the efficacy of drugs to enhance their absorption by the human body [23]. To date, an increasing number of FDA-approved liposome-based biologics and clinical therapeutics have been developed in a wide range of fields, including anticancer, antimicrobial, etc. [24].

In this study, we developed a nanoliposome delivery system (Lip-Cur/Ba) co-encapsulating curcumin and baicalin; characterized the morphology, size and structure of Lip-Cur/Ba; demonstrated the successful encapsulation of the drugs in liposomes; evaluated their in vitro release and in vivo antitumor activity; and proved the synergistic inhibitory effect of Lip-Cur/Ba on A549 cells by in vitro experiments and the antitumor activity by intravitreal injection in BALB/c mice with no obvious toxic side effects.

2. Materials and Methods

2.1. Materials

Curcumin and baicalin were purchased from Baoji Chenguang Biological Co., Ltd. (Baoji, China); egg yolk lecithin (EYL) was purchased from Shanghai Yuanye Biotechnology Co., Ltd. (Shanghai, China); cholesterol (Chol) was purchased from Solebaum Biotechnology Co., Ltd. (Beijing, China); methanol and chloroform were purchased from McLean Biochemical Co., Ltd. (Shanghai, China); Dulbecco's minimum essential medium (DMEM) was obtained from Pricella Biotechnology Co., Ltd. (Shanghai, China); fetal bovine serum (FBS) was obtained from Thermo Fisher Scientific Co., Ltd. (Shanghai, China); the A549 cell line was purchased from Punosai Life Science and Technology Co., Ltd. (Wuhan, China); the ROS assay kit was purchased from Beyotime Biological Co., Ltd. (Shanghai, China); and the BALB/c mice (male, 5 weeks old) were purchased from Guosheng Zhongyuan Science and Technology Company (Tianjin, China) under the license no. SCXK(Beijing)2019-0008. All the animal experiments complied with the guidelines of the Tianjin Medical Experimental Animal Care, and animal protocols were approved by the Institutional Animal Care and Use Committee of Yi Shengyuan Gene Technology (Tianjin) Co., Ltd. (protocol number YSY-DWLL-2023251).

2.2. Methods

2.2.1. Preparation of Lip-Cur/Ba, Lip-Cur, Lip-Ba and Blank Liposomes (B-Lip)

Lip-Cur/Ba was prepared using a thin-film hydration-ultrasonic method [25–27]. EYL (140 mg), Chol (20 mg), Cur (5 mg) and Ba (6 mg) were dissolved in a mixture of methanol

(6 mL) and chloroform (6 mL) and stirred until complete dissolution. The mixture was then added to a round-bottomed flask and all the solvent was evaporated at 42 °C using a rotary evaporator to form a homogeneous film inside the flask wall. Then, 10 mL of PBS solution preheated to 40 °C was added so that the film was completely dissolved in the PBS solution and hydrated to obtain the liposome suspension. Next, the liposome suspension was magnetically stirred at 40 °C for 1 h. This was to make the liposome suspension more homogeneous and completely dissolved. Finally, the liposome suspension was sonicated using a cell crusher for 10 min to obtain an aqueous solution of Lip-Cur/Ba. Blank-Lip(B-Lip) without drugs and single-drug loaded Lip-Cur and Lip-Ba were prepared according to the same method.

2.2.2. Encapsulation Efficiency and Loading Capacity Determination of Lip-Cur/Ba

The encapsulation efficiency and loading capacity were determined using UV spectrophotometry. The Lip-Cur/Ba was centrifuged at 10,000 r/min for 5 min at a high speed. At this time, the drugs not encapsulated into the liposome were free in the water to form crystals precipitation, the high-speed centrifugation aggregated these drugs into the precipitate [28], the supernatant was taken and methanol was added to completely dissolve the liposomes and the encapsulated drug, the contents of Cur and Ba were determined using an ultraviolet spectrophotometer (Shimadzu, UV2600) at 425 nm and 278 nm [29,30] and Lip-Cur and Lip-Ba were determined using the same method. In addition, the encapsulation efficiency (EE) and the loading capacity (LC) were calculated according to the following equation:

$$EE(\%) = \frac{\mathrm{W_1 + W_2}}{\mathrm{W_d}} \times 100\%$$

$$LC(\%) = \frac{\mathrm{W_1 + W_2}}{\mathrm{W_m}} \times 100\%$$

where $\mathrm{W_1}$ and $\mathrm{W_2}$ are the mass of Cur and Ba embedded in the liposome, $\mathrm{W_d}$ is the total amount of both drugs added to the liposome and $\mathrm{W_m}$ is the total mass of the entire drug-loaded liposome.

2.2.3. Characterization of Lip-Cur/Ba

The morphology of Lip-Cur/Ba was observed using transmission electron microscopy. The Lip-Cur/Ba solution was diluted 5 times, held in a test tube using an ultrasonic cleaner to treat the sample at a low power for 15 min and then dripped onto a copper mesh, allowed to dry and then mounted on a machine and observed by imaging at 80 kV.

2.2.4. Size and Zeta Potential

The particle size, PDI and zeta potential of Lip-Cur/Ba were determined using a laser particle sizer. The appropriate amount of the Lip-Cur/Ba solution was diluted and added into the cuvette then placed into the instrument, the temperature was set at 25 °C and the determination was repeated three times to take the average value.

2.2.5. Fourier-Transform Infrared (FT-IR) Spectroscopy

Infrared spectral analysis of B-Lip, Cur, Ba and Lip-Cur/Ba was performed using a Fourier-transform infrared (FT-IR) spectrometer. The liposome samples of B-Lip and Lip-Cur/Ba were lyophilized to a powder form. The samples were taken separately and mixed with an appropriate amount of KBr and pressed into tablets using a tablet press. The tablets were then examined on the machine and scanned in the range of 400–4000 cm^{-1}.

2.2.6. Thermogravimetric Analysis

The weight losses of B-Lip, Cur, Ba and Lip-Cur/Ba were determined using a thermogravimetric analyzer. The samples of B-Lip and Lip-Cur/Ba were lyophilized to a dry powder form. The samples were heated from room temperature to 800 °C in nitrogen at a rate of 20 °C/min to test the heating curves.

2.2.7. Differential Scanning Calorimetry (DSC) Analysis

Thermal analyses of B-Lip, Cur, Ba and Lip-Cur/Ba were carried out using a differential scanning calorimeter. Samples (5 mg) were separately packed in pure aluminum crucibles and analyzed by heating from room temperature to 200 °C at 10 °C/min in nitrogen gas and later cooling down to 20 °C [27].

2.2.8. In Vitro Releasing Assay of Lip-Cur/Ba

In vitro release kinetic studies were carried out using dialysis. The release medium was PBS solution containing 20% ethanol. A solution of 1 mL of Lip-Cur/Ba was placed into a dialysis bag (10 KDa), tied at both ends with string, placed into 80 mL of the release solution and placed in a shaker at a temperature of 37 °C at 130 rpm. The control was the same concentration of solution of Cur and Ba dissolved using methanol. At the 2 h, 4 h, 6 h, 8 h, 12 h, 24 h and 48 h of dialysis, 1 mL was taken from the release solution and then supplemented with 1 mL of fresh release solution [31]. The content of Cur and Ba in the removed release solution was determined using a UV spectrophotometer and the release rate was calculated.

2.2.9. Cell Cytotoxicity Assays

MTT assay (3-(4,5-dimethyl-2-thiazolyl)-2, 5-diphenyl-2H-tetrazolium bromide) was used to evaluate the toxicity of Lip-Cur/Ba to A549 cells in vitro. B-Lip, Lip-Cur, Lip-Ba and Lip-Cur/Ba solutions were prepared separately, free Cur, Ba and Cur/Ba were dissolved in DMSO as controls and gradient dilutions were performed using DMEM culture medium. A549 cells in a logarithmic growth phase were selected and then digested with 1 mL of EDTA-containing trypsin. Then, the concentration of cell suspension was diluted to 1×10^5 cells/mL, added to 96-well plates at 100 μL per well and 100 μL PBS was added in the peripheral-most wells to prevent evaporation and cultured until the cells were completely adherent to the wall. After wall attachment, the culture medium in the 96-well plate was discarded, the prepared culture medium containing the drug at different concentration gradients was added and each group was repeated for 6 wells, while the blank control group was added with culture medium without drugs. After a certain time of co-culture between the drug and the cells, the original culture medium in the wells was discarded and washed with PBS solution 2–3 times, 100 μL DMEM culture medium was reintroduced and then 10 μL MMTT solution was added to each well and continued to be incubated at 37 °C for 3 h. At the end of the incubation, the supernatant was aspirated out, 100 μL DMSO was added to each well and then the wells were shaken in the shaking table at 37 °C for 10 min, so as to completely dissolve the purple crystals. Finally, the absorbance was detected at 490 nm using an enzyme marker [32]. The cell viability was calculated according to the following formula:

$$Cell\ viability(\%) = \frac{\text{OD-test}}{\text{OD-control}} \times 100\%$$

where OD-test is the absorbance of the drug addition experimental group and OD-control is the absorbance of the control group. The IC50 of Lip-Cur/Ba was calculated based on the cell viability and the CI of the combination of the two drugs was calculated according to the following equation:

$$CI = \frac{(\mathrm{D})_1}{(\mathrm{D_x})_1} + \frac{(\mathrm{D})_2}{(\mathrm{D_x})_2}$$

where $(D_x)_1$ and $(D_x)_2$ are the doses of Lip-Cur or Lip-Ba, respectively, required to achieve a given survival rate, and D_1 and D_2 are the doses of Cur and Ba, respectively, required to achieve the same survival rate when combined (Lip-Cur/Ba).

2.2.10. Cell Scratch Assays

A cell scratch assay was used to evaluate the lateral antimigration ability of Lip-Cur/Ba for A549 cells. A549 cells were inoculated in six-well plates, and after all the cells had grown all over the whole plate bottom, the old culture medium was discarded and a serum-free culture medium was added to starve the cells for 24 h. A 20 μL lance tip was used to draw a line along the ruler on the bottom of the six-well plate, three lines were drawn in each well and then some PBS was added to clean the cells that had fallen out of the wells. Lip-Cur, Lip-Ba and Lip-Cur/Ba solutions were prepared separately and diluted to a concentration of 80 μg/mL using serum-free culture medium, and then added into the six-well plate to co-culture with the cells [33]. At 0 h and 48 h of culture, three fields of view were selected at the same position using an inverted microscope to photograph the scratches, and the area of the scratches was counted using Image J to calculate the migration rate. The migration rate was calculated according to the following formula:

$$\text{Scratch healing rate}(\%) = \frac{\text{0 h scratch areas} - \text{48 h scratch areas}}{\text{0 h scratch areas}} \times 100\%$$

2.2.11. Cellular Transwell Assays

A cellular Transwell assay was used to evaluate the longitudinal antimigration ability of Lip-Cur/Ba for A549 cells. A549 cells grown to a logarithmic phase were starved with serum-free culture medium for 24 h, digested with EDTA-free trypsin and then the cells were resuspended to a concentration of 5×10^4 cells/mL using serum-free culture medium by adding 100 μL of cell suspension to the upper chamber of the Transwell and 1 mL of culture medium with a serum concentration of 20% to the lower chamber. At the same time, Lip-Cur, Lip-Ba and Lip-Cur/Ba solutions were prepared and added to the upper chamber so that the drug concentration in the upper chamber was finally 80 μg/mL, and then placed in the incubator for 48 h. At the end of the incubation, the culture solution in the upper and lower chambers of the Transwell were discarded, the upper chamber was washed with PBS three times and the migrated cells on the upper surface of the upper chamber were gently wiped away with a clean cotton swab. Then, an appropriate amount of methanol was added into the upper and lower chambers of the Transwell, respectively, and the cells were fixed for 20 min and washed with PBS three times after fixation. Finally, the Transwell upper chamber was dipped in 0.1% crystal violet dye solution for 20 min and washed with water to remove the excess dye [34]. After drying, the cell migration on the outer membrane of the upper chamber of the Transwell was observed and photographed under an inverted microscope to record the cell migration, and the number of cells migrated was counted by Image J. The cell migration rate was calculated according to the following formula:

$$\text{migration rate}(\%) = \frac{\text{Number of cells migrating in the Lip-Cur/Ba}}{\text{Number of cells migrating in the Control}} \times 100\%$$

2.2.12. Detection of the Intracellular Reactive Oxygen Species (ROS) Level

The effect of Lip-Cur/Ba on the accumulation of reactive oxygen species in A549 cells was detected using an ROS assay kit. A549 cells grown in a logarithmic phase were inoculated in glass-bottomed culture dishes, and the number of cells was controlled at 5×10^5 cells/mL. Lip-Cur, Lip-Ba and Lip-Cur/Ba solutions were prepared separately and diluted with cell culture medium to a drug concentration of 80 μg/mL, and incubated for 24 h. Then, the culture medium containing the drug was discarded and DCFH-DA was diluted with a serum-free culture medium at a ratio of 1:1000. Then, the culture medium containing the drug was discarded, DCFH-DA was diluted with the serum-free culture medium at a ratio of 1:1000 and 1 mL of DCFH-DA solution was added to each dish and incubated for 30 min [35], protected from the light. The solution was then discarded and washed with serum-free culture medium three times to remove the residual probes. Then, the probes were observed and photographed with a laser confocal microscope and recorded and the fluorescence intensity was measured using Image J. The fluorescence intensity of the probes was measured with a laser confocal microscope.

2.2.13. In Vivo Antitumor Activity and Histological Analysis

Five-week-old male BALB/c mice were selected as animal models for the test and were housed in an SPF environmental system with a temperature of 20–26 °C, a humidity of 40–70%, circulating ventilation and light. Mice were acclimatized for 7 days prior to testing. A549 cells in a logarithmic growth phase were collected and digested using trypsin, the cell suspension was adjusted to 5×10^7/mL and each mouse was injected subcutaneously with 0.1 mL of cell suspension. When the subcutaneous tumor grew to an obvious mass, the length (L) and width (W) of the tumor were measured daily and the volume was calculated ($V = L \times W^2/2$), and when the volume grew to 100 mm^3 and the mouse's weight was not significantly reduced, the administration of the drug was started.

All mice were randomly divided into the following two groups ($n = 3$): one group was injected with PBS solution and one group was injected with Lip-Cur/Ba (at a dose of 20 mg/kg). The administration method was intravenous and the frequency of administration was once every 2 days, for a total of seven times. The mice were terminated at the end of drug administration and the tumors were stripped off and weighed. The tumors were then soaked in formalin and sectioned by paraffin embedding. The sectioned tumor tissues were used for hematoxylin and eosin staining (H&E), terminal deoxynucleotidyl transferase-mediated dUTP nick-end labeling (TUNEL) and Ki67 staining, which were used to observe the structural and physiological changes of the cells within the tumor tissues, cell proliferation and apoptosis.

2.2.14. Statistical Analysis

Data were analyzed by one-way analysis of variance (ANOVA) and Duncan's multiple range test. Statistical analysis was performed with the software package SPSS® 26.0 and $p < 0.05$ was deemed statistically significant.

3. Results

3.1. Morphology and Size of Lip-Cur/Ba

As shown in Figure 1A,B, which shows the images of Lip-Cur/Ba under a transmission electron microscope, it can be seen that Lip-Cur/Ba is mostly a regular round shape, and the magnified observation reveals that there are multiple vesicle structures within the Lip-Cur/Ba [36–38] and this structure can encapsulate more drugs to achieve a good encapsulation efficiency and loading capacity [39]. The samples of Lip-Cur/Ba were yellow, translucent and opalescent (Figure 1D). The average particle size measured by the particle sizer was 268 nm (Figure 1C), the zeta potential was −15.23 (mv) and the PDI was 0.104. Usually, the smaller the PDI is, the more homogeneous the molecular distribution in the system [40], which also proves that the prepared Lip-Cur/Ba has a certain stability [41].

3.2. Encapsulation Efficiency and Loading Capacity of Lip-Cur/Ba

In order to verify whether the B-Lip could successfully load two drugs, the concentrations of Cur and Ba were detected using UV spectrophotometry. According to the experimental results, the encapsulation efficiency of Cur in Lip-Cur/Ba was 97.23% and that of Ba was 94.06%, and the loading capacity of the whole system was 6.87%. This indicates that the B-Lip can be used as a drug-carrying system for Cur and Ba and can achieve good encapsulation efficiency and loading capacity of the drug, which can be continued for subsequent exploratory experiments. The encapsulation efficiency and loading capacity of Lip-Cur and Lip-Ba were also detected. The encapsulation efficiency of Lip-Cur was 86.45% and the loading capacity of Lip-Cur was 3.22%. The encapsulation efficiency of Lip-Ba was 68.52% and the loading capacity of Lip-Ba was 2.64%.

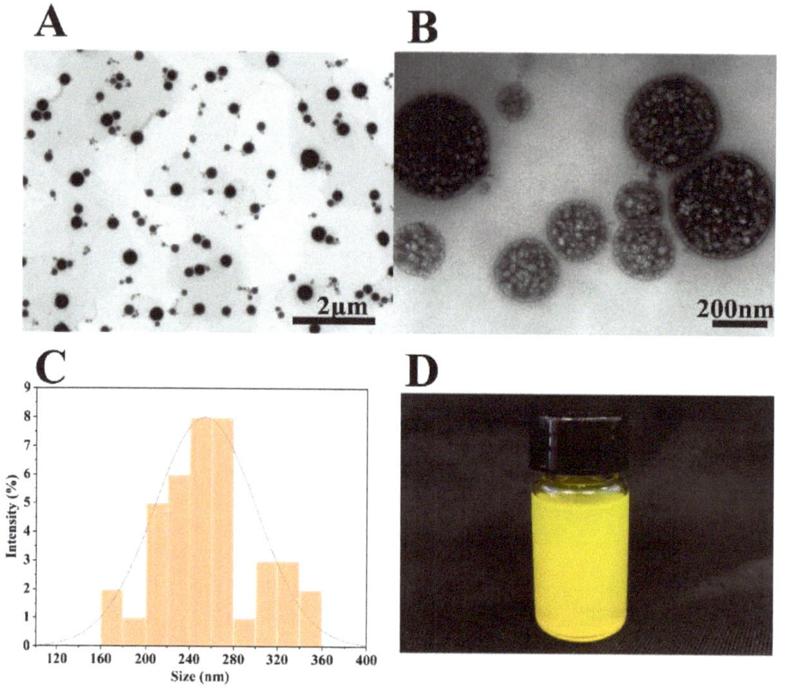

Figure 1. (**A**,**B**) TEM image of Lip-Cur/Ba at different magnifications; (**C**) the size of Lip-Cur/Ba; (**D**) appearance of Lip-Cur/Ba.

3.3. FT-IR Analysis

FT-IR spectroscopy is commonly used to analyze functional groups and structures in unknown substances. As shown in Figure 2, for the FT-IR spectroscopy of B-Lip, the absorption peaks at 2924 cm^{-1} and 2853 cm^{-1} are attributed to the stretching vibration of C-H in the low-end hydroxyl group of YL, the absorption peaks at 1242 cm^{-1} and 1090 cm^{-1} are attributed to the stretching vibration of the head group of Chol, PO^{2-} and the absorption peak at 970 cm^{-1} is attributed to the stretching vibration of N^{+}-CH_3 [42]. For the FT-IR spectroscopy of Cur, the absorption peak at 1628 cm^{-1} is attributed to the mixed vibration of C=O and C=C, the absorption peak at 1509 cm^{-1} is attributed to the telescopic vibration of C-O and C-C, the absorption peak at 1427 cm^{-1} is attributed to the bending vibration of the olefinic structure C-H and the absorption peak at 1375 cm^{-1} is attributed to the telescopic vibration of the C-O-C of the aromatic ring [43]. For the FT-IR spectroscopy of Ba, the absorption peak at 3500 cm^{-1} is attributed to the stretching vibration of the intermolecular hydroxyl group of baicalein, the absorption peaks at 1600–1700 cm^{-1} are attributed to the C=C and benzene ring C-H stretching vibration, the absorption peak at 1247 cm^{-1} is attributed to the stretching vibration of the benzene ring C=C and the absorption peak at 1072 cm^{-1} is attributed to the stretching vibration of the C-O-C [44]. Compared with the profiles of the above three substances, the FT-IR spectroscopy of Lip-Cur/Ba retained the characteristic peaks at 1375 cm^{-1} belonging to Cur and 1247 cm^{-1} to Ba, which indicated that Cur and Ba were successfully encapsulated into liposomes.

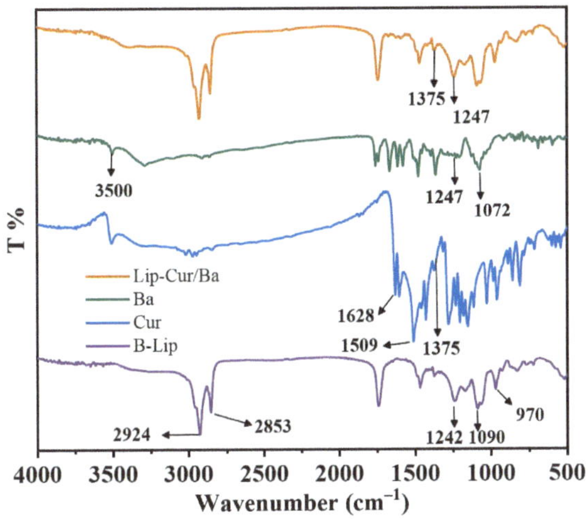

Figure 2. FT-IR spectra of B-Lip, Cur, Ba and Lip-Cur/Ba.

3.4. Thermogravimetric Analysis

As shown in Figure 3A,B, the thermal decomposition of B-Lip is concentrated between 220 °C and 420 °C, and the mass loss within this temperature is due to the loss of choline groups within the EYL [45]. The thermal decomposition of Cur occurs mainly at 398 °C. There are two loss platforms for Ba, and its thermal decomposition occurs mainly at 230 °C and 348 °C. Lip-Cur/Ba occurs mainly at 351 °C due to the weight loss peaks that occur as a result of the combined action of Cur and Ba, and the combined effect of EYL [46]. This indicates that Cur and Ba were successfully encapsulated into liposomes.

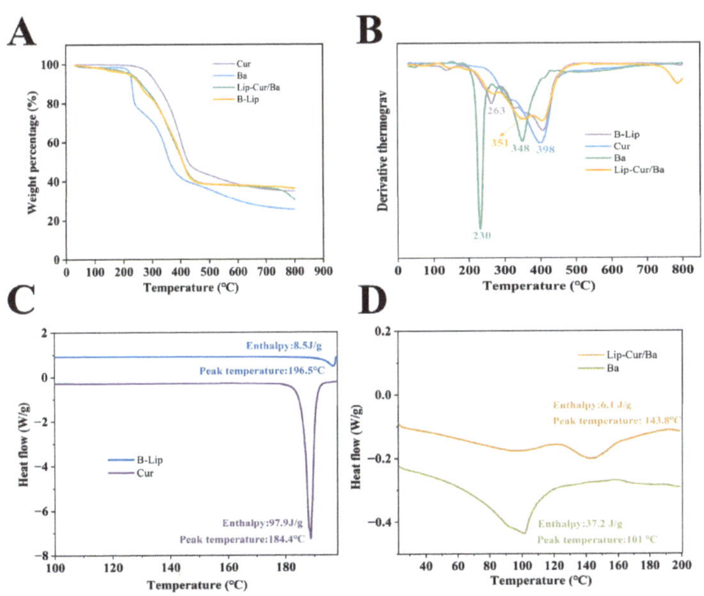

Figure 3. (**A**) TGA curves of Cur, Ba, Lip-Cur/Ba and B-Lip. (**B**) DTG curves of Cur, Ba, Lip-Cur/Ba and B-Lip. (**C**) DSC curves of B-Lip and Cur. (**D**) DSC curves of Lip-Cur/Ba and Ba.

3.5. DSC Analysis

As shown in Figure 3C,D, the characteristic absorption peaks of B-Lip, Cur and Ba were 196 °C, 184 °C and 101 °C, and those of LIP-Cur/Ba were 94.19 °C and 143.83 °C. The characteristic peaks of Cur and Ba were not shown, which proved that the two drugs existed in liposomes in an amorphous form [47]. The lower enthalpy of absorption of 6.11 J/g for Lip-Cur/Ba compared to that of 8.52 J/g for B-LIP indicated that the drug was embedded in the hydrophobic inner layer of the phospholipid bilayer [48], which further demonstrated the successful encapsulation of the drug in liposomes.

3.6. In Vitro Releasing Assay Analysis

As shown in Figure 4, the in vitro drug release profile of Lip-Cur/Ba shows the release behavior of Cur and Ba over a fixed period of time. For Cur and Ba, the control group had a fast release rate in the first 6 h phase, and the release had reached 78.52% and 81.94% in the first 8 h phase. The subsequent release rate gradually slowed down in the 12–48 h phase. Moreover, the drug was almost fully released in the first 48 h phase with a final release degree of 95.23% and 98.22%. For Cur and Ba in Lip-Cur/Ba, the release was only 33.54% and 40.28% at the first 8 h phase, and the release rate continued to increase steadily from 12 to 48 h. The final release was 68.76% and 67% at the first 48 h phase. This suggests that Lip-Cur/Ba has a slow release effect on the drug, thus prolonging the drug's holding period, which is conducive to the utilization and efficacy of the drug in the treatment.

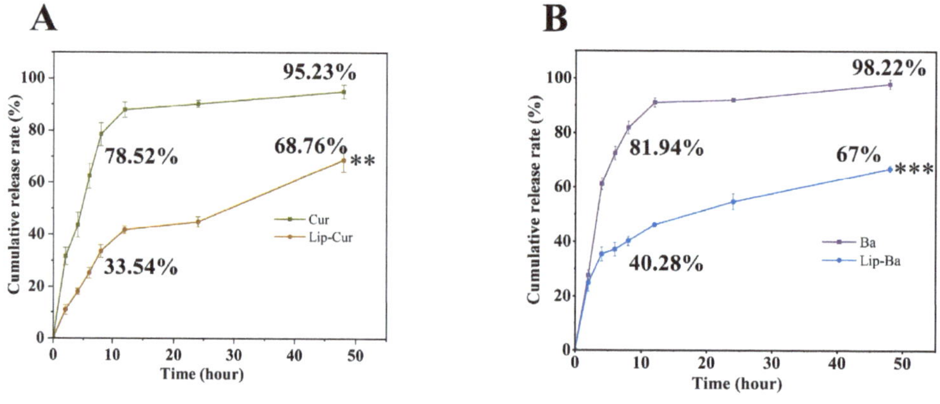

Figure 4. (**A**) Release behaviors of Lip-Cur and Cur (**: $p < 0.01$). (**B**) Release behaviors of Lip-Ba and Ba (***: $p < 0.001$).

3.7. Cell Cytotoxicity of Lip-Cur/Ba

MTT can be reduced to formazan by succinate dehydrogenase in the mitochondria of living cells and DMSO can dissolve this water-insoluble blue-violet crystal and measure its absorbance at 490 nm with an enzyme marker. The number of living cells within a certain range is directly proportional to the magnitude of absorbance, which is able to respond to the proportion of living cells [49], thus inferring the cell-killing effect of Lip-Cur/Ba.

3.7.1. Time-Dependence of Lip-Cur/Ba Action on A549

In order to investigate the inhibitory effect of Lip-Cur/Ba on A549 cells at different times and concentrations, different concentrations of Lip-Cur/Ba were co-cultured with A549 cells for 6, 12, 24 and 48 h, and the cell survival rate was determined by the MTT assay. As shown in Figure 5, the survival rate of the A549 cells showed concentration-time dependence. At the same time (6 h, 24 h, 48 h), the higher the concentration of Lip-Cur/Ba, the lower the survival rate of the A549 cells. At the same concentration, the cell viability gradually decreased with the increase in time. In all groups, the cell viability was still high at 6 h of co-culture, which was above 70%, and the inhibitory effect on the A549 cells was weak. When the co-culture time was delayed to 48 h, the survival rate of the Lip-Cur/Ba cells at a concentration of 160 μg/mL was only 7.74%, and the inhibitory effect on the A549 cells reached the maximum at this time, so that Lip-Cur/Ba was able to effectively eliminate hepatocellular carcinoma cells and exert the maximum efficacy of the drug. This result is consistent with the results of the previous in vitro release experiments, because the drug encapsulated in liposomes has the property of slow release, which results in less drug release in a short period of time, and the release of the drug has already reached more than 60% after 48 h, and thus can achieve the best drug effect. Based on the above results, 48 h of co-culture between the drug and the cells was chosen as the time point for the subsequent experiments.

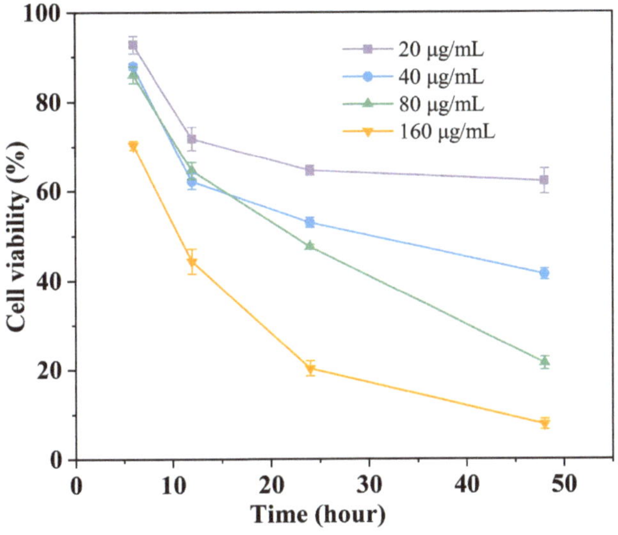

Figure 5. Time-dependence of Lip-Cur/Ba action on A549.

3.7.2. Cell Cytotoxicity of Lip-Cur/Ba on A549

To investigate whether Cur and Ba co-embedded in liposomes were more effective in promoting apoptosis of A549, the cytotoxicity of B-Lip, Cur, Ba, Cur/Ba, Lip-Cur, Lip-Ba, Lip-Cur/Ba against A549 was evaluated using the MTT method. The IC50 values of each group and the combination index (CI) of the two drugs were also calculated. As shown in Figure 6A, the blank liposome B-Lip without drug loading had little toxic effect on cells at different concentrations, and the cell survival rates were all greater than 90%, which proved that the liposome carriers were safe and nontoxic for subsequent experiments. The cell survival rates of Cur and Ba dissolved with DMSO at the same concentration were significantly greater ($p < 0.001$) than those of Lip-Cur and Lip-Ba. Similarly, the cell survival rates of Cur/Ba dissolved and physically mixed with DMSO at the same concentration were greater than those of Lip-Cur/Ba, which suggests that the prepared B-Lip is effective for the encapsulation of drugs. In order to further determine whether Cur and Ba have a synergistic effect, this experiment also compared the cytotoxicity magnitude of dual-loaded and single-loaded liposomes, and it can be seen from Figure 6A that the cell survival rate of Lip-Cur/Ba was only 4.3%, which was significantly smaller ($p < 0.001$) than that of the Lip-Cur and Lip-Ba groups. In order to compare the effects of each group of drugs on cell survival more intuitively, the IC50 values of each group of experiments were calculated (Figure 6B), and it can be seen that the IC50 of free Cur, Ba and mixtures were greater than that of the liposome-loaded group, and that the IC50 value of Lip-Cur/Ba was 16.5 (μg/mL) and was significantly smaller than that of ($p < 0.001$) Lip-Cur and Lip-Ba

IC50 values. According to the formula proposed by Chou and Talaay [50], the CI of the association index of Cur and Ba was calculated to be 0.5, when CI > 1 is antagonistic, CI = 1 is additive and CI < 1 is synergistic, and at this time, CI < 1 proves the synergistic effect of Cur and Ba. These results showed that the co-encapsulation of curcumin and baicalin into liposomes (Lip-Cur/Ba) were more effective in killing A549 than an individual agent (Lip-Cur and Lip-Ba), and verified the synergistic effect of the Cur/Ba combination.

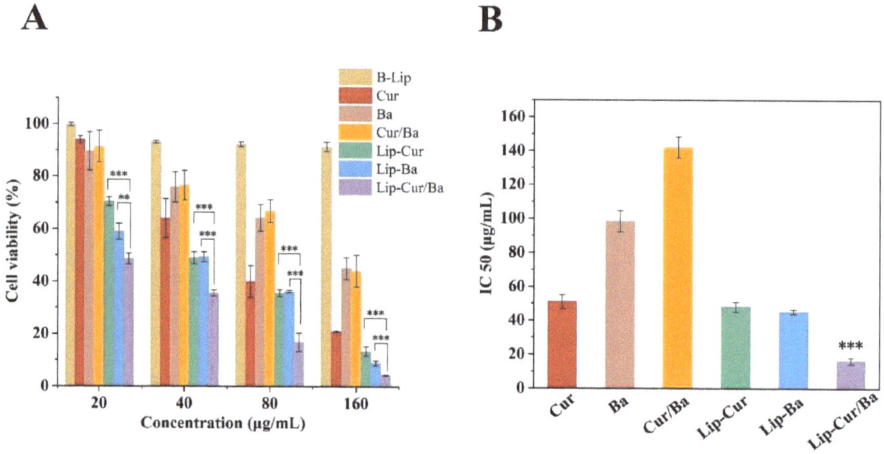

Figure 6. (**A**) Cell cytotoxicity of B-Lip, Cur, Ba, Cur/Ba, Lip-Cur, Lip-Ba and Lip-Cur/Ba. (**B**) IC50 of Cur, Ba, Cur/Ba, Lip-Cur, Lip-Ba and Lip-Cur/Ba (**: $p < 0.01$, ***: $p < 0.001$).

3.8. Antimigration Capacity of Lip-Cur/Ba

Tumor cells can proliferate indefinitely in the body and have the ability to migrate, which leads to the proliferation and metastasis of cancer foci and is one of the most important reasons for the aggravation of cancer [51]. Therefore, analyzing the characteristics of cell migration has great significance to cancer research. Evaluation of antimigratory ability is also an important point in the evaluation of drug efficacy. We used the cell scratch assay and Transwell assay to evaluate the antilateral migration and antilongitudinal migration abilities of Lip-Cur/Ba.

3.8.1. Results of Cell Scratching Experiments

In this experiment, a scratch was artificially created on the monolayer cells, and the cells at the edge of the scratch had a tendency to migrate to the blank area, thus simulating the environment of cell migration, and the area of the scratch was photographed and recorded at regular intervals so as to calculate the Lip-Cur/Ba anticell migration rate. As shown in Figure 7A, in the control group, the cells were not treated with any drugs, and after 48 h of incubation, the area of the cell scratches decreased and the borders appeared irregularly extending inward with new cells, which had an obvious tendency to migrate. The scratched area of cells treated with Lip-Cur, Lip-Ba and Lip-Cur/Ba in the experimental group was larger than that of the control group. And by quantifying the scratch area and cell migration rate, it can be found that the cell migration rate of Lip-Cur/Ba was only 4.43%, which was significantly smaller ($p < 0.001$) than that of the Lip-Cur and Lip-Ba groups. In addition, the healing rate of Lip-Cur/Ba was reduced by 91.3%, 82.6% and 89.5% compared with the control group, Lip-Cur group and Lip-Ba group (Figure 7B). This indicates that Lip-Cur/Ba can effectively inhibit the lateral migration of A549 and is more effective than single-carrier liposomes.

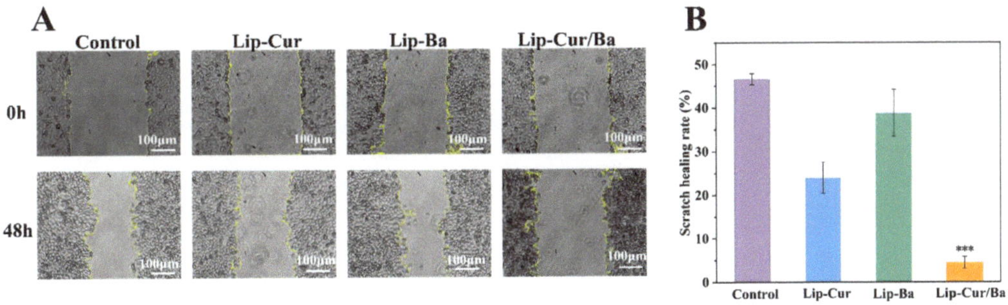

Figure 7. (**A**) Micrograph of the scratch experiments on A549 cells of Lip-Cur, Lip-Ba and Lip-Cur/Ba. (**B**) Scratch healing rate of Lip-Cur, Lip-Ba and Lip-Cur/Ba (***: $p < 0.001$).

3.8.2. Results of the Cell Transwell Assay

The Transwell chamber is divided into an upper chamber and a lower chamber with a polycarbonate membrane with small holes at the bottom of the upper chamber. Different culture solutions were added to the upper and lower chambers so that the effect of the components in the culture solution on cell movement and migration could be investigated. As shown in Figure 8A, the experimental group migrated significantly fewer cells into the lower chamber than the control group. The number of migrated cells was quantified using ImageJ. It can be found that the longitudinal migration rate of Lip-Cur/Ba was only 18.04%, which was significantly less ($p < 0.001$) than that of the Lip-Cur and Lip-Ba groups. Moreover, the migration rate of Lip-Cur/Ba was reduced by 82.06%, 79.53% and 76.62% compared with that of the control group, Lip-Cur group and Lip-Ba group (Figure 8B). This indicates that Lip-Cur/Ba can effectively inhibit the longitudinal migration of A549 and is more effective than single-carrier liposomes. Based on the above results, we can preliminarily deduce that Lip-Cur/Ba has a certain inhibitory effect on the migratory movement of A549 cells, and Lip-Cur/Ba has the best antimigration ability.

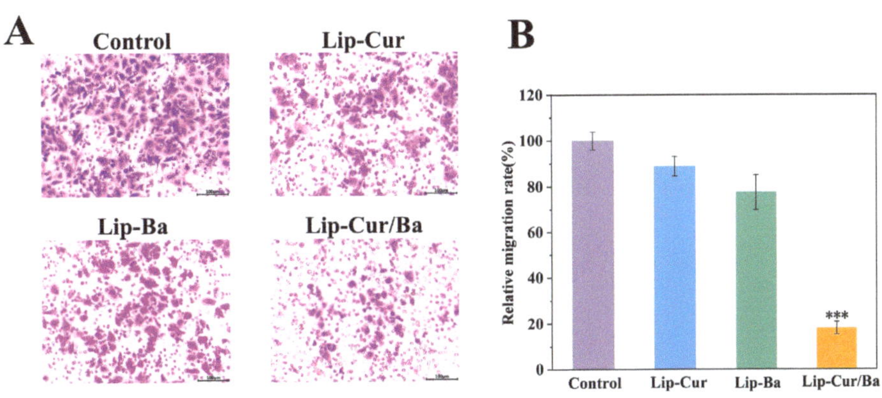

Figure 8. (**A**) Micrograph of the Transwell assay of Lip-Cur, Lip-Ba and Lip-Cur/Ba. (**B**) Relative migration rate of Lip-Cur, Lip-Ba and Lip-Cur/B (***: $p < 0.001$).

3.9. Results of ROS Level Detection

Elevation of intracellular ROS can affect the viability status of cells and even lead to damage or apoptosis [52]. The DCFH-DA in the ROS assay kit used is nonfluorescent and can cross the cell membrane into the cell and be hydrolyzed by esterase to DCFH, whereas intracellular ROS can oxidize nonfluorescent DCFH to fluorescent DCF, and the stronger the fluorescent signal, the higher the intracellular ROS level. As shown in Figure 9A, in the control group without any drug treatment, the green fluorescence signal was almost invisible, which indicated that the cells in the control group were in a good state, the ROS level was very low and there was no apoptotic tendency. However, after the treatment of the liposome administration group, the green fluorescence signal could be observed to be enhanced, and the green fluorescence signal was the strongest in the Lip-Cur/Ba group. Therefore, we speculated that the liposome administration group might cause apoptosis by affecting the elevated intracellular ROS level, and the effect of the Lip-Cur/Ba group was significantly stronger ($p < 0.001$) than that of the Lip-Cur and Lip-Ba groups (Figure 9B).

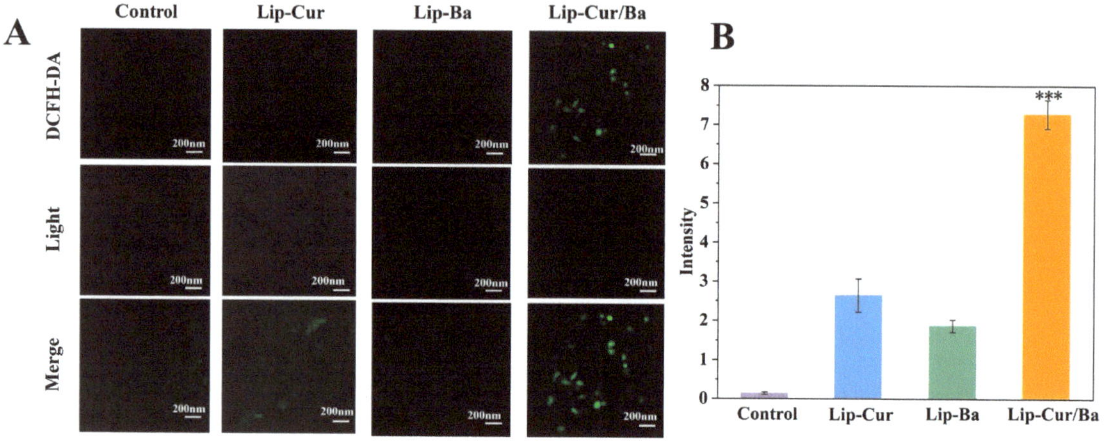

Figure 9. (**A**) Intracellular ROS levels photographed by an inverted-type laser scanning confocal microscope. (**B**) Quantitative analysis of intracellular ROS levels (***: $p < 0.001$).

3.10. In Vivo Antitumor Activity

The antitumor activity of Lip-Cur/Ba was assessed by subcutaneous injection of A549 cells in BALB/c mice to form tumors to mimic the in vivo experimental setting. The results of in vitro experiments have demonstrated that Lip-Cur/Ba is significantly more potent than Lip-Cur and Lip-Ba in killing A549 cells, so the in vivo experiments mainly explored the antitumor activity of Lip-Cur/Ba. As shown in Figure 10A, which shows the change in tumor volume of each mouse, the tumors of control mice injected with PBS increased in volume over time, from only 169 mm^3 on the first day at the start of the injections until the tumors had grown to 1905 mm^3 on the 14th day at the end of the treatment, which is a more than 10-fold increase in volume. The tumor volume of Lip-Cur/Ba mice was 148 mm^3 on the first day of the injections, and the subsequent growth rate was significantly inhibited, with a tumor volume of 745 mm^3 at the end of 14 days, which was significantly smaller than that of the control group. After 14 days of treatment, the mice were terminated and the tumor tissues were stripped and weighed. The average mass of the tumors in the control group was 1629 g and that of the injected group was 485 g (Figure 10B), which proved that Lip-Cur/Ba had a certain inhibitory effect on the tumors. Moreover, the weight of the mice increased within 14 days of treatment, and there was no weight loss and other side effects, which proves the safety of Lip-Cur/Ba.

To further confirm the therapeutic effect of Lip-Cur/Ba, tumor tissue was sectioned and examined. Hematoxylin and eosin (H&E) staining can reflect the structural and physiological changes of the cells in the tumor tissues, as shown in Figure 11A. In the sections of the control group, it can be seen that the tumor cells are arranged neatly and closely, the nuclei of the cells are in blue color and the majority of the cells are structurally intact, with regular shapes and no rupture phenomenon, from which it can be inferred that the tumor cells in the control group have a good growth status. In the sections injected with Lip-Cur/Ba, it can be seen that the tumor cells in the field of view are arranged in a crowded and disordered way, with inconsistent morphology and size, and there are obvious vacuoles in the cells and the nuclei of some cells are ruptured with no cytoplasm visible. This proved that under the action of Lip-Cur/Ba, the proliferation of tumor cells was obviously inhibited, and there was some necrosis.

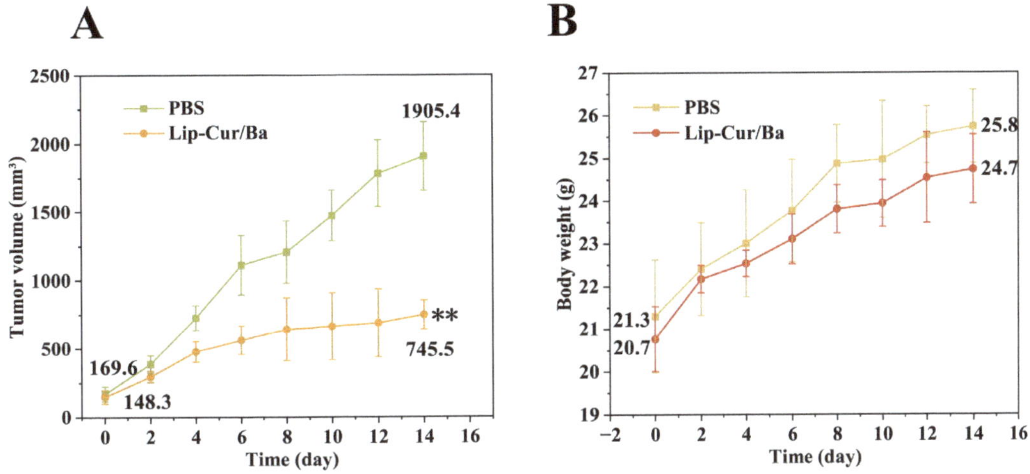

Figure 10. (**A**) Tumor volumes (mm^3) and (**B**) body weights (g) of the A549 tumor-bearing mice in the different treatment groups (**: $p < 0.01$).

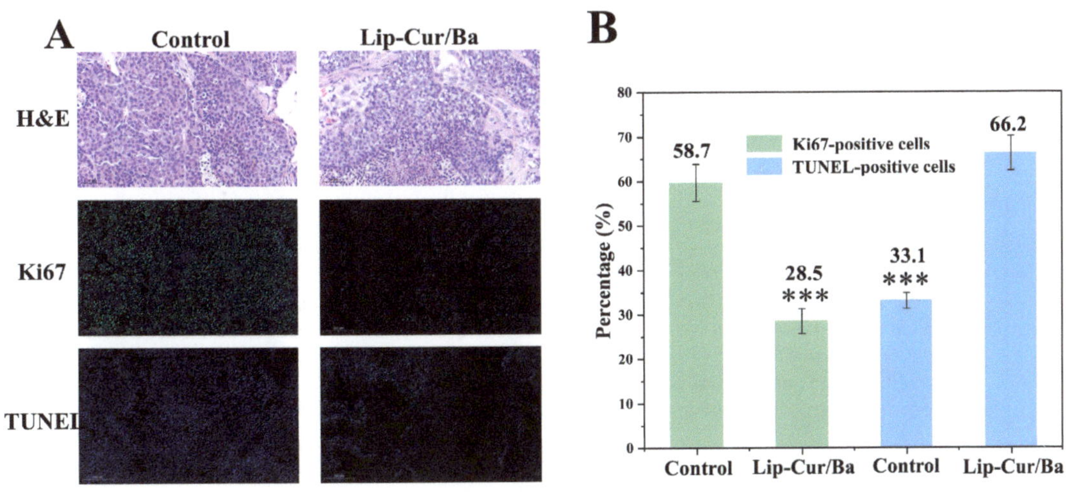

Figure 11. (**A**) Hematoxylin and eosin (H&E), Ki67 staining and terminal deoxynucleotidyl transferase-mediated dUTP nick-end labeling (TUNEL) of Lip-Cur/Ba tumor tissues on day 14. (**B**) Percentage of Ki67-positive and TUNEL-positive cells in tumor sections (***: $p < 0.001$).

The expression of Ki67 marks the level of tumor cell proliferation, as shown in Figure 11A. The expression of green signals was stronger in the control group and weaker and less in Lip-Cur/Ba, which proved that the proliferation of tumor cells was inhibited after the injection of Lip-Cur/Ba in mice. This was further confirmed in the TUNEL assay, where there was little green signal in the control group, indicating less apoptosis, whereas a large area of green fluorescence expression could be observed in Lip-Cur/Ba, proving that apoptosis was greatly increased. By analyzing the percentage of positive cells

(Figure 11B), it can be seen that the percentage of Ki67-positive cells in Lip-Cur/Ba (28.54%) was significantly smaller than that in the control group (59.68%), and the percentage of TUNEL-positive cells in Lip-Cur/Ba (66.21%) was about twice as high as that in the control group (33.09%). These above results consistently demonstrated the inhibitory effect of Lip-Cur/Ba on tumor cells in vivo.

4. Discussion

Natural medical components show great potential in cancer treatment, whereas their poor solubility and low bioavailability limit their clinical application. In particular, some insoluble drugs such as curcumin and baicalin are difficult to absorb after direct oral administration or injection, and quickly degrade due to their instability [12,53]. Curcumin and baicalin have been found to suppress cancer progression and metastasis by blocking metalloprotease [54,55], and Cur/Bai-based combination therapy showed better anticancer effects than individual Cur application [20,21]. Hence, in the present study, the double-loaded nanoliposomes (Lip-Cur/Ba) have been developed for co-delivering curcumin and baicalin, aiming to overcome the application shortcomings. After preparation, optimization and characterization, the encapsulation efficiency of Cur in nanoliposomes was 97.23% and that of Ba was 94.06%, and the loading capacity of the whole system was 6.87%. In addition, Lip-Cur/Ba exhibited good physicochemical stabilities and sustained release property, as well as improved A549 cell inhibitory and antitumor activities. Moreover, in vitro and in vivo experiments verified the synergistic effect of the combination of curcumin and baicalin. In the following study, more in-depth research should be continued to explore the mechanism of the synergistic effect. Further chemical modification on the surface of liposome, such as functional groups and targeting substances, could be improved to achieve targeted delivery and to strengthen therapeutic effects. Additionally, the mass production method should be optimized for the wider application in clinical research.

5. Conclusions

In this study, we prepared a new drug-carrying system with a certain stability and slow-release function, Lip-Cur/Ba, which can effectively solve the drawbacks of curcumin and baicalin's poor solubility and low bioavailability. The mean size, PDI and zeta potential of Lip-Cur/Ba were 268 nm, 0.104 and −15.23 mV. Meanwhile, the cytotoxicity test showed that Lip-Cur/Ba had good biosafety at the recommended dose. In addition, in vitro experiments showed that the co-encapsulated liposome of the two drugs has higher cytotoxicity and inhibition of cell migration against A549 cells, compared with the free-drug and single-drug carrier. Furthermore, in vivo experiments demonstrate the good antitumor activity of Lip-Cur/Ba in mice, which confirmed the strong inhibitory effect of Lip-Cur/Ba on non-small cell carcinoma. Moreover, these results verified the synergistic effect of the combination of curcumin and baicalin. In conclusion, Lip-Cur/Ba showed good therapeutic effects and potential research value on NSCLC, and this co-encapsulated liposome system should be applied in extended exploring.

Author Contributions: Conceptualization and methodology, J.P., M.Z. and C.W.; data analysis, Q.S.; writing-original draft, Q.S. and J.P.; writing-review and editing, X.Z. and J.P.; funding acquisition, C.W., H.C. and X.Z. All authors have read and agreed to the published version of the manuscript.

Funding: We are grateful for the financial support from the National Key R&D Program of China (2023YFD1700301), the National Natural Science Foundation of China (22378421), the Basic Scientific Research Foundation of National non-Profit Scientific Institute of China (BSRF202203, BSRF202223) and the Key Technologies R&D Program of Guangdong Province (2023B0202080002).

Institutional Review Board Statement: All the animal experiments were complied with the guidelines of the Tianjin Medical Experimental Animal Care, and animal protocols were approved by the Institutional Animal Care and Use Committee of Yi Shengyuan Gene Technology (Tianjin) Co., Ltd. (protocol number YSY-DWLL-2023251).

Informed Consent Statement: Not applicable.

Data Availability Statement: The data presented in this study are contained in the article.

Conflicts of Interest: The authors declare no conflicts of interest.

References

1. Siegel, R.L.; Miller, K.D.; Fuchs, H.E.; Jemal, A. Cancer Statistics, 2021. *CA Cancer J. Clin.* **2021**, *71*, 7–33. [CrossRef] [PubMed]
2. Antonia, S.J.; Villegas, A.; Daniel, D.; Vicente, D.; Murakami, S.; Hui, R.; Yokoi, T.; Chiappori, A.; Lee, K.H.; de Wit, M.; et al. Durvalumab after Chemoradiotherapy in Stage III Non-Small-Cell Lung Cancer. *N. Engl. J. Med.* **2017**, *377*, 1919–1929. [CrossRef] [PubMed]
3. Carbone, D.P.; Reck, M.; Paz-Ares, L.; Creelan, B.; Horn, L.; Steins, M.; Felip, E.; van den Heuvel, M.M.; Ciuleanu, T.E.; Badin, F.; et al. First-Line Nivolumab in Stage IV or Recurrent Non-Small-Cell Lung Cancer. *N. Engl. J. Med.* **2017**, *376*, 2415–2426. [CrossRef] [PubMed]
4. Long, H.; Tan, Q.Y.; Luo, Q.Q.; Wang, Z.; Jiang, G.N.; Situ, D.R.; Lin, Y.B.; Su, X.D.; Liu, Q.; Rong, T.H. Thoracoscopic Surgery Versus Thoracotomy for Lung Cancer: Short-Term Outcomes of a Randomized Trial. *Ann. Thorac. Surg.* **2018**, *105*, 386–392. [CrossRef]
5. Antonia, S.J.; Villegas, A.; Daniel, D.; Vicente, D.; Murakami, S.; Hui, R.; Kurata, T.; Chiappori, A.; Lee, K.H.; de Wit, M.; et al. Overall Survival with Durvalumab after Chemoradiotherapy in Stage III NSCLC. *N. Engl. J. Med.* **2018**, *379*, 2342–2350. [CrossRef] [PubMed]
6. Haratani, K.; Hayashi, H.; Chiba, Y.; Kudo, K.; Yonesaka, K.; Kato, R.; Kaneda, H.; Hasegawa, Y.; Tanaka, K.; Takeda, M.; et al. Association of Immune-Related Adverse Events With Nivolumab Efficacy in Non-Small Cell Lung Cancer. *Jama Oncol.* **2018**, *4*, 374–378. [CrossRef] [PubMed]
7. Mulvenna, P.; Nankivell, M.; Barton, R.; Faivre-Finn, C.; Wilson, P.; McColl, E.; Moore, B.; Brisbane, I.; Ardron, D.; Holt, T.; et al. Dexamethasone and supportive care with or without whole brain radiotherapy in treating patients with non-small cell lung cancer with brain metastases unsuitable for resection or stereotactic radiotherapy (QUARTZ): Results from a phase 3, non-inferiority, randomised trial. *Lancet* **2016**, *388*, 2004–2014. [CrossRef]
8. Huang, C.-Y.; Ju, D.-T.; Chang, C.-F.; Reddy, P.M.; Velmurugan, B.K. A review on the effects of current chemotherapy drugs and natural agents in treating non-small cell lung cancer. *BioMedicine* **2017**, *7*, 12–23. [CrossRef] [PubMed]
9. Nafees, B.; Lloyd, A.J.; Dewilde, S.; Rajan, N.; Lorenzo, M. Health state utilities in non-small cell lung cancer: An international study. *Asia-Pac. J. Clin. Oncol.* **2017**, *13*, E195–E203. [CrossRef]
10. Videtic, G.M.M.; Hu, C.; Singh, A.K.; Chang, J.Y.; Parker, W.; Olivier, K.R.; Schild, S.E.; Komaki, R.; Urbanic, J.J.; Choy, H. A Randomized Phase 2 Study Comparing 2 Stereotactic Body Radiation Therapy Schedules for Medically Inoperable Patients With Stage I Peripheral Non-Small Cell Lung Cancer: NRG Oncology RTOG 0915 (NCCTG N0927). *Int. J. Radiat. Oncol. Biol. Phys.* **2015**, *93*, 757–764. [CrossRef]
11. Wang, X.; Hang, Y.; Liu, J.; Hou, Y.; Wang, N.; Wang, M. Anticancer effect of curcumin inhibits cell growth through miR-21/PTEN/Akt pathway in breast cancer cell. *Oncol. Lett.* **2017**, *13*, 4825–4831. [CrossRef]
12. Memon, H.; Patel, B.M. Immune checkpoint inhibitors in non-small cell lung cancer: A bird's eye view. *Life Sci.* **2019**, *233*, 116713. [CrossRef] [PubMed]
13. Wen, Y.Q.; Wang, Y.Z.; Zhao, C.X.; Zhao, B.Y.; Wang, J.G. The Pharmacological Efficacy of Baicalin in Inflammatory Diseases. *Int. J. Mol. Sci.* **2023**, *24*, 9317. [CrossRef] [PubMed]
14. Wang, L.; Feng, T.; Su, Z.L.; Pi, C.; Wei, Y.M.; Zhao, L. Latest research progress on anticancer effect of baicalin and its aglycone baicalein. *Arch. Pharmacal Res.* **2022**, *45*, 535–557. [CrossRef] [PubMed]
15. Cheng, C.S.; Chen, J.; Tan, H.Y.; Wang, N.; Chen, Z.; Feng, Y.B. *Scutellaria baicalensis* and Cancer Treatment: Recent Progress and Perspectives in Biomedical and Clinical Studies. *Am. J. Chin. Med.* **2018**, *46*, 25–54. [CrossRef] [PubMed]
16. Chang, H.-T.; Chou, C.-T.; Kuo, D.-H.; Shieh, P.; Jan, C.-R.; Liang, W.-Z. The mechanism of Ca2+ movement in the involvement of baicalein-induced cytotoxicity in ZR-75-1 human breast cancer cells. *J. Nat. Prod.* **2015**, *78*, 1624–1634. [CrossRef]
17. Bie, B.; Sun, J.; Guo, Y.; Li, J.; Jiang, W.; Yang, J.; Huang, C.; Li, Z. Baicalein: A review of its anti-cancer effects and mechanisms in Hepatocellular Carcinoma. *Biomed. Pharmacother.* **2017**, *93*, 1285–1291. [CrossRef] [PubMed]
18. Yu, M.; Qi, B.; Xiaoxiang, W.; Xu, J.; Liu, X. Baicalein increases cisplatin sensitivity of A549 lung adenocarcinoma cells via PI3K/Akt/NF-κB pathway. *Biomed. Pharmacother.* **2017**, *90*, 677–685. [CrossRef] [PubMed]
19. Sharawi, Z.W.; Ibrahim, I.M.; Abd-Alhameed, E.K.; Althagafy, H.S.; Jaber, F.A.; Harakeh, S.; Hassanein, E.H. Baicalin and lung diseases. *Naunyn-Schmiedeberg's Arch. Pharmacol.* **2023**, *397*, 1405–1419. [CrossRef]
20. Wang, X.; Chang, X.; Zhan, H.; Li, C.; Zhang, Q.; Li, S.; Sun, Y. Curcumin combined with Baicalin attenuated ethanol-induced hepatitis by suppressing p38 MAPK and TSC1/eIF-2α/ATF4 pathways in rats. *Food Biosci.* **2021**, *40*, 100851. [CrossRef]
21. Wang, B.; Zhang, W.; Zhou, X.; Liu, M.; Hou, X.; Cheng, Z.; Chen, D. Development of dual-targeted nano-dandelion based on an oligomeric hyaluronic acid polymer targeting tumor-associated macrophages for combination therapy of non-small cell lung cancer. *Drug Deliv.* **2019**, *26*, 1265–1279. [CrossRef] [PubMed]
22. Large, D.E.; Abdelmessih, R.G.; Fink, E.A.; Auguste, D.T. Liposome composition in drug delivery design, synthesis, characterization, and clinical application. *Adv. Drug Deliv. Rev.* **2021**, *176*, 113851. [CrossRef] [PubMed]

23. Li, M.Y.; Du, C.Y.; Guo, N.; Teng, Y.O.; Meng, X.; Sun, H.; Li, S.S.; Yu, P.; Galons, H. Composition design and medical application of liposomes. *Eur. J. Med. Chem.* **2019**, *164*, 640–653. [CrossRef] [PubMed]
24. Filipczak, N.; Pan, J.Y.; Yalamarty, S.S.K.; Torchilin, V.P. Recent advancements in liposome technology. *Adv. Drug Deliv. Rev.* **2020**, *156*, 4–22. [CrossRef] [PubMed]
25. Li, Z.R.; Qiao, W.M.; Wang, C.H.; Wang, H.Q.; Ma, M.C.; Han, X.Y.; Tang, J.L. DPPC-coated lipid nanoparticles as an inhalable carrier for accumulation of resveratrol in the pulmonary vasculature, a new strategy for pulmonary arterial hypertension treatment. *Drug Deliv.* **2020**, *27*, 736–744. [CrossRef] [PubMed]
26. Du, Q.; Ding, X.Q.; Gao, F.; Cui, B.; Wang, T.Y.; Chen, F.Y.; Chen, L.; Chen, H.Y.; Cui, H.X.; Wang, Y.; et al. Thermo-responsive liposome nano-vesicles for co-delivery of emamectin benzoate and nitenpyram with synergistic pest control. *Chem. Eng. J.* **2024**, *479*, 147548. [CrossRef]
27. Du, Q.; Chen, L.; Ding, X.; Cui, B.; Chen, H.; Gao, F.; Wang, Y.; Cui, H.; Zeng, Z. Development of emamectin benzoate-loaded liposome nano-vesicles with thermo-responsive behavior for intelligent pest control. *J. Mater. Chem. B* **2022**, *10*, 9896–9905. [CrossRef] [PubMed]
28. Ong, S.G.M.; Ming, L.C.; Lee, K.S.; Yuen, K.H. Influence of the Encapsulation Efficiency and Size of Liposome on the Oral Bioavailability of Griseofulvin-Loaded Liposomes. *Pharmaceutics* **2016**, *8*, 25. [CrossRef] [PubMed]
29. Liu, Y.; Liu, D.; Zhu, L.; Gan, Q.; Le, X. Temperature-dependent structure stability and in vitro release of chitosan-coated curcumin liposome. *Food Res. Int.* **2015**, *74*, 97–105. [CrossRef]
30. Chen, Y.; Le Van, M.; Liu, J.; Angelov, B.; Drechsler, M.; Garamus, V.M.; Willumeit-Roemer, R.; Zou, A. Baicalin loaded in folate-PEG modified liposomes for enhanced stability and tumor targeting. *Colloids Surf. B-Biointerfaces* **2016**, *140*, 74–82. [CrossRef]
31. Jiang, L.; Li, L.; He, X.D.; Yi, Q.Y.; He, B.; Cao, J.; Pan, W.S.; Gu, Z.W. Overcoming drug-resistant lung cancer by paclitaxel loaded dual-functional liposomes with mitochondria targeting and pH-response. *Biomaterials* **2015**, *52*, 126–139. [CrossRef] [PubMed]
32. Angius, F.; Floris, A. Liposomes and MTT cell viability assay: An incompatible affair. *Toxicol. Vitr.* **2015**, *29*, 314–319. [CrossRef] [PubMed]
33. Giannakopoulos, E.; Katopodi, A.; Rallis, M.; Politopoulos, K.; Alexandratou, E. The effects of low power laser light at 661 nm on wound healing in a scratch assay fibroblast model. *Lasers Med. Sci.* **2022**, *38*, 27. [CrossRef] [PubMed]
34. Kang, X.; Zheng, Z.; Liu, Z.; Wang, H.; Zhao, Y.; Zhang, W.; Shi, M.; He, Y.; Cao, Y.; Xu, Q.; et al. Liposomal Codelivery of Doxorubicin and Andrographolide Inhibits Breast Cancer Growth and Metastasis. *Mol. Pharm.* **2018**, *15*, 1618–1626. [CrossRef] [PubMed]
35. Jhaveri, A.; Deshpande, P.; Pattni, B.; Torchilin, V. Transferrin-targeted, resveratrol-loaded liposomes for the treatment of glioblastoma. *J. Control. Release* **2018**, *277*, 89–101. [CrossRef] [PubMed]
36. Paleos, C.M.; Tsiourvas, D.; Sideratou, Z.; Pantos, A. Formation of artificial multicompartment vesosome and dendrosome as prospected drug and gene delivery carriers. *J. Control. Release* **2013**, *170*, 141–152. [CrossRef]
37. Hamada, T.; Miura, Y.; Ishii, K.-i.; Araki, S.; Yoshikawa, K.; Vestergaard, M.d.; Takagi, M. Dynamic processes in endocytic transformation of a raft-exhibiting giant liposome. *J. Phys. Chem. B* **2007**, *111*, 10853–10857. [CrossRef] [PubMed]
38. Zong, W.; Ma, S.; Zhang, X.; Wang, X.; Li, Q.; Han, X. A Fissionable Artificial Eukaryote-like Cell Model. *J. Am. Chem. Soc.* **2017**, *139*, 9955–9960. [CrossRef] [PubMed]
39. Zhong, Y.; Wang, J.; Wang, Y.; Wu, B. Preparation and evaluation of liposome-encapsulated codrug LMX. *Int. J. Pharm.* **2012**, *438*, 240–248. [CrossRef]
40. Danaei, M.; Dehghankhold, M.; Ataei, S.; Davarani, F.H.; Javanmard, R.; Dokhani, A.; Khorasani, S.; Mozafari, M.R. Impact of Particle Size and Polydispersity Index on the Clinical Applications of Lipidic Nanocarrier Systems. *Pharmaceutics* **2018**, *10*, 57. [CrossRef]
41. Luo, M.; Zhang, R.; Liu, L.; Chi, J.; Huang, F.; Dong, L.; Ma, Q.; Jia, X.; Zhang, M. Preparation, stability and antioxidant capacity of nano liposomes loaded with procyandins from lychee pericarp. *J. Food Eng.* **2020**, *284*, 110065. [CrossRef]
42. Eloy, J.O.; Petrilli, R.; Topan, J.F.; Ribeiro Antonio, H.M.; Abriata Barcellos, J.P.; Chesca, D.L.; Serafini, L.N.; Tiezzi, D.G.; Lee, R.J.; Marchetti, J.M. Co-loaded paclitaxel/rapamycin liposomes: Development, characterization and in vitro and in vivo evaluation for breast cancer therapy. *Colloids Surf. B-Biointerfaces* **2016**, *141*, 74–82. [CrossRef] [PubMed]
43. Roy, S.; Rhim, J.-W. Carboxymethyl cellulose-based antioxidant and antimicrobial active packaging film incorporated with curcumin and zinc oxide. *Int. J. Biol. Macromol.* **2020**, *148*, 666–676. [CrossRef] [PubMed]
44. Yu, Y.; Feng, R.; Li, J.; Wang, Y.; Song, Y.; Tan, G.; Liu, D.; Liu, W.; Yang, X.; Pan, H.; et al. A hybrid genipin-crosslinked dual-sensitive hydrogel/nanostructured lipid carrier ocular drug delivery platform. *Asian J. Pharm. Sci.* **2019**, *14*, 423–434. [CrossRef] [PubMed]
45. Hashemi, M.; Omidi, M.; Muralidharan, B.; Tayebi, L.; Herpin, M.J.; Mohagheghi, M.A.; Mohammadi, J.; Smyth, H.D.C.; Milner, T.E. Layer-by-layer assembly of graphene oxide on thermosensitive liposomes for photo-chemotherapy. *Acta Biomater.* **2018**, *65*, 376–392. [CrossRef]
46. Chen, M.H.; Chiang, B.H. Modification of curcumin-loaded liposome with edible compounds to enhance ability of crossing blood brain barrier. *Colloids Surf. A-Physicochem. Eng. Asp.* **2020**, *599*, 124862. [CrossRef]

47. Handali, S.; Moghimipour, E.; Rezaei, M.; Ramezani, Z.; Kouchak, M.; Amini, M.; Angali, K.A.; Saremy, S.; Dorkoosh, F.A. A novel 5-Fluorouracil targeted delivery to colon cancer using folic acid conjugated liposomes. *Biomed. Pharmacother.* **2018**, *108*, 1259–1273. [CrossRef] [PubMed]
48. Tai, K.D.; Rappolt, M.; Mao, L.K.; Gao, Y.X.; Yuan, F. Stability and release performance of curcumin-loaded liposomes with varying content of hydrogenated phospholipids. *Food Chem.* **2020**, *326*, 126973. [CrossRef] [PubMed]
49. Hong, C.; Wang, D.; Liang, J.M.; Guo, Y.Z.; Zhu, Y.; Xia, J.X.; Qin, J.; Zhan, H.X.; Wang, J.X. Novel ginsenoside-based multifunctional liposomal delivery system for combination therapy of gastric cancer. *Theranostics* **2019**, *9*, 4437–4449. [CrossRef]
50. Chou, T.-C.; Talalay, P. Quantitative analysis of dose-effect relationships: The combined effects of multiple drugs or enzyme inhibitors. *Adv. Enzym. Regul.* **1984**, *22*, 27–55. [CrossRef]
51. Liang, T.; Wang, B.; Li, J.; Liu, Y. LINC00922 Accelerates the Proliferation, Migration and Invasion of Lung Cancer Via the miRNA-204/CXCR4 Axis. *Med. Sci. Monit.* **2019**, *25*, 5075–5086. [CrossRef] [PubMed]
52. Hayes, J.D.; Dinkova-Kostova, A.T.; Tew, K.D. Oxidative Stress in Cancer. *Cancer Cell* **2020**, *38*, 167–197. [CrossRef] [PubMed]
53. Zhang, W.; Bai, W.; Zhang, W. MiR-21 suppresses the anticancer activities of curcumin by targeting PTEN gene in human non-small cell lung cancer A549 cells. *Clin. Transl. Oncol.* **2014**, *16*, 708–713. [CrossRef] [PubMed]
54. Gupta, P.B.; Pastushenko, I.; Skibinski, A.; Blanpain, C.; Kuperwasser, C. Phenotypic Plasticity: Driver of Cancer Initiation, Progression, and Therapy Resistance. *Cell Stem Cell* **2019**, *24*, 65–78. [CrossRef]
55. Wang, D.; Li, Y. Pharmacological effects of baicalin in lung diseases. *Front. Pharmacol.* **2023**, *24*, 1188202. [CrossRef]

Disclaimer/Publisher's Note: The statements, opinions and data contained in all publications are solely those of the individual author(s) and contributor(s) and not of MDPI and/or the editor(s). MDPI and/or the editor(s) disclaim responsibility for any injury to people or property resulting from any ideas, methods, instructions or products referred to in the content.

pharmaceutics

Review

Colorectal Cancer Stem Cells and Targeted Agents

Haobin Zhao [1,2], Ruining Han [3], Zhankun Wang [4], Junfang Xian [1] and Xiaosu Bai [2,*]

1 Department of General Practice, People's Hospital of Longhua, 38 Jinglong Jianshe Road, Shenzhen 518109, China; 635274465@mail.nwpu.edu.cn (H.Z.); xianjunfang2022@163.com (J.X.)
2 Endocrinology Department, People's Hospital of Longhua, 38 Jinglong Jianshe Road, Shenzhen 518109, China
3 Obstetric Department, The Eighth Affiliated Hospital, Sun Yat-Sen University, Shenzhen 518033, China; guyuansiyu@163.com
4 Emergency Department, People's Hospital of Longhua, 38 Jinglong Jianshe Road, Shenzhen 518109, China; liuzhishusheng.001@163.com
* Correspondence: bxsllb@163.com; Tel.: +86-755-29407559

Abstract: Since their discovery, cancer stem cells have become a hot topic in cancer therapy research. These cells possess stem cell-like self-renewal and differentiation capacities and are important factors that dominate cancer metastasis, therapy-resistance and recurrence. Worse, their inherent characteristics make them difficult to eliminate. Colorectal cancer is the third-most common cancer and the second leading cause of cancer death worldwide. Targeting colorectal cancer stem cells (CR-CSCs) can inhibit colorectal cancer metastasis, enhance therapeutic efficacy and reduce recurrence. Here, we introduced the origin, biomarker proteins, identification, cultivation and research techniques of CR-CSCs, and we summarized the signaling pathways that regulate the stemness of CR-CSCs, such as Wnt, JAK/STAT3, Notch and Hh signaling pathway. In addition to these, we also reviewed recent anti-CR-CSC drugs targeting signaling pathways, biomarkers and other regulators. These will help researchers gain insight into the current agents targeting to CR-CSCs, explore new cancer drugs and propose potential therapies.

Keywords: colorectal cancer stem cells; Lgr5; Wnt signaling pathway; single-cell omics technology

1. Introduction

In 1994, John and Bonnet isolated and identified cancer cells with stemness from leukemia cells and proposed the concept of "leukemia stem cells (LSCs)" [1]. This was the first confirmation of the existence of stem cells in cancer, a major breakthrough in the field of cancer stem cell (CSC) research. In 2003, Dontu and colleagues isolated CSCs from breast cancer cells [2], providing the first proof of the existence of CSCs in solid tumors. In the following years, CSCs were found in brain tumors, prostate cancer, lung cancer, colorectal cancer and other tumors [3–6]. Nowadays, the theory of CSCs has gained consensus and has attracted much attention in cancer treatment research. CSCs are a small population of cancer cells with stemness like stem cells. They can achieve self-renewal through symmetrical division and asymmetric division to produce daughter cells with stemness or normal cancer cells [7]. Moreover, CSCs are capable of forming cancer cells with different degrees of differentiation and reassembling the complete cancer cell repertoire of the original cancer. In addition, normal cancer cells without CSC properties can dedifferentiate back into CSCs through a bidirectional interconversion process [8,9]. Normal cancer cells without CSC properties can dedifferentiate back into CSCs through a bidirectional interconversion process [10]. This is a major reason for cancer cell heterogeneity [11]. Cancer cells with or without CSC characteristics must be eradicated to achieve good therapeutic effects. During cancer development, CSCs are important factors that lead to metastasis, therapy-resistance and recurrence [12–14]. CSCs are often accompanied by an epithelial to mesenchymal transition phenotype, and they interact with stromal cells, endothelial cells and others to promote angiogenesis, promote stem-like cancer cell differentiation and accelerate metastasis [15]. The cell cycle of CSCs arrests in the G0 phase, so they are resistant to cycle specific chemotherapy drugs [16]. Due to their DNA synthesis asynchrony and enhanced DNA repair, CSCs are resistant to DNA damaging drugs [16]. Moreover, CSCs highly express drug transporters and anti-apoptotic proteins such as Bcl-2, which endows them with the ability to pump chemotherapy drugs out of the cell and resist programmed cell death [16]. Recent research has suggested that resting cancer stem cells can evade immune surveillance and lay the seeds for cancer recurrence [17,18]. This makes CSCs more difficult to eliminate than other cancer cells.

Colorectal cancer (CRC) is the third most common malignant tumor type. In recent years, with the popularization of early screening for colorectal cancer and the advancement of treatment methods, the mortality rate associated with colorectal cancer has decreased [19]. However, metastasis and recurrence are still the leading causes of death in most end-stage CRC patients. Reducing metastasis and recurrence remains an urgent problem in CRC therapy. Colorectal cancer stem cells (CR-CSCs) may be the initial cells of colon cancer [20], promoting colon cancer metastasis [21,22] and also one of the main culprits of therapy-resistance and recurrence [23] (Figure 1). Eliminating CR-CSCs can promote therapeutic effects against colon cancer [24–26]. Here, we reviewed the origin and identification of colorectal stem cells, and we summarized the potential therapeutic targets of CR-CSCs and the current research status of agents targeting CR-CSCs. This will help researchers to gain insight into the current agents targeting CR-CSCs, explore new drugs and propose potential therapies.

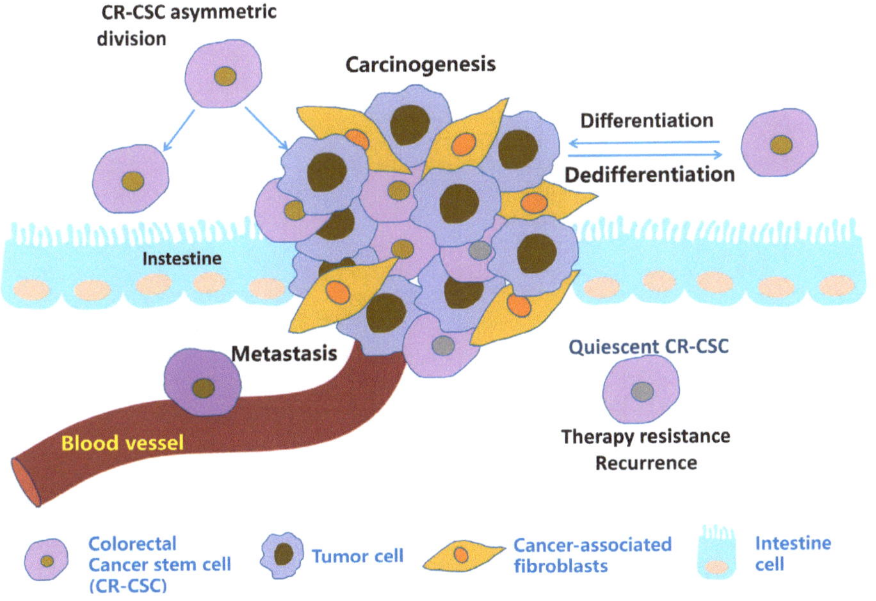

Figure 1. Illustration of metastasis, therapy resistance and recurrence promoted by CR-CSCs.

CR-CSCs not only divide into CR-CSCs, but can also produce ordinary cancer cells through proliferation or differentiation. Due to their quiescent state, high differentiation activity, secreting cytokines to make normal cells malignant and other properties, CR-CSCs can promote metastasis, therapeutic resistance and recurrence.

2. Colorectal Cancer Stem Cells

2.1. Origin of CR-CSCs

Researchers generally consider CSCs to have two main origins, derivation from normal cells that acquire mesenchymal properties [27] or transformation from normal adult stem cells [28]. The same holds true for the origin of CR-CSCs. In intestine, leucine-rich repeat-containing G-protein coupled receptor 5 (Lgr5) is expressed selectively in the crypt-base columnar cells [29] and was the first proven biomarker of CR-CSCs. In mouse models, genetic inactivation of the key colorectal cancer (CRC) driver gene Adenomatous Polyposis Coli (Apc) in Lgr5+ cells precipitated rapid tumor induction [30]. By downregulating β-Catenin and YAP signaling pathways, Protein kinase C ζ (PKC ζ) can inhibit intestinal stem cell function. PKC ζ deficiency can lead to an increase in stem cell activity in organoid cultures. Furthermore, tumorigenic activity increased in Lgr5+PKC ζ deficient mice [31]. This evidence suggests that CR-CSCs seem to originate from intestinal stem cells. However, selective and effective killing of Lgr5+ cells had no impact on primary tumor growth [24], and cells that disseminate and colonize distant organs were frequently Lgr5− [32]. Recent research using single cell sequencing technology has shown that the rDNA transcription and protein synthesis of Lgr5+ and Lgr5− cancer cell subsets were increased, which showed the characteristics of functional stem cells [33] and that lineage conversion between cell types can be driven by a combination of key CRC driver genes and microenvironmental extracellular signaling [34].Vazquez and colleagues also confirmed that the intestine contains two types of stem cells, Lgr5+ crypt-base columnar stem cells (CBCs) and Lgr5 regenerative stem cells (RSCs) using single cell sequencing technology. The two stem cell populations can coexist during tumorigenesis, exhibit dynamic plasticity, and complement each other to achieve homeostasis. The relative abundance of CBC-RSC is related to epithelial mutation and microenvironment signal destruction [35]. With the advancement of research technology, it is certain to uncover the origin of CR-CSCs.

2.2. Identification of CR-CSCs

The sorting of cancer stem cells mainly relies on flow cytometry and magnetic activation sorting. The most commonly used basis is for sorting cancer stem cell biomarker proteins. Previous studies have found that CSCs have specific biomarkers, including CD133, ALDH1, CD44 and EpCAM [36]. CSC biomarkers vary with the tumor type. There are also some biomarkers for CR-CSCs. The marker proteins located on the cell membrane include Lgr5 [37], CD133 [38,39], CD44 [40], CD26 [41], CD24 [42], CD29 [43], CD166 [44] and EpCAM [45]. Aldehyde dehydrogenase1 (ALDH1) is an intracellular enzyme that oxidizes aldehydes and mediates the control of differentiation pathways. It is currently widely used as a marker for identifying and isolating various types of normal stem cells and CSCs [44,46]. Oct4 [47], Sox2 [48] and Nanog [49] are transcription factors used as biomarker located in the nucleus (Figure 2). The biological functions of most biomarkers are related to cell stemness.

Biomarker proteins and regulators in the pathway are the most prominent targets in CR-CSC therapy.

By combining fluorescent labeled antibodies with cancer stem cell biomarkers, flow cytometry can be used to select CSCs expressing the related biomarkers from cancer cells. The side population (SP) cells with strong drug resistance are also considered to have the stemness of tumor stem cells. The characteristic of these cells is that they can expel the fluorescent dye hoechst33342 out of the cell, and it is shown as a non-fluorescent cell when detected via flow cytometry. CSCs with strong drug resistance in SP cells can be obtained by flow sorting [50]. Magnetic activated cell sorting utilizes antibodies attached to magnetic beads to bind to CSC biomarkers, adsorbing the corresponding cancer stem cells onto a separation column, while unbound cells pass through the separation column. Cancer stem cells with positive surface labeling can be obtained by mean of elution from the separation column [51,52] Single-cell omics technology is a powerful tool for exploring CSCs [53,54].

Single-cell omics technology can characterize and type CSCs in tumors, and establishing a stemness model has prospective clinical implications for prognostic evaluation [35,55].

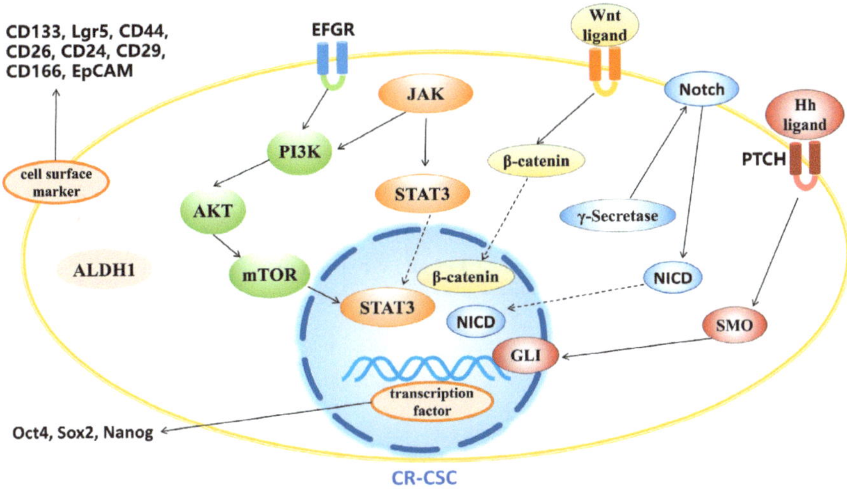

Figure 2. Biomarker proteins and regulators in pathways in CR-CSCs.

2.3. Cultivation of CR-CSCs

It is worth emphasizing that although the research results on cancer stem cells have broad prospects for practical clinical applications, they are still in the initial stage. In order to successfully unleash the enormous potential of cancer stem cell research achievements, there are still many urgent issues to address. To understand the physiological activity of CSCs, the first step is to obtain them. For solid tumors, the most commonly used method to enrich cancer stem cells is non-adhesive culture with serum-free culture [56,57]. CSCs with self-renewal capacity are able to survive under non-adherent conditions and maintain clonogenic activity, whereas non-CSCs undergo anoikis by loss of anchorage.

Three-dimensional (3D) culture has emerged as a cell culture method in vitro in recent years. By using hydrogel to mimic the extracellular matrix and applying different culture conditions, 3D culture can mimic in vivo microenvironment [58]. Different gel materials have different porosity, permeability, surface chemical and mechanical properties, which will have different effects on cell growth and differentiation [59]. Three-dimensional culture can be used to enrich stem cells or study cell differentiation [60]. Organoid is an advanced version of 3D culture, which is a 3D micro cell cluster formed by directional differentiation of stem cells [61]. Organoids have the abilities to self-renew and self-organize, and can highly mimic the structure and function of organs in vivo. They have been widely used in the study of organ diseases, drug toxicity and cancer therapy [62,63].

3. Agents Targeting CR-CSCs

3.1. Targeting CR-CSC Biomarkers

Biomarker proteins are targets for the rapid screening of CRCs. In order to enhance the specificity of therapeutic strategies, researchers often choose ligands or antibodies against CSC surface makers (Table 1). MCLA-158 is an EGFR and Lgr5 targeting bispecific antibody with strong growth inhibitory effects on CRC organoids. Simultaneously, it exhibits strong anti-tumor activity in xenograft models derived from patients with high expression of Lgr5 and EGFR [64]. In mouse orthotopic xenograft models derived from CRC patients, MCLA-158 treatment not only reduced the size of the primary tumor but also effectively suppressed metastasis, including that of KRAS mutant tumors resistant to Cetuximab. Currently, researchers are conducting clinical trials of MCLA-158 in various solid tumors (NCT03526835) [64]. Catumaxomab was the first T cell binding bispecific antibody approved by the European Medicines Agency (EMA) in 2009 for the treatment of malignant ascites [65]. Catumaxomab is a trifunctional bispecific antibody that binds to EpCAM on cancer cells and CD3 on T cells. It also binds to FcγR to recruit immune helper cells [65]. Catumaxomab can effectively eliminate CD133+/EpCAM+CSCs in malignant ascites in patients with advanced ovarian cancer, gastric cancer and pancreatic cancer, which indicates that it has potential therapeutic applications in eradicating CSCs of epithelial cancers [66,67]. Similar to catumaxomab, solidomab is also a bispecific antibody targeting EpCAM and CD3. Solidomab treatment was found to effectively eradicated EpCAM+CSCs, originating from colon or pancreatic cancer patients that were inoculated into NOD/SCID mice [68,69].

Table 1. Agents targeting to CR-CSC biomarkers and Wnt pathway.

Agents	Targets of CR-CSCs	Efficacy	References
MCLA-158	EFGR and Lgr5	Effective in preclinical models	[64]
Catumaxomab	EpCAM	Approved in the European Union for the treatment of malignant ascites	[65–67]
Solidomab	EpCAM	Effective in vitro	[68,69]
CD133-directed CAR T cells	CD133	Effective in a phase I trial	[70]
Cetuximab	EFGR	Effective in combination therapies	[71–73]
CD133-targeted oncolyticvirus	CD133	Effective in mice	[74]
NCB0846	Wnt pathway	Effective in mice	[75]
Epigallocatechin gallate	Wnt pathway	Effective in mice	[76,77]
XAV939	Wnt pathway	Effective in vitro	[78]
Phenethyl isothiocyanate and sulforaphane	Wnt pathway	Not proven effective in trials	[79–81]
Salinomycin	Wnt pathway	Effective in mice	[82]
JIB04	Wnt pathway	Effective in mice	[83]
CBB1003	Wnt pathway	Effective in vitro	[84]
YW2065	Wnt pathway	Effective in mice	[85]
LF3	Wnt pathway	Effective in mice	[86]
Dickkopf-2	Wnt pathway	Effective in vitro	[87]
ICG-001	Wnt pathway	Effective in vitro	[88]
4-Acetyl-antroquinonol B	Wnt pathway and JAK-STAT pathway	Effective in mice	[89,90]
Diallyl trisulfide	Wnt pathway	Effective in vitro	[91]
36-077	Wnt pathway	Effective in vitro	[92]
Evodiamine	Wnt and Notch pathway	Effective in vitro	[93]
Farnesyl dimethyl chromanol	Wnt pathway	Effective in mice	[94]
FH535	Wnt pathway	Effective in vitro	[95]

In addition to antibodies, there are oncolytic virotherapies and CSC vaccines for targeted biomarker therapies. Oncolytic viruses are a class of viruses with tumor-killing functions. Oncolytic virotherapy is an emerging new tumor treatment that utilizes oncolytic viruses to selectively destroy tumor cells while leaving normal cells intact. Using the properties of oncolytic viruses combined with receptors on tumor cells, researchers have screened or engineered oncolytic viruses that target cancer stem cells [96]. Due to the characteristics of virus vectors, oncolytic virotherapy can trigger immunogenic cell death, release tumor-related antigens and elicit anti-tumor immune response, which can exert stronger anti-cancer effect [96]. Oncolytic viruses with a CD133-targeting motif effectively infected and killed CD133+CR-CSCs, and inhibited the growth of CRC xenotransplantation models [74]. Oncolytic virotherapy is one potential therapy strategy, but it still needs further research. CSCs vaccines are also a type of immunotherapy under research. For example, B16F10 CD133+/CD44+CSCs vaccine can effectively inhibit melanoma growth in mice and reduce the CSC population within tumors [97]. Although no cancer stem cell vaccine has entered clinical trials at this time, the demonstrated efficacy of a vaccine targeting metastatic CRC is reassuring and raises hope [98].

3.2. *Targeting Signaling Pathway*

Multiple signaling pathways are involved in the self-renewal, proliferation, apoptosis and angiogenesis processes of CR-CSCs. Currently, it is believed that specifically targeting cell signaling pathways to inhibit the effects of CR-CSCs is a major development direction for CRC therapy.

3.2.1. Wnt Signaling Pathway

The Wnt pathway plays a critical role in controlling epithelial stem cell self-renewal, and its dysregulation causes colorectal carcinogenesis [99,100]. The canonical Wnt pathway downstream signaling is regulated by the level of β-catenin (Figure 2). TRAF2- and NCK-interacting kinase (TNIK) is an essential activator of Wnt target genes [99]. The inhibitory activity of TNIK inhibitors such as NCB0846 on CR-CSCs has been confirmed [75]. Epigallocatechin gallate (EGCG) is a kind of the catechins found in green tea. It has been proven to effectively inhibit stem cells from various cancers [101,102]. EGCG can inhibit the stemness of CRC cells by downregulating the expression of biomarkers such as CD133, CD44, NANOG, OCT4, ALDH1 and Wnt/β-catenin signaling pathway [76,77]. The small molecule inhibitor XAV939 was shown to significantly downregulate CSC biomarkers in colon cancer cells and increased apoptosis induced by chemotherapy drugs [78]. Phenethyl isothiocyanate (PEITC) and sulforaphane are natural products extracted from cruciferae plants with anti-cancer activities [79,103]. PEITC suppressed the characteristics of CR-CSCs by reducing the activity of the Wnt/β-catenin pathway, leading to a decline in the proportion of CD133+ cells [79,80]. Salinomycin, an anti-bacterial polyether isolated from Streptomyces albus, was found to selectively eliminate CD133+ cells in CRC [104]. Salinomycin induced apoptosis of human CR-CSCs by activating caspase, increasing DNA damage and disrupting of the Wnt/β-catenin/TCF complex. Tumor growth and expression of CSC-related Wnt genes, including Lgr5 were decreased [82,105]. In addition to these, there are many drugs that reduce CSC stemness by targeting the Wnt signaling pathway, such as pan-inhibitor of histone demethylases JIB04 [83] and lysine-specific demethylase 1 inhibitor CBB1003 [84] (Table 1).

3.2.2. Hedgehog Signaling Pathway

The Hedgehog (Hh) signaling pathway plays an essential role in the growth and differentiation of gastrointestinal tissue [106]. The canonical Hh signal involves Hh ligands (sonic Hh, Indian Hh or desert Hh) binding to the patched (PTCH) receptor, releasing smoothened (SMO) and causing the receptor to activate. In this process, GLI protein will be activated and become transcriptional activators of the downstream targets of the Hh signaling pathway. The Hh-GLI pathway is involved in maintaining the self-renewal ability of CR-CSCs [107,108] (Figure 2).

Vismodegib (also named Ericdge, GDC-0449) is a Hedgehog signaling pathway inhibitor used in clinical practice and approved by the US Food and Drug Administration for the treatment of basal cell carcinoma. Vismodegib targets a subpopulation of CSCs in basal cell carcinoma [109]. Studies have shown that vismodegib can inhibit the stemness of CR-CSC and the expression of biomarkers CD44 and ALDH1 [110]. Cyclopamine is a natural alkaloid that can inhibit the Hh-GLI signaling pathway by inhibiting SMO. After cyclopamine treatment, the mRNA levels of CSC biomarkers and genes related to Hh signaling, including PTCH1, SMO and GLI1 were found to decreased in stem cells derived from HCT116 [111]. Given the regulation of CR-CSCs by Hh signaling pathway, more new inhibitors are being developed (Table 2).

Table 2. Agents targeting to signaling pathway.

Agents	Targets of CR-CSCs	Efficacy	Reference
Vismodegib	SMO of Hedgehog pathway	Approved by FDA for the treatment of basal cell carcinoma	[110,112]
Cyclopamine	SMO of Hedgehog pathway	Effective in vitro	[111]
RO4929097	γ-secretase of Notch pathway	Not proven effective in a phase II trial	[113]
Anti-DLL4	DLL4 of Notch pathway	Effective in a phase I trial	[114]
Honokiol	γ-secretase of Notch pathway	Effective in mice	[115]
Quercetin	γ-secretase of Notch pathway	Effective in mice	[116]
α-Mangostine	Notch pathway	Effective in vitro	[117]
BEZ235	PI3K/Akt/mTOR pathway	Not proven effective in a phase Ib trial	[118,119]
LY294002	PI3K/Akt/mTOR pathway	Effective in vitro	[120]
Piplartine	PI3K/Akt/mTOR pathway	Not proven effective in trials	[121,122]
Rapamycin	mTOR of PI3K/Akt/mTOR pathway	Not proven effective in trials	[123,124]
Metformin	mTOR of PI3K/Akt/mTOR pathway	Effective in combination therapies	[125]
Atractylenolide I	PI3K/Akt/mTOR pathway	Effective in mice	[126]
Torin-1	PI3K/Akt/mTOR pathway	Effective in vitro	[127]
Buparlisib	Akt of PI3K/Akt/mTOR pathway	Effective in a phase Ib trial	[128,129]
MK-2206	Akt of PI3K/Akt/mTOR pathway	Not proven effective in a phase II trial	[130,131]
Curcumin and GO-Y030	STAT3 of JAK/STAT3 signaling pathway	Effective in mice	[132]
Napabucasin	STAT3 of JAK/STAT3 signaling pathway	Not proven effective in a phase III trial	[133]

3.2.3. Notch Signaling Pathway

Notch signaling is involved in the regulation of cell differentiation, proliferation and tumorigenesis [134]. The pathway consists of four receptors (Notch1-4) and five ligands (Jagged-1, Jagged-2, Delta-1, Delta-3, Delta-4) and DNA-binding proteins. The interaction between receptors and ligands initiates protein cleavage cascade reactions, leading to the activation of Notch target genes [135]. Gamma secretase inhibitors (GSIs) can inhibit Notch signaling by preventing the proteolytic cleavage of Notch receptors [136] (Figure 2). However, RO4929097, one of the GSIs, failed to achieve excellent results in clinical trials [113]. More GSIs are under investigation. DLL4 is an activator protein of the non-canonical Notch signaling pathway.DLL4 antibody was confirmed to be effective against both KRAS wild-type and mutant CRC cells, effectively eradicating CR-CSCs and enhancing the antitumor effect of irinotecan [114,137]. In addition, Honokiol, Quercetin and others have also been shown to have the ability to inhibit CR-CSC stemness [115,116] (Table 2).

3.2.4. PI3K/Akt/mTOR Signaling Pathway

The PI3K/Akt/mTOR signaling pathway plays a crucial role in cell metabolism and proliferation, and it is closely related to the CR-CSC phenotype [138]. Studies have demonstrated that components of the PI3K/Akt signaling pathway are overexpressed in CRC in vitro and in vivo [130,139]. PI3K and MEK inhibitors used in combination can induce CR-CSC death and the regression of tumor xenografts [140]. BEZ235, a dual pathway inhibitor of mTOR and PI3K, could inhibit the proliferation of CR-CSCs and the expression of its biomarkers CD133 and Lgr5, thus suppressing the stemness of CR-CSCs [118]. LY294002 is a PI3K inhibitor based on the flavonoid quercetin. LY294002 blocked Akt phosphorylation through the PI3K/Akt signaling pathway and inhibited liver CSC proliferation and tumorigenicity in vitro and in vivo [120]. LY294002 treatment led to a decrease in proliferation, spheroid formation and self-renewal properties, as well as a decrease in Akt phosphorylation and cyclin D1 expression in CR-CSCs in vitro [120]. Piplartine is an alkaloid amide isolated from peppers. It was reported to inhibit stemness properties in leukemia and oral cancer [121,140]. In combination with auranofin, piplartine reduced the expression levels of surface biomarker CD44v9, eliminated CR-CSCs and inhibited CRC growth [121]. Rapamycin is an mTOR inhibitor and is used clinically as an immunosuppressive drug. In CRC cell lines, it has the potential to decrease the spheroid-forming ability and ALDH1 activity [123]. In cotreatment with 5-FU and oxaliplatin, rapamycin reduced the CR-CSCs subpopulation. Metformin is also reported to reduce the CSC population in different types of cancers [141]. Metformin not only reduced the proliferation of CSC population in mouse xenografts [125], but also effectively reduced CSC population in colorectal and other gastrointestinal cancers in a pilot clinical trial [142]. There are also many drugs that target the PI3K/Akt/mTOR signaling pathway to inhibit CR-CSCs, such as Atractylenolide I and Torin-1 [126,127].

3.2.5. JAK/STAT3 Signaling Pathway

JAK/STAT signaling is closely related to cancer growth and metastasis. In cancer cells, JAK/STAT signaling can be activated by multiple mechanisms, most notably by STAT3 activation [143]. High STAT3 activity was found in CRC-SCs, but not in normal colon epithelial cells [144]. Another study revealed that the JAK2/STAT3 signaling pathway promoted the persistence and radio-resistance of CR-CSCs [145]. Curcumin is a polyphenol from Curcuma longa, and GO-Y030 is a novel curcumin analog. Curcumin and its analog GO-Y030 were proposed drug candidates to eliminate CR-CSCs by suppressing STAT3 activity [132]. Napabucasin, also named BBI608, is an orally administered STAT3 inhibitor with anti-CSC activity against various types of cancer [146,147]. However, unfortunately, napabucasin failed to achieve satisfactory results in phase 3 clinical trials for the treatment of colorectal cancer [133]. ls. Napabucasin may be the first anti-CRC drug approved for clinical use targeting CSCs

There are other signaling pathways such as TGF-β and Hippo, regulating CSCs stemness. These various signaling pathways do not operate independently and often act via crosstalk to influence cancer progression [22,106,148–150] (Table 2).

3.3. Other Agents Targeting CR-CSCs

FBXL5 E3 ligase plays an important role in maintaining the stemness of CR-CSCs. The anandamide uptake inhibitor AM404 can suppress FBXL5 expression and inhibit CR-CSC dedifferentiation, migration and drug resistance [151]. Prexasertib, also named LY2606368, is an investigational checkpoint kinase inhibitor. By inhibiting checkpoint kinase (CHK) 1, LY2606368 affected DNA replication in most CR-CSCs [152]. ASR352 and NSC30049 are both CHK1 inhibitor [153,154]. RAB5/7, which is associated with the endo lysosomal pathway, plays an important role in the survival and maintenance of CSCs through the mitophagic pathway. Mefloquine, an anti-malaria drug, has been identified as a new inhibitor of RAB. In the PDX model of colorectal cancer, mefloquine can target RAB5/7 to inhibit the mitophagic pathway and induce mitochondrial-induced apoptosis, thereby exerting anti-tumor effects without significant side effects [155]. At present, there are many other types of CR-CSC antagonists, such as pitavastatin [156], histone deacetylase inhibitor trichostatin A [157] and inhibitors of the post-translational sumoylation modification pathway [158]. They may play an important role in targeting CR-CSCs in future (Table 3).

Table 3. Agents targeting CR-CSCs.

Agents	Targets of CR-CSCs	Efficacy	Reference
AM404	FBXL5	Effective in mice	[151]
LY2606368	Checkpoint kinase 1	Effective in a phase II trial of ovarian cancer	[152,159]
ASR352	Checkpoint kinase 1	Effective in vitro	[153]
NCS30049	Checkpoint kinase 1	Effective in vitro	[154]
Mefloquine	RAB5/7	Effective in vitro	[155]
Pitavastatin	——	Effective in vitro	[156]
Trichostatin A	histone deacetylase	Effective in vitro	[157]
Dabrafenib	BRAF	Approved by FDA for the treatment of elanoma	[160]
Mithramycin A	SP1	Effective in vitro	[161]
Parthenolide	USP47	Effective in vitro	[162]
Gambogic acid	ZFP36	Effective in a phase IIa trial	[163,164]

4. Future Prospects

Despite significant progress in research on therapeutic drugs for CR-CSCs, cancer treatment still faces many challenges. Tumor microenvironment (TME) plays a major role in determining cell fate and behavioral choices [165,166]. Under the complex interaction of the TME, reversible transformation can be achieved between tumorigenic and non-tumorigenic cells. This is the reason why it is difficult to completely remove CSCs [167]. Cancer-associated fibroblasts (CAFs) play a significant positive role in the development and transfer of CR-CSCs [168]. A tumor is an entity composed of multiple heterogeneous cells. Different subtypes of CSCs may have different resistance mechanisms, and therefore, each cancer subtype may require unique therapies [169]. The plethora of contributing factors in cancer and the complex regulatory network make it difficult to eradicate cancer via a single therapeutic intervention.

Fortunately, researchers never give up. In order to achieve effective treatment, more extensive and in-depth research has been conducted to examine molecular and cellular aspects, including the synergistic targeting of CR-CSCs and TME in cancer treatment. Fibroblast activation protein (FAP) is a type II membrane-bound glycoprotein that is overexpressed in CAFs and activated fibroblasts at wound healing/inflammatory sites. FAP inhibitor has been developed to target CAFs to improve TME [170]. In response to the problem of tumor stem cell heterogeneity, anti CSC drugs with diverse targets have been or are currently being developed. Many of them have been incorporated into clinical or preclinical trials. In the face of the differing responses of different patients to therapeutic approaches, prognosis prediction and personalized treatment are the best solutions. Single cell omics and organoid technology can assist in achieving this goal. Using large-scale omics technologies, we can subtype cancers and build predictive models for treatment response [35,55]. In vitro culture of patient derived tumor organoids can enable prediction of drug sensitivity and resistance, and achieve precision treatment [171]. In summary, in the face of differing treatment responses in patients, the heterogeneity of cancer stem cells and the complex regulatory mechanisms of cancer, researchers have been struggling to decipher them.

5. Conclusions

CR-CSCs are a small group of stem cells in colon cancer that have unlimited proliferation, self-renewal and differentiation ability, playing an important role in drug resistance, metastasis and recurrence. CSCs are like cancer seeds, which cannot be ignored in cancer treatment. The advancement of modern medical technology has given us a certain level of understanding of colon cancer stem cells, but we have not yet fully understood them. Regarding the current situation of CR-CSCs targeted inhibitors, it is important to strengthen the synergistic effect between drugs. By combining drugs targeting CR-CSCs with other treatment methods, we can prevent cancer metastasis and recurrence while reducing the occurrence of drug resistance, which will improve the effectiveness of current CRC treatment. Cancer and the tissue involved are integrated, and treatment should adopt a systematic approach, striving to completely eliminate the seeds to prevent metastasis and recurrence. Targeted inhibitors of CRCSCs are an emerging treatment method for CRC. Although there are still many unclear mechanisms to be discovered, it can be expected that in the future, these drugs will play an undeniable role in preventing colon cancer metastasis and recurrence. Certainly, a complete cancer treatment requires not only targeted treatment for CR-CSCs, but also targeted combination therapy for non-CR-CSCs and TME, as well as the entire tumor. In order to benefit all patients, personalized therapy is the ultimate goal. Single-cell omics technology and organoid technology have contributed to a deeper understanding of the different aspects of cancer stem cells and to the development of more effective treatments for cancer. Achieving this goal still requires considerable efforts and collaboration from researchers.

Author Contributions: X.B. proposed the theme of the manuscript. H.Z. and R.H. searched, consulted the literature, and wrote the manuscript, while Z.W. and J.X. revised the manuscript. H.Z. and R.H. made the same contribution to the manuscript. All authors have read and agreed to the published version of the manuscript.

Funding: This research was supported by Shenzhen Science and Technology Program (JCYJ20210324133602007), Construction Funds of Key Medical Disciplines in Longhua District, Shenzhen (MKD202007090211), Inflammation and Immune Mediated Diseases Laboratory of Anhui Province Open Project (IMMDL20220009) and Special project of medical research of Medical Association of Longhua District, Shenzhen (2023LHMA03).

Institutional Review Board Statement: Not Applicable.

Informed Consent Statement: Not Applicable.

Data Availability Statement: Not Applicable.

Acknowledgments: We acknowledge Zhifu Zhang for assistance, support and significant contributions during the revisions of the paper. We would like to thank the Support from the Shenzhen "Healthcare San Ming Project".

Conflicts of Interest: The authors declare no conflict of interest.

References

1. Lapidot, T.; Sirard, C.; Vormoor, J.; Murdoch, B.; Hoang, T.; Caceres-Cortes, J.; Minden, M.; Paterson, B.; Caligiuri, M.A.; Dick, J.E. A cell initiating human acute myeloid leukaemia after transplantation into SCID mice. *Nature* **1994**, *367*, 645–648. [CrossRef] [PubMed]
2. Dontu, G.; Al-Hajj, M.; Abdallah, W.M.; Clarke, M.F.; Wicha, M.S. Stem cells in normal breast development and breast cancer. *Cell Prolif.* **2003**, *36* (Suppl. 1), 59–72. [CrossRef] [PubMed]
3. Singh, S.K.; Clarke, I.D.; Terasaki, M.; Bonn, V.E.; Hawkins, C.; Squire, J.; Dirks, P.B. Identification of a cancer stem cell in human brain tumors. *Cancer Res.* **2003**, *63*, 5821–5828. [PubMed]
4. Maitland, N.J.; Collins, A. A tumour stem cell hypothesis for the origins of prostate cancer. *BJU Int.* **2005**, *96*, 1219–1223. [CrossRef] [PubMed]
5. Lam, J.S.; Yamashiro, J.; Shintaku, I.P.; Vessella, R.L.; Jenkins, R.B.; Horvath, S.; Said, J.W.; Reiter, R.E. Prostate stem cell antigen is overexpressed in prostate cancer metastases. *Clin. Cancer Res.* **2005**, *11*, 2591–2596. [CrossRef]
6. O'Brien, C.A.; Pollett, A.; Gallinger, S.; Dick, J.E. A human colon cancer cell capable of initiating tumour growth in immunodeficient mice. *Nature* **2007**, *445*, 106–110. [CrossRef] [PubMed]
7. Boman, B.M.; Wicha, M.S. Cancer stem cells: A step toward the cure. *J. Clin. Oncol.* **2008**, *26*, 2795–2799. [CrossRef] [PubMed]
8. Reya, T.; Morrison, S.J.; Clarke, M.F.; Weissman, I.L. Stem cells, cancer, and cancer stem cells. *Nature* **2001**, *414*, 105–111. [CrossRef]
9. Chen, K.; Huang, Y.H.; Chen, J.L. Understanding and targeting cancer stem cells: Therapeutic implications and challenges. *Acta Pharmacol. Sin.* **2013**, *34*, 732–740. [CrossRef]
10. Chaffer, C.L.; Brueckmann, I.; Scheel, C.; Kaestli, A.J.; Wiggins, P.A.; Rodrigues, L.O.; Brooks, M.; Reinhardt, F.; Su, Y.; Polyak, K.; et al. Normal and neoplastic nonstem cells can spontaneously convert to a stem-like state. *Proc. Natl. Acad. Sci. USA* **2011**, *108*, 7950–7955. [CrossRef]
11. Prasetyanti, P.R.; Medema, J.P. Intra-tumor heterogeneity from a cancer stem cell perspective. *Mol. Cancer* **2017**, *16*, 41. [CrossRef] [PubMed]
12. Bütof, R.; Dubrovska, A.; Baumann, M. Clinical perspectives of cancer stem cell research in radiation oncology. *Radiother. Oncol.* **2013**, *108*, 388–396. [CrossRef] [PubMed]
13. Rich, J.N. Cancer stem cells in radiation resistance. *Cancer Res.* **2007**, *67*, 8980–8984. [CrossRef] [PubMed]
14. Hermann, P.C.; Huber, S.L.; Herrler, T.; Aicher, A.; Ellwart, J.W.; Guba, M.; Bruns, C.J.; Heeschen, C. Distinct populations of cancer stem cells determine tumor growth and metastatic activity in human pancreatic cancer. *Cell Stem Cell* **2007**, *1*, 313–323. [CrossRef] [PubMed]
15. Oskarsson, T.; Batlle, E.; Massagué, J. Metastatic stem cells: Sources, niches, and vital pathways. *Cell Stem Cell* **2014**, *14*, 306–321. [CrossRef] [PubMed]
16. Abdullah, L.N.; Chow, E.K. Mechanisms of chemoresistance in cancer stem cells. *Clin. Transl. Med.* **2013**, *2*, 3. [CrossRef]
17. Yao, J.; Liu, Y.; Yang, J.; Li, M.; Li, S.; Zhang, B.; Yang, R.; Zhang, Y.; Cui, X.; Feng, C. Single-Cell Sequencing Reveals that DBI is the Key Gene and Potential Therapeutic Target in Quiescent Bladder Cancer Stem Cells. *Front. Genet.* **2022**, *13*, 904536. [CrossRef]
18. Antonica, F.; Santomaso, L.; Pernici, D.; Petrucci, L.; Aiello, G.; Cutarelli, A.; Conti, L.; Romanel, A.; Miele, E.; Tebaldi, T.; et al. A slow-cycling/quiescent cells subpopulation is involved in glioma invasiveness. *Nat. Commun.* **2022**, *13*, 4767. [CrossRef]
19. Sung, H.; Ferlay, J.; Siegel, R.L.; Laversanne, M.; Soerjomataram, I.; Jemal, A.; Bray, F. Global Cancer Statistics 2020: GLOBOCAN Estimates of Incidence and Mortality Worldwide for 36 Cancers in 185 Countries. *CA Cancer J. Clin.* **2021**, *71*, 209–249. [CrossRef]
20. Marhaba, R.; Klingbeil, P.; Nuebel, T.; Nazarenko, I.; Buechler, M.W.; Zoeller, M. CD44 and EpCAM: Cancer-initiating cell markers. *Curr. Mol. Med.* **2008**, *8*, 784–804. [CrossRef]
21. Gaiser, M.R.; Lämmermann, T.; Feng, X.; Igyarto, B.Z.; Kaplan, D.H.; Tessarollo, L.; Germain, R.N.; Udey, M.C. Cancer-associated epithelial cell adhesion molecule (EpCAM; CD326) enables epidermal Langerhans cell motility and migration in vivo. *Proc. Natl. Acad. Sci. USA* **2012**, *109*, E889–E897. [CrossRef] [PubMed]
22. Cheung, P.; Xiol, J.; Dill, M.T.; Yuan, W.C.; Panero, R.; Roper, J.; Osorio, F.G.; Maglic, D.; Li, Q.; Gurung, B.; et al. Regenerative Reprogramming of the Intestinal Stem Cell State via Hippo Signaling Suppresses Metastatic Colorectal Cancer. *Cell Stem Cell* **2020**, *27*, 590–604.e9. [CrossRef] [PubMed]
23. Shimokawa, M.; Ohta, Y.; Nishikori, S.; Matano, M.; Takano, A.; Fujii, M.; Date, S.; Sugimoto, S.; Kanai, T.; Sato, T. Visualization and targeting of LGR5(+) human colon cancer stem cells. *Nature* **2017**, *545*, 187–192. [CrossRef] [PubMed]
24. de Sousa e Melo, F.; Kurtova, A.V.; Harnoss, J.M.; Kljavin, N.; Hoeck, J.D.; Hung, J.; Anderson, J.E.; Storm, E.E.; Modrusan, Z.; Koeppen, H.; et al. A distinct role for Lgr5(+) stem cells in primary and metastatic colon cancer. *Nature* **2017**, *543*, 676–680. [CrossRef] [PubMed]
25. Wang, H.; Gong, P.; Chen, T.; Gao, S.; Wu, Z.; Wang, X.; Li, J.; Marjani, S.L.; Costa, J.; Weissman, S.M.; et al. Colorectal Cancer Stem Cell States Uncovered by Simultaneous Single-Cell Analysis of Transcriptome and Telomeres. *Adv. Sci.* **2021**, *8*, 2004320. [CrossRef] [PubMed]
26. Ohta, Y.; Fujii, M.; Takahashi, S.; Takano, A.; Nanki, K.; Matano, M.; Hanyu, H.; Saito, M.; Shimokawa, M.; Nishikori, S.; et al. Cell-matrix interface regulates dormancy in human colon cancer stem cells. *Nature* **2022**, *608*, 784–794. [CrossRef] [PubMed]
27. Perekatt, A.O.; Shah, P.P.; Cheung, S.; Jariwala, N.; Wu, A.; Gandhi, V.; Kumar, N.; Feng, Q.; Patel, N.; Chen, L.; et al. SMAD4 Suppresses WNT-Driven Dedifferentiation and Oncogenesis in the Differentiated Gut Epithelium. *Cancer Res.* **2018**, *78*, 4878–4890. [CrossRef]

28. Mani, S.A.; Guo, W.; Liao, M.J.; Eaton, E.N.; Ayyanan, A.; Zhou, A.Y.; Brooks, M.; Reinhard, F.; Zhang, C.C.; Shipitsin, M.; et al. The epithelial-mesenchymal transition generates cells with properties of stem cells. *Cell* **2008**, *133*, 704–715. [CrossRef]
29. Barker, N.; van Es, J.H.; Kuipers, J.; Kujala, P.; van den Born, M.; Cozijnsen, M.; Haegebarth, A.; Korving, J.; Begthel, H.; Peters, P.J.; et al. Identification of stem cells in small intestine and colon by marker gene Lgr5. *Nature* **2007**, *449*, 1003–1007. [CrossRef]
30. Barker, N.; Ridgway, R.A.; van Es, J.H.; van de Wetering, M.; Begthel, H.; van den Born, M.; Danenberg, E.; Clarke, A.R.; Sansom, O.J.; Clevers, H. Crypt stem cells as the cells-of-origin of intestinal cancer. *Nature* **2009**, *457*, 608–611. [CrossRef]
31. Llado, V.; Nakanishi, Y.; Duran, A.; Reina-Campos, M.; Shelton, P.M.; Linares, J.F.; Yajima, T.; Campos, A.; Aza-Blanc, P.; Leitges, M.; et al. Repression of Intestinal Stem Cell Function and Tumorigenesis through Direct Phosphorylation of β-Catenin and Yap by PKCζ. *Cell Rep.* **2015**, *10*, 740–754. [CrossRef] [PubMed]
32. Fumagalli, A.; Oost, K.C.; Kester, L.; Morgner, J.; Bornes, L.; Bruens, L.; Spaargaren, L.; Azkanaz, M.; Schelfhorst, T.; Beerling, E.; et al. Plasticity of Lgr5-Negative Cancer Cells Drives Metastasis in Colorectal Cancer. *Cell Stem Cell* **2020**, *26*, 569–578.e7. [CrossRef]
33. Morral, C.; Stanisavljevic, J.; Hernando-Momblona, X.; Mereu, E.; Álvarez-Varela, A.; Cortina, C.; Stork, D.; Slebe, F.; Turon, G.; Whissell, G.; et al. Zonation of Ribosomal DNA Transcription Defines a Stem Cell Hierarchy in Colorectal Cancer. *Cell Stem Cell* **2020**, *26*, 845–861.e12. [CrossRef] [PubMed]
34. Han, T.; Goswami, S.; Hu, Y.; Tang, F.; Zafra, M.P.; Murphy, C.; Cao, Z.; Poirier, J.T.; Khurana, E.; Elemento, O.; et al. Lineage Reversion Drives WNT Independence in Intestinal Cancer. *Cancer Discov.* **2020**, *10*, 1590–1609. [CrossRef] [PubMed]
35. Vasquez, E.G.; Nasreddin, N.; Valbuena, G.N.; Mulholland, E.J.; Belnoue-Davis, H.L.; Eggington, H.R.; Schenck, R.O.; Wouters, V.M.; Wirapati, P.; Gilroy, K.; et al. Dynamic and adaptive cancer stem cell population admixture in colorectal neoplasia. *Cell Stem Cell* **2022**, *29*, 1213–1228.e8. [CrossRef] [PubMed]
36. Makena, M.R.; Ranjan, A.; Thirumala, V.; Reddy, A.P. Cancer stem cells: Road to therapeutic resistance and strategies to overcome resistance. *Biochim. Biophys. Acta Mol. Basis Dis.* **2020**, *1866*, 165339. [CrossRef]
37. Sato, T.; Vries, R.G.; Snippert, H.J.; van de Wetering, M.; Barker, N.; Stange, D.E.; van Es, J.H.; Abo, A.; Kujala, P.; Peters, P.J.; et al. Single Lgr5 stem cells build crypt-villus structures in vitro without a mesenchymal niche. *Nature* **2009**, *459*, 262–265. [CrossRef]
38. Ricci-Vitiani, L.; Lombardi, D.G.; Pilozzi, E.; Biffoni, M.; Todaro, M.; Peschle, C.; De Maria, R. Identification and expansion of human colon-cancer-initiating cells. *Nature* **2007**, *445*, 111–115. [CrossRef]
39. Li, G.; Liu, C.; Yuan, J.; Xiao, X.; Tang, N.; Hao, J.; Wang, H.; Bian, X.; Deng, Y.; Ding, Y. CD133(+) single cell-derived progenies of colorectal cancer cell line SW480 with different invasive and metastatic potential. *Clin. Exp. Metastasis* **2010**, *27*, 517–527. [CrossRef]
40. Greve, B.; Kelsch, R.; Spaniol, K.; Eich, H.T.; Götte, M. Flow cytometry in cancer stem cell analysis and separation. *Cytom. Part A* **2012**, *81*, 284–293. [CrossRef]
41. Pang, R.; Law, W.L.; Chu, A.C.; Poon, J.T.; Lam, C.S.; Chow, A.K.; Ng, L.; Cheung, L.W.; Lan, X.R.; Lan, H.Y.; et al. A subpopulation of CD26+ cancer stem cells with metastatic capacity in human colorectal cancer. *Cell Stem Cell* **2010**, *6*, 603–615. [CrossRef]
42. Choi, D.; Lee, H.W.; Hur, K.Y.; Kim, J.J.; Park, G.S.; Jang, S.H.; Song, Y.S.; Jang, K.S.; Paik, S.S. Cancer stem cell markers CD133 and CD24 correlate with invasiveness and differentiation in colorectal adenocarcinoma. *World J. Gastroenterol.* **2009**, *15*, 2258–2264. [CrossRef]
43. Fujimoto, K.; Beauchamp, R.D.; Whitehead, R.H. Identification and isolation of candidate human colonic clonogenic cells based on cell surface integrin expression. *Gastroenterology* **2002**, *123*, 1941–1948. [CrossRef] [PubMed]
44. Dalerba, P.; Dylla, S.J.; Park, I.K.; Liu, R.; Wang, X.; Cho, R.W.; Hoey, T.; Gurney, A.; Huang, E.H.; Simeone, D.M.; et al. Phenotypic characterization of human colorectal cancer stem cells. *Proc. Natl. Acad. Sci. USA* **2007**, *104*, 10158–10163. [CrossRef] [PubMed]
45. Munz, M.; Baeuerle, P.A.; Gires, O. The emerging role of EpCAM in cancer and stem cell signaling. *Cancer Res.* **2009**, *69*, 5627–5629. [CrossRef]
46. Huang, E.H.; Hynes, M.J.; Zhang, T.; Ginestier, C.; Dontu, G.; Appelman, H.; Fields, J.Z.; Wicha, M.S.; Boman, B.M. Aldehyde dehydrogenase 1 is a marker for normal and malignant human colonic stem cells (SC) and tracks SC overpopulation during colon tumorigenesis. *Cancer Res.* **2009**, *69*, 3382–3389. [CrossRef]
47. Chen, Y.C.; Hsu, H.S.; Chen, Y.W.; Tsai, T.H.; How, C.K.; Wang, C.Y.; Hung, S.C.; Chang, Y.L.; Tsai, M.L.; Lee, Y.Y.; et al. Oct-4 expression maintained cancer stem-like properties in lung cancer-derived CD133-positive cells. *PLoS ONE* **2008**, *3*, e2637. [CrossRef] [PubMed]
48. Tang, Q.; Chen, J.; Di, Z.; Yuan, W.; Zhou, Z.; Liu, Z.; Han, S.; Liu, Y.; Ying, G.; Shu, X.; et al. TM4SF1 promotes EMT and cancer stemness via the Wnt/β-catenin/SOX2 pathway in colorectal cancer. *J. Exp. Clin. Cancer Res.* **2020**, *39*, 232. [CrossRef]
49. Yao, C.; Su, L.; Shan, J.; Zhu, C.; Liu, L.; Liu, C.; Xu, Y.; Yang, Z.; Bian, X.; Shao, J.; et al. IGF/STAT3/NANOG/Slug Signaling Axis Simultaneously Controls Epithelial-Mesenchymal Transition and Stemness Maintenance in Colorectal Cancer. *Stem Cells* **2016**, *34*, 820–831. [CrossRef]
50. Wu, A.; Oh, S.; Wiesner, S.M.; Ericson, K.; Chen, L.; Hall, W.A.; Champoux, P.E.; Low, W.C.; Ohlfest, J.R. Persistence of CD133+ cells in human and mouse glioma cell lines: Detailed characterization of GL261 glioma cells with cancer stem cell-like properties. *Stem Cells Dev.* **2008**, *17*, 173–184. [CrossRef]
51. Elkashty, O.A.; Abu Elghanam, G.; Su, X.; Liu, Y.; Chauvin, P.J.; Tran, S.D. Cancer stem cells enrichment with surface markers CD271 and CD44 in human head and neck squamous cell carcinomas. *Carcinogenesis* **2020**, *41*, 458–466. [CrossRef]

52. Liu, L.; Borlak, J. Advances in Liver Cancer Stem Cell Isolation and their Characterization. *Stem Cell Rev. Rep.* **2021**, *17*, 1215–1238. [CrossRef] [PubMed]
53. Kharchenko, P.V. The triumphs and limitations of computational methods for scRNA-seq. *Nat. Methods* **2021**, *18*, 723–732. [CrossRef] [PubMed]
54. Frank, M.H.; Wilson, B.J.; Gold, J.S.; Frank, N.Y. Clinical Implications of Colorectal Cancer Stem Cells in the Age of Single-Cell Omics and Targeted Therapies. *Gastroenterology* **2021**, *160*, 1947–1960. [CrossRef] [PubMed]
55. Zheng, H.; Liu, H.; Li, H.; Dou, W.; Wang, J.; Zhang, J.; Liu, T.; Wu, Y.; Liu, Y.; Wang, X. Characterization of stem cell landscape and identification of stemness-relevant prognostic gene signature to aid immunotherapy in colorectal cancer. *Stem Cell Res. Ther.* **2022**, *13*, 244. [CrossRef] [PubMed]
56. Chen, S.F.; Chang, Y.C.; Nieh, S.; Liu, C.L.; Yang, C.Y.; Lin, Y.S. Nonadhesive culture system as a model of rapid sphere formation with cancer stem cell properties. *PLoS ONE* **2012**, *7*, e31864. [CrossRef] [PubMed]
57. Zhang, J.; Zhang, Y.; Cheng, L.; Li, C.; Dai, L.; Zhang, H.; Yan, F.; Shi, H.; Dong, G.; Ning, Z.; et al. Enrichment and characterization of cancer stem-like cells in ultra-low concentration of serum and non-adhesive culture system. *Am. J. Transl. Res.* **2018**, *10*, 1552–1561.
58. Chaicharoenaudomrung, N.; Kunhorm, P.; Noisa, P. Three-dimensional cell culture systems as an in vitro platform for cancer and stem cell modeling. *World J. Stem Cells* **2019**, *11*, 1065–1083. [CrossRef]
59. Hoarau-Véchot, J.; Rafii, A.; Touboul, C.; Pasquier, J. Halfway between 2D and Animal Models: Are 3D Cultures the Ideal Tool to Study Cancer-Microenvironment Interactions? *Int. J. Mol. Sci.* **2018**, *19*, 181. [CrossRef]
60. Guo, X.; Chen, Y.; Ji, W.; Chen, X.; Li, C.; Ge, R. Enrichment of cancer stem cells by agarose multi-well dishes and 3D spheroid culture. *Cell Tissue Res.* **2019**, *375*, 397–408. [CrossRef]
61. Gjorevski, N.; Sachs, N.; Manfrin, A.; Giger, S.; Bragina, M.E.; Ordóñez-Morán, P.; Clevers, H.; Lutolf, M.P. Designer matrices for intestinal stem cell and organoid culture. *Nature* **2016**, *539*, 560–564. [CrossRef] [PubMed]
62. Clevers, H. Modeling Development and Disease with Organoids. *Cell* **2016**, *165*, 1586–1597. [CrossRef]
63. Huang, L.; Holtzinger, A.; Jagan, I.; BeGora, M.; Lohse, I.; Ngai, N.; Nostro, C.; Wang, R.; Muthuswamy, L.B.; Crawford, H.C.; et al. Ductal pancreatic cancer modeling and drug screening using human pluripotent stem cell- and patient-derived tumor organoids. *Nat. Med.* **2015**, *21*, 1364–1371. [CrossRef] [PubMed]
64. Herpers, B.; Eppink, B.; James, M.I.; Cortina, C.; Cañellas-Socias, A.; Boj, S.F.; Hernando-Momblona, X.; Glodzik, D.; Roovers, R.C.; van de Wetering, M.; et al. Functional patient-derived organoid screenings identify MCLA-158 as a therapeutic EGFR × LGR5 bispecific antibody with efficacy in epithelial tumors. *Nat. Cancer* **2022**, *3*, 418–436. [CrossRef] [PubMed]
65. Frampton, J.E. Catumaxomab: In malignant ascites. *Drugs* **2012**, *72*, 1399–1410. [CrossRef]
66. Bezan, A.; Hohla, F.; Meissnitzer, T.; Greil, R. Systemic effect of catumaxomab in a patient with metastasized colorectal cancer: A case report. *BMC Cancer* **2013**, *13*, 618. [CrossRef]
67. Ströhlein, M.A.; Lordick, F.; Rüttinger, D.; Grützner, K.U.; Schemanski, O.C.; Jäger, M.; Lindhofer, H.; Hennig, M.; Jauch, K.W.; Peschel, C.; et al. Immunotherapy of peritoneal carcinomatosis with the antibody catumaxomab in colon, gastric, or pancreatic cancer: An open-label, multicenter, phase I/II trial. *Onkologie* **2011**, *34*, 101–108. [CrossRef]
68. Bellone, S.; Black, J.; English, D.P.; Schwab, C.L.; Lopez, S.; Cocco, E.; Bonazzoli, E.; Predolini, F.; Ferrari, F.; Ratner, E.; et al. Solitomab, an EpCAM/CD3 bispecific antibody construct (BiTE), is highly active against primary uterine serous papillary carcinoma cell lines in vitro. *Am. J. Obstet. Gynecol.* **2016**, *214*, 99.e1–99.e8. [CrossRef]
69. Herrmann, I.; Baeuerle, P.A.; Friedrich, M.; Murr, A.; Filusch, S.; Rüttinger, D.; Majdoub, M.W.; Sharma, S.; Kufer, P.; Raum, T.; et al. Highly efficient elimination of colorectal tumor-initiating cells by an EpCAM/CD3-bispecific antibody engaging human T cells. *PLoS ONE* **2010**, *5*, e13474. [CrossRef]
70. Wang, Y.; Chen, M.; Wu, Z.; Tong, C.; Dai, H.; Guo, Y.; Liu, Y.; Huang, J.; Lv, H.; Luo, C.; et al. CD133-directed CAR T cells for advanced metastasis malignancies: A phase I trial. *Oncoimmunology* **2018**, *7*, e1440169. [CrossRef]
71. Silva Galbiatti-Dias, A.L.; Fernandes, G.M.M.; Castanhole-Nunes, M.M.U.; Hidalgo, L.F.; Nascimento Filho, C.H.V.; Kawasaki-Oyama, R.S.; Ferreira, L.A.M.; Biselli-Chicote, P.M.; Pavarino, É.C.; Goloni-Bertollo, E.M. Relationship between CD44(high)/CD133(high)/CD117(high) cancer stem cells phenotype and Cetuximab and Paclitaxel treatment response in head and neck cancer cell lines. *Am. J. Cancer Res.* **2018**, *8*, 1633–1641. [PubMed]
72. Yaeger, R.; Weiss, J.; Pelster, M.S.; Spira, A.I.; Barve, M.; Ou, S.I.; Leal, T.A.; Bekaii-Saab, T.S.; Paweletz, C.P.; Heavey, G.A.; et al. Adagrasib with or without Cetuximab in Colorectal Cancer with Mutated KRAS G12C. *N. Engl. J. Med.* **2023**, *388*, 44–54. [CrossRef]
73. Tabernero, J.; Grothey, A.; Van Cutsem, E.; Yaeger, R.; Wasan, H.; Yoshino, T.; Desai, J.; Ciardiello, F.; Loupakis, F.; Hong, Y.S.; et al. Encorafenib Plus Cetuximab as a New Standard of Care for Previously Treated BRAF V600E-Mutant Metastatic Colorectal Cancer: Updated Survival Results and Subgroup Analyses from the BEACON Study. *J. Clin. Oncol.* **2021**, *39*, 273–284. [CrossRef] [PubMed]
74. Sato-Dahlman, M.; Miura, Y.; Huang, J.L.; Hajeri, P.; Jacobsen, K.; Davydova, J.; Yamamoto, M. CD133-targeted oncolytic adenovirus demonstrates anti-tumor effect in colorectal cancer. *Oncotarget* **2017**, *8*, 76044–76056. [CrossRef] [PubMed]
75. Masuda, M.; Uno, Y.; Ohbayashi, N.; Ohata, H.; Mimata, A.; Kukimoto-Niino, M.; Moriyama, H.; Kashimoto, S.; Inoue, T.; Goto, N.; et al. TNIK inhibition abrogates colorectal cancer stemness. *Nat. Commun.* **2016**, *7*, 12586. [CrossRef]

76. Chen, Y.; Wang, X.Q.; Zhang, Q.; Zhu, J.Y.; Li, Y.; Xie, C.F.; Li, X.T.; Wu, J.S.; Geng, S.S.; Zhong, C.Y.; et al. (-)-Epigallocatechin-3-Gallate Inhibits Colorectal Cancer Stem Cells by Suppressing Wnt/β-Catenin Pathway. *Nutrients* **2017**, *9*, 572. [CrossRef] [PubMed]
77. Toden, S.; Tran, H.M.; Tovar-Camargo, O.A.; Okugawa, Y.; Goel, A. Epigallocatechin-3-gallate targets cancer stem-like cells and enhances 5-fluorouracil chemosensitivity in colorectal cancer. *Oncotarget* **2016**, *7*, 16158–16171. [CrossRef]
78. Wu, X.; Luo, F.; Li, J.; Zhong, X.; Liu, K. Tankyrase 1 inhibitior XAV939 increases chemosensitivity in colon cancer cell lines via inhibition of the Wnt signaling pathway. *Int. J. Oncol.* **2016**, *48*, 1333–1340. [CrossRef]
79. Chen, Y.; Wang, M.H.; Zhu, J.Y.; Xie, C.F.; Li, X.T.; Wu, J.S.; Geng, S.S.; Han, H.Y.; Zhong, C.Y. TAp63α targeting of Lgr5 mediates colorectal cancer stem cell properties and sulforaphane inhibition. *Oncogenesis* **2020**, *9*, 89. [CrossRef]
80. Chen, Y.; Li, Y.; Wang, X.Q.; Meng, Y.; Zhang, Q.; Zhu, J.Y.; Chen, J.Q.; Cao, W.S.; Wang, X.Q.; Xie, C.F.; et al. Phenethyl isothiocyanate inhibits colorectal cancer stem cells by suppressing Wnt/β-catenin pathway. *Phytother. Res. PTR* **2018**, *32*, 2447–2455. [CrossRef]
81. Alumkal, J.J.; Slottke, R.; Schwartzman, J.; Cherala, G.; Munar, M.; Graff, J.N.; Beer, T.M.; Ryan, C.W.; Koop, D.R.; Gibbs, A.; et al. A phase II study of sulforaphane-rich broccoli sprout extracts in men with recurrent prostate cancer. *Investig. New Drugs* **2015**, *33*, 480–489. [CrossRef]
82. Wang, Z.; Zhou, L.; Xiong, Y.; Yu, S.; Li, H.; Fan, J.; Li, F.; Su, Z.; Song, J.; Sun, Q.; et al. Salinomycin exerts anti-colorectal cancer activity by targeting the β-catenin/T-cell factor complex. *Br. J. Pharmacol.* **2019**, *176*, 3390–3406. [CrossRef] [PubMed]
83. Wang, L.; Chang, J.; Varghese, D.; Dellinger, M.; Kumar, S.; Best, A.M.; Ruiz, J.; Bruick, R.; Peña-Llopis, S.; Xu, J.; et al. A small molecule modulates Jumonji histone demethylase activity and selectively inhibits cancer growth. *Nat. Commun.* **2013**, *4*, 2035. [CrossRef] [PubMed]
84. Hsu, H.C.; Liu, Y.S.; Tseng, K.C.; Yang, T.S.; Yeh, C.Y.; You, J.F.; Hung, H.Y.; Chen, S.J.; Chen, H.C. CBB1003, a lysine-specific demethylase 1 inhibitor, suppresses colorectal cancer cells growth through down-regulation of leucine-rich repeat-containing G-protein-coupled receptor 5 expression. *J. Cancer Res. Clin. Oncol.* **2015**, *141*, 11–21. [CrossRef] [PubMed]
85. Yang, W.; Li, Y.; Ai, Y.; Obianom, O.N.; Guo, D.; Yang, H.; Sakamuru, S.; Xia, M.; Shu, Y.; Xue, F. Pyrazole-4-Carboxamide (YW2065): A Therapeutic Candidate for Colorectal Cancer via Dual Activities of Wnt/β-Catenin Signaling Inhibition and AMP-Activated Protein Kinase (AMPK) Activation. *J. Med. Chem.* **2019**, *62*, 11151–11164. [CrossRef]
86. Fang, L.; Zhu, Q.; Neuenschwander, M.; Specker, E.; Wulf-Goldenberg, A.; Weis, W.I.; von Kries, J.P.; Birchmeier, W. A Small-Molecule Antagonist of the β-Catenin/TCF4 Interaction Blocks the Self-Renewal of Cancer Stem Cells and Suppresses Tumorigenesis. *Cancer Res.* **2016**, *76*, 891–901. [CrossRef]
87. Shin, J.H.; Jeong, J.; Choi, J.; Lim, J.; Dinesh, R.K.; Braverman, J.; Hong, J.Y.; Maher, S.E.; Amezcua Vesely, M.C.; Kim, W.; et al. Dickkopf-2 regulates the stem cell marker LGR5 in colorectal cancer via HNF4α1. *iScience* **2021**, *24*, 102411. [CrossRef] [PubMed]
88. Roy, S.; Zhao, Y.; Yuan, Y.C.; Goel, A. Metformin and ICG-001 Act Synergistically to Abrogate Cancer Stem Cells-Mediated Chemoresistance in Colorectal Cancer by Promoting Apoptosis and Autophagy. *Cancers* **2022**, *14*, 1281. [CrossRef] [PubMed]
89. Bamodu, O.A.; Yang, C.K.; Cheng, W.H.; Tzeng, D.T.W.; Kuo, K.T.; Huang, C.C.; Deng, L.; Hsiao, M.; Lee, W.H.; Yeh, C.T. 4-Acetyl-Antroquinonol B Suppresses SOD2-Enhanced Cancer Stem Cell-Like Phenotypes and Chemoresistance of Colorectal Cancer Cells by Inducing hsa-miR-324 re-Expression. *Cancers* **2018**, *10*, 269. [CrossRef]
90. Chang, T.C.; Yeh, C.T.; Adebayo, B.O.; Lin, Y.C.; Deng, L.; Rao, Y.K.; Huang, C.C.; Lee, W.H.; Wu, A.T.; Hsiao, M.; et al. 4-Acetylantroquinonol B inhibits colorectal cancer tumorigenesis and suppresses cancer stem-like phenotype. *Toxicol. Appl. Pharmacol.* **2015**, *288*, 258–268. [CrossRef]
91. Zhang, Q.; Li, X.T.; Chen, Y.; Chen, J.Q.; Zhu, J.Y.; Meng, Y.; Wang, X.Q.; Li, Y.; Geng, S.S.; Xie, C.F.; et al. Wnt/β-catenin signaling mediates the suppressive effects of diallyl trisulfide on colorectal cancer stem cells. *Cancer Chemother. Pharmacol.* **2018**, *81*, 969–977. [CrossRef]
92. Kumar, B.; Ahmad, R.; Sharma, S.; Gowrikumar, S.; Primeaux, M.; Rana, S.; Natarajan, A.; Oupicky, D.; Hopkins, C.R.; Dhawan, P.; et al. PIK3C3 Inhibition Promotes Sensitivity to Colon Cancer Therapy by Inhibiting Cancer Stem Cells. *Cancers* **2021**, *13*, 2168. [CrossRef]
93. Kim, H.; Yu, Y.; Choi, S.; Lee, H.; Yu, J.; Lee, J.H.; Kim, W.Y. Evodiamine Eliminates Colon Cancer Stem Cells via Suppressing Notch and Wnt Signaling. *Molecules* **2019**, *24*, 4520. [CrossRef]
94. Husain, K.; Coppola, D.; Yang, C.S.; Malafa, M.P. Farnesyl dimethyl chromanol targets colon cancer stem cells and prevents colorectal cancer metastasis. *Sci. Rep.* **2021**, *11*, 2185. [CrossRef]
95. Chen, Y.; Rao, X.; Huang, K.; Jiang, X.; Wang, H.; Teng, L. FH535 Inhibits Proliferation and Motility of Colon Cancer Cells by Targeting Wnt/β-catenin Signaling Pathway. *J. Cancer* **2017**, *8*, 3142–3153. [CrossRef]
96. Lin, D.; Shen, Y.; Liang, T. Oncolytic virotherapy: Basic principles, recent advances and future directions. *Signal Transduct. Target. Ther.* **2023**, *8*, 156. [CrossRef]
97. Zhao, F.; Zhang, R.; Wang, J.; Wu, D.; Pan, M.; Li, M.; Guo, M.; Dou, J. Effective tumor immunity to melanoma mediated by B16F10 cancer stem cell vaccine. *Int. Immunopharmacol.* **2017**, *52*, 238–244. [CrossRef] [PubMed]
98. Hubbard, J.M.; Tőke, E.R.; Moretto, R.; Graham, R.P.; Youssoufian, H.; Lőrincz, O.; Molnár, L.; Csiszovszki, Z.; Mitchell, J.L.; Wessling, J.; et al. Safety and Activity of PolyPEPI1018 Combined with Maintenance Therapy in Metastatic Colorectal Cancer: An Open-Label, Multicenter, Phase Ib Study. *Clin. Cancer Res.* **2022**, *28*, 2818–2829. [CrossRef] [PubMed]

99. Katoh, M. Canonical and non-canonical WNT signaling in cancer stem cells and their niches: Cellular heterogeneity, omics reprogramming, targeted therapy and tumor plasticity (Review). *Int. J. Oncol.* **2017**, *51*, 1357–1369. [CrossRef] [PubMed]
100. Silva, V.R.; Santos, L.S.; Dias, R.B.; Quadros, C.A.; Bezerra, D.P. Emerging agents that target signaling pathways to eradicate colorectal cancer stem cells. *Cancer Commun.* **2021**, *41*, 1275–1313. [CrossRef]
101. Sun, X.; Song, J.; Li, E.; Geng, H.; Li, Y.; Yu, D.; Zhong, C. (-)-Epigallocatechin-3-gallate inhibits bladder cancer stem cells via suppression of sonic hedgehog pathway. *Oncol. Rep.* **2019**, *42*, 425–435. [CrossRef] [PubMed]
102. Jiang, P.; Xu, C.; Zhang, P.; Ren, J.; Mageed, F.; Wu, X.; Chen, L.; Zeb, F.; Feng, Q.; Li, S. Epigallocatechin-3-gallate inhibits self-renewal ability of lung cancer stem-like cells through inhibition of CLOCK. *Int. J. Mol. Med.* **2020**, *46*, 2216–2224. [CrossRef]
103. Wang, D.; Upadhyaya, B.; Liu, Y.; Knudsen, D.; Dey, M. Phenethyl isothiocyanate upregulates death receptors 4 and 5 and inhibits proliferation in human cancer stem-like cells. *BMC Cancer* **2014**, *14*, 591. [CrossRef] [PubMed]
104. Dong, T.T.; Zhou, H.M.; Wang, L.L.; Feng, B.; Lv, B.; Zheng, M.H. Salinomycin selectively targets 'CD133+' cell subpopulations and decreases malignant traits in colorectal cancer lines. *Ann. Surg. Oncol.* **2011**, *18*, 1797–1804. [CrossRef]
105. Zhang, C.; Tian, Y.; Song, F.; Fu, C.; Han, B.; Wang, Y. Salinomycin inhibits the growth of colorectal carcinoma by targeting tumor stem cells. *Oncol. Rep.* **2015**, *34*, 2469–2476. [CrossRef]
106. Takebe, N.; Miele, L.; Harris, P.J.; Jeong, W.; Bando, H.; Kahn, M.; Yang, S.X.; Ivy, S.P. Targeting Notch, Hedgehog, and Wnt pathways in cancer stem cells: Clinical update. *Nat. Rev. Clin. Oncol.* **2015**, *12*, 445–464. [CrossRef] [PubMed]
107. Varjosalo, M.; Taipale, J. Hedgehog: Functions and mechanisms. *Genes Dev.* **2008**, *22*, 2454–2472. [CrossRef]
108. Cochrane, C.R.; Szczepny, A.; Watkins, D.N.; Cain, J.E. Hedgehog Signaling in the Maintenance of Cancer Stem Cells. *Cancers* **2015**, *7*, 1554–1585. [CrossRef]
109. Frampton, J.E.; Basset-Séguin, N. Vismodegib: A Review in Advanced Basal Cell Carcinoma. *Drugs* **2018**, *78*, 1145–1156. [CrossRef]
110. Wu, C.; Hu, S.; Cheng, J.; Wang, G.; Tao, K. Smoothened antagonist GDC-0449 (Vismodegib) inhibits proliferation and triggers apoptosis in colon cancer cell lines. *Exp. Ther. Med.* **2017**, *13*, 2529–2536. [CrossRef]
111. Batsaikhan, B.E.; Yoshikawa, K.; Kurita, N.; Iwata, T.; Takasu, C.; Kashihara, H.; Shimada, M. Cyclopamine decreased the expression of Sonic Hedgehog and its downstream genes in colon cancer stem cells. *Anticancer Res.* **2014**, *34*, 6339–6344.
112. Smith, D.C.; Eisenberg, P.D.; Manikhas, G.; Chugh, R.; Gubens, M.A.; Stagg, R.J.; Kapoun, A.M.; Xu, L.; Dupont, J.; Sikic, B. A phase I dose escalation and expansion study of the anticancer stem cell agent demcizumab (anti-DLL4) in patients with previously treated solid tumors. *Clin. Cancer Res.* **2014**, *20*, 6295–6303. [CrossRef]
113. Strosberg, J.R.; Yeatman, T.; Weber, J.; Coppola, D.; Schell, M.J.; Han, G.; Almhanna, K.; Kim, R.; Valone, T.; Jump, H.; et al. A phase II study of RO4929097 in metastatic colorectal cancer. *Eur. J. Cancer* **2012**, *48*, 997–1003. [CrossRef]
114. Fischer, M.; Yen, W.C.; Kapoun, A.M.; Wang, M.; O'Young, G.; Lewicki, J.; Gurney, A.; Hoey, T. Anti-DLL4 inhibits growth and reduces tumor-initiating cell frequency in colorectal tumors with oncogenic KRAS mutations. *Cancer Res.* **2011**, *71*, 1520–1525. [CrossRef]
115. Ponnurangam, S.; Mammen, J.M.; Ramalingam, S.; He, Z.; Zhang, Y.; Umar, S.; Subramaniam, D.; Anant, S. Honokiol in combination with radiation targets notch signaling to inhibit colon cancer stem cells. *Mol. Cancer Ther.* **2012**, *11*, 963–972. [CrossRef]
116. Li, Y.; Wang, Z.; Jin, J.; Zhu, S.X.; He, G.Q.; Li, S.H.; Wang, J.; Cai, Y. Quercetin pretreatment enhances the radiosensitivity of colon cancer cells by targeting Notch-1 pathway. *Biochem. Biophys. Res. Commun.* **2020**, *523*, 947–953. [CrossRef]
117. Chandra Boinpelly, V.; Verma, R.K.; Srivastav, S.; Srivastava, R.K.; Shankar, S. α-Mangostin-encapsulated PLGA nanoparticles inhibit colorectal cancer growth by inhibiting Notch pathway. *J. Cell. Mol. Med.* **2020**, *24*, 11343–11354. [CrossRef] [PubMed]
118. Chen, J.; Shao, R.; Li, F.; Monteiro, M.; Liu, J.P.; Xu, Z.P.; Gu, W. PI3K/Akt/mTOR pathway dual inhibitor BEZ235 suppresses the stemness of colon cancer stem cells. *Clin. Exp. Pharmacol. Physiol.* **2015**, *42*, 1317–1326. [CrossRef]
119. Wise-Draper, T.M.; Moorthy, G.; Salkeni, M.A.; Karim, N.A.; Thomas, H.E.; Mercer, C.A.; Beg, M.S.; O'Gara, S.; Olowokure, O.; Fathallah, H.; et al. A Phase Ib Study of the Dual PI3K/mTOR Inhibitor Dactolisib (BEZ235) Combined with Everolimus in Patients with Advanced Solid Malignancies. *Target. Oncol.* **2017**, *12*, 323–332. [CrossRef] [PubMed]
120. Peng, Y.C.; Lu, S.D.; Zhong, J.H.; Xie, Z.B.; You, X.M.; Peng, N.F.; Li, L.Q. Combination of 5-fluorouracil and 2-morphilino-8-phenyl-4H-chromen-4-one may inhibit liver cancer stem cell activity. *Tumour Biol.* **2016**, *37*, 10943–10958. [CrossRef] [PubMed]
121. Tanaka, G.; Inoue, K.; Shimizu, T.; Akimoto, K.; Kubota, K. Dual pharmacological inhibition of glutathione and thioredoxin systems synergizes to kill colorectal carcinoma stem cells. *Cancer Med.* **2016**, *5*, 2544–2557. [CrossRef]
122. Kumar, S.; Agnihotri, N. Piperlongumine, a piper alkaloid targets Ras/PI3K/Akt/mTOR signaling axis to inhibit tumor cell growth and proliferation in DMH/DSS induced experimental colon cancer. *Biomed. Pharmacother.* **2019**, *109*, 1462–1477. [CrossRef]
123. Cai, Z.; Ke, J.; He, X.; Yuan, R.; Chen, Y.; Wu, X.; Wang, L.; Wang, J.; Lan, P.; Wu, X. Significance of mTOR signaling and its inhibitor against cancer stem-like cells in colorectal cancer. *Ann. Surg. Oncol.* **2014**, *21*, 179–188. [CrossRef]
124. Ji, N.; Mukherjee, N.; Reyes, R.M.; Gelfond, J.; Javors, M.; Meeks, J.J.; McConkey, D.J.; Shu, Z.J.; Ramamurthy, C.; Dennett, R.; et al. Rapamycin enhances BCG-specific γδ T cells during intravesical BCG therapy for non-muscle invasive bladder cancer: A randomized, double-blind study. *J. Immunother. Cancer* **2021**, *9*, e001941. [CrossRef]
125. Seo, Y.; Kim, J.; Park, S.J.; Park, J.J.; Cheon, J.H.; Kim, W.H.; Kim, T.I. Metformin Suppresses Cancer Stem Cells through AMPK Activation and Inhibition of Protein Prenylation of the Mevalonate Pathway in Colorectal Cancer. *Cancers* **2020**, *12*, 2554. [CrossRef]

126. Wang, K.; Huang, W.; Sang, X.; Wu, X.; Shan, Q.; Tang, D.; Xu, X.; Cao, G. Atractylenolide I inhibits colorectal cancer cell proliferation by affecting metabolism and stemness via AKT/mTOR signaling. *Phytomedicine Int. J. Phytother. Phytopharm.* **2020**, *68*, 153191. [CrossRef]
127. Francipane, M.G.; Lagasse, E. Selective targeting of human colon cancer stem-like cells by the mTOR inhibitor Torin-1. *Oncotarget* **2013**, *4*, 1948–1962. [CrossRef] [PubMed]
128. Mangiapane, L.R.; Nicotra, A.; Turdo, A.; Gaggianesi, M.; Bianca, P.; Di Franco, S.; Sardina, D.S.; Veschi, V.; Signore, M.; Beyes, S.; et al. PI3K-driven HER2 expression is a potential therapeutic target in colorectal cancer stem cells. *Gut* **2022**, *71*, 119–128. [CrossRef] [PubMed]
129. Goodwin, R.; Jonker, D.; Chen, E.; Kennecke, H.; Cabanero, M.; Tsao, M.S.; Vickers, M.; Bohemier, C.; Lim, H.; Ritter, H.; et al. A phase Ib study of a PI3Kinase inhibitor BKM120 in combination with panitumumab in patients with KRAS wild-type advanced colorectal cancer. Invest. *New Drugs* **2020**, *38*, 1077–1084. [CrossRef] [PubMed]
130. Malkomes, P.; Lunger, I.; Luetticke, A.; Oppermann, E.; Haetscher, N.; Serve, H.; Holzer, K.; Bechstein, W.O.; Rieger, M.A. Selective AKT Inhibition by MK-2206 Represses Colorectal Cancer-Initiating Stem Cells. *Ann. Surg. Oncol.* **2016**, *23*, 2849–2857. [CrossRef] [PubMed]
131. Do, K.; Speranza, G.; Bishop, R.; Khin, S.; Rubinstein, L.; Kinders, R.J.; Datiles, M.; Eugeni, M.; Lam, M.H.; Doyle, L.A.; et al. Biomarker-driven phase 2 study of MK-2206 and selumetinib (AZD6244, ARRY-142886) in patients with colorectal cancer. *Investig. New Drugs* **2015**, *33*, 720–728. [CrossRef] [PubMed]
132. Lin, L.; Liu, Y.; Li, H.; Li, P.K.; Fuchs, J.; Shibata, H.; Iwabuchi, Y.; Lin, J. Targeting colon cancer stem cells using a new curcumin analogue, GO-Y030. *Br. J. Cancer* **2011**, *105*, 212–220. [CrossRef] [PubMed]
133. Jonker, D.J.; Nott, L.; Yoshino, T.; Gill, S.; Shapiro, J.; Ohtsu, A.; Zalcberg, J.; Vickers, M.M.; Wei, A.C.; Gao, Y.; et al. Napabucasin versus placebo in refractory advanced colorectal cancer: A randomised phase 3 trial. *Lancet Gastroenterol. Hepatol.* **2018**, *3*, 263–270. [CrossRef] [PubMed]
134. Yuan, X.; Wu, H.; Xu, H.; Xiong, H.; Chu, Q.; Yu, S.; Wu, G.S.; Wu, K. Notch signaling: An emerging therapeutic target for cancer treatment. *Cancer Lett.* **2015**, *369*, 20–27. [CrossRef]
135. Bray, S.J. Notch signalling in context. *Nat. Rev. Mol. Cell Biol.* **2016**, *17*, 722–735. [CrossRef] [PubMed]
136. BeLow, M.; Osipo, C. Notch Signaling in Breast Cancer: A Role in Drug Resistance. *Cells* **2020**, *9*, 2204. [CrossRef]
137. Hoey, T.; Yen, W.C.; Axelrod, F.; Basi, J.; Donigian, L.; Dylla, S.; Fitch-Bruhns, M.; Lazetic, S.; Park, I.K.; Sato, A.; et al. DLL4 blockade inhibits tumor growth and reduces tumor-initiating cell frequency. *Cell Stem Cell* **2009**, *5*, 168–177. [CrossRef]
138. Polivka, J., Jr.; Janku, F. Molecular targets for cancer therapy in the PI3K/AKT/mTOR pathway. *Pharmacol. Ther.* **2014**, *142*, 164–175. [CrossRef]
139. Chen, S.; Fisher, R.C.; Signs, S.; Molina, L.A.; Shenoy, A.K.; Lopez, M.C.; Baker, H.V.; Koomen, J.M.; Chen, Y.; Gittleman, H.; et al. Inhibition of PI3K/Akt/mTOR signaling in PI3KR2-overexpressing colon cancer stem cells reduces tumor growth due to apoptosis. *Oncotarget* **2017**, *8*, 50476–50488. [CrossRef]
140. Pei, S.; Minhajuddin, M.; Callahan, K.P.; Balys, M.; Ashton, J.M.; Neering, S.J.; Lagadinou, E.D.; Corbett, C.; Ye, H.; Liesveld, J.L.; et al. Targeting aberrant glutathione metabolism to eradicate human acute myelogenous leukemia cells. *J. Biol. Chem.* **2013**, *288*, 33542–33558. [CrossRef]
141. Song, C.W.; Lee, H.; Dings, R.P.; Williams, B.; Powers, J.; Santos, T.D.; Choi, B.H.; Park, H.J. Metformin kills and radiosensitizes cancer cells and preferentially kills cancer stem cells. *Sci. Rep.* **2012**, *2*, 362. [CrossRef]
142. Saif, M.W.; Rajagopal, S.; Caplain, J.; Goodman, M.D.; Popowich, D.; Orkin, B.A.; Tsichlis, P.N.; Martell, R. The First Study Evaluating the Safety of Pre-Surgery Administration of Metformin in Patients with Colorectal and other Gastrointestinal Cancers and Effect on Cancer Stem Cells. *Cancer Med. J.* **2021**, *4* (Suppl. 4), 1–10.
143. Brooks, A.J.; Putoczki, T. JAK-STAT Signalling Pathway in Cancer. *Cancers* **2020**, *12*, 1971. [CrossRef] [PubMed]
144. Quintás-Cardama, A.; Verstovsek, S. Molecular pathways: Jak/STAT pathway: Mutations, inhibitors, and resistance. *Clin. Cancer Res.* **2013**, *19*, 1933–1940. [CrossRef] [PubMed]
145. Park, S.Y.; Lee, C.J.; Choi, J.H.; Kim, J.H.; Kim, J.W.; Kim, J.Y.; Nam, J.S. The JAK2/STAT3/CCND2 Axis promotes colorectal Cancer stem cell persistence and radioresistance. *J. Exp. Clin. Cancer Res.* **2019**, *38*, 399. [CrossRef] [PubMed]
146. Li, Y.; Rogoff, H.A.; Keates, S.; Gao, Y.; Murikipudi, S.; Mikule, K.; Leggett, D.; Li, W.; Pardee, A.B.; Li, C.J. Suppression of cancer relapse and metastasis by inhibiting cancer stemness. *Proc. Natl. Acad. Sci. USA* **2015**, *112*, 1839–1844. [CrossRef] [PubMed]
147. Li, Y.; Han, Q.; Zhao, H.; Guo, Q.; Zhang, J. Napabucasin Reduces Cancer Stem Cell Characteristics in Hepatocellular Carcinoma. *Front. Pharmacol.* **2020**, *11*, 597520. [CrossRef] [PubMed]
148. Yang, B.; Bai, H.; Sa, Y.; Zhu, P.; Liu, P. Inhibiting EMT, stemness and cell cycle involved in baicalin-induced growth inhibition and apoptosis in colorectal cancer cells. *J. Cancer* **2020**, *11*, 2303–2317. [CrossRef]
149. Song, L.; Li, Z.Y.; Liu, W.P.; Zhao, M.R. Crosstalk between Wnt/β-catenin and Hedgehog/Gli signaling pathways in colon cancer and implications for therapy. *Cancer Biol. Ther.* **2015**, *16*, 1–7. [CrossRef]
150. van den Brink, G.R.; Hardwick, J.C. Hedgehog Wnteraction in colorectal cancer. *Gut* **2006**, *55*, 912–914. [CrossRef]
151. Ahmed, M.; Jinks, N.; Babaei-Jadidi, R.; Kashfi, H.; Castellanos-Uribe, M.; May, S.T.; Mukherjee, A.; Nateri, A.S. Repurposing Antibacterial AM404 as a Potential Anticancer Drug for Targeting Colorectal Cancer Stem-Like Cells. *Cancers* **2019**, *12*, 106. [CrossRef]

152. Manic, G.; Signore, M.; Sistigu, A.; Russo, G.; Corradi, F.; Siteni, S.; Musella, M.; Vitale, S.; De Angelis, M.L.; Pallocca, M.; et al. CHK1-targeted therapy to deplete DNA replication-stressed, p53-deficient, hyperdiploid colorectal cancer stem cells. *Gut* **2018**, *67*, 903–917. [CrossRef]
153. Narayan, S.; Ramisetti, S.; Jaiswal, A.S.; Law, B.K.; Singh-Pillay, A.; Singh, P.; Amin, S.; Sharma, A.K. ASR352, A potent anticancer agent: Synthesis, preliminary SAR, and biological activities against colorectal cancer bulk, 5-fluorouracil/oxaliplatin resistant and stem cells. *Eur. J. Med. Chem.* **2019**, *161*, 456–467. [CrossRef] [PubMed]
154. Narayan, S.; Jaiswal, A.S.; Sharma, R.; Nawab, A.; Duckworth, L.V.; Law, B.K.; Zajac-Kaye, M.; George, T.J.; Sharma, J.; Sharma, A.K.; et al. NSC30049 inhibits Chk1 pathway in 5-FU-resistant CRC bulk and stem cell populations. *Oncotarget* **2017**, *8*, 57246–57264. [CrossRef] [PubMed]
155. Takeda, M.; Koseki, J.; Takahashi, H.; Miyoshi, N.; Nishida, N.; Nishimura, J.; Hata, T.; Matsuda, C.; Mizushima, T.; Yamamoto, H.; et al. Disruption of Endolysosomal RAB5/7 Efficiently Eliminates Colorectal Cancer Stem Cells. *Cancer Res.* **2019**, *79*, 1426–1437. [CrossRef] [PubMed]
156. Zhang, Z.Y.; Zheng, S.H.; Yang, W.G.; Yang, C.; Yuan, W.T. Targeting colon cancer stem cells with novel blood cholesterol drug pitavastatin. *Eur. Rev. Med. Pharmacol. Sci.* **2017**, *21*, 1226–1233.
157. Huang, T.H.; Wu, S.Y.; Huang, Y.J.; Wei, P.L.; Wu, A.T.; Chao, T.Y. The identification and validation of Trichosstatin A as a potential inhibitor of colon tumorigenesis and colon cancer stem-like cells. *Am. J. Cancer Res.* **2017**, *7*, 1227–1237. [PubMed]
158. Bogachek, M.V.; Park, J.M.; De Andrade, J.P.; Lorenzen, A.W.; Kulak, M.V.; White, J.R.; Gu, V.W.; Wu, V.T.; Weigel, R.J. Inhibiting the SUMO Pathway Represses the Cancer Stem Cell Population in Breast and Colorectal Carcinomas. *Stem Cell Rep.* **2016**, *7*, 1140–1151. [CrossRef]
159. Konstantinopoulos, P.A.; Lee, J.M.; Gao, B.; Miller, R.; Lee, J.Y.; Colombo, N.; Vergote, I.; Credille, K.M.; Young, S.R.; McNeely, S.; et al. A Phase 2 study of prexasertib (LY2606368) in platinum resistant or refractory recurrent ovarian cancer. *Gynecol. Oncol.* **2022**, *167*, 213–225. [CrossRef]
160. Wu, Z.; Huang, M.; Gong, Y.; Lin, C.; Guo, W. BRAF and EGFR inhibitors synergize to increase cytotoxic effects and decrease stem cell capacities in BRAF(V600E)-mutant colorectal cancer cells. *Acta Biochim. Biophys. Sin.* **2018**, *50*, 355–361. [CrossRef]
161. Quarni, W.; Dutta, R.; Green, R.; Katiri, S.; Patel, B.; Mohapatra, S.S.; Mohapatra, S. Mithramycin A Inhibits Colorectal Cancer Growth by Targeting Cancer Stem Cells. *Sci. Rep.* **2019**, *9*, 15202. [CrossRef] [PubMed]
162. Zhang, S.; Ju, X.; Yang, Q.; Zhu, Y.; Fan, D.; Su, G.; Kong, L.; Li, Y. USP47 maintains the stemness of colorectal cancer cells and is inhibited by parthenolide. *Biochem. Biophys. Res. Commun.* **2021**, *562*, 21–28. [CrossRef] [PubMed]
163. Wei, F.; Zhang, T.; Yang, Z.; Wei, J.C.; Shen, H.F.; Xiao, D.; Wang, Q.; Yang, P.; Chen, H.C.; Hu, H.J.C.P. Biochemistry, Gambogic Acid Efficiently Kills Stem-Like Colorectal Cancer Cells by Upregulating ZFP36 Expression. *Cell. Physiol. Biochem.* **2018**, *46*, 829–846. [CrossRef] [PubMed]
164. Chi, Y.; Zhan, X.K.; Yu, H.; Xie, G.R.; Wang, Z.Z.; Xiao, W.; Wang, Y.G.; Xiong, F.X.; Hu, J.F.; Yang, L.; et al. An open-labeled, randomized, multicenter phase IIa study of gambogic acid injection for advanced malignant tumors. *Chin. Med. J. Engl.* **2013**, *126*, 1642–1646.
165. Ferguson, L.P.; Diaz, E.; Reya, T. The Role of the Microenvironment and Immune System in Regulating Stem Cell Fate in Cancer. *Trends Cancer* **2021**, *7*, 624–634. [CrossRef]
166. Antonio, N.; Bønnelykke-Behrndtz, M.L.; Ward, L.C.; Collin, J.; Christensen, I.J.; Steiniche, T.; Schmidt, H.; Feng, Y.; Martin, P. The wound inflammatory response exacerbates growth of pre-neoplastic cells and progression to cancer. *EMBO J.* **2015**, *34*, 2219–2236. [CrossRef]
167. Meacham, C.E.; Morrison, S.J. Tumour heterogeneity and cancer cell plasticity. *Nature* **2013**, *501*, 328–337. [CrossRef]
168. Kobayashi, H.; Gieniec, K.A.; Lannagan, T.R.M.; Wang, T.; Asai, N.; Mizutani, Y.; Iida, T.; Ando, R.; Thomas, E.M.; Sakai, A.; et al. The Origin and Contribution of Cancer-Associated Fibroblasts in Colorectal Carcinogenesis. *Gastroenterology* **2022**, *162*, 890–906. [CrossRef] [PubMed]
169. Kozovska, Z.; Gabrisova, V.; Kucerova, L. Colon cancer: Cancer stem cells markers, drug resistance and treatment. *Biomed. Pharmacother.* **2014**, *68*, 911–916. [CrossRef]
170. Li, M.; Younis, M.H.; Zhang, Y.; Cai, W.; Lan, X. Clinical summary of fibroblast activation protein inhibitor-based radiopharmaceuticals: Cancer and beyond. *Eur. J. Nucl. Med. Mol. Imaging* **2022**, *49*, 2844–2868. [CrossRef] [PubMed]
171. Drost, J.; van Jaarsveld, R.H.; Ponsioen, B.; Zimberlin, C.; van Boxtel, R.; Buijs, A.; Sachs, N.; Overmeer, R.M.; Offerhaus, G.J.; Begthel, H.; et al. Sequential cancer mutations in cultured human intestinal stem cells. *Nature* **2015**, *521*, 43–47. [CrossRef] [PubMed]

Disclaimer/Publisher's Note: The statements, opinions and data contained in all publications are solely those of the individual author(s) and contributor(s) and not of MDPI and/or the editor(s). MDPI and/or the editor(s) disclaim responsibility for any injury to people or property resulting from any ideas, methods, instructions or products referred to in the content.

cancers

MDPI

Article

Novel Thienopyrimidine-Hydrazinyl Compounds Induce DRP1-Mediated Non-Apoptotic Cell Death in Triple-Negative Breast Cancer Cells

Saloni Malla [1], Angelique Nyinawabera [1], Rabin Neupane [1], Rajiv Pathak [2], Donghyun Lee [1], Mariam Abou-Dahech [1], Shikha Kumari [1], Suman Sinha [3], Yuan Tang [4], Aniruddha Ray [5], Charles R. Ashby, Jr. [6], Mary Qu Yang [7], R. Jayachandra Babu [8] and Amit K. Tiwari [1,2,*]

1 Department of Pharmacology and Experimental Therapeutics, College of Pharmacy and Pharmaceutical Sciences, University of Toledo, Toledo, OH 43614, USA; saloni.malla@rockets.utoledo.edu (S.M.); angelique.nyinawabera@rockets.utoledo.edu (A.N.); rabin.neupane@rockets.utoledo.edu (R.N.); donghyun.lee@rockets.utoledo.edu (D.L.); mariam.aboudahech@rockets.utoledo.edu (M.A.-D.); shikha.kumari@rockets.utoledo.edu (S.K.)

2 Department of Pharmaceutical Sciences, College of Pharmacy, University of Arkansas for Medical Sciences, Little Rock, AR 72205, USA; rpathak2@uams.edu

3 Institute of Pharmaceutical Research, GLA University, Mathura 281406, UP, India; suman.sinha@gla.ac.in

4 Department of Bioengineering, College of Engineering, University of Toledo, Toledo, OH 43606, USA; yuan.tang@utoledo.edu

5 Department of Physics, College of Math's and Natural Sciences, University of Toledo, Toledo, OH 43606, USA; aniruddha.ray@utoledo.edu

6 Department of Pharmaceutical Sciences, College of Pharmacy, St. John's University, Queens, NY 11439, USA; cnsratdoc@optonline.net

7 MidSouth Bioinformatics Center and Joint Bioinformatics Graduate Program of University of Arkansas at Little Rock, University of Arkansas for Medical Sciences, Little Rock, AR 72204, USA; mqyang@ualr.edu

8 Department of Drug Discovery & Development, Harrison School of Pharmacy, Auburn University, Auburn, AL 36849, USA; ramapjb@auburn.edu

* Correspondence: atiwari@uams.edu; Tel.: +1-501-526-7833

Simple Summary: Triple-negative breast cancer (TNBC) is characterized by the absence of estrogen receptors, progesterone receptors, and human epidermal receptors. This lack of receptors renders TNBC unsuitable for targeted-based treatment, making it the most fatal and aggressive subtype of breast cancer. TNBC has a greater relapse rate, worse prognosis, and increased metastasis rate compared to non-TNBC because of its tendency to resist apoptosis, a programmed cell death triggered by most chemotherapeutic drugs, producing anticancer efficacy. This work describes two new drugs, TPH104c, and TPH104m, that induce a non-apoptotic form of cell death in TNBC. The incubation of TNBC cells with TPH104c or TPH104m causes cellular expansion and rupture without producing apoptotic characteristics, such as nuclear fragmentation, apoptotic blebbing, or caspase activation. TPH104c and TPH104m decreased the mitochondrial protein, division regulator, and dynamin-related protein 1 (DRP1). The level of DRP1 in TNBC cells affects the magnitude of cytotoxicity produced by TPH104c and TPH104m.

Abstract: Apoptosis induction with taxanes or anthracyclines is the primary therapy for TNBC. Cancer cells can develop resistance to anticancer drugs, causing them to recur and metastasize. Therefore, non-apoptotic cell death inducers could be a potential treatment to circumvent apoptotic drug resistance. In this study, we discovered two novel compounds, TPH104c and TPH104m, which induced non-apoptotic cell death in TNBC cells. These lead compounds were 15- to 30-fold more selective in TNBC cell lines and significantly decreased the proliferation of TNBC cells compared to that of normal mammary epithelial cell lines. TPH104c and TPH104m induced a unique type of non-apoptotic cell death, characterized by the absence of cellular shrinkage and the absence of nuclear fragmentation and apoptotic blebs. Although TPH104c and TPH104m induced the loss of the mitochondrial membrane potential, TPH104c- and TPH104m-induced cell death did not increase the levels of cytochrome c and intracellular reactive oxygen species (ROS) and caspase activation, and cell death was not rescued by incubating cells with the pan-caspase inhibitor, carbobenzoxy-valyl-alanyl-aspartyl-[O-methyl]-fluoromethylketone (Z-VAD-FMK). Furthermore, TPH104c and TPH104m significantly downregulated the expression of the mitochondrial fission protein, DRP1, and their levels determined their cytotoxic efficacy. Overall, TPH104c and TPH104m induced non-apoptotic cell death, and further determination of their cell death mechanisms will aid in the development of new potent and efficacious anticancer drugs to treat TNBC.

Keywords: triple-negative breast cancer; multidrug resistance; non-apoptotic cell death; thienopyrimidines; mitochondrial membrane potential; dynamin-related protein 1 (DRP1)

1. Introduction

Triple-negative breast cancer (TNBC) is a subtype of breast cancer that does not express estrogen, progesterone, and HER2 receptors and accounts for 15–20% of breast cancer cases [1]. TNBC exhibits a wide range of morphological, genetic, and clinical variations, and has significant aggressive characteristics [2,3]. TNBC patients have a worse survival rate than non-TNBC patients due to a poorer prognosis and a greater recurrence rate [4,5]. Furthermore, TNBC cannot be treated with hormonal therapy, such as selective estrogen receptor modulators (SERMS), HER2 antagonists, or aromatase inhibitors, which limits treatment options [6]. Currently, there are only limited combinations of immunotherapy and chemotherapy for the treatment of metastatic TNBC (mTNBC). These include atezolizumab (Tecentriq) in combination with nab-paclitaxel and pembrozulizumab (Keytruda) and in combination with paclitaxel-carboplatin, doxorubicin-cyclophosphamide, or epirubicin-cyclophosphamide [7–10]. Similarly, sacituzumab govitecan (Trodelvy) has been approved for patients previously treated for mTNBC with two targeted therapies, and talazoparib (Talzenna) and olaparib (Lynparza) have been approved for mTNBC that contain germline BRCA mutations [11]. Nevertheless, over the past three decades, neoadjuvant anthracyclines, such as doxorubicin and epirubicin, and taxane-based chemotherapeutic regimens, such as paclitaxel and docetaxel, are still the main therapeutic options for patients with early stage TNBC and higher mortality risk [12–14]. Although TNBC patients initially have a therapeutic response to chemotherapy, treatment eventually becomes ineffective after the tumor metastasizes or becomes resistant to chemotherapy [13]. Therefore, treatment will not be therapeutically optimal due to an increase in chemoresistance as well as the occurrence of severe toxicity [15–17].

Resistance to anticancer drugs can be produced by various mechanisms, such as (1) increased expression of certain ATP-binding cassette (ABC) and other efflux transporters [18], (2) resistance to or evasion of apoptosis [19], (3) impairment or decrease in anticancer drug uptake into cells [20], (4) increased DNA damage response and repair [21], (5) increased tolerance of cancer cells to a stressful or non-homeostatic tumor microenvironment [22], (6) mutations in drug targets that significantly decrease or abrogate the interaction of drugs with their cellular targets [23], (7) sequestration of drugs by certain cellular organelles, which decreases the amount of drug that can interact with their cellular target(s) [24–26], and (8) increased systemic or intracellular metabolism of drugs to less efficacious or inactive metabolites [27]. Currently, there is an urgent demand for novel anticancer therapies that can circumvent resistance in cancer cells.

Recently, there has been an increase in the discovery and development of anticancer treatments that induce cancer cell death by mechanisms independent of apoptosis, also known as non-apoptotic cell death, which can surmount resistance to drugs that produce their efficacy by inducing apoptosis [28–30]. Mitochondrial dynamics have garnered attention as a potential target for the treatment of cancer [31–34]. Mitochondrial fission and fusion events, the main processes in mitochondrial dynamics, are involved in maintaining cellular homeostasis [35]. Through this process, cells regulate the number, location, and shape of their mitochondria to meet their energy demands [36]. Dynamin—related protein 1 (DRP1) belongs to the dynamin family of GTPases and regulates mitochondrial dynamics. Upregulation of DRP1, a key protein in mitochondrial fission and a fragmented mitochondrial pattern, occurs in a number of different types of cancer [37–40]. DRP1 has been implicated in increasing the proliferation, migration, and invasiveness of cancers of different origins [31], including breast cancer [38]. In addition, enhanced mitochondrial fission caused by the upregulation of DRP1 has been correlated with poor prognosis in TNBC [40]. Therefore, the development of a potential pharmacophore to target DRP1 and induce non-apoptotic death could be a milestone in addressing drug resistance related to apoptotic cell death.

Heterocyclic compounds containing fused thiophene and pyrimidine rings, such as thieno [2,3-d]pyrimidine, possess structural similarities to purine bases and have been reported to be effective as antibiotics [41], antiviral [42], anti-inflammatory [43], antimicrobial [44], anti-tuberculosis [45], antioxidant [46], and anticancer drugs [38–44]. Furthermore, these compounds can inhibit certain kinases and efflux transporters [47]. Currently, three thieno-pyrimidine-based lead compounds, apitolisib (phosphoinositide-3-kinase (PI3K) and mammalian target of rapamycin (mTOR) kinase inhibitor), SNA-314 Ph1 and pictilisib (inhibitor of PI3Kα and PI3Kδ), are being evaluated for their anticancer efficacy in clinical trials [48–52]. These compounds highlight the importance of thieno-pyrimidine pharmacophores in the development of novel chemotherapeutic molecules. Therefore, in this study, our group has synthesized TPH104c and TPH104m, derived from the parent compound, (*E*)-4-methoxy-2-((2-(5-(*p*-tolyl)thieno [2,3-*d*]pyrimidin-4-yl)hydrazineylidene)methyl)phenol (TPH104) [53,54] and evaluated whether they induce non-apoptotic cell death in TNBC and whether these compounds we found that these compounds dysregulated mitochondrial dynamics by downregulating the protein, DRP1.

2. Materials and Methods

2.1. Cell Lines and Cell Culture

All triple-negative breast cancer (TNBC) cell lines (MDA-MB-231, MDA-MB-468, and BT-20), non-TNBC cell lines (ZR-75-1 and MCF-7), and mouse embryonic fibroblast line (MEF) were generously provided by the late Dr. Gary Kruh (University of Illinois at Chicago, Chicago, IL, USA). The normal human mammary epithelial cell line (HMEC) (Cat: PCS-600- 010), MCF-10A (Cat: CRL10317), and MCF-12A (Cat: CRL10782) were purchased from the American Type Culture Collection (ATCC, Manassas, VA, USA). Likewise, Paclitaxel-resistant SUM159 (PAC200) was developed in collaboration with Dr. Dayanidhi Raman (University of Toledo, Toledo, OH, USA) [55]. TNBC cells were cultured as adherent monolayers in Dulbecco's modified Eagle medium (DMEM) (Corning, Tewksbury, MA, USA). HMEC and MCF-12A were cultured in Mammary Epithelial Cell Basal Medium (ATCC) and Mammary Epithelial Cell Growth Basal Medium (Lonza, Basel, Switzerland), whereas MCF-10A was cultured in DMEM:F12 medium along with supplements as described in this study [56]. These culture media were supplemented with 10% fetal bovine serum (FBS) (Biotechne, Minneapolis, MN, USA), 1% penicillin and streptomycin (Cytiva, Marlborough, MA, USA), and 0.1% plasmocin (Invivogen, San Diego, CA, USA) in a humidified incubator with 5% CO_2 at 37 °C. All cells tested negative for fungus and mycoplasma.

2.2. Cell Cytotoxicity Assay

The cytotoxic efficacy of thienopyrimidine derivatives was determined as previously described, using 3 different assays: (1) (3-(4,5-dimethylthiazol-2-yl)-2,5-diphenyltetrazolium bromide) (MTT) (Avantor, Radnor, PA, USA), (2) CellTiter-Blue (CTB) (Promega, Madison, WI, USA), and (3) sulforhodamine B (SRB) (TargetMol, Boston, MA, USA) assay. For these assays, cells were harvested using 0.05% trypsin-ethylenediamine-tetraacetic acid (EDTA) (Corning, Corning, NY, USA), seeded at a density of 3000–5000 cells/well in a 96-well plate, and incubated at 37 °C overnight. The next day, the cells were incubated with different concentrations of the test compounds (0.1, 0.3, 1, 3, 10, 30, or 100 μM) and incubated for 72 h.

TPH104c and TPH104m were prepared in dimethylsulfoxide (DMSO) (Avantor, Radnor, PA, USA) and then diluted in media to achieve the desired concentration. In contrast, vehicle control (cells incubated in drug-free medium) contained less than 0.1% of DMSO.

For the MTT assay, 4 mg/mL MTT was added to the cells and incubated for 3 h to allow for the conversion of MTT (yellow) to formazan crystals (dark blue). Following incubation, the media was aspirated and DMSO was added to solubilize the formazan crystals. The Cytation 7 Cell Imaging Multi-Mode Reader (Agilent Technologies, Winooski, VT, USA) was used to measure the absorbance at 570 nm.

For the SRB assay, the cells were fixed with 50% (*w*/*v*) tri-chloroacetic acid (TCA) (Avantor, Radnor, PA, USA) and incubated at 4 °C for 1 h. The cells were washed 4 times with deionized, distilled water, and air-dried at room temperature. The next day, the cells were stained with 0.04% (*w*/*v*) SRB solution for 1 h at room temperature and washed 4 times with 1% (*v*/*v*) acetic acid (Avantor, Radnor, PA, USA). After airdrying the plates overnight, 10 mM Tris base solution (pH 10.5) was added to each well and pipetted thoroughly to dissolve the dye, and absorbance was read at 510 nm.

For the CTB assay, the CTB reagent was added to cells and incubated for 3 h to allow the reduction of resazurin (emits a blue color and low fluorescence) by metabolically active cells to resorufin (emits a pink color and high fluorescence). Finally, the plates were shaken for 10 s in a plate shaker, and fluorescence was measured at 560/590 nm.

2.3. *Real-Time Cytotoxicity Assays*

2.3.1. IncuCyte™ Live-Cell Morphology Study

Real-time morphological assessment of the cells was performed using the IncuCyte® S3 Live-Cell Analysis System (Essen BioScience, Ann Arbor, MI, USA), as previously described [53]. Briefly, BT-20 TNBC cells were plated at a cell density of 3000/well and incubated overnight. The next day, cells were incubated in media with or without different concentrations of TPH104c and TPH104m. The plate was incubated in the IncuCyte® S3 Live-Cell Analysis System to capture images every 6 h for 72 h. The integrated IncuCyte S3 software version 2020B was used to analyze the images.

2.3.2. IncuCyte™ Cytotox Green Assay

The real-time assessment of dead BT-20 cells was conducted using the IncuCyte cytotox green reagent (Essence BioScience, Ann Arbor, MI, USA), as described previously [57]. This reagent enters dead or non-viable cells, due to structurally compromised cell membranes and binds to nuclear DNA, resulting in green fluorescence [58]. BT-20 cells were cultured at a density of 3000 cells/well and incubated overnight. The cells were incubated with different concentrations of the test compounds or vehicle, prepared at a 3X concentration in cytotox dye—containing media. The plate was placed in an IncuCyte® S3 Live-Cell Analysis System, which was programmed to obtain images of BT-20 cells, every 6 h for 72 h. Finally, the integrated IncuCyte S3 software version 2020B was used to analyze the mean fluorescence intensity of the cytotox dye in the BT-20 cells.

2.4. *β-Galactosidase Staining*

BT-20 cells were plated at 4000/well into a 96-well plate and incubated overnight. The next day, the cells were incubated with 2 or 5 µM of TPH104c and TPH104m. Four thousand cells/well of senescent MEFs were also seeded. The plate was incubated for 24 h. Once 80–100% confluency was obtained, mouse embryonic fibroblast (MEF) cells were incubated with 250 nM of doxorubicin for 24 h to induce senescence (positive control), followed by a change in media. The cells were incubated for another week and the media was changed every 3–4 days.

The next day, the cells were washed with PBS and fixed with 3% formaldehyde for 5 min. The cells were washed with PBS twice, followed by an addition of β-galactosidase (Research Products International, Racine, WI, USA) stain. The cells were placed in a 37 °C incubator with no CO_2 overnight and imaged to detect β-galactosidase staining the next day using the Color Brightfield channel on the Cytation 7 Imaging Multi-Mode Reader.

2.5. Colony Formation Assay

BT-20 cells were cultured at a density of 500 cells/well into a 6-well plate overnight. The following day, the cells were incubated with 0.1, 0.3, or 1 μM of TPH104c or TPH104m, as well as media containing no test compounds (vehicle control). The vehicle or test compounds were added every 72 h over a 10-day period. The media was carefully aspirated on the tenth day, and the colonies formed in each plate were fixed using 100% methanol. The colonies were stained with crystal violet dye prepared at 0.1% concentration for 15 min in the dark. Finally, the colonies were visualized, using an EVOS microscope at 4 and 20× (Thermo Fisher Scientific, Wayne, MI, USA), and the area covered by colonies was calculated using ImageJ software Version 1.53k (National Institutes of Health, Bethesda, MD, USA).

2.6. Cell Cycle Analysis

Briefly, 250,000 cells/well of BT-20 cells were plated in a 6-well plate and allowed to grow overnight. The next day, the cells were incubated with vehicle, 0.5, 1, or 2 μM of TPH104c or TPH104m. Twenty-four hours later, the cells were washed with DPBS, trypsinized using 0.05% trypsin and 2.21mM EDTA, re-washed one time, and suspended in 1ml of ice-cold PBS. Subsequently, 200 μL of propidium iodide (PI), prepared at a stock concentration of 50 μg/mL, was added to each sample, and each sample was incubated for at least 15 min to stain the cellular DNA. The distribution of BT-20 cells incubated with media, TPH104c or TPH104m, was determined in the Go, S, G1, and G2 phases of the cell cycle using a BD Accuri™ flow cytometer (BD Biosciences, Becton-Dickinson, San Jose, CA, USA). One hundred thousand cellular events were collected, with a maximum rate of 1000 events per second, and the results were generated by analyzing the raw instrument files, using FCS express 7 plus De Novo software (Glendale, CA, USA).

2.7. Nuclear Staining

To determine whether our lead compounds induced nuclear fragmentation, nuclear staining was conducted according to a previous study [59], using the dye Hoechst 33342 (2′-(4-Ethoxyphenyl)-5-(4-methyl-1-piperazinyl)-2,5′-bi-1H-benzimidazole trihydrochloride) (Immunochemistry Technologies, Davis, CA, USA). Briefly, 100,000 cells/well of BT-20 cells were plated in a 6-well plate containing clear sterile coverslips. Cells were incubated with vehicle or TPH104c (2 or 5 μM), TPH104m (2 or 5 μM), or paclitaxel (1 μM; an anticancer drug that induces fragmentation of cancer cells) [60,61], for 24 h. Next, the cells were stained with 0.5% *v*/*v* of the Hoechst 33342 dye for 15 min. 4% paraformaldehyde at a concentration of 4%, was used to fix cells at room temperature for another 15 min. After 1 wash with PBS, the cells were mounted on a clear slide, using Fluoromount-G (SouthernBiotech, Birmingham, AL, USA). The slides were visualized to detect nuclear fragmentation using the Cytation 7 Cell Imaging Multi-Mode Reader (Agilent Technologies, Winooski, VT, USA), which provided data related to nuclear fragmentation.

2.8. Apoptosis and Mitochondrial Membrane Potential

Alexa Flour 488-conjugated Annexin V (Molecular Probes Inc., Invitrogen, Eugene, OR, USA) staining was used to quantitatively assess apoptosis by flow cytometry, according to a previous study [62]. Briefly, 250,000 cells/well of BT-20 cells were plated in a 6-well plate and incubated with vehicle or lead compounds, TPH104c or TPH104m, at several concentrations (0.5, 2.5, or 5 μM), for 24 h, on the following day. Subsequently, the cells were collected, subjected to a cold PBS wash and resuspended in 1X Annexin-binding buffer. Following a 15 min incubation with 5% Annexin V, 400 μL of 1X Annexin-binding buffer was added. The cells were mixed gently and analyzed for Annexin V staining, using a BD FACSCalibur Flow Cytometer. One hundred thousand cellular events were collected, with a maximum rate of 1000 events per second and the raw data were analyzed using FCS express 7 plus De Novo software.

The mitochondrial membrane potential (MMP) was determined using fluorescence microscopy by staining cellular mitochondria with tetramethylrhodamine ethyl ester (TMRE) dye (Invitrogen, Waltham, MA, USA). Briefly, 3000 cells/well of BT-20 cells were seeded in a 96-well plate and incubated with 2 or 5 μM TPH104c or TPH104m, for 24 h. As a positive control, cells were incubated with carbonyl cyanide 3-chlorophenylhydrazone (CCCP) (TargetMol, Boston, MA, USA), a compound that uncouples mitochondrial oxidative phosphorylation [63], at a concentration of 200 μM, for 4 h. After incubation with the test compounds, the media was carefully removed from each well and incubated for 20 min with 0.4 μM of TMRE in PBS. Finally, the dye was carefully removed and replaced with fresh PBS. The cells were then imaged to detect MMP using a Cytation 7 Cell Imaging Multi-Mode Reader.

2.9. Cell Lysis and Western Blot Analysis

Western blot assays were conducted to determine the effect of TPH104c and TPH104m on the levels of cleaved and full-length caspases (-3, -7, -8, -9), B-cell lymphoma-2 (BCL-2)—associated X (BAX), BCL-2 homologous antagonist/killer (BAK), BCL-2, cleaved and full-length Poly (ADP-ribose) polymerase (PARP), which are increased during apoptosis [64]. Briefly, cells were seeded and incubated with vehicle, TPH104c, or TPH104m (0.5, 1, 2, or 5 μM) for 12 h. Subsequently, the cells were washed with ice-cold PBS. The subcellular fraction was obtained by scraping the cells using a cell scrapper in ice-cold cytosolic lysis buffer [65]. Next, the lysates were left on ice for 15 min. Nonyl phenoxypolyethoxylethanol (NP-40) (10% *v*/*v*) was introduced in the lysates and subjected to 2–3 min incubation. The lysates were then centrifuged for 10 min at 4 °C and 14,000 rpm. The resultant protein concentration in the lysates was determined using bicinchoninic acid (BCA) assay. Thirty micrograms of the proteins were loaded and separated on a 10% acrylamide SDS-PAGE gel, transferred to a PVDF membrane, and incubated overnight at 4 °C, with primary antibodies against cleaved caspase-3, caspase-3, cleaved caspase-7, caspase-7, cleaved caspase-9, caspase-9, cleaved caspase-8, caspase-8, BAX, BAK, BCL-2, cleaved PARP, PARP, p-DRP1, DRP1, p-MFF, MFF, FIS1, MFN1, MFN2, OPA1, and β-actin. Apart from β-actin, which was prepared at a dilution of 1:2000, all antibodies were prepared at a dilution of 1:1000 in 5% Bovine serum albumin (BSA). Horseradish peroxidase (HRP)-labeled anti-rabbit or anti-mouse secondary antibodies (1:4000) were added the next day for 1.5 h. G:BOX Chemi XX6/XX9, obtained from Syngene (Frederick, MD, USA), was used for protein band detection in the blots. ImageJ software (National Institutes of Health, Bethesda, MD, USA) was used to quantify the protein. Cellular proteins were quantified as a ratio to β-actin and were normalized to the vehicle control. The densitometry readings/intensity ratio of each band, andthe original whole western blot (uncropped blots) showing all the bands with the molecular weight markers, is shown in the Supplemental Materials.

2.10. Caspase-3/7 Activity Assay

Caspase-Glo® 3/7 Assay (Promega, Madison, WI, USA) was used to study the caspase 3/7 activity in BT-20 cells incubated with lead compounds. Briefly, 3000 BT-20 TNBC cells/well were plated in an opaque 96-well plate. The cells were incubated the following day with the vehicle, TPH104c (0.3, 1, or 3 μM), or TPH104m (0.3, 1, or 3 μM) for 24 h. Next, a mixture of Caspase-Glo® 3/7 buffer and lyophilized Caspase-Glo® 3/7 substrate was equilibrated to room temperature. The plates were removed from the incubator and allowed to adjust to room temperature for 30 min. Next, 100 μL of the Caspase-Glo® 3/7 reagent was added to each well, and the samples were placed in a shaker for 30 s. After 3 h of incubation at room temperature, luminescence, which indicates cleavage of initiator caspases (caspase-3 and -7), was measured using a microplate reader (Agilent Technologies, Winooski, VT, USA).

2.11. Immunofluorescence Staining and Analysis

Immunofluorescence assays were conducted as previously described [66]. In total, 100,000 BT-20 cells per well were plated on coverslips in a 6-well plate. On the following day, cells were incubated with either vehicle, TPH104c (2 or 5 μM), or TPH104m (2 or 5 μM) for 24 h. After the incubation period, the media was carefully removed, and the cells were fixed using 1 mL of 4% paraformaldehyde for 15 min at room temperature. The cells were rinsed three times with PBS for 5 min. Five hundred microliters of 0.2% Trition-X100 was added to each well for 10 min to permeabilize the cells. The cells were washed three times with PBS for 5 min each. The cells were then blocked with 3% bovine serum albumin (BSA) in PBS, containing 0.1% Tween, for 2 h at room temperature before incubation with either cytochrome c (1:250), DRP1 (1:50), or phosphorylated-DRP1(1:450) monoclonal antibodies (Cell Signaling Technology, Danvers, MA, USA) overnight at 4 °C. The cells were incubated with either anti-mouse Alexa Fluor™ 594 (Invitrogen, Waltham, MA, USA) or anti-rabbit Alexa Fluor™ 488 at room temperature for 1 h. Nuclei were finally stained with Hoechst 33342 (ImmunoChemistry Technologies, Davis, CA, USA) for 10 min. Images were captured using a Cytation 7 Cell Imaging Multi-Mode Reader.

2.12. Molecular Docking Studies

The interaction between the Drp1 protein and ligands (TPH104c and TPH104m) was examined through a docking simulation conducted using the AceDock program accessed through the Playmolecule platform (https://www.playmolecule.com/AceDock/). AceDock is a set of protein-ligand docking protocols that run rDock [67] in the backend. Docking software was used to predict the binding mode of a given ligand to a defined binding site in a protein. The protein data bank (http://www.rcsb.org) was used to retrieve the X-ray crystal structure of DRP1 (PDB-ID: 4H1V) [68]. Subsequently, the protein underwent various optimizations, including dehydration, hydrogenation, refinement of loop regions and selection of the binding site based on the natural ligand in 4H1V. Subsequently, TPH104c and TPH104m were docked into the active binding site of the DRP1 protein using the same parameters. Both compounds were observed to occupy the same pocket (Figure S4a). The starting point for our simulations was determined by extracting coordinates from previously docked structures. We conducted Molecular Dynamics (MD) simulations using GROMACS software (version 2023.1) [69,70] and applied the CHARMM36m force field [71]. To prepare the systems, we utilized the CHARMM-GUI web server [72–74]. We used a cubic box with dimensions of 10.10 nm^3, which was subsequently filled with TIP3P water molecules [75], and the system's charge was neutralized with potassium chloride counter ions, at 0.15 mol/liter. The system underwent optimization, using the steepest descent algorithm [76], to reach its lowest energy state. To maintain the positions of both the ligand and protein atoms, we imposed a position restraint of 1000 $kJ/mol \cdot nm^2$. The entire system was equilibrated under the NVT ensemble for 1 nanosecond, during which the V-rescale thermostat was used to regulate the temperature at approximately 310 K. After the NVT step, we proceeded to equilibrate the system under the NPT ensemble for an additional 1 nanosecond, ensuring that the system's pressure stabilized at 1 atm. Subsequently, we conducted two sets of production MD runs for each ligand, utilizing a 3 fs timestep with hydrogen mass repartitioning [77] and the leap-frog integrator. The only difference between these runs was the assignment of the initial velocity seeds, both starting from the well-equilibrated system at 310 °K and a pressure of 1 atm. For calculating long-range electrostatic effects, we used the Particle-mesh Ewald (PME) algorithm [78], and the length of covalent bonds was constrained using the LINCS algorithm [79], known for its computational efficiency, compared to the SHAKE algorithm [80]. We also used the analytical SETTLE algorithm [81] to reset the positions and velocities to satisfy the holonomic constraints on the rigid water model. Finally, 100 nanoseconds of unbiased simulations were run to examine the ligand dynamics and corresponding protein conformations. Upon completion of the simulations, the protein was repositioned at the center of the simulation box, and the periodic boundary conditions were removed from the trajectory.

2.13. Surface Plasmon Resonance (SPR) Binding Assay

The binding of TPH compounds to DRP1 protein was validated, using surface plasmon resonance (SPR) (Nicoya Lifesciences, Kitchener, ON, Canada). His-tagged recombinant Drp1 protein was generously gifted by Dr. Blake Hill (Medical College of Wisconsin). The protein was diluted in a solution of immobilization buffer (pH 7.2) that consisted of HEPES (10 mM), NaCl (0.15 M), Tween 20 (0.05%), and then tethered to a high-sensitivity nitrilotriacetic acid (NTA) sensor chip (Nicoya Lifesciences, Kitchener, ON, Canada) at a final surface concentration of 10,000 RU. The TPH analogs were prepared in a two-fold concentration series from 100–6.25 μM in an immobilization buffer, and 150 μL was injected across the chip at a rate of 50 μL/min for 1 min. Finally, the binding constant KD value was calculated, using Tracedrawer software Version 1.9.2 (Tracedrawer, Uppsala, Sweden).

2.14. Generation of Partial and Complete DRP1-KO Gene Models

Partial and complete *DRP1* knockout models of PAC200 (paclitaxel-resistant variant of SUM159) were generated using the CRISPR/Cas9 system (Santa Cruz Biotechnology, Dallas, TX, USA). Briefly, 200,000 cells/well of PAC200 cells were plated in a 6-well plate in 3 mL of DMEM media. After 24 h incubation, the mixture of plasmid transfection medium containing plasmid DNA (CRISPR control (sc-418922) and *DRP1* (sc-400459)) and plasmid transfection medium containing transfection reagent was introduced into each well and allowed to incubate for 48 h. The cells were sorted based on the detection of green fluorescent protein (GFP) with a BD FACSAria™ III High-Speed Cell Sorter manufactured by BD Biosciences (Franklin Lakes, NJ, USA). Dulbecco's phosphate-buffered saline (DPBS), modified without Ca^{2+} and Mg^{2+} ions, was utilized as a sheath fluid, as recommended by BD Biosciences.

The sorted cells were grown in a small Petri dish. After reaching confluency, the cells were placed in a 96-well plate to allow the development of single-cell colonies. Western blotting was performed to confirm the complete and partial knockout of DRP1 in PAC200 cells.

2.15. Statistical Analysis

All experiments were performed at least in triplicate. Results are presented as the mean ± standard error of the mean (SEM). GraphPad Prism (San Diego, CA, USA) was used to analyze the data. The data from colony assay, cell cycle assay, ROS assay, Annexin V staining, caspase-3/7 activity assay, western blotting analysis, and comparison of IC_{50} values of control wild-type, partial, and complete DRP KO PAC200 cells were analyzed using a two-way ANOVA, and post hoc comparisons were performed using Dunnett's test. The analysis of the IC_{50} data for BT-20 cells preincubated with or without z-VAD-FMK was performed using an unpaired, 2-tailed t-test. The mitochondrial membrane potential analysis data were analyzed using one-way ANOVA with Dunnett's post hoc test. The a priori significance level was $p < 0.05$.

3. Results

3.1. TPH104c and TPH104m Selectively Decreased the Proliferation of Cancer Cell Lines

Using the MTT assay, we determined the antiproliferative efficacy of the two lead compounds, TPH104c and TPH104m, in the (1) TNBC cell lines, BT-20, MDA-MB-231, and MDA-MB-468 and (2) normal human mammary epithelial cell line, HMEC, MCF-10A, and MCF12A (Table 1). The IC_{50} values of TPH104c for BT-20, MDA-MB-231, and MDA-MB-468 TNBC cells were 0.22 ± 0.06 μM, 0.48 ± 0.16 μM, and 0.45 ± 0.17 μM, respectively. The IC50 values of TPH104m were: (1) 0.18 ± 0.03 μM, 0.47 ± 0.15 μM, and 0.27 ± 0.14 μM for BT-20, MDA-MB-231, and MDA-MB-468 cells, respectively.

Neither TPH104c nor TPH104m resulted in a significant decrease in the proliferation of non-cancerous HMEC cells (IC_{50} values for TPH104c and TPH104m were >5 μM). (Figure 1a,b). The TPH compounds were 15-to 30-fold more selective in decreasing in vitro tumor growth, compared to the normal cells, HMEC, MCF-10A, and MCF-12A. We also determined cellular viability using the CellTiter-Blue® (CTB) and Sulforhodamine B (SRB) assays. The IC_{50} values of TPH104c and TPH104m in the CTB assays for the BT-20 cell line were 0.23 ± 0.06 µM and 0.19 ± 0.08 µM, respectively (Table 2). In the SRB assay, the IC_{50} values of TPH104c and TPH104m for the BT-20 cell line were 0.30 ± 0.07 µM and 0.32 ± 0.16 µM, respectively (Table 2).

Table 1. The efficacy of the thieno-pyrimidin-4-yl-hydrazylidene (TPH) derivatives, TPH104c and TPH104m, in the TNBC cell line, BT-20, MDA-MB-231, and MDA-MB-468, and the normal human mammary epithelial cell lines HMEC, MCF-10A and MCF-12A.

Compounds	IC_{50} ± SD (µM)					
	TNBC			Normal		
	BT-20	MDA-MB-231	MDA-MB-468	HMEC	MCF-10A	MCF-12A
TPH104c	0.22 ± 0.06	0.48 ± 0.16	0.45 ± 0.17	6.74 ± 0.97	5.84 ± 1.81	6.04 ± 1.56
TPH104m	0.18 ± 0.03	0.47 ± 0.15	0.27 ± 0.14	5.67 ± 0.23	5.24 ± 2.47	6.13 ± 1.30

Cell survival assay was performed using the MTT assay. IC_{50} values represent the concentration required to inhibit cell proliferation by 50%. These values are presented as the average ± SD of three separate experiments conducted in triplicate. The efficacy of TPH104c and TPH104m was determined in TNBC cell lines: BT-20, MDA-MB-231, MDA-MB-468, and normal mammary epithelial cell lines: primary HMEC, MCF-10A, and MCF-12A.

BT-20 cancer cells reached their maximum confluence (~95%) after 72 h of incubation with the vehicle (Figure 1c). The incubation of BT-20 cells with 0.1 µM of TPH104c and TPH104m did not produce a marked cytotoxic effect in BT-20 cells. After incubation with TPH104c at a concentration lower than the IC_{50}, the number of BT-20 cells increased from 20% to 50% to 95% at 24 h, 48 h, and 72 h, respectively. Similarly, following the incubation of BT-20 cells with TPH104m at a concentration lower than IC_{50}, the number of BT-20 cells increased from 20% to 60% to 90% at 24 h, 48 h, and 72 h, respectively. However, at concentrations greater than the IC_{50} value, i.e., 0.3 µM, the level of BT-20 cell confluence was only increased by a smaller percentage, i.e., from 18% to 25% to 40% at 24 h, 48 h, and 72 h, respectively, for TPH104c and from 20% to 30% to 35% at 24 h, 48 h, and 72 h, respectively, for TPH104m. At 1 µM of either TPH104c or TPH104m, the proliferation of BT-20 cells was approximately 20% at 24, 48, and 72 h) (Figure 1c). These results suggest that BT-20 cell proliferation was significantly decreased over time by incubation with either TPH104c or TPH104m at 0.3 and 1 µM ($p < 0.0001$) for 48 and 72 h, compared to the vehicle control.

We also used the Incucyte™ Cytotox Green assay to further validate the effects of TPH104c and TPH104m on TNBC cell viability. In this assay, the highly sensitive cyanine nucleic acid dye, Cytotox green, penetrates and stains dead or non-viable cells due to a compromised cellular membrane, and upon binding to deoxyribose nucleic acid (DNA), it emits green fluorescence [57]. The incubation of BT-20 cells for 72 h with 0.1 µM of either TPH104c or TPH104m did not significantly alter the level of green fluorescence, compared to the vehicle control (Figure 1d). In contrast, after the incubation of BT-20 cells with 1 µM of TPH104c and TPH104m, for 72 h, there was a significant increase in the fluorescence intensity ($p < 0.0001$), compared to the vehicle control (Figure 1c,d). These in vitro results indicated that TPH104c and TPH104m significantly decreased the growth of BT-20 cells and increased the percentage of dead cells, after 72 h of incubation. This was in contrast to the cells incubated with the vehicle control, which continued to grow, multiply, and remained healthy over time, as shown by the low fluorescence intensity of cytotox green dye in the cells.

Similar to the cytotoxicity findings, TPH104c and TPH104m produced a concentration-dependent decrease in BT-20 colony formation (Figure 1e,f). The incubation of BT-20 cells with 0.3 or 1 µM of TPH104c for 10 days, significantly decreased the colony formation area ($p < 0.05$ for 0.3 and 1 µM), compared to the vehicle control. TPH104m also significantly decreased the area of the BT-20 colonies, compared to vehicle control ($p < 0.05$ for 0.3 µM and $p < 0.1$ for 1 µM). TPH104c and TPH104m significantly decreased BT-20 cell division, resulting in smaller, less dense colonies, compared to the control cells, where the cells proliferated rapidly and formed larger colonies (Figure 1e,f).

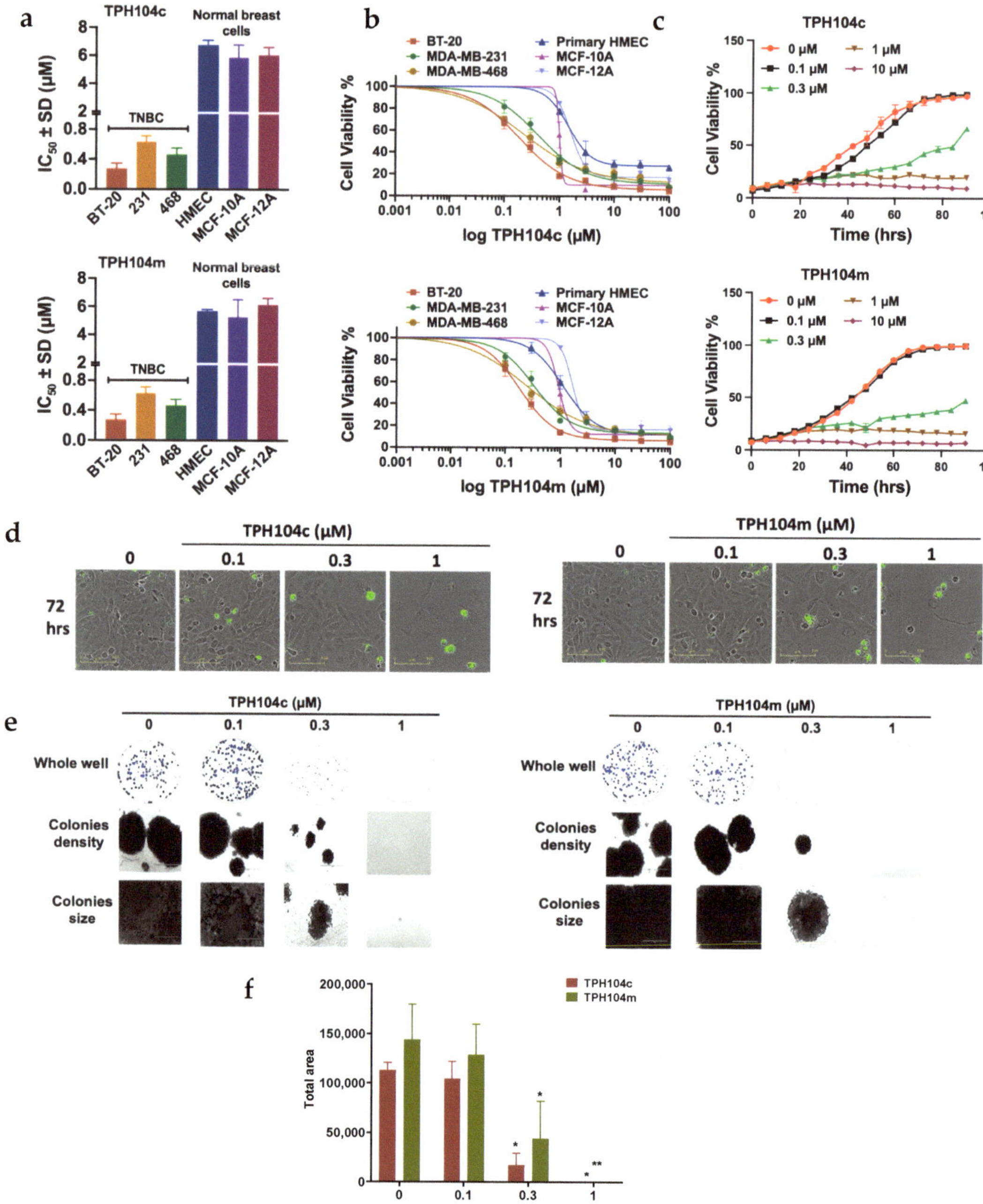

Figure 1. The cytotoxicity (i.e., anticancer efficacy) of TPH104c and TPH104m in different breast cancer cell lines. (a) The selectivity of TPH104c and TPH104m for TNBC, compared to normal, non-TNBC cell lines and TNBC, compared to normal breast cell line. (b) The cell viability curves of

BT-20 cells after incubation for 72 h, with varying concentrations of TPH104c or TPH104m, using the MTT, CTB, or SRB assays, respectively. (**c**) Quantitative graphs of percent (%) cell viability data obtained using IncuCyte S3 software based on phase-contrast images of BT-20 cells incubated for 72 h with vehicle or varying concentrations of TPH104c, TPH104m and media. (**d**) Real-time live-cell imaging pictures of BT-20 cells after incubation with TPH104c and TPH104m for 72 hrs, in an Incucyte Cytotox green reagent—containing media. The images show the green fluorescence intensity of cytotox green dye, which stains dead or non-viable cells. (**e**) Colony formation assay for BT-20 cells that were incubated with vehicle (0 μM), 0.1, 0.3, or 1 μM of TPH104c or TPH104m. The images show the effect of TPH104c and TPH104m on colony density and size. (**f**) Bar graph summarizing the effect of different concentrations of TPH104c or TPH104m on the size of the colonies formed by BT-20 cells. The results represent the mean ± SD of three independent experiments. * $p < 0.05$, ** $p < 0.01$.

Table 2. The efficacy of TPH104c and TPH104m in inhibiting the proliferation of BT-20 cells, as determined using the MTT, CTB and SRB assays.

Compounds	IC_{50} ± SD (μM)		
	MTT Assay	**CTB Assay**	**SRB Assay**
TPH104c	0.22 ± 0.06	0.23 ± 0.06	0.30 ± 0.07
TPH104m	0.18 ± 0.03	0.19 ± 0.08	0.32 ± 0.16
PTX	0.05 ± 0.00	0.07 ± 0.03	0.05 ± 0.00

BT-20 cell survival was further confirmed with CTB and SRB assays and compared with the MTT assay. Paclitaxel was used as the positive control. IC_{50} values represent the average concentration ± SD required to suppress cell proliferation by 50% and are the average of three separate experiments performed in triplicate.

3.2. *TPH104c and TPH104m Arrest the Cell Cycle of BT-20 Cells in the S/G2 Phase*

It is well known that anticancer drugs can significantly disrupt the cell cycle of cancer cells [82,83]. Therefore, we stained cells with PI to study the effects of TPH104c and TPH104m on the cell cycle. PI stains the DNA and this allows for the determination of the cell distribution in different phases of the cell cycle: G1, S, and G2 phases, using flow cytometry [84]. The vehicle control had a normal cell cycle distribution, where 6.3%, 81.4%, 5.8%, and 5.1% of the cells were in the subG1, G1, S, and G2 phases, respectively (Figure 2a–d).

However, there was a significant decrease in the % of cells in the G1 phase, following incubation with 2 μM of TPH104c, compared to vehicle control (81.4% and 69.15% at 0 and 2 μM, respectively, $p < 0.001$ at 2 μM, Figure 2a,b). BT-20 cells incubated with TPH104c significantly shifted the cell cycle toward the S (15.4% and 21.4% for 1 and 2 μM, respectively, with $p < 0.01$ and $p < 0.0001$ for 1 and 2 μM, respectively) and G2 phases (14.1% and 12.9% for 1 and 2 μM, respectively, with $p < 0.01$ and $p < 0.05$ for 1 and 2 μM, respectively, Figure 2a,b). Similarly, the percentage of cells in the G1 phase, following incubation with 1 and 2 μM of TPH104m, was significantly decreased, compared to the vehicle control (81.4%, 68.4%, and 61.3% at 0, 1, and 2 μM, respectively, $p < 0.05$ at 1 μM and $p < 0.0001$ at 2 μM, Figure 2c,d). BT-20 cells incubated with TPH104m significantly shifted the cell cycle toward the S (18.4% and 22.1% for 1 and 2 μM, respectively, with $p < 0.05$ and $p < 0.001$ for 1 and 2 μM, respectively, Figure 2c,d) and G2 phases (19.7% and 19.5% for 1 and 2 μM, respectively, with $p < 0.05$ for 1 and 2 μM, Figure 2c,d). Overall, these results indicate that BT-20 cells are arrested in the S and G2 stages of the cell cycle after incubation with TPH104c and TPH104m.

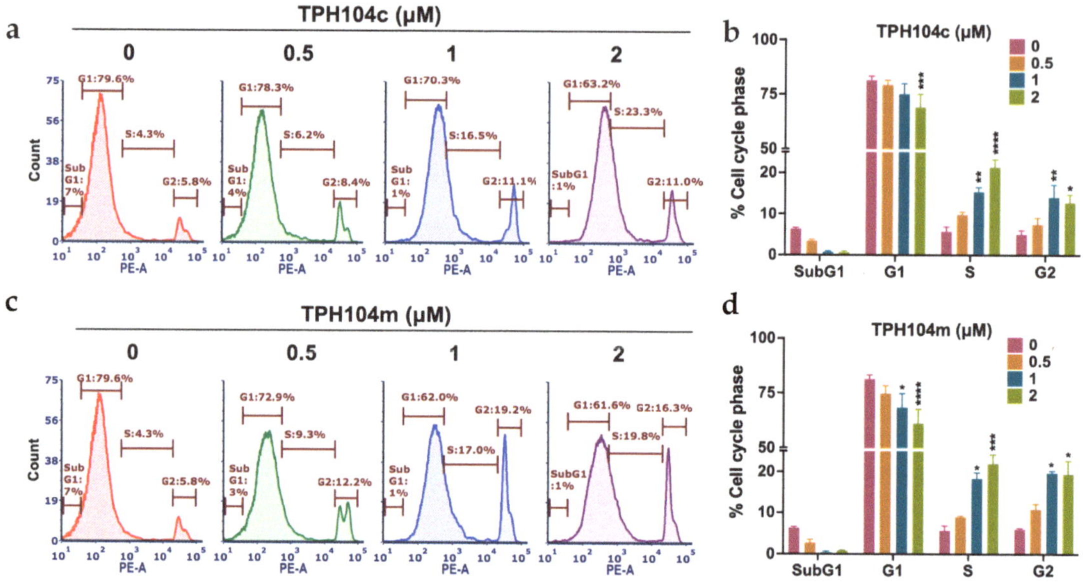

Figure 2. The effect of TPH104c or TPH104m on the cell cycle in BT-20 cells. Representative figures showing the distribution of BT-20 cells in different phases of the cell cycle after incubation with vehicle (0 µM), (**a**) TPH104c, or (**c**) TPH104m (0.5, 1, and 2 µM). BT-20 cells were stained with PI and subjected to flow cytometry. Count (*y*-axis) represents the cell population used in the flow cytometric analysis, and PE-A (*x*-axis) represents the cells stained with PI. Quantitative histograms depicting the percent change in BT-20 cells in the SubG1, G1, S, and G2 phases of the cell cycle upon treatment with (**b**) TPH104c or (**d**) TPH104m. * $p < 0.05$, ** $p < 0.01$, *** $p < 0.001$, **** $p < 0.0001$. The data represent the average ± SD of three separate experiments performed in triplicate.

3.3. TPH104c and TPH104m-Mediated Cell Death Occurs Independent of Intrinsic and Extrinsic Apoptosis

Our morphological experiments indicated that the incubation of BT-20 cells with 0.1, 0.3, or 1 µM of TPH104c and 0.1, 0.3, or 1 µM of TPH104m did not produce cellular features indicative of apoptosis, such as a decrease in cell size, blebbing of the cytoplasmic membrane, nuclear fragmentation, and apoptotic body formation (Figures 3a and 4a) [62,63]. However, TPH104c and TPH104m produced an increase in the surface area of BT-20 cells (Figures 3a and 4a) that resembled swelling, which ultimately led to cell death by bursting (Videos S1–S3). Alternatively, senescence, defined as a state of permanent cell growth arrest, produces a flattened, enlarged cellular morphology [85,86]. Therefore, to confirm whether TPH104c and TPH104m induced senescence, we performed β-galactosidase staining. Senescent cells had β-galactosidase activity, known as SA-G-gal, a biomarker of senescence [87]. Our positive control, MEF cells incubated with doxorubicin, appeared flatter and much larger than the BT-20 cells and stained blue, which indicated SA-G-gal staining and the presence of senescence. However, there was no β-galactosidase staining in BT-20 cells incubated with TPH compounds. This finding confirmed that TPH104c and TPH104m do not induce senescence in BT-20 cells (Figure S1).

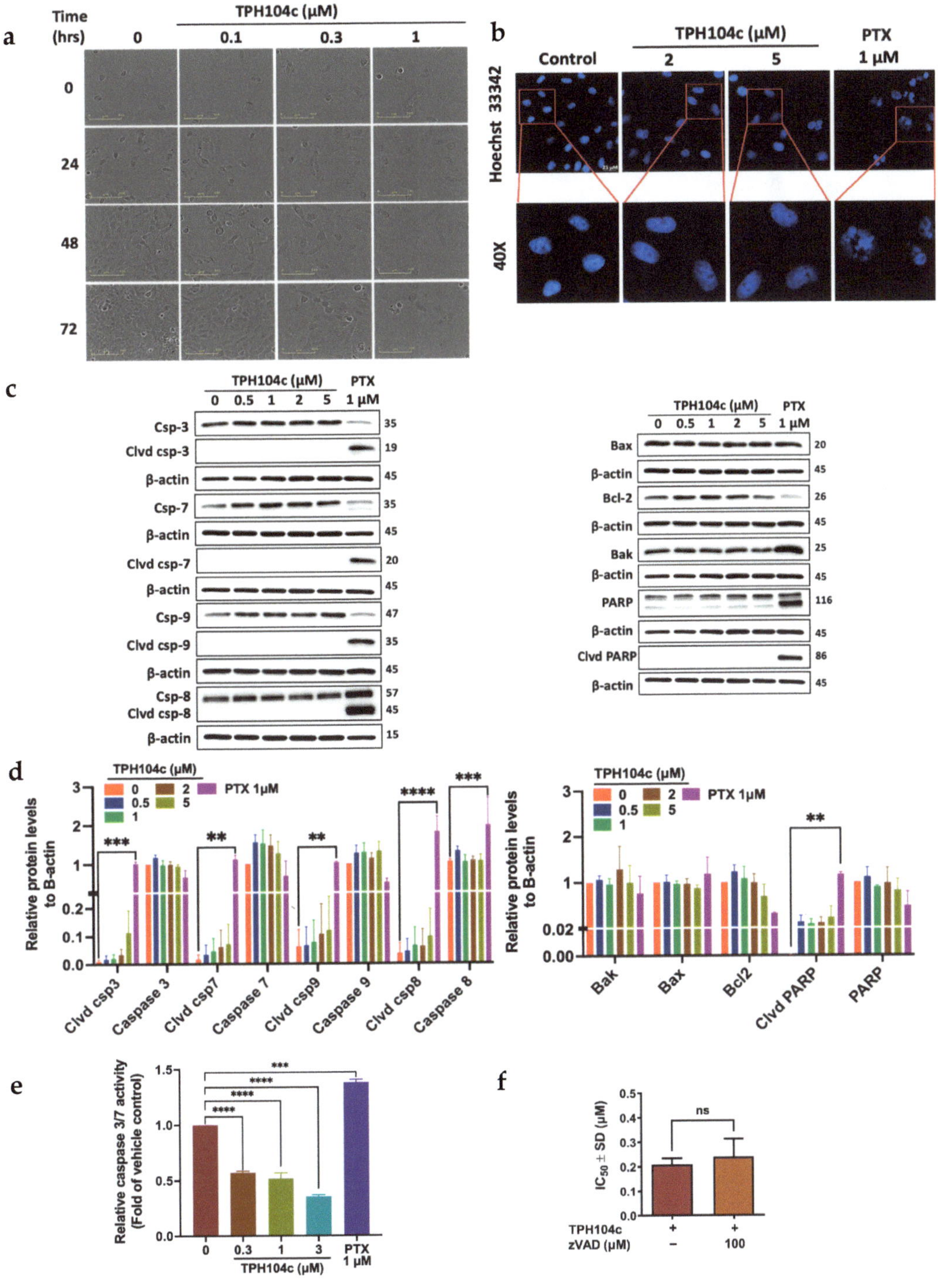

Figure 3. The effect of TPH104c on the levels of apoptotic and anti-apoptotic proteins in BT-20 cells. (**a**) Representative images featuring morphological changes in BT-20 cells (under 20× magnification)

after incubation with vehicle (0 μM, media without drug), 0.1, 0.3, or 1 μM of TPH104c for 0, 24, 48 or 72 h. (**b**) Representative images of BT-20 cells with vehicle (0 μM), 2, or 5 μM of TPH104c for 24 h or paclitaxel (PTX, 1 μM, a positive control) and stained with Hoechst 33342 dye. TPH104c did not produce condensed or fragmented nuclei compared to cells incubated with paclitaxel (PTX). Scale bar = 25 μM. (**c**) Western blot images representing the levels of the apoptotic molecules, cleaved caspase-3, caspase-3, cleaved caspase-7, caspase-7, cleaved caspase-9, caspase-9, cleaved caspase-8, caspase-8, BAX, BAK, BCL-2, cleaved PARP and PARP, following incubation with vehicle (0 μM), 0.5, 1, 2 or 5 μM of TPH104c. The proteins are expressed as a ratio to β-actin, followed by normalization to the vehicle control. (**d**) The level of each protein is shown by histograms. Clvd = cleaved; Csp = caspase. The data represent the average ± SEM of four separate studies. (**e**) Caspase-Glo 3/7 assay results are represented as a bar graph and curve, showing a decrease in the levels of caspase-3 and caspase-7 by TPH104c, in a concentration dependent manner in BT-20 cells, after 24 h of incubation. In contrast, 1 μMof PTX induced caspase- 3 and 7 activity (n = 2). (**f**) The IC_{50} values, using the MTT assay, for TPH104c in BT-20 cells that were preincubated with zVAD-FMK (a pan-caspase inhibitor) and then incubated with varying concentrations of TPH104c for 72 h. The data were obtained from three independent experiments conducted in triplicate and represent the average ± SD. ** $p < 0.01$, *** $p < 0.001$, **** $p < 0.0001$ and ns means non-significant. Original Western Blot images can be found in Supplementary Materials.

Therefore, to further validate our hypothesis that TPH104c and TPH104m do not induce apoptosis, we incubated BT-20 cells with a fluorophore-labeled Annexin V dye, which binds to phosphatidylserine that is translocated from the inner plasma membrane to the outer membrane during the early stage of apoptosis [88]. BT-20 cells incubated with 0.5, 2.5, or 5 μM of TPH104c or TPH104m did not significantly increase in the percentage of Annexin V positive cells, compared to the vehicle control (Figure S2). Approximately 90% of the vehicle control cells were viable, whereas only 11% of cells that had Annexin V incorporated into their membranes, i.e., they were undergoing apoptosis. Similar to the vehicle group, BT-20 cells incubated with 0.5, 2.5, or 5 μM of TPH104c and TPH104m did not have significant changes in the percentage of PS exposure. BT-20 cells incubated with 0.5, 2.5, or 5 μM of TPH104c, resulted in 12.1%, 13.9%, and 14.8% Annexin V positive cells, whereas BT-20 cells incubated with 0.5, 2.5, or 5 μM of TPH104m resulted in only 14.0%, 15.6% and 15.6% Annexin V positive cells. These results indicate that neither TPH104c nor TPH104m produced a level of apoptosis that was significantly greater than that of the vehicle, i.e., these compounds did not cause cancer cell death by inducing apoptosis.

We also studied the effect of TPH104c and TPH104m on nuclear fragmentation, another hallmark of apoptosis, where nuclear chromatin condensation begins at the peripheral surface of the nuclear membrane and ultimately produces fragmentation of the nucleus, known as karyorrhexis [89]. BT-20 cells were incubated with Hoechst 33342 dye, which can penetrate into live or viable cells, where it binds to DNA in adenine-thymine regions and produces a measurable blue fluorescence when exposed to light at 460–490 nm [90]. The incubation of BT-20 cells with 2 or 5 μM of either TPH104c or TPH104m for 24 h did not significantly alter the level of blue fluorescence or the shape of the nucleus, compared to the vehicle control (Figures 3b and 4b). However, BT-20 cells incubated with the positive control, 1 μM of paclitaxel, which has been previously reported to produce nuclear fragmentation [91], significantly increased the level of nuclear fragmentation (Figures 3b and 4b). Thus, these results suggest that at the concentrations and incubation times used in this study, TPH104c and TPH104m did not induce nuclear fragmentation, a process that occurs in the later stage of apoptosis.

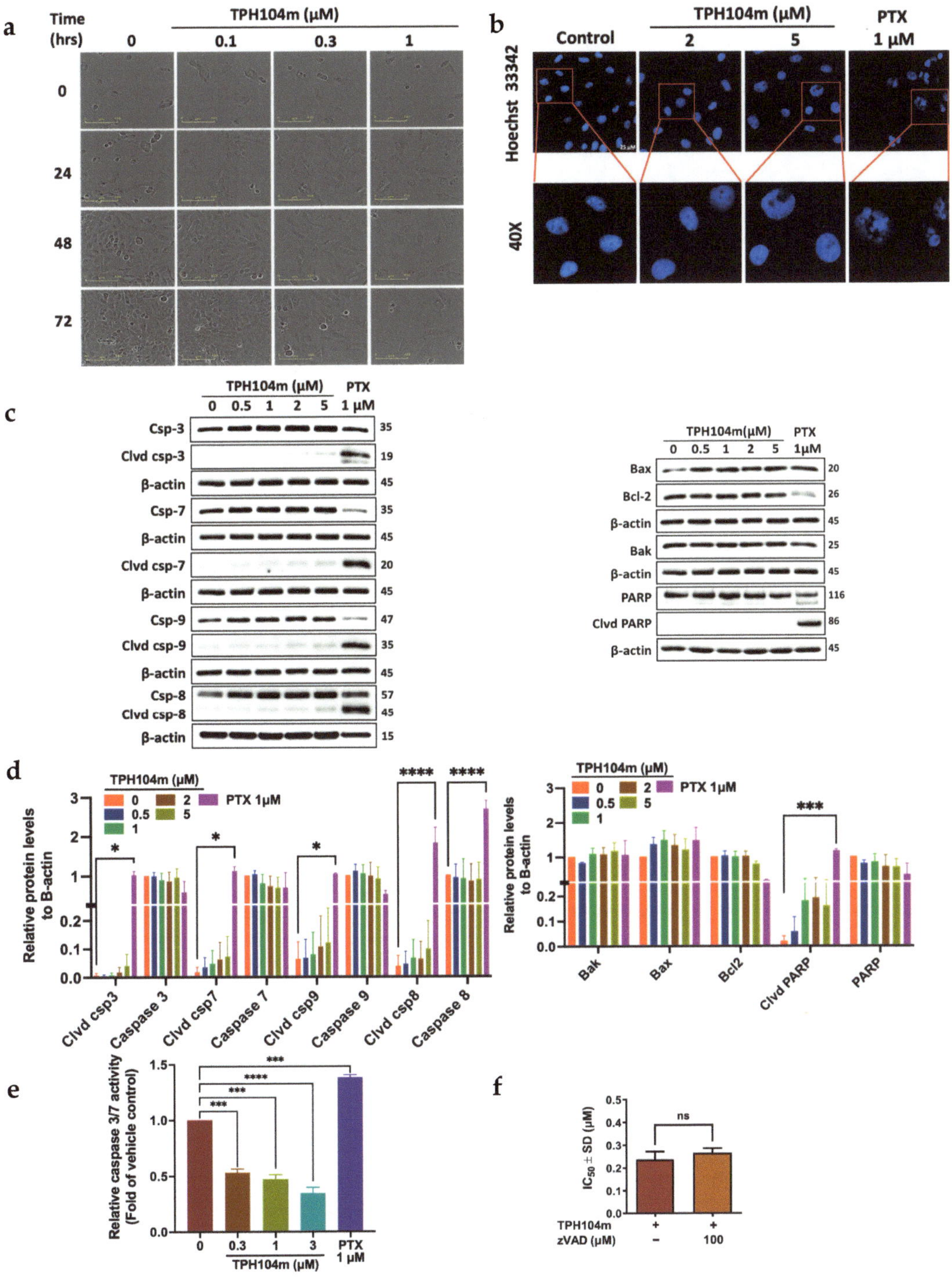

Figure 4. The effect of TPH104c on apoptotic and anti-apoptotic proteins in BT-20 cells. (a) Representative images featuring morphological changes in BT-20 cells (20× magnification) after incubation

with vehicle (media without the TPH compounds or paclitaxel (PTX)), 0.1, 0.3, or 1 μM of TPH104m, at 0, 24, 48 or 72 h post-incubation. (**b**) Representative images of BT-20 cells incubated with 2 or 5 μM of TPH104m or PTX (1 μM,) a positive control) or vehicle control and stained with Hoechst 33342 dye. TPH104c did not produce condensed or fragmented nuclei, compared to cells incubated with PTX. Scale bar = 25 μM. (**c**) Western blot images for the apoptotic molecules, cleaved caspase-3, caspase-3, cleaved caspase-7, caspase-7, cleaved caspase-9, caspase-9, cleaved caspase-8, caspase-8, BAX, BAK, BCL-2, cleaved PARP, and PARP, following incubation with vehicle (0 μM), 0.5, 1, 2, or 5 μM of TPH104m. The data are expressed as the ratio to β-actin, followed by normalization to the vehicle control. (**d**) The level of each protein is shown by histograms. Clvd = cleaved; Csp = caspase. The data represent the average ± SEM of four separate studies. (**e**) Caspase-Glo 3/7 assay results are presented as a bar graph and as a curve, showing that incubation of BT-20 cells with TPH104m for 24 h decreased the levels of caspase 3/7 in a concentration-dependent manner. In contrast, PTX (1 μM) increased the levels of caspase 3 and 7 (n = 2). (**f**) IC_{50} values, using the MTT assay, for TPH104c in BT-20 cells that were preincubated with z-VADfmk and then incubated with varying concentrations of TPH104c for 72 h. The data is obtained from three independent experiments conducted in triplicates and represents the average ± SD. * $p < 0.05$, *** $p < 0.001$, **** $p < 0.0001$ and ns means non-significant. Original Western Blot images can be found in Supplementary Materials.

We also determined the effect of the TPH compounds on the levels of key regulators of apoptosis, including initiator and executioner caspases, caspase-8, caspase-9, caspase-3, and caspase-7, pro-apoptotic proteins, BAK and BAX, anti-apoptotic protein, Bcl-2, and PARP, using western blot assay. BT-20 cells were also incubated with 1 μM of paclitaxel, which alters the levels of certain apoptotic proteins [85]. BT-20 cells incubated with paclitaxel, significantly upregulated the levels of cleaved caspase-3 ($p < 0.001$), caspase-7 ($p <0.01$), caspase-8 ($p < 0.0001$), caspase-9 ($p < 0.01$),) and total caspase-8 (***, $p <0.001$), compared to the vehicle control (Figures 3c,d and 4c,d). In contrast, the incubation of BT-20 cells with 0.5, 1, 2, or 5 μM of TPH104c or TPH104m did not significantly alter the level of cleaved and total caspases (both initiator and executioner caspases), compared to the vehicle control (Figures 3c,d and 4c,d). Since TPH104c and TPH104m did not induce the cleavage of caspase-3 and caspase-7, it is unlikely that they activated the intrinsic or mitochondrial pathway of apoptosis. Furthermore, there was no caspase-8 cleavage in cells incubated with TPH104c and TPH104m, indicating that TPH104c- and TPH104m-induced cell death is not mediated through the extrinsic apoptotic pathway, as activation of initiator caspase-8 is required to cleave and activate caspase-3 and caspase-7 to induce extrinsic apoptosis [92]. Also, the incubation of BT-20 cells with TPH104c or TPH104m did not significantly alter the levels of (1) BAK; (2) BAX, (3) cleaved PARP, and (4) total PARP, compared to the vehicle control. There was no significant change in the levels of Bcl-2 in BT-20 cells incubated with TPH104c and TPH104m (0.5, 1, 2, or 5 μM), compared to the vehicle control. In contrast, there was a significant decrease in Bcl-2 levels in BT-20 cells incubated with paclitaxel, compared to vehicle control cells.

We used the Caspase-Glo® 3/7 assay, which involves incubating cells with the caspase-3/7 substrate, Z-DEVD-aminoluciferin, a substrate for luciferase that is cleaved by active caspase-3 and caspase-7 [93], to further validate the above results, indicating that the TPH compounds do not induce apoptosis. The cleavage of Z-DEVD-aminoluciferin by caspase-3 or caspase-7, releases aminoluciferin, a substrate for luciferase, which produces luminescence [94]. The incubation of BT-20 cells with 0.3, 1, or 3 μM of TPH104c or TPH104m for 24 h did not significantly induce the activation of caspase 3/7, compared to the vehicle control (Figures 3e and 4e). However, BT-20 cells treated with 0.1 μM of paclitaxel, a compound that activates the intrinsic apoptotic pathway [95,96], significantly increased the level of bioluminescence, indicating activation of caspase-3 and caspase-7 (Figures 3e and 4e). We conducted an additional experiment to show that TPH104c and TPH104m do not induce BT-20 cell death by apoptosis. The pre-incubation of BT-20 cells with 100 μM of benzyloxycarbonyl-valine-alanine-aspartate-FMK (Z-VAD-FMK), an irreversible pan-caspase inhibitor [68], did not prevent cell death after incubation with 0.1, 0.3, or 1 μM of TPH104c or TPH104m, compared to vehicle control (Figure S3). There was no significant difference between the IC_{50} values of BT-20 cells treated with Z-VAD-FMK and BT-20 cells treated with either TPH104c or TPH104m (Figures 3f and 4f). These results suggested that neither TPH104c nor TPH104m induced cell death by activating caspase-3 and caspase-7, i.e., they did not induce apoptosis by the intrinsic pathway. It is important to note that although the incubation of BT-20 cells with TPH104c and TPH104m resulted in a significant loss of the mitochondrial membrane potential, it is possible that the level of cytochrome c release in the cytoplasm was not sufficient to activate caspases and cause apoptotic cell death.

3.4. TPH104c and TPH104m-Mediated Cell Death Induced the Loss of the Mitochondrial Membrane Potential, Independent of Cytochrome c Release and Reactive Oxygen Species (ROS) Production

As previously discussed, the majority of clinically used anticancer drugs induce the apoptosis of cancer cells [97]. Apoptosis can be activated through the intrinsic/mitochondrial or extrinsic/death receptor pathways [64,98]. Intrinsic apoptosis is mediated by the apoptotic regulator family known as the B-cell lymphoma-2 (BCL-2) family. This family includes pro-apoptotic proteins such as BAX, BAK, and BCL-2 related ovarian killer (BOK), as well as BH3-only proteins like BCL-2 associated agonist of cell death (BAD), BH3 interacting domain death agonist (BID), BCL-2 interacting killer (BIK), BCL-2 modifying factor (BMF), BCL-2-like 11 (BIM), activator of apoptosis hara-kiri (HRK), NOVA, p53 upregulated modulator of apoptosis (PUMA), and SOUL. Additionally, there are anti-apoptotic survival proteins in this family, such as BCL-2, BCL-extra-large (BCL-X_{L}), BCL-2-like protein (BCL2-L-2) or BCL-W, B-cell lymphoma 2 (BCL-B), BCL-2-related protein A1 (BCL-2-A1), and myeloid cell leukemia-1 (MCL-1) [99]. Numerous studies indicate that intrinsic stimuli, such as cellular stress, DNA damage, excessive levels of reactive oxygen species (ROS), and pro-apoptotic proteins, such as BAK and BAX, are activated either transcriptionally or post-transcriptionally and are translocated to the outer mitochondrial membrane [64]. Due to pore formation on the outer surface of the mitochondria, apoptogenic factors such as cytochrome c and diablo IAP-binding mitochondrial protein (DIABLO/Smac) are released into the cytosol, leading to mitochondrial outer membrane permeabilization (MOMP) [100,101]. Subsequently, cytochrome c binds to the apoptotic peptidase activating factor 1 (APAF1) and pro-caspase 9, to form an apoptosome complex [102]. Caspase-9, an initiator caspase, is activated by the apoptosome via heterodimerization with APAF1 and a self-homodimerization process [103,104]. This complex activates caspase-3 and caspase-7, which produce DNA fragmentation, phosphatidylserine (PS) externalization and apoptotic blebs [105–108]. In contrast, extrinsic apoptosis is mediated by transmembrane death receptors, TNF receptor superfamily members 1A (TNFR1), 10a (TRAILR1 or DR4), and 10b (TRAILR2 or DR5), and the Fas cell surface death receptor (Fas/CD95/APO1) [64]. The binding of the endogenous ligands, FAS l to the Fas receptor and TRAIL to the TRAIL receptor, recruits the adaptor proteins Fas-associated via death domain (FADD) and TNFR1 associated via death domain (TRADD), respectively, and forms an intracellular multiprotein complex known as the death-inducing signaling complex (DISC) [109]. This process enables the recruitment and activation of caspase-8 or caspase -10 through homodimerization, leading to the corresponding activation of the executioner caspase cascade, ultimately resulting in cell death [110].

Using the dye, TMRE, we determined the effect of TPH compounds on the mitochondrial membrane potential in BT-20 cells. This positively the charged dye is taken up by negatively charged viable mitochondria with an intact mitochondrial membrane potential, resulting in the emission of red fluorescence when exposed to the TPH compounds [111]. The vehicle control cells emitted high levels of red fluorescence (Figure 5a). However, BT-20 cells incubated with 2 and 5 μM of TPH104c or TPH104m, for 24 h, had significantly lower levels of red fluorescence, compared to the vehicle control (**, $p < 0.01$, for both concentrations of TPH104c and **, $p < 0.01$ and ***, $p < 0.001$ for 2 and 5 μM of TPH104m, respectively) (Figure 5a,b). Carbonyl cyanide m-chlorophenyl hydrazone (CCCP), an inhibitor of oxidative phosphorylation [112], was used as the positive control for this assay. BT-20 cells incubated with 200 μM of CCCP had a significantly lower level of fluorescence, compared to the vehicle control and 2 or 5 μM of TPH104c and TPH104m (Figure 5a,b; $p < 0.0001$) [113]. These results indicated that TPH104c and TPH104 caused a loss of mitochondrial membrane potential. The loss of mitochondrial membrane potential results in the release of apoptogenic factors, such as cytochrome c, from the mitochondria, which is crucial for the activation of specific caspases to initiate apoptosis [114–116]. Therefore, to determine whether TPH compounds release cytochrome c, which mediates apoptosis, we determined the effect of TPH104c and TPH104m (2 and 5 μM) on the level of cytochrome c using immunofluorescence. Interestingly, TPH104c and TPH104m, at 2 or 5 μM, significantly decreased the fluorescence of cytochrome c ($p < 0.0001$ and $p < 0.001$ for 2 and 5 μM of TPH104c, respectively; $p < 0.0001$ and $p < 0.0001$ for 2 and 5 μM of TPH104m, respectively (Figure 5c,d), indicating that the levels of cytochrome c were lower in BT-20 cells incubated with TPH104c and TPH104m, for 24 h, compared to the vehicle control. In contrast, BT-20 cells incubated with 1 μM of paclitaxel, known to induce apoptotic cell death, significantly enhanced cytochrome c release (**** $p < 0.0001$), compared to the vehicle control, TPH104c, or TPH104m. These results suggest that TPH104c and TPH104m did not induce cell death by increasing the levels of cytochrome c in the cytosol of BT-20 cells.

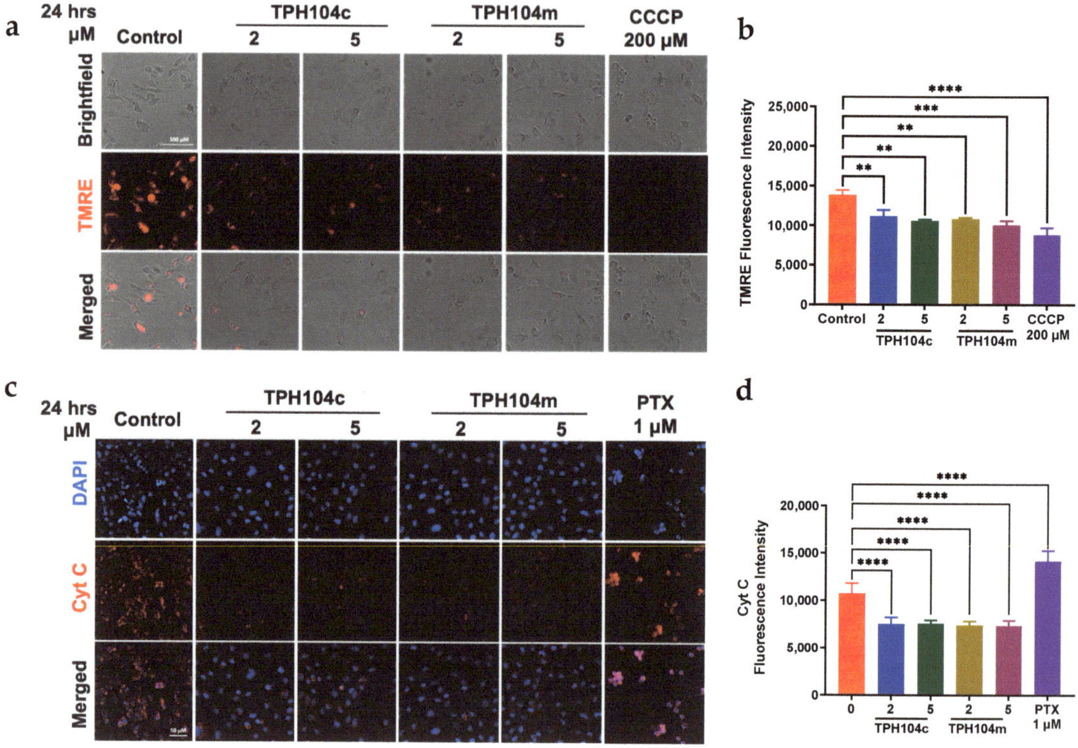

Figure 5. *Cont.*

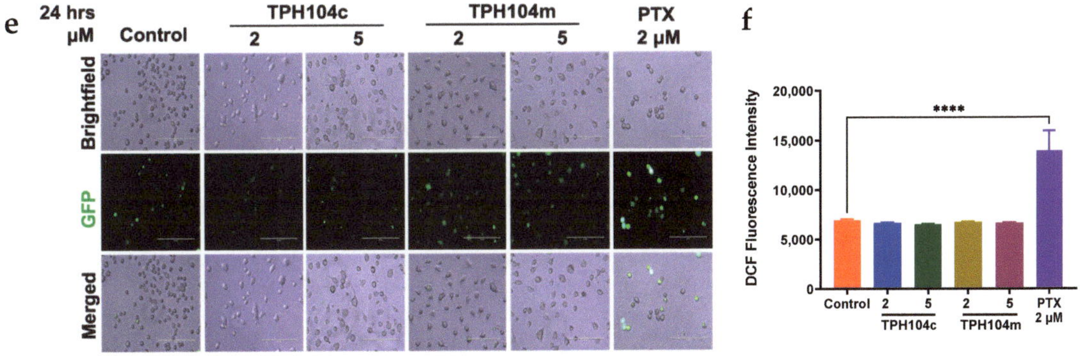

Figure 5. TPH104c and TPH104m induced the loss of the mitochondrial membrane potential but did not induce oxidative stress in BT-20 cells. (**a**) Fluorescent microscopic images of BT-20 cells stained with TMRE dye after incubation with the vehicle for 24 h (0 µM), 2 or 5 µM of TPH104c or TPH104m, and CCCP as a positive control. The TMRE dye is retained in cells with normal structural and functioning mitochondria, producing a high level of red fluorescence, whereas weak or no fluorescence occurred in cells without MMP. Scale bar = 200 µm. (**b**) Quantitative bar graph illustrating the change in the percentage of red fluorescence in BT-20 cells incubated with 2, or 5 µM of TPH104c and TPH104m or CCCP, compared to cells incubated with media. The results are shown as mean ± SD in triplicate. CCCP = Carbonyl cyanide 3-chlorophenylhydrazone. (**c**) Immunofluorescence analysis of cytochrome c levels in BT-20 cells incubated with 2 or 5 µM of TPH104c or TPH104m or PTX or vehicle control (0 µM), for 24 h. PTX = Paclitaxel. Scale bar = 50 µm. (**d**) Bar graphs illustrating the fluorescence intensity of cytochrome c in BT-20 cells incubated with 2 and 5 µM TPH104c and TPH104m or vehicle control (0 µM) for 24 h. (**e**) Representative images and (**f**) bar graphs depicting the level of dichlorofluorescein (DCF) fluorescence in BT-20 cells incubated with TPH104c and TPH104m (0 µM (vehicle), 2, or 5 µM) for 24 h, or paclitaxel (2 µM) for 2 h. Images were captured at 20× magnification. Scale bar = 200 µm. Relative fluorescence units of H_2DCFA in BT-20 cells. The data are expressed as the average fluorescence ± SEM of three separate experiments. ** $p < 0.01$, *** $p < 0.001$, **** $p < 0.0001$, compared to the vehicle control cells.

It has been reported that ROS can cause the death of cancer cells by inducing apoptosis [29,117–119]. Indeed, high levels of ROS activate the p53 enzyme system, which promotes late-stage apoptosis by upregulating the levels of pro-apoptotic proteins such as BAK and BAX and downregulating the levels of anti-apoptotic proteins such as BCL-2, BCL-xL, and MCL-1 [120]. In addition, ROS induce permeabilization of the outer mitochondrial membrane by opening the mitochondrial permeability transition pore (mPTP) [121,122]. This alters the electrochemical proton gradient across the mitochondria, causing the release of pro-apoptotic molecules into the cytoplasm, which are involved in apoptotic cell death [100,123]. To determine if an increase in ROS levels is the primary cause of the loss of mitochondrial membrane permeability, we determined the effect of TPH104c and TPH104m on the intracellular levels of ROS in BT-20 cells, using the dye 2′,7′-dichlorodihydrofluorescein diacetate (H_2DCFDA). Cellular esterases hydrolyze the acetyl groups after the dye is taken up by cells, resulting in the formation of H_2DCF [124]. Subsequently, intracellular ROS oxidize H_2DCF to produce 2′,7′-dichlorofluorescein, which emits green fluorescence (excitation and emission wavelengths of 485 nm and 522 nm, respectively) [125]. The incubation of BT-20 cells with 2 and 5 µM of TPH104c or 2 and 5 µM of TPH104m for 24 h did not significantly alter ROS levels compared to the vehicle control (Figure 5e,f). However, as previously reported [126], BT-20 cells incubated with 2 µM of paclitaxel significantly elevated the ROS levels (**** $p < 0.0001$), compared to the vehicle control, TPH104c, or TPH104m (Figure 5). These findings suggest that at the concentrations and incubation times used in this study, TPH104c and TPH104m did not produce their anticancer efficacy by increasing ROS levels.

3.5. TPH104c and TPH104m-Mediated Cell Death Is Regulated by the Protein, DRP1, a Mitochondrial Marker

The loss of mitochondrial membrane potential and decrease in cytochrome c release prompted us to determine whether TPH104c and TPH104m altered the levels of mitochondrial dynamic proteins. Mitochondria undergo continuous cycles of fission and fusion to maintain mitochondrial homeostasis and quality, and balance their population and cellular function [127]. In mitochondrial fission, DRP1 is recruited from the cytoplasm to the mitochondrial outer membrane (MOM) receptor, Fis1, in a complex with the mitochondrial fission factor (MFF) [128]. This produces an incision in the mitochondrial membrane in a GTP-dependent manner, resulting in mitochondrial fission [129]. Mitochondrial fusion is mediated by the proteins mitofusin 1 (MFN1) and mitofusin 2 (MFN2), located on the MOM, and Optic atrophy 1 (OPA1) proteins, located in the inner mitochondrial membrane [130]. BT-20 cells incubated with 2 and 5 μM of TPH104c and TPH104m significantly decreased the phospho-DRP1 to DRP1 ratio ($p < 0.0001$ for 2 and 5 μM of TPH104c, respectively, and $p < 0.0001$ for 2 and 5 μM of TPH104m, respectively), compared to the vehicle-incubated cells (Figure 6a,b). Interestingly, when compared to the vehicle control, the levels of phospho-MFF to MFF were increased in BT-20 cells incubated with 2 and 5 μM of TPH104c and TPH104m, compared to the controls but were not significant. The levels of Fis1 in BT-20 cells were not significantly altered after incubation with 2 or 5 μM of TPH104c and TPH104m, compared to the vehicle-incubated cells (Figure 6a). Furthermore, BT-20 cells incubated with 2 and 5 μM of TPH104c and TPH104m, did not significantly alter the level of the mitochondrial fusion proteins, MFN1, MFN2, and OPA1, compared to the vehicle control (Figures 6a and S4a). We also conducted immunofluorescence experiments to determine the effect of TPH compounds on the levels of DRP1 and phospho-DRP1 in BT-20 cells. The incubation of BT-20 cells with 2 and 5 μM of TPH104c and TPH104m for 24 h significantly decreased the levels of DRP1 ($p < 0.01$ and $p < 0.05$ for 2 and 5 μM of TPH104c, respectively; Figure 6c,d). Similarly, the levels of phosphorylated DRP1 were significantly decreased in BT-20 cells after incubation with 2 ($p < 0.01$) and 5 μM ($p < 0.05$) of TPH104c and 2 ($p < 0.05$) and 5 μM ($p < 0.001$) of TPH104m, compared to vehicle-incubated cells (Figure 6e,f).

Molecular docking studies suggested that the TPH104c and TPH104m (i.e., the ligands) adopt a highly stable configuration within the binding pocket, facilitated by numerous intermolecular interactions, including hydrogen bonding with neighboring residues. Molecular dynamics simulations revealed that the aryl moiety of both molecules reside near a deeply concealed hydrophobic subpocket, enveloped by LEU51, PRO52, ILE57, ILE111, THR59 and ILE63, and this moiety progressively penetrates deeper into this subpocket over time (Figure S4b,c). Furthermore, these compounds interact with the nearby residues, GLY37, GLY149, LYS38, SER39 and SER35, forming hydrogen bonds. Analysis conducted with the VMD program indicated that LYS38 and ASP146 have the highest hydrogen bond occupancy, underscoring their crucial role in stabilizing the ligands within the binding pocket (Table S1). Due to the presence of a hydroxyl group, TPH104c forms a strong hydrogen bond with the carbonyl group in the main chain, specifically between residues ARG61 and PRO62, ensuring stability. In addition to hydrogen bonds and hydrophobic interactions, both TPH104c and TPH104m consistently exhibit carbon-π and donor-π interactions [131] with PRO148 and GLN34 residues throughout the simulation trajectories. These interactions are visually represented in (Figure 6g–j). Similarly, the dose-response binding kinetics of the DRP1 recombinant protein and TPH compounds were studied using Nicoya OpenSPR. These results confirmed that DRP1 binds with the TPH compounds. TPH104c and TPH104m have a direct binding interaction with the recombinant DRP1 protein, as indicated by a binding constant (KD) of 3. 57 ± 0.7 μM, 3.89 ± 1.64 μM, and 25.2 ± 3.6 μM, respectively (Figure 6k,l)

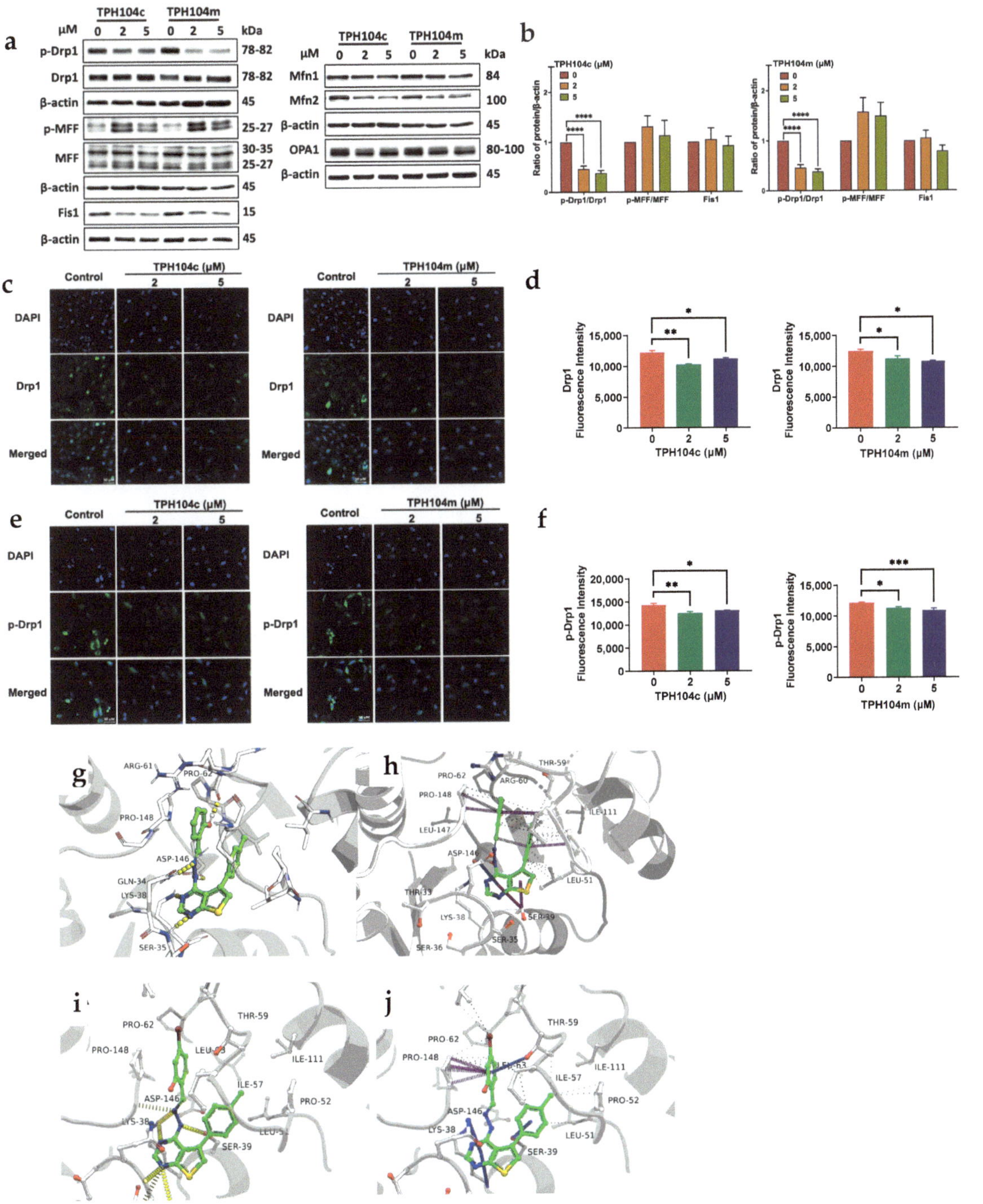

Figure 6. *Cont.*

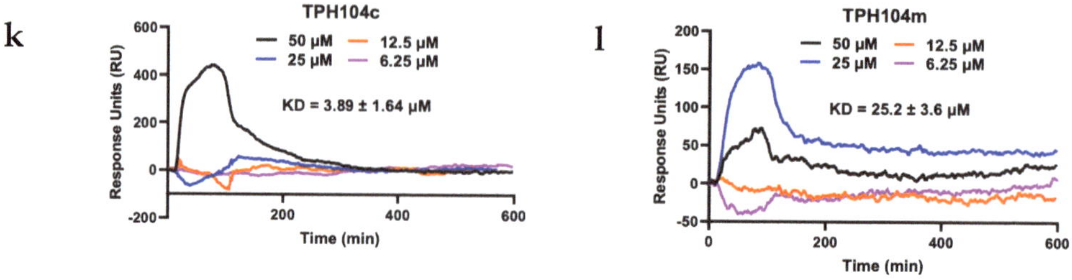

Figure 6. The effect of TPH104c and TPH104m on the levels of mitochondrial proteins, DRP1 and phosphorylated DRP1 (p-DRP1). (**a**) Western blot images for the mitochondrial fission proteins, p-DRP1, DRP1, p-MFF, MFF, and Fis1, and the mitochondrial fusion proteins, MFN1, MFN2, or OPA1, following incubation with vehicle (0 μM), 2, or 5 μM of TPH104c and TPH104m. All proteins were expressed as a ratio to β-actin, followed by normalization to the vehicle control. (**b**) Histograms showing the ratio of phosphorylated proteins to total proteins and individual proteins. All data are presented as the mean ± SEM of 4-5 independent studies. Immunofluorescence analysis of DRP1 (**c**) and p-DRP1 (**e**) at Serine 616C in BT-20 cells incubated for 24 h with vehicle (0 μM), 2, or 5 μM of TPH104c or TPH104m. Bar graphs showing the quantification of the fluorescence intensity of DRP1 (**d**) and p-DRP1 (**f**). Scale bar = 50 μm. * $p < 0.05$, ** $p < 0.01$, *** $p < 0.001$, **** $p < 0.0001$. Predicted non-covalent interactions of ligands TPH104c and TPH104m. (**g**) Hydrogen bonds (yellow) shared between TPH104c and DRP-1; (**h**) Carbon-π and donor-π interactions between TPH104c and DRP-1 (**i**) Hydrogen bonds (yellow) shared between TPH104m and DRP-1; (**j**) Carbon-π and donor-π interactions between TPH104m and DRP1. Representative graphs obtained from a Nicoya SPR assay, where a direct drug-protein binding interaction occurred between the Drp1 recombinant protein and varying concentrations of (**k**) TPH104c (**l**) TPH104m. Results are shown as the mean ± SD of triplicate experiments. Original Western Blot images can be found in Supplementary Materials.

To further determine the role of DRP1 protein in the non-apoptotic cell death induced by TPH104c and TPH104m, we generated complete and partial *DRP1* knockout models, using the TNBC cell line PAC200 (a paclitaxel-resistant variant of SUM159 cells) (Figure 7a). Because TPH104c and TPH104m decreased DRP1 levels and induced non-apoptotic cell death in TNBC cell lines, we hypothesized that knocking out the *DRP1* gene in TNBC cell lines would increase TNBC cell viability. The results of this experiment supported our hypothesis, as the IC_{50} values of TPH104c and TPH104m were increased in the *DRP1* knockout (partial KO and complete KO) PAC200 cell lines. We conducted four different cell viability assays, MTT, CTB, CTG, and SRB, to confirm the above results (Figure S4d). MTT assays indicated that the cytotoxic efficacy of TPH104c increased by 1.9- ($p < 0.01$) and 2.9-fold ($p < 0.001$) in partial and complete *DRP1* KO PAC200 cells, respectively (Figure 7b). Similarly, the TPH104m IC_{50} value was increased by 2.0 ($p < 0.01$) and 2.7-fold ($p < 0.001$) in the partial KO and *DRP1* KO PAC200 cells, respectively. In the CTB assay (Figure 7c), the IC_{50} values of TPH104c in partial *DRP1* KO cells were increased by 1.3-fold in partial *DRP1* KO cells and 2.1-fold ($p < 0.05$) in complete *DRP1* KO cells. There was a 0.9-fold increase in the TPH104m IC_{50} value in the -partial *DRP1* KO cells, compared to 3.3-fold ($p < 0.05$) in the partial *DRP1* KO cells treated with TPH104m. Similarly, in the CTG assay, the IC_{50} values for the TPH compounds were significantly increased in the complete *DRP1* KO PAC200 cells after incubation with TPH104c (2.7-fold, $p < 0.01$) and TPH104m (4.7-fold, $p < 0.05$), compared to the partial *DRP1* KO PAC200 cells (1.9-fold increase for TPH104c and 3.2-fold increase for TPH104m) (Figure 7d). Finally, the SRB assay (Figure 7e) results indicated that the IC_{50} values for TPH104c (3.0-fold, $p < 0.001$) and TPH104m (6.7-fold, $p < 0.01$) were significantly increased compared to the partial *DRP1* KO cells (0.6-fold increase for TPH104c and 0.8-fold increase for TPH104m) and control PAC200 cells. Thus, the increase in the viability of TNBC cells after partial and complete *DRP1* knockout suggests that TPH104c and TPH104m induce cell death by affecting the levels of the DRP1 protein.

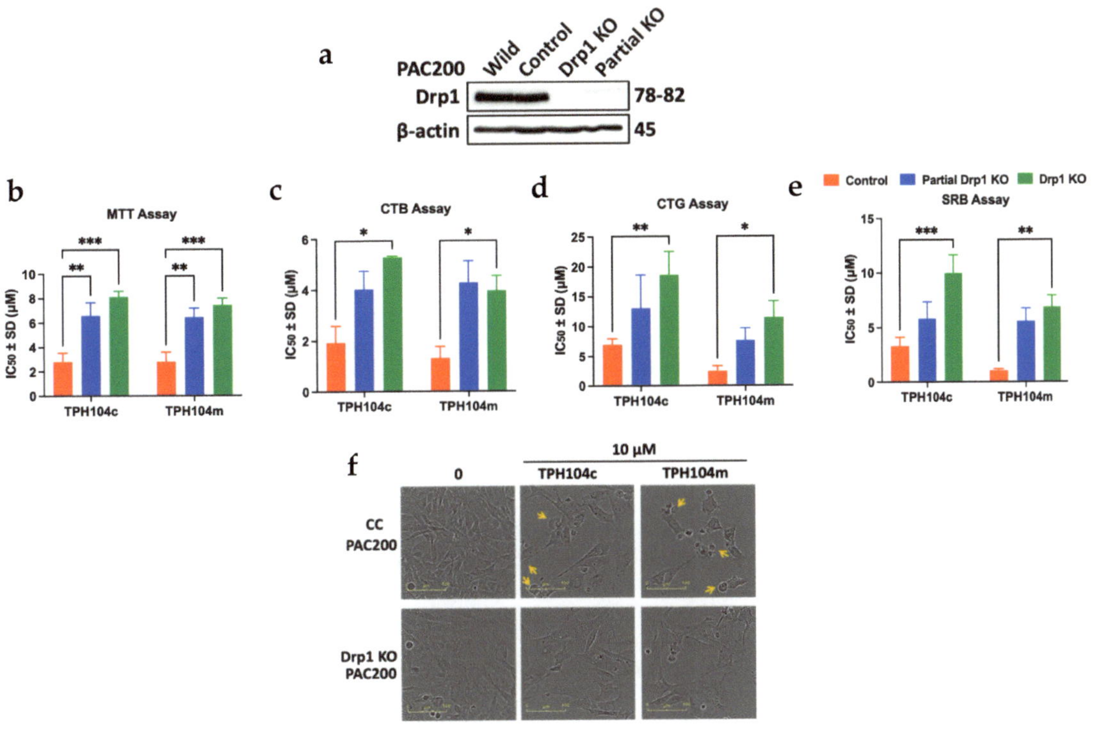

Figure 7. The cytotoxic efficacy of TPH104c and TPH104m on CRISPR (wild-type control) and partial and complete *DRP1* knockout (KO) PAC200 cells. (**a**) Western blot images of DRP1 levels in CRISPR wild-type (control) PAC200 cells PAC200 and complete and partial *DRP1* KO cells. Bar graphs depicting the IC_{50} values of TPH104c and TPH104m in CRISPR wild-type, partial *DRP1* KO, and complete *DRP1* KO PAC200 cells after 72 h of incubation, calculated using (**b**) MTT assay, (**c**) CTB assay, (**d**) CTG assay, and (**e**) SRB assay. (**f**) Morphological images of CRISPR wild-type and complete DRP1 KO PAC200 cells incubated with 10 µM of TPH104c and TPH104m, for 72 h. Yellow arrows represent a bubble-like formation that indicates bursting. Scale bar, 100 µm. * $p < 0.05$, ** $p < 0.01$, *** $p < 0.001$. Original Western Blot images can be found in Supplementary Materials.

Furthermore, we conducted additional experiments to determine the mechanism by which TPH104c- and TPH104m-induced cell death in control wild-type and complete *DRP1* KO PAC200 cells, by performing a morphological experiment, using the Incucyte live-cell analysis system (Figure 7f). Both cell lines were incubated with 10 µM TPH104c and TPH104m for 72 h, and images were captured using an Incucyte instrument. The control (wild-type) PAC200 cells underwent death in a process similar to that of BT-20 cells: the size of the cells incubated with 10 µM TPH104c or TPH104m gradually increased, and this ultimately caused bursting (indicated by yellow arrows in Figure 7f) and detachment from the growth surface, followed by death. Interestingly, the death of the *DRP1* knockout PAC200 cells was different from that of the control PAC200 cells, as the *DRP1* KO PAC200 cells were larger in size but died without bursting, as there were no bubble-like formations in these cells. Overall, these data indicated that the decrease in DRP1 levels by TPH104c and TPH104m played a significant part in triggering a unique non-apoptotic-like cell death.

4. Discussion

In this study, we investigated the mechanism by which the thienopyrimidine derivates, TPH104c and TPH104m, induced the in vitro death of TNBC cells. Our data suggested that TPH104c and TPH104m induced non-apoptotic cell death in TNBC cell lines that was characterized by the absence of apoptotic morphology (i.e., no nuclear fragmentation, no cell shrinkage or apoptotic cell bodies, and the absence of rounded cells). TPH104c and TPH104m produced cell cycle arrest at the S/G2 phases and did not significantly alter the levels of ROS. TPH104c and TPH104m did not activate either initiator or executioner caspases, and cell death was not rescued by the pan-caspase inhibitor, Z-VAD-FMK. Interestingly, TPH104c and TPH104m increased mitochondrial membrane permeabilization but significantly decreased the release of total cytochrome c. Cytochrome c is an essential component of the electron transport chain, which is involved in the transfer of electrons between complexes III and IV that generates a proton gradient across the inner membrane [132,133]. Thus, the generated proton gradient is involved in ATP synthesis through the action of ATP synthase [132,133]. Therefore, a decrease in cytochrome c levels can decrease ATP production and impair mitochondrial function. Furthermore, TPH104c and TPH104m significantly decreased the levels of the mitochondrial fission protein, DRP1, and its phosphorylated form, p-DRP1. Studies have reported that inhibiting DRP1 induces apoptosis in cancer cells and may also prevent cytochrome c release, although it induces apoptosis. [134,135]. However, here, we report the non-apoptotic cell death induced by our lead compounds that bind to DRP1, result in its downregulation, as well as cytochrome c, in TNBC. Interestingly, the anticancer efficacy of our compounds was dependent on the amount of DRP1 present in TNBC cells, compared to the wild-PAC200. Indeed, the reversal of cytotoxicity was non-significant in partial *DRP1* KO PAC200 cells and significant in complete *DRP1* KO PAC200 cells. To our knowledge, the results of our study describe a novel mechanism of thienopyrimidine compound-induced non-apoptotic cell death in TNBC via decreasing Drp1 levels.

Although an increase in mitochondrial membrane potential and loss of mitochondrial membrane potential are two major events in apoptotic cell death [136], the release of the apoptogenic factor cytochrome c is required to activate the initiator caspases, followed by activation of the executioner caspases [64,98]. In this study, TPH014c and TPH104m significantly decreased cytochrome c levels, which is an apoptogenic factor released by mitochondria when cells undergo apoptotic cell death. Clearly, TPH104c and TPH104m did not induce apoptotic cell death by increasing the levels of cytochrome c. It has been reported that the loss of the mitochondrial membrane potential and subsequent mitochondrial damage are characteristics of the Fas-associated protein with death domain (FADD)-mediated necrotic death pathway; however, cytochrome c is not released [137,138]. Further investigations must be conducted to determine if Fas contributes to cell death triggered by TPH104c and TPH104m.

In addition, our findings revealed that the incubation of TNBC cells with TPH104c and TPH104m decreased DRP1 expression, whereas there was a trend (non-significant) in the increase in MFF expression, after cells were incubated with TPH104c and TPH104m. The upregulation of MFF has been shown to facilitate the recruitment of DRP1 to the mitochondria and initiate mitochondrial fission, independent of Fis1 [128]. Our results indicate that TPH104c and TPH104m have a minimal impact on MFF-mediated DRP1 recruitment to the mitochondria. However, DRP1 is inhibited once it is recruited to the mitochondria. It is also possible that MFF is upregulated to compensate for the decrease in DRP1 levels. Studies report that DRP1 inhibition, via *DRP1* knockout, can produce in vivo tumor suppression in pancreatic cells [139] and decrease metastasis after DRP1 silencing [38]. Qian et al. reported that loss of *DRP1* in the TNBC cell line MDA-MB-231 arrested the G2/M phase of the cell cycle, produced replication stress mediated by mitochondrial hyperfusion, and led to aneuploidy [140]. Similarly, *DRP1* knockdown and mdivi-1-induced inhibition of DRP1 suppressed mitochondrial fission and decreased TNBC cell migration [141]. The depletion of DRP1 has been reported to facilitate apoptosis in human cancer cells [135,142]. However, other studies suggest that DRP1 is necessary to trigger apoptosis, and its downregulation prevents cytochrome c release and the occurrence of apoptosis [134,143,144]. Interestingly, DRP1 mediates another form of non-apoptotic cell death, necroptosis, either by activating mitochondrial phosphatase, PGAM5 [145] or through interaction with retinoblastoma [146]. TPH104c- and TPH104m-induced cell death in BT-20 cells was not rescued upon incubation with Necrostatin-1 (RIPK1 inhibitor) [147] and necrosulfonamide (MLKL inhibitor) [148] (Figure S5a,b), which inhibit proteins required for necroptosis. Additionally, activation of DRP1 is crucial for initiating ferroptosis, another form of programmed non-apoptotic cell death, as either mitochondrial inactivation or DRP1 ablation decreases ferroptosis [149]. In accordance with this, our data indicated that the incubation of cells with Ferrostatin-1 (an inhibitor of ferroptosis [150]) did not rescue TPH104c- and TPH104m-induced cell death (Figure S5c). Further studies need to be performed to rule out the possibility of other forms of non-apoptotic cell death induced by TPH104c and TPH104m. However, considering the significant impact of TPH104c and TPH104m on the levels of DRP1 and MFF, additional studies will be required to determine whether these compounds also affect the structure of TNBC mitochondria, disrupt energy-producing processes, such as mitochondrial respiration and glycolysis or cause damage to the mitochondria.

5. Conclusions

In conclusion, our study results suggest that TPH104c- and TPH104m-mediated TNBC cell death is independent of apoptosis and regulated by DRP1, and thus, it is possible that these compounds could be used to treat cancer cells that are resistant to apoptosis, although this remains to be determined. TNBC tumors are characterized by increased mitochondrial fission and levels of DRP1 compared to peritumor tissues, and this is positively correlated with a poorer prognosis in TNBC patients [40]. Thus, it is possible that targeting DRP1 may be beneficial in the treatment of TNBC [151,152]. Therefore, the thienopyrimidine derivatives TPH104c and TPH104m could be potential candidates for treating TNBC by inducing non-apoptotic, DRP1-mediated TNBC cell death. Additional experiments must be conducted to elucidate how TPH104c and TPH104m induce non-apoptotic cell death in TNBC tumors, as this will assist us in obtaining optimal lead molecules for future preclinical development.

Supplementary Materials: The following supporting information can be downloaded at https://www.mdpi.com/article/10.3390/cancers16152621/s1, Original Western Blot images; Densitometry readings of Western Blot; Figure S1: TPH104c and TPH104m do not induce senescence in BT-20 cells, as shown by the morphological images of MEF cells treated with 250 nM of Doxorubicin for 24 h and BT-20 cells treated with 0.1, 0.3 or 1 μM of TPH104c and TPH104m for 24 h and stained with β-galactosidase. Scale bar = 200 μm; Figure S2: Bar graph illustrating the percentage of Annexin V positive BT-20 cells treated with TPH104c and TPH104m or vehicle that correlates to phosphatidyl serine exposure on the surface of apoptotic cells; Figure S3: The impact of pan-caspase inhibitor, Z-VAD-FMK and TPH104c and TPH104m on caspase activity. (a) Morphological images of BT-20 cells pre-treated with 100 μM Z-VAD-FMK and incubated with 0.1, 0.3, or 1 μM TPH104c and TPH104m captured at 0, 24, 48, and 72 h. Scale bar = 100 μm. (b) Cell viability curves of BT-20 cells pre-treated with Z-VAD-FMK and then incubated with varying concentrations of TPH104c or TPH104m over 72 h obtained using IncuCyte S3 software based on phase-contrast images of BT-20 cells; Figure S4: Effect of mitochondrial fusion proteins on TPH104c- and TPH104m-induced cell death. (a) Histograms summarizing the ratio of fusion proteins (MFN1, MFN2, and OPA1) to β-actin normalized to the vehicle control. The data are presented as the mean ± SEM of three separate studies. Predicted non-covalent interactions of ligands TPH104c and TPH104m. (b) TPH104c-magenta; TPH104m-cyan (c) TPH104m migration to a deeper hydrophobic pocket; ligand initial pose-gray; ligand final pose-cyan; the aryl moiety was observed to delve deeper into the hydrophobic subpocket guarded by LEU51, PRO52, ILE57, ILE111, THR59, and ILE63) (d) IC50 values of TPH104c and TPH104m in control wild-type, partial *DRP1* KO, and complete *DRP1* KO PAC200 cells by means of MTT, Cell Titer Blue assay, Cell Titer Blue assay, and SRB assay after 72 h post-incubation. Data are mean ± SEM of four independent experiments, each performed in triplicate; Figure S5: The impact of Necrostatin-1 (RIPK1 inhibitor), Necrosulfonamide (MLKL inhibitor), and Ferrostatin-1 (ferroptosis inhibitor) on TPH104c and TPH104m-induced cell death. Morphological images of BT-20 cells pre-incubated with (a) 50 μM of Necrostatin-1, (b) 1 μM of necrosulfonamide (NSA), and (c) 2 μM of Ferrostatin-1 and incubated with 1 μM TPH104c and TPH104m, captured at 72 h post-incubation. Scale bar = 100 μm. The respective cell viability curves were obtained using IncuCyte S3 software based on phase-contrast images of BT-20 cells. The data represent the mean ± SD of three independent experiments performed in triplicate; Table S1: The hydrogen bond occupancy table; Video S1: Time-lapse bright field movie shows the morphology of BT-20 cells during 48 h of incubation with control; Video S2: Time-lapse bright field movie shows the morphology of BT-20 cells during 48 h of incubation with TPH104c (5 μM); Video S3: Time-lapse bright field movie shows the morphology of BT-20 cells during 48 h of incubation with TPH104m (5 μM).

Author Contributions: Conceptualization, A.K.T. and R.J.B.; methodology, S.M., A.N., R.N., D.L., A.K.T. and S.K.; software, S.M., S.S. and A.K.T.; validation, S.K., A.R., R.J.B., R.P. and Y.T.; formal analysis, A.K.T., A.R. and Y.T.; investigation, S.M. and A.K.T.; resources, A.R., S.K. and Y.T.; data curation, S.M., D.L., A.N., M.A.-D. and R.J.B.; writing—original draft preparation, S.M. and A.K.T.; writing—review and editing, R.P., M.Q.Y., R.J.B., R.N. and C.R.A.J.; visualization, S.M. and A.K.T.; supervision, A.K.T. and R.J.B.; project administration and funding acquisition, A.K.T. All authors have read and agreed to the published version of the manuscript.

Funding: This research was funded by the Susan G. Komen Breast Cancer Foundation, grant number CCR18548498, and the Department of Defense, grant number W81XWH-21-1-0053. The views expressed in this article are those of the authors and may not reflect the official policy or position of the Susan G. Komen Breast Cancer Foundation or of the Department of the Army, Department of Defense, or the US Government.

Institutional Review Board Statement: Not applicable.

Informed Consent Statement: Not applicable.

Data Availability Statement: The data presented in this study are available in this article and Supplementary Materials.

Acknowledgments: We would like to acknowledge trainees in Tiwari's Lab, including Diwakar Tukaram, David Terrero, Noor Hussein, and Karthikeyan Chandrabose, for their contribution to maintaining cell lines and conducting chemical synthesis work. The graphical abstract was created with Biorender.com.

Conflicts of Interest: The authors declare no conflicts of interest.

References

1. Font-Clos, F.; Zapperi, S.; La Porta, C.A. Classification of triple negative breast cancer by epithelial mesenchymal transition and the tumor immune microenvironment. *Sci. Rep.* **2022**, *12*, 9651.
2. Geyer, F.C.; Pareja, F.; Weigelt, B.; Rakha, E.; Ellis, I.O.; Schnitt, S.J.; Reis-Filho, J.S. The spectrum of triple-negative breast disease: High-and low-grade lesions. *Am. J. Pathol.* **2017**, *187*, 2139–2151. [CrossRef]
3. Ensenyat-Mendez, M.; Llinàs-Arias, P.; Orozco, J.I.; Íñiguez-Muñoz, S.; Salomon, M.P.; Sesé, B.; DiNome, M.L.; Marzese, D.M. Current Triple-Negative Breast Cancer Subtypes: Dissecting the Most Aggressive Form of Breast Cancer. *Front. Oncol.* **2021**, *2311*, 681476. [CrossRef] [PubMed]
4. Dent, R.; Trudeau, M.; Pritchard, K.I.; Hanna, W.M.; Kahn, H.K.; Sawka, C.A.; Lickley, L.A.; Rawlinson, E.; Sun, P.; Narod, S.A. Triple-negative breast cancer: Clinical features and patterns of recurrence. *Clin. Cancer Res.* **2007**, *13*, 4429–4434. [CrossRef] [PubMed]
5. Aysola, K.; Desai, A.; Welch, C.; Xu, J.; Qin, Y.; Reddy, V.; Matthews, R.; Owens, C.; Okoli, J.; Beech, D.J. Triple negative breast cancer—An overview. *Hered. Genet. Curr. Res.* **2013**, *2013*, 1.
6. Joensuu, H.; Gligorov, J. Adjuvant treatments for triple-negative breast cancers. *Ann. Oncol.* **2012**, *23*, vi40–vi45. [CrossRef] [PubMed]
7. Mavratzas, A.; Seitz, J.; Smetanay, K.; Schneeweiss, A.; Jäger, D.; Fremd, C. Atezolizumab for use in PD-L1-positive unresectable, locally advanced or metastatic triple-negative breast cancer. *Future Oncol.* **2020**, *16*, 4439–4453. [CrossRef] [PubMed]
8. Bagegni, N.A.; Davis, A.A.; Clifton, K.K.; Ademuyiwa, F.O. Targeted Treatment for High-Risk Early-Stage Triple-Negative Breast Cancer: Spotlight on Pembrolizumab. *Breast Cancer Targets Ther.* **2022**, *14*, 113–123. [CrossRef] [PubMed]
9. Schmid, P.; Cortes, J.; Dent, R.; Pusztai, L.; McArthur, H.; Kümmel, S.; Bergh, J.; Denkert, C.; Park, Y.H.; Hui, R. Event-free survival with pembrolizumab in early triple-negative breast cancer. *N. Engl. J. Med.* **2022**, *386*, 556–567. [CrossRef] [PubMed]
10. Schmid, P.; Cortes, J.; Pusztai, L.; McArthur, H.; Kümmel, S.; Bergh, J.; Denkert, C.; Park, Y.H.; Hui, R.; Harbeck, N. Pembrolizumab for early triple-negative breast cancer. *N. Engl. J. Med.* **2020**, *382*, 810–821. [CrossRef]
11. Nagayama, A.; Vidula, N.; Bardia, A. Novel Therapies for Metastatic Triple-Negative Breast Cancer: Spotlight on Immunotherapy and Antibody-Drug Conjugates. *Oncology* **2021**, *35*, 249–254. [CrossRef] [PubMed]

12. Costa, R.L.; Gradishar, W.J. Triple-negative breast cancer: Current practice and future directions. *J. Oncol. Pract.* **2017**, *13*, 301–303. [CrossRef] [PubMed]
13. Lebert, J.; Lester, R.; Powell, E.; Seal, M.; McCarthy, J. Advances in the systemic treatment of triple-negative breast cancer. *Curr. Oncol.* **2018**, *25*, S142. [CrossRef]
14. Škubník, J.; Pavlíčková, V.; Ruml, T.; Rimpelová, S. Current perspectives on taxanes: Focus on their bioactivity, delivery and combination therapy. *Plants* **2021**, *10*, 569. [CrossRef]
15. McGee, S. Understanding metastasis: Current paradigms and therapeutic challenges in breast cancer progression. *RCSI Stud. Med. J.* **2010**, *3*, 56–60.
16. Saloustros, E.; Nikolaou, M.; Kalbakis, K.; Polyzos, A.; Christofillakis, C.; Kentepozidis, N.; Pistamaltzian, N.; Kourousis, C.; Vamvakas, L.; Georgoulias, V. Weekly paclitaxel and carboplatin plus bevacizumab as first-line treatment of metastatic triple-negative breast cancer. A Multicenter Phase II Trial by the Hellenic Oncology Research Group. *Clin. Breast Cancer* **2018**, *18*, 88–94. [CrossRef] [PubMed]
17. Wahba, H.A.; El-Hadaad, H.A. Current approaches in treatment of triple-negative breast cancer. *Cancer Biol. Med.* **2015**, *12*, 106.
18. Choi, C.H. ABC transporters as multidrug resistance mechanisms and the development of chemosensitizers for their reversal. *Cancer Cell Int.* **2005**, *5*, 30. [CrossRef]
19. Fulda, S. Evasion of apoptosis as a cellular stress response in cancer. *Int. J. Cell Biol.* **2010**, *2010*, 370835. [CrossRef] [PubMed]
20. Pisco, A.O.; Jackson, D.A.; Huang, S. Reduced intracellular drug accumulation in drug-resistant leukemia cells is not only solely due to MDR-mediated efflux but also to decreased uptake. *Front. Oncol.* **2014**, *4*, 306. [CrossRef]
21. Helleday, T.; Petermann, E.; Lundin, C.; Hodgson, B.; Sharma, R.A. DNA repair pathways as targets for cancer therapy. *Nat. Rev. Cancer* **2008**, *8*, 193–204. [CrossRef] [PubMed]
22. Trédan, O.; Galmarini, C.M.; Patel, K.; Tannock, I.F. Drug Resistance and the Solid Tumor Microenvironment. *JNCI J. Natl. Cancer Inst.* **2007**, *99*, 1441–1454. [CrossRef] [PubMed]
23. Mansoori, B.; Mohammadi, A.; Davudian, S.; Shirjang, S.; Baradaran, B. The Different Mechanisms of Cancer Drug Resistance: A Brief Review. *Adv. Pharm. Bull.* **2017**, *7*, 339–348. [CrossRef] [PubMed]
24. Gong, Y.; Duvvuri, M.; Krise, J.P. Separate roles for the Golgi apparatus and lysosomes in the sequestration of drugs in the multidrug-resistant human leukemic cell line HL-60. *J. Biol. Chem.* **2003**, *278*, 50234–50239. [CrossRef] [PubMed]
25. Hraběta, J.; Belhajová, M.; Šubrtová, H.; Merlos Rodrigo, M.A.; Heger, Z.; Eckschlager, T. Drug Sequestration in Lysosomes as One of the Mechanisms of Chemoresistance of Cancer Cells and the Possibilities of Its Inhibition. *Int. J. Mol. Sci.* **2020**, *21*, 4392. [CrossRef] [PubMed]
26. Ouar, Z.; Lacave, R.; Bens, M.; Vandewalle, A. Mechanisms of altered sequestration and efflux of chemotherapeutic drugs by multidrug-resistant cells. *Cell Biol. Toxicol.* **1999**, *15*, 91–100. [CrossRef]
27. Zaal, E.A.; Berkers, C.R. The Influence of Metabolism on Drug Response in Cancer. *Front. Oncol.* **2018**, *8*, 500. [CrossRef] [PubMed]
28. Tait, S.W.; Ichim, G.; Green, D.R. Die another way–non-apoptotic mechanisms of cell death. *J. Cell Sci.* **2014**, *127*, 2135–2144. [CrossRef] [PubMed]
29. Woo, S.M.; Seo, S.U.; Min, K.J.; Im, S.S.; Nam, J.O.; Chang, J.S.; Kim, S.; Park, J.W.; Kwon, T.K. Corosolic Acid Induces Non-Apoptotic Cell Death through Generation of Lipid Reactive Oxygen Species Production in Human Renal Carcinoma Caki Cells. *Int. J. Mol. Sci.* **2018**, *19*, 1309. [CrossRef]
30. Kornienko, A.; Mathieu, V.; Rastogi, S.K.; Lefranc, F.; Kiss, R. Therapeutic Agents Triggering Nonapoptotic Cancer Cell Death. *J. Med. Chem.* **2013**, *56*, 4823–4839. [CrossRef]
31. Rodrigues, T.; Ferraz, L.S. Therapeutic potential of targeting mitochondrial dynamics in cancer. *Biochem. Pharmacol.* **2020**, *182*, 114282. [CrossRef] [PubMed]
32. Srinivasan, S.; Guha, M.; Kashina, A.; Avadhani, N.G. Mitochondrial dysfunction and mitochondrial dynamics-The cancer connection. *Biochim. Biophys. Acta Bioenerg.* **2017**, *1858*, 602–614. [CrossRef] [PubMed]
33. Kumar, S.; Ashraf, R.; Aparna, C.K. Mitochondrial dynamics regulators: Implications for therapeutic intervention in cancer. *Cell Biol. Toxicol.* **2022**, *38*, 377–406. [CrossRef] [PubMed]
34. Chen, H.; Chan, D.C. Mitochondrial Dynamics in Regulating the Unique Phenotypes of Cancer and Stem Cells. *Cell Metab.* **2017**, *26*, 39–48. [CrossRef] [PubMed]
35. Tilokani, L.; Nagashima, S.; Paupe, V.; Prudent, J. Mitochondrial dynamics: Overview of molecular mechanisms. *Essays Biochem.* **2018**, *62*, 341–360. [CrossRef] [PubMed]
36. Wai, T.; Langer, T. Mitochondrial Dynamics and Metabolic Regulation. *Trends Endocrinol. Metab.* **2016**, *27*, 105–117. [CrossRef] [PubMed]
37. Rehman, J.; Zhang, H.J.; Toth, P.T.; Zhang, Y.; Marsboom, G.; Hong, Z.; Salgia, R.; Husain, A.N.; Wietholt, C.; Archer, S.L. Inhibition of mitochondrial fission prevents cell cycle progression in lung cancer. *FASEB J.* **2012**, *26*, 2175. [CrossRef] [PubMed]
38. Zhao, J.; Zhang, J.; Yu, M.; Xie, Y.; Huang, Y.; Wolff, D.W.; Abel, P.W.; Tu, Y. Mitochondrial dynamics regulates migration and invasion of breast cancer cells. *Oncogene* **2013**, *32*, 4814–4824. [CrossRef] [PubMed]
39. Xie, Q.; Wu, Q.; Horbinski, C.M.; Flavahan, W.A.; Yang, K.; Zhou, W.; Dombrowski, S.M.; Huang, Z.; Fang, X.; Shi, Y. Mitochondrial control by DRP1 in brain tumor initiating cells. *Nat. Neurosci.* **2015**, *18*, 501–510. [CrossRef]

40. Chen, L.; Zhang, J.; Lyu, Z.; Chen, Y.; Ji, X.; Cao, H.; Jin, M.; Zhu, J.; Yang, J.; Ling, R. Positive feedback loop between mitochondrial fission and Notch signaling promotes survivin-mediated survival of TNBC cells. *Cell Death Dis.* **2018**, *9*, 1050. [CrossRef]
41. Lagardère, P.; Fersing, C.; Masurier, N.; Lisowski, V. Thienopyrimidine: A Promising Scaffold to Access Anti-Infective Agents. *Pharmaceuticals* **2022**, *15*, 35. [CrossRef]
42. Bassetto, M.; Leyssen, P.; Neyts, J.; Yerukhimovich, M.M.; Frick, D.N.; Brancale, A. Computer-aided identification, synthesis and evaluation of substituted thienopyrimidines as novel inhibitors of HCV replication. *Eur. J. Med. Chem.* **2016**, *123*, 31–47. [CrossRef]
43. Rizk, O.H.; Shaaban, O.G.; El-Ashmawy, I.M. Design, synthesis and biological evaluation of some novel thienopyrimidines and fused thienopyrimidines as anti-inflammatory agents. *Eur. J. Med. Chem.* **2012**, *55*, 85–93. [CrossRef]
44. El-Sayed, W.A.; Ali, O.M.; Zyada, R.; Mohamed, A.A.; Abdel-Rahman, A. Synthesis and antimicrobial activity of new substituted thienopyrimidines, their tetrazolyl and sugar derivatives. *Acta Pol. Pharm.* **2012**, *69*, 439–447.
45. Li, S.-G.; Vilchèze, C.; Chakraborty, S.; Wang, X.; Kim, H.; Anisetti, M.; Ekins, S.; Rhee, K.Y.; Jacobs, W.R., Jr.; Freundlich, J.S. Evolution of a thienopyrimidine antitubercular relying on medicinal chemistry and metabolomics insights. *Tetrahedron Lett.* **2015**, *56*, 3246–3250. [CrossRef]
46. Kotaiah, Y.; Harikrishna, N.; Nagaraju, K.; Rao, C.V. Synthesis and antioxidant activity of 1, 3, 4-oxadiazole tagged thieno [2, 3-d] pyrimidine derivatives. *Eur. J. Med. Chem.* **2012**, *58*, 340–345. [CrossRef]
47. Bugge, S.; Buene, A.F.; Jurisch-Yaksi, N.; Moen, I.U.; Skjønsfjell, E.M.; Sundby, E.; Hoff, B.H. Extended structure–activity study of thienopyrimidine-based EGFR inhibitors with evaluation of drug-like properties. *Eur. J. Med. Chem.* **2016**, *107*, 255–274. [CrossRef]
48. Powles, T.; Lackner, M.R.; Oudard, S.; Escudier, B.; Ralph, C.; Brown, J.E.; Hawkins, R.E.; Castellano, D.; Rini, B.I.; Staehler, M.D. Randomized open-label phase II trial of apitolisib (GDC-0980), a novel inhibitor of the PI3K/mammalian target of rapamycin pathway, versus everolimus in patients with metastatic renal cell carcinoma. *J. Clin. Oncol.* **2016**, *34*, 1660. [CrossRef]
49. Makker, V.; Recio, F.O.; Ma, L.; Matulonis, U.A.; Lauchle, J.O.; Parmar, H.; Gilbert, H.N.; Ware, J.A.; Zhu, R.; Lu, S. A multicenter, single-arm, open-label, phase 2 study of apitolisib (GDC-0980) for the treatment of recurrent or persistent endometrial carcinoma (MAGGIE study). *Cancer* **2016**, *122*, 3519–3528. [CrossRef]
50. Shapiro, G.I.; LoRusso, P.; Kwak, E.; Pandya, S.; Rudin, C.M.; Kurkjian, C.; Cleary, J.M.; Pilat, M.J.; Jones, S.; de Crespigny, A. Phase Ib study of the MEK inhibitor cobimetinib (GDC-0973) in combination with the PI3K inhibitor pictilisib (GDC-0941) in patients with advanced solid tumors. *Investig. New Drugs* **2020**, *38*, 419–432. [CrossRef]
51. Robert, F.; Verschraegen, C.; Hurwitz, H.; Uronis, H.; Advani, R.; Chen, A.; Taverna, P.; Wollman, M.; Fox, J.; Michelson, G. A phase I trial of sns-314, a novel and selective pan-aurora kinase inhibitor, in advanced solid tumor patients. *J. Clin. Oncol.* **2009**, *27*, 2536. [CrossRef]
52. Shyyka, O.; Pokhodylo, N.; Finiuk, N.; Matiychuk, V.; Stoika, R.; Obushak, M. Anticancer Activity Evaluation of New Thieno [2, 3-d] pyrimidin-4 (3 H)-ones and Thieno [3, 2-d] pyrimidin-4 (3 H)-one Derivatives. *Sci. Pharm.* **2018**, *86*, 28. [CrossRef]
53. Tukaramrao, D.B.; Malla, S.; Saraiya, S.; Hanely, R.A.; Ray, A.; Kumari, S.; Raman, D.; Tiwari, A.K. A Novel Thienopyrimidine Analog, TPH104, Mediates Immunogenic Cell Death in Triple-Negative Breast Cancer Cells. *Cancers* **2021**, *13*, 1954. [CrossRef]
54. Tiwari, A.K.; Karthikeyan, C.; Nyinawabera, A. Necroptosis Inducers or Autophagy Inhibitors or a Combination Thereof. U.S. Patent US17/047,155, 12 April 2019.
55. Sridharan, S.; Robeson, M.; Bastihalli-Tukaramrao, D.; Howard, C.M.; Subramaniyan, B.; Tilley, A.M.; Tiwari, A.K.; Raman, D. Targeting of the eukaryotic translation initiation factor 4A against breast cancer stemness. *Front. Oncol.* **2019**, *9*, 1311. [CrossRef]
56. Debnath, J.; Muthuswamy, S.K.; Brugge, J.S. Morphogenesis and oncogenesis of MCF-10A mammary epithelial acini grown in three-dimensional basement membrane cultures. *Methods* **2003**, *30*, 256–268. [CrossRef]
57. Amawi, H.; Hussein, N.A.; Ashby, C.R., Jr.; Alnafisah, R.; Sanglard, L.M.; Manivannan, E.; Karthikeyan, C.; Trivedi, P.; Eisenmann, K.M.; Robey, R.W. Bax/tubulin/epithelial-mesenchymal pathways determine the efficacy of silybin analog HM015k in colorectal cancer cell growth and metastasis. *Front. Pharmacol.* **2018**, *9*, 520. [CrossRef]
58. O'Clair, L.; Artymovich, K.; Roddy, M.; Appledorn, D.M. *Quantification of Cytotoxicity Using the IncuCyte® Cytotoxicity Assay*; Essen BioScience: Ann Arbor, MI, USA, 2017; pp. 1–5.
59. Len, J.M.; Hussein, N.; Malla, S.; Mcintosh, K.; Patidar, R.; Elangovan, M.; Chandrabose, K.; Moorthy, N.S.H.N.; Pandey, M.; Raman, D.; et al. A Novel Dialkylamino-Functionalized Chalcone, DML6, Inhibits Cervical Cancer Cell Proliferation, In Vitro, via Induction of Oxidative Stress, Intrinsic Apoptosis and Mitotic Catastrophe. *Molecules* **2021**, *26*, 4214. [CrossRef]
60. Heney, M.; Alipour, M.; Vergidis, D.; Omri, A.; Mugabe, C.; Th'ng, J.; Suntres, Z. Effectiveness of liposomal paclitaxel against MCF-7 breast cancer cells. *Can. J. Physiol. Pharmacol.* **2010**, *88*, 1172–1180. [CrossRef]
61. Fang, L.; Cheng, Q.; Bai, J.; Qi, Y.-D.; Liu, J.-J.; Li, L.-T.; Zheng, J.-N. An oncolytic adenovirus expressing interleukin-24 enhances antitumor activities in combination with paclitaxel in breast cancer cells. *Mol. Med. Rep.* **2013**, *8*, 1416–1424. [CrossRef]
62. Neupane, R.; Malla, S.; Abou-Dahech, M.S.; Balaji, S.; Kumari, S.; Waiker, D.K.; Moorthy, N.H.N.; Trivedi, P.; Ashby, C.R., Jr.; Karthikeyan, C. Antiproliferative Efficacy of N-(3-chloro-4-fluorophenyl)-6, 7-dimethoxyquinazolin-4-amine, DW-8, in Colon Cancer Cells Is Mediated by Intrinsic Apoptosis. *Molecules* **2021**, *26*, 4417. [CrossRef] [PubMed]
63. Chen, L.; Ma, K.; Han, J.; Chen, Q.; Zhu, Y. Monitoring mitophagy in mammalian cells. In *Methods in Enzymology*; Elsevier: Amsterdam, The Netherlands, 2017; Volume 588, pp. 187–208.

64. Galluzzi, L.; Vitale, I.; Aaronson, S.A.; Abrams, J.M.; Adam, D.; Agostinis, P.; Alnemri, E.S.; Altucci, L.; Amelio, I.; Andrews, D.W. Molecular mechanisms of cell death: Recommendations of the Nomenclature Committee on Cell Death 2018. *Cell Death Differ.* **2018**, *25*, 486–541. [PubMed]
65. Kabir, M.A.; Kharel, A.; Malla, S.; Kreis, Z.J.; Nath, P.; Wolfe, J.N.; Hassan, M.; Kaur, D.; Sari-Sarraf, H.; Tiwari, A.K. Automated detection of apoptotic versus nonapoptotic cell death using label-free computational microscopy. *J. Biophotonics* **2022**, *15*, e202100310. [CrossRef] [PubMed]
66. Amawi, H.; Hussein, N.A.; Karthikeyan, C.; Manivannan, E.; Wisner, A.; Williams, F.E.; Samuel, T.; Trivedi, P.; Ashby, C.R., Jr.; Tiwari, A.K. HM015k, a novel silybin derivative, multi-targets metastatic ovarian cancer cells and is safe in zebrafish toxicity studies. *Front. Pharmacol.* **2017**, *8*, 498. [CrossRef]
67. Ruiz-Carmona, S.; Alvarez-Garcia, D.; Foloppe, N.; Garmendia-Doval, A.B.; Juhos, S.; Schmidtke, P.; Barril, X.; Hubbard, R.E.; Morley, S.D. rDock: A fast, versatile and open source program for docking ligands to proteins and nucleic acids. *PLoS Comput. Biol.* **2014**, *10*, e1003571. [CrossRef]
68. Wenger, J.; Klinglmayr, E.; Fröhlich, C.; Eibl, C.; Gimeno, A.; Hessenberger, M.; Puehringer, S.; Daumke, O.; Goettig, P. Functional mapping of human dynamin-1-like GTPase domain based on x-ray structure analyses. *PLoS ONE* **2013**, *8*, e71835. [CrossRef] [PubMed]
69. Van Der Spoel, D.; Lindahl, E.; Hess, B.; Groenhof, G.; Mark, A.E.; Berendsen, H.J. GROMACS: Fast, flexible, and free. *J. Comput. Chem.* **2005**, *26*, 1701–1718. [CrossRef] [PubMed]
70. Abraham, M.J.; Murtola, T.; Schulz, R.; Páll, S.; Smith, J.C.; Hess, B.; Lindahl, E. GROMACS: High performance molecular simulations through multi-level parallelism from laptops to supercomputers. *SoftwareX* **2015**, *1*, 19–25. [CrossRef]
71. Huang, J.; Rauscher, S.; Nawrocki, G.; Ran, T.; Feig, M.; De Groot, B.L.; Grubmüller, H.; MacKerell, A.D., Jr. CHARMM36m: An improved force field for folded and intrinsically disordered proteins. *Nat. Methods* **2017**, *14*, 71–73. [CrossRef] [PubMed]
72. Jo, S.; Kim, T.; Iyer, V.G.; Im, W. CHARMM-GUI: A web-based graphical user interface for CHARMM. *J. Comput. Chem.* **2008**, *29*, 1859–1865. [CrossRef]
73. Lee, J.; Cheng, X.; Jo, S.; MacKerell, A.D.; Klauda, J.B.; Im, W. CHARMM-GUI input generator for NAMD, GROMACS, AMBER, OpenMM, and CHARMM/OpenMM simulations using the CHARMM36 additive force field. *Biophys. J.* **2016**, *110*, 641a. [CrossRef]
74. Lee, J.; Hitzenberger, M.; Rieger, M.; Kern, N.R.; Zacharias, M.; Im, W. CHARMM-GUI supports the Amber force fields. *J. Chem. Phys.* **2020**, *153*, 035103. [CrossRef] [PubMed]
75. Jorgensen, W.L.; Chandrasekhar, J.; Madura, J.D.; Impey, R.W.; Klein, M.L. Comparison of simple potential functions for simulating liquid water. *J. Chem. Phys.* **1983**, *79*, 926–935. [CrossRef]
76. Haug, E.; Arora, J.; Matsui, K. A steepest-descent method for optimization of mechanical systems. *J. Optim. Theory Appl.* **1976**, *19*, 401–424. [CrossRef]
77. Hopkins, C.W.; Le Grand, S.; Walker, R.C.; Roitberg, A.E. Long-time-step molecular dynamics through hydrogen mass repartitioning. *J. Chem. Theory Comput.* **2015**, *11*, 1864–1874. [CrossRef] [PubMed]
78. Darden, T.; York, D.; Pedersen, L. Particle mesh Ewald: An N· log (N) method for Ewald sums in large systems. *J. Chem. Phys.* **1993**, *98*, 10089–10092. [CrossRef]
79. Hess, B.; Bekker, H.; Berendsen, H.J.; Fraaije, J.G. LINCS: A linear constraint solver for molecular simulations. *J. Comput. Chem.* **1997**, *18*, 1463–1472. [CrossRef]
80. Elber, R.; Ruymgaart, A.P.; Hess, B. SHAKE parallelization. *Eur. Phys. J. Spec. Top.* **2011**, *200*, 211–223. [CrossRef] [PubMed]
81. Miyamoto, S.; Kollman, P.A. Settle: An analytical version of the SHAKE and RATTLE algorithm for rigid water models. *J. Comput. Chem.* **1992**, *13*, 952–962. [CrossRef]
82. Shapiro, G.I.; Harper, J.W. Anticancer drug targets: Cell cycle and checkpoint control. *J. Clin. Investig.* **1999**, *104*, 1645–1653. [CrossRef]
83. Sun, Y.; Liu, Y.; Ma, X.; Hu, H. The Influence of Cell Cycle Regulation on Chemotherapy. *Int. J. Mol. Sci.* **2021**, *22*, 6923. [CrossRef]
84. Nunez, R. DNA measurement and cell cycle analysis by flow cytometry. *Curr. Issues Mol. Biol.* **2001**, *3*, 67–70. [CrossRef] [PubMed]
85. Zhao, H.; Darzynkiewicz, Z. Biomarkers of cell senescence assessed by imaging cytometry. In *Cell Senescence. Methods in Molecular Biology*; Humana Press: Totowa, NJ, USA, 2013; pp. 83–92.
86. Lee, B.Y.; Han, J.A.; Im, J.S.; Morrone, A.; Johung, K.; Goodwin, E.C.; Kleijer, W.J.; DiMaio, D.; Hwang, E.S. Senescence-associated β-galactosidase is lysosomal β-galactosidase. *Aging Cell* **2006**, *5*, 187–195. [CrossRef] [PubMed]
87. Itahana, K.; Campisi, J.; Dimri, G.P. Methods to detect biomarkers of cellular senescence: The senescence-associated β-galactosidase assay. *Biol. Aging Methods Protoc.* **2007**, *371*, 21–31.
88. Zhang, G.; Gurtu, V.; Kain, S.R.; Yan, G. Early detection of apoptosis using a fluorescent conjugate of annexin V. *Biotechniques* **1997**, *23*, 525–531. [CrossRef] [PubMed]
89. Ziegler, U.; Groscurth, P. Morphological features of cell death. *Physiology* **2004**, *19*, 124–128. [CrossRef]
90. Chazotte, B. Labeling nuclear DNA with hoechst 33342. *Cold Spring Harb. Protoc.* **2011**, *2011*, pdb.prot5557. [CrossRef] [PubMed]
91. Wang, F.; Chen, Y.; Zhang, D.; Zhang, Q.; Zheng, D.; Hao, L.; Liu, Y.; Duan, C.; Jia, L.; Liu, G. Folate-mediated targeted and intracellular delivery of paclitaxel using a novel deoxycholic acid-O-carboxymethylated chitosan–folic acid micelles. *Int. J. Nanomed.* **2012**, *7*, 325–337.

92. Tummers, B.; Green, D.R. Caspase-8: Regulating life and death. *Immunol. Rev.* **2017**, *277*, 76–89. [CrossRef]
93. Hickson, J.; Ackler, S.; Klaubert, D.; Bouska, J.; Ellis, P.; Foster, K.; Oleksijew, A.; Rodriguez, L.; Schlessinger, S.; Wang, B. Noninvasive molecular imaging of apoptosis in vivo using a modified firefly luciferase substrate, Z-DEVD-aminoluciferin. *Cell Death Differ.* **2010**, *17*, 1003–1010. [CrossRef]
94. Riss, T.L.; Moravec, R.A.; O'Brien, M.A.; Hawkins, E.M.; Niles, A. Homogeneous Multiwell Assays for Measuring Cell Viabiltiy, Cytotoxicity, and Apoptosis. In *Handbook of Assay Development in Drug Discovery*; CRC Press: Boca Raton, FL, USA, 2006; pp. 403–424.
95. Kutuk, O.; Letai, A. Alteration of the mitochondrial apoptotic pathway is key to acquired paclitaxel resistance and can be reversed by ABT-737. *Cancer Res.* **2008**, *68*, 7985–7994. [CrossRef]
96. Kutuk, O.; Letai, A. Displacement of Bim by Bmf and Puma rather than increase in Bim level mediates paclitaxel-induced apoptosis in breast cancer cells. *Cell Death Differ.* **2010**, *17*, 1624–1635. [CrossRef]
97. Pistritto, G.; Trisciuoglio, D.; Ceci, C.; Garufi, A.; D'Orazi, G. Apoptosis as anticancer mechanism: Function and dysfunction of its modulators and targeted therapeutic strategies. *Aging* **2016**, *8*, 603. [CrossRef] [PubMed]
98. Elmore, S. Apoptosis: A review of programmed cell death. *Toxicol. Pathol.* **2007**, *35*, 495–516. [CrossRef] [PubMed]
99. Kale, J.; Osterlund, E.J.; Andrews, D.W. BCL-2 family proteins: Changing partners in the dance towards death. *Cell Death Differ.* **2018**, *25*, 65–80. [CrossRef] [PubMed]
100. Redza-Dutordoir, M.; Averill-Bates, D.A. Activation of apoptosis signalling pathways by reactive oxygen species. *Biochim. Biophys. Acta BBA-Mol. Cell Res.* **2016**, *1863*, 2977–2992. [CrossRef]
101. Martinou, J.-C.; Youle, R.J. Mitochondria in apoptosis: Bcl-2 family members and mitochondrial dynamics. *Dev. Cell* **2011**, *21*, 92–101. [CrossRef]
102. Li, P.; Nijhawan, D.; Budihardjo, I.; Srinivasula, S.M.; Ahmad, M.; Alnemri, E.S.; Wang, X. Cytochrome c and dATP-dependent formation of Apaf-1/caspase-9 complex initiates an apoptotic protease cascade. *Cell* **1997**, *91*, 479–489. [CrossRef]
103. Hu, Q.; Wu, D.; Chen, W.; Yan, Z.; Yan, C.; He, T.; Liang, Q.; Shi, Y. Molecular determinants of caspase-9 activation by the Apaf-1 apoptosome. *Proc. Natl. Acad. Sci. USA* **2014**, *111*, 16254–16261. [CrossRef]
104. Wu, C.-C.; Lee, S.; Malladi, S.; Chen, M.-D.; Mastrandrea, N.J.; Zhang, Z.; Bratton, S.B. The Apaf-1 apoptosome induces formation of caspase-9 homo-and heterodimers with distinct activities. *Nat. Commun.* **2016**, *7*, 1–14. [CrossRef]
105. Julien, O.; Wells, J.A. Caspases and their substrates. *Cell Death Differ.* **2017**, *24*, 1380–1389. [CrossRef]
106. Nagata, S. DNA degradation in development and programmed cell death. *Annu. Rev. Immunol.* **2005**, *23*, 853–875. [CrossRef] [PubMed]
107. Naito, M.; Nagashima, K.; Mashima, T.; Tsuruo, T. Phosphatidylserine Externalization Is a Downstream Event of Interleukin-1β–Converting Enzyme Family Protease Activation during Apoptosis. *Blood J. Am. Soc. Hematol.* **1997**, *89*, 2060–2066. [CrossRef]
108. Sebbagh, M.; Renvoizé, C.; Hamelin, J.; Riché, N.; Bertoglio, J.; Bréard, J. Caspase-3-mediated cleavage of ROCK I induces MLC phosphorylation and apoptotic membrane blebbing. *Nat. Cell Biol.* **2001**, *3*, 346–352. [CrossRef] [PubMed]
109. Dickens, L.S.; Powley, I.R.; Hughes, M.A.; MacFarlane, M. The 'complexities' of life and death: Death receptor signalling platforms. *Exp. Cell Res.* **2012**, *318*, 1269–1277. [CrossRef] [PubMed]
110. Kischkel, F.C.; Hellbardt, S.; Behrmann, I.; Germer, M.; Pawlita, M.; Krammer, P.H.; Peter, M.E. Cytotoxicity-dependent APO-1 (Fas/CD95)-associated proteins form a death-inducing signaling complex (DISC) with the receptor. *EMBO J.* **1995**, *14*, 5579–5588. [CrossRef] [PubMed]
111. Crowley, L.C.; Christensen, M.E.; Waterhouse, N.J. Measuring mitochondrial transmembrane potential by TMRE staining. *Cold Spring Harb. Protoc.* **2016**, *2016*, pdb.prot087361. [CrossRef] [PubMed]
112. Goldsby, R.; Heytler, P. Uncoupling of oxidative phosphorylation by carbonyl cyanide phenylhydrazones. II. Effects of carbonyl cyanide m-chlorophenylhydrazone on mitochondrial respiration. *Biochemistry* **1963**, *2*, 1142–1147. [CrossRef] [PubMed]
113. Perry, S.W.; Norman, J.P.; Barbieri, J.; Brown, E.B.; Gelbard, H.A. Mitochondrial membrane potential probes and the proton gradient: A practical usage guide. *BioTechniques* **2011**, *50*, 98–115. [CrossRef] [PubMed]
114. Seervi, M.; Joseph, J.; Sobhan, P.; Bhavya, B.; Santhoshkumar, T. Essential requirement of cytochrome c release for caspase activation by procaspase-activating compound defined by cellular models. *Cell Death Dis.* **2011**, *2*, e207. [CrossRef]
115. Renz, A.; Berdel, W.E.; Kreuter, M.; Belka, C.; Schulze-Osthoff, K.; Los, M. Rapid extracellular release of cytochrome c is specific for apoptosis and marks cell death in vivo. *Blood J. Am. Soc. Hematol.* **2001**, *98*, 1542–1548. [CrossRef]
116. Ricci, J.-E.; Muñoz-Pinedo, C.; Fitzgerald, P.; Bailly-Maitre, B.; Perkins, G.A.; Yadava, N.; Scheffler, I.E.; Ellisman, M.H.; Green, D.R. Disruption of mitochondrial function during apoptosis is mediated by caspase cleavage of the p75 subunit of complex I of the electron transport chain. *Cell* **2004**, *117*, 773–786. [CrossRef] [PubMed]
117. Simon, H.-U.; Haj-Yehia, A.; Levi-Schaffer, F. Role of reactive oxygen species (ROS) in apoptosis induction. *Apoptosis* **2000**, *5*, 415–418. [CrossRef]
118. Woo, C.C.; Hsu, A.; Kumar, A.P.; Sethi, G.; Tan, K.H.B. Thymoquinone inhibits tumor growth and induces apoptosis in a breast cancer xenograft mouse model: The role of p38 MAPK and ROS. *PLoS ONE* **2013**, *8*, e75356. [CrossRef] [PubMed]
119. Dai, X.; Wang, L.; Deivasigamni, A.; Looi, C.Y.; Karthikeyan, C.; Trivedi, P.; Chinnathambi, A.; Alharbi, S.A.; Arfuso, F.; Dharmarajan, A. A novel benzimidazole derivative, MBIC inhibits tumor growth and promotes apoptosis via activation of ROS-dependent JNK signaling pathway in hepatocellular carcinoma. *Oncotarget* **2017**, *8*, 12831. [CrossRef] [PubMed]

120. Yoshida, K.; Miki, Y. The cell death machinery governed by the p53 tumor suppressor in response to DNA damage. *Cancer Sci.* **2010**, *101*, 831–835. [CrossRef] [PubMed]
121. Hausenloy, D.; Wynne, A.; Duchen, M.; Yellon, D. Transient mitochondrial permeability transition pore opening mediates preconditioning-induced protection. *Circulation* **2004**, *109*, 1714–1717. [CrossRef] [PubMed]
122. Varanyuwatana, P.; Halestrap, A.P. The mitochondrial permeability transition pore and its modulators. *BBA-Bioenerg.* **2010**, *1797*, 130–131. [CrossRef]
123. Giorgio, M.; Migliaccio, E.; Orsini, F.; Paolucci, D.; Moroni, M.; Contursi, C.; Pelliccia, G.; Luzi, L.; Minucci, S.; Marcaccio, M. Electron transfer between cytochrome c and p66Shc generates reactive oxygen species that trigger mitochondrial apoptosis. *Cell* **2005**, *122*, 221–233. [CrossRef] [PubMed]
124. Yang, C.; Jiang, L.; Zhang, H.; Shimoda, L.A.; DeBerardinis, R.J.; Semenza, G.L. Analysis of hypoxia-induced metabolic reprogramming. *Methods Enzymol.* **2014**, *542*, 425–455.
125. Kim, H.; Xue, X. Detection of Total Reactive Oxygen Species in Adherent Cells by 2′,7′-Dichlorodihydrofluorescein Diacetate Staining. *J. Vis. Exp. JoVE* **2020**, *160*, 60682. [CrossRef]
126. Li, M.; Yin, L.; Wu, L.; Zhu, Y.; Wang, X. Paclitaxel inhibits proliferation and promotes apoptosis through regulation ROS and endoplasmic reticulum stress in osteosarcoma cell. *Mol. Cell. Toxicol.* **2020**, *16*, 377–384. [CrossRef]
127. Ren, L.; Chen, X.; Chen, X.; Li, J.; Cheng, B.; Xia, J. Mitochondrial dynamics: Fission and fusion in fate determination of mesenchymal stem cells. *Front. Cell Dev. Biol.* **2020**, *8*, 580070. [CrossRef] [PubMed]
128. Otera, H.; Wang, C.; Cleland, M.M.; Setoguchi, K.; Yokota, S.; Youle, R.J.; Mihara, K. Mff is an essential factor for mitochondrial recruitment of Drp1 during mitochondrial fission in mammalian cells. *J. Cell Biol.* **2010**, *191*, 1141–1158. [CrossRef] [PubMed]
129. Smirnova, E.; Griparic, L.; Shurland, D.-L.; Van Der Bliek, A.M. Dynamin-related protein Drp1 is required for mitochondrial division in mammalian cells. *Mol. Biol. Cell* **2001**, *12*, 2245–2256. [CrossRef] [PubMed]
130. Berman, S.; Pineda, F.; Hardwick, J. Mitochondrial fission and fusion dynamics: The long and short of it. *Cell Death Differ.* **2008**, *15*, 1147–1152. [CrossRef] [PubMed]
131. Wang, J.; Yao, L. Dissecting C– H··· π and N– H··· π interactions in two proteins using a combined experimental and computational approach. *Sci. Rep.* **2019**, *9*, 20149. [CrossRef] [PubMed]
132. Ow, Y.-L.P.; Green, D.R.; Hao, Z.; Mak, T.W. Cytochrome c: Functions beyond respiration. *Nat. Rev. Mol. Cell Biol.* **2008**, *9*, 532–542. [CrossRef] [PubMed]
133. Fontanesi, F.; Soto, I.C.; Barrientos, A. Cytochrome c oxidase biogenesis: New levels of regulation. *IUBMB Life* **2008**, *60*, 557–568. [CrossRef] [PubMed]
134. Estaquier, J.; Arnoult, D. Inhibiting Drp1-mediated mitochondrial fission selectively prevents the release of cytochrome c during apoptosis. *Cell Death Differ.* **2007**, *14*, 1086–1094. [CrossRef]
135. Inoue-Yamauchi, A.; Oda, H. Depletion of mitochondrial fission factor DRP1 causes increased apoptosis in human colon cancer cells. *Biochem. Biophys. Res. Commun.* **2012**, *421*, 81–85. [CrossRef]
136. Tsujimoto, Y.; Shimizu, S. Role of the mitochondrial membrane permeability transition in cell death. *Apoptosis* **2007**, *12*, 835–840. [CrossRef] [PubMed]
137. Holler, N.; Zaru, R.; Micheau, O.; Thome, M.; Attinger, A.; Valitutti, S.; Bodmer, J.-L.; Schneider, P.; Seed, B.; Tschopp, J. Fas triggers an alternative, caspase-8–independent cell death pathway using the kinase RIP as effector molecule. *Nat. Immunol.* **2000**, *1*, 489–495. [CrossRef]
138. Matsumura, H.; Shimizu, Y.; Ohsawa, Y.; Kawahara, A.; Uchiyama, Y.; Nagata, S. Necrotic death pathway in Fas receptor signaling. *J. Cell Biol.* **2000**, *151*, 1247–1256. [CrossRef] [PubMed]
139. Yu, M.; Nguyen, N.D.; Huang, Y.; Lin, D.; Fujimoto, T.N.; Molkentine, J.M.; Deorukhkar, A.; Kang, Y.a.; San Lucas, F.A.; Fernandes, C.J. Mitochondrial fusion exploits a therapeutic vulnerability of pancreatic cancer. *JCI Insight* **2019**, *4*, 126915. [CrossRef]
140. Qian, W.; Choi, S.; Gibson, G.A.; Watkins, S.C.; Bakkenist, C.J.; Van Houten, B. Mitochondrial hyperfusion induced by loss of the fission protein Drp1 causes ATM-dependent G2/M arrest and aneuploidy through DNA replication stress. *J. Cell Sci.* **2012**, *125*, 5745–5757. [CrossRef] [PubMed]
141. Han, X.-J.; Yang, Z.-J.; Jiang, L.-P.; Wei, Y.-F.; Liao, M.-F.; Qian, Y.; Li, Y.; Huang, X.; Wang, J.-B.; Xin, H.-B. Mitochondrial dynamics regulates hypoxia-induced migration and antineoplastic activity of cisplatin in breast cancer cells. *Int. J. Oncol.* **2015**, *46*, 691–700. [CrossRef] [PubMed]
142. Hu, J.; Zhang, H.; Li, J.; Jiang, X.; Zhang, Y.; Wu, Q.; Shi, J.; Gao, N. ROCK1 activation-mediated mitochondrial translocation of Drp1 and cofilin are required for arnidiol-induced mitochondrial fission and apoptosis. *J. Exp. Clin. Cancer Res.* **2020**, *39*, 1–16. [CrossRef] [PubMed]
143. Jenner, A.; Peña-Blanco, A.; Salvador-Gallego, R.; Ugarte-Uribe, B.; Zollo, C.; Ganief, T.; Bierlmeier, J.; Mund, M.; Lee, J.E.; Ries, J. DRP1 interacts directly with BAX to induce its activation and apoptosis. *EMBO J.* **2022**, *41*, e108587. [CrossRef]
144. Milani, M.; Byrne, D.P.; Greaves, G.; Butterworth, M.; Cohen, G.M.; Eyers, P.A.; Varadarajan, S. DRP-1 is required for BH3 mimetic-mediated mitochondrial fragmentation and apoptosis. *Cell Death Dis.* **2018**, *8*, e2552. [CrossRef] [PubMed]
145. Wang, Z.; Jiang, H.; Chen, S.; Du, F.; Wang, X. The mitochondrial phosphatase PGAM5 functions at the convergence point of multiple necrotic death pathways. *Cell* **2012**, *148*, 228–243. [CrossRef]
146. Zhang, S.; Che, L.; He, C.; Huang, J.; Guo, N.; Shi, J.; Lin, Y.; Lin, Z. Drp1 and RB interaction to mediate mitochondria-dependent necroptosis induced by cadmium in hepatocytes. *Cell Death Dis.* **2019**, *10*, 523. [CrossRef] [PubMed]

147. Degterev, A.; Hitomi, J.; Germscheid, M.; Ch'en, I.L.; Korkina, O.; Teng, X.; Abbott, D.; Cuny, G.D.; Yuan, C.; Wagner, G. Identification of RIP1 kinase as a specific cellular target of necrostatins. *Nat. Chem. Biol.* **2008**, *4*, 313–321. [CrossRef] [PubMed]
148. Sun, L.; Wang, H.; Wang, Z.; He, S.; Chen, S.; Liao, D.; Wang, L.; Yan, J.; Liu, W.; Lei, X. Mixed lineage kinase domain-like protein mediates necrosis signaling downstream of RIP3 kinase. *Cell* **2012**, *148*, 213–227. [CrossRef] [PubMed]
149. Basit, F.; Van Oppen, L.M.; Schöckel, L.; Bossenbroek, H.M.; Van Emst-de Vries, S.E.; Hermeling, J.C.; Grefte, S.; Kopitz, C.; Heroult, M.; HGM Willems, P. Mitochondrial complex I inhibition triggers a mitophagy-dependent ROS increase leading to necroptosis and ferroptosis in melanoma cells. *Cell Death Dis.* **2017**, *8*, e2716. [CrossRef] [PubMed]
150. Miotto, G.; Rossetto, M.; Di Paolo, M.L.; Orian, L.; Venerando, R.; Roveri, A.; Vučković, A.-M.; Travain, V.B.; Zaccarin, M.; Zennaro, L. Insight into the mechanism of ferroptosis inhibition by ferrostatin-1. *Redox Biol.* **2020**, *28*, 101328. [CrossRef]
151. Simula, L.; Campanella, M.; Campello, S. Targeting Drp1 and mitochondrial fission for therapeutic immune modulation. *Pharmacol. Res.* **2019**, *146*, 104317. [CrossRef]
152. Weiner-Gorzel, K.; Murphy, M. Mitochondrial dynamics, a new therapeutic target for Triple Negative Breast Cancer. *Biochim. Biophys. Acta BBA-Rev. Cancer* **2021**, *1875*, 188518. [CrossRef]

Disclaimer/Publisher's Note: The statements, opinions and data contained in all publications are solely those of the individual author(s) and contributor(s) and not of MDPI and/or the editor(s). MDPI and/or the editor(s) disclaim responsibility for any injury to people or property resulting from any ideas, methods, instructions or products referred to in the content.

pharmaceutics MDPI

Article

Cytotoxic Effects of Doxorubicin on Cancer Cells and Macrophages Depend Differently on the Microcarrier Structure

Daria Kalenichenko [1], Irina Kriukova [2,3], Alexander Karaulov [4], Igor Nabiev [1,2,3,4,*] and Alyona Sukhanova [1,*]

1 Université de Reims Champagne-Ardenne, BIOSPECT, 51100 Reims, France; daria.kalenichenko@univ-reims.fr
2 Life Improvement by Future Technologies (LIFT) Center, Skolkovo, 143025 Moscow, Russia; irina.kryukova.mephi@gmail.com
3 Laboratory of Nano-Bioengineering, National Research Nuclear University MEPhI (Moscow Engineering Physics Institute), 115409 Moscow, Russia
4 Department of Clinical Immunology and Allergology, Institute of Molecular Medicine, Sechenov First Moscow State Medical University (Sechenov University), 119146 Moscow, Russia; drkaraulov@mail.ru
* Correspondence: igor.nabiev@univ-reims.fr (I.N.); alyona.sukhanova@univ-reims.fr (A.S.)

Abstract: Microparticles are versatile carriers for controlled drug delivery in personalized, targeted therapy of various diseases, including cancer. The tumor microenvironment contains different infiltrating cells, including immune cells, which can affect the efficacy of antitumor drugs. Here, prototype microparticle-based systems for the delivery of the antitumor drug doxorubicin (DOX) were developed, and their cytotoxic effects on human epidermoid carcinoma cells and macrophages derived from human leukemia monocytic cells were compared in vitro. DOX-containing calcium carbonate microparticles with or without a protective polyelectrolyte shell and polyelectrolyte microcapsules of about 2.4–2.5 μm in size were obtained through coprecipitation and spontaneous loading. All the microstructures exhibited a prolonged release of DOX. An estimation of the cytotoxicity of the DOX-containing microstructures showed that the encapsulation of DOX decreased its toxicity to macrophages and delayed the cytotoxic effect against tumor cells. The DOX-containing calcium carbonate microparticles with a protective polyelectrolyte shell were more toxic to the cancer cells than DOX-containing polyelectrolyte microcapsules, whereas, for the macrophages, the microcapsules were most toxic. It is concluded that DOX-containing core/shell microparticles with an eight-layer polyelectrolyte shell are optimal drug microcarriers due to their low toxicity to immune cells, even upon prolonged incubation, and strong delayed cytotoxicity against tumor cells.

Keywords: microparticles; microcapsules; doxorubicin; cancer cells; macrophages

1. Introduction

Cancer is the leading cause of death worldwide, accounting for almost 10 million deaths in 2020, or about one in six deaths [1]. A malignant tumor is a complex "ecosystem" consisting of cancer cells, as well as infiltrating immune, endothelial, and stromal cells. There is increasing evidence that the tumor microenvironment is involved in many oncogenic processes, including tumor cell proliferation and survival, immune evasion, metastatic process, angiogenesis, and resistance to therapy. Thus, the tumor microenvironment plays a key role in tumor development and drug resistance [2–5]. Therefore, chemotherapy, one of the most effective treatments, has a number of inherent drawbacks and limitations, with low selectivity of the drugs toward cancer cells being the most critical of them [6,7]. The development of controlled and targeted antitumor-drug delivery systems is one of the challenges of personalized cancer therapy. Controlled delivery and release could reduce the side effects of antitumor drugs and their toxicity to normal cells while ensuring selectivity for cancer cells [8–10].

Multilayer polymer microstructures have been shown to be promising candidate carriers for targeted delivery and the modified release of drugs, as well as contrast and fluorescent detection probes for the in vitro and in vivo imaging of the delivery system [11–15]. Currently, this is one of the most promising approaches in the field of personalized tumor diagnosis and therapy.

Doxorubicin (DOX) is a common antitumor antibiotic of the anthracycline group, widely used in the chemotherapy of various primary and metastatic cancers [16]. Specifically, DOX can be used for chemotherapy of most types of invasive breast cancer, including triple-negative breast cancer. It can also be used together with targeted drugs, such as trastuzumab (Herceptin®), in the treatment of HER2-positive breast cancer. Despite its proven high efficacy in the treatment of cancer, DOX has a wide range of undesirable side effects, including strong cardiotoxicity [17,18]. Due to its high amphiphilicity and its fluorescent properties, DOX may be a useful model anticancer drug for incorporation into microcarriers in order to obtain an effective delivery system. Encapsulation of DOX in microcarriers, together with targeted delivery to the tumor site, can ensure a controlled release of the drug, thereby reducing its side effects on normal cells [19,20]. We have previously discussed the difficulty of DOX encapsulation using traditional methods (the emulsion method and the addition of organic solvents) [21,22]. The novelty of our approach to the preparation of DOX-containing microstructures is the efficient encapsulation of DOX in the aqueous phase without the use of additional components or equipment.

Optimal selection of the physicochemical properties of microstructures, such as their shape, size, and structure (the number of polymer layers in the shell, the presence or absence of a core, integration of other functional components, etc.) [23], can contribute to a prolonged release of the antitumor agent [19,24,25], an increased time of its circulation in the body, and decreased side effects on healthy tissues and organs [26], as well as ensure its targeted delivery to the tumor site without loss of its pharmacological properties [27].

The mechanical properties of the particles, including their stiffness and surface characteristics, may also influence their behavior and interaction with cells [28,29]. The rigidity of the microstructures significantly affects their internalization by cancer cells: rigid or strengthened particles are uptaken more rapidly than soft ones [28]. It has been found that the cellular uptake and subsequent endosomal transport of biodegradable and non-biodegradable microstructures strongly depend on the particle stiffness rather than the shell composition. At the same time, the rate of release of encapsulated components from microstructures may be influenced by the composition of the polymer shell. The shell of the microstructures containing non-degradable polymers, such as poly(sodium 4-styrene sulfonate) (PSS) and poly(allylamine hydrochloride) (PAH), exhibited a pH sensitivity in a pH range from 3.0 to 7.5. The experiments have shown that the shell of these microstructures is highly permeable in the slightly acidic tumor microenvironment (6.5–6.8) [15,30].

Therefore, in this study, we prepared different types of microstructures—calcium carbonate microbeads (MBs) (rigid microstructures), MBs coated with layers of oppositely charged polyelectrolytes (PAH and PSS) (rigid microstructures with a polymer shell), and polyelectrolyte microcapsules (MCs) (soft microstructures) containing DOX—in order to determine how the structure of the microcarriers affect their cytotoxicity against human tumor cells and immune cells (macrophages) when in vitro.

2. Materials and Methods

2.1. Materials

Sodium chloride (NaCl), sodium carbonate (Na_2CO_3), calcium chloride ($CaCl_2$), glycerol, poly(allylamine hydrochloride) (PAH, Mw $\approx$ 17,500 Da), poly(sodium-4-styrenesulfonate) (PSS, Mw $\approx$ 70,000 Da), phorbol 12-myristate 13-acetate (PMA), dimethylsulfoxide (DMSO), and DOX (suitable for fluorescence, 98.0–102.0%) were purchased from Sigma-Aldrich Chimie S.a.r.l. (Merck), Saint-Quentin-Fallavier, France. UltraPure™ 0.5 M EDTA (pH 8.0) was purchased from Thermo Fischer Scientific, Illkirch, France.

All polymer and buffer solutions were prepared using Milli-Q water (18.2 mΩ·cm) and additionally filtered through the sterile Millex-GV filters (0.22 μm) obtained from Sigma-Aldrich Chimie S.a.r.l. (Merck), Saint-Quentin-Fallavier, France.

Roswell Park Memorial Institute (RPMI) 1640 medium with phenol red and without L-glutamine, heat-inactivated fetal bovine serum (FBS), 10,000 U/mL of solution of penicillin–streptomycin, 100 mM solution of sodium pyruvate, 200 mM solution of L-glutamine, Dulbecco's phosphate-buffered saline (DPBS), sterile PBS (pH 7.4), (3-(4,5-dimethylthiazol-2-yl)-2,5-diphenyltetrazolium bromide) (MTT), and 0.05% solution of Trypsin-EDTA were purchased from Thermo Fischer Scientific, Illkirch, France.

The A-431 human epidermoid carcinoma cell line was obtained from ATCC. The THP-1 human leukemia monocytic cell line was kindly provided by Prof. Halima Kerdjoudj (EA-4691 BIOS, Université de Reims Champagne-Ardenne, Reims, France).

2.2. Methods

2.2.1. Fabrication of Microstructures of Different Types

Synthesis of Calcium Carbonate Microbeads

Calcium carbonate MBs were further used as cores for the assembly of core/shell microstructures, and the microcapsules were obtained by mixing 7.5 mL of 0.33 M Na_2CO_3 and 7.5 mL of 0.33 M $CaCl_2$ with an equivalent volume of 44 wt% aqueous solution of glycerol (Sigma-Aldrich Chimie S.a.r.l. (Merck), Saint-Quentin-Fallavier, France) serving as a thickening agent, as described earlier [22]. The reaction mixture was placed onto a magnetic stirrer at 500 rpm for 60 min. The obtained MBs were washed to remove excess glycerol four times with ultrapure water by sequential centrifugation at 3000× *g* for 15 min. After the final centrifugation, the resultant MB precipitate was dried at 90 °C overnight.

Preparation of Core/Shell Microparticles and Microcapsules

Core/shell microparticles consisting of the MBs coated with eight-layer polymer shells (MB(+8L)) and MC consisting of the polymer shell alone (MC(8L)) were obtained by means of layer-by-layer adsorption of oppositely charged polyelectrolytes (the polycation PAH and the polyanion PSS) onto the MB surface [22,23,31].

About 10^8 MBs, dried after the synthesis, were resuspended in 0.5 mL of ultrapure water. The suspension was sonicated on an ultrasonic bath to separate the aggregated particles. Then, 0.5 mL of a PAH solution (2 mg/mL) in 0.5 M NaCl was added to 0.5 mL of the suspension. The resulting mixture was stirred on a vortex and sonicated on an ultrasonic bath for 60 s. The suspension was incubated on a rotary shaker for 20 min at room temperature and then centrifuged at 1377× *g* for 3 min. The supernatant was withdrawn, and the pellet was resuspended in 0.5 mL of water. To apply the next layer, 0.5 mL of a PSS solution (2 mg/mL) in 0.5 M NaCl was added to 0.5 mL of the mixture. The suspension was sonicated and incubated under the conditions described above. The microstructures were washed to remove excess polyelectrolyte three times with ultrapure water by centrifugation at 1377× *g* for 3 min. The polyelectrolytes were applied onto the MB surface in the following order: PAH/PSS/PAH/PSS/PAH/PSS/PAH/PSS.

After the last layer was applied and the last washing step was performed, the obtained MBs(+8L) were resuspended in 0.5 mL of ultrapure water and stored at +4 °C until use.

The hollow MC(8L) was obtained by incubating 10^7 MB(+8L) in 0.5 M EDTA (pH 8.0) (Thermo Fischer Scientific, Illkirch, France) for 4 h to remove the calcium carbonate core. The resulting MC(8L) was sedimented by centrifugation for 5 min at 8609× *g* and resuspended in ultrapure water. The washing with ultrapure water was repeated three more times; after the last washing, the MC(8L) was resuspended in 0.5 mL of water.

The size distributions of the prepared microstructures were analyzed by means of dynamic light scattering using a Zetasizer NanoZS (Malvern Panalytical, Palaiseau, France). The deposition of polyelectrolytes was controlled by means of laser Doppler electrophoresis using a Zetasizer NanoZS. Each measurement was made at least five times, and the results were estimated using standard statistical methods.

Loading of Doxorubicin into the Microstructures

The DOX-containing MBs were obtained by coprecipitation at the step of MB synthesis. First, 1 mL of a 10 mg/mL DOX solution was added to 14.5 mL of a mixture of 0.33 M $CaCl_2$ and 44 wt% glycerol. The resulting mixture was stirred on a magnetic stirrer, and then 14.5 mL of a mixture of 0.33 M Na_2CO_3 and 44 wt% glycerol was added. The reaction mixture was stirred for 60 min at 500 rpm. The synthesized MB-DOX were washed from the residual reaction mixture two times with ultrapure water. The obtained MB-DOX precipitate was dried at 90 °C overnight.

The MB-DOX were subsequently used as substrates to obtain core/shell microparticles containing DOX (MB(+8L)-DOX). They were also obtained through layer-by-layer adsorption of polyelectrolytes, as described above. The polyelectrolytes were applied in the order PAH/PSS/PAH/PSS/PAH/PSS/PAH/PSS.

The DOX-containing microcapsules (MC(8L)-DOX) were obtained via spontaneous loading of the anticancer drug into the MC(8L). For this purpose, 0.5 mL of a mixture of 0.05 M phosphate buffer solution (pH 8.0) containing 0.5 M NaCl and 0.032 mg/mL DOX was added to a precipitate containing ~6×10^6 previously obtained MC(8L). The suspension was incubated for 16 h at 25 °C on a rotary shaker in test tubes wrapped in foil. After incubation, the sample was centrifuged at $8609\times g$ for 5 min, the supernatant was withdrawn, and the resulting MC(8L)-DOX was resuspended in 0.5 mL of ultrapure water.

The amount of DOX loaded into MB, MB(+8L), and MC(8L) was determined spectrophotometrically at the wavelength of the maximum absorption of DOX (485 nm) using a Spark™ 10M model of multimode microplate reader Tecan (Männedorf, Switzerland) as described earlier [22].

The release of DOX from the obtained microstructures was analyzed under the following physiological conditions: a temperature of 37 °C and a pH of 7.4. For this purpose, samples containing 6×10^6 microstructures in the release medium (0.05 M phosphate buffer solution, pH 7.4) were incubated at 37 °C under constant stirring on a shaker at 500 rpm, the supernatants were collected at fixed time intervals (45 min, 1.5 h, 3 h, 6 h, 12 h, 24 h, 48 h, and 72 h) by centrifugation at $1900\times g$ for 10 min, and the DOX content of the samples was determined by spectrophotometry at the wavelength of the maximum absorbance of DOX (485 nm).

The size distributions of the DOX-containing microstructures were analyzed by dynamic light scattering using a Zetasizer NanoZS (Malvern Panalytical, Palaiseau, France). The deposition of polyelectrolytes was monitored by laser Doppler electrophoresis using a Zetasizer NanoZS. Each measurement was made at least five times, and the results were estimated using standard statistical methods.

2.2.2. Scanning Electron Microscopy

A scanning electron microscope with an SU8030 field emission gun (Hitachi, Tokyo, Japan) at the NANO'MAT platform (University of Technology of Troyes, Troyes, France) was used. The powder of dried microstructures was applied onto a conductive carbon adhesive tape and scanned at an accelerating voltage of 3.0 kV, a working distance of 8.5–8.6 mm, and an emission current of 9000 nA.

2.2.3. Cell Culture

Human epidermoid carcinoma A-431 cells were cultured in a complete RPMI-1640 medium supplemented with 10% heat-inactivated FBS, 2 mM L-glutamine, 1% penicillin–streptomycin solution, and 0.1% sodium pyruvate at 37 °C (Thermo Fischer Scientific, Illkirch, France) in a 5% CO_2 atmosphere under sterile conditions. THP-1 macrophages were obtained by incubating THP-1 human monocytic leukemia cells in a complete RPMI-1640 medium supplemented with 150 ng/mL of PMA for 48 h at 37 °C in a 5% CO_2 atmosphere. After PMA stimulation, the THP-1 cells were cultured in a complete RPMI-1640 medium. When the cells had formed a monolayer, they were detached from culture flasks with a 0.05% Trypsin–EDTA solution (Thermo Fischer Scientific, Illkirch, France).

The cell suspension was centrifuged at 302× *g* for 5 min, the cell pellet was resuspended in complete growth medium, and the cells were counted in a KOVA™Glasstic™ slide (Thermo Fisher Scientific, Illkirch, France) and placed into a fresh culture flask. Both cell lines were cultured for no more than 20 passages.

2.2.4. MTT Assay

Cell viability was estimated using the MTT assay according to the manufacturer's instructions (Thermo Fischer Scientific, Illkirch, France). The cells were seeded into a 96-well microplate, ~3.2 × 10^4 cells per well (in 0.18 mL of complete working medium) in the case of A-431 cells and ~5.3 × 10^4 cells per well in the case of differentiated THP-1m cells. These amounts were so selected that confluence would be achieved within 24 h of incubation. The cells were incubated under sterile conditions at 37 °C in an atmosphere of 5% CO_2.

After 80% confluence was reached, 0.2 mL of the sample suspension in the complete medium was added to the microplate wells. The samples tested are listed below.

- Microstructures containing DOX in the final concentration range from 0 to 9 μM: MB-DOX; MB(+8L)-DOX; MC(8L)-DOX.
- Microstructures not containing DOX (control samples) at a ratio from 0 to 50 microstructures per cell: MB; MB(+8L); MC(8L).
- A DOX solution in the concentration range from 0 to 9 μM in the complete medium.

Wells containing only 0.2 mL of the complete working medium and empty (blank) wells were also used as controls. Each experiment was repeated three times in three replicates.

After incubation for 24 h, 48 h, 72 h, or 96 h, 0.02 mL of a 12 mM MTT solution was added to the microplate wells, and the microplates were incubated for 4 h in an incubator under sterile conditions at 37 °C in an atmosphere of 5% CO_2. After incubation, the microplates were centrifuged at 1500× *g* for 10 min at room temperature. Then, the supernatant was carefully withdrawn, with the pipette tip not touching the bottom of the well, 0.15 mL of DMSO was added to each well, and the microplates were incubated for 10 min at 37 °C in an atmosphere of 5% CO_2. The microplates were then incubated on a microplate shaker for 20 min with stirring at 200 rpm until the formazan crystals were completely dissolved. The optical density was estimated in each well at the formazan absorbance peak wavelength of 540 nm using a Spark™ 10M multimode microplate reader (Tecan, Männedorf, Switzerland) according to the manufacturer's protocol.

The cell survival rate was calculated by following the equation:

$$Cell\ viability = \frac{A_i}{A_0} \times 100\% \tag{1}$$

where A_i is the average optical density in the wells containing cells and the sample suspension; A_0 is the average optical density in the control wells containing only cells, with the optical densities in the control wells containing the complete medium and the blank ones taken into account.

2.2.5. Inhibitory Dose Estimation and Statistical Analysis of Data

The Origin Pro version 8.5.0 SR1, Data Analysis, and Graphing software (OriginLab Corporation, Northampton, MA, USA, 2010) were used for the estimation of the inhibitory concentration and statistical analyses of the data (Student's *t*-test). The results are presented as the mean and standard deviation for three independent experiments if not indicated otherwise.

3. Results and Discussion

3.1. Preparation and Characterization of Microstructures of Different Types

In order to use the microstructures for targeted drug delivery, their size should be no more than several micrometers, and they should have well-defined shape and surface properties, ensuring optimal distribution, release kinetics, degradation rate, and elimination time [32,33]. In addition, the microstructure material should allow their loading with drug substances. Here, we engineered DOX-containing core microbeads with a regular spherical shape (MB-DOX), core/polymer-shell structures (MB(+8L)-DOX), and soft shell-type hollow microcapsules (MC(8L)-DOX). In addition, similar microstructures not containing DOX were synthesized and used as controls (Figure 1).

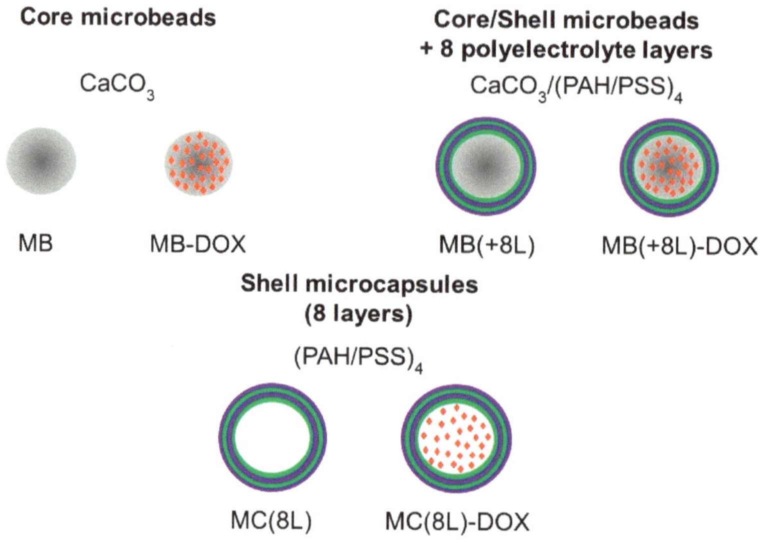

Figure 1. Synthesized microstructures. Designations: MB, core microbeads; MB-DOX, doxorubicin-containing core MBs with a regular spherical shape; MB(+8L), core/shell MBs with a shell of eight polyelectrolyte layers; MB(+8L)-DOX, doxorubicin-containing MB(+8L); MC(8L), soft hollow microcapsules with a shell of eight polyelectrolyte layers; and MC(8L)-DOX, MC(8L) loaded with doxorubicin.

The size of the obtained microstructures was determined by the size of the synthesized calcium carbonate matrix core, which had good biocompatibility, biodegradability, and pyrogenicity.

The core MBs represented calcium carbonate microparticles obtained by crystallization from mixed sodium carbonate and calcium chloride solutions. Glycerol was added to the reaction mixture as a thickener [21,22,34]. This approach yielded spherical microparticles (of the vaterite type) that were smaller than those synthesized without a thickener. The MBs obtained in this study had a porous structure, a narrow size distribution (~2.4 ± 0.5 μm), and a negative surface charge (-16.3 ± 0.8 mV); they were used as a matrix for obtaining highly homogeneous MB(+8L).

The subsequent layer-by-layer adsorption of oppositely charged polyelectrolytes onto the core yielded microparticles with several protective layers of polymers on the surface, as well as, after an additional procedure of core removal, hollow MC. The core/shell microstructures MB(+8L) were formed via layer-by-layer adsorption of oppositely charged polyelectrolytes, PAH and PSS, onto calcium carbonate MBs. This technique allowed for obtaining microstructures of uniform size, which is important in terms of their passive transport because carriers of the same size are transported and accumulated in the body uniformly. The size of the synthesized MB(+8L) was 2.5 ± 0.3 μm, and the surface charge was more negative (-32.1 ± 2.2 mV). Soft hollow microstructures (MC(8L)) were obtained by treating MB(+8L) with 0.5 M EDTA to dissolve the calcium carbonate core while preserving the polymer shell; the size and surface properties remained unchanged. However, the obtained MC(8L) lost the regular spherical structure, although they remained rounded.

The main advantage of the obtained microstructures is the possibility of controlled modification of the release of the loaded compounds, as well as the protection of these compounds from external factors that can cause their degradation.

The amphiphilicity of the anticancer drug DOX and the hydrophilicity of its salt form, DOX hydrochloride, preclude using standard approaches for its loading into the microcarriers. Currently, the most common approaches are the spontaneous loading of DOX [35] and its encapsulation at the stage of synthesis of these microcarriers, e.g., by the coprecipitation method [36]. It should be noted that DOX-loading methods that use only the aqueous phase are of particular interest because they do not require organic solvents, an oil phase, or special equipment for dispersion and emulsification.

We used different microstructures, for which the optimal methods of DOX loading were also different. Specifically, the coprecipitation method was optimal for loading DOX into MB and MB(+8L), whereas the spontaneous loading ensured the highest loading efficiency in the case of MC(8L). Loading the same quantities of DOX into all microcarriers was also important for our subsequent experiments on cell viability using the same number of microstructures per cell with a normalized DOX concentration.

The synthesized MB-DOX had a porous structure (Figure 2a,d), a narrow size distribution (2.7 ± 0.5 μm), and a negative ζ-potential (−11.3 ± 1.8 mV). The efficiency of DOX loading by this method was 76.4 ± 2.9% (Table 1).

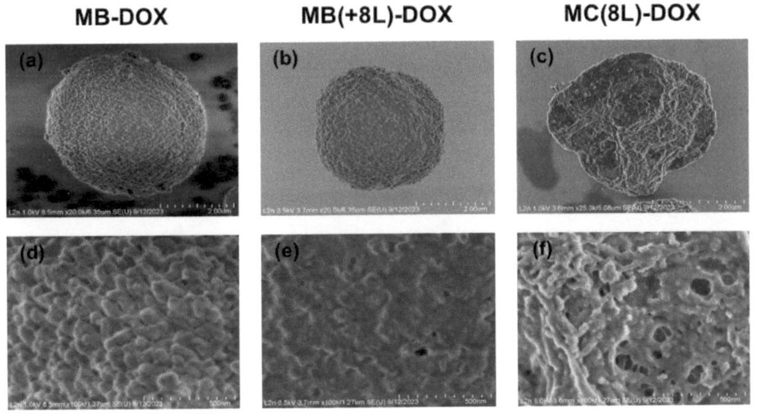

Figure 2. Scanning electron microscopy images of the microstructures loaded with doxorubicin. (**a**,**d**) Core microbeads (MB-DOX); (**b**,**e**) microbeads coated with eight polyelectrolyte layers (MB(+8L)-DOX); (**c**,**f**) microcapsules with a shell of eight polyelectrolyte layers (MC(8L)-DOX).

Table 1. Efficiency of doxorubicin loading into the engineered microcarriers.

Sample [1]	Loading Efficiency, %	Amount of DOX per Microcarrier, μg
MB-DOX	76.4 ± 2.9	$2 \times 10^{-6} \pm 5.8 \times 10^{-7}$
MB(+8L)-DOX	74.3 ± 4.8	$1.96 \times 10^{-6} \pm 1.3 \times 10^{-7}$
MC(8L)-DOX	73.9 ± 3.9	$1.9 \times 10^{-6} \pm 1 \times 10^{-7}$

[1] Microstructures loaded with doxorubicin (DOX): MB-DOX, microbeads; MB(+8L)-DOX, microbeads coated with eight polyelectrolyte layers; MC(8L)-DOX, microcapsules with eight polyelectrolyte layers shell.

The MB-DOX was used as a matrix for the engineering of MB(+8L)-DOX. The resultant MB(+8L)-DOX (Figure 2b,e) were within the same size range as the original MBs ($p > 0.05$, Student's *t*-test), 2.7 ± 0.3 μm. In order to obtain MB(+8L)-DOX with a standardized amount of DOX per microcarrier, it was necessary to take into account the loss of DOX during the application of the polyelectrolyte shell. However, an experimental estimation showed that the loss of DOX was negligible (2–6%). The efficiency of DOX loading by this method was 74.3 ± 4.8 (Table 1).

The preliminarily fabricated control MC(8L) (2.7 ± 0.4 μm) was used for obtaining MC(8L)-DOX by spontaneous loading. The mean size of the MC(8L)-DOX (Figure 2c,f) did not differ significantly from that of the original MCs (2.7 ± 0.4 μm) ($p > 0.05$, Student's *t*-test). The efficiency of DOX encapsulation by this method was 73.9 ± 3.9% (Table 1).

Thus, the coprecipitation and spontaneous loading methods used in this study for preparing DOX-containing microstructures provided a higher efficiency of DOX loading into microstructures in the aqueous phase compared to the previously reported ones (~29–44% [36,37] and ~50% [20], respectively).

3.2. Release of Doxorubicin from the Microcarriers

To further analyze the synergistic effect of the microcarrier structure and released DOX on cell viability, the rate of DOX release from the prepared microcarriers under the conditions used for the cell culture at 37 °C and a pH of 7.4 was preliminarily evaluated (Figure 3). As seen in Figure 3, a prolonged release of DOX from all microcarriers was demonstrated. In the case of MBs, an explosive release was observed, but the cumulative release of DOX did not exceed 75% within 72 h, as we have already shown earlier [22]. The plots shown in Figure 3 demonstrate that the polyelectrolyte shell inhibited the explosive release of the drug from MB(+8L) and MC(8L) at the initial stages. The cumulative release of DOX from MB(+8L) and MC(8L) did not exceed 40% within 72 h. Slow release of the anticancer compound at the physiologic pH may facilitate the preservation of the functional properties of the compound, as well as reduce toxicity to healthy cells of the human body. Apparently, the core/shell microstructures and MCs are the most promising drug carriers because they exhibited a longer release of DOX compared to the MBs.

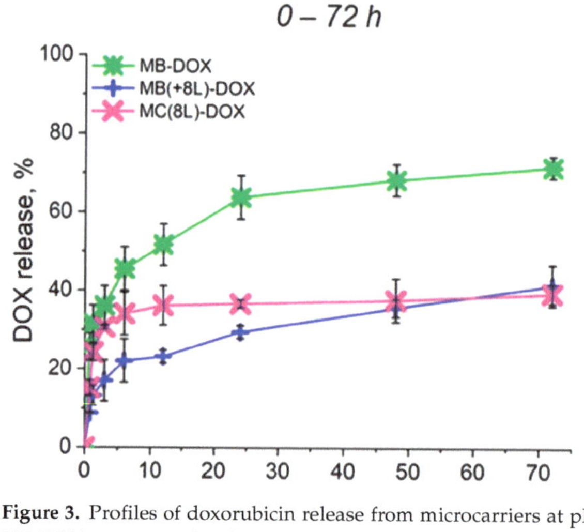

Figure 3. Profiles of doxorubicin release from microcarriers at pH 7.4 during 72 h. Designations: MB-DOX, core microbeads containing doxorubicin; MB(+8L)-DOX, core microbeads containing doxorubicin and coated with eight polyelectrolyte layers; MC(8L)-DOX, microcapsules with a shell of eight polyelectrolyte layers containing doxorubicin.

3.3. Cell Viability in the Presence of the Microstructures

The main objective in the preparation of microcarriers for antitumor therapy is to reduce the toxic effect on healthy cells while preserving or enhancing the toxic effect on tumor cells. Thus, cell viability analysis is essential to assess the applicability of microcarriers for in vitro drug delivery, as well as to evaluate the functional activity of the compound loaded into the microcarriers. We analyzed the cytotoxicity of DOX-containing microstructures in comparison with the cytotoxicity of DOX-free microstructures by the MTT method using tumor cells (epidermoid carcinoma A-431 cells) and immune cells (THP-1 human peripheral blood monocytes differentiated into macrophages).

The viability of cells in the presence of different microcarriers was assessed under the same conditions by varying the microcarrier-to-cell ratio from 1:1 to 50:1. The loading conditions for different types of microcarriers were preliminarily determined in order to load the same amounts of DOX into different types of microcarriers (Table 2).

Table 2. Doxorubicin concentrations corresponding to different numbers of microcarriers.

Number of Particles per Cell	1	2	5	10	20	30	50
Average Concentration of DOX [1], μM	0.175 ± 0.004	0.371 ± 0.008	0.878 ± 0.019	1.79 ± 0.039	3.55 ± 0.075	5.06 ± 0.111	8.78 ± 0.192

[1] Doxorubicin (DOX).

The results showed that the control DOX-free microstructures insignificantly affected the proliferation rate of both the tumor and immune cells. A slight decrease in cell viability after prolonged incubation to 70–80%, depending on the type of microcarriers, was observed. It is also of interest that spherical microparticles with a regular structure (MBs) had the highest cytotoxic effect on tumor cells ($p < 0.05$, Student's t-test), while the maximum cytotoxic effect on immune cells was exerted by soft hollow MCs ($p < 0.05$, Student's t-test), whose wall consisted of eight polyelectrolyte layers. At the same time, spherical microparticles with a regular structure of the core that was coated with eight polyelectrolyte layers (MB(+8L)) were practically nontoxic for immune cells ($p < 0.05$, Student's t-test) (Figures 4 and 5; Tables 3 and 4).

Table 3. Inhibitory concentrations of microcarriers for A-431 cells.

Sample [1]	IC Values, Particles per Cell			
Agent Type	**24 h**	**48 h**	**72 h**	**96 h**
MB	IC_{20} = 5.5 ± 0.03	IC_{20} = 3.5 ± 0.06	IC_{20} = 3.25 ± 0.05	IC_{20} = 0.5 ± 0.2
MB(+8L)	IC_{20} –	IC_{20} = 33.3 ± 0.04	IC_{20} = 10.8 ± 0.08	IC_{20} = 11.01 ± 0.03
MC(8L)	IC_{20} –	IC_{20} –	IC_{20} –	IC_{20} = 22.2 ± 0.05

[1] MB, core microbeads; MB(+8L), core microbeads coated with eight polyelectrolyte layers; MC(8L), microcapsules with a shell of eight polyelectrolyte layers.

Table 4. Inhibitory concentrations of microcarriers for THP-1 cells.

Sample [1]	IC Values, Particles per Cell			
Agent Type	**24 h**	**48 h**	**72 h**	**96 h**
MB	IC_{20} –	IC_{20} = 42.4 ± 0.08	IC_{20} = 22.5 ± 0.06	IC_{20} = 7.2 ± 0.02
MB(+8L)	IC_{20} –	IC_{20} –	IC_{20} –	IC_{20} –
MC(8L)	IC_{20} = 32.3 ± 0.03	IC_{20} = 31.2 ± 0.05	IC_{20} = 6.2 ± 0.09	IC_{20} = 0.6 ± 0.03

[1] MB, core microbeads; MB(+8L), core microbeads coated with eight polyelectrolyte layers; MC(8L), microcapsules with a shell of eight polyelectrolyte layers.

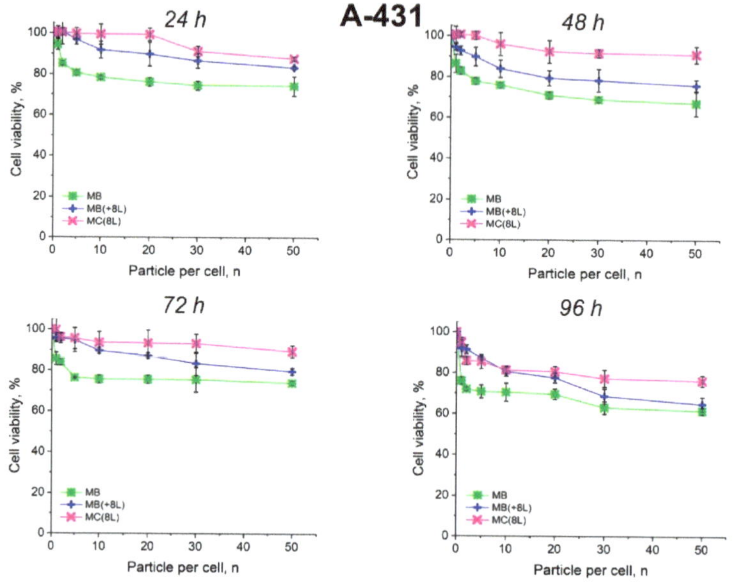

Figure 4. Viability of A-431 cells as estimated by the MTT assay. Designations: MB, core microbeads; MB(+8L), core microbeads coated with eight polyelectrolyte layers; MC(8L), microcapsules with a shell of eight polyelectrolyte layers.

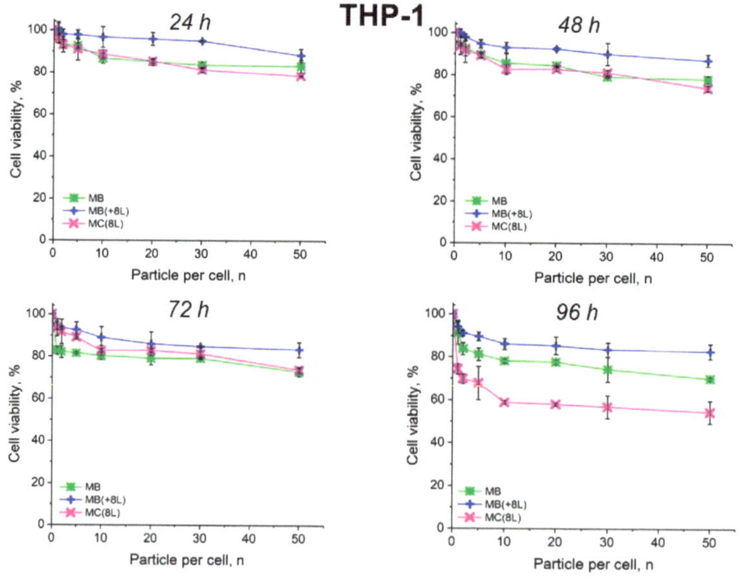

Figure 5. Viability of THP-1 cells as estimated by the MTT assay. Designations: MB, core microbeads; MB(+8L), core microbeads coated with eight polyelectrolyte layers; MC(8L), microcapsules with a shell of eight polyelectrolyte layers.

Unencapsulated DOX was highly toxic for both A-431 and THP-1 cells, with the survival rate of the macrophages in the presence of free DOX being lower than that of the tumor cells (Figures 6 and 7, Tables 5 and 6).

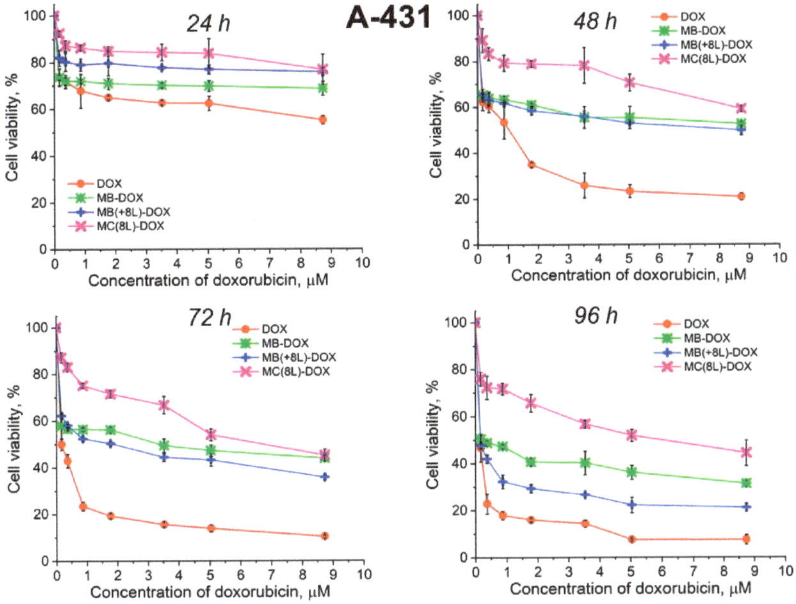

Figure 6. Viability of A-431 cells as estimated by the MTT assay. Designations: DOX, doxorubicin; MB-DOX, core microbeads containing doxorubicin; MB(+8L)-DOX, core microbeads containing doxorubicin and coated with eight polyelectrolyte layers; MC(8L)-DOX, microcapsules with a shell of eight polyelectrolyte layers containing doxorubicin.

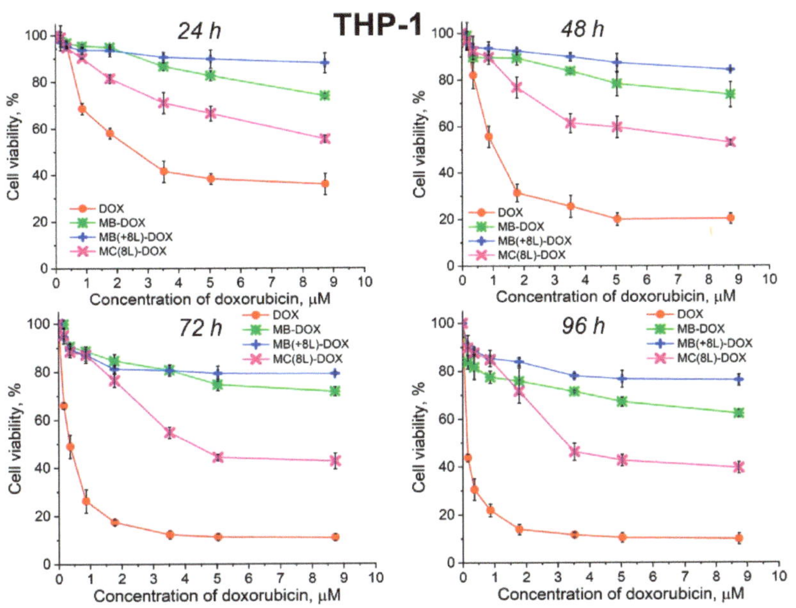

Figure 7. Viability of THP-1 cells as estimated by the MTT assay. Designations: DOX, doxorubicin; MB-DOX, core microbeads containing doxorubicin; MB(+8L)-DOX, core microbeads containing doxorubicin and coated with eight polyelectrolyte layers; MC(8L)-DOX, microcapsules with a shell of eight polyelectrolyte layers containing doxorubicin.

Table 5. Inhibitory concentrations of doxorubicin for A-431 cells.

Sample [1]	IC Values			
Agent Type	24 h	48 h	72 h	96 h
DOX	$IC_{20} = 0.06 \pm 0.017$ IC_{50} –	$IC_{20} = 0.03 \pm 0.02$ $IC_{50} = 1.09 \pm 0.07$	$IC_{20} = 0.018 \pm 0.04$ $IC_{50} = 0.17 \pm 0.03$	$IC_{20} = 0.01 \pm 0.05$ $IC_{50} = 0.085 \pm 0.04$
MB-DOX	$IC_{20} = 0.08 \pm 0.03$ IC_{50} –	$IC_{20} = 0.04 \pm 0.02$ IC_{50} –	$IC_{20} = 0.02 \pm 0.04$ $IC_{50} = 3.22 \pm 0.03$	$IC_{20} = 0.005 \pm 0.002$ $IC_{50} = 0.15 \pm 0.015$
MB(+8L)-DOX	$IC_{20} = 0.36 \pm 0.06$ IC_{50} –	$IC_{20} = 0.08 \pm 0.05$ $IC_{50} = 7.56 \pm 0.43$	$IC_{20} = 0.04 \pm 0.025$ $IC_{50} = 1.71 \pm 0.02$	$IC_{20} = 0.02 \pm 0.003$ $IC_{50} = 0.12 \pm 0.07$
MC(8L)-DOX	$IC_{20} = 5.14 \pm 0.04$ IC_{50} –	$IC_{20} = 0.75 \pm 0.35$ IC_{50} –	$IC_{20} = 0.47 \pm 0.08$ $IC_{50} = 6.24 \pm 0.52$	$IC_{20} = 0.08 \pm 0.04$ $IC_{50} = 5.33 \pm 0.07$

[1] DOX, doxorubicin; MB-DOX, microbeads containing doxorubicin; MB(+8L)-DOX, microbeads containing doxorubicin and coated with eight polyelectrolyte layers; MC(8L)-DOX, microcapsules with a shell of eight polyelectrolyte layers containing doxorubicin.

Table 6. Inhibitory concentrations of doxorubicin for THP-1 cells.

Sample [1]	IC Values			
Agent Type	24 h	48 h	72 h	96 h
DOX	$IC_{20} = 0.54 \pm 0.05$ $IC_{50} = 2.83 \pm 0.06$	$IC_{20} = 0.38 \pm 0.08$ $IC_{50} = 0.91 \pm 0.04$	$IC_{20} = 0.19 \pm 0.06$ $IC_{50} = 0.35 \pm 0.05$	IC_{20} – $IC_{50} = 0.17 \pm 0.04$
MB-DOX	$IC_{20} = 4.89 \pm 0.03$ IC_{50} –	$IC_{20} = 4.81 \pm 0.03$ IC_{50} –	$IC_{20} = 1.78 \pm 0.1$ IC_{50} –	$IC_{20} = 0.81 \pm 0.06$ IC_{50} –
MB(+8L)-DOX	IC_{20} – IC_{50} –	IC_{20} – IC_{50} –	$IC_{20} = 3.45 \pm 0.04$ IC_{50} –	$IC_{20} = 3.44 \pm 0.34$ IC_{50} –
MC(8L)-DOX	$IC_{20} = 1.54 \pm 0.2$ IC_{50} –	$IC_{20} = 1.61 \pm 0.03$ IC_{50} –	$IC_{20} = 1.25 \pm 0.04$ $IC_{50} = 4.05 \pm 0.01$	$IC_{20} = 0.94 \pm 0.02$ $IC_{50} = 2.55 \pm 0.6$

[1] DOX, doxorubicin, MB-DOX, core microbeads containing doxorubicin; MB(+8L)-DOX, core microbeads containing doxorubicin and coated with eight polyelectrolyte layers; MC(8L)-DOX, microcapsules with a shell of eight polyelectrolyte layers containing doxorubicin.

It was found that the encapsulation of DOX in microcarriers considerably increased the survival rate of both the tumor and immune cells. At the same time, the toxic effect of encapsulated DOX on the cancer cells was delayed, but it was stronger than that on immune cells. This can be explained by its more rapid transport into cancer cells and the lack of attenuation of the toxic effect of the transported DOX by the drug resistance mechanisms of cancer cells. The differences between the cancer cell cytotoxicities of free DOX and DOX encapsulated in different microcarriers increased with time, which was due to the difference between the rates of DOX release from different types of microcarriers (Figures 6 and 7, Tables 5 and 6). On the other hand, the delayed toxic effect of encapsulated DOX on tumor cells was comparable to the effect of unencapsulated DOX ($p > 0.05$, Student's t-test) (Figure 6, Table 5).

An interesting finding was that the microcarriers themselves influenced the cytotoxic effect of DOX. MC(8L)-DOX were less toxic for tumor cells compared to MB-DOX and MB(+8L)-DOX ($p < 0.05$, Student's t-test) (Figure 6, Table 5). The cytotoxic effect of MB(+8L)-DOX during the first 24 h was slightly weaker than that of MC(8L)-DOX. However, the cytotoxicity of MB(+8L)-DOX was similar to that of MB-DOX after 48 h of incubation ($p > 0.05$, Student's t-test) and became stronger than the cytotoxicities of all other microstructures after 96 h of incubation ($p < 0.05$, Student's t-test). This was probably because their core/polymer-shell structure favored the biphasic release of encapsulated DOX and was more rigid compared to MC(8L)-DOX [28].

In contrast, MB-DOX and MB(+8L)-DOX exhibited lower cytotoxicity towards the macrophages than MC(8L)-DOX did ($p < 0.05$, Student's t-test) (Figure 7, Table 6), even upon prolonged incubation. This can be explained by the soft structure of MC(8L)-DOX, which determined their more rapid uptake by macrophages compared to cancer cells [35], probably because they more readily change shape when uptaken by the cells [28]. It is also possible that macrophages and cancer cells use different mechanisms for uptaking different types of microstructures: micropinocytosis or clathrin- or caveolin-mediated phagocytosis [38].

Thus, the study of the viability of A-431 tumor cells and differentiated THP-1 human macrophages in the presence of the microstructures loaded with DOX has shown that encapsulation of this antitumor drug decreases its cytotoxicity against normal cells and delays its toxic effect against tumor cells. The DOX-containing microstructures can provide a longer action of DOX on tumor cells, comparable in strength to that of unencapsulated DOX, thus reducing its nonselective side effects on the body while preserving its pharmacological activity. The rigid microstructures with a polymer shell (MB(+8L)-DOX) are the most attractive among the microstructures studied because they exhibit lower cytotoxicity against normal human cells, even upon prolonged incubation, and a strong delayed cytotoxic effect against tumor cells.

The results of this study could serve as a basis for the development of new drug delivery systems because the approach used here allows for obtaining microstructures with different physical and chemical properties. The optimal size of the microstructures for intravenous/intramuscular administration is known to be about several micrometers, their optimal shape being spherical [39,40]. The size can also determine the biodistribution of microstructures in different organs (spleen, liver, or lungs) after their injection [39,41]. Furthermore, the presence of a polyelectrolyte shell is expected to be important because it can significantly increase the circulation time of the microstructures in the bloodstream and provide a controlled prolonged release of the loaded drug from the microstructures in the vicinity of cancer cells. All these properties together could play a key role in future in vivo applications. Therefore, the next stage of our study will be aimed at evaluating the in vivo behavior of the microstructures and determining the parameters that affect the efficacy of the microstructures as drug delivery agents for the treatment of cancer.

4. Conclusions

The results of this study show that the microcarrier structural characteristics, such as the stiffness and regularity of the microcarrier structure, should be taken into account in the development of delivery systems for antitumor drugs. It has been demonstrated that regular rigid spherical microcarriers containing an additional protective shell of oppositely charged polyelectrolyte layers on the surface are promising drug delivery tools that can be adapted for use as antitumor therapeutic agents. Conversely, softer hollow microcapsules of the same size are highly cytotoxic for human macrophages and may induce undesirable effects on the immune system. The core/shell microstructures with an eight-layer polyelectrolyte shell designed in this study represent a promising platform for further development of theranostic agents for the diagnosis and treatment of tumors.

Author Contributions: Conceptualization, D.K., I.N. and A.S.; methodology, D.K., I.K. and A.S.; formal analysis, D.K., I.K., A.K. and A.S.; investigation, D.K., I.K. and A.S.; data curation, D.K. and A.S.; writing—original draft preparation, D.K., I.N. and A.S.; writing—review and editing, D.K., I.K., A.K., I.N. and A.S.; supervision, I.N. and A.S. All authors have read and agreed to the published version of the manuscript.

Funding: This research was funded by the ITMO Cancer of Aviesan in the framework of the 2021–2030 Cancer Control Strategy; the French National Institute of Health and Medical Research, grant No. 22CP174-00 Smart-Nano; the Université de Reims Champagne-Ardenne (I.N., A.S.); and the Russian Science Foundation (RSF), grant No. 22-75-10103 in the part of research related to the synthesis of microparticles (I.K.), and grant No. 21-79-30048 in the part of the work related to the microparticles functionalization.

Institutional Review Board Statement: Not applicable.

Informed Consent Statement: Not applicable.

Data Availability Statement: The data presented in this study are available on request from the corresponding authors.

Acknowledgments: We thank Galina Nifontova for the technical assistance, Sergei Kostcheev for performing scanning electron microscopy, and Vladimir Ushakov for proofreading the manuscript.

Conflicts of Interest: The authors declare no conflicts of interest. The funders had no role in the design of the study, in the collection, analyses, or interpretation of data, in the writing of the manuscript, or in the decision to publish the results. The company Life Improvement by Future Technologies (LIFT) Center had no role in the design of the study, in the collection, analyses, or interpretation of data, in the writing of the manuscript, or in the decision to publish the results.

References

1. Ferlay, J.; Ervik, M.; Lam, F.; Laversanne, M.; Colombet, M.; Mery, L.; Piñeros, M.; Znaor, A.; Soerjomataram, I.; Bray, F. *Global Cancer Observatory: Cancer Today*; International Agency for Research on Cancer: Lyon, France, 2024. Available online: https://gco.iarc.who.int/today (accessed on 8 February 2024).
2. Sylvestre, M.; Tarte, K.; Roulois, D. Epigenetic mechanisms driving tumor supportive microenvironment differentiation and function: A role in cancer therapy? *Epigenomics* **2020**, *12*, 157–169. [CrossRef] [PubMed]
3. Dagogo-Jack, I.; Shaw, A. Tumour heterogeneity and resistance to cancer therapies. *Nat. Rev. Clin. Oncol.* **2018**, *15*, 81–94. [CrossRef] [PubMed]
4. Danenberg, E.; Bardwell, H.; Zanotelli, V.R.T.; Provenzano, E.; Chin, S.-F.; Rueda, O.M.; Green, A.; Rakha, E.; Aparicio, S.; Ellis, I.O.; et al. Breast tumor microenvironment structures are associated with genomic features and clinical outcome. *Nat. Genet.* **2022**, *54*, 660–669. [CrossRef] [PubMed]
5. Malta, T.M.; Noushmehr, H. The cancer genome atlas research Network. The immune landscape of cancer. *Immunity* **2018**, *48*, 812–830. [CrossRef] [PubMed]
6. Xia, Y.; Sun, M.; Huang, H.; Jin, W.L. Drug repurposing for cancer therapy. *Signal Transduct. Target. Ther.* **2024**, *9*, 92. [CrossRef] [PubMed]
7. Wei, G.; Wang, Y.; Yang, G.; Wang, Y.; Ju, R. Recent progress in nanomedicine for enhanced cancer chemotherapy. *Theranostics* **2021**, *11*, 6370. [CrossRef] [PubMed]
8. Manzari, M.T.; Shamay, Y.; Kiguchi, H.; Rosen, N.; Scaltriti, M.; Heller, D.A. Targeted drug delivery strategies for precision medicines. *Nat. Rev. Mater.* **2021**, *6*, 351–370. [CrossRef] [PubMed]
9. Di Nardo, P.; Lisanti, C.; Garutti, M.; Buriolla, S.; Alberti, M.; Mazzeo, R.; Puglisi, F. Chemotherapy in patients with early breast cancer: Clinical overview and management of long-term side effects. *Expert Opin. Drug Saf.* **2022**, *21*, 1341–1355. [CrossRef]
10. Shi, J.; Kantoff, P.W.; Wooster, R.; Farokhzad, O.C. Cancer nanomedicine: Progress, challenges and opportunities. *Nat. Rev. Cancer* **2017**, *17*, 20–37. [CrossRef]
11. Timin, A.S.; Gao, H.; Voronin, D.V.; Gorin, D.A.; Sukhorukov, G.B. Inorganic/organic multilayer capsule composition for improved functionality and external triggering. *Adv. Mater. Interfaces* **2017**, *4*, 1600338. [CrossRef]
12. Novoselova, M.V.; Loh, H.M.; Trushina, D.B.; Ketkar, A.; Abakumova, T.O.; Zatsepin, T.S.; Kakran, M.; Brzozowska, A.M.; Lau, H.H.; Gorin, D.A.; et al. Biodegradable polymeric multilayer capsules for therapy of lung cancer. *ACS Appl. Mater. Interfaces* **2020**, *12*, 5610–5623. [CrossRef]
13. Kudryavtseva, V.; Boi, S.; Read, J.; Guillemet, R.; Zhang, J.; Udalov, A.; Shesterikov, E.; Tverdokhlebov, S.; Pastorino, L.; Gould, D.J.; et al. Biodegradable defined shaped printed polymer microcapsules for drug delivery. *ACS Appl. Mater. Interfaces* **2021**, *13*, 2371–2381. [CrossRef]
14. Nifontova, G.; Krivenkov, V.; Zvaigzne, M.; Efimov, A.; Korostylev, E.; Zarubin, S.; Karaulov, A.; Nabiev, I.; Sukhanova, A. Nanoparticle-doped hybrid polyelectrolyte microcapsules with controlled photoluminescence for potential bioimaging applications. *Polymers* **2021**, *13*, 4076. [CrossRef]
15. Nifontova, G.; Tsoi, T.; Karaulov, A.; Nabiev, I.; Sukhanova, A. Structure-function relationships in polymeric multilayer capsules designed for cancer drug delivery. *Biomater. Sci.* **2022**, *10*, 5092–5115. [CrossRef] [PubMed]
16. Sritharan, S.; Sivalingam, N. A comprehensive review on time-tested anticancer drug doxorubicin. *Life Sci.* **2021**, *278*, 119527. [CrossRef] [PubMed]
17. Fraczkowska, K.; Bacia, M.; Przybyło, M.; Drabik, D.; Kaczorowska, A.; Rybka, J.; Stefanko, E.; Drobczynski, S.; Masajada, J.; Podbielska, H.; et al. Alterations of biomechanics in cancer and normal cells induced by doxorubicin. *Biomed. Pharmacother.* **2018**, *97*, 1195–1203. [CrossRef]
18. Christidi, E.; Brunham, L.R. Regulated cell death pathways in doxorubicin-induced cardiotoxicity. *Cell Death Dis.* **2021**, *12*, 339. [CrossRef]
19. Wang, J.; Hao, H.; Cai, J.H. Amphiphilic drug delivery microcapsules via layer-by-layer self-assembly. *J. Polym. Sci. Part B Polym. Phys.* **2019**, *58*, 535–550. [CrossRef]
20. Trushina, D.B.; Akasov, R.A.; Khovankina, A.V.; Borodina, T.N.; Bukreeva, T.V.; Markvicheva, E.A. Doxorubicin-loaded biodegradable capsules: Temperature induced shrinking and study of cytotoxicity in vitro. *J. Mol. Liq.* **2019**, *284*, 215–224. [CrossRef]

21. Kalenichenko, D.; Nifontova, G.; Sukhanova, A.; Nabiev, I. Design and characterisation of calcium carbonate microspheres for anticancer drug delivery. *J. Phys. Conf. Ser.* **2021**, *2058*, 012009. [CrossRef]
22. Kalenichenko, D.; Nifontova, G.; Karaulov, A.; Sukhanova, A.; Nabiev, I. Designing functionalized polyelectrolyte microcapsules for cancer treatment. *Nanomaterials* **2021**, *11*, 3055. [CrossRef]
23. Nifontova, G.; Kalenichenko, D.; Kriukova, I.; Terryn, C.; Audonnet, S.; Karaulov, A.; Nabiev, I.; Sukhanova, A. Impact of macrophages on the interaction of cetuximab-functionalized polyelectrolyte capsules with EGFR-expressing cancer cells. *ACS Appl. Mater. Interfaces* **2023**, *15*, 52137–52149. [CrossRef]
24. Kim, A.L.; Musin, E.V.; Oripova, M.J.; Oshchepkova, Y.I.; Salikhov, S.I.; Tikhonenko, S.A. Polyelectrolyte microcapsules—A promising target delivery system of amiodarone with the possibility of prolonged release. *Int. J. Mol. Sci.* **2023**, *24*, 3348. [CrossRef]
25. Hu, Y.; Zhang, J.; Hu, H.; Xu, S.; Xu, L.; Chen, E. Gefitinib encapsulation based on nano-liposomes for enhancing the curative effect of lung cancer. *Cell Cycle* **2020**, *19*, 3581–3594. [CrossRef]
26. Mattiazzi, J.; Sari, M.H.M.; Araujo, P.C.O.; Englert, A.V.; Nadal, J.M.; Farago, P.V.; Nogueira, C.W.; Cruz, L. Ethylcellulose microparticles enhance 3,3′-diindolylmethane anti-hypernociceptive action in an animal model of acute inflammatory pain. *J. Microencapsul.* **2020**, *37*, 528–541. [CrossRef]
27. Meng, Q.; Zhong, S.; Wang, J.; Gao, Y.; Cui, X. 10-hydroxycamptothecin-loaded starch-based microcapsules with the stepwise responsive release strategy for targeted controlled release. *Int. J. Biol. Macromol.* **2023**, *252*, 126424. [CrossRef] [PubMed]
28. Sun, H.; Wong, E.H.; Yan, Y.; Cui, J.; Dai, Q.; Guo, J.; Qiao, G.G.; Caruso, F. The role of capsule stiffness on cellular processing. *Chem. Sci.* **2015**, *6*, 3505–3514. [CrossRef] [PubMed]
29. Palomba, R.; Palange, A.L.; Rizzuti, I.F.; Ferreira, M.; Cervadoro, A.; Barbato, M.G.; Canale, C.; Decuzzi, P. Modulating phagocytic cell sequestration by tailoring nanoconstruct softness. *ACS Nano* **2018**, *12*, 1433–1444. [CrossRef] [PubMed]
30. Hartmann, R.; Weidenbach, M.; Neubauer, M.; Fery, A.; Parak, W.J. Stiffness-dependent in vitro uptake and lysosomal acidification of colloidal particles. *Angew. Chem. Int. Ed. Engl.* **2015**, *54*, 1365–1368. [CrossRef]
31. Akdeniz, B.; Wood, J.A.; Lammertink, R.G.H. Diffusiophoretic behavior of polyelectrolyte-coated particles. *Langmuir* **2024**, *40*, 5934–5944. [CrossRef]
32. Shekunov, B.Y.; Chattopadhyay, P.; Tong, H.H.; Chow, A.H. Particle size analysis in pharmaceutics: Principles, methods and applications. *Pharm. Res.* **2007**, *24*, 203–227. [CrossRef]
33. Komatsu, S.; Yamada, S.; Kikuchi, A. Preparation of degradable and transformable core–corona-type particles that control cellular uptake by thermal shape change. *ACS Biomater. Sci. Eng.* **2024**, *10*, 897–904. [CrossRef] [PubMed]
34. Trushina, D.B.; Bukreeva, T.V.; Antipina, M.N. Size-controlled synthesis of vaterite calcium carbonate by the mixing method: Aiming for nanosized particles. *Cryst. Growth Des.* **2016**, *16*, 1311–1319. [CrossRef]
35. Ma, Y.; Wang, A.; Li, J.; Li, Q.; Han, Q.; Jing, Y.; Zheng, X.; Cao, H.; Yan, X.; Bai, S. Surface self-assembly of dipeptides on porous $CaCO_3$ particles promoting cell internalization. *ACS Appl. Mater. Interfaces* **2023**, *15*, 2486–2497. [CrossRef]
36. Bosio, V.E.; Cacicedo, M.L.; Calvignac, B.; León, I.; Beuvier, T.; Boury, F.; Castro, G.R. Synthesis and characterization of $CaCO_3$–biopolymer hybrid nanoporous microparticles for controlled release of doxorubicin. *Colloids Surf. B Biointerfaces* **2014**, *123*, 158–169. [CrossRef]
37. Pallaeva, T.N.; Mikheev, A.V.; Khmelenin, D.N.; Eurov, D.A.; Kurdyukov, D.A.; Popova, V.K.; Dmitrienko, E.V.; Trushina, D.B. High-capacity calcium carbonate particles as pH-sensitive containers for doxorubicin. *Crystallogr. Rep.* **2023**, *68*, 309–315. [CrossRef]
38. Kastl, L.; Sasse, D.; Wulf, V.; Hartmann, R.; Mircheski, J.; Ranke, C.; Carregal-Romero, S.; Martínez-López, J.A.; Fernández-Chacón, R.; Parak, W.J.; et al. Multiple internalization pathways of polyelectrolyte multilayer capsules into mammalian cells. *ACS Nano* **2013**, *7*, 6605–6618. [CrossRef] [PubMed]
39. Navolokin, N.A.; German, S.V.; Bucharskaya, A.B.; Godage, O.S.; Zuev, V.V.; Maslyakova, G.N.; Pyataev, N.A.; Zamyshliaev, P.S.; Zharkov, M.N.; Terentyuk, G.S.; et al. Systemic administration of polyelectrolyte microcapsules: Where do they accumulate and when? In vivo and ex vivo study. *Nanomaterials* **2018**, *8*, 812. [CrossRef]
40. Choukrani, G.; Maharjan, B.; Park, C.H.; Kim, C.S.; Kurup Sasikala, A.R. Biocompatible superparamagnetic sub-micron vaterite particles for thermo-chemotherapy: From controlled design to in vitro anticancer synergism. *Mater. Sci. Eng. C Mater. Biol. Appl.* **2020**, *106*, 110226. [CrossRef]
41. Zhang, Y.; Cai, L.; Li, D.; Lao, Y.-H.; Liu, D.; Li, M.; Ding, J.; Chen, X. Tumor microenvironment-responsive hyaluronate-calcium carbonate hybrid nanoparticle enables effective chemotherapy for primary and advanced osteosarcomas. *Nano Res.* **2018**, *11*, 4806–4822. [CrossRef]

Disclaimer/Publisher's Note: The statements, opinions and data contained in all publications are solely those of the individual author(s) and contributor(s) and not of MDPI and/or the editor(s). MDPI and/or the editor(s) disclaim responsibility for any injury to people or property resulting from any ideas, methods, instructions or products referred to in the content.

cancers

MDPI

Review

FLASH Radiotherapy and the Use of Radiation Dosimeters

Sarkar Siddique [1], Harry E. Ruda [2,3] and James C. L. Chow [4,5,*]

1 Department of Physics, Toronto Metropolitan University, Toronto, ON M5B 2K3, Canada; sarkar.siddique@torontomu.ca
2 Centre of Advance Nanotechnology, Faculty of Applied Science and Engineering, University of Toronto, Toronto, ON M5S 3E4, Canada; harry.ruda@utoronto.ca
3 Department of Materials Science and Engineering, University of Toronto, Toronto, ON M5S 3E4, Canada
4 Radiation Medicine Program, Princess Margaret Cancer Centre, University Health Network, Toronto, ON M5G 1X6, Canada
5 Department of Radiation Oncology, University of Toronto, Toronto, ON M5T 1P5, Canada
* Correspondence: james.chow@uhn.ca; Tel.: +1-416-946-4501

Simple Summary: FLASH radiotherapy (RT) delivering ultra-high dose rate radiation can reduce normal tissue toxicity while effectively treating tumors. However, implementing FLASH RT in clinical settings faces challenges like limited depth penetration and complex treatment planning. Monte Carlo simulation is a valuable tool to optimize FLASH RT. Radiation detectors, including diamond detectors like microDiamond and ionization chambers, play a crucial role in accurately measuring dose delivery. Moreover, optically stimulated luminescence dosimeters and radiochromic films are used for validation. Advancements are being made to improve detector accuracy in FLASH RT. Further research is needed to refine treatment planning and detector performance for widespread FLASH RT implementation, which can potentially revolutionize cancer treatment.

Abstract: Radiotherapy (RT) using ultra-high dose rate (UHDR) radiation, known as FLASH RT, has shown promising results in reducing normal tissue toxicity while maintaining tumor control. However, implementing FLASH RT in clinical settings presents technical challenges, including limited depth penetration and complex treatment planning. Monte Carlo (MC) simulation is a valuable tool for dose calculation in RT and has been investigated for optimizing FLASH RT. Various MC codes, such as EGSnrc, DOSXYZnrc, and Geant4, have been used to simulate dose distributions and optimize treatment plans. Accurate dosimetry is essential for FLASH RT, and radiation detectors play a crucial role in measuring dose delivery. Solid-state detectors, including diamond detectors such as microDiamond, have demonstrated linear responses and good agreement with reference detectors in UHDR and ultra-high dose per pulse (UHDPP) ranges. Ionization chambers are commonly used for dose measurement, and advancements have been made to address their response nonlinearities at UHDPP. Studies have proposed new calculation methods and empirical models for ion recombination in ionization chambers to improve their accuracy in FLASH RT. Additionally, strip-segmented ionization chamber arrays have shown potential for the experimental measurement of dose rate distribution in proton pencil beam scanning. Radiochromic films, such as Gafchromic™ EBT3, have been used for absolute dose measurement and to validate MC simulation results in high-energy X-rays, triggering the FLASH effect. These films have been utilized to characterize ionization chambers and measure off-axis and depth dose distributions in FLASH RT. In conclusion, MC simulation provides accurate dose calculation and optimization for FLASH RT, while radiation detectors, including diamond detectors, ionization chambers, and radiochromic films, offer valuable tools for dosimetry in UHDR environments. Further research is needed to refine treatment planning techniques and improve detector performance to facilitate the widespread implementation of FLASH RT, potentially revolutionizing cancer treatment.

Keywords: FLASH radiotherapy; ultra-high dose rate radiotherapy; detectors; dosimetry

1. Introduction

While radiotherapy (RT) utilizes ionizing radiation to damage and eliminate cancer cells, radiation-induced toxicity restricts the maximum deliverable dose [1,2]. Ultra-high dose rate (UHDR) RT, known as FLASH RT, can solve this problem, as it delivers radiation at a rate several orders of magnitude higher than conventional clinical RT [3]. The FLASH effect, referred to as UHDR (≥40 Gy/s) RT, reduces damage to healthy tissues while maintaining antitumor effectiveness [4]. The flash effect, now termed FLASH RT, was initially reported by Dewey and Boag in 1959, but gained prominence after 2014 with in vivo studies demonstrating reduced normal tissue toxicity while achieving similar tumor control compared to conventional RT [5].

The first patient treated with FLASH RT was a 75-year-old individual with multiresistant CD30+ T-cell cutaneous lymphoma that had disseminated throughout the skin surface. FLASH treatment was delivered using a specialized 5.6 MeV LINAC, designed specifically for FLASH RT. The prescribed dose to the planning target volume was 15 Gy delivered in 90 milliseconds (ms). Dosimetric measurements using GafChromic films and alanine were performed to ensure dose consistency [6].

Numerous in vivo studies have investigated the FLASH effect and its potential benefits. For instance, a study evaluated lung fibrogenesis in mice subjected to UHDR irradiation and conventional dose rate irradiation, demonstrating improved outcomes and spared normal smooth muscles and epithelial cells from acute radiation-induced apoptosis with UHDR irradiation [7]. FLASH RT shows promise as a treatment option with significant potential for improving outcomes, particularly for pancreatic cancer, which currently faces limitations due to gastrointestinal toxicity [8].

However, the clinical implementation of FLASH RT presents technical challenges. Conventional linear accelerators are unable to generate therapeutic doses beyond a 15 cm depth, limiting FLASH RT to skin cancers or tumors located close to the body surface [9]. Treatment planning for FLASH RT is complex and currently under investigation to determine the best methods and optimization techniques. Several studies have explored the application of Monte Carlo (MC) codes for dose calculation in FLASH RT [10]. Moreover, dosimetry in FLASH RT is challenging due to the delivery of high instantaneous doses, necessitating a comprehensive understanding of factors influencing detector response [11].

Although FLASH RT has primarily been studied using X-rays, the FLASH effect has been validated in preclinical experiments using electrons and protons, with both particle types operated at mean dose rates above 40 Gy/s [12]. Notably, the immunological memory response in mice was found to be similar between electron and proton beams, independent of dose rate [13]. Fractional delivery in FLASH RT typically involves a sequence of pulses with a frequency of approximately 100 Hz (interval between pulses $\approx$ 10 ms) and a dose per pulse greater than 1 Gy, enabling fraction delivery within a few tenths of a second [14].

The sparing effect of FLASH RT on normal cells is influenced by oxygen depletion, with varying oxygen levels in tumors and normal tissues affecting the efficacy of the FLASH effect [15]. Determining the precise dose required to induce the effect is crucial and requires further investigation [16]. Studies using carbon ion irradiation explored the response of CHO-K1 cells to irradiation at different dose rates under various levels of oxygenation. FLASH irradiation with a dose rate of 70 Gy/s demonstrated a significant FLASH effect and oxygenation dependence [17]. Furthermore, FLASH RT has been found to spare normal tissue temporarily due to hypoxia resulting from oxygen depletion induced by UHDR irradiation [18]. Depleting cellular oxygen at the FLASH dose rate was shown to be achievable with an oxygen concentration of 0.4% and a dose rate of 5–10 Gy [19]. Dosimetry performance and optimization of FLASH dose rates have been systematically evaluated in hypofractionated lung cancer patients, enabling the optimization of Bragg Peak and transmission plans to achieve acceptable plan quality [19].

Moreover, FLASH irradiation induces different cell death mechanisms, including pyroptosis, apoptosis, and necrosis, with varying ratios in cancer stem cells and normal cancer cells. Cancer stem cells exhibit greater resistance to radiation under FLASH irradiation, potentially due to increased lysosome-mediated autophagy and decreased necrosis, apoptosis, and pyroptosis. Further investigations are warranted to better understand the radioresistance of cancer stem cells [20].

2. Monte Carlo Simulation

MC simulation is recognized as one of the most accurate methods for dose calculation in RT [21]. Bazalova-Carter et al. investigated the application of MC methods in percentage depth dose calculation using electron beams of different sizes (50 and 70 MeV). The EGSnrc/BEAMnrc and DOSXYZnrc MC codes were employed to calculate the dose in a polystyrene phantom. The simulation results exhibited good agreement (within 5%) with the measured data for depth–dose curves and beam profiles. However, there was a discrepancy of 42% between the calculated and measured doses [21].

Palma et al. utilized the same MC codes (EGSnrc/BEAMnrc and DOSXYZnrc [22,23]) to perform dose distribution calculations for very high-energy electron beams in five clinical cases. Additionally, MC simulation was employed for dose calculation using two 160 kV X-ray tubes, where the difference between experimental results and simulations was within 3.6% [24]. Geant4 is another widely used software for simulating particle transport in matter and has been employed for dose calculation and new hardware design in FLASH research [24]. In another study, BEAMnrc MC codes were used to model a LINAC. The resulting phase-space file from the simulation was fed into DOSXYZnrc to calculate the 3D dose distribution in a voxel-based phantom. Comparison between the simulated and experimentally measured results showed good agreement for different maximum dose ranges (R_{max}, R_{90}, R_{80}, and R_{50}). The deviation between the MC-calculated percent depth dose (PDD) curves and the measurements was 5.2% [25]. EGSnrc (release v2023) MC software modules, namely BEAMnrc and DOSXYZnrc, were employed to create a treatment plan for whole-brain RT. The simulation demonstrated that two lateral opposing 40 MeV electron beams could be used to deliver a FLASH dose rate of >115 Gy/s for whole-brain RT, highlighting its potential for clinical application [26].

The UHDR of FLASH therapy presents new challenges, such as the need for a new shielding system. MC simulation can provide a solution for simulating such a shielding system, as explored in a study [27]. Another investigation focused on ionizing radiation acoustic imaging through simulation and its potential as a dosimetric tool for FLASH RT. Ionizing radiation acoustic imaging is an imaging technique that creates dose-related images by utilizing acoustic waves generated through the thermoacoustic effect in response to ionizing radiation. A full 3D dose distribution was simulated using the EGSnrc (BEAMnrc/DOSXYZnrc [22,23]) MC simulation code in a phantom with a 1×1 cm^2 field. The simulation results were verified using Gafchromic films. The experimental measurements and dose simulation agreed within an approximately 5% relative error for the central beam region at up to 80% dose, both for the central profile region and the percentage depth dose. This study demonstrates the feasibility of utilizing ionizing radiation acoustic imaging as a dosimeter for depth–dose measurement and beam localization in FLASH RT [28]. These studies highlight the use of MC simulation in dose calculation, treatment planning, hardware design, shielding system simulation, and dosimetry for various aspects of RT, including both conventional and FLASH techniques.

3. Radiation Dose Detectors

Radiation detectors play a vital role in various fields, including medical physics, radiation protection, and high-energy sensitive imaging [29]. Recent advancements in detector technology have introduced exciting developments, such as the photon counting detector that utilizes semiconductor materials to generate electronic signals in response to incident X-ray photons [30]. Another noteworthy innovation is the pressurized ionization chamber detector, which enables the characterization of alpha and beta radioactive sources and can measure radioactive sources in internal 2π or 4π geometry [31]. Furthermore, the availability of 2D and 3D ionization chamber arrays allows for real-time dose verification [32]. The application of these novel dosimetric technologies in UHDR dose delivery holds significant promise.

In the context of FLASH RT, UHDR per pulse is necessary to achieve the FLASH effect. However, real-time dosimetry poses a significant challenge. Conventional vented ionization chambers used for dosimetry exhibit substantial deviation from linearity as the dose rate per pulse increases, primarily due to recombination losses in the sensitive air volume. Solid-state detectors offer good response stability with respect to accumulated dose and present a promising alternative. Diamond detectors, among other solid-state detectors, have been extensively utilized in RT applications [33].

These advancements in radiation detector technology enhance the accuracy and reliability of dose measurements, allowing for improved outcomes in various fields, including FLASH RT and conventional RT.

3.1. Diamond Detector

Diamond detectors possess high radiosensitivity and offer excellent spatial resolution, making them well suited for applications involving large dose gradients and small fields [34]. The viability of diamond detectors, such as microDiamond, is being investigated for their potential use in FLASH RT. The microDiamond detector functions as a Schottky diode, where the sensitive volume of a diamond is positioned between a metallic contact and a p-type diamond structure that serves as the back contact. This arrangement generates a depletion region in the contact area, which possesses an inherent potential and serves as the sensitive volume. As a result, there is no need for an external bias voltage to operate the detector. Figure 1 illustrates the equivalent circuit of this diode [35].

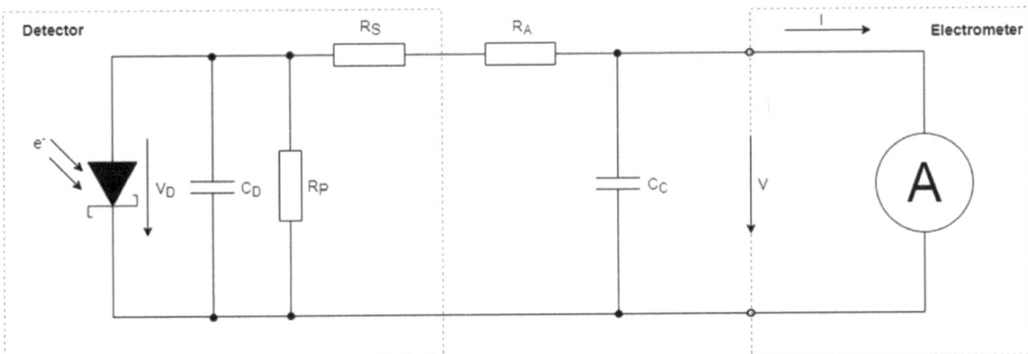

Figure 1. Circuit diagram for a diode representation of a diamond detector. Reproduced from reference [35] under the Creative Commons Attribution 4.0 International License (https://creativecommons.org/licenses/by/4.0/ (accessed on 1 July 2023)).

In the context of FLASH RT, a specific diamond detector designed for dosimetry purposes was introduced. The study focused on its application in both ultra-high dose per pulse (UHDPP) and UHDR beams utilized in FLASH RT. The detector was successfully implemented in an electron FLASH LINAC, and it exhibited linearity within the dose per pulse range. The study demonstrated strong agreement between dose per pulse, output factor (ratio of the dose in air for a given field to that for a reference field), and beam profile measurements when compared to a reference detector [36].

To address the inherent response nonlinearities observed in conventional detectors, a novel diamond-based Schottky diode detector was developed. The prototype's response linearity was influenced by the size of its active volume and series resistance. However, through proper tuning and adjustment, the detector layout was able to achieve linearity up to at least 20 Gy/pulse [37].

The unique properties of diamond detectors, along with their improved linearity and dose measurement capabilities, make them promising candidates for enhancing dosimetry accuracy in both FLASH RT and conventional RT settings.

3.2. Ionization Chamber

In clinical practice, ionization chambers are commonly used for both absolute and relative dose measurements in radiation therapy. These chambers are particularly useful in regions with high dose gradients [38]. For FLASH RT, specific ionization chambers such as the 2D strip segmented ionization chamber array were developed for the experimental measurement of 2D dose rate distributions [39]. However, the standard ionization chamber can be significantly affected by UHDR per pulse due to the electric field generated by the large density of charges from the dose pulse [40].

To address the dosimetric challenges associated with UHDR per-pulse irradiation, researchers have explored modifications and calculation methods for ionization chambers. A study introduced a new calculation method for the free electron fraction in an ionization chamber. By modeling the capture process of electrons and evaluating the free electron fraction, they were able to estimate the response of the ionization chamber after irradiation [41]. Another study proposed an empirical model of ion recombination in an ionization chamber for UHDR per pulse electron beams. The study compared the observed ion recombination output with various theoretical models and found that taking ion recombination into account enables the ionization chamber to function for dose measurements at UHDR per pulse [42].

In the context of proton therapy and FLASH irradiation, different models of ionization chambers have been evaluated. One study investigated the response of four ionization chamber models for spread-out Bragg peak proton FLASH irradiation. The study found that plane-parallel chambers with smaller gaps between electrodes are more favorable for FLASH RT dose measurements [43]. Furthermore, efforts have been made to improve the ion collection efficiency of ionization chambers to make them suitable for FLASH RT. For example, the ion collection efficiency of vented ionization chambers was studied for the UHDR electron beam, and the dependences of the sensitive air volume on the design of chamber and electric field were evaluated. The results indicated a decrease in ion collection efficiency within the UHDR range. The extent of the decrease varied depending on factors such as electrode distribution, electric field strength, and chamber voltage in the sensitive air volume [44]. Another study developed and characterized an ultra-thin parallel plate ionization chamber that showed potential for extending the dose rate operating range to the ultra-high dose per pulse range used in FLASH RT. To accommodate the ultra-thin ionization chamber (UTIC) and a specifically modified diamond detector (referred to as flash-diamond) for UHDR, a polymethyl methacrylate (PMMA) phantom was constructed. The flash-diamond served as a reference dosimeter for the experiment, as shown in Figure 2 [45].

Figure 2. The experimental setup at SIT (Italy). On the left side, there is the ElectronFlash, a linear accelerator (1), which is utilized with a 100 mm diameter applicator (2). On the right side is the PMMA phantom (1) accompanied by the flash-diamond (2) and the ultra-thin ionization chamber (3) that are prepared for irradiation with the 35 mm diameter applicator (4). Reproduced from reference [45] under the Creative Commons Attribution 4.0 International License (https://creativecommons.org/licenses/by/4.0/ (accessed on 1 July 2023)).

Additionally, novel ionization chamber technologies have been explored for online dosimetry in FLASH RT. The RazorTM Nano Chamber, with its small sensitive volume, has demonstrated higher ion collection efficiency compared to larger chambers, making it a potential tool for online dosimetry in FLASH RT [46].

The development and refinement of specialized ionization chambers, calculation methods, and online dosimetry tools are essential for advancing the field of radiation dosimetry in FLASH RT. These advancements aim to ensure accurate and reliable dose measurements in the context of UHDR delivery, facilitating the safe and effective implementation of FLASH RT in clinical practice.

3.3. Radiochromic Film

Radiochromic film is a dosimeter that possesses desirable characteristics for radiation responses, such as independence from radiation energy and dose rate, as well as a negligible volume effect [47]. The effectiveness of the different types of radiochromic film depends on their dose sensitivity, accuracy, and response to environmental conditions [48].

In the context of FLASH RT a study utilized Gafchromic^{TM} EBT3 radiochromic film to measure the dose in high-energy X-rays capable of triggering the FLASH effect in mice. The film was placed between the mice and the PMMA holder to measure the dose, and it was also used to validate MC simulation results [49]. Another investigation performed a dosimetric characterization of a plane-parallel ionization chamber under UHDR conditions using radiochromic films. Radiochromic films were used to verify the beamline setup, measure depth–dose distribution and dose profile, and serve as a reference for ionization chamber characterization. The study revealed significant recombination losses and polarity effects in the ionization chamber [50].

An electron-scattering device was created for the practical use of UHDR electron beams in FLASH preclinical research at the Dongnam Institute of Radiological and Medical Sciences [51]. The scattering device's geometry for a 6-MeV linear accelerator was determined using Monte Carlo N-particle transport simulations. Radiochromic films were used to measure the off-axis and depth dose distributions with the scattering device. The measured dose per pulse varied from 4.0 to 0.2 Gy/pulse at different source-to-surface distances (SSD) ranging from 20 cm to 90 cm. At an SSD of 30 cm and a repetition rate of 100 Hz, the dose rate reached 180 Gy/s, providing a sufficient dose rate for conducting small-animal FLASH studies.

Furthermore, radiochromic film has been employed in various applications within the establishment of FLASH RT. In a study involving canine cancer patients, radiochromic film (GafChromic EBT-XD) was utilized for dose measurements on a phantom and to measure dose per pulse. The film was also used for in vivo dose measurements at the skin's surface to verify the delivered dose. The experimental configuration depicted in Figure 3 illustrates the setup utilized for conducting measurements using radiochromic film to determine both the total dose and dose per pulse [52]. These measurements were correlated with the signal obtained from a Farmer-type ionization chamber (NE 2505/3-3A), which was positioned within a specially designed holder placed in the applicator.

Figure 3. Experimental arrangement employed in the preparation of each patient's treatment. Radiochromic film was utilized to conduct measurements on phantoms that simulated the treatment geometry. These measurements encompassed the total dose, number of pulses, and dose per pulse intended for delivery to the patients. A Farmer-type ionization chamber was employed as the output monitor. Reproduced from reference [52] under the Creative Commons Attribution 4.0 International Li-cense (https://creativecommons.org/licenses/by/4.0/ (accessed on 1 July 2023)).

In addition, radiochromic film was used in conjunction with the MC FLUKA code to measure dose in FLASH irradiation and investigate the enhancement of radio-resistance in normal fibroblast cells under conditions of hypoxia and mitochondrial dysfunction [53].

In proton FLASH dosimetry, different radiochromic films have been compared for their dose rate dependency. A study conducted at the ARRONAX cyclotron facility evaluated GAFchromic™ EBT-XD, GAFchromic™ EBT3, and OrthoChromic OC-1 films after proton irradiation. The study found that OC-1 films exhibited dose rate independence in proton beams up to 7500 Gy/s, while caution should be exercised when using EBT-XD and EBT3 films at dose rates exceeding 10 Gy [54]. Another study focused on dosimetry in proton pencil beam scanning FLASH RT, employing MC codes for simulations and Gafchromic® EBT3 films for dose measurements. The investigation aimed to determine the absolute dose for FLASH proton beam radiotherapy using a primary standard proton calorimeter, achieving an uncertainty of 0.9% through the application of correction factors [55].

By leveraging the capabilities of radiochromic film and its compatibility with various dosimetric techniques and simulations, researchers continue to advance the field of dosimetry in FLASH RT, enabling accurate and precise dose measurements necessary for the safe and effective implementation of this promising treatment modality.

3.4. Alanine

Alanine dosimetry is a widely used method in high-dose dosimetry, relying on irradiated crystalline alanine that is measured using electron paramagnetic resonance (EPR) spectrometry. It is renowned for its exceptional stability in post-irradiation response [56]. Alanine dosimeters are commonly employed for calibration services and are suitable for a wide range of industrial applications due to their energy independence (above 100 keV) and minimal dose rate effects [57].

While alanine dosimetry is accurate, its application in FLASH RT for biological experiments and clinical use requires a reduction in reading time. One study focused on optimizing an alanine dosimeter by improving the acquisition of EPR spectra using a Bruker spectrometer. Parameters such as the number of scans, time constraints, conversion time, microwave power, and modulation amplitude of the magnetic field were investigated for optimization purposes [58].

In the context of specific radiation sources, another study compared an alanine detector with a PTW PinPoint ionization chamber (used as a reference) for an orthovoltage X-ray source with an average dose rate of 11.6 kGy/s. The study concluded that the alanine dosimeter is suitable for the UHDR calibration of orthovoltage X-ray sources [59]. Elsewhere, a study examined the use of an alanine-based dosimetry system to precisely evaluate absorbed dose to water in UHDR per pulse electron beams. The electron beam used in the study had a range of 0.15–6.2 Gy/pulse, and MC simulation was employed to calculate the conversion factor required for alanine dosimetry and determine the beam quality [60]. The absolute dosimetry of the Oriatron eRT6 linear accelerator was examined using alanine, thermo-luminescent dosimeters (TLD), radiochromic films, and an ionization chamber for relative stability [61]. A comparison of results between alanine, films, and TLD demonstrated a dose agreement within 3% for dose rates ranging from 0.078 Gy/s to 1050 Gy/s. This indicates that such dosimeters are suitable for absolute dosimetry in FLASH RT. A comparison was made between the reference dosimetry using the PinPoint ionization chamber and alanine dosimetry for synchrotron X-ray sources [59]. The results revealed a relative response of 0.932 ± 0.027 (1σ) for the alanine pellets irradiated at the European Synchrotron Radiation Facility (ESRF) compared to the ^{60}Co facility at National Centre for Radiation Research and Technology. These findings took into account corrections for the ESRF polychromatic spectrum and the different field sizes used. Therefore, it can be confirmed that alanine is a suitable dosimeter for calibrating orthovoltage X-ray sources operating at UHDR.

Furthermore, research has demonstrated the applicability of alanine dosimeters and TLDs for dosimetry in FLASH RT. By imposing specific requirements on the procedure, such as optimizing conversion time, time constant, microwave power, modulation amplitude of the magnetic field, and the number of scans, a maximum dose deviation of 1.8% was achieved for the dose range of 10 Gy–100 Gy, while keeping the deviation to the reference within $\pm 2\%$ [58]. Moreover, studies have shown that alanine dosimeters exhibit good agreement with TLDs, and alanine dosimetry provides the closest match between the expected and measured doses. Figure 4 presents the bias of various detectors, including alanine, film, and TLD, in relation to the expected doses in both conventional RT and UHDR RT [62].

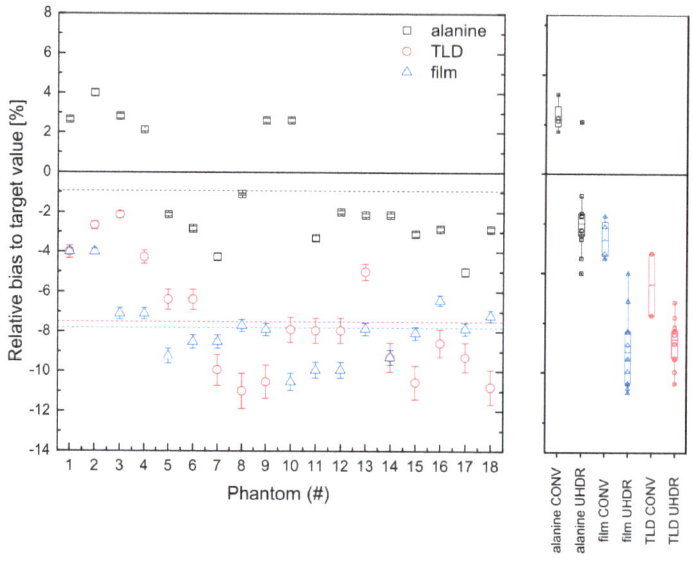

Figure 4. The (**left**) plot shows the relative bias to target value in phantom for alanine, film and TLD in conventional RT and UHDR RT. The (**right**) plot shows the biases for each dose detector and dose rate mode. Reproduced from reference [62] under the Creative Commons Attribution 4.0 International License (https://creativecommons.org/licenses/by/4.0/ (accessed on 1 July 2023)).

For the irradiation of biological models with pulsed electron beams at UHDR, dosimetry procedures involving alanine dosimeters, films, and TLDs have been investigated. These methods demonstrated dose agreements within 3% for dose rates ranging from 0.078 Gy/s to 1050 Gy/s, making them suitable for FLASH RT. The studies also emphasized the importance of appropriate setup and correction factors, as active dosimetry without them can lead to dose deviations of up to 15% of the prescribed dose. However, by following the proposed study setup and procedure, the deviations can be reduced to less than 3% [61].

The ongoing research and optimization efforts in alanine dosimetry highlight its potential for accurate and reliable dose measurements in the context of FLASH RT, paving the way for its integration into clinical practice and biological studies.

3.5. Radioluminescence, Cherenkov Radiation Dosimetry, and Others

Recently, there have been significant advancements in utilizing Cherenkov energy as a monitoring tool for biological changes, such as oxygen levels, during radiotherapy. Cherenkov emission occurs naturally as a byproduct of RT when high-energy charged particles surpass the local phase velocity of light within a dielectric medium, resulting in the emission of optical photons [63].

Studies have explored spatial-temporal beam profiling for electrons in UHDR conditions using Cherenkov emission, radioluminescence imaging, and complementary metal oxide semiconductor (CMOS) cameras. Surface dosimetry was investigated by imaging scintillation or Cherenkov emission from a solid water phantom (Gd_2O_2S:Tb) and comparing the optical imaging results with the response measured by Gafchromic film at various depths. The pulse-per-beam output from Cherenkov imaging agreed within 3% with photomultiplier tube Cherenkov output. Scintillation and Cherenkov emission showed linearity with dose (R^2 = 0.995 and 0.987, respectively) and were independent of dose rate in the range of approximately 50 Gy/s to 300 Gy/s (0.18–0.91 Gy/pulse) [64].

In another study, a nitrogen-doped, silica-based multimodal optical fiber was examined for monitoring very UHDR conditions through radiation-induced emission. The findings indicated that the emission of radiation from this fiber exhibited a linear dependence on the dose rate over a broad range of dose rates (10^{-2} Gy(SiO_2)/s to a few 10^9 Gy(SiO_2)/s) and photon energies (40 keV to 19 MeV). This is depicted in Figure 5, highlighting its significant potential for beam monitoring in UHDR scenarios [65].

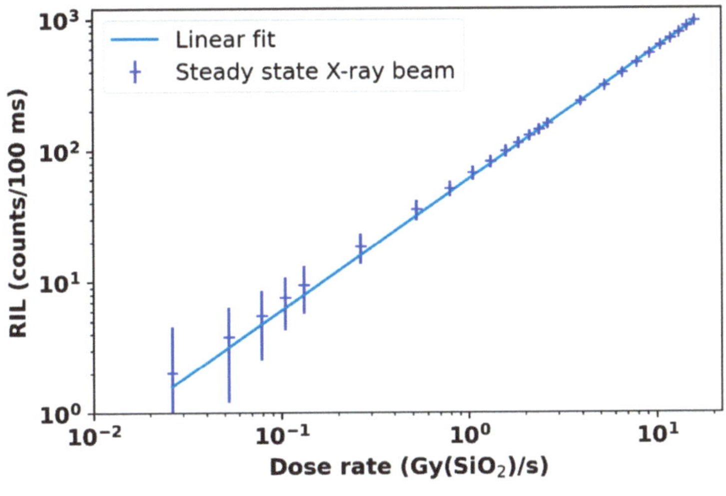

Figure 5. The dose rate dependence of radiation-induced luminescence (RIL) in nitrogen-doped optical fiber was investigated in response to X-ray radiation. Reproduced from reference [65] under the Creative Commons Attribution 4.0 International Li-cense (https://creativecommons.org/licenses/by/4.0/ (accessed on 1 July 2023)).

Fricke or ferrous ammonium sulphate detectors, which are chemical-based dosimeters, rely on the oxidation of ferrous and ferric ions, followed by their interaction with ionizing radiation. These dosimeters possess properties similar to water since they consist of 96% water by weight. They can serve as absorbed doses to water primary standards in high-energy electron beams [66].

A novel plastic scintillator capable of resolving individual pulses with a temporal resolution as short as 2.5 ms was investigated in a study. The plastic scintillator's response measurement exhibited linearity with ionization chamber measurement (within $\leq$1%) over a dose range of 4–20 Gy and pulse frequencies of 18–180 Hz. Under reference conditions, the plastic scintillator maintained its dose–response even under ultra-high pulsed dose rate conditions and agreed with EBT-XD film dose measurements within >4%. It demonstrated a linear and reproducible response, accurately measuring the absorbed dose from a 16 MeV electron beam with an ultrahigh pulsed dose rate [67].

One study focused on the first characterization of six real-time point scintillation dosimeters using five phosphors (Al_2O_3:C, Mg; Y_2O_3:Eu; Al_2O_3:C; ($C_{38}H_{34}P_2$)$MnBr_4$ and ($C_{38}H_{34}P_2$)$MnCl_4$) in an ultra-high pulsed dose rate electron beam. The linearity of response with dose was tested by varying the number of pulses, and a linearity with R2 > 0.9989 was observed up to at least 200 Gy [68].

The response of three detectors, Gafchromic EBT-XD film, optically stimulated luminescence (OSL), and the CC13 ionization chamber was investigated in UHDR conditions. Experimental results showed that EBT-XD film can be used in FLASH experiments without requiring any dose rate correction up to at least 2×10^4 Gy/s. The agreement between the doses measured with film at different distances from the scattering foil and the doses computed using the effective inverse square law confirmed this. OSL measurements also exhibited agreement with the inverse square law, maintaining independence up to 280 Gy/s. The ionization chamber achieved reasonable agreement between the modeled and measured chamber efficiency; however, the discrepancies exceeded the clinically used tolerance of 2% [69]. Over the years, OSL has emerged as a strong competitor for thermoluminescence dosimetry and other dosimetry systems [70]. In spite of the promise that OSL offers in terms of UHDR conditions, it is limited by available materials, many of which (e.g., Al_2O_3:C) were first introduced in the 1960′s. The key will be to identify new materials specifically designed for FLASH—that is, with tuned bandgap, radiation hardness, high radiative recombination efficiency of trapped carriers, linearity in deep state creation as a function of dose up to high doses, and excellent minority carrier lifetime and transport. It is likely that such materials will rely on nanostructured materials where size quantization of electronic states can allow for tailored spectral output, enhanced exciton binding energies, and polarization anisotropy to provide for higher performance and more versatile materials and likely the next generation of OSL for FLASH.

The potential of lead-doped scintillator dosimeters for use in FLASH-capable UHDR X-ray beams was investigated. The study demonstrated that the lead-doped scintillators were independent of dose rate for UHDR X-rays in the range of 1.1 Gy/s to 40.1 Gy/s. When compared with MC simulations, the dose to water measured with the lead-doped (5%) scintillator detector agreed within 0.6% [71].

In the first positron emission tomography imaging and dosimetry study of a FLASH proton beam, the radiation environment was characterized using cadmium-zinc-telluride and a plastic scintillator counter [72].

A fiber optic radiation sensor created with a plastic scintillator, an optical filter, and a plastic optical fiber was explored for use in FLASH RT. The sensor detected radiation-induced emissions such as fluorescence and Cherenkov radiation generated within the transmitting optical fiber. The sensor's output was measured at different distances from an electron scattering device and compared with the output of an ionization chamber and radiochromic films [73].

The EDGE detector, based on diodes, was also studied to characterize FLASH beams and its response compared to other detectors. The EDGE detector showed agreement with film measurements within 2% on average over the measured range of varying doses (up to 70 Gy), dose per pulse (up to 0.63 Gy/pulse), and dose rate (nearly 200 Gy/s). It also agreed with the W1 scintillation detector for dose per pulse (up to 0.78 Gy/pulse) within 2% on average. The EDGE detector demonstrated the ability to quantify the beam spatially and temporally with sub-millisecond resolution, making it suitable for in vivo studies [74].

These studies contribute to the advancement of dosimetry methods for FLASH RT and provide valuable insights into the performance and potential applications of various detectors in ultra-high dose rate scenarios.

4. Future Prospective

The future prospects of radiation dosimetry in FLASH RT hold significant promise for advancing this emerging treatment modality. Dosimetry plays a crucial role in accurately measuring and monitoring the dose delivered during RT, and its importance is further magnified in the context of FLASH RT, which involves ultra-high dose rates and unique delivery techniques.

One of the key areas of focus for future dosimetry in FLASH RT is the development of specialized detectors capable of accurately measuring the high dose rates associated with this treatment. Conventional dosimeters may exhibit limitations in their response time and saturation effects at such extreme dose rates. Research efforts are underway to explore novel dosimetry technologies that can provide real-time measurements and maintain accuracy in the presence of rapid dose delivery.

Additionally, there is a need to investigate the dosimetric properties of various radiation modalities used in FLASH RT, including electron beams, proton beams, and X-rays. Each modality may have distinct dosimetric characteristics, and understanding their behavior in the context of FLASH RT is crucial for optimizing treatment planning and ensuring accurate dose delivery. Comparative studies and advancements in MC simulation techniques can contribute to a deeper understanding of the dosimetric aspects specific to FLASH RT.

The development and validation of comprehensive dosimetry systems specifically designed for FLASH RT are also anticipated in the future. These systems would encompass not only dose measurement devices, but also data acquisition, analysis, and quality assurance tools tailored to the unique requirements of FLASH RT. Such systems would facilitate precise and reliable dose calculations, treatment verification, and patient safety in clinical implementations of FLASH RT.

Moreover, the exploration of advanced imaging techniques integrated with dosimetry in FLASH RT holds great potential. Real-time imaging modalities, such as in vivo dosimetry using electronic portal imaging devices or onboard imaging systems, can provide valuable information on dose distribution during treatment delivery. Combining imaging data with dosimetric measurements can enable continuous monitoring and adaptive strategies to further enhance the accuracy and safety of FLASH RT.

The future prospects of radiation dosimetry in FLASH RT are centered around the development of specialized detectors, comprehensive dosimetry systems, and integration with advanced imaging technologies. Continued research and collaboration between radiation oncologists, medical physicists, and engineers is vital to address the dosimetric challenges and unlock the full potential of FLASH RT as an innovative and effective cancer treatment option.

5. Conclusions

FLASH RT demonstrates tremendous potential as a cancer treatment option; however, further investigation is needed before it can be widely adopted. Future FLASH devices may require the ability to perform multiple-field conformal radiation to reduce toxicity in healthy tissues compared to single-field approaches [2]. While most of the current FLASH studies have focused on electron beams, proton beams, and X-ray beams, they have shown beneficial effects [75]. In addition to the dosimetry challenges associated with FLASH RT, further research is required for its successful clinical implementation [76]. Caution should be exercised during the clinical application of FLASH RT until a comprehensive understanding of the biological effects and a thoroughly tested dosimetry system are established [77]. Ongoing research endeavors to unravel the fundamental mechanisms responsible for the distinctive tissue-sparing benefits of FLASH radiation. By comprehending how FLASH RT influences biological responses in both healthy tissues and cancer cells, researchers hope to develop enhanced treatment protocols to enhance patient outcomes.

In particular, the FLASH effect is influenced by various factors such as total dose, dose rate, pulse rate, radiation modality, and fractionation. Hence, accurate dose monitoring is vital in delivering the desired effect. Continued research and investigation into suitable dosimeters for FLASH RT will facilitate its further development and implementation in diverse types of cancer treatments [78,79].

Author Contributions: Conceptualization, J.C.L.C. and H.E.R.; methodology, S.S., J.C.L.C. and H.E.R.; resources, J.C.L.C. and H.E.R.; writing—original draft preparation, S.S.; writing—review and editing, S.S., J.C.L.C. and H.E.R.; visualization, S.S.; project administration, J.C.L.C. and H.E.R.; funding acquisition, J.C.L.C. and H.E.R. All authors have read and agreed to the published version of the manuscript.

Funding: This research was supported by the Government of Canada's New Frontiers in Research Fund—Exploration (Grant number: NFRFE-2022-00707), through the three federal research funding agencies (CIHR, NSERC and SSHRC).

Conflicts of Interest: The authors declare no conflict of interest.

References

1. Lv, Y.; Lv, Y.; Wang, Z.; Lan, T.; Feng, X.; Chen, H.; Zhu, J.; Ma, X.; Du, J.; Hou, G.; et al. FLASH radiotherapy: A promising new method for radiotherapy (Review). *Oncol. Lett.* **2022**, *24*, 419. [CrossRef]
2. Lin, B.; Gao, F.; Yang, Y.; Wu, D.; Zhang, Y.; Feng, G.; Dai, T.; Du, X. FLASH Radiotherapy: History and Future. *Front. Oncol.* **2021**, *11*, 644400. [CrossRef]
3. Hughes, J.R.; Parsons, J.L. FLASH Radiotherapy: Current Knowledge and Future Insights Using Proton-Beam Therapy. *Int. J. Mol. Sci.* **2020**, *21*, 6492. [CrossRef] [PubMed]
4. Lin, B.; Huang, D.; Gao, F.; Yang, Y.; Wu, D.; Zhang, Y.; Feng, G.; Dai, T.; Du, X. Mechanisms of FLASH effect. *Front. Oncol.* **2022**, *12*, 995612. [CrossRef]
5. Esplen, N.; Mendonca, M.S.; Bazalova-Carter, M. Physics and biology of ultrahigh dose-rate (FLASH) radiotherapy: A topical review. *Phys. Med. Biol.* **2020**, *65*, 23TR03. [CrossRef] [PubMed]
6. Bourhis, J.; Sozzi, W.J.; Jorge, P.G.; Gaide, O.; Bailat, C.; Duclos, F.; Patin, D.; Ozsahin, M.; Bochud, F.; Germond, J.-F.; et al. Treatment of a first patient with FLASH-radiotherapy. *Radiother. Oncol.* **2019**, *139*, 18–22. [CrossRef]
7. Favaudon, V.; Caplier, L.; Monceau, V.; Pouzoulet, F.; Sayarath, M.; Fouillade, C.; Poupon, M.-F.; Brito, I.; Hupé, P.; Bourhis, J.; et al. Ultrahigh dose-rate FLASH irradiation increases the differential response between normal and tumor tissue in mice. *Sci. Transl. Med.* **2014**, *6*, 245ra93. [CrossRef]
8. Okoro, C.M.; Schüler, E.; Taniguchi, C.M. The Therapeutic Potential of FLASH-RT for Pancreatic Cancer. *Cancers* **2022**, *14*, 1167. [CrossRef]
9. Matuszak, N.; Suchorska, W.M.; Milecki, P.; Kruszyna-Mochalska, M.; Misiarz, A.; Pracz, J.; Malicki, J. FLASH radiotherapy: An emerging approach in radiation therapy. *Rep. Pract. Oncol. Radiother.* **2022**, *27*, 343–351. [CrossRef]
10. Rahman, M.; Trigilio, A.; Franciosini, G.; Moeckli, R.; Zhang, R.; Böhlen, T.T. FLASH radiotherapy treatment planning and models for electron beams. *Radiother. Oncol.* **2022**, *175*, 210–221. [CrossRef] [PubMed]
11. Subiel, A.; Romano, F. Recent developments in absolute dosimetry for FLASH radiotherapy. *Br. J. Radiol.* **2023**, *96*, 20220560. [CrossRef] [PubMed]
12. Montay-Gruel, P.; Corde, S.; Laissue, J.A.; Bazalova-Carter, M. FLASH radiotherapy with photon beams. *Med. Phys.* **2022**, *49*, 2055–2067. [CrossRef]
13. Almeida, A.; Togno, M.; Ballesteros-Zebadua, P.; Franco-Perez, J.; Geyer, R.; Schaefer, R.; Petit, B.; Grilj, V.; Meer, D.; Safai, S.; et al. Dosimetric and biologic intercomparison between electron and proton FLASH beams. *bioRxiv* **2023**. *preprint*. [CrossRef]
14. El Naqa, I.; Pogue, B.W.; Zhang, R.; Oraiqat, I.; Parodi, K. Image guidance for FLASH radiotherapy. *Med. Phys.* **2022**, *49*, 4109–4122. [CrossRef]
15. Moon, E.J.; Petersson, K.; Olcina, M.M. The importance of hypoxia in radiotherapy for the immune response, metastatic potential and FLASH-RT. *Int. J. Radiat. Biol.* **2022**, *98*, 439–451. [CrossRef]
16. Abolfath, R.; Grosshans, D.; Mohan, R. Oxygen depletion in FLASH ultra-high-dose-rate radiotherapy: A molecular dynamics simulation. *Med. Phys.* **2020**, *47*, 6551–6561. [CrossRef]
17. Tinganelli, W.; Sokol, O.; Quartieri, M.; Puspitasari, A.; Dokic, I.; Abdollahi, A.; Durante, M.; Haberer, T.; Debus, J.; Boscolo, D.; et al. Ultra-High Dose Rate (FLASH) Carbon Ion Irradiation: Dosimetry and First Cell Experiments. *Int. J. Radiat. Oncol.* **2022**, *112*, 1012–1022. [CrossRef]
18. Alanazi, A.; Meesungnoen, J.; Jay-Gerin, J.-P. A Computer Modeling Study of Water Radiolysis at High Dose Rates. Relevance to FLASH Radiotherapy. *Radiat. Res.* **2020**, *195*, 149–162. [CrossRef] [PubMed]
19. Wei, S.; Lin, H.; Choi, J.I.; Simone, C.B.; Kang, M. A Novel Proton Pencil Beam Scanning FLASH RT Delivery Method Enables Optimal OAR Sparing and Ultra-High Dose Rate Delivery: A Comprehensive Dosimetry Study for Lung Tumors. *Cancers* **2021**, *13*, 5790. [CrossRef]
20. Yang, G.; Lu, C.; Mei, Z.; Sun, X.; Han, J.; Qian, J.; Liang, Y.; Pan, Z.; Kong, D.; Xu, S.; et al. Association of Cancer Stem Cell Radio-Resistance Under Ultra-High Dose Rate FLASH Irradiation With Lysosome-Mediated Autophagy. *Front. Cell Dev. Biol.* **2021**, *9*, 672693. [CrossRef]
21. Li, Y.; Sun, X.; Liang, Y.; Hu, Y.; Liu, C. Monte Carlo simulation of linac using PRIMO. *Radiat. Oncol.* **2022**, *17*, 185. [CrossRef] [PubMed]
22. Kawrakow, I.; Rogers, D.W. *The EGSnrc Code System*; NRC Report PIRS-701; NRC: Ottawa, ON, Canda, 2000; Volume 17, p. 108.
23. Walters, B.R.; Kawrakow, I.; Rogers, D.W. *DOSXYZnrc Users Manual*; NRC Report Pirs; NRC: Ottawa, ON, Canda, 2005; Volume 794, pp. 57–58.
24. Gao, Y.; Liu, R.; Chang, C.; Charyyev, S.; Zhou, J.; Bradley, J.D.; Liu, T.; Yang, X. A potential revolution in cancer treatment: A topical review of FLASH radiotherapy. *J. Appl. Clin. Med. Phys.* **2022**, *23*, e13790. [CrossRef]
25. Lazarus, G.L.; van Eeden, D.; du Plessis, F.C. Validation of Monte Carlo-based calculations for megavolt electron beams for IORT and FLASH-IORT. *Heliyon* **2022**, *8*, e10682. [CrossRef]
26. Breitkreutz, D.Y.; Shumail, M.; Bush, K.K.; Tantawi, S.G.; Maxime, P.G.; Loo, B.W. Initial Steps Towards a Clinical FLASH Radiotherapy System: Pediatric Whole Brain Irradiation with 40 MeV Electrons at FLASH Dose Rates. *Radiat. Res.* **2020**, *194*, 594–599. [CrossRef]

27. Rosenstrom, A.; Santana-Leitner, M.; Rokni, S.H.; Shumail, M.; Tantawi, S.; Dewji, S.; Loo, B.W. Monte Carlo simulation of shielding designs for a cabinet form factor preclinical MV-energy photon FLASH radiotherapy system. *Med. Phys.* **2023**, *50*, 3055–3065. [CrossRef] [PubMed]
28. Sunbul, N.H.B.; Zhang, W.; Oraiqat, I.; Litzenberg, D.W.; Lam, K.L.; Cuneo, K.; Moran, J.M.; Carson, P.L.; Wang, X.; Clarke, S.D.; et al. A simulation study of ionizing radiation acoustic imaging (iRAI) as a real-time dosimetric technique for ultra-high dose rate radiotherapy (UHDR-RT). *Med. Phys.* **2021**, *48*, 6137–6151. [CrossRef]
29. Brunbauer, F.; Lupberger, M.; Oliveri, E.; Resnati, F.; Ropelewski, L.; Streli, C.; Thuiner, P.; van Stenis, M. Radiation imaging with optically read out GEM-based detectors. *J. Instrum.* **2018**, *13*, T02006. [CrossRef]
30. Esquivel, A.; Ferrero, A.; Mileto, A.; Baffour, F.; Horst, K.; Rajiah, P.S.; Inoue, A.; Leng, S.; McCollough, C.; Fletcher, J.G. Photon-Counting Detector CT: Key Points Radiologists Should Know. *Korean J. Radiol.* **2022**, *23*, 854–865. [CrossRef]
31. Calin, M.R. Gas spherical ionization chamber. *J. Radioanal. Nucl. Chem.* **2011**, *290*, 361–366. [CrossRef]
32. Yoosuf, A.M.; Jeevanandam, P.; Whitten, G.; Workman, G.; McGarry, C.K. Verification of high-dose-rate brachytherapy treatment planning dose distribution using liquid-filled ionization chamber array. *J. Contemp. Brachytherapy* **2018**, *10*, 142–154. [CrossRef]
33. Ashraf, M.R.; Rahman, M.; Zhang, R.; Williams, B.B.; Gladstone, D.J.; Pogue, B.W.; Bruza, P. Dosimetry for FLASH Radiotherapy: A Review of Tools and the Role of Radioluminescence and Cherenkov Emission. *Front. Phys.* **2020**, *8*, 328. [CrossRef]
34. Ravichandran, R.; Binukumar, J.P.; Al Amri, I.; Davis, C.A. Diamond detector in absorbed dose measurements in high-energy linear accelerator photon and electron beams. *J. Appl. Clin. Med. Phys.* **2016**, *17*, 291–303. [CrossRef]
35. Kranzer, R.; Schüller, A.; Bourgouin, A.; Hackel, T.; Poppinga, D.; Lapp, M.; Looe, H.K.; Poppe, B. Response of diamond detectors in ultra-high dose-per-pulse electron beams for dosimetry at FLASH radiotherapy. *Phys. Med. Biol.* **2022**, *67*, 075002. [CrossRef]
36. Rinati, G.V.; Felici, G.; Galante, F.; Gasparini, A.; Kranzer, R.; Mariani, G.; Pacitti, M.; Prestopino, G.; Schüller, A.; Vanreusel, V.; et al. Application of a novel diamond detector for commissioning of FLASH radiotherapy electron beams. *Med. Phys.* **2022**, *49*, 5513–5522. [CrossRef]
37. Marinelli, M.; Felici, G.; Galante, F.; Gasparini, A.; Giuliano, L.; Heinrich, S.; Pacitti, M.; Prestopino, G.; Vanreusel, V.; Verellen, D.; et al. Design, realization, and characterization of a novel diamond detector prototype for FLASH radiotherapy dosimetry. *Med. Phys.* **2022**, *49*, 1902–1910. [CrossRef]
38. Polaczek-Grelik, K.; Kawa-Iwanicka, A.; Michalecki, Ł. Dosimetric accuracy of a cross-calibration coefficient for plane-parallel ionization chamber obtained in low-energy electron beams using various cylindrical dosimeters. *Pol. J. Med. Phys. Eng.* **2021**, *27*, 303–313. [CrossRef]
39. Yang, Y.; Shi, C.; Chen, C.; Tsai, P.; Kang, M.; Huang, S.; Lin, C.; Chang, F.; Chhabra, A.M.; Choi, J.I.; et al. A 2D strip ionization chamber array with high spatiotemporal resolution for proton pencil beam scanning FLASH radiotherapy. *Med. Phys.* **2022**, *49*, 5464–5475. [CrossRef]
40. Di Martino, F.; Del Sarto, D.; Bisogni, M.G.; Capaccioli, S.; Galante, F.; Gasperini, A.; Linsalata, S.; Mariani, G.; Pacitti, M.; Paiar, F.; et al. A new solution for UHDP and UHDR (Flash) measurements: Theory and conceptual design of ALLS chamber. *Phys. Medica* **2022**, *102*, 9–18. [CrossRef]
41. Di Martino, F.; Del Sarto, D.; Barone, S.; Bisogni, M.G.; Capaccioli, S.; Galante, F.; Gasparini, A.; Mariani, G.; Masturzo, L.; Montefiori, M.; et al. A new calculation method for the free electron fraction of an ionization chamber in the ultra-high-dose-per-pulse regimen. *Phys. Medica* **2022**, *103*, 175–180. [CrossRef]
42. Petersson, K.; Jaccard, M.; Germond, J.-F.; Buchillier, T.; Bochud, F.; Bourhis, J.; Vozenin, M.-C.; Bailat, C. High dose-per-pulse electron beam dosimetry—A model to correct for the ion recombination in the Advanced Markus ionization chamber. *Med. Phys.* **2017**, *44*, 1157–1167. [CrossRef]
43. Darafsheh, A.; Hao, Y.; Zhao, X.; Zwart, T.; Wagner, M.; Evans, T.; Reynoso, F.; Zhao, T. Spread-out Bragg peak proton FLASH irradiation using a clinical synchrocyclotron: Proof of concept and ion chamber characterization. *Med. Phys.* **2021**, *48*, 4472–4484. [CrossRef] [PubMed]
44. Kranzer, R.; Poppinga, D.; Weidner, J.; Schüller, A.; Hackel, T.; Looe, H.K.; Poppe, B. Ion collection efficiency of ionization chambers in ultra-high dose-per-pulse electron beams. *Med. Phys.* **2021**, *48*, 819–830. [CrossRef]
45. Gómez, F.; Gonzalez-Castaño, D.M.; Fernández, N.G.; Pardo-Montero, J.; Schüller, A.; Gasparini, A.; Vanreusel, V.; Verellen, D.; Felici, G.; Kranzer, R.; et al. Development of an ultra-thin parallel plate ionization chamber for dosimetry in FLASH radiotherapy. *Med. Phys.* **2022**, *49*, 4705–4714. [CrossRef]
46. Cavallone, M.; Jorge, P.G.; Moeckli, R.; Bailat, C.; Flacco, A.; Prezado, Y.; Delorme, R. Determination of the ion collection efficiency of the Razor Nano Chamber for ultra-high dose-rate electron beams. *Med. Phys.* **2022**, *49*, 4731–4742. [CrossRef] [PubMed]
47. Gonzalez-Lopez, A.; Lago-Martin, J.-D.; Vera-Sanchez, J.-A. Small fields measurements with radiochromic films. *J. Med. Phys.* **2015**, *40*, 61–67. [CrossRef]
48. Aldweri, F.M.; Abuzayed, M.H.; Al-Ajaleen, M.S.; Rabaeh, K.A. Characterization of Thymol blue Radiochromic dosimeters for high dose applications. *Results Phys.* **2018**, *8*, 1001–1005. [CrossRef]
49. Gao, F.; Yang, Y.; Zhu, H.; Wang, J.; Xiao, D.; Zhou, Z.; Dai, T.; Zhang, Y.; Feng, G.; Li, J.; et al. First demonstration of the FLASH effect with ultrahigh dose rate high-energy X-rays. *Radiother. Oncol.* **2022**, *166*, 44–50. [CrossRef] [PubMed]
50. Poppinga, D.; Kranzer, R.; Farabolini, W.; Gilardi, A.; Corsini, R.; Wyrwoll, V.; Looe, H.K.; Delfs, B.; Gabrisch, L.; Poppe, B. VHEE beam dosimetry at CERN Linear Electron Accelerator for Research under ultra-high dose rate conditions. *Biomed. Phys. Eng. Express* **2020**, *7*, 015012. [CrossRef] [PubMed]

51. Jeong, D.H.; Lee, M.; Lim, H.; Kang, S.K.; Lee, S.J.; Kim, H.C.; Lee, K.; Kim, S.H.; Lee, D.E.; Jang, K.W. Electron beam scattering device for FLASH preclinical studies with 6-MeV LINAC. *Nucl. Eng. Technol.* **2020**, *53*, 1289–1296. [CrossRef]
52. Konradsson, E.; Arendt, M.L.; Jensen, K.B.; Børresen, B.; Hansen, A.E.; Bäck, S.; Kristensen, A.T.; Rosenschöld, P.M.A.; Ceberg, C.; Petersson, K. Establishment and Initial Experience of Clinical FLASH Radiotherapy in Canine Cancer Patients. *Front. Oncol.* **2021**, *11*, 658004. [CrossRef]
53. Han, J.; Mei, Z.; Lu, C.; Qian, J.; Liang, Y.; Sun, X.; Pan, Z.; Kong, D.; Xu, S.; Liu, Z.; et al. Ultra-High Dose Rate FLASH Irradiation Induced Radio-Resistance of Normal Fibroblast Cells Can Be Enhanced by Hypoxia and Mitochondrial Dysfunction Resulting From Loss of Cytochrome C. *Front. Cell Dev. Biol.* **2021**, *9*, 672929. [CrossRef]
54. Villoing, D.; Koumeir, C.; Bongrand, A.; Guertin, A.; Haddad, F.; Métivier, V.; Poirier, F.; Potiron, V.; Servagent, N.; Supiot, S.; et al. Technical note: Proton beam dosimetry at ultra-high dose rates (FLASH): Evaluation of GAFchromic™ (EBT3, EBT-XD) and OrthoChromic (OC-1) film performances. *Med. Phys.* **2022**, *49*, 2732–2745. [CrossRef] [PubMed]
55. Lourenço, A.; Subiel, A.; Lee, N.; Flynn, S.; Cotterill, J.; Shipley, D.; Romano, F.; Speth, J.; Lee, E.; Zhang, Y.; et al. Absolute dosimetry for FLASH proton pencil beam scanning radiotherapy. *Sci. Rep.* **2023**, *13*, 2054. [CrossRef] [PubMed]
56. Desrosiers, M.F. Optical Passive Sensor Calibration for Satellite Remote Sensing and the Legacy of NOAA and NIST Cooperation. *J. Res. Natl. Inst. Stand. Technol.* **2014**, *119*, 277–295. [CrossRef]
57. Desrosiers, M.F.; Publ, J.M.; Cooper, S.L. An absorbed-dose/dose-rate dependence for the alanine-EPR dosimetry system and its implications in high-dose ionizing radiation metrology. *J. Res. Natl. Inst. Stand. Technol.* **2008**, *113*, 79–95. [CrossRef]
58. Gondré, M.; Jorge, P.G.; Vozenin, M.-C.; Bourhis, J.; Bochud, F.; Bailat, C.; Moeckli, R. Optimization of Alanine Measurements for Fast and Accurate Dosimetry in FLASH Radiation Therapy. *Radiat. Res.* **2020**, *194*, 573–579. [CrossRef]
59. Soliman, Y.S.; Pellicioli, P.; Beshir, W.; Abdel-Fattah, A.A.; Fahim, R.A.; Krisch, M.; Bräuer-Krisch, E. A comparative dosimetry study of an alanine dosimeter with a PTW PinPoint chamber at ultra-high dose rates of synchrotron radiation. *Phys. Medica* **2020**, *71*, 161–167. [CrossRef]
60. Bourgouin, A.; Hackel, T.; Marinelli, M.; Kranzer, R.; Schüller, A.; Kapsch, R.-P. Absorbed-dose-to-water measurement using alanine in ultra-high-pulse-dose-rate electron beams. *Phys. Med. Biol.* **2022**, *67*, 205011. [CrossRef]
61. Jorge, P.G.; Jaccard, M.; Petersson, K.; Gondré, M.; Durán, M.T.; Desorgher, L.; Germond, J.-F.; Liger, P.; Vozenin, M.-C.; Bourhis, J.; et al. Dosimetric and preparation procedures for irradiating biological models with pulsed electron beam at ultra-high dose-rate. *Radiother. Oncol.* **2019**, *139*, 34–39. [CrossRef] [PubMed]
62. Jorge, P.G.; Melemenidis, S.; Grilj, V.; Buchillier, T.; Manjappa, R.; Viswanathan, V.; Gondré, M.; Vozenin, M.-C.; Germond, J.-F.; Bochud, F.; et al. Design and validation of a dosimetric comparison scheme tailored for ultra-high dose-rate electron beams to support multicenter FLASH preclinical studies. *Radiother. Oncol.* **2022**, *175*, 203–209. [CrossRef]
63. Rickard, A.G.; Yoshikawa, H.; Palmer, G.M.; Liu, H.Q.; Dewhirst, M.W.; Nolan, M.W.; Zhang, X. Cherenkov emissions for studying tumor changes during radiation therapy: An exploratory study in domesticated dogs with naturally-occurring cancer. *PLoS ONE* **2020**, *15*, e0238106. [CrossRef]
64. Rahman, M.; Ashraf, M.R.; Zhang, R.; Gladstone, D.J.; Cao, X.; Williams, B.B.; Hoopes, P.J.; Pogue, B.W.; Bruza, P. Spatial and temporal dosimetry of individual electron FLASH beam pulses using radioluminescence imaging. *Phys. Med. Biol.* **2021**, *66*, 135009. [CrossRef] [PubMed]
65. Vidalot, J.; Campanella, C.; Dachicourt, J.; Marcandella, C.; Duhamel, O.; Morana, A.; Poujols, D.; Assaillit, G.; Gaillardin, M.; Boukenter, A.; et al. Monitoring of Ultra-High Dose Rate Pulsed X-ray Facilities with Radioluminescent Nitrogen-Doped Optical Fiber. *Sensors* **2022**, *22*, 3192. [CrossRef]
66. Romano, F.; Bailat, C.; Jorge, P.G.; Lerch, M.L.F.; Darafsheh, A. Ultra-high dose rate dosimetry: Challenges and opportunities for FLASH radiation therapy. *Med. Phys.* **2022**, *49*, 4912–4932. [CrossRef]
67. Poirier, Y.; Xu, J.; Mossahebi, S.; Therriault-Proulx, F.; Sawant, A. Technical note: Characterization and practical applications of a novel plastic scintillator for online dosimetry for an ultrahigh dose rate (FLASH). *Med. Phys.* **2022**, *49*, 4682–4692. [CrossRef]
68. Vanreusel, V.; Gasparini, A.; Galante, F.; Mariani, G.; Pacitti, M.; Cociorb, M.; Giammanco, A.; Reniers, B.; Reulens, N.; Shonde, T.B.; et al. Point scintillator dosimetry in ultra-high dose rate electron "FLASH" radiation therapy: A first characterization. *Phys. Medica* **2022**, *103*, 127–137. [CrossRef] [PubMed]
69. Szpala, S.; Huang, V.; Zhao, Y.; Kyle, A.; Minchinton, A.; Karan, T.; Kohli, K. Dosimetry with a clinical linac adapted to FLASH electron beams. *J. Appl. Clin. Med. Phys.* **2021**, *22*, 50–59. [CrossRef] [PubMed]
70. Pradhan, A.; Lee, J.; Kim, J. Recent developments of optically stimulated luminescence materials and techniques for radiation dosimetry and clinical applications. *J. Med. Phys.* **2008**, *33*, 85–99. [CrossRef]
71. Hart, A.; Cecchi, D.; Giguère, C.; Larose, F.; Therriault-Proulx, F.; Esplen, N.; Beaulieu, L.; Bazalova-Carter, M. Lead-doped scintillator dosimeters for detection of ultrahigh dose-rate X-rays. *Phys. Med. Biol.* **2022**, *67*, 105007. [CrossRef]
72. Abouzahr, F.; Cesar, J.P.; Crespo, P.; Gajda, M.; Hu, Z.; Kaye, W.; Klein, K.; Kuo, A.S.; Majewski, S.; Mawlawi, O.; et al. The first PET glimpse of a proton FLASH beam. *Phys. Med. Biol.* **2023**, *68*, 125001. [CrossRef]
73. Jeong, D.-H.; Lee, M.; Lim, H.; Kang, S.-K.; Lee, K.; Lee, S.-J.; Kim, H.; Han, W.-K.; Kang, T.-W.; Jang, K.-W. Optical Filter-Embedded Fiber-Optic Radiation Sensor for Ultra-High Dose Rate Electron Beam Dosimetry. *Sensors* **2021**, *21*, 5840. [CrossRef] [PubMed]

74. Rahman, M.; Kozelka, J.; Hildreth, J.; Schönfeld, A.; Sloop, A.M.; Ashraf, M.R.; Bruza, P.; Gladstone, D.J.; Pogue, B.W.; Simon, W.E.; et al. Characterization of a diode dosimeter for UHDR FLASH radiotherapy. *Med. Phys.* **2023**. *ahead of print*. [CrossRef] [PubMed]
75. De Kruijff, R.M. FLASH radiotherapy: Ultra-high dose rates to spare healthy tissue. *Int. J. Radiat. Biol.* **2020**, *96*, 419–423. [CrossRef]
76. Diffenderfer, E.S.; Sørensen, B.S.; Mazal, A.; Carlson, D.J. The current status of preclinical proton FLASH radiation and future directions. *Med. Phys.* **2022**, *49*, 2039–2054. [CrossRef]
77. Marcu, L.G.; Bezak, E.; Peukert, D.D.; Wilson, P. Translational Research in FLASH Radiotherapy—From Radiobiological Mechanisms to In Vivo Results. *Biomedicines* **2021**, *9*, 181. [CrossRef] [PubMed]
78. Petersson, K. Collaborators FLASH radiotherapy: What, how and why? *Res. Outreach* **2020**, *2020*, 66–69. [CrossRef] [PubMed]
79. Chow, J.C.L.; Ruda, H.E. Flash Radiotherapy: Innovative Cancer Treatment. *Encyclopedia* **2023**, *3*, 808–823. [CrossRef]

Disclaimer/Publisher's Note: The statements, opinions and data contained in all publications are solely those of the individual author(s) and contributor(s) and not of MDPI and/or the editor(s). MDPI and/or the editor(s) disclaim responsibility for any injury to people or property resulting from any ideas, methods, instructions or products referred to in the content.

cancers

MDPI

Systematic Review

Combination of Local Ablative Techniques with Radiotherapy for Primary and Recurrent Lung Cancer: A Systematic Review

Paolo Bonome [1,*,†], Donato Pezzulla [1,†], Valentina Lancellotta [2,‡], Anna Rita Scrofani [3,‡], Gabriella Macchia [1], Elena Rodolfino [4], Luca Tagliaferri [2], György Kovács [5], Francesco Deodato [1,6] and Roberto Iezzi [3]

1 Radiation Oncology Unit, Responsible Research Hospital, 86100 Campobasso, Italy; donato.pezzulla@responsible.hospital (D.P.); gabriella.macchia@responsible.hospital (G.M.); francesco.deodato@responsible.hospital (F.D.)
2 Dipartimento di Diagnostica per Immagini, Radioterapia Oncologica ed Ematologia, UOC Radioterapia Oncologica, Fondazione Policlinico Universitario "A. Gemelli" IRCCS, 00168 Rome, Italy; valentina.lancellotta@policlinicogemelli.it (V.L.); luca.tagliaferri@policlinicogemelli.it (L.T.)
3 Dipartimento di Diagnostica per Immagini, Radioterapia Oncologica ed Ematologia, UOC Radiologia d'Urgenza ed Interventistica, Fondazione Policlinico Universitario "A. Gemelli" IRCCS, 00168 Rome, Italy; annarita.scrofani@guest.policlinicogemelli.it (A.R.S.); roberto.iezzi@policlinicogemelli.it (R.I.)
4 Dipartimento di Diagnostica per Immagini, Radioterapia Oncologica ed Ematologia, UOC Radiologia Addomino-Pelvica, Fondazione Policlinico Universitario "A. Gemelli" IRCCS, 00168 Rome, Italy; elena.rodolfino@policlinicogemelli.it
5 Gemelli-INTERACTS, Università Cattolica del Sacro Cuore, 20123 Rome, Italy; kovacsluebeck@gmail.com
6 Radiology Institute, Università Cattolica del Sacro Cuore, 00135 Rome, Italy
* Correspondence: paolo.bonome@libero.it; Tel.: +39-0874-312261
† These authors contributed equally to this work.
‡ These authors also contributed equally to this work.

Simple Summary: The aim of this review was to evaluate the feasibility and the effectiveness of radiation therapy combined with local tumor ablation therapy in the treatment of primary and recurrent lung cancer in terms of toxicity profile and local control rate. Six studies featuring a total of 115 patients and 119 lesions were selected, showing encouraging outcomes that appear to be promising in terms of toxicity profile. Further prospective studies are need to better delineate combining LTA-RT treatment benefits in this setting.

Abstract: In patients with early-stage or recurrent NSCLC who are unable to tolerate surgery, a benefit could derive only from a systemic therapy or another few forms of local therapy. A systematic review was performed to evaluate the feasibility and the effectiveness of radiotherapy combined with local ablative therapies in the treatment of primary and recurrent lung cancer in terms of toxicity profile and local control rate. Six studies featuring a total of 115 patients who met eligibility criteria and 119 lesions were included. Three studies evaluated lung cancer patients with a medically inoperable condition treated with image-guided local ablative therapies followed by radiotherapy: their local control rate (LC) ranged from 75% to 91.7% with only 15 patients (19.4%) reporting local recurrence after combined modality treatment. The other three studies provided a salvage option for patients with locally recurrent NSCLC after RT: the median follow-up period varied from 8.3 to 69.3 months with an LC rate ranging from 50% to 100%. The most common complications were radiation pneumonitis (9.5%) and pneumothorax (29.8%). The proposed intervention appears to be promising in terms of toxicity profile and local control rate. Further prospective studies are need to better delineate combining LTA-RT treatment benefits in this setting.

Keywords: lung cancer; SBRT; RT; percutaneous image-guided local tumor ablation (LTA); combining LTA-RT

1. Introduction

Lung cancer is one of the most frequent cancers in the world and the main cause of cancer mortality [1]. Traditional treatment for early stage non-small cell lung cancer (NSCLC) is surgical excision with or without thorough lymph node assessment. However, due to severe medical comorbidities, 20% of early-stage NSCLCs have been estimated to be unable to tolerate surgery [2,3]. Only systemic therapy or a few other forms of local therapy could aid these people. As a result, novel local ablative method modalities have emerged to strengthen our therapeutic arsenal [4].

Percutaneous image-guided local tumor ablation (LTA), which includes radiofrequency (RFA), microwave ablation (MWA), and cryoablation (CA), is one of them. LTA, which was first described in clinical trials in 2000 [5], is a minimally invasive approach for the local therapy of lung cancer with encouraging results [6,7]. Another option, as indicated by the National Comprehensive Cancer Network (NCCN) guidelines [8], is stereotactic body radiation (SBRT): a conventional treatment for medically inoperable patients whose efficacy, minimal toxicity, and satisfying local disease control are supported by multiple studies [9–11].

Indeed, radiotherapy (RT) and LTA use completely different mechanisms: the former is most effective against well-oxygenated cells in the periphery of the tumor and less effective at eradicating more hypoxic cells in the core, whereas LAT targets the core but is less effective in the periphery due to increasing heat sink effects [12–14]. In particular, because of the complimentary activities of these two techniques, some authors hypothesized that combining them in different settings, including pulmonary diseases, could result in a probable synergic result [15–17].

Despite these initial intriguing findings, the role and process of integration between RT and LAT are not completely characterized in the existing research, and the available data are inadequate, as they are characterized by a small sample size and heterogenous procedures.

In light of this, we conducted a systematic analysis to assess the feasibility and effectiveness of RT combined with LAT in the treatment of primary and recurrent lung cancer in terms of toxicity profile and local control rate.

2. Materials and Methods

2.1. Eligibility Criteria

Prospective and retrospective studies were included in this analysis. We used the following inclusion criteria: English language, full-text articles, patients treated with combined LTA-RT, presence of detailed toxicity and local control data. In addition, we used the following exclusion criteria: only abstracts, letters, proceedings from scientific meetings, editorials, expert opinions, reviews without original data, studies lacking toxicity and/or safety outcomes, repetitive data, animal studies, studies with fewer than 5 patients, and studies that included combination different than LAT and SBRT, such as chemotherapy, immunotherapy, or surgery.

2.2. Information Sources

This systematic review was performed following recommendations from the Preferred Reporting Items for Systematic Reviews and Meta-Analyses (PRISMA). A comprehensive search was conducted in PUBMED, MEDLINE, SCOPUS and Google Scholar to identify relevant published studies that confirmed the feasibility of integration between January 1999 and December 2022.

2.3. Search Strategy

Keywords used were: (NSCLC or lung cancer or lung neoplasm) AND (integration or combination or followed) AND (early stage or primary) AND (recurrent or relapse) AND (radiotherapy or radiation therapy or SBRT or IMRT) AND (LTA or radiofrequency ablation or microwave ablation or cryoablation). The computer search was supplemented manually using reference lists for all available review articles, primary studies, meeting abstracts, and bibliographies of books to identify studies not encountered in the computer search.

2.4. Selection Process

Retrieved records underwent title-and-abstract review and then full-text review. Two independent researchers (PB and AS) screened all the studies in duplicate using the eligibility criteria reported above. A third reviewer (DP) rechecked the articles when confronted with discrepancies. Three independent reviewers performed data extraction (PB, AS, DP). Reasons for exclusion at full-text review were recorded. Disagreements among reviewers were infrequent (<20%) and were resolved by discussion.

2.5. Data Items

The following data were included: author, year, study design, LTA techniques data (RFA or MWA or Cryoablation), radiation treatment data (i.e., type, fractionation, total dose), clinical/radiological treatment responses, follow-up time, toxicities, local control (LC), defined as response to the treatment until last follow-up or patient's exitus and overall survival (OS), calculated from the time of treatment until the last follow-up or patient's exitus survival time at the moment of the treatment.

2.6. Quality Assessment

The quality assessment score of included studies was assessed according to a checklist for the quality appraisal of case series studies produced by The Institute of Health Economics (IHE) [18].

2.7. Statistical Analysis

Statistical analysis was performed using Review Manager (RevMan) (computer program) Version 5.

Heterogeneity across studies was examined by I^2 statistic. Studies with I^2 statistic values of 0–50%, 50–75%, and >75% were considered to have low, moderate, and high heterogeneity, respectively [19]. A forest plot for a post hoc meta-analysis to display the association between lesions size and LC after the combined therapy was generated. We used random-effects models because there was great subjectivity given the lack of related control groups in the non-comparative studies and a tendency toward high heterogeneity.

2.8. Review Registration

The review was registered on the Open Science Framework (OSF), obtaining the following registration DOI: https://doi.org/10.17605/OSF.IO/VXGK9 (accessed on 3 November 2023).

3. Results

A total of 634 citations were retrieved; 600 of these were removed because they were limited to LTA or RT and focused on integration between the two techniques. The remaining 34 studies were evaluated using their entire texts. Following the rejection of studies with an inappropriate population, therapy, or providing insufficient data (N = 28), six papers were finally selected based on the inclusion criteria outlined above; more information is shown in Figure 1.

Except for Steber et al. [15], a prospective phase 2 study that closed early due to delayed enrollment, all of the studies chosen [16,17,20–22] were retrospective. The investigations included 115 patients and 119 lesions in total. The sample size for the majority of these experiences ranged from six patients [22] to 41 patients [16]. Except for Brooks et al. [22], all of the studies included age and gender information. The median age ranged from 55 to 93 years with a 62/47 male/female ratio.

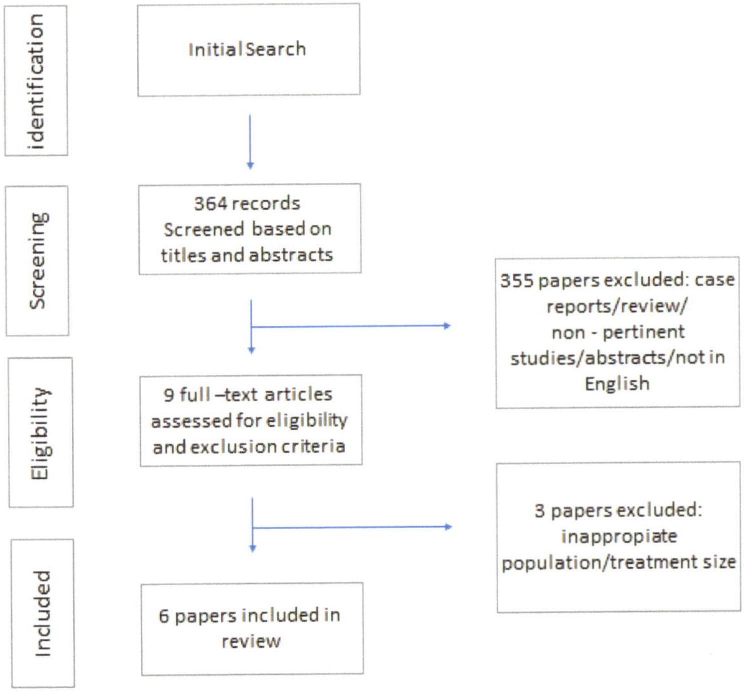

Figure 1. PRISMA literature search.

Three studies [15–17] evaluated lung cancer patients with a medically inoperable condition treated with LAT followed by radiotherapy, while another three studies [20–22] experienced LTA as a salvage option for patients with locally recurrent NSCLC after RT. More details on the patients' characteristics are reported in Table 1.

3.1. First Group: Image-Guided LAT Followed by Radiotherapy

In the first group of studies, 77 patients with early-stage NSCLC were assessed with a male/female ratio of 42/35 and a median age ranging from 55 to 93 years. The patients were staged as follows: stage IA (43 points), stage I B (28 points), stage II B (3 points), and staging data were unavailable for three patients. All patients received image-guided LAT (73 RFA and 4 MWA) before radiotherapy.

RFA was employed by Dupuy et al. [17]: the mean impedance was 72 ohms (range 42 to 11), the mean current was 1.6 amps (range 1.2 to 2.0 amps), and the post-RFA temperatures were greater than 60 °C (range 76.4 °C/62 to 85 °C) with a treatment time of 6.8 min (range 2 to 12). Grieco et al. [16] used RFA with a baseline impedance of 72.7 ohms (range 40–69), power 128.8 W (range 10–196) achieving temperature >70 °C (range 38–94 °C) with a mean treatment time of 6.3 min (range 1–12), whereas MWA had a power (W) of 47.5 (range 45–60) and treatment time of 8.4 min (range 2–10).

Table 1. Selected studies characteristics.

Author	Study Design	No of Patients	Sex	Median Age	Stage	Treat.	RT	LTA	Time Start II Treatment	Size	Dose RT	Median Follow-Up	PFS	IR	LP	LC Rate	OS	TOX
Steber [15]	PII	12	8 M/ 4 W	71 (60–93)	IA (11) IB (1)	LAT + RT	EBRT	RFA 12	36 days (27–60)	≤35 mm	HFRT (10 pts) 70.2 Gy-fSBRT (3 pts) 54 Gy	51.7 (12.3–130.9)	37.8 months	PET CT	3 (25)% at 6.8, 49.7 and 135.4 m CILP at 5 year 16.7%	75%	53.6 months (median)	G3 skin (1 pts 8%—full thickness thermal burn) G1 hemorrhage (3 pta 25%) G2 hemorrhage (1 pts 8%) G1 Pnx (4 pts 33%) G2 pneumothorax (4 pts 33%) G1 pneumonitis (10 pts 83%) G2 gastrointestinal (1 pts 8%)
Grieco [16]	R	41	24 M/ 17 W	76 (55–81)	IA (21) IB (17) II B (3)	LAT + RT (27 PTS) LAT + BT (14 pts)	EBRT (27) IRT-BT (14)	RFA ablation: 37 MWA ablation: 4	EBRT 24 days (5–53) after LTA IRT-BT 1–2 h after RFA	≤30 mm (17 pts) ≥30 mm (24 pts)	CFRT 66 Gy (26 pts)—CFRT 50 Gy 1 pts IRT-BT: 13 pts HDR ^{192}Ir/1 pts LDR ^{125}I	19.5 (1.0–73)	NA	PET CT 41/41	10/41 (24.4%) 2/17 < 30 mm 8/24 > 30 mm; average local recurrence: (11.8%) 45.6 ± 4.1 m. <30 mm vs. (33%) 34 ± 7.8 > 30 mm	75.6%	Average OS 34.7 ± 5.4 m for LTA + BT (14 pts) vs. 42 ± 6 m for LTA + RT (27 pts) CSS rates 97.6% at 6 m, 86.8% at 12 m and 57.1% at 36 m—average survival time 44.4 ± 5.3 months < 30 mm vs 34.6 ± 7 > 30 mm	Pneumothorax 15 pts (G2 9/15 22%—chest tube placement)—Acute respiratory distress 2 pts/41 (4.9%) (admission to respiratory intensive care unit)
Dupuy [17]	R	24	10 M/ 14 W	76 (58–85)	IA (11) IB (10) NA (3)	LAT + RT	EBRT	RFA 24	NA	median size: 34 mm (1.5–7.5)	CFRT 66 Gy	26.7 (6–65)	NA	PET CT (17 pts) CT (7 pts)	2/24 pts (8.3%)	91.7%	Mean follow-up period 26.7 CSS at 12, 24, 60 m was 83%, 50%, 39%; according to tumor stage CSS: stage IA: 12, 24, and 56 m were 92%, 62%, and 46% stage IB: 12, 24, 60 months were 73%, 42%, and 31%, respectively.	Pneumothorax 7 pts-29% (G2 3 pts—12.5%—chest tube placement), Radiation fibrosis 2 pts (8.3%)
Cheng [20]	R	12 pts	8 M/ F 4	71 ± 7	I (5) II (6) III (1)	LTA local salvage	RT (50–63 Gy) 11 EBRT + 1 fS-BRT	RFA 4/MWA 13	NA	34 mm ± 13 mm	RT (50–63 Gy)	19 ± 11 months	NA	CT within 1 month and 3 months and PET TC every 6 m.	TTLP 14 median months: 6/12 pts --> 5 re-ablation → 1/5 pts III ablations (tumor size ≤ 30 mm TTLP 23 months—tumor size ≥ 30 mm TTLP 14 mm), local progression rate at 1 year was 45%	50%	35 (median CI 12.58) mean survival tumor < 30 mm: 38 m, tumor > 30 mm: 35 m	Pneumothorax 5 post- RFA 29% (2 chest tube placement (12%))
Leung [21]	R	20	12 M/ 8 F	70.5	IA-IV	LTA local salvage	RT 60.4	RFA 17/MWA 6/CA 2	NA	40 mm	RT 60.4 Gy (50.4–77.4)	3.1 to 67.7 m (median, 10.4 m)	NA	CT within 1 month and 3 months and PET TC every 6 m.	8/20 (40%) TTLP 3.3 months (1.1–12.2) 5/8 re-ablation	60%	13.1 ± SE1.2 m 10.4 months (3.1–67.7) CSS at 6.12 24 months was 100%, 56%, 28%	G3 pseudoaneurysm/hemoptysis 1 pts (4%) (embolization)—G2 pneumothorax 1 pts (4%) (chest tube placement)—G2 pleural effusion 1 pts (4%) (chest tube placement—G2 empyema 1 pts [4%]
Brooks [22]	R	6	NA	NA	NA	LTA local salvage	SABR	NA	14.9 (1.5–91.9)	NA	NA	38.5 (19.9–69.3)	NA	NA	0/6	100%	51.6 m	NA

Legend: R (Retrospective), PII (Phase II), M (Male), W (Woman), NA (Not available), Treat. (Treatment), IR (Imaging response), EBRT (External beam radiotherapy), IRT-BT (Interventional radiotherapy–Brachytherapy), LTA (Local thermal ablation), RFA (Radiofrequency ablation), MWA (Microwave ablation) CA (Cryoablation), HFRT (Hypofractionated radiotherapy), CFRT (Conventional fractionated radiotherapy), fSBRT (Fractionated Stereotactic Body Radiotherapy), LP (Local progression), LC (Local control), CSS (Cancer-specific survival), OS (Overall survival), TOX (Toxicity), TTLP (Time To Local Progression), CT (Computed Tomography), PET (Positron Emission Tomography). SABR: Stereotactic ablative radiotherapy.

Information on the RT technique was available in all three analyzed studies. In the majority of cases (63/77, 81.8%), external beam radiotherapy (EBRT) was performed as three-dimensional conformal radiotherapy (3DCRT) in 51 patients [16,17], hypofractionated radiotherapy (HFRT) without any indication on the type of radiotherapy technique in 9 [15], and stereotactic body radiotherapy (SBRT) in three [15]. In addition, 14 out of 77 patients (18.1%) underwent interventional radiotherapy (IRT, also called brachytherapy). Thirteen patients received high-dose rate IRT with an Iridium ^{192}Ir source through an interstitial catheter, and one patient received low-dose rate IRT with 12 permanent iodine ^{125}I seeds placed through an interstitial applicator [16]. In all papers, data on total dose and fractionation were described. The most commonly used RT regimen was 66 Gy in 33 fractions (fx) (79.3%) [16,17], which was followed by nine patients receiving 70.2 Gy in 26 fx (14.2%) [15] and one patient receiving 50 Gy in 25 fx [16]. An approach with SBRT was used in three cases with a total dose of 54 Gy in three fractions [15].

Data on tumor size, radiological response evaluation, and median follow-up time are shown in Table 1.

The local control rate (LC) ranged from 75% to 91.7% [15–17], with only 15 patients (19.4%) reporting local recurrence after combined modality treatment [15–17]. In the study of Grieco et al. [16], local recurrence occurred in 11.8% of lesions smaller than 3 cm after an average of 45.6 ± 4.1 months and in 33.3% of the larger lesions after an average of 34 ± 7.8 months.

Steber et al. [15] reported a median OS value of 53.6 months, while Dupuy et al. [17] reported a mean OS of 26.7 months and rates of cancer-specific survival (CSS) at 12, 24, and 60 months of 83%, 50%, and 39%, respectively. Grieco et al. showed an average OS rate of 34.7 ± 5.4 months if LAT was combined with IRT and of 42 ± 6 months if it was associated with RT [16].

The adverse events and the associated grade of toxicity were evaluated using CTCAE v3.0. No ≥ grade 4 toxicity was recorded. The most frequent complication after LTA+RT was pneumothorax (G1/G2) in 26/77 (33%) patients [15–17], with 16 patients (20.7%) requiring intervention with chest tube placement [16,17]. The second most frequent toxicity was acute respiratory distress (grade not specified) in two patients (2.5%), requiring admission to a respiratory intensive care unit [16]. No ≥ grade 2 acute radiation pneumonitis was recorded. Other complications are reported in Table 1.

3.2. Second Group: Radiotherapy Followed by Image-Guided LAT

Thirty-eight patients were evaluated with a male/female ratio of 20/12 (we do not have data on gender in the works of Brooks et al.) [20–22]. Median age was described only in two papers and ranged from 64 to 78 years (median 70 years) [20,21]. Initial clinical stage data were reported only in one experience [20], reporting stage I in 5 patients, stage II in 6 patients, and stage III in 1 patient. More details are described in Table 1.

The three papers analyzed a total of 43 LTA sessions after previous radiotherapy in 38 patients. Thirty-one patients underwent EBRT (without any indication on the type of radiotherapy technique) [20,21] and seven SBRT [20,22], but the precise time interval between RT and LAT was not specified except for Brooks et al. [22], where the described median time was 14.9 months.

Only two studies described the type of LAT procedure [19,20]. Twenty-one treatments were RFA procedures [20,21], ten were MWA procedures [20,21], and two were CA procedures [20,21]. Technical parameters were reported only by Leung et al. [21]. The power (W) was 145.5 (range 90–198), the baseline impedance was 59 ohms (range 36–117), the time per lesion was 5 min (range 1–20), and the maximum temperature was 78 °C (range 63–98) for the RFA procedure. Power (W): 52.5 (range 45–60) and time per lesion: 10 min (range 5–10) for the MWA procedure, while the minimum temperature is 128 °C (range −117 to −132) and time per lesion: 8.5 min (range 7–10) for the cryoablation procedure.

Only two papers reported data on RT [20,21]. Variable radiation fractionations were used with a delivered median dose ranging from 50 to 63 Gy. Further data on lesion size and radiological response evaluation are shown in Table 1.

The median follow-up period varied from 8.3 to 69.3 months with an LC rate ranging from 50% to 100% [20–22]. Fourteen patients (36.8%) reported local failure after salvage LTA, and in 10 patients (26.3%), a second LTA was required. Among these 10 patients, one recurrence was registered [20,21]. Leung et al. reported a tumor time local progression (TTLP) of 3.3 months (range 1.1–12.2 months), and they showed that a size inferior to 30 mm had a longer TTLP compared to ones with bigger dimensions (23 months vs. 14 months) [20].

In terms of OS, the median OS ranges from 35 to 51.6 months. Cheng et al. [20] reported that a slightly higher mean survival in smaller tumors (<30 mm) could be observed (38 months vs. 35 months). Leung et al. showed rates of CSS at 12, 24, and 60 months of 100%, 56%, and 28%, respectively [21].

The most frequent adverse event after the procedure of LTA was pneumothorax (G1/G2), which was experienced in 8/38 (21%) patients [20,21]. Of these patients, three (20.7%) developed a pneumothorax requiring intervention with chest tube placement [19,20]. Moreover, one patient (2.6%) developed a pseudoaneurysm of a segmental pulmonary artery requiring an embolization intervention (grade 3) [21], and one patient (2.6%) developed a grade 2 pleural effusion that required a thoracentesis [21]. Regarding the RT toxicity profile, there was no acute radiation pneumonitis $\geq$ grade 2. Other complications are reported in Table 1.

3.3. Local Control and Tumor Dimensions

Data on tumor size and LC were both available only in three papers [16,20,21].

Figure 2 depicts the association between lesions size and LC after the combined therapy, using a random-effects model. Lesions up to 30 mm in diameter seem to have a higher possibility to reach local control after the combined therapy, but this was not statistically significant (OR 0.33, CI: 0.06–1.85, p: 0.21).

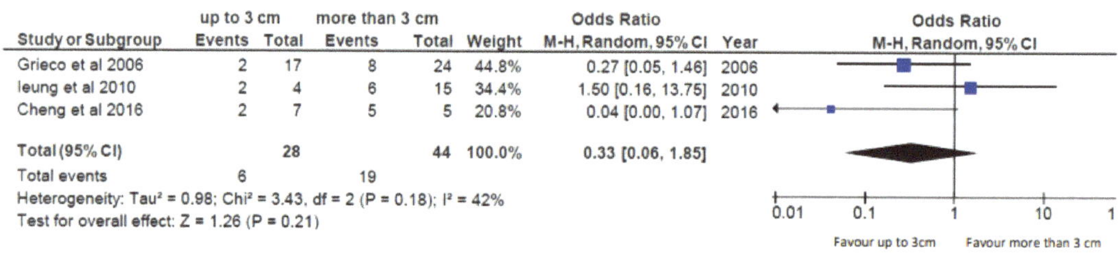

Figure 2. Forest plot investigating the relationship between lesions size and LC after the combined therapy [16,20,21].

4. Discussion

In the last few years, the possibility of a combination strategy between RT and other loco-regional approaches gained more and more attention. In particular, some authors theorized that a possible synergic result combining RT and LAT could be obtained using their different action mechanisms [15–17,20–22].

Encouraging data were provided by the experiences reported on hepatocellular carcinoma (HCC) or renal cancer. A recent meta-analysis [23] about HCC reported that the combination of SBRT and transcatheter arterial chemoembolization (TACE) might be an excellent choice for HCC with portal vein tumor thrombus (PVTT) rather than SBRT or TACE alone (monotherapy) with significant results in terms of OS and time to progression (TTP). In another setting, Blitzer et al. [24] performed the combination between SBRT and MWA in the treatment of renal cell carcinoma (RCC). The results were promising, indicating that SBRT combined with MW ablation appears to be a safe and feasible therapeutic modality for patients with large volume or vascular invasive RCC with an excellent rate of LC (100%).

These combinations could also be applied for pulmonary lesions due to their characteristics. RT depends on oxygen for cytotoxicity induction and is most effective against well-oxygenated cells, but it is less effective at destroying the hypoxic cells that make up the irregularly vascularized core of a solid neoplasm. Moreover, it is thought that hypoxic cells in the center of many tumors become progressively radiation resistant, contributing to tumor repopulation during RT of extended duration [12–14,25–27].

In contrast, LTA is most effective at the tumor central zone where the active zone of heating is focused, but it is less effective at damaging the tumor periphery, which tends to have impaired conduction due to the heat sink effect of large, high flow vessels and the insulation effect of aerated lung parenchyma [12–14,25–27]. Moreover, according to the works of Singh et al. [28,29], the heterogenous temperature distribution in the peripheral regions could also depend on the slight variations in the thermal-diffusion-mediated heat transfer, the blood-perfusion-mediated heat loss across the tumor tissue for the heat sink, and the irregular shape of the lesion.

To our knowledge, this is the first systematic review focused on combined treatment between RT and LTA in lung cancer lesions.

4.1. LAT Technique

The three most image-guided lung ablation techniques widely used are RFA, MWA and CA.

The lung is highly susceptible to the RFA technique because the air acts as an insulator, like a low electrical conductivity area. Therefore, it obtains a greater tissue volume ablation for the same energy than any other tissue [30]. The first published retrospective study reported that the 1-, 2-, and 3-year overall survival (OS) rates after the RFA of early NSCLC were 78%, 57% and 36%, respectively, and the local recurrence rates were 12%, 18%, and 21%, respectively [31,32]. According to the prospective multicenter clinical trial (RAPTUR study), NSCLC patients treated with RFA had a 1-year OS of 70% and a 2-year OS of 48% with stage I NSCLC patients having a 2-year OS and cancer-specific survival rate of 75% and 92%, respectively [33]. The main advantage of RFA is the extensive literature, as numerous studies have been conducted to evaluate the safety and efficacy of this treatment [34]. RFA provides an ablation volume with only one probe that can be activated at a time. The RFA is not generally recommended for central or near large vessel tumors or hilar lesions for the heat dissipation effects of neighboring blood vessels. Another disadvantage is that RFA may interfere with the heart's conduction system and is classically related to cardiac pacemakers' interference [35]. RFA treatment could be useful in an ideal patient with a peripherical lesion smaller than 3 cm.

Although not as extensively researched as RFA, MWA is becoming increasingly popular for image-guided percutaneous lung ablation. According to the literature, Yang et al. reported a median OS of 33.8 months after MWA among 47 patients with stage I NSCLC. The OS rates at 1, 3, and 5 years were 89%, 43%, and 16%, respectively, and the local control rates at 1, 3, and 5 years were 96%, 64%, and 48%, respectively [36].

Yao et al. found that MVA has similar outcomes to lobectomy for stage I NSCLC, with 1-, 3-, and 5-year OS rates of 100%, 92.6, and 50% for MWA and 100%, 90.7%, and 46.3% for lobectomy, respectively [37]. However, there is evidence that MWA is a promising therapeutic option for advanced lung cancer [38].

MWA may allow the treatment of larger tumors than RFA since tissue impedance does not limit the action of MWA [39]. In particular, MWA may be more effective for central or near large vessel tumors or hilar lesions, as the heat dissipation effect does not interfere with its therapeutic effect. However, it is difficult to control the ablation zone, and there is an increased risk of bronchial fistula when used near the pulmonary hilum. Microwave ablation could be useful in an ideal patient with a peripheral or central lesion larger than 3 cm without limitation regarding pacemaker disposal.

The CA is effective without damaging structures containing a collagenous matrix, such as blood vessels and bronchial tubes, with an advantage for the treatment of tumors near the pulmonary hilum or major vessels treatments [40].

The CA often requires the placement of two or more probes within the lesion, which increases the procedure's difficulty but allows the customization of the treated area's morphology. Both MWA and cryoablation (CA) allow for the simultaneous delivery of energy through several probes activated at the same time with a synergistic effect versus subsequent activation of the same probe [35].

However, unlike RFA and MWA, experience with CA is limited. Yamauchi et al. reported the first results of CA for inoperable stage I NSCLC patients with a total of 25 treatments in 22 patients. They found a local control rate of 97%, a median OS of 68 months, and a 3-year OS of 88% [41]. McDevitt et al. reported 1- and 3-year OS rates of 100% and 63%, respectively, in 25 patients with stage I NSCLC treated with CA [42]. One limitation of CA is that the procedure is longer than RFA and MWA with available protocols describing the need for up to three freeze–thaw cycles to achieve a correct ablative treatment [43]. Another disadvantage is that it is not recommended in a patient with coagulopathy due to the increased frequency and severity of pulmonary bleeding and hemoptysis. Cryoablation is an effective alternative in tumors near the great vessels, airways, pericardium, and subpleural lesions, as it tends to cause less pain than RFA and MWA. Another advantage is evaluating the ablation site during the procedure, optimizing the treatment in real time.

According to the literature, these ablative techniques have similar therapeutical results. Therefore, the choice is based on the tumor features and the patient's characteristics.

Another interesting possible approach is represented by the use of magnetic nanoparticle-based hyperthermia: a new cancer treatment technology that destroys tumors under an external alternating magnetic field [44]. Magnetic nanoparticle-based hyperthermia is a promising therapeutic strategy for non-invasive local tumor treatment, but the clinical use of this remains rare [44,45]. Only one paper [46] resulted from the review of Farzanegan et al. [44] on applying MNPs-based hyperthermia for lung cancer treatment. This study reported that hyperthermia using targeted superparamagnetic iron oxide (SPIO) nanoparticles significantly inhibited in vivo tumor growth. It highlights the potential for developing magnetic hyperthermia as an effective anticancer treatment modality for non-small cell lung cancer treatments [46]. But further studies are needed to evaluate the effectiveness, challenges, and probable defects of magnetic nanoparticle-based hyperthermia for cancer treatment in clinical practice.

4.2. RT Techniques

Historically, radiotherapy was delivered with conventional fractionation 1.8–2 Gy for a total dose of 90 Gy. Local recurrence rates were 40%, and 3-year overall and cancer-specific survival rates were 34% and 39%, respectively, which were significantly worse than surgical outcomes [47]. Over the years, SBRT has become the standard treatment in this patient setting, allowing notable improvements to be achieved compared to conventional radiotherapy. SBRT is a non-invasive radiotherapy technique that allows a high biological dose to be administered in a few sessions with extreme precision to a target of limited size thanks to the control of organ movement and an accurate definition of the target volumes. Specifically, SBRT is characterized by the delivery of high doses, greater than 5 Gy per fraction, in a limited number of fractions, and by the rapid drop in dose around the target, resulting in a maximum sparing of surrounding healthy tissues at risk of toxicity. SBRT is a local ablative treatment like a surgical intervention associated with a minimal incidence of local toxicity potentially capable of improving long-term survival without negatively impacting the patient's quality of life [48,49].

With outstanding outcomes in terms of local control and survival, SBRT is the radiation treatment now used for inoperable primary lung malignancies. Its efficacy has clearly exceeded that of conventional radiotherapy. In the randomized phase III CHISEL study, the risk of disease progression was found to be lower with SBRT (54 Gy in 3 fractions of 18 Gy, or 48 Gy in 4 fractions of 12 Gy) compared to conventional radiotherapy (66 Gy in 33 fractions of 2 Gy) with a favorable toxicity profile (14% vs. 31% HR 0.32 [95% CI 0.13–0.77], $p = 0.008$). There were no treatment-related deaths with only one case of G4 toxicity (dyspnea) in the SBRT arm; grade 3 toxicity was recorded in seven patients (10%) in the experimental arm and in two patients (6%) in the conventional RT arm. Local control at 2 years was 89% in the group of patients undergoing SBRT versus 65% in the patients enrolled in conventional RT [50].

Multiple studies investigated the feasibility and the effectiveness of SBRT for the treatment of lung cancer using a variety of dosing and fractionation schedules.

In the first phase I lung SBRT conducted by Timmerman and colleagues, we reported that doses of 20 Gy per fraction were tolerable and feasible, showing impressive rates of local control [51]. Two and three-year local control rates of 95% and 88%, respectively, were observed in a phase 2 study in which 70 patients were treated with 60–66 Gy [52].

Successively, Timmerman [53] reported in the first multi-institutional phase II trial 3 and 5-year local control rates of 97.6% and 92.7%, respectively, in a cohort of 55 patients treated at a dose of 54 Gy in three fractions with one local failure observed. In another prospective study, Ricardi et al. [10] analyzed 62 patients observing 3.2% of local relapse (2 pts) with a local control rate of 87.8%. In the same papers, the authors showed a significant correlation between tumor diameter and the probability of achieving a complete response, confirming that smaller lesions have a higher chance of being fully controlled and potentially cured.

Furthermore, in a recent review, a direct correlation was demonstrated between the administered dose and local disease control when 100 Gy in BED 10 (Biological Equivalent Dose) was exceeded. From this analysis, it can be seen that the percentage of local relapses is 8% for doses higher than 100 Gy and rises to 27% for lower doses with an impact also on survival (88% vs. 70%) [54].

The prescription dose of SBRT in thoracic tumors is conditioned not only by the tumor volume but also by the site of the disease, as it can influence the response and toxicity of the treatment itself.

4.3. Combined Approach

We reported interesting data on LC: the overall LC rate was 74.7% (range: 50–100%) with only 26 pts (24.7%) that reported local failure. These results can be compared with the ones regarding SBRT and LTA alone in the same setting in the current literature (30–55).

In our analysis, the combined treatment shows a limited risk of severe complications. Regarding toxicity profile, we registered pneumothorax (29.8%, with 18 patients requiring interventional therapy), pneumonitis (9.5%), pleural effusion (0.8%), and hemorrhage (0.8%).

Regarding the pneumothorax, the results are in line with the ones described in the literature on LAT alone, ranging from 29% to 34.3%, and about 11% to 12.3% of patients require interventional therapy (chest tube placement) [55]. Pleural effusion generally occurs in 5.2% to 9.6% of patients, and only 0.3% to 0.6% of patients had several pleural effusion requiring intervention in previous studies [56,57].

RT alone can lead to pulmonary toxicity, and the most common side effect of radiation alone is pneumonitis, which has been reported to occur in 5% to 15% of patients. In particular, SBRT presents negligible toxicity: the ratio of patients with grade 3 acute or late adverse event is less than 10%; in our series, no grade 3 or late toxicity was recorded [31,57–59].

Tumor size may be still considered a significant factor in the treatment response to combined treatment: we observed that tumors <30 mm had a longer tumor time local progression (TTLP) compared to tumors >30 mm having a shorter TTLP, but it was not statistically significative, which remains a key factor of technical success and clinical efficacy [16,19,20]. In Figure 2, forest plots visually demonstrate the overall relationship between lesions size and LC after the combined therapy. The trend association of tumor size with LC and TTLP obtained in our analysis was concordant with data literature. We have observed for primary NSCLC an average local recurrence of 45.6 ± 4.1 months for lesions <30 mm versus 34 ± 7.8 months for lesions >30 mm [16]. For recurrent NSCLC, we reported a TTLP of 23 months for tumor size ≤30 mm, whereas for tumors >30 mm, it was 14 months [20]. Simon et al. [31] reported a median TTLP for tumors ≤30 mm of 45 months versus 12 months for tumors >30 mm. In another study, Lanuti et al. [60] reported a recurrence rate of 50% for lesions >30 mm compared to 44% for lesions 20–30 mm. Schoellnast et al. [61] observed a median TTLP of 14 months for tumors with a mean size of 28 mm.

It should be noted that we examined case studies including patients who were not deemed the best candidates for surgery, which was most likely due to substantial morbidities, and with a median age ranging from 55 to 93 years.

As describe in Supplementary Table S1, the quality of the selected works ranged from the medium to low level. Moreover, we have to acknowledge that concerning the used RT techniques, not all the experiences used SBRT, with many using conventional radiotherapy instead.

Another aspect of these studies that needs further investigation is the sequence in which LAT and RT should be combined. In all the reported experiences, LAT was followed by RT; however, the hypoxia provided by LAT could make the cancerous tissue more radioresistant. Thus, RT, and in particular SBRT, should be performed before the LAT for radiobiological reasons.

Another point we have to consider in evaluating these results is the effect that blood perfusion can have on the efficacy of thermal ablation cancer treatments due to the heat-sink effect. This is due to heterogeneously perfused tumor regions that cause such a variability in thermal response to heating and thermal ablation, playing a crucial role in heat transfer within tissues. In fact, a heterogeneous blood perfusion can lead to significant variations in temperature distribution within tumors, and regions with lower blood perfusion may exhibit different sensitivity to therapies compared to areas with higher perfusion [62].

Even though the present systemic review had some limitations (small sample sizes, retrospective nature of the considered studies, their heterogeneity in terms of radiation treatment schedules and LTA and the short follow-up period), the data showed interesting results in terms of LC and toxicity. Our review could be considered a starting point for a further randomized controlled clinical study regarding the combination between RT and LAT in the treatment of primary or secondary lung cancer. However, we must remember that the key element in this treatment strategy should always be a harmonized multidisciplinary approach.

5. Conclusions

The proposed intervention demonstrated encouraging local control rates as well as low toxicity profiles. Despite these promising outcomes, it should be noted that these data come from retrospective studies with a significant level of heterogeneity, making it impossible to recommend an a priori strategy involving RT + LTA for patients in this context. While we await further randomized trials to verify this method, we propose a case-by-case evaluation based on tumor and patient characteristics.

Supplementary Materials: The following supporting information can be downloaded at https://www.mdpi.com/article/10.3390/cancers15245869/s1; Table S1: Quality appraisal score by Institute of Health Economics (IHE) for the selected studies.

Author Contributions: Conceptualization, F.D., R.I. and P.B.; methodology, D.P. and V.L.; validation, data collection, P.B., D.P. and A.R.S.; formal analysis, P.B., D.P. and G.M.; investigation, P.B., A.R.S. and D.P.; resources, F.D. and R.I.; data curation, P.B., D.P. and A.R.S.; writing—original draft preparation, P.B., D.P. and A.R.S.; writing—review and editing, all authors; visualization, R.I., F.D., V.L., G.K., G.M., E.R. and L.T.; supervision, R.I. and F.D. All authors have read and agreed to the published version of the manuscript.

Funding: This research received no external funding.

Conflicts of Interest: The authors declare no conflict of interest.

References

1. Sung, H.; Ferlay, J.; Siegel, R.L.; Laversanne, M.; Soerjomataram, I.; Jemal, A.; Bray, F.; Bsc, M.F.B.; Me, J.F.; Soerjomataram, M.I.; et al. Global Cancer Statistics 2020: GLOBOCAN Estimates of Incidence and Mortality Worldwide for 36 Cancers in 185 Countries. *CA Cancer J. Clin.* **2021**, *71*, 209–249. [CrossRef] [PubMed]
2. Duma, N.; Santana-Davila, R.; Molina, J.R. Non-small cell lung cancer: Epidemiology, screening, diagnosis, and treatment. *Themat. Rev. Neoplast. Hematol. Med. Oncol.* **2019**, *94*, 1623–1640. [CrossRef] [PubMed]
3. Jones, G.C.; Kehrer, J.D.; Kahn, J.; Koneru, B.N.; Narayan, R.; Thomas, T.O.; Camphausen, K.; Mehta, M.P.; Kaushal, A. Primary Treatment Options for High-Risk/Medically Inoperable Early Stage NSCLC Patients. *Clin. Lung Cancer* **2015**, *16*, 413–430. [CrossRef] [PubMed]
4. Olive, G.; Yung, R.; Marshall, H.; Fong, K.M. Alternative methods for local ablation—Interventional pul-monology: A narrative review. *Transl. Lung Cancer Res.* **2021**, *10*, 3432–3445. [CrossRef] [PubMed]
5. Dupuy, D.E.; Zagoria, R.J.; Akerley, W.; Mayo-Smith, W.W.; Kavanagh, P.V.; Safran, H. Percutaneous Radiofrequency Ablation of Malignancies in the Lung. *AJR Am. J. Roentgenol.* **2000**, *174*, 57–59. [CrossRef] [PubMed]
6. Thomas, J.V.; Naguib, N.N.N.; Lehnert, T.; Nour-Eldin, N.E.A. Radiofrequency, microwave and laser ablation of pulmonary neoplasms: Clinical studies and technical considerations—Review article. *Eur. J. Radiol.* **2011**, *77*, 346–357.
7. Ye, X.; Fan, W.; Wang, Z.; Wang, J.; Wang, H.; Niu, L.; Fang, Y.; Gu, S.; Liu, L.; Liu, B.; et al. Clinical practice guidelines on image-guided thermal ablation of primary and metastatic lung tumors (2022 edition). *J. Cancer Res. Ther.* **2022**, *18*, 1213–1230. [CrossRef]
8. NCCN Clinical Practice Guidelines in Oncology. Non-Small Cell Lung Cancer Versions 5.2023. Available online: https://www.nccn.org/guidelines/guidelines-detail?category=1&id=1450 (accessed on 3 November 2023).
9. Timmerman, R.; McGarry, R.; Yiannoutsos, C.; Papiez, L.; Tudor, K.; DeLuca, J.; Ewing, M.; Abdulrahman, R.; DesRosiers, C.; Williams, M.; et al. Excessive Toxicity When Treating Central Tumors in a Phase II Study of Stereotactic Body Radiation Therapy for Medically Inoperable Early-Stage Lung Cancer. *J. Clin. Oncol.* **2006**, *24*, 4833–4839. [CrossRef]
10. Ricardi, U.; Filippi, A.R.; Guarneri, A.; Giglioli, F.R.; Ciammella, P.; Franco, P.; Mantovani, C.; Borasio, P.; Scagliotti, G.V.; Ragona, R. Stereotactic body radiation therapy for early stage non-small cell lung cancer: Results of a prospective trial. *Lung Cancer* **2010**, *68*, 72–77. [CrossRef]
11. Buchberger, D.S.; Videtic, G.M. Stereotactic Body Radiotherapy for the Management of Early-Stage Non–Small-Cell Lung Cancer: A Clinical Overview. *JCO Oncol. Pr.* **2023**, *19*, 239–249. [CrossRef]
12. Wachsberger, P.; Burd, R.; Dicker, A.P. Tumor response to ionizing radiation combined with antiangiogenesis or vascular targeting agents: Exploring mechanisms of interaction. *Clin. Cancer Res.* **2003**, *9*, 1957–1971. [PubMed]
13. DiPetrillo, T.A.; Dupuy, D.E. Radiofrequency Ablation and Radiotherapy: Complementing Treatments for Solid Tumors. *Semin. Interv. Radiol.* **2003**, *20*, 341–345. [CrossRef]
14. Gadaleta, C.; Mattioli, V.; Colucci, G.; Cramarossa, A.; Lorusso, V.; Canniello, E.; Timurian, A.; Ranieri, G.; Fiorentini, G.; De Lena, M.; et al. Radiofrequency Ablation of 40 Lung Neoplasms: Preliminary Results. *Am. J. Roentgenol.* **2004**, *183*, 361–368. [CrossRef] [PubMed]
15. Steber, C.R.; Hughes, R.T.; Urbanic, J.; Clark, H.; Petty, W.J.; Blackstock, A.W.; Farris, M.K. Long-Term Outcomes from a Phase 2 Trial of Radiofrequency Ablation Combined with External Beam Radiation Therapy for Patients With Inoperable Non-Small Cell Lung Cancer. *Int. J. Radiat. Oncol. Biol. Phys.* **2021**, *111*, 152–156. [CrossRef] [PubMed]
16. Grieco, C.A.; Simon, C.J.; Mayo-Smith, W.W.; DiPetrillo, T.A.; Ready, N.E.; Dupuy, D.E. Percutaneous Image-guided Thermal Ablation and Radiation Therapy: Outcomes of Combined Treatment for 41 Patients with Inoperable Stage I/II Non–Small-Cell Lung Cancer. *J. Vasc. Interv. Radiol.* **2006**, *17*, 1117–1124. [CrossRef]
17. Dupuy, D.E.; DiPetrillo, T.; Gandhi, S.; Ready, N.; Ng, T.; Donat, W.; Mayo-Smith, W.W. Radiofrequency Ablation Followed by Conventional Radiotherapy for Medically Inoperable Stage I Non-small Cell Lung Cancer. *Chest* **2006**, *129*, 738–745. [CrossRef]
18. Institute of Health Economics (2016) Case Series Studies Quality Appraisal Checklist. Available online: https://www.ihe.ca/research-programs/rmd/cssqac/cssqac-about (accessed on 11 May 2018).
19. Higgins, J.P.T.; Thompson, S.G.; Deeks, J.J.; Altman, D.G. Measuring inconsistency in meta-analyses. *Br. Med. J.* **2003**, *327*, 557–560. [CrossRef]
20. Cheng, M.; Fay, M.; Steinke, K. Percutaneous CT-guided thermal ablation as salvage therapy for recurrent non-small cell lung cancer after external beam radiotherapy: A retrospective study. *Int. J. Hyperth.* **2016**, *32*, 316–323. [CrossRef]
21. Leung, V.A.; DiPetrillo, T.A.; Dupuy, D.E. Image-guided tumor ablation for the treatment of recurrent non-small cell lung cancer within the radiation field. *Eur. J. Radiol.* **2011**, *80*, e491–e499. [CrossRef]
22. Brooks, E.D.; Sun, B.; Feng, L.; Verma, V.; Zhao, L.; Gomez, D.R.; Liao, Z.; Jeter, M.; O'reilly, M.; Welsh, J.W.; et al. Association of Long-term Outcomes and Survival with Multidisciplinary Salvage Treatment for Local and Regional Recurrence After Stereotactic Ablative Radiotherapy for Early-Stage Lung Cancer. *JAMA Netw. Open* **2018**, *1*, e181390. [CrossRef]

23. Zhang, X.-F.; Lai, L.; Zhou, H.; Mo, Y.-J.; Lu, X.-Q.; Liu, M.; Lu, Y.-X.; Hou, E.-C. Stereotactic body ra-diotherapy plus transcatheter arterial chemoembolization for inoperable hepatocellular carcinoma patients with portal vein tumour thrombus: A meta analysis. *PLoS ONE* **2022**, *17*, e0268779.
24. Blitzer, G.C.; Wojcieszynski, A.; Abel, E.J.; Best, S.; Lee, F.T., Jr.; Hinshaw, J.L.; Wells, S.; Ziemlewicz, T.J.; Lubner, M.G.; Alexander, M.; et al. Com-bining Stereotactic Body Radiotherapy and Microwave Ablation Appears Safe and Feasible for Renal Cell Carcinoma in an Early Series. *Clin. Genitourin Cancer* **2021**, *19*, e313–e318. [CrossRef] [PubMed]
25. Horkan, C.; Dalal, K.; Coderre, J.A.; Kiger, J.L.; Dupuy, D.E.; Signoretti, S.; Halpern, E.F.; Goldberg, S.N. Reduced Tumor Growth with Combined Radiofrequency Ablation and Radiation Therapy in a Rat Breast Tumor Model. *Radiology* **2005**, *235*, 81–88. [CrossRef] [PubMed]
26. Jain, S.K.; Dupuy, D.E.; Cardarelli, G.A.; Zheng, Z.; DiPetrillo, T.A. Percutaneous radiofrequency ablation of pulmonary malignancies: Combined treatment with brachytherapy. *Am. J. Roentgenol.* **2003**, *181*, 711–715. [CrossRef] [PubMed]
27. Kosterev, V.V.; Kramer-Ageev, E.A.; Mazokhin, V.N.; van Rhoon, G.C.; Crezee, J. Development of a novel method to enhance the therapeutic effect on tumours by simultaneous action of radiation and heating. *Int. J. Hyperth.* **2015**, *31*, 443–452. [CrossRef] [PubMed]
28. Singh, M. Incorporating vascular-stasis based blood perfusion to evaluate the thermal signatures of cell-death using modified Arrhenius equation with regeneration of living tissues during nanoparticle-assisted thermal therapy. *Int. Commun. Heat Mass Transf.* **2022**, *135*, 106046. [CrossRef]
29. Singh, M.; Singh, T.; Soni, S. Pre-operative Assessment of Ablation Margins for Variable Blood Perfusion Metrics in a Magnetic Resonance Imaging Based Complex Breast Tumour Anatomy: Simulation Paradigms in Thermal Therapies. *Comput. Methods Programs Biomed.* **2021**, *198*, 105781. [CrossRef]
30. Seror, O. Ablative therapies: Advantages and disadvantages of radiofrequency, cryotherapy, microwave and electroporation methods, or how to choose the right method for an individual patient. *Diagn. Interv. Imaging* **2015**, *96*, 617–624. [CrossRef]
31. Simon, C.J.; Dupuy, D.E.; DiPetrillo, T.A.; Safran, H.P.; Grieco, C.A.; Ng, T.; Mayo-Smith, W.W. Pulmonary Radiofrequency Ablation: Long-term Safety and Efficacy in 153 Patients. *Radiology* **2007**, *243*, 268–275. [CrossRef]
32. Zhu, J.C.; Yan, T.D.; Morris, D.L. A systematic review of radiofrequency ablation for lung tumours. *Ann. Surg. Oncol.* **2008**, *15*, 1765.e74. [CrossRef]
33. Lencioni, R.; Crocetti, L.; Cioni, R.; Suh, R.; Glenn, D.; Regge, D.; Helmberger, T.; Gillams, A.R.; Frilling, A.; Ambrogi, M.; et al. Response to radiofrequency ablation of pulmonary tumours: A prospective, intention-to-treat, multicentre clinical trial (the RAPTURE study). *Lancet Oncol.* **2008**, *9*, 621.e8. [CrossRef] [PubMed]
34. Alzubaidi, S.J.; Liou, H.; Saini, G.; Segaran, N.; Kriegshauser, J.S.; Naidu, S.G.; Patel, I.J.; Oklu, R. Percutaneous Image-Guided Ablation of Lung Tumors. *J. Clin. Med.* **2021**, *10*, 5783. [CrossRef] [PubMed]
35. De Baere, T.; Tselikas, L.; Gravel, G.; Deschamps, F. Lung ablation: Best practice/results/response assessment/role alongside other ablative Therapies. *Clin. Radiol.* **2017**, *72*, 657–664. [CrossRef] [PubMed]
36. Yang, X.; Ye, X.; Zheng, A.; Huang, G.; Ni, X.; Wang, J.; Han, X.; Li, W.; Wei, Z. Percutaneous microwave ablation of stage I medically inoperable non-small cell lung cancer: Clinical evaluation of 47 cases. *J. Surg. Oncol.* **2014**, *110*, 758–763. [CrossRef] [PubMed]
37. Yao, W.; Lu, M.; Fan, W.; Huang, J.; Gu, Y.; Gao, F.; Wang, Y.; Li, J.; Zhu, Z. Comparison between microwave ablation and lobectomy for stage I non-small cell lung cancer: A propensity score analysis. *Int. J. Hyperth.* **2018**, *34*, 1329–1336. [CrossRef]
38. Pusceddu, C.; Melis, L.; Sotgia, B.; Guerzoni, D.; Porcu, A.; Fancellu, A. Usefulness of percutaneous microwave ablation for large non-small cell lung cancer: A preliminary report. *Oncol. Lett.* **2019**, *18*, 659–666. [CrossRef]
39. Aufranc, V.; Farouil, G.; Abdel-Rehim, M.; Smadja, P.; Tardieu, M.; Aptel, S.; Guibal, A. Percutaneous thermal ablation of primary and secondary lung tumors: Comparison between microwave and radiofrequency ablation. *Diagn. Interv. Imaging* **2019**, *100*, 781–791. [CrossRef]
40. Aarts, B.M.; Klompenhouwer, E.G.; Rice, S.L.; Imani, F.; Baetens, T.; Bex, A.; Horenblas, S.; Kok, M.; Haanen, J.B.A.G. Cryoablation and immunotherapy: An overview of evidence on its synergy. *Insights Imaging* **2019**, *10*, 1–12. [CrossRef]
41. Yamauchi, Y.; Izumi, Y.; Hashimoto, K.; Yashiro, H.; Inoue, M.; Nakatsuka, S.; Goto, T.; Anraku, M.; Ohtsuka, T.; Kohno, M.; et al. Percutaneous cryoablation for the treatment of medically in-operable stage I nonsmall cell lung cancer. *PLoS ONE* **2012**, *7*, e33223. [CrossRef]
42. McDevitt, J.L.; Mouli, S.K.; Nemcek, A.A.; Lewandowski, R.J.; Salem, R.; Sato, K.T. Percutaneous Cryoablation for the Treatment of Primary and Metastatic Lung Tumors: Identification of Risk Factors for Recurrence and Major Complications. *J. Vasc. Int. Radiol.* **2016**, *27*, 1371–1379. [CrossRef]
43. Hinshaw, J.L.; Lee, F.T., Jr.; Laeseke, P.F.; Sampson, L.A.; Brace, C. Temperature isotherms during pulmonary cryoablation and their correlation with the zone of ablation. *J. Vasc. Interv. Radiol.* **2010**, *21*, 1424–1428. [CrossRef] [PubMed]
44. Farzanegan, Z.; Tahmasbi, M. Evaluating the applications and effectiveness of magnetic nanoparticle-based hyperthermia for cancer treatment: A systematic review. *Appl. Radiat. Isot.* **2023**, *198*, 110873. [CrossRef] [PubMed]
45. Yang, N.; Gong, F.; Cheng, L.; Lei, H.; Li, W.; Sun, Z.; Ni, C.; Wang, Z.; Liu, Z. Biodegradable magnesium alloy with eddy thermal effect for effective and accurate magnetic hyperthermia ablation of tumors. *Natl. Sci. Rev.* **2020**, *8*, nwaa122. [CrossRef] [PubMed]
46. Sadhukha, T.; Wiedmann, T.S.; Panyam, J. Inhalable magnetic nanoparticles for targeted hyperthermia in lung cancer therapy. *Biomaterials* **2013**, *34*, 5163–5171. [CrossRef]

47. Qiao, X.; Tullgren, O.; Lax, I.; Sirzén, F.; Lewensohn, R. The role of radiotherapy in the treatment of stage I non-small cell lung cancer. *Lung Cancer* **2003**, *41*, 1–11. [CrossRef] [PubMed]
48. Dilling, T.J.; Hoffe, S.E. Stereotactic body radiation therapy: Transcending the conventional to improve outcomes. *Cancer Control.* **2008**, *15*, 104–111. [CrossRef] [PubMed]
49. Sutera, P.; Clump, D.A.; Kalash, R.; D'Ambrosio, D.; Mihai, A.; Wang, H.; Petro, D.P.; Burton, S.A.; Heron, D.E. Initial Results of a Multicenter Phase 2 Trial of Stereotactic Ablative Radiation Therapy for Oligometastatic Cancer. *Int. J. Radiat. Oncol. Biol. Phys.* **2019**, *103*, 116–122. [CrossRef]
50. Ball, D.; May, G.D.; Vinol, S.; Babington, S.; Ruben, J.; Kron, T. Stereotactic ablative radiotherapy versus standard radiotherapy in stage I non small cell lung cancer (TROG 09.02 CHISEL): A phase 3, open label, randomized controlled trial. *Lancet Oncol.* **2019**, *20*, 494–503. [CrossRef]
51. Timmerman, R.; Paplez, L.; McGarry, R.; Likes, L.; DesRosiers, C.; Frost, S.; Williams, M. Extracranial stereotactic radioablation: Result of a phase I study in. medically inoperable stage I non-small cell lung cancer. *Chest* **2003**, *124*, 1946–1955. [CrossRef]
52. Fakiris, A.J.; McGarry, R.C.; Yiannoutsos, C.T.; Papiez, L.; Williams, M.; Henderson, M.A.; Timmerman, R. Stereotactic body radiation therapy for early-stage non small-cell lung carcinoma: Four-year results of A prospective phase II study. *Int. J. Rad. Oncol. Biol. Phys.* **2009**, *75*, 677–682. [CrossRef]
53. Timmerman, R.; Paulus, R.; Galvin, J.; Michalski, J.; Straube, W.; Bradley, J.; Fakiris, A.; Bezjak, A.; Videtic, G.; Johnstone, D.; et al. Sterotactic body radiation therapy for inoperable early stage lung cancer. *JAMA* **2010**, *303*, 1070–1076. [CrossRef] [PubMed]
54. Lagerwaard, F.J.; Haasbeek, C.J.; Smit, E.F.; Slotman, B.J.; Senan, S. Outcomes of risk adapted fractionated stereotactic radiotherapy for stage I non-small cell lung cancer. *Int. J. Radiat. Biol. Phys.* **2008**, *70*, 685–692. [CrossRef] [PubMed]
55. Grasso, R.F.; Andresciani, F.; Altomare, C.; Pacella, G.; Castiello, G.; Carassiti, M.; Quattrocchi, C.C.; Faiella, E.; Beomonte Zobel, B. Radiofrequency ablation of stage IA non-small cell lung cancer in medically inoperable patients: Results from the American College of Surgeons Oncology Group Z4033 (Alliance) trial. *Cancer* **2015**, *121*, 3491–3498.
56. Palussière, J.; Chomy, F.; Savina, M.; Deschamps, F.; Gaubert, J.Y.; Renault, A.; Bonnefoy, O.; Laurent, F.; Meunier, C.; Bellera, C.; et al. Radiofrequency ablation of stage IA non–small cell lung cancer in patients ineligible for surgery: Results of a prospective multicenter phase II trial. *J. Cardiothorac. Surg.* **2018**, *13*, 1–9. [CrossRef] [PubMed]
57. Lanuti, M.; Sharma, A.; Willers, H.; Digumarthy, S.R.; Mathisen, D.J.; Shepard, J.-A.O. Radiofrequency Ablation for Stage I Non-Small Cell Lung Cancer: Management of Locoregional Recurrence. *Ann. Thorac. Surg.* **2012**, *93*, 921–988. [CrossRef] [PubMed]
58. Hiraki, T.; Gobara, H.; Mimura, H.; Matsui, Y.; Toyooka, S.; Kanazawa, S. Percutaneous radiofrequency ablation of clinical stage I non–small cell lung cancer. *J. Thorac. Cardiovasc. Surg.* **2011**, *142*, 24–30. [CrossRef] [PubMed]
59. Huang, B.-Y.; Li, X.-M.; Song, X.-Y.; Zhou, J.-J.; Shao, Z.; Yu, Z.-Q.; Lin, Y.; Guo, X.-Y.; Liu, D.-J.; Li, L. Long-term results of CT-guided percutaneous radiofrequency ablation of inoperable patients with stage Ia non-small cell lung cancer: A retrospective cohort study. *Int. J. Surg.* **2018**, *53*, 143–150. [CrossRef]
60. Lanuti, M.; Sharma, A.; Digumarthy, S.R.; Wright, C.D.; Donahue, D.M.; Wain, J.C.; Mathisen, D.J.; Shepard, J.-A.O. Radiofrequency ablation for treatment of medically inoperable stage I non–small cell lung cancer. *J. Thorac. Cardiovasc. Surg.* **2009**, *137*, 160–166. [CrossRef]
61. Schoellnast, H.; Deodhar, A.; Hsu, M.; Moskowitz, C.; Nehmeh, A.S.; Thornton, R.H.; Sofocleous, C.T.; Alago, W.; Downey, R.J.; Azzoli, C.G.; et al. Recurrent non-small cell lung cancer: Evaluation of CT-guided radiofrequency ablation as salvage therapy. *Acta Radiol.* **2012**, *53*, 893–899. [CrossRef]
62. Singh, M. Modified Pennes bioheat equation with heterogeneous blood perfusion: A newer perspective. *Int. J. Heat Mass Transf.* **2024**, *218*, 124698. [CrossRef]

Disclaimer/Publisher's Note: The statements, opinions and data contained in all publications are solely those of the individual author(s) and contributor(s) and not of MDPI and/or the editor(s). MDPI and/or the editor(s) disclaim responsibility for any injury to people or property resulting from any ideas, methods, instructions or products referred to in the content.

cancers

MDPI

Review

Emerging Treatment Options for Neuroendocrine Neoplasms of Unknown Primary Origin: Current Evidence and Future Perspectives

Francesca Corti [1,*], Roberta Elisa Rossi [2], Pietro Cafaro [1], Gaia Passarella [1], Antonella Turla [1], Sara Pusceddu [3], Jorgelina Coppa [4], Simone Oldani [3], Alessandro Guidi [1], Raffaella Longarini [1] and Diego Luigi Cortinovis [1]

1 Medical Oncology Unit, Fondazione IRCCS San Gerardo dei Tintori, Via G.B. Pergolesi 33, 20900 Monza, Italy; p.cafaro@unibs.it (P.C.); g.passarella@unibs.it (G.P.); a.turla@unibs.it (A.T.); alessandro.guidi@irccs-sangerardo.it (A.G.); raffaella.longarini@irccs-sangerardo.it (R.L.); diegoluigi.cortinovis@irccs-sangerardo.it (D.L.C.)
2 Gastroenterology and Endoscopy Unit, IRCCS Humanitas Research Hospital, Via Manzoni 56, Rozzano, 20089 Milan, Italy; robertaelisa.rossi@gmail.com
3 Gastro-Entero-Pancreatic and Neuroendocrine Unit 1, Department of Medical Oncology, ENETS Center of Excellence, Fondazione IRCCS Istituto Nazionale dei Tumori, Via Venezian 1, 20133 Milan, Italy; sara.pusceddu@istitutotumori.mi.it (S.P.); simone.oldani@istitutotumori.mi.it (S.O.)
4 Hepatology and Hepato-Pancreatic-Biliary Surgery and Liver Transplantation Unit, Fondazione IRCCS, Istituto Nazionale Tumori, Via Venezian 1, 20133 Milan, Italy; jorgelina.coppa@istitutotumori.mi.it
* Correspondence: francesca.corti@irccs-sangerardo.it; Tel.: +39-0392339575

Simple Summary: Sufferers of neuroendocrine neoplasms (NENs) of unknown primary origin are a poor prognostic group with largely unmet clinical needs. In the absence of standard therapeutic algorithms, treatment should be based on tumor clinical-pathological characteristics, disease burden, and patient conditions. The aim of this review is to explore the evidence relating to available treatment options for NENs of unknown primary and to offer insights into future perspectives. Particular attention is given to molecular characterization and genomic profiling of NENs with potential therapeutic implications, mainly through the identification of druggable targets for agnostic treatments. Moreover, a treatment algorithm for both well-differentiated and poorly differentiated NENs of unknown primary is proposed.

Abstract: Among neuroendocrine neoplasms (NENs), a non-negligible proportion (9–22%) is represented by sufferers of NENs of unknown primary origin (UPO), a poor prognostic group with largely unmet clinical needs. In the absence of standard therapeutic algorithms, current guidelines suggest that the treatment of UPO-NENs should be based on tumor clinical-pathological characteristics, disease burden, and patient conditions. Chemotherapy represents the backbone for the treatment of high-grade poorly differentiated UPO-NENs, usually providing deep but short-lasting responses. Conversely, the spectrum of available systemic therapy options for well-differentiated UPO-NENs may range from somatostatin analogs in indolent low-grade tumors, to peptide receptor radioligand therapy, tyrosine kinase inhibitors (TKIs), or chemotherapy for more aggressive tumors or in case of high disease burden. In recent years, molecular profiling has provided deep insights into the molecular landscape of UPO-NENs, with both diagnostic and therapeutic implications. Although preliminary, interesting activity data have been provided about upfront chemoimmunotherapy, the use of immune checkpoint inhibitors (ICIs), and the combination of ICIs plus TKIs in this setting. Here, we review the literature from the last 30 years to examine the available evidence about the treatment of UPO-NENs, with a particular focus on future perspectives, including the expanding scenario of targeted agents in this setting.

Keywords: neuroendocrine neoplasms; unknown primary origin; treatment; molecular biology; targeted therapy

1. Introduction

Neuroendocrine neoplasms (NENs) are a heterogeneous group of rare malignant neoplasms that arise from diffuse neuroendocrine cells. According to the 2022 World Health Organization (WHO) classification, NENs are classified into well-differentiated neuroendocrine tumors (NETs) and poorly differentiated neuroendocrine carcinomas (NECs) based on morphological features and the proliferation rate. Gastroenteropancreatic (GEP) NENs account for 62–67% of cases and include well-differentiated grade (G) 1–2 NETs (Ki-67 $\leq$ 20%), G3 NETs (Ki-67 index > 20% and well-differentiated morphology), and G3 NECs (Ki-67 index > 20% and poorly differentiated morphology). Thoracic NENs account for 22–27% of cases, including well-differentiated typical carcinoids of the lung and thymus (<2 mitoses/2 mm^2 and absence of necrosis), atypical carcinoids (2–10 mitoses/2 mm^2 and/or presence of necrosis), and poorly differentiated small cell (SC) and large cell neuroendocrine carcinomas (LCNECs) (>10 mitoses/2 mm^2 and presence of necrosis). In the absence of a clinically or radiologically identifiable primary site despite the use of gold standard diagnostic techniques so far, a non-negligible proportion of histologically documented NENs (9–22%) are of unknown primary origin (UPO) [1–6].

Compared to other NENs, UPO-NENs represent a significant diagnostic and therapeutic challenge due to their rarity, their complex clinical presentation, and the lack of definite therapeutic algorithms.

According to the Surveillance, Epidemiology, and End Results (SEER) program, the incidence of UPO NETs was 0.84/100,000 persons per year between 2000 and 2012, with a relatively scant prognosis (median overall survival of 33–48 months) compared to other NET groups [7,8].

UPO-NENs present, by definition, with advanced or metastatic disease, the most frequently involved sites being the liver, followed by the peritoneum, the lymph nodes, the bones, and the lung [9]. Although the gastrointestinal and thoracic origin are the most likely sites of origin of UPO-NENs, unusual locations such as the genitourinary tract or the head and neck district have to be considered [10–20].

If the primary tumor site remains unknown despite extensive workup, the initial treatment strategy should be based on the presumptive site of origin and on tumor clinical-pathological characteristics as suggested by the main international guidelines [21,22]. However, in the absence of definite treatment algorithms based on high-quality evidence from randomized phase III trials, an optimal therapeutic approach to UPO-NENs still represents an unmet clinical need.

This review aims to address current evidence about the treatment landscape of UPO-NENs, and to provide an insight into future perspectives, with a particular focus on the potential therapeutic implications of molecular characterization and genomic profiling of these neoplasms.

2. Materials and Methods

We conducted a comprehensive search on PubMed and the ClinicalTrials.gov website using the following search keywords: "neuroendocrine", with "tumor-" or "neoplasm-", combined with "unknown primary", "unknown origin" and "treatment" or "therapy" or "clinical trial" or "molecular biology". The reference list of the most important papers and abstract communications from relevant conferences were also examined in order to further check the existing data in the literature. We limited the search to English language publications in the last 30 years. Searches were last updated on December 2023. A total of 379 articles were found. A manual selection of relevant articles based on title and/or abstract content was performed. The full versions of all relevant reports were analyzed, with a total of 103 works included in this review. Figure 1 reports the flow diagram for the identification of relevant manuscripts included in the review.

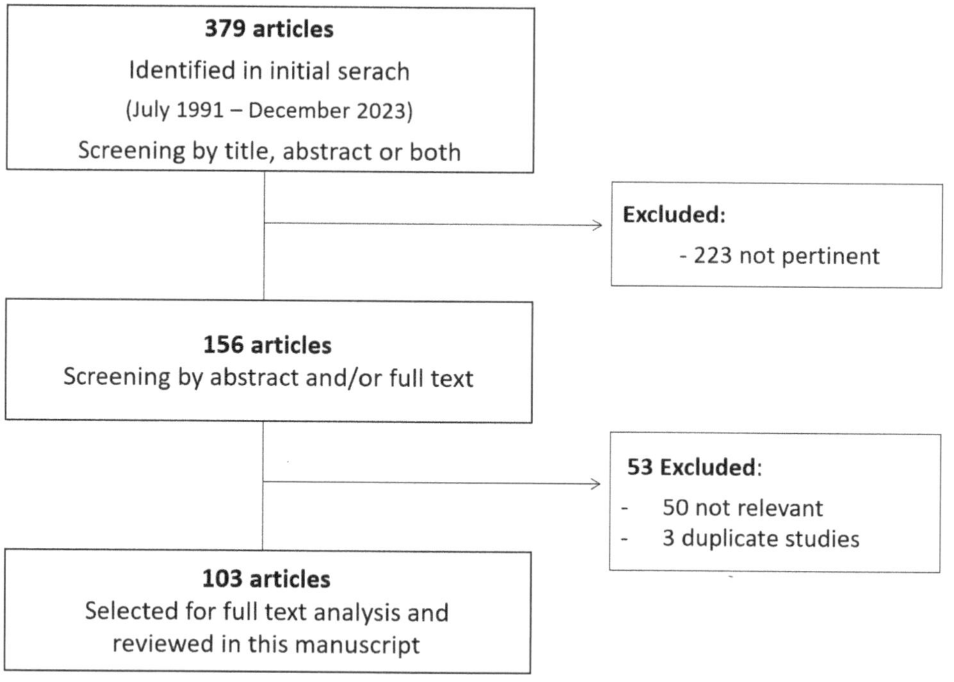

Figure 1. Flow diagram of review manuscript.

3. Diagnostic Approach to UPO-NEN

At the first evidence of UPO-NEN, every effort should be made to identify the primary site of origin, as it could lead to surgical treatment with curative intent and/or to the access to systemic treatment strategies for which primary site identification is required by specific registration boundaries [22]. According to available evidence, the resection of midgut and pancreatic primary tumors is independently associated with improved survival outcomes in NET patients with liver metastases. Moreover, primary tumor surgery may reduce the risk of local complications such as occlusion, bleeding, or perforation, especially in the case of small-bowel NETs [23–26].

A comprehensive assessment for primary site identification should include an extensive clinical evaluation (e.g., pattern of metastatic spread, presence of clinical syndromes), morphological and metabolic imaging, endoscopic procedures, and a thorough immunohistochemical (IHC) evaluation with the possible integration of molecular pathology. Clinical presentation, including the pattern of metastatic organ involvement and the presence of a functional syndrome, might be fundamental as a hint for primary site identification. For example, carcinoid syndrome is usually related to small-bowel NEN, whereas Zollinger–Ellison syndrome and insulinoma and glucagonoma syndromes, should prompt the investigation of the duodenal-pancreatic area, and ectopic ACTH production may suggest lung or thymus primaries [27].

An accurate pathological evaluation is pivotal both to orient primary site identification and to provide tumor grading to guide therapeutic choices. NENs are classified into well differentiated NETs and poorly differentiated NECs based on morphological features and proliferation rate. This classification accounts for critical differences in terms of genomic and biological characteristics, as well as clinical behavior. NETs display a morphological organoid and nesting pattern, with very rare cytological atypia, whereas NECs are characterized by a solid growth pattern with marked atypia and diffuse necrosis. The neuroendocrine phenotype is identified through the assessment of definite immunohistochemical features. NETs usually display Chromogranin A (CgA) and synaptophysin staining, as well as strongly positive somatostatin receptor (SSTR) staining, while NECs retain synaptophysin staining, but may display only focal or absent CgA and SSTR staining. Insulinoma-associated protein-1 (INSM1) is highly specific for NEN independently of primary site and differentiation grade.

The classification of NENs was recently updated in the 2022 WHO classification system. NECs (every site of origin) are poorly differentiated with a high proliferation rate (Ki-67 > 20%, usually >55%) and further distinguished into the small cell and large cell subtypes. The NET nomenclature has been standardized as a three-tiered grading system according to morphological differentiation, grading, and proliferation rate. GEP NETs are distinguished as well-differentiated low-grade G1 NETs (Ki-67 $\leq$ 2% and mitotic index < 2 mitoses/2 mm^2), well-differentiated intermediate-grade G2 NETs (Ki-67 between 3–20% and/or mitotic index between 2 and 20/2 mm^2), and well-differentiated G3 NETs (Ki67 > 20% and/or mitotic index > 20/2 mm^2). Similarly, thoracic NETs have been categorized into well-differentiated G1 NETs/typical carcinoids (mitotic index < 2/2 mm^2 and no necrosis), well-differentiated G2 NETs/atypical carcinoids (mitotic index between 2 and 10/2 mm^2 and/or necrosis), and well-differentiated NETs with elevated mitotic counts (atypical carcinoid morphology and >10 mitoses/2 mm^2 and/or Ki67 > 30%). The WHO classification is specifically intended for surgical specimens. Therefore, the limitations of diagnoses obtained from core biopsies or cytological specimens should be taken into account. Whereas the diagnosis of NEC on biopsies may be more reproducible, the diagnosis of NET has inherent limitations in terms of accuracy for the evaluation of the Ki-67 labeling index and mitotic index, potentially affecting tumor grading [1].

Comprehensive IHC evaluation encompassing multiple markers may orient primary site identification. For example, CDX2 is a transcription factor associated with gastrointestinal differentiation, and a possible marker for intestinal or pancreatic origin. CDX2 yields a 90% sensitivity for midgut origin, although it is also expressed in 15% of pancreatic primaries. Paired Box (PAX)-8, PAX6 and Islet-1 are markers for both pancreatic and rectal NENs. Even though Islet-1 is a 70%-sensitive pancreatic (p)NEN marker, it is also expressed in rectal NENs and in up to 10% of lung primaries. Pancreatic and duodenal homeobox (PDX)-1, progesteron receptor (Pr), and neuroendocrine secretory protein (NESP)-55 staining are suggestive of pancreatic primary. Conversely, special AT-rich sequence-binding protein (SATB)2 positivity is typical of rectal (96%) and appendiceal (79%) NETs. Thyroid Transcription Factor (TTF)-1 positivity may suggest a thoracic primary, even though its sensitivity is low, whereas CK7 yields high sensitivity but less specificity for pulmonary NENs. Orthopedia Homeobox Protein (OTP), in contrast, represents a highly specific marker for pulmonary carcinoids, with a 60–80% sensitivity [6,28]. Several IHC algorithms have been built for the presumptive primary site identification in case of UPO-NEN [28,29]. Indeed, sequential IHC staining algorithms may help to identify the presumptive primary site with a stepwise approach. Performing baseline CDX2, Pr, PAX8, TTF-1 and SATB2 staining may lead to the identification of a midgut pattern (CDX2 positive, other markers negative), pancreatic pattern (Pr/PAX8 positive, SATB2 negative, CDX2 positive/negative), rectum/appendix pattern (SATB2 positive, TTF1-negative), or lung pattern (TTF-1 positive) which can be further investigated with the addition of other markers (such as Islet-1, PAX6, OTP, PDX-1, NESP-55) [6,28,29].

Although conventional radiology (computed tomography [CT] or magnetic resonance imaging [MRI]) is of utmost importance for patients' staging, it might fail to detect the primary tumor if the lesions are small, especially in the case of a GEP primary. Therefore, metabolic imaging represents an essential tool in patient's staging and primary site detection. Less recent reports evaluated the diagnostic impact of In-pentetreotide somatostatin receptor scintigraphy (SRS) in the detection of GEP occult primaries. In a small series of 36 patients by Savelli and Colleagues, SRS was suggestive of the possible site of the primary lesion in 39% of patients and prompted surgical management in 17% of cases [30]. Due to its higher sensitivity, 68-Gallium [^{68}Ga]-labeled somatostatin analogs positron emission tomography (PET) is the gold standard for the detection of low-grade well-differentiated NETs, whereas fluorodeoxyglucose (FDG)-PET is recommended in high-grade poorly differentiated forms and for prognostication. In the case where pheochromocytoma/paraganglioma is suspected, other imaging modalities such as DOPA PET or metaiodobenzylguanidine (MIBG) scanning may also be considered [31–33]. According to the available literature, the true positive detection rates for an occult primary with ^{68}Ga-DOTA-D Phe1-Tyr3-Octreotide (DOTATOC) PET imaging ranges from 38% to 61%, with overall sensitivity and specificity of 82–92% and 55–82%, respectively. ^{68}Ga-DOTATOC PET imaging produces an alteration in patient management in 20–50% of cases [34–39]. Moreover, the use of radiolabeled somatostatin analogs has been exploited for intra-operative localization of UPO-NETs suspected to be of GEP primary, to improve intra-operative detection rates of small primaries and/or metastatic sites [40].

In cases where morphological or functional imaging has failed to detect the primary site, other investigations should be considered. If a gastrointestinal primary is suspected based on clinical-pathological assessments, endoscopic workout should be performed (including esophagogastroduodenoscopy, colonoscopy, and endoscopic ultrasonography). Since most UPO-NETs are of jejunoileal origin, an accurate study of the small intestine should be performed. Even though data concerning the use of capsule endoscopy (CE) or double balloon enteroscopy (DBE) for UPO-NEN assessment in clinical practice are scant, these assessments may allow the visualization of small intestinal lesions undetectable with conventional radiological imaging. DBE is more invasive when compared with capsule endoscopy; however, it may allow biopsies to be performed to obtain a pathological sample [27]. Moreover, surgical exploration of the abdomen may lead to the identification of the tumor primary in a non-negligible percentage of cases when GEP-NETs are suspected, potentially leading to surgery with radical intent [41].

If other more unusual areas are suspected, a thorough examination of the otolaryngologic and urogenital tracts, as well as full skin, eye, and breast assessments, should be performed [10–18,20]. For example, a very aggressive disease with limited therapeutic options is represented by neuroendocrine prostate cancer, which can emerge under the pressure of androgen deprivation treatment or arise de novo in a small percentage of cases [14].

In conclusion, the localization of the primary tumor is of paramount importance for the patient's management and prognosis. Not only may primary tumor resection have a radical and curative intent, but it has also been associated with improved survival outcomes in midgut and p-NET patients with liver metastases [23–26]. Moreover, after primary tumor identification and resection, excision or ablation with curative intent of metastatic sites may be pursued as part of a curative strategy (especially in liver-limited disease). Surgery can also decrease the risk of complications related to the primary lesion (such as bleeding, occlusion, or compression of adjacent structures). Finally, identification of the site of origin may allow access to registered systemic treatments which require the primary tumor to be identified [27].

Figure 2 depicts a possible diagnostic algorithm for UPO-NEN.

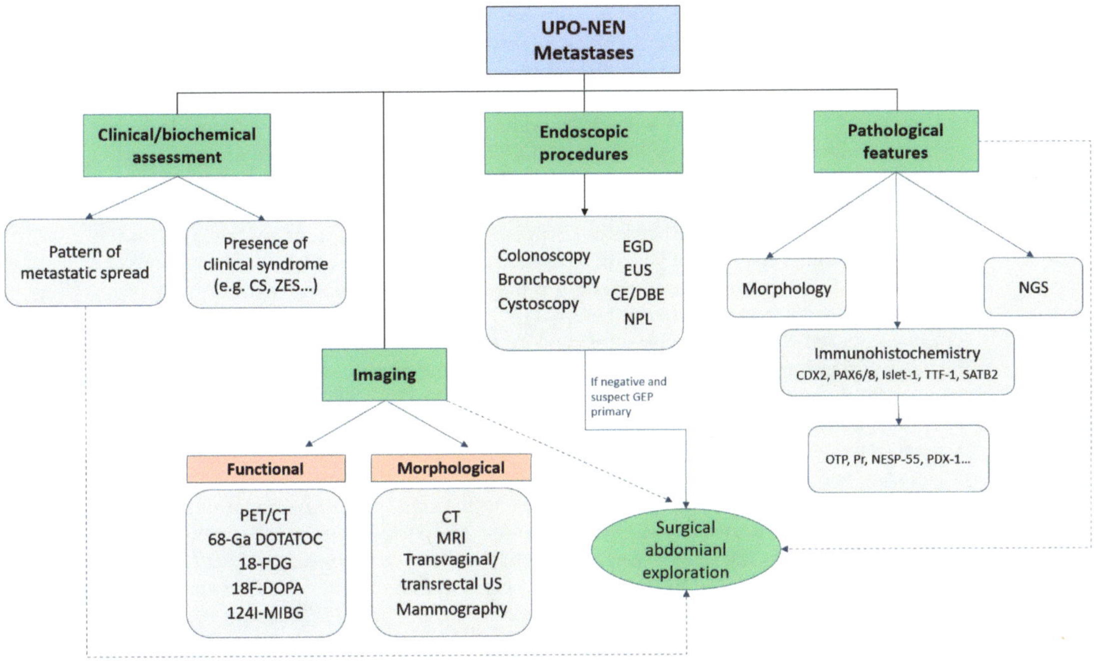

Figure 2. Diagnostic algorithm for UPO-NEN. CE: capsule endoscopy; CS: Carcinoid syndrome; CT: computed tomography; DBE: double-balloon enteroscopy; EGD: Esophagogastroduodenoscopy; EUS: endoscopic ultrasonography; FDG: fluorodeoxyglucose; GEP: gastroenteropancreatic; MIBG: metaiodobenzylguanidine; MRI: magnetic resonance imaging; NESP-55: neuroendocrine secretory protein-55; NGS: next generation sequencing; NPL: naso-pharyngeal-laryngoscopy; OTP: Orthopedia Homeobox Protein; PAX: paired Box; PDX-1: Pancreatic and duodenal homeobox-1; PET: positron emission tomography; Pr: progesterone receptor; SATB2: special AT-rich sequence-binding protein 2; TTF-1: thyroid transcription factor; UPO-NEN: neuroendocrine neoplasm of unknown primary origin; US: ultrasonography; ZES: Zollinger-Ellison syndrome; 68-Ga DOTATOC: ^{68}Gallium- DOTA-D Phe1-Tyr3-Octreotide.

4. Therapeutic Approach to UPO-NEN

No definite therapeutic algorithms are currently defined for UPO-NENs, mainly due to the lack of high-quality evidence from randomized phase III trials.

Therapeutic decision making for UPO-NENs is essentially based on tumor histology and grading, presumptive site of origin (based on histopathological and immunohistochemical characteristics), SSTR status, functionality, tumor burden, and progression rate, as well as the patient's general condition and comorbidities [21].

4.1. Treatment of Poorly Differentiated NEC of Unknown Origin

4.1.1. First-Line Setting

The frontline therapeutic approach to poorly differentiated UPO-NECs is primarily based on the use of platinum-based chemotherapy regimens. In the first-line setting, cisplatin plus etoposide represents the preferred regimen, providing response rates up to ~40–70%, progression-free survival (PFS) rates up to 9 months, and overall survival (OS) rates up to 19 months in historical series [42–45]. In an analogy with the treatment of SCLC, the combination of platinum agents and irinotecan may be evaluated as a possible alternative to cisplatin and etoposide with some differences in clinical outcomes by ethnicity (Asiatic versus non-Asiatic populations) [46]. A recent study by Zhang and colleagues assessed the non-inferiority of cisplatin plus etoposide vs. cisplatin plus irinotecan in terms of safety and efficacy as a first-line treatment in advanced NEC patients, including UPO-NEC (eight patients), with different toxicity profiles. The overall response rate (ORR) was 42.4% in both arms, with median PFS of 6.4 months and 5.8 months ($p = 0.81$), and median OS of 11.3 months and 10.2 months ($p = 0.37$) for platinum–etoposide and platinum-irinotecan, respectively [47]. The NORDIC-NEC trial retrospectively evaluated the prognostic and predictive factors for survival and treatment outcomes in 305 patients with G3 NEN (32% of whom had UPO-NEN) receiving palliative chemotherapy (including cisplatin-etoposide and carboplatin–etoposide with or without vincristine). ORR to first-line chemotherapy was 31%, with a disease stabilization rate of 33%. The response rates did not differ among different platinum-based regimens. Patients with Ki-67 < 55% had a lower response rate to chemotherapy (15% vs. 42%, $p < 0.001$), but displayed better OS compared to patients with Ki-67 ≥ 55% (14 vs. 10 months, $p < 0.001$) [48]. On the basis of these results, platinum–etoposide containing regimens may not be the most appropriate chemotherapeutic approach for NEN G3 with Ki-67 <55% and alternative regimens (e.g., fluoropyrimidines, temozolomide, and oxaliplatin-containing regimens) should be considered. Recently, the randomized phase II EA2142 trial was designed to assess the efficacy and activity of a regimen with capecitabine and temozolomide (CAPTEM) compared to cisplatin plus etoposide in patients with previously untreated unresectable or metastatic G3 NEN with a Ki-67 labeling index 20–100%. A total of 67 patients with tumors of suspected GEP origin were enrolled. The study was prematurely closed due to futility at 57.7% information time, showing median PFS of 2.43 vs. 5.36 months, OS of 12.6 vs. 13.6 months, and response rate of 9% vs. 10% with CAPTEM and platinum–etoposide, respectively. CAPTEM did not appear to be superior to platinum–etoposide chemotherapy, but was associated with a more favorable toxicity profile [49]. Overall, prospective data assessing G3 NETs independently of G3 NECs are needed to establish the optimal front-line treatment strategy.

Due to the poor prognosis of these tumors, treatment intensification with three-drug therapeutic regimens has been attempted. The combination of carboplatin, etoposide, and paclitaxel was evaluated in two trials including patients with UPO-NECs, yielding ORR of 47–53% and median OS of 13.4–14.5 months, at the cost of moderate toxicity [50,51]. The FOLFIRINEC randomized phase II trial, with the aim of assessing the efficacy and activity of the FOLFIRINOX (5-fluorouracil, irinotecan, oxaliplatin) regimen compared to platinum plus etoposide in a population of patients with metastatic GEP or UPO NEC, is currently ongoing (NCT04325425) [52].

The combination of frontline chemotherapy with immunotherapy has been recently explored with the aim of improving outcomes in this poor-prognosis population. The non-randomized open-label phase II NICE-NEC trial (EudraCT: 2019-001546-18) evaluated the combination of carboplatin–etoposide with nivolumab as a first-line treatment for patients with advanced or metastatic G3 GEP and UPO NEN. Overall, 38 patients were enrolled. With a median follow-up of 18.6 months (range: 2.2–24.6), ORR was 54.1%, the disease control rate (DCR) was 83.8%, median PFS was 5.7 months (95% confidence interval [CI]: 5.1–9), and median OS was 13.9 months (with 32.4% of patients surviving more than 18 months) [53].

4.1.2. Second-Line Setting

For cases of UPO-NEC progressing on platinum–etoposide, regimens containing irinotecan, fluoropyrimidines, temozolomide, or oxaliplatin (e.g., CAPTEM; FOLFIRI [5-fluorouracil-irinotecan]; FOLFOX [5-fluorouracil-oxaliplatin]) may be considered, mostly based on retrospective data showing ORR rates of ~30% [54–57].

The randomized, multicenter, non-comparative, open-label, phase 2 BEVANEC trial evaluated the efficacy of FOLFIRI plus bevacizumab, or FOLFIRI alone in patients with advanced NEC (including UPO-NEC) progressing on first-line platinum–etoposide-based chemotherapy. Of the 126 patients included in the intent-to-treat population, 18% had UPO-

NEC. After a median follow-up of 25.7 months, no clinically significant survival benefit was evidenced with the addition of bevacizumab to the FOLFIRI backbone, with a 6-month OS rate of 53% in the FOLFIRI plus bevacizumab group and 60% in the FOLFIRI group. Moreover, one fatal toxicity (ischemic stroke) occurred in the FOLFIRI-bevacizumab cohort [58]. The NET-02 randomized, non-comparative, phase II trial evaluated the efficacy of liposomal irinotecan (nal-IRI) plus 5-fluorouracil (arm A) or docetaxel (arm B) in patients with poorly differentiated extrapulmonary NECs progressing on first-line platinum–etoposide chemotherapy. Of the 58 enrolled patients, 10% had UPO-NECs. The trial met its primary endpoint in arm A, with a 6-month PFS rate of 29.6% (95% lower confidence limit: 15.7%) that exceeded the prespecified threshold for efficacy, but not in arm B (6 months PFS rate of 13.8%). ORR was 11.1% in arm A and 10.3% in arm B, with similar median PFS (3 months and 2 months) and OS (6 months and 6 months) in patients receiving nal-IRI plus 5-fluorouracil and docetaxel, respectively. According to the authors, 5-fluorouracil plus nal-IRI may represent a viable therapeutic option in this setting, whereas the poor performance of docetaxel, with the poor associated tolerability profile, should discourage further investigation of this regimen in this setting [59]. Another recent phase II trial aimed at evaluating the activity of temozolomide monotherapy in patients with extrapulmonary NECs progressing on first-line platinum–etoposide treatment. The trial enrolled 13 patients, 1 of whom had UPO-NEC. ORR was 15.4%, with median PFS of 1.8 months (95% CI, 1.0–2.7) and median OS of 7.8 months (95% CI, 6.0–9.5). O6-methylguanine-DNA methyltransferase (MGMT) deficiency was observed in one patient, who displayed partial response as the best response [57]. Of note, in the absence of other viable therapeutic options, some authors recently evaluated the opportunity of etoposide rechallenge in patients with a relapse-free interval of $\geq$3 months after first-line platinum–etoposide treatment. The retrospective RBNEC trial including 121 NEC patients (12% of whom with UPO-NEC) reported DCR of 62%, and median PFS and OS of 3.2 and 11.7 months, respectively, among the 31 patients receiving this treatment strategy [60].

Besides standard chemotherapy regimens, other treatment strategies employing immunotherapeutic agents and small molecules have been recently evaluated in order to expand the therapeutic armamentarium in high-grade NENs including UPO-NENs.

As immunotherapy has produced a paradigm shift in the treatment landscape of specific NENs such as Merkel cell carcinoma, immune checkpoint inhibitors (ICIs) have been recently tested in this setting [61,62]. Anti-programmed death (PD)- (ligand [L])1 monotherapy has shown limited activity in molecularly unselected G3 NENs including UPO-NECs, with ORR of 0–7%, median PFS range of 1.8–2.0 months, and median OS range of 4.2–7.8 months [63–67]. The combination of pembrolizumab plus mono-chemotherapy (weekly paclitaxel or weekly irinotecan) in high-grade pretreated extrapulmonary NECs (including 23% of UPO-NECs) also showed unsatisfactory activity (ORR 9%) and poor survival outcomes (median PFS: 2 months, median OS: 4 months) in unselected patients [63,68].

Conversely, dual anti-Cytotoxic T-Lymphocyte Antigen (CTLA)-4/anti-PD-1 blockade yielded more clinically significant results in high-grade NEN patients. The high-grade NEN cohort of the phase II DART-SWOG S1609 trial assessed the activity of the combination of the anti-CTLA-4 agent ipilimumab at the dose of 1 mg/kg every 6 weeks plus anti-PD-1 nivolumab in microsatellite-stable advanced G3 NEN patients (mostly with poorly differentiated tumors). A total of 19 patients were included, 4 (21%) of whom had UPO-NEC. Most of the included patients were pretreated for metastatic disease with a median of 1 (0–3) prior line. ORR was 26% (95% CI, 11–45%), with median PFS of 2.0 months and median OS of 8.7 months. Among the four patients with UPO-NEC, two achieved stable disease as the best response [69]. Another study, the NEN subgroup analysis of the CA209-538 trial of ipilimumab (at the dose of 1 mg/kg every 3 weeks for a total of four doses) and nivolumab in rare cancers, evaluated the outcome of 29 patients with advanced NEN (90% pretreated patients, 45% high grade NEN, 7% UPO-NEN). ORR was 24%, with DCR of 72% in the entire cohort. ORR was 31% and 23% in patients with G3 and G2 NEN, respectively. No responses were observed in the two enrolled patients with

UPO-NEC. Median PFS was 4.82 (95% CI 2.71–10.53) months and median OS was 14.78 (95% CI: 4.07–21.25) months [70]. No unexpected toxicities have been documented in both trials combining ipilimumab and nivolumab.

Another ICI combination, durvalumab plus tremelimumab, was evaluated in advanced pretreated NENs in the multicohort phase II DUNE trial, showing only limited activity in advanced G3 GEP and UPO-NENs progressing to platinum-based first-line chemotherapy (cohort 4). In this cohort, ORR was 9.1%, 9-month OS rate was 36.1%, and median OS was 5.9 (95% CI: 2–9.7) months. Even though the prespecified futility threshold for OS was surpassed, response rates and survival outcomes were poor. PD-L1 expression by combined positive score (CPS) did not correlate with treatment activity. In analyzed patients, no microsatellite instability (MSI)-high status was reported [71].

Targeted agents with well-known activity in well-differentiated NENs have also been evaluated in the setting of high-grade progressive NENs. The EVINEC phase II trial evaluated the safety and efficacy of second-line everolimus in NEN G3 patients progressing on platinum chemotherapy. Of the 36 enrolled patients, 13 (36%) had NET G3, 14 (39%) had NEC, and 9 (25%) had mixed-neuroendocrine/non-neuroendocrine neoplasm (MiNEN) with a NEC G3 component. Six patients (16%) had UPO-NEN. No unexpected safety events occurred. Efficacy was promising (ORR 7.7%, median PFS and OS of 5.2 and 23.9 months, respectively) in the NET G3 group. However, results were poor in NECs (ORR 0%, median PFS and OS of 1.8 and 5.6 months, respectively), and in MiNENs (ORR 0%, median PFS and OS of 2.2 and 7.0 months, respectively) [72].

An alternative treatment strategy that is currently being explored in ongoing trials is the combination of small molecules (tyrosine kinase inhibitors-TKIs) and ICIs. Weber and colleagues recently reported the activity and safety of cabozantinib (a c-MET, vascular endothelial growth factor receptor [VEGFR]2, RET, KIT, AXL, and Fms Related Tyrosine Kinase 3 inhibitor) in combination with avelumab in patients with G3 NEN, reporting ORR of 21% and median PFS of 48.1 weeks, with a manageable toxicity profile [73]. Conversely, results of the CABATEN/GETNE-T1914 trial, evaluating the activity of cabozantinib plus the anti-PD-L1 agent atezolizumab, showed limited activity and poor survival outcomes in progressive NENs including high grade NECs [74].

Surufatinib (a VEGFR 1, 2, 3, fibroblast growth factor receptor [FGFR]-1, and colony-stimulating-factor-1 receptor inhibitor), combined with the anti PD-1 sintilimab and the anti-CTLA-4 IBI310, is currently being evaluated for the treatment of high-grade NENs (NCT05165407) [75].

Of note, most of the aforementioned trials included patients with high-grade (G3) NEN, without specifically addressing tumor differentiation. In the future, subgroup analyses assessing NECs independently of G3 NETs are warranted to establish the activity of novel treatment options in these different populations.

4.2. Treatment of Well-Differentiated NETs of Unknown Origin

Therapeutic options for well-differentiated UPO-NETs potentially encompass the available agents registered for site-specific disease, ranging from somatostatin analogs (SSAs) to targeted agents (such as everolimus or TKIs), peptide-receptor radio-ligand therapy (PRRT) and chemotherapy. In this setting, therapeutic choices should be tailored according to tumor grading and functionality, SSTR status, tumor burden, and progression rate, as well as the patient's general condition and comorbidities.

SSA monotherapy may be considered for patients with well-differentiated, low-grade NETs expressing SSTRs, with low tumor burden and/or indolent disease behavior. Moreover, its use must always be considered in functioning tumors for symptomatic control.

UPO-NETs (13%) were included in the pivotal phase III randomized double-blind, placebo-controlled CLARINET trial, evaluating the efficacy of lanreotide in patients with well-differentiated advanced or metastatic, nonfunctioning, SSTR–positive NETs with Ki-67 < 10%. Progression-free survival was significantly improved in the lanreotide group compared to the placebo arm (median PFS not reached [NR] vs. 18.0 months, respectively;

hazard ratio [HR] 0.47; 95% CI, 0.30–0.73; $p < 0.001$). Overall survival did not significantly differ between the two arms, although the results' interpretation may have been impacted by crossover from the placebo to the lanreotide group that occurred in the extension study (CLARINET OLE) and by the long life expectancy of patients with indolent disease [76,77].

Faiss and Colleagues conducted a prospective randomized trial assessing the efficacy of subcutaneous lanreotide (at the dose of 1 mg three times a day), interferon alpha, or their combination in 80 patients with advanced progressive treatment-naïve NETs, including 11 (14%) UPO-NETs, showing a 32% DCR in the lanreotide group [78].

More recently, a phase II study in Japanese patients investigated lanreotide autogel in 28 patients with well-differentiated G1–2 NETs including 5 patients (18%) with UPO-NETs, reporting DCR of 64.3%, ORR of 3.6%, and median PFS of 36.3 weeks (95% CI: 24.1–53.1) [79].

PRRT is a valuable therapeutic option for NETs expressing SSTRs, with a good safety profile and limited acute and medium-term toxicities. PRRT employs radiolabeled, beta-emitting SSAs (^{90}Yttrium[Y]-DOTATOC and ^{177}Lutetium-[DOTA°, Tyr3] octreotate [^{177}Lu-Dotatate]) that bind to SSTRs on the surface of tumor cells, with consequent radiopeptide internalization and cell death [80]. The landmark NETTER-1 phase III trial demonstrated the superiority of PRRT with ^{177}Lu-Dotatate (in association with octreotide long-acting release [LAR] 30 mg every 28 days) versus high-dose octreotide LAR (60 mg every 28 days) in SSTR-positive midgut NET patients progressing on octreotide treatment, with a significant improvement in terms of PFS and ORR, and a clinically meaningful (~11 months) trend to improved OS in the PRRT arm [81,82]. Even though the phase III NETTER-1 trial only enrolled patients with well-differentiated midgut NETs, the activity of PRRT in other GEP NETs and UPO-NETs has been explored in several retrospective studies. In a meta-analysis of 18 studies considering 1920 patients with unresectable metastatic NETs treated with ^{177}Lu-Dotatate, PRRT exhibited a pooled disease response rate of ~30% and a combined DCR of 74–81% [83]. Another systematic review, including one publication addressing eight patients with UPO-NEN, reported ORR of 38% and DCR of 88%, with median PFS of 17.5 months (95% CI 7–34) and median OS of 43 months (95% CI 15 months–NR) [84]. Moreover, data from non-randomized trials of PRRT have consistently shown high response rates and long-term PFS outcomes in heterogeneous patient populations, including UPO-NETs [85–87]. PRRT may be the treatment of choice for patients with high STTR expression and/or high tumor burden, in whom tumor shrinkage and symptomatic response, rather than tumor stabilization, represent the therapeutic goal. Moreover, PRRT may also be considered in selected cases in the setting of NEN G3. Data deriving from retrospective studies of PRRT in patients with G3 NEN (including UPO-NEN) highlight disease control rates of 30–80%, median PFS ranging from 9 to 23 months, and median OS ranging from 19 to 53 months. However, reported outcomes were unsatisfactory in patients with Ki-67 > 55% [88–91].

Targeted therapies with demonstrated efficacy in NEN treatment encompass the mammalian target of rapamycin (mTOR) inhibitor everolimus and TKIs. Few data are currently available about the use of targeted therapies in UPO-NENs.

Yao and Colleagues evaluated the activity of everolimus (at the dose of either 5 mg/day or 10 mg/day) in combination with octreotide LAR in 60 patients with well-differentiated NETs, including 5 patients with UPO-NETs (8%). In the intent to-treat population, ORR was 20% (13% in the 5 mg cohort and 30% in the 10 mg cohort). Median PFS was 60 weeks (95% CI, 54–66 weeks), with a 3-year OS rate of 78% [92]. The Italian Trials in Medical Oncology (ITMO) trial enrolled 50 patients with treatment-naïve NETs (including 14 patients with UPO-NETs) to receive octreotide LAR plus everolimus. ORR was 18%, with a complete response rate of 2%, a partial response rate of 16% (including three patients with UPO-NETs), and a disease stabilization rate of 74%. In all patients experiencing a clinical benefit, disease control lasted more than 6 months. In the 5-year updated analysis of this study, 17 (34%) of patients had received treatment for more than 2 years, with a median time to progression of 33.6 months (95% CI 18.7–41.2) and a median OS of 61.0 months (95% CI 49.8-NR) [93].

A subgroup analysis of the RADIANT-4 trial of everolimus vs. placebo in G1–G2 advanced non-functional NETs, specifically focusing on patients with gastrointestinal carcinoids (175 patients) and UPO-NETs (36 patients), showed a clinically meaningful PFS advantage (13.6 months versus 7.5 months) for everolimus vs. placebo (HR 0.60; 95% CI, 0.24–1.51) in the UPO-NET setting [94].

The SANET-ep trial evaluated the efficacy and safety of surufatinib in patients with well-differentiated advanced extra-pancreatic NETs, including 27 (14%) UPO-NETs, evidencing a PFS advantage of surufatinib over placebo (9.2 vs. 3.8 months, HR 0.33; 95% CI, 0.22–0.49, $p < 0.0001$). A specific subgroup analysis of patients with UPO-NETs or NETs of uncommon tumor origin showed median PFS of 13.9 vs. 7.4 months (HR 0.5, 95% CI 0.24–1.06, p: 0.069) in the surufatinib and placebo groups, respectively [95].

More recently, the double-blinded phase III Alliance A021602-CABINET trial evaluated the efficacy of cabozantinib versus placebo in patients with advanced NETs progressing on prior therapy. In the extra-pancreatic NET cohort including patients with UPO-NETs, despite modest ORR rates (4% vs. 1% for cabozantinib versus placebo), a statistically significant improvement in PFS (8.2 vs. 3.2 months, HR 0.41, 95% CI 0.27–0.62, $p < 0.0001$) was evidenced in the cabozantinib group over the placebo arm [96].

Cytotoxic chemotherapy also remains an option for patients with well-differentiated UPO-NETs and may be the preferred treatment strategy in patients with high disease burden, higher Ki-67, poor ^{68}GaPET, and/or significant FDG-PET uptake, or in patients for whom rapid tumor shrinkage is a desirable goal. In fit patients, polychemotherapy is a preferred option over mono-chemotherapy in terms of activity. Regimens containing alkylating agents (streptozotocin, temozolomide), fluoropyrimidines (5-fluorouracil, capecitabine), oxaliplatin, and irinotecan proved active in NETs.

Chan and colleagues evaluated the activity of temozolomide in association with bevacizumab in 34 patients with carcinoids, including 7 UPO-NETs (21%), and pNETs. ORR was 15% in the whole study population, even though all responses occurred in the pNET cohort and none in the carcinoid group. However, 12 patients in the carcinoid cohort (63%) experienced some degree of tumor shrinkage. Median PFS was 7.3 months (95% CI, 3.9-NR) and median OS was 18.8 months (95% CI, 8.5–36.1) for carcinoid tumors [97]. Chauhan and colleagues reported median PFS of 10.8 and 7 months, respectively, on CAPTEM in G2 and G3 UPO-NETs [98]. A retrospective real-world experience on 170 patients with GEP, lung, and UPO NETs treated with the CAPTEM combination or temozolomide monotherapy showed clinically meaningful ORR (15.4%) and median PFS (16.9 months, 95% CI 6.0–30.4) and OS (35.7 months, 95% CI 16.2–63.0) results among the 16 (9%) patients with UPO-NETs (4 of whom were diagnosed with NET G3) [99]. Although higher response rates have been reported in patients with MGMT deficiency or promoter methylation treated with temozolomide, the use of MGMT status for preselection of patients remains controversial [99–101]. Recently, Walter and colleagues showed increased ORR, PFS, and OS outcomes in patients with methylated compared to unmethylated MGMT NETs (including UPO-NETs) treated with alkylating agents, but not oxaliplatin-based chemotherapy [102].

The NET-01 study randomized 86 patients with advanced GEP and UPO NETs to receive capecitabine and streptozotocin with or without cisplatin. ORR was similar between the two arms (12% vs. 16%), as well as median PFS (10.2 vs. 9.7 months) and OS (26.7 vs. 27.5 months) for the doublet vs. triplet arm, respectively. However, patients enrolled in the triplet group experienced a non-negligible proportion of $G \geq 3$ adverse events (68%), compared to the lower rate of high-grade toxicities of patients receiving capecitabine and streptozotocin (44%) [103].

Another valuable treatment option in the setting of well-differentiated NETs is represented by platinum derivates (oxaliplatin) in combination with fluoropyrimidines, with reported ORRs of ~13–30% and median PFS outcomes of 8–20 months [104–106].

Immunotherapy has yielded poor results in well-differentiated NENs, with only modest signals of activity in thoracic NENs. Translational studies are needed in order to identify subgroup of patients who are more likely to respond to this treatment strategy [66,70,107,108]. Only the anti-PD-1 agent toripalimab yielded promising response rates (ORR 20%) in Asian patients with G2–3 pretreated NEN. The subgroups of PD-L1-positive, tumor mutational burden (TMB)-high, or *ARID1A*-mutated tumors were enriched in responders [109].

Figure 3 depicts the clinical and pathological determinants of therapeutic choices in UPO-NEN.

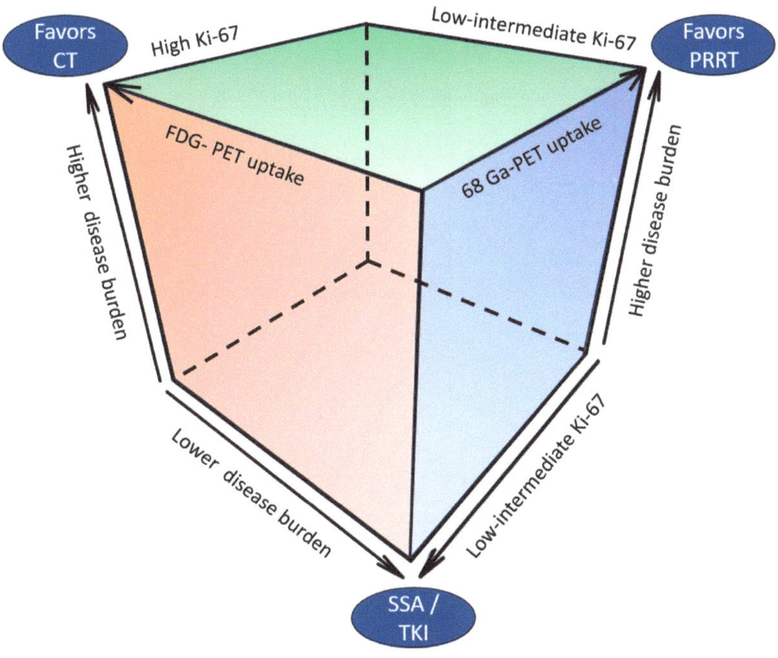

Figure 3. Clinical and pathological determinants of therapeutic choices in UPO-NEN. CT: chemotherapy: FDG: fluorodeoxyglucose; PET: positron emission tomography; PRRT: peptide receptor radioligand therapy; SSA: somatostatin analog; TKI: tyrosine kinase inhibitor.

Whenever possible, due to the exiguity of the therapeutic armamentarium and country-specific restrictions in the use of approved treatment options, patients should be considered for enrollment in clinical trials. Table 1 reports ongoing clinical trials including patients with UPO-NEN.

Table 1. Ongoing clinical trials including UPO-NEN.

Trial Identifier	Phase	Treatments	Setting	Primary Endpoint	Status	Estimated Completion Date
NCT04325425 (FOLFIRINEC)	II	mFOLFIRINOX vs. Platinum–Etoposide	1st line GEP or UPO NEC	PFS	Recruiting	September 2024
NCT03980925 (NICE-NEC)	II	Nivolumab/Carboplatin–Etoposide	1st line G3 GEP or UPO NEN	12 months-OS	Active, not recruiting	December 2023
NCT02820857 (BEVANEC)	II	FOLFIRI/Bevacizumab vs. FOLFIRI	Pretreated GEP or UPO NEC	Proportion of pts alive after 6 months	Active, not recruiting	September 2024

Table 1. *Cont.*

Trial Identifier	Phase	Treatments	Setting	Primary Endpoint	Status	Estimated Completion Date
NCT03736720	II	Liposomal Irinotecan/Fluorouracil/Leucovorin	Pretreated GEP or UPO NEC	ORR	Active, not recruiting	June 2026
NCT04412629	II	Cabozantinib	Pretreated High Grade NENs including UPO	ORR	Recruiting	November 2024
NCT04525638	II	Nivolumab plus ^{177}Lu-Dotatate	Pretreated SSTR positive NET/NEC G3 including UPO	ORR	Recruiting	September 2024
NCT02628067 (Keynote 158)	II	Pembrolizumab	TMB-high /MSI-H solid tumors including NEN	ORR	Recruiting	October 2026
NCT05882058 (DAREON™-5)	II	BI 764532	NECs	ORR, TEAEs	Recruiting	July 2025
NCT02925234 (DRUP)	II	Targeted therapies Basket trial	Solid tumors including NEN	% pts treated based on molecular profile; ORR; $G \geq 3$/serious TRAEs	Recruiting	December 2027
NCT04589845 (TAPISTRY)	II	Targeted therapies or immunotherapies Basket trial	Solid tumors including NEN	ORR	Recruiting	September 2032
NCT02568267 (STARTRK-2)	II	Entrectinib	NTRK 1/2/3, ROS1, or ALK rearranged solid tumors including NEN	ORR	Active, not recruiting	April 2025
NCT03157128 (LIBRETTO-001)	I/II	Selpercatinib	RET Fusion-Positive solid tumors including NEN	MTD, RP2D, ORR	Recruiting	February 2026
NCT03037385 (ARROW)	I/II	Pralsetinib	RET altered solid tumors including NEN	MTD, safety, ORR	Active, not recruiting	December 2023
NCT04427787 (LOLA)	II	Lanreotide/ Cabozantinib	Pretreated/not pretreated GEP, thoracic or UPO-NET	Safety, ORR	Recruiting	November 2023
NCT04544098	Early I	intraarterial/ intravenous ^{177}Lu-DOTATATE	GEP, Bronchial or UPO NET	nr of pts who completed 2 IA injections; ORR	Recruiting	September 2024
NCT05249114	I	Cabozantinib plus ^{177}Lu-Dotatate	SSTR2 positive NET including UPO NET	MTD	Recruiting	December 2027
NCT05554003 (MeTe)	II	Metronomic Temozolomide	NETs including UPO NETs in unfit patients	PFS	Recruiting	December 2024

^{177}Lu-DOTATATE: ^{177}Lutetium-[DOTA°,Tyr3]octreotate; ALK: Anaplastic lymphoma kinase; G: grade; GEP: gastroenteropancreatic; IA: intraarterial; mFOLFIRINOX: modified folinic acid/5-fluorouracil/irinotecan/oxaliplatin; MSI-H: microsatellite instability high; MTD: maximum tolerated dose; NEC: neuroendocrine carcinoma; NEN: neuroendocrine neoplasm; NET: neuroendocrine tumor; nr: number; NTRK: neurotrophic tyrosine receptor kinase; ORR: overall response rate; OS: overall survival; PFS: progression-free survival; pts: patients; RET: Rearranged during Transfection; RP2D: recommended Phase 2 dose; SSTR: somatostatin receptor; TMB: tumor mutational burden; TEAE: treatment emergent adverse event; TRAE: treatment related adverse event; UPO: unknown primary origin; vs.: versus.

4.3. Special Situations: Liver-Limited Disease

Even in the case of UPO-NETs, locoregional treatments may be employed as part of the therapeutic strategy. In particular, liver-directed locoregional therapies, alone or in combination with systemic treatments, may be considered in selected cases to improve local disease control, reduce hepatic tumor burden, and possibly improve patient prognosis [110]. Kim and colleagues conducted a phase 1b dose-finding study of pasireotide, everolimus, and selective internal radioembolization therapy (SIRT) in 13 patients with NET and secondary liver involvement (including 2 patients with UPO-NETs). No dose-limiting toxicities were reported; median PFS was 18.6 months and OS was 46.3 months [111]. Another study of systemic 5-fluorouracil combined with ^{90}Y-SIRT in 34 NEN patients with liver metastases showed radiologic ORR of 50% and mean survival of 27.6 months. Among enrolled patients with UPO-NEN, 3 out of 8 (37.5%) experienced a radiologic response [112].

In patients with liver-limited disease, several potentially curative treatment options may be considered, including liver resections or liver transplant. Few cases of liver transplant in patients with UPO-NET have been reported, with alternate outcomes. More data are needed in order to possibly extend the transplant strategy in the setting of UPO-NEN, provided an accurate selection based on patient features, disease behavior, and characteristics [113,114].

5. Unraveling Molecular Characterization of UPO-NENs: Time for an Agnostic Approach?

Molecular biology and gene expression profiling represent an area of increasing interest for the characterization of UPO-NENs, with both diagnostic and potential therapeutic implications. In recent years, a deeper insight has been achieved in subtype-specific NEN molecular landscape characterization. These findings, if appropriately integrated with clinical and pathological data, may help to determine tumor origin in UPO-NENs and/or identify druggable molecular targets.

With regard to GEP-NENs, a recent comprehensive genomic profiling analysis confirmed the differences in terms of genomic background of high grade versus low grade GEP-NENs. Among low-grade tumors, the most frequently mutated genes are *ATRX* (13%), *ARID1A* (10%), and *MEN1* (10%), whereas high-grade tumors exhibit *TP53* (51%), *KRAS* (30%), *APC* (27%), and *ARID1A* (23%) mutations and a higher prevalence of *BRAF* (5.4–70%) alterations. Moreover, immune-related biomarkers such as the MSI-high status (4–12% vs. 0–3%), PD-L1 overexpression (6% vs. 1%), and high TMB (7% vs. 1%) are prevalent in high-grade compared to low-grade tumors [115,116]. Among NENs of pancreatic primary, loss of DAXX or ATRX protein expression defines well-differentiated NETs, whereas abnormal p53, Rb, and SMAD4 define poorly differentiated NECs [117].

Similarly to GEP-NENs, genomic profiling provides further insight into thoracic NENs biology. Carcinoids generally display low TMB (<1 mutations/megabase [Mb]) and few recurrently mutated genes, including alterations in chromatin remodeling genes and genes in the phosphoinositide 3-kinase (PI3K)/Akt/mTOR pathway. Indeed, mutations in genes involved in chromatin remodeling are detected with a high frequency (~40%) in carcinoids, the most frequent being *MEN1* (11–22%), genes of the SWI/SNF complex mostly affecting *ARID1A* (6–7% of cases) and *KMT2C/MLL3* (8%). Other frequently mutated genes in carcinoids include *TP53* (10%), *NOTCH2* (5%), and *PIK3CA*. Of note, atypical carcinoids usually carry more alterations in the *MEN1* (22% vs. 6%) and *PIK3CA* genes (39% vs. 13%) compared to typical carcinoids. Furthermore, amplification of *MYCL*, *BCL2*, and *SRC* is almost exclusively described in atypical carcinoids [118]. Small cell NECs and LCNECs have higher TMB rates (8.5–10.5 mutations/Mb) compared to carcinoids. The most frequently described LCNEC alterations lie in tumor suppression genes such as *TP53*, *RB1*, and *STK11*, and genes of the RAS pathway. Indeed, two mutually exclusive genomic subtypes have been identified in LCNECs: the first, which is similar to SCLC, shows concurrent mutation of *TP53* and *RB1*, whereas the other subtype, more similar to non-small cell lung cancer, is predominantly *RB1* wild-type, harboring *STK11/KEAP1* alteration [119]. Preliminary data indicate that *RB1* wild-type tumors may have better outcomes when receiving NSCLC-type chemotherapy (platinum–gemcitabine or paclitaxel) than platinum–etoposide SCLC-like chemotherapy [118].

Thus, genomic profiling may provide insights into tumor biological characteristics that segregate with the anatomic primary site and guide therapeutic choices. For example, pulmonary and pancreatic NENs are frequently mutated in chromatin-remodeling genes, whereas midgut NETs exhibit cell cycle and Wnt pathway mutations, such as *CTNNB1*, *MEN1*, or *APC* alterations [29]. Recently, commercially available gene-expression profiling platforms have been implemented with the aim to assist clinicians in the prediction of tumor origin in cases of diagnostic uncertainty [120]. A validated real-time polymerase chain reaction 92-gene cancer ID analysis, able to categorize NENs according to putative primary site and differentiation, was recently shown to yield accuracy in primary site identification of metastatic UPO-NENs, with a likely impact on patient treatment and outcome [120,121]. As previously pointed out, NETs have a lower number of somatic mutations compared to epithelial tumors, while epigenetic modifications due to the mutation or loss of expression of chromatin modifiers are more common. Methylation array data have recently been used in order to create an algorithm for predicting the tissue of origin in UPO-NENs, based on a training set of 97 pNENs and small intestinal NENs [6].

Extensive molecular characterization through commercially available next generation sequencing (NGS) platforms may also lead to the identification of druggable targets for approved "agnostic" treatments. Potentially targetable rare molecular alterations in NENs, including UPO-NENs, encompass *BRAF* and *KRAS* mutations, *RET*, Anaplastic Lymphoma Kinase (*ALK*) and Neurotrophic tyrosine receptor kinase (*NTRK*) rearrangements, Delta-like ligand 3 (DLL-3) expression, and MSI-high or TMB-high status.

BRAF V600E mutations, although rare overall in NENs, are usually enriched in high-grade NENs of GEP origin (being reported in up to 70% of right-colon NECs) and have been associated with promising activity of combined BRAF-MEK inhibition [116]. The Food and Drug Administration (FDA) recently approved combined BRAF/MEK inhibition with dabrafenib and trametinib for the treatment of patients with advanced solid tumors harboring *BRAF* V600E mutations, based on the outcomes of basket trials enrolling patients with 24 tumor types (including 2 patients with MiNEN and 2 patients with colon NEC) [116]. Different case series have reported clinically significant responses in pretreated NEC patients harboring *BRAF* V600E mutations with BRAF/MEK targeted agents, even though no specific information about UPO-NENs has been reported so far to our knowledge [122–124]. Moreover, in a recent report, a LCNEC patient harboring a non-V600E *BRAF* activating mutation (G469R) showed durable disease control (>15 months) with the combination of dabrafenib and trametinib [125].

Since the development of the KRAS G12C inhibitors sotorasib and adagrasib, few case reports have addressed the potential use of these molecules in the setting of NENs harboring *KRAS* G12C mutations. One case, showing some clinical benefit of sotorasib in a patient with *KRAS* G12C mutant atypical lung carcinoid, has been recently reported [126,127]. More data are required to address the impact of KRAS inhibitors in the setting of NENs, and patients whose tumors harbor *KRAS*-actionable mutations should be referred for enrollment in clinical trials.

ALK fusions seem characteristic of thoracic NENs, with a reported incidence of ~0.9–3%, and correlate with high-grade and advanced stages. Few case series have reported significant disease responses of crizotinib and alectinib in lung NECs harboring *ALK* fusion, with a manageable toxicity profile [128–131].

In a large dataset of 2417 NEN patients, the incidence of *NTRK* rearrangements was 0.3% (including 2 patients with UPO-NEN) in the absence of site-specific prevalence [132]. Recently, entrectinib and larotrectinib received agnostic FDA approval for advanced adult or pediatric tumors bearing *NTRK* fusions based on results of the ALKA-372-001, STARTRK-1, and STARTRK-2 trials. ORR for the five patients with NENs enrolled in these trials was 40% [116,133]. Updated results of entrectinib in 121 patients with *NTRK*-rearranged solid tumors showed ORR of 61.2%, median PFS of 13.8 months (95% CI 10.1–19.9), median OS of 33.8 months (95% CI, 23.4–46.4), and intracranial ORR of 63.6% in the whole population. Among the five patients with NEN, ORR was 40%, median PFS was 15.6 months (95% CI 0.9-not estimable), and median OS was 40.5 months (95% CI 28.6–40.5) [134]. In a phase I trial of taletrectinib, a ROS1/NTRK inhibitor, 1 partial response (8.3%) and 7/12 (58%) disease stabilizations were observed among 12 molecularly unselected NEN patients, with median PFS of 10.2 months [135].

RET alterations include mutations (typical of medullary thyroid cancer and MEN2-related tumors) and rearrangements. The NCT03157128 and NCT03037385 studies of solid tumors (including NENs) harboring *RET* alterations are currently evaluating the safety and activity of the selective inhibitors selpercatinib and pralsetinib, respectively. Pralsetinib is a RET kinase inhibitor, including RET fusion proteins. The phase I/II ARROW trial reported the activity of pralsetinib in patients with *RET*-fusion-positive solid tumors, evidencing 67% ORR among the three enrolled patients with NEN [136]. Other case reports described the clinical activity of selpercatinib and cabozantinib in patients with NECs harboring *RET* alterations, underlying the possibility of an agnostic approach with anti-RET drugs in patients with *RET*-positive NEN [137,138].

DLL3, a negative regulator of Notch signaling, is frequently overexpressed in poorly differentiated NECs, but not in well-differentiated NETs [139]. A DLL3-targeted antibody-drug conjugate linked to a pyrrolobenzodiazepine dimer toxin, Rovalpituzumab tesirine, achieved a 17% ORR in 35 DLL3-overexpressing NEN (NEC and NET) patients (including UPO-NEN) in a phase I/II trial. Median PFS was 4.3 (2.7–6.1) months and median OS was 7.4 (5.6–13.1) months. [140] Further data are, however, required to fully elucidate the effectiveness of Rovalpituzumab tesirine in this setting, as this drug failed to demonstrate an OS benefit over placebo in SCLC patients as maintenance after platinum-based therapy [141] and over topotecan in second-line setting in phase III trials, at the cost of significant toxicity [142]. The DLL3-targeting T Cell engager BI 764532 is currently being evaluated in the DAREON™-5 open-label, multicenter phase II dose-selection trial, in patients with relapsed/refractory neuroendocrine carcinomas (NCT05882058).

With regard to immunotherapeutic agents, few data are currently available about prognostic and/or predictive immune-response biomarkers. In recent years, the anti-PD-1 agent pembrolizumab received agnostic FDA approval for pretreated solid tumors bearing the MSI-H phenotype or a high TMB status ($\geq$10 mutations/Mb). The prevalence of the MSI-H phenotype has been reported in up to 12% of NEN cases, being enriched in cases in gastrointestinal NECs and MiNEN [143].

The updated results of cohort K of the phase II Keynote 158 trial considering 351 patients with MSI-high/deficient mismatch repair (dMMR) non-colorectal cancers, including 12 (3.4%) patients with NEN, showed 30.8% ORR, with a median duration of response of 47.5 months, median PFS of 3.5 (95% CI 2.3–4.2) months, and median OS of 20.1 (95% CI 14.1–27.1) months in the entire cohort, with a manageable safety profile. No separate data on the 12 NEN patients have been specifically reported [144]. These results were recently confirmed in the tumor-agnostic cohort of the DRUP trial (NCT02925234), evaluating the activity of the anti-PD-L1 agent durvalumab in heavily pretreated patients with dMMR/MSI-H solid tumors, including one patient with NEN. ORR was 29%, median PFS was 5 months (95% CI 2-NR), and median OS was 26 months (95% CI 9-NR) in the entire cohort [145]. The Keynote-158 (NCT02628067) phase II study and the NCT04272034 phase I study are currently evaluating the activity and safety of the anti-PD-1 agent pembrolizumab and the anti-PDL-1 inhibitor INCB099318, respectively, in patients with MSI-H solid tumors (potentially including NENs).

High TMB has been detected in up to 45.6% of LCNEC, 11.8% of colon NEN, and 5.9% of patients with small intestinal NEN [146]. Agnostic approval of pembrolizumab in this molecular subset was based on the results of a pre-planned retrospective analysis of the Keynote-158 trial in patients with TMB $\geq$ 10 mutations/Mb, showing ORR of 29% among the 102 patients included in the efficacy analysis. Notably, among the five patients with

NEN (primary site not specified), ORR was 40% [116,147]. Table 2 summarized potential agnostic targets for the treatment of UPO-NEN.

Table 2. Novel biomarkers in UPO-NENs and the relative potential therapeutic strategies.

Molecular Target	Targeted Therapies	Level of Evidence	References
BRAF V600E	BRAF-MEK inhibitors	Phase I/II trials Case reports	[122–125]
KRAS	KRAS G12C inhibitors	Case-reports	[126,127]
ALK	ALK inhibitors	Case-series	[128–131]
NTRK	NTRK inhibitors, NTRK/ROS1 inhibitors	Phase II trials	[132–135]
RET	RET kinase inhibitors	Phase I/II trials	[136–138]
DLL3	DLL3-targeted antibody-drug conjugate, DLL3-targeting T-cell engager	Phase I/II trials Phase III trials	[140–142]
H-MSI	ICIs	Phase II trials	[144,145]
TMB	ICIs	Phase II trials	[147]

ALK: Anaplastic Lymphoma Kinase; DLL3, Delta-like protein 3; H-MSI, high microsatellite instability; KRAS: Kirsten rat sarcoma; ICI: immune checkpoint inhibitor; NTRK, Neurotrophic receptor tyrosine kinase; RET, Rearranged during Transfection; TMB, tumor mutational burden.

6. Discussion

In recent decades, the incidence and prevalence of NENs has dramatically risen across all primary sites, stages, and grades, mainly as a result of increased detection rates and advances in systemic therapies. In this scenario, a non-negligible proportion (up to 22% of cases) is represented by sufferers of UPO-NENs, a poor prognostic group with largely unmet clinical needs [7]. UPO NENs present, by definition, with advanced or metastatic disease. No standard therapeutic algorithms are defined, as this population is usually poorly represented in registration randomized phase III trials. Current guidelines suggest that treatment of UPO-NENs should be based on the presumptive site of origin, tumor clinical-pathological characteristics, disease burden, and the patient's conditions and comorbidities, thus requiring a case-by-case therapeutic individualization [21,22].

The differentiation between well- and poorly differentiated UPO-NEN represents one of the main criteria to orient therapeutic choices. This dichotomous morphological classification reflects underlying differences in terms of genomic characteristics and clinical and biological behavior. Chemotherapy still represents the backbone for the treatment of high-grade, poorly differentiated UPO-NECs, an approach that usually provides deep but short-lasting responses with poor survival outcomes. Attempts to improve survival in this particularly poor prognostic group include treatment intensification with three-drug chemotherapeutic regimens [50–52], chemo-immunotherapy combinations [53,63,68], ICIs, or a combination of ICIs and TKIs [63–71,73–75]. ICI monotherapy has provided unsatisfactory results in unselected patients' populations in recent clinical trials [63–67]. Although preliminary, interesting activity data have been recently provided about upfront chemoimmunotherapy [53], the use of anti-CTLA-4 plus anti-PD-L1 agents [69,70], and ICI plus TKI combinations [73]. However, such treatment strategies have not been directly compared with standard platinum-based chemotherapy and their development should entail more accurate patient selection based on predictive molecular biomarkers. Indeed, the differences observed in ICI activity between low- and high-grade NENs may rely on the higher TMB and neoantigen burden, and the higher PD-L1 expression in the latter group. To date, conflicting data are available about the role of PD-L1 expression in predicting response to ICIs in UPO-NEN [64,66,109], and the DART-SWOG and CA209–538 trials did not provide activity data of the ipilimumab/nivolumab combination stratified by PD-L1 expression [69,70]. Conversely, MSI-high and TMB-high status in addition to POLε alterations are more reproducible biomarkers of ICI-related benefits across different tumor types [139,146,147].

In recent years, molecular profiling has provided deep insights into the molecular landscape of UPO-NENs, with both diagnostic and therapeutic implications. Overall, about 20% of high-grade NECs may harbor one druggable molecular alteration (including *BRAF* and *KRAS* mutations, *RET*, *ALK*, and *NTRK* 1/2/3 rearrangements, and MSI-high or TMB-high status), so that comprehensive NGS analysis should be advocated in this poor-prognosis subset to orient agnostic target therapies [116].

Although well differentiated UPO-NETs harbor few somatic druggable alterations, molecular profiling platforms providing primary-site specific genomic profiles have been recently developed, with potential clinical applications in the near future [6,120,121]. The integration of molecular biology with standard pathology and imaging approaches may significantly contribute to primary site identification, potentially leading to surgical approaches with radical intent.

The spectrum of available systemic therapy options for well-differentiated UPO-NETs may range from SSA monotherapy in indolent low-grade NETs, to TKIs, PRRT, or chemotherapy for more aggressive tumors or in the case of a symptomatic disease burden.

Novel TKIs have shown promising activity and efficacy in the setting of well-differentiated UPO-NETs. Cabozantinib and surufatinib are multitargeted small molecules with high-spectrum biological activity against multiple and non-redundant oncogenic pathways responsible for tumor growth and neoangiogenesis, which yielded improved PFS outcomes compared to placebo in phase III trials including UPO-NETs. In the CABINET and SANET-ep trials, the PFS advantage was evidenced despite poor objective response rates, suggesting that TKI monotherapy may represent a valuable therapeutic option whenever tumor stabilization rather than tumor shrinkage is the therapeutic goal [95,96]. In the case of high tumor burden or symptomatic disease, PRRT or chemotherapy represent the treatments of choice, depending on tumor grade and SSTR expression. Chemotherapy, for example, is a valuable choice for G3 NETs or for NETs with low SSTR on functional imaging [85–91,97–106].

Even though immunotherapy showed limited efficacy in well-differentiated NETs, the anti-CTLA-4/anti PD-1 combination or the anti PD-L1 plus TKI combination showed signs of activity in G3 NETs, a subset of tumors with a higher biological aggressiveness and in which multidrug immune modulation may represent a promising therapeutic approach [69,70,73].

Figure 4 depicts a possible future therapeutic algorithm for UPO-NENs, integrating molecular biology profiling, agnostic, and multimodal treatment strategies.

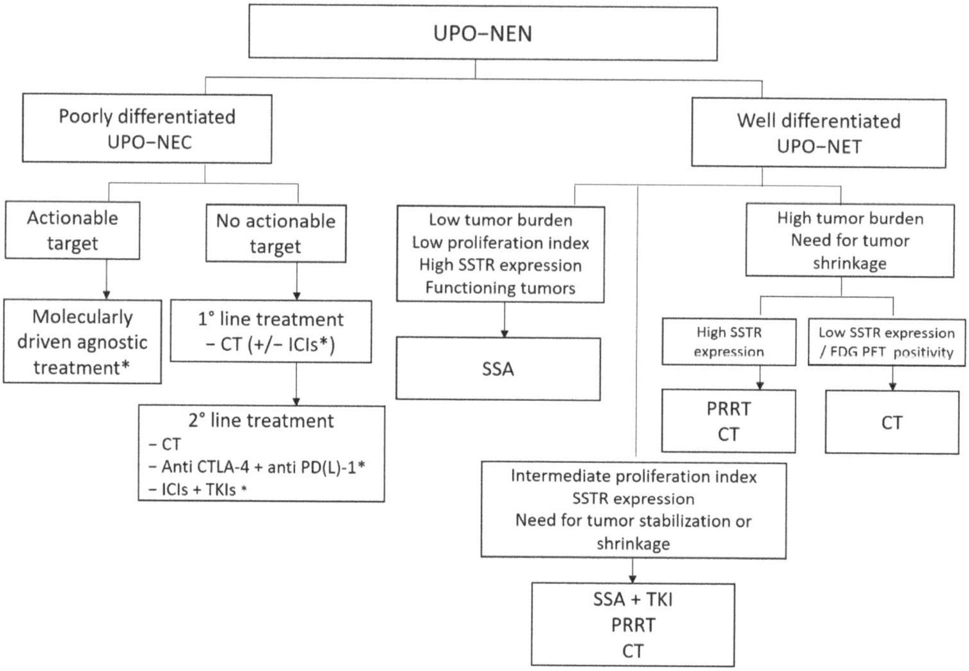

Figure 4. Possible therapeutic algorithm for UPO-NEN. CT: chemotherapy; CTLA-4: anti-Cytotoxic T-Lymphocyte Antigen 4; ICI: immune checkpoint inhibitor; FDG PET: fluorodeoxyglucose positron emission tomography; NEC: neuroendocrine carcinoma; NEN: neuroendocrine neoplasm; NET: neuroendocrine tumor; PD-(L)-1: programmed death (Ligand)-1; PRRT: peptide receptor radioligand therapy; SSA: somatostatin analog; SSTR: somatostatin receptor; TKI: Tyrosine kinase inhibitor; UPO: unknown primary origin. *: under investigation.

7. Conclusions and Future Directions

In conclusion, UPO-NENs represent a rare and heterogeneous disease with limited treatment options. Due to their rarity, we claim the possibility of a change in UPO-NEN management, moving from morphologically driven therapeutic choices, or those presuming the site of origin, to the integration of molecular biology. This opportunity, coupled with agnostic treatments, may pave the way to the definition of personalized therapeutic strategies, particularly when lacking clinical trials specifically drawn for this rare entity. In-development treatment approaches include multidrug combinations (e.g., combinations of ICIs, TKIs, and PRRT) and the implementation of genomic profiling in order to identify druggable molecular alterations, especially in high-grade disease. Improvement in diagnostic and surgical techniques may lead to enhanced locoregional treatments with radical intent. Multidisciplinarity and referral in high-volume centers is of utmost importance to optimize patients' management.

Author Contributions: Conceptualization, F.C., R.E.R. and S.P.; methodology, F.C., R.E.R., P.C., G.P., A.T. and S.P.; validation, F.C., R.E.R., P.C., G.P., A.T., S.P., A.G., R.L. and D.L.C.; formal analysis, F.C., R.E.R., P.C., G.P. and A.T.; investigation, F.C., R.E.R., P.C., G.P., A.T., S.P., J.C., S.O., A.G., R.L. and D.L.C.; resources: not applicable; data curation, F.C., R.E.R., P.C., G.P., A.T. and S.P.; writing—original draft preparation, F.C., R.E.R., P.C., G.P., A.T. and S.P.; writing—review and editing, F.C., R.E.R., P.C., G.P., A.T., S.P., J.C., S.O., A.G., R.L. and D.L.C.; visualization, F.C., R.E.R., P.C., G.P., A.T., S.P., J.C., S.O., A.G., R.L. and D.L.C.; supervision, F.C., R.E.R., S.P., J.C., R.L. and D.L.C.; project administration, F.C., R.E.R., S.P. and D.L.C. All authors have read and agreed to the published version of the manuscript.

Funding: This research received no external funding.

Conflicts of Interest: F.C. received travel grants from Ipsen, Advanced Accelerator Applications, Istituto Gentili, Wave Pharma outside the submitted work; S.P. received honoraria from Novartis, Ipsen, Pfizer, Merck Serono, and Advanced Accelerator Applications (AAA), received grants from Ipsen and Pfizer, and received personal fees from AAA, Novartis, and Merck outside the submitted work; D.L.C. received honoraria as a speaker bureau/scientific advisor from MSD, BMS, Astra Zeneca, Sanofi Genzyme, Seagen, Novartis, Amgen, Roche, and Takeda outside the submitted work. The remaining authors declare no conflicts of interest.

References

1. Rindi, G.; Mete, O.; Uccella, S.; Basturk, O.; La Rosa, S.; Brosens, L.A.A.; Ezzat, S.; de Herder, W.W.; Klimstra, D.S.; Papotti, M.; et al. Overview of the 2022 WHO Classification of Neuroendocrine Neoplasms. *Endocr. Pathol.* **2022**, *33*, 115–154. [CrossRef] [PubMed]
2. Taal, B.; Visser, O. Epidemiology of neuroendocrine tumours. *Neuroendocrinology* **2004**, *80* (Suppl. S1), 3–7. [CrossRef] [PubMed]
3. Polish, A.; Vergo, M.T.; Agulnik, M. Management of neuroendocrine tumors of unknown origin. *J. Natl. Compr. Cancer Netw.* **2011**, *9*, 1397–1402. [CrossRef] [PubMed]
4. Perren, A.; Couvelard, A.; Scoazec, J.-Y.; Costa, F.; Borbath, I.; Fave, G.D.; Gorbounova, V.; Gross, D.; Grossman, A.; Jensen, R.T.; et al. ENETS consensus guidelines for the standards of care in neuroendocrine tumors: Pathology-diagnosis and prognostic stratification. *Neuroendocrinology* **2017**, *105*, 196–200. [CrossRef]
5. Fernandez, C.J.; Agarwal, M.; Pottakkat, B.; Haroon, N.N.; George, A.S.; Pappachan, J.M. Gastroenteropancreatic neuroendocrine neoplasms: A clinical snapshot. *World J. Gastrointest. Surg.* **2021**, *13*, 231–255. [CrossRef] [PubMed]
6. Berner, A.M.; Pipinikas, C.; Ryan, A.; Dibra, H.; Moghul, I.; Webster, A.; Luong, T.V.; Thirlwell, C. Diagnostic Approaches to Neuroendocrine Neoplasms of Unknown Primary Site. *Neuroendocrinology* **2020**, *110*, 563–573. [CrossRef]
7. Dasari, A.; Shen, C.; Halperin, D.; Zhao, B.; Zhou, S.; Xu, Y.; Shih, T.; Yao, J.C. Trends in the Incidence, Prevalence, and Survival Outcomes in Patients with Neuroendocrine Tumors in the United States. *JAMA Oncol.* **2017**, *3*, 1335–1342. [CrossRef] [PubMed]
8. Garcia-Carbonero, R.; Capdevila, J.; Crespo-Herrero, G.; Díaz-Pérez, J.A.; del Prado, M.P.M.; Orduña, V.A.; Sevilla-García, I.; Villabona-Artero, C.; Beguiristain-Gómez, A.; Llanos-Muñoz, M.; et al. Incidence, patterns of care and prognostic factors for outcome of gastroenteropancreatic neuroendocrine tumors (GEP-NETs): Results from the National Cancer Registry of Spain (RGETNE). *Ann. Oncol.* **2010**, *21*, 1794–1803. [CrossRef]
9. Bhosale, P.; Shah, A.; Wei, W.; Varadhachary, G.; Johnson, V.; Shah, V.; Kundra, V. Carcinoid tumours: Predicting the location of the primary neoplasm based on the sites of metastases. *Eur. Radiol.* **2013**, *23*, 400–407. [CrossRef]
10. Kurl, S.; Rytkönen, H.; Farin, P.; Ala-Opas, M.; Soimakallio, S. A primary carcinoid tumor of the kidney: A case report and review of the literature. *Abdom. Imaging* **1996**, *21*, 464–467. [CrossRef]
11. Stroosma, O.B.; Delaere, K.P. Carcinoid tumours of the testis. *BJU Int.* **2008**, *101*, 1101–1105. [CrossRef] [PubMed]
12. Radfar, L.; Fatahzadeh, M. Neuroendocrine carcinoma of the oral cavity: A case report and review of the literature. *Gen. Dent.* **2008**, *56*, 714–718. [PubMed]
13. Widmeier, E.; Fuellgraf, H.; Waller, C.F. Complete remission of Cdx-2 positive primary testicular carcinoid tumor: 10-years follow-up and literature review. *BMC Urol.* **2020**, *20*, 197. [CrossRef] [PubMed]
14. Okasho, K.; Ogawa, O.; Akamatsu, S. Narrative review of challenges in the management of advanced neuroendocrine prostate cancer. *Transl. Androl. Urol.* **2021**, *10*, 3953–3962. [CrossRef] [PubMed]
15. Jagiella-Lodise, O.; Jagiella, V.; Weitman, E. An abdominal wall neuroendocrine tumor of unknown primary origin: A case report and review of the literature. *Cancer Rep.* **2022**, *5*, e1610. [CrossRef] [PubMed]
16. Agarwal, S.; van Zante, A.; Granados, M.L. Combined Neuroendocrine and Squamous Cell Carcinoma of the Sinonasal Tract: A Morphologic and Immunohistochemical Analysis and Review of Literature. *Head Neck Pathol.* **2022**, *16*, 1019–1033. [CrossRef] [PubMed]
17. Sun, H.; Dai, S.; Xu, J.; Liu, L.; Yu, J.; Sun, T. Primary Neuroendocrine Tumor of the Breast: Current Understanding and Future Perspectives. *Front. Oncol.* **2022**, *12*, 848485. [CrossRef] [PubMed]
18. Miquelestorena-Standley, E.; Dujardin, F.; Arbion, F.; Touzé, A.; Machet, L.; Velut, S.; Guyétant, S. Recurrent primary cutaneous mucinous carcinoma with neuroendocrine differentiation: Case report and review of the literature. *J. Cutan. Pathol.* **2014**, *41*, 686–691. [CrossRef] [PubMed]
19. Haq, S.; Batra, V.V.; Majumdar, K.; Javed, A.; Agarwal, A.K.; Sakhuja, P. Signet ring cell neuroendocrine tumor liver with mesenteric metastasis: Description of a rare phenomenon, with literature review. *J. Cancer Res. Ther.* **2015**, *11*, 658. [CrossRef]
20. La Salvia, A.; Persano, I.; Trevisi, E.; Parlagreco, E.; Muratori, L.; Scagliotti, G.V.; Brizzi, M.P. Ocular metastases from neuroendocrine tumors: A literature review. *Semin. Oncol.* **2020**, *47*, 144–147. [CrossRef]
21. Pavel, M.; O'Toole, D.; Costa, F.; Capdevila, J.; Gross, D.; Kianmanesh, R.; Krenning, E.; Knigge, U.; Salazar, R.; Pape, U.-F.; et al. ENETS Consensus Guidelines Update for the Management of Distant Metastatic Disease of Intestinal, Pancreatic, Bronchial Neuroendocrine Neoplasms (NEN) and NEN of Unknown Primary Site. *Neuroendocrinology* **2016**, *103*, 172–185. [CrossRef] [PubMed]

22. Pavel, M.; de Herder, W.W. ENETS Consensus Guidelines for the Standard of Care in Neuroendocrine Tumors. *Neuroendocrinology* **2017**, *105*, 193–195. [CrossRef] [PubMed]
23. Ahmed, A.; Turner, G.; King, B.; Jones, L.; Culliford, D.; McCance, D.; Ardill, J.; Johnston, B.T.; Poston, G.; Rees, M.; et al. Midgut neu-roendocrine tumours with liver metastases: Results of the UKINETS study. *Endocr. Relat. Cancer* **2009**, *16*, 885–894. [CrossRef]
24. Citterio, D.; Pusceddu, S.; Facciorusso, A.; Coppa, J.; Milione, M.; Buzzoni, R.; Bongini, M.; Debraud, F.; Mazzaferro, V. Primary tumour resection may improve survival in functional well-differentiated neuroendocrine tumours metastatic to the liver. *Eur. J. Surg. Oncol. (EJSO)* **2016**, *43*, 380–387. [CrossRef] [PubMed]
25. Capurso, G.; Rinzivillo, M.; Bettini, R.; Boninsegna, L.; Fave, G.D.; Falconi, M. Systematic review of resection of primary midgut carcinoid tumour in patients with unresectable liver metastases. *Br. J. Surg.* **2012**, *99*, 1480–1486. [CrossRef] [PubMed]
26. Keutgen, X.M.; Nilubol, N.; Glanville, J.; Sadowski, S.M.; Liewehr, D.J.; Venzon, D.J.; Steinberg, S.M.; Kebebew, E. Resection of primary tumor site is associated with prolonged survival in metastatic nonfunctioning pancreatic neuroendocrine tumors. *Surgery* **2016**, *159*, 311–319. [CrossRef] [PubMed]
27. Rossi, R.E.; Corti, F.; Pusceddu, S.; Milione, M.; Coppa, J.; Masoni, B.; Oldani, S.; Sabella, G.; Cafaro, P.; Repici, A. Multidisciplinary Approach to the Diagnosis of Occult Primary Neuroendocrine Neoplasm: A Clinical Challenge. *J. Clin. Med.* **2023**, *12*, 5537. [CrossRef]
28. Bellizzi, A.M. Immunohistochemistry in the diagnosis and classification of neuroendocrine neoplasms: What can brown do for you? *Hum. Pathol.* **2020**, *96*, 8–33. [CrossRef] [PubMed]
29. Juhlin, C.C.; Zedenius, J.; Höög, A. Metastatic Neuroendocrine Neoplasms of Unknown Primary: Clues from Pathology Workup. *Cancers* **2022**, *14*, 2210. [CrossRef] [PubMed]
30. Savelli, G.; Lucignani, G.; Seregni, E.; Marchian, A.; Serafini, G.; Aliberti, G.; Villano, C.; Maccauro, M.; Bombardieri, E. Feasibility of somatostatin receptor scintigraphy in the detection of occult primary gastro-entero-pancreatic (GEP) neuroendocrine tumours. *Nucl. Med. Commun.* **2004**, *25*, 445–449. [CrossRef]
31. Santhanam, P.; Chandramahanti, S.; Kroiss, A.; Yu, R.; Ruszniewski, P.; Kumar, R.; Taïeb, D. Nuclear imaging of neuroendocrine tumors with unknown primary: Why, when and how? *Eur. J. Nucl. Med. Mol. Imaging* **2015**, *42*, 1144–1155. [CrossRef] [PubMed]
32. Ambrosini, V.; Kunikowska, J.; Baudin, E.; Bodei, L.; Bouvier, C.; Capdevila, J.; Cremonesi, M.; de Herder, W.W.; Dromain, C.; Falconi, M.; et al. Consensus on molecular imaging and theranostics in neuroendocrine neoplasms. *Eur. J. Cancer* **2021**, *146*, 56–73. [CrossRef] [PubMed]
33. Balogova, S.; Talbot, J.-N.; Nataf, V.; Michaud, L.; Huchet, V.; Kerrou, K.; Montravers, F. 18F-Fluorodihydroxyphenylalanine vs other radiopharmaceuticals for imaging neuroendocrine tumours according to their type. *Eur. J. Nucl. Med. Mol. Imaging* **2013**, *40*, 943–966. [CrossRef] [PubMed]
34. Menda, Y.; O'Dorisio, T.M.; Howe, J.R.; Schultz, M.; Dillon, J.S.; Dick, D.; Watkins, G.L.; Ginader, T.; Bushnell, D.L.; Sunderland, J.J.; et al. Localization of Unknown Primary Site with 68Ga-DOTATOC PET/CT in Patients with Metastatic Neuroendocrine Tumor. *J. Nucl. Med.* **2017**, *58*, 1054–1057. [CrossRef] [PubMed]
35. Graham, M.M.; Gu, X.; Ginader, T.; Breheny, P.; Sunderland, J.J. ^{68}Ga-DOTATOC Imaging of Neuroendocrine Tumors: A Systematic Review and Metaanalysis. *J. Nucl. Med.* **2017**, *58*, 1452–1458. [CrossRef]
36. Sanli, Y.; Garg, I.; Kandathil, A.; Zanetti, M.J.B.; Kuyumcu, S.; Subramaniam, R.M. Neuroendocrine Tumor Diagnosis and Man-agement: 68Ga-DOTATATE PET/CT. *AJR Am. J. Roentgenol.* **2018**, *211*, 267–277. [CrossRef]
37. De Dosso, S.; Treglia, G.; Pascale, M.; Tamburello, A.; Santhanam, P.; Kroiss, A.S.; Mestre, R.P.; Saletti, P.; Giovanella, L. Detection rate of unknown primary tumour by using somatostatin receptor PET/CT in patients with metastatic neuroendocrine tumours: A meta-analysis. *Endocrine* **2019**, *64*, 456–468. [CrossRef] [PubMed]
38. Pollard, J.; McNeely, P.; Menda, Y. Nuclear Imaging of Neuroendocrine Tumors. *Surg. Oncol. Clin. N. Am.* **2020**, *29*, 209–221. [CrossRef]
39. Ma, H.; Kan, Y.; Yang, J.-G. Clinical value of ^{68}Ga-DOTA-SSTR PET/CT in the diagnosis and detection of neuroendocrine tumors of unknown primary origin: A systematic review and meta-analysis. *Acta Radiol.* **2021**, *62*, 1217–1228. [CrossRef]
40. Hubalewska-Dydejczyk, A.; Kulig, J.; Szybinski, P.; Mikolajczak, R.; Pach, D.; Sowa-Staszczak, A.; Fröss-Baron, K.; Huszno, B. Radio-guided surgery with the use of [99mTc-EDDA/HYNIC]octreotate in intra-operative detection of neuroendocrine tumours of the gastrointestinal tract. *Eur. J. Nucl. Med. Mol. Imaging* **2007**, *34*, 1545–1555. [CrossRef]
41. Wang, Y.Z.; Chauhan, A.; Rau, J.; Diebold, A.E.; Opoku-Boateng, A.; Ramcharan, T.; Boudreaux, J.P.; Woltering, E.A. Neuroendocrine tumors (NETs) of unknown primary: Is early surgical exploration and aggressive debulking justifiable? *Chin. Clin. Oncol.* **2016**, *5*, 4. [CrossRef] [PubMed]
42. Moertel, C.G.; Kvols, L.K.; O'Connell, M.J.; Rubin, J. Treatment of neuroendocrine carcinomas with combined etoposide and cisplatin. Evidence of major therapeutic activity in the anaplastic variants of these neoplasms. *Cancer* **1991**, *68*, 227–232. [CrossRef] [PubMed]
43. Mitry, E.; Baudin, E.; Ducreux, M.; Sabourin, J.-C.; Rufié, P.; Aparicio, T.; Lasser, P.; Elias, D.; Duvillard, P.; Schlumberger, M.; et al. Treatment of poorly differentiated neuroendocrine tumours with etoposide and cisplatin. *Br. J. Cancer* **1999**, *81*, 1351–1355. [CrossRef] [PubMed]
44. Fjällskog, M.L.; Granberg, D.P.; Welin, S.L.; Eriksson, C.; Oberg, K.E.; Janson, E.T.; Eriksson, B.K. Treatment with cisplatin and etoposide in patients with neuroendocrine tumors. *Cancer* **2001**, *92*, 1101–1107. [CrossRef] [PubMed]

45. Brandi, G.; Paragona, M.; Campana, D. Good performance of platinum-based chemotherapy for high-grade gastroentero-pancreatic and unknown primary neuroendocrine neoplasms. *J. Chemother.* **2018**, *30*, 53–58. [CrossRef] [PubMed]
46. Lobins, R.; Floyd, J. Small cell carcinoma of unknown primary. *Semin. Oncol.* **2007**, *34*, 39–42. [CrossRef]
47. Zhang, P.; Li, J.; Li, J.; Zhang, X.; Zhou, J.; Wang, X.; Peng, Z.; Shen, L.; Lu, M. Etoposide and cisplatin versus irinotecan and cisplatin as the first-line therapy for patients with advanced, poorly differentiated gastroenteropancreatic neuroendocrine carcinoma: A randomized phase 2 study. *Cancer* **2020**, *126* (Suppl. S9), 2086–2092. [CrossRef] [PubMed]
48. Sorbye, H.; Welin, S.; Langer, S.W.; Vestermark, L.W.; Holt, N.; Osterlund, P.; Dueland, S.; Hofsli, E.; Guren, M.G.; Ohrling, K.; et al. Predictive and prognostic factors for treatment and survival in 305 patients with advanced gastrointestinal neuroendocrine carcinoma (WHO G3): The NORDIC NEC study. *Ann. Oncol.* **2012**, *24*, 152–160. [CrossRef] [PubMed]
49. Eads, J.R.; Catalano, P.J.; Fisher, G.A.; Rubin, D.; Iagaru, A.; Klimstra, D.S.; Konda, B.; Kwong, M.S.; Chan, J.A.; De Jesus-Acosta, A.; et al. Randomized phase II study of platinum and etoposide (EP) versus temozolomide and capecitabine (CAPTEM) in patients (pts) with advanced G3 non-small cell gastroenteropancreatic neuroendocrine neoplasms (GEPNENs): ECOG-ACRIN EA2142. *J. Clin. Oncol.* **2022**, *40* (Suppl. S16), 4020. [CrossRef]
50. Hainsworth, J.D.; Erland, J.B.; Kalman, L.A.; Schreeder, M.T.; Greco, F.A. Carcinoma of unknown primary site: Treatment with 1-hour paclitaxel, carboplatin, and extended-schedule etoposide. *J. Clin. Oncol.* **1997**, *15*, 2385–2393. [CrossRef]
51. Hainsworth, J.D.; Spigel, D.R.; Litchy, S.; Greco, F.A. Phase II Trial of Paclitaxel, Carboplatin, and Etoposide in Advanced Poorly Differentiated Neuroendocrine Carcinoma: A Minnie Pearl Cancer Research Network Study. *J. Clin. Oncol.* **2006**, *24*, 3548–3554. [CrossRef] [PubMed]
52. Hadoux, J.; Afchain, P.; Walter, T.; Tougeron, D.; Hautefeuille, V.; Monterymard, C.; Lorgis, V.; Thuillier, F.; Baudin, E.; Scoazec, J.Y.; et al. FOLFIRINEC: A randomized phase II trial of mFOLFIRINOX vs platinum-etoposide for metastatic neuroendocrine carcinoma of gastroenteropancreatic or unknown origin. *Dig. Liver Dis.* **2021**, *53*, 824–829. [CrossRef] [PubMed]
53. Riesco Martinez, M.C.; Capdevila Castillon, J.; Alonso, V.; Jimenez-Fonseca, P.; Teule, A.; Grande, E.; Sevilla, I.; Benavent, M.; Alonso-Gordoa, T.; Custodio, A.; et al. Final overall survival results from the NICE-NEC trial (GETNE-T1913): A phase II study of nivolumab and platinum-doublet chemotherapy (CT) in untreated advanced G3 neuroendocrine neoplasms (NENs) of gastro-enteropancreatic (GEP) or unknown (UK) origin. *Ann. Oncol.* **2022**, *33* (Suppl. S7), S769. [CrossRef]
54. Hentic, O.; Hammel, P.; Couvelard, A.; Rebours, V.; Zappa, M.; Palazzo, M.; Maire, F.; Goujon, G.; Gillet, A.; Lévy, P.; et al. FOLFIRI regimen: An effective second-line chemotherapy after failure of etoposide–platinum combination in patients with neuroendocrine carcinomas grade 3. *Endocr. Relat. Cancer* **2012**, *19*, 751–757. [CrossRef]
55. Welin, S.; Sorbye, H.; Sebjornsen, S.; Knappskog, S.; Busch, C.; Öberg, K. Clinical effect of temozolomide-based chemotherapy in poorly differentiated endocrine carcinoma after progression on first-line chemotherapy. *Cancer* **2011**, *117*, 4617–4622. [CrossRef] [PubMed]
56. Hadoux, J.; Malka, D.; Planchard, D.; Scoazec, J.Y.; Caramella, C.; Guigay, J.; Boige, V.; Leboulleux, S.; Burtin, P.; Berdelou, A.; et al. Post-first-line FOLFOX chemotherapy for grade 3 neuroendocrine carcinoma. *Endocr. Relat. Cancer* **2015**, *22*, 289–298. [CrossRef] [PubMed]
57. Kobayashi, N.; Takeda, Y.; Okubo, N.; Suzuki, A.; Tokuhisa, M.; Hiroshima, Y.; Ichikawa, Y. Phase II study of temozolomide monotherapy in patients with extrapulmonary neuroendocrine carcinoma. *Cancer Sci.* **2021**, *112*, 1936–1942. [CrossRef]
58. Walter, T.; Lievre, A.; Coriat, R.; Malka, D.; Elhajbi, F.; Di Fiore, F.; Hentic, O.; Smith, D.; Hautefeuille, V.; Roquin, G.; et al. Bevacizumab plus FOLFIRI after failure of platinum-etoposide first-line chemotherapy in patients with advanced neuroendocrine carcinoma (PRODIGE 41-BEVANEC): A randomised, multicentre, non-comparative, open-label, phase 2 trial. *Lancet Oncol.* **2023**, *24*, 297–306. [CrossRef]
59. McNamara, M.G.; Swain, J.; Craig, Z.; Sharma, R.; Faluyi, O.; Wadsley, J.; Morgan, C.; Wall, L.R.; Chau, I.; Reed, N.; et al. NET-02: A randomised, non-comparative, phase II trial of nal-IRI/5-FU or docetaxel as second-line therapy in patients with progressive poorly differentiated extra-pulmonary neuroendocrine carcinoma. *eClinicalMedicine* **2023**, *60*, 102015. [CrossRef]
60. Hadoux, J.; Walter, T.; Kanaan, C.; Hescot, S.; Hautefeuille, V.; Perrier, M.; Tauveron, I.; Laboureau, S.; Cao, C.D.; Petorin, C.; et al. Second-line treatment and prognostic factors in neuroendocrine carcinoma: The RBNEC study. *Endocr. Relat. Cancer* **2022**, *29*, 569–580. [CrossRef]
61. Kaufman, H.L.; Russell, J.; Hamid, O.; Bhatia, S.; Terheyden, P.; D'Angelo, S.P.; Shih, K.C.; Lebbé, C.; Linette, G.P.; Milella, M.; et al. Avelumab in Patients with Chemotherapy-Refractory Metastatic Merkel Cell Carcinoma: A Multicentre, Single-Group, Open-Label, Phase 2 Trial. *Lancet Oncol.* **2016**, *17*, 1374–1385. [CrossRef] [PubMed]
62. D'Angelo, S.P.; Russell, J.; Lebbé, C.; Chmielowski, B.; Gambichler, T.; Grob, J.J.; Kiecker, F.; Rabinowits, G.; Terheyden, P.; Zwiener, I.; et al. Efficacy and Safety of First-Line Avelumab Treatment in Patients with Stage IV Metastatic Merkel Cell Carcinoma: A Pre-planned Interim Analysis of a Clinical Trial. *JAMA Oncol.* **2018**, *4*, e180077. [CrossRef] [PubMed]
63. Raj, N.; Chan, J.A.; Wang, S.J.; Aggarwal, R.R.; Calabrese, S.; DeMore, A.; Fong, L.; Grabowsky, J.; Hope, T.A.; Kolli, K.P.; et al. Pembrolizumab alone and pembrolizumab plus chemotherapy in previously treated, extrapulmonary poorly differentiated neuroendocrine carcinomas. *Br. J. Cancer* **2023**, *129*, 291–300. [CrossRef] [PubMed]
64. Vijayvergia, N.; Dasari, A.; Deng, M.; Litwin, S.; Al-Toubah, T.; Alpaugh, R.K.; Dotan, E.; Hall, M.J.; Ross, N.M.; Runyen, M.M.; et al. Pembrolizumab monotherapy in patients with previously treated metastatic high-grade neuroendocrine neoplasms: Joint analysis of two prospective, non-randomised trials. *Br. J. Cancer* **2020**, *122*, 1309–1314. [CrossRef] [PubMed]

65. Fottner, C.; Apostolidis, L.; Ferrata, M.; Krug, S.; Michl, P.; Schad, A.; Roth, W.; Jaeger, D.; Galle, P.R.; Weber, M.M. A phase II, open label, multicenter trial of avelumab in patients with advanced, metastatic high-grade neuroendocrine carcinomas NEC G3 (WHO 2010) progressive after first-line chemotherapy (AVENEC). *J. Clin. Oncol.* **2019**, *37* (Suppl. S15), 4103. [CrossRef]
66. Yao, J.C.; Strosberg, J.; Fazio, N.; Pavel, M.E.; Bergsland, E.; Ruszniewski, P.; Halperin, D.M.; Li, D.; Tafuto, S.; Raj, N.; et al. Spartalizumab in metastatic, well/poorly-differentiated neuroendocrine neoplasms. *Endocr.-Relat. Cancer* **2021**, *28*, 161–172. [CrossRef] [PubMed]
67. Chan, D.L.; Rodriguez-Freixinos, V.; Doherty, M.; Wasson, K.; Iscoe, N.; Raskin, W.; Hallet, J.; Myrehaug, S.; Law, C.; Thawer, A.; et al. Avelumab in unresectable/metastatic, progressive, grade 2-3 neuroendocrine neoplasms (NENs): Combined results from NET-001 and NET-002 trials. *Eur. J. Cancer* **2022**, *169*, 74–81. [CrossRef] [PubMed]
68. Chan, J.A.; Raj, N.P.; Aggarwal, R.R.; Calabrese, S.; DeMore, A.; Dhawan, M.S.; Fattah, D.; Fong, L.; Grabowsky, J.; Hope, T.A.; et al. Phase II study of pembrolizumab-based therapy in previously treated extrapulmonary poorly differentiated neuroendocrine carcinomas: Results of Part B (pembrolizumab + chemotherapy). *J. Clin. Oncol.* **2021**, *39* (Suppl. S15), 4148. [CrossRef]
69. Patel, S.P.; Mayerson, E.; Chae, Y.K.; Strosberg, J.; Wang, J.; Konda, B.; Hayward, J.; McLeod, C.M.; Chen, H.X.; Sharon, E.; et al. A phase II basket trial of Dual Anti-CTLA-4 and Anti-PD-1 Blockade in Rare Tumors (DART) SWOG S1609: High-grade neuroendocrine neoplasm cohort. *Cancer* **2021**, *127*, 3194–3201. [CrossRef]
70. Klein, O.; Kee, D.; Markman, B.; Michael, M.; Underhill, C.; Carlino, M.S.; Jackett, L.; Lum, C.; Scott, C.; Nagrial, A.; et al. Immunotherapy of ipilimumab and nivolumab in patients with advanced neuroendocrine tumours: A subgroup analysis of the CA209–538 clinical trial for rare cancers. *Clin. Cancer Res.* **2020**, *26*, 4454–4459. [CrossRef]
71. Capdevila, J.; Hernando, J.; Teule, A.; Lopez, C.; Garcia-Carbonero, R.; Benavent, M.; Custodio, A.; Garcia-Alvarez, A.; Cubillo, A.; Alonso, V.; et al. Durvalumab plus tremelimumab for the treatment of advanced neuroendocrine neoplasms of gastroentero-pancreatic and lung origin. *Nat. Commun.* **2023**, *14*, 2973. [CrossRef]
72. Pavel, M.E.; Fischer von Weikersthal, L.; Klöppel, G.; Krause, K.; Apostolidis, L. Safety and efficacy of everolimus (EVE) as second–line treatment in neuroendocrine neoplasms G3 (NEN G3)—An AIO phase II study (EVINEC). *Ann. Oncol.* **2023**, *34* (Suppl. S2), S702. [CrossRef]
73. Weber, M.; Apostolidis, L.; Krug, S.; Rinke, A.; Gruen, B.; Michl, P.; Gress, T.; Wagner, D.; Roth, W.; Mettler, E.; et al. Activity and safety of avelumab alone or in combination with cabozantinib in patients with advanced high grade neuroendocrine neoplasias (NEN G3) progressing after chemotherapy. The phase II, open-label, multicenter AVENEC and CABOAVENEC trials. *Ann. Oncol.* **2023**, *34* (Suppl. S2), S702. [CrossRef]
74. Capdevila Castillon, J.; Molina-Cerrillo, J.; Benavent Viñuales, M.; Garcia-Carbonero, R.; Teule, A.; Custodio, A.; Jimenez-Fonseca, P.; Lopez, C.; Hierro, C.; Carmona-Bayonas, A.; et al. Cabozantinib plus Atezolizumab in Advanced and Progressive Neoplasms of the Endocrine System: A multi-cohort Basket Phase II Trial (CABATEN/GETNE-T1914). *Ann. Oncol.* **2023**, *34* (Suppl. S2), S498. [CrossRef]
75. Lu, M.; Wang, Y.; Zhang, P.; Shen, L. Surufatinib combined with sintilimab and IBI310 in the treatment of high-grade advanced-neuroendocrine neoplasm: A single arm, open-label, multicenter study. *Ann. Oncol.* **2022**, *33* (Suppl. S7), S770. [CrossRef]
76. Caplin, M.E.; Pavel, M.; Ćwikła, J.B.; Phan, A.T.; Raderer, M.; Sedláčková, E.; Cadiot, G.; Wolin, E.M.; Capdevila, J.; Wall, L.; et al. Lanreotide in metastatic enteropancreatic neuroendocrine tumors. *N. Engl. J. Med.* **2014**, *371*, 224–233. [CrossRef] [PubMed]
77. Caplin, M.E.; Pavel, M.; Phan, A.T.; Ćwikła, J.B.; Sedláčková, E.; Thanh, X.T.; Wolin, E.M.; Ruszniewski, P.; CLARINET Investigators. Lanreotide autogel/depot in advanced enteropancreatic neuroendocrine tumours: Final results of the CLARINET openlabel ex-tension study. *Endocrine* **2021**, *71*, 502–551. [CrossRef] [PubMed]
78. Faiss, S.; Pape, U.F.; Böhmig, M.; Dörffel, Y.; Mansmann, U.; Golder, W.; Riecken, E.O.; Wiedenmann, B.; International Lanreotide and Interferon Alfa Study Group. Prospective, randomized, multicenter trial on the antiproliferative effect of lanreotide, interferon alfa, and their combination for therapy of metastatic neuroendocrine gastroenteropancreatic tumors—The International Lanreo-tide and Interferon Alfa Study Group. *J. Clin. Oncol.* **2003**, *21*, 2689–2696.
79. Ito, T.; Honma, Y.; Hijioka, S.; Kudo, A.; Fukutomi, A.; Nozaki, A.; Kimura, Y.; Motoi, F.; Isayama, H.; Komoto, I.; et al. Phase II study of lanreotide autogel in Japanese patients with unresectable or metastatic well-differentiated neuroendocrine tumors. *Investig. New Drugs* **2017**, *35*, 499–508. [CrossRef]
80. Kwekkeboom, D.J.; Mueller-Brand, J.; Paganelli, G.; Anthony, L.B.; Pauwels, S.; Kvols, L.K.; O'Dorisio, T.M.; Valkema, R.; Bodei, L.; Chinol, M.; et al. Overview of results of peptide receptor radionuclide therapy with 3 radiolabeled somatostatin analogs. *J. Nucl. Med.* **2005**, *46*, 62S–66S.
81. Strosberg, J.; El-Haddad, G.; Wolin, E.; Hendifar, A.; Yao, J.; Chasen, B.; Mittra, E.; Kunz, P.L.; Kulke, M.H.; Jacene, H.; et al. Phase 3 Trial of ^{177}Lu-Dotatate for Midgut Neuroendocrine Tumors. *N. Engl. J. Med.* **2017**, *376*, 125–135. [CrossRef] [PubMed]
82. Strosberg, J.R.; Caplin, M.E.; Kunz, P.L.; Kunz, P.L.; Ruszniewski, P.B.; Bodei, L.; Hendifar, A.; Mittra, E.; Wolin, E.M.; Yao, J.C.; et al. ^{177}Lu-Dotatate plus long-acting octreotide versus high-dose long-acting octreotide in patients with midgut neuroendocrine tumours (NETTER-1): Final overall survival and long-term safety results from an open-label, randomised, controlled, phase 3 trial. *Lancet Oncol.* **2021**, *22*, 1752–1763. [CrossRef] [PubMed]
83. Saravana-Bawan, B.; Bajwa, A.; Paterson, J.; McEwan, A.J.B.; McMullen, T.P.W. Efficacy of 177Lu Peptide Receptor Radionuclide Therapy for the Treatment of Neuroendocrine Tumors: A Meta-analysis. *Clin. Nucl. Med.* **2019**, *44*, 719–727. [CrossRef] [PubMed]

84. Hertelendi, M.; Belguenani, O.; Cherfi, A.; Folitar, I.; Kollar, G.; Polack, B.D. Efficacy and Safety of [177Lu]Lu-DOTA-TATE in Adults with Inoperable or Metastatic Somatostatin Receptor-Positive Pheochromocytomas/Paragangliomas, Bronchial and Unknown Origin Neuroendocrine Tumors, and Medullary Thyroid Carcinoma: A Systematic Literature Review. *Biomedicines* **2023**, *11*, 1024. [CrossRef] [PubMed]
85. Forrer, F.; Waldherr, C.; Maecke, H.R.; Mueller-Brand, J. Targeted radionuclide therapy with 90Y-DOTATOC in patients with neuroendocrine tumors. *J. Anticancer Res.* **2006**, *26*, 703–707.
86. Seregni, E.; Maccauro, M.; Chiesa, C.; Mariani, L.; Pascali, C.; Mazzaferro, V.; De Braud, F.; Buzzoni, R.; Milione, M.; Lorenzoni, A.; et al. Treatment with tandem [90Y]DOTATATE and [177Lu]DOTA-TATE of neuroendocrine tumours refractory to conventional therapy. *Eur. J. Nucl. Med. Mol. Imaging* **2014**, *41*, 223–230. [CrossRef] [PubMed]
87. Frilling, A.; Weber, F.; Saner, F.; Bockisch, A.; Hofmann, M.; Mueller-Brand, J.; Broelsch, C.E. Treatment with (90)Y- and (177)Lu-DOTATOC in patients with metastatic neuroendocrine tumors. *Surgery* **2006**, *140*, 968–977; Discussion 976–977. [CrossRef] [PubMed]
88. Thang, S.P.; Lung, M.S.; Kong, G.; Hofman, M.S.; Callahan, J.; Michael, M.; Hicks, R.J. Peptide receptor radionuclidetherapy (PRRT) in European Neuroendocrine Tumour Society (ENETS)grade 3 (G3) neuroendocrine neoplasia (NEN)–a single-institution retro-spective analysis. *Eur. J. Nucl. Med. Mol. Imaging* **2018**, *45*, 262–277. [CrossRef]
89. Carlsen, E.A.; Fazio, N.; Granberg, D.; Grozinsky-Glasberg, S.; Ahmadzadehfar, H.; Grana, C.M.; Zandee, W.T.; Cwikla, J.; Walter, M.A.; Oturai, P.S.; et al. Peptide receptor radionuclidetherapy in gastroenteropancreatic NEN G3: A multicenter cohortstudy. *Endocr. Relat. Cancer* **2019**, *26*, 227–239. [CrossRef] [PubMed]
90. Nicolini, S.; Severi, S.; Ianniello, A.; Sansovini, M.; Ambrosetti, A.; Bongiovanni, A.; Scarpi, E.; Di Mauro, F.; Rossi, A.; Matteucci, F.; et al. Investigation of receptor radionuclide therapy with (177)Lu-DOTATATE in patients with GEP-NEN and a high Ki-67 proliferation index. *Eur. J. Nucl. Med. Mol. Imaging* **2018**, *45*, 923–930. [CrossRef]
91. Zhang, J.; Kulkarni, H.R.; Singh, A.; Niepsch, K.; Müller, D.; Baum, R.P. Peptide receptor radionuclide therapy in grade 3 neuro-endocrine neoplasms: Safety and survival analysis in 69 patients. *J. Nucl. Med.* **2019**, *60*, 377–385. [CrossRef] [PubMed]
92. Yao, J.C.; Phan, A.T.; Chang, D.Z.; Wolff, R.A.; Hess, K.; Gupta, S.; Jacobs, C.; Mares, J.E.; Landgraf, A.N.; Rashid, A.; et al. Efficacy of RAD001 (everolimus) and octreotide LAR in advanced low- to intermediate-grade neuroendocrine tumors: Results of a phase II trial. *J. Clin. Oncol.* **2008**, *26*, 4311–4318. [CrossRef] [PubMed]
93. Bajetta, E.; Catena, L.; Pusceddu, S.; Spada, F.; Iannacone, C.; Sarno, I.; Di Menna, G.; Dottorini, L.; Marte, A.M. Everolimus in Combination with Octreotide Long-Acting Repeatable in a First-Line Setting for Patients with Neuroendocrine Tumors: A 5-Year Update. *Neuroendocrinology* **2018**, *106*, 307–311. [CrossRef] [PubMed]
94. Singh, S.; Carnaghi, C.; Buzzoni, R.; Pommier, R.F.; Raderer, M.; Tomasek, J.; Lahner, H.; Valle, J.W.; Voi, M.; Bubuteishvili-Pacaud, L.; et al. Everolimus in Neuroendocrine Tumors of the Gastrointestinal Tract and Unknown Primary. *Neuroendocrinology* **2018**, *106*, 211–220. [CrossRef] [PubMed]
95. Xu, J.; Shen, L.; Zhou, Z.; Li, J.; Bai, C.; Chi, Y.; Li, Z.; Xu, N.; Li, E.; Liu, T.; et al. Surufatinib in advanced extrapancreatic neuroendocrine tumours (SANET-ep): A randomised, double-blind, placebo-controlled, phase 3 study. *Lancet Oncol.* **2020**, *21*, 1500–1512. [CrossRef] [PubMed]
96. Chan, J.A.; Geyer, S.; Ou, F.S.; Knopp, M.; Behr, S.; Zemla, T.; Acoba, J.; Shergill, A.; Wolin, E.M.; Halfdanarson, T.R.; et al. Alliance A021602: Phase III, double-blinded study of cabozantinib versus placebo for advanced neuroendocrine tumors (NET) after progression on prior therapy (CABINET). *Ann. Oncol.* **2023**, *34* (Suppl. S2), S1292. [CrossRef]
97. Chan, J.A.; Stuart, K.; Earle, C.C.; Clark, J.W.; Bhargava, P.; Miksad, R.; Blaszkowsky, L.; Enzinger, P.C.; Meyerhardt, J.A.; Zheng, H.; et al. Prospective study of bevacizumab plus temozolomide in patients with advanced neuroendocrine tumors. *J. Clin. Oncol.* **2012**, *30*, 2963–2968. [CrossRef] [PubMed]
98. Chauhan, A.; Farooqui, Z.; Murray, L.A.; Weiss, H.L.; Myint, Z.W.; Raajasekar, A.K.A.; Evers, B.M.; Arnold, S.; Anthony, L. Capecitabine and Temozolomide in Neuroendocrine Tumor of Unknown Primary. *J. Oncol.* **2018**, *2018*, 3519247. [CrossRef] [PubMed]
99. Spada, F.; Maisonneuve, P.; Fumagalli, C.; Marconcini, R.; Gelsomino, F.; Antonuzzo, L.; Campana, D.; Puliafito, I.; Rossi, G.; Faviana, P.; et al. Temozolomide alone or in combination with capecitabine in patients with advanced neuroendocrine neoplasms: An Italian multicenter real-world analysis. *Endocrine* **2020**, *72*, 268–278. [CrossRef]
100. Cives, M.; Ghayouri, M.; Morse, B.; Brelsford, M.; Black, M.; Rizzo, A.; Meeker, A.; Strosberg, J. Analysis of potential response pre-dictors to capecitabine/temozolomide in metastatic pancreatic neuroendocrine tumors. *Endocr. Relat. Cancer* **2016**, *23*, 759–767. [CrossRef]
101. Kulke, M.H.; Hornick, J.L.; Frauenhoffer, C.; Hooshmand, S.; Ryan, D.P.; Enzinger, P.C.; Meyerhardt, J.A.; Clark, J.W.; Stuart, K.; Fuchs, C.S.; et al. *O* 6-methylguanine DNA methyltransferase deficiency and response to temozolomide-based therapy in patients with neuroendocrine tumors. *Clin. Cancer Res.* **2009**, *15*, 338–345. [CrossRef] [PubMed]
102. Walter, T.; Lecomte, T.; Hadoux, J.; Niccoli, P.; Saban-Roche, L.; Gaye, E.; Guimbaud, R.; Baconnier, M.; Hautefeuille, V.; Cao, C.D.; et al. Alkylating agent-based vs oxaliplatin-based chemotherapy in neuroendocrine tumours according to the O6-methylguanine-DNA methyltransferase (MGMT) status: A randomized phase II study (MGMT-NET) on behalf of the French Group of Endocrine Tumors (GTE) and ENDOCAN-RENATEN network. *Ann. Oncol.* **2023**, *34* (Suppl. S2), S1292–S1293.

103. Meyer, T.; Qian, W.; Caplin, M.E.; Armstrong, G.; Lao-Sirieix, S.-H.; Hardy, R.; Valle, J.W.; Talbot, D.C.; Cunningham, D.; Reed, N.; et al. Capecitabine and streptozocin±cisplatin in advanced gastroenteropancreatic neuroendocrine tumours. *Eur. J. Cancer* **2014**, *50*, 902–911. [CrossRef] [PubMed]
104. Bajetta, E.; Catena, L.; Procopio, G.; De Dosso, S.; Bichisao, E.; Ferrari, L.; Martinetti, A.; Platania, M.; Verzoni, E.; Formisano, B.; et al. Are capecitabine and oxaliplatin (XELOX) suitable treatments for progressing low-grade and high-grade neuroendocrine tumours? *Cancer Chemother. Pharmacol.* **2007**, *59*, 637–642. [CrossRef] [PubMed]
105. Spada, F.; Antonuzzo, L.; Marconcini, R.; Radice, D.; Antonuzzo, A.; Ricci, S.; Di Costanzo, F.; Fontana, A.; Gelsomino, F.; Luppi, G.; et al. Oxaliplatin-Based Chemotherapy in Advanced Neuroendocrine Tumors: Clinical Outcomes and Preliminary Correlation with Biological Factors. *Neuroendocrinology* **2016**, *103*, 806–814. [CrossRef] [PubMed]
106. Ollivier, S.; Fonck, M.; Bécouarn, Y.; Brunet, R. Dacarbazine, fluorouracil, and leucovorin in patients with advanced neuroendocrine tumors: A phase II trial. *Am. J. Clin. Oncol.* **1998**, *21*, 237–240. [CrossRef]
107. Strosberg, J.R.; Mizuno, N.; Doi, T.; Grande, E.; Delord, J.P.; Shapira-Frommer, R.; Bergsland, E.; Shah, M.; Fakih, M.; Takahashi, S.; et al. Efficacy and safety of pembrolizumab in previously treated advanced neuroendocrine tumors: Results from the phase 2 KEYNOTE-158 study. *Clin. Cancer Res.* **2020**, *26*, 2124–2130. [CrossRef] [PubMed]
108. Patel, S.P.; Othus, M.; Chae, Y.K.; Giles, F.J.; Hansel, D.E.; Singh, P.P.; Fontaine, A.; Shah, M.H.; Kasi, A.; Baghdadi, T.A.; et al. A phase II basket trial of dual anti–CTLA-4 and anti–PD-1 blockade in rare tumors (DART SWOG 1609) in patients with non-pancreatic neuroendocrine tumors. *Clin. Cancer Res.* **2020**, *26*, 2290–2296. [CrossRef] [PubMed]
109. Lu, M.; Zhang, P.; Zhang, Y.; Li, Z.; Gong, J.; Li, J.; Li, J.; Li, Y.; Zhang, X.; Lu, Z.; et al. Efficacy, safety, and biomarkers of toripalimab in patients with recurrent or metastatic neuroendocrine neoplasms: A multiple-center phase Ib trial. *Clin. Cancer Res.* **2020**, *26*, 2337–2345. [CrossRef]
110. Cavalcoli, F.; Rausa, E.; Conte, D.; Nicolini, A.F.; Massironi, S. Is there still a role for the hepatic locoregional treatment of metastatic neuroendocrine tumors in the era of systemic targeted therapies? *World J. Gastroenterol.* **2017**, *23*, 2640–2650. [CrossRef]
111. Kim, H.S.; Shaib, W.L.; Zhang, C.; Nagaraju, G.P.; Wu, C.; Alese, O.B.; Chen, Z.; Brutcher, E.; Renfroe, M.; El-Rayes, B.F. Phase 1b study of pasireotide, everolimus, and selective internal radioembolization therapy for unresectable neuroendocrine tumors with hepatic metastases. *Cancer* **2018**, *124*, 1992–2000. [CrossRef] [PubMed]
112. King, J.; Quinn, R.; Glenn, D.M.; Janssen, J.; Tong, D.; Liaw, W.; Morris, D.L. Radioembolization with selective internal radiation microspheres for neuroendocrine liver metastases. *Cancer* **2008**, *113*, 921–929. [CrossRef]
113. Blonski, W.C.; Reddy, K.R.; Shaked, A.; Siegelman, E.; Metz, D.C. Liver transplantation for metastatic neuroendocrine tumor: A case report and review of the literature. *World J. Gastroenterol.* **2005**, *11*, 7676–7683. [CrossRef] [PubMed]
114. Moradi, A.; Lamsehchi, N.; Khaki, S.; Nasiri-Toosi, M.; Jafarian, A. Liver Transplant for Patients with Neuroendocrine Tumor: A Report of 2 Exceptional Cases and Literature Review. *Exp. Clin. Transplant.* **2023**, *21*, 578–585.
115. Puccini, A.; Poorman, K.; Salem, M.E.; Soldato, D.; Seeber, A.; Goldberg, R.M.; Shields, A.F.; Xiu, J.; Battaglin, F.; Berger, M.D.; et al. Comprehensive Genomic Profiling of Gastroenteropancreatic Neuroendocrine Neoplasms (GEP-NENs). *Clin. Cancer Res.* **2020**, *26*, 5943–5951. [CrossRef]
116. Garcia-Carbonero, R.; Anton-Pascual, B.; Modrego, A.; Del Carmen Riesco-Martinez, M.; Lens-Pardo, A.; Carretero-Puche, C.; Ru-bio-Cuesta, B.; Soldevilla, B. Advances in the Treatment of Gastroenteropancreatic Neuroendocrine Carcinomas: Are we Moving Forward? *Endocr. Rev.* **2023**, *44*, 724–736. [CrossRef] [PubMed]
117. Tang, L.H.; Basturk, O.; Sue, J.J.B.; Klimstra, D.S. A Practical Approach to the Classification of WHO Grade 3 (G3) Well-differentiated Neuroendocrine Tumor (WD-NET) and Poorly Differentiated Neuroendocrine Carcinoma (PD-NEC) of the Pancreas. *Am. J. Surg. Pathol.* **2016**, *40*, 1192–1202. [CrossRef]
118. Derks, J.L.; Leblay, N.; Lantuejoul, S.; Dingemans, A.C.; Speel, E.M.; Fernandez-Cuesta, L. New Insights into the Molecular Characteristics of Pulmonary Carcinoids and Large Cell Neuroendocrine Carcinomas, and the Impact on Their Clinical Management. *J. Thorac. Oncol.* **2018**, *13*, 752–766. [CrossRef] [PubMed]
119. Pusceddu, S.; Corti, F.; Milione, M.; Centonze, G.; Prinzi, N.; Torchio, M.; de Braud, F. Are Cyclin-Dependent Kinase 4/6 Inhibitors Without Future in Neuroendocrine Tumors? *Oncologist* **2020**, *25*, e1257–e1258. [CrossRef]
120. Hendifar, A.E.; Ramirez, R.A.; Anthony, L.B.; Liu, E. Current Practices and Novel Techniques in the Diagnosis and Management of Neuroendocrine Tumors of Unknown Primary. *Pancreas* **2019**, *48*, 1111–1118. [CrossRef]
121. Saller, J.J.; Haider, M.; Al-Diffalha, S.; Coppola, D. Benefit of Gene Expression Profiling in Gastrointestinal Neuroendocrine Tumors of Unknown Primary Origin. *Anticancer Res.* **2022**, *42*, 1381–1396. [CrossRef] [PubMed]
122. Klempner, S.J.; Gershenhorn, B.; Tran, P.; Lee, T.K.; Erlander, M.G.; Gowen, K.; Schrock, A.B.; Morosini, D.; Ross, J.S.; Miller, V.A.; et al. BRAFV600E Mutations in High-Grade Colorectal Neuroendocrine Tumors May Predict Responsiveness to BRAF-MEK Combination Therapy. *Cancer Discov.* **2016**, *6*, 594–600. [CrossRef] [PubMed]
123. Burkart, J.; Owen, D.; Shah, M.H.; Abdel-Misih, S.R.Z.; Roychowdhury, S.; Wesolowski, R.; Haraldsdottir, S.; Reeser, J.W.; Samorodnitsky, E.; Smith, A.; et al. Targeting BRAF Mutations in High-Grade Neuroendocrine Carcinoma of the Colon. *J. Natl. Compr. Cancer Netw.* **2018**, *16*, 1035–1040. [CrossRef] [PubMed]
124. Ricco, G.; Seminerio, R.; Andrini, E.; Malvi, D.; Gruppioni, E.; Altimari, A.; Zagnoni, S.; Campana, D.; Lamberti, G. BRAF V600E-mutated large cell neuroendocrine carcinoma responding to targeted therapy: A case report and review of the literature. *Anti-Cancer Drugs* **2023**, *34*, 1076–1084. [CrossRef] [PubMed]

125. Chae, Y.K.; Tamragouri, K.B.; Chung, J.; Lin, X.; Miller, V.; Ali, S.M.; Giles, F.J. Large-Cell Neuroendocrine Carcinoma of the Lung: A Focused Analysis of *BRAF* Alterations and Case Report of a *BRAF* Non-V600–Mutated Tumor Responding to Targeted Therapy. *JCO Precis. Oncol.* **2018**, *2*, 1–12. [CrossRef] [PubMed]
126. Balbach, M.L.; Eisenberg, R.; Iams, W.T. De Novo KRAS G12C-Mutant SCLC: A Case Report. *JTO Clin. Res. Rep.* **2022**, *3*, 100306. [CrossRef] [PubMed]
127. Saiki, M.; Omori, C.; Morikawa, H.; Shinohara, K.; Shimamura, S.; Ohkoshi, H.; Uchida, Y.; Inoue, T.; Kondo, T.; Ikemura, S.; et al. The First Case Report of Effective Treatment with Sotorasib for Metastatic Atypical Lung Carcinoid Harboring KRAS G12C Mutation and Aggressive Disseminated Lung Metastasis: A Case Report. *JTO Clin. Res. Rep.* **2023**, *5*, 100620. [CrossRef] [PubMed]
128. Zheng, Q.; Zheng, M.; Jin, Y.; Shen, X.; Shan, L.; Shen, L.; Sun, Y.; Chen, H.; Li, Y. ALK-Rearrangement Neuroendocrine Carcinoma of the Lung: A Comprehensive Study of a Rare Case Series and Review of Literature. *OncoTargets Ther.* **2018**, *11*, 4991–4998. [CrossRef] [PubMed]
129. Hayashi, N.; Fujita, A.; Saikai, T.; Takabatake, H.; Sotoshiro, M.; Sekine, K.; Kawana, A. Large Cell Neuroendocrine Carcinoma Harboring an Anaplastic Lymphoma Kinase (ALK) Rearrangement with Response to Alectinib. *Intern. Med.* **2018**, *57*, 713–716. [CrossRef]
130. Shimizu, N.; Akashi, Y.; Fujii, T.; Shiono, H.; Yane, K.; Kitahara, T.; Ohta, Y.; Kakudo, K.; Wakasa, T. Use of ALK Immunohistochemistry for Optimal Therapeutic Strategy of Pulmonary Large-Cell Neuroendocrine Carcinoma and Identification of a Novel *KIF5B–ALK* Fusion Oncokinase. *Anticancer Res.* **2019**, *39*, 413–420. [CrossRef]
131. Nakajima, M.; Uchiyama, N.; Shigemasa, R.; Matsumura, T.; Matsuoka, R.; Nomura, A. Atypical Carcinoid Tumor with Anaplastic Lymphoma Kinase (ALK) Rearrangement Successfully Treated by an ALK Inhibitor. *Intern. Med.* **2016**, *55*, 3151–3153. [CrossRef] [PubMed]
132. Sigal, D.S.; Bhangoo, M.S.; Hermel, J.A.; Pavlick, D.C.; Frampton, G.; Miller, V.A.; Ross, J.S.; Ali, S.M. Comprehensive Genomic Profiling Identifies Novel NTRK Fusions in Neuroendocrine Tumors. *Oncotarget* **2018**, *9*, 35809–35812. [CrossRef] [PubMed]
133. Bazhenova, L.; Liu, S.; Lin, J.; Lu, S.; Drilon, A.; Chawla, S.; Fakih, M.; Krzakowski, M.; Paz-Ares, L.; Blakely, C.; et al. Efficacy and safety of entrectinib in patients with locally advanced/metastatic NTRK fusion-positive (NTRK-FP) solid tumours. *Ann. Oncol.* **2021**, *32* (Suppl. S5), S598–S599. [CrossRef]
134. Demetri, G.D.; De Braud, F.; Drilon, A.; Siena, S.; Patel, M.R.; Cho, B.C.; Liu, S.; Ahn, M.-J.; Chiu, C.-H.; Lin, J.J.; et al. Updated Integrated Analysis of the Efficacy and Safety of Entrectinib in Patients With NTRK Fusion-Positive Solid Tumors. *Clin. Cancer Res.* **2022**, *28*, 1302–1312. [CrossRef] [PubMed]
135. Papadopoulos, K.P.; Borazanci, E.; Shaw, A.T.; Katayama, R.; Shimizu, Y.; Zhu, V.W.; Sun, T.Y.; Wakelee, H.A.; Madison, R.; Schrock, A.B.; et al. Phase I First-In-Human Study of Taletrectinib (DS-6051b/AB-106), a ROS1/TRK Inhibitor, in Patients With Advanced Solid Tumors. *Clin. Cancer Res.* **2020**, *26*, 4785–4794. [CrossRef] [PubMed]
136. Subbiah, V.; Cassier, P.A.; Siena, S.; Garralda, E.; Paz-Ares, L.; Garrido, P.; Nadal, E.; Vuky, J.; Lopes, G.; Kalemkerian, G.P.; et al. Pan-cancer efficacy of pralsetinib in patients with RET fusion-positive solid tumors from the phase 1/2 ARROW trial. *Nat. Med.* **2022**, *28*, 1640–1645. [CrossRef] [PubMed]
137. Geiger, J.L.; Chiosea, S.I.; Challinor, S.M.; Nikiforova, M.N.; Bauman, J.E. Primary RET-mutated lung neuroendocrine carcinoma in MEN2B: Response to RET-targeted therapy. *Endocr. Relat. Cancer* **2015**, *22*, L19–L22. [CrossRef] [PubMed]
138. Arora, A.; Zaemes, J.; Ozdemirli, M.; Kim, C. Response to selpercatinib in a patient with RET fusion-positive pulmonary large-cell neuroendocrine carcinoma: A case report. *Front. Oncol.* **2023**, *13*, 1134151. [CrossRef] [PubMed]
139. Prisciandaro, M.; Antista, M.; Raimondi, A.; Corti, F.; Morano, F.; Centonze, G.; Sabella, G.; Mangogna, A.; Randon, G.; Pagani, F.; et al. Biomarker Landscape in Neuroendocrine Tumors with High-Grade Features: Current Knowledge and Future Perspective. *Front. Oncol.* **2022**, *12*, 780716. [CrossRef]
140. Mansfield, A.S.; Hong, D.S.; Hann, C.L.; Farago, A.F.; Beltran, H.; Waqar, S.N.; Hendifar, A.E.; Anthony, L.B.; Taylor, M.H.; Bryce, A.H.; et al. A phase I/II study of rovalpituzumab tesirine in delta-like 3—Expressing advanced solid tumors. *npj Precis. Oncol.* **2021**, *5*, 74. [CrossRef]
141. Johnson, M.L.; Zvirbule, Z.; Laktionov, K.; Helland, A.; Cho, B.C.; Gutierrez, V.; Colinet, B.; Lena, H.; Wolf, M.; Gottfried, M.; et al. Rovalpituzumab tesirine as a maintenance therapy after first-line platinum-based chemotherapy in patients with exten-sive-stage-SCLC: Results from the phase 3 MERU study. *J. Thorac. Oncol. Off. Publ. Int. Assoc. Study Lung Cancer* **2021**, *16*, 1570–1581.
142. Blackhall, F.; Jao, K.; Greillier, L.; Cho, B.C.; Penkov, K.; Reguart, N.; Majem, M.; Nackaerts, K.; Syrigos, K.; Hansen, K.; et al. Efficacy and safety of rovalpituzumab tesirine compared with topotecan as second-line therapy in DLL3-high SCLC: Results from the phase 3 TAHOE study. *J. Thorac. Oncol.* **2021**, *16*, 1547–1558. [CrossRef] [PubMed]
143. Sahnane, N.; Furlan, D.; Monti, M.; Romualdi, C.; Vanoli, A.; Vicari, E.; Solcia, E.; Capella, C.; Sessa, F.; La Rosa, S. Microsatellite Unstable Gastrointestinal Neuroendocrine Carcinomas: A New Clinicopathologic Entity. *Endocr.-Relat. Cancer* **2014**, *22*, 35–45. [CrossRef] [PubMed]
144. Maio, M.; Ascierto, P.A.; Manzyuk, L.; Motola-Kuba, D.; Penel, N.; Cassier, P.A.; Bariani, G.M.; Acosta, A.D.J.; Doi, T.; Longo, F.; et al. Pembrolizumab in microsatellite instability high or mismatch repair deficient cancers: Updated analysis from the phase II KEYNOTE-158 study. *Ann. Oncol.* **2022**, *33*, 929–938. [CrossRef] [PubMed]

145. Geurts, B.; Battaglia, T.; Henegouwen, J.v.B.; Zeverijn, L.; Hoes, L.; van der Wijngaart, H.; de Wit, G.; Roepman, P.; Jansen, A.; de Leng, W.; et al. Durvalumab in advanced, pre-treated microsatellite instability-high solid tumors: Results of a tumor-agnostic DRUP trial cohort. *Ann. Oncol.* **2022**, *33* (Suppl. S7), S594. [CrossRef]
146. Shao, C.; Li, G.; Huang, L.; Pruitt, S.; Castellanos, E.; Frampton, G.; Carson, K.R.; Snow, T.; Singal, G.; Fabrizio, D.; et al. Prevalence of High Tumor Mutational Burden and Association with Survival in Patients With Less Common Solid Tumors. *JAMA Netw. Open* **2020**, *3*, e2025109. [CrossRef]
147. Marabelle, A.; Fakih, M.; Lopez, J.; Shah, M.; Shapira-Frommer, R.; Nakagawa, K.; Chung, H.C.; Kindler, H.L.; Lopez-Martin, J.A.; Miller, W.H., Jr.; et al. Association of Tumour Mutational Burden with Outcomes in Patients with Advanced Solid Tumours Treated with Pembrolizumab: Prospective Biomarker Analysis of the Multicohort, Open-Label, Phase 2 KEYNOTE-158 Study. *Lancet Oncol.* **2020**, *21*, 1353–1365. [CrossRef]

Disclaimer/Publisher's Note: The statements, opinions and data contained in all publications are solely those of the individual author(s) and contributor(s) and not of MDPI and/or the editor(s). MDPI and/or the editor(s) disclaim responsibility for any injury to people or property resulting from any ideas, methods, instructions or products referred to in the content.

biomedicines

MDPI

Article

Randomized Phase II Cancer Clinical Trials to Validate Predictive Biomarkers

Baoshan Zhang [1], Jong-Mu Sun [2], Myung-Ju Ahn [2] and Sin-Ho Jung [1,*]

1 Department of Biostatistics and Bioinformatics, Duke University, Durham, NC 27705, USA
2 Division of Hematology-Oncology, Department of Medicine, Samsung Medical Center, Sungkyunkwan University School of Medicine, Gangnam-gu, Seoul 135-710, Republic of Korea; jongmu.sun@samsung.com (J.-M.S.)
* Correspondence: sinho.jung@duke.edu

Abstract: Objectives: The design of cancer clinical trials incorporating biomarkers depends on various factors, including the trial phase, the type of biomarker and whether its role has been validated. This article aims to present a method for designing and analyzing phase II cancer clinical trials that validate predictive biomarkers. Methods: We propose a randomized trial design where patients are allocated between a targeted therapy and a non-targeted therapy stratified by biomarker status. Tumor response is used as the primary endpoint to validate the biomarker through interaction testing between treatment and biomarker positivity. Additionally we propose a sample size calculation method for this design, considering two types of interaction: one based on logit-transformed response rates and the other on raw response rates. Results: The proposed sample size method is applied to the design of a real randomized phase II trial. Extensive simulations are conducted to evaluate the performance of the test statistic and the sample size method under different scenarios. Conclusions: Our method provides a practical approach to validating predictive biomarkers in phase II cancer trials. The simulations demonstrate robust performance for both interaction models, offering guidance for the sample size selection and analysis strategy in biomarker-stratified trials.

Keywords: interaction; logistic regression; sample size calculation; stratified randomization trial

1. Introduction

Cancer clinical trials often integrate a range of biomarkers that are derived from various sources including tumor tissues, blood, or urine samples. Depending on the sources, biomarkers are assessed using different methods, such as molecular, biochemical, physiological, anatomical, and imaging techniques, either at the onset of a trial or during its course. The utility of these biomarkers is multifaceted in the context of cancer diagnosis and treatment. Diagnostic biomarkers are used to diagnose cancers. For instance, carcinoembryonic antigen (CEA) is considered a diagnostic biomarker of colon cancer and rectal cancer [1]. Prognostic biomarkers are used to measure the aggressiveness of disease for patients with no or non-targeted treatment. BRAF mutation is known to be a diagnostic and prognostic biomarker for melanoma [2,3]. A predictive biomarker forecasts how well a patient might respond to a particular treatment. While BRAF mutation is a diagnostic and prognostic biomarker, it may be a predictive biomarker concerning tyrosine kinase inhibitors (TKIs), such as vemurafenib and dabrafenib, for lung cancer and melanoma patients [4].

In this paper, we focus on predictive biomarkers. Since a predictive biomarker plays a critical role in guiding therapeutic decisions for patients, it is crucial to ensure that the biomarker undergoes comprehensive validation before being employed as a treatment choice in clinical trials since an unvalidated predictive biomarker can lead to a wrong treatment for patients. In cases in which a biomarker has not yet undergone validation, it can be utilized as a stratification factor in randomized clinical trials since, by this design, the biomarker does not play any role in the selection of a treatment for patients. In such scenarios, the primary objective is to validate the biomarker rather than to use it as a basis for selecting a treatment approach. This approach ensures a more rigorous and scientifically sound application of biomarkers in clinical trial settings.

The approach to designing and analyzing clinical trials involving biomarkers can vary depending on the clinical role of the biomarker employed, its stage of development, the objectives of the study, etc. The intricate design considerations for randomized clinical trials that incorporate biomarkers were extensively explored by a group of biostatisticians [5]. Building upon this, they introduced a comprehensive set of statistical methodologies tailored for phase II randomized trials [6]. These methodologies are particularly relevant for trials involving predictive biomarkers that have yet to undergo stringent validation.

Phase II trials are pivotal and act as gatekeepers that filter out ineffective treatments before advancing to more extensive phase III studies. To be completed as quickly as possible, these trials typically select small sample sizes and a surrogate endpoint (an indicator or sign used in place of a definitive endpoint to tell if a treatment works), like tumor response or progression-free survival (PFS), rather than definitive endpoints requiring longer follow-up times, like overall survival. This approach facilitates more efficient progression through the critical phases of clinical research. In our paper, the primary endpoint is tumor response: a binary outcome.

To validate a predictive biomarker, we investigate a design method for phase II cancer clinical trials by randomizing patients between a targeted therapy and a non-targeted therapy stratified based on biomarker status (negative vs. positive). For such a trial, validation of a candidate predictive biomarker requires statistical testing of the interaction between the treatment allocation (a targeted therapy vs. a non-targeted therapy) and the biomarker status (positive vs. negative). Some investigators proposed sample size methods for case-controlled studies to test an interaction term in a logistic regression model when an exposure variable, like a biomarker, is categorical [7] and binary [8]. Their methods require inversion of a 4×4 information matrix to derive the variance of the interaction term. Using a binary predictive biomarker, we simply derive the variance using the delta method, which gives the same variance formula as the latter [8] without any matrix algebra.

In Section 2.1, we propose a sample size formula for testing the interaction between a treatment allocation and the positivity of the predictive biomarker to be validated using a logistic regression model. A logistic regression model defines an interaction in terms of the differences in logit-transformed response rates (RRs). In Section 2.2, we also present statistical testing and its sample size methods for an interaction defined by the difference between raw RRs. We demonstrate our sample size methods with the design of a real biomarker-guided trial in Section 3.1. Comprehensive numerical analyses are conducted to investigate the performance of the proposed methods in Section 3.2.

2. Material and Methods

Predictive biomarkers are vital for assessing the potential effectiveness of specific chemotherapy treatments. A preclinical study demonstrated that elevated levels of thymidylate synthase (TS) in tumors could indicate resistance to pemetrexed [9]. However, this hypothesis remained to be confirmed by prospective clinical research before using TS to select or deselect pemetrexed to treat patients with non-small-cell lung cancer (NSCLC). To explore this further, a phase II clinical trial was proposed to evaluate TS positivity as a predictive marker for pemetrexed/cisplatin (PC) treatment in NSCLC [10]. The trial aimed to compare the PC regimen against the standard non-targeted gemcitabine/cisplatin (GC) regimen. Participants were randomly assigned to one of the two treatment arms and were stratified based on TS status (positive vs. negative). This approach was intended to yield clearer insights into the role of TS status in predicting the efficacy of PC. The primary study endpoint was the overall response, i.e., partial response or complete response measured by RECIST [11].

2.1. Interaction Based on Logit-Transformed RRs

Let $y = 0$ for non-response and 0 for response, $z_1 = 0$ for GC (non-targeted regimen) and 1 for PC (targeted regimen), and $z_2 = 0$ for TS positivity and 1 for TS negativity (the favorable biomarker status for the targeted regimen). To validate TS as a predictive biomarker for PC, we have to prove that the RR of PC depends on TS positivity, while that of GC does not. In order to test this hypothesis, we consider a logistic regression model:

$$\text{logit}\,\Pr(y = 1|z_1, z_2) = \beta_0 + \beta_1 z_1 + \beta_2 z_2 + \beta_3 z_1 z_2 \tag{1}$$

By model (1), the RR is $\text{logit}(p) = \beta_0 + \beta_2 z_2$ for GC ($z_1 = 0$) and $\text{logit}(p) = \beta_0 + (\beta_2 + \beta_3)z_2$ for PC ($z_1 = 1$). Since GC is not a targeted treatment, we expect its RR not to depend on the TS status (z_2), so that $\beta_2 = 0$. With $\beta_2 = 0$, β_3 should take a positive value if TS negativity is favorable for PC. Hence, validation of TS as a predictive biomarker of PC requires testing of $H_0 : \beta_3 = 0$ against $H_0 : \beta_3 > 0$.

Let p_{kl} denote the RR of the patient group, with $(z_1, z_2) = (k, l)$ for $k, l = 0$ or 1. For the four combinations of (z_1, z_2), model (1) results in

$$\text{logit}(p_{00}) = \beta_0, \quad \text{logit}(p_{10}) = \beta_0 + \beta_1, \quad \text{logit}(p_{01}) = \beta_0 + \beta_2, \quad \text{logit}(p_{11}) = \beta_0 + \beta_1 + \beta_2 + \beta_3$$

Solving these equations for $(\beta_0, \beta_1, \beta_2, \beta_3)$ yields

$$\begin{aligned} &\beta_0 = \text{logit}(p_{00}), \quad \beta_1 = \text{logit}(p_{10}) - \text{logit}(p_{00}), \qquad \beta_2 = \text{logit}(p_{01}) - \text{logit}(p_{00}), \\ &\beta_3 = \{\text{logit}(p_{11}) - \text{logit}(p_{10})\} - \{\text{logit}(p_{01}) - \text{logit}(p_{00})\} \end{aligned} \tag{2}$$

From Formula (2), β_3 is the interaction expressed in terms of logit-transformed RRs. Note that $\exp(\beta_3) = \text{OR}_1/\text{OR}_0$, where $\text{OR}_k = p_{k1}(1 - p_{k0})$ is the odds ratio of regimen $k(= 0, 1)$ between TS positivity and TS negativity. Also, by Formula (2), we can specify regression coefficients $(\beta_0, \beta_1, \beta_2, \beta_3)$ in terms of RRs $(p_{00}, p_{01}, p_{10}, p_{11})$.

We derive a test statistic for $H_0 : \beta_3 = 0$. Let y_{kl} denote the number of responders among n_{kl} patients with $(z_1, z_2) = (k, l)$, $\hat{p}_{kl} = y_{kl}/n_{kl}$, and $n = n_{00} + n_{01} + n_{10} + n_{11}$ being the total number of patients.

From Formula (2), the maximum likelihood estimator (MLE) of β_3 is given as

$$\hat{\beta}_3 = \text{logit}(\hat{p}_{11}) - \text{logit}(\hat{p}_{10}) - \text{logit}(\hat{p}_{01}) + \text{logit}(\hat{p}_{00})$$

because $\hat{p}_{kl}$ is the MLE of p_{kl}.

Since $\sqrt{n_{kl}}(\hat{p}_{kl} - p_{kl})$ is approximately normal with mean 0 and variance $p_{kl}(1 - p_{kl})$, we can show that $\sqrt{n_{kl}}\{\text{logit}(\hat{p}_{kl}) - \text{logit}(p_{kl})\}$ is asymptotically normal with mean 0 and variance $1/\{p_{kl}(1 - p_{kl})\}$ using the delta method. Hence, $\sqrt{n}(\hat{\beta}_3 - \beta_3)$ is asymptotically normal with mean 0 and variance

$$n\Big\{\frac{1}{n_{11}p_{11}(1 - p_{11})} + \frac{1}{n_{10}p_{10}(1 - p_{10})} + \frac{1}{n_{01}p_{01}(1 - p_{01})} + \frac{1}{n_{00}p_{00}(1 - p_{00})}\Big\}$$

which converges to

$$\sigma_3^2 = \Big\{\frac{1}{r_{11}p_{11}(1 - p_{11})} + \frac{1}{r_{10}p_{10}(1 - p_{10})} + \frac{1}{r_{01}p_{01}(1 - p_{01})} + \frac{1}{r_{00}p_{00}(1 - p_{00})}\Big\} \tag{3}$$

and is consistently estimated by

$$\hat{\sigma}_3^2 = n\Big\{\frac{1}{n_{11}\hat{p}_{11}(1 - \hat{p}_{11})} + \frac{1}{n_{10}\hat{p}_{10}(1 - \hat{p}_{10})} + \frac{1}{n_{01}\hat{p}_{01}(1 - \hat{p}_{01})} + \frac{1}{n_{00}\hat{p}_{00}(1 - \hat{p}_{00})}\Big\} \tag{4}$$

This variance formula is identical to the (4,4)-component of the inverse of the information matrix for model (1) after complicated matrix computations by Demidenko [8]. Note that σ_3^2 decreases as the RRs, p_{kl}, are closer to 0.5.

Based on this result, we reject $H_0 : \beta_3 = 0$ in favor of $H_1 : \beta_3 > 0$ if $\sqrt{n}\hat{\beta}_3/\hat{\sigma}_3 > z_{1-\alpha}$, where $z_{1-\alpha}$ is the $100(1 - \alpha)$ percentile of the standard normal distribution.

We want to derive a sample size formula under $H_1 : \bar{\beta}_3(> 0)$. From Formula (2), β_3 is expressed in terms of RRs, $p_{00}, p_{01}, p_{10}, p_{11}$, so that $\bar{\beta}_3 = \text{logit}(p_{11}) - \text{logit}(p_{10}) - \text{logit}(p_{01}) + \text{logit}(p_{00})$ is determined once the RRs are specified. Let a_k denote the allocation proportion to arm k in randomization $(a_0 + a_1 = 1)$ and b_l denote the prevalence of biomarker status l $(b_0 + b_1 = 1)$. Then, with stratified randomization, we have $r_{kl} = P(z_1 = k, z_2 = l) = P(z_1 = k)P(z_2 = l) = a_k b_l$.

For a sample size calculation, we need to specify the following input parameters.

- Type I error rate and power: $(\alpha, 1 - \beta)$;
- Expected RRs: $(p_{00}, p_{01}, p_{10}, p_{11})$;
- Allocation proportion for arm $k(= 0, 1)$: a_k;
- Prevalence of biomarker status $l(= 0, 1)$: b_l.

Assume that n, the power for $H_1 : \beta_3 = \bar{\beta}_3(> 0)$, is given by

$$\begin{aligned} 1 - \beta &= P\left\{ \frac{\sqrt{n}\hat{\beta}_3}{\hat{\sigma}_3} > z_{1-\alpha} \middle| H_1 \right\} \\ &= P\left\{ \frac{\sqrt{n}(\hat{\beta}_3 - \bar{\beta}_3)}{\sigma_3} > z_{1-\alpha} - \frac{\sqrt{n}\bar{\beta}_3}{\sigma_3} \middle| H_1 \right\} \end{aligned} \tag{5}$$

Here, the second equality holds because $\hat{\sigma}_3^2$ is a consistent estimator of σ_3^2.

Since $\sqrt{n}(\hat{\beta}_3 - \bar{\beta}_3)/\sigma_3$ is asymptotically $N(0, 1)$ under H_1, from Formula (5), we have

$$z_{1-\alpha} - \frac{\bar{\beta}_3\sqrt{n}}{\sigma_3} = -z_{1-\beta}. \tag{6}$$

By solving this equation with respect to n, we obtain the required sample size

$$n = \frac{\sigma_3^2(z_{1-\alpha} + z_{1-\beta})^2}{\bar{\beta}_3^2} \tag{7}$$

Recall that by Formula (3), σ_3^2 is expressed in terms of $(p_{00}, p_{01}, p_{10}, p_{11})$, a_0, and b_0.

2.2. Interaction Based on Raw RRs

We considered an interaction in terms of logit-transformed RRs in Section 2.1. In this section, we consider an interaction in terms of raw RRs, $\theta = (p_{11} - p_{10}) - (p_{01} - p_{00})$. We have $\theta = 0$ if the biomarker is not a predictive biomarker for regimen $z_1 = 1$. So we derive a test statistic and its sample size formula for testing $H_0 : \theta = 0$.

The interaction θ is estimated by

$$\hat{\theta} = \hat{p}_{11} - \hat{p}_{10} - \hat{p}_{01} + \hat{p}_{00}$$

By the binomial theory, $\sqrt{n_{kl}}(\hat{p}_{kl} - p_{kl})$ is approximately normal with mean 0 and variance $p_{kl}(1 - p_{kl})$ for large values of n; so for $H_0 : \theta = 0$, $\sqrt{n}\hat{\theta}$ is asymptotically normal with mean 0 and variance

$$\sigma_n^2 = n\left\{ \frac{p_{11}(1 - p_{11})}{n_{11}} + \frac{p_{10}(1 - p_{10})}{n_{10}} + \frac{p_{01}(1 - p_{01})}{n_{01}} + \frac{p_{00}(1 - p_{00})}{n_{00}} \right\}$$

which is consistently estimated by

$$\hat{\sigma}^2 = n\left\{ \frac{\hat{p}_{11}(1 - \hat{p}_{11})}{n_{11}} + \frac{\hat{p}_{10}(1 - \hat{p}_{10})}{n_{10}} + \frac{\hat{p}_{01}(1 - \hat{p}_{01})}{n_{01}} + \frac{\hat{p}_{00}(1 - \hat{p}_{00})}{n_{00}} \right\}$$

Note that $\theta > 0$ if the biomarker is predictive for regimen $z_1 = 1$. So we reject $H_0 : \theta = 0$ in favor of $H_1 : \theta > 0$ if $\sqrt{n}\hat{\theta}/\hat{\sigma} > z_{1-\alpha}$. Similarly to Section 2.1, we can derive the required sample size for $H_1 : \theta = \bar{\theta}(> 0)$

$$n = \frac{\sigma^2 (z_{1-\alpha} + z_{1-\beta})^2}{\bar{\theta}^2} \tag{8}$$

where

$$\sigma^2 = \frac{p_{11}(1-p_{11})}{r_{11}} + \frac{p_{10}(1-p_{10})}{r_{10}} + \frac{p_{01}(1-p_{01})}{r_{01}} + \frac{p_{00}(1-p_{00})}{r_{00}}$$

is the limit of σ_n^2. Unlike the variance of $\hat{\beta}_3$, σ^2 increases as the RRs, p_{kl}, are closer to 0.5.

3. Numerical Analysis

3.1. Real Study Example

We apply our sample size calculation methods to the design of the randomized phase II trial between GC and PC stratified by TS status (positive vs. negative) [10]. Patients are randomized between the two treatment arms in a one-to-one ratio, i.e., $a_0 = a_1 = 1/2$, and are stratified by TS status to make sure that the two treatment arms are balanced within both the TS positive and TS negative cohorts. The cutoff value for TS positivity is selected as the median value from a previous study by Sun et al. [12], so we expect $b_0 = b_1 = 1/2$ and $r_{kl} = a_k b_l = 1/4$ for $k, l = 0, 1$. From this previous study, the investigators observed $\hat{p}_{00} = 0.37$, $\hat{p}_{10} = 0.24$, $\hat{p}_{01} = 0.32$, and $\hat{p}_{11} = 0.48$. The fact that $\hat{p}_{00} \approx \hat{p}_{01}$ implies that GC ($z_1 = 0$) is a non-targeted treatment, whereas $\hat{p}_{11} > \hat{p}_{10}$ implies that TS negativity ($z_2 = 1$) is favorable for PC ($z_1 = 1$). We use these estimates as the true RRs specified for our sample size calculation to test if TS is a predictive biomarker for PC or not.

Using the interaction defined in terms of logit-transformed RRs, we calculate the sample size for $H_1 : \beta_3 = \bar{\beta}_3(> 0)$. Based on the specified RRs, we have $\bar{\beta}_3 = 1.294$ from Formula (2). Additionally, by incorporating $r_{kl} = 1/4$, we obtain $\sigma_3^2 = 73.50$ from Formula (3). Hence, for $(\alpha, 1-\beta) = (0.1, 0.9)$, the required sample size is

$$n = \frac{73.50 \times (1.282 + 1.282)^2}{1.294^2} = 289$$

from Formula (7).

Now, we calculate the sample size for testing $H_0 : \theta = 0$ using the interaction based on the differences among raw RRs. For the specified RRs and $r_{kl} = 1/4$, we have $\bar{\theta} = 0.290$ and $\sigma^2 = 3.531$. Hence, for $(\alpha, 1-\beta) = (0.1, 0.9)$, the required sample size is

$$n = \frac{3.531 \times (1.282 + 1.282)^2}{0.290^2} = 276$$

3.2. Simulations

In this subsection, we conduct extensive simulations to show that the statistical test of the interaction term accurately controls the type I error rate and that a calculated sample size is appropriately powered.

At first, the sample size n is calculated for a given design setting under H_1 and for 10,000 simulation samples of size n under the design setting. Statistical testing is applied to each sample to calculate the empirical power $1 - \hat{\beta}$ by the proportion of samples rejecting H_0 among the 10,000 simulation samples. We will conclude that our sample size formula is accurate if the empirical power is close to the nominal one. We also generate 10,000 samples of size n under H_0 and calculate the empirical type I error rate $\hat{\alpha}$ similarly. If the empirical type I error rate $\hat{\alpha}$ is close to the nominal α, we will conclude that the test statistic controls the type I error rate accurately for the calculated sample size.

We set $(\alpha, 1-\beta) = (0.1, 0.9)$ and $a_{00} = a_{01} = a_{10} = a_{11} = 1/4$. In addition, we consider three different scenarios (A, B, and C) for H_0 and H_1. In Table 1, four sets of

$(p_{00}, p_{01}, p_{10}, p_{11})$ values are given for H_0 and H_1 for each scenario. Figure 1 displays a typical set of RRs for each scenario. Since the line of GC (connecting p_{00} and p_{01}) is horizontal under both H_0 and H_1, it is a non-targeted treatment. The line of PC (connecting p_{10} and p_{11}) is also horizontal under H_0 but not under H_1, so we want to test if PC is a targeted treatment or not. In scenarios A and B under H_0, we assume that the relative risk (RR) values for GC and PC are equal, and in scenario C, we assume both lines are horizontal but have different values. Under H_1, in scenarios A and C, we assume the RR value of PC is lower than that of GC for TS+ patients but higher for TS− patients. In scenario B under H_1, we assume that PC and GC have the same RR value for TS+ patients but that PC has a higher RR value than GC for TS− patients. More details about the parameter settings for the simulations can be found in Table 1.

Table 2 summarizes the odds ratios under H_1, the sample sizes, and the simulation results under these design settings. Note that sample size decreases based on the size of the interaction for both types of interaction. If the interaction under H_1 is identical, the sample size decreases (increases) if the RRs are closer to 0.5 for θ (for θ) because of the relationship between the variance of the interaction estimator and the RRs. We observe that for each design scenario, the sample size for testing $H_0 : \theta = 0$ is smaller than that for testing $H_0 : \theta = 0$, probably because the RRs under each H_1 exactly satisfy the interaction based on the raw RRs. For all of the H_1 scenarios, the empirical power $1 - \hat{\beta}$ is close to the nominal $1 - \beta = 0.9$, so we conclude that our sample size formulas are accurate. The empirical type I error rates $\hat{\alpha}$ are close to the nominal $\alpha = 0.1$, so we conclude that the test statistics control the type I error rate accurately for the wide range of sample sizes we have considered.

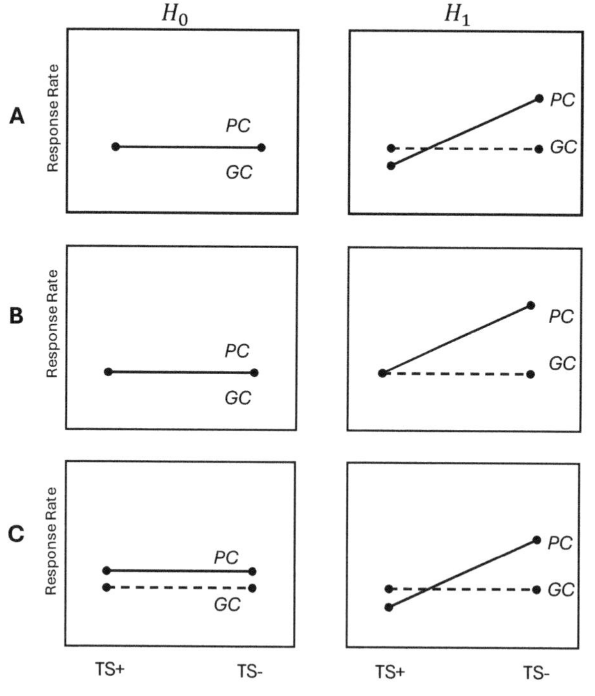

Figure 1. Three scenarios (**A–C**) of RRs for GC and PC depending on TS status under H_0 and H_1.

Table 1. Hypothesis settings under different scenarios.

	H_0				H_1			
Scenario	p_{00}	p_{01}	p_{10}	p_{11}	p_{00}	p_{01}	p_{10}	p_{11}
A1	0.2	0.2	0.2	0.2	0.2	0.2	0.1	0.4
A2	0.3	0.3	0.3	0.3	0.3	0.3	0.2	0.5
A3	0.4	0.4	0.4	0.4	0.4	0.4	0.3	0.6
A4	0.5	0.5	0.5	0.5	0.5	0.5	0.4	0.7
B1	0.2	0.2	0.2	0.2	0.2	0.2	0.2	0.55
B2	0.3	0.3	0.3	0.3	0.3	0.3	0.3	0.65
B3	0.4	0.4	0.4	0.4	0.4	0.4	0.4	0.75
B4	0.5	0.5	0.5	0.5	0.5	0.5	0.5	0.85
C1	0.2	0.2	0.3	0.3	0.2	0.2	0.1	0.5
C2	0.3	0.3	0.4	0.4	0.3	0.3	0.2	0.6
C3	0.4	0.4	0.5	0.5	0.4	0.4	0.3	0.7
C4	0.5	0.5	0.6	0.6	0.5	0.5	0.4	0.8

Table 2. Interactions under H_1, sample size, empirical type I error rate $\hat{\alpha}$, and power $1-\hat{\beta}$ under different design settings.

	$H_0: \beta_3 = 0$				$H_0: \theta = 0$			
Scenario	$\bar{\beta}_3$	n	$\hat{\alpha}$	$1-\hat{\beta}$	$\bar{\theta}$	n	$\hat{\alpha}$	$1-\hat{\beta}$
A1	1.792	228	0.1005	0.9180	0.30	188	0.1048	0.9033
A2	1.386	272	0.1013	0.9028	0.30	244	0.1038	0.8932
A3	1.253	288	0.1043	0.9086	0.30	272	0.0984	0.8983
A4	1.253	284	0.1077	0.9074	0.30	276	0.1030	0.8958
B1	1.587	236	0.1023	0.9004	0.35	156	0.1091	0.8949
B2	1.466	228	0.1004	0.9095	0.35	184	0.1025	0.8986
B3	1.504	208	0.0974	0.9094	0.35	196	0.1092	0.9001
B4	1.735	172	0.0979	0.9142	0.35	188	0.1003	0.8974
C1	1.792	152	0.1011	0.8962	0.30	108	0.1085	0.8912
C2	2.197	164	0.0997	0.9057	0.40	136	0.1088	0.902
C3	1.792	164	0.096	0.9056	0.40	148	0.1083	0.8972
C4	1.792	152	0.108	0.9143	0.40	148	0.1019	0.8969

4. Discussion

A biomarker cannot be used to select a treatment until it is validated because it is very risky to select a patient's treatment based on a wrong biomarker. However, a biomarker can be used as a stratification factor for a randomization trial even before validated. We investigated design and analysis methods for a randomized trial stratifying for biomarker positivity. This trial tests whether or not the biomarker is a predictive biomarker for a treatment by using a non-targeted treatment as a control. The analysis of the trial requires statistical testing on the interaction between treatment allocation and biomarker positivity.

We derived statistical tests and their sample size methods for two different forms of interactions: one based on the logit-transformed RRs and the other based on the raw RRs of subgroups defined by (z_1, z_2). Although we presented our methods for phase II trials, they can be used for phase III trials, too.

Extensive simulations were conducted under scenarios of alternative hypotheses for which the required sample sizes were reasonable for a real phase II trial to validate a potential predictive biomarker. The sample sizes calculated using our formulas were found to be appropriately powered. Also, from simulations under H_0, our test statistic controlled the type I error rate accurately for the range of sample sizes calculated.

In our paper, we wanted to test if a treatment is a targeted therapy for a biomarker or not. A simple design for this objective might be a single-arm design using a treatment group and a test group if the RR of the treatment is different between the biomarker positive group and the biomarker negative group. Instead, we selected a randomized trial design between a candidate targeted therapy arm and a non-targeted therapy arm (control) stratified by the status of the biomarker. By this design, the required sample size will increase, but as a secondary objective, we tested if the selected control treatment was really a non-targeted therapy with respect to the biomarker or not. This can be done by testing β_2 in model (1). Furthermore, by the stratification based on the biomarker status, the biomarker outcome was not used for the selection of the treatment for each patient. If the biomarker is shown to be a predictive biomarker for a treatment, then we can consider proceeding to a randomized phase III trial between a biomarker-guided treatment selection arm as an experimental therapy and a control arm using a treatment selected at the discretion of the treating physician and blinded in terms of biomarker status. If the biomarker is proven to be predictive for the targeted therapy through these trials, patients with a biomarker status that is beneficial in terms of the therapy will be treated with this therapy, resulting in personalized medicine for the target population.

Our computer programs for sample size calculation and simulations were developed in R and are available upon request.

Author Contributions: Methodology, B.Z. and S.-H.J.; Software, B.Z.; Investigation, J.-M.S., M.-J.A. and S.-H.J.; Writing—original draft, B.Z.; Writing—review & editing, J.-M.S., M.-J.A. and S.-H.J.; Supervision, M.-J.A. and S.-H.J. All authors have read and agreed to the published version of the manuscript.

Funding: This research received no external funding.

Institutional Review Board Statement: Not applicable.

Informed Consent Statement: Not applicable.

Data Availability Statement: Not applicable.

Conflicts of Interest: The authors declare no conflicts of interest.

Abbreviations

The following abbreviations are used in this manuscript:

TS	Thymidylate Synthase
PC	Pemetrexed/Cisplatin
GC	Gemcitabin/Cisplatin
NSCLC	Non-small-cell Lung Cancer
RR	Response Rate

References

1. Yang, Z.-Y.; Zhao, K.; Luo, D.; Yin, Z.; Zhou, C.; Chen, J.; Zhang, C. Carcinoembryonic antigen levels are increased with pulmonary output in pulmonary hypertension due to congenital heart disease. *J. Int. Med. Res.* **2020**, *48*, 0300060520964378.
2. Tolmeijer, S.H.; Koornstra, R.H.; de Groot, J.W.B.; Geerlings, M.J.; van Rens, D.H.; Boers-Sonderen, M.J.; Schalken, J.A.; Gerritsen, W.R.; Ligtenberg, M.J.; Mehra, N. Plasma BRAF mutation detection for the diagnostic and monitoring trajectory of patients with LDH-high stage IV melanoma. *Cancers* **2021**, *13*, 3913. [CrossRef] [PubMed]
3. Yang, G.; Liu, S.; Maghsoudloo, M.; Shasaltaneh, M.D.; Kaboli, P.J.; Zhang, C.; Deng, Y.; Heidari, H.; Entezari, M.; Fu, S.; et al. PLA1A expression as a diagnostic marker of BRAF-mutant metastasis in melanoma cancer. *Sci. Rep.* **2021**, *11*, 6056. [CrossRef] [PubMed]
4. Malapelle, U.; Rossi, G.; Pisapia, P.; Barberis, M.; Buttitta, F.; Castiglione, F.; Cecere, F.L.; Grimaldi, A.M.; Iaccarino, A.; Marchetti, A.; et al. BRAF as a positive predictive biomarker: Focus on lung cancer and melanoma patients. *Crit. Rev. Oncol.* **2020**, *156*, 103118. [CrossRef] [PubMed]
5. Freidlin, B.; McShane, L.M.; Korn, E.L. Randomized clinical trials with biomarkers: Design issues. *J. Natl. Cancer Inst.* **2010**, *102*, 152–160. [CrossRef] [PubMed]
6. Freidlin, B.; McShane, L.M.; Polley, M.Y.C.; Korn, E.L. Randomized phase II trial designs with biomarkers. *J. Clin. Oncol.* **2012**, *30*, 3304. [CrossRef] [PubMed]
7. Foppa, I.; Spiegelman, D. Power and sample size calculations for case-control studies of gene-environment interactions with a polytomous exposure variable. *Am. J. Epidemiol.* **1997**, *146*, 596–604. [CrossRef] [PubMed]
8. Demidenko, E. Sample size and optimal design for logistic regression with binary interaction. *Stat. Med.* **2008**, *27*, 36–46. [CrossRef] [PubMed]

9. Ozasa, H.; Oguri, T.; Uemura, T.; Miyazaki, M.; Maeno, K.; Sato, S.; Ueda, R. Significance of thymidylate synthase for resistance to pemetrexed in lung cancer. *Cancer Sci.* **2010**, *101*, 161–166. [CrossRef] [PubMed]
10. Sun, J.M.; Ahn, J.S.; Jung, S.H.; Sun, J.; Ha, S.Y.; Han, J.; Park, K.; Ahn, M.J. Pemetrexed plus cisplatin versus gemcitabine plus cisplatin according to thymidylate synthase expression in nonsquamous non–small-cell lung cancer: A biomarker-stratified randomized phase II trial. *J. Clin. Oncol.* **2015**, *33*, 2450–2456. [CrossRef] [PubMed]
11. Eisenhauer, E.A.; Therasse, P.; Bogaerts, J.; Schwartz, L.H.; Sargent, D.; Ford, R.; Dancey, J.; Arbuck, S.; Gwyther, S.; Mooney, M.; et al. New response evaluation criteria in solid tumours: Revised RECIST guideline (version 1.1). *Eur. J. Cancer* **2009**, *45*, 228–247. [CrossRef] [PubMed]
12. Sun, J.M.; Han, J.; Ahn, J.S.; Park, K.; Ahn, M.J. Significance of thymidylate synthase and thyroid transcription factor 1 expression in patients with nonsquamous non-small cell lung cancer treated with pemetrexed-based chemotherapy. *J. Thorac. Oncol.* **2011**, *6*, 1392–1399. [CrossRef] [PubMed]

Disclaimer/Publisher's Note: The statements, opinions and data contained in all publications are solely those of the individual author(s) and contributor(s) and not of MDPI and/or the editor(s). MDPI and/or the editor(s) disclaim responsibility for any injury to people or property resulting from any ideas, methods, instructions or products referred to in the content.

cancers

MDPI

Systematic Review

Intraoperative Techniques That Define the Mucosal Margins of Oral Cancer In-Vivo: A Systematic Review

Klijs J. de Koning *,†, Carleen M. E. M. Adriaansens †, Rob Noorlag, Remco de Bree and Robert J. J. van Es

Department of Head and Neck Surgical Oncology, University Medical Center Utrecht, Heidelberglaan 100, 3584 CX Utrecht, The Netherlands
* Correspondence: k.j.dekoning@umcutrecht.nl; Tel.: +31-88-75-67805
† These authors contributed equally to this work.

Simple Summary: This systematic review evaluates techniques defining adequate mucosal margins during the resection of oral squamous cell carcinoma (SCC). Residual SCC and dysplasia demand distinct adjuvant treatment, such as re-resection and radiation for SCC or CO_2-laser evaporation for severe dysplasia, necessitating accurate differentiation between SCC and dysplasia during surgery. The study includes eight investigations into margin visualization techniques—autofluorescence, iodine staining, and narrow-band imaging—concluding that, except for autofluorescence, there is considerable variability in negative predictive values. Autofluorescence does not significantly enhance margin outcomes compared to conventional white light-guided surgery, while iodine does. Studies on narrow-band imaging did not report a comparison with a white light-guided surgery cohort. The review advocates for more comprehensive studies comparing the diagnostic accuracy of iodine staining or narrow-band imaging, with a specific focus on diagnostic accuracy and the discrimination between SCC and dysplasia.

Abstract: Background: This systematic review investigates techniques for determining adequate mucosal margins during the resection of oral squamous cell carcinoma (SCC). The primary treatment involves surgical removal with ≥5 mm margins, highlighting the importance of accurate differentiation between SCC and dysplasia during surgery. Methods: A comprehensive Embase and PubMed literature search was performed. Studies underwent quality assessment using QUADAS-2. Results: After the full-text screening and exclusion of studies exhibiting high bias, eight studies were included, focusing on three margin visualization techniques: autofluorescence, iodine staining, and narrow-band imaging (NBI). Negative predictive value (NPV) was calculable across the studies, though reference standards varied. Results indicated NPVs for autofluorescence, iodine, and NBI ranging from 61% to 100%, 92% to 99%, and 86% to 100%, respectively. Autofluorescence did not significantly enhance margins compared to white light-guided surgery, while iodine staining demonstrated improvement for mild or moderate dysplasia. NBI lacked comparison with a white light-guided surgery cohort. Conclusions: We recommend studying and comparing the diagnostic accuracy of iodine staining and NBI in larger cohorts of patients with oral SCC, focusing on discriminating between SCC and (severe) dysplasia. Furthermore, we advise reporting the diagnostic accuracy alongside the treatment effects to improve the assessment of these techniques.

Keywords: oral squamous cell carcinoma; systematic review; mucosal margin; diagnostic accuracy autofluorescence; iodine; narrow band imaging

1. Introduction

Approximately one-third of all head and neck cancers are oral squamous cell carcinoma (SCC) [1]. The preferred choice of treatment is complete surgical removal with histopathological adequate resection margins of the primary tumor to establish local control [2,3].

There is still a discussion about the definition of an adequate margin. Several studies investigated the ideal histopathological cutoff margin [3–8]. Most guidelines define a free margin as $\geq$5 mm between the SCC and the resection plane [9,10]. There is a general consensus that margins between 0 and 1 mm from the resection plane adversely affect locoregional survival [7,11,12] and are an indication for adjuvant treatment. This could either be radiotherapy or a re-resection, both having their drawbacks. Radiotherapy has several side effects [13], while a re-resection requires extra operating time and sometimes general anesthesia during a second procedure. Furthermore, problems in localizing the inadequate margin in an already closed wound bed introduce uncertainty about the definitive margin status [14].

The existence of (severe) dysplasia in the resection margin adds a different aspect to the discussion of adequate margins. In many patients, the oral SCC develops in an area of (severe) dysplasia, also known as "field cancerization" [15]. There is evidence that when there is residual severe dysplasia after SCC resection, there is a high chance of local recurrence or new primaries [16,17]. There is little consensus about the appropriate treatment in case of severe dysplasia in the resection margin. This could either be CO_2-laser evaporation or an additional surgical resection [18]. However, surgical resection of all mucosal dysplasia in the case of extensive field cancerization may be an unnecessary overtreatment, potentially leading to increased morbidity. Nevertheless, it is important to differentiate between SCC and (severe) dysplasia in the resection margins, given the varied consequences of residual dysplasia in the resection margins. These consequences encompass differences in locoregional recurrence and the severity of adjuvant treatment.

In the past decade, an increasing amount of research into intraoperative margin assessment has been conducted that could improve the final margin status. For example, frozen section analysis (FSA) can be used to identify SCC and distinguish it from (severe) dysplasia. This technique uses tissue samples of the wound bed or specimen, which are rapidly assessed for SCC or dysplastic cells through histopathological examination. This allows for the immediate revision of surgical margins, if necessary. However, only 0.1–1% of the specimen and/or wound bed is sampled; therefore, a frozen section may lead to sampling errors, resulting in a low sensitivity for inadequate margins [12,19,20]. Bulbul et al. concluded in a meta-analysis that margin revision indicated by FSA does not lead to better local control [21].

In our center, the application of an intraoperative ultrasound has been investigated for SCC of the buccal mucosa and oral tongue [22,23]. Although it contributed to an enhanced assessment of deep and submucosal margins, it proved difficult to differentiate the tumor and (severe) dysplasia from normal mucosa. Also, intra-operative ex-vivo MRI, which is able to image deep and submucosal margins, has limitations in imaging the mucosal resection plane [24]. However, a margin visualization technique that ensures adequate mucosal margins is equally crucial as achieving adequate submucosal and deep margins. This is preferably a technique that determines the mucosal margin with a high sensitivity for both SCC and dysplasia.

There are several systematic reviews evaluating margin visualization techniques that may contribute to a higher number of adequate resection margins [25–28]. However, these reviews discuss only deep margins [28,29] or a combination of deep and superficial margins [26]. Some also include pre-clinical research, research that includes technologies that require sampling of the resection specimen and/or wound bed, or ex-vivo examination of the resection specimen [26,27,29].

This systematic review aims to provide an overview of publications evaluating the diagnostic accuracy of recently investigated mucosal margin visualization techniques that aim for adequate mucosal margins, both in the context of SCC and dysplasia. These techniques should be combined with deep margin visualization techniques. We specifically focus on in vivo technologies that are already applied in clinical practice and are suitable for defining the mucosal margin before incisions are made.

2. Materials and Methods

This systematic review was conducted following the guidelines outlined in the Preferred Reporting Items for Systematic Reviews and Meta-Analyses (PRISMA) [30] and has not been registered in PROSPERO.

2.1. Eligibility Criteria

The criteria for inclusion were: (1) the study population consisted of patients with a SCC of the head and neck area with a sub-group of oral SCC; (2) an in vivo intraoperatively technique (i.e., directly before the incision, during the resection or directly after the resection) was studied that was able to visualize the entire extent of the mucosal margin during surgery; (3) it aimed to assess or improve resection margin status; and (4) the sensitivity, specificity, positive predictive value (PPV), negative predictive value (NPV), number of free margins, or number of positive margins (in terms of SCC or dysplasia) were mentioned or could be extracted from the publication.

The criteria for exclusion were: (1) non-clinical studies; (2) publications before 2010; (3) publications that described techniques that only used white light (WL) for tumor/margin visualization, e.g., trans-oral robotic surgery without visual enhancement; (4) publications that described head and neck cancers with <50% oral cancers or without a subgroup analysis of oral cancer in the intervention group; (5) publications that described margin visualization techniques that only work with samples of the resection specimen; (6) publications that described techniques that only identified the presence of SCC or severe (dysplasia) rather than defining a positive or free margin; (7) reviews, case reports, book chapters, editorials, oral presentations, technical notes, and scientific posters; and (8) publications in a language other than English, Dutch, or German.

2.2. Search Strategy

A systematic search for relevant publications was performed on PubMed and Embase on 31 August 2023 (K.J.d.K.). The main focus was to find margin visualization techniques that helped the surgeon identify adequate SCC-free and/or dysplasia-fee margins during surgery. Therefore, search terms focused on the title, abstract, and MeSH terms and included "carcinoma," all subsites of the oral cavity, and "margins of excision". The same search terms were used in Embase, but instead of the Mesh terms, the "explode function" was used. Records predating 2010 were excluded from the search based on the assumption that techniques emerging before 2010 lack clinical relevance in the absence of subsequent publications after 2010. The search syntax is shown in Supplementary Materials.

De-duplication was conducted using the method described by Bramer et al. in EndNote (Version 19.3.3, Clarivate Analytics, Philadelphia, PA, USA) [31]. Afterwards, data were exported to Rayyan QCRI (Hamad Bin Khalifa University, Al Rayyan University, Qatar). Two of the three screening authors (C.M.A, K.J.d.K, R.N.) independently assessed the relevance of all titles and abstracts based on the predetermined inclusion and exclusion criteria. Consensus was reached through discussion. Two screening authors (C.M.A, K.J.d.K) reviewed the full texts to determine inclusion or exclusion. Additionally, a reference and citation check was conducted on the selected publications to ensure comprehensive coverage of the entire field of interest.

2.3. Data Extraction

The information extracted from the included publications included the following: year of publication, study methodology (i.e., intervention vs. control or diagnostic accuracy test), sort of index tests (i.e., margin visualization technique), sort of reference-standard (i.e., frozen section analysis or final histopathology), consistency of the cohort (i.e., types of SCC), number of included tumors and/or margins, safety margin distance around the SCC and/or (severe) dysplasia visible under white light safety margin around the area showing positive for the index test, immediate revision based on imaging modality, use of FSA (and whether it was guided by the technique), definition of histopathological positive margin and number of histopathological free margins.

Areas that were indicated by the index test as positive and showed a SCC and/or (severe) dysplasia in that area during the histopathological examination were considered "true positive"(TP), and in the case that no SCC and/or dysplasia was found, "false positive"(FP). Areas beyond the positive index test were considered negative (Figure 1). Depending on whether or not this index-negative area showed SCC and/or (severe) dysplasia, it was deemed false negative (FN) or true negative (TN), respectively. We registered when these variables were determined per resected specimen (specimen-based) or with multiple FSA samples per specimen (sample-based).

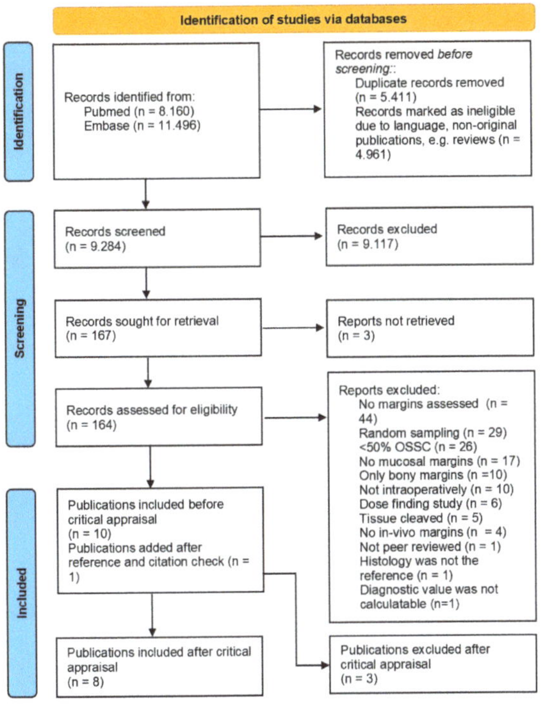

Figure 1. Prisma chart for inclusion and exclusion of publications. From: Page, 2021 [30].

If possible, sensitivity (TP cases divided by positive cases according to histopathology), specificity (TN cases divided by negative cases according to histopathology), positive predictive value (PPV) (TP divided by positive cases according to the index test), and negative predictive value (NPV) (TN divided by negative cases according to the index test) were calculated. This was performed, if possible, for the detection of (1) SCC only, (2) SCC in combination with severe dysplasia, and (3) SCC in combination with all types of dysplasia.

2.4. Critical Appraisal

Two screening authors (CA, KK) separately critically appraised the included publications using the Quality Assessment of Diagnostics Accuracy Studies (QUADAS-2) tool [32]. Elements making part of the following categories were assessed to score the risk of bias: (1) 'patient selection': a consecutive cohort of patients had been used, the optional control cohort was relevant, and inappropriate exclusions had been avoided; (2) 'index-test': the index test was interpreted without knowledge of the reference-standard; (3) 'reference-standard': the reference-standard was the final histopathology and the pathologist was blinded for the index test; (4) 'flow and timing': the reference-standard and index test were executed equally in each patient and all included patients were analyzed. Applicability was evaluated on the following categories by their elements: (1) 'patient selection': oral SCC of both small (T1-T2) and large (T3-T4) tumors were included; (2) 'index-test': there was a definition of a positive index, i.e., it used an observer-independent cutoff value and the needed devices and or doses had been described; (3) 'reference-standard': a clear definition of a positive margin was given and the reference-standard (i.e. final histopathology) was not affected by additional frozen sections that were not indicated by the margin visualization technique. All items were scored as sufficient: 2 points, unclear: 1 point, or bad: 0 points. The score for each category was determined by summing the points and then dividing the total by the number of items. Overall scores were categorized as 'insufficient' within the range of 0–0.5, 'intermediate' within the range of 0.6–1.4, and 'sufficient' within the range of 1.5–2.0.

3. Results

3.1. Search Strategy and Article Selection

The search revealed 19,656 citations (Figure 1). After removing duplicates and records that were marked ineligible because of language (e.g., non-English, non-Dutch, or non-German) or not being an original journal paper (e.g., conference abstract, review, book chapter), 9284 records remained and were screened on title and abstract, leading to 164 records that were screened full text. Eventually, ten records were included and used for the reference standards and citation checks. This led to one additional inclusion, resulting in eleven articles considered eligible for this review.

3.2. Critical Appraisal

An overview of the critical appraisal can be found in Table 1. Considering the risk of bias, none of the studies had a risk of bias for the category 'index-test'. For 'patient selection' and 'flow and timing', an intermediate risk of bias was found. Regarding the category 'reference-standard,' Baj et al. [33] and Sun et al. [34] scored insufficiently since only FSA or small samples were used to determine diagnostic accuracy, and no final histopathology was used.

Considering applicability, only two studies scored sufficiently in the category 'patient selection'; Baj et al. [33] and Sun et al. [34] included both early and advanced-stage oral SCC. Durham scored insufficiently for this category, as they did only include small (T1 and T2) tumors or "high grade lesions" defined as dysplasia or in situ carcinoma.

Table 1. Critical appraisal of included studies after text screening.

	Risk of Bias				Applicability		
	Patient Selection	Index Test	Reference	Flow and Timing	Patient Selection	Index Test	Reference
Morikawa, 2019 [35]	!	✓	✓	!	!	!	✗
Durham, 2020 [36]	!	✓	!	✓	✗	!	✓
Sun, 2021 [34]	✓	✓	✗	!	✓	!	✓
Morikawa, 2023 [37]	✓	✓	!	!	!	!	✗
McMahon, 2010 [38]	✓	✓	✓	✓	!	!	✓
Umeda, 2011 [39]	!	✓	✓	✓	!	!	✓
Tirelli, 2015 [40]	✓	✓	!	✓	!	!	✓

Table 1. *Cont.*

	Risk of Bias				Applicability		
	Patient Selection	Index Test	Reference	Flow and Timing	Patient Selection	Index Test	Reference
Tirelli, 2017 [41]	✓	✓	!	✓	!	!	✓
Tirelli, 2018 [42]	!	✓	!	✓	!	!	✓
Tirelli, 2019 [43]	✓	✓	✓	✓	!	✗	!
Baj, 2019 [33]	!	✓	✗	✓	✓	!	✓

Green check marks: 'sufficient.' Yellow exclamation marks: 'intermediate.' Red cross marks: 'insufficient.'

Tirelli et al.'s 2019 study [43] scored insufficiently for the category 'index-test.' They did not clearly define a positive index test while using narrow-band imaging (NBI), possibly because the validation of the NBI technique was not the primary goal of this study. Other studies thoroughly described the definition of a positive index test. However, their description was still observer-dependent and subjective, leading to an 'intermediate' score.

Both studies of Morikawa et al. [35,37] scored insufficiently for the category 'reference-standard', considering applicability. Both studies did not give a clear definition of a "positive" margin. Moreover, they applied frozen sections in addition to their margin visualization technique but did not discriminate the contribution of the FSA-indicated revisions from the margin visualization technique to the frequency of free margins. The latter issue was also the case for the 2019 study of Tirelli et al. [43]. However, they gave a clear definition of a positive margin. Therefore, they scored 'intermediate' for this category.

The fact that the studies of Morikawa et al. [35,37] and Tirelli et al. from 2019 [43] did not discriminate the contribution of the FSA-indicated revisions from the margin visualization technique made it impossible to determine the diagnostic accuracy of the margin visualization technique. Therefore, these studies were excluded from further analysis (Figure 1). Despite other studies scoring 'insufficient' on other categories as well [33,34,36], we decided to evaluate their margin visualization technique in this systematic review since it was possible to determine their diagnostic accuracy. This left eight studies for final evaluation. An overview of all studies and their methods of conducting their research can be found in Table 2.

3.3. Margin Visualization Techniques

Two included studies investigated autofluorescence [34,36]. Two studies assessed iodine staining [38,39]. Four included studies analyzed NBI [33,40–42].

In general, the methodology of all studies could be categorized as follows (Figure 2):

- Method A: Interventional studies (with or without a WL-safety margin control group). Surgical margins were enlarged when the index-positive area exceeded the WL-safety margin. SCC and/or dysplasia determined the TN or FN in the index-negative areas surrounding the index-positive areas. Index-positive areas were not analyzed; hence, only the NPV could be calculated. Three studies used this methodology [36,38,39].
- Method B: Interventional studies with diagnostic accuracy. In these studies, the index test was either smaller or larger than the WL-safety margin, and a specimen was either considered index test negative (index $\leq$ WL) or positive (index > WL). Tumors were excised according to the largest area. Histopathology determined the diagnostic accuracy in these areas. In contrast to Method A, the TP and FP could also be evaluated. In case the index-positive area was as large as the WL-safety margin, the case was considered negative. Two studies used this methodology [41,42].
- Method C: Diagnostic accuracy studies. In these studies, all tumors were excised according to the WL-safety margin. Index-positive areas extending beyond the WL-safety

margin were sampled and assessed on the TP or FP. Areas not extending further than the WL-safety margin were also sampled, indicating either the TN or FN. The overlap between the WL-safety margin and positive index test was considered a plausible situation, in contrast to 'Method C'. Three studies used this methodology [33,34,40].

3.3.1. Autofluorescence

Autofluorescence is one of the multiple imaging techniques that use the fluorescent properties of certain biomaterials. These materials can be excited by absorbing light of a particular wavelength and subsequently emitting this light by a different wavelength. These wavelengths are visible using fluorescence cameras. Instead of external contrast agents with fluorescent properties, autofluorescence margin visualization techniques use the fluorescent properties of biomaterials found within the body, especially those of collagen crosslinks and flavin adenine dinucleotide. When blue light (wavelength 400–460 nm) is absorbed by normal tissue, it subsequently re-emits light that appears green when observed through a filter. Abnormal tissue, such as neoplastic, dysplastic, and inflammatory tissue, cannot be excited and does not emit green light but appears brown through the filter [44]. These so-called fluorescence visualization loss (FVL) areas can be delineated with a certain margin to obtain the free margin status.

One interventional study by Durham et al. ('Method A') performed a randomized controlled trial with a minimal 10 mm WL-safety margin and minimal 10 mm FVL-safety margin [36]. They included OSCCs (n = 261) and high-grade lesions (i.e., severe dysplasia, n = 182). This study only reported the "first-pass margin"; margins found "positive for severe dysplasia or greater histopathologic change" and thus seemed not to make a difference between SCC and (severe) dysplasia. Additional revisions were possibly conducted but not described, resulting in an unknown number of free margins in final histopathology. The NPV of their test cohort (70%) was similar to that of their conventional cohort (70%).

One study by Sun et al. performed a 'Method C' study on autofluorescence by applying a demarcation on the boundary of the FVL-positive area [34]. They included only SCC patients. Then, they resected the specimen with a 15–20 mm WL-safety margin. In all cases, the FVL-positive area fell within this WL-safety margin. Samples (n = 126) collected from random locations between the FVL-based demarcation and resection plane were assessed on the frequency of SCC and/or (severe) dysplasia beyond the FVL-positive area. For SCC in the samples, this frequency was 0% (NPV 100%). For severe dysplasia, the frequency was 18% (NPV 82%). For mild dysplasia, the frequency was 21%. As no moderate dysplasia was found, for all types of dysplasia, the frequency was 39% (NPV was 61%).

An overview of autofluorescence's diagnostic accuracy can be found in Table 3.

3.3.2. Iodine Staining

Iodine staining has been widely used for the detection of intraepithelial neoplasia of the esophagus but can also be used to detect oral SCC and dysplasia [38]. Iodine stains healthy tissue and creates an iodine unstained (IU) area on the SCC or dysplastic tissue. Similar to autofluorescence, an IU-safety margin around the IU boundary can be applied to achieve free margin status. Only two interventional studies using 'Method A' were included that assessed this method [38,39].

One study by McMahon et al. used a 10 mm WL-safety margin and a 0 mm IU-safety margin [38]. They compared their prospective iodine-guided surgery cohort, consisting of 40/50 (80%) patients with oral SCC, with a retrospective WL-guided surgery cohort, consisting of 42/50 (84%) patients with oral SCC. They found no SCC-positive margins in the iodine-guided cohort (NPV of 100%) and 2/50 (4%) SCC-positive margins (NPV of 96%) in the WL-guided surgery cohort. They found 1/50 (2%) severe dysplasia and 1/50 (2%) other types of dysplasia in the iodine-guided cohort and 1/50 (2%) severe dysplasia and 13/50 (26%) other types of dysplasia in the WL-guided cohort. The NPV for dysplasia (all types) was 96% in the iodine cohort and 68% in the WL-guided cohort.

Table 2. Methods from included studies.

Author	Method	Technique	Cohorts/Survival Analysis	No. of Tumors/No. of Margin Samples	Consistency	Demarcation of Safety-Margin	Positive Margin Defined by Publication	Definition of Free Margin by Authors	Acquisition Time	Technique Influence on the Final Histopathology	Free Margin Status on the Final Histopathology
Durham, 2020 [36]	A	Autofluorescence	Autofluorescence (R) vs. WL-guided surgery (R)/survival analysis	443	Autofluorescence: 277 OSCC + HGL, control: 216 OSCC + HGL	At least 10 mm from the boundary of the WL-positive and FVL-positive areas	"Positive margin for severe dysplasia or greater histologic change".	Not given	Undefined	Yes	Undefined, only the "first pass margin" is given, defined as the positive margin before re-resections are taken from the tumor bed.
Sun, 2021 [34]	C	Autofluorescence	Diagnostic accuracy of autofluorescence (P)	30/126	30 OSCC	15-20 mm from the boundary of the WL-positive area, no resections based on the FVL-positive area	Carcinoma in situ, invasive carcinoma, and severe dysplasia in mucosal samples	Normal epithelium in mucosal samples	Undefined	No	Undefined, only margins within random samples were reported
McMahon, 2010 [38]	A	Iodine	Iodine (P) vs. WL-guided surgery ®	100	Iodine: 40 OSCC and 10 OPSCC, control: 42 OSCC, 8 OPSCC	10 mm from the boundary of the WL-positive area and 0 mm from the IU-positive areas were included	"Intraepithelial neoplasia in mucosal margin".	"Mucosal margins free from dysplasia, carcinoma in situ and invasive carcinoma"	Undefined	Yes	Iodine: 96% (48/50), WL 96% (34/50)
Umeda, 2011 [39]	A	Iodine	Iodine (R)/Survival analysis.	93	93 OSCC of the tongue	At least 10 mm from the boundary of the WL-positive areas and at least 5 mm from the boundary of the IU-positive areas	"Positive for SCC" or "positive for dysplasia".	SCC ≥ 1 mm from the deep or mucosal margin	Undefined	Yes	81/93 (87%)
Tirelli, 2015 [40]	C	NBI	NBI (P)	16	8 OSCC, 8 OPSCC	15 mm from the boundary of the WL-positive areas and including the boundary of the NBI-positive areas.	SCC < 0.1 mm from the mucosal margin	SCC > 3 mm from the mucosal margin	5 min	Yes, technique-directed FSA did not influence diagnostic accuracy	94% (15/16)/yes
Tirelli, 2017 [41]	B	NBI	NBI (P)	31	20 OSCC, 11 OPSCC (of 2 the result of the reference test was not clear)	15 mm from the boundary of the WL-positive areas and including the boundary of the NBI-positive areas.	SCC < 0.1 mm from the mucosal margin	SCC > 3 mm from the mucosal margin	5 min	Yes, FSA, in addition to the technique, did not influence diagnostic accuracy	77% (24/31)/yes
Tirelli, 2018 [42]	B	NBI	NBI (P)	61	39 OSCC, 22 OPSCC	15 mm from the boundary of the WL-positive areas and including the boundary of the NBI-positive areas.	SCC < 0.1 mm from the mucosal margin	SCC > 3 mm from the mucosal margin	5 min	Yes, FSA, in addition to the technique, did not influence diagnostic accuracy	85% (52/61)/yes
Baj, 2019 [33]	C	NBI	NBI (P)	16/ 88	16 OSCC	15-20 mm from the boundary of the WL-positive area, no resections based on the NBI-positive area	Tumor or dysplasia in the FSA biopsy	No tumor or dysplasia in FSA biopsy	Undefined	No	Undefined, only FSA biopsy status reported

WL: white light, NBI: narrow band imaging, FVL: fluorescence visualization loss, OSCC: oral squamous cell carcinoma, OPSCC: oropharyngeal squamous cell carcinoma, SCC: squamous cell carcinoma, R: retrospective, P: prospective, FSA: frozen section analysis, HGL: high-grade lesions.

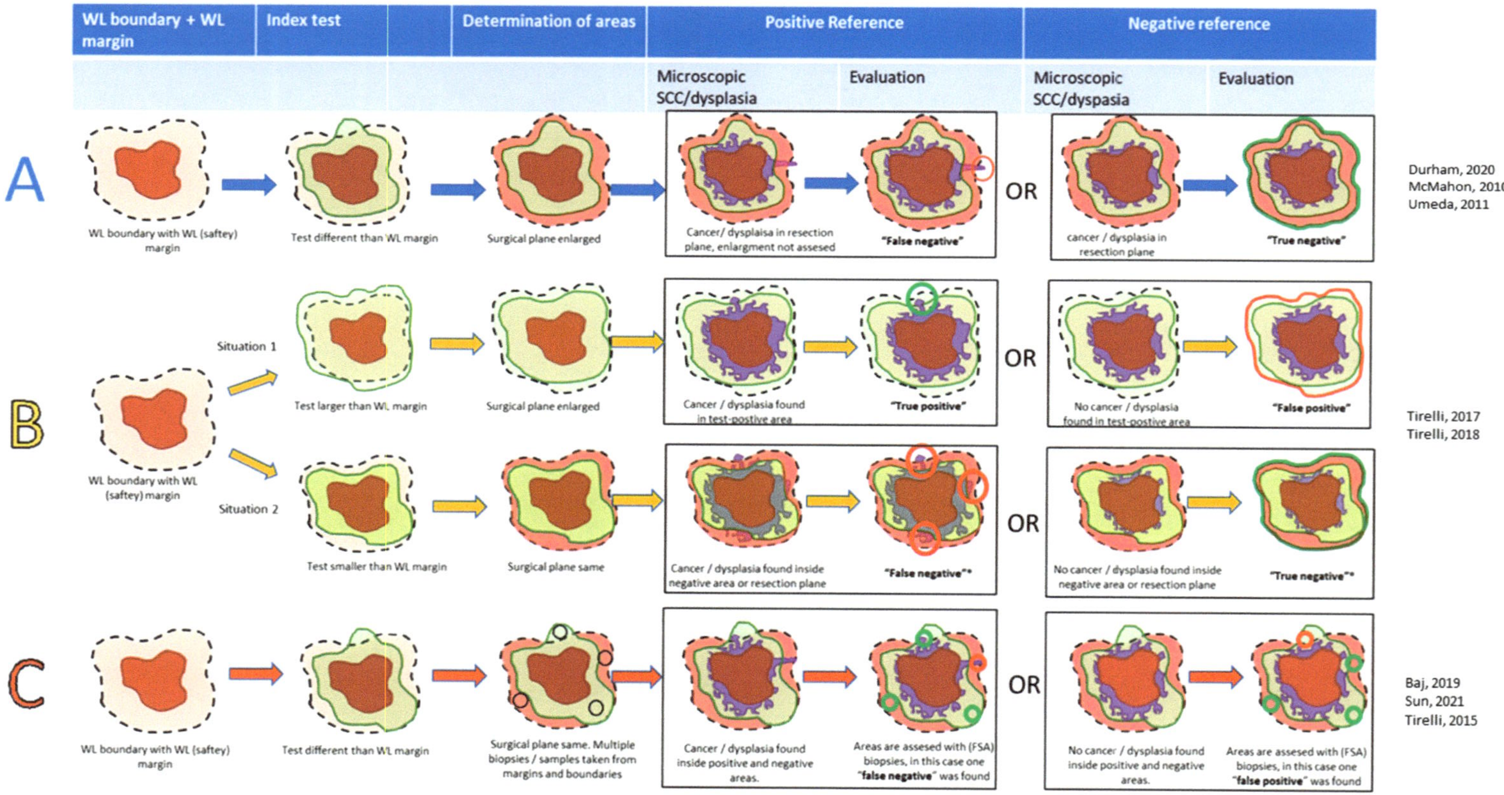

Figure 2. Scheme of the analyzed methods in this review: interventional study (method (**A**), blue arrows), interventional with diagnostic accuracy (method (**B**), yellow arrows), and diagnostic accuracy (method (**C**), red arrows). Dotted line: planned resection margin, which may be changed by the index-test in case of methods (**A**,**B**), light green: positive index-test. Light red: negative index-test (area outside positive area). Dark red: macroscopic tumor. Purple: microscopic tumor or (severe) dysplasia. Bright red: false tests. Bright green: true tests. * In type B studies, if the positive-index test was as large as the WL-safety margin, the specimen was denoted as 'negative' [33,34,36,38–42].

Table 3. Results from studies about autofluorescence.

Author	Evaluation	Reference Results Based on	Test Positive/Negative	Ref Positive/Negative	NPV SCC (Test/WL Control Group)	NPV SCC + Severe Dysplasia (Test/WL Control Group)	NPV SCC + Dysplasia (Test/WL Control Group)	Bias or Concern
Durham, 2020 [36]	Interventional (with WL-guided control group)	Full specimen (OSCC or HGL)	NA/10 mm from the WL-positive area and 10 mm from the FVL-positive area (whichever was wider)	"Severe dysplasia or greater histologic change" in the resection plane on the final histopathology/normal tissue in the resection plane on the final histopathology	Not given	Test: 70% (151/216) Control: 70% (159/227)	Not given	Unknown reason for certain exclusions; patients with small tumors and "High-grade lesions" were included as well.
Sun, 2021 [34]	Diagnostic accuracy	Samples from margin	Sample within the FVL-positive area exceeding the WL-positive area/sample within the FVL-positive area inside the WL-positive area	SCC or dysplasia (all types) in the sample of the FVL-positive area/normal tissue in the sample of the FVL-positive area	100% (126/126)	82% (103/126)	61% (77/126)	126 samples were taken and analyzed from random locations between the boundary of the FVL-positive area and the surgical margin of 30 tumors

WL: white light surgery, FVL: fluorescence visualization loss, FSA: frozen section analysis, NPV: negative predictive value, SCC: squamous cell carcinoma, NA: not applicable.

One single-arm study by Umeda et al. used a 10 mm WL-safety margin and a 5 mm IU-safety margin in a cohort consisting of 93 SCCs of the tongue [39]. They found in their retrospective cohort that only 1/93 (1%) of the patients had SCC-positive mucosal margins, leading to an NPV of 99% for SCC. They found that 6/93 (6%) of the patients had mucosal margins positive for mild dysplasia, leading to an NPV of 94%. The NPV for dysplasia and SCC combined was 86/93 (92%).

Both studies suggest that using iodine is excellent for determining mucosal safety margins and results in most margins free of SCC and dysplasia. The NPV for SCC and dysplasia (all types) of McMahon et al.'s iodine-guided surgery cohort [38] suggest that iodine has the potential to rule out moderate and mild dysplasia in the resection margin when compared to the results of the WL-guided surgery cohort. However, these results assessed the impact of iodine staining in conjunction with the IU-safety margin, lacking specific information on the sensitivity and specificity of the IU area alone.

An overview of iodine's diagnostic accuracy can be found in Table 4.

Table 4. Results from studies about iodine.

Author	Evaluation	Reference Results Based on	Test Positive/Negative	Ref Positive/Negative	NPV SCC (Test Group/WL Control Group)	NPV SCC + Severe Dysplasia or (Test/WL Control Group)	NPV SCC + Dysplasia (Test/WL Control Group)	Bias of Concern
McMahon, 2020 [38]	Interventional (with WL-guided control group)	Full specimen	NA/10 mm from the boundary of the WL-positive area, 0 mm from the IU-positive area	Dysplasia (all types)or SCC in the resection plane	Test: 100% (50/50) Control: 96% (48/50)	Test: 98% (49/50) Control: 96% (47/50)	Test: 96% (48/50) Control: 68% (34/50)	None.
Umeda, 2011 [39]	Interventional (no WL-guided surgery control group)	Full specimen	NA/ 10 mm from the boundary of the WL-positive area and 5 mm from the IU-positive area	Dysplasia or SCC in the resection plane	99% (92/93)	Not given, only mild dysplasia in the resection plane	92% (86/93)	None.

WL: white light, FSA: frozen section analysis, NPV: negative predictive value, CIS: carcinoma in situ, IU: iodine unstained, SCC: squamous cell carcinoma, NA: not applicable.

3.3.3. Narrow Band Imaging

NBI is a technique where the surgical field is illuminated by WL, but the reflection is filtered to only two specific wavelengths (415 and 540 nm) that enhance the visualization of the capillary bed and the intrapapillary loop pattern in the superficial mucosa [41]. Changes in the architecture of the capillaries may indicate SCC or dysplasia in the oral cavity. NBI can be applied to an endoscope and is therefore applicable in surgeries of both the oral and oropharyngeal mucosa. Two 'Method B' [41,42] studies and two 'Method C' [33,40] assessing NBI were included.

The two 'Method B' studies were conducted by Tirelli et al.: one from 2017 [41] and one from 2018 [42]. In their 2017 study, Tirelli et al. [41] evaluated a cohort that consisted of 20/31 (65%) oral SCC patients. In 28/31 (90%) of the patients, the safety margin was expanded, as the NBI-positive area was larger than the 15 mm WL-safety margin, which was considered to be a positive index test. Of these 28 cases, 20 were TPs (i.e., SCC and/or dysplasia of all types found in the extended margin), and 8 were FPs (i.e., no SCC and/or dysplasia of all types found in the extended margin). In 2/31 cases (7%), the NBI-positive area was similar to the 15 mm WL-safety margin, and in only 1/31 (3%) cases, the NBI-positive area was smaller than the 15 mm WL-safety margin. For these three cases, an extension of the safety margin was not needed. Hence, there were three negative index tests, although the authors only reported the presence of SCC and/or dysplasia (all types) in the case with the smaller NBI margin, resulting in one TN case and no FN case. These results yielded a sensitivity of 100% (CI: 83–100%), specificity of 11% (CI: 0–29%), PPV of 71% (CI: 66–76%), and NPV of 100% (CI: 3–100%), for SCC and dysplasia (all types).

Tirelli et al.'s 2018 study [42], used exactly the same method as their 2017 study [41] in a cohort of 39/61 (64%) oral SCC patients. Of 43/61 (70%) cases, an extension of the safety margin was needed, as the NBI-positive area was larger than the 15 mm WL-safety margin (i.e., positive index test). Of these 43 cases, 34 were TPs (i.e., SCC and/or dysplasia of all types in the extended margin), and 9 were FPs (i.e., no SCC and/or dysplasia of all types in the extended margin). In 18/61 (30%) cases, no extension of the safety margin was indicated by NBI, i.e., a negative index test. Sixteen of these 18 cases were TNs, and 2 were FNs. These results yielded a sensitivity of 94% (CI: 81–99%), specificity of 64% (CI: 42–82%), PPV of 79% (CI: 69–87%), and NPV of 89% (CI: 67–97%) for SCC and dysplasia (all types).

Two 'Method C' studies analyzed the diagnostic accuracy of NBI, one by Baj et al. [33] and one by Tirelli et al. from 2015 [40]. Baj et al. [33] assessed a cohort that consisted entirely of oral SCC patients (n = 16). They varied the distance of the WL-safety margin between 15 and 20 mm and took three to eight biopsies per specimen, situated at the border of the NBI-positive areas and of those of the WL-safety margin. After the FSA examination, biopsies were classified as positive or negative for "SCC or dysplasia (all types)". The authors did not discriminate SCC from dysplasia. Three TPs, 5 FNs, 14 FPs, and 32 TNs were found to yield a sensitivity, specificity, PPV, and NPV of 38% (CI: 9–76%), 70% (CI: 54–82%), 18% (CI: 7–37%), and 86% (CI: 78–92%), respectively. Contours of the NBI-positive areas were within the WL-safety margin in 50% of the cases.

Tirelli et al. [40] found in their 'Method C' study from 2015 that the 15 mm WL-safety margin was surrounded by a NBI-positive area in every case. This contrasts with the results from Baj et al. [33], who reported this situation in only 50% of the cases. They performed an FSA in the NBI-positive area and extended the surgical margin according to the NBI in case dysplasia or a SCC was found. In every case, SCC and/or dysplasia were found beyond the 15 mm WL safety margin. For SCC only, it resulted in 12 TPs, 0 FNs, 4 FPs, and 0 TNs cases, yielding a PPV of 75%, a sensitivity of 100%, and a specificity of 0%, but no calculable NPV. For SCC and dysplasia (all types), it resulted in 16 TPs, 0 FNs, 0 FPs, and 0 TNs cases, yielding a PPV of 100%, a sensitivity of 100%, but no calculable specificity or NPV. Although the safety margins were enlarged when FSA confirmed TP, there was still one specimen with SCC-positive margins (6%) and one specimen with margins positive for dysplasia.

NBI is the only assessed technique in this review, of which three out of four studies report both a calculable PPV, NPV sensitivity, and specificity. However, a wide variety of methods are employed to obtain these outcome measurements across the studies.

An overview can be found in Table 5.

Table 5. Results from studies about NBI.

Author	Evaluation	Reference Results Based on	Test Positive/Negative	Ref Positiv/Negative	Sens/Spec Cancer	PPV/NPV Cancer	Sens/Spec SCC + Sdys	PPV/NPV SCC + Sdys	Sens/Spec SCC + Dys (all Types)	PPV/NPV SCC + Dys (All Types)	Bias of Concern
Tirelli, 2015 [40]	Diagnostic accuracy	FSA-samples	The NBI-positive area beyond the 15 mm WL-safety margin/NBI-positive area between the boundary of the WL-positive area and 15 mm WL-safety margin	SCC and/or dysplasia/no SCC and/or dysplasia in the NBI-positive or negative area	Sens: 100% (12/12) Spec: 0% (0/4)	PPV: 75% (12/16) NPV: undefined (0/0)	NA	NA	Sens: 100% (16/16) Spec: undefined (0/0)	PPV: 100% (16/16) NPV: undefined (0/0)	Only the NBI-positive areas were assessed with biopsies, while the NBI-negative areas, (mucosa within the 15 mm W-safety margin, but outside the boundary of the NBI-positive area) did not receive a biopsy. Also, the NBI-positive area seemed too small, since dysplasia and SCC were found in the resection plane. Possible overlap with Tirelli 2017 and Tirelli 2018.
Tirelli, 2017 [41]	Interventional with diagnostic accuracy	Final histopathology	NBI-positive area beyond the 15 mm WL-safety margin/ NBI-positive area between the boundary of the WL-positive area and 15 mm WL-safety margin	SCC and/or dysplasia/no SCC and/or dysplasia in the NBI-positive or negative area	Sens: 100% (12/12) Spec: 6% (1/17)	PPV: 43% (12/28) NPV: 100% (1/1)	Sens: 100% (16/16) Spec: 8% (1/13)	PPV: 57% (16/28) NPV: 100% (1/1)	Sens: 100% (20/20) Spec: 11% (1/9)	PPV: 71% (20/28) NPV: 100% (1/1)	Only one specimen with NBI-negative findings (specimen with the boundary of the NBI-positive area within the WL margin). Of two specimens, the NBI-positive areas were as large as the WL-safety margin, but it was unclear whether the resection planes were free from SCC/dysplasia. Hence, only 29 cases could be evaluated. Possible overlap with Tirelli 2015 and Tirelli 2018.
Tirelli, 2018 [42]	Interventional with diagnostic accuracy	Final histopathology	NBI-positive area beyond the 15 mm WL-safety margin/ NBI-positive area between the boundary of the WL-positive area and 15 mm WL-safety margin	SCC and/or dysplasia/no SCC and/or dysplasia in the NBI-positive or negative area	Sens: 96% (23/24) Spec: 46% (17/37)	PPV: 53% (23/43) NPV: 94% (17/18)	Sens: 93% (28/30) Spec: 52% (16/31)	PPV: 65% (28/43) NPV: 89% (16/18)	Sens: 94% (34/36) Spec: 64% (16/25)	PPV: 79% (34/43) NPV: 89% (16/18)	Possible overlap with Tirelli 2015 and Tirelli 2017.
Baj, 2019 [33]	Diagnostic accuracy	FSA-samples	NBI boundary outside 15–20 mm from the WL boundary/NBI-positive area between the boundary of WL-positive area and 15 mm WL-safety margin	Dysplasia or SCC in FSA biopsy from a positive test situation/no dysplasia or SCC in FSA biopsy	Not given	Not given	Not given	Not given	Sens: 38% (3/8) Spec: 70% (32/46)	PPV: 18% (3/17) NPV: 86% (32/37)	Only small biopsies were taken for certain areas. The WL-safety margin was not from a consistent distance from the WL-positive boundary (varying between 15 and 20 mm).

WL: white light, NBI: narrow band imaging, FSA: frozen section analysis, SCC: squamous cell carcinoma, Sens: sensitivity, Spec: specificity, NPV: negative predictive value, PPV: positive predictive value, Dys: dysplasia, Sdys: Severe dysplasia, NA: not applicable.

4. Discussion

This systematic review highlights techniques that try to define the optimal mucosal surgical resection margins in the treatment of oral SCC. The demarcation of the mucosal surgical margin is an essential part of oral cancer surgery because it serves as a critical reference point for the surgeon to achieve tumor-free (i.e., ≥5 mm) histopathological margins in all dimensions. In the past years, more attention has been given to margin visualization techniques that aid the surgeon in estimating the deep extension of the tumor. Although several systematic reviews assess these techniques, to our knowledge, no reviews specifically illuminate the currently evaluated techniques that enhance the demarcation of the mucosal surgical margin in oral cancer surgery. This systematic review tries to fill in this gap in the literature.

During the setup of this review's methodology, we attempted to assess the visualization techniques by their diagnostic value in identifying positive margins and free margins as defined by the Royal College of Pathologists [10], i.e., <1 mm and ≥5 mm SCC free margins, respectively. However, no studies were found assessing the diagnostic accuracy for close margins with respect to SCC (1–5 mm). Instead, all studies seemed to focus on the presence of SCC or (severe) dysplasia in the resection plane, some of them not making a difference between the SCC or (severe) dysplasia. Indeed, several studies suggest that residual dysplasia has similar effects on disease-free survival as close margins [16,17]. Hence, dysplasia is preferably resected during SCC surgery. However, when compared to residual dysplasia, residual SCC has a far greater impact on patient survival. Moreover, residual SCC requires adjuvant treatments (radiotherapy or re-resections) with higher risks and complication rates compared to CO_2-laser evaporation for residual dysplasia [12,13,18,45]. Unfortunately, none of the included studies discussed the incidence of close mucosal resection margins (1–5 mm free of SCC), and some did not differentiate between SCC and (severe) dysplasia in the resection plane.

This systematic review included studies to examine the benefits of margin visualization techniques in a surgical context. Consequently, studies that specifically reported negative or clear margins were included, while those that solely assessed the presence of tumors were not included. As a result, three of the selected studies primarily consisted of interventional research ('Type A' studies) [36,38,39]. These studies do not generate a positive index test, as the surgical goal is to achieve a negative index test. Therefore, calculating a meaningful sensitivity, specificity, or PPV is impossible. For these studies, we cannot determine whether the implementation of these margin visualization techniques will result in potential over-treatment, i.e., unnecessary wide resection margins. Nevertheless, although strongly dependent on the incidence of histologically positive margins, the NPV indicates the effectiveness of the margin visualization technique for the resection of SCC and/or dysplasia.

In one 'Method C' study that investigated autofluorescence, conducted by Sun et al., NPV was the only measurement for diagnostic accuracy that could be reported, as the authors found that all FVL-areas were smaller than the 15–20 mm WL-safety margin (i.e. negative-index-test) [34]. This means that also, for this study, no valuable comparison between the diagnostic accuracy for identification of SCC-positive margins and dysplastic-positive margins was possible. While the authors used the WL-safety margin during the resection, their NPV of 100% for SCC in the resection plane showed that if an FVL-safety margin had been used, no SCC would have been found in the resection plane. However, for severe dysplasia and all types of dysplasia, the NPV would have been 28% and 39%, respectively. The presented numbers are comparable with the multicenter randomized controlled trial of Durham et al. [36], who found severe dysplasia in the resection plane in 30% when autofluorescence guidance was used. The frequency of positive margins and 5-year local recurrence were not lower in the autofluorescence-guided cohort when compared to the WL-guided cohort. According to the authors, these unexpected results were most likely caused by the relative inexperience in using autofluorescence of the participating centers outside the coordinating center. In the studies by Morikawa et al., larger FVL-safety margins were used (in combination with iodine), yet there was a considerable amount of FSA-positive rate for SCC and/or dysplasia (all types), namely 19% and 18%.

Two interventional ('Method A') studies using iodine-guided surgery reported a positive margin rate per specimen. McMahon et al. [38] compared an iodine-guided cohort with a WL-guided control cohort. They only found a significant difference between both cohorts when all types of dysplasia were considered positive (96% in the iodine-guided cohort vs. 68% in the WL-guided control cohort), which suggests that iodine-guided surgery makes the most difference in the detection of moderate or mild dysplasia. Umeda et al. found comparable results and reported no local recurrence in their single-arm study [39].

All studies examined NBI guidance assessed dysplasia (all types) in the resection plane, but only several studies did this specifically for SCC and/or severe dysplasia [40–42]. Baj et al. [33] reported a lower sensitivity for SCC and dysplasia (combined) in the resection plane (38%) compared to Tirelli et al.'s studies, which ranged from 94% to 100%. The reduced TP rate in Baj et al. may be subject to their sampling strategy—taking samples from the borders of NBI-positive areas, unlike Tirelli et al., who sampled within NBI-positive areas. In the diagnostic accuracy study ('Type B') of Tirelli from 2017, only one negative index test was found [41]. Interestingly, their subsequent study showed a much higher number of negative index tests [42]. This figure might have been the result of a learning curve.

Based on the included studies, it is impossible to determine whether autofluorescence, iodine guidance, or NBI is more accurate than WL-guided surgery to determine a safe surgical mucosal margin and also in terms of distinguishing (severe) dysplasia from SCC. There are several reasons.

Firstly, there is a high variety in the definition of a positive reference-standard dysplasia: i.e., SCC, SCC in combination with severe dysplasia, or SCC in combination with all types of dysplasia in the resection plane. Several studies do not differentiate between SCC and (severe) dysplasia.

Secondly, the index tests of all studies were not designed to distinguish (severe) dysplasia from SCC but rather tissue that was divergent from normal mucosa. For autofluorescence, neoplastic, dysplastic, and inflammatory tissue all show FVL [44]. Staining with Lugol's iodine is based on the fact that iodine is glycophilic and does not bind to cells that lack glycogen, leading to iodine unstained areas. However, SCC and dysplasia both lack glycogen; therefore, Lugol's iodine cannot differentiate between tissue types [38]. Finally, NBI is based on detecting alternations in the interpapillary capillary loops, which can underlie histopathologic changes, but this accounts for both SCC and all types of dysplasia [40].

Thirdly, all studies are possibly subject to high inter and intra-observer variability, requiring expertise and experience to achieve a sufficient diagnostic value. None of the studies presented a clear cutoff value to define a positive or negative index test. In the studies of Tirelli et al., NBI experts needed to be consulted to determine the NBI-safety margin, suggesting that finding alterations in the intrapapillary capillary loop patterns is difficult. Hence, they have found a variety of diagnostic accuracies [40–42].

Fourthly, the included studies have a relatively small number of included patients or conducted retrospective studies. Only Durham et al. [36] conducted a randomized clinical trial and may pose the highest level of evidence that autofluorescence guidance does not influence obtaining more adequate margins or more local control than WL guidance. However, the inexperience of certain observers and the surgeons' awareness of obtaining adequate margins in the WL-guided control cohort might have influenced the results.

Lastly, in most studies, only the NPV could be calculated. The sensitivity, specificity and PPV remain unknown for autofluorescence and iodine guidance. The lack of this information complicates the assessment of their potential impact on a "tailored-made" approach. Without these data, it remains unclear how the adjustment of the safety margin around a positive index test could affect surgical margins, either by expanding or reducing them. Only two studies suggested that NBI guidance could lead to more tailored-made resections. Tirelli et al. have shown a specificity of 64%, meaning that 64% of the margins positive for SCC or dysplasia were rightfully made smaller if only a resection plane free of SCC or dysplasia is considered acceptable [42]. For Baj et al., this number was 70% [33].

There are several other margin visualization techniques that could lead to new insights when investigated in a surgical setting. Optical coherence tomography (OCT), for instance, works essentially in the same manner as an ultrasound but uses light instead of sound waves. Because of the short wavelength of light, its penetration depth is not more than 0.5 mm for mucosa, but it can provide highly detailed images [46]. At the moment, the setup of OCT devices mostly does not allow intraoral assessment [47]. In one study by Sunny et al. [48], a hand-held OCT device was introduced for intraoral use. The authors captured images of multiple zones around the tumor and compared them with the histopathological report. The observers of the OCT data were blinded for the surgical procedure. They found that OCT was able to detect SCC inside the tumor and the area around the visible tumor with a sensitivity and specificity of 100%. For dysplasia, the sensitivity and specificity were 93% and 69%, respectively. The study was not included in this review because of the limited field of view of the device [48]. Further development is needed to eventually assess the whole mucosal part of a tumor with OCT.

Other fluorescence-guided techniques exist besides autofluorescence. Contrast-agent-based fluorescence uses a near-infrared fluorescent label for SCC-specific antigens, such as cetuximab [49] or panitumumab [50]. This technique can be used intra-orally but mostly to check the wound bed on any residual fluorescent signal [49]. The scope of most studies researching this technique is an ex vivo assessment of the resection specimen. FSA biopsies can be taken from the spot with the highest fluorescent signal and analyzed to determine whether this margin is close or positive. If not, it may suggest that the other fluorescent spots on the specimen are free margins as well [50]. One major advantage of this technique is that it can produce objective values for the index test, i.e., the signal-to-background ratio of the fluorescence signal, which eliminates inter-observer dependence, as presented by de Wit et al [49]. As autofluorescence does not yield significant improvements in obtaining mucosal margins when compared to WL-guided surgery, it would be interesting to investigate the impact of contrast-agent-based fluorescence on mucosal margins in randomized control trials, following a similar setup as Durham et al. [36].

Apart from iodine staining, staining with toluidine blue has also been researched. However, the studies of concern [51,52] stained the resection specimen, but only after the resection was completed. These studies concluded that this stain is highly sensitive to SCC in the resection margins but has a low PPV. Kerawala et al. [53] performed a study on the intra-oral use of toluidine blue as a margin visualization technique, but this study was also not included since it was published before 2010. They concluded that Toluidine blue is a suitable adjunct in identifying invasive tumors but has no benefit in identifying dysplastic tissue at the surgical margins. Unfortunately, their findings did not result in further research on the intraoperative application of Toluidine blue in the past decade.

Several limitations should be acknowledged in this review. Firstly, the inclusion of various methodologies (such as 'Method A') and diverse outcome measures (including diagnostic accuracy for both 'SCC and dysplasia' or 'SCC alone') poses a challenge in assessing potential publication bias. This complexity makes it difficult to employ standard methods like funnel plots or Egger's test for a comprehensive evaluation. Secondly, as some included articles have the same author (i.e., Tirelli et al.) and were published within four years while assessing the same technique, it cannot be ruled out that there may be some overlap between the described cohorts. However, evidence is lacking to confirm or refute this possibility.

We suggest that future studies on margin visualization techniques should focus more on the differentiation between (severe) dysplasia and SCC. Moreover, the evaluation of diagnostic accuracy should go beyond the goal to achieve only a negative index test. Ideally, a setup presented by Sunny et al. [48] would give a broader insight into the diagnostic accuracy for SCC and severe dysplasia. Independent observers designated the images obtained from the OCT device as "normal," "potentially malignant," and "malignant". This was conducted at different zones from the tumor border, which makes it feasible to determine the diagnostic accuracy for SCC and/or dysplasia in the resection plane but also for close margins (SCC at 1–5 mm from the resection plane). If technically possible, the margin visualization technique should also be as inter-observer-independent as possible. An example is the signal-to-background ratio-based fluorescence of de Wit et al. [49], where the author used an objective value to determine tumor presence.

5. Conclusions

Three margin visualization techniques for oral SCC have been reviewed in a pre-incision surgical setting to determine a safe mucosal margin demarcation: autofluorescence, iodine staining, and NBI. Most of these studies did not assess the frequency of free margins (≥5 mm) but only the presence of dysplasia and SCC in the resection plane. Apart from fluorescence, the margin visualization techniques found a wide variety in diagnostic accuracy, possibly due to learning curves and inter- or intra-observer variability. Autofluorescence guidance seems to make no difference in obtaining better margins than WL guidance. However, contrast-agent-based autofluorescence might be more effective, and testing this technique in large randomized controlled trials is advisable. We also recommend continuing to investigate iodine and NBI-guided surgery in more extensive cohorts, with a larger focus on differentiation between (severe) dysplasia and SCC, as the consequences of the treatment of residual dysplasia and SCC are highly different. Apart from reporting the treatment effect of the technique in terms of margins 'free from SCC and (severe) dysplasia', the presence of close (1–5 mm) or free (≥5 mm) margins should be reported as well, according to the standard guidelines. Finally, we recommend a larger focus on actual diagnostic accuracy rather than treatment effect only. This strategy would allow for determining a meaningful sensitivity, specificity, and PPV, in addition to negative predictive value (NPV). Such an approach will lead to a better understanding of the value of these techniques.

Supplementary Materials: The following supporting information can be downloaded at: https://www.mdpi.com/article/10.3390/cancers16061148/s1". PubMed search term and Embase search term.

Author Contributions: Conceptualization: K.J.d.K., C.M.E.M.A., R.N., R.d.B. and R.J.J.v.E.; Methodology: K.J.d.K., C.M.E.M.A., R.N., R.d.B. and R.J.J.v.E.; Formal analysis: K.J.d.K., C.M.E.M.A. and R.N.; Investigation: K.J.d.K., C.M.E.M.A. and R.N.; Resources: R.N., R.d.B. and R.J.J.v.E.; Data curation: K.J.d.K. and C.M.E.M.A.; Writing—Original draft: K.J.d.K. and C.M.E.M.A.; Writing—Review and Editing: R.N., R.d.B. and R.J.J.v.E.; Visualization: K.J.d.K. and C.M.E.M.A.; Supervision: R.N., R.d.B. and R.J.J.v.E.; Project administration: K.J.d.K. and C.M.E.M.A.; Funding acquisition: R.N. All authors have read and agreed to the published version of the manuscript.

Funding: This work was supported by KWF, the Dutch Cancer Society, grant number 11906. KWF (the Dutch Cancer Society) funded this work but had no influence on the research.

Conflicts of Interest: The authors declare no conflicts of interest.

References

1. Fitzmaurice, C.; Dicker, D.; Pain, A.; Hamavid, H.; Moradi-Lakeh, M.; MacIntyre, M.; Allen, C.; Hansen, G.; Woodbrook, R.; Wolfe, C.; et al. The Global Burden of Cancer 2013. *JAMA Oncol.* **2015**, *1*, 505–527. [CrossRef]
2. Chinn, S.B.; Myers, J.N. Oral cavity carcinoma: Current management, controversies, and future directions. *Am. Soc. Clin. Oncol.* **2015**, *33*, 3269–3276. [CrossRef]
3. Daniell, J.; Udovicich, C.; Rowe, D.; McDowell, L.; Vital, D.; Bressel, M.; Magarey, M.; Iseli, T.; Wong, T.; Lekgabe, E.; et al. Impact of histological Oral Tongue Cancer margins on locoregional recurrence: A multi-centre retrospective analysis. *Oral Oncol.* **2020**, *111*, 105004. [CrossRef]
4. Lee, D.Y.; Kang, S.H.; Kim, J.H.; Kim, M.; Oh, K.H.; Woo, J.; Kwon, S.; Jung, K.; Baek, S. Survival and recurrence of resectable tongue cancer: Resection margin cutoff value by T classification. *Head Neck* **2018**, *40*, 283–291. [CrossRef]

5. Brinkman, D.; Callanan, D.; O'Shea, R.; Jawad, H.; Feeley, L.; Sheahan, P. Impact of 3 mm margin on risk of recurrence and survival in oral cancer. *Oral Oncol.* **2020**, *110*, 104883. [CrossRef]
6. Singh, A.; Mishra, A.; Singhvi, H.; Sharin, F.; Bal, M.; Laskar, S.; Prabhash, K.; Chaturvedi, P. Optimum surgical margins in squamous cell carcinoma of the oral tongue: Is the current definition adequate? *Oral Oncol.* **2020**, *111*, 10948. [CrossRef] [PubMed]
7. Bajwa, M.S.; Houghton, D.; Java, K.; Triantafyllou, A.; Khattak, O.; Bekiroglu, F.; Schache, A.G.; Brown, J.S.; McCaul, J.A.; Rogers, S.N.; et al. The relevance of surgical margins in clinically early oral squamous cell carcinoma. *Oral Oncol.* **2020**, *110*, 104913. [CrossRef] [PubMed]
8. Dik, E.A.; Willems, S.M.; Ipenburg, N.A.; Adriaansens, S.O.; Rosenberg, A.J.W.P.; Van Es, R.J.J. Resection of early oral squamous cell carcinoma with positive or close margins: Relevance of adjuvant treatment in relation to local recurrence: Margins of 3 mm as safe as 5 mm. *Oral Oncol.* **2014**, *50*, 611–615. [CrossRef] [PubMed]
9. Haddad, R.; Hicks, W.; Hitchcock, Y.; Jimeno, A.; Leizman, D.; Pinto, H.; Rocco, J.; Rodriguez, C.; Schwartz, D.; Shah, J.; et al. NCCN Guidelines Version 2.2023 Head and Neck Cancers. 2023. Available online: https://www.nccn.org/home/member- (accessed on 2 February 2023).
10. Helliwell, T.; Woolgar, J. Standards and Datasets for Reporting Cancers. 2013. Available online: www.nice.org.uk/accreditation (accessed on 2 February 2023).
11. Varvares, M.A.; Poti, S.; Kenyon, B.; Christopher, K.; Walker, R.J. Surgical margins and primary site resection in achieving local control in oral cancer resections. *Laryngoscope* **2015**, *125*, 2298–2307. [CrossRef]
12. Ettl, T.; El-Gindi, A.; Hautmann, M.; Gosau, M.; Weber, F.; Rohrmeier, C.; Gerken, M.; Müller, S.; Reichert, T.; Klingelhöffer, C. Positive frozen section margins predict local recurrence in R0-resected squamous cell carcinoma of the head and neck. *Oral Oncol.* **2016**, *55*, 17–23. [CrossRef] [PubMed]
13. Jehn, P.; Stier, R.; Tavassol, F.; Dittmann, J.; Zimmerer, R.; Gellrich, N.; Krüskemper, G. Spalthoff SPhysical and Psychological Impairments Associated with Mucositis after Oral Cancer Treatment and Their Impact on Quality of Life. *Oncol Res. Treat.* **2019**, *42*, 342–348. [CrossRef] [PubMed]
14. Kubik, M.; Sridharan, S.; Varvares, M.; Zandberg, D.; Skinner, H.; Seethala, R.; Chiosea, S. Intraoperative Margin Assessment in Head and Neck Cancer: A Case of Misuse and Abuse? *Head Neck Pathol.* **2020**, *14*, 291–302. [CrossRef] [PubMed]
15. Slaughter, D.P.; Southwick, H.W.; Smejkal, W. "Field cancerization" in oral stratified squamous epithelium. Clinical implications of multicentric origin. *Cancer* **1953**, *6*, 963–968. [CrossRef]
16. Gokavarapu, S.; Parvataneni, N.; Pavagada, S.; Rao, L.C.; Raju, K.; Rao, T.S. Mild to moderate dysplasia at surgical margin is a significant indicator of survival in patients with oral cancer. *Oral Surg. Oral Med. Oral Pathol. Oral Radiol.* **2017**, *123*, 330–337. [CrossRef]
17. Singh, A.; Mair, M.; Singhvi, H.; Ramalingam, N.; Bal, M.; Lamba, K.; Nair, D.; Nair, S.; Chaturvedi, P. Incidence and impact of dysplasia at final resection margins in cancers of the oral cavity. *Acta Oto-Laryngol.* **2020**, *140*, 963–969. [CrossRef]
18. Mogedas-Vegara, A.; Hueto-Madrid, J.-A.; Chimenos-Küstner, E.; Bescós-Atín, C. Oral leukoplakia treatment with the carbon dioxide laser: A systematic review of the literature. *J. Cranio-Maxillofac. Surg.* **2016**, *44*, 331–336. [CrossRef]
19. Smits, R.W.H.; Koljenović, S.; Hardillo, J.A.; Hove, I.T.; Meeuwis, C.A.; Sewnaik, A.; Dronkers, E.A.; Schut, T.C.B.; Langeveld, T.P.M.; Molenaar, J.; et al. Resection margins in oral cancer surgery: Room for improvement. *Head Neck* **2016**, *38* (Suppl. S1), E2197–E2203. [CrossRef] [PubMed]
20. DiNardo, L.J.; Lin, J.; Karageorge, L.S.; Powers, C.N. Accuracy, Utility, and Cost of Frozen Section Margins in Head and Neck Cancer Surgery. *Laryngoscope* **2000**, *110*, 1773–1776. [CrossRef]
21. Bulbul, M.G.; Tarabichi, O.; Sethi, R.K.; Parikh, A.S.; Varvares, M.A. Does Clearance of Positive Margins Improve Local Control in Oral Cavity Cancer? A Meta-analysis. *Otolaryngol. Head Neck Surg.* **2019**, *161*, 235–244. [CrossRef]
22. de Koning, K.J.; van Es, R.J.; Klijn, R.J.; Breimer, G.E.; Dankbaar, J.W.; Braunius, W.W.; van Cann, E.M.; Dieleman, F.J.; Rijken, J.A.; Tijink, B.M.; et al. Application and accuracy of ultrasound-guided resections of tongue cancer. *Oral Oncol.* **2022**, *133*, 106023. [CrossRef]
23. Adriaansens, C.M.E.M.; de Koning, K.J.; de Bree, R.; Dankbaar, J.W.; Breimer, G.E.; van Es, R.J.J.; Noorlag, R. Ultrasound-guided resection for squamous cell carcinoma of the buccal mucosa: A feasibility study. *Head Neck* **2023**, *45*, 647–657. [CrossRef]
24. Heidkamp, J.; Weijs, W.L.J.; Grunsven, A.C.H.v.E.; Vries, I.d.L.; Maas, M.C.; Rovers, M.M.; Fütterer, J.J.; Steens, S.C.A.; Takes, R.P. Assessment of surgical tumor-free resection margins in fresh squamous-cell carcinoma resection specimens of the tongue using a clinical MRI system. *Head Neck* **2020**, *42*, 2039–2049. [CrossRef] [PubMed]
25. Brouwer de Koning, S.G.; Schaeffers, A.W.M.A.; Schats, W.; van den Brekel, M.W.M.; Ruers, T.J.M.; Karakullukcu, M.B. Assessment of the deep resection margin during oral cancer surgery: A systematic review. *Eur. J. Surg. Oncol.* **2021**, *47*, 2220–2232. [CrossRef]
26. Kain, J.J.; Birkeland, A.C.; Udayakumar, N.; Morlandt, A.B.; Stevens, T.M.; Carroll, W.R.; Rosenthal, E.L.; Warram, J.M. Surgical margins in oral cavity squamous cell carcinoma: Current practices and future directions. *Laryngoscope* **2020**, *130*, 128–138. [CrossRef] [PubMed]
27. Young, K.; Ma, E.; Kejriwal, S.; Nielsen, T.; Aulakh, S.S.; Birkeland, A.C. Intraoperative In Vivo Imaging Modalities in Head and Neck Cancer Surgical Margin Delineation: A Systematic Review. *Cancers* **2022**, *14*, 3416. [CrossRef]

28. Carnicelli, G.; Disconzi, L.; Cerasuolo, M.; Casiraghi, E.; Costa, G.; De Virgilio, A.; Esposito, A.A.; Ferreli, F.; Fici, F.; Casto, A.L.; et al. Image-Guided Intraoperative Assessment of Surgical Margins in Oral Cavity Squamous Cell Cancer: A Diagnostic Test Accuracy Review. *Diagnostics* **2023**, *13*, 1846. [CrossRef]
29. de Koning, S.G.B.; Karakullukcu, M.B.; Lange, C.A.; Ruers, T.J. The oral cavity tumor thickness: Measurement accuracy and consequences for tumor staging. *Eur. J. Surg. Oncol.* **2019**, *45*, 2131–2136. [CrossRef]
30. Page, M.J.; McKenzie, J.E.; Bossuyt, P.M.; Boutron, I.; Hoffmann, T.C.; Mulrow, C.D.; Shamseer, L.; Tetzlaff, J.M.; Akl, E.A.; Brennan, S.E.; et al. The PRISMA 2020 statement: An updated guideline for reporting systematic reviews. *Syst. Rev.* **2021**, *10*, 89. [CrossRef] [PubMed]
31. Bramer, W.M.; Giustini, D.; De Jong, G.B.; Holland, L.; Bekhuis, T. De-duplication of database search results for systematic reviews in endnote. *J. Med. Libr. Assoc.* **2016**, *104*, 240–243. [CrossRef]
32. Whiting, P.; Rutjes, A.; Westwood, M.; Mallett, S.; Deeks, J.; Reitsma, J.; Leeflang, M.; Sterne, J.; Bossuyt, M. QUADAS-2: A Revised Tool for the Quality Assessment of Diagnostic Accuracy Studies. 2011. Available online: https://annals.org (accessed on 1 September 2023).
33. Baj, A.; Fusco, N.; Bolzoni, A.; Carioli, D.; Mazzucato, C.; Faversani, A.; Bresciani, L.; Maggioni, M.; Capaccio, P. A novel inte-grated platform for the identification of surgical margins in oral squamous cell carcinoma: Results from a prospective single-institution series. *BMC Cancer* **2019**, *19*, 467. [CrossRef]
34. Sun, L.-F.; Wang, C.-X.; Cao, Z.-Y.; Han, W.; Guo, S.-S.; Wang, Y.-Z.; Meng, Y.; Hou, C.-X.; Zhu, Q.-H.; Tang, Y.-T.; et al. Evaluation of autofluorescence visualization system in the delineation of oral squamous cell carcinoma surgical margins. *Photodiagnosis Photodyn. Ther.* **2021**, *36*, 102487. [CrossRef] [PubMed]
35. Morikawa, T.; Bessho, H.; Nomura, T.; Kozakai, A.; Kosugi, A.; Shibahara, T. Setting of the surgical margin using optical in-strument for treatment of early tongue squamous cell carcinoma. *J. Oral Maxillofac. Surg. Med. Pathol.* **2019**, *31*, 8–12. [CrossRef]
36. Durham, J.; Brasher, P.; Anderson, D.; Yoo, J.; Hart, R.; Dort, J.; Seikaly, H.; Kerr, P.; Rosin, M.; Poh, C. Effect of Fluorescence Visualization-Guided Surgery on Local Recurrence of Oral Squamous Cell Carcinoma: A Randomized Clinical Trial. *JAMA Otolaryngol. Head Neck Surg.* **2020**, *146*, 1149–1155. [CrossRef] [PubMed]
37. Morikawa, T.; Shibahara, T.; Takano, M. Combination of fluorescence visualization and iodine solution-guided surgery for local control of early tongue cancer. *Int. J. Oral Maxillofac. Surg.* **2023**, *52*, 161–167. [CrossRef] [PubMed]
38. McMahon, J.; Devine, J.C.; McCaul, J.A.; McLellan, D.R.; Farrow, A. Use of Lugol's iodine in the resection of oral and oropharyngeal squamous cell carcinoma. *Br. J. Oral Maxillofac. Surg.* **2010**, *48*, 84–87. [CrossRef] [PubMed]
39. Umeda, M.; Shigeta, T.; Takahashi, H.; Minamikawa, T.; Komatsubara, H.; Oguni, A.; Shibuya, Y.; Komori, T. Clinical evaluation of Lugol's iodine staining in the treatment of stage I–II squamous cell carcinoma of the tongue. *Int. J. Oral Maxillofac. Surg.* **2011**, *40*, 593–596. [CrossRef] [PubMed]
40. Tirelli, G.; Piovesana, M.; Gatto, A.; Tofanelli, M.; Biasotto, M.; Nata, F.B. Narrow band imaging in the intra-operative definition of resection margins in oral cavity and oropharyngeal cancer. *Oral Oncol.* **2015**, *51*, 908–913. [CrossRef]
41. Tirelli, G.; Piovesana, M.; Gatto, A.; Torelli, L.; Di Lenarda, R.; Nata, F.B. NBI utility in the pre-operative and intra-operative assessment of oral cavity and oropharyngeal carcinoma. *Am. J. Otolaryngol.* **2017**, *38*, 65–71. [CrossRef]
42. Tirelli, G.; Piovesana, M.; Marcuzzo, A.V.; Gatto, A.; Biasotto, M.; Bussani, R.; Zandonà, L.; Giudici, F.; Nata, F.B. Tailored resections in oral and oropharyngeal cancer using narrow band imaging. *Am. J. Otolaryngol.* **2018**, *39*, 197–203. [CrossRef]
43. Tirelli, G.; Nata, F.B.; Gatto, A.; Bussani, R.; Spinato, G.; Zacchigna, S.; Piovesana, M. Intraoperative Margin Control in Transoral Approach for Oral and Oropharyngeal Cancer. *Laryngoscope* **2019**, *129*, 1810–1815. [CrossRef]
44. Lane, P.M.; Gilhuly, T.; Whitehead, P.; Zeng, H.; Poh, C.F.; Ng, S.; Williams, P.M.; Zhang, L.; Rosin, M.P.; MacAulay, C.E. Simple device for the direct visualization of oral-cavity tissue fluorescence. *J. Biomed. Opt.* **2006**, *11*, 024006. [CrossRef]
45. Yang, Z.-H.; Chen, W.-L.; Huang, H.-Z.; Pan, C.-B.; Li, J.-S. Quality of Life of Patients With Tongue Cancer 1 Year After Surgery. *J. Oral Maxillofac. Surg.* **2010**, *68*, 2164–2168. [CrossRef] [PubMed]
46. De Leeuw, F.; Abbaci, M.; Casiraghi, O.; Ben Lakhdar, A.; Alfaro, A.; Breuskin, I.; Laplace-Builhé, C. Value of Full-Field Optical Coherence Tomography Imaging for the Histological Assessment of Head and Neck Cancer. *Lasers Surg. Med.* **2020**, *52*, 768–778. [CrossRef] [PubMed]
47. Hamdoon, Z.; Jerjes, W.; McKenzie, G.; Jay, A.; Hopper, C. Optical coherence tomography in the assessment of oral squamous cell carcinoma resection margins. *Photodiagnosis Photodyn. Ther.* **2016**, *13*, 211–217. [CrossRef] [PubMed]
48. Sunny, S.P.; Agarwal, S.; James, B.L.; Heidari, E.; Muralidharan, A.; Yadav, V.; Pillai, V.; Shetty, V.; Chen, Z.; Hedne, N.; et al. Intra-operative point-of-procedure delineation of oral cancer margins using optical coherence tomography. *Oral Oncol.* **2019**, *92*, 12–19. [CrossRef]
49. De Wit, J.; Vonk, J.; Voskuil, F.; de Visscher, S.; Schepman, K.; Hooghiemstra, W.; Linssen, M.; Elias, S.; Halmos, G.; Plaat, B.; et al. EGFR-targeted fluorescence molecular imaging for in-traoperative margin assessment in oral cancer patients: A phase II trial. *Nat. Commun.* **2023**, *14*, 4952. [CrossRef]
50. Van Keulen, S.; Nishio, N.; Birkeland, A.; Fakurnejad, S.; Martin, B.; Forouzanfar, T.; Cunanan, K.; Colevas, A.; Van Den Berg, N.; Rosenthal, E. The sentinel margin: Intraoperative ex vivo specimen mapping using relative fluorescence intensity. *Clin. Cancer Res.* **2019**, *25*, 4656–4662. [CrossRef]
51. Junaid, M.; Choudhary, M.M.; A Sobani, Z.; Murtaza, G.; Qadeer, S.; Ali, N.S.; Khan, M.J.; Suhail, A. A comparative analysis of toluidine blue with frozen section in oral squamous cell carcinoma. *World J. Surg. Oncol.* **2012**, *10*, 57. [CrossRef]

52. Algadi, H.H.; Abou-Bakr, A.A.-E.; Jamali, O.M.; Fathy, L.M. Toluidine blue versus frozen section for assessment of mucosal tumor margins in oral squamous cell carcinoma. *BMC Cancer* **2020**, *20*, 1147. [CrossRef]
53. Kerawala, C.J.; Beale, V.; Reed, M.; Martin, C. The role of vital tissue staining the marginal control of oral squamous cell carcinoma Oncology. *Int. J. Oral Maxillofac. Surg.* **2000**, *29*, 32–35. [CrossRef]

Disclaimer/Publisher's Note: The statements, opinions and data contained in all publications are solely those of the individual author(s) and contributor(s) and not of MDPI and/or the editor(s). MDPI and/or the editor(s) disclaim responsibility for any injury to people or property resulting from any ideas, methods, instructions or products referred to in the content.

Current Oncology

MDPI

Article

Comparison of Weekly Paclitaxel Regimens in Recurrent Platinum-Resistant Ovarian Cancer: A Single Institution Retrospective Study

Laurence Morin [1], Louis-Philippe Grenier [2], Nicolas Foucault [3], Éric Lévesque [1], François Fabi [4], Eve-Lyne Langlais [5], Alexandra Sebastianelli [5], Marianne Lavoie [1], Marc Lalancette [1], Marie Plante [5], Mahukpe Narcisse Ulrich Singbo [6] and Vincent Castonguay [1,*]

[1] Medical Oncology Division, Centre Hospitalier Universitaire de Québec-Université Laval, Québec, QC G1J 5B3, Canada; lamor82@ulaval.ca (L.M.); eric.levesque.med@ssss.gouv.qc.ca (É.L.); marianne.lavoie.med@ssss.gouv.qc.ca (M.L.); marc.lalancette.med@ssss.gouv.qc.ca (M.L.)

[2] Medical Oncology Pharmacy Department, Centre Hospitalier Universitaire de Québec-Université Laval, Québec, QC G1J 5B3, Canada; louis-philippe.grenier@chudequebec.ca

[3] Pharmacy Department, Unité de Formation et de Recherche en Santé de Rouen, 76183 Normandie, France; nicolasfoucault96@gmail.com

[4] Radio-Oncology Division, Centre Hospitalier Universitaire de Québec-Université Laval, Québec, QC G1J 5B3, Canada; francois.fabi.med@ssss.gouv.qc.ca

[5] Gynecologic Oncology Division, Centre Hospitalier Universitaire de Québec-Université Laval, Québec, QC G1J 5B3, Canada; alexandra.sebastianelli.med@ssss.gouv.qc.ca (A.S.); marie.plante.med@ssss.gouv.qc.ca (M.P.)

[6] Centre de Recherche du Centre Hospitalier Universitaire de Québec-Université Laval, Québec, QC G1E 6W2, Canada; narcisse.singbo@crchudequebec.ulaval.ca

* Correspondence: vincent.castonguay.med@ssss.gouv.qc.ca; Tel.: +418-525-4444

Abstract: Weekly paclitaxel (WP) is a chemotherapeutic cornerstone in the management of patients with platinum-resistant ovarian carcinoma. Multiple WP dosing regimens have been used clinically and studied individually. However, no formal comparison of these regimens is available to provide objective guidance in clinical decision making. The primary objective of this study was to compare the cumulative dose of paclitaxel delivered using 80 mg/m^2/week, administered using either a 3 weeks out of 4 (WP3) or a 4 weeks out of 4 (WP4) regimen. The secondary objective was to evaluate the clinical outcomes associated with both regimens, including efficacy and toxicity parameters. Our retrospective cohort comprised 149 patients harboring platinum-resistant ovarian cancer treated at the CHU de Québec from January 2012 to January 2023. WP3 and WP4 reached a similar cumulative dose (1353.7 vs. 1404.2 mg/m^2; $p = 0.29$). No significant differences in the clinical outcomes were observed. The frequency of dose reduction was significantly higher for WP4 than WP3 (44.7% vs. 4.9%; $p < 0.01$), mainly due to treatment intolerance from toxicity (34.0% vs. 3.9%; $p < 0.01$). Our data suggest that a WP3 regimen delivers a similar cumulative dose to WP4, hence offering a better tolerability profile without compromising efficacy.

Keywords: paclitaxel; ovarian carcinoma; platinum-resistant

1. Introduction

In 2023, approximately 3100 Canadian women received a diagnosis of ovarian cancer [1]. Notwithstanding its low incidence, ovarian cancer represents the fifth leading cause of cancer-related death in this population and is the most lethal of all gynecological malignancies [1]. Survival rates are highly variable and are mainly related to the stage at diagnosis. While the 5-year pooled survival rate is 51%, at stage IV, the rate falls to 32% [2]. Moreover, owing in great part to the asymptomatic nature of the disease, approximately 50% of all ovarian cancer cases will be diagnosed at an advanced stage [2]. In almost all cases, the first line of treatment involves cytoreductive surgery combined with adjuvant chemotherapy, most frequently through the combination of platinum and taxane agents [3]. However, while primarily effective, most patients will relapse following initial treatment. Their disease will then demonstrate progressive resistance to further chemotherapeutic interventions, partly due to various molecular alterations, intratumoral heterogeneity and the emergence of resistant subpopulations [4,5]. More specifically, platinum-resistant ovarian carcinoma, which lies within a spectrum of resistance profiles, is broadly defined by the recurrence or progression within 6 months of exposure to platinum salts [6]. In patients exhibiting disease with such resistance, treatment options are limited.

There is currently no consensus on the optimal therapeutic strategy once platinum-resistance has emerged [3,7,8]. Weekly paclitaxel remains central to the available arsenal in this context, with the reported response rate oscillating between 20% and 62% [8–15]. However, chronic exposure to chemotherapeutic compounds is also thought to possess potent anti-angiogenic effects, underlining the potential benefit of metronomic dosing regimens [16]. In order to establish if the reduced frequency of treatments would translate into comparable effectiveness coupled with reduced toxicities, alternative schedules have been investigated. The 3 weeks out of 4 regimen (WP3) has been used in platinum-resistant ovarian carcinoma with good results [10,13,17]. Nonetheless, no prospective nor retrospective studies have directly compared the continuous weekly regimen (4 weeks out of 4; WP4) to WP3.

In this paper, we present retrospective data comparing the efficacy and safety of paclitaxel 80 mg/m^2 administered as WP3 and WP4 regimens in 149 patients with platinum-resistant ovarian carcinoma treated at our center over the last ten years. Our results add to the paucity of data available to guide clinical decision making in this challenging population.

The primary endpoint is the cumulative dose of paclitaxel received for WP3 and WP4. Secondary endpoints are related to the occurrence of paclitaxel dose reduction, the mean paclitaxel dose received per week and the dose intensity administered (% of the maximum expected dose infused). Additional secondary endpoints are time to next treatment (TTNT), overall survival (OS), mean duration of treatment, CA-125 response, occurrence of treatment delays, hospitalizations, neurotoxicity and the need for blood transfusions.

Our hypothesis was that WP4 would not lead to a higher cumulative dose since it would require more dose reductions and lead to more toxicities than WP3. We transposed this hypothesis from a similar study with Bortezomib, where a weekly administration schedule demonstrated equivalent progression free survival (PFS) and OS with a better tolerability profile than bi-weekly administration [18].

No formal statistical hypothesis was made and all the available patients were included.

Our results demonstrate a similar cumulative dose for WP3 and WP4 with a comparable efficacy profile and better tolerability of WP3.

2. Materials and Methods

We have retrospectively studied a cohort of 149 patients treated at CHU de Quebec-Université Laval who received WP for platinum-resistant ovarian carcinoma between January 2012 and January 2023. The paclitaxel regimen choice (WP3 or WP4) was based on the clinicians' personal preferences, patients' comorbidities and clinical trends. Inclusion criteria included a diagnosis of ovarian, tubal or primary peritoneal metastatic or locally advanced carcinoma. The platinum resistance was defined as progressing within 6 months after platinum-compound exposure.

Exclusion criteria included patients receiving WP before 2012 or after January 2023, treatment with WP for another type of cancer or administration of less than one full cycle of treatment. Finally, if WP was administered and withheld for several weeks/months then reintroduced for progression as a new line, only the first treatment was used for analyses.

Patients were identified retrospectively through the chemotherapy prescription and administration database of the CHU de Quebec-Université Laval. All patients receiving WP were screened with the inclusion and exclusion criteria mentioned above. Retrospective data were then analyzed comparing the two groups head-to-head (WP3 vs. WP4). Patients were allocated to WP3 and WP4 in an intention-to-treat manner.

Main characteristics of the study population were compiled for each group (WP3 and WP4), such as age, ECOG Performance Status [19], tumor origin, histology, surgical cytoreduction, BRCA status, number of previous lines of treatment, taxane-free interval, Bevacizumab and PARP inhibitors (PARPi) exposition. The cumulative and mean dose administered, dose reduction, treatment delay and dose intensity were the collected dosing parameters. The toxicity parameters were hospitalizations, neurotoxicity, blood transfusions and treatment intolerance. The efficacy parameters were median OS, TTNT, duration of treatment and CA-125 response based on the Gynecologic Cancer Intergroup (GCIG) criteria.

The study was approved by the local ethical research committee of the CHU de Québec-Université Laval (2023–6722) and was conducted conforming to the Declaration of Helsinki. Data were double-anonymized.

Descriptive statistics (mean with standard deviation or median with interquartile range, or proportions) were used as appropriate. Wilcoxon Mann–Whitney, Pearson's Chi Square and Student T-tests were used to compare groups. All tests were two-sided and the threshold of <0.05 for p values was considered to be statistically significant. The Kaplan–Meier method was used to estimate OS and TTNT. The analysis was conducted using the SAS® 9.4 software.

3. Results

Of the 149 patients corresponding to the aforementioned inclusion and exclusion criteria, 102 formed the WP3 and 47 the WP4 group. When dividing the studied period in half, 42/102 patients received WP3 between 2012 and 2017, and 60/102 between 2018 and 2023. In parallel, 36/47 patients received WP4 between 2012 and 2017 and 11/47 between 2018 and 2023. The median follow-up time was 13.0 months. As presented in Table 1, the WP3 and WP4 patient populations were essentially comparable. The majority of patients were BRCA-negative, diagnosed with high-grade serous carcinoma and had good performance status (ECOG = 1) at initiation of WP. The median number of previous treatment lines was 3 in both groups. The taxane and platinum-free intervals were similar. The descriptive demographics of the studied cohorts are detailed in Table 1.

Table 1. Main characteristics of the study population.

Variables	WP3 (n = 102)	WP4 (n = 47)	p
Treatment period			<0.01
2012–2017	42	36	
2018–2023	60	11	
Age (years)	69.0	64.0	0.06
ECOG (%)			0.47
0–1	87 (85.3)	44 (93.6)	
2–3	15 (14.7)	3 (6.4)	
Tumor origin (%)			0.18
Ovary	85 (83.3)	33 (70.2)	
Peritoneum	5 (4.9)	7 (14.9)	
Tubal	12 (11.8)	7 (14.9)	
Histology (%)			0.05
High-grade serous	91 (89.2)	36 (76.6)	
Others	11 (10.8)	11 (33.4)	
Surgical cytoreduction (%)			0.02
None	19 (18.6)	2 (4.3)	
Suboptimal	20 (19.6)	16 (34.0)	
Optimal	62 (60.8)	27 (57.4)	
Non-specified	1 (1.0)	2 (4.3)	

Table 1. *Cont.*

Variables	WP3 ($n = 102$)	WP4 ($n = 47$)	p
Germinal BRCA status (%)			0.42
Negative	75 (73.5)	29 (61.7)	
BRCA1	3 (2.9)	1 (2.1)	
BRCA2	2 (2.0)	2 (4.3)	
Unknown	22 (21.6)	15 (31.9)	
#previous lines of treatments (%)			0.40
1	7 (6.9)	1 (2.1)	
2	25 (24.5)	11 (23.4)	
3	40 (39.2)	14 (29.8)	
4	17 (16.7)	15 (31.9)	
5	8 (7.8)	4 (8.5)	
6	1 (1.0)	1 (2.1)	
7	4 (3.9)	1 (2.1)	
Taxane-free interval (months)	17.0	18.5	0.96
Platinum-free interval (months)	8.0	8.0	0.94
Bevacizumab (%)	10 (9.8)	5 (10.6)	1.0
PARPi (%)	17 (16.7)	6 (12.8)	0.75

Regimens were administered using weekly paclitaxel either 3 weeks out of 4 (WP3) or 4 weeks out of 4 (WP4). Maximal dosage regimens were WP3 = 60 mg/m^2/week (80 mg/m^2/week 3 weeks out of 4, thus 60 mg/m^2 when distributed on a 4-week schedule) and WP4 = 80 mg/m^2/week. The percentage represents proportion of patients presenting the specified characteristics within their respective groups. Age, taxane-free and platinum-free intervals are presented as medians. Bevacizumab and PARPi represent the percentage of patients with a prior exposure to these drugs.

There was no difference in the delivered cumulative dose between the two treatment regimens (1353.7 vs. 1404.2 mg/m^2; $p = 0.29$). An expected statistically significant difference in the mean weekly dose received between the two groups was observed (59.1 vs. 70.2 mg/m^2/week; $p < 0.01$), since the 80 mg/m^2/week in WP3 reduces to 60 mg/m^2/week when reported on a 4-week schedule. There was also a significant difference in the dose intensity received (98.5 vs. 87.8% of planned dose respectively; $p < 0.01$). Still, there was no difference in the treatment delays (27.5 vs. 23.4%; $p = 0.69$) was noted (Table 2).

Table 2. Comparison of WP3 and WP4 dosing parameters.

Variables	WP3	WP4	p
Cumulative dose (mg/m^2)	1353.7	1404.2	0.29
At least one dose reduction (%)	4.9	44.7	<0.01
At least one treatment delay (%)	27.5	23.4	0.69
Mean dose (mg/m^2/week)	59.1	70.2	<0.01
Dose intensity (%)	98.5	87.8	<0.01

Maximal dosage regimens were WP3 = 60 mg/m^2/week and WP4 = 80 mg/m^2/week. Cumulative dose is expressed as a mean. Percentage for dose reduction and treatment delay represents proportion of patients who required these interventions. Dose intensity is expressed as percentage of maximal dose received.

However, there was a significant difference in the dose reductions, with 4.9% of patients receiving WP3 requiring a dose reduction compared to 44.7% of patients receiving WP4 ($p < 0.01$) (Table 2). These dose reductions were mainly due to a difficulty in tolerating the treatment as per the clinician assessment (3.9 vs. 34.0%; $p < 0.01$) (Table 3). Nevertheless, when analyzed individually, there was no significant difference in hospitalizations (22.5 vs. 31.9%; $p = 0.33$), the occurrence of neurotoxicity (66.6 vs. 60%; $p = 0.93$) or the percentage of patients receiving packed red blood cells transfusion (4.9 vs. 10.6%; $p = 0.29$) (Table 3).

Table 3. Comparison of WP3 and WP4 toxicity parameters.

Variables	WP3	WP4	*p*
Hospitalizations (%)	22.5	31.9	0.33
Neurotoxicity (%)	66.6	66.0	0.93
Blood transfusions (%)	4.9	10.6	0.29
Toxicity-related dose reductions (%)	3.9	34.0	<0.01

The percentage represents the proportion of patients experiencing the adverse effect. Toxicity-related dose reduction is defined as any treatment intolerance causing a reduction in the administered dose.

As demonstrated in Table 4, the median TTNT was not statistically different between both groups (6.3 vs. 6.2 months; p = 0.28) (Figure 1a). The median OS was also not statistically different between WP3 and WP4 (14.6 vs. 13.6 months; p = 0.43) (Figure 1b). The median duration of treatment was comparable in both groups with 20.4 weeks for WP3 versus 17.0 weeks for WP4 (p = 0.52), respectively. A 50% or more CA-125 reduction was observed in 61.5% of WP3 vs. 64.1% of WP4 (p = 0.79).

Table 4. Comparison of WP3 and WP4 efficacy parameters.

Variables	WP3	WP4	*p*
Overall survival (months)	14.6	13.6	0.43
Time to next treatment (months)	6.3	6.2	0.28
Duration of treatment (weeks)	20.4	17.0	0.52
CA-125 > 50% response (%)	61.5	64.1	0.79

Overall survival, time to next treatment and duration of treatment are presented as medians. CA-125 response is based on the Gynecologic Cancer Intergroup (GCIG) criteria.

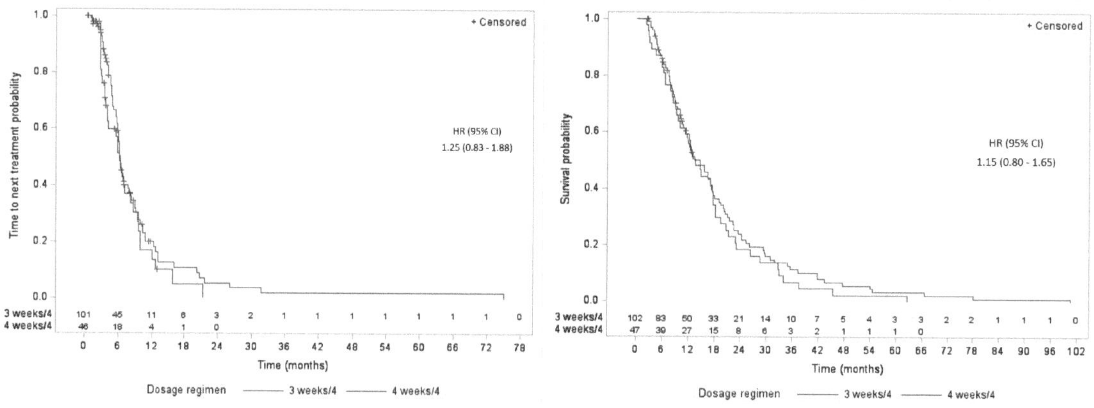

(a) (b)

Figure 1. (**a**) Time to next treatment according to the paclitaxel regimen used; (**b**) overall survival according to the paclitaxel regimen used.

4. Discussion

The results of this retrospective analysis suggest that the administration of WP3 delivers a similar cumulative dose with a comparable efficacy to WP4, which confirms our hypothesis. The collected results did not identify a specific toxicity pattern. However, the proportion of patients requiring dose reduction with WP4 was significantly higher than with WP3, mainly due to treatment intolerance. Given the inherent limitations of the retrospective collection of the toxicity data, we hypothesize that the greater number of dose reductions is a surrogate of the increased toxicity of the WP4 regimen, even if our results do not show this explicitly in the various individually collected adverse events.

As toxicity data were not collected prospectively, the retrospective assessment from the clinical notes of subjective symptoms such as fatigue, neuropathy, dyspnea, inappetence or nausea was of limited value. Nevertheless, we believe that increased toxicity is the more plausible explanation for the most frequent dose reductions with the WP4 regimen. This difference in tolerance between the two groups is also reflected in the planned dose intensity administered. Furthermore, the larger proportion of patients receiving WP4 in the first half of the time period seems to demonstrate a change in clinical practices, probably based on the observed toxicities in the WP4 group.

When compared to pre-existing data, two European studies published in 2002 used WP4 [12,20]. The first one included 57 patients treated with WP4 for platinum-resistant disease, with a response rate of 49–56%, an OS of 13.7 months and a PFS of 4 to 5 months [12]. The second study, comparing WP4 and paclitaxel every 3 weeks in 208 patients, demonstrated a 41% response rate for WP4 with a median complete response of 4.5 months. The median response duration was 9.4 months in the WP4 group, with a time to progression of 6.1 months and a median OS of 13.6 months. It should be noted that half of the patients in this study did not have platinum-resistant tumors [20]. Lastly, a study of 37 patients from 2004 administering WP3 to platinum-refractory patients demonstrated a total response rate of 45.9% with an initial improvement of the CA-125 of 56%, using Gynecological Cancer Intergroup (GCIG) response criteria [13]. The results also showed that as the number of previous lines of treatment increases, the response to treatment decreases [13]. It should be reminded that in our study, the median number of previous lines of treatment was 3, hence our patients were more likely to be multidrug-resistant. That being said, despite the differences in the populations and outcome definitions, the performance of our WP4 and WP3 regimens seems globally similar to the literature, suggesting that the comparable results between our two groups are unlikely to be attributable to an underperformance of the WP4 cohort [12,13,20].

The strength of our study is that it is, to our knowledge, the first retrospective trial to directly address the question of the optimal WP administration regimen in platinum-resistant ovarian carcinoma. Although an indirect analysis of phase II studies or a control arm of phase III studies [8–15] may inform us of the efficacy and toxicity of these two regimens, population and study design differences make inter-study comparisons biased and thus potentially less useful than the data presented in our study.

There are limitations to our study that need to be recognized, including mainly the retrospective nature of data collection. As discussed above, we believed that it specifically impacted the exhaustivity of the collected toxicity details. In addition, there may have been biases in the clinicians' selection of the chemotherapy regimen. However, it is probable that the frailest patients would have been assigned to the lowest dose-dense regimen (WP3), which is reassuring for the validity of the results observed. Also, the choice of a weekly, more tolerated regimen may result from frailty but also depends on the degree of toxicity of the previous treatment. Lastly, the use of growth factor was not collected, which is also a limitation that could influence the results in both groups.

Since the WP4 regimen did not lead to a greater cumulative dose administered compared to WP3, the addition of a therapeutic break without compromising the effectiveness of treatment in terms of TTNT, OS, CA-125 response and the total duration of treatment is clinically appealing. This monthly week off can potentially free up chemotherapy chair time, which is a major issue in the context of human resource shortages in North America. This could inform institutional decisions to provide wiser resource utilization. In addition, this pause offered with WP3 may be attractive for patients with a chronic and incurable disease who often seek ways to optimize their quality of life by alleviating treatment burden and toxicity. In addition, it was estimated that the cost of one week of WP at the CHU de Québec was about CAD 252, including the nursing staff, pharmacist and medication fees. Even if not transposable to other centers due to local variations, this could potentially lead to a substantial financial advantage for the healthcare system.

5. Conclusions

In summary, our data support a comparable cumulative dose administered for a similar efficacy between WP3 and WP4 regimens as well as a possible advantage with regard to the toxicity profile of WP3, as implicitly reflected by a lower proportion of dose reductions in this group.

Author Contributions: Conceptualization, L.M., L.-P.G. and V.C.; data curation, L.M. and N.F.; formal analysis, L.M., L.-P.G., M.N.U.S. and V.C.; funding acquisition, V.C.; investigation, L.M., L.-P.G. and V.C.; methodology, L.M., L.-P.G. and V.C.; project administration, V.C.; resources, L.M., L.-P.G. and V.C.; software, M.N.U.S.; supervision, V.C.; validation, L.M., L.-P.G. and V.C.; visualization, L.M., L.-P.G. and V.C.; writing—original draft, L.M., L.-P.G., É.L., F.F. and V.C.; writing—review & editing, L.M., L.-P.G., N.F., É.L., F.F., E.-L.L., A.S., M.L. (Marianne Lavoie), M.L. (Marc Lalancette), M.P., M.N.U.S. and V.C. All authors have read and agreed to the published version of the manuscript.

Funding: This study received funding from the consolidated funds for clinical research of the Hematology-Oncology department at the CHU de Québec.

Institutional Review Board Statement: The study was approved by the local ethical research committee of the CHU de Québec-Université Laval (2023–6722) and the study was performed in accordance with the Declaration of Helsinki.

Informed Consent Statement: Not applicable.

Data Availability Statement: The raw data supporting the conclusions of this article will be made available by the authors on request.

Acknowledgments: The authors would like to thank the patients and their families.

Conflicts of Interest: The authors have no conflicts of interest to disclose.

References

1. Canadian Cancer Statistics Advisory Committee. *Canadian Cancer Statistics 2023*; Canadian Cancer Society: Toronto, ON, Canada, 2023.
2. Siegel, R.L.; Giaquinto, A.N.; Jemal, A. Cancer statistics, 2024. *CA Cancer J. Clin.* **2024**, *74*, 12–49. [CrossRef] [PubMed]
3. National Comprehensive Cancer Network. NCCN Clinical Practice Guidelines in Oncology—Ovarian Cancer. 2024. Available online: https://www.nccn.org/patients/guidelines/content/PDF/ovarian-patient.pdf (accessed on 1 July 2024).
4. Kim, S.; Han, Y.; Kim, S.I.; Kim, H.S.; Kim, S.J.; Song, Y.S. Tumor evolution and chemoresistance in ovarian cancer. *NPJ Precis. Oncol.* **2018**, *2*, 20. [CrossRef] [PubMed]
5. Li, S.-S.; Ma, J.; Wong, A.S.T. Chemoresistance in ovarian cancer: Exploiting cancer stem cell metabolism. *J. Gynecol. Oncol.* **2018**, *29*, e32. [CrossRef] [PubMed]
6. Wilson, M.K.; Pujade-Lauraine, E.; Aoki, D.; Mirza, M.R.; Lorusso, D.; Oza, A.; du Bois, A.; Vergote, I.; Reuss, A.; Bacon, M.; et al. Fifth Ovarian Cancer Consensus Conference of the Gynecologic Cancer InterGroup: Recurrent disease. *Ann. Oncol.* **2017**, *28*, 727–732. [CrossRef] [PubMed]
7. Colombo, N.; Sessa, C.; Bois, A.D.; Ledermann, J.; McCluggage, W.G.; McNeish, I.; Morice, P.; Pignata, S.; Ray-Coquard, I.; Vergote, I.; et al. ESMO-ESGO consensus conference recommendations on ovarian cancer: Pathology and molecular biology, early and advanced stages, borderline tumours and recurrent disease. *Ann. Oncol.* **2019**, *30*, 672–705. [CrossRef] [PubMed]
8. Kumar, A.; Hoskins, P.; Tinker, A. Dose-dense Paclitaxel in Advanced Ovarian Cancer. *Clin. Oncol.* **2015**, *27*, 40–47. [CrossRef] [PubMed]
9. Baird, R.D.; Tan, D.S.P.; Kaye, S.B. Weekly paclitaxel in the treatment of recurrent ovarian cancer. *Nat. Rev. Clin. Oncol.* **2010**, *7*, 575–582. [CrossRef] [PubMed]
10. Dunder, I.; Berker, B.; Atabekoglu, C.; Bilgin, T. Preliminary experience with salvage weekly paclitaxel in women with advanced recurrent ovarian carcinoma. *Eur. J. Gynaecol. Oncol.* **2005**, *26*, 79–82.
11. Ghamande, S.; Lele, S.; Marchetti, D.; Baker, T.; Odunsi, K. Weekly paclitaxel in patients with recurrent or persistent advanced ovarian cancer. *Int. J. Gynecol. Cancer* **2003**, *13*, 142–147. [CrossRef] [PubMed]
12. Kaern, J.; Baekelandt, M.; Tropé, C.G. A phase II study of weekly paclitaxel in platinum and paclitaxel-resistant ovarian cancer patients. *Eur. J. Gynaec. Oncol.-IssN* **2002**, *23*, 383–389.
13. Kita, T.; Kikuchi, Y.; Takano, M.; Suzuki, M.; Oowada, M.; Konno, R.; Yamamoto, K.; Inoue, H.; Seto, H.; Yamamoto, T.; et al. The effect of single weekly paclitaxel in heavily pretreated patients with recurrent or persistent advanced ovarian cancer. *Gynecol. Oncol.* **2004**, *92*, 813–818. [CrossRef]

14. Markman, M.; Blessing, J.; Rubin, S.C.; Connor, J.; Hanjani, P.; Waggoner, S. Phase II trial of weekly paclitaxel (80 mg/m^2) in platinum and paclitaxel-resistant ovarian and primary peritoneal cancers: A Gynecologic Oncology Group study. *Gynecol. Oncol.* **2006**, *101*, 436–440. [CrossRef]
15. Markman, M.; Hall, J.; Spitz, D.; Weiner, S.; Carson, L.; Van Le, L.; Baker, M. Phase II Trial of Weekly Single-Agent Paclitaxel in Platinum/Paclitaxel-Refractory Ovarian Cancer. *J. Clin. Oncol.* **2002**, *20*, 2365–2369. [CrossRef] [PubMed]
16. Cazzaniga, M.E.; Cordani, N.; Capici, S.; Cogliati, V.; Riva, F.; Cerrito, M.G. Metronomic Chemotherapy. *Cancers* **2021**, *13*, 2236. [CrossRef]
17. Takano, M.; Kikuchi, Y.; Kita, T.; Suzuki, M.; Ohwada, M.; Yamamoto, T.; Yamamoto, K.; Inoue, H.; Shimizu, K. Phase I and pharmacological study of single paclitaxel administered weekly for heavily pre-treated patients with epithelial ovarian cancer. *Anticancer Res.* **2002**, *22*, 1833–1838.
18. Hoff, F.W.; Banerjee, R.; Khan, A.M.; McCaughan, G.; Wang, B.; Wang, X.; Roose, J.; Anderson, L.D.; Cowan, A.J.; Rajkumar, S.V.; et al. Once-weekly versus twice-weekly bortezomib in newly diagnosed multiple myeloma: A real-world analysis. *Blood Cancer J.* **2024**, *14*, 52. [CrossRef]
19. Oken, M.M.; Creech, R.H.; Tormey, D.C.; Horton, J.; Davis, T.E.; McFadden, E.T.; Carbone, P.P. Toxicity and response criteria of the Eastern Cooperative Oncology Group. *Am. J. Clin. Oncol.* **1982**, *5*, 649–655. [CrossRef]
20. Rosenberg, P.; Andersson, H.; Boman, K.; Ridderheim, M.; Sorbe, B.; Puistola, U.; Parö, G. Randomized Trial of Single Agent Paclitaxel Given Weekly Versus Every Three Weeks and with Peroral Versus Intravenous Steroid Premedication to Patients with Ovarian Cancer Previously Treated with Platinum. *Acta Oncol.* **2002**, *41*, 418–424. [CrossRef]

Disclaimer/Publisher's Note: The statements, opinions and data contained in all publications are solely those of the individual author(s) and contributor(s) and not of MDPI and/or the editor(s). MDPI and/or the editor(s) disclaim responsibility for any injury to people or property resulting from any ideas, methods, instructions or products referred to in the content.

Current Oncology

Review

Current Advances in Radioactive Iodine-Refractory Differentiated Thyroid Cancer

Fabio Volpe, Carmela Nappi *, Emilia Zampella, Erica Di Donna, Simone Maurea, Alberto Cuocolo and Michele Klain

Department of Advanced Biomedical Sciences, University of Naples "Federico II", 80138 Naples, Italy; fabio.volpe@unina.it (F.V.); emilia.zampella@gmail.com (E.Z.); ericadidonna5@gmail.com (E.D.D.); maurea@unina.it (S.M.); cuocolo@unina.it (A.C.); michele.klain@unina.it (M.K.)
* Correspondence: c.nappi@unina.it

Abstract: Background: Differentiated thyroid cancer (DTC) patients have an outstanding overall long-term survival rate, and certain subsets of DTC patients have a very high likelihood of disease recurrence. Radioactive iodine (RAI) therapy is a cornerstone in DTC management, but cancer cells can eventually develop resistance to RAI. Radioactive iodine-refractory DTC (RAIR-DTC) is a condition defined by ATA 2015 guidelines when DTC cannot concentrate RAI ab initio or loses RAI uptake ability after the initial therapy. The RAIR condition implies that RAI cannot reveal new met-astatic foci, so RAIR-DTC metabolic imaging needs new tracers. ^{18}F-FDG PET/CT has been widely used and has demonstrated prognostic value, but ^{18}F-FDG DTC avidity may remain low. Fibroblast activation protein inhibitors (FA-Pi)s, prostatic-specific membrane antigen (PSMA), and somatostatin receptor (SSTR) tracers have been proposed as theragnostic agents in experimental settings and Arg-Gly-Asp (RGD) peptides in the diagnostic trial field. Multi-targeted tyrosine kinase inhibitors are relatively new drugs approved in RAIR-DTC therapy. Despite the promising targeted setting, they relate to frequent adverse-event onset. Sorafenib and trametinib have been included in re-differentiation protocols aimed at re-inducing RAI accumulation in DTC cells. Results appear promising, but not excellent. Conclusions: RAIR-DTC remains a challenging nosological entity. There are still controversies on RAIR-DTC definition and post-RAI therapy evaluation, with post-therapy whole-body scan (PT-WBS) the only validated criterion of response. The recent introduction of multiple diagnostic and therapeutic agents obliges physicians to pursue a multidisciplinary approach aiming to correct drug introduction and timing choice.

Keywords: radioactive iodine; therapy; theragnostics; differentiated thyroid cancer; refractory DTC

1. Introduction

While differentiated thyroid cancer (DTC) patients have an outstanding overall long-term survival rate, certain subsets of DTC patients have a very high likelihood of disease recurrence [1–3]. To evaluate the likelihood of recurrent or chronic illness in DTC patients, the American Thyroid Association (ATA) initial risk classification system has been proposed. Three risk categories (low, middle, and high) are assigned to patients. Furthermore, the ATA has suggested a dynamic risk categorization approach that considers imaging, biochemical, and clinical data gathered during follow-up. Radioiodine (RAI) diagnostic whole-body scanning (WBS) has been utilized in the past for DTC disease status assessment, but it has been replaced by a combination of neck ultrasonography (US) and serum thyroglobulin (Tg) measurement [1].

The current data demonstrate that patients with undetectable serum Tg levels have a high chance of achieving complete remission, and that a diagnostic workup may not be necessary in these cases [4,5]. Moreover, serum Tg, after some months of detectable levels, can tend to zero with no further actions.

An adequate uptake of RAI in the target tissue, defined as RAI avidity (RAI-A), is mandatory to obtain a successful RAI therapy. Low-risk disease and a post-surgical thyroid remnant are usually highly iodine-avid targets as they usually retain sodium–iodine symporter (NIS) expression.

Recently, the clinical application of RAI therapy has experienced a gradual decrease [6,7]. In particular, low-risk DTC should not be treated with post-surgery RAI ablation according to ATA guidelines [1]. Nevertheless, intermediate- and high-risk DTC may take advantage of RAI therapy administered for ablation purposes, or in cases of advanced disease, for metastasis therapy or palliation purposes [1].

The primary tumor size and the eventual lymph node metastases determine the administered radioiodine activity, but RAI-A is not guaranteed, especially in high-risk DTC or in the presence of known metastases [8–10].

Several factors have been associated with lower RAI-A of metastatic tissue, such as patient age, large tumor, histological type and high [^{18}F]fluorodeoxyglucose uptake [11,12]. Furthermore, tumors exhibiting BRAF V600E or TERT promoter mutations are less likely to spawn iodine-avid metastases and are associated with poorer patient outcomes. The co-occurrence of these two mutational events in papillary thyroid cancer (PTC) has been found to be especially indicative of aggressive tumor features [8,13,14].

2. Defining Radioactive Iodine-Refractory Differentiated Thyroid Cancer

Despite the possibility of iodine uptake being altered ab initio in DTC [15], RAI therapy is still a cornerstone for the success of medium- and high-risk DTC treatment [1,2,16]. Iodine uptake may decrease with disease progression until further RAI administration becomes ineffective from a clinical point of view. In this condition, DTC can be considered refractory to RAI. RAIR-DTC is a relatively uncommon condition (four to five cases/million/year). RAIR-DTC is associated with a bad prognosis, and less than 10% of patients survive at 10 years (mean 3–5 years) [17].

Radioactive iodine-refractory DTC (RAIR-DTC) is defined by the ATA 2015 guidelines as a condition where DTC cannot concentrate radioactive iodine (RAI) at the time of initial treatment or loses its ability to concentrate RAI after initial therapy. RAIR-DTC also includes cases where only the local lesion concentrates RAI or there is disease progression and metastatic spread after high-dose treatment despite the ability to concentrate RAI [1].

While the refractory condition of DTC patients who lose the capability to concentrate RAI into the target lesion is well understood, more controversy surrounds cases where RAIR is associated with disease progression despite good RAI uptake. For these patients, evaluating the risk-to-reward ratio is crucial. After a cumulative dose of 600 mCi, the risk of side effects increases, while the likelihood of achieving a cure decreases. Therefore, the decision to continue RAI treatment should be made on a case-by-case basis, considering the patient's previous response to RAI administration [18–20]. Table 1 summarizes all the conditions where the ATA 2015 guidelines define a DTC as RAIR.

Table 1. ATA 2015 RAIR categories.

I.	Malignant/metastatic tissue cannot concentrate RAI on a diagnostic radioiodine scan.
II.	Malignant tissue cannot concentrate RAI on a post-^{131}I therapy scan.
III.	The tumor loses the ability to concentrate RAI after previous evidence of RAI-avid disease.
IV.	RAI is concentrated in some lesions only.
V.	Metastasis progression even with significant RAI uptake.
VI.	>600 mCi of cumulated ^{131}I therapy.

Radioactive iodine-refractory (RAIR); radioactive iodine (RAI).

Nevertheless, RAIR categories defined by ATA 2015 may appear over-restrictive in the view of a personalized medicine approach and should not be considered definitive. Martinique principles were proposed in 2019 when some experts proposed that the feasibility of RAI therapy in DTC patients should be discussed case by case, not excluding it a priori when a DTC patient falls in an ATA 2015 RAIR category. Indeed, RAIR definition criteria will be subject to evolution due to recent introduction of re-differentiation therapies [21].

The risk of RAIR-DTC can rise in elderly patients with an aggressive histological DTC subtype and with metastatic disease at the time of diagnosis. In these patients, cancer heterogeneity increases with RAI uptake inhomogeneity into target lesions, so RAI therapy can be less effective [3,22]. The prevalence of RAIR-DTC amounts to approximately 15% of DTC patients, particularly those with distant metastases at diagnosis and older age. BRAF and RAS kinase mutations are the more frequent alterations in follicular thyroid cancer (FTC) [8,14,23]. Extracellular signal-regulated kinase (ERK) or mammalian target of rapamycin (mTOR) activation pathways are the main mechanisms involved in RAIR with under-expression of sodium–iodine symporter (NIS) and the overexpression of glucose transporter 1 (GLUT1) [2,10,24,25]. From a functional point of view, DTC cells progressively lose the capability of accumulating iodine, but gain extra energetic substrates that can sustain the increased metabolic requirement of cancer cells.

3. Identifying RAIR

^{131}I gamma emission can be used for diagnostic purposes with a whole-body scan (WBS) performed by a gamma camera. According to the ^{131}I dose administered, WBS can be defined as diagnostic WBS (D-WBS) or post-therapy WBS (PT-WBS) according to low or high activity used. While PT-WBS can be considered a good negative detector of RAIR, the same consideration cannot be reserved to diagnostic ^{131}I-whole-body scan (D-WBS). RAI activity, acquisition time, γ-camera model and TSH stimulation play a role in D-WBS accuracy and sensibility. In particular, low-administered-RAI activity for D-WBS acquisition would not allow the detection of all the RAI-avid foci [26–28].

Nevertheless, the added value of performing ^{131}I-single-photon emission computed tomography (SPECT)–computed tomography (CT) has been debated since the introduction of this hybrid method. Some authors put the light on the better detection ability derived from the attenuation correction algorithms and from the morphological imaging acquired simultaneously [29–31]. In cases of equivocal findings on planar WBS images, PT-^{131}I-SPECT/CT can differentiate remnant thyroid from lymph-nodal accumulation. Indeed, focal uptake of uncertain source may be defined as para-physiological or metastatic with fine body district localization [31–33]. Thus, the initial staging of DTC, as with patient risk assessment, can be corrected by additional imaging findings.

Patients who present negative imaging of ^{131}I-WBS (despite D-WBS or PT-WBS) and abnormally elevated serum Tg levels should receive adequate attention, because this always indicates the presence of RAI-refractory disease.

RAIR often occurs in advanced DTC patients, when cancer heterogeneity increases along with aggressiveness. Additionally, RAI accumulation can vary lesion by lesion [34,35].

Molecular imaging reflects these changes accordingly. RAI accumulation decreases while ^{18}F-fluorodeoxyglucose (FDG) uptake increases. This is called the "flip-flop" phenomenon and it is directly correlated with DTC dedifferentiation and aggressiveness [11,12,36,37].

^{18}F-FDG positron emission tomography (PET)/computed tomography (TC) can be evaluated qualitatively by visual uptake detection and quantitatively by SUV estimation.

In RAIR-DTC, usually ^{18}F-FDG uptake and SUV are increased compared to DTC. Nevertheless, SUV may be considered a good predictor of cancer growth speed in DTC [38,39].

^{18}F-FDG DTC-positive findings are also correlated with poorer prognosis, as demonstrated by various scientific papers [2,12,36,39–41]. Some authors also suggest a good correlation between ^{18}F-FDG uptake and the presence of BRAF v600e mutation in DTC cells [42,43].

4. Current Molecular Imaging and Care Options

Routine RAI imaging in clinical settings involves both regional and planar WBS and SPECT methods. However, there are no standardized quantitative methods for assessing response. Instead, response criteria often rely on visually assessed decreases in tumor uptake during post-treatment follow-up. It is important to consider the potential for functional tumor de-differentiation over the course of the disease when interpreting decreased RAI uptake in follow-up scans. To assess this possibility, ^{18}F-FDG PET/CT scans, which reflect tumor glycolytic activity, should be used.

It is now possible to target aberrant cellular pathways and to provide additional treatment options for patients with otherwise poor prognoses due to the identification of multiple molecular alterations in advanced thyroid cancer.

For RAIR-DTC, the current standard of care involves treatment with tyrosine kinase inhibitors (TKIs).

The first-line setting includes both sorafenib and lenvatinib, as established by the National Comprehensive Cancer Network (NCCN) guidelines [44]. However, some patients manifest RET or NTRK fusions, and the standard of care has to be changed accordingly. More than half of patients show BRAF mutation, but the efficacy of BRAF inhibitors is not better than lenvatinib, and they are reserved to later therapy options [45].

Before initiating lenvatinib, blood pressure must be under control, but in cases of difficulty, sorafenib should be adopted. Selective RET inhibitors such as selpercatinib or larotrectinib should be preferred in patients with fusion detection. However, in cases of BRAF positivity, lenvatinib remains preferable, with BRAF inhibitors reserved for later lines of therapy. In the second-line setting, cabozantinib is also authorized and considered standard therapy.

The main challenges in managing RAI-refractory differentiated thyroid cancer (RAIR-DTC) include the onset of resistance and adverse events. To extend the efficacy of systemic therapy, local treatments such as surgery or external radiation should be considered for single progressing lesions. Although sorafenib and lenvatinib therapies are associated with adverse events, patients may achieve optimal outcomes and should be encouraged to adhere to treatment to avoid unnecessary dose reductions or treatment withdrawal.

5. Future Diagnostic and Therapeutic Perspectives

RAIR-DTC biochemical characteristics imply the need to research alternative targeted imaging tracers to iodine. Advanced cancer cells show some molecular pathway activation and mechanism similarities, so some tracers used in other cancer imaging could be adopted.

Integrin $\alpha v\beta 3$ is involved in tumor angiogenesis and can be a potential imaging target for cancer growth using radiolabeled arginylglycylaspartic acid (RGD) peptides in DTC patients who had negative ^{131}I-WBS, but elevated Tg levels [46–49]. Additionally, it has been suggested that ^{99m}Tc-3PRGD2 uptake can predict the disease progression after initial RAI therapy in high-risk DTC patients [50]. RGD peptides can also be labeled with positron-emitting radionuclides for PET/TC application [51]. Chernaya et al. reported that BRAF mutation is linked with different expression levels of integrin receptors in DTC. In this scenario RGD imaging can be proposed under individualized conditions [52].

Prostate-specific membrane antigen (PSMA) ligands are a recent introduction in prostate cancer theragnostics [53–55]. PSMA overexpression has also been found in tumor neovasculature in various other tumors [56,57]. The expression of PSMA in thyroid tissue has been examined by some authors. Bychkov et al. enrolled 267 patients and found that PSMA was expressed in DTC neovasculature, but not in healthy tissue [58]. Similar results were found by Heitkotter and coworkers when comparing PSMA expression in thyroid cancer and benign thyroid diseases [59]. Hence, PSMA imaging in RAIR-DTC should be feasible. One study investigated PSMA uptake prospectively in 10 patients with 32 DTC metastatic lesions: 68Ga-PSMA PET/TC uptake was consistent (30/32 detected metastasis) and performance was superior to ^{18}F-FDG PET/CT (23/32 detected metastasis) [60]. Verburg et al. in 2015 [61] and Lütje et al. in 2017 [62] demonstrated a possible role of

^{68}Ga-HBED-CC-PSMA PET/CT for staging patients with RAIR-DTC metastases and for select patients eligible for PSMA radioactive labeled therapy. More recently, de Vries and coworkers explored the possible use of ^{177}Lu-PSMA-617 therapy in five RAIR-DTC patients that showed ^{68}Ga-PSMA PET/CT uptake in distant metastasis foci. Only two of them were considered eligible for ^{177}Lu-PSMA-617 administration and only one of them established a temporary response [63]. These results need to be used to better define the possible role of PSMA ligands as a basis for future studies.

Somatostatin receptor (SSTR) types 2, 3, and 5 have been demonstrated in various studies in DTC cells and also in normal thyroid tissue and benign thyroid diseases [64–68]. Radiolabeled somatostatin analogues, such as octreotide and lanreotide marked with 68Ga-DOTA, have seen reasonably large use in PET/CT SSTR imaging in recent years, especially in neuroendocrine tumor (NET) imaging [69–73]. However, the role of SSTR tracers in RAIR-DTC remains unclear. In 2020, Donohoe and colleagues published a document on the appropriate use of the available nuclear medicine methods, including 68Ga-DOTATATE PET/CT and 177Lu-labeled SSTR tracers in RAIR-DTC. The committee stated that there was insufficient evidence to correlate Tg increase with 68Ga-DOTATATE PET/CT imaging positivity. Therefore 177Lu-labeled SSTR tracers should be considered in the therapeutic choices of RAIR-DTC patients that have demonstrated SSTR tracer imaging positivity [74].

Similarly to PSMA, radiolabeled choline PET/CT has found consistency in the diagnosis of prostate cancer. Thyroid uptake has been recorded in some ^{18}F-choline PET/CT for prostate cancer diagnosis and staging [75,76]. ^{18}F-choline PET/CT has also been investigated for detection of DTC metastases negative on ^{18}F-FDG PET/CT. Piccardo et al. evaluated 25 patients with high-risk RAIR-DTC with both ^{18}F-FDG and ^{18}F-choline PET/CT. They found a good correlation with Tg doubling time and ^{18}F-choline uptake. Thus, ^{18}F-choline outperformed ^{18}F-FDG in terms of sensitivity, specificity, and negative predictive value [77]. ^{18}F-choline PET/CT should be considered in addition to ^{18}F-FDG PET/CT DTC lesions.

More recently, attention has also moved to the tumor microenvironment (TME), a complex system composed of extracellular matrix, immune cells, fibroblast, endothelial cells, and signaling compounds. It has been demonstrated that the TME plays an important role in tumorigenesis and progression [78]. Of note, fibroblast function is shifted and promotes tumor growth, so these can be defined as cancer-associated fibroblasts (CAFs) and express the fibroblast activation protein (FAP) [78,79]. FAP can be targeted by FAP inhibitors (FAPis) and used in nuclear medicine theragnostic applications [80].

A possible RAIR-DTC application for FAPi has been explored by Chen and coworkers, who studied a population of 24 patients [81]. All of them underwent ^{68}Ga-DOTA-FAPi-04 PET/CT and the detection rate was fairly good (87.5%). Ballal and co-workers compared ^{68}Ga-DOTA-FAPi-04 PET/CT versus ^{18}F-FDG PET/CT in 117 patients with RAIR-DTC and demonstrated superior performance in metastasis detection of radiolabeled FAPi over ^{18}F-FDG [82]. After these results, Ballal et al. performed a pilot study aimed at evaluating a possible therapeutic use of ^{177}Lu-DOTAGA.(SA.FAPi)2 in 15 RAIR-DTC patients that had failed on all of the standard options of systemic drugs [83]. At the end of the therapy cycles, the response rate was 92% and a complete response was achieved in 23% of patients.

^{177}Lu-EB-FAPI was studied by Fu and coworkers in 12 patients with RAIR-DTC in a dose-escalation trial. The results, evaluated with RECIST 1.1 criteria [84], were a partial response in 25% of patients, stable disease in 58% of patients, and progression in 17% of patients [85].

Retinoic acids have been studied in thyroid function, and their impairment is often associated with iodine deficit and thyroid autoimmune disorders. Some authors suggested that retinoids are involved in gene regulation and NIS expression and potentially could be used in DTC treatment when RAI avidity decreases [86,87]. Pak and coworkers [88] and Groener et al. [89] explored the retinoic acid administration in RAIR-DTC patients for re-differentiation purposes and RAI administration eligibility. Both studies reported that a minority of patients responded to retinoid administration.

Selumetinib is an MAPK kinase (MEK) 1 and MEK2 inhibitor that has been proposed to reverse refractoriness to RAI. A cluster of RAIR-DTC patients were included in experimental selumetinib administration by Ho et al. [90]. Patient RAI uptake was studied by a ^{124}I-PET/TC scan, performed before and after 4 weeks of selumetinib treatment, for dosimetry purposes. Eight (four with BRAF mutation and five with NRAS mutation) of the twenty patients received RAI due to the optimal RAI dose to lesions ($\geq$2000 cGy). Five of eight obtained a partial response, while three achieved stability of disease [90].

Larson and coworkers also found an increase in RAI uptake after selumetinib administration in 20 RAIR-DTC patients studied with ^{124}I-PET/TC scan [91].

The ASTRA phase III trial investigated selumetinib and RAI synergic administration in 233 high-risk DTC patients with high likelihood of RAIR. In sum, 78 patients received placebo and 155 patients received selumetinib and RAI adjuvant therapy. The tandem drug administration failed to improve the complete response rate in this patient cluster [92].

Sorafenib and lenvatinib are multi-targeted tyrosine kinase inhibitors (mTKIs) recently approved for use in RAIR-DTC [93–96]. Progression-free survival (PFS) achieved using these drugs is good, but neither overall survival (OS) nor quality of life (QOL) would match the patient's needs. Numerous adverse events have been reported and the treatment is usually prolonged until progression, so the development of resistance has to be expected [94,95]. There is expanding evidence that mTKIs can induce a sort of re-differentiation in RAIR-DTC cells, promoting NIS exposition on cell membranes and re-inducing a possible RAI sensibility. Iravani et al. studied a re-differentiation protocol in six RAIR-DTC patients harboring the BRAF v600e mutation. The therapy was targeted to MEK with trametinib and the v600e mutation of BRAF with dabrafenib and trametinib. RAI uptake was demonstrated in four of six patients, and one of them achieved a complete response after therapeutic RAI administration [97]. Leboulleux and coworkers developed a phase II prospective trial based on re-differentiation therapy with dabrafenib and trametinib, followed by a fixed RAI administration of 5550 MBq. The RAIR-DTC status was demonstrated by a D-WBS prior to mTKI administration [98]. Eleven patients were enrolled and ten of them received RAI therapy. After 6 months, RECIST criteria defined a partial response in 20% of patients and stable disease in 70% of patients. Unfortunately, 10% of patients showed a progression of the disease. Metabolic assessment was performed with ^{18}F-FDG PET/CT and results were similar to RECIST evaluation (partial response in 25%, stable disease in 63%, and progression in 13% of patients) [98]. Balakirouchenane et coworkers studied 22 patients undergoing re-differentiation therapy followed by RAI administration. They found a linkage between lower mTKi plasma concentration and RAI uptake [99]. Leboulleux et al. studied 24 patients with RAIR-DTC (confirmed by D-WBS) with small metastases that underwent a re-differentiation protocol with dabrafenib–trametinib tandem administration for 42 days [95]. A 5550 MBq RAI therapy was administered at day 28 after rh-TSH stimulation and a first evaluation of response was assessed by RECIST criteria after 6 months. If a partial response was reached, a second RAI could be administered after 6 or 12 months. Progression was diagnosed in 10% of patients, while partial or stable disease was achieved in 38% and 52% of patients, respectively. Ten patients received a second RAI administration: one of them obtained a complete response and six obtained a partial response at 6-month evaluation. One patient died because of progressive disease within 24 months. Despite the evidence of adverse events being common (96% of patients), the re-differentiation protocol was considered a good option for RAIR-DTC patients with small metastases.

6. A Case of Re-Differentiation

A 59-year-old man underwent total thyroidectomy in 2016 and a subsequent left cervical lymphadenectomy based on evidence of papillary thyroid carcinoma with lymph node metastases (pT1b N1b Mx). 5550 MBq of RAI were administered within 6 months from surgery. Nevertheless, Tg levels returned, detectable after some years from the first RAI therapy, so a second dose of 5550 MBq if ^{131}I was administered. The PT-WBS did not show abnormal uptake foci (Figure 1), while Tg blood level was 378 pg/dL after FT4 withdrawal TSH stimulation and there was evidence of pulmonary nodules on CT examination.

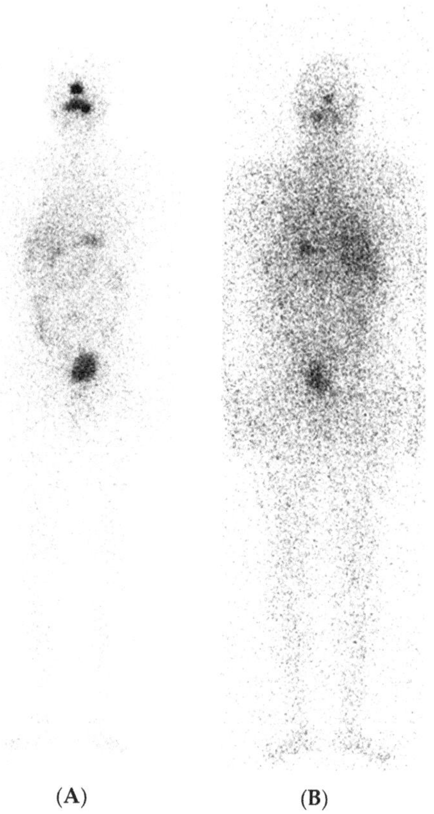

Figure 1. No evidence of pathological RAI uptake foci. (**A**) PT-WBS anterior view; (**B**) PT-WBS posterior view.

The patient was defined as RAIR and the presence of BRAF v600e mutation was identified by molecular investigation. A re-differentiation protocol was attempted with the administration of dabrafenib and trametinib for 42 days. A third dose of 5550 MBq RAI was administered at the 28th day of dabrafenib and trametinib administration, under rhTSH stimulation.

A PT-WBS scan demonstrated high RAI uptake in the pulmonary area and left cervical region (Figure 2). PT-SPECT/TC demonstrated RAI diffuse uptake in pulmonary parenchyma and left posterior mandibular lymph node (Figure 3). Tg blood levels also increased to 3183 pg/dL after rhTSH stimulation, suggesting that the re-differentiation protocol must have worked at different molecular levels.

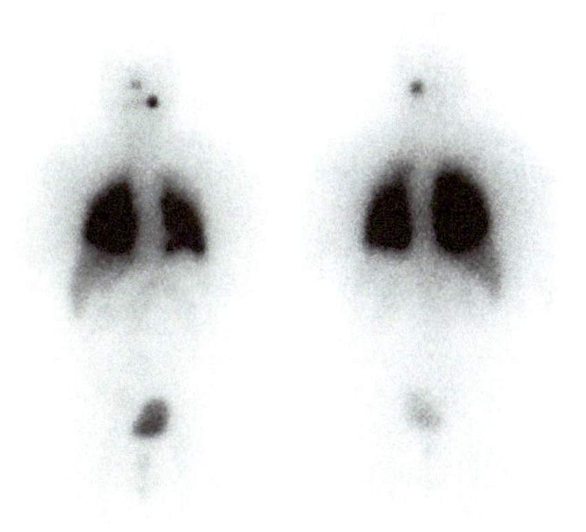

(**A**) (**B**)

Figure 2. Focal RAI accumulation in upper-left cervical region: diffuse and intense RAI uptake in pulmonary field. (**A**) PT-WBS anterior view; (**B**) PT-WBS posterior view.

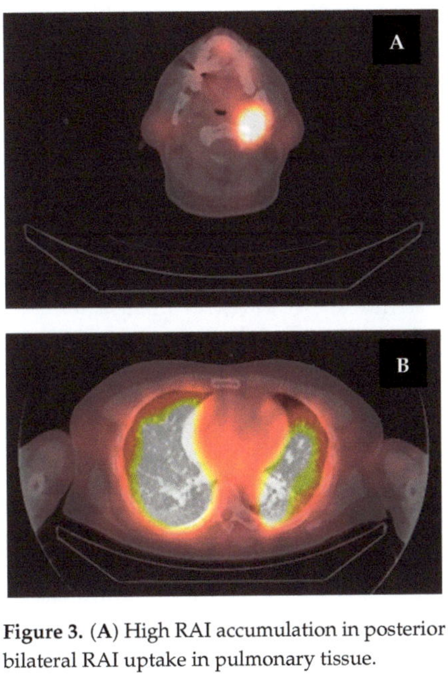

Figure 3. (**A**) High RAI accumulation in posterior mandibular lymph node. (**B**) Diffuse, intense, and bilateral RAI uptake in pulmonary tissue.

7. Advanced RAIR-DTC Treatment

When cancer progresses, it accumulates mutations and acquires multiple drug resistance. In this setting, different molecular targets have to be explored to obtain a clinical benefit. In RAIR-DTC, MAPK pathway alterations are involved in cancer de-differentiation and proliferation, so several drugs have been tested in this condition [100].

Lenvatinib is a broad-spectrum TKI directed at vascular endothelial growth factor receptors (VEGFRs), fibroblast growth factor receptor (FGFR) 1–4, C-KIT, RET protooncogene, and platelet-derived growth factor receptor α (PDGFR-α). It was first approved for advanced hepatocellular carcinoma, but recently it has been introduced in RAIR-DTC therapy options. While overall response rate and disease control are acceptable, the main lenvatinib shortcoming is the onset of important adverse events that can interfere with therapy continuation [101].

Similarly to lenvatinib, sorafenib is an oral antiangiogenetic agent. In the DECISION trial, sorafenib resulted in a significant improvement in progression-free survival over placebo in a setting of RAIR-DTC patients who showed progression after RAI therapy [102]. Cabozantinib is a relatively new entrant to broad-spectrum TKIs. In the COSMIC-311 trial, it was compared to placebo in previously TKI-treated RAIR-DTC patients, demonstrating superior efficacy with acceptable side effect onset [103].

Vandetanib was tested in RAIR-DTC patients versus placebo in the VERIFY study. Researchers found that this compound failed to obtain an improvement over placebo and in addition introduced an increase in adverse events and deaths [104].

The need for new molecular targets has led to the introduction of sarco/endoplasmic reticulum calcium ATPase (SERCA) inhibitors when RAIR-DTC develops resistance to TKIs. In some studies, SERCAi reached in vitro tumor control after TKI therapy failed [105,106].

In this scenario, the role of single-stranded mature microRNAs (miRNAs) has been investigated. MiRNAs are small sequences of nucleotides that lack coding capability, but are involved in post-transcriptional gene expression. Some miRNAs have been linked to DTC tumorigenesis [107], others have been proposed as biomarker for relapse detection [107,108], and others, such as miR-139-5p, have been suggested as an RAIR pathogenesis explanation [109]. When DTC cells take the way of de-differentiation, this leads to increased aggressivity, metastasis onset, and worse prognosis [2,40,110].

8. Conclusions

Understanding DTC functional differentiation requires understanding of its complexity, and it is necessary to build clear criteria for response evaluation. Tumor genomics insights are progressing rapidly, and the chimera of individualized therapy becomes more perceivable real time progresses. Despite that, RAIR-DTC still represents a challenging nosological entity. There are still controversies on RAIR-DTC definition, and post-RAI therapy evaluation with PT-WBS is the only validated criterion of response. Avoiding unnecessary RAI radiation exposure and sub-optimal interventions for patients are current concerns. There is a current need to predict RAIR-DTC before RAI therapy and individualizing therapeutic choices. Thus, molecular imaging is advancing with molecular biochemistry research and should aim for RAIR-DTC prediction, targeted therapy, and optimal onset timing to select second-line treatment strategies in advance.

Author Contributions: Conceptualization, F.V. and C.N.; methodology, F.V.; validation, S.M., E.D.D. and E.Z.; formal analysis, F.V.; investigation, F.V.; resources, F.V.; data curation, F.V.; writing—original draft preparation, F.V.; writing—review and editing, F.V. and C.N.; visualization, M.K.; supervision, M.K.; project administration, C.N.; funding acquisition, A.C. All authors have read and agreed to the published version of the manuscript.

Funding: This research received no external funding.

Conflicts of Interest: The authors declare no conflicts of interest.

References

1. Haugen, B.R.; Alexander, E.K.; Bible, K.C.; Doherty, G.M.; Mandel, S.J.; Nikiforov, Y.E.; Pacini, F.; Randolph, G.W.; Sawka, A.M.; Schlumberger, M.; et al. 2015 American Thyroid Association Management Guidelines for Adult Patients with Thyroid Nodules and Differentiated Thyroid Cancer: The American Thyroid Association Guidelines Task Force on Thyroid Nodules and Differentiated Thyroid Cancer. *Thyroid Off. J. Am. Thyroid Assoc.* **2016**, *26*, 1–133. [CrossRef] [PubMed]
2. Klain, M.; Nappi, C.; Zampella, E.; Cantoni, V.; Green, R.; Piscopo, L.; Volpe, F.; Manganelli, M.; Caiazzo, E.; Petretta, M.; et al. Ablation Rate after Radioactive Iodine Therapy in Patients with Differentiated Thyroid Cancer at Intermediate or High Risk of Recurrence: A Systematic Review and a Meta-Analysis. *Eur. J. Nucl. Med. Mol. Imaging* **2021**, *48*, 4437–4444. [CrossRef] [PubMed]
3. Worden, F.; Rajkovic-Hooley, O.; Reynolds, N.; Milligan, G.; Zhang, J. Real-World Treatment Patterns and Clinical Outcomes in Patients with Radioiodine-Refractory Differentiated Thyroid Cancer (RAI-R DTC) Treated with First Line Lenvatinib Monotherapy in the United States. *Endocrine* **2023**, *84*, 663–669. [CrossRef] [PubMed]
4. Chou, R.; Dana, T.; Brent, G.A.; Goldner, W.; Haymart, M.; Leung, A.M.; Ringel, M.D.; Sosa, J.A. Serum Thyroglobulin Measurement Following Surgery Without Radioactive Iodine for Differentiated Thyroid Cancer: A Systematic Review. *Thyroid Off. J. Am. Thyroid Assoc.* **2022**, *32*, 613–639. [CrossRef]
5. Schlumberger, M.; Leboulleux, S. Current Practice in Patients with Differentiated Thyroid Cancer. *Nat. Rev. Endocrinol.* **2021**, *17*, 176–188. [CrossRef] [PubMed]
6. Gordon, A.J.; Dublin, J.C.; Patel, E.; Papazian, M.; Chow, M.S.; Persky, M.J.; Jacobson, A.S.; Patel, K.N.; Suh, I.; Morris, L.G.T.; et al. American Thyroid Association Guidelines and National Trends in Management of Papillary Thyroid Carcinoma. *JAMA Otolaryngol. Neck Surg.* **2022**, *148*, 1156–1163. [CrossRef] [PubMed]
7. Schlumberger, M.; Leboulleux, S.; Catargi, B.; Deandreis, D.; Zerdoud, S.; Bardet, S.; Rusu, D.; Godbert, Y.; Buffet, C.; Schvartz, C.; et al. Outcome after Ablation in Patients with Low-Risk Thyroid Cancer (ESTIMABL1): 5-Year Follow-up Results of a Randomised, Phase 3, Equivalence Trial. *Lancet Diabetes Endocrinol.* **2018**, *6*, 618–626. [CrossRef] [PubMed]
8. Liu, J.; Liu, R.; Shen, X.; Zhu, G.; Li, B.; Xing, M. The Genetic Duet of BRAF V600E and TERT Promoter Mutations Robustly Predicts Loss of Radioiodine Avidity in Recurrent Papillary Thyroid Cancer. *J. Nucl. Med.* **2020**, *61*, 177–182. [CrossRef] [PubMed]
9. Nakanishi, K.; Kikumori, T.; Miyajima, N.; Takano, Y.; Noda, S.; Takeuchi, D.; Iwano, S.; Kodera, Y. Impact of Patient Age and Histological Type on Radioactive Iodine Avidity of Recurrent Lesions of Differentiated Thyroid Carcinoma. *Clin. Nucl. Med.* **2018**, *43*, 482–485. [CrossRef] [PubMed]
10. Simões-Pereira, J.; Mourinho, N.; Ferreira, T.C.; Limbert, E.; Cavaco, B.M.; Leite, V. Avidity and Outcomes of Radioiodine Therapy for Distant Metastasis of Distinct Types of Differentiated Thyroid Cancer. *J. Clin. Endocrinol. Metab.* **2021**, *106*, e3911–e3922. [CrossRef]
11. Pace, L.; Klain, M.; Salvatore, B.; Nicolai, E.; Zampella, E.; Assante, R.; Pellegrino, T.; Storto, G.; Fonti, R.; Salvatore, M. Prognostic Role of 18F-FDG PET/CT in the Postoperative Evaluation of Differentiated Thyroid Cancer Patients. *Clin. Nucl. Med.* **2015**, *40*, 111. [CrossRef] [PubMed]
12. Salvatore, B.; Klain, M.; Nicolai, E.; D'Amico, D.; De Matteis, G.; Raddi, M.; Fonti, R.; Pellegrino, T.; Storto, G.; Cuocolo, A.; et al. Prognostic Role of FDG PET/CT in Patients with Differentiated Thyroid Cancer Treated with 131-Iodine Empiric Therapy. *Medicine* **2017**, *96*, e8344. [CrossRef] [PubMed]
13. Celik, M.; Bulbul, B.Y.; Ayturk, S.; Durmus, Y.; Gurkan, H.; Can, N.; Tastekin, E.; Ustun, F.; Sezer, A.; Guldiken, S. The Relation between BRAFV600E Mutation and Clinicopathological Characteristics of Papillary Thyroid Cancer. *Med. Glas. Ljek. Komore Zenicko-Doboj. Kantona* **2020**, *17*, 30–34. [CrossRef] [PubMed]
14. Wu, Y.; Shi, L.; Zhao, Y.; Chen, P.; Cui, R.; Ji, M.; He, N.; Wang, M.; Li, G.; Hou, P. Synergistic Activation of Mutant TERT Promoter by Sp1 and GABPA in BRAFV600E-Driven Human Cancers. *Npj Precis. Oncol.* **2021**, *5*, 1–11. [CrossRef] [PubMed]
15. Schlumberger, M.; Lacroix, L.; Russo, D.; Filetti, S.; Bidart, J.-M. Defects in Iodide Metabolism in Thyroid Cancer and Implications for the Follow-up and Treatment of Patients. *Nat. Clin. Pract. Endocrinol. Metab.* **2007**, *3*, 260–269. [CrossRef] [PubMed]
16. Namwongprom, S.; Dejkhamron, P.; Unachak, K. Success Rate of Radioactive Iodine Treatment for Children and Adolescent with Hyperthyroidism. *J. Endocrinol. Investig.* **2021**, *44*, 541–545. [CrossRef] [PubMed]
17. Shogbesan, G.; Muzahir, S.; Bridges, A. Radioiodine Refractory Differentiated Thyroid Cancer: Albatross of Patients and Physicians. *J. Nucl. Med.* **2022**, *63*, 2693.
18. Schlumberger, M.; Brose, M.; Elisei, R.; Leboulleux, S.; Luster, M.; Pitoia, F.; Pacini, F. Definition and Management of Radioactive Iodine-Refractory Differentiated Thyroid Cancer. *Lancet Diabetes Endocrinol.* **2014**, *2*, 356–358. [CrossRef] [PubMed]
19. Finessi, M.; Liberini, V.; Deandreis, D. Definition of Radioactive Iodine Refractory Thyroid Cancer and Redifferentiation Strategies. In *Integrated Diagnostics and Theranostics of Thyroid Diseases*; Giovanella, L., Ed.; Springer International Publishing: Cham, Germany, 2023; pp. 143–156. ISBN 978-3-031-35213-3.
20. Kiyota, N.; Robinson, B.; Shah, M.; Hoff, A.O.; Taylor, M.H.; Li, D.; Dutcus, C.E.; Lee, E.K.; Kim, S.-B.; Tahara, M. Defining Radioiodine-Refractory Differentiated Thyroid Cancer: Efficacy and Safety of Lenvatinib by Radioiodine-Refractory Criteria in the SELECT Trial. *Thyroid* **2017**, *27*, 1135–1141. [CrossRef] [PubMed]
21. Van Nostrand, D. Selected Controversies of Radioiodine Imaging and Therapy in Differentiated Thyroid Cancer. *Endocrinol. Metab. Clin. N. Am.* **2017**, *46*, 783–793. [CrossRef] [PubMed]

22. Deandreis, D.; Rubino, C.; Tala, H.; Leboulleux, S.; Terroir, M.; Baudin, E.; Larson, S.; Fagin, J.A.; Schlumberger, M.; Tuttle, R.M. Comparison of Empiric Versus Whole-Body/-Blood Clearance Dosimetry–Based Approach to Radioactive Iodine Treatment in Patients with Metastases from Differentiated Thyroid Cancer. *J. Nucl. Med.* **2017**, *58*, 717–722. [CrossRef] [PubMed]
23. Mu, Z.-Z.; Zhang, Y.-Q.; Sun, D.; Lu, T.; Lin, Y.-S. Effect of BRAFV600E and TERT Promoter Mutations on Thyroglobulin Response in Patients With Distant-Metastatic Differentiated Thyroid Cancer. *Endocr. Pract. Off. J. Am. Coll. Endocrinol. Am. Assoc. Clin. Endocrinol.* **2022**, *28*, 265–270. [CrossRef]
24. Sgouros, G.; Bodei, L.; McDevitt, M.R.; Nedrow, J.R. Radiopharmaceutical Therapy in Cancer: Clinical Advances and Challenges. *Nat. Rev. Drug Discov.* **2020**, *19*, 589–608. [CrossRef] [PubMed]
25. Dotinga, M.; Vriens, D.; van Velden, F.H.P.; Stam, M.K.; Heemskerk, J.W.T.; Dibbets-Schneider, P.; Pool, M.; Rietbergen, D.D.D.; de Geus-Oei, L.-F.; Kapiteijn, E. Reinducing Radioiodine-Sensitivity in Radioiodine-Refractory Thyroid Cancer Using Lenvatinib (RESET): Study Protocol for a Single-Center, Open Label Phase II Trial. *Diagnostics* **2022**, *12*, 3154. [CrossRef] [PubMed]
26. Jeong, E.; Yoon, J.-K.; Lee, S.J.; Soh, E.Y.; Lee, J.; An, Y.-S. Risk Factors for Indeterminate Response After Radioactive Iodine Therapy in Patients With Differentiated Thyroid Cancer. *Clin. Nucl. Med.* **2019**, *44*, 714–718. [CrossRef] [PubMed]
27. Tramontin, M.Y.; Nobre, G.M.; Lopes, M.; Carneiro, M.P.; Alves, P.A.G.; de Andrade, F.A.; Vaisman, F.; Corbo, R.; Bulzico, D. High Thyroglobulin and Negative Whole-Body Scan: No Long-Term Benefit of Empiric Radioiodine Therapy. *Endocrine* **2021**, *73*, 398–406. [CrossRef] [PubMed]
28. Rosario, P.W.; Mineiro Filho, A.F.C.; Lacerda, R.X.; dos Santos, D.A.; Calsolari, M.R. The Value of Diagnostic Whole-Body Scanning and Serum Thyroglobulin in the Presence of Elevated Serum Thyrotropin during Follow-up of Anti-Thyroglobulin Antibody-Positive Patients with Differentiated Thyroid Carcinoma Who Appeared to Be Free of Disease after Total Thyroidectomy and Radioactive Iodine Ablation. *Thyroid Off. J. Am. Thyroid Assoc.* **2012**, *22*, 113–116. [CrossRef]
29. Al Hatmi, A.; Jain, A.; Mittal, A.K.; Hussain, S. Evaluation of Diagnostic Value of SPECT/CT Imaging in Post-Radioiodine Therapy in Thyroid Cancer. *Sultan Qaboos Univ. Med. J.* **2022**, *22*, 74–81. [CrossRef] [PubMed]
30. Spanu, A.; Nuvoli, S.; Marongiu, A.; Gelo, I.; Mele, L.; Piras, B.; Madeddu, G. Neck Lymph Node Metastasis Detection in Patients with Differentiated Thyroid Carcinoma (DTC) in Long-Term Follow-up: A 131I-SPECT/CT Study. *BMC Cancer* **2020**, *20*, 239. [CrossRef] [PubMed]
31. Zilioli, V.; Peli, A.; Panarotto, M.B.; Magri, G.; Alkraisheh, A.; Wiefels, C.; Rodella, C.; Giubbini, R. Differentiated Thyroid Carcinoma: Incremental Diagnostic Value of 131I SPECT/CT over Planar Whole Body Scan after Radioiodine Therapy. *Endocrine* **2017**, *56*, 551–559. [CrossRef]
32. Blum, M.; Tiu, S.; Chu, M.; Goel, S.; Friedman, K. I-131 SPECT/CT Elucidates Cryptic Findings on Planar Whole-Body Scans and Can Reduce Needless Therapy with I-131 in Post-Thyroidectomy Thyroid Cancer Patients. *Thyroid Off. J. Am. Thyroid Assoc.* **2011**, *21*, 1235–1247. [CrossRef] [PubMed]
33. Jiang, L.; Xiang, Y.; Huang, R.; Tian, R.; Liu, B. Clinical Applications of Single-Photon Emission Computed Tomography/Computed Tomography in Post-Ablation 131iodine Scintigraphy in Children and Young Adults with Differentiated Thyroid Carcinoma. *Pediatr. Radiol.* **2021**, *51*, 1724–1731. [CrossRef] [PubMed]
34. Jannin, A.; Lamartina, L.; Moutarde, C.; Djennaoui, M.; Lion, G.; Chevalier, B.; Vantyghem, M.C.; Deschamps, F.; Hadoux, J.; Baudin, E.; et al. Bone Metastases from Differentiated Thyroid Carcinoma: Heterogenous Tumor Response to Radioactive Iodine Therapy and Overall Survival. *Eur. J. Nucl. Med. Mol. Imaging* **2022**, *49*, 2401–2413. [CrossRef] [PubMed]
35. Zhu, C.; Zhang, M.; Wang, Q.; Jen, J.; Liu, B.; Guo, M. Intratumor Epigenetic Heterogeneity-A Panel Gene Methylation Study in Thyroid Cancer. *Front. Genet.* **2021**, *12*, 714071. [CrossRef] [PubMed]
36. Wang, H.; Dai, H.; Li, Q.; Shen, G.; Shi, L.; Tian, R. Investigating 18F-FDG PET/CT Parameters as Prognostic Markers for Differentiated Thyroid Cancer: A Systematic Review. *Front. Oncol.* **2021**, *11*, 648658. [CrossRef] [PubMed]
37. Albano, D.; Dondi, F.; Mazzoletti, A.; Bellini, P.; Rodella, C.; Bertagna, F. Prognostic Role of 2-[18F]FDG PET/CT Metabolic Volume Parameters in Patients Affected by Differentiated Thyroid Carcinoma with High Thyroglobulin Level, Negative 131I WBS and Positive 2-[18F]-FDG PET/CT. *Diagnostics* **2021**, *11*, 2189. [CrossRef]
38. Terroir, M.; Borget, I.; Bidault, F.; Ricard, M.; Deschamps, F.; Hartl, D.; Tselikas, L.; Dercle, L.; Lumbroso, J.; Baudin, E.; et al. The Intensity of 18FDG Uptake Does Not Predict Tumor Growth in Patients with Metastatic Differentiated Thyroid Cancer. *Eur. J. Nucl. Med. Mol. Imaging* **2017**, *44*, 638–646. [CrossRef] [PubMed]
39. Singh, I.; Bikas, A.; Garcia, C.A.; Desale, S.; Wartofsky, L.; Burman, K.D. 18F-FDG-PET SUV as a Prognostic Marker of Increasing Size in Thyroid Cancer Tumors. *Endocr. Pract. Off. J. Am. Coll. Endocrinol. Am. Assoc. Clin. Endocrinol.* **2017**, *23*, 182–189. [CrossRef] [PubMed]
40. Klain, M.; Zampella, E.; Piscopo, L.; Volpe, F.; Manganelli, M.; Masone, S.; Pace, L.; Salvatore, D.; Schlumberger, M.; Cuocolo, A. Long-Term Prognostic Value of the Response to Therapy Assessed by Laboratory and Imaging Findings in Patients with Differentiated Thyroid Cancer. *Cancers* **2021**, *13*, 4338. [CrossRef] [PubMed]
41. Klain, M.; Maurea, S.; Gaudieri, V.; Zampella, E.; Volpe, F.; Manganelli, M.; Piscopo, L.; De Risi, M.; Cuocolo, A. The Diagnostic Role of Total-Body 18F-FDG PET/CT in Patients with Multiple Tumors: A Report of the Association of Thyroid Cancer with Lung or Renal Tumors. *Quant. Imaging Med. Surg.* **2021**, *11*, 4211–4215. [CrossRef] [PubMed]
42. Santhanam, P.; Khthir, R.; Solnes, L.B.; Ladenson, P.W. The Relationship of Brafv600e Mutation Status to Fdg Pet/Ct Avidity in Thyroid Cancer: A Review and Meta-Analysis. *Endocr. Pract. Off. J. Am. Coll. Endocrinol. Am. Assoc. Clin. Endocrinol.* **2018**, *24*, 21–26. [CrossRef] [PubMed]

43. Chang, J.W.; Park, K.W.; Heo, J.H.; Jung, S.-N.; Liu, L.; Kim, S.M.; Kwon, I.S.; Koo, B.S. Relationship Between 18F-Fluorodeoxyglucose Accumulation and the BRAF V600E Mutation in Papillary Thyroid Cancer. *World J. Surg.* **2018**, *42*, 114–122. [CrossRef] [PubMed]
44. Haddad, R.I.; Bischoff, L.; Ball, D.; Bernet, V.; Blomain, E.; Busaidy, N.L.; Campbell, M.; Dickson, P.; Duh, Q.-Y.; Ehya, H.; et al. Thyroid Carcinoma, Version 2.2022, NCCN Clinical Practice Guidelines in Oncology. *J. Natl. Compr. Canc. Netw.* **2022**, *20*, 925–951. [CrossRef] [PubMed]
45. Cortas, C.; Charalambous, H. Tyrosine Kinase Inhibitors for Radioactive Iodine Refractory Differentiated Thyroid Cancer. *Life* **2024**, *14*, 22. [CrossRef] [PubMed]
46. Zhao, J.; Liu, P.; Yu, Y.; Zhi, J.; Zheng, X.; Yu, J.; Gao, M. Comparison of Diagnostic Methods for the Detection of a BRAF Mutation in Papillary Thyroid Cancer. *Oncol. Lett.* **2019**, *17*, 4661–4666. [CrossRef]
47. Solomon, J.P.; Hechtman, J.F. Detection of *NTRK* Fusions: Merits and Limitations of Current Diagnostic Platforms. *Cancer Res.* **2019**, *79*, 3163–3168. [CrossRef]
48. Zhang, Y.; Li, Y.; Lin, Z.; Chen, W. Can 99 Tc m -3PRGD 2 (α v β 3) and 18 F-FDG Dual-Tracer Molecular Imaging Change the Therapeutic Strategy for Progressive Refractory Differentiated Thyroid Cancer: Case Report. *Medicine* **2023**, *102*, e32751. [CrossRef] [PubMed]
49. Gao, R.; Zhang, G.-J.; Wang, Y.-B.; Liu, Y.; Wang, F.; Jia, X.; Liang, Y.-Q.; Yang, A.-M. Clinical Value of 99mTc-3PRGD2 SPECT/CT in Differentiated Thyroid Carcinoma with Negative 131I Whole-Body Scan and Elevated Thyroglobulin Level. *Sci. Rep.* **2018**, *8*, 473. [CrossRef] [PubMed]
50. Liang, Y.; Jia, X.; Wang, Y.; Liu, Y.; Yao, X.; Bai, Y.; Han, P.; Chen, S.; Yang, A.; Gao, R. Evaluation of Integrin Avβ3-Targeted Imaging for Predicting Disease Progression in Patients with High-Risk Differentiated Thyroid Cancer (Using 99mTc-3PRGD2). *Cancer Imaging* **2022**, *22*, 72. [CrossRef] [PubMed]
51. Parihar, A.S.; Mittal, B.R.; Kumar, R.; Shukla, J.; Bhattacharya, A. ^{68}Ga-DOTA-RGD$_2$ Positron Emission Tomography/Computed Tomography in Radioiodine Refractory Thyroid Cancer: Prospective Comparison of Diagnostic Accuracy with ^{18}F-FDG Positron Emission Tomography/Computed Tomography and Evaluation Toward Potential Theranostics. *Thyroid* **2020**, *30*, 557–567. [CrossRef] [PubMed]
52. Chernaya, G.; Mikhno, N.; Khabalova, T.; Svyatchenko, S.; Mostovich, L.; Shevchenko, S.; Gulyaeva, L. The Expression Profile of Integrin Receptors and Osteopontin in Thyroid Malignancies Varies Depending on the Tumor Progression Rate and Presence of BRAF V600E Mutation. *Surg. Oncol.* **2018**, *27*, 702–708. [CrossRef] [PubMed]
53. Volpe, F.; Nappi, C.; Piscopo, L.; Zampella, E.; Mainolfi, C.G.; Ponsiglione, A.; Imbriaco, M.; Cuocolo, A.; Klain, M. Emerging Role of Nuclear Medicine in Prostate Cancer: Current State and Future Perspectives. *Cancers* **2023**, *15*, 4746. [CrossRef] [PubMed]
54. Hofman, M.S.; Emmett, L.; Sandhu, S.; Iravani, A.; Joshua, A.M.; Goh, J.C.; Pattison, D.A.; Tan, T.H.; Kirkwood, I.D.; Ng, S.; et al. [177Lu]Lu-PSMA-617 versus Cabazitaxel in Patients with Metastatic Castration-Resistant Prostate Cancer (TheraP): A Randomised, Open-Label, Phase 2 Trial. *Lancet Lond. Engl.* **2021**, *397*, 797–804. [CrossRef] [PubMed]
55. Alan-Selcuk, N.; Beydagi, G.; Demirci, E.; Ocak, M.; Celik, S.; Oven, B.B.; Toklu, T.; Karaaslan, I.; Akcay, K.; Sonmez, O.; et al. Clinical Experience with [225Ac]Ac-PSMA Treatment in Patients with [177Lu]Lu-PSMA–Refractory Metastatic Castration-Resistant Prostate Cancer. *J. Nucl. Med.* **2023**, *64*, 1574–1580. [CrossRef] [PubMed]
56. Demirci, E.; Ocak, M.; Kabasakal, L.; Decristoforo, C.; Talat, Z.; Halaç, M.; Kanmaz, B. (68)Ga-PSMA PET/CT Imaging of Metastatic Clear Cell Renal Cell Carcinoma. *Eur. J. Nucl. Med. Mol. Imaging* **2014**, *41*, 1461–1462. [CrossRef] [PubMed]
57. Chang, S.S.; Reuter, V.E.; Heston, W.D.; Bander, N.H.; Grauer, L.S.; Gaudin, P.B. Five Different Anti-Prostate-Specific Membrane Antigen (PSMA) Antibodies Confirm PSMA Expression in Tumor-Associated Neovasculature. *Cancer Res.* **1999**, *59*, 3192–3198. [PubMed]
58. Bychkov, A.; Vutrapongwatana, U.; Tepmongkol, S.; Keelawat, S. PSMA Expression by Microvasculature of Thyroid Tumors–Potential Implications for PSMA Theranostics. *Sci. Rep.* **2017**, *7*, 5202. [CrossRef]
59. Heitkötter, B.; Steinestel, K.; Trautmann, M.; Grünewald, I.; Barth, P.; Gevensleben, H.; Bögemann, M.; Wardelmann, E.; Hartmann, W.; Rahbar, K.; et al. Neovascular PSMA Expression Is a Common Feature in Malignant Neoplasms of the Thyroid. *Oncotarget* **2018**, *9*, 9867–9874. [CrossRef]
60. Verma, P.; Malhotra, G.; Agrawal, R.; Sonavane, S.; Meshram, V.; Asopa, R.V. Evidence of Prostate-Specific Membrane Antigen Expression in Metastatic Differentiated Thyroid Cancer Using 68Ga-PSMA-HBED-CC PET/CT. *Clin. Nucl. Med.* **2018**, *43*, e265–e268. [CrossRef] [PubMed]
61. Verburg, F.A.; Krohn, T.; Heinzel, A.; Mottaghy, F.M.; Behrendt, F.F. First Evidence of PSMA Expression in Differentiated Thyroid Cancer Using [68Ga]PSMA-HBED-CC PET/CT. *Eur. J. Nucl. Med. Mol. Imaging* **2015**, *42*, 1622–1623. [CrossRef] [PubMed]
62. Lütje, S.; Gomez, B.; Cohnen, J.; Umutlu, L.; Gotthardt, M.; Poeppel, T.D.; Bockisch, A.; Rosenbaum-Krumme, S. Imaging of Prostate-Specific Membrane Antigen Expression in Metastatic Differentiated Thyroid Cancer Using 68Ga-HBED-CC-PSMA PET/CT. *Clin. Nucl. Med.* **2017**, *42*, 20–25. [CrossRef] [PubMed]
63. de Vries, L.H.; Lodewijk, L.; Braat, A.J.A.T.; Krijger, G.C.; Valk, G.D.; Lam, M.G.E.H.; Borel Rinkes, I.H.M.; Vriens, M.R.; de Keizer, B. 68Ga-PSMA PET/CT in Radioactive Iodine-Refractory Differentiated Thyroid Cancer and First Treatment Results with 177Lu-PSMA-617. *EJNMMI Res.* **2020**, *10*, 18. [CrossRef] [PubMed]
64. Pishdad, R.; Treglia, G.; Mehta, A.; Santhanam, P. Somatostatin Receptor Imaging of Thyroid Tissue and Differentiated Thyroid Cancer Using Gallium-68-Labeled Radiotracers—A Review of Clinical Studies. *Endocrine* **2024**. [CrossRef] [PubMed]

65. Sancak, S.; Hardt, A.; Singer, J.; Klöppel, G.; Eren, F.T.; Güllüoglu, B.M.; Sen, L.S.; Sever, Z.; Akalin, N.S.; Eszlinger, M.; et al. Somatostatin Receptor 2 Expression Determined by Immunohistochemistry in Cold Thyroid Nodules Exceeds That of Hot Thyroid Nodules, Papillary Thyroid Carcinoma, and Graves' Disease. *Thyroid Off. J. Am. Thyroid Assoc.* **2010**, *20*, 505–511. [CrossRef] [PubMed]
66. Pisarek, H.; Stepień, T.; Kubiak, R.; Borkowska, E.; Pawlikowski, M. Expression of Somatostatin Receptor Subtypes in Human Thyroid Tumors: The Immunohistochemical and Molecular Biology (RT-PCR) Investigation. *Thyroid Res.* **2009**, *2*, 1. [CrossRef] [PubMed]
67. Klagge, A.; Krause, K.; Schierle, K.; Steinert, F.; Dralle, H.; Fuhrer, D. Somatostatin Receptor Subtype Expression in Human Thyroid Tumours. *Horm. Metab. Res. Horm. Stoffwechselforschung Horm. Metab.* **2010**, *42*, 237–240. [CrossRef] [PubMed]
68. Teunissen, J.J.M.; Kwekkeboom, D.J.; Kooij, P.P.M.; Bakker, W.H.; Krenning, E.P. Peptide Receptor Radionuclide Therapy for Non-Radioiodine-Avid Differentiated Thyroid Carcinoma. *J. Nucl. Med. Off. Publ. Soc. Nucl. Med.* **2005**, *46* (Suppl. S1), 107S–114S.
69. Piscopo, L.; Zampella, E.; Pellegrino, S.; Volpe, F.; Nappi, C.; Gaudieri, V.; Fonti, R.; Vecchio, S.D.; Cuocolo, A.; Klain, M. Diagnosis, Management and Theragnostic Approach of Gastro-Entero-Pancreatic Neuroendocrine Neoplasms. *Cancers* **2023**, *15*, 3483. [CrossRef] [PubMed]
70. Park, H.; Subramaniam, R.M. Diagnosis and Treatment of Lung Neuroendocrine Neoplasms: Somatostatin Receptor PET Imaging and Peptide Receptor Radionuclide Therapy. *PET Clin.* **2023**, *18*, 223–231. [CrossRef] [PubMed]
71. Gallicchio, R.; Giordano, A.; Milella, M.; Storto, R.; Pellegrino, T.; Nardelli, A.; Nappi, A.; Tarricone, L.; Storto, G. Ga-68-Edotreotide Positron Emission Tomography/Computed Tomography Somatostatin Receptors Tumor Volume Predicts Outcome in Patients With Primary Gastroenteropancreatic Neuroendocrine Tumors. *Cancer Control* **2023**, *30*, 10732748231152328. [CrossRef] [PubMed]
72. Fortunati, E.; Bonazzi, N.; Zanoni, L.; Fanti, S.; Ambrosini, V. Molecular Imaging Theranostics of Neuroendocrine Tumors. *Semin. Nucl. Med.* **2023**, *53*, 539–554. [CrossRef] [PubMed]
73. Duan, H.; Ferri, V.; Fisher, G.; Shaheen, S.; Davidzon, G.; Moradi, F.; Nguyen, J.; Franc, B.; Iagaru, A.; Aparici, C.M. Evaluation of Interim 68Ga-Dotatate PET after Two Cycles of Peptide Receptor Radionuclide Therapy (PRRT) in Neuroendocrine Tumors (NET). *Clin. Nucl. Med.* **2023**, *48*, e276.
74. Donohoe, K.J.; Aloff, J.; Avram, A.M.; Bennet, K.G.; Giovanella, L.; Greenspan, B.; Gulec, S.; Hassan, A.; Kloos, R.T.; Solórzano, C.C.; et al. Appropriate Use Criteria for Nuclear Medicine in the Evaluation and Treatment of Differentiated Thyroid Cancer. *J. Nucl. Med.* **2020**, *61*, 375–396. [CrossRef] [PubMed]
75. Bertagna, F.; Albano, D.; Giovanella, L.; Giubbini, R.; Treglia, G. F18-Choline/C11-Choline PET/CT Thyroid Incidentalomas. *Endocrine* **2019**, *64*, 203–208. [CrossRef] [PubMed]
76. Albano, D.; Durmo, R.; Bertagna, F.; Giubbini, R. 18F-Choline PET/CT Incidental Thyroid Uptake in Patients Studied for Prostate Cancer. *Endocrine* **2019**, *63*, 531–536. [CrossRef] [PubMed]
77. Piccardo, A.; Trimboli, P.; Puntoni, M.; Foppiani, L.; Treglia, G.; Naseri, M.; Bottoni, G.L.; Massollo, M.; Sola, S.; Ferrarazzo, G.; et al. Role of 18F-Choline Positron Emission Tomography/Computed Tomography to Detect Structural Relapse in High-Risk Differentiated Thyroid Cancer Patients. *Thyroid Off. J. Am. Thyroid Assoc.* **2019**, *29*, 549–556. [CrossRef] [PubMed]
78. Fozzatti, L.; Cheng, S. Tumor Cells and Cancer-Associated Fibroblasts: A Synergistic Crosstalk to Promote Thyroid Cancer. *Endocrinol. Metab.* **2020**, *35*, 673–680. [CrossRef] [PubMed]
79. Dvorak, H.F. Tumors: Wounds That Do Not Heal. *N. Engl. J. Med.* **1986**, *315*, 1650–1659. [CrossRef] [PubMed]
80. Kratochwil, C.; Flechsig, P.; Lindner, T.; Abderrahim, L.; Altmann, A.; Mier, W.; Adeberg, S.; Rathke, H.; Röhrich, M.; Winter, H.; et al. ^{68}Ga-FAPI PET/CT: Tracer Uptake in 28 Different Kinds of Cancer. *J. Nucl. Med.* **2019**, *60*, 801. [CrossRef]
81. Chen, Y.; Zheng, S.; Zhang, J.; Yao, S.; Miao, W. 68Ga-DOTA-FAPI-04 PET/CT Imaging in Radioiodine-Refractory Differentiated Thyroid Cancer (RR-DTC) Patients. *Ann. Nucl. Med.* **2022**, *36*, 610–622. [CrossRef] [PubMed]
82. Ballal, S.; Yadav, M.P.; Roesch, F.; Satapathy, S.; Moon, E.S.; Martin, M.; Wakade, N.; Sheokand, P.; Tripathi, M.; Chandekar, K.R.; et al. Head-to-Head Comparison of [68Ga]Ga-DOTA.SA.FAPi with [18F]F-FDG PET/CT in Radioiodine-Resistant Follicular-Cell Derived Thyroid Cancers. *Eur. J. Nucl. Med. Mol. Imaging* **2023**, *51*, 233–244. [CrossRef] [PubMed]
83. Ballal, S.; Yadav, M.P.; Moon, E.S.; Rösch, F.; ArunRaj, S.T.; Agarwal, S.; Tripathi, M.; Sahoo, R.K.; Bal, C. First-in-Human Experience With 177Lu-DOTAGA.(SA.FAPi)2 Therapy in an Uncommon Case of Aggressive Medullary Thyroid Carcinoma Clinically Mimicking as Anaplastic Thyroid Cancer. *Clin. Nucl. Med.* **2022**, *47*, e444–e445. [CrossRef] [PubMed]
84. Eisenhauer, E.A.; Therasse, P.; Bogaerts, J.; Schwartz, L.H.; Sargent, D.; Ford, R.; Dancey, J.; Arbuck, S.; Gwyther, S.; Mooney, M.; et al. New Response Evaluation Criteria in Solid Tumours: Revised RECIST Guideline (Version 1.1). *Eur. J. Cancer* **2009**, *45*, 228–247. [CrossRef] [PubMed]
85. Fu, H.; Huang, J.; Zhao, T.; Wang, H.; Chen, Y.; Xu, W.; Pang, Y.; Guo, W.; Sun, L.; Wu, H.; et al. Fibroblast Activation Protein-Targeted Radioligand Therapy with 177Lu-EB-FAPI for Metastatic Radioiodine-Refractory Thyroid Cancer: First-in-Human, Dose-Escalation Study. *Clin. Cancer Res.* **2023**, *29*, 4740–4750. [CrossRef]
86. Farasati Far, B.; Broomand Lomer, N.; Gharedaghi, H.; Sahrai, H.; Mahmoudvand, G.; Karimi Rouzbahani, A. Is Beta-Carotene Consumption Associated with Thyroid Hormone Levels? *Front. Endocrinol.* **2023**, *14*, 1089315. [CrossRef] [PubMed]
87. Capriello, S.; Stramazzo, I.; Bagaglini, M.F.; Brusca, N.; Virili, C.; Centanni, M. The Relationship between Thyroid Disorders and Vitamin A.: A Narrative Minireview. *Front. Endocrinol.* **2022**, *13*, 968215. [CrossRef] [PubMed]

88. Pak, K.; Shin, S.; Kim, S.-J.; Kim, I.-J.; Chang, S.; Koo, P.; Kwak, J.; Kim, J.-H. Response of Retinoic Acid in Patients with Radioactive Iodine-Refractory Thyroid Cancer: A Meta-Analysis. *Oncol. Res. Treat.* **2018**, *41*, 100–104. [CrossRef] [PubMed]
89. Groener, J.; Gelen, D.; Mogler, C.; Herpel, E.; Toth, C.; Kender, Z.; Peichl, M.; Haufe, S.; Haberkorn, U.; Sulaj, A.; et al. BRAF V600E and Retinoic Acid in Radioiodine-Refractory Papillary Thyroid Cancer. *Horm. Metab. Res.* **2019**, *51*, 69–75. [CrossRef] [PubMed]
90. Ho, A.L.; Grewal, R.K.; Leboeuf, R.; Sherman, E.J.; Pfister, D.G.; Deandreis, D.; Pentlow, K.S.; Zanzonico, P.B.; Haque, S.; Gavane, S.; et al. Selumetinib-Enhanced Radioiodine Uptake in Advanced Thyroid Cancer. *N. Engl. J. Med.* **2013**, *368*, 623–632. [CrossRef]
91. Larson, S.M.; Osborne, J.R.; Grewal, R.K.; Tuttle, R.M. Redifferentiating Thyroid Cancer: Selumetinib-Enhanced Radioiodine Uptake in Thyroid Cancer. *Mol. Imaging Radionucl. Ther.* **2017**, *26*, 80–86. [CrossRef] [PubMed]
92. Ho, A.L.; Dedecjus, M.; Wirth, L.J.; Tuttle, R.M.; Inabnet, W.B.; Tennvall, J.; Vaisman, F.; Bastholt, L.; Gianoukakis, A.G.; Rodien, P.; et al. Selumetinib Plus Adjuvant Radioactive Iodine in Patients With High-Risk Differentiated Thyroid Cancer: A Phase III, Randomized, Placebo-Controlled Trial (ASTRA). *J. Clin. Oncol.* **2022**, *40*, 1870–1878. [CrossRef] [PubMed]
93. Schlumberger, M.; Tahara, M.; Wirth, L.J.; Robinson, B.; Brose, M.S.; Elisei, R.; Habra, M.A.; Newbold, K.; Shah, M.H.; Hoff, A.O.; et al. Lenvatinib versus Placebo in Radioiodine-Refractory Thyroid Cancer. *N. Engl. J. Med.* **2015**, *372*, 621–630. [CrossRef] [PubMed]
94. Porcelli, T.; Luongo, C.; Sessa, F.; Klain, M.; Masone, S.; Troncone, G.; Bellevicine, C.; Schlumberger, M.; Salvatore, D. Long-Term Management of Lenvatinib-Treated Thyroid Cancer Patients: A Real-Life Experience at a Single Institution. *Endocrine* **2021**, *73*, 358–366. [CrossRef] [PubMed]
95. Wirth, L.J.; Durante, C.; Topliss, D.J.; Winquist, E.; Robenshtok, E.; Iwasaki, H.; Luster, M.; Elisei, R.; Leboulleux, S.; Tahara, M. Lenvatinib for the Treatment of Radioiodine-Refractory Differentiated Thyroid Cancer: Treatment Optimization for Maximum Clinical Benefit. *Oncologist* **2022**, *27*, 565–572. [CrossRef] [PubMed]
96. Lieberman, L.; Worden, F. Novel Therapeutics for Advanced Differentiated Thyroid Cancer. *Endocrinol. Metab. Clin. N. Am.* **2022**, *51*, 367–378. [CrossRef] [PubMed]
97. Iravani, A.; Solomon, B.; Pattison, D.A.; Jackson, P.; Ravi Kumar, A.; Kong, G.; Hofman, M.S.; Akhurst, T.; Hicks, R.J. Mitogen-Activated Protein Kinase Pathway Inhibition for Redifferentiation of Radioiodine Refractory Differentiated Thyroid Cancer: An Evolving Protocol. *Thyroid* **2019**, *29*, 1634–1645. [CrossRef] [PubMed]
98. Leboulleux, S.; Benisvy, D.; Taieb, D.; Attard, M.; Bournaud, C.; Terroir, M.; Ghuzlan, A.A.; Lamartina, L.; Schlumberger, M.J.; Godbert, Y.; et al. MERAIODE: A Redifferentiation Phase II Trial with Trametinib Followed by Radioactive Iodine for Metastatic Radioactive Iodine Refractory Differentiated Thyroid Cancer Patients with a RAS Mutation. *Ann. Oncol.* **2021**, *32*, S1204. [CrossRef]
99. Balakirouchenane, D.; Seban, R.; Groussin, L.; Puszkiel, A.; Cottereau, A.S.; Clerc, J.; Vidal, M.; Goldwasser, F.; Arrondeau, J.; Blanchet, B.; et al. Pharmacokinetics/Pharmacodynamics of Dabrafenib and Trametinib for Redifferentiation and Treatment of Radioactive Iodine-Resistant Mutated Advanced Differentiated Thyroid Cancer. *Thyroid* **2023**, *33*, 1327–1338. [CrossRef] [PubMed]
100. Boucai, L.; Zafereo, M.; Cabanillas, M.E. Thyroid Cancer: A Review. *JAMA* **2024**, *331*, 425. [CrossRef]
101. Hamidi, S.; Boucher, A.; Lemieux, B.; Rondeau, G.; Lebœuf, R.; Ste-Marie, L.-G.; Le, X.K.; Mircescu, H. Lenvatinib Therapy for Advanced Thyroid Cancer: Real-Life Data on Safety, Efficacy, and Some Rare Side Effects. *J. Endocr. Soc.* **2022**, *6*, bvac048. [CrossRef] [PubMed]
102. Brose, M.S.; Nutting, C.M.; Jarzab, B.; Elisei, R.; Siena, S.; Bastholt, L.; de la Fouchardiere, C.; Pacini, F.; Paschke, R.; Shong, Y.K.; et al. Sorafenib in Radioactive Iodine-Refractory, Locally Advanced or Metastatic Differentiated Thyroid Cancer: A Randomised, Double-Blind, Phase 3 Trial. *Lancet* **2014**, *384*, 319–328. [CrossRef] [PubMed]
103. Brose, M.S.; Robinson, B.G.; Sherman, S.I.; Jarzab, B.; Lin, C.-C.; Vaisman, F.; Hoff, A.O.; Hitre, E.; Bowles, D.W.; Sen, S.; et al. Cabozantinib for Previously Treated Radioiodine-Refractory Differentiated Thyroid Cancer: Updated Results from the Phase 3 COSMIC-311 Trial. *Cancer* **2022**, *128*, 4203–4212. [CrossRef] [PubMed]
104. Brose, M.S.; Capdevila, J.; Elisei, R.; Bastholt, L.; Führer-Sakel, D.; Leboulleux, S.; Sugitani, I.; Taylor, M.H.; Wang, Z.; Wirth, L.J.; et al. Vandetanib in Locally Advanced or Metastatic Differentiated Thyroid Cancer Refractory to Radioiodine Therapy. *Endocr. Relat. Cancer* **2024**, *31*, e230354. [CrossRef]
105. Chang, H.-S.; Kim, Y.; Lee, S.Y.; Yun, H.J.; Chang, H.-J.; Park, K.C. Anti-Cancer SERCA Inhibitors Targeting Sorafenib-Resistant Human Papillary Thyroid Carcinoma. *Int. J. Mol. Sci.* **2023**, *24*, 7069. [CrossRef] [PubMed]
106. Kim, Y.; Yun, H.J.; Choi, K.H.; Kim, C.W.; Lee, J.H.; Weicker, R.; Kim, S.-M.; Park, K.C. Discovery of New Anti-Cancer Agents against Patient-Derived Sorafenib-Resistant Papillary Thyroid Cancer. *Int. J. Mol. Sci.* **2023**, *24*, 16413. [CrossRef] [PubMed]
107. Rosignolo, F.; Sponziello, M.; Giacomelli, L.; Russo, D.; Pecce, V.; Biffoni, M.; Bellantone, R.; Lombardi, C.P.; Lamartina, L.; Grani, G.; et al. Identification of Thyroid-Associated Serum microRNA Profiles and Their Potential Use in Thyroid Cancer Follow-Up. *J. Endocr. Soc.* **2017**, *1*, 3–13. [CrossRef] [PubMed]
108. Celano, M.; Rosignolo, F.; Maggisano, V.; Pecce, V.; Iannone, M.; Russo, D.; Bulotta, S. MicroRNAs as Biomarkers in Thyroid Carcinoma. *Int. J. Genom.* **2017**, *2017*, 6496570. [CrossRef]

109. Pecce, V.; Sponziello, M.; Verrienti, A.; Grani, G.; Abballe, L.; Bini, S.; Annunziata, S.; Perotti, G.; Salvatori, M.; Zagaria, L.; et al. The Role of miR-139-5p in Radioiodine-Resistant Thyroid Cancer. *J. Endocrinol. Invest.* **2023**, *46*, 2079–2093. [CrossRef] [PubMed]
110. Huang, I.-C.; Chou, F.-F.; Liu, R.-T.; Tung, S.-C.; Chen, J.-F.; Kuo, M.-C.; Hsieh, C.-J.; Wang, P.-W. Long-Term Outcomes of Distant Metastasis from Differentiated Thyroid Carcinoma. *Clin. Endocrinol.* **2012**, *76*, 439–447. [CrossRef] [PubMed]

Disclaimer/Publisher's Note: The statements, opinions and data contained in all publications are solely those of the individual author(s) and contributor(s) and not of MDPI and/or the editor(s). MDPI and/or the editor(s) disclaim responsibility for any injury to people or property resulting from any ideas, methods, instructions or products referred to in the content.

Current Oncology

MDPI

Review

^{177}Lu-PSMA-617 in Metastatic Castration-Resistant Prostate Cancer: A Review of the Evidence and Implications for Canadian Clinical Practice

Kim N. Chi [1,*], Steven M. Yip [2], Glenn Bauman [3], Stephan Probst [4], Urban Emmenegger [5], Christian K. Kollmannsberger [1], Patrick Martineau [6], Tamim Niazi [7], Frédéric Pouliot [8,9], Ricardo Rendon [10], Sebastien J. Hotte [11], David T. Laidley [12] and Fred Saad [13,14]

1 Department of Medical Oncology, BC Cancer—Vancouver, University of British Columbia, Vancouver, BC V5Z 1M9, Canada; ckollmannsberger@bccancer.bc.ca
2 Department of Oncology, Tom Baker Cancer Centre and Cumming School of Medicine, University of Calgary, Calgary, AB T2N 4N1, Canada; steven.yip@albertahealthservices.ca
3 London Regional Cancer Program, Department of Oncology, Western University, London, ON N6A 5W9, Canada; glenn.bauman@lhsc.on.ca
4 Department of Nuclear Medicine, Jewish General Hospital, McGill University, Montreal, QC H3A 0G4, Canada
5 Department of Medicine, Odette Cancer Centre, University of Toronto, Toronto, ON M5S 1A8, Canada; uemmengg@sri.utoronto.ca
6 Department of Radiology, BC Cancer—Vancouver, University of British Columbia, Vancouver, BC V5Z 1M9, Canada; patrick.martineau@bccancer.bc.ca
7 Department of Radiation Oncology, Jewish General Hospital, McGill University, Montréal, QC H3T 1E2, Canada; mohammad.tamim.niazi.med@ssss.gouv.qc.ca
8 Department of Urology, Centre Hospitalier Universitaire de Québec, Université Laval, Québec, QC G1V 0A6, Canada; frederic.pouliot@crchudequebec.ulaval.ca
9 Department of Surgery, Université Laval, Québec, QC G1V 0A6, Canada
10 Department of Urology, Queen Elizabeth II Health Sciences Centre, Dalhousie University, Halifax, NS B3H 4R2, Canada
11 Department of Oncology, Juravinski Cancer Centre, McMaster University, Hamilton, ON L8S 4L8, Canada; hotte@hhsc.ca
12 Department of Medical Imaging-Nuclear Medicine, London Health Sciences Centre, Western University, London, ON N6A 3K7, Canada
13 Division of Urology, Centre Hospitalier de l'Université de Montréal, Université de Montréal, Montréal, QC H2X 0A9, Canada; fred.saad@umontreal.ca
14 Department of Surgery, Université de Montréal, Montréal, QC H2X 0A9, Canada
* Correspondence: kchi@bccancer.bc.ca

Abstract: Prostate-specific membrane antigen (PSMA) is highly expressed in prostate cancer and a therapeutic target. Lutetium-177 (^{177}Lu)-PSMA-617 is the first radioligand therapy to be approved in Canada for use in patients with metastatic castration-resistant prostate cancer (mCRPC). As this treatment represents a new therapeutic class, guidance regarding how to integrate it into clinical practice is needed. This article aims to review the evidence from prospective phase 2 and 3 clinical trials and meta-analyses of observational studies on the use of ^{177}Lu-PSMA-617 in prostate cancer and discuss how Canadian clinicians might best apply these data in practice. The selection of appropriate patients, the practicalities of treatment administration, including necessary facilities for treatment procedures, the assessment of treatment response, and the management of adverse events are considered. Survival benefits were observed in clinical trials of ^{177}Lu-PSMA-617 in patients with progressive, PSMA-positive mCRPC who were pretreated with androgen receptor pathway inhibitors and taxanes, as well as in taxane-naïve patients. However, the results of ongoing trials are awaited to clarify questions regarding the optimal sequencing of ^{177}Lu-PSMA-617 with other therapies, as well as the implications of predictive biomarkers, personalized dosimetry, and combinations with other therapies.

Keywords: prostate cancer; mCRPC; radioligand therapy; ^{177}Lu-PSMA-617; ^{177}Lu vipivotide tetraxetan

1. Introduction

Prostate cancer accounts for approximately 10% of cancer mortality among males in Canada [1]. Historically, nearly all of these deaths were due to metastatic disease, which in 2011–2019 had a five-year relative survival rate of 34%, as compared to almost 100% for localized or regional disease [2]. The results of recent clinical trials suggest that median overall survival (OS) for patients with previously untreated metastatic castration-resistant prostate cancer (mCRPC) ranges from 31 to 41 months [3–6], with real-world data revealing a slightly shorter median OS of 21 months [7]. Research into therapeutics leveraging novel targets such as prostate-specific membrane antigen (PSMA) has aimed to improve survival in patients with metastatic prostate cancer [8–10]. PSMA is a transmembrane enzyme that has low levels of expression in normal prostate, kidney, and small intestine tissue, as well as salivary and lachrymal glands, but is overexpressed by 100- to 1000-fold in over 90% of metastatic prostate cancers, with particularly elevated levels in mCRPC [8–10]. Various strategies targeting PSMA in prostate cancer have been investigated, including monoclonal antibodies and small-molecule radioligand therapy (RLT) [9,10]. Of these, the only PSMA-directed therapeutic currently approved in Canada is lutetium-177 (^{177}Lu)-PSMA-617, also known as ^{177}Lu vipivotide tetraxetan, although alternative RLTs utilizing different PSMA-binding molecules and/or radionuclides are being evaluated in clinical trials [11,12].

^{177}Lu-PSMA-617 is a small-molecule RLT consisting of the radionuclide ^{177}Lu linked to a PSMA-binding ligand [12]. The radionuclide ^{177}Lu has a half-life of 6.6 days and emits primarily beta rays, which have an average range of 0.23 mm in soft tissue [13]. The PSMA-binding ligand, PSMA-617, is a chemically modified PSMA inhibitor demonstrated to have high inhibition potency and efficient internalization into PSMA-positive cells [14]. Binding of ^{177}Lu-PSMA-617 to PSMA-expressing cells delivers radiation in a target-specific manner, leading to cell death of PSMA-positive cells, as well as of surrounding cells due to the cross-fire effect [12,15]. Following promising preclinical results with radiolabeled PSMA-617 developed at the German Cancer Research Center in Heidelberg, Germany [14], ^{177}Lu-PSMA-617 was successfully used on a compassionate basis in patients with metastatic prostate cancer treated at German centres [16–21]. This paved the way for formal phase 1 dose-escalation trials in mCRPC to determine the recommended phase 2 dose [22,23], and subsequently for the phase 3 VISION trial [24], which allowed regulatory approval across numerous jurisdictions [12,25,26]. More recently, the results of the phase 3 PSMAfore trial evaluating ^{177}Lu-PSMA-617 earlier in the mCRPC treatment course have been reported [27].

In Canada, ^{177}Lu-PSMA-617 administered for up to six cycles was approved by Health Canada in 2022 for the treatment of adult patients with PSMA-positive mCRPC who have received at least one androgen receptor pathway inhibitor (ARPI) and at least one taxane-based chemotherapy regimen [12]. The treatment subsequently received a recommendation in the 2022 Canadian Urological Association–Canadian Uro-Oncology Group guideline [28]. The Canadian Agency for Drugs and Technologies in Health also recommended it be reimbursed by public drug plans, though with the caveat that the suggested pricing be reduced as list pricing would result in additional costs of $122,489 per patient [29]. However, as the first RLT to be approved for use in metastatic prostate cancer, there are practical challenges relating to integrating ^{177}Lu-PSMA-617 into clinical practice. This article aims to review the existing evidence and to discuss how Canadian clinicians might best apply these data for their patients.

2. Materials and Methods

Prospective phase 2 and 3 clinical trials and meta-analyses of observational studies on the use of ^{177}Lu-PSMA-617 in prostate cancer were identified through a search of the English language literature and recent major congress abstracts. Databases searched included PubMed and Google Scholar, which were used to identify publications from January 2013 to August 2023, as well as the repositories of abstracts presented at the American Society of Clinical Oncology (ASCO), ASCO Genitourinary Cancers (ASCO-GU), European Society for Medical Oncology (ESMO), and Society of Nuclear Medicine and Molecular Imaging (SNMMI) congresses from 2020 to 2023 (Appendix A). Abstracts were evaluated to identify potentially relevant data sources for full review.

3. Results

3.1. Results of Literature Review

The searches of the Google Scholar and PubMed databases identified 357 and 65 articles, respectively, while 8, 7, and 410 abstracts were identified from searches of the ASCO/ASCO-GU, ESMO, and SNMMI congress abstracts, respectively. After removal of duplicates, a total of 668 records were reviewed, 649 of which were removed after abstract review. A total of 17 publications and 9 congress abstracts/posters were reviewed (Figure 1). Five additional sources not meeting the original search criteria were also proposed by the authors.

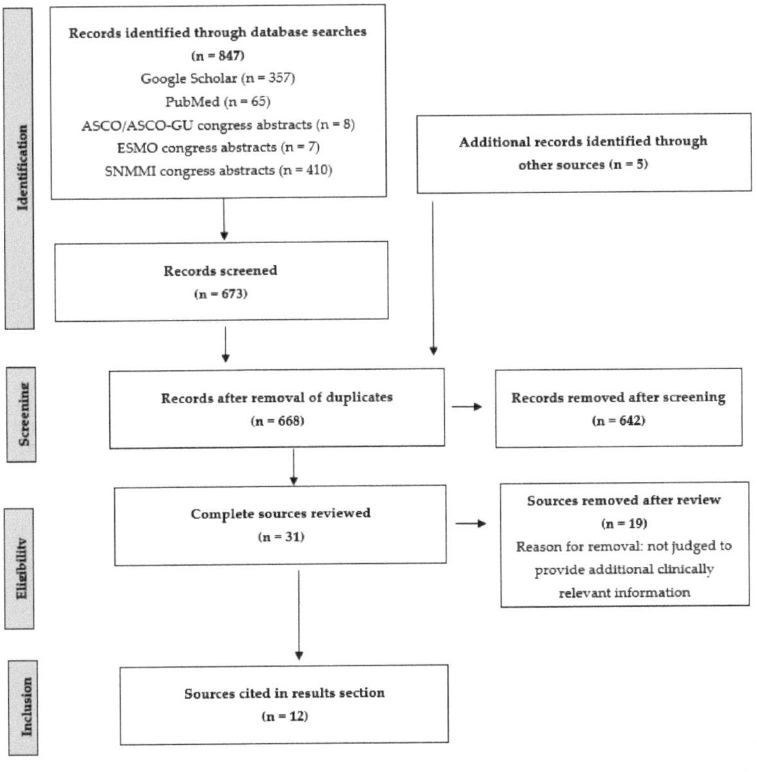

Figure 1. PRISMA flow diagram of literature review. ASCO, American Society of Clinical Oncology; ASCO-GU, American Society of Clinical Oncology Genitourinary Cancers; ESMO, European Society for Medical Oncology; PRISMA, Preferred Reporting Items for Systematic Reviews and Meta-Analyses; SNMMI, Society of Nuclear Medicine and Molecular Imaging.

3.2. Patients Treated with ^{177}Lu-PSMA-617

More than 850 patients with progressive mCRPC have been treated with ^{177}Lu-PSMA-617 in the context of three randomized phase 2 and 3 clinical trials [23,24,27]. While the majority of patients in these trials had an Eastern Cooperative Oncology Group (ECOG) performance status (PS) of 0 or 1 and the median age ranged from 70 to 72 years, there was considerable variation between the trials in other disease characteristics (Table 1). These differences were partly due to differing inclusion criteria. For instance, median prostate-specific antigen (PSA) levels in the ARPI-treated, taxane-naïve patients in the PSMAfore study were <20 µg/L [27], in contrast to median PSA levels of 75–110 µg/L in the TheraP and VISION trials' taxane-exposed patients [23,24]. The definition of PSMA-positivity criteria also varied across trials, with the TheraP trial mandating both PSMA-based and fluorodeoxyglucose (FDG)-based positron emission tomography (PET) scans [23], as compared to the VISION and PSMAfore trials, which used PSMA PET and contrast computed tomography (CT) scan correlation to determine study eligibility [24,27].

Table 1. Baseline patient characteristics in selected randomized phase 2 and 3 studies of ^{177}Lu-PSMA-617 in progressive PSMA-positive mCRPC.

	TheraP [23]		VISION [24]		PSMAfore [27]	
Study type	Phase 2		Phase 3		Phase 3	
PSMA PET eligibility criteria	^{68}Ga-PSMA-11, SUV$_{max}$ ≥ 20 at ≥1 disease site and >10 at all other metastatic disease sites		^{68}Ga-PSMA-11 uptake greater than liver parenchyma at ≥1 disease site and no PSMA-negative metastatic lesions		^{68}Ga-PSMA-11 uptake greater than liver parenchyma at ≥1 disease site and no PSMA-negative metastatic lesions	
FDG PET eligibility criteria	No sites with discordant FDG-positive/ PSMA-negative lesions		N/A		N/A	
Study arms	LuPSMA	Cabazitaxel	LuPSMA	SOC	LuPSMA	ARPI change
Patients, n	99	101	551	280	234	234
Median age, years	72.1	71.8	70.0	71.5	71	72
ECOG PS 0 or 1, %	96	96	92.6	92.1	99.1	97.9
Median PSA level, µg/L	93.5	110	77.5	74.6	18.4	14.9
Median ALP level, IU/L	111	130	105.0	94.5	100.0	103.5
Disease sites, %						
Bone	90.9	89.1	91.5	91.4	87.6	86.8
Liver	7.11 [1]	12.91 [1]	11.4	13.6	5.6	3.0
Lymph node	52.5	46.5	49.7	50.4	32.5	31.6
Previous treatments, %						
ARPI	92	90	100	100	100	100
Cabazitaxel	0	0	37.9	38.2	0	0
Docetaxel	100	100	96.9	97.5	0	0

[1] Includes all visceral disease sites (lung, liver, and other), not just liver. ^{68}Ga, gallium-68; ^{177}Lu, lutetium-177; ALP, alkaline phosphatase; ARPI, androgen receptor pathway inhibitor; ECOG, Eastern Cooperative Oncology Group; FDG, fluorodeoxyglucose; LuPSMA, ^{177}Lu-PSMA-617; mCRPC; metastatic castration-resistant prostate cancer; N/A, not applicable; PET, positron emission tomography; PS, performance status; PSA, prostate-specific antigen; PSMA, prostate-specific membrane antigen; SOC, standard of care; SUV$_{max}$, maximum standard uptake value.

Outside of clinical trials, the use of ^{177}Lu-PSMA-617 has been reported in more than 2500 patients with progressive mCRPC in real-world settings [30]. The reported median age of patients in one systematic review of observational studies ranged from 65 to 72 years [31]. In contrast to clinical trials, these patients had higher median PSA levels ranging from 59 to 1000 µg/L, along with a greater proportion of liver metastases (18%) [32]. Approximately 70% of the patients included in such observational studies had previously been treated with a taxane [32].

3.3. Survival Outcomes with ^{177}Lu-PSMA-617

In the VISION trial, which enrolled patients with mCRPC who had received at least one line of ARPI treatment and one line of chemotherapy, ^{177}Lu-PSMA-617 improved imaging-based progression-free survival (PFS) by 60% (hazard ratio [HR] = 0.40; 95% confidence interval [CI] 0.29–0.57; $p < 0.001$) and OS by 38% (HR = 0.62; 95% CI 0.52–0.74; $p < 0.001$) vs. trial-permitted best standard of care (SOC) (Table 2) [24]. The median imaging-based PFS was 8.7 months and median OS was 15.3 months for the ^{177}Lu-PSMA-617 arm, vs. 3.4 months and 11.3 months, respectively, for the SOC arm. In the TheraP trial, which enrolled patients with mCRPC who had received prior docetaxel chemotherapy, treatment with ^{177}Lu-PSMA-617 also significantly increased PFS (defined as the interval from randomization to first evidence of PSA progression) vs. cabazitaxel (HR = 0.63; 95% CI 0.46–0.86; $p = 0.0028$) [23]. In PSMAfore, which enrolled patients who were chemotherapy-naïve, at the time of the second interim analysis median imaging-based PFS was 6.4 months longer in the ^{177}Lu-PSMA-617 arm vs. the ARPI change arm (HR = 0.43; 95% CI 0.33–0.54; $p < 0.0001$), while there was no significant difference in median OS, which was 19.25 vs. 19.71 months in the ^{177}Lu-PSMA-617 and ARPI change arms, respectively (HR = 1.18; 95% CI 0.83–1.64) [27]. It is important to note that a high crossover rate occurred, with 84.2% of patients who progressed in the ARPI change arm subsequently receiving ^{177}Lu-PSMA-617, thus likely diminishing the between-arm differences [27].

Table 2. Survival and quality of life outcomes in selected randomized phase 2 and 3 studies of ^{177}Lu-PSMA-617 in progressive PSMA-positive mCRPC.

	TheraP [23]		**VISION [24,33]**		**PSMAfore [27]**	
Study arms	**LuPSMA**	**Cabazitaxel**	**LuPSMA**	**SOC**	**LuPSMA**	**ARPI Change**
Patients, n	99	101	551	280	234	234
Median imaging-based PFS, months	NR	NR	8.7	3.4	12.0	5.6
HR (95% CI)	0.63 (10.46–0.86)		0.40 (0.29–0.57)		0.41 (0.33–0.54)	
p value	0.0028		<0.001		<0.0001	
Median OS, months	NR	NR	15.3	11.3	19.2	19.7
HR (95% CI)	NR		0.62 (0.52–0.75)		1.16 (0.83–1.64)	
p value			<0.001		NR	
Median time to HRQOL worsening, months [1]	NR	NR	14.3	2.9	7.5	4.3
HR (95% CI)	NR		0.45 (0.33–0.60)		0.59 (0.47–0.72)	
p value			<0.001		NR	
Median time to pain worsening, months [2]	NR	NR	1.0	0.5	5.0	3.7
HR (95% CI)	NR		0.65 (0.54–0.78)		0.69 (0.56–0.85)	
p value			<0.001		NR	

[1] As measured by FACT-P score; [2] As measured on BPI-SF scale. ^{177}Lu, lutetium-177; LuPSMA, ^{177}Lu-PSMA-617; ARPI, androgen receptor pathway inhibitor; BPI-SF, Brief Pain Inventory-Short Form; CI, confidence interval; FACT-P, Functional Assessment of Cancer Therapy-Prostate; HR, hazard ratio; HRQOL, health-related quality of life; mCRPC; metastatic castration-resistant prostate cancer; NR, not reported; OS, overall survival; PFS, progression-free survival; PSMA, prostate-specific membrane antigen; SOC, standard of care.

A meta-analysis of observational studies of ^{177}Lu-PSMA RLT found that median OS in the real-world setting was 16 months [31]. This meta-analysis concluded that survival was longer in chemotherapy-naïve vs. chemotherapy-resistant patients, those with an ECOG PS of 0 vs. 1–2, those with only lymph node metastases vs. those with bone, lung, or liver metastases, those with normal vs. elevated serum alkaline phosphatase (ALP), those with higher vs. lower average standard uptake values ($SUV_{average}$) and minimal SUV (SUV_{min}), those who received an intensified vs. conventional schedule of RLT, and those who had a PSA decline of at least 50% [31]. Other meta-analyses confirmed the negative impact of visceral metastases and prior taxane-based chemotherapy on OS following ^{177}Lu-PSMA RLT [32,34].

Similar results were seen in phase 2 and 3 clinical trials. For instance, while no OS benefit has yet been shown in taxane-naïve patients treated with ^{177}Lu-PSMA-617 vs. ARPI change, possibly due to high levels of crossover in the phase 3 PSMAfore trial [27], subgroup analyses from the VISION trial suggested that both imaging-based PFS and OS benefits were potentially greater in patients who had previously been treated with one vs. two or more taxanes [35]. The same analyses also suggested greater survival benefits in patients who had been treated with at least two vs. only one ARPI, as well as those not on concurrent ARPI vs. on concurrent ARPI [35]. Additionally, the results of both TheraP and VISION suggested patients with higher whole-body tumour mean SUV on PSMA PET

($SUV_{mean} \geq 10$) were more likely to derive imaging-based PFS benefit from treatment with ^{177}Lu-PSMA-617 than those with lower SUV_{mean}, although all subgroups benefitted [36,37].

A multicentre retrospective study analyzed data from 176 patients treated with ^{177}Lu-PSMA RLT in order to incorporate these predictive markers into nomograms, which were then validated in another cohort of 74 patients [38]. Factors in the OS nomogram included time since diagnosis, use of previous chemotherapy, tumour SUV, and presence of pelvic nodal, bone, and liver metastases [38].

3.4. *Quality of Life with ^{177}Lu-PSMA-617*

Quality of life analyses of the VISION trial found that treatment with ^{177}Lu-PSMA-617 in addition to SOC delayed time to worsening vs. SOC alone in terms of measures of health-related quality of life (HRQOL) and pain, such as the Functional Assessment of Cancer Therapy-Prostate (FACT-P) score and Brief Pain Inventory-Short Form (BPI-SF) pain intensity score ($p < 0.001$ for all comparisons, Table 2) [33]. Quality of life analyses of the PSMAfore study found similar benefits in delaying time to worsening HRQOL and pain in the ^{177}Lu-PSMA-617 vs. ARPI change arms [27].

3.5. *Adverse Events Associated with ^{177}Lu-PSMA-617*

The adverse events of any grade that were most commonly increased in the ^{177}Lu-PSMA-617 + SOC arm vs. the SOC alone arm in the VISION trial included dry mouth, fatigue, nausea, anemia, and diarrhea, while the most commonly increased grade ≥3 adverse events were anemia, thrombocytopenia, and lymphopenia, which were generally infrequent (Figure 2) [24]. In this study, treatment-emergent adverse events occurred with similar frequency during cycles 1–5, which had median durations of 6 weeks each, with more adverse events being observed during cycle 6, which had a median duration of 26 weeks since the period of observation continued beyond week 6, reflecting an ascertainment bias due to the longer observation period [39]. Increases of ≥10% in the incidence of dry mouth with ^{177}Lu-PSMA-617 vs. control were also observed in the other randomized clinical trials, TheraP and PSMAfore, which employed cabazitaxel and ARPI change as controls, respectively [23,27]. Increases of ≥10% in the incidence of thrombocytopenia was also noted in TheraP [23], while in PSMAfore, nausea and anemia were increased ≥10% with ^{177}Lu-PSMA-617 vs. ARPI change (Figure 3) [27].

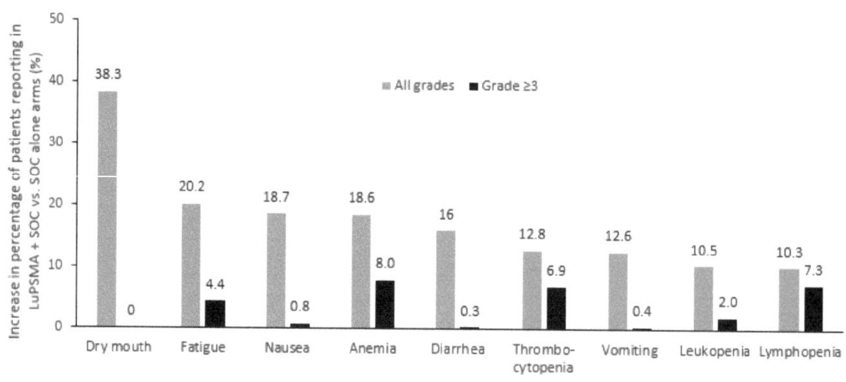

Figure 2. Adverse events most commonly increased in patients treated with ^{177}Lu-PSMA-617 + SOC vs. SOC alone in the phase 3 VISION trial ($\Delta \geq 10\%$) [24]. LuPSMA, ^{177}Lu-PSMA-617; SOC, standard of care.

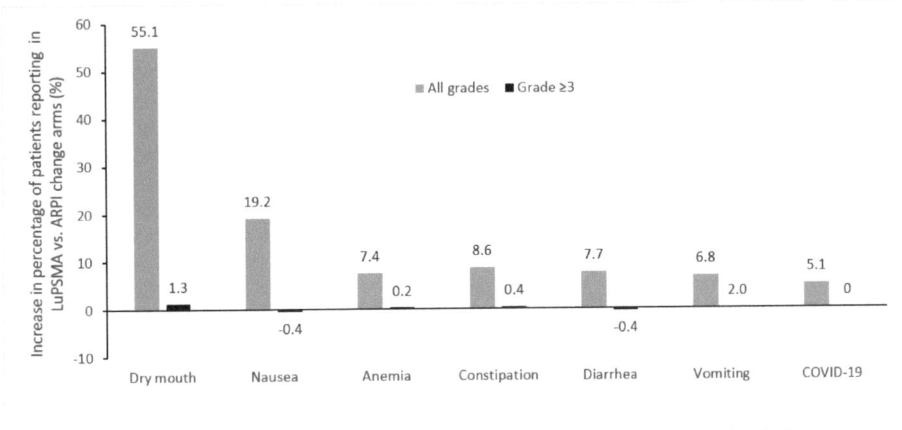

Figure 3. Adverse events most commonly increased in patients treated with ^{177}Lu-PSMA-617 vs. ARPI change in the phase 3 PSMAfore trial ($\Delta \geq 5\%$) [27]. ARPI, androgen receptor pathway inhibitor; LuPSMA, ^{177}Lu-PSMA-617.

4. Discussion

Clinical trials have demonstrated that ^{177}Lu-PSMA-617 improves imaging-based PFS and OS in patients with progressive, PSMA PET-positive mCRPC who have been pretreated with ARPIs and taxanes [23,24]. Improved imaging-based PFS vs. ARPI change was also demonstrated earlier in the disease course in taxane-naïve patients [27]. With health regulatory approval of ^{177}Lu-PSMA-617, the challenge is now to incorporate these clinical trial data into clinical practice.

4.1. Treatment Sequencing and Patient Selection Criteria

Selection of appropriate patients is key to fully realizing the potential benefits of RLT. While the Health Canada indication for ^{177}Lu-PSMA-617 requires that patients have been previously treated with at least one ARPI and one taxane [12], the optimal place of this therapy in the treatment sequence for mCRPC has yet to be determined. The current regulatory requirement for prior taxane exposure is based on the VISION clinical trial, which demonstrated the benefits of ^{177}Lu-PSMA-617 over SOC in taxane-exposed patients, including those who had received docetaxel as well as those who had received both docetaxel and cabazitaxel [24]. The TheraP trial demonstrated the superiority of ^{177}Lu-PSMA-617 for PFS as well as tolerability, although these patients were more highly selected for PSMA positivity by more stringent PSMA-PET criteria than the criteria used in the VISION study [23]. In addition, the current regulatory requirement for prior chemotherapy treatment is problematic as it has been demonstrated in population-based studies that the majority of patients with mCRPC within Canada never receive taxane chemotherapy during their disease course due to comorbidities that are common in this patient population, which is generally of advanced age [40]. Moreover, while patients who had been treated with radium-223 within six months were excluded from the VISION trial, real-world data suggest that treatment with radium-223 is feasible both before and after ^{177}Lu-PSMA-617 [41,42]. Other sequencing issues that have yet to be clarified include the benefits of RLT vs. docetaxel and its place in chemotherapy-naïve patients. Ongoing studies, such as Canadian Clinical Trials Group (CCTG) PR.21, PSMAddition, and PSMAfore, should help to address the optimal sequencing of ^{177}Lu-PSMA-617 in the current treatment paradigms for advanced prostate cancer [11].

While the results of these trials are awaited, no single criterion should preclude a patient who has already received ARPI and taxane treatment from consideration for treatment with ^{177}Lu-PSMA-617. Nonetheless, the European Association of Nuclear Medicine

(EANM)/SNMMI guideline for the use of ^{177}Lu-PSMA RLT suggests several factors that should be considered relative contraindications to treatment, such as life expectancy of less than six months, ECOG PS of more than two, severe myelosuppression, acute infections, acute bone complications (e.g., fracture, spinal cord compression), risk of multiorgan failure, untreated acute urinary tract obstruction, unmanageable urinary incontinence, unmanageable psychiatric comorbidities, and other severe comorbidities [43]. These factors should be considered in conjunction with the patient's overall health and cancer history, including time since diagnosis and the extent and location of metastases. An online risk calculator developed based on real-world nomograms (https://uclahealth.org/nuc/nomograms, accessed on 1 March 2024) [38] may assist oncologists with the selection of patients who should be considered with nuclear medicine for ^{177}Lu-PSMA-617, following prior ARPI and taxane treatment.

The results of PET imaging are also critical for determining patient suitability for therapy with ^{177}Lu-PSMA-617. While studies such as TheraP used dual PSMA and FDG PET imaging to determine PSMA-positivity [23], the VISION trial used PSMA PET/CT imaging for the inclusion of patients with at least one PSMA-positive metastatic lesion and no PSMA-negative lesions (Figure 4) [24,44]. This may be a reasonable alternative given that when a single-centre study examined 89 patients referred for ^{177}Lu-PSMA-617 with FDG and PSMA PET within two weeks, only three patients had an FDG/PSMA mismatch not detected by the PSMA PET-only (VISION-like) analysis [45], although the prevalence of $\geq$1 FDG-positive/PSMA-negative lesion in the TheraP trial was 28% [23]. The EANM/SNMMI guideline suggests that while simultaneous FDG PET may be useful in certain cases, it is not mandatory for all patients [43]. From a Canadian perspective, dual PET imaging in all patients is not practical for many hospital centres given the limited availability of PET scanners and associated infrastructure [29]. However, while dual PET imaging is not necessary, a separate diagnostic contrast CT scan remains important as liver disease maybe not be evident on non-contrast CT acquired as part of PET/CT scans.

Regardless of the imaging methods used, higher SUVs ($SUV_{mean} \geq 10$) may be a prognostic or predictive biomarker that helps identify patients with more favourable prognosis [36,37]. Conversely, caution should be used and alternative therapies considered if available and applicable in patients with rapidly progressing disease or progressive visceral disease. In addition to appropriate imaging to determine RLT eligibility, multidisciplinary evaluation and discussion are important to determining whether to proceed with RLT for a specific patient given the existing and emerging spectrum of systemic therapy options [28].

4.2. *Necessary Facilities for Treatment Procedures*

The administration of ^{177}Lu-PSMA-617 requires dedicated treatment facilities for the administration of unsealed radiation sources. In particular, dedicated radiopharmacy facilities and treatment rooms are necessary, as well as standard operating procedures for patient isolation immediately after infusion and the management of contaminated materials after treatment until any residual radioactivity has decayed to safe levels for disposal through usual hospital waste streams. Drug administration should be performed by qualified technical personnel in appropriately licensed facilities supervised by physicians with appropriate training in the administration of radiopharmaceuticals. In most cases, treatments will be administered within nuclear medicine departments under the supervision of nuclear medicine physicians. In some jurisdictions, radiopharmaceutical administration may fall under the purview of radiation oncologists as this speciality is also well positioned to oversee these treatments given their training in therapeutic radiotherapy and dosimetry with external beam radiation as well as sealed and unsealed brachytherapy materials. Guidance documents for the administration of RLT have been issued by professional organizations such as the EANM, SNMMI, and American Society for Radiation Oncology (ASTRO), among others [43,46].

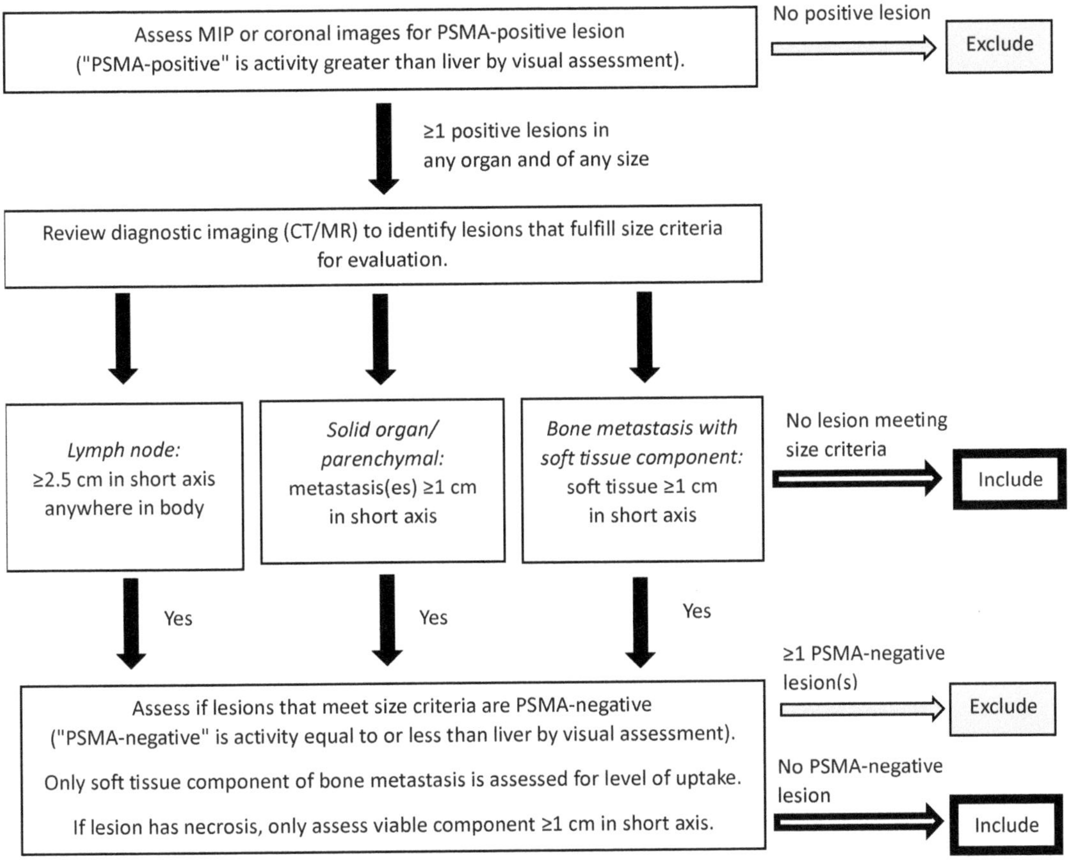

Figure 4. PSMA PET/CT selection criteria for the VISION trial [44]. A version of this figure was originally published in JNM. Kuo PH, Benson T, Messmann R, Groaning M. Why we did what we did: PSMA PET/CT selection criteria for the VISION trial. *J Nucl Med* **2022**, *63*, 816–818. © SNMMI [44]. CT, computed tomography; MIP, maximum intensity projection; MR, magnetic resonance; PET, positron emission tomography; PSMA, prostate-specific membrane antigen.

4.3. Counselling Patients on the Practicalities of Administration

Given the novelty of this therapeutic class in prostate cancer, patients who have been referred for ^{177}Lu-PSMA-617 may have numerous questions regarding the real-world experience of RLT treatment. ^{177}Lu-PSMA-617 is administered intravenously, often as an intravenous push given within one minute, with up to six doses being given at six-week intervals [12]. Typically, patients can expect to remain in the nuclear medicine department for 30–60 min. Although the radioactive nature of the therapy means certain precautions need to be taken in order to minimize radiation exposure to others, no hospitalization or prolonged isolation of patients is required due to radiation safety concerns and radioprotection may be managed by the patients at home, as outlined in sample patient instructions (Appendix A).

4.4. Assessment of Treatment Response

PSA should be monitored at each cycle in patients treated with ^{177}Lu-PSMA-617 as PSA response becomes a reliable proxy for response 2–3 weeks after the second cycle [43]. In addition, the EANM/SNMMI guideline recommends that imaging-based restaging be conducted every 12 weeks during treatment and at the end of each series of ^{177}Lu-PSMA RLT, with additional restaging conducted in cases of PSA rise (i.e., PSA increase of >25%) [43]. As in all mCRPC patients, the backbone of imaging restaging remains contrast CT scans of the chest, abdomen, and pelvis, and whole-body radionuclide bone scanning. Additionally, while restaging patients with PSMA PET or FDG PET was not carried out in the VISION trial and evidence supporting the post-therapeutic use of this strategy is limited, it may be useful in select patients where response or resistance would need to be determined in order to guide treatment decisions. Whole-body single photon emission computed tomography (SPECT) planar imaging, conducted 1–4 days post-therapy, may be another alternative to PSMA PET reimaging and response schemes based on SPECT imaging have been proposed [47,48]. In addition, the use of serial SPECT imaging for personalized ^{177}Lu-PSMA-617 dosimetry has been proposed to optimize treatment response [49]. However, at this time, such personalized dosimetry is not the standard of care as approvals for ^{177}Lu-PSMA-617 are for fixed dose administration, it is not yet possible to order and deliver patient-specific ^{177}Lu-PSMA-617 doses, and the benefits vs. fixed per patient dosing have yet to be established.

Therapy with ^{177}Lu-PSMA-617 may be continued until disease progression, unacceptable toxicity, or six cycles have been given [12]. However, there is no widely accepted definition as to what constitutes disease progression on PSMA imaging; for example, it is unclear whether the presence of one or two new lesions or, alternatively, increases in SUV in the absence of new lesions, would be considered progression. Additionally, it should be noted that if the imaging modality changes between staging and restaging, it can be difficult to differentiate true progression from pseudo-progression. In fact, in general, assessment of progression can be challenging in patients with mCRPC and discordant changes may be seen between PSA, imaging, and symptoms. Careful assessment and multidisciplinary review of cases is thus required to integrate all available information and make treatment decisions so as to not discontinue therapy too quickly in patients who may be benefiting.

4.5. Management of Adverse Events

As compared to SOC, the most common symptomatic adverse events seen with ^{177}Lu-PSMA-617 included dry mouth, fatigue, nausea, diarrhea, and cytopenias. Prophylactic antiemetic medication, such as ondansetron and/or corticosteroids, may help minimize nausea, and diarrhea may be managed through dietary changes and the use of medications such as loperamide or diphenoxylate/atropine [43]. Unfortunately, no effective strategies to manage treatment-related dry mouth or non-hematologic fatigue have yet been identified.

The treatment-modifying grade ≥ 3 adverse events most commonly observed with ^{177}Lu-PSMA-617 are hematologic in nature. Monitoring of hematologic parameters is thus advised before and during treatment with ^{177}Lu-PSMA-617 [12]. Treatment should be postponed or withheld in cases of grade ≥ 2 myelosuppression until recovery to baseline or grade 1 is observed [12,43]. Transfusion and/or erythropoietin may be used to manage anemia, while the use of growth factors may be appropriate for neutropenia [12,43].

It is important that RLT therapy be integrated into the multidisciplinary care of the patient with clear lines of communication and well-described roles and responsibilities regarding patient monitoring and treatment modification. For example, patients receiving RLT will be transitioning from prior ARPI and docetaxel chemotherapy and subsequently monitored by oncologists and nuclear medicine specialists. As patients move into a phase of treatment with RLT, it must be clear who is responsible for the monitoring and management of RLT toxicity; in most cases this will be the provider supervising RLT prescription and delivery. At the same time, co-management with the other specialties is required in order to ensure other oncologic issues, such as the administration of bone-modifying agents and intervention in cases of acute oncologic complications, are appropriately managed. Most patients will eventually experience treatment-limiting disease progression or toxicity and appropriate transition back to other oncologic specialties for alternate systemic therapies and to palliative care specialists for supportive care treatments must occur efficiently and seamlessly.

4.6. Ongoing Questions

Despite the clear benefits seen in clinical trials of ^{177}Lu-PSMA-617, a number of questions remain, including the identification of additional biomarkers to predict response, the implications of personalized dosimetry, the potential benefits of combination with other treatments, and the optimal sequencing with other therapies, including use earlier in the metastatic disease setting. Ongoing studies, such as CCTG PR.21, PSMAddition, and PSMAfore, among others, may help answer some of these questions [11]. Ongoing trials are also investigating the use of novel RLTs in progressive mCRPC, including treatments using ^{177}Lu linked to different PSMA-binding or other prostate cancer-specific ligands as well as treatments using different radionuclides, such as actinium-225, iodine-131, and lead-212 [11]. The announcement of statistically significant topline results from the phase 3 SPLASH study of the PSMA-targeted RLT ^{177}Lu-PNT2002 in patients with chemotherapy-naïve mCRPC who had progressed on an ARPI presages the advent of additional RLTs for patients with mCRPC [50].

5. Conclusions

^{177}Lu-PSMA-617 represents not just a new therapy but a new therapeutic class for the treatment of prostate cancer. As such, clinical pathways need to be developed and clinicians involved in the treatment of mCRPC must become familiar with these new processes in order to realize the benefits of RLT for their patients. While not all the suggestions included in this discussion are strictly evidence-based, it is the hope of the authors that this review of the evidence and associated expert opinions help practitioners translate these data into the current Canadian practice setting. Finally, as the therapeutic landscape for mCRPC continues to evolve, new treatments and emerging data will need to be considered when making treatment decisions.

Author Contributions: Conceptualization, G.B., K.N.C., U.E., S.J.H., C.K.K., D.T.L., T.N., F.P., R.R., F.S. and S.M.Y.; methodology, G.B., K.N.C., U.E., S.J.H., T.N., F.S. and S.M.Y.; validation, S.J.H. and S.P.; formal analysis, U.E., S.J.H., F.S. and S.M.Y.; investigation, F.S. and S.M.Y.; data curation, C.K.K. and S.M.Y.; writing—original draft preparation, K.N.C., U.E., F.P., S.P., F.S. and S.M.Y.; writing—review and editing, G.B., K.N.C., U.E., S.J.H., C.K.K., D.T.L., P.M., T.N., F.P., S.P., R.R., F.S. and S.M.Y.; visualization, T.N.; supervision, C.K.K., S.P., F.S. and S.M.Y.; project administration, C.K.K. All authors have read and agreed to the published version of the manuscript.

Funding: Financial support for medical writing assistance was provided by Novartis Pharmaceuticals Ltd. Canada. The authors had full control of the content and made the final decision for all aspects of this article.

Acknowledgments: We thank Rebecca Cowan for their medical editorial assistance with this manuscript.

Conflicts of Interest: G.B. has received compensation from Advanced Accelerator Applications/Novartis and the Ontario Institute for Cancer Research. K.N.C. has served as a consultant and received honoraria from Advanced Accelerator Applications/Novartis, Astellas Pharma, AstraZeneca, Genentech/Roche, Janssen, Merck, Pfizer, and POINT Biopharma, and received grants and research funding from Advanced Accelerator Applications/Novartis, AstraZeneca, Genentech/Roche, Janssen, Pfizer, and POINT Biopharma. U.E. has received personal fees for serving as an advisor/consultant for Advanced Accelerator Applications/Novartis, Amgen, Astellas Pharma, AstraZeneca, Bayer, Ferring Pharmaceuticals, Janssen, Knight Therapeutics, Merck, and Pfizer, research funding from Astellas Pharma, Bayer, and Janssen, and institutional funding for the conduct of clinical studies from Advanced Accelerator Applications/Novartis, Astellas Pharma, AstraZeneca, Bayer, Genentech/Roche, Janssen, Merck, and POINT Biopharma. S.J.H. has received honoraria for advisory activities and has conducted research with funding paid to the institution from Advanced Accelerator Applications/Novartis. C.K.K. has received honoraria for presentations from Astellas Pharma, Bayer, Bristol-Myers Squibb, Eisai, Ipsen, Janssen, Merck, Pfizer, and Seagen, and for ad-hoc advisory boards from Advanced Accelerator Applications/Novartis, Astellas Pharma, Bayer, BioNTech, Bristol-Myers Squibb, Eisai, Ipsen, Janssen, Merck, Pfizer, Seagen, and Sanofi. D.T.L. has participated in advisory meetings for Advanced Accelerator Applications/Novartis, Bayer, and Ipsen, has participated in research studies sponsored by Advanced Accelerator Applications/Novartis, POINT Biopharma, and Progenics, and has received consultancy fees from Advanced Accelerator Applications/Novartis and Ipsen. P.M. has served as a consultant and received honoraria from Advanced Accelerator Applications/Novartis. T.N. has received research/educational funding from AbbVie, Amgen, Astellas Pharma, AstraZeneca, Bayer, Janssen, Sanofi, TerSera, and Tolmar, and honoraria from AbbVie, Advanced Accelerator Applications/Novartis, Amgen, Astellas Pharma, AstraZeneca, Bayer, Ferring Pharmaceuticals, Janssen, Knight Therapeutics, Merck, Sanofi, TerSera, and Tolmar. F.P. has received honoraria and/or was a consultant for AbbVie, Advanced Accelerator Applications/Novartis, Amgen, Astellas Pharma, AstraZeneca, Bayer, Janssen, Merck, Sanofi, TerSera, and Tolmar. S.P has received speaking and consulting fees from Advanced Accelerator Applications/Novartis, Bayer, and POINT Biopharma. R.R. has served on advisory boards and speaker bureaus for AbbVie, Amgen, Astellas Pharma, AstraZeneca, Bayer, Ferring Pharmaceuticals, Janssen, McKesson, Sanofi, and TerSera, and has participated in clinical trials funded by Advanced Accelerator Applications/Novartis, Astellas Pharma, AstraZeneca, Bayer, Ferring Pharmaceuticals, Janssen, Myovant Sciences, Pfizer, POINT Biopharma, and Sanofi. F.S. has acted in a consulting/advisory role for and received honoraria from AbbVie, Advanced Accelerator Applications/Novartis, AstraZeneca, Astellas Pharma, Bayer, Janssen, Merck, Pfizer, and Tolmar, and has conducted research with funding paid to the institution from Advanced Accelerator Applications/Novartis, AstraZeneca, Astellas Pharma, Bayer, Janssen, Merck, and Pfizer. S.M.Y. has received consultant, advisory board, or sponsorship honoraria from Advanced Accelerator Applications/Novartis, AstraZeneca, Bayer, Bristol-Myers Squibb, Genentech/Roche, Ipsen, Janssen, Merck, OncoHelix, and Pfizer. Financial support for medical writing assistance was provided by Novartis Pharmaceuticals Ltd. Canada. The funder had no role in the design of the study, in the collection, analyses, or interpretation of the data, in the writing of the manuscript, or in the decision to publish the results.

Appendix A. Literature Search Strategy

- Objective: to identify clinical trials and observational studies on the use of ^{177}Lu-PSMA-617 in patients with prostate cancer that were published in the literature within the last 10 years or presented at a major congress within the last 3 years.
- Searches conducted:
    - Google Scholar
        - Search string: allintitle: (177Lu OR "lutetium-177" OR Lu OR lutetium) AND (PSMA OR "PSMA-617" OR "prostate specific membrane antigen" OR "vipivotide tetraxetan")
        - Limits: 2013 or more recent; terms in title
    - PubMed
        - Search string: ("prostate cancer" or "Prostatic Neoplasms" [Mesh]) AND (177Lu OR lutetium-177 OR Lu OR lutetium OR "Lutetium" [Mesh]) AND (PSMA OR PSMA-617 OR "prostate-specific membrane antigen" OR "vipivotide tetraxetan")
        - Limits: English language; article types: case reports, clinical study, clinical trial, comparative study, meta-analysis, observational study, randomized controlled trial; 2013 or more recent
    - ASCO database:
        - Search strings:
            i. 177Lu
            ii. Lutetium
        - Limits: ASCO and ASCO-GU conferences; years 2020, 2021, 2022, and 2023; topic: prostate cancer
    - ESMO database:

- Search strings:
  - i. 177Lu
  - ii. Lutetium
- Limits: meeting resources; tumour site: prostate cancer; years 2020, 2021, 2022, and 2023

○ SNMMI congress abstract supplements:
- Search string: 177Lu OR lutetium
- Years searched: 2020, 2021, 2022, and 2023.

Appendix A. 1777Lu-PSMA Therapy Instructions for Patients

Your doctors have determined that ^{177}Lu-PSMA therapy is the best way to treat your prostate cancer. Although safe, we need your help to minimize radiation exposure to the general population and members of your family following your therapy.

Instructions

1. Preferably, drive home alone after your treatment. If this is not possible, keep as much distance as possible between yourself and the driver.
2. To minimize radiation exposure to other people, keep a maximum distance and a minimum exposure time between yourself and anyone else. Spend the least amount of time necessary in close contact (stay more than 2 m away) with other people for the next 3 days. For example, sleep alone for the first 3 nights.
3. Avoid all contact with children less than 10 years of age for 7 days and with pregnant women for 15 days.
4. You can return to daily activities or work as early as 3 days after treatment, while avoiding contact with pregnant women and children less than 10 years of age.
5. Drink lots of water after the treatment and for the next 24 h (eight 8-ounce glasses).
6. Always follow good hygiene practices. Take at least one shower per day. You must use toilet paper each time you urinate. Wash your hands thoroughly after using the toilet. You should sit while urinating to avoid splashing. Flush the toilet twice after each use for the first 24 h. Caregivers must wear disposable gloves for 3 days after treatment if there is a risk of contact with bodily fluids.
7. If you have any nausea or vomiting, take the medication prescribed to you.
8. If you are planning to travel outside of the country by any means or to go to an airport in the next 3 months, please inform the Nuclear Medicine Department and you will be provided with a document explaining the therapy you just received.
9. Keep this document on you for the next week, and show it to your health care provider(s) should you require any urgent care in the next 7 days. Outside of working hours, health care providers can contact a nuclear medicine physician at TELEPHONE NUMBER.
10. Should you have questions regarding your treatment, you can contact someone during working hours at the Department of Nuclear Medicine at TELEPHONE NUMBER.

References

1. Canadian Cancer Statistics Advisory Committee; Canadian Cancer Society; Statistics Canada; Public Health Agency of Canada. *Canadian Cancer Statistics 2021*; Canadian Cancer Society: Toronto, ON, Canada, 2021. Available online: https://cancer.ca/en/research/cancer-statistics/canadian-cancer-statistics (accessed on 20 September 2023).
2. Cancer Stat Facts: Prostate Cancer. Available online: https://seer.cancer.gov/statfacts/html/prost.html (accessed on 20 September 2023).
3. Armstrong, A.J.; Lin, P.; Tombal, B.; Saad, F.; Higano, C.S.; Joshua, A.M.; Parli, T.; Rosbrook, B.; van Os, S.; Beer, T.M. Five-year survival prediction and safety outcomes with enzalutamide in men with chemotherapy-naïve metastatic castration-resistant prostate cancer from the PREVAIL trial. *Eur. Urol.* **2020**, *78*, 347–357. [CrossRef]
4. Saad, F.; Efstathiou, E.; Attard, G.; Flaig, T.W.; Franke, F.; Goodman, O.B.; Oudard, S.; Steuber, T.; Suzuki, H.; Wu, D.; et al. Apalutamide plus abiraterone acetate and prednisone versus placebo plus abiraterone and prednisone in metastatic, castration-resistant prostate cancer (ACIS): A randomised, placebo-controlled, double-blind, multinational, phase 3 study. *Lancet Oncol.* **2021**, *22*, 1541–1559. [CrossRef]

5. Morris, M.J.; Heller, G.; Hillman, D.W.; Bobek, O.; Ryan, C.; Antonarakis, E.S.; Bryce, A.H.; Hahn, O.; Beltran, H.; Armstrong, A.J.; et al. Randomized phase III study of enzalutamide compared with enzalutamide plus abiraterone for metastatic castration-resistant prostate cancer (Alliance A031201 trial). *J. Clin. Oncol.* **2023**, *41*, 3352–3362. [CrossRef]
6. Clarke, N.W.; Armstrong, A.J.; Thiery-Vuillemin, A.; Oya, M.; Shore, N.D.; Procopio, G.; Guedes, J.D.C.; Arslan, C.; Mehra, N.; Parnis, F.; et al. Final overall survival (OS) in PROpel: Abiraterone (abi) and olaparib (ola) versus abiraterone and placebo (pbo) as first-line (1L) therapy for metastatic castration-resistant prostate cancer (mCRPC). In Proceedings of the 2023 ASCO Genitourinary Cancers Symposium, San Francisco, CA, USA, 16–18 February 2023.
7. George, D.J.; Sartor, O.; Miller, K.; Saad, F.; Tombal, B.; Kalinovský, J.; Jiao, X.; Tangirala, K.; Sternberg, C.N.; Higano, C.S. Treatment patterns and outcomes in patients with metastatic castration-resistant prostate cancer in a real-world clinical practice setting in the United States. *Clin. Genitourin. Cancer* **2020**, *18*, 284–294. [CrossRef] [PubMed]
8. Paschalis, A.; Sheehan, B.; Riisnaes, R.; Rodrigues, D.N.; Gurel, B.; Bertan, C.; Ferreira, A.; Lambros, M.B.; Seed, G.; Yuan, W.; et al. Prostate-specific membrane antigen heterogeneity and DNA repair defects in prostate cancer. *Eur. Urol.* **2019**, *76*, 469–478. [CrossRef]
9. Donin, N.M.; Reiter, R.E. Why targeting PSMA is a game changer in the management of prostate cancer. *J. Nucl. Med.* **2018**, *59*, 177–182. [CrossRef]
10. Giraudet, A.L.; Kryza, D.; Hofman, M.; Moreau, A.; Fizazi, K.; Flechon, A.; Hicks, R.J.; Tran, B. PSMA targeting in metastatic castration-resistant prostate cancer: Where are we and where are we going? *Ther. Adv. Med. Oncol.* **2021**, *13*, 17588359211053898. [CrossRef] [PubMed]
11. ClinicalTrials.gov Search Results. Available online: https://www.clinicaltrials.gov/search?cond=PROSTATE%20CANCER&term=radioligand&aggFilters=status:act%20rec%20not (accessed on 7 November 2023).
12. Advanced Accelerator Applications USA, Inc. *PLUVICTOTM (Lutetium [177Lu] Vipivotide Tetraxetan Injection) Product Monograph Including Patient Medication Information*; Advanced Accelerator Applications USA, Inc.: Millburn, NJ, USA, 2022; Available online: https://pdf.hres.ca/dpd_pm/00067158.PDF (accessed on 20 September 2023).
13. Hosono, M.; Ikebuchi, H.; Nakamura, Y.; Nakamura, N.; Yamada, T.; Yanagida, S.; Kitaoka, A.; Kojima, K.; Sugano, H.; Kinuya, S.; et al. Manual on the proper use of lutetium-177-labeled somatostatin analogue (Lu-177-DOTA-TATE) injectable in radionuclide therapy (2nd ed.). *Ann. Nucl. Med.* **2018**, *32*, 217–235. [CrossRef] [PubMed]
14. Benešová, M.; Schäfer, M.; Bauder-Wüst, U.; Afshar-Oromieh, A.; Kratochwil, C.; Mier, W.; Haberkorn, U.; Kopka, K.; Eder, M. Preclinical evaluation of a tailor-made DOTA-conjugated PSMA inhibitor with optimized linker moiety for imaging and endoradiotherapy of prostate cancer. *J. Nucl. Med.* **2015**, *56*, 914–920. [CrossRef] [PubMed]
15. Haberkorn, U.; Giesel, F.; Morgenstern, A.; Kratochwil, C. The future of radioligand therapy: α, β, or both? *J. Nucl. Med.* **2017**, *58*, 1017–1018. [CrossRef] [PubMed]
16. Ahmadzadehfar, H.; Rahbar, K.; Kürpig, S.; Bögemann, M.; Claesener, M.; Eppard, E.; Gärtner, F.; Rogenhofer, S.; Schäfers, M.; Essler, M. Early side effects and first results of radioligand therapy with $_{177}$Lu-DKFZ-617 PSMA of castrate-resistant metastatic prostate cancer: A two-centre study. *EJNMMI Res.* **2015**, *5*, 114. [CrossRef]
17. Ahmadzadehfar, H.; Eppard, E.; Kürpig, S.; Fimmers, R.; Yordanova, A.; Schlenkhoff, C.D.; Gärtner, F.; Rogenhofer, S.; Essler, M. Therapeutic response and side effects of repeated radioligand therapy with ^{177}Lu-PSMA-DKFZ-617 of castrate-resistant metastatic prostate cancer. *Oncotarget* **2016**, *7*, 12477–12488. [CrossRef]
18. Kratochwil, C.; Giesel, F.L.; Stefanova, M.; Benešová, M.; Bronzel, M.; Afshar-Oromieh, A.; Mier, W.; Eder, M.; Kopka, K.; Haberkorn, U. PSMA-targeted radionuclide therapy of metastatic castration-resistant prostate cancer with Lu-177 labeled PSMA-617. *J. Nucl. Med.* **2016**, *57*, 1170–1176. [CrossRef]
19. Rahbar, K.; Schmidt, M.; Heinzel, A.; Eppard, E.; Bode, A.; Yordanova, A.; Claesener, M.; Ahmadzadehfar, H. Response and tolerability of a single dose of ^{177}Lu-PSMA-617 in patients with metastatic castration-resistant prostate cancer: A multicenter retrospective analysis. *J. Nucl. Med.* **2016**, *57*, 1334–1338. [CrossRef]
20. Rahbar, K.; Bode, A.; Weckesser, M.; Avramovic, N.; Claesener, M.; Stegger, L.; Bögemann, M. Radioligand therapy with ^{177}Lu-PSMA-617 as a novel therapeutic option in patients with metastatic castration resistant prostate cancer. *Clin. Nucl. Med.* **2016**, *41*, 522–528. [CrossRef]
21. Rahbar, K.; Ahmadzadehfar, H.; Kratochwil, C.; Haberkorn, U.; Schäfers, M.; Essler, M.; Baum, R.P.; Kulkarni, H.R.; Schmidt, M.; Drzezga, A.; et al. German multicenter study investigating ^{177}Lu-PSMA-617 radioligand therapy in advanced prostate cancer patients. *J. Nucl. Med.* **2017**, *58*, 85–90. [CrossRef]
22. Tagawa, S.T.; Vallabhajosula, S.; Christos, P.J.; Jhanwar, Y.S.; Batra, J.S.; Lam, L.; Osborne, J.; Beltran, H.; Molina, A.M.; Goldsmith, S.J.; et al. Phase 1/2 study of fractionated dose lutetium-177-labeled anti-prostate-specific membrane antigen monoclonal antibody J591 (177 Lu-J591) for metastatic castration-resistant prostate cancer. *Cancer* **2019**, *125*, 2561–2569. [CrossRef] [PubMed]
23. Hofman, M.S.; Emmett, L.; Sandhu, S.; Iravani, A.; Joshua, A.M.; Goh, J.C.; Pattison, D.A.; Tan, T.H.; Kirkwood, I.D.; Ng, S.; et al. [^{177}Lu]Lu-PSMA-617 versus cabazitaxel in patients with metastatic castration-resistant prostate cancer (TheraP): A randomised, open-label, phase 2 trial. *Lancet* **2021**, *397*, 797–804. [CrossRef] [PubMed]
24. Sartor, O.; De Bono, J.; Chi, K.N.; Fizazi, K.; Herrmann, K.; Rahbar, K.; Tagawa, S.T.; Nordquist, L.T.; Vaishampayan, N.; El-Haddad, G.; et al. Lutetium-177–PSMA-617 for metastatic castration-resistant prostate cancer. *N. Engl. J. Med.* **2021**, *385*, 1091–1103. [CrossRef] [PubMed]

25. Advanced Accelerator Applications USA, Inc. *PLUVICTOTM (Lutetium Lu 177 Vipivotide Tetraxetan) Injection, for Intravenous Use Full Prescribing Information*; Advanced Accelerator Applications USA, Inc.: Millburn, NJ, USA, 2022. Available online: https://www.accessdata.fda.gov/drugsatfda_docs/label/2022/215833s000lbl.pdf (accessed on 20 September 2023).
26. Novartis Europharm Limited. *PLUVICTOTM (Lutetium [177Lu] Vipivotide Tetraxetan) Summary of Product Characteristics*; Novartis Europharm Limited: Dublin, Ireland, 2023; Available online: https://www.ema.europa.eu/en/documents/product-information/pluvicto-epar-product-information_en.pdf (accessed on 20 September 2023).
27. Sartor, O.; Gauna, D.C.; Herrmann, K.; de Bono, J.S.; Shore, N.D.; Chi, K.N.N.; Crosby, M.; Rodriguez, J.P.; Flechon, A.; Wei, X.X.; et al. Phase 3 trial of [^{177}Lu]Lu-PSMA-617 in taxane-naive patients with metastatic castration-resistant prostate cancer (PSMAfore). In Proceedings of the ESMO Congress 2023, Madrid, Spain, 20–24 October 2023.
28. Saad, F.; Aprikian, A.; Finelli, A.; Fleshner, N.E.; Gleave, M.; Kapoor, A.; Niazi, T.; North, S.A.; Pouliot, F.; Rendon, R.A.; et al. 2022 Canadian Urological Association (CUA)-Canadian Uro Oncology Group (CUOG) guideline: Management of castration-resistant prostate cancer (CRPC). *Can. Urol. Assoc. J.* **2022**, *16*, E506–E515. [CrossRef] [PubMed]
29. Canadian Agency for Drugs and Technologies in Health. CADTH reimbursement recommendation: Lutetium (^{177}Lu) vipivotide tetraxetan (Pluvicto). *Can. J. Health Technol.* **2023**, *3*, 1–26.
30. Sadaghiani, M.S.; Sheikhbahaei, S.; Werner, R.A.; Pienta, K.J.; Pomper, M.G.; Gorin, M.A.; Solnes, L.B.; Rowe, S.P. ^{177}Lu-PSMA radioligand therapy effectiveness in metastatic castration-resistant prostate cancer: An updated systematic review and meta-analysis. *Prostate* **2022**, *82*, 826–835. [CrossRef]
31. von Eyben, F.E.; Bauman, G.; von Eyben, R.; Rahbar, K.; Soydal, C.; Haug, A.R.; Virgolini, I.; Kulkarni, H.; Baum, R.; Paganelli, G. Optimizing PSMA radioligand therapy for patients with metastatic castration-resistant prostate cancer. A systematic review and meta-analysis. *Int. J. Mol. Sci.* **2020**, *21*, 9054. [CrossRef] [PubMed]
32. Satapathy, S.; Sahoo, R.K.; Bal, C. [^{177}Lu]Lu-PSMA-radioligand therapy efficacy outcomes in taxane-naïve versus taxane-treated patients with metastatic castration-resistant prostate cancer: A systematic review and metaanalysis. *J. Nucl. Med.* **2023**, *64*, 1266–1271. [CrossRef]
33. Fizazi, K.; Herrmann, K.; Krause, B.J.; Rahbar, K.; Chi, K.N.; Morris, M.J.; Sartor, O.; Tagawa, S.T.; Kendi, A.T.; Vogelzang, N.; et al. Health-related quality of life and pain outcomes with [^{177}Lu]Lu-PSMA-617 plus standard of care versus standard of care in patients with metastatic castration-resistant prostate cancer (VISION): A multicentre, open-label, randomised, phase 3 trial. *Lancet Oncol.* **2023**, *24*, 597–610. [CrossRef]
34. Satapathy, S.; Mittal, B.R.; Sood, A. Visceral metastases as predictors of response and survival outcomes in patients of castration-resistant prostate cancer treated with ^{177}Lu-labeled prostate-specific membrane antigen radioligand therapy: A systematic review and meta-analysis. *Clin. Nucl. Med.* **2020**, *45*, 935–942. [CrossRef]
35. Vaishampayan, N.; Morris, M.J.; Krause, B.J.; Vogelzang, N.J.; Kendi, A.T.; Nordquist, L.T.; Calais, J.; Nagarajah, J.; Beer, T.M.; El-Haddad, G.; et al. [^{177}Lu]Lu-PSMA-617 in PSMA-positive metastatic castration-resistant prostate cancer: Prior and concomitant treatment subgroup analyses of the VISION trial. In Proceedings of the 2022 ASCO Annual Meeting, Chicago, IL, USA, 3–7 June 2022.
36. Buteau, J.P.; Martin, A.J.; Emmett, L.; Iravani, A.; Sandhu, S.; Joshua, A.M.; Francis, R.J.; Zhang, A.Y.; Scott, A.M.; Lee, S.T.; et al. PSMA and FDG-PET as predictive and prognostic biomarkers in patients given [^{177}Lu]Lu-PSMA-617 versus cabazitaxel for metastatic castration-resistant prostate cancer (TheraP): A biomarker analysis from a randomised, open-label, phase 2 trial. *Lancet Oncol.* **2022**, *23*, 1389–1397. [CrossRef] [PubMed]
37. Kuo, P.; Hesterman, J.; Rahbar, K.; Kendi, A.T.; Wei, X.X.; Fang, B.; Adra, N.; Armstrong, A.J.; Garje, R.; Michalski, J.M.; et al. [^{68}Ga]Ga-PSMA-11 PET baseline imaging as a prognostic tool for clinical outcomes to [^{177}Lu]Lu-PSMA-617 in patients with mCRPC: A VISION substudy. In Proceedings of the 2022 ASCO Annual Meeting, Chicago, IL, USA, 3–7 June 2022.
38. Gafita, A.; Calais, J.; Grogan, T.R.; Hadaschik, B.; Wang, H.; Weber, M.; Sandhu, S.; Kratochwil, C.; Esfandiari, R.; Tauber, R.; et al. Nomograms to predict outcomes after ^{177}Lu-PSMA therapy in men with metastatic castration-resistant prostate cancer: An international, multicentre, retrospective study. *Lancet Oncol.* **2021**, *22*, 1115–1125. [CrossRef]
39. Tagawa, S.T.; Armstrong, A.J.; Krause, B.J.; Herrmann, K.; Rahbar, K.; De Bono, J.S.; Adra, N.; Desilvio, M.; Messmann, R.; Holder, G.; et al. Tolerability of [^{177}Lu]Lu-PSMA-617 by treatment exposure in patients with metastatic castration-resistant prostate cancer (mCRPC): A VISION study subgroup analysis. In Proceedings of the 2022 ASCO Annual Meeting, Chicago, IL, USA, 3–7 June 2022.
40. Shayegan, B.; Wallis, C.J.; Malone, S.; Cagiannos, I.; Hamilton, R.J.; Ferrario, C.; Gotto, G.T.; Basappa, N.S.; Morgan, S.C.; Fernandes, R.; et al. Real-world use of systemic therapies in men with metastatic castration resistant prostate cancer (mCRPC) in Canada. *Urol. Oncol.* **2022**, *40*, 192.e1–192.e9. [CrossRef] [PubMed]
41. Rahbar, K.; Essler, M.; Eiber, M.; la Fougère, C.; Prasad, V.; Fendler, W.P.; Rassek, P.; Hasa, E.; Dittmann, H.; Bundschuh, R.A.; et al. ^{177}Lu-prostate-specific membrane antigen therapy in patients with metastatic castration-resistant prostate cancer and prior ^{223}Ra (RALU study). *J. Nucl. Med.* **2023**, *64*, 1925–1931. [CrossRef]
42. Sartor, O.; la Fougère, C.; Essler, M.; Ezziddin, S.; Kramer, G.; Ellinger, J.; Nordquist, L.; Sylvester, J.; Paganelli, G.; Peer, A.; et al. ^{177}Lu-prostate-specific membrane antigen ligand after ^{223}Ra treatment in men with bone-metastatic castration-resistant prostate cancer: Real-world clinical experience. *J. Nucl. Med.* **2022**, *63*, 410–414. [CrossRef] [PubMed]
43. Kratochwil, C.; Fendler, W.P.; Eiber, M.; Hofman, M.S.; Emmett, L.; Calais, J.; Osborne, J.R.; Iravani, A.; Koo, P.; Lindenberg, L.; et al. Joint EANM/SNMMI procedure guideline for the use of ^{177}Lu-labeled PSMA-targeted radioligand-therapy (^{177}Lu-PSMA-RLT). *Eur. J. Nucl. Med. Mol. Imaging* **2023**, *50*, 2830–2845. [CrossRef] [PubMed]

44. Kuo, P.H.; Benson, T.; Messmann, R.; Groaning, M. Why we did what we did: PSMA PET/CT selection criteria for the VISION trial. *J. Nucl. Med.* **2022**, *63*, 816–818. [CrossRef] [PubMed]
45. Seifert, R.; Telli, T.; Hadaschik, B.; Fendler, W.P.; Kuo, P.H.; Herrmann, K. Is ^{18}F-FDG PET needed to assess ^{177}Lu-PSMA therapy eligibility? A VISION-like, single-center analysis. *J. Nucl. Med.* **2023**, *64*, 731–737. [CrossRef] [PubMed]
46. Buatti, J.M.; Pryma, D.A.; Kiess, A.P.; Mailman, J.; Ennis, R.D.; Menda, Y.; White, G.A.; Pandit-Taskar, N. A framework for patient-centered pathways of care for radiopharmaceutical therapy: An ASTRO consensus document. *Int. J. Radiat. Oncol. Biol. Phys.* **2021**, *109*, 913–922. [CrossRef]
47. Straub, M.; Kupferschläger, J.; Higuita, L.M.S.; Weissinger, M.; Dittmann, H.; la Fougère, C.; Fiz, F. Dual-time-point posttherapy ^{177}Lu-PSMA-617 SPECT/CT describes the uptake kinetics of mCRPC lesions and prognosticates patients' outcome. *J. Nucl. Med.* **2023**, *64*, 1431–1438. [CrossRef]
48. Pathmanandavel, S.; Crumbaker, M.; Ho, B.; Yam, A.O.; Wilson, P.; Niman, R.; Ayers, M.; Sharma, S.; Hickey, A.; Eu, P.; et al. Evaluation of ^{177}Lu-PSMA-617 SPECT/CT quantitation as a response biomarker within a prospective ^{177}Lu-PSMA-617 and NOX66 combination trial (LuPIN). *J. Nucl. Med.* **2023**, *64*, 221–226. [CrossRef]
49. Jackson, P.A.; Hofman, M.S.; Hicks, R.J.; Scalzo, M.; Violet, J. Radiation dosimetry in ^{177}Lu-PSMA-617 therapy using a single posttreatment SPECT/CT scan: A novel methodology to generate time- and tissue-specific dose factors. *J. Nucl. Med.* **2020**, *61*, 1030–1036. [CrossRef]
50. Lantheus and POINT Biopharma Announce Positive Topline Results from Pivotal SPLASH Trial in Metastatic Castration-Resistant Prostate Cancer. Available online: https://www.globenewswire.com/en/news-release/2023/12/18/2797729/0/en/Lantheus-and-POINT-Biopharma-Announce-Positive-Topline-Results-from-Pivotal-SPLASH-Trial-in-Metastatic-Castration-Resistant-Prostate-Cancer.html (accessed on 21 December 2023).

Disclaimer/Publisher's Note: The statements, opinions and data contained in all publications are solely those of the individual author(s) and contributor(s) and not of MDPI and/or the editor(s). MDPI and/or the editor(s) disclaim responsibility for any injury to people or property resulting from any ideas, methods, instructions or products referred to in the content.

Current Oncology

MDPI

Article

Prognostic Impact of Histologic Subtype and Divergent Differentiation in Patients with Metastatic Urothelial Carcinoma Treated with Enfortumab Vedotin: A Multicenter Retrospective Study

Akinori Minato [1,*], Nobuki Furubayashi [2], Yujiro Nagata [1], Toshihisa Tomoda [3], Hiroyuki Masaoka [4], Yoohyun Song [4], Yoshifumi Hori [5], Keijiro Kiyoshima [6], Takahito Negishi [2], Kentaro Kuroiwa [5], Narihito Seki [4], Ikko Tomisaki [1], Kenichi Harada [1], Motonobu Nakamura [2] and Naohiro Fujimoto [1]

1 Department of Urology, School of Medicine, University of Occupational and Environmental Health, Kitakyushu 807-8555, Japan; harada311@med.uoeh-u.ac.jp (K.H.); n-fuji@med.uoeh-u.ac.jp (N.F.)
2 Department of Urology, National Hospital Organization Kyushu Cancer Center, Fukuoka 811-1395, Japan; furubayashi.nobuki.yc@mail.hosp.go.jp (N.F.)
3 Department of Urology, Oita Prefectural Hospital, Oita 870-8511, Japan
4 Department of Urology, Kyushu Central Hospital of the Mutual Aid Association of Public School Teachers, Fukuoka 815-8588, Japan
5 Department of Urology, Miyazaki Prefectural Miyazaki Hospital, Miyazaki 880-8510, Japan
6 Department of Urology, Japanese Red Cross Fukuoka Hospital, Fukuoka 815-8555, Japan
* Correspondence: a-minato@med.uoeh-u.ac.jp

Abstract: Subtype of urothelial carcinoma (SUC), defined here as urothelial carcinoma with any histologic subtype or divergent differentiation, is a clinically aggressive disease. However, the efficacy of enfortumab vedotin (EV) against SUC remains unclear. Hence, this study aimed to assess the oncological outcomes of patients with SUC treated with EV for metastatic disease. We retrospectively evaluated consecutive patients with advanced lower and upper urinary tract cancer who received EV after platinum-based chemotherapy and immune checkpoint blockade therapy at six institutions. The objective response rate (ORR), progression-free survival (PFS), and overall survival (OS) were compared between patients with pure urothelial carcinoma (PUC) and those with SUC. We identified 44 and 18 patients with PUC and SUC, respectively. Squamous differentiation was the most common subtype element, followed by glandular differentiation and sarcomatoid subtype. Although patients with SUC had a comparable ORR to those with PUC, the duration of response for SUC was short. Patients with SUC had poorer PFS than those with PUC; however, no significant difference was observed in OS. Multivariate analysis revealed that SUC was significantly associated with shorter PFS. Although the response of metastatic SUC to EV was similar to that of PUC, SUC showed faster progression than PUC.

Keywords: enfortumab vedotin; antibody–drug conjugate; histologic subtype; metastatic urothelial carcinoma; prognosis; survival; divergent differentiation; variant histology

1. Introduction

Urothelial carcinoma (UC) is a common malignancy of the genitourinary system, typically affecting the bladder, renal pelvis, and the ureter. However, bladder cancer accounts for the majority of the UC cases. In 2020, 573,200 new cases of bladder cancer and 212,500 related deaths were recorded worldwide according to the GLOBOCAN estimates [1]. In recent years, immune checkpoint inhibitors (ICIs) have become the standard treatment for advanced UC as an adjuvant, maintenance, or second-line therapy after platinum-based chemotherapy [2–4]. However, most cases of advanced UC tend to progress. In the EV-301 phase 3 clinical trial, enfortumab vedotin (EV), which is an antibody–drug conjugate (ADC) directed against nectin-4, improved the survival of patients after platinum-based chemotherapy and ICI therapy failure [5]. Thus, in November 2021 in Japan, EV monotherapy was approved as a third-line regimen for patients with advanced UC. In 2023, we reported our early experience with the high effectiveness and tolerability of EV monotherapy for metastatic UC in a single-center cohort [6].

Pure conventional UC (PUC) is a predominant histology of upper or lower urinary tract malignancies, and it also has different morphologic categories within a tumor type. Owing to improved pathologic recognition [7], a subtype of UC (SUC), defined here as UC with any histologic subtype or divergent differentiation, has been frequently observed [8]. Thus, we previously reported that SUC accounted for approximately 31% of muscle-invasive bladder cancers, 12% of upper tract urinary cancers, and 34% of metastatic diseases [9]. SUC generally presents with an already advanced stage at diagnosis, indicating an aggressive biological behavior [10]. Recent studies have focused on the morphologic category in UC as a prognosticator in patients with locally advanced bladder cancer [11] and upper urinary tract cancer [12]. Ultimately, the results regarding prognosis in the surgical setting for patients with SUC are conflicting. Additionally, evidence of survival from systemic therapy for patients with metastatic SUC is insufficient [13,14] as the efficacy of EV on SUC has rarely been reported, thereby remaining unclear. Therefore, the therapeutic effect of EV in patients with SUC must be investigated further.

This study aimed to assess the oncological outcomes of patients with metastatic SUC who received EV monotherapy in real-world clinical practice from the Uro-Oncology Group in Kyushu (UROKYU) study population.

2. Materials and Methods

2.1. Patient Population

We retrospectively reviewed 63 consecutive patients with histologically confirmed metastatic PUC or SUC in the upper or lower urinary tract who had received EV after chemotherapy and immunotherapy at six institutions between December 2021 and August 2023, using the UROKYU study population. In this study, SUC was defined as the mixed presence of UC and a histologic subtype or divergent differentiation based on the World Health Organization Classification of Tumors [8]. The histomorphological subgroup was determined based on reports provided by dedicated pathologists at each institution without a central review. Prior radical surgeries included cystectomy and nephroureterectomy. In our cohort, no patient underwent metastasectomy or cytoreductive surgery. Some patients were diagnosed with PUC or SUC solely based on a small biopsy specimen for primary or metastatic tumor sites, including transurethral resection of bladder tumors and ureteroscopic biopsy of the renal pelvis or the ureter. All patients showed radiologically confirmed disease progression after undergoing platinum-based chemotherapy and subsequent ICI therapy for metastatic disease. After excluding one patient for whom the therapeutic effect of EV could not be evaluated, we included 62 patients for the analysis. Our study protocol was approved by the University of Occupational and Environmental Health Institutional Review Board (approval no. CRG23-017) and the ethics committee of each institution.

2.2. Patient Management

EV was administered intravenously at a dose of 1.25 mg/kg on days 1, 8, and 15, and the cycle was repeated every 28 days until disease progression, unacceptable adverse events, or consent withdrawal occurred. No upper limit was put on the number of cycles in the case of no progression. Moreover, EV treatment was stopped immediately in the case of unacceptable adverse events or consent withdrawal. Follow-up evaluation included physical examination, laboratory tests, and chest–abdominal–pelvic computed tomography, which was performed at baseline and after every two to three cycles of EV. If symptoms appeared, appropriate additional examinations were conducted.

2.3. Evaluation

Tumor response was assessed as the best response according to the Response Evaluation Criteria in Solid Tumors, version 1.1. [15]. We defined objective response rate (ORR) as the proportion of patients with a complete response (CR) or a partial response (PR), and the disease control rate as the proportion of patients with CR, PR, or stable disease (SD) without progressive disease (PD). The duration of response was the time from PR or CR onset until progression or death from any cause, whichever was earlier.

Moreover, progression-free survival (PFS) was calculated from the date of EV introduction to the date of disease progression or death, whichever occurred earlier, or to the last follow-up in patients without disease progression. Overall survival (OS) was calculated from the date of administration to the date of death from any cause or to the last follow-up in patients who survived.

2.4. Statistical Analysis

All statistical data were analyzed using EZR ver. 1.40 (Easy R; Saitama Medical Center, Jichi Medical University, Saitama, Japan), which is a graphical user interface for R (The R Foundation for Statistical Computing, Vienna, Austria) [16]. Between-group differences were assessed using Fisher's exact test for categorical variables and Mann–Whitney *U* test for continuous variables. Response duration, PFS, and OS were estimated using the Kaplan–Meier method and compared using the log-rank test. For the univariate and multivariate analyses of clinicopathological factors, we used the Cox proportional hazard models. The significant factors influencing the cause of progression or death as the dependent outcome were recruited in multivariate analyses. A p value less than 0.05 was considered statistically significant.

3. Results

3.1. Patient Characteristics

Of the 62 patients enrolled, 44 (71%) and 18 (29%) had PUC and SUC, respectively. The most common subtype element was squamous differentiation (16.1%), followed by glandular differentiation (6.5%) and sarcomatoid subtype (3.2%) (Table 1).

Table 1. Histologic type of patients treated with enfortumab vedotin.

Histologic Type	Number of Patients (%)	Primary Tumor Site Lower/Upper Urinary Tract
PUC	44 (71)	20/24
SUC	18 (29)	12/6
SUC subgroup		
Squamous differentiation	10 (16.1)	6/4
Glandular differentiation	4 (6.5)	4/0
Sarcomatoid subtype	2 (3.2)	0/2
Plasmacytoid subtype	1 (1.6)	1/0
Neuroendocrine differentiation	1 (1.6)	1/0

Abbreviations: PUC, pure urothelial carcinoma; SUC, subtype of urothelial carcinoma.

Table 2 compares the baseline characteristics of patients with PUC and SUC. Age, sex, Eastern Cooperative Oncology Group performance status (ECOG-PS), primary tumor site, anemia occurrence, proportion of liver metastasis, and prior treatment pattern did not significantly differ between the two patient groups. Furthermore, the dosing cycles of EV administered were comparable between the groups. Withdrawal of EV resulting in adverse events and consent withdrawal occurred in five patients and one patient, respectively. Regardless of their severity, we did not note any deaths caused by adverse events during the EV treatment.

Table 2. Patient characteristics.

	PUC (n = 44)	SUC (n = 18)	p Value
Age, median (IQR)	73 (68–76)	73 (71–79)	0.415
Sex, n (%)			0.355
Male	31 (70.5)	15 (83.3)	
Female	13 (29.5)	3 (16.7)	
ECOG-PS score, n (%)			0.667
0	19 (43.2)	7 (38.9)	
1	18 (40.9)	8 (44.4)	
2	4 (9.1)	3 (16.7)	
3	3 (6.8)	0 (0)	
Primary tumor site, n (%)			0.166
Lower urinary tract	20 (45.5)	12 (66.7)	
Upper urinary tract	24 (54.5)	6 (33.3)	
Histologic diagnosis, n (%)			0.412
Prior radical surgery	24 (54.5)	12 (66.7)	
Biopsy	20 (45.5)	6 (33.3)	
Anemia (Hb < 10 g/dL), n (%)	14 (31.8)	7 (38.9)	0.768
Liver metastasis, n (%)	9 (20.5)	4 (22.2)	1.00
Number of prior lines of therapy, n (%)			0.842
2	32 (72.7)	13 (72.2)	
≥3	12 (27.3)	5 (27.8)	
Prior immune checkpoint blockade, n (%)			1.00
Anti-PD-1	28 (63.6)	11 (61.1)	
Anti-PD-L1	16 (36.4)	7 (38.9)	
EV cycles, median (IQR)	4 (3–7)	4 (2–7)	0.365

Abbreviations: IQR, interquartile range; ECOG-PS, Eastern Cooperative Oncology Group performance status; Hb, hemoglobin; PD-1, programmed cell death protein 1; PD-L1, programmed death-ligand 1; EV, enfortumab vedotin; PUC, pure urothelial carcinoma; SUC, subtype of urothelial carcinoma.

3.2. Response

Table 3 shows the best overall response in the PUC and SUC groups. The ORR and disease control rate were similar between the two groups. The detailed response in patients with SUC was as follows: squamous differentiation (PR in eight and PD in two patients); glandular differentiation (SD in two and PD in two patients); sarcomatoid subtype (PD in two patients); plasmacytoid subtype (PD in one patient); and neuroendocrine differentiation (SD in one patient). Among the 33 patients evaluated as PR or CR, the response duration for patients with SUC was significantly shorter than for patients with PUC (median, 3.7 months vs. 7.3 months, p = 0.003) (Figure 1).

Table 3. Observed efficacy of enfortumab vedotin stratified by histologic type.

	PUC (n = 44)	SUC (n = 18)	p Value
Response, n (%)			0.475
CR	3 (6.8)	0 (0)	
PR	22 (50.0)	8 (44.4)	
SD	10 (22.7)	3 (16.7)	
PD	9 (20.5)	7 (38.9)	
Objective response rate (CR + PR), n (%)	25 (56.8)	8 (44.4)	0.413
Disease control rate (CR + PR + SD), n (%)	35 (79.5)	11 (61.1)	0.20

Abbreviations: CR, complete response; PR, partial response; SD, stable disease; PD, progressive disease; PUC, pure urothelial carcinoma; SUC, subtype of urothelial carcinoma.

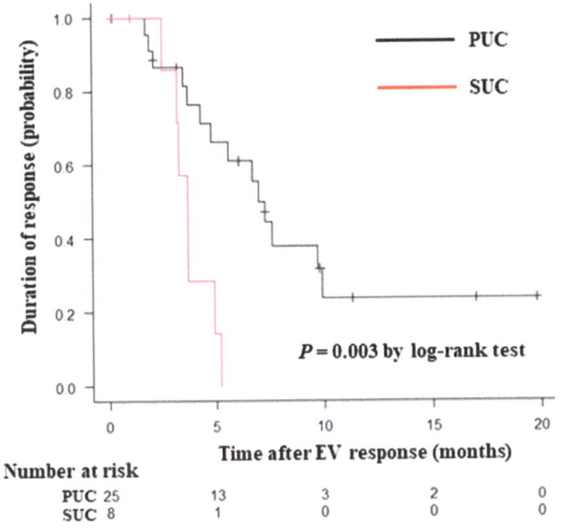

Figure 1. Kaplan–Meier curves for the duration of response (complete or partial responders) to enfortumab vedotin in patients with PUC and SUC. Abbreviations: PUC, pure urothelial carcinoma; SUC, subtype of urothelial carcinoma.

3.3. Survival

The median follow-up time was 7.1 months (interquartile range, 4.0–11.8), during which 47 (75.8%) patients experienced progression and 30 (48.4%) patients died. PFS was poorer in patients with SUC than in those with PUC (median, 4.2 months vs. 5.9 months; $p = 0.045$) (Figure 2a), whereas OS showed no significant difference between such groups (median, 7.3 months vs. 16.1 months; $p = 0.065$) (Figure 2b).

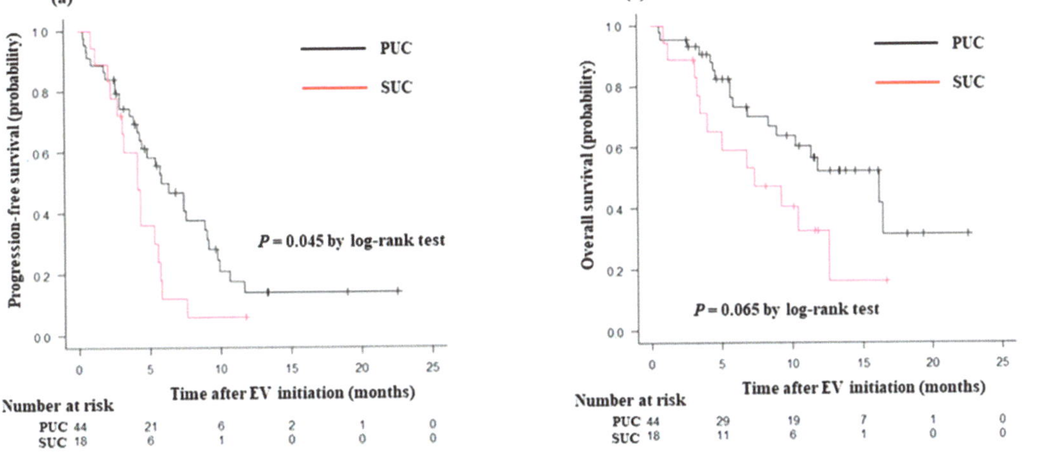

Figure 2. Kaplan–Meier curves for (**a**) progression-free survival and (**b**) overall survival after enfortumab vedotin initiation in patients with PUC and SUC. Abbreviations: PUC, pure urothelial carcinoma; SUC, subtype of urothelial carcinoma.

In the univariate and multivariate Cox proportional hazards regression analyses predicting PFS after adjusting for clinicopathological characteristics (Table 4), the presence of histologic subtype or divergent differentiation was identified as a significant independent predictor of PFS. Additionally, poor ECOG-PS was significantly associated with PFS.

Table 4. Results of univariate and multivariate analyses for progression-free survival.

Variable	Univariate		Multivariate	
	HR (95% CI)	*p* Value	HR (95% CI)	*p* Value
Age, years				
<73	1			
≥73	1.21 (0.67–2.16)	0.529		
Sex				
Male	1			
Female	0.97 (0.49–1.91)	0.932		
ECOG-PS score				
0	1		1	
1	1.35 (0.71–2.59)	0.361	1.27 (0.66–2.45)	0.467
2	2.01 (0.83–4.86)	0.123	1.73 (0.70–4.25)	0.233
3	3.77 (1.08–13.2)	0.038	4.54 (1.27–16.2)	0.019
Primary tumor site				
Lower urinary tract	1			
Upper urinary tract	0.83 (0.47–1.48)	0.527		
Prior radical surgery				
No	1			
Yes	0.69 (0.38–1.22)	0.201		
Anemia				
No	1			
Yes	1.54 (0.83–2.84)	0.169		
Liver metastasis				
No	1			
Yes	1.50 (0.75–2.99)	0.252		
Prior immune checkpoint blockade				
Anti-PD-1	1			
Anti-PD-L1	0.67 (0.36–1.23)	0.193		
Histologic type				
PUC	1		1	
SUC	1.86 (1.01–3.45)	0.049	1.90 (1.01–3.61)	0.048

Abbreviations: ECOG-PS, Eastern Cooperative Oncology Group performance status; PD-1, programmed cell death protein 1; PD-L1, programmed death-ligand 1; PUC, pure urothelial carcinoma; SUC, subtype of urothelial carcinoma; HR, hazard ratio; CI, confidence interval.

4. Discussion

To assess the efficacy of EV—an ADC directed against nectin-4—on clinical outcomes according to the histologic types, this study evaluated the therapeutic response to EV monotherapy and its survival outcome in patients with PUC and SUC after platinum-based chemotherapy and ICI therapy. In our cohort, squamous differentiation was the most common subtype element. Although patients with SUC had similar ORR and disease control rate to those with PUC, the duration of response for SUC was short. Patients with SUC had poorer PFS than those with PUC, but no significant difference was observed in OS. Multivariate analysis showed that the presence of histologic subtype or divergent differentiation was an independent predictor of progression after EV initiation. SUC might harbor more aggressive biological features in metastatic disease than in locally advanced disease.

Currently, the efficacy of EV monotherapy as a third-line treatment for patients with advanced UC remains insufficiently investigated in a real-world setting. In the United States, only approximately 3–7% of patients with newly diagnosed metastatic disease receive third-line therapy [17]. Moreover, the role of EV against SUC has been less explored. Although the EV-301 trial included 15% (n = 45) of patients with SUC who received EV, clinical data regarding the response and survival in patients with SUC are still unavailable [5]. The Urothelial Cancer Network to Investigate Therapeutic Experience (UNITE) study has the largest retrospective cohort of patients treated with EV in the United States (n = 260), of which 66 patients have SUC [18]. The ORR to EV in patients with PUC and SUC was 58% and 42%, which is consistent with our results. The responses in patients with squamous differentiation (n = 28) were CR and PR in one (3.6%) and thirteen (46.4%) patients, respectively. However, compared with our cohort, the UNITE study population included both platinum-pretreated and platinum-naïve patients. In particular, 86 patients (33%) received EV monotherapy as the second or earlier line of treatment [18]. Additionally, response duration and PFS for patients with SUC were not analyzed in the EV-301 trial. Conversely, the duration of response in our PUC cohort is consistent with that in the EV-201 phase 2 trial (median, 7.6 months) [19]. Recently, Zschabitz et al. [20] reported the clinical experience of EV treatment in the largest European study population (n = 125); however, only two patients were included in the SUC group.

In our study, the number of other histologic subtypes or divergent differentiation was insufficient. Consequently, we did not include histologic subtypes, such as micropapillary and nested. The heterogeneity in SUC populations may affect the EV therapeutic effect and patient survival. When evaluating the efficacy of platinum-based chemotherapy as the first-line treatment, the duration of PFS or OS in patients with squamous differentiation was comparable to that in patients with other histologic subgroups [9].

Nectin-4 expression is consistently very high in PUC, but prior studies showed lower nectin-4 expression in SUC than in PUC [21]. Although current clinical trials exploring EV in UC do not require nectin-4 expression as a stratifying factor [5], preclinical data have suggested that its expression is necessary for a response to EV [22]. Klümper et al. [23] recently revealed that nectin-4 expression decreased during metastatic spread in 59% of their cases. Interestingly, low nectin-4 expression was associated with reduced PFS duration on EV treatment. In Fan et al.'s immunohistochemical analysis of 161 surgical specimens stained for nectin-4 [24], membranous positive expression was observed in 79.2%, 100%, 65.2%, 21.1%, 78.9%, and 88.9% of conventional UC, squamous, glandular, neuroendocrine differentiation, micropapillary, and nested subtypes, respectively. Moreover, a single-center retrospective analysis on radical cystectomy for SUC showed that sarcomatoid subtypes had low nectin-4 expression [25]. In 2023, Ghali et al. reported the prominent cytoplasmic staining of nectin-4 by a rapid autopsy study [26]. Interestingly, nectin-4 accumulates in the cytoplasm within squamous differentiation or plasmacytoid subtype in bladder cancer, especially within metastatic specimens, but not neuroendocrine differentiation. Currently, changes in nectin-4 expression according to the histologic types during EV treatment remain unevaluated; this evaluation is a major challenge for future studies, including ours. Additionally, in daily practice, the expression of nectin-4 for SUC is difficult to identify in metastatic lesions.

Given that there is still no effective treatment strategy for metastatic SUC because of the exclusion of its analysis from clinical studies, its pharmaceutical therapy is performed according to PUC. Our previous study showed a similar ORR of gemcitabine plus cisplatin (or carboplatin) therapy between the PUC (n = 86) and SUC (n = 45) groups. However, the SUC group had significantly worse PFS (median, 4.9 months vs. 7.9 months) and OS (median, 10.9 months vs. 18.2 months) than the PUC group [9]. In 2022, we conducted a multicenter retrospective study showing the survival outcomes of pembrolizumab therapy in patients with chemotherapy-resistant SUC [14]. Interestingly, the PFS or OS from the start of pembrolizumab did not significantly differ between the PUC and SUC groups. Therefore, early sequential therapy from platinum-based chemotherapy to ICI therapy may be beneficial for patients with SUC. Evaluating the efficacy of avelumab maintenance therapy or nivolumab adjuvant therapy in patients with SUC is suggested. Moreover, we expect the EV plus pembrolizumab as a regimen in the ongoing clinical EV 302 trial (NCT04223856) to yield a positive effect for SUC.

ECOG-PS is a well-known prognostic factor concerning chemotherapy response. Patients with poor ECOG-PS (>1) have been excluded from the current clinical trial [27]. In our previous study, the response to EV was observed irrespective of ECOG-PS (proportion of patients with PS score of ≥2 was 26.9%), and the health-related quality of life in patients remained stable from baseline to post-EV introduction [6]. However, the present study suggests that patients with an ECOG-PS score of 3 are poor candidates for EV treatment.

Although surgery was not associated with a better prognosis in this study, previous studies have demonstrated that the treatment of the primary tumor can provide some survival benefit to patients with metastatic UC [28,29]. In the context of improved systemic therapies, aggressive local treatment in well-selected patients could improve the typically poor prognosis of these patients.

This study has certain limitations, such as its retrospective nonrandomized design, small sample size, and short observation period. Histologic assessment of small biopsies potentially has a false-negative risk in the detection of subtype histology, except for prior radical surgery. Given the limited number of patients in our cohort, we could not compare the patients according to the SUC subgroup or primary organ stratified by bladder or upper urinary tract. Moreover, the timing of EV monotherapy was not uniform, with most patients receiving two regimens and the rest receiving three or more before EV introduction. However, EV treatment outcomes depending on histomorphologic groups have not been described in larger populations to date.

Nevertheless, our data suggest that these clinically aggressive histologic types are promising prognosticators for EV treatment regardless of the response. Although multivariate analysis for OS was not estimated, prognostic factors such as late-line treatment should be further explored in the ADC era. The results of response or OS rates for SUC may be attributed to the lack of statistical power. More studies with larger cohorts are needed to further validate our results. Particularly, the difference in the oncological outcomes among subgroups within the SUC group should be evaluated.

5. Conclusions

The duration of response and survival after treatment with EV in patients with SUC tended to be shorter than in those with PUC with metastatic disease. However, patients with SUC were few, thus necessitating further investigation.

Author Contributions: Conceptualization, A.M. and N.F. (Nobuki Furubayashi); methodology, A.M. and N.F. (Nobuki Furubayashi); formal analysis, A.M. and N.F. (Nobuki Furubayashi); investigation, A.M., N.F. (Nobuki Furubayashi), Y.N., T.T., H.M., Y.S., Y.H., K.K. (Keijiro Kiyoshima) and T.N.; data curation, A.M., N.F. (Nobuki Furubayashi), T.T., H.M., Y.S., Y.H., K.K. (Keijiro Kiyoshima) and T.N.; writing—original draft preparation, A.M.; supervision, M.N. and N.F. (Naohiro Fujimoto); editing, A.M., N.F. (Nobuki Furubayashi) and Y.N.; reviewing, N.F. (Nobuki Furubayashi), Y.N., K.K. (Kentaro Kuroiwa), N.S., I.T. and K.H. All authors have read and agreed to the published version of the manuscript.

Funding: This research was funded by JSPS KAKENHI grant number JP23K15773.

Institutional Review Board Statement: This study protocol was approved by the University of Occupational and Environmental Health Institutional Review Board (approval no. CRG23-017).

Informed Consent Statement: Informed consent was obtained through an opt-out process due to the retrospective study.

Data Availability Statement: The data presented in this study are available on request from the corresponding author.

Conflicts of Interest: The authors declare no conflicts of interest.

References

1. Sung, H.; Ferlay, J.; Siegel, R.L.; Laversanne, M.; Soerjomataram, I.; Jemal, A.; Bray, F. Global cancer statistics 2020: GLOBOCAN estimates of incidence and mortality worldwide for 36 cancers in 185 countries. *CA Cancer J. Clin.* **2021**, *71*, 209–249. [CrossRef]
2. Bajorin, D.F.; Witjes, J.A.; Gschwend, J.E.; Schenker, M.; Valderrama, B.P.; Tomita, Y.; Bamias, A.; Lebret, T.; Shariat, S.F.; Park, S.H.; et al. Adjuvant nivolumab versus placebo in muscle-invasive urothelial carcinoma. *N. Engl. J. Med.* **2021**, *384*, 2102–2114. [CrossRef]
3. Powles, T.; Park, S.H.; Voog, E.; Caserta, C.; Valderrama, B.P.; Gurney, H.; Kalofonos, H.; Radulović, S.; Demey, W.; Ullén, A.; et al. Avelumab maintenance therapy for advanced or metastatic urothelial carcinoma. *N. Engl. J. Med.* **2020**, *383*, 1218–1230. [CrossRef] [PubMed]
4. Bellmunt, J.; de Wit, R.; Vaughn, D.J.; Fradet, Y.; Lee, J.L.; Fong, L.; Vogelzang, N.J.; Climent, M.A.; Petrylak, D.P.; Choueiri, T.K.; et al. Pembrolizumab as second-line therapy for advanced urothelial carcinoma. *N. Engl. J. Med.* **2017**, *376*, 1015–1026. [CrossRef]
5. Powles, T.; Rosenberg, J.E.; Sonpavde, G.P.; Loriot, Y.; Durán, I.; Lee, J.L.; Matsubara, N.; Vulsteke, C.; Castellano, D.; Wu, C.; et al. Enfortumab vedotin in previously treated advanced urothelial carcinoma. *N. Engl. J. Med.* **2021**, *384*, 1125–1135. [CrossRef] [PubMed]
6. Minato, A.; Kimuro, R.; Ohno, D.; Tanigawa, K.; Kuretake, K.; Matsukawa, T.; Takaba, T.; Jojima, K.; Harada, M.; Higashijima, K.; et al. Efficacy and tolerability of enfortumab vedotin for metastatic urothelial carcinoma: Early experience in the real world. *Anticancer Res.* **2023**, *43*, 4055–4060. [CrossRef]
7. Mantica, G.; Simonato, A.; Du Plessis, D.E.; Maffezzini, M.; De Rose, A.F.; van der Merwe, A.; Terrone, C. The pathologist's role in the detection of rare variants of bladder cancer and analysis of the impact on incidence and type detection. *Minerva Urol. Nefrol.* **2018**, *70*, 594–597. [CrossRef] [PubMed]
8. Netto, G.J.; Amin, M.B.; Berney, D.M.; Compérat, E.M.; Gill, A.J.; Hartmann, A.; Menon, S.; Raspollini, M.R.; Rubin, M.A.; Srigley, J.R.; et al. The 2022 World Health Organization classification of tumors of the urinary system and male genital organs-part B: Prostate and urinary tract tumors. *Eur. Urol.* **2022**, *82*, 469–482. [CrossRef]
9. Minato, A.; Murooka, K.; Okumura, Y.; Takaba, T.; Higashijima, K.; Nagata, Y.; Tomisaki, I.; Harada, K.; Fujimoto, N. Efficacy of platinum-based chemotherapy in patients with metastatic urothelial carcinoma with variant histology. *In Vivo*, 2024, *in press*.
10. Lobo, N.; Shariat, S.F.; Guo, C.C.; Fernandez, M.I.; Kassouf, W.; Choudhury, A.; Gao, J.; Williams, S.B.; Galsky, M.D.; Taylor, J.A.; et al. What is the significance of variant histology in urothelial carcinoma? *Eur. Urol. Focus* **2020**, *6*, 653–663. [CrossRef]
11. Mori, K.; Abufaraj, M.; Mostafaei, H.; Quhal, F.; Karakiewicz, P.I.; Briganti, A.; Kimura, S.; Egawa, S.; Shariat, S.F. A systematic review and meta-analysis of variant histology in urothelial carcinoma of the bladder treated with radical cystectomy. *J. Urol.* **2020**, *204*, 1129–1140. [CrossRef] [PubMed]
12. Mori, K.; Janisch, F.; Parizi, M.K.; Mostafaei, H.; Lysenko, I.; Kimura, S.; Enikeev, D.V.; Egawa, S.; Shariat, S.F. Prognostic value of variant histology in upper tract urothelial carcinoma treated with nephroureterectomy: A systematic review and meta-analysis. *J. Urol.* **2020**, *203*, 1075–1084. [CrossRef] [PubMed]
13. Hsieh, M.C.; Sung, M.T.; Chiang, P.H.; Huang, C.H.; Tang, Y.; Su, Y.L. The prognostic impact of histopathological variants in patients with advanced urothelial carcinoma. *PLoS ONE* **2015**, *10*, e0129268. [CrossRef] [PubMed]
14. Minato, A.; Furubayashi, N.; Harada, M.; Negishi, T.; Sakamoto, N.; Song, Y.; Hori, Y.; Tomoda, T.; Tamura, S.; Kuroiwa, K.; et al. Efficacy of pembrolizumab in patients with variant urothelial carcinoma: A multicenter retrospective study. *Clin. Genitourin. Cancer* **2022**, *20*, 499.e1–499.e8. [CrossRef] [PubMed]
15. Eisenhauer, E.A.; Therasse, P.; Bogaerts, J.; Schwartz, L.H.; Sargent, D.; Ford, R.; Dancey, J.; Arbuck, S.; Gwyther, S.; Mooney, M.; et al. New response evaluation criteria in solid tumours: Revised RECIST guideline, version 1.1. *Eur. J. Cancer* **2009**, *45*, 228–247. [CrossRef] [PubMed]
16. Kanda, Y. Investigation of the freely available easy-to-use software "EZR" for medical statistics. *Bone Marrow Transpl.* **2013**, *48*, 452–458. [CrossRef] [PubMed]
17. Swami, U.; Grivas, P.; Pal, S.K.; Agarwal, N. Utilization of systemic therapy for treatment of advanced urothelial carcinoma: Lessons from real world experience. *Cancer Treat. Res. Commun.* **2021**, *27*, 100325. [CrossRef]
18. Koshkin, V.S.; Henderson, N.; James, M.; Natesan, D.; Freeman, D.; Nizam, A.; Su, C.T.; Khaki, A.R.; Osterman, C.K.; Glover, M.J.; et al. Efficacy of enfortumab vedotin in advanced urothelial cancer: Analysis from the urothelial cancer network to investigate therapeutic experiences (UNITE) study. *Cancer* **2022**, *128*, 1194–1205. [CrossRef]
19. Rosenberg, J.E.; O'Donnell, P.H.; Balar, A.V.; McGregor, B.A.; Heath, E.I.; Yu, E.Y.; Galsky, M.D.; Hahn, N.M.; Gartner, E.M.; Pinelli, J.M.; et al. Pivotal trial of enfortumab vedotin in urothelial carcinoma after platinum and anti-programmed death 1/programmed death ligand 1 therapy. *J. Clin. Oncol.* **2019**, *37*, 2592–2600. [CrossRef]
20. Zschäbitz, S.; Biernath, N.; Hilser, T.; Höllein, A.; Zengerling, F.; Cascucelli, J.; Paffenholz, P.; Seidl, D.; Lutz, C.; Schlack, K.; et al. Enfortumab vedotin in metastatic urothelial carcinoma: Survival and safety in a European multicenter real-world patient cohort. *Eur. Urol. Open Sci.* **2023**, *53*, 31–37. [CrossRef] [PubMed]
21. Hoffman-Censits, J.H.; Lombardo, K.A.; Parimi, V.; Kamanda, S.; Choi, W.; Hahn, N.M.; McConkey, D.J.; McGuire, B.M.; Bivalacqua, T.J.; Kates, M.; et al. Expression of Nectin-4 in bladder urothelial carcinoma, in morphologic variants, and nonurothelial histotypes. *Appl. Immunohistochem. Mol. Morphol.* **2021**, *29*, 619–625. [CrossRef]

22. Chu, C.E.; Sjöström, M.; Egusa, E.A.; Gibb, E.A.; Badura, M.L.; Zhu, J.; Koshkin, V.S.; Stohr, B.A.; Meng, M.V.; Pruthi, R.S.; et al. Heterogeneity in NECTIN4 expression across molecular subtypes of urothelial cancer mediates sensitivity to enfortumab vedotin. *Clin. Cancer Res.* **2021**, *27*, 5123–5130. [CrossRef] [PubMed]
23. Klümper, N.; Ralser, D.J.; Ellinger, J.; Roghmann, F.; Albrecht, J.; Below, E.; Alajati, A.; Sikic, D.; Breyer, J.; Bolenz, C.; et al. Membranous NECTIN-4 expression frequently decreases during metastatic spread of urothelial carcinoma and is associated with enfortumab vedotin resistance. *Clin. Cancer Res.* **2023**, *29*, 1496–1505. [CrossRef] [PubMed]
24. Fan, Y.; Li, Q.; Shen, Q.; Liu, Z.; Zhang, Z.; Hu, S.; Yu, W.; He, Z.; He, Q.; Zhang, Q. Head-to-head comparison of the expression differences of nectin-4, TROP-2, and HER2 in urothelial carcinoma and its histologic variants. *Front. Oncol.* **2022**, *12*, 858865. [CrossRef] [PubMed]
25. Rodler, S.; Eismann, L.; Schlenker, B.; Casuscelli, J.; Brinkmann, I.; Sendelhofert, A.; Waidelich, R.; Buchner, A.; Stief, C.; Schulz, G.B.; et al. Expression of nectin-4 in variant histologies of bladder cancer and its prognostic value-need for biomarker testing in high-risk patients? *Cancers* **2022**, *14*, 4411. [CrossRef] [PubMed]
26. Ghali, F.; Vakar-Lopez, F.; Roudier, M.P.; Garcia, J.; Arora, S.; Cheng, H.H.; Schweizer, M.T.; Haffner, M.C.; Lee, J.K.; Yu, E.Y.; et al. Metastatic bladder cancer expression and subcellular localization of Nectin-4 and Trop-2 in variant histology: A rapid autopsy study. *Clin. Genitourin. Cancer* **2023**, *21*, 669–678. [CrossRef] [PubMed]
27. Rosenberg, J.E.; Powles, T.; Sonpavde, G.P.; Loriot, Y.; Duran, I.; Lee, J.L.; Matsubara, N.; Vulsteke, C.; Castellano, D.; Mamtani, R.; et al. EV-301 long-term outcomes: 24-month findings from the phase III trial of enfortumab vedotin versus chemotherapy in patients with previously treated advanced urothelial carcinoma. *Ann. Oncol.* **2023**, *34*, 1047–1054. [CrossRef] [PubMed]
28. Paciotti, M.; Nguyen, D.D.; Modonutti, D.; Haeuser, L.; Lipsitz, S.; Mossanen, M.; Kibel, A.S.; Lughezzani, G.; Trinh, Q.D.; Cole, A.P. Impact of high-intensity local treatment on overall survival in stage IV upper tract urothelial carcinoma. *Urol. Oncol.* **2021**, *39*, 436.e1–436.e10. [CrossRef]
29. Seisen, T.; Sun, M.; Leow, J.J.; Preston, M.A.; Cole, A.P.; Gelpi-Hammerschmidt, F.; Hanna, N.; Meyer, C.P.; Kibel, A.S.; Lipsitz, S.R.; et al. Efficacy of high-intensity local treatment for metastatic urothelial carcinoma of the bladder: A propensity score-weighted analysis from the national cancer data base. *J. Clin. Oncol.* **2016**, *34*, 3529–3536. [CrossRef]

Disclaimer/Publisher's Note: The statements, opinions and data contained in all publications are solely those of the individual author(s) and contributor(s) and not of MDPI and/or the editor(s). MDPI and/or the editor(s) disclaim responsibility for any injury to people or property resulting from any ideas, methods, instructions or products referred to in the content.

MDPI AG
Grosspeteranlage 5
4052 Basel
Switzerland
Tel.: +41 61 683 77 34

MDPI Books Editorial Office
E-mail: books@mdpi.com
www.mdpi.com/books

Disclaimer/Publisher's Note: The title and front matter of this reprint are at the discretion of the Topic Editors. The publisher is not responsible for their content or any associated concerns. The statements, opinions and data contained in all individual articles are solely those of the individual Editors and contributors and not of MDPI. MDPI disclaims responsibility for any injury to people or property resulting from any ideas, methods, instructions or products referred to in the content.

www.ingramcontent.com/pod-product-compliance
Lightning Source LLC
Chambersburg PA
CBHW041434210926
51850CB00013B/3421
* 9 7 8 3 7 2 5 8 4 2 1 7 9 *